F /UT

1929

C000026262

O.

THE PLAYS OF
JOHN GALSWORTHY

THE PLAYS

OF

JOHN GALSWORTHY

DUCKWORTH
3 Henrietta Street, London, W.C.
1929

DEDICATIONS

"The Silver Box," "Joy," and "Strife"
are dedicated to H. Granville-Barker;

"The Eldest Son," "The Little Dream," and "Justice"
to John Masefield;

"The Fugitive," "The Pigeon," and "The Mob"
to Dolores and Frank Lucas;

"A Bit o' Love," "The Foundations," and "The Skin Game"
to H. W. Massingham;

"A Family Man," "Loyalties," and "Windows"
to Thomas Blair Reynolds;

"The Forest," "Old English," and "The Show"
to John Drinkwater;

The "Six Short Plays" are dedicated to Stacy Aumonier.

CONTENTS

CONTENTS

THE SILVER BOX

CAST OF THE ORIGINAL PRODUCTION AT THE ROYAL
COURT THEATRE, LONDON, ON SEPTEMBER 25, 1906

JOHN BARTHWICK, M.P.	Mr. James Hearn
MRS. BARTHWICK	Miss Frances Ivor
JACK BARTHWICK	Mr. A. E. Matthews
ROPER	Mr. A. Goodsall
MRS. JONES	Miss Irene Rooke
MARLOW	Mr. Frederick Lloyd
WHEELER	Miss Gertrude Henriques
JONES	Mr. Norman McKinnell
MRS. SEDDON	Mrs. Charles Maltby
SNOW	Mr. Trevor Lowe
A POLICE MAGISTRATE	Mr. Athol Forde
AN UNKNOWN LADY	Miss Sydney Fairbrother
LIVENS	Mr. Edmund Gurney
RELIEVING OFFICER	Mr. Edmund Gwenn
MAGISTRATE'S CLERK	Mr. Lewis Casson
USHER	Mr. Norman Page

ACT I

SCENE I

The curtain rises on the BARTHWICKS' *dining-room, large, modern, and well furnished; the window curtains drawn. Electric light is burning. On the large round dining-table is set out a tray with whisky, a syphon, and a silver cigarette-box. It is past midnight.*

A fumbling is heard outside the door. It is opened suddenly; JACK BARTHWICK *seems to fall into the room. He stands holding by the door knob, staring before him, with a beatific smile. He is in evening dress and opera hat, and carries in his hand a sky-blue velvet lady's reticule. His boyish face is freshly coloured and clean-shaven. An overcoat is hanging on his arm.*

JACK. Hallo! I've got home all ri—— [*Defiantly.*] Who says I sh'd never've opened th' door without 'sistance. [*He staggers in, fumbling with the reticule. A lady's handkerchief and purse of crimson silk fall out.*] Serve her joll' well right—everything droppin' out. Th' cat. I've scored her off—I've got her bag. [*He swings the reticule.*] Serves her joll' well right. [*He takes a cigarette out of the silver box and puts it in his mouth.*] Never gave tha' fellow anything! [*He hunts through all his pockets and pulls a shilling out; it drops and rolls away. He looks for it.*] Beastly shilling! [*He looks again.*] Base ingratitude! Absolutely nothing. [*He laughs.*] Mus' tell him I've got absolutely nothing.

　　　　[*He lurches through the door and down a corridor, and presently returns, followed by* JONES, *who is advanced in liquor.* JONES, *about thirty years of age, has hollow cheeks, black circles round his eyes, and rusty clothes. He looks as though he might be unemployed, and enters in a hang-dog manner.*

JACK. Sh! sh! sh! Don't you make a noise, whatever you do. Shu' the door, an' have a drink. [*Very solemnly.*] You helped me to open the door—I've got nothin' for you. This is my house. My father's name's Barthwick; he's Member of Parliament—Liberal Member of Parliament: I've told you that before. Have a drink! [*He pours out whisky and drinks it up.*] I'm not drunk—— [*Subsiding on a sofa.*] Tha's all right. Wha's your name? My name's Barthwick, so's my father's; *I'm* a Liberal too—wha're you?

3

JONES. [*In a thick, sardonic voice*] I'm a bloomin' Conser*vative*. My name's Jones ! My wife works 'ere ; she's the char ; she works 'ere.

JACK. Jones ? [*He laughs.*] There's 'nother Jones at college with me. I'm not a Socialist myself ; I'm a Liberal—there's ve-lill difference, because of the principles of the Lib—Liberal Party. We're all equal before the law—tha's rot, tha's silly. [*Laughs.*] Wha' was I about to say ? Give me some whisky.

> [JONES *gives him the whisky he desires, together with a squirt of syphon.*

Wha' I was goin' tell you was—I've had a row with her. [*He waves the reticule.*] Have a drink, Jones—sh'd never have got in without you —tha's why I'm giving you a drink. Don' care who knows I've scored her off. Th' cat ! [*He throws his feet up on the sofa.*] Don' you make a noise, whatever you do. You pour out a drink—you make yourself good long, long drink—you take cigarette—you take anything you like. Sh'd never have got in without you. [*Closing his eyes.*] You're a Tory—you're a Tory Socialist. I'm Liberal myself—have a drink— I'm an excel'nt chap.

> [*His head drops back. He, smiling, falls asleep, and* JONES *stands looking at him ; then, snatching up* JACK'S *glass, he drinks it off. He picks the reticule from off* JACK'S *shirt-front, holds it to the light, and smells at it.*

JONES. Been on the tiles and brought 'ome some of yer cat's fur. [*He stuffs it into* JACK'S *breast pocket.*]

JACK. [*Murmuring*] I've scored you off ! You cat !

> [JONES *looks around him furtively ; he pours out whisky and drinks it. From the silver box he takes a cigarette, puffs at it, and drinks more whisky. There is no sobriety left in him.*

JONES. Fat lot o' things they've got 'ere ! [*He sees the crimson purse lying on the floor.*] More cat's fur. Puss, puss ! [*He fingers it, drops it on the tray, and looks at* JACK.] Calf ! Fat calf ! [*He sees his own presentment in a mirror. Lifting his hands, with fingers spread, he stares at it ; then looks again at* JACK, *clenching his fist as if to batter in his sleeping, smiling face. Suddenly he tilts the rest of the whisky into the glass and drinks it. With cunning glee he takes the silver box and purse and pockets them.*] I'll score *you* off too, that's wot I'll do !

> [*He gives a little snarling laugh and lurches to the door. His shoulder rubs against the switch ; the light goes out. There is a sound as of a closing outer door.*

The curtain falls.

The curtain rises again at once.

SCENE II

In the BARTHWICKS' *dining-room.* JACK *is still asleep; the morning light is coming through the curtains. The time is half-past eight.* WHEELER, *brisk person, enters with a dust-pan, and* MRS. JONES *more slowly with a scuttle.*

WHEELER. [*Drawing the curtains*] That precious husband of yours was round for you after you'd gone yesterday, Mrs. Jones. Wanted your money for drink, I suppose. He hangs about the corner here half the time. I saw him outside the " Goat and Bells " when I went to the post last night. If I were you I wouldn't live with him. I wouldn't live with a man that raised his hand to me. I wouldn't put up with it. Why don't you take the children and leave him? If you put up with 'im it'll only make him worse. I never can see why, because a man's married you, he should knock you about.

MRS. JONES. [*Slim, dark-eyed, and dark-haired; oval-faced, and with a smooth, soft, even voice; her manner patient, her way of talking quite impersonal; she wears a blue linen dress, and boots with holes*] It was nearly two last night before he come home, and he wasn't himself. He made me get up, and he knocked me about; he didn't seem to know *what* he was saying or doing. Of course I *would* leave him, but I'm really afraid of what he'd do to me. He's such a violent man when he's not himself.

WHEELER. Why don't you get him locked up? You'll never have any peace until you get him locked up. If I were you I'd go to the police court to-morrow. That's what I would do.

MRS. JONES. Of course I ought to go, because he does treat me so badly when he's not himself. But you see, Bettina, he has a very hard time—he's been out of work two months, and it preys upon his mind. When he's in work he behaves himself much better. It's when he's out of work that he's so violent.

WHEELER. Well, if you won't take any steps you'll never get rid of him.

MRS. JONES. Of course it's very wearing to me; I don't get my sleep at nights. And it's not as if I were getting help from him, because I have to do for the children and all of us. And he throws such dreadful things up at me, talks of my having men to follow me about. Such a thing never happens; no man ever speaks to me. And of course it's just the other way. It's what he does that's wrong and makes me so unhappy. And then he's always threatenin' to cut my throat if I leave him. It's all the drink, and things preying on his mind; he's not a bad man really. Sometimes he'll speak quite kind to me, but I've stood so much from him, I don't feel it in me to speak kind back, but just keep myself to myself.   And he's all right with the children too, except when he's not himself.

WHEELER. You mean when he's drunk, the beauty.

MRS. JONES. Yes. [*Without change of voice.*] There's the young gentleman asleep on the sofa.

[*They both look silently at* JACK.

MRS. JONES. [*At last, in her soft voice*] He doesn't look quite himself.

WHEELER. He's a young limb, that's what he is.   It's my belief he was tipsy last night, like your husband.   It's another kind of bein' out of work that sets *him* to drink.   I'll go and tell Marlow.   This is his job.   [*She goes.*

[MRS. JONES, *upon her knees, begins a gentle sweeping.*

JACK. [*Waking*] Who's there ?   What is it ?

MRS. JONES. It's me, sir, Mrs. Jones.

JACK. [*Sitting up and looking round*] Where is it—what—what time is it ?

MRS. JONES. It's getting on for nine o'clock, sir.

JACK. For nine !   Why—what !   [*Rising, and loosening his tongue ; putting hand to his head, and staring hard at* MRS. JONES.] Look here, you, Mrs.—Mrs. Jones—don't you say you caught me asleep here.

MRS. JONES. No, sir, of course I won't, sir.

JACK. It's quite an accident ; I don't know how it happened.   I must have forgotten to go to bed.   It's a queer thing.   I've got a most beastly headache.   Mind you don't say anything, Mrs. Jones.

[*Goes out and passes* MARLOW *in the doorway.*   MARLOW *is young and quiet ; he is clean-shaven, and his hair is brushed high from his forehead in a coxcomb.   Incidentally a butler, he is first a man.   He looks at* MRS. JONES, *and smiles a private smile.*

MARLOW. Not the first time, and won't be the last.   Looked a bit dicky, eh, Mrs. Jones ?

MRS. JONES. He didn't look quite himself.   Of course I didn't take notice.

MARLOW. You're used to them.   How's your old man ?

MRS. JONES. [*Softly as throughout*] Well, he was very bad last night ; he didn't seem to know what he was about.   He was very late, and he was most abusive.   But now, of course, he's asleep.

MARLOW. That's his way of finding a job, eh ?

MRS. JONES. As a rule, Mr. Marlow, he goes out early every morning looking for work, and sometimes he comes in fit to drop— and of course I can't say he doesn't try to get it, because he does. Trade's very bad.   [*She stands quite still, her pan and brush before her, at the beginning and the end of long vistas of experience, traversing them with her impersonal eye.*] But he's not a good husband to me—last night he hit me, and he was so dreadfully abusive.

MARLOW. Bank 'oliday, eh! He's too fond of the "Goat and Bells," that's what's the matter with him. I see him at the corner late every night. He hangs about.

MRS. JONES. He gets to feeling very low walking about all day after work, and being refused so often, and then when he gets a drop in him it goes to his head. But he shouldn't treat his wife as he treats me. Sometimes I've had to go and walk about at night, when he wouldn't let me stay in the room; but he's sorry for it afterwards. And he hangs about after me, he waits for me in the street; and I don't think he ought to, because I've always been a good wife to him. And I tell him Mrs. Barthwick wouldn't like him coming about the place. But that only makes him angry, and he says dreadful things about the gentry. Of course it was through me that he first lost his place, through his not treating me right; and that's made him bitter against the gentry. He had a very good place as groom in the country; but it made such a stir, because of course he didn't treat me right.

MARLOW. Got the sack?

MRS. JONES. Yes; his employer said he couldn't keep him, because there was a great deal of talk; and he said it was such a bad example. But it's very important for me to keep my work here; I have the three children, and I don't want him to come about after me in the streets, and make a disturbance as he sometimes does.

MARLOW. [*Holding up the empty decanter*] Not a drain! Next time he hits you get a witness and go down to the court——

MRS. JONES. Yes, I think I've made up my mind. I think I ought to.

MARLOW. That's right. Where's the ciga——?

[*He searches for the silver box; he looks at* MRS. JONES, *who is sweeping on her hands and knees; he checks himself and stands reflecting. From the tray he picks two half-smoked cigarettes, and reads the name of them.*

Nestor—where the deuce——?

[*With a meditative air he looks again at* MRS. JONES, *and, taking up* JACK'S *overcoat, he searches in the pockets.* WHEELER, *with a tray of breakfast things, comes in.*

MARLOW. [*Aside to* WHEELER] Have you seen the cigarette-box?

WHEELER. No.

MARLOW. Well, it's gone. I put it on the tray last night. And he's been smoking [*Showing her the ends of cigarette.*] It's not in these pockets. He can't have taken it upstairs this morning! Have a good look in his room when he comes down. Who's been in here?

WHEELER. Only me and Mrs. Jones.

MRS. JONES. I've finished here; shall I do the drawing-room now?

WHEELER. [*Looking at her doubtfully*] Have you seen—— Better do the boudwower first.

[MRS. JONES *goes out with pan and brush.* MARLOW *and* WHEELER *look each other in the face.*

MARLOW. It'll turn up.

WHEELER. [*Hesitating*] You don't think she—— [*Nodding at the door.*]

MARLOW. [*Stoutly*] I don't—I never believes anything of anybody.

WHEELER. But the master'll have to be told.

MARLOW. You wait a bit, and see if it don't turn up. Suspicion's no business of ours. I set my mind against it.

The curtain falls.

The curtain rises again at once.

SCENE III

BARTHWICK *and* MRS. BARTHWICK *are seated at the breakfast table. He is a man between fifty and sixty; quietly important, with a bald forehead, and pince-nez, and " The Times " in his hand. She is a lady of nearly fifty, well dressed, with greyish hair, good features, and a decided manner. They face each other.*

BARTHWICK. [*From behind his paper*] The Labour man has got in at the by-election for Barnside, my dear.

MRS. BARTHWICK. Another Labour? I can't think what on earth the country is about.

BARTHWICK. I predicted it. It's not a matter of vast importance.

MRS. BARTHWICK. Not? How can you take it so calmly, John? To me it's simply outrageous. And there you sit, you Liberals, and pretend to encourage these people!

BARTHWICK. [*Frowning*] The representation of all parties is necessary for any proper reform, for any proper social policy.

MRS. BARTHWICK. I've no patience with your talk of reform—all that nonsense about social policy. We know perfectly well what it is they want; they want things for themselves. Those Socialists and Labour men are an absolutely selfish set of people. They have no sense of patriotism, like the upper classes, *they simply want what we've got.*

BARTHWICK. Want what we've got! [*He stares into space.*] My dear, what are you talking about? [*With a contortion.*] I'm no alarmist.

MRS. BARTHWICK. Cream! Quite uneducated men! Wait until they begin to tax our investments. I'm convinced that when they once get a chance they will tax everything—they've no feeling for the country. You Liberals and Conservatives, you're all alike; you don't see an inch before your noses. You've no imagination, not a scrap of imagination between you. You ought to join hands and nip it in the bud.

BARTHWICK. You're talking nonsense ! How is it possible for Liberals and Conservatives to join hands, as you call it ? That shows how absurd it is for women—— Why, the very essence of a Liberal is to trust in the people !

MRS. BARTHWICK. Now, John, eat your breakfast. As if there were any real difference between you and the Conservatives. All the upper classes have the same interests to protect, and the same principles. [*Calmly.*] Oh ! you're sitting upon a volcano, John.

BARTHWICK. What !

MRS. BARTHWICK. I read a letter in the paper yesterday. I forget the man's name, but it made the whole thing perfectly clear. You don't look things in the face.

BARTHWICK. Indeed ! [*Heavily.*] I am a Liberal. Drop the subject, please !

MRS. BARTHWICK. Toast ? I quite agree with what this man says : Education is simply ruining the lower classes. It unsettles them, and that's the worst thing for us all. I see an enormous difference in the manner of servants.

BARTHWICK. [*With suspicious emphasis*] I welcome any change that will lead to something better. [*He opens a letter.*] H'm ! This is that affair of Master Jack's again. " High Street, Oxford. Sir, We have received Mr. John Barthwick, Senior's, draft for forty pounds." Oh ! the letter's to him ! " We now enclose the cheque you cashed with us, which, as we stated in our previous letter, was not met on presentation at your bank. We are, Sir, yours obediently, Moss and Sons, Tailors." H'm ! [*Staring at the cheque.*] A pretty business altogether ! The boy might have been prosecuted.

MRS. BARTHWICK. Come, John, you know Jack didn't mean anything ; he only thought he was overdrawing. I still think his bank ought to have cashed that cheque. They must know your position.

BARTHWICK. [*Replacing in the envelope the letter and the cheque*] Much good that would have done him in a court of law. [*He stops as* JACK *comes in, fastening his waistcoat and staunching a razor cut upon his chin.*]

JACK. [*Sitting down between them, and speaking with an artificial joviality*] Sorry I'm late. [*He looks lugubriously at the dishes.*] Tea, please, mother. Any letters for me ? [BARTHWICK *hands the letter to him.*] But look here, I say, this has been opened ! I do wish you wouldn't——

BARTHWICK. [*Touching the envelope*] I suppose I'm entitled to this name.

JACK. [*Sulkily*] Well, I can't help having your name, father ! [*He reads the letter, and mutters.*] Brutes.

BARTHWICK. [*Eyeing him*] You don't deserve to be so well out of that.

JACK. Haven't you ragged me enough, dad?

MRS. BARTHWICK. Yes, John, let Jack have his breakfast.

BARTHWICK. If you hadn't had me to' come to, where would you have been? It's the merest accident—suppose you had been the son of a poor man or a clerk. Obtaining money with a cheque you knew your bank could not meet. It might have ruined you for life. I can't see what's to become of you if these are your principles. I never did anything of the sort myself.

JACK. I expect you always had lots of money. If you've got plenty of money, of course——

BARTHWICK. On the contrary, I had not your advantages. My father kept me very short of money.

JACK. How much had you, dad?

BARTHWICK. It's not material. The question is, do you feel the gravity of what you did?

JACK. I don't know about the gravity. Of course, I'm very sorry if you think it was wrong. Haven't I said so! I should never have done it at all if I hadn't been so jolly hard up.

BARTHWICK. How much of that forty pounds have you got left, Jack?

JACK. [Hesitating] I don't know—not much.

BARTHWICK. How much?

JACK. [Desperately] I haven't got any.

BARTHWICK. What?

JACK. I know I've got the most beastly headache.

[He leans his head on his hand.

MRS. BARTHWICK. Headache? My dear boy! Can't you eat any breakfast?

JACK. [Drawing in his breath] Too jolly bad!

MRS. BARTHWICK. I'm so sorry. Come with me, dear; I'll give you something that will take it away at once.

[They leave the room; and BARTHWICK, tearing up the letter, goes to the fireplace and puts the pieces in the fire. While he is doing this MARLOW comes in, and, looking round him, is about quietly to withdraw.

BARTHWICK. What's that? What d'you want?

MARLOW. I was looking for Mr. John, sir.

BARTHWICK. What d'you want Mr. John for?

MARLOW. [With hesitation] I thought I should find him here, sir.

BARTHWICK. [Suspiciously] Yes, but what do you want him for?

MARLOW. [Offhandedly] There's a lady called—asked to speak to him for a minute, sir.

BARTHWICK. A lady, at this time of the morning. What sort of a lady?

MARLOW. [Without expression in his voice] I can't tell, sir; no particular sort.   She might be after charity.   She might be a Sister of Mercy, I should think, sir.

BARTHWICK.   Is she dressed like one ?

MARLOW.   No, sir, she's in plain clothes, sir.

BARTHWICK.   Didn't she say what she wanted ?

MARLOW.   No, sir.

BARTHWICK.   Where did you leave her ?

MARLOW.   In the hall, sir.

BARTHWICK.   In the hall ?   How do you know she's not a thief— not got designs on the house ?

MARLOW.   No, sir, I don't fancy so, sir.

BARTHWICK.   Well, show her in here ; I'll see her myself.

> [MARLOW *goes out with a private gesture of dismay.   He soon returns, ushering in a young pale lady with dark eyes and pretty figure, in a modish, black, but rather shabby dress, a black and white trimmed hat with a bunch of Parma violets wrongly placed, and fuzzy-spotted veil.   At the sight of* MR. BARTHWICK *she exhibits every sign of nervousness.*   MARLOW *goes out.*

UNKNOWN LADY.   Oh ! but—I beg pardon—there's some mistake —I—— [*She turns to fly.*]

BARTHWICK.   Whom did you want to see, madam ?

UNKNOWN.   [*Stopping and looking back*] It was Mr. *John* Barthwick I wanted to see.

BARTHWICK.   I am John Barthwick, madam.   What can I have the pleasure of doing for you ?

UNKNOWN.   Oh !   I—I don't—— [*She drops her eyes.* BARTHWICK *scrutinizes her, and purses his lips.*]

BARTHWICK.   It was my son, perhaps, you wished to see ?

UNKNOWN.   [*Quickly*] Yes, of course, it's your son.

BARTHWICK.   May I ask whom I have the pleasure of speaking to ?

UNKNOWN.   [*Appeal and hardiness upon her face*] My name is—oh ! it doesn't matter—I don't want to make any fuss.   I just want to see your son for a minute. [*Boldly.*]   In fact, I *must* see him.

BARTHWICK.   [*Controlling his uneasiness*] My son is not very well. If necessary, no doubt I could attend to the matter ; be so kind as to let me know——

UNKNOWN.   Oh ! but I *must* see him—I've come on purpose—— [*She bursts out nervously.*]   I don't want to make any fuss, but the fact is, last—last night your son took away—he took away my——

> [*She stops.*

BARTHWICK.   [*Severely*] Yes, madam, what ?

UNKNOWN.   He took away my—my reticule.

BARTHWICK.   Your reti——— ? "

UNKNOWN.   I don't care about the reticule   it's not *that* I want

—I'm sure I don't want to make any fuss—[*her face is quivering*]—but —but—all my money was in it !

BARTHWICK. In what—in what ?

UNKNOWN. In my purse, in the reticule. It was a crimson silk purse. Really, I wouldn't have come—I don't want to make any fuss. But I must get my money back—mustn't I ?

BARTHWICK. Do you tell me that my son——?

UNKNOWN. Oh ! well you see, he wasn't quite—I mean he was——
[*She smiles mesmerically.*

BARTHWICK. I beg your pardon.

UNKNOWN. [*Stamping her foot*] Oh ! don't you see—tipsy ! We had a quarrel.

BARTHWICK. [*Scandalized*] How ? Where ?

UNKNOWN. [*Defiantly*] At my place. We'd had supper at the—— and your son——

BARTHWICK. [*Pressing the bell*] May I ask how you knew this house ? Did he give you his name and address ?

UNKNOWN. [*Glancing sidelong*] I got it out of his overcoat.

BARTHWICK. [*Sardonically*] Oh ! you got it out of his overcoat. And may I ask if my son will know you by daylight ?

UNKNOWN. Know me ? I should jolly—I mean, of course he will !
[MARLOW *comes in.*

BARTHWICK. Ask Mr. John to come down.
[MARLOW *goes out, and* BARTHWICK *walks uneasily about.*
And how long have you enjoyed his acquaintanceship ?

UNKNOWN. Only since—only since Good Friday.

BARTHWICK. I am at a loss—I repeat I am at a loss——
[*He glances at this unknown lady, who stands with eyes cast down, twisting her hands. And suddenly* JACK *appears. He stops on seeing who is here, and the unknown lady hysterically giggles. There is a silence.*

BARTHWICK. [*Portentously*] This young—er—lady says that last night—I think you said last night, madam—you took away——

UNKNOWN. [*Impulsively*] My reticule, and all my money was in a crimson silk purse.

JACK. Reticule. [*Looking round for any chance to get away.*] I don't know anything about it.

BARTHWICK. [*Sharply*] Come, do you deny seeing this young lady last night ?

JACK. Deny ? No, of course. [*Whispering.*] Why did you give me away like this ? What on earth did you come here for ?

UNKNOWN. [*Tearfully*] I'm sure I didn't want to—it's not likely, is it ? You snatched it out of my hand—you know you did—and the purse had all my money in it. I didn't follow you last night because I didn't want to make a fuss and it was so late, and you were so——

BARTHWICK. Come, sir, don't turn your back on me—explain!

JACK. [*Desperately*] I don't remember anything about it. [*In a low voice to his friend.*] Why on earth couldn't you have written?

UNKNOWN. [*Sullenly*] I want it now; I must have it—I've got to pay my rent to-day. [*She looks at* BARTHWICK.] They're only too glad to jump on people who are not—not *well off*.

JACK. I don't remember anything about it, really I don't remember anything about last night at all. [*He puts his hand up to his head.*] It's all—cloudy, and I've got such a beastly headache.

UNKNOWN. But you *took* it; you know you did. You said you'd score me off.

JACK. Well, then, it must be here. I remember now—I remember something. Why did I take the beastly thing?

BARTHWICK. Yes, why did you take the beastly——

[*He turns abruptly to the window.*

UNKNOWN. [*With her mesmeric smile*] You weren't quite——were you?

JACK. [*Smiling pallidly*] I'm *awfully* sorry. If there's anything I can do——

BARTHWICK. Do? You can restore this property, I suppose.

JACK. I'll go and have a look, but I really don't think I've got it.

[*He goes out hurriedly. And* BARTHWICK, *placing a chair, motions to the visitor to sit; then, with pursed lips, he stands and eyes her fixedly. She sits, and steals a look at him; then turns away, and, drawing up her veil, stealthily wipes her eyes. And* JACK *comes back.*

JACK. [*Ruefully holding out the empty reticule*] Is that the thing? I've looked all over—I can't find the purse anywhere. Are you sure it was there?

UNKNOWN. [*Tearfully*] Sure? Of course I'm sure. A crimson silk purse. It was all the money I had.

JACK. I really am awfully sorry—my head's so jolly bad. I've asked the butler, but he hasn't seen it.

UNKNOWN. I *must* have my money——

JACK. Oh! Of course—that'll be all right; I'll see that that's all right. How much?

UNKNOWN. [*Sullenly*] Seven pounds—twelve—it's all I've got in the world.

JACK. That'll be all right; I'll—send you a—cheque.

UNKNOWN. [*Eagerly*] No; now, please. Give me what was in my purse; I've got to pay my rent this morning. They won't give me another day; I'm a fortnight behind already.

JACK. [*Blankly*] I'm awfully sorry; I really haven't a penny in my pocket.

[*He glances stealthily at* BARTHWICK.

UNKNOWN. [*Excitedly*] Come, I say you must—it's my money, and you took it. I'm not going away without it. They'll turn me out of my place.

JACK. [*Clasping his head*] But I can't give you what I haven't got. Don't I tell you I haven't a beastly penny?

UNKNOWN. [*Tearing at her handkerchief*] Oh! do give it me! [*She puts her hands together in appeal; then, with sudden fierceness.*] If you don't I'll summons you. It's stealing, that's what it is!

BARTHWICK. [*Uneasily*] One moment, please. As a matter of—er —principle, I shall settle this claim. [*He produces money.*] Here is eight pounds; the extra will cover the value of the purse and your cab fares. I need make no comment—no thanks are necessary.

> [*Touching the bell, he holds the door ajar in silence. The unknown lady stores the money in her reticule, she looks from* JACK *to* BARTHWICK, *and her face is quivering faintly with a smile. She hides it with her hand, and steals away. Behind her* BARTHWICK *shuts the door.*

BARTHWICK. [*With solemnity*] H'm! This is a nice thing to happen!

JACK. [*Impersonally*] What awful luck!

BARTHWICK. So this is the way that forty pounds has gone! One thing after another! Once more I should like to know where you'd have been if it hadn't been for me! You don't seem to have any principles. You—you're one of those who are a nuisance to society; you—you're dangerous! What your mother would say I don't know. Your conduct, as far as I can see, is absolutely unjustifiable. It's—it's criminal. Why, a poor man who behaved as you've done . . . d'you think he'd have any mercy shown him? What you want is a good lesson. You and your sort are—[*he speaks with feeling*]— a nuisance to the community. Don't ask me to help you next time. You're not fit to be helped.

JACK. [*Turning upon his sire, with unexpected fierceness*] All right, I won't then, and see how you like it. You wouldn't have helped me this time, I know, if you hadn't been scared the thing would get into the papers. Where are the cigarettes?

BARTHWICK. [*Regarding him uneasily*] Well—I'll say no more about it. [*He rings the bell.*] I'll pass it over for this once, but——

[MARLOW *comes in.*

You can clear away.   [*He hides his face behind "The Times."*

JACK. [*Brightening*] I say, Marlow, where are the cigarettes?

MARLOW. I put the box out with the whisky last night, sir, but this morning I can't find it anywhere.

JACK. Did you look in my room?

MARLOW. Yes, sir; I've looked all over the house. I found two Nestor ends in the tray this morning, so you must have been smokin' last night, sir. [*Hesitating.*] I'm really afraid some one's purloined the box.

JACK. [*Uneasily*] Stolen it!

BARTHWICK. What's that? The cigarette-box! Is anything else missing?

MARLOW. No, sir; I've been through the plate.

BARTHWICK. Was the house all right this morning? None of the windows open?

MARLOW. No, sir. [*Quietly to* JACK.] You left your latchkey in the door last night, sir.   [*He hands it back, unseen by* BARTHWICK.

JACK. Tst!

BARTHWICK. Who's been in the room this morning?

MARLOW. Me and Wheeler, and Mrs. Jones is all, sir, as far as I know.

BARTHWICK. Have you asked Mrs. Barthwick? [*To* JACK.] Go and ask your mother if she's had it; ask her to look and see if she's missed anything else.   [JACK *goes upon his mission.*] Nothing is more disquieting than losing things like this.

MARLOW. No, sir.

BARTHWICK. Have you any suspicions?

MARLOW. No, sir.

BARTHWICK. This Mrs. Jones—how long has she been working here?

MARLOW. Only this last month, sir.

BARTHWICK. What sort of person?

MARLOW. I don't know much about her, sir; seems a very quiet respectable woman.

BARTHWICK. Who did the room this morning?

MARLOW. Wheeler and Mrs. Jones, sir.

BARTHWICK. [*With his forefinger upraised*] Now, was this Mrs. Jones in the room alone at any time?

MARLOW. [*Expressionless*] Yes, sir.

BARTHWICK. How do you know that?

MARLOW. [*Reluctantly*] I found her here, sir.

BARTHWICK. And has Wheeler been in the room alone?

MARLOW. No, sir, she's not, sir. I should say, sir, that Mrs. Jones seems a very honest——

BARTHWICK. [*Holding up his hand*] I want to know this: Has this Mrs. Jones been here the whole morning?

MARLOW. Yes, sir—no, sir—she stepped over to the greengrocer's for cook.

BARTHWICK. H'm! Is she in the house now?

MARLOW. Yes, sir.

BARTHWICK. Very good. I shall make a point of clearing this up. On principle I shall make a point of fixing the responsibility; it goes to the foundations of security. In all your interests——

MARLOW. Yes, sir.

BARTHWICK. What sort of circumstances is this Mrs. Jones in? Is her husband in work?

MARLOW. I believe not, sir.

BARTHWICK. Very well. Say nothing about it to anyone. Tell Wheeler not to speak of it, and ask Mrs. Jones to step up here.

MARLOW. Very good, sir.

[MARLOW *goes out, his face concerned; and* BARTHWICK *stays, his face judicial and a little pleased, as befits a man conducting an inquiry.* MRS. BARTHWICK *and her son come in.*

BARTHWICK. Well, my dear, you've not seen it, I suppose?

MRS. BARTHWICK. No. But what an extraordinary thing, John! Marlow, of course, is out of the question. I'm certain none of the maids—— As for cook!

BARTHWICK. Oh, cook!

MRS. BARTHWICK. Of course! It's perfectly detestable to me to suspect anybody.

BARTHWICK. It is not a question of one's feelings. It's a question of justice. On principle——

MRS. BARTHWICK. I shouldn't be a bit surprised if the charwoman knew something about it. It was Laura who recommended her.

BARTHWICK. [*Judicially*] I am going to have Mrs. Jones up. Leave it to me; and—er—remember that nobody is guilty until they're proved so. I shall be careful. I have no intention of frightening her; I shall give her every chance. I hear she's in poor circumstances. If we are not able to do much for them we are bound to have the greatest sympathy with the poor.   [MRS. JONES *comes in.* [*Pleasantly.*] Oh! good morning, Mrs. Jones.

MRS. JONES. [*Soft, and even, unemphatic*] Good morning, sir! Good morning, ma'am!

BARTHWICK. About your husband—he's not in work, I hear?

MRS. JONES. No, sir; of course he's not in work just now.

BARTHWICK. Then I suppose he's earning nothing.

MRS. JONES. No, sir, he's not earning anything just now, sir.

BARTHWICK. And how many children have you?

MRS. JONES. Three children; but of course they don't eat very much, sir.   [*A little silence.*

BARTHWICK. And how old is the eldest?

MRS. JONES. Nine years old, sir.

BARTHWICK. Do they go to school?

MRS. JONES. Yes, sir, they all three go to school every day.

BARTHWICK. [*Severely*] And what about their food when you're out at work.

MRS. JONES. Well, sir, I have to give them their dinner to take with them. Of course I'm not always able to give them anything; some-times I have to send them without; but my husband is very good about the children when he's in work. But when he's not in work of course he's a very difficult man.

BARTHWICK. He drinks, I suppose?

MRS. JONES. Yes, sir. Of course I can't say he doesn't drink, because he does.

BARTHWICK. And I suppose he takes all your money?

MRS. JONES. No, sir, he's very good about my money, except when he's not himself, and then, of course, he treats me very badly.

BARTHWICK. Now what is he—your husband?

MRS. JONES. By profession, sir, of course he's a groom.

BARTHWICK. A groom! How came he to lose his place?

MRS. JONES. He lost his place a long time ago, sir, and he's never had a very long job since; and now, of course, the motor-cars are against him.

BARTHWICK. When were you married to him, Mrs. Jones?

MRS. JONES. Eight years ago, sir—that was in——

MRS. BARTHWICK. [*Sharply*] Eight? You said the eldest child was nine.

MRS. JONES. Yes, ma'am; of course that was why he lost his place. He didn't treat me rightly, and of course his employer said he couldn't keep him because of the example.

BARTHWICK. You mean he—ahem——

MRS. JONES. Yes, sir; and of course after he lost his place he married me.

MRS. BARTHWICK. You actually mean to say you—you were——

BARTHWICK. My dear——

MRS. BARTHWICK. [*Indignantly*] How disgraceful!

BARTHWICK. [*Hurriedly*] And where are you living now, Mrs. Jones?

MRS. JONES. We've not got a home, sir. Of course we've been obliged to put away most of our things.

BARTHWICK. Put your things away! You mean to—to—er—to pawn them?

MRS. JONES. Yes, sir, to put them away. We're living in Merthyr Street—that is close by here, sir—at No. 34. We just have the one room.

BARTHWICK. And what do you pay a week?

MRS. JONES. We pay six shillings a week, sir, for a furnished room.

BARTHWICK. And I suppose you're behind in the rent?

MRS. JONES. Yes, sir, we're a little behind in the rent.

BARTHWICK. But *you're* in good work, aren't you?

MRS. JONES. Well, sir, I have a day in Stamford Place Thursdays. And Mondays and Wednesdays and Fridays I come here. But to-day, of course, is a half-day, because of yesterday's Bank Holiday.

BARTHWICK. I see; four days a week, and you get half a crown a day, is that it?

MRS. JONES. Yes, sir, and my dinner; but sometimes it's only half a day, and that's eighteenpence.

BARTHWICK. And when your husband earns anything he spends it in drink, I suppose?

MRS. JONES. Sometimes he does, sir, and sometimes he gives it to me for the children. Of course he would work if he could get it, sir, but it seems there are a great many people out of work.

BARTHWICK. Ah! Yes. We—er—won't go into that. [*Sympathetically.*] And how about your work here? Do you find it hard?

MRS. JONES. Oh! no, sir, not very hard, sir; except, of course, when I don't get my sleep at night.

BARTHWICK. Ah! And you help do all the rooms? And sometimes, I suppose, you go out for cook?

MRS. JONES. Yes, sir.

BARTHWICK. And you've been out this morning?

MRS. JONES. Yes, sir, of course I had to go to the greengrocer's.

BARTHWICK. Exactly. So your husband earns nothing? And he's a bad character.

MRS. JONES. No, sir, I don't say that, sir. I think there's a great deal of good in him; though he does treat me very bad sometimes. And of course I don't like to leave him, but I think I ought to, because really I hardly know how to stay with him. He often raises his hand to me. Not long ago he gave me a blow here [*touches her breast*] and I can feel it now. So I think I ought to leave him, don't *you*, sir?

BARTHWICK. Ah! I can't help you there. It's a very serious thing to leave your husband. Very serious thing.

MRS. JONES. Yes, sir, of course I'm afraid of what he might do to me if I were to leave him; he can be so very violent.

BARTHWICK. H'm! Well, that I can't pretend to say anything about. It's the bad principle I'm speaking of——

MRS. JONES. Yes, sir; I know nobody can help me. I know I must decide for myself, and of course I know that he has a very hard life. And he's fond of the children, and it's very hard for him to see them going without food.

BARTHWICK. [*Hastily*] Well—er—thank you, I just wanted to hear about you. I don't think I need detain you any longer, Mrs.—Jones.

MRS. JONES. No, sir, thank you, sir.

BARTHWICK. Good morning, then.

MRS. JONES. Good morning, sir; good morning, ma'am.

BARTHWICK. [*Exchanging glances with his wife*] By the way, Mrs. Jones—I think it is only fair to tell you, a silver cigarette-box—er—is missing.

MRS. JONES. [*Looking from one face to the other*] I am very sorry, sir.

BARTHWICK. Yes ; you have not seen it, I suppose ?

MRS. JONES. [*Realizing that suspicion is upon her ; with an uneasy movement*] Where was it, sir ; if you please, sir ?

BARTHWICK. [*Evasively*] Where did Marlow say ? Er—in this room, yes, in *this* room.

MRS. JONES. No, sir, I haven't seen it—of course if I'd seen it I should have noticed it.

BARTHWICK. [*Giving her a rapid glance*] You—you are sure of that ?

MRS. JONES. [*Impassively*] Yes, sir. [*With a slow nodding of her head.*] I have not seen it, and of course I *don't* know where it is.

[*She turns and goes quietly out.*

BARTHWICK. H'm !

[*The three* BARTHWICKS *avoid each other's glances*

The curtain falls.

ACT II

SCENE I

The JONES' *lodgings, Merthyr Street, at half-past two o'clock.*
The bare room, with tattered oilcloth and damp, distempered walls, has an air of tidy wretchedness. On the bed lies JONES, *half-dressed; his coat is thrown across his feet, and muddy boots are lying on the floor close by. He is asleep. The door is opened and* MRS. JONES *comes in, dressed in a pinched black jacket and old black sailor hat; she carries a parcel wrapped up in "The Times." She puts her parcel down, unwraps an apron, half a loaf, two onions, three potatoes, and a tiny piece of bacon. Taking a teapot from the cupboard, she rinses it, shakes into it some powdered tea out of a screw of paper, puts it on the hearth, and sitting in a wooden chair quietly begins to cry.*

JONES. [*Stirring and yawning*] That you? What's the time?

MRS. JONES. [*Drying her eyes, and in her usual voice*] Half-past two.

JONES. What you back so soon for?

MRS. JONES. I only had the half-day to-day, Jem.

JONES. [*On his back, and in a drowsy voice*] Got anything for dinner?

MRS. JONES. Mrs. Barthwick's cook gave me a little bit of bacon. I'm going to make a stew. [*She prepares for cooking.*] There's fourteen shillings owing for rent, James, and of course I've only got two and fourpence. They'll be coming for it to-day.

JONES. [*Turning towards her on his elbow*] Let 'em come and find my surprise packet. I've had enough o' this tryin' for work. Why should I go round and round after a job like a bloomin' squirrel in a cage. "Give us a job, sir"—"Take a man on"—"Got a wife and three children." Sick of it I am! I'd sooner lie here and rot. "Jones, you come and join the demonstration; come and 'old a flag, and listen to the ruddy orators, and go 'ome as empty as you came." There's some that seems to like *that*—the sheep! When I go seekin' for a job now, and see the brutes lookin' me up an' down, it's like a thousand serpents in me. I'm not arskin' for any treat. A man wants to sweat hisself silly and not allowed—that's a rum start, ain't it? A man wants to sweat his soul out to keep the breath in him and ain't allowed—that's justice—that's freedom and all the rest of it. [*He turns his face towards the wall.*] You're so milky mild; you don't know what goes on inside o' me. I'm done with the silly game. If they want me, let 'em come for me!

[MRS. JONES *stops cooking and stands unmoving at the table.*]

20

I've tried and done with it, I tell you. I've never been afraid of what's before *me*. You mark my words—if you think they've broke my spirit, you're mistook. I'll lie and rot sooner than arsk 'em again. What makes you stand like that—you long-sufferin', Gawd-forsaken image—that's why I can't keep my hands off you. So now you know. Work! You can work, but you haven't the spirit of a louse!

MRS. JONES. [*Quietly*] You talk more wild sometimes when you're yourself, James, than when you're not. If you don't get work, how are we to go on? They won't let us stay here; they're looking to their money to-day, I know.

JONES. I see this Barthwick o' yours every day goin' down to Pawlyment snug and comfortable to talk his silly soul out; an' I see that young calf, his son, swellin' it about, and goin' on the razzle-dazzle. Wot 'ave they done that makes 'em any better than wot I am? They never did a day's work in their lives. I see 'em day after day——

MRS. JONES. And I wish you wouldn't come after me like that, and hang about the house. You don't seem able to keep away at all, and whatever you do it for I can't think, because of course they notice it.

JONES. I suppose I may go where I like. Where *may* I go? The other day I went to a place in the Edgware Road. " Guv'nor," I says to the boss, " take me on," I says. " I 'aven't done a stroke o' work not these two months; it takes the heart out of a man," I says; " I'm one to work; I'm not afraid of anything you can give me! " " My good man," 'e says, " I've had thirty of you here this morning. I took the first two," he says, " and that's all I want." " Thank you, then rot the world! " I says. " Blasphemin'," he says, " is not the way to get a job. Out you go, my lad! " [*He laughs sardonically.*] Don't you raise your voice because you're starvin'; don't yer even think of it; take it lyin' down! Take it like a sensible man, carn't you? And a little way down the street a lady says to me: [*Pinching his voice.*] " D'you want to earn a few pence, my man? " and gives me her dog to 'old outside a shop—fat as a butler 'e was —tons o' meat had gone to the makin' of *him*. It did 'er good, it did, made 'er feel 'erself that *charitable*, but I see 'er lookin' at the copper standin' alongside o' me, for fear I should make off with 'er bloomin' fat dog. [*He sits on the edge of the bed and puts a boot on. Then looking up.*] What's in that head o' yours? [*Almost pathetically.*] Carn't you speak for once?

[*There is a knock, and* MRS. SEDDON, *the landlady, appears, an anxious, harassed, shabby woman in working clothes.*]

MRS. SEDDON. I thought I 'eard you come in, Mrs. Jones. I've spoke to my 'usband, but he says he really can't afford to wait another day.

JONES. [*With scowling jocularity*] Never you mind what your 'usband says, you go your own way like a proper independent woman. Here, Jenny, chuck her that.

> [*Producing a sovereign from his trousers pocket, he throws it to his wife, who catches it in her apron with a gasp.* JONES *resumes the lacing of his boots.*

MRS. JONES. [*Rubbing the sovereign stealthily*] I'm very sorry we're so late with it, and of course it's fourteen shillings, so if you've got six that will be right.

> [MRS. SEDDON *takes the sovereign and fumbles for the change.*

JONES. [*With his eyes fixed on his boots*] Bit of a surprise for yer, ain't it?

MRS. SEDDON. Thank you, and I'm sure I'm very much obliged. [*She does indeed appear surprised.*] I'll bring you the change.

JONES. [*Mockingly*] Don't mention it.

MRS. SEDDON. Thank you, and I'm sure I'm very much obliged.
> [*She slides away.*

> [MRS. JONES *gazes at* JONES, *who is still lacing up his boots.*

JONES. I've had a bit of luck. [*Pulling out the crimson purse and some loose coins.*] Picked up a purse—seven pound and more.

MRS. JONES. Oh, James!

JONES. Oh, James! What about Oh, James! I picked it up I tell you. This is lost property, this is!

MRS. JONES. But isn't there a name in it, or something?

JONES. Name? No, there ain't no name. This don't belong to such as 'ave visitin' cards. This belongs to a perfec' lidy. Tike an' smell it. [*He pitches her the purse, which she puts gently to her nose.*] Now, you tell me what I ought to have done. You tell me that. You can always tell me what I ought to ha' done, can't yer?

MRS. JONES. [*Laying down the purse*] I can't say what you ought to have done, James. Of course the money wasn't yours; you've taken somebody else's money.

JONES. Finding's keeping. I'll take it as wages for the time I've gone about the streets asking for what's my rights. I'll take it for what's *overdue*, d'ye hear? [*With strange triumph.*] I've got money in my pocket, my girl.

> [MRS. JONES *goes on again with the preparation of the meal,* JONES *looking at her furtively.*]

Money in my pocket! And I'm not goin' to waste it. With this 'ere money I'm goin' to Canada. I'll let you have a pound. [*A silence.*] You've often talked of leavin' me. You've often told me I treat you badly—well, I 'ope you'll be glad when I'm gone.

MRS. JONES. [*Impassively*] You *have* treated me very badly, James, and of course I can't prevent your going; but I can't tell whether I shall be glad when you're gone.

JONES. It'll change my luck. I've 'ad nothing but bad luck since I first took up with you. [*More softly.*] And you've 'ad no bloomin' picnic.

MRS. JONES. Of course it would have been better for us if we had never met. We weren't meant for each other. But you're set against me, that's what you are, and you *have* been for a long time. And you treat me so badly, James, going after that Rosie and all. You don't ever seem to think of the children that I've had to bring into the world, and of all the trouble I've had to keep them, and what'll become of them when you're gone.

JONES. [*Crossing the room gloomily*] If you think I want to leave the little beggars you're bloomin' well mistaken.

MRS. JONES. Of course I know you're fond of them.

JONES. [*Fingering the purse, half angrily*] Well, then, you stow it, old girl. The kids'll get along better with you than when I'm here. If I'd ha' known as much as I do now, I'd never ha' had one o' them. What's the use o' bringin' 'em into a state o' things like this ? It's a crime, that's what it is ; but you find it out too late ; that's what's the matter with this 'ere world.

[*He puts the purse back in his pocket.*

MRS. JONES. Of course it would have been better for them, poor little things ; but they're your own children, and I wonder at you talkin' like that. I should miss them dreadfully if I was to lose them.

JONES. [*Sullenly*] An' you ain't the only one. If I make money out there—— [*Looking up, he sees her shaking out his coat—in a changed voice.*] Leave that coat alone !

[*The silver box drops from the pocket, scattering the cigarettes upon the bed. Taking up the box, she stares at it ; he rushes at her and snatches the box away.*

MRS. JONES. [*Cowering back against the bed*] Oh, Jem ! oh, Jem !

JONES. [*Dropping the box on to the table*] You mind what you're sayin' ! When I go out I'll take and chuck it in the water along with that there purse. I 'ad it when I was in liquor, and for what you do when you're in liquor you're not responsible—and that's Gawd's truth as you ought to know. I don't want the thing—I won't have it. I took it out o' spite. I'm no thief, I tell you ; and don't you call me one, or it'll be the worse for you.

MRS. JONES. [*Twisting her apron strings*] It's Mr. Barthwick's ! You've taken away my reputation. Oh, Jem, whatever made you ?

JONES. What d'you mean ?

MRS. JONES. It's been missed ; they think it's me. Oh ! whatever made you do it, Jem ?

JONES. I tell you I was in liquor. I don't want it ; what's the good of it to me ? If I were to pawn it they'd only nab me. I'm no thief. I'm no worse than wot that young Barthwick is ; he brought 'ome that

purse that I picked up—a lady's purse—'ad it off 'er in a row, kept
sayin' 'e'd scored 'er off. Well, I scored 'im off. Tight as an owl 'e
was ! And d'you think anything'll happen to him ?

MRS. JONES. [*As though speaking to herself*] Oh, Jem ! it's the bread
out of our mouths !

JONES. Is it then ? I'll make it hot for 'em yet. What about that
purse ? What about young Barthwick ?

[MRS. JONES *comes forward to the table and tries to take the box ;*
JONES *prevents her.*

What do you want with that ? You drop it, I say !

MRS. JONES. I'll take it back and tell them all about it.

[*She attempts to wrest the box from him.*

JONES. Ah, would yer ?

[*He drops the box, and rushes on her with a snarl. She slips back*
past the bed. He follows ; a chair is overturned. The door
is opened ; SNOW *comes in, a detective in plain clothes and*
bowler hat, with clipped moustaches. JONES *drops his arms,*
MRS. JONES *stands by the window gasping ;* SNOW, *advancing*
swiftly to the table, puts his hand on the silver box.

SNOW. Doin' a bit o' skylarkin' ? Fancy this is what I'm after.
J.B., the very same. [*He gets back to the door, scrutinizing the crest and*
cypher on the box. To MRS. JONES.] I'm a police officer. Are you
Mrs. Jones ?

MRS. JONES. Yes, sir.

SNOW. My instructions are to take you on a charge of stealing this
box from J. Barthwick, Esquire, M.P., of 6, Rockingham Gate.
Anything you say may be used against you. Well, missis ?

MRS. JONES. [*In her quiet voice, still out of breath, her hand upon her*
breast] Of course I did *not* take it, sir. I never have taken anything
that didn't belong to me ; and of course I know nothing about it.

SNOW. You were at the house this morning ; you did the room in
which the box was left ; you were alone in the room. I find the box
'ere. You say you didn't take it ?

MRS. JONES. Yes, sir, of course I say I did not take it, because I
did *not*.

SNOW. Then how does the box come to be here ?

MRS. JONES. I would rather not say anything about it.

SNOW. Is this your husband ?

MRS. JONES. Yes, sir, this is my husband, sir.

SNOW. Do you wish to say anything before I take her ?

[JONES *remains silent, with his head bent down.*]

Well then, Missis, I'll just trouble you to come along with me
quietly.

MRS. JONES. [*Twisting her hands*] Of course I wouldn't say I hadn't
taken it if I had—and I *didn't* take it, indeed I didn't. Of course I

know appearances are against me, and I can't tell you what really happened. But my children are at school, and they'll be coming home—and I don't know what they'll do without me !

Snow. Your 'usband'll see to them, don't you worry.

[*He takes the woman gently by the arm.*

Jones. You drop it—she's all right ! [*Sullenly.*] I took the thing myself.

Snow. [*Eyeing him*] There, there, it does you credit. Come along, Missis.

Jones. [*Passionately*] Drop it, I say, you blooming teck. She's my wife ; she's a respectable woman. Take her if you dare !

Snow. Now, now. What's the good of this ? Keep a civil tongue, and it'll be the better for all of us.

[*He puts his whistle in his mouth and draws the woman to the door.*

Jones. [*With a rush*] Drop her, and put up your 'ands, or I'll soon make yer. You leave her alone, will yer ! Don't I tell yer, I took the thing myself !

Snow. [*Blowing his whistle*] Drop your hands, or I'll take you too. Ah, would you ?

[Jones, *closing, deals him a blow. A Policeman in uniform appears ; there is a short struggle and* Jones *is overpowered.* Mrs. Jones *raises her hands and drops her face on them.*

The curtain falls.

SCENE II

The Barthwicks' *dining-room the same evening. The* Barthwicks *are seated at dessert.*

Mrs. Barthwick. John ! [*A silence broken by the cracking of nuts.*] John !

Barthwick. I wish you'd speak about the nuts—they're uneatable.

[*He puts one in his mouth.*

Mrs. Barthwick. It's not the season for them. I called on the Holyroods. [Barthwick *fills his glass with port.*

Jack. Crackers, please, dad.

[Barthwick *passes the crackers. His demeanour is reflective.*

Mrs. Barthwick. Lady Holyrood has got very stout. I've noticed it coming for a long time.

Barthwick. [*Gloomily*] Stout ? [*He takes up the crackers—with transparent airiness.*] The Holyroods had some trouble with their servants, hadn't they ?

Jack. Crackers, please, dad.

Barthwick. [*Passing the crackers*] It got into the papers. The cook, wasn't it ?

2

Mrs. Barthwick. No, the lady's-maid. I was talking it over with Lady Holyrood. The girl used to have her young man to see her.

Barthwick. [*Uneasily*] I'm not sure they were wise——

Mrs. Barthwick. My dear John, what are you talking about? How could there be any alternative? Think of the effect on the other servants!

Barthwick. Of course in principle—I wasn't thinking of that.

Jack. [*Maliciously*] Crackers, please, dad.

[Barthwick *is compelled to pass the crackers.*

Mrs. Barthwick. Lady Holyrood told me: "I had her up," she said; "I said to her, 'You'll leave my house at once; I think your conduct disgraceful. I can't tell, I don't know, and I don't wish to know, what you were doing. I send you away on principle; you need not come to me for a character.' And the girl said: 'If you don't give me my notice, my lady, I want a month's wages. I'm perfectly respectable. I've done nothing.' "—Done nothing!

Barthwick. H'm!

Mrs. Barthwick. Servants have too much licence. They hang together so terribly you never can tell what they're really thinking; it's as if they were all in a conspiracy to keep you in the dark. Even with Marlow, you feel that he never lets you know what's really in his mind. I hate that secretiveness; it destroys all confidence. I feel sometimes I should like to shake him.

Jack. Marlow's a most decent chap. It's simply beastly every one knowing your affairs.

Barthwick. The less you say about that the better!

Mrs. Barthwick. It goes all through the lower classes. You can *not* tell when they are speaking the truth. To-day when I was shopping after leaving the Holyroods, one of these unemployed came up and spoke to me. I suppose I only had twenty yards or so to walk to the carriage, but he seemed to spring up in the street.

Barthwick. Ah! You must be very careful whom you speak to in these days.

Mrs. Barthwick. I didn't answer him, of course. But I could see at once that he wasn't telling the truth.

Barthwick. [*Cracking a nut*] There's one very good rule—look at their eyes.

Jack. Crackers, please, dad.

Barthwick. [*Passing the crackers*] If their eyes are straightforward I sometimes give them sixpence. It's against my principles, but it's most difficult to refuse. If you see that they're desperate, and dull, and shifty-looking, as so many of them are, it's certain to mean drink, or crime, or something unsatisfactory.

Mrs. Barthwick. This man had dreadful eyes. He looked as if

he could commit a murder. " I've 'ad nothing to eat to-day," he said. Just like that.

BARTHWICK. What was William about ? He ought to have been waiting.

JACK. [*Raising his wineglass to his nose*] Is this the '63, Dad ?

[BARTHWICK, *holding his wineglass to his eye, lowers it and passes it before his nose.*

MRS. BARTHWICK. I hate people that can't speak the truth. [*Father and son exchange a look behind their port.*] It's just as easy to speak the truth as not. I've always found it easy enough. It makes it impossible to tell what is genuine ; one feels as if one were continually being taken in.

BARTHWICK. [*Sententiously*] The lower classes are their own enemies. If they would only trust us, they would get on so much better.

MRS. BARTHWICK. But even then it's so often their own fault. Look at that Mrs. Jones this morning.

BARTHWICK. I only want to do what's right in that matter. I had occasion to see Roper this afternoon. I mentioned it to him. He's coming in this evening. It all depends on what the detective says. I've had my doubts. I've been thinking it over.

MRS. BARTHWICK. The woman impressed me most unfavourably. She seemed to have no shame. That affair she was talking about— she and the man when they were young, so immoral ! And before you and Jack ! I could have put her out of the room !

BARTHWICK. Oh ! I don't want to excuse them, but in looking at these matters one must consider——

MRS. BARTHWICK. Perhaps you'll say the man's employer was wrong in dismissing him ?

BARTHWICK. Of course not. It's not there that I feel doubt. What I ask myself is——

JACK. Port, please, Dad.

BARTHWICK. [*Circulating the decanter in religious imitation of the rising and setting of the sun*] I ask myself whether we are sufficiently careful in making inquiries about people before we engage them, especially as regards moral conduct.

JACK. Pass the port, please, Mother !

MRS. BARTHWICK. [*Passing it*] My dear boy, aren't you drinking too much ?   [JACK *fills his glass.*

MARLOW. [*Entering*] Detective Snow to see you, sir.

BARTHWICK. [*Uneasily*] Ah ! say I'll be with him in a minute.

MRS. BARTHWICK. [*Without turning*] Let him come in here, Marlow.

[SNOW *enters in an overcoat, his bowler hat in hand.*

BARTHWICK. [*Half rising*] Oh ! Good evening !

SNOW. Good evening, sir ; good evening, ma'am. I've called round to report what I've done, rather late, I'm afraid—another case took me away. [*He takes the silver box out of his pocket, causing a sensation in the* BARTHWICK *family*.] This is the identical article, I believe.

BARTHWICK. Certainly, certainly.

SNOW. Havin' your crest and cypher, as you described to me, sir, I'd no hesitation in the matter.

BARTHWICK. Excellent. Will you have a glass of—[*he glances at the waning port*]—er—sherry? [*Pours out sherry.*] Jack, just give Mr. Snow this.

[JACK *rises and gives the glass to* SNOW ; *then, lolling in his chair, regards him indolently.*

SNOW. [*Drinking off wine and putting down the glass*] After seeing you I went round to this woman's lodgings, sir. It's a low neighbourhood, and I thought it as well to place a constable below—and not without 'e was wanted, as things turned out.

BARTHWICK. Indeed !

SNOW. Yes, sir, I 'ad some trouble. I asked her to account for the presence of the article. She could give me no answer, except to deny the theft ; so I took her into custody ; then her husband came for me, so I was obliged to take him, too, for assault. He was very violent on the way to the station—very violent—threatened you and your son, and altogether he was a handful, I can tell you.

MRS. BARTHWICK. What a ruffian he must be !

SNOW. Yes, ma'am, a rough customer.

JACK. [*Sipping his wine, bemused*] Punch the beggar's head.

SNOW. Given to drink, as I understand, sir.

MRS. BARTHWICK. It's to be hoped he will get a severe punishment.

SNOW. The odd thing is, sir, that he persists in sayin' he took the box himself.

BARTHWICK. Took the box himself ! [*He smiles.*] What does he think to gain by that ?

SNOW. He says the young gentleman was intoxicated last night— [JACK *stops the cracking of a nut, and looks at* SNOW. BARTHWICK, *losing his smile, has put his wineglass down ; there is a silence*—SNOW, *looking from face to face, remarks*]—took him into the house and gave him whisky ; and under the influence of an empty stomach the man says he took the box.

MRS. BARTHWICK. The impudent wretch !

BARTHWICK. D'you mean that he—er—intends to put this forward to-morrow——

SNOW. That'll be his line, sir ; but whether he's endeavouring to shield his wife, or whether [*he looks at* JACK] there's something in it, will be for the magistrate to say.

MRS. BARTHWICK. [*Haughtily*] Something in what? I don't understand you. As if my son would bring a man like that into the house !

BARTHWICK. [*From the fireplace, with an effort to be calm*] My son can speak for himself, no doubt.—Well, Jack, what do you say?

MRS. BARTHWICK. [*Sharply*] What does he say? Why, of course, he says the whole story's stuff!

JACK. [*Embarrassed*] Well, of course, I—of course, I don't know anything about it.

MRS. BARTHWICK. I should think not, indeed! [*To* SNOW.] The man is an audacious Ruffian!

BARTHWICK. [*Suppressing jumps*] But in view of my son's saying there's nothing in this—this fable—will it be necessary to proceed against the man under the circumstances?

SNOW. We shall have to charge him with the assault, sir. It would be as well for your son to come down to the Court. There'll be a remand, no doubt. The queer thing is there was quite a sum of money found on him, and a crimson silk purse. [BARTHWICK *starts ;* JACK *rises and sits down again.*] I suppose the lady hasn't missed her purse?

BARTHWICK. [*Hastily*] Oh no! Oh, No!

JACK. No!

MRS. BARTHWICK. [*Dreamily*] No! [*To* SNOW.] I've been inquiring of the servants. This man *does* hang about the house. I shall feel much safer if he gets a good long sentence ; I do think we ought to be protected against such ruffians.

BARTHWICK. Yes, yes, of course, on principle—but in this case we have a number of things to think of. [*To* SNOW.] I suppose, as you say, the man *must* be charged, eh?

SNOW. No question about that, sir.

BARTHWICK. [*Staring gloomily at* JACK] This prosecution goes very much against the grain with me. I have great sympathy with the poor. In my position I'm bound to recognize the distress there is amongst them. The condition of the people leaves much to be desired. D'you follow me? I wish I could see my way to drop it.

MRS. BARTHWICK. [*Sharply*] John! it's simply not fair to other people. It's putting property at the mercy of anyone who likes to take it.

BARTHWICK. [*Trying to make signs to her aside*] I'm not defending him, not at all. I'm trying to look at the matter broadly.

MRS. BARTHWICK. Nonsense, John, there's a time for everything.

SNOW. [*Rather sardonically*] I might point out, sir, that to withdraw the charge of stealing would not make much difference, because the facts must come out [*he looks significantly at* JACK] in reference to the assault ; and, as I said, that charge will have to go forward.

BARTHWICK. [*Hastily*] Yes, oh! exactly! It's entirely on the woman's account—entirely a matter of my own private feelings.

SNOW. If I were you, sir, I should let things take their course.

It's not likely there'll be much difficulty. These things are very quick settled.

BARTHWICK. [*Doubtfully*] You think so—you think so ?

JACK. [*Rousing himself*] I say, what shall I have to swear to ?

SNOW. That's best known to yourself, sir. [*Retreating to the door.*] Better employ a solicitor, sir, in case anything should arise. We shall have the butler to prove the loss of the article. You'll excuse me going, I'm rather pressed to-night. The case may come on any time after eleven. Good evening, sir ; good evening, ma'am. I shall have to produce the box in court to-morrow, so if you'll excuse me, sir, I may as well take it with me.

[*He takes the silver box and leaves them with a little bow.*
[BARTHWICK *makes a move to follow him, then dashing his hands beneath his coat tails, speaks with desperation.*

BARTHWICK. I do wish you'd leave me to manage things myself. You *will* put your nose into matters you know nothing of. A pretty mess you've made of this !

MRS. BARTHWICK. [*Coldly*] I don't in the least know what you're talking about. If you can't stand up for your rights, I can. I've no patience with your principles, it's such nonsense.

BARTHWICK. Principles ! Good Heavens ! What have principles to do with it, for goodness' sake ? Don't you know that Jack was drunk last night !

JACK. Dad !

MRS. BARTHWICK. [*In horror rising*] Jack !

JACK. Look here, mother—I had supper. Everybody does. I mean to say—you know what I mean—it's absurd to call it being drunk. At Oxford everybody gets a bit " on " sometimes——

MRS. BARTHWICK. Well I think it's most dreadful ! If that is really what you do at Oxford——

JACK. [*Angrily*] Well, why did you send me there ? One must do as other fellows do. It's such nonsense, I mean, to call it being drunk. Of course I'm awfully sorry. I've had such a beastly headache all day.

BARTHWICK. Tcha ! If you'd only had the common decency to remember what happened when you came in. Then we should know what truth there was in what this fellow says—as it is, it's all the most confounded darkness.

JACK. [*Staring as though at half-formed visions*] I just get a—and then —it's gone——

MRS. BARTHWICK. Oh, Jack ! do you mean to say you were so tipsy you can't even remember——

JACK. Look here, mother ! Of course I remember I came—I must have come——

BARTHWICK. [*Unguardedly, and walking up and down*] Tcha !—and that infernal purse ! Good Heavens ! It'll get into the papers.

Who on earth could have foreseen a thing like this ?   Better to have lost a dozen cigarette-boxes, and said nothing about it. [*To his wife.*] It's all your doing.   I told you so from the first.   I wish to goodness Roper would come !

MRS. BARTHWICK. [*Sharply*] I don't know what you're talking about, John.

BARTHWICK. [*Turning on her*] No, you—you—you don't know anything !   [*Sharply.*] Where the devil is Roper ?   If he can see a way out of this he's a better man than I take him for.   I defy *anyone* to see a way out of it.   *I* can't.

JACK. Look here, don't excite, Dad—I can simply say I was too beastly tired, and don't remember anything except that I came in and [*in a dying voice*] went to bed the same as usual.

BARTHWICK. Went to bed ?   Who knows where you went ?—I've lost all confidence.   For all I know you slept on the floor.

Jack. [*Indignantly*] I didn't, I slept on the——

BARTHWICK. [*Sitting on the sofa*] Who cares where you slept ; what does it matter if he mentions the—the—a perfect disgrace ?

MRS. BARTHWICK. *What ?* [*A silence.*] I *insist* on knowing.

JACK. Oh ! nothing——

MRS. BARTHWICK. Nothing ?   What do you mean by nothing, Jack ?   There's your father in such a state about it——

JACK. It's only my purse.

MRS. BARTHWICK. Your purse !   You know perfectly well you haven't got one.

JACK. Well, it was somebody else's—It was all a joke—I didn't want the beastly thing——

MRS. BARTHWICK. Do you mean that you had another person's purse, and that this man took it too ?

BARTHWICK. Tcha !   Of course he took it too !   A man like that Jones will make the most of it.   It'll get into the papers.

MRS. BARTHWICK. I don't understand.   What on earth is all the fuss about ? [*Bending over* JACK, *and softly.*] Jack now, tell me dear ! Don't be afraid.   What is it ?   Come !

JACK. Oh, don't, mother !

MRS. BARTHWICK. But don't what, dear ?

JACK. It was pure sport.   I don't know how I got the thing.   Of course I'd had a bit of a row—I didn't know what I was doing—I was—I was—well, you know—I suppose I must have pulled the bag out of her hand.

MRS. BARTHWICK. Out of her hand ?   Whose hand ?   What bag —whose bag ?

JACK. Oh ! I don't know—*her* bag—it belonged to—[*in a desperate and rising voice*] a woman.

MRS. BARTHWICK. A woman ?   *Oh ! Jack ! No !*

JACK. [*Jumping up*] You *would* have it. I didn't want to tell you. It's not my fault.

> [*The door opens and* MARLOW *ushers in a man of middle age, inclined to corpulence, in evening dress. He has a ruddy, thin moustache, and dark, quick-moving little eyes. His eyebrows are Chinese.*

MARLOW. Mr. Roper, sir.   [*He leaves the room.*

ROPER. [*With a quick look round*] How do you do?
                              [*But neither* JACK *nor* MRS. BARTHWICK *make a sign.*

BARTHWICK. [*Hurrying*] Thank goodness you've come, Roper. You remember what I told you this afternoon; we've just had the detective here.

ROPER. Got the box?

BARTHWICK. Yes, yes, but look here—it wasn't the charwoman at all; her drunken loafer of a husband took the things—he says that fellow there [*he waves his hand at* JACK, *who with his shoulder raised, seems trying to ward off a blow*] let him into the house last night. Can you imagine such a thing?   [*Roper laughs.*

BARTHWICK. [*With excited emphasis*] It's no laughing matter, Roper. I told you about that business of Jack's too—don't you see—the brute took both the things—took that infernal purse. It'll get into the papers.

ROPER. [*Raising his eyebrows*] H'm! The purse! Depravity in high life! What does your son say?

BARTHWICK. He remembers nothing. D——n! Did you ever see such a mess? It'll get into the papers.

MRS. BARTHWICK. [*With her hand across her eyes*] No! it's not that——   [BARTHWICK *and* ROPER *turn and look at her.*

BARTHWICK. It's the idea of that woman—she's just heard——

> [ROPER *nods. And* MRS. BARTHWICK, *setting her lips, gives a slow look at* JACK, *and sits down at the table.*]

What on earth's to be done, Roper? A ruffian like this Jones will make all the capital he can out of that purse.

MRS. BARTHWICK. I don't believe that Jack took that purse.

BARTHWICK. What—when the woman came here for it this morning?

MRS. BARTHWICK. Here? She had the impudence? Why wasn't I told?

> [*She looks round from face to face—no one answers her, there is a pause.*

BARTHWICK. [*Suddenly*] What's to be done, Roper?

ROPER. [*Quietly to* JACK] I suppose you didn't leave your latch-key in the door?

JACK. [*Sullenly*] Yes, I did.

BARTHWICK. Good heavens! What next?

MRS. BARTHWICK. I'm certain you never let that man into the house, Jack, it's a wild invention. I'm sure there's not a word of truth in it, Mr. Roper.

ROPER. [*Very suddenly*] Where did you sleep last night?

JACK. [*Promptly*] On the sofa, there—[*hesitating*] that is—I——

BARTHWICK. On the sofa? D'you mean to say you didn't go to bed?

JACK. [*Sullenly*] No.

BARTHWICK. If you don't remember anything, how can you remember that?

JACK. Because I woke up there in the morning.

MRS. BARTHWICK. Oh, Jack!

BARTHWICK. Good Gracious!

JACK. And Mrs. Jones saw me. I wish you wouldn't bait me so.

ROPER. Do you remember giving anyone a drink?

JACK. By Jove, I do seem to remember a fellow with—a fellow with—— [*He looks at Roper*] I say, d'you want me——?

ROPER. [*Quick as lightning*] With a dirty face?

JACK. [*With illumination*] I do—I distinctly remember his——

[BARTHWICK *moves abruptly;* MRS. BARTHWICK *looks at* ROPER *angrily, and touches her son's arm.*

MRS. BARTHWICK. You don't remember, it's ridiculous! I don't believe the man was ever here at all.

BARTHWICK. You must speak the truth, if it *is* the truth. But you *do* remember such a dirty business, I shall wash my hands of you altogether.

JACK. [*Glaring at them*] Well, what the devil——

MRS. BARTHWICK. Jack!

JACK. Well, mother, I—I don't know what you *do* want.

MRS. BARTHWICK. We want you to speak the truth and say you never let this low man into the house.

BARTHWICK. Of course if you think that you really gave this man whisky in that disgraceful way, and let him see what you'd been doing, and were in such a disgusting condition that you don't remember a word of it——

ROPER. [*Quick*] I've no memory myself—never had.

BARTHWICK. [*Desperately*] I don't know what you're to say.

ROPER. [*To* JACK] Say nothing at all! Don't put yourself in a false position. The man stole the things or the woman stole the things, you had nothing to do with it. You were asleep on the sofa.

MRS. BARTHWICK. Your leaving the latchkey in the door was quite bad enough, there's no need to mention anything else. [*Touching his forehead softly.*] My dear, how hot your head is!

JACK. But I want to know what I'm to do. [*Passionately.*] I won't be badgered like this. [MRS. BARTHWICK *recoils from him.*

2*

ROPER. [*Very quickly*] You forget all about it.   You were asleep.

JACK. Must I go down to the Court to-morrow ?

ROPER. [*Shaking his head*] No.

BARTHWICK. [*In a relieved voice*] Is that so ?

ROPER. Yes.

BARTHWICK. But *you'll* go, Roper.

ROPER. Yes.

JACK. [*With wan cheerfulness*] Thanks, awfully ! So long as I don't have to go. [*Putting his hand up to his head.*] I think if you'll excuse me—I've had a most beastly day.

> [*He looks from his father to his mother.*

MRS. BARTHWICK. [*Turning quickly*] Good night, my boy.

JACK. Good-night, mother.

> [*He goes out. MRS. BARTHWICK heaves a sigh. There is a silence.*

BARTHWICK. He gets off too easily.   But for my money that woman would have prosecuted him.

ROPER. You find money useful.

BARTHWICK. I've my doubts whether we ought to hide the truth——

ROPER. There'll be a remand.

BARTHWICK. What !   D'you mean he'll have to *appear* on the remand ?

ROPER. Yes.

BARTHWICK. H'm, I thought you'd be able to——   Look here, Roper, you *must* keep that purse out of the papers.

> [ROPER *fixes his little eyes on him and nods.*

MRS. BARTHWICK. Mr. Roper, don't you think the magistrate ought to be told what sort of people these Joneses are ; I mean about their immorality before they were married.   I don't know if John told you.

ROPER. Afraid it's not material.

MRS. BARTHWICK. Not material ?

ROPER. Purely private life !   May have happened to the magistrate.

BARTHWICK. [*With a movement as if to shift a burden*] Then you'll take the thing into your hands ?

ROPER. If the gods are kind.   [*He holds his hand out.*

BARTHWICK. [*Shaking it dubiously*] Kind—eh ? What ? You going ?

ROPER. Yes. I've another case, something like yours—most unexpected.

> [*He bows to* MRS. BARTHWICK *and goes out, followed by* BARTHWICK, *talking to the last.* MRS. BARTHWICK *at the table bursts into smothered sobs.* BARTHWICK *returns.*

BARTHWICK. [*To himself*] There'll be a scandal.

MRS. BARTHWICK. [*Disguising her grief at once*] I simply can't imagine what Roper means by making a joke of a thing like that !

BARTHWICK. [*Staring strangely*] You ! You can't imagine anything ! You've no more imagination than a fly !

MRS. BARTHWICK. [*Angrily*] You dare to tell me that I have no imagination.

BARTHWICK. [*Flustered*] I—I'm upset. From beginning to end, the whole thing has been utterly against my principles.

MRS. BARTHWICK. Rubbish ! You haven't any ! Your principles are nothing in the world but sheer—fright !

BARTHWICK. [*Walking to the window*] I've never been frightened in my life. You heard what Roper said. It's enough to upset anyone when a thing like this happens. Everything one says and does seems to turn in one's mouth—it's—it's uncanny. It's not the sort of thing I've been accustomed to. [*As though stifling, he throws the window open. The faint sobbing of a child comes in.*] What's that ?   [*They listen.*

MRS. BARTHWICK. [*Sharply*] I can't stand that crying. I must send Marlow to stop it. My nerves are all on edge. [*She rings the bell.*]

BARTHWICK. I'll shut the window ; you'll hear nothing. [*He shuts the window. There is silence.*]

MRS. BARTHWICK. [*Sharply*] That's no good ! It's on my nerves. Nothing upsets me like a child's crying. [MARLOW *comes in.*] What's that noise of crying, Marlow ? It sounds like a child.

BARTHWICK. It is a child. I can see it against the railings.

MARLOW. [*Opening the window, and looking out—quietly*] It's Mrs. Jones's little boy, ma'am ; he came here after his mother.

MRS. BARTHWICK. [*Moving quickly to the window*] Poor little chap ! John, we oughtn't to go on with this !

BARTHWICK. [*Sitting heavily in a chair*] Ah ! but it's out of our hands !

[MRS. BARTHWICK *turns her back to the window. There is an expression of distress on her face. She stands motionless, compressing her lips. The crying begins again.* BARTHWICK *covers his ears with his hands, and* MARLOW *shuts the window. The crying ceases.*

The curtain falls.

ACT III

*Eight days have passed, and the scene is a London Police Court at one o'clock.
A canopied seat of Justice is surmounted by the lion and unicorn. Before
the fire a worn-looking* MAGISTRATE *is warming his coat-tails, and
staring at two little girls in faded blue and orange rags, who are placed
before the dock. Close to the witness-box is a* RELIEVING OFFICER
*in an overcoat, and a short brown beard. Beside the little girl stands a
bald* POLICE CONSTABLE. *On the front bench are sitting* BARTHWICK
and ROPER, *and behind them* JACK. *In the railed enclosure are seedy-
looking men and women. Some prosperous constables sit or stand about.*

MAGISTRATE. [*In his paternal and ferocious voice, hissing his s's*] Now
let us dispose of these young ladies.

USHER. Theresa Livens, Maud Livens.

[*The bald* CONSTABLE *indicates the little girls, who remain silent,
disillusioned, inattentive.*

Relieving Officer! [*The* RELIEVING OFFICER *steps into the witness-box.*

USHER. The evidence you give to the Court shall be the truth, the
whole truth, and nothing but the truth, so help you God! Kiss the
book!   [*The book is kissed.*

RELIEVING OFFICER. [*In a monotone, pausing slightly at each sentence
end, that his evidence may be inscribed*] About ten o'clock this morning,
your Worship, I found these two little girls in Blue Street, Pulham,
crying outside a public-house. Asked where their home was, they said
they had no home. Mother had gone away. Asked about their
father. Their father had no work. Asked where they slept last
night. At their aunt's. I've made inquiries, your Worship. The
wife has broken up the home and gone on the streets. The husband
is out of work and living in common lodging-houses. The husband's
sister has eight children of her own, and says she can't afford to keep
these little girls any longer.

MAGISTRATE. [*Returning to his seat beneath the canopy of Justice*]
Now, let me see. You say the mother is on the streets; what evidence
have you of that?

RELIEVING OFFICER. I have the husband here, your Worship.

MAGISTRATE. Very well; then let us see him.

[*There are cries of "* LIVENS." *The* MAGISTRATE *leans forward,
and stares with hard compassion at the little girls.* LIVENS
*comes in. He is quiet, with grizzled hair, and a muffler for a
collar. He stands beside the witness-box.*

36

And you are their father? Now, why don't you keep your little girls at home. How is it you leave them to wander about the streets like this?

LIVENS. I've got no home, your Worship. I'm living from 'and to mouth. I've got no work; and nothin' to keep them on.

MAGISTRATE. How is that?

LIVENS. [Ashamedly] My wife, she broke my 'ome up, and pawned the things.

MAGISTRATE. But what made you let her?

LEVINS. Your Worship, I'd no chance to stop 'er; she did it when I was out lookin' for work.

MAGISTRATE. Did you ill-treat her?

LIVENS. [Emphatically] I never raised my 'and to her in my life, your Worship.

MAGISTRATE. Then what was it—did she drink?

LIVENS. Yes, your Worship.

MAGISTRATE. Was she loose in her behaviour?

LIVENS. [In a low voice] Yes, your Worship.

MAGISTRATE. And where is she now?

LIVENS. I don't know, your Worship. She went off with a man, and after that I——

MAGISTRATE. Yes, yes. Who knows anything of her? [To the bald CONSTABLE.] Is she known here?

RELIEVING OFFICER. Not in this district, your Worship; but I have ascertained that she is well known——

MAGISTRATE. Yes—yes; we'll stop at that. Now [to the Father] you say that she has broken up your home, and left these little girls. What provision can you make for them? You look a strong man.

LIVENS. So I am, your Worship. I'm willin' enough to work, but for the life of me I can't get anything to do.

MAGISTRATE. But have you tried?

LIVENS. I've tried everything, your Worship—I've tried my 'ardest.

MAGISTRATE. Well, well—— [There is a silence.

RELIEVING OFFICER. If your Worship thinks it's a case, my people are willing to take them.

MAGISTRATE. Yes, yes, I know; but I've no evidence that this man is not the proper guardian for his children.

[He rises and goes back to the fire.

RELIEVING OFFICER. The mother, your Worship, is able to get access to them.

MAGISTRATE. Yes, yes; the mother, of course, is an improper person to have anything to do with them. [To the Father.] Well, now what do you say?

LIVENS. Your Worship, I can only say that if I could get work I should be only too willing to provide for them. But what can I do, your Worship ? Here I am obliged to live from 'and to mouth in these 'ere common lodging-houses. I'm a strong man—I'm willing to work—I'm half as alive again as some of 'em—but you see, your Worship, my 'air's turned a bit, owing to the fever—[*Touches his hair.*] —and that's against me ; and I don't seem to get a chance anyhow.

MAGISTRATE. Yes—yes. [*Slowly.*] Well, I think it's a case. [*Staring his hardest at the little girls.*] Now are you willing that these little girls should be sent to a home ?

LIVENS. Yes, your Worship, I should be very willing.

MAGISTRATE. Well, I'll remand them for a week. Bring them again to-day week ; if I see no reason against it then, I'll make an order.

RELIEVING OFFICER. To-day week, your Worship.

[*The bald* CONSTABLE *takes the little girls out by the shoulders. The Father follows them. The* MAGISTRATE, *returning to his seat, bends over and talks to his* CLERK *inaudibly.*

BARTHWICK. [*Speaking behind his hand*] A painful case, Roper ; very distressing state of things.

ROPER. Hundreds like this in the Police Courts.

BARTHWICK. Most distressing ! The more I see of it, the more important this question of the condition of the people seems to become. I shall certainly make a point of taking up the cudgels in the House. I shall move——

[*The* MAGISTRATE *ceases talking to his* CLERK.

CLERK. Remands.

[BARTHWICK *stops abruptly. There is a stir and* MRS. JONES *comes in by the public door ;* JONES, *ushered by policemen, comes from the prisoner's door. They file into the dock.*

CLERK. James Jones, Jane Jones.

USHER. Jane Jones.

BARTHWICK. [*In a whisper*] The purse—the purse *must* be kept out of it, Roper. Whatever happens you must keep that out of the papers.

[ROPER *nods.*

BALD CONSTABLE. Hush !

[MRS. JONES, *dressed in her thin, black, wispy dress, and black straw hat, stands motionless with hands crossed on the front rail of the dock.* JONES *leans against the back rail of the dock, and keeps half turning, glancing defiantly about him. He is haggard and unshaven.*

CLERK. [*Consulting with his papers*] This is the case remanded from last Wednesday, sir. Theft of a silver cigarette-box and assault on the police ; the two charges were taken together. Jane Jones ! James Jones !

MAGISTRATE. [*Staring*] Yes, yes ; I remember.

CLERK. Jane Jones.

MRS. JONES. Yes, sir.

CLERK. Do you admit stealing a silver cigarette-box valued at five pounds, ten shillings, from the house of John Barthwick, M.P., between the hours of 11 P.M. on Easter Monday and 8.45 A.M. on Easter Tuesday last? Yes or no?

MRS. JONES. [*In a low voice*] No, sir, I do not, sir.

CLERK. James Jones? Do you admit stealing a silver cigarette-box valued at five pounds, ten shillings, from the house of John Barthwick, M.P., between the hours of 11 P.M. on Easter Monday and 8.45 a.m. on Easter Tuesday last? And further making an assault on the police when in the execution of their duty at 3 p.m. on Easter Tuesday? Yes or no?

JONES. [*Sullenly*] Yes, but I've a lot to say about it.

MAGISTRATE. [*To the* CLERK] Yes—yes. But how comes it that these two people are charged with the same offence? Are they husband and wife?

CLERK. Yes, sir. You remember you ordered a remand for further evidence as to the story of the male prisoner.

MAGISTRATE. Have they been in custody since?

CLERK. You released the woman on her own recognizances, sir.

MAGISTRATE. Yes, yes, this is the case of the silver box; I remember now. Well?

CLERK. Thomas Marlow.

[*The cry of* "THOMAS MARLOW" *is repeated.* MARLOW *comes in, and steps into the witness-box, and is sworn. The silver box is handed up, and placed on the rail.*

CLERK. [*Reading from his papers*] Your name is Thomas Marlow? Are you butler to John Barthwick, M.P., of 6, Rockingham Gate?

MARLOW. Yes, sir.

CLERK. Did you between 10.45 and 11 o'clock on the night of Easter Monday last place a silver cigarette-box on a tray on the dining-room table at 6, Rockingham Gate? Is that the box?

MARLOW. Yes, sir.

CLERK. And did you miss the same at 8.45 on the following morning, on going to remove the tray?

MARLOW. Yes, sir.

CLERK. Is the female prisoner known to you?

[MARLOW *nods.*

Is she the charwoman employed at 6, Rockingham Gate?

[*Again* MARLOW *nods.*

Did you at the time of your missing the box find her in the room alone?

MARLOW. Yes, sir.

CLERK. Did you afterwards communicate the loss to your employer, and did he send you to the police station?

MARLOW. Yes, sir.

CLERK. [*To* Mrs. JONES.] Have you anything to ask him ?

MRS. JONES. No, sir, nothing, thank you, sir.

CLERK. [*To* JONES] James Jones, have you anything to ask this witness ?

JONES. I don't know 'im.

MAGISTRATE. Are you sure you put the box in the place you say at the time you say ?

MARLOW. Yes, your Worship.

MAGISTRATE. Very well ; then now let us have the officer.

[MARLOW *leaves the box, and* SNOW *goes into it.*

USHER. The evidence you give to the court shall be the truth, the whole truth, and nothing but the truth, so help you God.

[*The book is kissed.*

CLERK. [*Reading from his papers*] Your name is Robert Snow ? You are a detective in the X. B. division of the Metropolitan police force ? According to instructions received, did you on Easter Tuesday last proceed to the prisoners' lodgings at 34, Merthyr Street, St. Soames' ? And did you on entering see the box produced, lying on the table ?

SNOW. Yes, sir.

CLERK. Is that the box ?

SNOW. [*Fingering the box*] Yes, sir.

CLERK. And did you thereupon take possession of it, and charge the female prisoner with theft of the box from 6, Rockingham Gate ? And did she deny the same ?

SNOW. Yes, sir.

CLERK. Did you take her into custody ?

SNOW. Yes, sir.

MAGISTRATE. What was her behaviour ?

SNOW. Perfectly quiet, your Worship. She persisted in the denial. That's all.

MAGISTRATE. Do you know her ?

SNOW. No, your Worship.

MAGISTRATE. Is she known here ?

BALD CONSTABLE. No, your Worship, they're neither of them known, we've nothing against them at all.

CLERK. [*To* MRS. JONES] Have you anything to ask the officer ?

MRS. JONES. No, sir, thank you, I've nothing to ask him.

MAGISTRATE. Very well then—go on.

CLERK. [*Reading from his papers*] And while you were taking the female prisoner did the male prisoner interpose, and endeavour to hinder you in the execution of your duty, and did he strike you a blow ?

SNOW. Yes, sir.

CLERK. And did he say, " You let her go, I took the box myself ? "

SNOW. He did.

CLERK. And did you blow your whistle and obtain the assistance of another constable, and take him into custody?

SNOW. I did.

CLERK. Was he violent on the way to the station, and did he use bad language, and did he several times repeat that he had taken the box himself? [SNOW *nods.*

Did you thereupon ask him in what manner he had stolen the box? And did you understand him to say that he had entered the house at the invitation of young Mr. Barthwick

[BARTHWICK, *turning in his seat, frowns at* ROPER.]
after midnight on Easter Monday, and partaken of whisky, and that under the influence of the whisky he had taken the box?

SNOW. I did, sir.

CLERK. And was his demeanour throughout very violent?

SNOW. It *was* very violent.

JONES. [*Breaking in*] Violent—of course it was. You put your 'ands on my wife when I kept tellin' you I took the thing myself.

MAGISTRATE. [*Hissing, with protruded neck*] Now—you will have your chance of saying what you want to say presently. Have you anything to ask the officer?

JONES. [*Sullenly*] No.

MAGISTRATE. Very well then. Now let us hear what the female prisoner has to say first.

MRS. JONES. Well, your Worship, of course I can only say what I've said all along, that I didn't take the box.

MAGISTRATE. Yes, but did you know that it was taken?

MRS. JONES. No, your Worship. And, of course, as to what my husband says, your Worship, I can't speak of my own knowledge. Of course, I know that he came home very late on the Monday night. It was past one o'clock when he came in, and he was not himself at all.

MAGISTRATE. Had he been drinking?

MRS. JONES. Yes, your Worship.

MAGISTRATE. And was he drunk?

MRS. JONES. Yes, your Worship, he was almost quite drunk.

MAGISTRATE. And did he say anything to you?

MRS. JONES. No, your Worship, only to call me names. And of course in the morning when I got up and went to work he was asleep. And I don't know anything more about it until I came home again. Except that Mr. Barthwick—that's my employer, your Worship—told me the box was missing.

MAGISTRATE. Yes, yes.

MRS. JONES. But of course when I was shaking out my husband's coat the cigarette-box fell out and all the cigarettes were scattered on the bed.

MAGISTRATE. You say all the cigarettes were scattered on the bed ? [*To* SNOW.] Did you see the cigarettes scattered on the bed ?

SNOW. No, your Worship, I did not.

MAGISTRATE. You see he says he didn't see them.

JONES. Well, they were there for all that.

SNOW. I can't say, your Worship, that I had the opportunity of going round the room ; I had all my work cut out with the male prisoner.

MAGISTRATE. [*To* MRS. JONES] Well, what more have you to say ?

MRS. JONES. Of course when I saw the box, your Worship, I was dreadfully upset, and I couldn't think why he had done such a thing ; when the officer came we were having words about it, because it is ruin to me, your Worship, in my profession, and I have three little children dependent on me.

MAGISTRATE. [*Protruding his neck*] Yes—yes—but what did he say to you ?

MRS. JONES. I asked him whatever came over him to do such a thing—and he said it was the drink. He said that he had had too much to drink, and something came over him. And of course, your Worship, he had had very little to eat all day, and the drink does go to the head when you have not had enough to eat. Your Worship may not know, but it is the truth. And I would like to say that all through his married life I have never known him to do such a thing before, though we have passed through great hardships, and [*speaking with soft emphasis*] I am quite sure he would not have done it if he had been himself at the time.

MAGISTRATE. Yes, yes. But don't you know that that is no excuse ?

MRS. JONES. Yes, your Worship. I know that it is no excuse.

[*The* MAGISTRATE *leans over and parleys with his* CLERK.

JACK. [*Leaning over from his seat behind*] I say, Dad——

BARTHWICK. Tsst ! [*Sheltering his mouth, he speaks to* ROPER.] Roper, you had better get up now and say that considering the circumstances and the poverty of the prisoners, we have no wish to proceed any further, and if the magistrate would deal with the case as one of disorder only on the part of——

BALD CONSTABLE. Hssshh !   [ROPER *shakes his head.*

MAGISTRATE. Now, supposing what you say and what your husband says is true, what I have to consider is—how did he obtain access to this house, and were you in any way a party to his obtaining access ? You are the charwoman employed at the house ?

MRS. JONES. Yes, your Worship, and of course if I had let him into the house it would have been very wrong of me ; and I have never done such a thing in any of the houses where I have been employed.

MAGISTRATE. Well—so you say. Now let us hear what story the male prisoner makes of it.

JONES. [*Who leans with his arms on the dock behind, speaks in a slow, sullen voice*] Wot I say is wot my wife says. I've never been 'ad up in a police court before, an' I can prove I took it when in liquor. I told her, an' she can tell you the same, that I was goin' to throw the thing into the water sooner than 'ave it on my mind.

MAGISTRATE. But how did you get into the *house*?

JONES. I was passin'. I was goin' 'ome from the " Goat and Bells."

MAGISTRATE. The " Goat and Bells,"—what is that? A public-house?

JONES. Yes, at the corner. It was Bank 'oliday, an' I'd 'ad a drop to drink. I see this young Mr. Barthwick tryin' to find the keyhole on the wrong side of the door.

MAGISTRATE. Well?

JONES. [*Slowly and with many pauses*] Well—I 'elped 'im to find it—drunk as a lord 'e was. He goes on, an' comes back again, and says, I've got nothin' for you, 'e says, but come in an' 'ave a drink. So I went in just as you might 'ave done yourself. We 'ad a drink o' whisky just as you might have 'ad, 'nd young Mr. Barthwick says to me, " Take a drink 'nd a smoke. Take anything you like," 'e says. And then he went to sleep on the sofa. I 'ad some more whisky— an' I 'ad a smoke—and I 'ad some more whisky—an' I carn't tell yer what 'appened after that.

MAGISTRATE. Do you mean to say you were so drunk that you can remember nothing?

JACK. [*Softly to his father*] I say, that's exactly what——

BARTHWICK. Tssh!

JONES. That's what I do mean.

MAGISTRATE. And yet you say you stole the box?

JONES. I never stole the box. I took it.

MAGISTRATE. [*Hissing, with protruded neck*] You did not steal it— you took it. Did it belong to you—what is that but stealing?

JONES. I took it.

MAGISTRATE. You took it—you took it away from their house and you took it to your house——

JONES. [*Sullenly breaking in*] I ain't got a house.

MAGISTRATE. Very well, let us hear what this young man Mr.— Mr. Barthwick—has to say to your story.

[SNOW *leaves the witness-box. The* BALD CONSTABLE *beckons* JACK, *who, clutching his hat, goes into the witness-box.* ROPER *moves to the table set apart for his profession.*

SWEARING CLERK. The evidence you give to the Court shall be the truth, the whole truth, and nothing but the truth, so help you God. Kiss the book.   [*The book is kissed.*

ROPER. [*Examining*] What is your name?

JACK. [*In a low voice*] John Barthwick, Junior.

[*The* CLERK *writes it down.*

ROPER. Where do you live?

JACK. At 6, Rockingham Gate.

[*All his answers are recorded by the* CLERK.

ROPER. You are the son of the owner?

JACK. [*In a very low voice*] Yes.

ROPER. Speak up, please. Do you know the prisoners?

JACK. [*Looking at the* JONESES, *in a low voice*] I've seen Mrs. Jones. I—[*in a loud voice*] don't know the man.

JONES. Well, I know you!

BALD CONSTABLE. Hssh!

ROPER. Now, did you come in late on the night of Easter Monday?

JACK. Yes.

ROPER. And did you by mistake leave your latchkey in the door?

JACK. Yes.

MAGISTRATE. Oh! You left your latchkey in the door?

ROPER. And is that all you can remember about your coming in?

JACK. [*In a loud voice*] Yes, it is.

MAGISTRATE. Now, you have heard the male prisoner's story, what do you say to that!

JACK. [*Turning to the* MAGISTRATE, *speaks suddenly in a confident, straightforward voice*] The fact of the matter is, sir, that I'd been out to the theatre that night, and had supper afterwards, and I came in late.

MAGISTRATE. Do you remember this man being outside when you came in?

JACK. No, sir. [*He hesitates.*] I don't think I do.

MAGISTRATE. [*Somewhat puzzled*] Well, did he help you to open the door, as he says? Did *any*one help you to open the door?

JACK. No, sir—I don't think so, sir—I don't know.

MAGISTRATE. You don't know? But you must know. It isn't a usual thing for you to have the door opened for you, is it?

JACK. [*With a shamefaced smile*] No.

MAGISTRATE. Very well, then——

JACK. [*Desperately*] The fact of the matter is, sir, I'm afraid I'd had too much champagne that night.

MAGISTRATE. [*Smiling*] Oh! you'd had too much champagne?

JONES. May I ask the gentleman a question?

MAGISTRATE. Yes—yes—you may ask him what questions you like.

JONES. Don't you remember you said you was a Liberal, same as your father, and you asked me wot I was?

JACK. [*With his hand against his brow*] I seem to remember——

JONES. And I said to you, " I'm a bloomin' Conserva*tive*," I said;

an' you said to me, " You look more like one of these 'ere Socialists. Take wotever you like," you said.

JACK. [*With sudden resolution*] No, I don't. I don't remember anything of the sort.

JONES. Well, I do, an' my word's as good as yours. I've never been had up in a police court before. Look 'ere, don't you remember you had a sky-blue bag in your 'and—— [BARTHWICK *jumps*.

ROPER. I submit to your worship that these questions are hardly to the point, the prisoner having admitted that he himself does not remember anything. [*There is a smile on the face of Justice.*] It is a case of the blind leading the blind.

JONES. [*Violently*] I've done no more than wot he 'as. I'm a poor man. I've got no money an' no friends—he's a toff—he can do wot I can't.

MAGISTRATE. Now, now! All this won't help you—you must be quiet. You say you took this box? Now, what made you take it? Were you pressed for money?

JONES. I'm always pressed for money.

MAGISTRATE. Was that the reason you took it?

JONES. No.

MAGISTRATE. [*To* SNOW] Was anything found on him?

SNOW. Yes, your Worship. There was six pounds twelve shillin's found on him, and this purse.

[*The red silk purse is handed to the* MAGISTRATE. BARTHWICK *rises in his seat, but hastily sits down again.*

MAGISTRATE. [*Staring at the purse*] Yes, yes—let me see—— [*There is a silence.*] No, no, I've nothing before me as to the purse. How did you come by all that money?

JONES. [*After a long pause, suddenly*] I declines to say.

MAGISTRATE. But if you had all that money, what made you take this box?

JONES. I took it out of spite.

MAGISTRATE. [*Hissing, with protruded neck*] You took it out of spite? Well now, that's something! But do you imagine you can go about the town taking things out of spite?

JONES. If you had my life, if you'd been out of work——

MAGISTRATE. Yes, yes; I know—because you're out of work you think it's an excuse for everything.

JONES. [*Pointing at* JACK] You ask '*im* wot made '*im* take the——

ROPER. [*Quietly*] Does your worship require this witness in the box any longer?

MAGISTRATE. [*Ironically*] I think not; he is hardly profitable.

[JACK *leaves the witness-box, and, hanging his head, resumes his seat.*

JONES. You ask 'im wot made 'im take the lady's——

[*But the* BALD CONSTABLE *catches him by the sleeve.*

BALD CONSTABLE. Sssh!

MAGISTRATE. [*Emphatically*] Now listen to me. I've nothing to do with what he may or may not have taken. Why did you resist the police in the execution of their duty?

JONES. It warn't their duty to take my wife, a respectable woman, that 'adn't done nothing.

MAGISTRATE. But I say it was. What made you strike the officer a blow?

JONES. Any man would a struck 'im a blow. I'd strike 'im again, I would.

MAGISTRATE. You are not making your case any better by violence. How do you suppose we could get on if everybody behaved like you?

JONES. [*Leaning forward, earnestly*] Well, wot about 'er; who's to make up to 'er for this? Who's to give 'er back 'er good name?

MRS. JONES. Your Worship, it's the children that's preying on his mind, because of course I've lost my work. And I've had to find another room owing to the scandal.

MAGISTRATE. Yes, yes, I know—but if he hadn't acted like this nobody would have suffered.

JONES. [*Glaring round at* JACK] I've done no worse than wot 'e 'as. Wot I want to know is wot's goin' to be done to '*im*.

[*The* BALD CONSTABLE *again says* "Hssh!"]

ROPER. Mr. Barthwick wishes it known, your Worship, that considering the poverty of the prisoners he does not press the charge as to the box. Perhaps your worship would deal with the case as one of disorder.

JONES. I don't want it smothered up, I want it all dealt with fair— I want my rights——

MAGISTRATE. [*Rapping his desk*] Now you have said all you have to say, and you will be quiet.

[*There is a silence; the* MAGISTRATE *bends over and parleys with his* CLERK.]

Yes, I think I may discharge the woman. [*In a kindly voice he addresses* MRS. JONES, *who stands unmoving with her hands crossed on the rail.*] It is very unfortunate for you that this man has behaved as he has. It is not the consequences to him but the consequences to you. You have been brought here twice, you have lost your work—[*He glares at* JONES] and this is what always happens. Now you may go away, and I am very sorry it was necessary to bring you here at all.

MRS. JONES. [*Softly*] Thank you very much, your Worship.

[*She leaves the dock, and looking back at* JONES, *twists her fingers and is still.*]

MAGISTRATE. Yes, yes, but I can't pass it over. Go away, there's a good woman.

[MRS. JONES *stands back. The* MAGISTRATE *leans his head on his hand; then raising it, he speaks to* JONES.]

Now, listen to me. Do you wish the case to be settled here, or do you wish it to go before a Jury?

JONES. [*Muttering*] I don't want no Jury.

MAGISTRATE. Very well then, I will deal with it here. [*After a pause.*] You have pleaded guilty to stealing this box——

JONES. Not to stealin'——

BALD CONSTABLE. Hssshh.

MAGISTRATE. And to assaulting the police——

JONES. Any man as was a man——

MAGISTRATE. Your conduct here has been most improper. You give the excuse that you were drunk when you stole the box. I tell you that is no excuse. If you choose to get drunk and break the law afterwards you must take the consequences. And let me tell you that men like you, who get drunk and give way to your spite or whatever it is that's in you, are—are—a *nuisance to the community*.

JACK. [*Leaning from his seat*] Dad! that's what you said to me?

BARTHWICK. Tsst.

[*There is a silence, while the* MAGISTRATE *consults his* CLERK; JONES *leans forward waiting.*

MAGISTRATE. This is your first offence, and I am going to give you a light sentence. [*Speaking sharply, but without expression.*] One month with hard labour.

[*He bends, and parleys with his* CLERK. *The* BALD CONSTABLE *and another help* JONES *from the dock.*

JONES. [*Stopping and twisting round*] Call this justice? What about 'im? 'E got drunk! 'E took the purse—'e took the purse but [*in a muffled shout*] it's 'is money got 'im off—*Justice!*

[*The prisoner's door is shut on* JONES, *and from the seedy-looking men and women comes a hoarse and whispering groan.*

MAGISTRATE. We will now adjourn for lunch! [*He rises from his seat.*]

[*The Court is in a stir.* ROPER *gets up and speaks to the reporter.* JACK, *throwing up his head, walks with a swagger to the corridor;* BARTHWICK *follows.*

MRS. JONES. [*Turning to him with a humble gesture*] Oh! Sir!——

[BARTHWICK *hesitates, then yielding to his nerves, he makes a shamefaced gesture of refusal, and hurries out of Court.* MRS. JONES *stands looking after him.*

The curtain falls.

JOY

CAST OF THE ORIGINAL PRODUCTION AT THE SAVOY THEATRE, LONDON, ON SEPTEMBER 24, 1907

COLONEL HOPE	*Mr. A. E. George*
MRS. HOPE	*Miss Henrietta Watson*
MISS BEECH	*Miss Florence Haydon*
LETTY	*Miss Mary Barton*
ERNEST BLUNT	*Mr. Frederick Lloyd*
MRS. GWYN	*Miss Wynne Matthison*
JOY	*Miss Dorothy Minto*
DICK MERTON	*Mr. Alan Wade*
HON. MAURICE LEVER	*Mr. Thalberg Corbet*
ROSE	*Miss Amy Lamborn*

ACT I

The time is morning, and the scene a level lawn, beyond which the river is running amongst fields. A huge old beech tree overshadows everything, in the darkness of whose hollow many things are hidden. A rustic seat encircles it. A low wall clothed in creepers, with two openings, divides this lawn from the flowery approaches to the house. Close to the wall there is a swing. The sky is clear and sunny. COLONEL HOPE *is seated in a garden-chair, reading a newspaper through pince-nez. He is fifty-five, and bald, with drooping grey moustaches and a weather-darkened face. He wears a flannel suit, and a hat from Panama ; a tennis racquet leans against his chair.* MRS. HOPE *comes quickly through the opening of the wall, with roses in her hands. She is going grey ; she wears tan gauntlets, and no hat. Her manner is decided, her voice emphatic, as though aware that there is no nonsense in its owner's composition. Screened by the hollow tree,* MISS BEECH *is seated ; and* JOY *is perched on a lower branch, concealed by foliage.*

MRS. HOPE. I told Molly in my letter that she'd have to walk up, Tom.

COLONEL. Walk up in this heat ? My dear, why didn't you order Benson's fly ?

MRS. HOPE. Expense for nothing ! Bob can bring up her things in the barrow. I've told Joy I won't have her going down to meet the train. She's so excited about her mother's coming there's no doing anything with her.

COLONEL. No wonder, after two months.

MRS. HOPE. Well, she's going home to-morrow ; she must just keep herself fresh for the dancing to-night. I'm not going to get people in to dance, and have Joy worn out before they begin.

COLONEL. [*Dropping his paper*] I don't like Molly's walking up.

MRS. HOPE. A great strong woman like Molly Gwyn ! It isn't half a mile.

COLONEL. I don't like it, Nell ; it's not hospitable.

MRS. HOPE. Rubbish ! If you want to throw away money, you must just find some better investment than those wretched three per cents. of yours. The green-fly are in my roses already ! Did you ever see anything so *disgusting* ? [*They bend over the roses they have grown, and lose all sense of everything.*] Where's the syringe ? I saw you mooning about with it last night, Tom.

51

COLONEL. [*Uneasily*] Mooning! [*He retires behind his paper.* MRS. HOPE *enters the hollow of the tree.*] There's an account of that West Australian swindle. Set of ruffians! Listen to this, Nell! "It is understood that amongst the shareholders are large numbers of women, clergymen, and Army officers." How people can be such fools!

[*Becoming aware that his absorption is unobserved, he drops his glasses, and reverses his chair towards the tree.*

MRS. HOPE. [*Reappearing with a garden syringe*] I simply won't have Dick keep his fishing things in the tree; there's a whole potful of disgusting worms. *I* can't touch them. *You* must go and take 'em out, Tom. [*In his turn the* COLONEL *enters the hollow of the tree.*

MRS. HOPE. [*Personally*] What on earth's the pleasure of it? I can't see! He never catches anything worth eating.

[*The* COLONEL *reappears with a paint-pot full of worms; he holds them out abstractedly.*

MRS. HOPE. [*Jumping*] Don't put them near me!

MISS BEECH. [*From behind the tree*] Don't hurt the poor creatures.

COLONEL. [*Turning*] Hallo, Peachey? What are *you* doing round there? [*He puts the worms down on the seat.*

MRS. HOPE. Tom, take the worms off that seat at once!

COLONEL. [*Somewhat flurried*] Good gad! *I* don't know what to do with the beastly worms!

MRS. HOPE. It's not *my* business to look after Dick's worms. Don't put them on the ground. I won't have them anywhere where they can crawl about. [*She flicks some green-fly off her roses.*

COLONEL. [*Looking into the pot as though the worms could tell him where to put them*] Dash!

MISS BEECH. Give them to me.

MRS. HOPE. [*Relieved*] Yes, give them to Peachey.

[*There comes from round the tree* MISS BEECH, *old-fashioned, barrel-shaped, balloony in the skirts. She takes the paint-pot, and sits beside it on the rustic seat.*

MISS BEECH. Poor creatures!

MRS. HOPE. Well, it's beyond *me* how you can make pets of worms —wriggling, crawling, horrible things!

[*ROSE, who is young and comely, in a pale print frock, comes from the house and places letters before her on a silver salver.*

[*Taking the letters.*] What about Miss Joy's frock, Rose?

ROSE. Please, 'm, I can't get on with the back without Miss Joy.

MRS. HOPE. Well, then you must just find her. *I* don't know where she is.

ROSE. [*In a slow, sidelong manner*] If you please, Mum, I think Miss Joy's up in the——

[*She stops, seeing* MISS BEECH *signing to her with both hands.*

MRS. HOPE. [*Sharply*] What is it, Peachy?

MISS BEECH. [*Selecting a finger*] Pricked meself!

MRS. HOPE. Let's look!

[*She bends to look, but* MISS BEECH *places the finger in her mouth.*

ROSE. [*Glancing askance at the* COLONEL] If you please, Mum, it's —below the waist, I think I can manage with the dummy.

MRS. HOPE. Well, you can try. [*Opening her letter as* ROSE *retires.*] Here's Molly about her train.

MISS BEECH. Is there a letter for me?

MRS. HOPE. No, Peachey.

MISS BEECH. There never is.

COLONEL. What's that? You got four by the first post.

MISS BEECH. Exceptions!

COLONEL. [*Looking over his glasses*] Why! You know, you get 'em every day!

MRS. HOPE. Molly says she'll be down by the eleven-thirty. [*In an injured voice.*] She'll be here in half an hour! [*Reading with disapproval from the letter*.] " MAURICE LEVER is coming down by the same train to see Mr. Henty about the Tocopala Gold Mine. Could you give him a bed for the night?" [*Silence, slight but ominous.*

COLONEL. [*Calling in to his aid his sacred hospitality*] Of course we must give him a bed!

MRS. HOPE. Just like a man! What room I should like to know!

COLONEL. Pink.

MRS. HOPE. As if *Molly* wouldn't have the Pink!

COLONEL. [*Ruefully*] I thought she'd have the Blue!

MRS. HOPE. You know perfectly well it's full of earwigs, Tom. I killed ten there yesterday morning.

MISS BEECH. Poor creatures!

MRS. HOPE. I don't know that I approve of this Mr. Lever's dancing attendance. Molly's only thirty-six.

COLONEL. [*In a high voice*] You can't refuse him a bed; I never heard of such a thing.

MRS. HOPE. [*Reading from the letter*] " This gold mine seems to be a splendid chance. [*She glances at the* COLONEL.] I've put all *my* spare cash into it. They're issuing some Preference shares now; if Uncle Tom wants an investment." [*She pauses, then in a changed, decided voice.*] Well, I suppose I shall have to screw him in somehow.

COLONEL. What's that about gold mines? Gambling nonsense! Molly ought to know my views.

MRS. HOPE. [*Folding the letter away out of her consciousness*] Oh! your views! This may be a specially good chance.

MISS BEECH. Ahem! Special case!

MRS. HOPE. [*Paying no attention*] I'm sick of these three per cent. dividends. When you've only got so little money, to put it all into that

India Stock, when it might be earning six per cent. at least, quite safely !
There are ever so many things I want.

COLONEL. There you go !

MRS. HOPE. As to Molly, *I* think it's high time her husband came
home to look after her, instead of sticking out there in that hot place.
In fact

[MISS BEECH *looks up at the tree and exhibits cerebral excitement.*]
I don't know what Geoff's about ; why doesn't he find something in
England, where they could live together.

COLONEL. Don't say anything against Molly, Nell !

MRS. HOPE. Well, I don't believe in husband and wife being
separated.   That's not my idea of married life.

[*The* COLONEL *whistles quizzically.*]
Ah, yes, she's *your* niece, not *mine !*   Molly's very——

MISS BEECH. Ouch ! [*She sucks her finger.*]

MRS. HOPE. Well, if I couldn't sew at your age, Peachey, without
pricking my fingers !   Tom, if I have Mr. Lever here, you'll just
attend to what I say and look into that mine !

COLONEL. Look into your grandmother !   I haven't made a study
of geology for nothing.   For every ounce you take out of a gold
mine, you put an ounce and a half in.   Any fool knows that, eh,
Peachey ?

MISS BEECH. I hate your horrid mines, with all the poor creatures
underground.

MRS. HOPE. Nonsense, Peachey !   As if they'd go there if they
didn't want to !

COLONEL. Why don't you read your paper, then you'd see what a
lot of wild-cat things there are about.

MRS. HOPE. [*Abstractedly*] I can't put Ernest and Letty in the
blue room, there's only the single bed.   Suppose I put Mr. Lever
there, and say nothing about the earwigs.   I daresay he'll never
notice.

COLONEL. Treat a guest like that !

MRS. HOPE. Then where am I to put him for goodness' sake ?

COLONEL. Put him in my dressing-room ; I'll turn out.

MRS. HOPE. Rubbish, Tom, I won't have you turned out, that's
flat.   He can have Joy's room, and she can sleep with the earwigs.

JOY. [*From her hiding-place upon a lower branch of the hollow tree*] I
won't.   [MRS. HOPE *and the* COLONEL *jump.*]

COLONEL. God bless my soul !

MRS. HOPE. You wretched girl !   I told you never to climb that
tree again.   Did *you* know, Peachey ?   [MISS BEECH *smiles.*]
She's always up there, spoiling all her frocks.   Come down now,
Joy ; there's a good child !

JOY. I don't want to sleep with earwigs, Aunt Nell.

MISS BEECH. *I'll* sleep with the poor creatures.

MRS. HOPE. [*After a pause*] Well, it would be a mercy if you would for once, Peachey.

COLONEL. Nonsense, I won't have Peachey——

MRS. HOPE. Well, who is to sleep there then?

JOY. [*Coaxingly*] Let me sleep with *Mother*, Aunt Nell, do!

MRS. HOPE. Litter her up with a great girl like you, as if we'd only one spare room! Tom, see that she comes down—I can't stay here, I must manage something.   [*She goes away towards the house.*

COLONEL. [*Moving to the tree, and looking up*] You heard what your Aunt said?

JOY. [*Softly*] Oh, Uncle Tom!

COLONEL. I shall have to come up after you.

JOY. Oh, *do*, and Peachey too!

COLONEL. [*Trying to restrain a smile*] Peachey, you talk to her. [*Without waiting for* MISS BEECH *however, he proceeds.*] What'll your Aunt say to me if I don't get you down?

MISS BEECH. Poor creature!

JOY. I don't want to be worried about my frock.

COLONEL. [*Scratching his bald head*] Well, *I* shall catch it.

JOY. Oh, Uncle Tom, your head is so beautiful from here!
          [*Leaning over, she fans it with a leafy twig.*

MISS BEECH. Disrespectful little toad.

COLONEL. [*Quickly putting on his hat*] You'll fall out, and a pretty mess that'll make on—[*he looks uneasily at the ground*]—*my* lawn!
          [*A voice is heard calling " Colonel! Colonel! "*

JOY. There's Dick calling you, Uncle Tom.   [*She disappears.*

DICK. [*Appearing in the opening of the wall*] Ernie's waiting to play you that single, Colonel!   [*He disappears.*

JOY. Quick, Uncle Tom! Oh! *do* go, before he finds I am up here.

MISS BEECH. Secret little creature!
          [*The* COLONEL *picks up his racquet, shakes his fist, and goes away.*

JOY. [*Calmly*] I'm coming down now, Peachey.
[*Climbing down.*] Look out! I'm dropping on your head.

MISS BEECH. [*Unmoved*] Don't hurt yourself!
          [JOY *drops on the rustic seat and rubs her shin.*]
Told you so! [*She hunts in a little bag for plaster.*] Let's see!

JOY. [*Seeing the worms*] Ugh!

MISS BEECH. What's the matter with the poor creatures?

JOY. They're so wriggly!
          [*She backs away and sits down in the swing. She is just seventeen, light and slim, brown-haired, fresh-coloured, and grey-eyed; her white frock reaches to her ankles, she wears a sun-bonnet.*]
Peachey, how long were you Mother's governess?

Miss Beech. Five years.

Joy. Was she as bad to teach as me?

Miss Beech. Worse! [Joy claps her hands.]
She was the worst girl I ever taught.

Joy. Then you weren't fond of her?

Miss Beech. Oh! yes, I was.

Joy. Fonder than of me?

Miss Beech. Don't you ask such a lot of questions!

Joy. Peachey, duckie, what was Mother's *worst* fault?

Miss Beech. Doing what she knew she oughtn't.

Joy. Was she ever sorry?

Miss Beech. Yes, but she always went on doin' it.

Joy. *I* think being sorry's stupid!

Miss Beech. Oh, do you?

Joy. It isn't any good. Was Mother revengeful, like me?

Miss Beech. Ah! Wasn't she?

Joy. And jealous?

Miss Beech. The most jealous girl I ever saw.

Joy. [*Nodding*] I *like* to be like her.

Miss Beech. [*Regarding her intently*] Yes! you've got all your troubles before *you*.

Joy. Mother was married at eighteen, wasn't she, Peachey? Was she—was she much in love with Father then?

Miss Beech. [*With a sniff*] About as much as usual.

> [*She takes the paint-pot, and walking round begins to release the worms.*

Joy. [*Indifferently*] They don't get on now, you know.

Miss Beech. What d'you mean by that, disrespectful little creature?

Joy. [*In a hard voice*] They haven't ever since *I've* known them.

Miss Beech. [*Looks at her, and turns away again*] Don't talk about such things.

Joy. I suppose you don't know Mr. Lever? [*Bitterly.*] He's such a cool beast. He never loses his temper.

Miss Beech. Is that why you don't like him?

Joy. [*Frowning*] No—yes—I don't know.

Miss Beech. Oh! perhaps you *do* like him?

Joy. I don't; I hate him.

Miss Beech. [*Standing still*] Fie! Naughty temper!

Joy. Well, so would you! He takes up all Mother's time.

Miss Beech. [*In a peculiar voice*] Oh! does he?

Joy. When he comes *I* might just as well go to bed. [*Passionately.*] And now he's chosen to-day to come down here, when I haven't seen her for two months! Why couldn't he come when Mother and I'd gone home. It's simply brutal!

Miss Beech. But your mother likes him?

Joy. [*Sullenly*] I don't *want* her to like him.

Miss Beech. [*With a long look at* Joy] I see!

Joy. What are you doing, Peachey?

Miss Beech. [*Releasing a worm*] Letting the poor creatures go.

Joy. If I tell Dick he'll never forgive you.

Miss Beech. [*Sidling behind the swing and plucking off* Joy's *sun-bonnet. With devilry*] Ah-h-h! You've done your hair up; so that's why you wouldn't come down!

Joy. [*Springing up and pouting*] I didn't want anyone to see before Mother. You *are* a pig, Peachey!

Miss Beech. I thought there was *something*!

Joy. [*Twisting round*] How does it look?

Miss Beech. I've seen better.

Joy. You tell anyone before Mother comes, and see what I do!

Miss Beech. Well, don't you tell about my worms, then!

Joy. Give me my hat! [*Backing hastily towards the tree, and putting her finger to her lips.*] Look out! Dick!

Miss Beech. Oh! dear!

[*She sits down on the swing concealing the paint-pot with her feet and skirts.*

Joy. [*On the rustic seat, and in a violent whisper*] I hope the worms will crawl up your legs!

[Dick, *in flannels and a hard straw hat, comes in. He is a quiet and cheerful boy of twenty. His eyes are always fixed on* Joy.

Dick. [*Grimacing*] The Colonel's getting licked. Hallo! Peachey, in the swing?

Joy. [*Chuckling*] Swing her, Dick.

Miss Beech. [*Quivering with emotion*] Little creature!

Joy. Swing her!   [Dick *takes the ropes.*

Miss Beech. [*Quietly*] It makes me sick, young man.

Dick. [*Patting her gently on the back*] All right, Peachey.

Miss Beech. [*Maliciously*] Could you get me my sewing from the seat! Just behind Joy.

Joy. [*Leaning her head against the tree*] If you do, I won't dance with you to-night.

[Dick *stands paralysed.* Miss Beech *gets off the swing, picks up the paint-pot and stands concealing it behind her.*

Joy. Look what she's got behind *her*, sly old thing!

Miss Beech. Oh! dear!

Joy. Dance with her, Dick.

Miss Beech. If he dare!

Joy. Dance with her, or I won't dance with you to-night.

[*She whistles a waltz.*

3

DICK. [*Desperately*] Come on then, Peachey. We *must*.

JOY. Dance, dance !

[DICK *seizes* MISS BEECH *by the waist. She drops the paint-pot. They revolve.*

[*Convulsed*] Oh, Peachey, oh !

[MISS BEECH *is dropped upon the rustic seat.* DICK *seizes* JOY'S *hands and drags her up.*]

No, no ! I won't !

MISS BEECH. [*Panting*] Dance, dance with the poor young man [*She moves her hands.*] La la—la *la* la—la *la* la !

[DICK *and* JOY *dance.*

DICK. By Jove, Joy, you've done your hair up. I say, how jolly ! You *do* look——

JOY. [*Throwing her hands up to her hair*] I didn't mean *you* to see !

DICK. [*In a hurt voice*] Oh ! didn't you ? I'm awfully sorry !

JOY. [*Flashing round*] Oh, you old Peachey ! [*She looks at the ground, and then again at* DICK.]

MISS BEECH. [*Sidling round the tree*] Oh ! dear !

JOY. [*Whispering*] She's been letting out your worms.

[MISS BEECH *disappears from view*.]

Look !

DICK. [*Quickly*] Hang the worms ! Joy, promise *me* the second and fourth and sixth and eighth and tenth and supper, to-night. Promise. Do ! [JOY *shakes her head.*] It's not much to ask.

JOY. I won't promise anything.

DICK. Why not ?

JOY. Because Mother's coming. I won't make any arrangements.

DICK. [*Tragically*] It's our last night.

JOY. [*Scornfully*] You don't understand ! [*Dancing and clasping her hands.*] Mother's coming, mother's coming !

DICK. [*Violently*] I wish—— Promise, Joy !

JOY. [*Looking over her shoulder*] Sly old thing ! If you'll pay Peachey out, I'll promise you supper !

MISS BEECH. [*From behind the tree*] I hear you.

JOY. [*Whispering*] Pay her out, pay her out ! She's let out all your worms !

DICK. [*Looking moodily at the paint-pot*] I say, is it true that Maurice Lever's coming with your mother ? I've met him playing cricket, he's rather a good sort.

JOY. [*Flashing out*] I hate him.

DICK. [*Troubled*] Do you ? Why ? I thought—I didn't know—if I'd *known* of course, I'd have——

[*He is going to say " hated him too ! " But the voices of* ERNEST BLUNT *and the* COLONEL *are heard approaching, in dispute.*

Joy. Oh! Dick, hide me, I don't want my hair seen till Mother comes.

[*She springs into the hollow tree. The* COLONEL *and* ERNEST *appear in the opening of the wall.*

ERNEST. The ball *was* out, Colonel.

COLONEL. Nothing of the sort.

ERNEST. A good foot out.

COLONEL. It was not, sir.   I saw the chalk fly.

[ERNEST *is twenty-eight, with a little moustache, and the positive cool voice of a young man who knows that he knows everything.   He is perfectly calm.*

ERNEST. I was nearer to it than you.

COLONEL. [*In a high, hot voice*] I don't care where you were, I hate a fellow who can't keep cool.

MISS BEECH. [*From behind the hollow tree*] Fie! Fie!

ERNEST. We're two to one ; Letty says the ball was out.

COLONEL. Letty's *your wife*, she'd say anything.

ERNEST. Well, look here, Colonel, I'll show you the very place it pitched.

COLONEL. Gammon! You've lost your temper, you don't know what you're talking about.

ERNEST. [*Coolly*] I suppose you'll admit the rule that one umpires one's own court.

COLONEL. [*Hotly*] Certainly not *in this case !*

MISS BEECH. [*From behind the hollow tree*] Special case !

ERNEST. [*Moving chin in collar—very coolly*] Well, of course if you won't play the game !

COLONEL. [*In a towering passion*] If you lose your temper like this, I'll never play with you again.

[*To* LETTY *a pretty soul in a linen suit, approaching through the wall.*]

Do you mean to say that ball was out, Letty ?

LETTY. Of course it was, Father.

COLONEL. You say that because he's *your husband*. [*He sits on the rustic seat.*] If your mother'd been there she'd have backed *me* up !

LETTY. Mother wants Joy, Dick, about her frock.

DICK. I—I don't know where she is.

MISS BEECH. [*From behind the hollow tree*] Ahem !

LETTY. What's the matter, Peachey ?

MISS BEECH. Swallowed a fly.   Poor creature !

ERNEST. [*Returning to his point*] Why I know the ball was out, Colonel, was because it pitched in a line with that arbutus tree——

COLONEL. [*Rising*] Arbutus tree ! [*To his daughter.*] Where's your mother ?

LETTY. In the blue room, Father.

ERNEST. The ball was a good foot out; at the height it was coming when it passed me——

COLONEL. [*Staring at him*] You're a—you're a—a theorist! From where you were you couldn't see the ball at all. [*To* LETTY.] Where's your mother?

LETTY. [*Emphatically*] In the *blue* room, Father!

[*The* COLONEL *glares confusedly, and goes away towards the blue room.*

ERNEST. [*In the swing, and with a smile*] Your old Dad'll never be a sportsman!

LETTY. [*Indignantly*] I wish you wouldn't call Father old, Ernie! What time's Molly coming, Peachey?

[ROSE *has come from the house, and stands waiting for a chance to speak.*

ERNEST. [*Breaking in*] Your old Dad's only got one fault: he can't take an *impersonal* view of things.

MISS BEECH. Can you find me anyone who can?

ERNEST. [*With a smile*] Well, Peachey!

MISS BEECH. [*Ironically*] Oh! of course, there's you!

ERNEST. I don't know about that! But——

ROSE. [*To* LETTY] Please, Miss, the Missis says will you and Mr. Ernest please to move your things into Miss Peachey's room.

ERNEST. [*Vexed*] Deuce of a nuisance havin' to turn out for this fellow Lever. What did Molly want to bring him for?

MISS BEECH. Course you've no personal feeling in the matter!

ROSE. [*Speaking to* MISS BEECH] The Missis says you're to please move your things into the blue room, please, Miss.

LETTY. Aha, Peachey! That settles you! Come on, Ernie!

[*She goes towards the house.* ERNEST, *rising from the swing, turns to* MISS BEECH, *who follows.*

ERNEST. [*Smiling, faintly superior*] Personal, not a bit! I only think while Molly's out at grass, she oughtn't to——

MISS BEECH. [*Sharply*] Oh! do you?

[*She hustles* ERNEST *out through the wall, but his voice is heard faintly from the distance: "I think it's jolly thin."*

ROSE. [*To* DICK] The Missis says you're to take all your worms and things, sir, and put them where they won't be seen.

DICK. [*Shortly*] Haven't got any!

ROSE. The Missis says she'll be very angry if you don't put your worms away; and would you come and help kill earwigs in the blue——?

DICK. Hang!   [*He goes, and* ROSE *is left alone.*

ROSE. [*Looking straight before her*] Please, Miss Joy, the Missis says will you go to her about your frock.

[*There is a little pause, then from the hollow tree* JOY'S *voice is heard.*

JOY. No—o!

ROSE. If you didn't come, I was to tell you she was going to put you in the blue—— [JOY *looks out of the tree.*]

[*Immovable, but smiling.*] Oh, Miss Joy, you've done your hair up! [JOY *retires into the tree.*]

Please, Miss, what shall I tell the Missis?

JOY. [JOY's *voice is heard*] Anything you like!

ROSE. [*Over her shoulder*] I shall be drove to tell her a story, Miss.

JOY. All right! Tell it.

[ROSE *goes away, and* JOY *comes out. She sits on the rustic seat and waits.* DICK, *coming softly from the house, approaches her.*

DICK. [*Looking at her intently*] Joy! I wanted to say something—— [JOY *does not look at him, but twists her fingers.*]

I shan't see you again, you know, after to-morrow till I come up for the 'Varsity match.

JOY. [*Smiling*] But that's next week.

DICK. *Must* you go home to-morrow? [JOY *nods three times.*]

[*Coming closer.*] I shall miss you so awfully. You don't know how I—— [JOY *shakes her head.*]

Do look at me! [JOY *steals a look.*] Oh! Joy! [*Again* JOY *shakes her head.*

JOY. [*Suddenly*] Don't!

DICK. [*Seizing her hand*] Oh, Joy! Can't you——

JOY. [*Drawing her hand away*] Oh! don't.

DICK. [*Bending his head*] It's—it's—so——

JOY. [*Quietly*] Don't, Dick!

DICK. But I can't help it! It's too much for me, Joy, I must tell you—— [MRS. GWYN *is seen approaching towards the house.*

JOY. [*Spinning round*] It's Mother—oh, *Mother!* [*She rushes at her.*

[MRS. GWYN *is a handsome creature of thirty-six, dressed in a muslin frock. She twists her daughter round, and kisses her.*

MRS. GWYN. How sweet you look with your hair up, Joy! Who's this? [*Glancing with a smile at* DICK.

JOY. Dick Merton—in my letters you know. [*She looks at* DICK *as though she wished him gone.*

MRS. GWYN. How do you do?

DICK. [*Shaking hands*] How d'you do? I think if you'll excuse me—I'll go in. [*He goes uncertainly.*

MRS. GWYN. What's the matter with him?

JOY. Oh, nothing! [*Hugging her.*] Mother! You *do* look such a duck. Why did you come by the towing-path, wasn't it *cooking?*

MRS. GWYN. [*Avoiding her eyes*] Mr. Lever wanted to go into Mr. Henty's. [*Her manner is rather artificially composed.*

JOY. [*Dully*] Oh! Is he—is he really coming *here*, Mother?

MRS. GWYN. [*Whose voice has hardened just a little*] If Aunt Nell's got a room for him—of course—why not?

JOY. [*Digging her chin into her mother's shoulder*] Why couldn't he choose some day when we'd gone? I wanted you all to myself.

MRS. GWYN. You *are* a quaint child—when I was your age——

JOY. [*Suddenly looking up*] Oh! Mother, you must have been a chook!

MRS. GWYN. Well, I was about twice as old as you, I know that.

JOY. Had you any—any other offers before you were married, Mother?

MRS. GWYN. [*Smilingly*] Heaps!

JOY. [*Reflectively*] Oh!

MRS. GWYN. Why? Have *you* been having any?

JOY. [*Glancing at* MRS. GWYN, *and then down*] N—o, of course not!

MRS. GWYN. Where are they all? Where's Peachey?

JOY. Fussing about somewhere; don't let's hurry! Oh! you duckie—duckie! Aren't there any letters from Dad?

MRS. GWYN. [*In a harder voice*] Yes, one or two.

JOY. [*Hesitating*] Can't I see?

MRS. GWYN. I didn't bring them. [*Changing the subject obviously.*] Help me to tidy—I'm so hot I don't know what to do.

[*She takes out a powder-puff bag, with a tiny looking-glass.*

JOY. How lovely it'll be to-morrow—going home!

MRS. GWYN. [*With an uneasy look*] London's dreadfully stuffy, Joy. You'll only get knocked up again.

JOY. [*With consternation*] Oh! but, Mother, I *must* come.

MRS. GWYN. [*Forcing a smile*] Oh, well, if you must, you must!

[JOY *makes a dash at her.*] Don't rumple me again. Here's Uncle Tom.

JOY. [*Quickly*] Mother, we're going to dance to-night, promise to dance with me; there are three more girls than men, at least, and don't dance too much with—with—you know—because I'm—[*dropping her voice and very still*]—jealous.

MRS. GWYN. [*Forcing a laugh*] You are funny!

JOY. [*Very quickly*] *I* haven't made any engagements because of *you*.   [*The* COLONEL *approaches through the wall.*

MRS. GWYN. Well, Uncle Tom?

COLONEL. [*Genially*] Why, Molly! [*He kisses her.*] What made you come by the towing-path?

JOY. Because it's so much cooler, of course.

COLONEL. Hallo! What's the matter with *you*? Phew! you've got your hair up! Go and tell your aunt your mother's on the lawn. Cut along!   [JOY *goes, blowing a kiss.*] Cracked about you, Molly! Simply cracked! We shall miss her when you take her off to-morrow. [*He places a chair for her.*] Sit down, sit down, you must be tired in this heat. I've sent Bob for your things with the wheelbarrow; what have you got—only a bag, I suppose?

MRS. GWYN. [*Sitting, with a smile*] That's all, Uncle Tom, except— my trunk and hat-box.

COLONEL. Phew! And what's-his-name brought a bag, I suppose?

MRS. GWYN. They're all together. I hope it's not too much, Uncle Tom.

COLONEL. [*Dubiously*] Oh! Bob'll manage! I suppose you see a good deal of—of—Lever. That's his brother in the Guards, isn't it?

MRS. GWYN. Yes.

COLONEL. Now what does this chap do?

MRS. GWYN. What should he do, Uncle Tom? He's a Director.

COLONEL. Guinea-pig! [*Dubiously.*] Your bringing him down was a good idea. [MRS. GWYN, *looking at him sidelong, bites her lips.*] I should like to have a look at him. But, I say, you know, Molly —mines, mines! There are a lot of these chaps about, whose business is to cook their own dinners. Your aunt thinks——

MRS. GWYN. Oh! Uncle Tom, don't tell me what Aunt Nell thinks!

COLONEL. Well—well! Look here, old girl! It's *my* experience never to—what I mean is—never to trust too much to a man who has to do with mining. *I've* always refused to have anything to do with mines. If your husband were in England, of course, I'd say nothing.

MRS. GWYN. [*Very still*] We'd better keep *him* out of the question, hadn't we?

COLONEL. Of course, if you wish it, my dear.

MRS. GWYN. Unfortunately, I do.

COLONEL. [*Nervously*] Ah! yes, I know; but look here, Molly, your aunt thinks you're in a very delicate position—in fact, she thinks you see too much of young Lever——

MRS. GWYN. [*Stretching herself like an angry cat*] Does she? And what do *you* think?

COLONEL. I? I make a point of not thinking. I only know that here he is, and I don't want you to go burning your fingers, eh?

[MRS. GWYN *sits with a vindictive smile.*]

A gold mine's a *gold* mine. I don't mean he deliberately—but they take in women and parsons, and—and all sorts of fools. [*Looking down.*] And then, you know, I can't tell your feelings, my dear, and I don't want to; but a man about town'll compromise a woman as soon as he'll look at her, and [*softly shaking his head*] I don't like that, Molly! It's not the thing!

[MRS. GWYN *sits unmoved, smiling the same smile, and the* COLONEL *gives her a nervous look.*]

If—if—you were any other woman—*I* shouldn't care—and if—if you were a plain woman, damme, you might do what you liked! I know you and Geoff don't get on; but here's this child of yours, devoted to you, and—and don't you see, old girl? Eh?

MRS. GWYN. [*With a little hard laugh*] Thanks! Perfectly! I suppose as you don't think, Uncle Tom, it never occurred to you that *I* have rather a lonely time of it.

COLONEL. [*With compunction*] Oh! my dear, yes, of course I know it must be beastly.

MRS. GWYN. [*Stonily*] It *is*.

COLONEL. Yes, yes! [*Speaking in a surprised voice*] I don't know what I am talking like this for! It's your Aunt! She goes on at me till she gets on my nerves. What d'you think she wants me to do now? Put money into this gold mine! Did you ever hear such folly?

MRS. GWYN. [*Breaking into laughter*] Oh! Uncle Tom.

COLONEL. All very well for you to laugh, Molly!

MRS. GWYN. [*Calmly*] And how much *are* you going to put in?

COLONEL. Not a farthing! Why, I've got nothing but my pension and three thousand India Stock!

MRS. GWYN. Only ninety pounds a year, besides your pension! D'you mean to say that's all you've got, Uncle Tom? I never knew that before. What a shame!

COLONEL. [*Feelingly*] It *is*—a d——d shame! I don't suppose there's another case in the army of a man being treated as *I've* been.

MRS. GWYN. But how on earth do you manage here on so little?

COLONEL. [*Brooding*] Your Aunt's very funny. She's a born manager. She'd manage the hind leg off a donkey; but if *I* want five shillings for a charity or what not, I have to whistle for it. And then all of a sudden, Molly, she'll take it into her head to spend good-ness knows what on some trumpery or other, and come to me for the money. If I haven't got it to give her, out she flies about three per cent., and worries me to invest in some wild-cat or other, like your friend's thing, the Jaco—what is it? I don't pay the slightest attention to her.

MRS. HOPE. [*From the direction of the house*] Tom!

COLONEL. [*Rising*] Yes, dear! [*Then dropping his voice.*] I say, Molly, don't you mind what I said about young Lever. I don't wan't you to imagine that I think harm of people—you know I don't —but so many women come to grief, and—[*hotly*]—I can't stand men about town; not that he of course——

MRS. HOPE. [*Peremptorily*] Tom!

COLONEL. [*In hasty confidence*] I find it best to let your Aunt run on. If she says anything——

MRS. HOPE. To-om!

COLONEL. Yes, dear!

[*He goes hastily.* MRS. GWYN *sits drawing circles on the ground with her charming parasol. Suddenly she springs to her feet, and stands waiting like an animal at bay. The* COLONEL *and* MRS. HOPE *approach her talking.*

MRS. HOPE. Well, how was *I* to know?

COLONEL. Didn't Joy come and tell you?

MRS. HOPE. I don't know what's the matter with that child? Well, Molly, so here you are. You're before your time—that train's always late.

MRS. GWYN. [*With faint irony*] I'm sorry, Aunt Nell!

[THEY *bob, seem to take fright, and kiss each other gingerly.*

MRS. HOPE. What have you done with Mr. Lever? I shall have to put him in Peachey's room. Tom's got no champagne.

COLONEL. They've a very decent brand down at the " George," Molly. I'll send Bob over——

MRS. HOPE. Rubbish, Tom! He'll just have to put up with what he can get!

MRS. GWYN. Of course! He's not a snob! For goodness' sake, Aunt Nell, don't put yourself out! I'm sorry I suggested his coming.

COLONEL. My dear, we *ought* to have champagne in the house—in case of accident.

MRS. GWYN. [*Shaking him gently by the coat*] No, *please,* Uncle Tom!

MRS. HOPE. [*Suddenly*] Now, I've told your Uncle, Molly, that he's not to go in for this gold mine without making certain it's a good thing. Mind, I think you've been very rash. I'm going to give you a good talking to; and that's not all—you oughtn't to go about like this with a young man; he's not at all bad looking. I remember him perfectly well at the Flemings' dance.

[*On* MRS. GWYN'S *lips there comes a little mocking smile.*

COLONEL. [*Pulling his wife's sleeve*] Nell!

MRS. HOPE. No, Tom, I'm going to talk to Molly; she's old enough to know better.

MRS. GWYN. Yes?

MRS. HOPE. Yes, and you'll get yourself into a mess; I don't approve of it, and when I see a thing I don't approve of——

COLONEL. [*Walking about, and pulling his moustache*] Nell, I won't have it, I simply won't have it.

MRS. HOPE. What rate of interest are these Preference Shares to pay?

MRS. GWYN. [*Still smiling*] Ten per cent.

MRS. HOPE. What did I tell you, Tom? And are they safe?

MRS. GWYN. You'd better ask Maurice.

MRS. HOPE. There, you see, you call him Maurice! Now supposing your Uncle went in for some of them——

3*

COLONEL. [*Taking off his hat—in a high, hot voice*] I'm not going in for anything of the sort.

MRS. HOPE. Don't swing your hat by the brim! Go and look if you can see him coming! [*The* COLONEL *goes.*] [*In a lower voice.*] Your Uncle's getting very bald. I've only shoulder of lamb for lunch, and a salad. It's lucky it's too hot to eat.

[MISS BEECH *has appeared while she is speaking.*]
Here she is, Peachey!

MISS BEECH. I see her. [*She kisses* MRS. GWYN, *and looks at her intently.*]

MRS. GWYN. [*Shrugging her shoulders*] Well, Peachey! What d'you make of me?

COLONEL. [*Returning from his search*] There's a white hat crossing the second stile. Is that your friend, Molly? [MRS. GWYN *nods.*

MRS. HOPE. Oh! before I forget, Peachey—Letty and Ernest can move their things back again. I'm going to put Mr. Lever in *your* room. [*Catching sight of the paint-pot on the ground.*] There's that disgusting paint-pot! Take it up at once, Tom, and put it in the tree.

[*The* COLONEL *picks up the pot and bears it to the hollow tree, followed by* MRS. HOPE; *he enters.*]

MRS. HOPE. [*Speaking into the tree*] Not *there!*

COLONEL. [*From within*] Well, where then?

MRS. HOPE. Why—up—oh! gracious!

[MRS. GWYN, *standing alone, is smiling.* LEVER *approaches from the towing-path. He is a man like a fencer's wrist, supple and steely. A man whose age is difficult to tell, with a quick, good-looking face, and a line between his brows; his darkish hair is flecked with grey. He gives the feeling that he has always had to spurt to keep pace with his own life.*

MRS. HOPE. [*Also entering the hollow tree.*] No—oh!

COLONEL. [*From the depths, in a high voice*] Well, dash it then! What *do* you want?

MRS. GWYN. Peachey, may I introduce Mr. Lever to you? Miss Beech, my old governess. [*They shake each other by the hand.*

LEVER. How do you do?

[*His voice is pleasant, his manner easy.*

MISS BEECH. Pleased to meet you.

[*Her manner is that of one who is not pleased. She watches.*

MRS. GWYN. [*Pointing to the tree—maliciously*] This is my uncle and my aunt. They're taking exercise, I think.

[*The* COLONEL *and* MRS. HOPE *emerge convulsively. They are very hot.* LEVER *and* MRS. GWYN *are very cool.*

MRS. HOPE. [*Shaking hands with him*] So you've got here! Aren't you very hot?—Tom!

COLONEL. Brought a splendid day with you !   Splendid !

[*As he speaks,* JOY *comes running with a bunch of roses ; seeing* LEVER, *she stops and stands quite rigid.*

MISS BEECH. [*Sitting in the swing*] Thunder !

COLONEL. Thunder ?   Nonsense, Peachey, you're always imagining something.   Look at the sky !

MISS BEECH. Thunder !   [MRS. GWYN's *smile has faded.*

MRS. HOPE. [*Turning*] Joy, don't you see Mr. Lever ?

[JOY, *turning to her mother, gives her the roses. With a forced smile,* LEVER *advances, holding out his hand.*

LEVER. How are you, Joy ?   Haven't seen you for an age !

JOY. [*Without expression*] I am very well, thank you.

[*She raises her hand, and just touches his.* MRS. GWYN's *eyes are fixed on her daughter.* MISS BEECH *is watching them intently ;* MRS. HOPE *is buttoning the* COLONEL's *coat.*

The curtain falls.

ACT II

It is afternoon, and at a garden-table placed beneath the hollow tree, the COLONEL *is poring over plans. Astride of a garden-chair,* LEVER *is smoking cigarettes.* DICK *is hanging Chinese lanterns to the hollow tree.*

LEVER. Of course, if this level [*pointing with his cigarette*] peters out to the West we shall be in a tightish place ; you know what a mine is at this stage, Colonel Hope ?

COLONEL. [*Absently*] Yes, yes. [*Tracing a line.*] What is there to prevent its running out here to the *East* ?

LEVER. Well, nothing, except that as a matter of fact it doesn't.

COLONEL. [*With some excitement*] I'm *very glad* you showed me these papers, very glad ! *I* say that it's a most astonishing thing if the ore suddenly stops there. [*A gleam of humour visits* LEVER's *face.*] I'm not an expert, but you ought to prove that ground to the East more thoroughly.

LEVER. [*Quizzically*] Of course, sir, if you advise that——

COLONEL. If it were *mine*, I'd no more sit down under the belief that the ore stopped there, than I'd—— There's a harmony in these things.

LEVER. I can only tell you what our experts say.

COLONEL. Ah ! Experts ! No faith in them—never had ! Miners, lawyers, theologians, cowardly lot—pays them to be cowardly. When they haven't their own axes to grind, they've got their theories; a theory's a dangerous thing. [*He loses himself in contemplation of the papers.*] Now *my* theory is, you're in strata here of what we call the Triassic Age.

LEVER. [*Smiling faintly*] Ah !

COLONEL. You've struck a fault, that's what's happened. The ore may be as much as thirty or forty yards out ; but it's there, depend on it.

LEVER. Would you back that opinion, sir ?

COLONEL. [*With dignity*] I never give an opinion that I'm not prepared to back. I want to get to the *bottom* of this. What's to prevent the gold going down *indefinitely* ?

LEVER. Nothing, so far as I know.

COLONEL. [*With suspicion*] Eh !

LEVER. All I can tell you is : This is as far as we've got, and we want more money before we can get any further.

COLONEL. [*Absently*] Yes, yes ; that's very usual.

LEVER. If you ask my personal opinion I think it's very doubtful that the gold does go down.

COLONEL. [*Smiling*] Oh ! a *personal* opinion—on a matter of this sort !

LEVER. [*As though about to take the papers*] Perhaps we'd better close the sitting, sir ; sorry to have bored you.

COLONEL. Now, now ! Don't be so touchy ! If I'm to put money in, I'm bound to look at it all round.

LEVER. [*With lifted brows*] Please don't imagine that I *want* you to put money in.

COLONEL. Confound it, sir ! D'you suppose I take you for a Company promoter ?

LEVER. Thank you !

COLONEL. [*Looking at him doubtfully*] You've got Irish blood in you—um ? You're so hasty !

LEVER. If you're really thinking of taking shares—my advice to you is, don't !

COLONEL. [*Regretfully*] If this were an ordinary gold mine, I wouldn't dream of looking at it, I want you to understand that. Nobody has a greater objection to gold mines than I.

LEVER. [*Looks down at his host with half-closed eyes*] But it *is* a gold mine, Colonel Hope.

COLONEL. I know, I know ; but I've been into it for *myself* ; I've formed my *opinion personally*. Now, what's the reason you don't want me to invest ?

LEVER. Well, if it doesn't turn out as you expect, you'll say it's my doing. I know what investors are.

COLONEL. [*Dubiously*] If it were a Westralian or a Kaffir I wouldn't touch it with a pair of tongs ! It's not as if I were going to put much in ! [*He suddenly bends above the papers as though magnetically attracted.*] *I like* these Triassic formations !

[DICK *who has hung the last lantern, moodily departs.*

LEVER. [*Looking after him*] That young man seems depressed.

COLONEL. [*As though remembering his principles*] I don't like mines, never have ! [*Suddenly absorbed again.*] I tell you what, Lever—this thing's got tremendous possibilities. You don't seem to believe in it enough. No mine's any good without faith ; until I see for *myself*, however, I shan't commit myself beyond a thousand.

LEVER. Are you serious, sir ?

COLONEL. Certainly ! I've been thinking it over ever since you told me Henty had fought shy. I've a poor opinion of Henty. He's one of those fellows that says one thing and does another. An opportunist !

LEVER. [*Slowly*] I'm afraid we're all that, more or less.

[*He sits beneath the hollow tree.*

COLONEL. A man never knows what he is himself. There's my wife. She thinks she's—— By the way, don't say anything to her about this, please. And, Lever [*nervously*], I don't think, you know, this is *quite* the sort of thing for my niece.

LEVER. [*Quietly*] I agree. I mean to get her out of it.

COLONEL. [*A little taken aback*] Ah! You know, she—she's in a very delicate position, living by herself in London. [LEVER *looks at him ironically.*] You [*very nervously*] see a good deal of her? If it hadn't been for Joy growing so fast, we shouldn't have had the child down here. Her Mother ought to have her with her. Eh! Don't you think so?

LEVER. [*Forcing a smile*] Mrs. Gwyn always seems to me to get on all right.

COLONEL. [*As though making a discovery*] You know, I've found that when a woman's living alone and unprotected, the very least thing will set a lot of hags and jackanapes talking. [*Hotly.*] The more unprotected and helpless a woman is, the more they revel in it. If there's anything I hate in this world, it's those wretched creatures who babble about their neighbours' affairs.

LEVER. I agree with you.

COLONEL. One ought to be very careful not to give them—that is [*checks himself confused; then hurrying on*]—I suppose you and Joy get on all right?

LEVER. [*Coolly*] Pretty well, thanks. I'm not exactly in Joy's line; haven't seen very much of her, in fact.

[MISS BEECH *and* JOY *have been approaching from the house. But seeing* LEVER, JOY *turns abruptly, hesitates a moment, and with an angry gesture goes away.*

COLONEL [*Unconscious*] Wonderfully affectionate little thing! Well, she'll be going home to-morrow!

MISS BEECH. [*Who has been gazing after* JOY] Talkin' business, poor creatures?

LEVER. Oh, no! If you'll excuse me, I'll wash my hands before tea.

[*He glances at the* COLONEL *poring over papers, and, shrugging his shoulders, strolls away.*

MISS BEECH. [*Sitting in the swing*] I see your horrid papers.

COLONEL. Be quiet, Peachey!

MISS BEECH. On a beautiful summer's day, too.

COLONEL. That'll do now.

MISS BEECH. [*Unmoved*] For every ounce you take out of a gold mine you put two in.

COLONEL. Who told you that rubbish?

Miss Beech. [*With devilry*] *You did !*

Colonel. This isn't an ordinary gold mine.

Miss Beech. Oh ! quite a *special* thing.

[Colonel *stares at her, but subsiding at her impassivity he pores again over the papers.*

[Rose *has approached with a tea cloth.*

Rose. If you please, sir, the missis told me to lay the tea.

Colonel. Go away ! Ten fives fifty. Ten 5-16ths, Peachey ?

Miss Beech. I hate your nasty sums !

[Rose *goes away. The* Colonel *writes.* Mrs. Hope's *voice is heard, " Now then, bring those chairs, you two. Not that one, Ernest."* Ernest *and* Letty *appear through the openings of the wall, each with a chair.*

Colonel. [*With dull exasperation*] What do *you* want !

Letty. Tea, father.   [*She places her chair and goes away.*

Ernest. That Johnny-bird Lever is too cocksure for me, Colonel. Those South American things are no good at all. I know all about *them* from young Scrotton. There's not one that's worth a red cent. If you want a flutter——

Colonel. [*Explosively*] Flutter ! I'm not a gambler, sir !

Ernest. Well, Colonel [*with a smile*] I only don't want you to chuck your money away on a stiff 'un. If you want anything good you should go to Mexico.

Colonel. [*Jumping up and holding out the map*] Go to—— [*He stops in time.*] What d'you call that, eh ? M-E-X——

Ernest. [*Not to be embarrassed*] It all depends on what part.

Colonel. You think you know everything—you think nothing's right unless it's your own idea ! Be good enough to keep your advice to yourself.

Ernest. [*Moving with his chair, and stopping with a smile*] If you ask me, I should say it wasn't playing the game to put Molly into a thing like that.

Colonel. What do you mean, sir ?

Ernest. Any Juggins can see that she's a bit gone on our friend.

Colonel. [*Freezingly*] Indeed !

Ernest. He's not at all the sort of Johnny that appeals to me.

Colonel. Really ?

Ernest. [*Unmoved*] If I were you, Colonel, I should tip her the wink. He was hanging about her at Ascot all the time. It's a bit thick !   [Mrs. Hope, *followed by* Rose, *appears from the house.*

Colonel. [*Stammering with passion*] Jackanapes !

Mrs. Hope. Don't stand there, Tom ; clear those papers, and let Rose lay the table. Now, Ernest, go and get another chair.

[*The* Colonel *looks wildly round and sits beneath the hollow tree, with his head held in his hands.* Rose *lays the cloth.*

MISS BEECH. [*Sitting beside the* COLONEL] Poor creature !

ERNEST. [*Carrying his chair about with him*] Ask any Johnny in the City, he'll tell you Mexico's a very tricky country—the people are awful rotters—

MRS. HOPE. Put that chair down, Ernest.

[ERNEST *looks at the chair, puts it down, opens his mouth, and goes away.* ROSE *follows him.*]

What's he been talking about ? You oughtn't to get so excited, Tom ; is your head bad, old man ? Here, take these papers ! [*She hands the papers to the* COLONEL.] Peachey, go in and tell them tea'll be ready in a minute, there's a good soul ! Oh ! and on my dressing-table you'll find a bottle of eau-de-Cologne——

MISS BEECH. Don't let him get in a temper again ? That's three times to-day !   [*She goes towards the house.*

COLONEL. Never met such a fellow in my life, the most opinionated, narrow-minded—thinks he knows everything. Whatever Letty could see in him I can't think. Pragmatical beggar !

MRS. HOPE. Now, Tom ! What have you been up to, to get into a state like this ?

COLONEL. [*Avoiding her eyes*] I shall lose my temper with him one of these days. He's got that confounded habit of thinking nobody can be right but himself.

MRS. HOPE. That's enough ! I want to talk to you seriously ! Dick's in love. I'm perfectly certain of it.

COLONEL. Love ! Who's he in love with—Peachey ?

MRS. HOPE. You can see it all over him. If I saw any signs of Joy's breaking out, I'd send them both away. I simply won't have it.

COLONEL. Why, she's a child !

MRS. HOPE. [*Pursuing her own thoughts*] But she isn't—not yet. I've been watching her very carefully. She's more in love with her Mother than anyone, follows her about like a dog ! She's been quite rude to Mr. Lever.

COLONEL. [*Pursuing his own thoughts*] I don't believe a word of it.

[*He rises and walks about.*

MRS. HOPE. Don't believe a word of what ?

[*The* COLONEL *is silent.*]

[*Pursuing his thoughts with her own.*] If I thought there were anything between Molly and Mr. Lever d'you suppose I'd have him in the house ?   [*The* COLONEL *stops, and gives a sort of grunt.*] He's a very nice fellow ; and I want you to pump him well, Tom, and see what there is in this mine.

COLONEL. [*Uneasily*] Pump !

MRS. HOPE. [*Looking at him curiously*] Yes, you've been up to something ! Now what is it ?

COLONEL. Pump my own guest ! I never heard of such a thing !

Mrs. Hope. There you are on your high horse! I do wish you had a little common sense, Tom!

Colonel. I'd as soon you ask me to sneak about eavesdropping! Pump!

Mrs. Hope. Well, what were you looking at these papers for? It does drive me so wild the way you throw away all the chances you have of making a little money. I've got you this opportunity, and you do nothing but rave up and down, and talk nonsense!

Colonel. [*In a high voice*] Much you know about it! I've taken a thousand shares in this mine! [*He stops dead. There is a silence.*

Mrs. Hope. You've—WHAT? Without consulting me? Well, then, you'll just go and take them out again!

Colonel. You want me to——?

Mrs. Hope. The idea! As if you could trust your judgment in a thing like that! You'll just go at once and say there was a mistake; then we'll talk it over calmly.

Colonel. [*Drawing himself up*] Go back on what I've said? Not if I lose every penny! First you worry me to take the shares, and then you worry me not—I won't have it, Nell, I won't have it!

Mrs. Hope. Well, if I'd thought you'd have forgotten what you said this morning and turned about like this, d'you suppose I'd have spoken to you at all? Now, *do* you?

Colonel. Rubbish! If you can't see that this is a special opportunity!

[*He walks away followed by* Mrs. Hope, *who endeavours to make him see her point of view.* Ernest *and* Letty *are now returning from the house armed with a third chair.*

Letty. What's the matter with everybody? Is it the heat?

Ernest. [*Preoccupied and sitting in the swing*] That sportsman, Lever, you know, ought to be warned off.

[Rose *has followed with the tea tray.*

Letty. [*Signing to* Ernest] Where's Miss Joy, Rose?

Rose. Don't know, Miss.   [*Putting down the tray, she goes.*

Letty. Ernie, be careful, you never know where Joy is.

Ernest. [*Preoccupied with his reflections*] Your old Dad's as mad as a hatter with me.

Letty. Why?

Ernest. Well, I merely said what I thought, that Molly ought to look out what she's doing, and he dropped on me like a cartload of bricks.

Letty. The Dad's very fond of Molly.

Ernest. But look here, d'you mean to tell me that she and Lever aren't——

Letty. Don't! Suppose they are! If Joy were to hear it'd be simply awful. I *like* Molly. *I'm* not going to believe anything against her. I don't see the use of it. If it is, it is, and if it isn't, it isn't.

ERNEST. Well, all I know is that when I told her the mine was probably a frost she went for me like steam.

LETTY. Well, so should I. She was only sticking up for her friends.

ERNEST. Ask the old Peachey-bird. She knows a thing or two. Look here, I don't mind a man's being a bit of a sportsman, but I think Molly's bringin' him down here is too thick. Your old dad's got one of his notions that because this Josser's his guest, he must keep him in a glass case, and take shares in his mine, and all the rest of it.

LETTY. I do think people are horrible, always thinking things. It's not as if Molly were a stranger. She's *my own cousin.* I'm not going to believe anything about my own cousin. I simply *won't.*

ERNEST. [*Reluctantly realizing the difference that this makes*] I suppose it *does* make a difference, her bein' your cousin.

LETTY. Of course it does! I only hope to goodness no one will make Joy suspect——

[*She stops and puts her finger to her lips, for* JOY *is coming towards them, as the tea-bell sounds. She is followed by* DICK *and* MISS BEECH *with the eau-de-Cologne. The* COLONEL *and* MRS. HOPE *are also coming back, discussing still each other's point of view.*

JOY. Where's Mother? Isn't she here?

MRS. HOPE. Now, Joy, come and sit down; your mother's been told tea's ready; if she lets it get cold it's her look out.

DICK. [*Producing a rug, and spreading it beneath the tree*] Plenty of room, Joy.

JOY. I don't believe Mother knows, Aunt Nell.

[MRS. GWYN *and* LEVER *appear in the opening of the wall.*

LETTY [*Touching* ERNEST's *arm*] Look, Ernie! Four couples and Peachey——

ERNEST. [*Preoccupied*] What couples?

JOY. Oh! Mums, here you are!

[*Seizing her, she turns her back on* LEVER. *They sit in various seats, and* MRS. HOPE *pours out the tea.*

MRS. HOPE. Hand the sandwiches to Mr. Lever, Peachey. It's our own jam, Mr. Lever.

LEVER. Thanks. [*He takes a bite.*] It's splendid!

MRS. GWYN. [*With forced gaiety*] It's the first time I've ever seen you eat jam.

LEVER. [*Smiling a forced smile*] Really! But I love it.

MRS. GWYN. [*With a little bow*] You always refuse mine.

Joy. [*Who has been staring at her enemy, suddenly*] I'm all burnt up! Aren't you simply boiled, Mother? [*She touches her Mother's forehead.*

Mrs. Gwyn. Ugh! You're quite clammy, Joy.

Joy. It's enough to make anyone clammy.

[*Her eyes go back to* Lever's *face as though to stab him.*

Ernest. [*From the swing*] I say, you know, the glass is going down.

Lever. [*Suavely*] The glass in the hall's steady enough.

Ernest. Oh, I never go by that; that's a rotten old glass.

Colonel. Oh! is it?

Ernest. [*Paying no attention*] I've got a little ripper—never puts you in the cart. Bet you what you like we have thunder before to-morrow night.

Miss Beech. [*Removing her gaze from* Joy *to* Lever] You don't think we shall have it before to-night, do you?

Lever. [*Suavely*] I beg your pardon; did you speak to me?

Miss Beech. I said, you don't think we shall have the thunder before to-night, do you? [*She resumes her watch on* Joy.

Lever. [*Blandly*] Really, I don't see any signs of it.

[Joy, *crossing to the rug, flings herself down. And* Dick *sits cross-legged, with his eyes fast fixed on her.*

Miss Beech. [*Eating*] People don't often see what they don't want to, do they? [Lever *only lifts his brows.*

Mrs. Gwyn. [*Quickly breaking in*] What *are* you talking about? The weather's perfect.

Miss Beech. Isn't it.

Mrs. Hope. You'd better make a good tea, Peachey; nobody'll get anything till eight, and then only cold shoulder. You must just put up with no hot dinner, Mr. Lever.

Lever. [*Bowing*] Whatever is good enough for Miss Beech is good enough for me.

Miss Beech. [*Sardonically—taking another sandwich*] So you think!

Mrs. Gwyn. [*With forced gaiety*] Don't be so absurd, Peachey.

[Miss Beech *grunts slightly.*

Colonel. [*Once more busy with his papers*] I see the name of your engineer is Rodriguez—Italian, eh?

Lever. Portuguese.

Colonel. Don't like that!

Lever. I believe he was born in England.

Colonel. [*Reassured*] Oh, was he? Ah!

Ernest. Awful rotters, those Portuguese!

Colonel. There you go!

Letty. Well, Father, Ernie only said what you said.

Mrs. Hope. Now I want to ask you, Mr. Lever, is this gold mine safe? If it isn't—I simply won't allow Tom to take these shares; he can't afford it.

LEVER. It rather depends on what you call safe, Mrs. Hope.

MRS. HOPE. I don't want anything extravagant, of course ; if they're going to pay their ten per cent. regularly, and Tom can have his money out at any time—— [*There is a faint whistle from the swing.*] I only want to know that it's a thoroughly genuine thing.

MRS. GWYN. [*Indignantly*] As if Maurice would be a director if it wasn't ?

MRS. HOPE. Now, Molly, I'm simply asking——

MRS. GWYN. Yes, you are !

COLONEL [*Rising*] I'll take two thousand of those shares, Lever. To have my wife talk like that—I'm quite ashamed.

LEVER. Oh, come, sir, Mrs. Hope only meant——
                    [MRS. GWYN *looks eagerly at* LEVER.

DICK. [*Quietly*] Let's go on the river, Joy.
                    [JOY *rises, and goes to her Mother's chair.*

MRS. HOPE. Of course ! What rubbish, Tom ! As if anyone ever invested money without making sure !

LEVER. [*Ironically*] It seems a little difficult to make sure in this case. There isn't the smallest necessity for Colonel Hope to take any shares, and it looks to me as if he'd better not. [*He lights a cigarette.*

MRS. HOPE. Now, Mr. Lever, don't be offended ! I'm very anxious for Tom to take the shares if you say the thing's so good.

LEVER. I'm afraid I must ask to be left out, please.

JOY. [*Whispering*] Mother, if you've finished, do come, I want to show you my room.

MRS. HOPE. I wouldn't say a word, only Tom's so easily taken in.

MRS. GWYN. [*Fiercely*] Aunt Nell, how *can* you ?
                    [JOY *gives a little savage laugh.*

LETTY. [*Hastily*] Ernie, will you play Dick and me ? Come on, Dick !   [*All three go out towards the lawn.*

MRS. HOPE. You ought to know your Uncle by this time, Molly. He's just like a child. He'd be a pauper to-morrow if I didn't see to things.

COLONEL. Understand once for all that I shall take two thousand shares in this mine. I'm—I'm humiliated.
                    [*He turns and goes towards the house.*

MRS. HOPE. Well, what on earth have I said ?
                    [*She hurries after him.*

MRS. GWYN. [*In a low voice as she passes*] You needn't insult my friends !
          [LEVER, *shrugging his shoulders, has strolled aside.* JOY, *with a passionate movement seen only by* MISS BEECH, *goes off towards the house.* MISS BEECH *and* MRS. GWYN *are left alone beside the remnants of the feast.*

MISS BEECH. Molly ! [MRS. GWYN *looks up startled.*] Take care,

Molly, take care! The child! Can't you see? [*Apostrophizing*
LEVER.] Take care, Molly, take care!

LEVER. [*Coming back*] Awfully hot, isn't it?

MISS BEECH. Ah! and it'll be hotter if we don't mind.

LEVER. [*Suavely*] Do we control these things?

   [MISS BEECH *looking from face to face, nods her head repeatedly ;*
      then gathering her skirts she walks towards the house. MRS.
      GWYN *sits motionless, staring before her.*]

Extraordinary old lady! [*He pitches away his cigarette.*] What's the
matter with her, Molly?

MRS. GWYN. [*With an effort*] Oh! Peachey's a character!

LEVER. [*Frowning*] So I see!   [*There is a silence.*

MRS. GWYN. Maurice!

LEVER. Yes.

MRS. GWYN. Aunt Nell's hopeless, you mustn't mind her.

LEVER. [*In a dubious and ironic voice*] My dear girl, I've too much
to bother me to mind trifles like that.

MRS. GWYN. [*Going to him suddenly*] Tell *me*, won't you?

                  [LEVER *shrugs his shoulders.*]
A month ago you'd have told me soon enough!

LEVER. Now, Molly!

MRS. GWYN. Ah! [*With a bitter smile.*] The Spring's soon over.

LEVER. It's always Spring between us.

MRS. GWYN. Is it?

LEVER. You didn't tell me what *you* were thinking about just now
when you sat there like stone.

MRS. GWYN. It doesn't do for a *woman* to say too much.

LEVER. Have I been so bad to you that you need feel like that,
Molly?

MRS. GWYN. [*With a little warm squeeze of his arm*] Oh! my *dear*,
it's only that I'm so——   [*She stops.*

LEVER. [*Gently*] So what?

MRS. GWYN. [*In a low voice*] It's hateful here.

LEVER. I didn't want to come. I don't understand why you
suggested it. [MRS. GWYN *is silent.*] It's been a mistake!

MRS. GWYN. [*Her eyes fixed on the ground*] Joy comes *home* to-morrow.
I thought if I brought you here—I should know——

LEVER. [*Vexedly*] Um!

MRS. GWYN. [*Losing her control*] Can't you *see?* It haunts me?
How are we to go on? I must know—I must know!

LEVER. I don't see that my coming——

MRS. GWYN. I thought I should have more confidence; I thought
I should be able to face it better in London, if you came down here
openly—and now—I feel I mustn't speak or look at you.

LEVER. You don't think your Aunt——

MRS. GWYN. [*Scornfully*] She ! It's only Joy I care about.

LEVER. [*Frowning*] We must be more careful, that's all. We mustn't give ourselves away again as we were doing just now.

MRS. GWYN. When anyone says anything horrid to you, I can't help it. [*She puts her hand on the lapel of his coat.*

LEVER. My dear child, take care !

[MRS. GWYN *drops her hand. She throws her head back, and her throat is seen to work as though she were gulping down a bitter draught. She moves away.*]

[*Following hastily.*] Don't dear, don't ! I only meant—— Come, Molly, let's be sensible. I want to tell you something about the mine.

MRS. GWYN. [*With a quavering smile*] Yes—let's talk sensibly, and walk properly in this sensible, proper place.

[LEVER *is seen trying to soothe her, and yet to walk properly. As they disappear, they are viewed by* JOY, *who like the shadow parted from its figure, has come to join it again. She stands now, foiled, a carnation in her hand ; then flings herself on a chair, and leans her elbows on the table.*]

JOY. I hate him ! Pig !

ROSE. [*Who has come to clear the tea things*] Did you call, Miss ?

JOY. Not you !

ROSE. [*Motionless*] No, Miss !

JOY. [*Leaning back and tearing the flower*] Oh ! do hurry up, Rose !

ROSE. [*Collects the tea things*] Mr. Dick's coming down the path ! Aren't I going to get you to do your frock, Miss Joy ?

JOY. No.

ROSE. What will the Missis say ?

JOY. Oh, *don't* be so stuck, Rose ! [ROSE *goes, but* DICK *has come.*

DICK. Come on the river, Joy, just for half an hour, as far as the kingfishers—do ! [JOY *shakes her head.*] Why not ? It'll be so jolly and cool. I'm most awfully sorry if I worried you this morning. I didn't mean to. I won't again, I promise. [JOY *slides a look at him, and from that look he gains a little courage.*] Do come ! It'll be the last time. *I* feel it awfully, Joy.

JOY. There's nothing to hurt *you !*

DICK. [*Gloomily*] Isn't there—when you're like this ?

JOY. [*In a hard voice*] If you don't like me, why do you follow me about ?

DICK. What *is* the matter ?

JOY. [*Looking up, as if for want of air*] Oh ! Don't !

DICK. Oh, Joy, what *is* the matter ? Is it the heat ?

JOY. [*With a little laugh*] Yes.

DICK. Have some eau-de-Cologne. I'll make you a bandage. [*He takes the eau-de-Cologne, and makes a bandage with his handkerchief.*] It's *quite* clean.

JOY. Oh, Dick, you are so funny!

DICK. [*Bandaging her forehead*] I can't bear *you* to feel bad; it puts me off completely. I mean I don't generally make a fuss about people, but when it's *you*——

JOY. [*Suddenly*] I'm all right.

DICK. Is that comfy?

JOY. [*With her chin up, and her eyes fast closed*] Quite.

DICK. I'm not going to stay and worry you. You ought to rest. Only, Joy! Look here! If you want me to do *anything* for you, *any* time——

JOY. [*Half opening her eyes*] Only to go away.

[DICK *bites his lips and walks away.*

Dick—[*softly*]—Dick! [DICK *stops.*] I didn't mean that; will you get me some water-irises for this evening?

DICK. Won't I? [*He goes to the hollow tree and from its darkness takes a bucket and a boat hook.*] I know where there are some rippers!

[JOY *stays unmoving with her eyes half closed.*]

Are you sure you're all right, Joy? You'll just rest here in the shade, won't you, till I come back; it'll do you no end of good. I shan't be twenty minutes.

[*He goes, but cannot help returning softly, to make sure.*]

You're *quite* sure you're all right?

[JOY *nods. He goes away towards the river. But there is no rest for* JOY. *The voices of* MRS. GWYN *and* LEVER *are heard returning.*

JOY. [*With a gesture of anger*] Hateful! Hateful! [*She runs away.*

[MRS. GWYN *and* LEVER *are seen approaching; they pass the tree, in conversation.*

MRS. GWYN. But I don't see why, Maurice.

LEVER. We mean to sell the mine; we must do some more work on it, and for that we must have money.

MRS. GWYN. If you only want a little, I should have thought you could have got it in a minute in the City.

LEVER. [*Shaking his head*] No, no; we must get it privately.

MRS. GWYN. [*Doubtfully*] Oh! [*She slowly adds.*] Then it isn't such a good thing! [*And she does not look at him.*

LEVER. Well, we mean to sell it.

MRS. GWYN. What about the people who buy?

LEVER. [*Dubiously regarding her*] My dear girl, they've just as much chance as *we* had. It's not my business to think of them. There's *your* thousand pounds——

MRS. GWYN. [*Softly*] Don't bother about *my* money, Maurice. I don't want you to do anything not quite——

LEVER. [*Evasively*] Oh! There's my brother's and my sister's too. I'm not going to let any of you run any risk. When we all went in for it the thing looked splendid ; it's only the last month that we've had doubts. What bothers me now is your Uncle. I don't want him to take these shares. It looks as if I'd come here on purpose.

MRS. GWYN. Oh ! he *mustn't* take them !

LEVER. That's all very well ; but it's not so simple.

MRS. GWYN. [*Shyly*] But, Maurice, have you told him about the selling ?

LEVER. [*Gloomily, under the hollow tree*] It's a Board secret. I'd no business to tell even you.

MRS. GWYN. But he thinks he's taking shares in a good—a permanent thing.

LEVER. You can't go in to a mining venture without some risk.

MRS. GWYN. Oh, yes, I know—but—but Uncle Tom is such a dear !

LEVER. [*Stubbornly*] I can't help his being the sort of man he is. I didn't want him to take these shares, I told him so in so many words. Put yourself in my place, Molly, how can I go to him and say—" This thing may turn out rotten," when he knows I got you to put your money into it ?

[*But* JOY, *the lost shadow, has come back. She moves forward resolutely. They are divided from her by the hollow tree ; she is unseen. She stops.*

MRS. GWYN. I think he *ought* to be told about the selling ; it's not fair.

LEVER. What on earth made him rush at the thing like that ? I don't understand that kind of man ?

MRS. GWYN. [*Impulsively*] I *must* tell him, Maurice ; I can't let him take the shares without——   [*She puts her hand on his arm.*

[JOY *turns, as if to go back whence she came, but stops once more.*

LEVER. [*Slowly and very quietly*] I didn't think you'd give *me* away, Molly.

MRS. GWYN. I don't think I quite understand.

LEVER. If you tell the Colonel about this sale the poor old chap will think me a man that you ought to have nothing to do with. Do you want that ?

[MRS. GWYN, *giving her lover a long look, touches his sleeve.* JOY, *slipping behind the hollow tree, has gone.*]

You can't act in a case like this as if you'd only a *principle* to consider. It's the—the *special circumstances*——

MRS. GWYN. [*With a faint smile*] But you'll be glad to get the money, won't you ?

LEVER. By George, if you're going to take it like this, Molly !

MRS. GWYN. Don't !

LEVER. We may not sell after all, dear, we may find it turn out trumps.

MRS. GWYN. [*With a shiver*] I don't want to hear any more. I know women don't understand. [*Impulsively.*] It's only that I can't bear anyone should think that *you*——

LEVER. [*Distressed*] For goodness' sake, don't look like that, Molly! Of course, I'll speak to your Uncle. I'll stop him somehow, even if I have to make a fool of myself. I'll do anything you want——

MRS. GWYN. I feel as if I were being smothered here.

LEVER. It's only for one day.

MRS. GWYN. [*With sudden tenderness*] It's not your fault, dear. I ought to have known how it would be. Well, let's go in!

> [*She sets her lips, and walks towards the house with* LEVER *following. But no sooner has she disappeared than* JOY *comes running after; she stops, as though throwing down a challenge. Her cheeks and ears are burning.*

JOY. Mother!

> [*After a moment* MRS. GWYN *reappears in the opening of the wall.*

MRS. GWYN. Oh! here you are!

JOY. [*Breathlessly*] Yes.

MRS. GWYN. [*Uncertainly*] Where—have you been? You look dreadfully hot; have you been running?

JOY. Yes—no.

MRS. GWYN. [*Looking at her fixedly*] What's the matter—you're trembling! [*Softly.*] Aren't you well, dear?

JOY. Yes—I don't know.

MRS. GWYN. What *is* it, darling?

JOY. [*Suddenly clinging to her*] Oh! Mother!

MRS. GWYN. I don't understand.

JOY. [*Breathlessly*] Oh, Mother, let me go back home with you now at once——

MRS. GWYN. [*Her face hardening*] Why? What on earth——

JOY. I can't stay here.

MRS. GWYN. But why?

JOY. I want to be with *you*—Oh! Mother, don't you love me?

MRS. GWYN. [*With a faint smile*] Of course I love you, Joy.

JOY. Ah! but you love *him* more.

MRS. GWYN. Love him—whom?

JOY. Oh! Mother, I didn't——[*She tries to take her Mother's hand, but fails.*] Oh! *don't.*

MRS. GWYN. You'd better explain what you mean, I think.

JOY. I want to get you to—he—he's—he's—not——!

MRS. GWYN. [*Frigidly*] Really, Joy!

JOY. [*Passionately*] I'll fight against him, and I know there's something wrong about——   [*She stops.*

MRS. GWYN. About what?

JOY. Let's tell Uncle Tom, Mother, and go away.

MRS. GWYN. Tell Uncle Tom—what?

JOY. [*Looking down and almost whispering*] About—about—the mine.

MRS. GWYN. What about the mine? What do you mean? [*Fiercely.*] Have you been spying on me?

JOY. [*Shrinking*] No! oh, no!

MRS. GWYN. Where were you?

JOY. [*Just above her breath*] I—I heard something.

MRS. GWYN. [*Bitterly*] But you were not spying?

JOY. I wasn't—I wasn't! I didn't want—to hear. I only heard a little. I couldn't help listening, Mother.

MRS. GWYN. [*With a little laugh*] Couldn't help listening?

JOY. [*Through her teeth*] I hate him. I didn't mean to listen, but I hate him.

MRS. GWYN. I see.   [*There is a silence.*] Why do you hate him?

JOY. He—he——   [*She stops.*]

MRS. GWYN. Yes?

JOY. [*With a sort of despair*] I don't know. Oh! I *don't know!* But I feel——

MRS. GWYN. I can't reason with you. As to what you heard, it's —ridiculous.

JOY. It's not that. It's—it's you!

MRS. GWYN. [*Stonily*] I don't know what you mean.

JOY. [*Passionately*] I wish Dad were here!

MRS. GWYN. Do you love your Father as much as me?

JOY. Oh! Mother, no—you *know* I don't.

MRS. GWYN. [*Resentfully*] Then why do you want him?

JOY. [*Almost under her breath*] Because of that man.

MRS. GWYN. Indeed!

JOY. I will never—never make friends with him.

MRS. GWYN. [*Cuttingly*] I have not asked you to.

JOY. [*With a blind movement of her hand*] Oh, Mother!

                   [MRS. GWYN *half turns away.*]

Mother—won't you? Let's tell Uncle Tom, and go away from him?

MRS. GWYN. If you were not a child, Joy, you wouldn't say such things.

JOY. [*Eagerly*] I'm not a child, I'm—I'm a woman. I *am.*

MRS. GWYN. No! You—are—*not* a woman, Joy.

    [*She sees* JOY *throw up her arms as though warding off a blow, and turning finds that* LEVER *is standing in the opening of the wall.*

LEVER. [*Looking from face to face*] What's the matter? [*There is no answer.*] What is it, Joy?

JOY. [*Passionately*] I heard you, I don't care who knows. I'd listen again.

LEVER. [*Impassively*] Ah! and what did I say that was so very dreadful?

JOY. You're a—a—you're a—coward!

MRS. GWYN. [*With a sort of groan*] Joy!

LEVER. [*Stepping up to* JOY, *and standing with his hands behind him— in a low voice*] Now, hit me in the face—hit me—hit me as hard as you can. Go on, Joy, it'll do you good.

[JOY *raises her clenched hand, but drops it, and hides her face.*] Why don't you? I'm not pretending! [JOY *makes no sign.*] Come, Joy; you'll make yourself ill, and that won't help, will it?

[*But* JOY *still makes no sign.*]

[*With determination.*] What's the matter; now come—tell me!

JOY. [*In a stifled, sullen voice*] Will you leave my mother alone?

MRS. GWYN. Oh! my dear Joy, don't be silly!

JOY. [*Wincing; then with sudden passion*] I defy you—I defy you!

[*She rushes from their sight.*]

MRS. GWYN. [*With a movement of distress*] Oh!

LEVER. [*Turning to* MRS. GWYN *with a protecting gesture*] Never mind, dear! It'll be—it'll be all right!

[*But the expression of his face is not the expression of his words.*]

The curtain falls.

ACT III

It is evening; a full yellow moon is shining through the branches of the hollow tree. The Chinese lanterns are alight. There is dancing in the house; the music sounds now loud, now soft. Miss Beech is sitting on the rustic seat in a black bunchy evening dress, whose inconspicuous opening is inlaid with white. She slowly fans herself.
Dick *comes from the house in evening dress. He does not see* Miss Beech.

Dick. Curse! [*A short silence.*] Curse!

Miss Beech. Poor young man!

Dick. [*With a start*] Well, Peachey, I can't help it.

[*He fumbles off his gloves.*

Miss Beech. Did you ever know anyone that could?

Dick. [*Earnestly*] It's such awfully hard lines on Joy. I can't get her out of my head, lying there with that beastly headache while everybody's jigging round.

Miss Beech. Oh! you don't mind about yourself—noble young man!

Dick. I should be a brute if I didn't mind more for her.

Miss Beech. So you think it's a headache, do you?

Dick. Didn't you hear what Mrs. Gwyn said at dinner about the sun? [*With inspiration.*] I say, Peachey, couldn't you—couldn't you just go up and give her a message from me, and find out if there's anything she wants, and say how brutal it is that she's seedy; it would be most awfully decent of you. And tell her the dancing's no good without her. Do, Peachey, now do! Ah! and look here!

[*He dives into the hollow of the tree, and brings from out of it a pail of water, in which are placed two bottles of champagne, and some yellow irises—he takes the irises.*]

You might give her these. I got them specially for her, and I haven't had a chance.

Miss Beech. [*Lifting a bottle*] What's this?

Dick. Fizz. The Colonel brought it from the "George." It's for supper; he put it in here because of—— [*Smiling faintly.*] Mrs. Hope, I think. Peachey, *do* take her those irises.

Miss Beech. D'you think they'll do her any good?

Dick. [*Crestfallen*] I thought she'd like—— I don't want to worry her—you might try. [Miss Beech *shakes her head.*]
Why not?

MISS BEECH. The poor little creature won't let me in.

DICK. You've *been* up then !

MISS BEECH. [*Sharply*] Of course I've been up. I've not got a stone for my heart, young man !

DICK. All right ! I suppose I shall just have to get along somehow.

MISS BEECH. [*With devilry*] That's what we've all got to do.

DICK. [*Gloomily*] But this is too brutal for anything.

MISS BEECH. Worse than ever happened to anyone !

DICK. I swear I'm not thinking of *myself*.

MISS BEECH. Did y'ever know anybody that swore they were ?

DICK. Oh ! shut up !

MISS BEECH. You'd better go in and get yourself a partner.

DICK. [*With pale desperation*] Look here, Peachey, I simply loathe all those girls.

MISS BEECH. Ah—h ! [*Ironically.*] Poor lot, aren't they ? .

DICK. All right ; chaff away, it's good fun, isn't it ? It makes me sick to dance when Joy's lying there. Her last night, too !

MISS BEECH. [*Sidling to him*] You're a good young man, and you've got a good heart.   [*She takes his hand and puts it to her cheek.*

DICK. Peachey—I say, Peachey—d'you think there's—I mean d'you think there'll ever be any chance for me ?

MISS BEECH. I *thought* that was coming ! I don't approve of your making love at your time of life ; don't you think I'm going to encourage you.

DICK. But I shall be of age in a year ; my money's my own, it's not as if I had to ask anyone's leave ; and I mean, I *do* know my own mind.

MISS BEECH. Of course you do. Nobody else would at your age, but *you* do.

DICK. I wouldn't ask her to promise, it wouldn't be fair when she's so young, but I do want her to know that I shall never change.

MISS BEECH. And suppose—only suppose—she's fond of you, and says *she'll* never change.

DICK. Oh ! Peachey ! D'you think there's a chance of that— *do* you ?

MISS BEECH. A—h—h !

DICK. I wouldn't let her bind herself, I swear I wouldn't. [*Solemnly.*] I'm not such a selfish brute as you seem to think.

MISS BEECH. [*Sidling close to him and in a violent whisper*] Well— have a go !

DICK. Really ? You *are* a brick, Peachey !   [*He kisses her.*

MISS BEECH. [*Yielding pleasurably ; then remembering her principles*] Don't you ever say I said so ! You're too young, both of you.

DICK. But it is exceptional, I mean in *my* case, isn't it ?

[*The* COLONEL *and* MRS. GWYN *are coming down the lawn.*

MISS BEECH. Oh! *very!* [*She sits beneath the tree and fans herself.*

COLONEL. The girls are all sitting out, Dick! I've been obliged to dance myself. Phew! [*He mops his brow.*]

[DICK, *swinging round, goes rushing off towards the house.*] [*Looking after him.*] Hallo! What's the matter with him? Cooling your heels, Peachey? By George! it's hot. Fancy the poor devils in London on a night like this, what? [*He sees the moon.*] It's a full moon. You're lucky to be down here, Molly.

MRS. GWYN. [*In a low voice*] Very!

MISS BEECH. Oh! so you think she's lucky, do you?

COLONEL. [*Expanding his nostrils*] Delicious scent to-night! Hay and roses—delicious. [*He seats himself between them.*] A shame that poor child has knocked up like this. Don't think it was the sun myself—more likely neuralgic—she's subject to neuralgia, Molly.

MRS. GWYN. [*Motionless*] I know.

COLONEL. Got too excited about your coming. I told Nell not to keep worrying her about her frock, and this is the result. But your Aunt—you know—she can't let a thing alone!

MISS BEECH. Ah! 'tisn't neuralgia.

[MRS. GWYN *looks at her quickly and averts her eyes.*

COLONEL. Excitable little thing. You don't understand her, Peachey.

MISS BEECH. Don't I?

COLONEL. She's all affection. Eh, Molly? I remember what I was like at her age, a poor affectionate little rat, and now look at me!

MISS BEECH. [*Fanning herself*] I see you.

COLONEL. [*A little sadly*] We forget what we were like when we were young. She's been looking forward to to-night ever since you wrote; and now to have to go to bed and miss the dancing. Too bad!

MRS. GWYN. Don't, Uncle Tom!

COLONEL. [*Patting her hand*] There, there, old girl, don't think about it. She'll be all right to-morrow.

MISS BEECH. If I were her mother I'd soon have her up.

COLONEL. Have her up with that headache! What are you talking about, Peachey?

MISS BEECH. *I* know a remedy.

COLONEL. Well, out with it.

MISS BEECH. Oh! Molly knows it too!

MRS. GWYN. [*Staring at the ground*] It's easy to advise.

COLONEL. [*Fidgeting*] Well, if you're thinking of morphia for her, don't have anything to do with it. I've always set my face against morphia; the only time I took it was in Burmah. I'd raging neuralgia for two days. I went to our old doctor, and I made him give me some. " Look here, doctor," I said, " I hate the idea of morphia, I've never taken it, and I never want to."

MISS BEECH. [*Looking at* MRS. GWYN] When a tooth hurts, you should have it out. It's only putting off the evil day.

COLONEL. You say that because it wasn't your own.

MISS BEECH. Well, it was hollow, and you broke your principles !

COLONEL. Hollow yourself, Peachey ; you're as bad as anyone !

MISS BEECH. [*With devilry*] Well, I know that ! [*She turns to* MRS. GWYN.] He should have had it out ! Shouldn't he, Molly ?

MRS. GWYN. I—don't—judge for other people.

[*She gets up suddenly, as though deprived of air.*

COLONEL. [*Alarmed*] Hallo, Molly ! Aren't *you* feeling the thing, old girl ?

MISS BEECH. Let her get some air, poor creature !

COLONEL. [*Who follows anxiously*] Your Aunt's got some first-rate sal volatile.

MRS. GWYN. It's all right, Uncle Tom. I felt giddy, it's nothing now.

COLONEL. That's the dancing. [*He taps his forehead.*] I know what it is when you're not used to it.

MRS. GWYN. [*With a sudden bitter outburst*] I suppose you think I'm a very bad mother to be amusing myself while Joy's suffering.

COLONEL. My dear girl, whatever put such a thought into your head ? We all know if there were anything you *could* do, you'd do it at once, wouldn't she, Peachey ?

[MISS BEECH *turns a slow look on* MRS. GWYN.

MRS. GWYN. Ah ! you see, Peachey knows me better.

COLONEL. [*Following up his thoughts*] I always think women are wonderful. There's your Aunt, she's very funny, but if there's anything the matter with me, she'll sit up all night ; but when she's ill herself, and you try to do anything for her, out she raps at once.

MRS. GWYN. [*In a low voice*] There's always *one* that a woman will do anything for.

COLONEL. Exactly what I say. With your Aunt it's me, and by George ! Molly, sometimes I wish it wasn't.

MISS BEECH. [*With meaning*] But is it ever for another *woman !*

COLONEL. You old cynic ! D'you mean to say Joy wouldn't do anything on earth for her Mother, or Molly for Joy ? You don't know human nature. What a wonderful night ! Haven't seen such a moon for years, she's like a great, great lamp !

[MRS. GWYN *hiding from* MISS BEECH'S *eyes, rises and slips her arm through his ; they stand together looking at the moon.*]

Don't like these Chinese lanterns, with that moon—tawdry ! eh ! By Jove, Molly, I sometimes think we humans are a rubbishy lot— each of us talking and thinking of nothing but our own potty little

affairs, and when you see a great thing like that up there—— [*Sighs.*]
But there's your Aunt, if I were to say a thing like that to her she'd—
she'd think me a lunatic ; and yet, you know, she's a *very good* woman.

MRS. GWYN. [*Half clinging to him*] Do *you* think me very selfish,
Uncle Tom ?

COLONEL. My dear—what a fancy ! Think you selfish—of *course*
I don't ; why should I ?

MRS. GWYN. [*Dully*] I don't know.

COLONEL. [*Changing the subject nervously*] I like your friend, Lever,
Molly. He came to me before dinner quite distressed about your
Aunt, beggin' me not to take those shares. She'll be the first to
worry me, but he made such a point of it, poor chap—in the end I
was obliged to say I wouldn't. I thought it showed very nice feeling.
[*Ruefully.*] It's a pretty tight fit to make two ends meet on my income
—I've missed a good thing, all owing to your Aunt. [*Dropping his
voice.*] I don't mind telling you, Molly, I think they've got a much
finer mine there than they've any idea of.

　　　　　[MRS. GWYN *gives way to laughter that is very near to sobs.*
[*With dignity.*] I can't see what there is to laugh at.

MRS. GWYN. I don't know what's the matter with me this evening.

MISS BEECH. [*In a low voice*] *I* do.

COLONEL. There, there ! Give me a kiss, old girl. [*He kisses her
on the brow.*] Why, you're forehead's as hot as fire. I know—I know
—you're fretting about Joy. Never mind—come ! [*He draws her
hand beneath his arm.*] Let's go and have a look at the moon on the
river. We all get upset at times ; eh ! [*Lifting his hand as if he had
been stung.*] Why, you're not crying, Molly ! I say ! Don't do that,
old girl, it makes me wretched. Look here, Peachey. [*Holding out
the hand on which the tear had dropped.*] This is dreadful !

MRS. GWYN. [*With a violent effort*] It's all right, Uncle Tom !

　　　　　[MISS BEECH *wipes her own eyes stealthily. From the house is
　　　　　heard the voice of* MRS. HOPE, *calling* " TOM."

MISS BEECH. Someone calling you !

COLONEL. There, there, my dear, you just stay here, and cool
yourself—I'll come back—shan't be a minute.　　　[*He turns to go.*]

　　　　　　　　　　　　　　　　　　[MRS. HOPE'S *voice sounds nearer.*

[*Turning back.*] And, Molly, old girl, don't you mind anything I said.
I don't remember what it was—it must have been *something*, I suppose.

　　　　　　　　　　　　　　　　　　　　　[*He hastily retreats.*

MRS. GWYN. [*In a fierce low voice*] Why do you torture me ?

MISS BEECH. [*Sadly*] I don't want to torture you.

MRS. GWYN. But you do. D'you think I haven't seen this coming
—all these weeks. I knew she must find out some time ! But even
a day counts——

MISS BEECH. I don't understand why you brought him down here.

Mrs. Gwyn. [*After staring at her, bitterly*] When day after day and night after night you've thought of nothing but how to keep them both, you might a little want to prove that it was possible, mightn't you? But *you don't* understand—how should you? You've never been a mother! [*And fiercely.*] You've never had a lov——

[Miss Beech *raises her face—it is all puckered.*]

[*Impulsively.*] Oh, I didn't mean that, Peachey!

Miss Beech. All right, my dear.

Mrs. Gwyn. I'm so dragged in two. [*She sinks into a chair.*] I knew it must come.

Miss Beech. Does she know everything, Molly?

Mrs. Gwyn. She guesses.

Miss Beech. [*Mournfully*] It's either him or her then, my dear; one or the other you'll have to give up.

Mrs. Gwyn. [*Motionless*] Life's very hard on women?

Miss Beech. Life's only just beginning for that child, Molly.

Mrs. Gwyn. You don't care if it ends for *me!*

Miss Beech. Is it as bad as that?

Mrs. Gwyn. Yes.

Miss Beech. [*Rocking her body*] Poor things! Poor things!

Mrs. Gwyn. Are you still fond of me?

Miss Beech. Yes, yes, my dear, of course I am.

Mrs. Gwyn. In spite of my—wickedness?   [*She laughs.*

Miss Beech. Who am I to tell what's wicked and what isn't? God knows you're both like daughters to me.

Mrs. Gwyn. [*Abruptly*] I can't.

Miss Beech. Molly.

Mrs. Gwyn. You don't know what you're asking.

Miss Beech. If I could save you suffering, my dear, I would. I hate suffering, if it's only a fly, I hate it.

Mrs. Gwyn. [*Turning away from her*] Life isn't fair. Peachey, go in and leave me alone.   [*She leans back motionless.*

[Miss Beech *gets off her seat, and stroking* Mrs. Gwyn's *arm in passing goes silently away. In the opening of the wall she meets* Lever, *who is looking for his partner. They make way for each other.*

Lever. [*Going up to* Mrs. Gwyn—*gravely*] The next is our dance, Molly.

Mrs. Gwyn. [*Unmoving*] Let's sit it out here, then.

[Lever *sits down.*

Lever. I've made it all right with your Uncle.

Mrs. Gwyn. [*Dully*] Oh?

Lever. I spoke to him about the shares before dinner.

Mrs. Gwyn. Yes, he told me, thank you.

Lever. There's nothing to worry over, dear.

4

Mrs. Gwyn. [*Passionately*] What does it matter about the wretched shares *now* ? I'm stifling. [*She throws her scarf off.*

Lever. I don't understand what you mean by " now."

Mrs. Gwyn. Don't you ?

Lever. We weren't—Joy can't *know*—why should she ? I don't believe for a minute——

Mrs. Gwyn. Because you don't want to.

Lever. Do you mean she does ?

Mrs. Gwyn. Her heart knows.

[Lever *makes a movement of discomfiture ; suddenly* Mrs. Gwyn *looks at him as though to read his soul.*]

I seem to bring you nothing but worry, Maurice. Are you tired of me ?

Lever. [*Meeting her eyes*] No, I am not.

Mrs. Gwyn. Ah, but would you tell me if you were ?

Lever. [*Softly*] Sufficient unto the day is the evil thereof.

[Mrs. Gwyn *struggles to look at him, then covers her face with her hands.*

Mrs. Gwyn. If I were to give you up, you'd forget me in a month.

Lever. Why do you say such things ?

Mrs. Gwyn. If only I could believe I was necessary to you !

Lever. [*Forcing the fervour of his voice*] But you *are* !

Mrs. Gwyn. Am I ? [*With the ghost of a smile.*] Midsummer day !

[*She gives a laugh that breaks into a sob.*
[*The music of a waltz sounds from the house.*

Lever. For God's sake, don't, Molly—I don't believe in going to meet trouble.

Mrs. Gwyn. It's staring me in the face.

Lever. Let the future take care of itself !

[Mrs. Gwyn *has turned away her face, covering it with her hands.*] Don't, Molly ! [*Trying to pull her hands away.*] Don't !

Mrs. Gwyn. Oh ! what *shall* I do ?

[*There is a silence ; the music of the waltz sounds louder from the house.*]

[*Starting up.*] Listen ! One can't sit it out and dance it too. Which is it to be, Maurice, dancing—or sitting out ? It must be one or the other, mustn't it ?

Lever. Molly ! Molly !

Mrs. Gwyn. Ah, my dear ! [*Standing away from him as though to show herself.*] How long shall I keep you ? This is all that's left of me. It's time I joined the wallflowers. [*Smiling faintly.*] It's time I played the mother, isn't it ? [*In a whisper.*] It'll be all sitting out then.

Lever. Don't ! Let's go and dance, it'll do you good.

[*He puts his hands on her arms, and in a gust of passion kisses her lips and throat.*

MRS. GWYN. I can't give you up—I can't. Love me, oh! love
me!

    [*For a moment they stand so ; then, with sudden remembrance of
       where they are, they move apart.*

LEVER. Are you all right now, darling?

MRS. GWYN. [*Trying to smile*] Yes, dear—quite.

LEVER. Then let's go, and dance.   [*They go.*

    [*For a few seconds the hollow tree stands alone ; then from the house
    ROSE comes and enters it. She takes out a bottle of champagne,
    wipes it, and carries it away ; but seeing MRS. GWYN's scarf
    lying across the chair, she fingers it, and stops, listening to the
    waltz. Suddenly draping it round her shoulders, she seizes the
    bottle of champagne, and waltzes with abandon to the music, as
    though avenging a long starvation of her instincts. Thus
    dancing, she is surprised by DICK, who has come to smoke a
    cigarette and think, at the spot where he was told to " have a
    go." ROSE, startled, stops and hugs the bottle.*

DICK. It's not claret, Rose, I shouldn't warm it.

    [ROSE, *taking off the scarf, replaces it on the chair ; then with the
    half-warmed bottle, she retreats. DICK, in the swing, sits
    thinking of his fate. Suddenly from behind the hollow tree, he
    sees JOY darting forward in her day dress with her hair about her
    neck, and her skirt all torn. As he springs towards her she
    turns at bay.*

DICK. Joy!

JOY. I want Uncle Tom.

DICK. [*In consternation*] But ought you to have got up—I thought
you were ill in bed ; oughtn't you to be lying down?

JOY. I haven't *been* in bed. Where's Uncle Tom?

DICK. But where have you been—your dress is all torn? Look!

                          [*He touches the torn skirt.*

JOY. [*Tearing it away*] In the fields. Where's Uncle Tom?

DICK. Aren't you really ill, then?

        [JOY *shakes her head.* DICK, *showing her the irises.*]

Look at these. They were the best I could get!

JOY. Don't! I want Uncle Tom!

DICK. Won't you take them?

JOY. I've got something else to do.

DICK. [*With sudden resolution*] What do you want the Colonel
for?

JOY. I want him.

DICK. Alone?

JOY. Yes.

DICK. Joy, what *is* the matter?

JOY. I've got something to tell him.

DICK. What? [*With sudden inspiration.*] Is it about Lever?

JOY. [*In a low voice*] The mine.

DICK. The mine?

JOY. It's not—not a proper one.

DICK. How do you mean, Joy?

JOY. I overheard. I don't care, I listened. I wouldn't if it had been anybody else, but I *hate* him.

DICK. [*Gravely*] What did you hear?

JOY. He's keeping back something Uncle Tom ought to know.

DICK. Are you sure?   [JOY *makes a rush to pass him.*] [*Barring the way.*] No, wait a minute—you must! Was it something that really matters, I don't want to know what.

JOY. Yes, it was.

DICK. What a beastly thing—are you quite certain, Joy?

JOY. [*Between her teeth*] Yes.

DICK. Then you *must* tell him, of course, even if you did overhear. You can't stand by and see the Colonel swindled. Whom was he talking to?

JOY. I won't tell you.

DICK. [*Taking her wrist*] Was it—was it your Mother?

[JOY *bends her head.*] But if it was your Mother, why doesn't she——

JOY. Let me go.

DICK. [*Still holding her*] I mean I can't see what——

JOY. [*Passionately*] Let me *go!*

DICK. [*Releasing her*] I'm thinking of your Mother, Joy. She would never——

JOY. [*Covering her face*] That man!

DICK. But, Joy, just think! There must be some mistake. It's so queer—it's *quite impossible!*

JOY. He won't let her.

DICK. Won't let her—won't *let* her? But—— [*Stopping dead, and in a very different voice.*] Oh!

JOY. [*Passionately*] Why d'you look at me like that? Why can't you speak?   [*She waits for him to speak, but he does not.*] I'm going to show what he is, so that mother shan't speak to him again. I can—can't I—if I tell Uncle Tom?—can't I——?

DICK. But, Joy—if your Mother knows a thing like—that——

JOY. She wanted to tell—she begged him—and he wouldn't.

DICK. But, Joy, dear, it means——

JOY. I hate him, I want to make her hate him, and I *will.*

DICK. But, Joy, dear, don't you see—if your Mother knows a thing like that, and doesn't speak of it, it means that she—it means that you can't *make* her hate him—it means—— If it were anybody else, but, well, you can't give *your own Mother* away!

JOY. How dare you ! How *dare* you ! [*Turning to the hollow tree.*] It isn't true——— Oh ! it *isn't* true ?

DICK. [*In deep distress*] Joy, dear, I never meant, I didn't really ! [*He tries to pull her hands down from her face.*

JOY. [*Suddenly*] Oh ! go away, go *away* !

> [MRS. GWYN *is seen coming back.* JOY *springs into the tree.* DICK *quickly steals away.* MRS. GWYN *goes up to the chair and takes the scarf that she has come for, and is going again when* JOY *steals out to her.*]

Mother ! [MRS. GWYN *stands looking at her with her teeth set on her lower lip.*]

Oh ! Mother, it isn't true ?

MRS. GWYN. [*Very still*] What isn't true ?

JOY. That you and he are———

> [*Searching her Mother's face, which is deadly still. In a whisper.*] Then it *is* true. Oh !

MRS. GWYN. That's enough, Joy ! What *I* am is *my* affair—not *yours*—do you understand ?

JOY. [*Low and fierce*] Yes, I *do*.

MRS. GWYN. You don't. You're only a child.

JOY. [*Passionately*] I understand that you've hurt——— [*She stops.*

MRS. GWYN. Do you mean your father ?

JOY. [*Bowing her head*] Yes, and—and me. [*She covers her face.*] I'm—I'm ashamed.

MRS. GWYN. I brought you into the world, and you say that to me ? Have I been a bad mother to you ?

JOY. [*In a smothered voice*] Oh ! Mother !

MRS. GWYN. Ashamed ? Am *I* to live all my life like a dead woman because you're ashamed ? Am I to live like the dead because you're a child that knows nothing of life ? Listen, Joy, you'd better understand this once for all. Your Father has no right over me and he knows it. We've been hateful to each other for years. *Can* you understand that ? Don't cover your face like a child—look at me.

> [JOY *drops her hands, and lifts her face.* MRS. GWYN *looks back at her, her lips are quivering; she goes on speaking with stammering rapidity.*]

D'you think—because I suffered when you were born and because I've suffered since with every ache you ever had, that that gives you the right to dictate to me now ? [*In a dead voice.*] I've been unhappy enough and I shall be unhappy enough in the time to come. [*Meeting the hard wonder in* JOY's *face.*] Oh ! you untouched things, you're as hard and cold as iron.

JOY. I would do anything for *you*, Mother.

MRS. GWYN. Except—let me live, Joy. That's the only thing you won't do for me, I quite understand.

Joy. Oh ! Mother, you *don't* understand—I *want* you so ; and I seem to be nothing to you now.

Mrs. Gwyn. Nothing to me ?   [*She smiles.*

Joy. Mother, darling, if you're so unhappy let's forget it all, let's go away and I'll be everything to you, I promise.

Mrs. Gwyn. [*With a ghost of a laugh*] Ah, Joy !

Joy. I would try so hard.

Mrs. Gwyn. [*With the same quivering smile*] My darling, I know you would, until you fell in love yourself.

Joy. Oh, Mother, I wouldn't, I never would, I swear it.

Mrs. Gwyn. There has never been a woman, Joy, that did not fall in love.

Joy. [*In a despairing whisper*] But it's wrong of you—it's wicked !

Mrs. Gwyn. If it's wicked, *I* shall pay for it, not *you !*

Joy. But I want to save you, Mother !

Mrs. Gwyn. Save me ?   [*Breaking into laughter.*

Joy. I can't bear it that *you*—if you'll only—I'll never leave you. You think I don't know what I'm saying, but I *do*, because even now I —I half love somebody. Oh, Mother ! [*Pressing her breast.*] I feel —I feel *so awful*—as if everybody knew.

Mrs. Gwyn. You think I'm a monster to hurt you. Ah ! yes. You'll understand better some day.

Joy. [*In a sudden outburst of excited fear*] I won't believe it—I—I— can't—you're *deserting me*, Mother.

Mrs. Gwyn. Oh, you untouched things ! You——

          [*Joy looks up suddenly, sees her face, and sinks down on her knees.*

Joy. Mother—it's for *me !*

Mrs. Gwyn. Ask for my life, Joy—don't be afraid !

          [*Joy turns her face away. Mrs. Gwyn bends suddenly and touches
          her daughter's hair ; Joy shrinks from that touch.*]

[*Recoiling as though she had been stung.*] I forgot—I'm deserting you.

          [*And swiftly without looking back she goes away. Joy left alone
          under the hollow tree, crouches lower, and her shoulders shake.
          Here Dick finds her, when he hears no longer any sound of
          voices. He falls on his knees beside her.*

Dick. Oh ! Joy, dear, don't cry. It's so dreadful to see you ! I'd do anything not to see you cry.   Say something.

          [*Joy is still for a moment, then the shaking of the shoulders begins
          again.*]

Joy, *darling !*   It's so awful, you'll make yourself ill, and it isn't worth it really.   I'd do anything to save you pain—won't you stop just for a minute ?   [*Joy is still again.*]

Nothing in the world's worth *your* crying, Joy.   Give me just a little look.

Joy. [*Looking ; in a smothered voice*] Don't.

DICK. You do look so sweet! Oh, Joy! I'll comfort you, I'll take it all on myself. I know all about it. [JOY *gives a sobbing laugh.*] I do. I've had trouble too, I swear I have. It gets better, it does really.

JOY. You don't know—it's—it's——

DICK. Don't think about it! No, no, no! I know exactly what it's like.   [*He strokes her arm.*

JOY. [*Shrinking, in a whisper*] You mustn't.

[*The music of a waltz is heard again.*

DICK. Look here, Joy! It's no good, we must talk it over calmly.

JOY. You don't *see*! It's the—it's the disgrace——

DICK Oh! as to disgrace—she's *your* Mother, whatever she does; I'd like to see anybody say anything about her—[*viciously*]—I'd punch his head.

JOY. [*Gulping her tears*] That doesn't help.

DICK. But if she doesn't love your Father——

JOY. But she's *married* to him!

DICK. [*Hastily*] Yes, of course, I know, marriage is awfully important; but a man understands these things.

[JOY *looks at him. Seeing the impression he has made, he tries again.*] I mean, he understands better than a woman. I've often argued about moral questions with men up at Oxford.

JOY. [*Catching at a straw*] But there's nothing to argue about.

DICK. [*Hastily*] Of course, *I* believe in morals. [*They stare solemnly at each other.*] Some men don't. But *I* can't help seeing marriage is awfully important.

JOY. [*Solemnly*] It's sacred.

DICK. Yes, I know, but there must be exceptions, Joy.

JOY. [*Losing herself a little in the stress of this discussion*] How can there be exceptions if a thing's sacred?

DICK. [*Earnestly*] All rules have exceptions; that's true, you know; it's a proverb.

JOY. It can't be true about marriage—how can it when——?

DICK. [*With intense earnestness*] But look here, Joy. I know a really clever man—an author. He says that if marriage is a failure people ought to be perfectly free; it isn't everybody who believes that marriage is everything. Of course, *I* believe it's sacred, but if it's a failure, I *do* think it seems awful—don't you?

JOY. I don't know—yes—if—— [*Suddenly.*] But *it's my own Mother*!

DICK. [*Gravely*] I know, of course. I can't expect *you* to see it in *your own case* like this. [*With desperation.*] But look here, Joy, this'll show you! If a person loves a person, they have to decide, haven't they? Well, then, you see, that's what your Mother's done.

JOY. But that doesn't show me anything !

DICK. But it does. The thing is to look at it as if it wasn't yourself. If it had been you and me in love, Joy, and it was wrong, like them, of course [*ruefully*] I know you'd have decided right. [*Fiercely.*] But I swear I should have decided wrong. [*Triumphantly.*] That's why I feel I understand your Mother.

JOY. [*Brushing her sleeve across her eyes*] Oh, Dick, you are so sweet —and—and—funny !

DICK. [*Sliding his arm about her*] I love you, Joy, that's why, and I'll love you till you don't feel it any more. I will. I'll love you all day and every day ; you shan't miss anything, I swear it. It's such a beautiful night—it's on purpose. Look ! [JOY *looks ; he looks at her.*] But it's not so beautiful as you.

JOY. [*Bending her head*] You mustn't. I don't know—what's coming.

DICK. [*Sidling closer*] Aren't your knees tired, darling ? I—I *can't* get near you properly.

JOY. [*With a sob*] Oh ! Dick, you are a funny—comfort !

DICK. We'll stick together, Joy, always ; nothing'll matter then.
                    [*They struggle to their feet—the waltz sounds louder.*]
You're missing it all ! I can't bear you to miss the dancing. It seems so queer ! Couldn't we ? Just a *little* turn ?

JOY. No, no !

DICK. Oh ! try ! [*He takes her gently by the waist, she shrinks back.*]

JOY. [*Brokenly*] No—no ! Oh ! Dick—to-morrow'll be so awful.

DICK. To-morrow shan't hurt you, Joy ; nothing shall ever hurt you again.

[*She looks at him, and her face changes ; suddenly she buries it against his shoulder.*

[*They stand so just a moment in the moonlight ; then turning to the river move slowly out of sight. Again the hollow tree is left alone. The music of the waltz has stopped. The voices of* MISS BEECH *and the* COLONEL *are heard approaching from the house. They appear in the opening of the wall. The* COLONEL *carries a pair of field-glasses with which to look at the moon.*

COLONEL. Charming to see Molly dance with Lever, their steps go so well together ! I can always tell when a woman's enjoying herself, Peachey.

MISS BEECH. [*Sharply*] Can you ? You're *very* clever.

COLONEL. Wonderful, that moon ! I'm going to have a look at her ! Splendid glasses these, Peachey [*he screws them out*], not a better pair in England. I remember in Burmah with these glasses I used to be able to tell a man from a woman at two miles and a quarter. And that's no joke, I can tell you. [*But on his way to the moon, he has taken*

a survey of the earth to the right along the river. In a low but excited voice.]
I say, I say—is it one of the maids ?—the baggage ! Why ! It's Dick !
By George, she's got her hair, down, Peachey ! It's *Joy !*
    [Miss Beech *goes to look. He makes as though to hand the glasses
        to her, but puts them to his own eyes instead—excitedly.*]
It is ! What about her headache ? By George, they're kissing. I
say, Peachey ! I shall have to tell Nell !
    Miss Beech. Are you sure they're kissing ? Well, that's some
comfort.
    Colonel. They're at the stile now. Oughtn't I to stop them, eh ?
[*He stands on tiptoe.*] We mustn't spy on them, dash it all. [*He drops
the glasses.*] They're out of sight now.
    Miss Beech. [*To herself*] He said he wouldn't let her.
    Colonel. *What !* have *you* been encouraging them.
    Miss Beech. Don't be in such a hurry !
                                        [*She moves towards the hollow tree.*
    Colonel. [*Abstractedly*] By George, Peachey, to think that Nell
and I were once—Poor Nell ! I remember just such a night as
this——   [*He stops, and stares before him, sighing.*
    Miss Beech. [*Impressively*] It's a comfort she's got that good young
man. She's found out that her mother and this Mr. Lever are—
you know.
    Colonel. [*Losing all traces of his fussiness, and drawing himself up
as though he were on parade*] You tell me that my niece——?
    Miss Beech. Out of her own mouth !
    Colonel. [*Bowing his head*] I never would have believed she'd
have forgotten herself.
    Miss Beech. [*Very solemnly*] Ah, my dear ! We're all the same ;
we're all as hollow as that tree ! When it's ourselves it's always a
special case !
    [*The* Colonel *makes a movement of distress, and* Miss Beech
        goes to him.]
Don't you take it so to heart, my dear !   [*A silence.*
    Colonel. [*Shaking his head*] I couldn't have believed Molly would
forget that child.
    Miss Beech. [*Sadly*] They must go their own ways, poor things !
She can't put herself in the child's place, and the child can't put herself
in Molly's. A woman and a girl—there's the tree of life between them !
    Colonel. [*Staring into the tree to see indeed if that were the tree alluded
to*] It's a grief to me, Peachey, it's a grief ! [*He sinks into a chair,
stroking his long moustaches. Then to avenge his hurt.*] Shan't tell Nell—
dashed if I do anything to make the trouble worse !
    Miss Beech. [*Nodding*] There's suffering enough, without adding
to it with our trumpery judgments ! If only things would last between
them !

4*

COLONEL. [*Fiercely*] Last! By George, they'd better—— [*He
stops, and looking up with a queer sorry look.*] I say, Peachey—*Life's
very funny!*

MISS BEECH. Men and women are! [*Touching his forehead tenderly.*]
There, there—take care of your poor, dear head! Tsst! The
blessed innocents!

       [*She pulls the* COLONEL'S *sleeve. They slip away towards the
house, as* JOY *and* DICK *come back. They are still linked
together, and stop by the hollow of the tree.*

JOY. [*In a whisper*] Dick, is love always like this!

DICK. [*Putting his arms round her, with conviction*] It's never been like
this before. It's you and me!

                              [*He kisses her on the lips.*

                The curtain falls.

STRIFE

A DRAMA IN THREE ACTS

ACT I., *The dining-room of the Manager's house.*

ACT II., SCENE I. *The kitchen of the Roberts' cottage near the works.*

SCENE II. *A space outside the works.*

ACT III., *The drawing-room of the Manager's house.*

The action takes place on February 7th between the hours of noon and six in the afternoon, close to the Trenartha Tin Plate Works, on the borders of England and Wales, where a strike has been in progress throughout the winter.

CAST OF THE ORIGINAL PRODUCTION
At the Duke of York's Theatre on March 9, 1909.

JOHN ANTHONY	*Mr. Norman McKinnel*
EDGAR ANTHONY	*Mr. C. M. Hallard*
FREDERIC WILDER	*Mr. Dennis Eadie*
WILLIAM SCANTLEBURY	*Mr. Luigi Lablache*
OLIVER WANKLIN	*Mr. Charles V. France*
HENRY TENCH	*Mr. O. P. Heggie*
FRANCIS UNDERWOOD	*Mr. A. S. Holmwood*
SIMON HARNESS	*Mr. George Ingleton*
DAVID ROBERTS	*Mr. J. Fisher White*
JAMES GREEN	*Mr. R. Luisk*
JOHN BULGIN	*Mr. P. L. Julian*
HENRY THOMAS	*Mr. H. R. Hignett*
GEORGE ROUS	*Mr. Owen Roughwood*
JAGO	*Mr. Charles Danvers*
EVANS	*Mr. Drelincourt Odlam*
FROST	*Mr. Edward Gwenn*
ENID UNDERWOOD	*Miss Ellen O'Malley*
ANNIE ROBERTS	*Miss Mary Barton*
MADGE THOMAS	*Miss Lillah McCarthy*
MRS. ROUS	*Miss Rose Cazalet*
MRS. BULGIN	*Miss Sidney Paxton*
MRS. YEO	*Miss Blanche Stanley*

ACT I

It is noon. In the Underwoods' dining-room a bright fire is burning. On one side of the fireplace are double doors leading to the drawing-room, on the other side a door leading to the hall. In the centre of the room a long dining-table without a cloth is set out as a board table. At the head of it, in the Chairman's seat, sits JOHN ANTHONY, *an old man, big, clean shaven, and high-coloured, with thick white hair, and thick dark eyebrows. His movements are rather slow and feeble, but his eyes are very much alive. There is a glass of water by his side. On his right sits his son* EDGAR, *an earnest-looking man of thirty, reading a newspaper. Next him* WANKLIN, *a man with jutting eyebrows, and silver-streaked light hair, is bending over transfer papers.* TENCH, *the secretary, a short and rather humble, nervous man, with side whiskers, stands helping him. On* WANKLIN'S *right sits* UNDERWOOD, *the Manager, a quiet man, with a long, stiff jaw, and steady eyes. Back to the fire is* SCANTLEBURY, *a very large, pale, sleepy man, with grey hair, rather bald. Between him and the Chairman are two empty chairs.*

WILDER. [*Who is lean, cadaverous, and complaining, with drooping grey moustaches, stands before the fire*] I say, this fire's the devil! Can I have a screen, Tench?

SCANTLEBURY. A screen, ah!

TENCH. Certainly, Mr. Wilder. [*He looks at* UNDERWOOD.] That is—perhaps the Manager—perhaps Mr. Underwood——

SCANTLEBURY. These fireplaces of yours, Underwood——

UNDERWOOD. [*Roused from studying some papers*] A screen? Rather! I'm sorry. [*He goes to the door with a little smile.*] We're not accustomed to complaints of too much fire down here just now.

[*He speaks as though he holds a pipe between his teeth, slowly, ironically.*

WILDER. [*In an injured voice*] You mean the men. H'm!

[UNDERWOOD *goes out.*

SCANTLEBURY. Poor devils!

WILDER. It's their own fault, Scantlebury.

EDGAR. [*Holding out his paper*] There's great distress amongst them, according to the *Trenartha News*.

WILDER. Oh, that rag! Give it to Wanklin. Suit his Radical views. They call us monsters, I suppose. The editor of that rubbish ought to be shot.

EDGAR. [*Reading*] " If the Board of worthy gentlemen who control the Trenartha Tin Plate Works from their armchairs in London, would condescend to come and see for themselves the conditions prevailing amongst their workpeople during this strike——"

WILDER. Well, we *have* come.

EDGAR. [*Continuing*] " We cannot believe that even their leg-of-mutton hearts would remain untouched."

[WANKLIN *takes the paper from him.*

WILDER. Ruffian! I remember that fellow when he hadn't a penny to his name; little snivel of a chap that's made his way by blackguarding everybody who takes a different view to himself.

[ANTHONY *says something that is not heard.*

WILDER. What does your father say?

EDGAR. He says " The kettle and the pot."

WILDER. H'm!   [*He sits down next to* SCANTLEBURY.

SCANTLEBURY. [*Blowing out his cheeks*] I shall boil if I don't get that screen.

[UNDERWOOD *and* ENID *enter with a screen, which they place before the fire.* ENID *is tall; she has a small, decided face, and is twenty-eight years old.*

ENID. Put it closer, Frank. Will that do, Mr. Wilder? It's the highest we've got.

WILDER. Thanks, capitally.

SCANTLEBURY. [*Turning, with a sigh of pleasure*] Ah! Merci, Madame!

ENID. Is there anything else you want, father? [ANTHONY *shakes his head.*] Edgar—anything?

EDGAR. You might give me a " J " nib, old girl.

ENID. There are some down there by Mr. Scantlebury.

SCANTLEBURY. [*Handing a little box of nibs*] Ah! your brother uses " J's." What does the manager use? [*With expansive politeness.*] What does your husband use, Mrs. Underwood?

UNDERWOOD. A quill!

SCANTLEBURY. The homely product of the goose.

[*He holds out quills.*

UNDERWOOD. [*Dryly*] Thanks, if you can spare me one. [*He takes a quill.*] What about lunch, Enid?

ENID. [*Stopping at the double doors and looking back*] We're going to have lunch here, in the drawing-room, so you needn't hurry with your meeting.   [WANKLIN *and* WILDER *bow, and she goes out.*

SCANTLEBURY. [*Rousing himself, suddenly*] Ah! Lunch! That hotel—— Dreadful! Did you try the whitebait last night? Fried fat!

WILDER. Past twelve! Aren't you going to read the minutes, Tench?

TENCH. [*Looking for the* CHAIRMAN'S *assent, reads in a rapid and monotonous voice*] " At a Board Meeting held the 31st of January at the Company's Offices, 512, Cannon Street, E.C. Present—Mr. Anthony in the chair, Messrs. F. H. Wilder, William Scantlebury, Oliver Wanklin, and Edgar Anthony. Read letters from the Manager dated January 20th, 23rd, 25th, 28th, relative to the strike at the Company's Works. Read letters to the Manager of January 21st, 24th, 26th, 29th. Read letter from Mr. Simon Harness, of the Central Union, asking for an interview with the Board. Read letter from the Men's Committee, signed David Roberts, James Green, John Bulgin, Henry Thomas, George Rous, desiring conference with the Board ; and it was resolved that a special Board Meeting be called for February 7th at the house of the Manager, for the purpose of discussing the situation with Mr. Simon Harness and the Men's Committee on the spot. Passed twelve transfers, signed and sealed nine certificates and one balance certificate."

[*He pushes the book over to the* CHAIRMAN.

ANTHONY. [*With a heavy sigh*] If it's your pleasure, sign the same.

[*He signs, moving the pen with difficulty.*

WANKLIN. What's the Union's game, Tench ? They haven't made up their split with the men. What does Harness want this interview for ?

TENCH. Hoping we shall come to a compromise, I think, sir ; he's having a meeting with the men this afternoon.

WILDER. Harness ! Ah ! He's one of those cold-blooded, cool-headed chaps. I distrust them. I don't know that we didn't make a mistake to come down. What time'll the men be here ?

UNDERWOOD. Any time now.

WILDER. Well, if we're not ready, they'll have to wait—won't do 'em any harm to cool their heels a bit.

SCANTLEBURY. [*Slowly*] Poor devils ! It's snowing. *What* weather !

UNDERWOOD. [*With meaning slowness*] This house'll be the warmest place they've been in this winter.

WILDER. Well, I hope we're going to settle this business in time for me to catch the 6.30. I've got to take my wife to Spain to-morrow. [*Chattily.*] My old father had a strike at his works in '69 ; just such a February as this. They wanted to shoot him.

WANKLIN. What ! In the close season ?

WILDER. By George, there was no close season for employers then ! He used to go down to his office with a pistol in his pocket.

SCANTLEBURY. [*Faintly alarmed*] Not seriously ?

WILDER. [*With finality*] Ended in his shootin' one of 'em in the legs.

SCANTLEBURY. [*Unavoidably feeling his thigh*] No ? God bless me !

ANTHONY. [*Lifting the agenda paper*] To consider the policy of the Board in relation to the strike.   [*There is a silence.*

WILDER. It's this infernal three-cornered duel—the Union, the men, and ourselves.

WANKLIN. We needn't consider the Union.

WILDER. It's my experience that you've always got to consider the Union, confound them ! If the Union were going to withdraw their support from the men, as they've done, why did they ever allow them to strike at all ?

EDGAR. We've had that over a dozen times.

WILDER. Well, I've never understood it ! It's beyond me. They talk of the engineers' and furnacemen's demands being excessive—so they are—but that's not enough to make the Union withdraw their support. What's behind it ?

UNDERWOOD. Fear of strikes at Harper's and Tinewell's.

WILDER. [*With triumph*] Afraid of other strikes—now, that's a reason ! Why couldn't we have been told that before ?

UNDERWOOD. You were.

TENCH. You were absent from the Board that day, sir.

SCANTLEBURY. The men must have seen they had no chance when the Union gave them up. It's madness.

UNDERWOOD. It's Roberts !

WILDER. Just our luck, the men finding a fanatical firebrand like Roberts for leader. [*A pause.*

WANKLIN. [*Looking at* ANTHONY] Well ?

WILDER. [*Breaking in fussily*] It's a regular mess. I don't like the position we're in ; I don't like it ; I've said so for a long time. [*Looking at* WANKLIN.] When Wanklin and I came down here before Christmas it looked as if the men must collapse. You thought so too, Underwood.

UNDERWOOD. Yes.

WILDER. Well, they haven't ! Here we are, going from bad to worse—losing our customers—shares going down !

SCANTLEBURY. [*Shaking his head*] M'm ! M'm !

WANKLIN. What loss have we made by this strike, Tench ?

TENCH. Over fifty thousand, sir !

SCANTLEBURY. [*Pained*] You don't say !

WILDER. We shall never get it back.

TENCH. No, sir.

WILDER. Who'd have supposed the men were going to stick out like this—nobody suggested that. [*Looking angrily at* TENCH.

SCANTLEBURY. [*Shaking his head*] I've never liked a fight—never shall.

ANTHONY. No surrender ! [*All look at him.*

WILDER. Who wants to surrender ? [ANTHONY *looks at him.*] I—I want to act reasonably. When the men sent Roberts up to the Board in December—then was the time. We ought to have humoured him; instead of that, the Chairman—[*Dropping his eyes before* ANTHONY'S]—er—we snapped his head off. We could have got them in then by a little tact.

ANTHONY. No compromise!

WILDER. There we are! This strike's been going on now since October, and as far as I can see it may last another six months. Pretty mess we shall be in by then. The only comfort is, the men'll be in a worse!

EDGAR. [*To* UNDERWOOD] What sort of state are they really in, Frank?

UNDERWOOD. [*Without expression*] Damnable!

WILDER. Well, who on earth would have thought they'd have held on like this without support!

UNDERWOOD. Those who know them.

WILDER. I defy anyone to know them! And what about tin? Price going up daily. When we do get started we shall have to work off our contracts at the top of the market.

WANKLIN. What do you say to that, Chairman?

ANTHONY. Can't be helped!

WILDER. Shan't pay a dividend till goodness knows when!

SCANTLEBURY. [*With emphasis*] We ought to think of the share-holders. [*Turning heavily.*] Chairman, I say we ought to think of the shareholders.   [ANTHONY *mutters.*

SCANTLEBURY. What's that?

TENCH. The Chairman says he *is* thinking of you, sir.

SCANTLEBURY. [*Sinking back into torpor*] Cynic!

WILDER. It's past a joke. *I* don't want to go without a dividend for years if the Chairman does. We can't go on playing ducks and drakes with the Company's prosperity.

EDGAR. [*Rather ashamedly*] I think we ought to consider the men.
          [*All but* ANTHONY *fidget in their seats.*

SCANTLEBURY. [*With a sigh*] We mustn't think of our private feelings, young man. That'll never do.

EDGAR. [*Ironically*] I'm not thinking of our feelings. I'm thinking of the men's.

WILDER. As to that—we're men of business.

WANKLIN. That *is* the little trouble.

EDGAR. There's no necessity for pushing things so far in the face of all this suffering—it's—it's cruel.

          [*No one speaks, as though* EDGAR *had uncovered something whose existence no man prizing his self-respect could afford to recognize.*

WANKLIN. [*With an ironical smile*] I'm afraid we mustn't base our policy on luxuries like sentiment.

EDGAR. I detest this state of things.

ANTHONY. We didn't seek the quarrel.

EDGAR. I know that, sir, but surely we've gone far enough.

ANTHONY. No.   [*All look at one another.*

WANKLIN. Luxuries apart, Chairman, we must look out what we're doing.

ANTHONY. Give way to the men once and there'll be no end to it.

WANKLIN. I quite agree, but——   [ANTHONY *shakes his head.*] You make it a question of bedrock principle ?   [ANTHONY *nods.*] Luxuries again, Chairman !   The shares are below par.

WILDER. Yes, and they'll drop to a half when we pass the next dividend.

SCANTLEBURY. [*With alarm*] Come, come ! Not so bad as that.

WILDER. [*Grimly*] You'll see !   [*Craning forward to catch* ANTHONY's *speech.*] I didn't catch——

TENCH. [*Hesitating*] The Chairman says, sir, " Fais que—que—devra——"

EDGAR. [*Sharply*] My father says : " Do what we ought—and let things rip."

WILDER. Tcha !

SCANTLEBURY. [*Throwing up his hands*] The Chairman's a Stoic— I always said the Chairman was a Stoic.

WILDER. Much good that'll do us.

WANKLIN. [*Suavely*] Seriously, Chairman, are you going to let the ship sink under you, for the sake of—a principle ?

ANTHONY. She won't sink.

SCANTLEBURY. [*With alarm*] Not while I'm on the Board I hope.

ANTHONY. [*With a twinkle*] Better rat, Scantlebury.

SCANTLEBURY. What a man !

ANTHONY. I've always fought them ; I've never been beaten yet.

WANKLIN. We're with you in theory, Chairman. But we're not all made of cast-iron.

ANTHONY. We've only to hold on.

WILDER. [*Rising and going to the fire*] And go to the devil as fast as we can !

ANTHONY. Better go to the devil than give in !

WILDER. [*Fretfully*] That may suit you, sir, but it doesn't suit me, or anyone else I should think.

                    [ANTHONY *looks him in the face—a silence.*

EDGAR. I don't see how we can get over it that to go on like this means starvation to the men's wives and families.

      [WILDER *turns abruptly to the fire, and* SCANTLEBURY *puts out a hand to push the idea away.*

WANKLIN. I'm afraid again that sounds a little sentimental.

EDGAR. Men of business are excused from decency, you think ?

WILDER. Nobody's more sorry for the men than I am, but if they [*lashing himself*] choose to be such a pig-headed lot, it's nothing to do with us ; we've quite enough on *our* hands to think of ourselves and the shareholders.

EDGAR. [*Irritably*] It won't kill the shareholders to miss a dividend or two ; I don't see that *that's* reason enough for knuckling under.

SCANTLEBURY. [*With grave discomfort*] You talk very lightly of your dividends, young man ; I don't know where we are.

WILDER. There's only one sound way of looking at it. We can't go on ruining *ourselves* with this strike.

ANTHONY. No caving in !

SCANTLEBURY. [*With a gesture of despair*] Look at him !

[ANTHONY *is leaning back in his chair. They do look at him.*

WILDER. [*Returning to his seat*] Well, all I can say is, if that's the Chairman's view, I don't know what we've come down here for.

ANTHONY. To tell the men that we've got nothing for them—— [*Grimly.*] They won't believe it till they hear it spoken in plain English.

WILDER. H'm ! Shouldn't be a bit surprised if that brute Roberts hadn't got us down here with the very same idea. I hate a man with a grievance.

EDGAR. [*Resentfully*] We didn't pay him enough for his discovery. I always said that at the time.

WILDER. We paid him five hundred and a bonus of two hundred three years later. If that's not enough ! What does he want for goodness' sake ?

TENCH. [*Complainingly*] Company made a hundred thousand out of his brains, and paid him seven hundred—that's the way he goes on, sir.

WILDER. The man's a rank agitator ! Look here, I hate the Unions. But now we've got Harness here let's get him to settle the whole thing.

ANTHONY. No !   [*Again they look at him.*

UNDERWOOD. Roberts won't let the men assent to that.

SCANTLEBURY. Fanatic ! Fanatic !

WILDER. [*Looking at* ANTHONY] And not the only one !

[FROST *enters from the hall.*

FROST. [*To* ANTHONY] Mr. Harness from the Union, waiting, sir. The men are here too, sir.

[ANTHONY *nods.* UNDERWOOD *goes to the door, returning with* HARNESS, *a pale, clean-shaven man with hollow cheeks, quick eyes and lantern jaw—*FROST *has retired.*

UNDERWOOD. [*Pointing to* TENCH'S *chair*] Sit there next the Chairman, Harness, won't you ?

[*At* HARNESS'S *appearance, the Board have drawn together, as it were, and turned a little to him, like cattle at a dog.*

HARNESS. [*With a sharp look round, and a bow*] Thanks ! [*He sits*

—*his accent is slightly nasal*.] Well, Gentlemen, we're going to do business at last, I hope.

WILDER. Depends on what you *call* business, Harness. Why don't you make the men come in ?

HARNESS. [*Sardonically*] The men are far more in the right than you are. The question with us is whether we shan't begin to support them again.

[*He ignores them all, except* ANTHONY, *to whom he turns in speaking.*

ANTHONY. Support them if you like ; we'll put in free labour and have done with it.

HARNESS. That won't do, Mr. Anthony. You can't get free labour, and you know it.

ANTHONY. We shall see that.

HARNESS. I'm quite frank with you. We were forced to withhold our support from your men because some of their demands are in excess of current rates. I expect to make them withdraw those demands to-day : if they do, take it straight from me, gentlemen, we shall back them again at once. Now, I want to see something fixed up before I go back to-night. Can't we have done with this old-fashioned tug-of-war business ? What good's it doing you ? Why don't you recognize once for all that these people are men like yourselves, and want what's good for them just as you want what's good for you—— [*Bitterly*.] Your motor-cars, and champagne, and eight-course dinners.

ANTHONY. If the men will come in, we'll do something for them.

HARNESS. [*Ironically*] Is that your opinion too, sir—and yours—and yours ? [*The Directors do not answer*.] Well, all I can say is : It's a kind of high and mighty aristocratic tone I thought we'd grown out of—seems I was mistaken.

ANTHONY. It's the tone the men use. Remains to be seen which can hold out longest—they without us, or we without them.

HARNESS. As business men, I wonder you're not ashamed of this waste of force, gentlemen. You know what it'll all end in.

ANTHONY. What ?

HARNESS. Compromise—it always does.

SCANTLEBURY. Can't you persuade the men that their interests are the same as ours ?

HARNESS. [*Turning ironically*] I could persuade them of that, sir, if they were.

WILDER. Come, Harness, you're a clever man, you don't believe all the Socialistic claptrap that's talked nowadays. There's no real difference between their interests and ours.

HARNESS. There's just one very simple little question I'd like to put to you. Will you pay your men one penny more than they force you to pay them ?   [WILDER *is silent.*

WANKLIN. [*Chiming in*] I humbly thought that not to pay more than was necessary was the A B C of commerce.

HARNESS. [*With irony*] Yes, that seems to be the A B C of commerce, sir; and the A B C of commerce is between your interests and the men's.

SCANTLEBURY. [*Whispering*] We ought to arrange something.

HARNESS. [*Dryly*] Am I to understand then, gentlemen, that your Board is going to make no concessions?

[*WANKLIN and WILDER bend forward as if to speak, but stop.*

ANTHONY. [*Nodding*] None.

[*WANKLIN and WILDER again bend forward, and SCANTLEBURY gives an unexpected grunt.*

HARNESS. You were about to say something, I believe?

[*But SCANTLEBURY says nothing.*

EDGAR. [*Looking up suddenly*] We're sorry for the state of the men.

HARNESS. [*Icily*] The men have no use for your pity, sir. What they want is justice.

ANTHONY. Then let *them* be just.

HARNESS. For that word " just " read " humble," Mr. Anthony. Why should they be humble? Barring the accident of money, aren't they as good men as you?

ANTHONY. Cant!

HARNESS. Well, I've been five years in America. It colours a man's notions.

SCANTLEBURY. [*Suddenly, as though avenging his uncompleted grunt*] Let's have the men in and hear what they've got to say!

[*ANTHONY nods, and UNDERWOOD goes out by the single door.*

HARNESS. [*Dryly*] As I'm to have an interview with them this afternoon, gentlemen, I'll ask you to postpone your final decision till that's over.

[*Again ANTHONY nods, and taking up his glass drinks.*

[*UNDERWOOD comes in again, followed by ROBERTS, GREEN, BULGIN, THOMAS, ROUS. They file in, hat in hand, and stand silent in a row. ROBERTS is lean, of middle height, with a slight stoop. He has a little rat-gnawn, brown-grey beard, moustaches, high cheek-bones, hollow cheeks, small fiery eyes. He wears an old and grease-stained, blue serge suit, and carries an old bowler hat. He stands nearest the Chairman. GREEN, next to him, has a clean, worn face, with a small grey, goatee beard and drooping moustaches, iron spectacles, and mild, straightforward eyes. He wears an overcoat, green with age, and a linen collar. Next to him is BULGIN, a tall, strong man, with a dark moustache, and fighting jaw, wearing a red muffler, who keeps changing his cap from one hand to the other. Next to him is THOMAS, an old man with a grey moustache,*

*full beard, and weatherbeaten, bony face, whose overcoat dis-
closes a lean, plucked-looking neck. On his right, ROUS,
the youngest of the five, looks like a soldier ; he has a glitter in
his eyes.*

UNDERWOOD. [*Pointing*] There are some chairs there against the
wall, Roberts ; won't you draw them up and sit down ?

ROBERTS. Thank you, Mr. Underwood ; we'll stand—in the
presence of the Board. [*He speaks in a biting and staccato voice, rolling
his r's, pronouncing his a's like an Italian a, and his consonants short and
crisp.*] How are you, Mr. Harness ? Didn't expect t' have the
pleasure of seeing you till this afternoon.

HARNESS. [*Steadily*] We shall meet again then, Roberts.

ROBERTS. Glad to hear that ; we shall have some news for you
to take to your people.

ANTHONY. What do the men want ?

ROBERTS. [*Acidly*] Beg pardon, I don't quite catch the Chairman's
remark.

TENCH. [*From behind the Chairman's chair*] The Chairman wishes
to know what the men have to say.

ROBERTS. It's what the Board has to say we've come to hear. It's
for the Board to speak first.

ANTHONY. The Board has nothing to say.

ROBERTS. [*Looking along the line of men*] In that case we're wasting
the Directors' time. We'll be taking our feet off this pretty carpet.

[*He turns, the men move slowly, as though hypnotically influenced.*

WANKLIN. [*Suavely*] Come, Roberts, you didn't give us this long
cold journey for the pleasure of saying that.

THOMAS. [*A pure Welshman*] No, sir, an' what I say iss——

ROBERTS. [*Bitingly*] Go on, Henry Thomas, go on. You're better
able to speak to the—Directors than me.   [THOMAS *is silent*.

TENCH. The Chairman means, Roberts, that it was the men who
asked for the Conference, the Board wish to hear what they have to
say.

ROBERTS. Gad ! If I was to begin to tell ye all they have to say,
I wouldn't be finished to-day. And there'd be some that'd wish
they'd never left their London palaces.

HARNESS. What's your proposition, man ? Be reasonable.

ROBERTS. You want reason, Mr. Harness ? Take a look round
this afternoon before the meeting. [*He looks at the men ; no sound
escapes them.*] You'll see some very pretty scenery.

HARNESS. All right, my friend ; you won't put me off.

ROBERTS. [*To the men*] We shan't put Mr. Harness off. Have
some champagne with your lunch, Mr. Harness ; you'll want it, sir.

HARNESS. Come, get to business, man !

THOMAS. What we're asking, look you, is just simple justice.

ROBERTS. [*Venomously*] Justice from London? What are you talking about, Henry Thomas? Have you gone silly? [THOMAS *is silent*.] We know very well what we are—discontented dogs—never satisfied. What did the Chairman tell me up in London? That I didn't know what I was talking about. I was a foolish, uneducated man, that knew nothing of the wants of the men I spoke for.

EDGAR. Do please keep to the point.

ANTHONY. [*Holding up his hand*] There can only be one master, Roberts.

ROBERTS. Then, be Gad, it'll be us.

[*There is a silence ;* ANTHONY *and* ROBERTS *stare at one another.*

UNDERWOOD. If you've nothing to say to the Directors, Roberts, perhaps you'll let Green or Thomas speak for the men.

[GREEN *and* THOMAS *look anxiously at* ROBERTS, *at each other, and the other men.*

GREEN. [*An Englishman*] If I'd been listened to, gentlemen——

THOMAS. What I'fe got to say iss what we'fe all got to say——

ROBERTS. Speak for yourself, Henry Thomas.

SCANTLEBURY. [*With a gesture of deep spiritual discomfort*] Let the poor men call their souls their own !

ROBERTS. Aye, they shall keep their souls, for it's not much body that you've left them, Mr. [*with biting emphasis, as though the word were an offence*] Scantlebury ! [*To the men.*] Well, will you speak, or shall I speak for you ?

ROUS. [*Suddenly*] Speak out, Roberts, or leave it to others.

ROBERTS. [*Ironically*] Thank you, George Rous. [*Addressing himself to* ANTHONY.] The Chairman and Board of Directors have honoured us by leaving London and coming all this way to hear what we've got to say ; it would not be polite to keep them any longer waiting.

WILDER. Well, thank God for that !

ROBERTS. Ye will not dare to thank Him when I have done, Mr. Wilder, for all your piety. May be your God up in London has no time to listen to the working man. I'm told He is a wealthy God ; but if He listens to what I tell Him, He will know more than ever He learned in Kensington.

HARNESS. Come, Roberts, you have your own God. Respect the God of other men.

ROBERTS. That's right, sir. We have another God down here ; I doubt He is rather different to Mr. Wilder's. Ask Henry Thomas ; he will tell you whether his God and Mr. Wilder's are the same.

[THOMAS *lifts his hand, and cranes his head as though to prophesy.*

WANKLIN. For goodness' sake, let's keep to the point, Roberts.

ROBERTS. I rather think it is the point, Mr. Wanklin. If you can get the God of Capital to walk through the streets of Labour, and pay attention to what he sees, you're a brighter man than I take you for, for all that you're a Radical.

ANTHONY. Attend to me, Roberts ! [ROBERTS *is silent.*] You are here to speak for the men, as I am here to speak for the Board.

[*He looks slowly round.*]

[WILDER, WANKLIN, *and* SCANTLEBURY *make movements of uneasiness, and* EDGAR *gazes at the floor. A faint smile comes on* HARNESS' *face.*]

Now then, what is it ?

ROBERTS. Right, sir !

[*Throughout all that follows, he and* ANTHONY *look fixedly upon each other. Men and Directors show in their various ways suppressed uneasiness, as though listening to words that they themselves would not have spoken.*]

The men can't afford to travel up to London ; and they don't trust you to believe what they say in black and white. They know what the post is [*he darts a look at* UNDERWOOD *and* TENCH], and what Directors' meetings are : " Refer it to the manager—let the manager advise us on the men's condition. Can we squeeze them a little more ? "

UNDERWOOD. [*In a low voice*] Don't hit below the belt, Roberts !

ROBERTS. Is it below the belt, Mr. Underwood ? The men know. When I came up to London, I told you the position straight. An' what came of it ? I was told I didn't know what I was talkin' about. I can't afford to travel up to London to be told that again.

ANTHONY. What have you to say for the men ?

ROBERTS. I have this to say—and first as to their condition. Ye shall 'ave no need to go and ask your manager. Ye can't squeeze them any more. Every man of us is well-nigh starving. [*A surprised murmur rises from the men.* ROBERTS *looks round.*] Ye wonder why I tell ye that ? Every man of us is going short. We can't be no worse off than we've been these weeks past. Ye needn't think that by waiting ye'll drive us to come in. We'll die first, the whole lot of us. The men have sent for ye to know, once and for all, whether ye are going to grant them their demands. I see the sheet of paper in the Secretary's hand. [TENCH *moves nervously.*] That's it, I think, Mr. Tench. It's not very large.

TENCH. [*Nodding*] Yes.

ROBERTS. There's not one sentence of writing on that paper that we can do without.

[*A movement amongst the men.* ROBERTS *turns on them sharply.*] Isn't that so ? "

[*The men assent reluctantly.* ANTHONY *takes from* TENCH *the paper and peruses it.*]

Not one single sentence. All those demands are fair. We have
not asked anything that we are not entitled to ask. What I said up
in London, I say again now : there is not anything on that piece of
paper that a just man should not ask, and a just man give. [*A pause.*

ANTHONY. There is not one single demand on this paper that we
will grant.

[*In the stir that follows on these words,* ROBERTS *watches the Directors and* ANTHONY *the men.* WILDER *gets up abruptly
and goes over to the fire.*

ROBERTS. D'ye mean that ?

ANTHONY. I do.

[WILDER *at the fire makes an emphatic movement of disgust.*

ROBERTS. [*Noting it, with dry intensity*] Ye best know whether the
condition of the Company is any better than the condition of the men.
[*Scanning the Directors' faces.*] Ye best know whether ye can afford
your tyranny—but this I tell ye : If ye think the men will give way
the least part of an inch, ye're making the worst mistake ye ever
made. [*He fixes his eyes on* SCANTLEBURY.] Ye think because the
Union is not supporting us—more shame to it !—that we'll be coming
on our knees to you one fine morning. Ye think because the men
have got their wives an' families to think of—that it's just a question
of a week or two——

ANTHONY. It would be better if you did not speculate so much on
what we think.

ROBERTS. Aye ! It's not much profit to us ! I will say this for
you, Mr. Anthony—ye know your own mind ! [*Staring at* ANTHONY.]
I can reckon on ye !

ANTHONY. [*Ironically*] I am obliged to you !

ROBERTS. And I know mine. I tell ye this. The men will send
their wives and families where the country will have to keep them ;
an' they will starve sooner than give way. I advise ye, Mr. Anthony,
to prepare yourself for the worst that can happen to your Company.
We are not so ignorant as you might suppose. We know the way
the cat is jumping. Your position is not all that it might be—not
exactly !

ANTHONY. Be good enough to allow us to judge of our position
for ourselves. Go back, and reconsider your own.

ROBERTS. [*Stepping forward*] Mr. Anthony, you are not a young man
now ; from the time that I remember anything ye have been an enemy
to every man that has come into your works. I don't say that ye're
a mean man, or a cruel man, but ye've grudged them the say of any
word in their own fate. Ye've fought them down four times. I've
heard ye say ye love a fight—mark my words—ye're fighting the
last fight ye'll ever fight——   [TENCH *touches* ROBERTS' *sleeve.*

UNDERWOOD. Roberts ! Roberts !

ROBERTS. Roberts! Roberts! I mustn't speak my mind to the Chairman, but the Chairman may speak his mind to me!

WILDER. What are things coming to?

ANTHONY. [*With a grim smile at* WILDER] Go on, Roberts; say what you like.

ROBERTS. [*After a pause*] I have no more to say.

ANTHONY. The meeting stands adjourned to five o'clock.

WANKLIN. [*In a low voice to* UNDERWOOD] We shall never settle anything like this.

ROBERTS. [*Bitingly*] We thank the Chairman and Board of Directors for their gracious hearing.

[*He moves towards the door; the men cluster together stupefied; then* ROUS, *throwing up his head, passes* ROBERTS *and goes out. The others follow.*

ROBERTS. [*With his hand on the door—maliciously*] Good day, gentlemen!   [*He goes out.*

HARNESS. [*Ironically*] I congratulate you on the conciliatory spirit that's been displayed. With your permission, gentlemen, I'll be with you again at half-past five. Good morning!

[*He bows slightly, rests his eyes on* ANTHONY, *who returns his stare unmoved, and, followed by* UNDERWOOD, *goes out. There is a moment of uneasy silence.* UNDERWOOD *reappears in the doorway.*

WILDER. [*With emphatic disgust*] Well!

[*The double doors are opened.*

ENID. [*Standing in the doorway*] Lunch is ready.

[EDGAR, *getting up abruptly, walks out past his sister.*

WILDER. Coming to lunch, Scantlebury?

SCANTLEBURY. [*Rising heavily*] I suppose so, I suppose so. It's the only thing we can do.   [*They go out through the double doors.*

WANKLIN. [*In a low voice*] Do you really mean to fight to a finish, Chairman?   [ANTHONY *nods.*

WANKLIN. Take care! The essence of things is to know when to stop.   [ANTHONY *does not answer.*

WANKLIN. [*Very gravely*] This way disaster lies. The ancient Trojans were fools to your father, Mrs. Underwood.

[*He goes out through the double doors.*

ENID. I want to speak to father, Frank.

[UNDERWOOD *follows* WANKLIN *out.* TENCH, *passing round the table, is restoring order to the scattered pens and papers.*

ENID. Aren't you coming, Dad?

[ANTHONY *shakes his head.* ENID *looks meaningly at* TENCH.

ENID. Won't you go and have some lunch, Mr. Tench.

TENCH. [*With papers in his hand*] Thank you, ma'am, thank you!

[*He goes slowly, looking back.*

ENID. [*Shutting the doors*] I *do* hope it's settled, father!

ANTHONY. No!

ENID. [*Very disappointed*] Oh! Haven't you done anything?

[ANTHONY *shakes his head.*

ENID. Frank says they all want to come to a compromise, really, except that man Roberts.

ANTHONY. *I* don't.

ENID. It's such a horrid position for us. If you were the wife of the manager, and lived down here, and saw it all. You can't realize, Dad!

ANTHONY. Indeed?

ENID. We see *all* the distress. You remember my maid Annie, who married Roberts? [ANTHONY *nods.*] It's so wretched, her heart's weak; since the strike began, she hasn't even been getting proper food. I know it for a fact, father.

ANTHONY. Give her what she wants, poor woman!

ENID. Roberts won't let her take anything from *us*.

ANTHONY. [*Staring before him*] I can't be answerable for the men's obstinacy.

ENID. They're all suffering. Father! Do stop it, for my sake!

ANTHONY. [*With a keen look at her*] You don't understand, my dear.

ENID. If I were on the Board, I'd do something.

ANTHONY. What would you do?

ENID. It's because you can't bear to give way. It's so——

ANTHONY. Well?

ENID. So unnecessary.

ANTHONY. What do *you* know about necessity? Read your novels, play your music, talk your talk, but don't try and tell *me* what's at the bottom of a struggle like this.

ENID. I live down here, and see it.

ANTHONY. What d'you imagine stands between you and your class and these men that you're so sorry for?

ENID. [*Coldly*] I don't know what you mean, father.

ANTHONY. In a few years you and your children would be down in the condition they're in, but for those who have the eyes to see things as they are and the backbone to stand up for themselves.

ENID. You don't know the state the men are in.

ANTHONY. I know it well enough.

ENID. You don't, father; if you did, you wouldn't——

ANTHONY. It's you who don't know the simple facts of the position. What sort of mercy do you suppose you'd get if no one stood between you and the continual demands of labour? This sort of mercy— [*he puts his hand up to his throat and squeezes it.*] First would go your sentiments, my dear; then your culture, and your comforts would be going all the time!

ENID. I don't believe in barriers between classes.

ANTHONY. You — don't — believe — in — barriers — between the classes ?

ENID. [*Coldly*] And I don't know what that has to do with this question.

ANTHONY. It will take a generation or two for you to understand.

ENID. It's only you and Roberts, father, and you know it !

[ANTHONY *thrusts out his lower lip.*] It'll ruin the Company.

ANTHONY. Allow me to judge of that.

ENID. [*Resentfully*] I won't stand by and let poor Annie Roberts suffer like this !   And think of the children, father !   I warn you.

ANTHONY. [*With a grim smile*] What do you propose to do ?

ENID. That's my affair.   [ANTHONY *only looks at her.*

ENID. [*In a changed voice, stroking his sleeve*] Father, you *know* you oughtn't to have this strain on you—you know what Dr. Fisher said !

ANTHONY. No old man can afford to listen to old women.

ENID. But you *have* done enough, even if it really is such a matter of principle with you.

ANTHONY. You think so ?

ENID. Don't, Dad !   [*Her face works.*] You—you might think of *us* !

ANTHONY. I am.

ENID. It'll break you down.

ANTHONY. [*Slowly*] My dear, I am not going to funk ; you may rely on that.

[*Re-enter* TENCH *with papers ; he glances at them, then plucking up courage.*

TENCH. Beg pardon, Madam, I think I'd rather see these papers were disposed of before I get my lunch.

[ENID, *after an impatient glance at him, looks at her father, turns suddenly, and goes into the drawing-room.*

TENCH. [*Holding the papers and a pen to* ANTHONY, *very nervously*] Would you sign these for me, please sir ?

[ANTHONY *takes the pen and signs.*

TENCH. [*Standing with a sheet of blotting-paper behind* EDGAR'S *chair, begins speaking nervously*] I owe my position to you, sir.

ANTHONY. Well ?

TENCH. I'm obliged to see everything that's going on, sir ; I—I depend upon the Company entirely.   If anything were to happen to it, it'd be disastrous for me.   [ANTHONY *nods.*] And, of course, my wife's just had another ;   and so it makes me doubly anxious just now. And the rates are really terrible down our way.

ANTHONY. [*With grim amusement*] Not more terrible than they are up mine.

TENCH. No, sir? [*Very nervously.*] I know the Company means a great deal to you, sir.

ANTHONY. It does; I founded it.

TENCH. Yes, sir. If the strike goes on it'll be very serious. I think the Directors are beginning to realize that, sir.

ANTHONY. [*Ironically*] Indeed?

TENCH. I know you hold very strong views, sir, and it's always your habit to look things in the face; but I don't think the Directors —like it, sir, now they—they see it.

ANTHONY. [*Grimly*] Nor you, it seems.

TENCH. [*With the ghost of a smile*] No, sir; of course I've got my children, and my wife's delicate; in my position I *have* to think of these things. [ANTHONY *nods.*] It wasn't *that* I was going to say, sir, if you'll excuse me [*hesitates*]——

ANTHONY. Out with it, then!

TENCH. I know—from my own father, sir, that when you get on in life you do feel things dreadfully——

ANTHONY. [*Almost paternally*] Come, out with it, Tench!

TENCH. I don't *like* to say it, sir.

ANTHONY. [*Stonily*] You must.

TENCH. [*After a pause, desperately bolting it out*] I think the Directors are going to throw you over, sir.

ANTHONY. [*Sits in silence*] Ring the bell!

[TENCH *nervously rings the bell and stands by the fire.*

TENCH. Excuse me saying such a thing. I was *only* thinking of you, sir.

[FROST *enters from the hall, he comes to the foot of the table, and looks at* ANTHONY; TENCH *covers his nervousness by arranging papers.*

ANTHONY. Bring me a whisky and soda.

FROST. Anything to eat, sir?

[ANTHONY *shakes his head—*FROST *goes to the sideboard, and prepares the drink.*

TENCH. [*In a low voice, almost supplicating*] If you *could* see your way, sir, it would be a great relief to my mind, it would indeed. [*He looks up at* ANTHONY, *who has not moved.*] It does make me so very anxious. I haven't slept properly for weeks, sir, and that's a fact.

[ANTHONY *looks in his face, then slowly shakes his head.*

TENCH. [*Disheartened*] No, sir? [*He goes on arranging papers.* FROST *places the whisky and soda on a salver and puts it down by* ANTHONY'S *right hand. He stands away, looking gravely at* ANTHONY.

FROST. *Nothing* I can get you, sir? [ANTHONY *shakes his head.*] You're aware, sir, of what the doctor said, sir?

ANTHONY. I am.

[*A pause.* FROST *suddenly moves closer to him, and speaks in a low voice.*

FROST. This strike, sir; puttin' all this strain on you. Excuse me, sir, is it—is it worth it, sir?

[ANTHONY *mutters some words that are inaudible.*]

Very good, sir!

[*He turns and goes out into the hall*—TENCH *makes two attempts to speak; but meeting his Chairman's gaze he drops his eyes, and turning dismally, he too goes out.* ANTHONY *is left alone. He grips the glass, tilts it, and drinks deeply; then sets it down with a deep and rumbling sigh, and leans back in his chair.*

The curtain falls.

ACT II

SCENE I

It is half-past three. In the kitchen of ROBERTS' *cottage a meagre little fire is burning. The room is clean and tidy, very barely furnished, with a brick floor and white-washed walls, much stained with smoke. There is a kettle on the fire. A door opposite the fireplace opens inwards from a snowy street. On the wooden table are a cup and saucer, a teapot, knife, and plate of bread and cheese. Close to the fireplace in an old armchair, wrapped in a rug, sits* MRS. ROBERTS, *a thin and dark-haired woman about thirty-five, with patient eyes. Her hair is not done up, but tied back with a piece of ribbon. By the fire, too, is* MRS. YEO; *a red-haired, broad-faced person. Sitting near the table is* MRS. ROUS, *an old lady, ashen-white, with silver hair; by the door, standing, as if about to go, is* MRS. BULGIN, *a little pale, pinched-up woman. In a chair, with her elbows resting on the table, and her face resting in her hands sits* MADGE THOMAS, *a good-looking girl, of twenty-two, with high cheekbones, deep-set eyes, and dark, untidy hair. She is listening to the talk but she neither speaks nor moves.*

MRS. YEO. So he give me a sixpence, and that's the first bit o' money *I* seen this week. There an't much 'eat to this fire. Come and warm yerself, Mrs. Rous, you're lookin' as white as the snow, you are.

MRS. ROUS. [*Shivering—placidly*] Ah! but the winter my old man was took was the proper winter. Seventy-nine that was, when none of you was hardly born—not Madge Thomas, nor Sue Bulgin. [*Looking at them in turn.*] Annie Roberts, 'ow old were you, dear?

MRS. ROBERTS. Seven, Mrs. Rous.

MRS. ROUS. Seven—well ther'! A tiny little thing!

MRS. YEO. [*Aggressively*] Well, I was ten myself, *I* remembers it.

MRS. ROUS. [*Placidly*] The Company hadn't been started three years. Father was workin' on the acid that's 'ow he got 'is pisoned leg. I kep' sayin' to 'im "Father, you've got a pisoned leg." "Well," 'e, said, "Mother, pison or no pison, I can't afford to go a-layin' up." An' two days after he was on 'is back, and never got up again. It was Providence! There wasn't none o' these Compension Acts then.

MRS. YEO. Ye hadn't no strike that winter! [*With grim humour.*] This winter's 'ard enough for me. Mrs. Roberts, you don't want no 'arder winter, do you? Wouldn't seem natural to 'ave a dinner, would it, Mrs. Bulgin?

Mrs. Bulgin. We've had bread and tea last four days.

Mrs. Yeo. You got that Friday's laundry job?

Mrs. Bulgin. [*Dispiritedly*] They said they'd give it me, but when I went last Friday, they were full up. I got to go again next week.

Mrs. Yeo. Ah! There's too many after that. I send Yeo out on the ice to put on the gentry's skates an' pick up what 'e can. Stops 'im from broodin' about the 'ouse.

Mrs. Bulgin. [*In a desolate, matter-of-fact voice*] Leavin' out the men—it's bad enough with the children. I keep 'em in bed, they don't get so hungry when they're not running about; but they're that restless in bed they worry your life out.

Mrs. Yeo. You're lucky they're all so small. It's the goin' to school that makes 'em 'ungry. Don't Bulgin give you *anythin'*?

Mrs. Bulgin. [*Shakes her head, then, as though by afterthought*] Would if he could, I s'pose.

Mrs. Yeo. [*Sardonically*] What! 'Aven't 'e got no shares in the Company?

Mrs. Rous. [*Rising with tremendous cheerfulness*] Well, good-bye, Annie Roberts, I'm going along home.

Mrs. Roberts. Stay an' have a cup of tea, Mrs. Rous?

Mrs. Rous. [*With the faintest smile*] Roberts'll want 'is tea when he comes in. I'll just go an' get to bed; it's warmer there than anywhere.
                    [*She moves very shakily towards the door.*

Mrs. Yeo. [*Rising and giving her an arm*] Come on, Mother, take my arm; we're all goin' the same way.

Mrs. Rous. [*Taking the arm*] Thank you, my dearies!
                    [*They go out, followed by* Mrs. Bulgin.

Madge. [*Moving for the first time*] There, Annie, you see that! I told George Rous, " Don't think to have my company till you've made an end of all this trouble. You ought to be ashamed," I said, " with your own mother looking like a ghost, and not a stick to put on the fire. So long as you're able to fill your pipes, you'll let us starve." " I'll take my oath, Madge," he said, " I've not had smoke nor drink these three weeks! " " Well, then, why do you go on with it? " " I can't go back on Roberts! " . . . That's it! Roberts, always Roberts! They'd all drop it but for him. When *he* talks it's the devil that comes into them.

[*A silence.* Mrs. Roberts *makes a movement of pain.*] Ah! *You* don't want him beaten! He's your man. With everybody like their own shadows! [*She makes a gesture towards* Mrs. Roberts.] If Rous wants me he must give up Roberts. If *he* gave him up—they all would. They're only waiting for a lead. Father's against him —they're all against him in their hearts.

MRS. ROBERTS. You won't beat Roberts! [*They look silently at each other.*]

MADGE. Won't I? The cowards—when their own mothers and their own children don't know where to turn.

MRS. ROBERTS. Madge!

MADGE. [*Looking searchingly at* MRS. ROBERTS] I wonder he can look *you* in the face. [*She squats before the fire, with her hands out to the flame.*] Harness is here again. They'll have to make up their minds to-day.

MRS. ROBERTS. [*In a soft, slow voice, with a slight West-country burr*] Roberts will never give up the furnacemen and engineers. 'Twouldn't be right.

MADGE. You can't deceive me. It's just his pride.

[*A tapping at the door is heard, the women turn as* ENID *enters. She wears a round fur cap, and a jacket of squirrel's fur. She closes the door behind her.*

ENID. Can I come in, Annie?

MRS. ROBERTS. [*Flinching*] Miss Enid! Give Mrs. Underwood a chair, Madge.   [MADGE *gives* ENID *the chair she has been sitting on.*

ENID. Thank you!

ENID. Are you any better?

MRS. ROBERTS. Yes, M'm; thank you, M'm.

ENID. [*Looking at the sullen* MADGE *as though requesting her departure*] Why did you send back the jelly? I call that really wicked of you!

MRS. ROBERTS. Thank you, M'm, I'd no need for it.

ENID. Of course! It was Roberts' doing, wasn't it? How can he let all this suffering go on amongst you?

MADGE. [*Suddenly*] What suffering?

ENID. [*Surprised*] I beg your pardon!

MADGE. Who said there was suffering?

MRS. ROBERTS. Madge!

MADGE. [*Throwing her shawl over her head*] Please to let us keep ourselves to ourselves. We don't want you coming here and spying on us.

ENID. [*Confronting her, but without rising*] I didn't speak to you.

MADGE. [*In a low, fierce voice*] Keep your kind feelings to yourself. You think you can come amongst us, but you're mistaken. Go back and tell the Manager that.

ENID. [*Stonily*] This is not your house.

MADGE. [*Turning to the door*] No, it is not my house; keep clear of my house, Mrs. Underwood.

                    [*She goes out.* ENID *taps her fingers on the table.*

MRS. ROBERTS. Please to forgive Madge Thomas, M'm; she's a bit upset to-day.   [*A pause.*

ENID. [*Looking at her*] Oh, I think they're so *stupid*, all of them.

5

MRS. ROBERTS. [*With a faint smile*] Yes, M'm.

ENID. Is Roberts out?

MRS. ROBERTS. Yes, M'm.

ENID. It is *his doing*, that they don't come to an agreement. Now isn't it, Annie?

MRS. ROBERTS. [*Softly, with her eyes on* ENID, *and moving the fingers of one hand continually on her breast*] They do say that your father, M'm——

ENID. My father's getting an old man, and you know what old men are.

MRS. ROBERTS. I am sorry, M'm.

ENID. [*More softly*] I don't expect *you* to feel sorry, Annie. I know it's his fault as well as Roberts'.

MRS. ROBERTS. I'm sorry for anyone that gets old, M'm; it's dreadful to get old, and Mr. Anthony was such a fine old man I always used to think.

ENID. [*Impulsively*] He always liked you, don't you remember? Look here, Annie, what can I do? I do so want to know. You don't get what you ought to have. [*Going to the fire, she takes the kettle off, and looks for coals.*] And you're so naughty sending back the soup and things!

MRS. ROBERTS. [*With a faint smile*] Yes, M'm?

ENID. [*Resentfully*] Why, you haven't even got coals?

MRS. ROBERTS. If you please, M'm, to put the kettle on again; Roberts won't have long for his tea when he comes in. He's got to meet the men at four.

ENID. [*Putting the kettle on*] That means he'll lash them into a fury again. Can't you stop his going, Annie? [MRS. ROBERTS *smiles ironically.*] Have you tried? [*A silence.*] Does he know how ill you are?

MRS. ROBERTS. It's only my weak 'eart, M'm.

ENID. You used to be so well when you were with us.

MRS. ROBERTS. [*Stiffening*] Roberts is always good to me.

ENID. But you ought to have everything you want, and you have nothing!

MRS. ROBERTS. [*Appealingly*] They tell me I don't look like a dyin' woman?

ENID. Of course you don't; if you could only have proper—— Will you see my doctor if I send him to you? I'm sure he'd do you good.

MRS. ROBERTS. [*With faint questioning*] Yes, M'm.

ENID. Madge Thomas oughtn't to come here; she only excites you. As if I didn't know what suffering there is amongst the men! I do feel for them dreadfully, but you know they *have* gone too far.

MRS. ROBERTS. [*Continually moving her fingers*] They say there's no other way to get better wages, M'm.

ENID. [*Earnestly*] But, Annie, that's why the Union won't help them. My husband's very sympathetic with the men, but he says they're not underpaid.

MRS. ROBERTS. No, M'm ?

ENID. They never think how the Company could go on if we paid the wages they want.

MRS. ROBERTS. [*With an effort*] But the dividends having been so big, M'm.

ENID. [*Taken aback*] You all seem to think the shareholders are rich men, but they're not—most of them are really no better off than working men. [MRS. ROBERTS *smiles.*] They have to keep up appearances.

MRS. ROBERTS. Yes, M'm ?

ENID. You don't have to pay rates and taxes, and a hundred other things that they do. If the men didn't spend such a lot in drink and betting they'd be quite well off !

MRS. ROBERTS. They say, workin' so hard, they must have some pleasure.

ENID. But surely not low pleasure like that.

MRS. ROBERTS. [*A little resentfully*] Roberts never touches a drop ; and he's never had a bet in his life.

ENID. Oh ! but he's not a com—— I mean he's an engineer— a superior man.

MRS. ROBERTS. Yes, M'm. Roberts says they've no chance of other pleasures.

ENID. [*Musing*] Of course, I know it's hard.

MRS. ROBERTS. [*With a spice of malice*] And they say gentlefolk's just as bad.

ENID. [*With a smile*] I go as far as most people, Annie, but you know, yourself, that's nonsense.

MRS. ROBERTS. [*With painful effort*] A lot o' the men never go near the Public ; but even they don't save but very little, and that goes if there's illness.

ENID. But they've got their clubs, haven't they ?

MRS. ROBERTS. The clubs only give up to eighteen shillin's a week, M'm, and it's not much amongst a family. Roberts says workin' folk have always lived from hand to mouth. Sixpence to-day is worth more than a shillin' to-morrow, that's what they say.

ENID. But that's the spirit of gambling.

MRS. ROBERTS. [*With a sort of excitement*] Roberts says a working man's life is all a gamble, from the time 'e's born to the time 'e dies.

> [ENID *leans forward, interested.* MRS. ROBERTS *goes on with a growing excitement that culminates in the personal feeling of the last words.*]

He says, M'm, that when a working man's baby is born, it's a toss-up from breath to breath whether it ever draws another, and so on all 'is life ; an' when he comes to be old, it's the workhouse or the grave. He says that without a man is very near, and pinches and stints 'imself and 'is children to save, there can't be neither surplus nor security.   That's why he wouldn't have no children [*she sinks back*], not though I *wanted* them.

ENID. Yes, yes, I know !

MRS. ROBERTS. No, you don't, M'm.   You've got your children, and you'll never need to trouble for them.

ENID. [*Gently*] You oughtn't to be talking so much, Annie. [*Then, in spite of herself.*] But Roberts was paid a lot of money, wasn't he, for discovering that process ?

MRS. ROBERTS. [*On the defensive*] All Roberts' savin's have gone. He's always looked forward to this strike.   He says he's no right to a farthing when the others are suffering.   'Tisn't so with all o' them ! Some don't seem to care no more than that—so long as they get their own.

ENID. I don't see how they can be expected to when they're suffering like this. [*In a changed voice.*] But Roberts ought to think of *you !*   It's all terrible !   The kettle's boiling.   Shall I make the tea ? [*She takes the teapot, and seeing tea there, pours water into it.*] Won't you have a cup ?

MRS. ROBERTS. No, thank you, M'm. [*She is listening, as though for footsteps.*] I'd sooner you didn't see Roberts, M'm, he gets so wild.

ENID. Oh ! but I must, Annie ; I'll be quite calm, I promise.

MRS. ROBERTS. It's life an' death to him, M'm.

ENID. [*Very gently*] I'll get him to talk to me outside, we won't excite you.

MRS. ROBERTS. [*Faintly*] No, M'm.

[*She gives a violent start.* ROBERTS *has come in, unseen.*

ROBERTS. [*Removing his hat—with subtle mockery*] Beg pardon for coming in ; you're engaged with a lady, I see.

ENID. Can I speak to you, Mr. Roberts ?

ROBERTS. Whom have I the pleasure of addressing, Ma'am ?

ENID. But surely you know me !   I'm Mrs. Underwood.

ROBERTS. [*With a bow of malice*] The daughter of our chairman.

ENID [*Earnestly*] I've come on purpose to speak to you ; will you come outside a minute ?   [*She looks at* MRS. ROBERTS.

ROBERTS. [*Hanging up his hat*] I have nothing to say, Ma'am.

ENID. But I *must* speak to you, please.   [*She moves towards the door.*

ROBERTS. [*With sudden venom*] I have not the time to listen !

MRS. ROBERTS. David !

ENID. Mr. Roberts, *please !*

ROBERTS. [*Taking off his overcoat*] I am sorry to disoblige a lady—Mr. Anthony's daughter.

ENID. [*Wavering, then with sudden decision*] Mr. Roberts, I know you've another meeting of the men.   [ROBERTS *bows.*] I came to appeal to you. Please, please try to come to some compromise ; give way a little, if it's only for your own sakes !

ROBERTS. [*Speaking to himself*] The daughter of Mr. Anthony begs me to give way a little, if it's only for our own sakes.

ENID. For everybody's sake ; for your wife's sake.

ROBERTS. For my wife's sake, for everybody's sake—for the sake of Mr. Anthony.

ENID. Why are you so bitter against my father ? He has never done anything to you.

ROBERTS. Has he not ?

ENID. He can't help his views, any more than you can help yours.

ROBERTS. I really didn't know that I had a right to views !

ENID. He's an old man, and you——
      [*Seeing his eyes fixed on her, she stops.*

ROBERTS. [*Without raising his voice*] If I saw Mr. Anthony going to die, and I could save him by lifting my hand, I would not lift the little finger of it.

ENID. You—you——   [*She stops again, biting her lips.*

ROBERTS. I would not, and that's flat !

ENID. [*Coldly*] You don't mean what you say, and you know it !

ROBERTS. I mean every word of it.

ENID. But why ?

ROBERTS. [*With a flash*] Mr. Anthony stands for tyranny ! That's why !

ENID. Nonsense !

[MRS. ROBERTS *makes a movement as if to rise, but sinks back in her chair.*

ENID. [*With an impetuous movement*] Annie !

ROBERTS. Please not to touch my wife !

ENID. [*Recoiling with a sort of horror*] I believe—you are mad.

ROBERTS. The house of a madman then is not the fit place for a lady.

ENID. I'm not afraid of you.

ROBERTS. [*Bowing*] I would not expect the daughter of Mr. Anthony to be afraid. Mr. Anthony is not a coward like the rest of them.

ENID. [*Suddenly*] I suppose you think it brave, then, to go on with this struggle.

ROBERTS. Does Mr. Anthony think it brave to fight against women and children ? Mr. Anthony is a rich man, I believe ; does he think it brave to fight against those who haven't a penny ? Does he think it brave to set children crying with hunger, an' women shivering with cold ?

ENID. [*Putting up her hand, as though warding off a blow*] My father is acting on his principles, and you know it!

ROBERTS. And so am I!

ENID. You hate us; and you can't bear to be beaten.

ROBERTS. Neither can Mr. Anthony, for all that he may say.

ENID. At any rate you might have pity on your wife.

[MRS. ROBERTS, *who has her hand pressed to her heart, takes it away, and tries to calm her breathing.*

ROBERTS. Madam, I have no more to say.

[*He takes up the loaf. There is a knock at the door, and* UNDER-WOOD *comes in. He stands looking at them,* ENID *turns to him, then seems undecided.*

UNDERWOOD. Enid!

ROBERTS. [*Ironically*] Ye were not needing to come for your wife, Mr. Underwood. We are not rowdies.

UNDERWOOD. I know that, Roberts. I hope Mrs. Roberts is better.

[ROBERTS *turns away without answering.*]

Come, Enid!

ENID. I make one more appeal to you, Mr. Roberts, for the sake of your wife.

ROBERTS. [*With polite malice*] If I might advise ye, Ma'am—make it for the sake of your husband and your father.

[ENID, *suppressing a retort, goes out.* UNDERWOOD *opens the door for her and follows.* ROBERTS, *going to the fire, holds out his hands to the dying glow.*

ROBERTS. How goes it, my girl? Feeling better, are you?

[MRS. ROBERTS *smiles faintly. He brings his overcoat and wraps it round her.*]

[*Looking at his watch.*] Ten minutes to four! [*As though inspired.*] I've seen their faces, there's no fight in them, except for that one old robber.

MRS. ROBERTS. Won't you stop and eat, David? You've 'ad nothing all day!

ROBERTS. [*Putting his hand to his throat*] Can't swallow till those old sharks are out o' the town. [*He walks up and down.*] I shall have a bother with the men—there's no heart in them, the cowards. Blind as bats, they are—can't see a day before their noses.

MRS. ROBERTS. It's the women, David.

ROBERTS. Ah! So they say! They can remember the women when their own bellies speak! The women never stops them from the drink; but from a little suffering to themselves in a sacred cause, the women stop them fast enough.

MRS. ROBERTS. But think o' the children, David.

ROBERTS. Ah! If they will go breeding themselves for slaves, without a thought o' the future o' them they breed——

MRS. ROBERTS. [*Gasping*] That's enough, David; don't begin to talk of that—I won't—I can't——

ROBERTS. [*Staring at her*] Now, now, my girl!

MRS. ROBERTS. [*Breathlessly*] No, no, David—I won't!

ROBERTS. There, there! Come, come! That's right. [*Bitterly.*] Not one penny will they put by for a day like this. Not they! Hand to mouth—Gad!—I know them! They've broke my heart. There was no holdin' them at the start, but now the pinch 'as come.

MRS. ROBERTS. How can you expect it, David? They're not made of iron.

ROBERTS. Expect it? Wouldn't I expect what I would do meself? Wouldn't I starve an' rot rather than give in? What one man can do, another can.

MRS. ROBERTS. And the women?

ROBERTS. This is not women's work.

MRS. ROBERTS. [*With a flash of malice*] No, the women may die for all you care. That's their work.

ROBERTS. [*Averting his eyes*] Who talks of dying? No one will die till we have beaten these——

[*He meets her eyes again, and again turns his away. Excitedly.*] This is what I've been waiting for all these months. To get the old robbers down, and send them home again without a farthin's worth o' change. I've seen their faces, I tell you, in the valley of the shadow of defeat.   [*He goes to the peg and takes down his hat.*

MRS. ROBERTS. [*Following with her eyes—softly*] Take your overcoat, David; it must be bitter cold.

ROBERTS. [*Coming up to her—his eyes are furtive*] No, no! There, there, stay quiet and warm. I won't be long, my girl!

MRS. ROBERTS. [*With soft bitterness*] You'd better take it.

[*She lifts the coat. But* ROBERTS *puts it back, and wraps it round her. He tries to meet her eyes, but cannot.* MRS. ROBERTS *stays huddled in the coat, her eyes, that follow him about, are half malicious, half yearning. He looks at his watch again, and turns to go. In the doorway he meets* JAN THOMAS, *a boy of ten in clothes too big for him, carrying a penny whistle.*

ROBERTS. Hallo, boy!

[*He goes,* JAN *stops within a yard of* MRS. ROBERTS, *and stares at her without a word.*

MRS. ROBERTS. Well, Jan!

JAN. Father's coming; sister Madge is coming.

[*He sits at the table, and fidgets with his whistle; he blows three vague notes; then imitates a cuckoo.*

[*There is a tap on the door. Old* THOMAS *comes in.*

THOMAS. A very coot tay to you, Ma'am. It is petter that you are.

MRS. ROBERTS. Thank you, Mr. Thomas.

THOMAS. [*Nervously*] Roberts in?

MRS. ROBERTS. Just gone on to the meeting, Mr. Thomas.

THOMAS. [*With relief, becoming talkative*] This is fery unfortunate, look you! I came to tell him that we must make terms with London. It is a fery great pity he is gone to the meeting. He will be kicking against the pricks, I am thinking.

MRS. ROBERTS. [*Half rising*] He'll never give in, Mr. Thomas.

THOMAS. You must not be fretting, that is very pat for you. Look you, there iss hartly any mans for supporting him now, but the engineers and George Rous. [*Solemnly.*] This strike is no longer coing with Chapel, look you! I have listened carefully, an' I have talked with her. [JAN *blows.*] Sst! I don't care what th' others say, I say that *Chapel means us* to be stopping the trouble, that is what I make of her; and it is my opinion that this is the fery best thing for all of us. If it wasn't my opinion, I ton't say—but it is my opinion, look you.

MRS. ROBERTS. [*Trying to suppress her excitement*] I don't know what'll come to Roberts, if you give in.

THOMAS. It iss no disgrace whateffer! All that a mortal man coult do he hass tone. It iss against Human Nature he hass gone; fery natural—any man may to that; but Chapel has spoken and he must not co against *her.* [JAN *imitates the cuckoo.*] Ton't make that squeaking! [*Going to the door.*] Here iss my taughter come to sit with you. A fery goot day, Ma'am—no fretting— rememper!

[MADGE *comes in and stands at the open door, watching the street.*

MADGE. You'll be late, Father; they're beginning. [*She catches him by the sleeve.*] For the love of God, stand up to him, Father—this time!

THOMAS. [*Detaching his sleeve with dignity*] Leave me to do what's proper, girl!

[*He goes out,* MADGE, *in the centre of the open doorway, slowly moves in, as though before the approach of someone.*

ROUS. [*Appearing in the doorway*] Madge!

[MADGE *stands with her back to* MRS. ROBERTS, *staring at him with her head up and her hands behind her.*

ROUS. [*Who has a fierce distracted look*] Madge! I'm going to the meeting.

[MADGE, *without moving, smiles contemptuously.*]
D'ye hear me?   [*They speak in quick low voices.*

MADGE. I hear! Go, and kill your own Mother, if you must.

[ROUS *seizes her by both her arms. She stands rigid, with her head bent back. He releases her, and he too stands motionless.*

ROUS. I swore to stand by Roberts. I swore that! Ye want me to go back on what I've sworn.

MADGE. [*With slow soft mockery*] You are a pretty lover!

Rous. Madge!

Madge. [*Smiling*] I've heard that lovers do what their girls ask them —[Jan *sounds the cuckoo's notes*]—but that's not true, it seems!

Rous. You'd make a blackleg of me!

Madge. [*With her eyes half-closed*] Do it for me!

Rous. [*Dashing his hand across his brow*] Damn! I can't!

Madge. [*Swiftly*] Do it for me!

Rous. [*Through his teeth*] Don't play the wanton with me!

Madge. [*With a movement of her hand towards* Jan—*quick and low*] I'd do *that* to get the children bread!

Rous. [*In a fierce whisper*] Madge! Oh, Madge!

Madge. [*With soft mockery*] But *you* can't break your word with me!

Rous. [*With a choke*] Then, Begod, I can!

[*He turns and rushes off.*

[Madge *stands with a faint smile on her face, looking after him. She moves to the table.*

Madge. I have done for Roberts!

[*She sees that* Mrs. Roberts *has sunk back in her chair.*

Madge. [*Running to her, and feeling her hands*] You're as cold as a stone! You want a drop of brandy. Jan, run to the " Lion " ; say I sent you for Mrs. Roberts.

Mrs. Roberts. [*With a feeble movement*] I'll just sit quiet, Madge. Give Jan—his—tea.

Madge. [*Giving* Jan *a slice of bread*] There, ye little rascal. Hold your piping. [*Going to the fire, she kneels.*] It's going out.

Mrs. Roberts. [*With a faint smile*] 'Tis all the same!

[Jan *begins to blow his whistle.*

Madge. Tsht! Tsht!—you—— [Jan *stops.*

Mrs. Roberts. [*Smiling*] Let 'im play, Madge.

Madge. [*On her knees at the fire, listening*] Waiting an' waiting. I've no patience with it ; waiting an' waiting—that's what a woman has to do! Can you hear them at it—I can!

[*She leans her elbows on the table, and her chin on her hands. Behind her,* Mrs. Roberts *leans forward, with painful and growing excitement, as the sounds of the strikers' meeting come in.*

The curtain falls.

SCENE II

It is past four. In a grey, failing light, an open muddy space is crowded with workmen. Beyond, divided from it by a barbed-wire fence, is the raised towing-path of a canal, on which is moored a barge. In the distance are marshes and snow-covered hills. The " Works' " high wall runs from

5*

the canal across the open space, and in the angle of this wall is a rude
platform of barrels and boards. On it, HARNESS *is standing.* ROBERTS,
a little apart from the crowd, leans his back against the wall. On
the raised towing-path two bargemen lounge and smoke indifferently.

HARNESS. [*Holding out his hand*] Well, I've spoken to you straight.
If I speak till to-morrow I can't say more.

JAGO. [*A dark, sallow, Spanish-looking man, with a short, thin beard*]
Mister, want to ask you ! Can they get blacklegs ?

BULGIN. [*Menacing*] Let 'em try.

[*There are savage murmurs from the crowd.*

BROWN. [*A round-faced man*] Where could they get 'em then ?

EVANS. [*A small restless, harassed man, with a fighting face*] There's
always blacklegs ; it's the nature of 'em. There's always men that'll
save their own skins.

[*Another savage murmur. There is a movement, and old* THOMAS,
joining the crowd, takes his stand in front.

HARNESS. [*Holding up his hand*] They can't get them. But that
won't help you. Now men, be reasonable. Your demands would
have brought on us the burden of a dozen strikes at a time when we
were not prepared for them. The Unions live by Justice, not to one,
but all. Any fair man will tell you—you were ill-advised ! I don't
say you go too far for that which you're entitled to, but you're going
too far for the moment ; you've dug a pit for yourselves. Are you
to stay there, or are you to climb out ? Come !

LEWIS. [*A clean-cut Welshman with a dark moustache*] You've hit it,
Mister ! Which is it to be ?

[*Another movement in the crowd, and* ROUS, *coming quickly, takes*
his stand next THOMAS.

HARNESS. Cut your demands to the right pattern, and we'll see you
through ; refuse, and don't expect me to waste my time coming down
here again. I'm not the sort that speaks at random, as you ought to
know by this time. If you're the sound men I take you for—no
matter who advises you against it—[*he fixes his eyes on* ROBERTS] you'll
make up your minds to come in, and trust to us to get your terms.
Which is it to be ? Hands together, and victory—or—the starvation
you've got now ?   [*A prolonged murmur from the crowd.*

JAGO. [*Sullenly*] Talk about what you know.

HARNESS. [*Lifting his voice above the murmur*] Know ? [*With cold
passion.*] All that you've been through, my friend, I've been through
—I was through it when I was no bigger than [*pointing to a youth*] that
shaver there ; the Unions then weren't what they are now. What's
made them strong ? It's hands together that's made them strong.
I've been through it all, I tell you, the brand's on my soul yet. I know
what you've suffered—there's nothing you can tell me that I don't

know; but the whole is greater than the part, and you are only the part.   Stand by us, and we will stand by you.

[*Quartering them with his eyes, he waits.   The murmuring swells; the men form little groups.* GREEN, BULGIN, *and* LEWIS *talk together.*

LEWIS. Speaks very sensible, the Union chap.

GREEN. [*Quietly*] Ah! if I'd a been *listened* to, you'd 'ave 'eard sense these two months past.   [*The bargemen are seen laughing.*

LEWIS. [*Pointing*] Look at those two blanks over the fence there!

BULGIN. [*With gloomy violence*] They'd best stop their cackle, or I'll break their jaws.

JAGO. [*Suddenly*] You say the furnace men's paid enough?

HARNESS. I did not say they were paid enough; I said they were paid as much as the furnace men in similar works elsewhere.

EVANS. That's a lie. [*Hubbub.*] What about Harper's?

HARNESS. [*With cold irony*] You may look at home for lies, my man.   Harper's shifts are longer, the pay works out the same.

HENRY ROUS. [*A dark edition of his brother George*] Will ye support us in double pay overtime Saturdays?

HARNESS. Yes, we will.

JAGO. What have ye done with our subscriptions?

HARNESS. [*Coldly*] I have told you what we *will* do with them.

EVANS. Ah! *will*, it's always will!   Ye'd have our mates desert us.   [*Hubbub.*

BULGIN. [*Shouting*] Hold your row!   [EVANS *looks round angrily.*

HARNESS. [*Lifting his voice*] Those who know their right hands from their lefts know that the Unions are neither thieves nor traitors. I've said my say.   Figure it out, my lads; when you want me you know where I shall be.

[*He jumps down, the crowd gives way, he passes through them, and goes away.   A bargeman looks after him, jerking his pipe with a derisive gesture.   The men close up in groups, and many looks are cast at* ROBERTS, *who stands alone against the wall.*

EVANS. He wants ye to turn blacklegs, that's what he wants.   He wants ye to go back on us.   Sooner than turn blackleg—I'd starve, I would.

BULGIN. Who's talkin' o' blacklegs—mind what you're saying, will you?

BLACKSMITH. [*A youth with yellow hair and huge arms*] What about the women?

EVANS. They can stand what we can stand, I suppose, can't they?

BLACKSMITH. Ye've no wife?

EVANS. An' don't want one.

THOMAS. [*Raising his voice*] Aye! Give us the power to come to terms with London, lads.

DAVIES. [*A dark, slow-fly, gloomy man*] Go up the platform, if you got anything to say, go up an' say it.

> [*There are cries of " Thomas ! " He is pushed towards the platform ; he ascends it with difficulty, and bares his head, waiting for silence. A hush !*

RED-HAIRED YOUTH. [*Suddenly*] Coot old Thomas !

> [*A hoarse laugh ; the bargemen exchange remarks ; a hush again, and* THOMAS *begins speaking.*

THOMAS. We are all in the tepth together, and it iss Nature that has put us there.

HENRY ROUS. It's London put us there !

EVANS. It's the Union.

THOMAS. It iss not Lonton ; not it iss not the Union—it iss Nature. It iss no disgrace whateffer to a potty to give in to Nature. For this Nature iss a fery pig thing ; it is pigger than what a man is. There iss more years to my hett than to the hett of any one here. It is fery pat, look you, this coing against Nature. It is pat to make other potties suffer, when there is nothing to pe cot py it.

> [*A laugh.* THOMAS *angrily goes on.*]

What are ye laughing at ? It is pat, I say ! We are fighting for a principle ; there is nopotty that shall say I am not a peliever in principle. Putt when Nature says " No further," then it is no coot snapping your fingers in her face.

> [*A laugh from* ROBERTS, *and murmurs of approval.*]

This Nature must pe humort. It is a man's pisiness to pe pure, honest, just and merciful. That's what Chapel tells you. [*To* ROBERTS, *angrily.*] And, look you, David Roberts, Chapel tells you ye can do that without coing against Nature.

JAGO. What about the Union ?

THOMAS. I ton't trust the Union ; they haf treated us like tirt. " Do what we tell you," said they. I haf peen captain of the furnace men twenty years, and I say to the Union—[*excitedly*]—" Can you tell me then, as well as I can tell you, what iss the right wages for the work that these men do ? " For fife and twenty years I haf paid my moneys to the Union and—[*with great excitement*]—for nothings ! What iss that but roguery, for all that this Mr. Harness says ! [*Murmurs.*

EVANS. Hear, hear.

HENRY ROUS. Get on with you ! Cut on with it then !

THOMAS. Look you, if a man toes not trust me, am I coing to trust him ?

JAGO. That's right.

THOMAS. Let them alone for rogues, and act for ourselves.

> [*Murmurs.*

BLACKSMITH. That's what we been doin', haven't we ?

THOMAS. [*With increased excitement*] I wass brought up to do for

meself. I wass brought up to go without a thing, if I hat not moneys
to puy it. There iss too much, look you, of doing things with other
people's moneys. We haf fought fair, and if we haf peen beaten, it
iss no fault of ours. Gif us the power to make terms with London
for ourself; if we ton't succeed, I say it iss petter to take our peating
like men, than to tie like togs, or hang on to others' coat-tails to make
them do our pusiness for us !

EVANS. [*Muttering*] Who wants to ?

THOMAS. [*Craning*] What's that ? If I stand up to a potty, and he
knocks me town, I am not to go hollering to other potties to help
me ; I am to stand up again ; and if he knocks me town properly, I
am to stay there, isn't that right ?   [*Laughter.*

JAGO. No Union !

HENRY ROUS. Union !   [*Others take up the shout.*

EVANS. Blacklegs !

        [BULGIN *and the* BLACKSMITH *shake their fists at* EVANS.

THOMAS. [*With a gesture*] I am an olt man, look you.

                [*A sudden silence, then murmurs again.*

LEWIS. Olt fool, with his " No Union ! "

BULGIN. Them furnace chaps ! For twopence I'd smash the faces
o' the lot of them.

GREEN. If I'd 'a been listened to at the first——

THOMAS. [*Wiping his brow*] I'm comin' now to what I was coing to
say——

DAVIES. [*Muttering*] An' time too !

THOMAS. [*Solemnly*] Chapel says : Ton't carry on this strike !
Put an end to it !

JAGO. That's a lie ! Chapel says go on !

THOMAS. [*Scornfully*] Inteet ! I haf ears to my head.

RED-HAIRED YOUTH. Ah ! long ones !   [*A laugh.*

JAGO. Your ears have misbeled you then.

THOMAS. [*Excitedly*] Ye cannot be right if I am, ye cannot haf it
both ways.

RED-HAIRED YOUTH. Chapel can though !

        [" *The Shaver* " *laughs ; there are murmurs from the crowd.*

THOMAS. [*Fixing his eyes on* " *The Shaver* "] Ah ! ye're coing
the roat to tamnation. An' so I say to all of you. If ye co
against Chapel I will not pe with you, nor will any other Got-fearing
man.

        [*He steps down from the patform.* JAGO *makes his way towards it.*
        There are cries of " *Don't let 'im go up !* "

JAGO. Don't let him go up ? That's free speech, that is. [*He
goes up.*] I ain't got much to say to you. Look at the matter plain ;
ye've come the road this far, and now you want to chuck the journey.
We've all been in one boat ; and now you want to pull in two. We

engineers have stood by you ; ye're ready now, are ye, to give us the go-by ? If we'd a-known that before, we'd not a-started out with you so early one bright morning ! That's all I've got to say. Old man Thomas a'n't got his Bible lesson right. If you give up to London, or to Harness, now, it's givin' us the chuck— to save your skins—you won't get over that, my boys ; it's a dirty thing to do.

[*He gets down ; during his little speech, which is ironically spoken, there is a restless discomfort in the crowd.* ROUS, *stepping forward, jumps on the platform. He has an air of fierce distraction. Sullen murmurs of disapproval from the crowd.*

ROUS. [*Speaking with great excitement*] I'm no blanky orator, mates, but wot I say is drove from me. What I say is yuman nature. Can a man set an' see 'is mother starve ? Can 'e now ?

ROBERTS. [*Starting forward*] Rous !

ROUS. [*Staring at him fiercely*] Sim 'Arness said fair ! I've changed my mind.

EVANS. Ah ! Turned your coat you mean !

[*The crowd manifests a great surprise.*

LEWIS. [*Apostrophizing* ROUS] Hallo ! What's turned him round ?

ROUS. [*Speaking with intense excitement*] 'E said fair. " Stand by us," 'e said, " and we'll stand by you." That's where we've been makin' our mistake this long time past ; and who's to blame for't ? [*He points at* ROBERTS.] That man there ! " No," 'e said, " fight the robbers," 'e said, " squeeze the breath out o' them ! " But it's not the breath out o' them that's being squeezed ; it's the breath out of *us* and *ours*, and that's the book of truth. I'm no orator, mates, it's the flesh and blood in me that's speakin', it's the heart o' me. [*With a menacing, yet half ashamed movement towards* ROBERTS.] He'll speak to you again, mark my words, but don't ye listen. [*The crowd groans.*] It's hell fire that's on that man's tongue. [ROBERTS *is seen laughing.*] Sim 'Arness is right. What are we without the Union— handful o' parched leaves—a puff o' smoke. I'm no orator, but I say : Chuck it up ! Chuck it up ! Sooner than go on starving the women and the children.

[*The murmurs of acquiescence almost drown the murmurs of dissent.*

EVANS. What's turned *you* to blacklegging ?

ROUS. [*With a furious look*] Sim 'Arness knows what he's talkin' about. Give us power to come to terms with London ; I'm no orator, but I say—have done wi' this black misery !

[*He gives his muffler a twist, jerks his head back and jumps off the platform. The crowd applauds and surges forward. Amid cries of " That's enough ! " " Up Union ! " " Up Harness ! "* ROBERTS *quietly ascends the platform. There is a moment of silence.*

BLACKSMITH. We don't want to hear you. Shut it!

HENRY ROUS. Get down!

[*Amid such cries they surge towards the platform.*

EVANS. [*Fiercely*] Let 'im speak! Roberts! Roberts!

BULGIN. [*Muttering*] He'd better look out that I don't crack 'is skull.

[ROBERTS *faces the crowd, probing them with his eyes till they gradually become silent. He begins speaking. One of the bargemen rises and stands.*

ROBERTS. You don't want to hear me, then? You'll listen to Rous and to that old man, but not to me. You'll listen to Sim Harness of the Union that's treated you *so fair;* maybe you'll listen to those men from London? Ah! You groan! What for? You love their feet on your necks, don't you? [*Then as* BULGIN *elbows his way towards the platform, with calm pathos.*] You'd like to break my jaw, John Bulgin. Let me speak, then do your smashing, if it gives you pleasure. [BULGIN *stands motionless and sullen.*] Am I a liar, a coward, a traitor? If only I were, ye'd listen to me, I'm sure. [*The murmurings cease, and there is now dead silence.*] Is there a man of you here that has less to gain by striking? Is there a man of you that had more to lose? Is there a man of you that has given up *eight hundred* pounds since this trouble here began? Come now, is there? How much has Thomas given up—ten pounds or five, or what? You listened to him, and what had he to say? "None can pretend," he said, "that I'm not a believer in principle—[*with biting irony*]—but when Nature says : 'No further, 'tes going agenst Nature.'" *I* tell you if a man cannot say to Nature : "Budge me from this if ye can!"—[*with a sort of exaltation*]—his principles are but his belly. "Oh, but," Thomas says, "a man can be pure and honest, just and merciful, and take off his hat to Nature!" *I* tell you Nature's neither pure nor honest, just nor merciful. You chaps that live over the hill, an' go home dead beat in the dark on a snowy night—don't ye fight your way every inch of it? Do ye go lyin' down an' trustin' to the tender mercies of this merciful Nature? Try it and you'll soon know with what ye've got to deal. 'Tes only by that—[*he strikes a blow with his clenched fist*]—in Nature's face that a man can be a man. "Give in," says Thomas, "go down on your knees ; throw up your foolish fight, an' perhaps," he said, "perhaps your enemy will chuck you down a crust."

JAGO. Never!

EVANS. Curse them!

THOMAS. I nefer said that.

ROBERTS. [*Bitingly*] If ye did not say it, man, ye meant it. An' what did ye say about Chapel? "Chapel's against it," ye said. "She's against it!" Well, if Chapel and Nature go hand in hand, it's the first I've ever heard of it. That young man there—[*pointing to* ROUS]—said I 'ad 'ell fire on my tongue. If I had I would use it all to scorch and wither this talking of surrender. Surrendering's the work of cowards and traitors.

HENRY ROUS. [*As* GEORGE ROUS *moves forward*] Go for him, George—don't stand his lip!

ROBERTS. [*Flinging out his finger*] Stop there, George Rous, it's no time this to settle personal matters. [ROUS *stops.*] But there was one other spoke to you—Mr. Simon Harness. We have not much to thank Mr. Harness and the Union for. They said to us "Desert your mates, or we'll desert you." An' they did desert us.

EVANS. They did.

ROBERTS. Mr. Simon Harness is a clever man, but he has come too late. [*With intense conviction.*] For all that Mr. Simon Harness says, for all that Thomas, Rous, for all that any man present here can say— *We've won the fight!*

[*The crowd sags nearer, looking eagerly up. With withering scorn.*] You've felt the pinch o't in your bellies. You've forgotten what that fight 'as been; many times I have told you; I will tell you now this once again. The fight o' the country's body and blood against a blood-sucker. The fight of those that spend theirselves with every blow they strike and every breath they draw, against a thing that fattens on them, and grows and grows by the law of *merciful* Nature. That thing is Capital! A thing that buys the sweat o' men's brows, and the tortures o' their brains, at its own price. *Don't I* know that? Wasn' the work o' *my* brains bought for seven hundred pounds, and hasn't one hundred thousand pounds been gained them by that seven hundred without the stirring of a finger? It is a thing that will take as much and give you as little as it can. That's *Capital!* A thing that will say—"I'm very sorry for you, poor fellows—you have a cruel time of it, I know," but will not give one sixpence of its dividends to help you have a better time. That's Capital! Tell me, for all their talk is there one of them that will consent to another penny on the Income Tax to help the poor? That's Capital! A white-faced, stony-hearted monster! Ye have got it on its knees; are ye to give up at the last minute to save your miserable bodies pain? When I went this morning to those old men from London, I looked into their very 'earts. One of them was sitting there—Mr. Scantlebury, a mass of flesh nourished on us: sittin' there for all the world like the shareholders in this Company, that sit not moving tongue nor finger, takin' dividends—a great dumb ox that can only be roused when its food is threatened. I looked into his eyes and I saw *he was afraid*—afraid for himself and his dividends, afraid for his fees, afraid of the very shareholders he stands for; and all but one of them's afraid—like children that get into a wood at night,

and start at every rustle of the leaves. I ask you, men—[*he pauses,
holding out his hand till there is utter silence*]—Give me a free hand to
tell them : " Go you back to London. The men have nothing for
you ! " [*A murmuring.*] Give me that, an' I swear to you, within
a week you shall have from London all you want.

EVANS, JAGO, AND OTHERS. A free hand ! Give him a free hand !
Bravo—bravo !

ROBERTS. 'Tis not for this little moment of time we're fighting
[*the murmuring dies*], not for ourselves, our own little bodies, and their
wants, 'tis for all those that come after throughout all time. [*With
intense sadness.*] Oh ! men—for the love o' them, don't roll up another
stone upon their heads, don't help to blacken the sky, an' let the bitter
sea in over them. They're welcome to the worst that can happen
to me, to the worst that can happen to us all, aren't they—aren't
they ? If we can shake [*passionately*] that white-faced monster with
the bloody lips, that has sucked the life out of ourselves, our wives
and children, since the world began. [*Dropping the note of passion,
but with the utmost weight and intensity.*] If we have not the hearts of
men to stand against it breast to breast, and eye to eye, and force it
backward till it cry for mercy, it will go on sucking life ; and we
shall stay for ever what we are [*in almost a whisper*] less than the very
dogs.

[*An utter stillness, and ROBERTS stands rocking his body slightly,
with his eyes burning the faces of the crowd.*

EVANS AND JAGO. [*Suddenly*] Roberts ! [*The shout is taken up.*]

[*There is a slight movement in the crowd, and MADGE passing below
the towing-path stops by the platform, looking up at ROBERTS.
A sudden doubting silence.*

ROBERTS. " Nature," says that old man, " give in to Nature."
I tell you, strike your blow in Nature's face — an' let it do
its worst !

[*He catches sight of MADGE, his brows contract, he looks
away.*

MADGE. [*In a low voice—close to the platform*] Your wife's dying !

[*ROBERTS glares at her as if torn from some pinnacle of exaltation.*

ROBERTS. [*Trying to stammer on*] I say to you—answer them—answer
them—— [*He is drowned by the murmur in the crowd.*

THOMAS. [*Stepping forward*] Ton't you hear her, then ?

ROBERTS. What is it ? [*A dead silence.*

THOMAS. Your wife, man !

[*ROBERTS hesitates, then with a gesture, he leaps down, and goes
away below the towing-path, the men making way for him.
The standing bargeman opens and prepares to light a lantern.
Daylight is fast failing.*

MADGE. He needn't have hurried ! Annie Roberts is dead. [*Then *in the silence, passionately.*] You pack of blinded hounds ! How many more women are you going to let die ?

> [*The crowd shrinks back from her, and breaks up in groups, with a confused, uneasy movement.* MADGE *goes quickly away below the towing-path. There is a hush as they look after her.*

LEWIS. There's a spitfire, for ye !

BULGIN. [*Growling*] I'll smash 'er jaw.

GREEN. If I'd a-been listened to, that poor woman——

THOMAS. It's a judgment on him for coing against Chapel. I toit him how 'twould be !

EVANS. All the more reason for sticking by 'im. [*A cheer.*] Are you goin' to desert him now 'e's down ? Are you goin' to chuck him over, now 'e's lost 'is wife ?

> [*The crowd is murmuring and cheering all at once.*

ROUS. [*Stepping in front of platform*] Lost his wife ! Aye ! Can't ye see ? Look at home, look at your own wives ! What's to save them ? Ye'll have the same in all your houses before long !

LEWIS. Aye, aye !

HENRY ROUS. Right ! George, right !

> [*There are murmurs of assent.*

ROUS. It's not us that's blind, it's Roberts. How long will ye put up with 'im !

HENRY ROUS, BULGIN, DAVIES. Give 'im the chuck !

> [*The cry is taken up.*

EVANS. [*Fiercely*] Kick a man that's down ? Down ?

HENRY ROUS. Stop his jaw there !

> [EVANS *throws up his arm at a threat from* BULGIN. *The bargeman, who has lighted the lantern, holds it high above his head.*

ROUS. [*Springing on to the platform*] What brought him down then, but 'is own black obstinacy ? Are ye goin' to follow a man that can't see better than that where he's goin' ?

EVANS. He's lost 'is wife.

ROUS. An' who's fault's that but his own ? 'Ave done with 'im, I say, before he's killed your own wives and mothers.

DAVIES. Down im !

HENRY ROUS. He's finished !

BROWN. We've had enough of 'im !

BLACKSMITH. Too much !

> [*The crowd takes up these cries, excepting only* EVANS, JAGO, *and* GREEN, *who is seen to argue mildly with the* BLACKSMITH.

ROUS. [*Above the hubbub*] We'll make terms with the Union, lads.

> [*Cheers.*

EVANS. [*Fiercely*] Ye blacklegs !

BULGIN. [*Savagely—squaring up to him*] Who are ye callin' black-legs, Rat ?

> [EVANS *throws up his fists, parries the blow, and returns it. They fight. The bargemen are seen holding up the lantern and enjoying the sight.* Old THOMAS *steps forward and holds out his hands.*

THOMAS. Shame on your strife !

> [*The* BLACKSMITH, BROWN, LEWIS, *and the* RED-HAIRED YOUTH *pull* EVANS *and* BULGIN *apart. The stage is almost dark.*

The curtain falls.

ACT III

It is five o'clock. In the UNDERWOOD'S *drawing-room, which is artistically furnished,* ENID *is sitting on the sofa working at a baby's frock.* EDGAR, *by a little spindle-legged table in the centre of the room, is fingering a china-box. His eyes are fixed on the double doors that lead into the dining-room.*

EDGAR. [*Putting down the china-box, and glancing at his watch*] Just on five, they're all in there waiting, except Frank.   Where's he?

ENID. He's had to go down to Gasgoyne's about a contract. Will you want him?

EDGAR. He can't help us. This is a directors' job. [*Motioning towards a single door half hidden by a curtain.*] Father in his room?

ENID. Yes.

EDGAR. I wish he'd stay there, Enid.   [ENID *looks up at him.*] This is a beastly business, old girl?

          [*He takes up the little box again and turns it over and over.*

ENID. I went to the Roberts's this afternoon, Ted.

EDGAR. That wasn't very wise.

ENID. He's simply killing his wife.

EDGAR. We are, you mean.

ENID. [*Suddenly*] Roberts *ought* to give way!

EDGAR. There's a lot to be said on the men's side.

ENID. I don't feel half so sympathetic with them as I did before I went. They just set up class feeling against you.   Poor Annie was looking dreadfully bad—fire going out, and nothing fit for her to eat.   [EDGAR *walks to and fro.*] But she would stand up for Roberts.   When you see all this wretchedness going on and feel you can do nothing, you have to shut your eyes to the whole thing.

EDGAR. If you can.

ENID. When I went I was all on their side, but as soon as I got there I began to feel quite different at once. People talk about sympathy with the working classes, they don't know what it means to try and put it into practice.   It seems hopeless.

EDGAR. Ah! well.

ENID. It's dreadful going on with the men in this state.   I do hope the Dad will make concessions.

EDGAR. He won't. [*Gloomily.*] It's a sort of religion with him. Curse it! I know what's coming! He'll be voted down.

ENID. They wouldn't dare !

EDGAR. They will—they're in a funk.

ENID. [*Indignantly*] He'd never stand it !

EDGAR. [*With a shrug*] My dear girl, if you're beaten in a vote, you've got to stand it.

ENID. Oh ! [*She gets up in alarm.*] But would he resign ?

EDGAR. Of course ! It goes to the roots of his beliefs.

ENID. But he's so *wrapped up in this company*, Ted ! There'd be nothing left for him ! It'd be dreadful !

[EDGAR *shrugs his shoulders.*]

Oh, Ted, he's so old now ! You mustn't let them !

EDGAR. [*Hiding his feelings in an outburst*] My sympathies in this strike are all on the side of the men.

ENID. He's been Chairman for more than thirty years ! He made the whole thing ! And think of the bad times they've had, it's always been he who pulled them through. Oh, Ted, you must——

EDGAR. What is it you want ? You said just now you hoped he'd make concessions. Now you want me to back him in not making them. This isn't a game, Enid !

ENID. [*Hotly*] It isn't a game to *me* that the Dad's in danger of losing all he cares about in life. If he won't give way, and he's beaten, it'll simply break him down !

EDGAR. Didn't you say it was dreadful going on with the men in this state ?

ENID. But can't you see, Ted, Father'll never get over it ! You must stop them somehow. The others are afraid of him. If you back him up——

EDGAR. [*Putting his hand to his head*] Against my convictions—against yours ! The moment it begins to pinch one personally——

ENID. It isn't personal, it's the Dad !

EDGAR. Your family or yourself, and over goes the show !

ENID. [*Resentfully*] If you don't take it seriously, I do.

EDGAR. I am as fond of him as you are; that's nothing to do with it.

ENID. We can't tell about the men ; it's all guess-work. But we know the Dad might have a stroke any day. D'you mean to say that he isn't more to you than——

EDGAR. Of course he is.

ENID. I don't understand you then.

EDGAR. H'm !

ENID. If it were for oneself it would be different, but for our own Father ! You don't seem to realize.

EDGAR. I realize perfectly.

ENID. It's your first duty to save him.

EDGAR. I wonder.

ENID. [*Imploring*] Oh, Ted! It's the only interest he's got left; it'll be like a death-blow to him!

EDGAR. [*Restraining his emotion*] I know.

ENID. Promise!

EDGAR. I'll do what I can.   [*He turns to the double doors.*

[*The curtained door is opened, and* ANTHONY *appears.* EDGAR *opens the double doors, and passes through.*

[SCANTLEBURY'S *voice is faintly heard:* "*Past five; we shall never get through—have to eat another dinner at that hotel!*" *The doors are shut.* ANTHONY *walks forward.*

ANTHONY. You've been seeing Roberts, I hear.

ENID. Yes.

ANTHONY. Do you know what trying to bridge such a gulf as this is like?   [ENID *puts her work on the little table, and faces him.*] Filling a sieve with sand!

ENID. Don't!

ANTHONY. You think with your gloved hands you can cure the trouble of the century.   [*He passes on.*

ENID. Father! [ANTHONY *stops at the double doors.*] I'm only thinking of you!

ANTHONY. [*More softly*] I can take care of myself, my dear.

ENID. Have you thought what'll happen if you're beaten—[*she points*]—in there?

ANTHONY. I don't mean to be.

ENID. Oh! Father, don't give them a chance. You're not well; need you go to the meeting at all?

ANTHONY. [*With a grim smile*] Cut and run?

ENID. But they'll outvote you!

ANTHONY. [*Putting his hand on the doors*] We shall see!

ENID. I beg you, Dad!   [ANTHONY *looks at her softly.*] Won't you?

[ANTHONY *shakes his head. He opens the doors. A buzz of voices comes in.*

SCANTLEBURY. Can one get dinner on that 6.30 train up?

TENCH. No, sir, I believe not, sir.

WILDER. Well, I shall speak out; I've had enough of this.

EDGAR. [*Sharply*] What?

[*It ceases instantly.* ANTHONY *passes through, closing the doors behind him.* ENID *springs to them with a gesture of dismay. She puts her hand on the knob, and begins turning it; then goes to the fireplace, and taps her foot on the fender. Suddenly she rings the bell.* FROST *comes in by the door that leads into the hall.*

FROST. Yes, M'm?

ENID. When the men come, Frost, please show them in here; the hall's cold.

FROST. I could put them in the pantry, M'm.

ENID. No.   I don't want to—to offend them; they're so touchy.

FROST. Yes, M'm.   [*Pause.*] Excuse me, Mr. Anthony's 'ad nothing to eat all day.

ENID. I know, Frost.

FROST. Nothin' but two whiskies and sodas, M'm.

ENID. Oh! you oughtn't to have let him have those.

FROST. [*Gravely*] Mr. Anthony is a little difficult, M'm.   It's not as if he were a younger man, an' knew what was good for 'im; he will have his own way.

ENID. I suppose we all want that.

FROST. Yes, M'm.   [*Quietly.*] Excuse me speakin' about the strike. I'm sure if the other gentlemen were to give up to Mr. Anthony, and quietly let the men 'ave what they want, afterwards, that'd be the best way.   I find that very useful with him at times, M'm.

[ENID *shakes her head.*]

If he's crossed, it makes him violent [*with an air of discovery*], and I've noticed in my own case, when I'm violent I'm always sorry for it afterwards.

ENID. [*With a smile*] Are *you* ever violent, Frost?

FROST. Yes, M'm; oh! sometimes very violent.

ENID. I've never seen you.

FROST. [*Impersonally*] No, M'm; that is so.

[ENID *fidgets towards the door's back.*]

[*With feeling.*] Bein' with Mr. Anthony, as you know, M'm, ever since I was fifteen, it worries me to see him crossed like this at his age.   I've taken the liberty to speak to Mr. Wanklin [*dropping his voice*]—seems to be the most sensible of the gentlemen—but 'e said to me: " That's all very well, Frost, but this strike's a very serious thing," 'e said.   " Serious for all parties, no doubt," I said, " but yumour 'im, sir," I said, " yumour 'im.   It's like this, if a man comes to a stone wall, 'e doesn't drive 'is 'ead against it, 'e gets over it." " Yes," 'e said, " you'd better tell your master that."   [FROST *looks at his nails.*] That's where it is, M'm.   I said to Mr. Anthony this morning : " Is it worth it, sir?"   " Damn it," he said to me, " Frost! Mind your own business, or take a month's notice!"   Beg pardon, M'm, for using such a word.

ENID. [*Moving to the double doors, and listening*] Do you know that man Roberts, Frost?

FROST. Yes, M'm; that's to say, not to speak to.   But to *look* at 'im you can tell what *he's* like.

ENID. [*Stopping*] Yes?

FROST. He's not one of these 'ere ordinary 'armless Socialists. 'E's violent; got a fire inside 'im.   What I call " personal."   A man may 'ave what opinion 'e likes, so long as 'e's not personal ; when 'e's that 'e's *not* safe.

ENID. I think that's what my Father feels about Roberts.

FROST. No doubt, M'm, Mr. Anthony has a feeling against him.

[ENID *glances at him sharply, but finding him in perfect earnest, stands biting her lips, and looking at the double doors.*]

It's a regular right down struggle between the two. I've no patience with this Roberts, from what I 'ear he's just an ordinary workin' man like the rest of 'em. If he did invent a thing he's no worse off than 'undreds of others. My brother invented a new kind o' dumb waiter—nobody gave *him* anything for it, an' there it is, bein' used all over the place. [ENID *moves closer to the double doors.*] There's a kind o' man that never forgives the world, because 'e wasn't born a gentleman. What I say is—no man that's a gentleman looks down on another man because 'e 'appens to be a class or two above 'im, no more than if 'e 'appens to be a class or two below.

ENID. [*With slight impatience*] Yes, I know, Frost, of course. Will you please go in and ask if they'll have some tea ; say I sent you.

FROST. Yes, M'm.

[*He opens the doors gently and goes in. There is a momentary sound of earnest, rather angry talk.*]

WILDER. I don't agree with you.

WANKLIN. We've had this over a dozen times.

EDGAR. [*Impatiently*] Well, what's the proposition ?

SCANTLEBURY. Yes, what does your Father say ? Tea ? Not for me, not for me !

WANKLIN. What I understand the Chairman to say is this——

[FROST *re-enters, closing the door behind him.*

ENID. [*Moving from the door*] Won't they have any tea, Frost ?

[*She goes to the little table, and remains motionless, looking at the baby's frock.* [*A parlourmaid enters from the hall.*

PARLOURMAID. A Miss Thomas, M'm.

ENID. [*Raising her head*] Thomas ? What Miss Thomas—d'you mean a—— ?

PARLOURMAID. Yes, M'm.

ENID. [*Blankly*] Oh ! Where is she ?

PARLOURMAID. In the porch.

ENID. I don't want—— [*She hesitates.*]

FROST. Shall I dispose of her, M'm ?

ENID. I'll come out. No, show her in here, Ellen.

[*The* PARLOURMAID *and* FROST *go out.* ENID *pursing her lips, sits at the little table, taking up the baby's frock. The* PARLOURMAID *ushers in* MADGE THOMAS *and goes out ;* MADGE *stands by the door.*

ENID. Come in. What is it ? What have you come for, please ?

MADGE. Brought a message from Mrs. Roberts.

ENID. A message? Yes.

MADGE. She asks you to look after her Mother.

ENID. I don't understand.

MADGE. [*Sullenly*] That's the message.

ENID. But—what—why?

MADGE. Annie Roberts is dead.   [*There is a silence.*

ENID. [*Horrified*] But it's only a little more than an hour since I saw her.

MADGE. Of cold and hunger.

ENID. [*Rising*] Oh! that's not true! the poor thing's heart—— What makes you look at me like that? I tried to help her.

MADGE. [*With suppressed savagery*] I thought you'd like to know.

ENID. [*Passionately*] It's so unjust! Can't you see that I want to help you all?

MADGE. I never harmed anyone that hadn't harmed me first.

ENID. [*Coldly*] What harm have I done you? Why do you speak to me like that?

MADGE. [*With the bitterest intensity*] You come out of your comfort to spy on us! A week of hunger, that's what *you* want!

ENID. [*Standing her ground*] Don't talk nonsense!

MADGE. I saw her die; her hands were blue with the cold.

ENID. [*With a movement of grief*] Oh! why wouldn't she let me help her? It's such senseless pride!

MADGE. Pride's better than nothing to keep your body warm.

ENID. [*Passionately*] I won't talk to you! How can you tell what I feel? It's not my fault that I was born better off than you.

MADGE. We don't want your money.

ENID. You don't understand, and you don't want to; please to go away!

MADGE. [*Balefully*] You've killed her, for all your soft words, you and your father——

ENID. [*With rage and emotion*] That's wicked! My father is suffering himself through this wretched strike.

MADGE. [*With sombre triumph*] Then tell him Mrs. Roberts is dead! That'll make him better.

ENID. Go away!

MADGE. When a person hurts us we get it back on them.

[*She makes a sudden and swift movement towards* ENID, *fixing her eyes on the child's frock lying across the little table.* ENID *snatches the frock up, as though it were the child itself. They stand a yard apart, crossing glances.*

MADGE. [*Pointing to the frock with a little smile*] Ah! You felt *that!* Lucky it's her mother—not her children—you've to look after, isn't it. *She* won't trouble you long!

ENID. Go away!

MADGE. I've given you the message.

[*She turns and goes out into the hall.* ENID, *motionless till she has gone, sinks down at the table, bending her head over the frock, which she is still clutching to her. The double doors are opened, and* ANTHONY *comes slowly in; he passes his daughter, and lowers himself into an arm-chair. He is very flushed.*

ENID. [*Hiding her emotion—anxiously*] What is it, Dad? ANTHONY *makes a gesture, but does not speak.*] Who was it?

[ANTHONY *does not answer.* ENID *going to the double doors meets* EDGAR *coming in. They speak together in low tones.*]

What is it, Ted?

EDGAR. That fellow Wilder! Taken to personalities! He was downright insulting.

ENID. What did he *say?*

EDGAR. Said, Father was too old and feeble to know what he was doing! The Dad's worth six of him!

ENID. Of course he is. [*They look at* ANTHONY.

[*The doors open wider,* WANKLIN *appears with* SCANTLEBURY.

SCANTLEBURY. [*Sotto voce*] I don't like the look of this!

WANKLIN. [*Going forward*] Come, Chairman! Wilder sends you his apologies. A man can't do more.

[WILDER, *followed by* TENCH, *comes in, and goes to* ANTHONY.

WILDER. [*Glumly*] I withdraw my words, sir. I'm sorry.

[ANTHONY *nods to him.*

ENID. You haven't come to a decision, Mr. Wanklin?

[WANKLIN *shakes his head.*

WANKLIN. We're all here, Chairman; what do you say? Shall we get on with the business, or shall we go back to the other room?

SCANTLEBURY. Yes, yes; let's get on. We must settle something.

[*He turns from a small chair, and settles himself suddenly in the largest chair, with a sigh of comfort.*

[WILDER *and* WANKLIN *also sit; and* TENCH, *drawing up a straight-backed chair close to his Chairman, sits on the edge of it with the minute-book and a stylographic pen.*

ENID. [*Whispering*] I want to speak to you a minute, Ted.

[*They go out through the double doors.*

WANKLIN. Really, Chairman, it's no use soothing ourselves with a sense of false security. If this strike's not brought to an end before the General Meeting, the shareholders will certainly haul us over the coals.

SCANTLEBURY. [*Stirring*] What—what's that?

WANKLIN. I know it for a fact.

ANTHONY. Let them!

WILDER. And get turned out?

WANKLIN. [*To* ANTHONY] I don't mind martyrdom for a policy in which I believe, but I object to being burnt for someone else's principles.

SCANTLEBURY. Very reasonable—you must see that, Chairman.

ANTHONY. We owe it to other employers to stand firm.

WANKLIN. There's a limit to that.

ANTHONY. You were all full of fight at the start.

SCANTLEBURY. [*With a sort of groan*] We thought the men would give in, but they—haven't !

ANTHONY. They will !

WILDER. [*Rising and pacing up and down*] I can't have my reputation as a man of business destroyed for the satisfaction of starving the men out. [*Almost in tears.*] I can't have it ! How can we meet the shareholders with things in the state they are ?

SCANTLEBURY. Hear, hear—hear, hear !

WILDER. [*Lashing himself*] If anyone expects me to say to them I've lost you fifty thousand pounds and sooner than put my pride in my pocket I'll lose you another—— [*Glancing at* ANTHONY.] It's —it's unnatural ! *I don't want to* go against you, sir——

WANKLIN. [*Persuasively*] Come, Chairman, we're *not* free agents. We're part of a machine. Our only business is to see the Company earns as much profit as it safely can. If you blame me for want of principle : I say that we're Trustees. Reason tells us we shall never get back in the saving of wages what we shall lose if we continue this struggle—really, Chairman, we *must* bring it to an end, on the best terms we can make.

ANTHONY. No ! [*There is a pause of general dismay.*

WILDER. It's a deadlock then. [*Letting his hands drop with a sort of despair.*] Now I shall never get off to Spain !

WANKLIN. [*Retaining a trace of irony*] You hear the consequences of your victory, Chairman ?

WILDER. [*With a burst of feeling*] My wife's *ill* !

SCANTLEBURY. Dear, dear ! You don't say so !

WILDER. If I don't get her out of this cold, I won't answer for the consequences.

[*Through the double doors* EDGAR *comes in looking very grave.*

EDGAR. [*To his Father*] Have you heard this, sir ? Mrs. Roberts is dead !

[*Everyone stares at him, as if trying to gauge the importance of this news.*

Enid saw her this afternoon, she had no coals, or food, or anything. It's enough !

[*There is a silence, everyone avoiding the other's eyes, except* ANTHONY, *who stares hard at his son.*

SCANTLEBURY. You don't suggest that we could have helped the poor thing?

WILDER. [*Flustered*] The woman was in bad health. Nobody can say there's any responsibility on us. At least—not on me.

EDGAR. [*Hotly*] I say that we *are* responsible.

ANTHONY. War is war!

EDGAR. Not on women!

WANKLIN. It not infrequently happens that women are the greatest sufferers.

EDGAR. If we knew that, all the more responsibility rests on us.

ANTHONY. This is no matter for amateurs.

EDGAR. Call me what you like, sir. It's sickened me. We had no right to carry things to such a length.

WILDER. I don't like this business a bit—that Radical rag will twist it to their own ends; see if they don't! They'll get up some cock-and-bull story about the poor woman's dying from starvation. I wash my hands of it.

EDGAR. You can't. None of us can.

SCANTLEBURY. [*Striking his fist on the arm of his chair*] But I protest against this——

EDGAR. Protest as you like, Mr. Scantlebury, it won't alter facts.

ANTHONY. That's enough.

EDGAR. [*Facing him angrily*] No, sir. I tell you exactly what I think. If we pretend the men are not suffering, it's humbug; and if they're suffering, we know enough of human nature to know the women are suffering more, and as to the children—well—it's damnable! [SCANTLEBURY *rises from his chair.*] I don't say that we meant to be cruel, I don't say anything of the sort; but I do say it's criminal to shut our eyes to the facts. We employ these men, and we can't get out of it. I don't care so much about the men, but I'd sooner resign my position on the Board than go on starving women in this way.

[*All except* ANTHONY *are now upon their feet,* ANTHONY *sits grasping the arms of his chair and staring at his son.*

SCANTLEBURY. I don't—I don't like the way you're putting it, young sir.

WANKLIN. You're rather overshooting the mark.

WILDER. I should think so indeed!

EDGAR. [*Losing control*] It's no use blinking things! if *you* want to have the death of women on your hands—*I* don't!

SCANTLEBURY. Now, now, young man!

WILDER. On *our* hands? Not on *mine*, I won't have it!

EDGAR. We are five members of this Board; if we were four against it, why did we let it drift till it came to this? You know perfectly well why—because we hoped we should starve the men out. Well, all we've done is to starve one woman out !

SCANTLEBURY. [*Almost hysterically*] I protest, I protest ! I'm a humane man—we're all humane men !

EDGAR. [*Scornfully*] There's nothing wrong with our *humanity*. It's our imaginations, Mr. Scantlebury.

WILDER. Nonsense ! My imagination's as good as yours.

EDGAR. If so, it isn't good enough.

WILDER. I foresaw this !

EDGAR. Then why didn't you put your foot down !

WILDER. Much good that would have done.

[*He looks at* ANTHONY.

EDGAR. If you, and I, and each one of us here who say that our imaginations are so good——

SCANTLEBURY. [*Flurried*] I never said so.

EDGAR. [*Paying no attention*] ——had put our feet down, the thing would have been ended long ago, and this poor woman's life wouldn't have been crushed out of her like this. For all we can tell there may be a dozen other starving women.

SCANTLEBURY. For God's sake, sir, don't use that word at a—at a Board meeting ; it's—it's monstrous.

EDGAR. I *will* use it, Mr. Scantlebury.

SCANTLEBURY. Then I shall not listen to you. I shall not listen ! It's painful to me.   [*He covers his ears.*

WANKLIN. None of us are opposed to a settlement, except your Father.

EDGAR. I'm certain that if the shareholders knew——

WANKLIN. I don't think you'll find their imaginations are any better than ours. Because a woman happens to have a weak heart——

EDGAR. A struggle like this finds out the weak spots in everybody. Any child knows that. If it hadn't been for this cut-throat policy, she needn't have died like this ; and there wouldn't be all this misery that anyone who isn't a fool can see is going on.

[*Throughout the foregoing* ANTHONY *has eyed his son ; he now moves as though to rise, but stops as* EDGAR *speaks again.*]
I don't defend the men, or myself, or anybody.

WANKLIN. You may have to ! A coroner's jury of disinterested sympathizers may say some very nasty things. We mustn't lose sight of our position.

SCANTLEBURY. [*Without uncovering his ears*] Coroner's jury ! No, no, it's not a case for that ?

EDGAR. I've had enough of cowardice.

WANKLIN. Cowardice is an unpleasant word, Mr. Edgar Anthony. It will look very like cowardice if we suddenly concede the men's demands when a thing like this happens ; we must be careful !

WILDER. Of course we must. We've no knowledge of this matter, except a rumour. The proper course is to put the whole thing into the hands of Harness to settle for us ; that's natural, that's what we *should* have come to any way.

SCANTLEBURY. [*With dignity*] Exactly ! [*Turning to* EDGAR.] And as to you, young sir, I can't sufficiently express my—my distaste for the way you've treated the whole matter. You ought to withdraw ! Talking of starvation, talking of cowardice ! Considering what our views are ! Except your own Father—we're all agreed the only policy is—is one of goodwill—it's most irregular, it's most improper, and all I can say is it's—it's given me pain——

[*He places his hand on the centre of his scheme.*

EDGAR. [*Stubbornly*] I withdraw nothing.

[*He is about to say more when* SCANTLEBURY *once more covers up his ears.* TENCH *suddenly makes a demonstration with the minute-book. A sense of having been engaged in the unusual comes over all of them, and one by one they resume their seats.* EDGAR *alone remains on his feet.*

WILDER. [*With an air of trying to wipe something out*] I pay no attention to what young Mr. Anthony has said. Coroner's Jury ! The idea's preposterous. I—I move this amendment to the Chairman's Motion : That the dispute be placed at once in the hands of Mr. Simon Harness for settlement, on the lines indicated by him this morning. Anyone second that ? [TENCH *writes in the book.*

WANKLIN. I do.

WILDER. Very well, then ; I ask the Chairman to put it to the Board.

ANTHONY. [*With a great sigh—slowly*] We have been made the subject of an attack. [*Looking round at* WILDER *and* SCANTLEBURY *with ironical contempt.*] I take it on *my* shoulders. I am seventy-six years old. I have been Chairman of this Company since its inception two-and-thirty years ago. I have seen it pass through good and evil report. My connection with it began in the year that this young man was born.

[EDGAR *bows his head.* ANTHONY, *gripping his chair, goes on.*] I have had to do with " men " for fifty years ; I've always stood up to them ; I have never been beaten yet. I have fought the men of this Company four times, and four times I have beaten them. It has been said that I am not the man I was. [*He looks at* WILDER.] However that may be, I am man enough to stand to my guns.

[*His voice grows stronger. The double doors are opened.* ENID *slips in, followed by* UNDERWOOD, *who restrains her.*] The men have been treated justly, they have had fair wages, we have always been ready to listen to complaints. It has been said that times have changed ; if they have, I have not changed with them.

Neither will I. It has been said that masters and men are equal! Cant! There can only be one master in a house! Where two men meet the better man will rule. It has been said that Capital and Labour have the same interests. Cant! Their interests are as wide asunder as the poles. It has been said that the Board is only part of a machine. Cant! We *are* the machine; its brains and sinews; it is for us to lead and to determine what is to be done, and to do it without fear or favour. Fear of the men! Fear of the shareholders! Fear of our own shadows! Before I am like that, I hope to die.

[*He pauses, and meeting his son's eyes, goes on.*] There is only one way of treating " men "—with *the iron hand.* This half-and-half business, the half-and-half manners of this generation has brought all this upon us. Sentiment and softness, and what this young man, no doubt, would call his social policy. You can't eat cake and have it! This middle-class sentiment, or socialism, or whatever it may be, is rotten. Masters are masters, men are men! Yield one demand, and they will make it six. They are [*he smiles grimly*] like Oliver Twist, asking for more. If I were in *their* place I should be the same. But I am not in their place. Mark my words: one fine morning, when you have given way here, and given way there—you will find you have parted with the ground beneath your feet, and are deep in the bog of bankruptcy; and with you, floundering in that bog, will be the very men you have given way to. I have been accused of being a domineering tyrant, thinking only of my pride— I am thinking of the future of this country, threatened with the black waters of confusion, threatened with mob government, threatened with what I cannot see. If by any conduct of mine I help to bring this on us, I shall be ashamed to look my fellows in the face.

[ANTHONY *stares before him, at what he cannot see, and there is perfect stillness.* FROST *comes in from the hall, and all but* ANTHONY *look round at him uneasily.*]

FROST. [*To his master*] The men are here, sir.

[ANTHONY *makes a gesture of dismissal.*]

Shall I bring them in, sir?

ANTHONY. Wait!

[FROST *goes out,* ANTHONY *turns to face his son.*]

I come to the attack that has been made upon me.

[EDGAR, *with a gesture of deprecation, remains motionless with his head a little bowed.*]

A woman has died. I am told that her blood is on my hands; I am told that on my hands is the starvation and the suffering of other women and of children.

EDGAR. I said " on *our* hands," sir.

ANTHONY. It is the same. [*His voice grows stronger and stronger, his feeling is more and more made manifest.*] I am not aware that if my adversary suffer in a fair fight not sought by me, it is *my* fault. If I fall under *his* feet—as fall I may—I shall not complain. That will be *my* look-out—and this is—his. I cannot separate, as I would, these men from their women and children. A fair fight is a fair fight ! Let them learn to think before they pick a quarrel !

EDGAR. [*In a low voice*] But is it a fair fight, Father ? Look at them, and look at us ! They've only this one weapon !

ANTHONY. [*Grimly*] And you're weak-kneed enough to teach them how to use it ! It seems the fashion nowadays for men to take their enemy's side. I have not learnt that art. Is it my fault that they quarrelled with their Union too ?

EDGAR. There is such a thing as Mercy.

ANTHONY. And Justice comes before it.

EDGAR. What seems just to one man, sir, is injustice to another.

ANTHONY. [*With suppressed passion*] You accuse me of injustice —of what amounts to inhumanity—of cruelty——

[EDGAR *makes a gesture of horror—a general frightened movement.*

WANKLIN. Come, come, Chairman !

ANTHONY. [*In a grim voice*] These are the words of my own son. They are the words of a generation that I don't understand ; the words of a soft breed.

[*A general murmur. With a violent effort* ANTHONY *recovers his control.*

EDGAR. [*Quietly*] I said it of *myself*, too, Father.

[*A long look is exchanged between them, and* ANTHONY *puts out his hand with a gesture as if to sweep the personalities away ; then places it against his brow, swaying as though from giddiness. There is a movement towards him. He waves them back.*

ANTHONY. Before I put this amendment to the Board, I have one more word to say. [*He looks from face to face.*] If it is carried, it means that we shall fail in what we set ourselves to do. It means that we shall fail in the duty that we owe to all Capital. It means that we we shall fail in the duty that we owe ourselves. It means that we shall be open to constant attack to which we as constantly shall have to yield. Be under no misapprehension—run this time, and you will never make a stand again ! You will have to fly like curs before the whips of your own men. If that is the lot you wish for, you will vote for this amendment.

[*He looks again from face to face, finally resting his gaze on* EDGAR ; *all sit with their eyes on the ground.* ANTHONY *makes a gesture, and* TENCH *hands him the book. He reads.*]

" Moved by Mr. Wilder, and seconded by Mr. Wanklin : ' That the men's demands be placed at once in the hands of Mr. Simon Harness for settlement on the lines indicated by him this morning.' " [*With sudden vigour.*] Those in favour : Signify the same in the usual way !

> [*For a minute no one moves ; then hastily, just as* ANTHONY *is about to speak,* WILDER'S *hand and* WANKLIN'S *are held up, then* SCANTLEBURY'S, *and last* EDGAR'S, *who does not lift his head.*]

Contrary ?   [ANTHONY *lifts his own hand.*]
[*In a clear voice.*] The amendment is carried.   I resign my position on this Board.

> [ENID *gasps, and there is dead silence.* ANTHONY *sits motionless, his head slowly drooping ; suddenly he heaves as though the whole of his life had risen up within him.*]

Fifty years !   You have disgraced me, gentlemen.   Bring in the men !

> [*He sits motionless, staring before him. The Board draws hurriedly together, and forms a group.* TENCH *in a frightened manner speaks into the hall.* UNDERWOOD *almost forces* ENID *from the room.*]

WILDER. [*Hurriedly*] What's to be said to them ? Why isn't Harness here ? Ought we to see the men before he comes ? I don't——

TENCH. Will you come in, please ?

> [*Enter* THOMAS, GREEN, BULGIN *and* ROUS, *who file up in a row past the little table.* TENCH *sits down and writes. All eyes are fixed on* ANTHONY, *who makes no sign.*]

WANKLIN. [*Stepping up to the little table, with nervous cordiality*] Well, Thomas, how's it to be ?   What's the result of your meeting ?

ROUS. Sim Harness has our answer.   He'll tell you what it is. We're waiting for him.   He'll speak for us.

WANKLIN. Is that so, Thomas ?

THOMAS. [*Sullenly*] Yes.   Roberts will not be coming, his wife is dead.

SCANTLEBURY. Yes, yes !   Poor woman !   Yes ! Yes !

FROST. [*Entering from the hall*] Mr. Harness, sir !

> [*As* HARNESS *enters he retires.*

> [HARNESS *has a piece of paper in his hand, he bows to the Directors, nods towards the men, and takes his stand behind the little table in the very centre of the room.*

HARNESS. Good evening, gentlemen.

> [TENCH, *with the paper he has been writing, joins him, they speak together in low tones.*

WILDER. We've been waiting for you, Harness.   Hope we shall come to some——

FROST. [*Entering from the hall*] Roberts.   [*He goes.*

> [ROBERTS *comes hastily in, and stands staring at* ANTHONY. *His face is drawn and old.*

6

ROBERTS. Mr. Anthony, I am afraid I am a little late. I would have been here in time but for something that—has happened. [*To the men.*] Has anything been said?

THOMAS. No! But, man, what made ye come?

ROBERTS. Ye told us this morning, gentlemen, to go away and reconsider our position. We have reconsidered it; we are here to bring you the men's answer. [*To* ANTHONY.] Go ye back to London. We have nothing for you. By no jot or tittle do we abate our demands, nor will we until the whole of those demands are yielded.

[ANTHONY *looks at him but does not speak. There is a movement amongst the men as though they were bewildered.*

HARNESS. Roberts!

ROBERTS. [*Glancing fiercely at him, and back to* ANTHONY] Is that clear enough for ye? Is it short enough and to the point? Ye made a mistake to think that we would come to heel. Ye may break the body, but ye cannot break the spirit. Get back to London, the men have nothing for ye?

[*Pausing uneasily he takes a step towards the unmoving* ANTHONY.

EDGAR. We're all sorry for you, Roberts, but——

ROBERTS. Keep your sorrow, young man. Let your Father speak!

HARNESS. [*With the sheet of paper in his hand, speaking from behind the little table*] Roberts!

ROBERTS. [*To* ANTHONY, *with passionate intensity*] Why don't ye answer?

HARNESS. Roberts!

ROBERTS. [*Turning sharply*] What is it?

HARNESS. [*Gravely*] You're talking without the book; things have travelled past you.

[*He makes a sign to* TENCH, *who beckons the Directors. They quickly sign his copy of the terms.*]

Look at this, man!   [*Holding up his sheet of paper.*]

'Demands conceded, *with the exception of those relating to the engineers and furnace men.* Double wages for Saturday's overtime. Night-shifts as they are.' These terms have been agreed. The men go back to work again to-morrow. The strike is at an end.

ROBERTS. [*Reading the paper, and turning on the men. They shrink back from him, all but* ROUS, *who stands his ground. With deadly stillness*] Ye have gone back on me? I stood by ye to the death; ye waited for *that* to throw me over!   [*The men answer, all speaking together.*

ROUS. It's a lie!

THOMAS. Ye were past endurance, man.

GREEN. If ye'd listen to me——

BULGIN. [*Under his breath*] Hold your jaw!

ROBERTS. Ye waited for *that*!

HARNESS. [*Taking the Directors' copy of the terms, and handing his own to* TENCH] That's enough, men.   You had better go.

[*The men shuffle slowly, awkwardly away.*

WILDER. [*In a low, nervous voice*] There's nothing to stay for now, I suppose. [*He follows to the door.*] I shall have a try for that train! Coming, Scantlebury?

SCANTLEBURY. [*Following with* WANKLIN] Yes, yes ; wait for me.

[*He stops as* ROBERTS *speaks.*

ROBERTS. [*To* ANTHONY] But *ye* have not signed them terms! They can't make terms without their Chairman!   Ye would never sign them terms !   [ANTHONY *looks at him without speaking.*] Don't tell me ye have ! for the love o' God ! [*With passionate appeal.*]   I reckoned on ye !

HARNESS. [*Holding out the Directors' copy of the terms*] The Board has signed !

[ROBERTS *looks dully at the signatures—dashes the paper from him, and covers up his eyes.*

SCANTLEBURY. [*Behind his hand to* TENCH] Look after the Chairman !   He's not well ; he's not well—he had no lunch.   If there's any fund started for the women and children, put me down for—for twenty pounds.

[*He goes out into the hall, in cumbrous haste ; and* WANKLIN, *who has been staring at* ROBERTS *and* ANTHONY *with twitchings of his face, follows.*   EDGAR *remains seated on the sofa, looking at the ground ;* TENCH, *returning to the bureau, writes in his minute-book.*   HARNESS *stands by the little table, gravely watching* ROBERTS.

ROBERTS. Then you're no longer Chairman of this Company ! [*Breaking into half-mad laughter.*] Ah ! ha—ah, ha, ha ! They've thrown ye over—thrown over their Chairman : Ah—ha—ha ! [*With a sudden dreadful calm.*] So—they've done us both down, Mr. Anthony ?

[ENID, *hurrying through the double doors, comes quickly to her father and bends over him.*

HARNESS. [*Coming down and laying his hands on* ROBERTS' *sleeve*] For shame, Roberts !   Go home quietly, man ; go home !

ROBERTS. [*Tearing his arm away*] Home ? [*Shrinking together— in a whisper.*] Home !

ENID. [*Quietly to her father*] Come away, dear !   Come to your room !

[ANTHONY *rises with an effort.   He turns to* ROBERTS, *who looks at him.   They stand several seconds, gazing at each other fixedly ;* ANTHONY *lifts his hand, as though to salute, but lets it fall.   The expression of* ROBERTS' *face changes from hostility to wonder.   They bend their heads in token of respect.* ANTHONY

*turns, and slowly walks towards the curtained door. Suddenly
he sways as though about to fall, recovers himself and is assisted
out by* ENID *and* EDGAR, *who has hurried across the room.*
ROBERTS *remains motionless for several seconds, staring
intently after* ANTHONY, *then goes out into the hall.*

TENCH. [*Approaching* HARNESS] It's a great weight off my mind,
Mr. Harness! But what a painful scene, sir!   [*He wipes his brow.*

[HARNESS, *pale and resolute, regards with a grim half-smile the
quavering* TENCH.]

It's all been so violent! What did he mean by: "Done us both
down?" If he has lost his wife, poor fellow, he oughtn't to have
spoken to the Chairman like that!

HARNESS. A woman dead; and the two best men both broken!
                                        [UNDERWOOD *enters suddenly.*

TENCH. [*Staring at* HARNESS—*suddenly excited*] D'you know, sir
—these terms, they're the *very same* we drew up together, you and I,
and put to both sides before the fight began? All this—all this—
and—and what for?

HARNESS. [*In a slow grim voice*] That's where the fun comes in!

[UNDERWOOD *without turning from the door makes a gesture of
assent.*

The curtain falls.

THE ELDEST SON

PERSONS OF THE PLAY

SIR WILLIAM CHESHIRE, *a baronet*
LADY CHESHIRE, *his wife*
BILL, *their eldest son*
HAROLD, *their second son*
RONALD KEITH (*in the Lancers*), *their son-in-law*
CHRISTINE (*his wife*), *their eldest daughter*
DOT, *their second daughter*
JOAN, *their third daughter*
MABEL LANFARNE, *their guest*
THE REVEREND JOHN LATTER, *engaged to Joan*
OLD STUDDENHAM, *the head-keeper*
FREDA STUDDENHAM, *the lady's-maid*
YOUNG DUNNING, *the under-keeper*
ROSE TAYLOR, *a village girl*
JACKSON, *the butler*
CHARLES, *a footman*

TIME : The present. The action passes on December 7 *and* 8 *at the Cheshires' country house, in one of the shires.*

ACT I., SCENE I. The hall ; before dinner
    SCENE II. The hall ; after dinner.

ACT II. Lady Cheshire's morning-room ; after breakfast.

ACT III. The smoking-room ; tea-time.

A night elapses between Acts I. and II.

ACT I

SCENE I

The scene is a well-lighted, and large, oak-panelled hall, with an air of being lived in, and a broad, oak staircase. The dining-room, drawing-room, billiard-room, all open into it; and under the staircase a door leads to the servants' quarters. In a huge fireplace a log fire is burning. There are tiger-skins on the floor, horns on the walls; and a writing-table against the wall opposite the fireplace. FREDA STUDDENHAM, *a pretty, pale girl with dark eyes, in the black dress of a lady's-maid, is standing at the foot of the staircase with a bunch of white roses in one hand, and a bunch of yellow roses in the other. A door closes above, and* SIR WILLIAM CHESHIRE, *in evening dress, comes downstairs. He is perhaps fifty-eight, of strong build, rather bull-necked, with grey eyes, and a well-coloured face, whose choleric autocracy is veiled by a thin urbanity. He speaks before he reaches the bottom.*

SIR WILLIAM. Well, Freda! Nice roses. Who are they for?

FREDA. My lady told me to give the yellow to Mrs. Keith, Sir William, and the white to Miss Lanfarne, for their first evening.

SIR WILLIAM. Capital. [*Passing on towards the drawing-room.*] Your father coming up to-night?

FREDA. Yes.

SIR WILLIAM. Be good enough to tell him I specially want to see him here after dinner, will you?

FREDA. Yes, Sir William.

SIR WILLIAM. By the way, just ask him to bring the game-book in, if he's got it.

> [*He goes out into the drawing-room; and* FREDA *stands restlessly tapping her foot against the bottom stair. With a flutter of skirts* CHRISTINE KEITH *comes rapidly down. She is a nice-looking, fresh-coloured young woman in a low-necked dress.*

CHRISTINE. Hullo, Freda! How are *you*?

FREDA. Quite well, thank you, Miss Christine—Mrs. Keith, I mean. My lady told me to give you these.

CHRISTINE. [*Taking the roses*] Oh! Thanks! How sweet of mother!

FREDA. [*In a quick toneless voice*] The others are for Miss Lanfarne. My lady thought white would suit her better.

CHRISTINE. They suit *you* in that black dress.

[FREDA *lowers the roses quickly.*]

What do you think of Joan's engagement?

FREDA. It's very nice for her.

CHRISTINE. I say, Freda, have they been going hard at rehearsals?

FREDA. Every day. Miss Dot gets very cross, stage-managing.

CHRISTINE. I do hate learning a part. Thanks awfully for unpacking. Any news?

FREDA. [*In the same quick, dull voice*] The under-keeper, Dunning, won't marry Rose Taylor, after all.

CHRISTINE. What a shame! But I say that's serious. I thought there was—she was—I mean——

FREDA. He's taken up with another girl, they say.

CHRISTINE. Too bad! [*Pinning the roses.*] D'you know if Mr. Bill's come?

FREDA. [*With a swift upward look*] Yes, by the six-forty.

[RONALD KEITH *comes slowly down, a weathered firm-lipped man, in evening dress, with eyelids half drawn over his keen eyes, and the air of a horseman.*

KEITH. Hallo! Roses in December. I say, Freda, your father missed a wigging this morning when they drew blank at Warnham's spinney. Where's that litter of little foxes?

FREDA. [*Smiling faintly*] I expect father knows, Captain Keith.

KEITH. You bet he does. Emigration? Or thin air? What?

CHRISTINE. Studdenham'd never shoot a fox, Ronny. He's been here since the flood.

KEITH. There's more ways of killing a cat—eh, Freda?

CHRISTINE. [*Moving with her husband towards the drawing-room*] Young Dunning won't marry that girl, Ronny.

KEITH. Phew! Wouldn't be in his shoes, then! Sir William'll never keep a servant who's made a scandal in the village. Bill come?

[*As they disappear from the hall,* JOHN LATTER, *in a clergyman's evening dress, comes sedately downstairs, a tall, rather pale young man, with something in him, as it were, both of heaven and a drawing-room. He passes* FREDA *with a formal little nod.*

HAROLD, *a fresh-cheeked, cheery-looking youth, comes down, three steps at a time.*

HAROLD. Hallo, Freda! Patience on the monument. Let's have a sniff! For Miss Lanfarne? Bill come down yet?

FREDA. No, Mr. Harold.

[HAROLD *crosses the hall, whistling, and follows* LATTER *into the drawing-room. There is the sound of a scuffle above, and a voice crying: " Shut up, Dot!" And* JOAN *comes down screwing her head back. She is pretty and small, with large clinging eyes.*

JOAN. Am I all right behind, Freda? That beast, Dot!

FREDA. Quite, Miss Joan.

[DOT'S *face, like a full moon, appears over the upper banisters.*
She too comes running down, a frank figure, with the face of a
rebel.

DOT. You little *being!*

JOAN. [*Flying towards the drawing-room, is overtaken at the door*] Oh!
Dot! You're pinching!

[*As they disappear into the drawing-room,* MABEL LANFARNE, *a*
tall girl with a rather charming Irish face, comes slowly down.
And at sight of her FREDA'S *whole figure becomes set and*
meaning-full.

FREDA. For you, Miss Lanfarne, from my lady.

MABEL. [*In whose speech is a touch of wilful Irishry*] How sweet!
[*Fastening the roses.*] And how are *you*, Freda?

FREDA. Very well, thank you.

MABEL. And your father? Hope he's going to let me come out
with the guns again.

FREDA. [*Stolidly*] He'll be delighted, I'm sure.

MABEL. Ye-es! I haven't forgotten his face—last time.

FREDA. You stood with Mr. Bill. He's better to stand with than
Mr. Harold, or Captain Keith?

MABEL. He didn't touch a feather, that day.

FREDA. People don't when they're anxious to do their best.

[*A gong sounds. And* MABEL LANFARNE, *giving* FREDA *a rather*
inquisitive stare, moves on to the drawing-room. Left alone
without the roses, FREDA *still lingers. At the slamming of*
a door above, and hasty footsteps, she shrinks back against the
stairs. BILL *runs down, and comes on her suddenly. He is*
a tall, good-looking edition of his father, with the same stubborn
look of veiled choler.

BILL. Freda! [*And as she shrinks still further back.*] What's the
matter? [*Then at some sound he looks round uneasily and draws away from*
her.] Aren't you glad to see me?

FREDA. I've something to say to you, Mr. Bill. After dinner.

BILL. Mister——?

[*She passes him, and rushes away upstairs. And* BILL, *who stands*
frowning and looking after her, recovers himself sharply as the
drawing-room door is opened, and SIR WILLIAM *and* MISS
LANFARNE *come forth, followed by* KEITH, DOT, HAROLD,
CHRISTINE, LATTER, *and* JOAN, *all leaning across each other,*
and talking. By herself, behind them, comes LADY CHESHIRE,
a refined-looking woman of fifty, with silvery dark hair, and
an expression at once gentle and ironic. They move across the
hall towards the dining-room.

6*

SIR WILLIAM. Ah! Bill.

MABEL. How do you do?

KEITH. How are you, old chap?

DOT. [*Gloomily*] Do you know your part?

HAROLD. Hallo, old man!

[CHRISTINE *gives her brother a flying kiss.* JOAN *and* LATTER *pause and look at him shyly without speech.*

BILL. [*Putting his hand on* JOAN'S *shoulder*] Good luck, you two! Well, mother?

LADY CHESHIRE. Well, my dear boy! Nice to see you at last. What a long time!

[*She draws his arm through hers, and they move towards the dining-room.*

The curtain falls.

The curtain rises again at once.

SCENE II

CHRISTINE, LADY CHESHIRE, DOT, MABEL LANFARNE, *and* JOAN *are returning to the hall after dinner.*

CHRISTINE. [*In a low voice*] Mother, is it true about young Dunning and Rose Taylor?

LADY CHESHIRE. I'm afraid so, dear.

CHRISTINE. But can't they be——

DOT. Ah! ah-h! [CHRISTINE *and her mother are silent.*] My child, I'm not the young person.

CHRISTINE. No, of course not—only—[*nodding towards* JOAN *and* MABEL].

DOT. Look here! This is just an instance of what I hate.

LADY CHESHIRE. My dear? Another one?

DOT. Yes, mother, and don't you pretend you don't understand, because you know you do.

CHRISTINE. Instance? Of what?

[JOAN *and* MABEL *have ceased talking, and listen, still at the fire.*

DOT. Humbug, of course. Why should you want them to marry, if he's tired of her?

CHRISTINE. [*Ironically*] Well! If your imagination doesn't carry you as far as that!

DOT. When people marry, do you believe they ought to be in love with each other?

CHRISTINE. [*With a shrug*] That's not the point.

DOT. Oh? Were you in love with Ronny?

CHRISTINE. Don't be idiotic!

DOT. Would you have married him if you hadn't been?

CHRISTINE. Of course not!

JOAN. Dot! You are!——

DOT. Hallo! my little snipe!

LADY CHESHIRE. Dot, dear!

DOT. Don't shut me up, mother! [*To* JOAN.] Are you in love with John? [JOAN *turns hurriedly to the fire.*] Would you be going to marry him if you were not?

CHRISTINE. You are a brute, Dot.

DOT. Is Mabel in love with—whoever she is in love with?

MABEL. And I wonder who that is.

DOT. Well, would you marry him if you weren't?

MABEL. No, I would *not*.

DOT. Now, mother; did you love father?

CHRISTINE. Dot, you really are awful.

DOT. [*Rueful and detached*] Well, it is a bit too thick, perhaps.

JOAN. Dot!

DOT. Well, mother, did you—I mean quite calmly?

LADY CHESHIRE. Yes, dear, quite calmly.

DOT. Would you have married him if you hadn't? [LADY CHESHIRE *shakes her head.*] Then we're all agreed!

MABEL. Except yourself.

DOT. [*Grimly*] Even if I loved him, he might think himself lucky if I married him.

MABEL. Indeed, and I'm not so sure.

DOT. [*Making a face at her*] What I was going to——

LADY CHESHIRE. But don't you think, dear, you'd better not?

DOT. Well, I won't say what I was going to say, but what I do say is—Why the devil——

LADY CHESHIRE. Quite so, Dot!

DOT. [*A little disconcerted*] If they're tired of each other, they ought not to marry, and if father's going to make them——

CHRISTINE. You don't understand in the least. It's for the sake of the——

DOT. Out with it, Old Sweetness! The approaching infant! God bless it!

[*There is a sudden silence, for* KEITH *and* LATTER *are seen coming from the dining-room.*

LATTER. That must be so, Ronny.

KEITH. No, John; not a bit of it!

LATTER. You don't *think*!

KEITH. Good Gad, who wants to think after dinner!

DOT. Come on! Let's play Pool. [*She turns at the billiard-room door.*] Look here! Rehearsal to-morrow is directly after breakfast; from " Eccles enters breathless " to the end.

MABEL. Whatever made you choose *Caste*, Dot? You know it's awfully difficult.

DOT. Because it's the only play that's not too advanced.

[*The girls all go into the billiard-room.*

LADY CHESHIRE. Where's Bill, Ronny?

KEITH. [*With a grimace*] I rather think Sir William and he are in Committee of Supply—Mem-Sahib.

LADY CHESHIRE. Oh!

[*She looks uneasily at the dining-room ; then follows the girls out.*

LATTER. [*In the tone of one resuming an argument*] There can't be two opinions about it, Ronny. Young Dunning's refusal is simply indefensible.

KEITH. I don't agree a bit, John.

LATTER. Of course, if you won't listen.

KEITH. [*Clipping a cigar*] Draw it mild, my dear chap. We've had the whole thing over twice at least.

LATTER. My point is this——

KEITH. [*Regarding* LATTER *quizzically with his half-closed eyes*] I know —I know—but the point is, how far your point is simply professional.

LATTER. If a man wrongs a woman, he ought to right her again. There's no answer to that.

KEITH. It all depends.

LATTER. That's rank opportunism.

KEITH. Rats! Look here—Oh! hang it, John, one can't argue this out with a parson.

LATTER. [*Frigidly*] Why not?

HAROLD. [*Who has entered from the dining-room*] Pull devil, pull baker!

KEITH. Shut up, Harold!

LATTER. " To play the game " is the religion even of the Army.

KEITH. Exactly, but what *is* the game?

LATTER. What else can it be in this case?

KEITH. You're too puritanical, young John. You can't help it —line of country laid down for you. All drag-huntin'! What!

LATTER. [*With concentration*] Look here!

HAROLD. [*Imitating the action of a man pulling at a horse's head*] " Come hup, I say, you hugly beast! "

KEITH. [*To* LATTER] You're not going to draw me, old chap. You don't see where you'd land us all. [*He smokes calmly.*]

LATTER. How do you imagine vice takes its rise? From precisely this sort of thing of young Dunning's.

KEITH. From human nature, I should have thought, John. I admit that I don't like a fellow's leavin' a girl in the lurch ; but I don't see the use in drawin' hard and fast rules. You only have to break 'em. Sir William and you would just tie Dunning and the girl up together, willy-nilly, to save appearances, and ten to one but there'll be the deuce to pay in a year's time. You can take a horse to the water, you can't make him drink.

LATTER. I entirely and absolutely disagree with you.

HAROLD. Good old John!

LATTER. At all events we know where your principles take you.

KEITH. [*Rather dangerously*] Where, please? [HAROLD *turns up his eyes, and points downwards.*] Dry up, Harold!

LATTER. Did you ever hear the story of Faust?

KEITH. Now look here, John; with all due respect to your cloth, and all the politeness in the world, you may go to—blazes.

LATTER. Well, I must say, Ronny—of all the rude boors——

[*He turns towards the billiard-room.*

KEITH. Sorry I smashed the glass, old chap.

[LATTER *passes out. There comes a mingled sound through the opened door, of female voices, laughter, and the click of billiard balls, clipped off by the sudden closing of the door.*

KEITH. [*Impersonally*] Deuced odd, the way a parson puts one's back up! Because you know I agree with him really; young Dunning *ought* to play the game; and I hope Sir William'll make him.

[*The butler* JACKSON *has entered from the door under the stairs followed by the keeper* STUDDENHAM, *a man between fifty and sixty, in a full-skirted coat with big pockets, cord breeches and gaiters; he has a steady self-respecting weathered face, with blue eyes and a short grey beard, which has obviously once been red.*

KEITH. Hullo! Studdenham!

STUDDENHAM. [*Touching his forehead*] Evenin', Captain Keith.

JACKSON. Sir William still in the dining-room with Mr. Bill, sir?

HAROLD. [*With a grimace*] He is, Jackson.

[JACKSON *goes out to the dining-room.*

KEITH. You've shot no pheasants yet, Studdenham?

STUDDENHAM. No, sir. Only birds. We'll be doin' the spinneys and the home covert while you're down.

KEITH. I say, talkin' of spinneys——

[*He breaks off sharply, and goes out with* HAROLD *into the billiard-room.* SIR WILLIAM *enters from the dining-room, applying a gold toothpick to his front teeth.*

SIR WILLIAM. Ah! Studdenham. Bad business this about young Dunning!

STUDDENHAM. Yes, Sir William.

SIR WILLIAM. He definitely refuses to marry her?

STUDDENHAM. He does that.

SIR WILLIAM. That won't do, you know. What reason does he give?

STUDDENHAM. Won't say other than that he don't want no more to do with her.

SIR WILLIAM. God bless me! That's not a reason. I can't have a keeper of mine playing fast and loose in the village like this. [*Turning to* LADY CHESHIRE, *who has come in from the billiard-room.*] That affair of young Dunning's, my dear.

LADY CHESHIRE. Oh! Yes! I'm *so* sorry, Studdenham. The poor girl!

STUDDENHAM. [*Respectfully*] Fancy he's got a feeling she's not his equal, now, my lady.

LADY CHESHIRE. [*To herself*] Yes, I suppose he *has* made her his superior.

SIR WILLIAM. What? Eh! Quite! Quite! I was just telling Studdenham the fellow must set the matter straight. We can't have open scandals in the village. If he wants to keep his place he must marry her at once.

LADY CHESHIRE. [*To her husband in a low voice*] Is it right to force them? Do you know what the girl wishes, Studdenham?

STUDDENHAM. Shows a spirit, my lady—says she'll have him—willin' or not.

LADY CHESHIRE. A spirit? I see. If they marry like that they're sure to be miserable.

SIR WILLIAM. What! Doesn't follow at all. Besides, my dear, you ought to know by this time, there's an unwritten law in these matters. They're perfectly well aware that when there are consequences, they have to take them.

STUDDENHAM. Some o' these young people, my lady, they don't put two and two together no more than an old cock pheasant.

SIR WILLIAM. I'll give him till to-morrow. If he remains obstinate, he'll have to go; he'll get no character, Studdenham. Let him know what I've said. I like the fellow, he's a good keeper. I don't want to lose him. But this sort of thing I won't have. He must toe the mark or take himself off. Is he up here to-night?

STUDDENHAM. Hangin' patridges, Sir William. Will you have him in?

SIR WILLIAM. [*Hesitating*] Yes—yes. I'll see him.

STUDDENHAM. Good-night to you, my lady.

LADY CHESHIRE. Freda's not looking well, Studdenham.

STUDDENHAM. She's a bit pernickitty with her food, that's where it is.

LADY CHESHIRE. I must try and make her eat.

SIR WILLIAM. Oh! Studdenham. We'll shoot the home covert first. What did we get last year?

STUDDENHAM. [*Producing the game-book; but without reference to it*]

Two hundred and fifty-three pheasants, eleven hares, fifty-two rabbits, three woodcock, sundry.

SIR WILLIAM. Sundry?   Didn't include a fox, did it? [*Gravely.*] I was seriously upset this morning at Warnham's spinney——

STUDDENHAM. [*Very gravely*] Yu don't say, Sir William; that four-year-old he du look a handful!

SIR WILLIAM. [*With a sharp look*] You know well enough what I mean.

STUDDENHAM. [*Unmoved*] Shall I send young Dunning, Sir William?

    [SIR WILLIAM *gives a short, sharp nod, and* STUDDENHAM *retires by the door under the stairs.*

SIR WILLIAM. Old fox!

LADY CHESHIRE. Don't be too hard on Dunning. He's very young.

SIR WILLIAM. [*Patting her arm*] My dear, you don't understand young fellows, how should you?

LADY CHESHIRE. [*With her faint irony*] A husband and two sons not counting.   [*Then as the door under the stairs is opened.*] Bill, now do——

SIR WILLIAM. I'll be gentle with him. [*Sharply.*] Come in!

    [LADY CHESHIRE *retires to the billiard-room. She gives a look back and a half smile at young* DUNNING, *a fair young man dressed in brown cords and leggings, and holding his cap in his hand; then goes out.*

SIR WILLIAM. Evenin', Dunning.

DUNNING. [*Twisting his cap*] Evenin', Sir William.

SIR WILLIAM. Studdenham's told you what I want to see you about?

DUNNING. Yes, Sir.

SIR WILLIAM. The thing's in your hands. Take it or leave it. I don't put pressure on you.   I simply won't have this sort of thing on my estate.

DUNNING. I'd like to say, Sir William, that she——   [*He stops.*]

SIR WILLIAM. Yes, I daresay—Six of one and half a dozen of the other.   Can't go into that.

DUNNING. No, Sir William.

SIR WILLIAM. I'm quite mild with you. This is your first place. If you leave here you'll get no character.

DUNNING. I never meant any harm, sir.

SIR WILLIAM. My good fellow, you know the custom of the country.

DUNNING. Yes, Sir William, but——

SIR WILLIAM. You should have looked before you leaped. I'm not forcing you.   If you refuse you must go, that's all.

DUNNING. Yes, Sir William.

SIR WILLIAM. Well, now go along and take a day to think it over.

[BILL, *who has sauntered moodily from the dining-room, stands by the stairs listening. Catching sight of him,* DUNNING *raises his hand to his forelock.*

DUNNING. Very good, Sir William. [*He turns, fumbles, and turns again.*] My old mother's dependent on me——

SIR WILLIAM. Now, Dunning, I've no more to say.

[DUNNING *goes sadly away under the stairs.*

SIR WILLIAM. [*Following*] And look here! Just understand this—— [*He too goes out.*

[BILL, *lighting a cigarette, has approached the writing-table. He looks very glum. The billiard-room door is flung open.* MABEL LANFARNE *appears, and makes him a little curtsey.*

MABEL. Against my will I am bidden to bring you in to pool.

BILL. Sorry! I've got letters.

MABEL. You seem to have become very conscientious.

BILL. Oh! I don't know.

MABEL. Do you remember the last day of the covert shooting?

BILL. I do.

MABEL. [*suddenly*] What a pretty girl Freda Studdenham's grown!

BILL. Has she?

MABEL. "She walks in beauty."

BILL. Really? Hadn't noticed.

MABEL. Have you been taking lessons in conversation?

BILL. Don't think so.

MABEL. Oh! [*There is a silence.*] Mr. Cheshire.

BILL. Miss Lanfarne!

MABEL. What's the matter with you? Aren't you rather queer, considering that I don't bite, and *was* rather a pal!

BILL. [*Stolidly*] I'm sorry.

[*Then seeing that his mother has come in from the billiard-room, he sits down at the writing-table.*

LADY CHESHIRE. Mabel, dear, do take my cue. Won't you play too, Bill, and try and stop Ronny, he's too terrible?

BILL. Thanks. I've go these letters.

[MABEL *taking the cue passes back into the billiard-room, whence comes out the sound of talk and laughter.*

LADY CHESHIRE. [*Going over and standing behind her son's chair*] Anything wrong, darling?

BILL. Nothing, thanks. [*Suddenly.*] I say, I wish you hadn't asked that girl here.

LADY CHESHIRE. Mabel! Why? She's wanted for rehearsals. I thought you got on so well with her last Christmas.

BILL. [*With a sort of sullen exasperation*] A year ago.

LADY CHESHIRE. The girls like her, so does your father ; personally I must say I think she's rather nice and Irish.

BILL. She's all right, I daresay.

[*He looks round as if to show his mother that he wishes to be left alone. But* LADY CHESHIRE, *having seen that he is about to look at her, is not looking at him.*

LADY CHESHIRE. I'm afraid your father's been talking to you, Bill.

BILL. He has.

LADY CHESHIRE. Debts ? Do try and make allowances. [*With a faint smile.*] Of course he is a little——

BILL. He is.

LADY CHESHIRE. I wish *I* could——

BILL. Oh, Lord ! Don't *you* get mixed up in it !

LADY CHESHIRE. It seems almost a pity that you told him.

BILL. He wrote and asked me point-blank what I owed.

LADY CHESHIRE. Oh ! [*Forcing herself to speak in a casual voice.*] I happen to have a little money, Bill—— I think it would be simpler if——

BILL. Now look here, mother, you've tried that before. I can't help spending money, I never *shall* be able, unless I go to the Colonies, or something of the kind.

LADY CHESHIRE. Don't talk like that !

BILL. I *would*, for two straws !

LADY CHESHIRE. It's only because your father thinks such a lot of the place, and the name, and your career. The Cheshires are all like that. They've been here so long ; they're all—root.

BILL. Deuced funny business my career will be, I expect !

LADY CHESHIRE. [*Fluttering, but restraining himself lest he should see*] But, Bill, why *must* you spend more than your allowance ?

BILL. Why—anything ? I didn't make myself.

LADY CHESHIRE. I'm afraid *we* did that. It *was* inconsiderate perhaps.

BILL. Yes, you'd better have left me out.

LADY CHESHIRE. But why are you so—— Only a little fuss about money !

BILL. Ye-es.

LADY CHESHIRE. You're not keeping anything from me, are you ?

BILL. [*Facing her*] No. [*He then turns very deliberately to the writing things, and takes up a pen.*] I must write these letters, please.

LADY CHESHIRE. Bill, if there's any real trouble, you will tell me, won't you ?

BILL. There's nothing whatever.

[*He suddenly gets up and walks about.*

[LADY CHESHIRE, *too, moves over to the fireplace, and after an uneasy look at him, turns to the fire. Then, as if trying to switch off his mood, she changes the subject abruptly.*

LADY CHESHIRE. Isn't it a pity about young Dunning? I'm so sorry for Rose Taylor.

[*There is a silence. Stealthily under the staircase* FREDA *has entered, and seeing only* BILL, *advances to speak to him.*

BILL. [*Suddenly*] Oh! well, you can't help these things in the country.

[*As he speaks,* FREDA *stops dead, perceiving that he is not alone;* BILL, *too, catching sight of her, starts.*

LADY CHESHIRE. [*Still speaking to the fire*] It seems dreadful to force him. I do so believe in people doing things of their own accord. [*Then seeing* FREDA *standing so uncertainly by the stairs.*] Do you want me, Freda?

FREDA. Only your cloak, my lady. Shall I—begin it?

[*At this moment* SIR WILLIAM *enters from the drawing-room.*

LADY CHESHIRE. Yes, yes.

SIR WILLIAM. [*Genially*] Can you give me another five minutes, Bill? [*Pointing to the billiard-room.*] We'll come directly, my dear.

[FREDA, *with a look at* BILL, *has gone back whence she came; and* LADY CHESHIRE *goes reluctantly away into the billiard-room.*

SIR WILLIAM. I shall give young Dunning short shrift. [*He moves over to the fireplace and divides his coat-tails.*] Now, about you, Bill! I don't want to bully you the moment you come down, but, you know, this can't go on. I've paid your debts twice. Shan't pay them this time unless I see a disposition to change your mode of life. [*A pause.*] You get your extravagance from your mother. She's very queer—[*A pause*]—All the Winterleghs are like that about money.

BILL. Mother's particularly generous, if that's what you mean.

SIR WILLIAM. [*Dryly*] We will put it that way. [*A pause.*] At the present moment you owe, as I understand it, eleven hundred pounds.

BILL. About that.

SIR WILLIAM. Mere flea-bite. [*A pause.*] I've a proposition to make.

BILL. Won't it do to-morrow, sir?

SIR WILLIAM. " To-morrow " appears to be your motto in life.

BILL. Thanks!

SIR WILLIAM. I'm anxious to change it to " To-day." [BILL *looks at him in silence.*] It's time you took your position seriously, instead of hanging about town, racing, and playing polo, and what not.

BILL. Go ahead!

[*At something dangerous in his voice,* SIR WILLIAM *modifies his attitude.*

SIR WILLIAM. The proposition's very simple. I can't suppose anything so rational and to your advantage will appeal to you, but [*dryly*] I mention it. Marry a nice girl, settle down, and stand for the division; you can have the Dower House and fifteen hundred a year, and I'll pay your debts into the bargain. If you're elected I'll make it two thousand. Plenty of time to work up the constituency before we kick out these infernal Rads. Carpet-bagger against you; if you go hard at it in the summer, it'll be odd if you don't manage to put in your three days a week, next season. You can take Rocketer and that four-year-old—he's well up to your weight, fully eight and a half inches of bone. You'll only want one other. And if Miss—if your wife means to hunt——

BILL. You've chosen my wife, then?

SIR WILLIAM. [*With a quick look*] I imagine, you've some girl in your mind.

BILL. Ah!

SIR WILLIAM. Used not to be unnatural at your age. I married your mother at twenty-eight. Here you are, eldest son of a family that stands for something. The more I see of the times the more I'm convinced that everybody who is anybody has got to buckle to, and save the landmarks left. Unless we're true to our caste, and prepared to work for it, the landed classes are going to go under to this infernal democratic spirit in the air. The outlook's very serious. We're threatened in a hundred ways. If you mean business, you'll want a wife. When I came into the property I should have been lost without your mother.

BILL. I thought this was coming.

SIR WILLIAM. [*With a certain geniality*] My dear fellow, I don't want to put a pistol to your head. You've had a slack rein so far. I've never objected to your sowing a few wild oats—so long as you—er— [*Unseen by* SIR WILLIAM, BILL *makes a sudden movement.*] Short of that—at all events, I've not inquired into your affairs. I can only judge by the—er—pecuniary evidence you've been good enough to afford me from time to time. I imagine you've lived like a good many young men in your position—I'm not blaming you, but there's a time for all things.

BILL. Why don't you say outright that you want me to marry Mabel Lanfarne?

SIR WILLIAM. Well, I do. Girl's a nice one. Good family—got a little money—rides well. Isn't she good-looking enough for you, or what?

BILL. Quite, thanks.

SIR WILLIAM. I understood from your mother that you and she were on good terms.

BILL. Please don't drag mother into it.

SIR WILLIAM. [*With dangerous politeness*] Perhaps you'll be good enough to state your objections.

BILL. Must we go on with this?

SIR WILLIAM. I've never asked you to do anything for me before;

I expect you to pay attention now. I've no wish to dragoon you into this particular marriage. If you don't care for Miss Lanfarne, marry a girl you're fond of.

BILL. I refuse.

SIR WILLIAM. In that case you know what to look out for. [*With a sudden rush of choler.*] You young . . . [*He checks himself and stands glaring at* BILL, *who glares back at him.*] This means, I suppose, that you've got some entanglement or other.

BILL. Suppose what you like, sir.

SIR WILLIAM. I warn you, if you play the blackguard——

BILL. You can't force me like young Dunning.

[*Hearing the raised voices* LADY CHESHIRE *has come back from the billiard-room.*

LADY CHESHIRE. [*Closing the door*] What is it ?

SIR WILLIAM. You deliberately refuse ! Go away, Dorothy.

LADY CHESHIRE. [*Resolutely*] I haven't seen Bill for two months.

SIR WILLIAM. What ! [*Hesitating.*] Well—we must talk it over again.

LADY CHESHIRE. Come to the billiard-room, both of you ! Bill, *do* finish those letters !

[*With a deft movement she draws* SIR WILLIAM *toward the billiard-room, and glances back at* BILL *before going out, but he has turned to the writing-table. When the door is closed,* BILL *looks into the drawing-room, then opens the door under the stairs ; and backing away towards the writing-table, sits down there, and takes up a pen.* FREDA *who has evidently been waiting, comes in and stands by the table.*

BILL. I say, this is dangerous, you know.

FREDA. Yes—but I must.

BILL. Well, then—— [*With natural recklessness.*] Aren't you going to kiss me ?

[*Without moving she looks at him with a sort of miserable inquiry.*

BILL. Do you know you haven't seen me for eight weeks ?

FREDA. Quite—long enough—for you to have forgotten.

BILL. Forgotten ! I don't forget people so soon.

FREDA. No ?

BILL. What's the matter with you, Freda ?

FREDA. [*After a long look*] It'll never be as it was.

BILL. [*Jumping up*] How d'you mean ?

FREDA. I've got something for you. [*She takes a diamond ring out of her dress and holds it out to him.*] I've not worn it since Cromer.

BILL. Now, look here——

FREDA. I've had my holiday ; I shan't get another in a hurry.

BILL. Freda !

FREDA. You'll be glad to be free. That fortnight's all you really loved me in.

BILL. [*Putting his hands on her arms*] I swear——

FREDA. [*Between her teeth*] Miss Lanfarne need never know about me.

BILL. So that's it! I've told you a dozen times—nothing's changed. [FREDA *looks at him and smiles.*

BILL. Oh! very well! If you *will* make yourself miserable.

FREDA. Everybody will be pleased.

BILL. At what?

FREDA. When you marry her.

BILL. This is too bad.

FREDA. It's what always happens—even when it's not a gentleman.

BILL. That's enough!

FREDA. But I'm not like that girl down in the village. You needn't be afraid I'll say anything when—it comes. That's what I had to tell you.

BILL. *What!*

FREDA. *I* can keep a secret.

BILL. Do you mean this? [*She bows her head.*

BILL. Good God!

FREDA. Father brought me up not to whine. Like the puppies when they hold them up by their tails. [*With a sudden break in her voice.*] Oh! Bill!

BILL. [*With his head down, seizing her hands*] Freda! [*He breaks away from her towards the fire.*] Good God!

    [*She stands looking at him, then quietly slips away by the door under the staircase.* BILL *turns to speak to her, and sees that she has gone. He walks up to the fireplace, and grips the mantelpiece.*

BILL. By Jove! This is——!

The curtain falls.

ACT II

The scene is LADY CHESHIRE'S *morning room, at ten o'clock on the following
day. It is a pretty room, with white panelled walls, and chrysanthemums
and carmine lilies in bowls. A large bow window overlooks the park
under a sou'-westerly sky. A piano stands open; a fire is burning;
and the morning's correspondence is scattered on a writing-table. Doors
opposite each other lead to the maid's workroom, and to a corridor.*
LADY CHESHIRE *is standing in the middle of the room, looking at an
opera cloak, which* FREDA *is holding out.*

LADY CHESHIRE. Well, Freda, suppose you just give it up!

FREDA. I don't like to be beaten.

LADY CHESHIRE. You're not to worry over your work. And by
the way, I promised your father to make you eat more.

[FREDA *smiles.*

LADY CHESHIRE. It's all very well to smile. You want bracing up.
Now don't be naughty. I shall give you a tonic. And I think you
had better put that cloak away.

FREDA. I'd rather have one more try, my lady.

LADY CHESHIRE. [*Sitting down at her writing-table*] Very well.

[FREDA *goes out into her workroom, as* JACKSON *comes in from the
corridor.*

JACKSON. Excuse me, my lady. There's a young woman from the
village, says you wanted to see her.

LADY CHESHIRE. Rose Taylor? Ask her to come in. Oh! and,
Jackson, the car for the meet, please, at half-past ten.

[JACKSON *having bowed and withdrawn,* LADY CHESHIRE *rises with
marked signs of nervousness, which she has only just suppressed
when* ROSE TAYLOR, *a stolid country girl, comes in and stands
waiting by the door.*

LADY CHESHIRE. Well, Rose. Do come in!

[ROSE *advances perhaps a couple of steps.*

LADY CHESHIRE. I just wondered whether you'd like to ask my
advice. Your engagement with Dunning's broken off, isn't it?

ROSE. Yes—but I've told him he's got to marry me.

LADY CHESHIRE. I see! And you think that'll be the wisest thing?

ROSE. [*Stolidly*] I don't know, my lady. He's *got* to.

LADY CHESHIRE. I do hope you're a little fond of him still.

ROSE. I'm *not*. He don't deserve it.

174

LADY CHESHIRE. And—do you think he's quite lost his affection for you?

ROSE. I suppose so, else he wouldn't treat me as he's done. He's after that—that—— He didn't ought to treat me as if I was dead.

LADY CHESHIRE. No, no—of course. But you *will* think it all well over, won't you?

ROSE. I've a-got nothing to think over, except what I know of.

LADY CHESHIRE. But for you both to marry in that spirit! You know it's for life, Rose. [*Looking into her face.*] I'm always ready to help you.

ROSE. [*Dropping a very slight curtsey*] Thank you, my lady, but I think he ought to marry me. I've told him he ought.

LADY CHESHIRE. [*Sighing*] Well, that's all I wanted to say. It's a question of your self-respect; I can't give you any real advice. But just remember that if you want a friend——

ROSE. [*With a gulp*] I'm not so 'ard, really. I only want him to do what's right by me.

LADY CHESHIRE. [*With a little lift of her eyebrows—gently*] Yes—yes —I see.

ROSE. [*Glancing back at the door*] I don't like meeting the servants.

LADY CHESHIRE. Come along, I'll take you out another way.

[*As they reach the door,* DOT *comes in.*

DOT. [*With a glance at* ROSE] Can we have this room for the mouldy rehearsal, Mother?

LADY CHESHIRE. Yes, dear, you can air it here.

[*Holding the door open for* ROSE, *she follows her out. And* DOT, *with a book of "Caste" in her hand, arranges the room according to a diagram.*

DOT. Chair—chair—table—chair—Dash! Table—piano—fire— window! [*Producing a pocket comb.*] Comb for Eccles. Cradle?— Cradle—[*She viciously dumps a waste-paper basket down, and drops a foot-stool into it.*] Brat! [*Then reading from the book gloomily.*] "Enter Eccles breathless. Esther and Polly rise—Esther puts on lid of bandbox." Bandbox!

[*Searching for something to represent a bandbox, she opens the work-room door.*

DOT. Freda?   [FREDA *comes in.*

DOT. I say, Freda. Anything the matter? You seem awfully down.   [FREDA *does not answer.*

DOT. You haven't looked anything of a lollipop lately.

FREDA. I'm quite all right, thank you, Miss Dot.

DOT. Has Mother been givin' you a tonic?

FREDA. [*Smiling a little*] Not yet.

DOT. That doesn't account for it then. [*With a sudden warm impulse.*] What *is* it, Freda?

FREDA. Nothing.

DOT. [*Switching off on a different line of thought*] Are you very busy this morning ?

FREDA. Only this cloak for my lady.

DOT. Oh ! that can wait. I may have to get you in to prompt, if I can't keep 'em straight. [*Gloomily.*] They stray so. Would you mind ?

FREDA. [*Stolidly*] I shall be very glad, Miss Dot.

DOT. [*Eyeing her dubiously*] All right. Let's see—what did I want ?

[JOAN *has come in.*

JOAN. Look here, Dot ; about the baby in this scene. I'm sure I ought to make more of it.

DOT. Romantic little beast ! [*She plucks the footstool out by one ear, and holds it forth*]. Let's see you try !

JOAN. [*Recoiling*] But, Dot, what are we really going to have for the baby ? I can't rehearse with that thing. Can't *you* suggest something, Freda ?

FREDA. Borrow a real one, Miss Joan. There are some that don't count much.

JOAN. Freda, how horrible !

DOT. [*Dropping the footstool back into the basket*] You'll just put up with what you're given.

[*Then as* CHRISTINE *and* MABEL LANFARNE *come in,* FREDA *turns abruptly and goes out.*

DOT. Buck up ! Where are Bill and Harold ? [*To* JOAN.] Go and find them, mouse-cat.

[*But* BILL *and* HAROLD, *followed by* LATTER, *are already in the doorway. They come in, and* LATTER, *stumbling over the waste-paper basket, takes it up to improve its position.*

DOT. Drop that cradle, John ! [*As he picks the footstool out of it.*] Leave the baby in ! Now then ! Bill, you enter there ! [*She points to the workroom door, where* BILL *and* MABEL *range themselves close to the piano ; while* HAROLD *goes to the window.*] John ! get off the stage ! Now then, " Eccles enters breathless, Esther and Polly rise." Wait a minute. I know now. [*She opens the workroom door.*] Freda, I wanted a bandbox.

HAROLD. [*Cheerfully*] I hate beginning to rehearse, you know, you feel such a fool.

DOT. [*With her bandbox—gloomily*] You'll feel more of a fool when you have begun. [*To* BILL, *who is staring into the workroom.*] Shut the door. Now. [BILL *shuts the door.*

LATTER. [*Advancing*] Look here ! I want to clear up a point of psychology before we start.

DOT. Good Lord !

LATTER. When I bring in the milk—ought I to bring it in seriously —as if I were accustomed—I mean, I maintain that if I'm——

JOAN. Oh! John, but I don't think it's meant that you should——

DOT. Shut up! Go back, John! Blow the milk! Begin, begin, begin! Bill!

LATTER. [*Turning round and again advancing*] But I think you underrate the importance of my entrance altogether.

MABEL. Oh! no, Mr. Latter.

LATTER. I don't in the least want to destroy the balance of the scene, but I do want to be clear about the spirit. What is the spirit?

DOT. [*With gloom*] Rollicking!

LATTER. Well, I don't think so. We shall run a great risk with this play, if we rollick.

DOT. Shall we? Now look here——!

MABEL. [*Softly to* BILL.] Mr. Cheshire!

BILL. [*Desperately*] Let's get on!

DOT. [*Waving* LATTER *back*] Begin, begin! At last!

[*But* JACKSON *has come in.*

JACKSON. [*To* CHRISTINE] Studdenham says, M'm, if the young ladies want to see the spaniel pups, he's brought 'em round.

JOAN. [*Starting up*] Oh! come on, John!

[*She flies towards the door, followed by* LATTER.

DOT. [*Gesticulating with her book*] Stop! You——!

[CHRISTINE *and* HAROLD *also rush past.*

DOT. [*Despairingly*] First pick! [*Tearing her hair.*] Pigs! Devils!

[*She rushes after them.*

[BILL *and* MABEL *are left alone.*

MABEL. [*Mockingly*] And don't *you* want one of the spaniel pups?

BILL. [*Painfully reserved and sullen, and conscious of the workroom door*] Can't keep a dog in town. You can have one, if you like. The breeding's all right.

MABEL. Sixth pick?

BILL. The girls'll give you one of theirs. They only fancy they want 'em.

MABEL. [*Moving nearer to him, with her hands clasped behind her*] You know, you remind me awfully of your father. Except that you're not nearly so polite. I don't understand you English—lords of the soil. The way you have of disposing of your females. [*With a sudden change of voice.*] What was the matter with you last night? [*Softly.*] Won't you tell me?

BILL. Nothing to tell.

MABEL. Ah! no, Mr. Bill.

BILL. [*Almost succumbing to her voice—then sullenly*] Worried, I suppose.

MABEL. [*Returning to her mocking*] Quite got over it?

BILL. Don't chaff me, please.

MABEL. You really are rather formidable.

BILL. Thanks.

MABEL. But, you know, I love to cross a field where there's a bull.

BILL. Really! Very interesting.

MABEL. The way of their only seeing one thing at a time. [*She moves back as he advances.*] And overturning people on the journey.

BILL. Hadn't you better be a little careful?

MABEL. And never to see the hedge until they're stuck in it. And then straight from that hedge into the opposite one.

BILL. [*Savagely*] What makes you bait me this morning of all mornings?

MABEL. The beautiful morning! [*Suddenly.*] It must be dull for poor Freda working in there with all this fun going on?

BILL. [*Glancing at the door*] Fun you call it?

MABEL. To go back to you, now—Mr. Cheshire.

BILL. No.

MABEL. You always make me feel so Irish. Is it because you're so English, d'you think? Ah! I can see him moving his ears. Now he's pawing the ground—He's started!

BILL. Miss Lanfarne!

MABEL. [*Still backing away from him, and drawing him on with her eyes and smile*] You can't help coming after me! [*Then with a sudden change to a sort of stern gravity.*] Can you? You'll feel that when I've gone.

[*They stand quite still, looking into each other's eyes, and* FREDA, *who has opened the door of the workroom, stares at them.*

MABEL. [*Seeing her*] Here's the stile. *Adieu, Monsieur le taureau!*

[*She puts her hand behind her, opens the door, and slips through, leaving* BILL *to turn, following the direction of her eyes, and see* FREDA *with the cloak still in her hand.*

BILL. [*Slowly walking towards her*] I haven't slept all night.

FREDA. No?

BILL. Have you been thinking it over?

[FREDA *gives a bitter little laugh.*

BILL. Don't! We must make a plan. I'll get you away. I won't let you suffer. I swear I won't.

FREDA. That will be clever.

BILL. I wish to Heaven my affairs weren't in such a mess.

FREDA. I shall be—all—right, thank you.

BILL. You *must* think me a blackguard. [*She shakes her head.*] Abuse me—say something! Don't look like that!

FREDA. Were you ever really fond of me?

BILL. Of course I was, I am now. Give me your hands.

[*She looks at him, then drags her hands from his, and covers her face.*

BILL. [*Clenching his fists*] Look here! I'll prove it. [*Then as she suddenly flings her arms round his neck and clings to him.*] There, there!
    [*There is a click of a door handle. They start away from each other, and see* LADY CHESHIRE *regarding them.*
LADY CHESHIRE. [*Without irony*] I beg your pardon.
    [*She makes as if to withdraw from an unwarranted intrusion, but suddenly turning, stands, with lips pressed together, waiting.*
LADY CHESHIRE. Yes?
    [FREDA *has muffled her face. But* BILL *turns and confronts his mother.*
BILL. Don't say anything against her!
LADY CHESHIRE. [*Tries to speak to him and fails—then to* FREDA] Please—go!
BILL. [*Taking* FREDA'S *arm*] No.
    [LADY CHESHIRE, *after a moment's hesitation, herself moves towards the door.*
BILL. Stop, mother!
LADY CHESHIRE. I think perhaps not.
BILL. [*Looking at* FREDA, *who is cowering as though from a blow*] It's a d—d shame!
LADY CHESHIRE. It is.
BILL. [*With sudden resolution*] It's not as you think. I'm engaged to be married to her.   [FREDA *gives him a wild stare, and turns away.*
LADY CHESHIRE. [*Looking from one to the other*] I—don't—think—I—quite—understand.
BILL. [*With the brutality of his mortification*] What I said was plain enough.
LADY CHESHIRE. Bill!
BILL. I tell you I am going to marry her.
LADY CHESHIRE. [*To* FREDA] Is that true?
                     [FREDA *gulps and remains silent.*
BILL. If you want to say anything, say it to *me*, mother.
LADY CHESHIRE. [*Gripping the edge of a little table*] Give me a chair, please.   [BILL *gives her a chair.*
LADY CHESHIRE. [*To* FREDA] Please sit down too.
    [FREDA *sits on the piano stool, still turning her face away.*
LADY CHESHIRE. [*Fixing her eyes on* FREDA] Now!
BILL. I fell in love with her. And she with me.
LADY CHESHIRE. When?
BILL In the summer.
LADY CHESHIRE. Ah!
BILL. It wasn't her fault.
LADY CHESHIRE. No?
BILL. [*With a sort of menace*] Mother!
LADY CHESHIRE. Forgive me, I am not quite used to the idea. You say that you—are engaged?

BILL. Yes.

LADY CHESHIRE. The reasons against such an engagement have occurred to you, I suppose? [*With a sudden change of tone.*] Bill! what does it mean?

BILL. If you think she's trapped me into this——

LADY CHESHIRE. I do not. Neither do I think she has been trapped. I think nothing. I understand nothing.

BILL. [*Grimly*] Good!

LADY CHESHIRE. How long has this—engagement lasted?

BILL. [*After a silence*] Two months.

LADY CHESHIRE. [*Suddenly*] This is—this is quite impossible.

BILL. You'll find it isn't.

LADY CHESHIRE. It's simple misery.

BILL. [*Pointing to the workroom*] Go and wait in there, Freda.

LADY CHESHIRE. [*Quickly*] And are you still in love with her?

[FREDA, *moving towards the workroom, smothers a sob.*

BILL. Of course I am.

[FREDA *has gone, and as she goes,* LADY CHESHIRE *rises suddenly, forced by the intense feeling she has been keeping in hand.*

LADY CHESHIRE. Bill! Oh, Bill! What does it all mean? [BILL, *looking from side to side, only shrugs his shoulders.*] You are *not* in love with her now. It's no good telling me you are.

BILL. I am.

LADY CHESHIRE. That's not exactly how you would speak if you were.

BILL. She's in love with me.

LADY CHESHIRE. [*Bitterly*] I suppose so.

BILL. I mean to see that nobody runs her down.

LADY CHESHIRE. [*With difficulty*] Bill! Am I a hard, or mean woman?

BILL. Mother!

LADY CHESHIRE. It's all your life—and—your father's—and—all of us. I want to understand—I must understand. Have you realized what an awful thing this would be for us all? It's quite impossible that it should go on.

BILL. I'm always in hot water with the Governor, as it is. She and I'll take good care not to be in the way.

LADY CHESHIRE. Tell me everything!

BILL. I have.

LADY CHESHIRE. I'm your mother, Bill.

BILL. What's the good of these questions?

LADY CHESHIRE. You won't give her away—I see!

BILL. I've told you all there is to tell. We're engaged, we shall be married quietly, and—and—go to Canada.

LADY CHESHIRE. If there weren't more than that to tell you'd be in love with her now.

BILL. I've told you that I am.

LADY CHESHIRE. You are *not*. [*Almost fiercely.*] I *know*—I *know* there's more behind.

BILL. There—is—nothing.

LADY CHESHIRE. [*Baffled, but unconvinced*] Do you mean that your love for her has been just what it might have been for a lady ?

BILL. [*Bitterly*] Why not ?

LADY CHESHIRE. [*With painful irony*] It is not so as a rule.

BILL. Up to now I've never heard you or the girls say a word against Freda. This isn't the moment to begin, please.

LADY CHESHIRE. [*Solemnly*] All such marriages end in wretchedness. You haven't a taste or tradition in common. You don't know what marriage is. Day after day, year after year. It's no use being senti-mental—for people brought up as we are, to have different manners is worse than to have different souls. Besides, it's poverty. Your father will never forgive you, and *I've* practically nothing. What can you do ? You have no profession. How are you going to stand it ; with a woman who——? It's the little things.

BILL. I know all that, thanks.

LADY CHESHIRE. Nobody does till they've been through it. Mar-riage is hard enough when people are of the same class. [*With a sudden movement towards him.*] Oh ! my dear—before it's too late !

BILL. [*After a struggle*] It's no good.

LADY CHESHIRE. It's not fair to her. It *can* only end in her misery.

BILL. Leave that to me, please.

LADY CHESHIRE. [*With an almost angry vehemence*] Only the very finest can do such things. And you—don't even know what trouble's like.

BILL. Drop it, please, mother.

LADY CHESHIRE. Bill, on your word of honour, are you acting of your own free will ?

BILL. [*Breaking away from her*] I can't stand any more.

[*He goes out into the workroom.*

LADY CHESHIRE. What in God's name shall I do ?

[*In her distress she stands quite still, then goes to the workroom door, and opens it.*

LADY CHESHIRE. Come in here, please, Freda.

[*After a second's pause,* FREDA, *white and trembling, appears in the doorway, followed by* BILL.

LADY CHESHIRE. No, Bill. I want to speak to her alone.

[BILL *does not move.*

LADY CHESHIRE. [*Icily*] I must ask you to leave us.

[BILL *hesitates ; then shrugging his shoulders, he touches* FREDA'S *arms, and goes back into the workroom, closing the door. There is silence.*

LADY CHESHIRE. How did it come about?

FREDA. I don't know, my lady.

LADY CHESHIRE. For heaven's sake, child, don't call me that again, whatever happens. [*She walks to the window, and speaks from there.*] I know well enough how love comes. I don't blame you. Don't cry. But, you see, it's my eldest son. [FREDA *puts her hand to her breast.*] Yes, I know. Women always get the worst of these things. That's natural. But it's not only you—is it? Does anyone guess?

FREDA. No.

LADY CHESHIRE. Not even your father? [FREDA *shakes her head.*] There's nothing more dreadful than for a woman to hang like a stone round a man's neck. How far has it gone? Tell me!

FREDA. I can't!

LADY CHESHIRE. Come!

FREDA. I—won't.

LADY CHESHIRE. [*Smiling painfully*] Won't give him away? Both of you the same. What's the use of that with me? Look at me! Wasn't he with you when you went for your holiday this summer?

FREDA. He's—always—behaved—like—a—gentleman.

LADY CHESHIRE. Like a *man*—you mean!

FREDA. It hasn't been his fault! I love him so.

[LADY CHESHIRE *turns abruptly, and begins to walk up and down the room. Then stopping, she looks intently at* FREDA.

LADY CHESHIRE. I don't know what to say to you. It's simple madness! It can't, and shan't go on.

FREDA. [*Sullenly*] I know I'm not his equal, but I am—somebody.

LADY CHESHIRE. [*Answering this first assertion of rights with a sudden steeliness*] Does he love you *now*?

FREDA. That's not fair—it's not fair.

LADY CHESHIRE. If men are like gunpowder, Freda, women are not. If you've lost him it's been your own fault.

FREDA. But he *does* love me, he must. It's only four months.

LADY CHESHIRE. [*Looking down, and speaking rapidly*] Listen to me. I love my son, but I know him—I know all his kind of man. I've lived with one for thirty years. I know the way their senses work. When they want a thing they must have it, and then—they're sorry.

FREDA. [*Sullenly*] He's *not* sorry.

LADY CHESHIRE. Is his love big enough to carry you both over everything? . . . You know it isn't.

FREDA. If I were a lady, you wouldn't talk like that.

LADY CHESHIRE. If you were a lady there'd be no trouble before either of you. You'll make him hate you.

FREDA. I won't believe it. I could make him happy—out there.

LADY CHESHIRE. I don't want to be so odious as to say all the things you must know. I only ask you to try and put yourself in our position.

FREDA. Ah, yes!

LADY CHESHIRE. You ought to know me better than to think I'm purely selfish.

FREDA. Would you like to put yourself in my position?

[*She throws up her head.*

LADY CHESHIRE. What!

FREDA. Yes. Just like Rose.

LADY CHESHIRE. [*In a low, horror-stricken voice*] Oh!

[*There is a dead silence; then going swiftly up to her, she looks straight into* FREDA'S *eyes.*

FREDA. [*Meeting her gaze*] Oh! yes—it's the truth. [*Then to* BILL, *who has come in from the workroom, she gasps out.*] I never meant to tell.

BILL. Well, are you satisfied?

LADY CHESHIRE. [*Below her breath*] This is terrible!

BILL. The Governor had better know.

LADY CHESHIRE. Oh! no; not yet!

BILL. Waiting won't cure it!

[*The door from the corridor is thrown open;* CHRISTINE *and* DOT *run in with their copies of the play in their hands; seeing that something is wrong, they stand still. After a look at his mother,* BILL *turns abruptly, and goes back into the workroom.* LADY CHESHIRE *moves towards the window.*

JOAN. [*Following her sisters*] The car's round. What's the matter?

DOT. Shut up!

[*Sir* WILLIAM'S *voice is heard from the corridor calling "Dorothy!"
As* LADY CHESHIRE, *passing her handkerchief over her face, turns round, he enters. He is in full hunting dress: well-weathered pink, buckskins, and mahogany tops.*

SIR WILLIAM. Just off, my dear. [*To his daughters, genially.*] Rehearsin'? What! [*He goes up to* FREDA, *holding out his gloved right hand.*] Button that for me, Freda, would you? It's a bit stiff!

[FREDA *buttons the glove:* LADY CHESHIRE *and the girls watching in hypnotic silence.*

SIR WILLIAM. Thank you! "Balmy as May"; scent ought to be first-rate. [*To* LADY CHESHIRE.] Good-bye, my dear! Sampson's Gorse—best day of the whole year. [*He pats* JOAN *on the shoulder.*] Wish you were comin' out, Joan.

[*He goes out, leaving the door open, and as his footsteps and the chink of his spurs die away,* FREDA *turns and rushes into the workroom.*

CHRISTINE. Mother! What——?

[*But* LADY CHESHIRE *waves the question aside, passes her daughter, and goes out into the corridor. The sound of a motor-car is heard.*

JOAN. [*Running to the window*] They've started!—Chris! What is it? Dot?

DOT. Bill, and her!

JOAN. But *what?*

DOT. [*Gloomily*] Heaven knows! Go away, you're not fit for this.

JOAN. [*Aghast*] I am fit.

DOT. I think not.

JOAN. Chris?

CHRISTINE. [*In a hard voice*] Mother ought to have told us.

JOAN. It can't be very awful. Freda's so *good*.

DOT. Call yourself in love, you—milky kitten!

CHRISTINE. It's horrible, not knowing anything! I *wish* Ronny hadn't gone.

JOAN. Shall I fetch John?

DOT. John!

CHRISTINE. Perhaps Harold knows.

JOAN. He went out with Studdenham.

DOT. It's always like this, women kept in blinkers. Rose-leaves and humbug! That awful old man!

JOAN. Dot!

CHRISTINE. Don't talk of father like that!

DOT. Well, he is! And Bill will be just like him at fifty! Heaven help Freda, whatever she's done! I'd sooner be a private in a German regiment than a woman.

JOAN. Dot, you're awful!

DOT. You—mouse-hearted—linnet!

CHRISTINE. Don't talk that nonsense about women!

DOT. You're married and out of it; and Ronny's not one of these terrific John Bulls. [*To* JOAN, *who has opened the door*.] Looking for John? No good, my dear; lath and plaster.

JOAN. [*From the door, in a frightened whisper*] Here's Mabel!

DOT. Heavens, and the waters under the earth!

CHRISTINE. If we only *knew!*

[*As* MABEL *comes in, the three girls are silent, with their eyes fixed on their books.*

MABEL. The silent company.

DOT. [*Looking straight at her*] We're chucking it for to-day.

MABEL. What's the matter?

CHRISTINE. Oh! nothing.

DOT. Something's happened.

MABEL. Really! I *am* sorry. [*Hesitating.*] Is it bad enough for me to go?

CHRISTINE. Oh! no, Mabel!

DOT. [*Sardonically*] I should think very likely.

[*While she is looking from face to face,* BILL *comes in from the workroom. He starts to walk across the room, but stops, and looks stolidly at the four girls.*

BILL. Exactly! Fact of the matter is, Miss Lanfarne, I'm engaged to my mother's maid.

[*No one moves or speaks. Suddenly* MABEL LANFARNE *goes towards him, holding out her hand.* BILL *does not take her hand, but bows. Then after a swift glance at the girls' faces* MABEL *goes out into the corridor, and the three girls are left staring at their brother.*

BILL. [*Coolly*] Thought you might like to know.

[*He, too, goes out into the corridor.*

CHRISTINE. Great heavens!

JOAN. How *awful!*

CHRISTINE. I never thought of anything as bad as that.

JOAN. Oh! Chris! Something must be done!

DOT. [*Suddenly to herself*] Ha! When Father went up to have his glove buttoned!

[*There is a sound,* JACKSON *has come in from the corridor.*

JACKSON. [*To* DOT] If you please, Miss, Studdenham's brought up the other two pups. He's just outside. Will you kindly take a look at them, he says?

[*There is silence.*

DOT [*Suddenly*] We can't.

CHRISTINE. Not just now, Jackson.

JACKSON. Is Studdenham and the pups to wait, M'm?

[DOT *shakes her head violently. But* STUDDENHAM *is seen already standing in the doorway, with a spaniel puppy in either side-pocket. He comes in, and* JACKSON *stands waiting behind him.*

STUDDENHAM. This fellow's the best, Miss Dot. [*He protrudes the right-hand pocket.*] I was keeping him for my girl—a proper breedy one—takes after his father.   [*The girls stare at him in silence.*

DOT. [*Hastily*] Thanks, Studdenham, I see.

STUDDENHAM. I won't take 'em out in here. They're rather bold yet.

CHRISTINE. [*Desperately*] No, no, of course.

STUDDENHAM. Then you think you'd like him, Miss Dot? The other's got a white chest; she's a lady.

[*He protrudes the left-hand pocket.*

DOT. Oh, yes! Studdenham; thanks, thanks awfully.

STUDDENHAM. Wonderful faithful creatures; follow you like a woman. You can't shake 'em off anyhow. [*He protrudes the right-hand pocket.*] My girl, she'd set her heart on *him*, but she'll just have to do without.

DOT. [*As though galvanized*] Oh! no, I can't take it away from *her*.

7

STUDDENHAM. Bless you, she won't mind! That's settled, then.
[*He turns to the door. To the puppy.*] Ah! would you! Tryin' to
wriggle out of it! Regular young limb!

[*He goes out, followed by* JACKSON.

CHRISTINE. How ghastly!

DOT. [*Suddenly catching sight of the book in her hand*] Caste!

[*She gives vent to a short sharp laugh.*

The curtain falls.

ACT III

*It is five o'clock of the same day. The scene is the smoking-room, with walls
of Leander red, covered by old steeplechase and hunting prints. Armchairs encircle a high-fendered hearth, in which a fire is burning. The
curtains are not yet drawn across mullioned windows; but electric
light is burning. There are two doors, leading, the one to the billiard-
room, the other to a corridor. BILL is pacing up and down; HAROLD,
at the fireplace, stands looking at him with commiseration.*

BILL. What's the time?

HAROLD. Nearly five. They won't be in yet, if that's any consolation.
Always a good meet—[*softly*] as the tiger said when he ate the man.

BILL. By Jove! You're the only person I can stand within a mile
of me, Harold.

HAROLD. Old boy! Do you seriously think you're going to make
it any better by marrying her?

[BILL *shrugs his shoulders, still pacing the room.*

HAROLD. Well, then?

BILL. Look here! I'm not the sort that finds it easy to say things.

HAROLD. No, old man.

BILL. But I've got a kind of self-respect though you wouldn't
think it!

HAROLD. My dear old chap!

BILL. This is about as low-down a thing as one could have done,
I suppose—one's own mother's maid; we've known her since she
was so high. I see it now that—I've got over the attack.

HAROLD. But, heavens! if you're no longer keen on her, Bill!
Do apply your reason, old boy.

[*There is silence; while* BILL *again paces up and down.*

BILL. If you think I care two straws about the morality of the
thing——

HAROLD. Oh! my dear old man! Of course not!

BILL. It's simply that I shall feel such a d—d skunk, if I leave her in
the lurch, with everybody knowing. Try it yourself; you'd soon see!

HAROLD. Poor old chap!

BILL. It's not as if she'd tried to force me into it. And she's a
soft little thing. Why I ever made such a sickening ass of myself,
I can't think. I never meant——

HAROLD. No, I know! But, don't do anything rash, Bill; keep
your head, old man!

187

BILL. I don't see what loss I should be, if I did clear out of the country. [*The sound of cannoning billiard balls is heard.*] Who's that knocking the balls about ?

HAROLD. John, I expect.   [*The sound ceases.*

BILL. He's coming in here. Can't stand that !

[*As* LATTER *appears from the billiard-room, he goes hurriedly out.*

LATTER. Was that Bill ?

HAROLD. Yes.

LATTER. Well ?

HAROLD. [*Pacing up and down in his turn*] Cat on hot bricks is nothing to him. This is the sort of thing you read of in books, John ! What price your argument with Ronny now ? Well, it's not too late for *you* luckily.

LATTER. What do you mean ?

HAROLD. You needn't connect yourself with this eccentric family !

LATTER. I'm not a bounder, Harold.

HAROLD. Good !

LATTER. It's terrible for your sisters.

HAROLD. Deuced lucky we haven't a lot of people staying here ! Poor mother ! John, I feel awfully bad about this. If something isn't done, pretty mess I shall be in.

LATTER. How ?

HAROLD. There's no entail. If the Governor cuts Bill off, it'll all come to me.

LATTER. Oh !

HAROLD. Poor old Bill ! I say, the play ! Nemesis ! What ? Moral ! Caste don't matter. Got us fairly on the hop.

LATTER. It's too bad of Bill. It really is. He's behaved disgracefully.

HAROLD. [*Warmly*] Well ! There are thousands of fellows who'd never dream of sticking to the girl, considering what it means.

LATTER. Perfectly disgusting !

HAROLD. Hang you, John ! Haven't you any human sympathy ? Don't you know how these things come about ? It's like a spark in a straw-yard.

LATTER. One doesn't take lighted pipes into straw-yards unless one's an idiot, or worse.

HAROLD. H'm ! [*With a grin.*] You're not allowed tobacco. In the good old days no one would have thought anything of this. My great-grandfather——

LATTER. Spare me your great-grandfather.

HAROLD. I could tell you of at least a dozen men I know who've been through this same business, and got off scot-free ; and now because Bill's going to play the game, it'll smash him up.

LATTER. Why didn't he play the game at the beginning ?

HAROLD. I can't stand your sort, John. When a thing like this happens, all you can do is to cry out: Why didn't he—? Why didn't she—? What's to be *done*—that's the point!

LATTER. Of course he'll have to——

HAROLD. Ha!

LATTER. What do you mean by—that?

HAROLD. Look here, John! You feel in your bones that a marriage'll be hopeless, just as I do, knowing Bill and the girl and everything! Now don't you?

LATTER. The whole thing is—is most unfortunate.

HAROLD. By Jove! I should think it was!

[*As he speaks* CHRISTINE *and* KEITH *come in from the billiard-room. He is still in splashed hunting clothes, and looks exceptionally weathered, thin-lipped, reticent. He lights a cigarette and sinks into an armchair. Behind them* DOT *and* JOAN *have come stealing in.*

CHRISTINE. I've told Ronny.

JOAN. This waiting for father to be told is awful.

HAROLD. [*To* KEITH] Where did you leave the old man?

KEITH. Clackenham. He'll be home in ten minutes.

DOT. Mabel's going. [*They all stir, as if at fresh consciousness of discomfiture.*] She walked into Gracely, and sent herself a telegram.

HAROLD. Phew!

DOT. And we shall say good-bye as if nothing had happened!

HAROLD. It's up to you, Ronny.

[KEITH, *looking at* JOAN, *slowly emits smoke; and* LATTER *passing his arm through* JOAN's, *draws her away with him into the billiard-room.*

KEITH. Dot?

DOT. *I'm* not a squeamy squirrel.

KEITH. Anybody seen the girl since?

DOT. Yes.

HAROLD. Well?

DOT. She's just sitting there.

CHRISTINE. [*In a hard voice*] As we're all doing.

DOT. She's so soft, that's what's so horrible. If one could only feel——!

KEITH. She's got to face the music like the rest of us.

DOT. Music! Squeaks! Ugh! The whole thing's like a concertina, and some one jigging it!

[*They all turn as the door opens, and a* FOOTMAN *enters with a tray of whisky, gin, lemons, and soda water. In dead silence the* FOOTMAN *puts the tray down.*

HAROLD. [*Forcing his voice*] Did you get a run, Ronny? [*As* KEITH *nods.*] What point?

KEITH. Eight mile.

FOOTMAN. Will you take tea, sir?

KEITH. No, thanks, Charles!

[*In dead silence again the* FOOTMAN *goes out, and they all look after him.*

HAROLD. [*Below his breath*] Good Gad! That's a queeze of it!

KEITH. What's our line of country to be?

CHRISTINE. All depends on father.

KEITH. Sir William's between the devil and the deep sea, as it strikes me.

CHRISTINE. He'll simply forbid it utterly, of course.

KEITH. H'm! Hard case! Man who reads family prayers, and lessons on Sunday forbids son to——

CHRISTINE. Ronny!

KEITH. Great Scot! I'm not saying Bill ought to marry her. She's got to stand the racket. But your Dad will have a tough job to take up that position.

DOT. Awfully funny!

CHRISTINE. What on earth d'you mean, Dot?

DOT. Morality in one eye, and your title in the other!

CHRISTINE. Rubbish!

HAROLD. You're all reckoning without your Bill.

KEITH. Ye-es. Sir William can cut him off; no mortal power can help the title going down, if Bill chooses to be such a——

[*He draws in his breath with a sharp hiss.*

HAROLD. I won't take what Bill ought to have; nor would any of you girls, I should think——

CHRISTINE AND DOT. Of course not!

KEITH. [*Patting his wife's arm*] Hardly the point, is it?

DOT. If it wasn't for mother! Freda's just as much of a lady as most girls. Why shouldn't he marry her, and go to Canada? It's what he's really fit for.

HAROLD. Steady on, Dot!

DOT. Well, imagine him in Parliament! That's what he'll come to, if he stays here—jolly for the country!

CHRISTINE. Don't be cynical! We must find a way of stopping Bill.

DOT. *Me* cynical!

CHRISTINE. Let's go and beg him, Ronny!

KEITH. No earthly! The only hope is in the girl.

DOT. She hasn't the stuff in her!

HAROLD. I say! What price young Dunning! Right about face! Poor old Dad!

CHRISTINE. It's past joking, Harold!

DOT. [*Gloomily*] Old Studdenham's better than most relations by marriage!

KEITH. Thanks !

CHRISTINE. It's ridiculous—monstrous ! It's fantastic !

HAROLD. [*Holding up his hand*] There's his horse going round. He's in !

> [*They turn from listening to the sound, to see* LADY CHESHIRE *coming from the billiard-room. She is very pale. They all rise and* DOT *puts an arm round her ; while* KEITH *pushes forward his chair.* JOAN *and* LATTER *too have come stealing back.*

LADY CHESHIRE. Thank you, Ronny !   [*She sits down.*

DOT. Mother, you're shivering ! Shall I get you a fur ?

LADY CHESHIRE. No, thanks, dear !

DOT. [*In a low voice*] Play up, mother darling !

LADY CHESHIRE. [*Straightening herself*] What sort of a run, Ronny ?

KEITH. Quite fair, M'm.   Brazier's to Caffyn's Dyke, good straight line.

LADY CHESHIRE. And the young horse ?

KEITH. Carries his ears in your mouth a bit, that's all.   [*Putting his hand on her shoulder.*] Cheer up, Mem-Sahib !

CHRISTINE. Mother, *must* anything be said to father ?   Ronny thinks it all depends on *her*.   Can't you use your influence ?

> [LADY CHESHIRE *shakes her head.*

CHRISTINE. But, mother, it's desperate.

DOT. Shut up, Chris ! Of course mother can't. We simply couldn't *beg* her to let us off !

CHRISTINE. There must be *some* way.   What do you think in your heart, mother ?

DOT. Leave mother alone !

CHRISTINE. It must be faced, now or never.

DOT. [*In a low voice*] Haven't you any self-respect ?

CHRISTINE. We shall be the laughing-stock of the whole county. Oh ! mother, do speak to her !   You know it'll be misery for both of them.   [LADY CHESHIRE *bows her head.*]   Well, then ?

> [LADY CHESHIRE *shakes her head.*

CHRISTINE. Not even for Bill's sake ?

DOT. Chris !

CHRISTINE. Well, for heaven's sake, speak to Bill again, mother ! We ought all to go on our knees to him.

LADY CHESHIRE. He's with your father now.

HAROLD. Poor old Bill !

CHRISTINE. [*Passionately*] He didn't think of *us !* That wretched girl !

LADY CHESHIRE. Chris !

CHRISTINE. There are limits.

LADY CHESHIRE. Not to self-control.

CHRISTINE. No, mother! I can't—I never shall—Something must be done! You know what Bill is. He rushes his fences so, when he gets his head down. Oh! do try! It's only fair to her, and all of us!

LADY CHESHIRE. [*Painfully*] There are things one can't do.

CHRISTINE. But it's Bill! I know you can make her give him up, if you'll only say all you can. And, after all, what's coming won't affect her as if she'd been a lady. Only *you* can do it, mother. Do back me up, all of you! It's the only way!

> [*Hypnotized by their private longing for what* CHRISTINE *has been urging, they have all fixed their eyes on* LADY CHESHIRE, *who looks from face to face, and moves her hands as if in physical pain.*

CHRISTINE. [*Softly* Mother!

> [LADY CHESHIRE *suddenly rises, looking towards the billiard-room door, listening. They all follow her eyes. She sits down again, passing her hand over her lips, as* SIR WILLIAM *enters. His hunting clothes are splashed; his face very grim and set. He walks to the fire without a glance at anyone, and stands looking down into it. Very quietly, everyone but* LADY CHESHIRE *steals away.*

LADY CHESHIRE. What have you done?

SIR WILLIAM. *You* there!

LADY CHESHIRE. Don't keep me in suspense!

SIR WILLIAM. The fool! My God! Dorothy! I didn't think I had a blackguard for a son, who was a fool into the bargain.

LADY CHESHIRE. [*Rising*] If he were a blackguard he would not be what you call a fool.

SIR WILLIAM. [*After staring angrily, makes her a slight bow*] Very well!

LADY CHESHIRE. [*In a low voice*] Bill, don't be harsh. It's all too terrible.

SIR WILLIAM. Sit down, my dear.

> [*She resumes her seat, and he turns back to the fire.*

SIR WILLIAM. In all my life I've never been face to face with a thing like this. [*Gripping the mantelpiece so hard that his hands and arms are seen shaking.*] You ask me to be calm. I am trying to be. Be good enough in turn not to take his part against me.

LADY CHESHIRE. Bill!

SIR WILLIAM. I am trying to think. I understand that you've known this—piece of news since this morning. I've known it ten minutes. Give me a little time, please. [*Then, after a silence.*] Where's the girl?

LADY CHESHIRE. In the workroom.

SIR WILLIAM. [*Raising his clenched fist*] What in God's name is he about?

LADY CHESHIRE. What have you said to him?

SIR WILLIAM. Nothing—by a miracle. [*He breaks away from the fire and walks up and down.*] My family goes back to the thirteenth century. Nowadays they laugh at that! I don't! Nowadays they laugh at everything—they even laugh at the word lady—I married *you*, and I don't. . . . Married his mother's maid! By George! Dorothy! I don't know what we've done to deserve this; it's a death blow! I'm not prepared to sit down and wait for it. By Gad! I am not. [*With sudden fierceness.*] There are plenty in these days who'll be glad enough for this to happen; plenty of these d——d Socialists and Radicals, who'll laugh their souls out over what they haven't the bowels to see's a—tragedy. I say it *would* be a tragedy; for you, and me, and all of us. You and I were brought up, and we've brought the children up, with certain beliefs, and wants, and habits. A man's past—his traditions—he can't get rid of them. They're—they're himself! [*Suddenly.*] It shan't go on.

LADY CHESHIRE. What's to prevent it?

SIR WILLIAM. I utterly forbid this piece of madness. I'll stop it.

LADY CHESHIRE. But the thing we can't stop.

SIR WILLIAM. Provision must be made.

LADY CHESHIRE. The unwritten law!

SIR WILLIAM. What! [*Suddenly perceiving what she is alluding to.*] You're thinking of young—young—— [*Shortly.*] I don't see the connection.

LADY CHESHIRE. What's so awful, is that the boy's trying to do what's loyal—and we—his father and mother——!

SIR WILLIAM. I'm not going to see my eldest son ruin his life. I must think this out.

LADY CHESHIRE. [*Beneath her breath*] I've tried that—it doesn't help.

SIR WILLIAM. This girl, who was born on the estate, had the run of the house—brought up with money earned from me—nothing but kindness from all of us; she's broken the common rules of gratitude and decency—she lured him on, I haven't a doubt!

LADY CHESHIRE. [*To herself*] In a way, I suppose.

SIR WILLIAM. What! It's ruin. We've always been here. Who the deuce are we if we leave this place? D'you think we could stay? Go out and meet everybody just as if nothing had happened? Good-bye to any prestige, political, social, or anything! This is the sort of business nothing can get over. I've seen it before. As to that other matter—it's soon forgotten—constantly happening—Why, my own grandfather——!

LADY CHESHIRE. Does he help?

7*

SIR WILLIAM. [*Stares before him in silence—suddenly*] You must go to the girl. She's soft. She'll never hold out against you.

LADY CHESHIRE. I did before I knew what was in front of her— I said all I could. I can't go again now. How can I, Bill?

SIR WILLIAM. What *are* you going to do, then—fold your hands? [*Then as* LADY CHESHIRE *makes a movement of distress.*] If he marries her, I've done with him. As far as I'm concerned he'll cease to exist. The title—I can't help. My God! Does that meet your wishes?

LADY CHESHIRE. [*With sudden fire*] You've no right to put such an alternative to me. I'd give ten years of my life to prevent this marriage. I'll go to Bill. I'll beg him on my knees.

SIR WILLIAM. Then why can't you go to the girl? She deserves no consideration. It's not a question of morality. Morality be d——d!

LADY CHESHIRE. But not self-respect.

SIR WILLIAM. What! You're his mother!

LADY CHESHIRE. I have been to her; I've tried; I [*putting her hand to her throat*] couldn't get it out.

SIR WILLIAM. [*Staring at her*] You won't?

LADY CHESHIRE. I can't, Bill. It seems so—caddish, so mean.

SIR WILLIAM. In the whole course of our married life, Dorothy, I've never known you set yourself up against me. I resent this, I warn you—I resent it. Send the girl to me.

[*With a look back at him,* LADY CHESHIRE *goes out into the corridor.*

SIR WILLIAM. This is a nice end to my day!

[*He takes a small china cup from off the mantelpiece; it breaks with the pressure of his hand, and falls into the fireplace. While he stands looking at it blankly, there is a knock.*

SIR WILLIAM. Come in!   [FREDA *enters from the corridor.*

SIR WILLIAM. I've asked you to be good enough to come, in order that— [*pointing to chair*] You may sit down.

[*But though she advances two or three steps, she does not sit down.*

SIR WILLIAM. This is a sad business.

FREDA. [*Below her breath*] Yes, Sir William.

SIR WILLIAM. [*Becoming conscious of the depths of feeling before him*] I—er—are you attached to my son?

FREDA. [*In a whisper*] Yes.

SIR WILLIAM. It's very painful to me to have to do this.

[*He turns away from her and speaks to the fire.*] I sent for you—to—ask— [*quickly*] How old are you?

FREDA. Twenty-two.

SIR WILLIAM. [*More resolutely*] Do you expect me to—sanction such a mad idea as a marriage?

FREDA. I don't expect anything.

SIR WILLIAM. You know—you haven't earned the right to be considered.

FREDA. Not yet!

SIR WILLIAM. What! That oughtn't to help you! On the contrary. Now brace yourself up, and listen to me!

> [*She stands waiting to hear her sentence.* SIR WILLIAM *looks at her; and his glance gradually wavers.*

SIR WILLIAM. I've not a word to say for my son. He's behaved like a scamp.

FREDA. Oh! no!

SIR WILLIAM. [*With a silencing gesture*] At the same time— What made you forget yourself? You've no excuse, you know.

FREDA. No.

SIR WILLIAM. You'll deserve all you'll get. Confound it! To expect me to— It's intolerable! Do you know where my son is?

FREDA. [*Faintly*] I think he's in the billiard-room with my lady.

SIR WILLIAM. [*With renewed resolution*] I wanted to—to put it to you—as a—as a—what! [*Seeing her stand so absolutely motionless, looking at him, he turns abruptly, and opens the billiard-room door.*] I'll speak to him first. Come in here, please! [*To* FREDA.] Go in, and wait!

> [LADY CHESHIRE *and* BILL *come in, and* FREDA *passing them, goes into the billiard-room to wait.*

SIR WILLIAM. [*Speaking with a pause between each sentence*] Your mother and I have spoken of this—calamity. I imagine that even you have some dim perception of the monstrous nature of it. I must tell you this : If you do this mad thing, you fend for yourself. You'll receive nothing from me now or hereafter. I consider that only due to the position our family has always held here. Your brother will take your place. We shall get on as best we can without you. [*There is a dead silence, till he adds sharply.*] Well!

BILL. I shall marry her.

LADY CHESHIRE. Oh! Bill! Without love—without anything!

BILL. All right, mother! [*To* SIR WILLIAM.] You've mistaken your man, sir. Because I'm a rotter in one way, I'm not necessarily a rotter in all. You put the butt end of the pistol to Dunning's head yesterday, you put the other end to mine to-day. Well! [*He turns round to go out.*] Let the d——d thing off!

LADY CHESHIRE. Bill!

BILL. [*Turning to her*] I'm not going to leave her in the lurch.

SIR WILLIAM. Do me the justice to admit that I have not attempted to persuade you to.

BILL. No! you've chucked me out. I don't see what else you could have done under the circumstances. It's quite all right. But if you wanted me to throw her over, father, you went the wrong way to work, that's all; neither you nor I are very good at seeing consequences.

SIR WILLIAM. Do you realize your position?

BILL. [*Grimly*] I've a fair notion of it.

SIR WILLIAM. [*With a sudden outburst*] You have none—not the faintest, brought up as you've been.

BILL. I didn't bring myself up.

SIR WILLIAM. [*With a movement of uncontrolled anger, to which his son responds*] You—ungrateful young dog!

LADY CHESHIRE. How can you—both?

[*They drop their eyes, and stand silent.*]

SIR WILLIAM. [*With grimly suppressed emotion*] I am speaking under the stress of very great pain—some consideration is due to me. This is a disaster which I never expected to have to face. It is a matter which I naturally can never hope to forget. I shall carry this down to my death. We shall all of us do that. I have had the misfortune all my life to believe in our position here—to believe that we counted for something—that the country wanted us. I have tried to do my duty by that position. I find in one moment that it is gone—smoke —gone. My philosophy is not equal to that. To countenance this marriage would be unnatural.

BILL. I know. I'm sorry. I've got her into this—I don't see any other way out. It's a bad business for me, father, as well as for you——

[*He stops, seeing that* JACKSON *has come in, and is standing there waiting.*]

JACKSON. Will you speak to Studdenham, Sir William? It's about young Dunning.

[*After a moment of dead silence,* SIR WILLIAM *nods, and the butler withdraws.*]

BILL. [*Stolidly*] He'd better be told.

SIR WILLIAM. He shall be.

[STUDDENHAM *enters, and touches his forehead to them all with a comprehensive gesture.*]

STUDDENHAM. Good evenin', my lady! Evenin', Sir William! Glad to be able to tell you, the young man's to do the proper thing. Asked me to let you know, Sir William. Banns'll be up next Sunday. [*Struck by the silence, he looks round at all three in turn, and suddenly seeing that* LADY CHESHIRE *is shivering.*] Beg pardon, my lady, you're shakin' like a leaf!

BILL. [*Blurting it out*] I've a painful piece of news for you, Studdenham; I'm engaged to your daughter. We're to be married at once.

STUDDENHAM. I—don't—understand you—sir.

BILL. The fact is, I've behaved badly; but I mean to put it straight.

STUDDENHAM. I'm a little deaf. Did you say—my daughter?

SIR WILLIAM. There's no use mincing matters, Studdenham. It's a thunderbolt—young Dunning's case over again.

STUDDENHAM. I don't rightly follow. She's— You've— ! I must see my daughter. Have the goodness to send for her, m'lady.

[LADY CHESHIRE *goes to the billiard-room, and calls:* "FREDA, *come here, please.*"

STUDDENHAM. [*To* SIR WILLIAM] You tell me that my daughter's in the position of that girl owing to your son? Men ha' been shot for less.

BILL. If you like to have a pot at me, Studdenham—you're welcome.

STUDDENHAM. [*Averting his eyes from* BILL *at the sheer idiocy of this sequel to his words*] I've been in your service five and twenty years, Sir William; but this is man to man—this is !

SIR WILLIAM. I don't deny that, Studdenham.

STUDDENHAM. [*With eyes shifting in sheer anger*] No—'twouldn't be very easy. Did I understand him to say that he offers her marriage?

SIR WILLIAM. You did.

STUDDENHAM. [*Into his beard*] Well—that's something! [*Moving his hands as if wringing the neck of a bird.*] I'm tryin' to see the rights o' this.

SIR WILLIAM. [*Bitterly*] You've all your work cut out for you, Studdenham.

[*Again* STUDDENHAM *makes the unconscious wringing movement with his hands.*

LADY CHESHIRE. [*Turning from it with a sort of horror*] Don't, Studdenham. Please !

STUDDENHAM. What's that, m'lady ?

LADY CHESHIRE. [*Under her breath*] Your—your—hands.

[*While* STUDDENHAM *is still staring at her,* FREDA *is seen standing in the doorway, like a black ghost.*

STUDDENHAM. Come here ! You ! [FREDA *moves a few steps towards her father.*] When did you start this?

FREDA. [*Almost inaudibly*] In the summer, father.

LADY CHESHIRE. Don't be harsh to her !

STUDDENHAM. Harsh ! [*His eyes again move from side to side as if pain and anger had bewildered them. Then looking sideways at* FREDA, *but in a gentler voice.*] And when did you tell him about—what's come to you?

FREDA. Last night.

STUDDENHAM. Oh ! [*With sudden menace.*] You young—— ! [*He makes a convulsive movement of one hand ; then, in the silence, seems to lose grip of his thoughts, and puts his hand up to his head.*] I want to clear me mind a bit—I don't see it plain at all. [*Without looking at* BILL.] 'Tis said there's been an offer of marriage?

BILL. I've made it, I stick to it.

STUDDENHAM. Oh? [*With slow, puzzled anger.*] I want time to get the pith o' this. You don't say anything, Sir William?

SIR WILLIAM. The facts are all before you.

STUDDENHAM. [*Scarcely moving his lips*] M'lady?

[LADY CHESHIRE *is silent.*

STUDDENHAM. [*Stammering*] My girl was—was good enough for any man. It's not for him that's—that's—to look down on her. [*To* FREDA.] You hear the handsome offer that's been made you? Well? [FREDA *moistens her lips and tries to speak, but cannot.*] If nobody's to speak a word, we won't get much forrarder. I'd like for you to say what's in your mind, Sir William.

SIR WILLIAM. I—If my son marries her he'll have to make his own way.

STUDDENHAM. [*Savagely*] I'm not puttin' thought to that.

SIR WILLIAM. I didn't suppose you were, Studdenham. It appears to rest with your daughter. [*He suddenly takes out his handkerchief, and puts it to his forehead.*] Infernal fires they make up here!

[LADY CHESHIRE, *who is again shivering desperately, as if with intense cold, makes a violent attempt to control her shuddering.*

STUDDENHAM. [*Suddenly*] There's luxuries that's got to be paid for. [*To* FREDA.] Speak up, now.

[FREDA *turns slowly and looks up at* SIR WILLIAM; *he involuntarily raises his hand to his mouth. Her eyes travel on to* LADY CHESHIRE, *who faces her, but so deadly pale that she looks as if she were going to faint. The girl's gaze passes on to* BILL, *standing rigid, with his jaw set.*

FREDA. I want— [*Then flinging her arm up over her eyes, she turns from him.*] No!

SIR WILLIAM. Ah!

[*At that sound of profound relief,* STUDDENHAM, *whose eyes have been following his daughter's, moves towards* SIR WILLIAM, *all his emotion turned into sheer angry pride.*

STUDDENHAM. Don't be afraid, Sir William! We want none of you! She'll not force herself where she's not welcome. She may ha' slipped her good name, but she'll keep her proper pride. I'll have no *charity marriage* in my family.

SIR WILLIAM. Steady, Studdenham!

STUDDENHAM. If the young gentleman has tired of her in three months, as a blind man can see by the looks of him—she's not for him!

BILL. [*Stepping forward*] I'm ready to make it up to her.

STUDDENHAM. Keep back, there? [*He takes hold of* FREDA, *and looks around him.*] Well! She's not the first this has happened to since the world began, an' she won't be the last. Come away, now, come away!

[*Taking* FREDA *by the shoulders, he guides her towards the door.*

SIR WILLIAM. D——n it, Studdenham! Give us credit for something!

STUDDENHAM. [*Turning—his face and eyes lighted up by a sort of smiling snarl*] Ah! I do that, Sir William. But there's things that can't be undone!   [*He follows* FREDA *out.*

> [*As the door closes,* SIR WILLIAM'S *calm gives way. He staggers past his wife, and sinks heavily, as though exhausted, into a chair by the fire.* BILL, *following* FREDA *and* STUDDENHAM, *has stopped at the shut door.* LADY CHESHIRE *moves swiftly close to him. The door of the billiard-room is opened, and* DOT *appears. With a glance round, she crosses quickly to her mother.*

DOT. [*In a low voice*] Mabel's just going, mother! [*Almost whispering.*] Where's Freda? Is it—— Has she really had the pluck?

> [LADY CHESHIRE *bending her head for "Yes," goes out into the billiard-room.* DOT *clasps her hands together, and standing there in the middle of the room, looks from her brother to her father, from her father to her brother. A quaint little pitying smile comes on her lips. She gives a faint shrug of her shoulders.*

The curtain falls.

THE LITTLE DREAM

CHARACTERS

SEELCHEN, *a mountain girl*
LAMOND, *a climber*
FELSMAN, *a guide*

CHARACTERS IN THE DREAM

THE GREAT HORN
THE COW HORN } *mountains*
THE WINE HORN

THE EDELWEISS
THE ALPENROSE
THE GENTIAN } *flowers*
THE MOUNTAIN DANDELION

FIGURES IN THE DREAM

MOTH CHILDREN
DANCING LIGHTS
DEATH BY SLUMBER
DEATH BY DROWNING

FLOWER CHILDREN
GOATHERD
GOAT BOYS
THE FORMS OF SLEEP

SCENE I

It is just after sunset of an August evening. The scene is a room in a mountain hut, furnished only with a dresser and a low broad window seat. Through this window three rocky peaks are seen by the light of a moon, which is slowly whitening the last hues of sunset. An oil lamp is burning. SEELCHEN, *a mountain girl, eighteen years old, is humming a folk-song, and putting away in a cupboard freshly washed soup-bowls and glasses. She is dressed in a tight-fitting black velvet bodice, square-cut at the neck, and partly filled in with a gay handkerchief, coloured rose-pink, blue, and golden, like the alpenrose, the gentian, and the mountain dandelion; alabaster beads, pale as edelweiss, are round her throat; her stiffened, white linen sleeves finish at the elbow; and her full well-worn skirt is of gentian blue. The two thick plaits of her hair are crossed, and turned round her head. As she puts away the last bowl, there is a knock; and* LAMOND *opens the outer door. He is young, tanned, and good-looking, dressed like a climber, and carries a plaid, a rucksack, and an ice-axe.*

LAMOND. Good evening!

SEELCHEN. Good evening, gentle Sir!

LAMOND. My name is Lamond. I'm very late I fear.

SEELCHEN. Do you wish to sleep here?

LAMOND. Please.

SEELCHEN. All the beds are full—it is a pity. I will call Mother.

LAMOND. I've come to go up the Great Horn at sunrise.

SEELCHEN. [*Awed*] The Great Horn! But he is impossible.

LAMOND. I am going to try that.

SEELCHEN. There is the Wine Horn, and the Cow Horn.

LAMOND. I have climbed them.

SEELCHEN. But he is so dangerous—it is perhaps—death.

LAMOND. Oh! that's all right! One must take one's chance.

SEELCHEN. And father has hurt his foot. For guide, there is only Hans Felsman.

LAMOND. The celebrated Felsman?

SEELCHEN. [*Nodding; then looking at him with admiration*] Are you that Herr Lamond who has climbed all our little mountains this year?

LAMOND. All but that big fellow.

SEELCHEN. We have heard of you. Will you not wait a day for father's foot?

LAMOND. Ah! no. I must go back home to-morrow.

SEELCHEN. The gracious Sir is in a hurry.

LAMOND. [*Looking at her intently*] Alas !

SEELCHEN. Are you from a great city ?   Is it very big ?

LAMOND. Six million souls.

SEELCHEN. Oh !   [*After a little pause.*] I have seen Cortina twice.

LAMOND. Do you live here all the year ?

SEELCHEN. In winter in the valley.

LAMOND. And don't you want to see the world ?

SEELCHEN. Sometimes.   [*Going to a door, she calls softly.*] Hans ! [*Then pointing to another door.*] There are seven German gentlemen asleep in there !

LAMOND. Oh, God !

SEELCHEN. Please !   They are here to see the sunrise.   [*She picks up a little book that has dropped from* LAMOND'*s pocket.*] I have read several books.

LAMOND. This is by a great poet.   Do you never make poetry here, and dream dreams, among your mountains ?

SEELCHEN. [*Slowly shaking her head*] See ! It is the full moon.
    [*While they stand at the window looking at the moon, there enters
        a lean, well-built, taciturn young man dressed in Loden.*

SEELCHEN. Hans !

FELSMAN. [*In a deep voice*] The gentleman wishes me ?

SEELCHEN. [*Awed*] The Great Horn for to-morrow.   [*Whispering to him.*] It is the celebrated city one.

FELSMAN. The Great Horn is not possible.

LAMOND. You say that ?   And you're the famous Felsman ?

FELSMAN. [*Grimly*] We start at dawn.

SEELCHEN. It is the first time for years !

LAMOND. [*Placing his plaid and rucksack on the window bench*] Can I sleep here ?

SEELCHEN. I will see !   [*She runs out.*

FELSMAN. [*Taking blankets from the cupboard and spreading them on the window seat*] So !

            [*As he goes out into the air,* SEELCHEN *comes slipping in again.*

SEELCHEN. There is still one bed.   This is too hard for you.

LAMOND. Oh !   thanks ; but that's all right.

SEELCHEN. To please me !

LAMOND. May I ask your name ?

SEELCHEN. Seelchen.

LAMOND. Little soul, that means—doesn't it ?   To please you I would sleep with seven German gentlemen.

SEELCHEN. Oh !   no ; it is not necessary.

LAMOND. [*With a grave bow*] At your service, then.

                                                [*He prepares to go.*

SEELCHEN. Is it very nice in towns, in the World, where you come from ?

LAMOND. When I'm there I would be here ; but when I'm here I would be there.

SEELCHEN. [*Clasping her hands*] That is like me—but *I* am always *here.*

LAMOND. Ah ! yes ; there is no one like you in towns.

SEELCHEN. In two places one cannot be.   [*Suddenly.*] In the towns there are theatres, and there is beautiful fine work, and—dancing, and—churches—and trains—and all the things in books—and——

LAMOND. Misery.

SEELCHEN. But there is life.

LAMOND. And there is death.

SEELCHEN. To-morrow, when you have climbed—will you not come back ?

LAMOND. No.

SEELCHEN. You have all the world ; and I have nothing.

LAMOND. Except Felsman, and the mountains.

SEELCHEN. It is not good to eat only bread.

LAMOND. [*Looking at her hard*] *I* would like to eat *you !*

SEELCHEN. But I am not nice ; I am full of big wants—like the cheese with holes.

LAMOND. I shall come again.

SEELCHEN. There will be no more hard mountains left to climb. And if it is not exciting, you do not care.

LAMOND. O wise little soul !

SEELCHEN. No.   I am not wise.   In here it is always aching.

LAMOND. For the moon ?

SEELCHEN. Yes.   [*Then suddenly.*] From the big world you will remember ?

LAMOND. [*Taking her hand*] There is nothing in the big world so sweet as this.

SEELCHEN. [*Wisely*] But there is the big world itself.

LAMOND. May I kiss you, for good night ?

[*She puts her face forward ; and he kisses her cheek, and, suddenly, her lips.   Then as she draws away.*

LAMOND. I am sorry, little soul.

SEELCHEN. That's all right !

LAMOND. [*Taking the candle*] Dream well !   Good night !

SEELCHEN. [*Softly*] Good night !

FELSMAN. [*Coming in from the air, and eyeing them*] It is cold—it will be fine.

    [LAMOND, *still looking back, goes ; and* FELSMAN *waits for him to pass.*

SEELCHEN. [*From the window seat*] It was hard for him here, I thought.

[*He goes up to her, stays a moment looking down, then bends and kisses her hungrily.*

SEELCHEN. Art thou angry?

[*He does not answer, but turning out the lamp, goes into an inner room.*

[SEELCHEN *sits gazing through the window at the peaks bathed in full moonlight. Then, drawing the blankets about her, she snuggles down on the window seat.*

SEELCHEN. [*In a sleepy voice*] They kissed me—both. [*She sleeps. The scene falls quite dark.*

SCENE II

The scene is slowly illuminated as by dawn. SEELCHEN *is still lying on the window seat. She sits up, freeing her face and hands from the blankets, changing the swathings of deep sleep for the filmy coverings of a dream. The wall of the hut has vanished; there is nothing between her and the three dark mist-veiled mountains save a trough of black space.*
Close to SEELCHEN, *on the edge of the trough of dark space that divides her from the mountains, are four little flower figures,* EDELWEISS *and* GENTIAN, MOUNTAIN DANDELION *and* ALPENROSE, *peering up at her through the darkness. On their heads are crowns of their several flowers, all powdered with dewdrops which ring like little bells.*

SEELCHEN. Oh! They have faces!
   [*All around the peaks there is nothing but almost blue-black sky. The peaks brighten.*

EDELWEISS. [*In a tiny voice*] Would you? Would you? Would you? Ah! ha!

GENTIAN, M. DANDELION, ALPENROSE. [*With their bells ringing enviously.*] Oo-oo-oo!
   [*And suddenly the Peak of* THE COW HORN *speaks in a voice as of one unaccustomed.*

THE COW HORN. I am the mountains. Amongst kine and my black-brown sheep I live; I am silence, and monotony; I am the solemn hills. I am fierceness, and the mountain wind; clean pasture, and wild rest. Look in my eyes, love *me* alone!

SEELCHEN. [*Breathless*] The Cow Horn! He is speaking—for Felsman and the mountains. It is the half of my heart!

   [THE FLOWERS *laugh happily.*

THE COW HORN. I stalk the eternal hills—I drink the mountain snows. My eyes are the colour of burned wine; in them lives melancholy. The lowing of the kine, the wind, the sound of falling rocks, the running of the torrents; no other talk know I. Thoughts simple, and blood hot, strength huge—the cloak of gravity.

SEELCHEN. Yes, yes, I want him. He is strong !

THE COW HORN. Little soul ! Hold to me ! Love me ! Live with me under the stars !

SEELCHEN. [*Below her breath*] I am afraid.

[*And suddenly the Peak of* THE WINE HORN *speaks in a youth's voice.*

THE WINE HORN. I am the town—the will-o'-the-wisp that dances through the streets ; I am the cooing dove, from the plane-trees' and the chestnuts' shade. From day to day all changes, where I burn my incense to my thousand little gods. In white palaces I dwell, and passionate dark alleys. The life of men in crowds is mine—of lamplight in the streets at dawn. [*Softly.*] I have a thousand loves, and never one too long ; for I am nimbler than your heifers playing in the sunshine.

[THE FLOWERS, *ringing in alarm, cry :* " *We know them !* "

THE WINE HORN. I hear the rustling of the birth and death of pleasure ; and the rattling of swift wheels. I hear the hungry oaths of men ; and love kisses in the airless night.   Without *me*, little soul, you starve and die.

SEELCHEN. He is speaking for the gentle Sir, and the big world of the Town. It pulls my heart.

THE WINE HORN. My thoughts surpass in number the flowers in your meadows ; they fly more swiftly than your eagles on the wind. I drink the wine of aspiration, and the drug of disillusion. Thus am I never dull !

SEELCHEN. I am afraid.

THE WINE HORN. Love *me*, little soul ! I paint life fifty colours. I make a thousand pretty things ! I twine about your heart.

SEELCHEN. He is honey !

[THE FLOWERS *ring their bells jealously and cry :* " *Bitter !* *Bitter !* "

THE COW HORN. *Stay* with me, Seelchen ! I wake thee with the crystal air.   [THE FLOWERS *laugh happily.*

THE WINE HORN. *Come* with me, Seelchen ! My fan, Variety, shall wake you !   [THE FLOWERS *moan.*

SEELCHEN. [*In grief*] My heart ! It is torn !

THE WINE HORN. With *me*, little soul, you shall race in the streets, and peep at all secrets. We will hold hands, and fly like the thistle-down.

M. DANDELION. My puff-balls fly faster !

THE WINE HORN. I will show you the sea.

GENTIAN. My blue is deeper !

THE WINE HORN. I will shower on you blushes.

ALPENROSE. I can blush redder !

THE WINE HORN. Little soul, listen ! My Jewels ! Silk ! Velvet !

EDELWEISS. I am softer than velvet!

THE WINE HORN. [*Proudly*] My wonderful rags!

THE FLOWERS. [*Moaning*] Of those we have none.

SEELCHEN. He has all things.

THE COW HORN. Mine are the clouds with the dark silvered wings; mine are the rocks on fire with the sun; and the dewdrops cooler than pearls. Away from my breath of snow and sweet grass, thou wilt droop, little soul.

THE WINE HORN. The dark Clove is *my* fragrance!

SEELCHEN. [*Distracted*] Oh! it is hard!

THE COW HORN. *I* will never desert thee.

THE WINE HORN. A hundred times *I* will desert you, a hundred times come back, and kiss you.

SEELCHEN. [*Whispering*] Peace for my heart!

THE COW HORN. With me thou shalt lie on the warm wild thyme.   [THE FLOWERS *laugh happily*.

THE WINE HORN. With me you shall lie on a bed of dove's feathers.
                                       [THE FLOWERS *moan*.

THE WINE HORN. *I* will give you old wine.

THE COW HORN. *I* will give thee new milk.

THE WINE HORN. Hear my song!
                    [*From far away comes a sound as of mandolins.*

SEELCHEN. [*Clasping her breast*] My heart—it is leaving me!

THE COW HORN. Hear my song!
          [*From the distance floats the piping of a Shepherd's reed.*

SEELCHEN. [*Curving her hand at her ears*] The piping! Ah!

THE COW HORN. *Stay* with me, Seelchen!

THE WINE HORN. *Come* with me, Seelchen!

THE COW HORN. I give thee certainty!

THE WINE HORN. I give you chance!

THE COW HORN. I give thee peace.

THE WINE HORN. I give you change.

THE COW HORN. I give thee stillness.

THE WINE HORN. I give you voice.

THE COW HORN. I give thee one love.

THE WINE HORN. I give you many.

SEELCHEN. [*As if the words were torn from her heart*] Both, both—I will love!
                    [*And suddenly the Peak of* THE GREAT HORN *speaks.*

THE GREAT HORN. And both thou shalt love, little soul! Thou shalt lie on the hills with Silence; and dance in the cities with Knowledge. Both shall possess thee! The sun and the moon on the mountains shall burn thee; the lamps of the Town singe thy wings, small Moth! Each shall seem all the world to thee, each shall seem as thy grave! Thy heart is a feather blown from one mouth to

the other. But be not afraid ! For the life of a man is for all loves
in turn. 'Tis a little raft moored, then sailing out into the blue ; a
tune caught in a hush, then whispering on ; a new-born babe, half
courage and half sleep. There is a hidden rhythm. Change, Quietude.
Chance, Certainty. The One, The Many. Burn on—thou pretty
flame, trying to eat the world ! Thou shalt come to me at last, my
little soul !

     [SEELCHEN, *enraptured, stretches her arms to embrace the sight and*
        sound, but all fades slowly into dark sleep.

SCENE III

The dark scene again becomes glamorous under a night sky. SEELCHEN *is*
standing with her hand stretched out towards the gateway of a Town from
which is streaming a pathway of light. On one side of the gate stands the
glowing figure of a youth. On the other side of the gateway is a cloaked
statue in shadow. Above the centre of the gateway is a dimly seen
sphynx-like stone head.

The Youth of THE WINE HORN *sings :*
  " *Little star soul*
    Through the frost fields of night
    Roaming alone, disconsolate—
    From out the cold
    I call thee in—
    Striking my dark mandolin—
    Beneath this moon of gold."
SEELCHEN. [*Whispering*] Is it the Town—the big world ?
  The Youth of THE WINE HORN *sings on :*
  " *Pretty grey moth,*
    Where the strange candles shine,
    Seeking for warmth, so desperate—
    Ah ! fluttering dove
    I bid thee win—
    Striking my dark mandolin—
    The crimson flame of love."
SEELCHEN. [*Gazing enraptured at the gateway*] In there it is warm
and light !

     [*As she speaks, from either side come moth-children, meeting and*
        fluttering up the path of light to the gateway ; then wheeling
        aside, they form again, and again flutter forward.
  SEELCHEN. [*Holding out her hands*] They are real— Their wings
are windy.

           [*They rush past her and vanish into the Town.*

The Youth of THE WINE HORN *sings on :*
> " *Lips of my song,*
> *To the white maiden's heart*
> *Go ye, and whisper, passionate,*
> *These words that burn—*
> ' *O listening one !*
> *Love that flieth past is gone,*
> *Nor ever may return !* ' "

[SEELCHEN *runs towards him—but the glow around him fades, he has become shadow. There in the gateway stands* LAMOND *in a dark cloak.*

SEELCHEN. It is *you !*

LAMOND. Without my little soul I am cold.   Come !

[*He holds out his arms to her.*

SEELCHEN. Shall I be safe ?

LAMOND. What is safety ?   Are you safe in your mountains ?

SEELCHEN. Where am I, here ?

LAMOND. The Town.

[*Smiling, he points to the gateway. There come dancing out all the firefly lights of the streets.*

SEELCHEN. [*Whispering*] What are they ?

LAMOND. The lights, little one—street lights.   The lamps—the gold of life !

SEELCHEN. Are they always so bright ?

[*The Youth of* THE WINE HORN *is again illumined. He strikes a loud chord ; then, as* SEELCHEN *moves towards that sound, the glow dies ; there is again only blue shadow, and all the firefly lights have vanished through the gateway.*

SEELCHEN. Is he laughing at me ?

LAMOND. Come !

SEELCHEN. I am afraid !

LAMOND. Of what is new ?   Would you know but one-half of the moon ?   Ah !   Little Soul will you live for ever with your goats— when I can show you such wonders ?

SEELCHEN. Are they good ?

LAMOND. They are everything.

SEELCHEN. [*Creeping a little nearer to the gateway*] It is so strange and bright in the Town !   Is it not dark in there too ?

LAMOND. I will keep the darkness from you with love.

SEELCHEN. Oh ! but I do not love.

LAMOND. Child !   To love is to live—seeking for wonder.   When a feather flies is it not loving the wind, the unknown ?   If darkness and light did not change, could we breathe ?   [*And as she draws nearer.*] To love is to peer over the edge, and, spying the little grey flower, to climb down !   It has wings ; it has flown—again you must climb ;

it shivers, 'tis but air in your hand—you must crawl, you must cling, you must leap, and still it is there and not there—for the grey flower flits like a moth, and the wind of its wings is all you shall catch.   But your eyes shall be shining, your cheeks shall be burning, your breast shall be panting.—Ah! little heart! [*The scene falls darker.*] And when the night comes—there it is still, thistledown blown on the dark, and your white hands will reach for it, and your honey breath waft it, and never, never, shall you grasp it—but life shall be lovely. [*His voice dies to a whisper.   He stretches out his arms.*] Come to my Town!— Come!

SEELCHEN. [*Touching his breast*] I will come.

LAMOND. [*Drawing her to the gateway*] Love me!

SEELCHEN. I love!

> [*The mandolin twangs out; they pass through into the Town. Illumined in his crimson glow, the Youth of* THE WINE HORN *is seen again.   And slowly to the chords of his mandolin he begins to sing :*

" *The windy hours through darkness fly—*
Canst hear them, little heart ?
New loves are born, and old loves die,
And kissing lips must part.
The dusky bees of passing years—
Canst see them, soul of mine—
From flower and flower supping tears,
And pale sweet honey wine ?

> [*His voice grows strange and passionate.*]

" *O flame that treads the marsh of time,*
Flitting for ever low,
Where, through the black enchanted slime,
We, desperate, following go—
Untimely fire, we bid thee stay !
Into dark air above,
The golden gipsy thins away—
So has it been with love ! "

> [*While he is singing it falls dark, save for the glow around him.   As his song ends he fades away, and the dawn breaks.   Then from the dark gateway of the Town, in the chill grey light,* SEELCHEN *comes forth.   She is pale, as if wan with living ; her eyes like pitch against the powdery whiteness of her face.*

SEELCHEN. My heart is old.

> [*But as she speaks from far away is heard a faint chiming of* COW- BELLS *; and whilst she stands listening,* LAMOND *appears in the gateway of the Town.*

LAMOND. Little soul !

SEELCHEN. You !   Always you !

LAMOND. I have new wonders. [SEELCHEN *shakes her head.*] I swear it. You have not tired of me, who am never the same. That cannot be.

SEELCHEN. Listen !   [*The chime of* THE COWBELLS *is heard again.*

LAMOND. [*Jealously*] The music of dull sleep ! Has life, then, with me been sorrow ?

SEELCHEN. I do not regret.

LAMOND. Come !

SEELCHEN. [*Pointing to her breast*] The bird is tired with flying. [*Touching her lips.*] The flowers have no dew.

LAMOND. Would you leave me ?

SEELCHEN. See !

> [*There, in a streak of the dawn, close to the gateway, but pointing away from the Town, the dim cloaked statue has turned into the* Shepherd *of* THE COW HORN.

LAMOND. What is it ?

SEELCHEN. My mountains !

LAMOND. There is nothing. [*He holds her fast.*] Do not go ! Do not go ! I have given you the marvels of my town. I will give you more ! [*But* SEELCHEN *turns from him.*] If with you I may no longer live, then together let us die ! See ! Here are sweet Deaths by Slumber and by Drowning !

> [*From the dim gateway of the Town come forth the shadowy forms,* DEATH BY SLUMBER *and* DEATH BY DROWNING, *who dance slowly towards* SEELCHEN, *stand smiling at her, and as slowly dance away.*

SEELCHEN. [*Following*] Yes. They are good and sweet.

> [*While she moves again towards the Town* LAMOND'S *face becomes transfigured with joy. But just as she reaches the gateway there is heard again the distant chime of* COWBELLS, *and the sound of the blowing of pipes; the Shepherd of* THE COW HORN *sings:*

> " To the wild grass come, and the dull far roar
> Of the falling rock ; to the flowery meads
> Of thy mountain home, where the eagles soar,
> And the grizzled flock in the sunshine feeds.
> To the Alp, where I, in the pale light crowned
> With the moon's thin horns, to my pasture roam,
> To the silent sky, and the wistful sound
> Of the rosy dawns—my daughter, come ! "

> [*While he sings, the sun has risen; and* SEELCHEN *has turned, with parted lips, and hands stretched out; and the Forms of Death have vanished back into the Town.*

SEELCHEN. I come.

LAMOND. [*Clasping her knees*] Little soul ! Must I then die, like a gnat when the sun goes down ? Without *you* I am nothing.

SEELCHEN. [*Releasing herself*] Poor heart—I am gone!

LAMOND. It is dark. [*He covers his face with his cloak, in the gateway of the Town.*]

[*Then as* SEELCHEN *reaches the Shepherd of* THE COW HORN, *there is blown a long note of a pipe; the scene falls black; and there rises a far, continual, mingled sound of Cowbells, and Flower-Bells, and Pipes.*]

SCENE IV

The scene slowly brightens with the misty flush of dawn. SEELCHEN *stands on a green alp, with, all around, nothing but blue sky. A slip of a crescent moon is lying on her back. On a low rock sits a brown-faced* GOATHERD *blowing on a pipe, and the four* FLOWER-CHILDREN *are dancing in their shifts of grey-white, and blue, rose-pink, and burnt gold. Their bells are ringing, as they pelt each other with flowers of their own colours; and each in turn, wheeling, flings one flower at* SEELCHEN, *who puts them to her lips and eyes.*

SEELCHEN. The dew. [*She moves towards the rock.*] Goatherd!

[*But* THE FLOWERS *encircle her; and when they wheel away he has vanished. She turns to* THE FLOWERS, *but they too vanish. The veils of mist are rising.*]

SEELCHEN. Gone! [*She rubs her eyes; then turning once more to the rock, sees* FELSMAN *standing there, with his arms folded.*] Thou!

FELSMAN. So thou hast come—like a sick heifer to be healed. Was it good in the Town—that kept thee so long?

SEELCHEN. I do not regret.

FELSMAN. Why then return?

SEELCHEN. I was tired.

FELSMAN. Never again shalt thou go from me!

SEELCHEN. [*Mocking*] With what wilt thou keep me?

FELSMAN. [*Grasping her*] Thus.

SEELCHEN. I have known Change—I am no timid maid.

FELSMAN. [*Moodily*] Aye, thou art different. Thine eyes are hollow—thou art white-faced.

SEELCHEN. [*Still mocking*] Then what hast thou here that shall keep me?

FELSMAN. The sun.

SEELCHEN. To burn me.

FELSMAN. The air.   [*There is a faint wailing of wind.*

SEELCHEN. To freeze me.

FELSMAN. The silence.   [*The noise of the wind dies away.*

SEELCHEN. Yes, it is *lonely*.

FELSMAN. The flowers shall dance to thee.

[*And to a ringing of their bells,* THE FLOWERS *come dancing ; till, one by one, they cease, and sink down, nodding, falling asleep.*

SEELCHEN. See ! Even they grow sleepy here !

FELSMAN. The goats shall wake them.

[THE GOATHERD *is seen again sitting upright on his rock and piping. And there come four little brown, wild-eyed, naked Boys, with Goat's legs and feet, who dance gravely in and out of the sleeping* FLOWERS ; *and* THE FLOWERS *wake, spring up, and fly ; till each Goat, catching his flower, has vanished, and* THE GOAT-HERD *has ceased to pipe, and lies motionless again on his rock.*

FELSMAN. Love me !

SEELCHEN. Thou art rude !

FELSMAN. Love me !

SEELCHEN. Thou art grim !

FELSMAN. Aye, I have no silver tongue. Listen ! This is my voice ! [*Sweeping his arm round all the still alp.*] From dawn to the first star all is quiet. [*Laying his hand on her heart.*] And the wings of the bird shall be still.

SEELCHEN. [*Touching his eyes*] Thine eyes are fierce. In them I see the wild beasts crouching. In them I see the distance. Are they always fierce ?

FELSMAN. Never—to look on thee, my flower.

SEELCHEN. [*Touching his hands*] Thy hands are rough to pluck flowers. [*She breaks away from him—to the rock where* THE GOATHERD *is lying.*] See ! Nothing moves. The very day stands still. Boy ! [*But* THE GOATHERD *neither stirs nor answers.*] He is lost in the blue. [*Passionately.*] Boy! He will not answer me. No one will answer me here.

FELSMAN. [*With fierce longing*] Am *I* no one ?

[*The scene darkens with evening.*

SEELCHEN. See ! Sleep has stolen the day ! It is night already.

[*There comes the female shadow-forms of* SLEEP, *in grey cobweb garments, waving their arms drowsily, wheeling round her.*

SEELCHEN. Are you Sleep ? My lover Sleep ! My love.—Rest !

[*Smiling, she holds out her arms to* FELSMAN. *He takes her swaying form. They vanish, encircled by the forms of* SLEEP. *It is dark, save for the light of the thin-horned moon suddenly grown bright. Then on his rock, to a faint piping* THE GOATHERD *sings :*

" *My goat, my little speckled one,*
My yellow-eyed, sweet-smelling,
Let moon and wind and golden sun
And stars beyond all telling
Make, every day, a sweeter grass,
And multiply thy leaping !

> *And may the mountain foxes pass*
> *And never scent thee sleeping !*
> *Oh ! let my pipe be clear and far,*
> *And let me find sweet water !*
> *No hawk, nor udder-seeking jar*
> *Come near thee, little daughter !*
> *May fiery rocks defend, at noon,*
> *Thy tender feet from slipping !*
> *Oh ! hear my prayer beneath the moon—*
> *Great Master, Goat-God—skipping !* "

[*With a long wail of the pipe* THE GOATHERD BOY *is silent. Then the moon fades, and all is black ; till, in the faint grisly light of the false dawn creeping up,* SEELCHEN *is seen rising from the side of the sleeping* FELSMAN. THE GOATHERD BOY *has gone ; but by the rock stands the Shepherd of* THE COW HORN *in his cloak.*

SEELCHEN. Years, years I have slept. My spirit is hungry. [*Then as she sees the Shepherd of* THE COW HORN *standing there.*] I know thee now—Life of the earth—the smell of thee, the sight of thee, the taste of thee, and all thy music. I have passed thee and gone by.

[*She moves away.*

FELSMAN. [*Waking*] Where wouldst thou go ?

SEELCHEN. To the edge of the world.

FELSMAN. [*Rising and trying to stay her*] Thou *shalt* not leave me !

[*But against her smiling gesture he struggles as though against solidity.*

SEELCHEN. Friend ! The time has come.

FELSMAN. Were my kisses, then, too rude ? Was I too dull ?

SEELCHEN. I do not regret, but I must go.

[*The Youth of* THE WINE HORN *is seen suddenly standing opposite the motionless Shepherd of* THE COW HORN ; *and his mandolin twangs out.*

FELSMAN. The cursed music of the Town. Is it to *him* thou wilt return ? [*Groping for sight of the hated figure.*] I cannot see.

SEELCHEN. Fear not ! I go ever onward.

FELSMAN. Do not leave me to the wind in the rocks ! Without thee love is dead, and I must die.

SEELCHEN. Poor heart ! I am gone.

FELSMAN. [*Crouching against the rock*] It is cold.

[*At the blowing of the Shepherd's pipe,* THE COW HORN *stretches forth his hand to her. The mandolin twangs out, and* THE WINE HORN *holds out his hand. She stands unmoving.*

SEELCHEN. Companions, I must go. In a moment it will be dawn.

[*In silence* THE COW HORN *and* THE WINE HORN *cover their faces. The false dawn dies. It falls quite dark.*

SCENE V

Then a faint glow stealing up, lights the snowy peak of THE GREAT HORN, *and streams forth on* SEELCHEN. *No other peak is visible, but to either side of that path of light, like shadows,* THE COW HORN *and* THE WINE HORN *stand with cloaked heads.*

SEELCHEN. Great One! I come!
> [*The Peak of* THE GREAT HORN *speaks in a far-away voice, growing with the light, clearer and stronger :*
> *Wandering flame, thou restless fever*
> *Burning all things, regretting none ;*
> *The winds of fate are stilled for ever—*
> *Thy little generous life is done,*
> *And all its wistful wonderings cease !*
> *Thou traveller to the tideless sea,*
> *Where light and dark, and change and peace,*
> *Are One—Come, little soul, to* MYSTERY *!*
> [SEELCHEN, *falling on her knees, bows her head to the ground. The glow slowly fades till the scene is black.*

SCENE VI

Then as the blackness lifts, in the dim light of the false dawn filtering through the window of the mountain hut, LAMOND *and* FELSMAN *are seen standing beside* SEELCHEN *looking down at her asleep on the window seat.*

FELSMAN. [*Putting out his hand to wake her*] In a moment it will be dawn.   [*She stirs, and her lips move, murmuring.*
LAMOND. Let her sleep. She's dreaming.
> [FELSMAN *raises a lantern, till its light falls on her face. Then the two men move stealthily towards the door, and, as she speaks, pass out.*
SEELCHEN. [*Rising to her knees, and stretching out her hands with ecstasy*] Great One, I come! [*Waking, she looks around, and struggles to her feet.*] My little dream!
> [*Through the open door, the first flush of dawn shows in the sky. There is a sound of goat-bells passing.*

The curtain falls.

JUSTICE: A TRAGEDY

CAST OF THE FIRST PRODUCTION AT THE DUKE OF YORK'S THEATRE, FEBRUARY 21, 1910

JAMES HOW	Mr. Sydney Valentin
WALTER HOW	Mr. Charles Maude
COKESON	Mr. Edmund Gwenne
FALDER	Mr. Dennis Eadie
THE OFFICE-BOY	Mr. George Hersee
THE DETECTIVE	Mr. Leslie Carter
THE CASHIER	Mr. C. E. Vernon
THE JUDGE	Mr. Dion Boucicault
THE OLD ADVOCATE . . .	Mr. Oscar Adye
THE YOUNG ADVOCATE . . .	Mr. Charles Bryant
THE PRISON GOVERNOR . . .	Mr. Grendon Bentley
THE PRISON CHAPLAIN . . .	Mr. Hubert Harben
THE PRISON DOCTOR . . .	Mr. Lewis Casson
WOODER	Mr. Frederick Lloyd
MOANEY	Mr. Robert Pateman
CLIPTON	Mr. O. P. Heggie
O'CLEARY	Mr. Whitford Kane
RUTH HONEYWILL	Miss Edyth Olive

ACT I

The scene is the managing clerk's room, at the offices of JAMES AND WALTER
How, *on a July morning. The room is old-fashioned, furnished with
well-worn mahogany and leather, and lined with tin boxes and estate plans.
It has three doors. Two of them are close together in the centre of a wall.
One of these two doors leads to the outer office, which is only divided from
the managing clerk's room by a partition of wood and clear glass; and
when the door into this outer office is opened there can be seen the wide
outer door leading out on to the stone stairway of the building. The other
of these two centre doors leads to the junior clerks' room. The third door
is that leading to the partners' room.*

The managing clerk, COKESON, *is sitting at his table adding up figures in a
pass-book, and murmuring their numbers to himself. He is a man of
sixty, wearing spectacles; rather short, with a bald head, and an honest,
pug-dog face. He is dressed in a well-worn black frock-coat and pepper-
and-salt trousers.*

COKESON. And five's twelve, and three—fifteen, nineteen, twenty-
three, thirty-two, forty-one—and carry four. [*He ticks the page, and
goes on murmuring.*] Five, seven, twelve, seventeen, twenty-four and
nine, thirty-three, thirteen and carry one.

    [*He again makes a tick. The outer office door is opened, and*
      SWEEDLE, *the office-boy, appears, closing the door behind him.
      He is a pale youth of sixteen, with spiky hair.*

COKESON. [*With grumpy expectation*] And carry one.

SWEEDLE. There's a party wants to see Falder, Mr. Cokeson.

COKESON. Five, nine, sixteen, twenty-one, twenty-nine—and carry
two. Sent him to Morris's. What name?

SWEEDLE. Honeywill.

COKESON. What's his business?

SWEEDLE. It's a woman.

COKESON. A lady?

SWEEDLE. No, a person.

COKESON. Ask her in. Take this pass-book to Mr. James.

                                [*He closes the pass-book.*

SWEEDLE. [*Reopening the door*] Will you come in, please?

    [RUTH HONEYWILL *comes in. She is a tall woman, twenty-six
      years old, unpretentiously dressed, with black hair and eyes, and an*

*ivory-white, clear-cut face. She stands very still, having a
natural dignity of pose and gesture.*

[SWEEDLE *goes out into the partners' room with the pass-book.*

COKESON. [*Looking round at* RUTH] The young man's out.
[*Suspiciously.*] State your business, please.

RUTH. [*Who speaks in a matter-of-fact voice, and with a slight West-
country accent*] It's a personal matter, sir.

COKESON. We don't allow private callers here. Will you leave a
message ?

RUTH. I'd rather see him, please.

[*She narrows her dark eyes and gives him a honeyed look.*

COKESON. [*Expanding*] It's all against the rules. Suppose I had
my friends here to see me ! It'd never do !

RUTH. No, sir.

COKESON. [*A little taken aback*] Exactly ! And here you are
wanting to see a *junior* clerk !

RUTH. Yes, sir ; I must see him.

COKESON. [*Turning full round to her with a sort of outraged interest*]
But this is a lawyer's office. Go to his private address.

RUTH. He's not there.

COKESON. [*Uneasy*] Are you related to the party ?

RUTH. No, sir.

COKESON. [*In real embarrassment*] I don't know what to say. It's
no affair of the office.

RUTH. But what am I to do ?

COKESON. Dear me ! I can't tell you that.

[SWEEDLE *comes back. He crosses to the outer office and passes
through into it, with a quizzical look at* COKESON, *carefully
leaving the door an inch or two open.*

COKESON. [*Fortified by this look*] This won't do, you know, this
won't do at all. Suppose one of the partners came in !

[*An incoherent knocking and chuckling is heard from the outer door
of the outer office.*

SWEEDLE. [*Putting his head in*] There's some children outside here.

RUTH. They're mine, please.

SWEEDLE. Shall I hold them in check ?

RUTH. They're quite small, sir. [*She takes a step towards* COKESON.

COKESON. You mustn't take up his time in office hours ; we're a
clerk short as it is.

RUTH. It's a matter of life and death.

COKESON. [*Again outraged*] Life and death !

SWEEDLE. Here *is* Falder.

[FALDER *has entered through the outer office. He is a pale, good-
looking young man, with quick, rather scared eyes. He moves
towards the door of the clerks' office, and stands there irresolute.*

COKESON. Well, I'll give you a minute. It's not regular.

[*Taking up a bundle of papers, he goes out into the partners' room.*

RUTH. [*In a low, hurried voice*] He's on the drink again, Will. He tried to cut my throat last night. I came out with the children before he was awake. I went round to you——

FALDER. I've changed my digs.

RUTH. Is it all ready for to-night ?

FALDER. I've got the tickets. Meet me 11.45 at the booking office. For God's sake don't forget we're man and wife ! [*Looking at her with tragic intensity.*] Ruth !

RUTH. You're not afraid of going, are you ?

FALDER. Have you got your things, and the children's ?

RUTH. Had to leave them, for fear of waking Honeywill, all but one bag. I can't go near home again.

FALDER. [*Wincing*] All that money gone for nothing. How much *must* you have ?

RUTH. Six pounds—I could do with that, I think.

FALDER. Don't give away where we're going. [*As if to himself.*] When I get out there I mean to forget it all.

RUTH. If you're sorry, say so. I'd sooner he killed me than take you against your will.

FALDER. [*With a queer smile*] We've *got* to go. I don't care ; I'll have *you*.

RUTH. You've just to say ; it's not too late.

FALDER. It *is* too late. Here's seven pounds. Booking office— 11.45 to-night. If you weren't what you are to me, Ruth——!

RUTH. Kiss me !

[*They cling together passionately, then fly apart just as* COKESON *re-enters the room.* RUTH *turns and goes out through the outer office.* COKESON *advances deliberately to his chair and seats himself.*

COKESON. This isn't right, Falder.

FALDER. It shan't occur again, sir.

COKESON. It's an improper use of these premises.

FALDER. Yes, sir.

COKESON. You quite understand—the party was in some distress ; and, having children with her, I allowed my feelings—— [*He opens a drawer and produces from it a tract.*] Just take this ! " Purity in the Home." It's a well-written thing.

FALDER. [*Taking it, with a peculiar expression*] Thank you, sir.

COKESON. And look here, Falder, before Mr. Walter comes, have you finished up that cataloguing Davis had in hand before he left ?

FALDER. I shall have done with it to-morrow, sir—for good.

COKESON. It's over a week since Davis went. Now it won't do,

Falder. You're neglecting your work for private life. I shan't mention about the party having called, but——

FALDER. [*Passing into his room*] Thank you, sir.

[COKESON *stares at the door through which* FALDER *has gone out ; then shakes his head, and is just settling down to write, when* WALTER HOW *comes in through the outer office. He is a rather refined-looking man of thirty-five, with a pleasant, almost apologetic voice.*

WALTER. Good-morning, Cokeson.

COKESON. Morning, Mr. Walter.

WALTER. My father here?

COKESON [*Always with a certain patronage as to a young man who might be doing better*] Mr. James has been here since eleven o'clock.

WALTER. I've been in to see the pictures, at the Guildhall.

COKESON. [*Looking at him as though this were exactly what was to be expected*] Have you now—ye-es. This lease of Boulter's—am I to send it to counsel?

WALTER. What does my father say?

COKESON. 'Aven't bothered him.

WALTER. Well, we can't be too careful.

COKESON. It's such a little thing—hardly worth the fees. I thought you'd do it yourself.

WALTER. Send it, please. I don't want the responsibility.

COKESON. [*With an indescribable air of compassion*] Just as you like. This " right-of-way " case—we've got 'em on the deeds.

WALTER. I know ; but the intention was obviously to exclude that bit of common ground.

COKESON. We needn't worry about that. We're the *right* side of the law.

WALTER. I don't like it.

COKESON. [*With an indulgent smile*] We shan't want to set ourselves up against the law. Your father wouldn't waste his time doing that.

[*As he speaks* JAMES HOW *comes in from the partners' room. He is a shortish man, with white side-whiskers, plentiful grey hair, shrewd eyes, and gold pince-nez.*

JAMES. Morning, Walter.

WALTER. How are you, father?

COKESON. [*Looking down his nose at the papers in his hand as though deprecating their size*] I'll just take Boulter's lease in to young Falder to draft the instructions.   [*He goes out into* FALDER'S *room.*

WALTER. About that right-of-way case?

JAMES. Oh, well, we must go forward there. I thought you told me yesterday the firm's balance was over four hundred.

WALTER. So it is.

JAMES. [*Holding out the pass-book to his son*] Three—five—one, no recent cheques.   Just get me out the cheque-book.

[WALTER *goes to a cupboard, unlocks a drawer, and produces a cheque-book.*

JAMES. Tick the pounds in the counterfoils.   Five, fifty-four, seven, five, twenty-eight, twenty, ninety, eleven, fifty-two, seventy-one. Tally ?

WALTER [*Nodding*] Can't understand.   Made sure it was over four hundred.

JAMES. Give me the cheque-book.   [*He takes the cheque-book and cons the counterfoils.*] What's this ninety ?

WALTER. Who drew it ?

JAMES. You.

WALTER. [*Taking the cheque-book*] July 7th ?   That's the day I went down to look over the Trenton Estate—last Friday week ; I came back on the Tuesday, you remember.   But look here, father, it was *nine* I drew a cheque for.   Five guineas to Smithers and my expenses.   It just covered all but half a crown.

JAMES. [*Gravely*] Let's look at that ninety cheque.   [*He sorts the cheque out from the bundle in the pocket of the pass-book.*] Seems all right.   There's no nine here.   This is bad.   Who cashed that nine-pound cheque ?

WALTER. [*Puzzled and pained*] Let's see !   I was finishing Mrs. Reddy's will—only just had time ; yes—I gave it to Cokeson.

JAMES. Look at that *t y* : that yours ?

WALTER. [*After consideration*] My *y's* curl back a little ; this doesn't.

JAMES. [*As* COKESON *re-enters from* FALDER'S *room*] We must ask him.   Just come here and carry your mind back a bit, Cokeson. D'you remember cashing a cheque for Mr. Walter last Friday week —the day he went to Trenton ?

COKESON. Ye-es.   Nine pounds.

JAMES. Look at this.   [*Handing him the cheque.*

COKESON. No !   Nine pounds.   My lunch was just coming in ; and of course I *like* it hot ; I gave the cheque to Davis to run round to the bank.   He brought it back, all notes—you remember, Mr. Walter, you wanted some silver to pay your cab.   [*With a certain contemptuous compassion.*] Here, let *me* see.   You've got the wrong cheque.   [*He takes cheque-book and pass-book from* WALTER.

WALTER. Afraid not.

COKESON. [*Having seen for himself*] It's funny.

JAMES. You gave it to Davis, and Davis sailed for Australia on Monday.   Looks black, Cokeson.

COKESON. [*Puzzled and upset*] Why this'd be a felony !   No, no ! there's some mistake.

JAMES. I hope so.

COKESON. There's never been anything of that sort in the office the twenty-nine years I've been here.

JAMES. [*Looking at cheque and counterfoil*] This is a very clever bit of work; a warning to you not to leave space after your figures, Walter.

WALTER. [*Vexed*] Yes, I know—I was in such a tearing hurry that afternoon.

COKESON. [*Suddenly*] This has upset me.

JAMES. The counterfoil altered too—very deliberate piece of swindling. What was Davis's ship?

WALTER. *City of Rangoon.*

JAMES. We ought to wire and have him arrested at Naples; he can't be there yet.

COKESON. His poor young wife. I liked the young man. Dear, oh dear ! In this office !

WALTER. Shall I go to the bank and ask the cashier ?

JAMES. [*Grimly*] Bring him round here. And ring up Scotland Yard.

WALTER. Really ?

> [*He goes out through the outer office.* JAMES *paces the room. He stops and looks at* COKESON, *who is disconsolately rubbing the knees of his trousers.*

JAMES. Well, Cokeson ! There's something in character, isn't there ?

COKESON. [*Looking at him over his spectacles*] I don't quite take you, sir.

JAMES. Your story would sound d——d thin to anyone who didn't know you.

COKESON. Ye-es ! [*He laughs. Then with sudden gravity.*] I'm sorry for that young man. I feel it as if it was my own son, Mr. James.

JAMES. A nasty business !

COKESON. It unsettles you. All goes on regular, and then a thing like this happens. Shan't relish my lunch to-day.

JAMES. As bad as that, Cokeson ?

COKESON. It makes you think. [*Confidentially.*] He must have had temptation.

JAMES. Not so fast. We haven't convicted him yet.

COKESON. I'd sooner have lost a month's salary than had this happen.   [*He broods.*

JAMES. I hope that fellow will hurry up.

COKESON. [*Keeping things pleasant for the cashier*] It isn't fifty yards, Mr. James. He won't be a minute.

JAMES. The idea of dishonesty about this office—it hits me hard, Cokeson.   [*He goes towards the door of the partners' room.*

SWEEDLE. [*Entering quietly, to* COKESON *in a low voice*] She's popped up again, sir—something she forgot to say to Falder.

COKESON. [*Roused from his abstraction*] Eh? Impossible. Send her away!

JAMES. What's that?

COKESON. Nothing, Mr. James. A private matter. Here, I'll come myself. [*He goes into the outer office as* JAMES *passes into the partners' room*.] Now, you really mustn't—we can't have anybody just now.

RUTH. Not for a minute, sir?

COKESON. Reely! Reely! I can't have it. If you want him, wait about; he'll be going out for his lunch directly.

RUTH. Yes, sir.

      [WALTER, *entering with the cashier, passes* RUTH *as she leaves the outer office.*

COKESON. [*To the cashier, who resembles a sedentary dragoon*] Good-morning. [*To* WALTER.] Your father's in there.

                   [WALTER *crosses and goes into the partners' room.*

COKESON. It's a nahsty, unpleasant little matter, Mr. Cowley. I'm quite ashamed to have to trouble you.

COWLEY. I remember the cheque quite well. [*As if it were a liver.*] Seemed in perfect order.

COKESON. Sit down, won't you? I'm not a sensitive man, but a thing like this about the place—it's not nice. I like people to be open and jolly together.

COWLEY. Quite so.

COKESON. [*Button-holing him, and glancing towards the partners' room*] Of course he's a young man. I've told him about it before now —leaving space after his figures, but he *will* do it.

COWLEY. I should remember the person's face—quite a youth.

COKESON. I don't think we shall be able to show him to you, as a matter of fact.

      [JAMES *and* WALTER *have come back from the partners' room.*

JAMES. Good-morning, Mr. Cowley. You've seen my son and myself, you've seen Mr. Cokeson, and you've seen Sweedle, my office-boy. It was none of us, I take it.

               [The cashier shakes his head with a smile.

JAMES. Be so good as to sit there. Cokeson, engage Mr. Cowley in conversation, will you?   [He goes towards FALDER'S room.

COKESON. Just a word, Mr. James.

JAMES. Well?

COKESON. You don't want to upset the young man in there, do you? He's a nervous young feller.

JAMES. This must be thoroughly cleared up, Cokeson, for the sake of Falder's name, to say nothing of yours.

COKESON. [*With some dignity*] That'll look after itself, sir. He's been upset once this morning; I don't want him startled again.

  8*

JAMES. It's a matter of form; but I can't stand upon niceness over a thing like this—too serious. Just talk to Mr. Cowley.

[*He opens the door of* FALDER's *room.*

JAMES. Bring in the papers in Boulter's lease, will you, Falder?

COKESON. [*Bursting into voice*] Do you keep dogs?

[*The cashier, with his eyes fixed on the door, does not answer.*

COKESON. You haven't such a thing as a bulldog pup you could spare me, I suppose?

[*At the look on the cashier's face his jaw drops, and he turns to see* FALDER *standing in the doorway, with his eyes fixed on* COWLEY, *like the eyes of a rabbit fastened on a snake.*

FALDER. [*Advancing with the papers*] Here they are, sir.

JAMES. [*Taking them*] Thank you.

FALDER. Do you want me, sir?

JAMES. No, thanks!

[FALDER *turns and goes back into his own room. As he shuts the door* JAMES *gives the cashier an interrogative look, and the cashier nods.*

JAMES. Sure? This isn't as we suspected.

COWLEY. Quite. He knew me. I suppose he can't slip out of that room?

COKESON. [*Gloomily*] There's only the window—a whole floor and a basement.

[*The door of* FALDER's *room is quietly opened, and* FALDER, *with his hat in his hand, moves towards the door of the outer office.*

JAMES. [*Quietly*] Where are you going, Falder?

FALDER. To have my lunch, sir.

JAMES. Wait a few minutes, would you? I want to speak to you about this lease.

FALDER. Yes, sir. [*He goes back into his room.*

COWLEY. If I'm wanted, I can swear that's the young man who cashed the cheque. It was the last cheque I handled that morning before my lunch. These are the numbers of the notes he had. [*He puts a slip of paper on the table; then, brushing his hat round.*] Good-morning!

JAMES. Good-morning, Mr. Cowley!

COWLEY. [*To* COKESON] Good-morning.

COKESON. [*With stupefaction*] Good-morning.

[*The cashier goes out through the outer office.* COKESON *sits down in his chair, as though it were the only place left in the morass of his feelings.*

WALTER. What are you going to do?

JAMES. Have him in. Give me the cheque and the counterfoil.

COKESON. I don't understand. I thought young Davis——

JAMES. We shall see.

WALTER. One moment, father : have you thought it out ?

JAMES. Call him in !

COKESON. [*Rising with difficulty and opening* FALDER'S *door ; hoarsely*] Step in here a minute.   [FALDER *comes in.*

FALDER. [*Impassively*] Yes, sir ?

JAMES. [*Turning to him suddenly with the cheque held out*] You know this cheque, Falder ?

FALDER. No, sir.

JAMES. Look at it.   You cashed it last Friday week.

FALDER. Oh ! yes, sir ; that one—Davis gave it me.

JAMES. I know.   And you gave Davis the cash ?

FALDER. Yes, sir.

JAMES. When Davis gave you the cheque was it exactly like this ?

FALDER. Yes, I think so, sir.

JAMES. You know that Mr. Walter drew that cheque for *nine* pounds ?

FALDER. No, sir—ninety.

JAMES. Nine, Falder.

FALDER. [*Faintly*] I don't understand, sir.

JAMES. The suggestion, of course, is that the cheque was altered ; whether by you or Davis is the question.

FALDER. I—I——

COKESON. Take your time, take your time.

FALDER. [*Regaining his impassivity*] Not by me, sir.

JAMES. The cheque was handed to Cokeson by Mr. Walter at one o'clock ; we know that because Mr. Cokeson's lunch had just arrived.

COKESON. I couldn't leave it.

JAMES. Exactly ; he therefore gave the cheque to Davis.   It was cashed by you at 1.15.   We know that because the cashier recollects it for the last cheque he handled before *his* lunch.

FALDER. Yes, sir, Davis gave it to me because some friends were giving him a farewell luncheon.

JAMES. [*Puzzled*] You accuse Davis, then ?

FALDER. I don't know, sir—it's very funny.

[WALTER, *who has come close to his father, says something to him in a low voice.*

JAMES. Davis was not here again after that Saturday, was he ?

COKESON. [*Anxious to be of assistance to the young man, and seeing faint signs of their all being jolly once more*] No, he sailed on the Monday.

JAMES. Was he, Falder ?

FALDER. [*Very faintly*] No, sir.

JAMES. Very well, then, how do you account for the fact that this nought was added to the nine in the counterfoil on or after *Tuesday* ?

COKESON. [*Surprised*] How's that ?

[FALDER *gives a sort of lurch ; he tries to pull himself together, but he has gone all to pieces.*

JAMES. [*Very grimly*] Out, I'm afraid, Cokeson.   The cheque-book remained in Mr. Walter's pocket till he came back from Trenton on Tuesday morning.   In the face of this, Falder, do you still deny that you altered both cheque and counterfoil ?

FALDER. No, sir—no, Mr. How.   I did it, sir ; I did it.

COKESON. [*Succumbing to his feelings*] Dear, dear ! what a thing to do !

FALDER. I wanted the money so badly, sir.   I didn't know what I was doing.

COKESON. However such a thing could have come into your head !

FALDER. [*Grasping at the words*] I can't think, sir, really !   It was just a minute of madness.

JAMES. A long minute, Falder.   [*Tapping the counterfoil.*] Four days at least.

FALDER. Sir, I swear I didn't know what I'd done till afterwards, and then I hadn't the pluck.   Oh ! sir, look over it !   I'll pay the money back—I will, I promise.

JAMES. Go into your room.

[FALDER, *with a swift imploring look, goes back into his room. There is silence.*

JAMES. About as bad a case as there could be.

COKESON. To break the law like that—in here !

WALTER. What's to be done ?

JAMES. Nothing for it.   Prosecute.

WALTER. It's his first offence.

JAMES. [*Shaking his head*] I've grave doubts of that.   Too neat a piece of swindling altogether.

COKESON. I shouldn't be surprised if he was tempted.

JAMES. Life's one long temptation, Cokeson.

COKESON. Ye-es, but I'm speaking of the flesh and the devil, Mr. James.   There was a woman come to see him this morning.

WALTER. The woman we passed as we came in just now.   Is it his wife ?

COKESON. No, no relation.   [*Restraining what in jollier circumstances would have been a wink.*] A married person, though.

WALTER. How do you know ?

COKESON. Brought her children.   [*Scandalized.*] There they were outside the office.

JAMES. A real bad egg.

WALTER. I should like to give him a chance.

JAMES. I can't forgive him for the sneaky way he went to work— counting on our suspecting young Davis if the matter came to light. It was the merest accident the cheque-book stayed in your pocket.

WALTER. It *must* have been the temptation of a moment.   He hadn't time.

JAMES. A man doesn't succumb like that in a moment, if he's a clean mind and habits. He's rotten ; got the eyes of a man who can't keep his hands off when there's money about.

WALTER. [*Dryly*] We hadn't noticed that before.

JAMES. [*Brushing the remark aside*] I've seen lots of those fellows in my time. No doing anything with them except to keep 'em out of harm's way. They've got a blind spot.

WALTER. It's penal servitude.

COKESON. They're *nahsty* places—prisons.

JAMES. [*Hesitating*] I don't see how it's possible to spare him. Out of the question to keep him in this office—honesty's the *sine qua non*.

COKESON. [*Hypnotized*] Of course it *is*.

JAMES. Equally out of the question to send him out amongst people who've no knowledge of his character. One must think of society.

WALTER. But to brand him like this ?

JAMES. If it had been a straightforward case I'd give him another chance. It's far from that. He has dissolute habits.

COKESON. I didn't say that—extenuating circumstances.

JAMES. Same thing. He's gone to work in the most cold-blooded way to defraud his employers, and cast the blame on an innocent man. If that's not a case for the law to take its course, I don't know what is.

WALTER. For the sake of his future, though.

JAMES. [*Sarcastically*] According to you, no one would ever prosecute.

WALTER. [*Nettled*] I hate the idea of it.

COKESON. We must have protection.

JAMES. This is degenerating into talk.

[*He moves towards the partners' room.*]

WALTER. Put yourself in his place, father.

JAMES. You ask too much of me.

WALTER. We can't possibly tell the pressure there was on him.

JAMES. You may depend on it, my boy, if a man is going to do this sort of thing he'll do it, pressure or no pressure ; if he isn't nothing'll make him.

WALTER. He'll never do it again.

COKESON. [*Fatuously*] S'pose I were to have a talk with him. We don't want to be hard on the young man.

JAMES. That'll do, Cokeson. I've made up my mind.

[*He passes into the partners' room.*]

COKESON. [*After a doubtful moment*] We must excuse your father. I don't want to go against your father ; if he thinks it right.

WALTER. Confound it, Cokeson ! why don't you back me up ? You know you feel——

COKESON. [*On his dignity*] I really can't say what I feel.

WALTER. We shall regret it.

COKESON. He must have known what he was doing.

WALTER. [*Bitterly*] " The quality of mercy is not strained."

COKESON. [*Looking at him askance*] Come, come, Mr. Walter. We must try and see it sensible.

SWEEDLE. [*Entering with a tray*] Your lunch, sir.

COKESON. Put it down !

> [*While* SWEEDLE *is putting it down on* COKESON'S *table, the detective,* WISTER, *enters the outer office, and, finding no one there, comes to the inner doorway. He is a square, medium-sized man, clean-shaved, in a serviceable blue serge suit and strong boots.*]

WISTER. [*To* WALTER] From Scotland Yard, sir. Detective-Sergeant Wister.

WALTER. [*Askance*] Very well ! I'll speak to my father.

> [*He goes into the partners' room.* JAMES *enters.*]

JAMES. Morning ! [*In answer to an appealing gesture from* COKESON.] I'm sorry ; I'd stop short of this if I felt I could. Open that door. [SWEEDLE, *wondering and scared, opens it.*] Come here, Mr. Falder.

> [*As* FALDER *comes shrinkingly out, the detective, in obedience to a sign from* JAMES, *slips his hand out and grasps his arm.*]

FALDER. [*Recoiling*] Oh ! no—oh ! no !

WISTER. Come, come, there's a good lad.

JAMES. I charge him with felony.

FALDER. Oh, sir ! There's someone—I did it for her. Let me be till to-morrow.

> [JAMES *motions with his hand. At that sign of hardness,* FALDER *becomes rigid. Then, turning, he goes out quietly in the detective's grip.* JAMES *follows, stiff and erect.* SWEEDLE, *rushing to the door with open mouth, pursues them through the outer office into the corridor. When they have all disappeared* COKESON *spins completely round and makes a rush for the outer office.*

COKESON. [*Hoarsely*] Here ! Here ! What are we doing ?

> [*There is silence. He takes out his handkerchief and mops the sweat from his face. Going back blindly to his table, he sits down, and stares blankly at his lunch.*]

The curtain falls.

ACT II

A Court of Justice, on a foggy October afternoon—crowded with barristers, solicitors, reporters, ushers, and jurymen. Sitting in the large, solid dock is FALDER, *with a warder on either side of him, placed there for his safe custody, but seemingly indifferent to and unconscious of his presence.* FALDER *is sitting exactly opposite to the* JUDGE, *who, raised above the clamour of the court, also seems unconscious of and indifferent to everything.* HAROLD CLEAVER, *the counsel for the Crown, is a dried, yellowish man, of more than middle age, in a wig worn almost to the colour of his face.* HECTOR FROME, *the counsel for the defence, is a young, tall man, clean-shaved, in a very white wig. Among the spectators, having already given their evidence, are* JAMES *and* WALTER HOW, *and* COWLEY, *the cashier.* WISTER, *the detective, is just leaving the witness-box.*

CLEAVER. That is the case for the Crown, me lud!

[*Gathering his robes together, he sits down.*

FROME. [*Rising and bowing to the* JUDGE] If it please your lordship and members of the jury. I am not going to dispute the fact that the prisoner altered this cheque, but I am going to put before you evidence as to the condition of his mind, and to submit that you would not be justified in finding that he was responsible for his actions at the time. I am going to show you, in fact, that he did this in a moment of aberration, amounting to temporary insanity, caused by the violent distress under which he was labouring. Gentlemen, the prisoner is only twenty-three years old. I shall call before you a woman from whom you will learn the events that led up to this act. You will hear from her own lips the tragic circumstances of her life, the still more tragic infatuation with which she has inspired the prisoner. This woman, gentlemen, has been leading a miserable existence with a husband who habitually ill-uses her, from whom she actually goes in terror of her life. I am not, of course, saying that it's either right or desirable for a young man to fall in love with a married woman, or that it's his business to rescue her from an ogre-like husband. I'm not saying anything of the sort. But we all know the power of the passion of love; and I would ask you to remember, gentlemen, in listening to her evidence, that, married to a drunken and violent husband, she has no power to get rid of him; for, as you know, another offence besides violence is necessary to

231

enable a woman to obtain a divorce ; and of this offence it does not appear that her husband is guilty.

JUDGE. Is this relevant, Mr. Frome ?

FROME. My lord, I submit, extremely—I shall be able to show your lordship that directly.

JUDGE. Very well.

FROME. In these circumstances, what alternatives were left to her ? She could either go on living with this drunkard, in terror of her life ; or she could apply to the Court for a separation order. Well, gentlemen, my experience of such cases assures me that this would have given her very insufficient protection from the violence of such a man ; and even if effectual would very likely have reduced her either to the workhouse or the streets—for it's not easy, as she is now finding, for an unskilled woman without means of livelihood to support herself and her children without resorting either to the Poor Law or—to speak quite plainly—to the sale of her body.

JUDGE. You are ranging rather far, Mr. Frome.

FROME. I shall fire point-blank in a minute, my lord.

JUDGE. Let us hope so.

FROME. Now, gentlemen, mark—and this is what I have been leading up to—this woman will tell you, and the prisoner will confirm her, that, confronted with such alternatives, she set her whole hopes on himself, knowing the feeling with which she had inspired him. She saw a way out of her misery by going with him to a new country, where they would both be unknown, and might pass as husband and wife. This was a desperate and, as my friend Mr. Cleaver will no doubt call it, an immoral resolution ; but, as a fact, the minds of both of them were constantly turned towards it. One wrong is no excuse for another, and those who are never likely to be faced by such a situation possibly have the right to hold up their hands—as to that I prefer to say nothing. But whatever view you take, gentlemen, of this part of the prisoner's story—whatever opinion you form of the right of these two young people under such circumstances to take the law into their own hands—the fact remains that this young woman in her distress, and this young man, little more than a boy, who was so devotedly attached to her, *did* conceive this—if you like—reprehensible design of going away together. Now, for that, of course, they required money, and—they had none. As to the actual events of the morning of July 7th, on which this cheque was altered, the events on which I rely to prove the defendant's irresponsibility—I shall allow those events to speak for themselves, through the lips of my witnesses. Robert Cokeson. [*He turns, looks round, takes up a sheet of paper, and waits.*]

[COKESON *is summoned into court, and goes into the witness-box, holding his hat before him. The oath is administered to him.*

FROME. What is your name?

COKESON. Robert Cokeson.

FROME. Are you managing clerk to the firm of solicitors who employ the prisoner?

COKESON. Ye-es.

FROME. How long had the prisoner been in their employ?

COKESON. Two years. No, I'm wrong there—all but seventeen days.

FROME. Had you him under your eye all that time?

COKESON. Except Sundays and holidays.

FROME. Quite so. Let us hear, please, what you have to say about his general character during those two years.

COKESON. [*Confidentially to the jury, and as if a little surprised at being asked*] He was a nice, pleasant-spoken young man. I'd no fault to find with him—quite the contrary. It was a *great* surprise to me when he did a thing like that.

FROME. Did he ever give you reason to suspect his honesty?

COKESON. No! To have dishonesty in our office, that'd never do.

FROME. I'm sure the jury fully appreciate that, Mr. Cokeson.

COKESON. Every man of business knows that honesty's the sign qua nonne.

FROME. Do you give him a good character all round, or do you not?

COKESON. [*Turning to the* JUDGE] Certainly. We were all very jolly and pleasant together, until this happened. Quite upset me.

FROME. Now, coming to the morning of the 7th of July, the morning on which the cheque was altered. What have you to say about his demeanour that morning?

COKESON. [*To the jury*] If you ask me, I don't think he was quite compos when he did it.

THE JUDGE. [*Sharply*] Are you suggesting that he was insane?

COKESON. Not compos.

THE JUDGE. A little more precision, please.

FROME. [*Smoothly*] Just tell us, Mr. Cokeson.

COKESON. [*Somewhat outraged*] Well, in my opinion—[*looking at the* JUDGE]—such as it is—he was jumpy at the time. The jury will understand my meaning.

FROME. Will you tell us how you came to that conclusion?

COKESON. Ye-es, I will. I have my lunch in from the restaurant, a chop and a potato—saves time. That day it happened to come just as Mr. Walter How handed me the cheque. Well, I like it hot; so I went into the clerks' office and I handed the cheque to Davis, the other clerk, and told him to get change. I noticed young Falder walking up and down. I said to him: "This is not the Zoological Gardens, Falder."

FROME. Do you remember what he answered?

COKESON. Ye-es: "I wish to God it were!" Struck me as funny.

FROME. Did you notice anything else peculiar?

COKESON. I did.

FROME. What was that?

COKESON. His collar was unbuttoned. Now, I like a young man to be neat. I said to him: "Your collar's unbuttoned."

FROME. And what did he answer?

COKESON. Stared at me. It wasn't nice.

THE JUDGE. Stared at you? Isn't that a very common practice?

COKESON. Ye-es, but it was the look in his eyes. I can't explain my meaning—it was funny.

FROME. Had you ever seen such a look in his eyes before?

COKESON. No. If I had I should have spoken to the partners. We can't have anything eccentric in our profession.

THE JUDGE. Did you speak to them on that occasion?

COKESON. [*Confidentially*] Well, I didn't like to trouble them without prime facey evidence.

FROME. But it made a very distinct impression on your mind?

COKESON. Ye-es. The clerk Davis could have told you the same.

FROME. Quite so. It's very unfortunate that we've not got him here. Now can you tell me of the morning on which the discovery of the forgery was made? That would be the 18th. Did anything happen that morning?

COKESON. [*With his hand to his ear*] I'm a little deaf.

FROME. Was there anything in the course of that morning—I mean before the discovery—that caught your attention?

COKESON. Ye-es—a woman.

THE JUDGE. How is *this* relevant, Mr. Frome?

FROME. I am trying to establish the state of mind in which the prisoner committed this act, my lord.

THE JUDGE. I quite appreciate that. But this was long after the act.

FROME. Yes, my lord, but it contributes to my contention.

THE JUDGE. Well!

FROME. You say a woman. Do you mean that she came to the office?

COKESON. Ye-es.

FROME. What for?

COKESON. Asked to see young Falder; he was out at the moment.

FROME. Did you see her?

COKESON. I did.

FROME. Did she come alone?

COKESON. [*Confidentially*] Well, there you put me in a difficulty. I mustn't tell you what the office-boy told me.

FROME. Quite so, Mr. Cokeson, quite so——

COKESON. [*Breaking in with an air of " You are young—leave it to me "*] But I think we can get round it. In answer to a question put to her by a third party the woman said to me : " They're mine, sir."

THE JUDGE. What are ? What were ?

COKESON. Her children. They were outside.

THE JUDGE. How do you know ?

COKESON. Your lordship mustn't ask me that, or I shall have to tell you what I was told—and that'd never do.

THE JUDGE. [*Smiling*] The office-boy made a statement.

COKESON. Egg-zactly.

FROME. What I want to ask you, Mr. Cokeson, is this. In the course of her appeal to see Falder, did the woman say anything that you specially remember ?

COKESON. [*Looking at him as if to encourage him to complete the sentence*] A leetle more, sir.

FROME. Or did she not ?

COKESON. She did. I shouldn't like you to have led me to the answer.

FROME. [*With an irritated smile*] Will you tell the jury what it was ?

COKESON. " It's a matter of life and death."

FOREMAN OF THE JURY. Do you mean the woman said that ?

COKESON. [*Nodding*] It's not the sort of thing you like to have said to you.

FROME. [*A little impatiently*] Did Falder come in while she was there ? [COKESON *nods*.] And she saw him, and went away ?

COKESON. Ah ! there I can't follow you. I didn't see her go.

FROME. Well, is she there now ?

COKESON. [*With an indulgent smile*] No !

FROME. Thank you, Mr. Cokeson.   [*He sits down.*

CLEAVER. [*Rising*] You say that on the morning of the forgery the prisoner was jumpy. Well, now, sir, what precisely do you mean by that word ?

COKESON. [*Indulgently*] I *want* you to understand. Have you ever seen a dog that's lost its master ? He was kind of everywhere at once with his eyes.

CLEAVER. Thank you ; I was coming to his eyes. You called them " funny." What are we to understand by that ? Strange, or what ?

COKESON. Ye-es, funny.

CLEAVER. [*Sharply*] Yes, sir, but what may be funny to you may not be funny to me, or to the jury. Did they look frightened, or shy, or fierce, or what ?

COKESON. You make it very hard for me. I give you the word, and you want me to give you another.

CLEAVER. [*Rapping his desk*] Does "funny" mean mad?

COKESON. Not mad, fun——

CLEAVER. Very well! Now you say he had his collar unbuttoned? Was it a hot day?

COKESON. Ye-es; I think it was.

CLEAVER. And did he button it when you called his attention to it?

COKESON. Ye-es, I think he did.

CLEAVER. Would you say that that denoted insanity?

> [*He sits down.* COKESON, *who has opened his mouth to reply, is left gaping.*

FROME. [*Rising hastily*] Have you ever caught him in that dishevelled state before?

COKESON. No! He was *always* clean and quiet.

FROME. That will do, thank you.

> [COKESON *turns blandly to the* JUDGE, *as though to rebuke counsel for not remembering that the* JUDGE *might wish to have a chance; arriving at the conclusion that he is to be asked nothing further, he turns and descends from the box, and sits down next to* JAMES *and* WALTER.

FROME. Ruth Honeywill.

> [RUTH *comes into court, and takes her stand stoically in the witness-box. She is sworn.*

FROME. What is your name, please?

RUTH. Ruth Honeywill.

FROME. How old are you?

RUTH. Twenty-six.

FROME. You are a married woman, living with your husband? A little louder.

RUTH. No, sir; not since July.

FROME. Have you any children?

RUTH. Yes, sir, two.

FROME. Are they living with you?

RUTH. Yes, sir.

FROME. You know the prisoner?

RUTH. [*Looking at him*] Yes.

FROME. What was the nature of your relations with him?

RUTH. We were friends.

THE JUDGE. Friends?

RUTH. [*Simply*] Lovers, sir.

THE JUDGE. [*Sharply*] In what sense do you use that word?

RUTH. We love each other.

THE JUDGE. Yes, but——

RUTH. [*Shaking her head*] No, your lordship—not yet.

THE JUDGE. Not yet! H'm! [*He looks from* RUTH *to* FALDER.] Well!

FROME. What is your husband?

RUTH. Traveller.

FROME. And what was the nature of your married life?

RUTH. [*Shaking her head*] It don't bear talking about.

FROME. Did he ill-treat you, or what?

RUTH. Ever since my first was born.

FROME. In what way?

RUTH. I'd rather not say. All sorts of ways.

THE JUDGE. I am afraid I must stop this, you know.

RUTH. [*Pointing to* FALDER] He offered to take me out of it, sir. We were going to South America.

FROME. [*Hastily*] Yes, quite—and what prevented you?

RUTH. I was outside his office when he was taken away. It nearly broke my heart.

FROME. You knew, then, that he had been arrested?

RUTH. Yes, sir. I called at his office afterwards, and [*pointing to* COKESON] that gentleman told me all about it.

FROME. Now, do you remember the morning of Friday, July 7th?

RUTH. Yes.

FROME. Why?

RUTH. My husband nearly strangled me that morning.

THE JUDGE. Nearly strangled you!

RUTH. [*Bowing her head*] Yes, my lord.

FROME. With his hands, or——?

RUTH. Yes, I just managed to get away from him. I went straight to my friend. It was eight o'clock.

THE JUDGE. In the morning? Your husband was not under the influence of liquor then?

RUTH. It wasn't always that.

FROME. In what condition were you?

RUTH. In very bad condition, sir. My dress was torn, and I was half choking.

FROME. Did you tell your friend what had happened?

RUTH. Yes. I wish I never had.

FROME. It upset him?

RUTH. Dreadfully.

FROME. Did he ever speak to you about a cheque?

RUTH. Never.

FROME. Did he ever give you any money?

RUTH. Yes.

FROME. When was that?

RUTH. On Saturday.

FROME. The 8th?

RUTH. To buy an outfit for me and the children, and get all ready to start.

FROME. Did that surprise you, or not?

RUTH. What, sir?

FROME. That he had money to give you.

RUTH. Yes, because on the morning when my husband nearly killed me my friend cried because he hadn't the money to get me away. He told me afterwards he'd come into a windfall.

FROME. And when did you last see him?

RUTH. The day he was taken away, sir. It was the day we were to have started.

FROME. Oh, yes, the morning of the arrest. Well, did you see him at all between the Friday and that morning? [RUTH *nods.*] What was his manner then?

RUTH. Dumb-like—sometimes he didn't seem able to say a word.

FROME. As if something unusual had happened to him?

RUTH. Yes.

FROME. Painful, or pleasant, or what?

RUTH. Like a fate hanging over him.

FROME. [*Hesitating*] Tell me, did you love the defendant very much?

RUTH. [*Bowing her head*] Yes.

FROME. And had he a very great affection for you?

RUTH. [*Looking at* FALDER] Yes, sir.

FROME. Now, ma'am, do you or do you not think that your danger and unhappiness would seriously affect his balance, his control over his actions?

RUTH. Yes.

FROME. His reason, even?

RUTH. For a moment like, I think it would.

FROME. Was he very much upset that Friday morning, or was he fairly calm?

RUTH. Dreadfully upset. I could hardly bear to let him go from me.

FROME. Do you still love him?

RUTH. [*With her eyes on* FALDER] He's ruined himself for me.

FROME. Thank you.

[*He sits down.* RUTH *remains stoically upright in the witness-box.*

CLEAVER. [*In a considerate voice*] When you left him on the morning of Friday the 7th you would not say that he was out of his mind, I suppose?

RUTH. No, sir.

CLEAVER. Thank you; I've no further questions to ask you.

RUTH. [*Bending a little forward to the jury*] I would have done the same for him; I would indeed.

THE JUDGE. Please, please! You say your married life is an unhappy one? Faults on both sides?

RUTH. Only that I never bowed down to him. I don't see why I should, sir, not to a man like that.

THE JUDGE. You refused to obey him?

RUTH. [*Avoiding the question*] I've always studied him to keep things nice.

THE JUDGE. Until you met the prisoner—was that it?

RUTH. No; even after that.

THE JUDGE. I ask, you know, because you seem to me to glory in this affection of yours for the prisoner.

RUTH. [*Hesitating*] I—I do. It's the only thing in my life now.

THE JUDGE. [*Staring at her hard*] Well, step down, please.

    [RUTH *looks at* FALDER, *then passes quietly down and takes her seat among the witnesses.*

FROME. I call the prisoner, my lord.

    [FALDER *leaves the dock; goes into the witness-box, and is duly sworn.*

FROME. What is your name?

FALDER. William Falder.

FROME. And age?

FALDER. Twenty-three.

FROME. You are not married?   [FALDER *shakes his head.*

FROME. How long have you known the last witness?

FALDER. Six months.

FROME. Is her account of the relationship between you a correct one?

FALDER. Yes.

FROME. You became devotedly attached to her, however?

FALDER. Yes.

THE JUDGE. Though you knew she was a married woman?

FALDER. I couldn't help it, your lordship.

THE JUDGE. Couldn't help it?

FALDER. I didn't seem able to.

    [*The* JUDGE *slightly shrugs his shoulders.*

FROME. How did you come to know her?

FALDER. Through my married sister.

FROME. Did you know whether she was happy with her husband?

FALDER. It was trouble all the time.

FROME. You knew her husband?

FALDER. Only through her—he's a brute.

THE JUDGE. I can't allow indiscriminate abuse of a person not present.

FROME. [*Bowing*] If your lordship pleases. [*To* FALDER.] You admit altering this cheque?   [FALDER *bows his head.*

FROME. Carry your mind, please, to the morning of Friday, July the 7th, and tell the jury what happened.

FALDER. [*Turning to the jury*] I was having my breakfast when she
came. Her dress was all torn, and she was gasping and couldn't
seem to get her breath at all; there were the marks of his fingers
round her throat; her arm was bruised, and the blood had got into
her eyes dreadfully. It frightened me, and then when she told me,
I felt—I felt—well—it was too much for me! [*Hardening suddenly.*]
If you'd seen it, having the feelings for her that I had, you'd have
felt the same, I know.

FROME. Yes?

FALDER. When she left me—because I had to go to the office—
I was out of my senses for fear that he'd do it again, and thinking what
I could do. I couldn't work—all the morning I was like that—
simply couldn't fix my mind on anything. I couldn't think at all.
I seemed to have to keep moving. When Davis—the other clerk—
gave me the cheque—he said: "It'll do you good, Will, to have a
run with this. You seem half off your chump this morning." Then
when I had it in my hand—I don't know how it came, but it just
flashed across me that if I put the *t y* and the nought there would be
the money to get her away. It just came and went—I never thought
of it again. Then Davis went out to his luncheon, and I don't really
remember what I did till I'd pushed the cheque through to the cashier
under the rail. I remember his saying "Notes?" Then I suppose
I knew what I'd done. Anyway, when I got outside I wanted to
chuck myself under a bus; I wanted to throw the money away; but
it seemed I was in for it, so I thought at any rate I'd save her. Of
course the tickets I took for the passage and the little I gave her's
been wasted, and all, except what I was obliged to spend myself, I've
restored. I keep thinking over and over however it was I came to
do it, and how I can't have it all again to do differently!

[FALDER *is silent, twisting his hands before him.*

FROME. How far is it from your office to the bank?

FALDER. Not more than fifty yards, sir.

FROME. From the time Davis went out to lunch to the time you
cashed the cheque, how long do you say it must have been?

FALDER. It couldn't have been four minutes, sir, because I ran all
the way.

FROME. During those four minutes you say you remember nothing?

FALDER. No, sir; only that I ran.

FROME. Not even adding the *t y* and the nought?

FALDER. No, sir. I don't really.

[FROME *sits down, and* CLEAVER *rises.*

CLEAVER. But you remember running, do you?

FALDER. I was all out of breath when I got to the bank.

CLEAVER. And you don't remember altering the cheque?

FALDER. [*Faintly*] No, sir.

CLEAVER. Divested of the romantic glamour which my friend is casting over the case, is this anything but an ordinary forgery? Come.

FALDER. I was half frantic all that morning sir.

CLEAVER. Now, now! You don't deny that the *t y* and the nought were so like the rest of the handwriting as to thoroughly deceive the cashier?

FALDER. It was an accident.

CLEAVER. [*Cheerfully*] Queer sort of accident, wasn't it? On which day did you alter the counterfoil?

FALDER. [*Hanging his head*] On the Wednesday morning.

CLEAVER. Was that an accident too?

FALDER. [*Faintly*] No.

CLEAVER. To do that you had to watch your opportunity, I suppose?

FALDER. [*Almost inaudibly*] Yes.

CLEAVER. You don't suggest that you were suffering under great excitement when you did that?

FALDER. I was haunted.

CLEAVER. With the fear of being found out?

FALDER. [*Very low*] Yes.

THE JUDGE. Didn't it occur to you that the only thing for you to do was to confess to your employers, and restore the money?

FALDER. I was afraid.   [*There is silence.*

CLEAVER. You desired, too, no doubt, to complete your design of taking this woman away?

FALDER. When I found I'd done a thing like that, to do it for nothing seemed so dreadful. I might just as well have chucked myself into the river.

CLEAVER. You knew that the clerk Davis was about to leave England—didn't it occur to you when you altered this cheque that suspicion would fall on him?

FALDER. It was all done in a moment. I thought of it afterwards.

CLEAVER. And that didn't lead you to avow what you'd done?

FALDER. [*Sullenly*] I meant to write when I got out there—I would have repaid the money.

THE JUDGE. But in the meantime your innocent fellow clerk might have been prosecuted.

FALDER. I knew he was a long way off, your lordship. I thought there'd be time. I didn't think they'd find it out so soon.

FROME. I might remind your lordship that as Mr. Walter How had the cheque-book in his pocket till after Davis had sailed, if the discovery had been made only one day later Falder himself would have left, and suspicion would have attached to him, and not to Davis, from the beginning.

THE JUDGE. The question is whether the prisoner knew that suspicion would light on himself, and not on Davis. [*To* FALDER *sharply*.] Did you know that Mr. Walter How had the cheque-book till after Davis had sailed ?

FALDER. I—I—thought—he——

THE JUDGE. Now speak the truth—yes or no !

FALDER. [*Very low*] No, my lord. I had no means of knowing.

THE JUDGE. That disposes of your point, Mr. Frome.

[FROME *bows to the* JUDGE.

CLEAVER. Has any aberration of this nature ever attacked you before ?

FALDER. [*Faintly*] No, sir.

CLEAVER. You had recovered sufficiently to go back to your work that afternoon ?

FALDER. Yes, I had to take the money back.

CLEAVER. You mean the *nine* pounds. Your wits were sufficiently keen for you to remember that ? And you still persist in saying you don't remember altering this cheque. [*He sits down.*

FALDER. If I hadn't been mad I should never have had the courage.

FROME. [*Rising*] Did you have your lunch before going back ?

FALDER. I never ate a thing all day ; and at night I couldn't sleep.

FROME. Now, as to the four minutes that elapsed between Davis's going out and your cashing the cheque : do you say that you recollect *nothing* during those four minutes ?

FALDER. [*After a moment*] I remember thinking of Mr. Cokeson's face.

FROME. Of Mr. Cokeson's face ! Had that any connection with what you were doing ?

FALDER. No, sir.

FROME. Was that in the office, before you ran out ?

FALDER. Yes, and while I was running.

FROME. And that lasted till the cashier said : " Will you have notes ? "

FALDER. Yes, and then I seemed to come to myself—and it was too late.

FROME. Thank you. That closes the evidence for the defence, my lord. [*The* JUDGE *nods, and* FALDER *goes back to his seat in the dock*.

FROME. [*Gathering up notes*] If it please your Lordship—Members of the Jury,—My friend in cross-examination has shown a disposition to sneer at the defence which has been set up in this case, and I am free to admit that nothing I can say will move you, if the evidence has not already convinced you that the prisoner committed this act in a moment when to all practical intents and purposes he was not responsible for his actions ; a moment of such mental and moral vacuity, arising from the violent emotional agitation under which he had been suffering, as to amount to temporary madness. My friend has alluded to the "romantic glamour" with which I have sought to invest this case. Gentlemen, I have done nothing of the kind. I have merely shown you the background of "life"—that palpitating life which, believe me—whatever my friend may say—always lies behind the commission of a crime. Now, gentlemen, we live in a highly civilized age, and the sight of brutal violence disturbs us in a very strange way, even when we have no personal interest in the matter. But when we see it inflicted on a woman whom we love— what then? Just think of what your own feelings would have been, each of you, at the prisoner's age; and then look at him. Well! he is hardly the comfortable, shall we say bucolic, person likely to contemplate with equanimity marks of gross violence on a woman to whom he was devotedly attached. Yes, gentlemen, look at him! He has not a strong face; but neither has he a vicious face. He is just the sort of man who would easily become the prey of his emotions. You have heard the description of his eyes. My friend may laugh at the word "funny"—*I* think it better describes the peculiar uncanny look of those who are strained to breaking-point than any other word which could have been used. I don't pretend, mind you, that his mental irresponsibility was more than a flash of darkness, in which all sense of proportion became lost; but I do contend, that, just as a man who destroys himself at such a moment may be, and often is, absolved from the stigma attaching to the crime of self-murder, so he may, and frequently does, commit other crimes while in this irresponsible condition, and that he may as justly be acquitted of criminal intent and treated as a patient. I admit that this is a plea which might well be abused. It is a matter for discretion. But here you have a case in which there is every reason to give the benefit of the doubt. You heard me ask the prisoner what he thought of during those four fatal minutes. What was his answer? "I thought of Mr. Cokeson's face?" Gentlemen, no man could invent an answer like that; it is absolutely stamped with truth. You have seen the great affection (legitimate or not) existing between him and this woman, who came here to give evidence for him at the risk of her life. It is impossible for you to doubt his distress on the morning when he committed this act. We well know what terrible havoc such distress can make in weak and highly nervous people. It was all the work of a moment. The rest has followed, as death follows a stab to the heart, or water drops if you hold up a jug to empty it. Believe me, gentlemen, there is nothing more tragic in life than the utter impossibility of changing what you have done. Once this cheque was altered and presented, the work of four minutes—four mad minutes—the rest has been silence. But in those four minutes the boy before you has slipped through a door, hardly opened, into

that great cage which never again quite lets a man go—the cage of
the Law. His further acts, his failure to confess, the alteration of
the counterfoil, his preparations for flight, are all evidence—not of
deliberate and guilty intention when he committed the prime act
from which these subsequent acts arose ; no—they are merely evidence of the weak character which is clearly enough his misfortune.
But is a man to be lost because he is bred and born with a weak
character ? Gentlemen, men like the prisoner are destroyed daily
under our law for want of that human insight which sees them as they
are, patients, and not criminals. If the prisoner be found guilty,
and treated as though he were a criminal type, he will, as all experience
shows, in all probability become one. I beg you not to return a
verdict that may thrust him back into prison and brand him for ever.
Gentlemen, Justice is a machine that, when someone has once given
it the starting push, rolls on of itself. Is this young man to be ground
to pieces under this machine for an act which at the worst was one of
weakness ? Is he to become a member of the luckless crews that man
those dark, ill-starred ships called prisons ? Is that to be his voyage
—from which so few return ? Or is he to have another chance, to
be still looked on as one who has gone a little astray, but who will
come back ? I urge you, gentlemen, do not ruin this young man !
For, as a result of those four minutes, ruin, utter and irretrievable,
stares him in the face. He can be saved now. Imprison him as a
criminal, and I affirm to you that he will be lost. He has neither the
face nor the manner of one who can survive that terrible ordeal.
Weigh in the scales his criminality and the suffering he has undergone.
The latter is ten times heavier already. He has lain in prison under
this charge for more than two months. Is he likely ever to forget
that ? Imagine the anguish of his mind during that time. He has
had his punishment, gentlemen, you may depend. The rolling of the
chariot-wheels of Justice over this boy began when it was decided to
prosecute him. We are now already at the second stage. If you
permit it to go on to the third I would not give—that for him.

    [*He holds up finger and thumb in the form of a circle, drops his hand,
        and sits down.*

    [*The jury stir, and consult each other's faces ; then they turn towards
        the counsel for the Crown, who rises, and, fixing his eyes on a
        spot that seems to give him satisfaction, slides them every now
        and then towards the jury.*

    CLEAVER. May it please your Lordship. [*Rising on his toes.*]
Gentlemen of the Jury,—The facts in this case are not disputed, and
the defence, if my friend will allow me to say so, is so thin that I don't
propose to waste the time of the Court by taking you over the evidence.
The plea is one of temporary insanity. Well, gentlemen, I daresay
it is clearer to me than it is to you why this rather—what shall we call

it ?—bizarre defence has been set up. The alternative would have been to plead guilty. Now, gentlemen, if the prisoner had pleaded guilty my friend would have had to rely on a simple appeal to his lordship. Instead of that, he has gone into the byways and hedges and found this—er—peculiar plea, which has enabled him to show you the proverbial woman, to put her in the box—to give, in fact, a romantic glow to this affair. I compliment my friend; I think it highly ingenious of him. By these means, he has—to a certain extent —got round the Law. He has brought the whole story of motive and stress out in court, at first hand, in a way that he would not other- wise have been able to do. But when you have once grasped that fact, gentlemen, you have grasped everything. [*With good-humoured contempt.*] For look at this plea of insanity; we can't put it lower than that. You have heard the woman. She has every reason to favour the prisoner, but what did she say ? She said that the prisoner was *not* insane when she left him in the morning. If he were going out of his mind through distress, that was obviously the moment when insanity would have shown itself. You have heard the managing clerk, another witness for the defence. With some difficulty I elicited from him the admission that the prisoner, though jumpy (a word that he seemed to think you would understand, gentlemen, and I'm sure I hope you do), was *not* mad when the cheque was handed to Davis. I agree with my friend that it's unfortunate that we have not got Davis here, but the prisoner has told you the words with which Davis in turn handed him the cheque; he obviously, therefore, was *not* mad when he received it, or he would not have remembered those words. The cashier has told you that he was certainly in his senses when he cashed it. We have therefore the plea that a man who is sane at ten minutes past one, and sane at fifteen minutes past, may, for the purposes of avoiding the consequences of a crime, call himself insane between those points of time. Really, gentlemen, this is so peculiar a proposition that I am not disposed to weary you with further argument. You will form your own opinion of its value. My friend has adopted this way of saying a great deal to you—and very eloquently—on the score of youth, temptation, and the like. I might point out, however, that the offence, with which the prisoner is charged is one of the most serious known to our law; and there are certain features in this case, such as the suspicion which he allowed to rest on his innocent fellow clerk, and his relations with this married woman, which will render it difficult for you to attach too much importance to such pleading. I ask you, in short, gentlemen, for that verdict of guilty which, in the circumstances, I regard you as, unfortunately, bound to record.

    [*Letting his eyes travel from the* JUDGE *and the jury to* FROME, *he sits down.*]

THE JUDGE. [*Bending a little towards the jury, and speaking in a business-like voice*] Members of the Jury, you have heard the evidence, and the comments on it.   My only business is to make clear to you the issues you have to try.   The facts are admitted, so far as the alteration of this cheque and counterfoil by the prisoner.   The defence set up is that he was not in a responsible condition when he committed the crime.   Well, you have heard the prisoner's story, and the evidence of the other witnesses—so far as it bears on the point of insanity.   If you think that what you have heard establishes the fact that the prisoner was insane at the time of the forgery, you will find him guilty but insane.   If, on the other hand, you conclude from what you have seen and heard that the prisoner was sane—and nothing short of insanity will count—you will find him guilty.   In reviewing the testimony as to his mental condition you must bear in mind very carefully the evidence as to his demeanour and conduct both before and after the act of forgery—the evidence of the prisoner himself, of the woman, of the witness—er—Cokeson, and—er—of the cashier. And in regard to that I especially direct your attention to the prisoner's admission that the idea of adding the *t y* and the nought did come into his mind at the moment when the cheque was handed to him ; and also to the alteration of the counterfoil, and to his subsequent conduct generally.   The bearing of all this on the question of premeditation (and premeditation will imply sanity) is very obvious.   You must not allow any considerations of age or temptation to weigh with you in the finding of your verdict.   Before you can come to a verdict guilty but insane, you must be well and thoroughly convinced that the condition of his mind was such as would have qualified him at the moment for a lunatic asylum.   [*He pauses ; then, seeing that the jury are doubtful whether to retire or no, adds :*] You may retire, gentlemen, if you wish to do so.

> [*The jury retire by a door behind the* JUDGE.   *The* JUDGE *bends over his notes.*   FALDER, *leaning from the dock, speaks excitedly to his solicitor, pointing down at* RUTH.   *The solicitor in turn speaks to* FROME.

FROME. [*Rising*] My lord.   The prisoner is very anxious that I should ask you if your lordship would kindly request the reporters not to disclose the name of the woman witness in the Press reports of these proceedings.   Your lordship will understand that the consequences might be extremely serious to her.

THE JUDGE. [*Pointedly—with the suspicion of a smile*] Well, Mr. Frome, you deliberately took this course which involved bringing her here.

FROME. [*With an ironic bow*] If your lordship thinks I could have brought out the full facts in any other way ?

THE JUDGE. H'm !   Well.

FROME. There is very real danger to her, your lordship.

THE JUDGE. You see, I have to take your word for all that.

FROME. If your lordship would be so kind. I can assure your lordship that I am not exaggerating.

THE JUDGE. It goes very much against the grain with me that the name of a witness should ever be suppressed. [*With a glance at* FALDER, *who is gripping and clasping his hands before him, and then at* RUTH, *who is sitting perfectly rigid with her eyes fixed on* FALDER.] I'll consider your application. It must depend. I have to remember that she may have come here to commit perjury on the prisoner's behalf.

FROME. Your lordship, I really——

THE JUDGE. Yes, yes—I don't suggest anything of the sort, Mr. Frome. Leave it at that for the moment.

[*As he finishes speaking, the jury return, and file back into the box.*

CLERK OF ASSIZE. Members of the Jury, are you agreed on your verdict ?

FOREMAN. We are.

CLERK OF ASSIZE. Is it Guilty, or Guilty, but insane ?

FOREMAN. Guilty.

[*The* JUDGE *nods ; then, gathering up his notes, he looks at* FALDER, *who sits motionless.*

FROME. [*Rising*] If your lordship would allow me to address you in mitigation of sentence. I don't know if your lordship thinks I can add anything to what I have said to the jury on the score of the prisoner's youth, and the great stress under which he acted.

THE JUDGE. I don't think you can, Mr. Frome.

FROME. If your lordship says so—I do most earnestly beg your lordship to give the utmost weight to my plea.   [*He sits down.*

THE JUDGE. [*To the Clerk*] Call upon him.

THE CLERK. Prisoner at the bar, you stand convicted of felony. Have you anything to say for yourself why the Court should not give you judgment according to Law ?   [FALDER *shakes his head.*

THE JUDGE. William Falder, you have been given fair trial and found guilty, in my opinion rightly found guilty, of forgery. [*He pauses ; then, consulting his notes, goes on.*] The defence was set up that you were not responsible for your actions at the moment of committing the crime. There is no doubt, I think, that this was a device to bring out at first hand the nature of the temptation to which you succumbed. For throughout the trial your counsel was in reality making an appeal for mercy. The setting up of this defence of course enabled him to put in some evidence that might weigh in that direction. Whether he was well advised to do so is another matter. He claimed that you should be treated rather as a patient than as a criminal. And this plea of his, which in the end amounted to a passionate appeal, he based in effect on an indictment of the march of Justice, which he practically accused of confirming and completing the process of criminality. Now, in considering how far I should allow weight to his appeal, I have a number of factors to take into account. I have to consider on the one hand the grave nature of your offence, the deliberate way in which you subsequently altered the counterfoil, the danger you caused to an innocent man—and that, to my mind, is a very grave point— and finally I have to consider the necessity of deterring others from following your example. On the other hand, I bear in mind that you are young, that you have hitherto borne a good character, that you were, if I am to believe your evidence and that of your witnesses, in a state of some emotional excitement when you committed this crime. I have every wish, consistently with my duty—not only to you, but to the community, to treat you with leniency. And this brings me to what are the determining factors in my mind in my consideration of your case. You are a clerk in a lawyer's office—that is a very serious aggravation in this case ; no possible excuse can be made for you on the ground that you were not fully conversant with the nature of the crime you were committing and the penalties that attach to it. It is said, however, that you were carried away by your emotions. The story has been told here to-day of your relations with this—er— Mrs. Honeywill ; on that story both the defence and the plea for mercy were in effect based. Now what is that story ? It is that you, a young man, and she a young woman unhappily married, had formed an attachment, which you both say—with what truth I am unable to gauge—had not yet resulted in immoral relations, but which you both admit was about to result in such relationship. Your counsel has made an attempt to palliate this, on the ground that the woman is in what he describes, I think, as " a hopeless position." As to that I can express no opinion. She is a married woman, and the fact is patent that you committed this crime with the view of furthering an immoral design. Now, however I might wish, I am not able to justify to my conscience a plea for mercy which has a basis inimical to morality. It is vitiated *ab initio*. Your counsel has made an attempt also to show that to punish you with further imprisonment would be unjust. I do not follow him in these flights. *The Law, is what it is*—a majestic edifice, sheltering all of us, each stone of which rests on another. I am concerned only with its administration. The crime you have committed is a very serious one. I cannot feel it in accordance with my duty to society to exercise the powers I have in your favour. You will go to penal servitude for three years.

> [FALDER, *who throughout the* JUDGE'S *speech has looked at him steadily, lets his head fall forward on his breast.* RUTH *starts up from her seat as he is taken out by the warders. There is a bustle in court.*

THE JUDGE. [*Speaking to the reporters*] Gentlemen of the Press, I think that the name of the female witness should not be reported.

                [*The reporters bow their acquiescence.*

THE JUDGE. [*To* RUTH, *who is staring in the direction in which* FALDER *has disappeared*] Do you understand, your name will not be mentioned?

COKESON. [*Pulling her sleeve*] The judge is speaking to you.

                [RUTH *turns, stares at the* JUDGE, *and turns away.*

THE JUDGE. I shall sit rather late to-day.   Call the next case.

CLERK OF ASSIZE. [*To a warder*] Put up John Booley.

To cries of "Witnesses in the case of Booley"

The curtain falls.

ACT III

SCENE I

*A prison.   A plainly furnished room, with two large barred windows, over-
looking the prisoners' exercise yard, where men, in yellow clothes marked
with arrows, and yellow brimless caps, are seen in single file at a distance
of four yards from each other, walking rapidly on serpentine white lines
marked on the concrete floor of the yard.   Two warders in blue uniforms,
with peaked caps and swords, are stationed amongst them.   The room
has distempered walls, a bookcase with numerous official-looking books,
a cupboard between the windows, a plan of the prison on the wall, a writing-
table covered with documents.   It is Christmas Eve.*

The GOVERNOR, *a neat, grave-looking man, with a trim, fair moustache,
the eyes of a theorist, and grizzled hair, receding from the temples, is
standing close to this writing-table looking at a sort of rough saw made
out of a piece of metal.   The hand in which he holds it is gloved, for two
fingers are missing.   The chief warder,* WOODER, *a tall, thin, military-
looking man of sixty, with grey moustache and melancholy, monkey-like
eyes, stands very upright two paces from him.*

THE GOVERNOR. [*With a faint, abstracted smile*] Queer-looking
affair, Mr. Wooder !   Where did you find it ?

WOODER. In his mattress, sir.   Haven't come across such a thing
for two years now.

THE GOVERNOR. [*With curiosity*] Had he any set plan ?

WOODER. He'd sawed his window-bar about that much. [*He holds
up his thumb and finger a quarter of an inch apart.*]

THE GOVERNOR. I'll see him this afternoon.   What's his name ?
Moaney !   An old hand, I think ?

WOODER. Yes, sir—fourth spell of penal.   You'd think an old lag
like him would have had more sense by now. [*With pitying contempt.*]
Occupied his mind, he said.   Breaking in and breaking out—that's
all they think about.

THE GOVERNOR. Who's next him ?

WOODER. O'Cleary, sir.

THE GOVERNOR. The Irishman.

WOODER. Next him again there's that young fellow, Falder—star
class—and next him old Clipton.

THE GOVERNOR. Ah, yes !   " The philosopher."   I want to see
him about his eyes.

WOODER. Curious thing, sir : they seem to know when there's one of these tries at escape going on. It makes them restive—there's a regular wave going through them just now.

THE GOVERNOR. [*Meditatively*] Odd things—those waves. [*Turning to look at the prisoners exercising.*] Seem quiet enough out here !

WOODER. That Irishman, O'Cleary, began banging on his door this morning. Little thing like that's quite enough to upset the whole lot. They're just like dumb animals at times.

THE GOVERNOR. I've seen it with horses before thunder—it'll run right through cavalry lines.

> [*The prison* CHAPLAIN *has entered. He is a dark-haired, ascetic man, in clerical undress, with a peculiarly steady, tight-lipped face and slow, cultured speech.*

THE GOVERNOR. [*Holding up the saw*] Seen this, Miller ?

THE CHAPLAIN. Useful-looking specimen.

THE GOVERNOR. Do for the Museum, eh ! [*He goes to the cupboard and opens it, displaying to view a number of quaint ropes, hooks, and metal tools with labels tied on them.*] That'll do, thanks, Mr. Wooder.

WOODER. [*Saluting*] Thank you, sir.   [*He goes out.*

THE GOVERNOR. Account for the state of the men last day or two, Miller ? Seems going through the whole place.

THE CHAPLAIN. No. I don't know of anything.

THE GOVERNOR. By the way, will you dine with us to-morrow ?

THE CHAPLAIN. Christmas Day ? Thanks very much.

THE GOVERNOR. Worries me to feel the men discontented. [*Gazing at the saw.*] Have to punish this poor devil. Can't help liking a man who tries to escape.

> [*He places the saw in his pocket and locks the cupboard again.*

THE CHAPLAIN. Extraordinary perverted will-power—some of them. Nothing to be done till it's broken.

THE GOVERNOR. And not much afterwards, I'm afraid. Ground too hard for golf ?   [WOODER *comes in again.*

WOODER. Visitor to speak to you, sir. I told him it wasn't usual.

THE GOVERNOR. What about ?

WOODER. Shall I put him off, sir ?

THE GOVERNOR. [*Resignedly*] No, no. Let's see him. Don't go, Miller.

> [WOODER *motions to someone without, and as the visitor comes in withdraws.*
>
> [*The visitor is* COKESON, *who is attired in a thick overcoat to the knees, woollen gloves, and carries a top hat.*

COKESON. I'm sorry to trouble you. But it's about a young man you've got here.

THE GOVERNOR. We have a good many.

COKESON. Name of Falder, forgery. [*Producing a card, and handing it to the* GOVERNOR.] Firm of James and Walter How. Well known in the law.

THE GOVERNOR. [*Receiving the card—with a faint smile.*] What do you want to see me about, sir?

COKESON. [*Suddenly seeing the prisoners at exercise*] Why! what a sight!

THE GOVERNOR. Yes, we have that privilege from here; my office is being done up. [*Sitting down at his table.*] Now, please!

COKESON. [*Dragging his eyes with difficulty from the window*] I *wanted* to say a word to you; I shan't keep you long. [*Confidentially.*] Fact is, I oughtn't to be here by rights. His sister came to me—he's got no father and mother—and she was in some distress. " My husband won't let me go and see him," she said; " says he's disgraced the family. And his other sister," she said, " is an invalid." And she asked me to come. Well, I take an interest in him. He was our junior—I go to the same chapel—and I didn't like to refuse.

THE GOVERNOR. I'm afraid he's not allowed a visitor yet—he's only here for his one month's separate confinement.

COKESON. You see, I saw him while he was shut up waiting for his trial and he was lonely.

THE GOVERNOR. [*With faint amusement*] Ring the bell—would you, Miller. [*To* COKESON.] You'd like to hear what the doctor says about him, perhaps.

THE CHAPLAIN. [*Ringing the bell*] You are not accustomed to prisons, it would seem, sir.

COKESON. No. But it's a pitiful sight. He's quite a young fellow. I said to him : " Be patient," I said. " Patient ! " he said. " A day," he said, " shut up in your cell thinking and brooding as I do, it's longer than a year outside, I can't help it," he said; " I try—but I'm built that way, Mr. Cokeson." And he held his hand up to his face. I could see the tears trickling through his fingers. It wasn't nice.

THE CHAPLAIN. He's a young man with rather peculiar eyes, isn't he? Not Church of England, I think?

COKESON. No.

THE CHAPLAIN. I know.

THE GOVERNOR. [*To* WOODER, *who has come in*] Ask the doctor to be good enough to come here for a minute. [WOODER *salutes, and goes out.*] Let's see, he's not married?

COKESON. No. [*Confidentially.*] But there's a party he's very much attached to, not altogether com-il-fo. It's a sad story.

THE CHAPLAIN. If it wasn't for drink and women, sir, this prison might be closed.

COKESON. [*Looking at the* CHAPLAIN *over his spectacles*] Ye-es, but I wanted to tell you about that, special. It preys on his mind.

THE GOVERNOR. Well!

COKESON. Like this. The woman had a nahsty, spiteful feller for a husband, and she'd left him. Fact is, she was going away with our young friend. It's not nice—but I've looked over it. Well, after the trial she said she'd earn her living apart, and wait for him to come out. That was a great consolation to him. But after a month she came to me—I *don't* know her personally—and she said: "I can't earn the children's living, let alone my own—I've got no friends. I'm obliged to keep out of everybody's way, else my husband'd get to know where I was. I'm very much reduced," she said. And she has lost flesh. "I'll have to go in the workhouse!" It's a painful story. I said to her: "No," I said, "not that! I've got a wife an' family, but sooner than you should do that I'll spare you a little myself." "Really," she said—she's a nice creature—"I don't like to take it from you. I think I'd better go back to my husband." Well, I know he's a nahsty, spiteful feller—drinks—but I didn't like to persuade her not to.

THE CHAPLAIN. Surely, no.

COKESON. Ye-es, but I'm sorry now. He's got his three years to serve. I *want* things to be pleasant for him.

THE CHAPLAIN. [*With a touch of impatience*] The Law hardly shares your view, I'm afraid.

COKESON. He's all alone there by himself. I'm afraid it'll turn him silly. And nobody wants that, I s'pose. He cried when I saw him. I don't like to see a man cry.

THE CHAPLAIN. It's a very rare thing for them to give way like that.

COKESON. [*Looking at him—in a tone of sudden dogged hostility*] I keep dogs.

THE CHAPLAIN. Indeed?

COKESON. Ye-es. And I say this: I wouldn't shut one of them up all by himself, week after week, not if he'd bit me all over.

THE CHAPLAIN. Unfortunately, the criminal is not a dog; he has a sense of right and wrong.

COKESON. But that's not the way to make him feel it.

THE CHAPLAIN. Ah! there I'm afraid we must differ.

COKESON. It's the same with dogs. If you treat 'em with kindness they'll do anything for you; but to shut 'em up alone, it only makes 'em savage.

THE CHAPLAIN. Surely you should allow those who have had a little more experience than yourself to know what is best for prisoners.

COKESON. [*Doggedly*] I know this young feller, I've watched him for years. He's eurotic—got no stamina. His father died of consumption. I'm thinking of his future. If he's to be kept there shut up by himself, without a cat to keep him company, it'll do him harm. I said to him: "Where do you feel it?" "I can't tell you, Mr.

Cokeson," he said, " but sometimes I could beat my head against the wall." It's not nice.

> [*During this speech the* DOCTOR *has entered. He is a medium-sized, rather good-looking man, with a quick eye. He stands leaning against the window.*]

THE GOVERNOR. This gentleman thinks the separate is telling on Q 3007—Falder, young thin fellow, star class. What do you say, Doctor Clements ?

THE DOCTOR. He doesn't like it, but it's not doing him any harm, it's only a month.

COKESON. But he was weeks before he came in here.

THE DOCTOR. We can always tell. He's lost no weight since he's been here.

COKESON. It's his state of mind I'm speaking of.

THE DOCTOR. His mind's all right so far. He's nervous, rather melancholy. I don't see signs of anything more. I'm watching him carefully.

COKESON. [*Nonplussed*] I'm glad to hear you say that.

THE CHAPLAIN. [*More suavely*] It's just at this period that we are able to make some impression on them, sir. I am speaking from my special standpoint.

COKESON. [*Turning bewildered to the* GOVERNOR] I *don't* want to be unpleasant, but I do feel it's awkward.

THE GOVERNOR. I'll make a point of seeing him to-day.

COKESON. I'm much obliged to you. I thought perhaps seeing him every day you wouldn't notice it.

THE GOVERNOR. [*Rather sharply*] If any sign of injury to his health shows itself his case will be reported at once. That's fully provided for. [*He rises.*]

COKESON. [*Following his own thoughts*] Of course, what you don't see doesn't trouble you ; but I don't want to have him on my mind.

THE GOVERNOR. I think you may safely leave it to us, sir.

COKESON. [*Mollified and apologetic*] I thought you'd understand me. I'm a plain man—never set myself up against authority. [*Expanding to the* CHAPLAIN.] Nothing personal meant. *Good*-morning.

> [*As he goes out the three officials do not look at each other, but their faces wear peculiar expressions.*]

THE CHAPLAIN. Our friend seems to think that prison is a hospital.

COKESON. [*Returning suddenly with an apologetic air*] There's just one little thing. This woman—I suppose I mustn't ask you to let him see her. It'd be a rare treat for them both. He'll be thinking about her all the time. Of course she's not his wife. But he's quite safe in here. They're a pitiful couple. You couldn't make an exception ?

THE GOVERNOR. [*Wearily*] As you say, my dear sir, I couldn't make an exception; he won't be allowed a visit till he goes to a convict prison.

COKESON. I see. [*Rather coldly.*] Sorry to have troubled you.

[*He again goes out.*

THE CHAPLAIN. [*Shrugging his shoulders*] The plain man indeed, poor fellow.   Come and have some lunch, Clements ?

[*He and the* DOCTOR *go out talking.*

[*The* GOVERNOR, *with a sigh, sits down at his table and takes up a pen.*

The curtain falls.

SCENE II

Part of the ground corridor of the prison.   The walls are coloured with greenish distemper up to a stripe of deeper green about the height of a man's shoulder, and above this line are whitewashed.   The floor is of blackened stones.   Daylight is filtering through a heavily barred window at the end. The doors of four cells are visible.   Each cell door has a little round peephole at the level of a man's eye, covered by a little round disc, which, raised upwards, affords a view of the cell.   On the wall, close to each cell door, hangs a little square board with the prisoner's name, number, and record.

Overhead can be seen the iron structures of the first-floor and second-floor corridors.

The WARDER INSTRUCTOR, *a bearded man in blue uniform, with an apron, and some dangling keys, is just emerging from one of the cells.*

INSTRUCTOR. [*Speaking from the door into the cell*] I'll have another bit for you when that's finished.

O'CLEARY. [*Unseen—in an Irish voice*] Little doubt o' that, sirr.

INSTRUCTOR. [*Gossiping*] Well, you'd rather have it than nothing, I s'pose.

O'CLEARY. An' that's the blessed truth.

[*Sounds are heard of a cell door being closed and locked, and of approaching footsteps.*

INSTRUCTOR. [*In a sharp, changed voice*] Look alive over it !

[*He shuts the cell door, and stands at attention.*

[*The* GOVERNOR *comes walking down the corridor, followed by* WOODER.

THE GOVERNOR. Anything to report ?

INSTRUCTOR. [*Saluting*] Q 3007. [*He points to a cell*] is behind with his work, sir.   He'll lose marks to-day.

[*The* GOVERNOR *nods and passes on to the end cell.   The* INSTRUCTOR *goes away.*

THE GOVERNOR. This is our maker of saws, isn't it?

[*He takes the saw from his pocket as* WOODER *throws open the door of the cell. The convict* MOANEY *is seen lying on his bed, athwart the cell, with his cap on. He springs up and stands in the middle of the cell. He is a raw-boned fellow, about fifty-six years old, with outstanding bat's ears and fierce, staring, steel-coloured eyes.*

WOODER. Cap off! [MOANEY *removes his cap.*] Out here!

[MOANEY *comes to the door.*

THE GOVERNOR. [*Beckoning him out into the corridor, and holding up the saw—with the manner of an officer speaking to a private*] Anything to say about this, my man? [MOANEY *is silent.*] Come!

MOANEY. It passed the time.

THE GOVERNOR. [*Pointing into the cell*] Not enough to do, eh?

MOANEY. It don't occupy your mind.

THE GOVERNOR. [*Tapping the saw*] You might find a better way than this.

MOANEY. [*Sullenly*] Well! What way? I must keep my hand in against the time I get out. What's the good of anything else to me at my time of life? [*With a gradual change to civility, as his tongue warms.*] Ye know that, sir. I'll be in again within a year or two, after I've done this lot. I don't want to disgrace meself when I'm out. *You've* got your pride keeping the prison smart; well, I've got mine. [*Seeing that the* GOVERNOR *is listening with interest, he goes on, pointing to the saw*], *I must* be doin' a little o' this. It's no harm to any one. I was five weeks makin' that saw—a bit of all right it is, too; now I'll get cells. I suppose, or seven days' bread and water. You can't help it, sir, I know that—I quite put meself in your place.

THE GOVERNOR. Now, look here, Moaney, if I pass it over will you give me your word not to try it on again? Think!

[*He goes into the cell, walks to the end of it, mounts the stool, and tries the window-bars.*

THE GOVERNOR. [*Returning*] Well?

MOANEY. [*Who has been reflecting*] I've got another six weeks to do in here, alone. I can't do it and think o' nothing. I must have something to interest me. You've made me a sporting offer, sir, but I can't pass my word about it. I shouldn't like to deceive a gentleman. [*Pointing into the cell.*] Another four hours' steady work would have done it.

THE GOVERNOR. Yes, and what then? Caught, brought back, punishment. Five weeks' hard work to make this, and cells at the end of it, while they put a new bar to your window. Is it worth it, Moaney?

MOANEY. [*With a sort of fierceness*] Yes, it is.

THE GOVERNOR. [*Putting his hand to his brow*] Oh, well! Two days' cells—bread and water.

MOANEY. Thank 'e, sir.

> [*He turns quickly like an animal and slips into his cell.*
> [*The* GOVERNOR *looks after him and shakes his head as* WOODER *closes and locks the cell door.*

THE GOVERNOR. Open Clipton's cell.

> [WOODER *opens the door of* CLIPTON'S *cell.* CLIPTON *is sitting on a stool just inside the door, at work on a pair of trousers. He is a small, thick, oldish man, with an almost shaven head, and smouldering little dark eyes behind smoked spectacles. He gets up and stands motionless in the doorway, peering at his visitors.*

THE GOVERNOR. [*Beckoning*] Come out here a minute, Clipton.

> [CLIPTON, *with a sort of dreadful quietness, comes into the corridor, the needle and thread in his hand. The* GOVERNOR *signs to* WOODER, *who goes into the cell and inspects it carefully.*

THE GOVERNOR. How are your eyes?

CLIPTON. I don't complain of them. I don't see the sun here. [*He makes a stealthy movement, protruding his neck a little.*] There's just one thing, Mr. Governor, as you're speaking to me. I wish you'd ask the cove next door here to keep a bit quieter.

THE GOVERNOR. What's the matter? I don't want any tales, Clipton.

CLIPTON. He keeps me awake. I don't know who he is. [*With contempt.*] One of this *star* class, I expect. Oughtn't to be here with *us*.

THE GOVERNOR. [*Quietly*] Quite right, Clipton. He'll be moved when there's a cell vacant.

CLIPTON. He knocks about like a wild beast in the early morning. I'm not used to it—stops me getting my sleep out. In the evening too. It's not fair, Mr. Governor, as you're speaking to me. Sleep's the comfort I've got here; I'm entitled to take it out full.

> [WOODER *comes out of the cell, and instantly, as though extinguished,* CLIPTON *moves with stealthy suddenness back into is cell.*

WOODER. All right, sir.

> [*The* GOVERNOR *nods. The door is closed and locked.*

THE GOVERNOR. Which is the man who banged on his door this morning?

WOODER. [*Going towards* O'CLEARY'S *cell*] This one, sir; O'Cleary.

> [*He lifts the disc and glances through the peep-hole.*

THE GOVERNOR. Open.

> [WOODER *throws open the door.* O'CLEARY, *who is seated at a little table by the door as if listening, springs up and stands at attention just inside the doorway. He is a broad-faced, middle-aged man, with a wide, thin, flexible mouth, and little holes under his high cheek-bones.*

THE GOVERNOR. Where's the joke, O'Cleary?

O'CLEARY. The joke, your honour? I've not seen one for a long time.

9*

THE GOVERNOR. Banging on your door?

O'CLEARY. Oh! that!

THE GOVERNOR. It's womanish.

O'CLEARY. An' it's that I'm becoming this two months past.

THE GOVERNOR. Anything to complain of?

O'CLEARY. No, sirr.

THE GOVERNOR. You're an old hand; you ought to know better.

O'CLEARY. Yes, I've been through it all.

THE GOVERNOR. You've got a youngster next door; you'll upset him.

O'CLEARY. It cam' over me, your honour. I can't always be the same steady man.

THE GOVERNOR. Work all right?

O'CLEARY. [*Taking up a rush mat he is making*] Oh! I can do it on my head. It's the miserablest stuff—don't take the brains of a mouse. [*Working his mouth.*] It's here I feel it—the want of a little noise—a terrible little wud aise me.

THE GOVERNOR. You know as well as I do that if you were out in the shops you wouldn't be allowed to talk.

O'CLEARY. [*With a look of profound meaning*] Not with my mouth.

THE GOVERNOR. Well, then?

O'CLEARY. But it's the great conversation I'd be havin'.

THE GOVERNOR. [*With a smile*] Well, no more conversation on your door.

O'CLEARY. No, sirr, I wud not have the little wit to repate meself.

THE GOVERNOR. [*Turning*] Good-night.

O'CLEARY. Good-night, your honour.

        [*He turns into his cell. The* GOVERNOR *shuts the door.*

THE GOVERNOR. [*Looking at the record card*] Can't help liking the poor blackguard.

WOODER. He's an amiable man, sir.

THE GOVERNOR. [*Pointing down the corridor*] Ask the doctor to come here, Mr. Wooder.

        [WOODER *salutes and goes away down the corridor.*

    [*The* GOVERNOR *goes to the door of* FALDER'S *cell. He raises his uninjured hand to uncover the peep-hole; but, without uncovering it, shakes his head and drops his hand; then, after scrutinizing the record board, he opens the cell door.* FALDER, *who is standing against it, lurches forward, with a gasp.*

THE GOVERNOR. [*Beckoning him out*] Now tell me; can't you settle down, Falder?

FALDER. [*In a breathless voice*] Yes, sir.

THE GOVERNOR. You know what I mean? It's no good running your head against a stone wall, is it?

FALDER. No, sir.

THE GOVERNOR. Well, come.

FALDER. I try, sir.

THE GOVERNOR. Can't you sleep?

FALDER. Very little. Between two o'clock and getting up's the worst time.

THE GOVERNOR. How's that?

FALDER. [*His lips twitch with a sort of smile*] I don't know, sir. I was always nervous. [*Suddenly voluble.*] Everything seems to get such a size then. I feel I'll never get out as long as I live.

THE GOVERNOR. That's morbid, my lad. Pull yourself together.

FALDER. [*With an equally sudden dogged resentment*] Yes—I've got to——

THE GOVERNOR. Think of all these other fellows?

FALDER. They're used to it.

THE GOVERNOR. They all had to go through it once for the first time, just as you're doing now.

FALDER. Yes, sir, I shall get to be like them in time, I suppose.

THE GOVERNOR. [*Rather taken aback*] H'm! Well! That rests with you. Now, come. Set your mind to it, like a good fellow. You're still quite young. A man can make himself what he likes.

FALDER. [*Wistfully*] Yes, sir.

THE GOVERNOR. Take a good hold of yourself. Do you read?

FALDER. I don't take the words in. [*Hanging his head.*] I know it's no good; but I can't help thinking of what's going on outside.

THE GOVERNOR. Private trouble?

FALDER. Yes.

THE GOVERNOR. You mustn't think about it.

FALDER. [*Looking back at his cell*] How can I help it, sir?

[*He suddenly becomes motionless as* WOODER *and the* DOCTOR *approach. The* GOVERNOR *motions to him to go back into his cell.*

FALDER. [*Quick and low*] I'm quite right in my head, sir.

[*He goes back into his cell.*

THE GOVERNOR. [*To the* DOCTOR] Just go in and see him, Clements.

[*The* DOCTOR *goes into the cell. The* GOVERNOR *pushes the door to, nearly closing it, and walks towards the window.*

WOODER. [*Following*] Sorry you should be troubled like this, sir. Very contented lot of men, on the whole.

THE GOVERNOR. [*Shortly*] You think so?

WOODER. Yes, sir. It's Christmas doing it, in my opinion.

THE GOVERNOR. [*To himself*] Queer, that!

WOODER. Beg pardon, sir?

THE GOVERNOR. Christmas!

[*He turns towards the window, leaving* WOODER *looking at him with a sort of pained anxiety.*

WOODER. [*Suddenly*] Do you think we make show enough, sir ?
If you'd like us to have more holly ?

THE GOVERNOR. Not at all, Mr. Wooder.

WOODER. Very good, sir.

> [*The* DOCTOR *has come out of* FALDER'S *cell, and the* GOVERNOR
> *beckons to him.*

THE GOVERNOR. Well ?

THE DOCTOR. I can't make anything much of him.   He's nervous,
of course.

THE GOVERNOR. Is there any sort of case to report ?   Quite
frankly, Doctor.

THE DOCTOR. Well, I don't think the separate's doing him any
good ; but then I could say the same of a lot of them—they'd get on
better in the shops, there's no doubt.

THE GOVERNOR. You mean you'd have to recommend others ?

THE DOCTOR. A dozen at least.   It's on his nerves.   There's
nothing tangible.   This fellow here [*pointing to* O'CLEARY's *cell*], for
instance—feels it just as much, in his way.   If I once get away from
physical facts—I shan't know where I am.   Conscientiously, sir, I
don't know how to differentiate him.   He hasn't lost weight.
Nothing wrong with his eyes.   His pulse is good.   Talks all right.
It's only another week before he goes.

THE GOVERNOR. It doesn't amount to melancholia ?

THE DOCTOR. [*Shaking his head*] I can report on him if you like ;
but if I do I ought to report on others.

THE GOVERNOR. I see.   [*Looking towards* FALDER's *cell.*] The poor
devil must just stick it then.

> [*As he says this he looks absently at* WOODER.

WOODER. Beg pardon, sir ?

> [*For answer the* GOVERNOR *stares at him, turns on his heel, and
> walks away.*

> [*There is a sound as of beating on metal.*

THE GOVERNOR. [*Stopping*] Mr. Wooder ?

WOODER. Banging on his door, sir.   I thought we should have
more of that.

> [*He hurries forward, passing the* GOVERNOR, *who follows slowly.*

> *The curtain falls.*

SCENE III

FALDER'S *cell, a whitewashed space thirteen feet broad by seven deep, and
nine feet high, with a rounded ceiling.   The floor is of shiny blackened
bricks.   The barred window, with a ventilator, is high up in the middle
of the end wall.   In the middle of the opposite end wall is the narrow
door.   In a corner are the mattress and bedding rolled up (two blankets,*

two sheets, and a coverlet). Above them is a quarter-circular wooden
shelf, on which is a Bible and several little devotional books, piled in
a symmetrical pyramid; there are also a black hair-brush, tooth-
brush, and a bit of soap. In another corner is the wooden frame of a
bed, standing on end. There is a dark ventilator under the window,
and another over the door. FALDER'S *work (a shirt to which he is*
putting button-holes) is hung to a nail on the wall over a small wooden
table, on which the novel "Lorna Doone" lies open. Low down
in the corner by the door is a thick glass screen, about a foot square,
covering the gas-jet let into the wall. There is also a wooden stool, and a
pair of shoes beneath it. Three bright round tins are set under the window.
In fast-failing daylight, FALDER, *in his stockings, is seen standing motionless,*
with his head inclined towards the door, listening. He moves a little
closer to the door, his stockinged feet making no noise. He stops at
the door. He is trying harder and harder to hear something, any little
thing that is going on outside. He springs suddenly upright—as if at a
sound—and remains perfectly motionless. Then, with a heavy sigh,
he moves to his work, and stands looking at it, with his head down;
he does a stitch or two, having the air of a man so lost in sadness that
each stitch is, as it were, a coming to life. Then, turning abruptly,
he begins pacing the cell, moving his head, like an animal pacing its
cage. He stops again at the door, listens, and, placing the palms of
his hands against it with his fingers spread out, leans his forehead against
the iron. Turning from it presently, he moves slowly back towards
the window tracing his way with his finger along the top line of the dis-
temper that runs round the walls. He stops under the window, and,
picking up the lid of one of the tins, peers into it, as if trying to make
a companion of his own face. It has grown very nearly dark. Suddenly
the lid falls out of his hand with a clatter—the only sound that has
broken the silence—and he stands staring intently at the wall where the
stuff of the shirt is hanging rather white in the darkness—he seems to
be seeing somebody or something there. There is a sharp tap and
click; the cell light behind the glass screen has been turned up. The
cell is brightly lighted. FALDER *is seen gasping for breath.*
A sound from far away, as of distant, dull beating on thick metal, is suddenly
audible. FALDER *shrinks back, not able to bear this sudden clamour.*
But the sound grows, as though some great tumbril were rolling towards
the cell. And gradually it seems to hypnotize him. He begins creeping
inch by inch nearer to the door. The banging sound, travelling from cell
to cell, draws closer and closer; FALDER'S *hands are seen moving*
as if his spirit had already joined in this beating, and the sound swells
till it seems to have entered the very cell. He suddenly raises his clenched
fists. Panting violently, he flings himself at his door, and beats on it.

The curtain falls.

ACT IV

The scene is again COKESON'S *room, at a few minutes to ten of a March morning, two years later. The doors are all open.* SWEEDLE, *now blessed with a sprouting moustache, is getting the offices ready. He arranges papers on* COKESON'S *table; then goes to a covered washstand, raises the lid, and looks at himself in the mirror. While he is gazing his fill* Ruth Honeywill *comes in through the outer office and stands in the doorway. There seems a kind of exultation and excitement behind her habitual impassivity.*

SWEEDLE. [*Suddenly seeing her, and dropping the lid of the washstand with a bang*] Hello! It's you!

RUTH. Yes.

SWEEDLE. There's only me here! They don't waste their time hurrying down in the morning. Why, it must be two years since we had the pleasure of seeing you. [*Nervously.*] What have you been doing with yourself?

RUTH. [*Sardonically*] Living.

SWEEDLE. [*Impressed*] If you want to see *him* [*he points to* COKESON'S *chair*], he'll be here directly—never misses—not much. [*Delicately.*] I hope our friend's back from the country. His time's been up these three months, if I remember. [RUTH *nods.*] I was awful sorry about that. The governor made a mistake—if you ask me.

RUTH. He did.

SWEEDLE. He ought to have given him a chanst. And, *I* say, the judge ought to ha' let him go after that. They've forgot what human nature's like. Whereas *we* know. [RUTH *gives him a honeyed smile.*]

SWEEDLE. They come down on you like a cartload of bricks, flatten you out, and when you don't swell up again they complain of it. I know 'em—seen a lot of that sort of thing in my time. [*He shakes his head in the plenitude of wisdom.*] Why, only the other day the governor——

[*But* COKESON *has come in through the outer office; brisk with east wind, and decidedly greyer.*

COKESON. [*Drawing off his coat and gloves*] Why! it's you! [*Then motioning* SWEEDLE *out, and closing the door.*] Quite a stranger! Must be two years. D'you want to see me? I can give you a minute. Sit down! Family well?

RUTH. Yes. I'm not living where I was.

COKESON. [*Eyeing her askance*] I hope things are more comfortable at home.

262

Ruth. I couldn't stay with Honeywill, after all.

Cokeson. You haven't done anything rash, I hope. I should be sorry if you'd done anything rash.

Ruth. I've kept the children with me.

Cokeson. [*Beginning to feel that things are not so jolly as he had hoped*] Well, I'm glad to have seen you. You've not heard from the young man, I suppose, since he came out ?

Ruth. Yes, I ran across him yesterday.

Cokeson. I hope he's well.

Ruth. [*With sudden fierceness*] He can't get anything to do. It's dreadful to see him. He's just skin and bone.

Cokeson. [*With genuine concern*] Dear me ! I'm sorry to hear that. [*On his guard again.*] Didn't they find him a place when his time was up ?

Ruth. He was only there three weeks. It got out.

Cokeson. I'm sure I don't know what I can do for you. I don't like to be snubby.

Ruth. I can't bear his being like that.

Cokeson. [*Scanning her not unprosperous figure*] I know his relations aren't very forthy about him. Perhaps *you* can do something for him, till he finds his feet.

Ruth. Not now. I could have—but not *now*.

Cokeson. I don't understand.

Ruth. [*Proudly*] I've seen *him* again—that's all over.

Cokeson. [*Staring at her—disturbed*] I'm a family man—I don't want to hear anything unpleasant. Excuse me—I'm very busy.

Ruth. I'd have gone home to my people in the country long ago, but they've never got over me marrying Honeywill. I never was waywise, Mr. Cokeson, but I'm proud. I was only a girl, you see, when I married him. I thought the world of him, of course . . . he used to come travelling to our farm.

Cokeson. [*Regretfully*] I did hope you'd have got on better, after you saw me.

Ruth. He used me worse than ever. He couldn't break my nerve, but I lost my health ; and then he began knocking the children about. . . . I couldn't stand that. I wouldn't go back now, if he were dying.

Cokeson. [*Who has risen and is shifting about as though dodging a stream of lava*] We mustn't be violent, must we ?

Ruth. [*Smouldering*] A man that can't behave better than that——

[*There is silence.*

Cokeson. [*Fascinated in spite of himself*] Then there you were ! And what did you do then ?

Ruth. [*With a shrug*] Tried the same as when I left him before . . . making shirts . . . cheap things. It was the best I could get, but I never made more than ten shillings a week, buying my own cotton and working all day; I hardly ever got to bed till past twelve. I kept at it for nine months. [*Fiercely.*] Well, I'm not fit for that; I wasn't made for it. I'd rather die.

COKESON. My dear woman! We mustn't talk like that.

RUTH. It was starvation for the children too—after what they'd always had. I soon got not to care. I used to be too tired.

[*She is silent.*

COKESON. [*With fearful curiosity*] And—what happened then?

RUTH. [*With a laugh*] My employer happened then—he's happened ever since.

COKESON. Dear! Oh dear! I never came across a thing like this.

RUTH. [*Dully*] He's treated me all right. But I've done with that. [*Suddenly her lips begin to quiver, and she hides them with the back of her hand.*] I never thought I'd see *him* again, you see. It was just a chance I met him by Hyde Park. We went in there and sat down, and he told me all about himself. Oh! Mr. Cokeson, give him another chance.

COKESON. [*Greatly disturbed*] Then you've both lost your livings! What a horrible position!

RUTH. If he could only get here—where there's nothing to find out about him!

COKESON. We can't have anything derogative to the firm.

RUTH. I've no one else to go to.

COKESON. I'll speak to the partners, but I don't think they'll take him, under the circumstances. I don't really.

RUTH. He came with me; he's down there in the street.

[*She points to the window.*

COKESON. [*On his dignity*] He shouldn't have done that until he's sent for. [*Then softening at the look on her face.*] We've got a vacancy, as it happens, but I can't promise anything.

RUTH. It would be the saving of him.

COKESON. Well, I'll do what I can, but I'm not sanguine. Now tell him that I don't want him here till I see how things are. Leave your address? [*Repeating her.*] 83, Mullingar Street? [*He notes it on blotting-paper.*] Good-morning.

RUTH. Thank you.

[*She moves towards the door, turns as if to speak but does not, and goes away.*

COKESON. [*Wiping his head and forehead with a large white cotton handkerchief*] What a business! [*Then, looking amongst his papers, he sounds his bell.* SWEEDLE *answers it.*]

COKESON. Was that young Richards coming here to-day after the clerk's place?

SWEEDLE. Yes.

COKESON. Well, keep him in the air; I don't want to see him yet.

SWEEDLE. What shall I tell him, sir?

COKESON. [*With asperity*] Invent something. Use your brains. Don't stump him off altogether.

SWEEDLE. Shall I tell him that we've got illness, sir?

COKESON. No! Nothing untrue. Say I'm not here to-day.

SWEEDLE. Yes, sir. Keep him hankering?

COKESON. Exactly. And look here. You remember Falder? I may be having him round to see me. Now, treat him like you'd have him treat you in a similar position.

SWEEDLE. I naturally should do.

COKESON. That's right. When a man's down never hit 'im. 'Tisn't necessary. Give him a hand up. That's a metaphor I recommend to you in life. It's sound policy.

SWEEDLE. Do you think the governors will take him on again, sir?

COKESON. Can't say anything about that. [*At the sound of someone having entered the outer office.*] Who's there?

SWEEDLE. [*Going to the door and looking*] It's Falder, sir.

COKESON. [*Vexed*] Dear me! That's very naughty of her. Tell him to call again. I don't want——

> [*He breaks off as* FALDER *comes in.* FALDER *is thin, pale, older, his eyes have grown more restless. His clothes are very worn and loose.*
>
>> [SWEEDLE, *nodding cheerfully, withdraws.*

COKESON. Glad to see you. You're rather previous. [*Trying to keep things pleasant.*] Shake hands! She's striking while the iron's hot. [*He wipes his forehead.*] I don't blame her. She's anxious.

> [FALDER *timidly takes* COKESON'S *hand and glances towards the partners' door.*

COKESON. No—not yet! Sit down! [FALDER *sits in the chair at the side of* COKESON'S *table, on which he places his cap.*] Now you are here I'd like you to give me a little account of yourself. [*Looking at him over his spectacles.*] How's your health?

FALDER. I'm alive, Mr. Cokeson.

COKESON. [*Preoccupied*] I'm glad to hear that. About this matter. I don't like doing anything out of the ordinary; it's not my habit. I'm a plain man, and I want everything smooth and straight. But I promised your friend to speak to the partners, and I always keep my word.

FALDER. I just want a chance, Mr. Cokeson. I've paid for that job a thousand times and more. I have, sir. No one knows. They say I weighed more when I came out than when I went in. They couldn't weigh me here [*he touches his head*] or here [*he touches his heart, and gives a sort of laugh*]. Till last night I'd have thought there was nothing in here at all.

COKESON. [*Concerned*] You've not got heart disease?

FALDER. Oh! they passed me sound enough.

COKESON. But they got you a place, didn't they?

FALDER. Yes; very good people, knew all about it—very kind to me. I thought I was going to get on first-rate. But one day, all of a sudden, the other clerks got wind of it. . . . I couldn't stick it, Mr. Cokeson, I couldn't, sir.

COKESON. Easy, my dear fellow, easy.

FALDER. I had one small job after that, but it didn't last.

COKESON. How was that?

FALDER. It's no good deceiving you, Mr. Cokeson. The fact is, I seem to be struggling against a thing that's all round me. I can't explain it: it's as if I was in a net; as fast as I cut it here, it grows up there. I didn't act as I ought to have, about references; but what are you to do? You must have them. And that made me afraid, and I left. In fact, I'm—I'm afraid all the time now.

[*He bows his head and leans dejectedly silent over the table.*]

COKESON. I feel for you—I do really. Aren't your sisters going to do anything for you?

FALDER. One's in consumption. And the other——

COKESON. Ye . . . es. She told me her husband wasn't quite pleased with you.

FALDER. When I went there—they were at supper—my sister wanted to give me a kiss—I know. But he just looked at her, and said: "What have you come for?" Well, I pocketed my pride and I said: "Aren't you going to give me your hand, Jim? Cis is, I know," I said. "Look here!" he said, "that's all very well, but we'd better come to an understanding. I've been expecting you, and I've made up my mind. I'll give you twenty-five pounds to go to Canada with." "I see," I said—"good riddance! No, thanks; keep your twenty-five pounds." Friendship's a queer thing when you've been where I have.

COKESON. I understand. Will you take the twenty-five pound from me? [*Flustered, as* FALDER *regards him with a queer smile.*] Quite without prejudice; I meant it kindly.

FALDER. They wouldn't let me in.

COKESON. Oh! Ah! No! You aren't looking the thing.

FALDER. I've slept in the Park three nights this week. The dawns aren't all poetry there. But meeting her—I feel a different man this morning. I've often thought the being fond of her's the best thing about me; it's sacred, somehow—and yet it did for me. That's queer, isn't it?

COKESON. I'm sure we're all very sorry for you.

FALDER. That's what I've found, Mr. Cokeson. Awfully sorry for me. [*With quiet bitterness.*] But it doesn't do to associate with criminals!

COKESON. Come, come, it's no use calling yourself names. That never did a man any good. Put a face on it.

FALDER. It's easy enough to put a face on it, sir, when you're independent. Try it when you're down like me. They talk about giving you your deserts. Well, I think I've had just a bit over.

COKESON. [*Eyeing him askance over his spectacles*] I hope they haven't made a Socialist of you.

[FALDER *is suddenly still, as if brooding over his past self ; he utters a peculiar laugh.*

COKESON. You must give them credit for the best intentions. Really you must. Nobody wishes you harm, I'm sure.

FALDER. I believe that, Mr. Cokeson. Nobody wishes you harm, but they down you all the same. This feeling—— [*He stares round him, as though at something closing in.*] It's crushing me. [*With sudden impersonality.*] I know it is.

COKESON. [*Horribly disturbed.*] There's nothing there ! We must try and take it quiet. I'm sure I've often had you in my prayers. Now leave it to me. I'll use my gumption and take 'em when they're jolly.   [*As he speaks the two partners come in.*

COKESON. [*Rather disconcerted, but trying to put them all at ease*] I didn't expect you quite so soon. I've just been having a talk with this young man. I think you'll remember him.

JAMES. [*With a grave, keen look*] Quite well. How are you, Falder ?

WALTER. [*Holding out his hand almost timidly*] Very glad to see you again, Falder.

FALDER. [*Who has recovered his self-control, takes the hand*] Thank you, sir.

COKESON. Just a word, Mr. James. [*To* FALDER, *pointing to the clerks' office.*] You might go in there a minute. You know your way. Our junior won't be coming this morning. His wife's just had a little family.   [FALDER *goes uncertainly out into the clerks' office.*

COKESON. [*Confidentially*] I'm bound to tell you all about it. He's quite penitent. But there's a prejudice against him. And you're not seeing him to advantage this morning ; he's under-nourished. It's very trying to go without your dinner.

JAMES. Is that so, Cokeson ?

COKESON. I wanted to ask you. He's had his lesson. Now *we* know all about him, and we want a clerk. There is a young fellow applying, but I'm keeping him in the air.

JAMES. A gaol-bird in the office, Cokeson ? I don't see it.

WALTER. " The rolling of the chariot-wheels of Justice ! " I've never got that out of my head.

JAMES. I've nothing to reproach myself with in this affair. What's he been doing since he came out ?

COKESON. He's had one or two places, but he hasn't kept them. He's sensitive—quite natural. Seems to fancy everybody's down on him.

JAMES. Bad sign. Don't like the fellow—never did from the first. " Weak character " 's written all over him.

WALTER. I think we owe him a leg up.

JAMES. He brought it all on himself.

WALTER. The doctrine of full responsibility doesn't quite hold in these days.

JAMES. [*Rather grimly*] You'll find it safer to hold it for all that, my boy.

WALTER. For oneself, yes—not for other people, thanks.

JAMES. Well! I don't want to be hard.

COKESON. I'm glad to hear you say that. He seems to see something [*spreading his arms*] round him. 'Tisn't healthy.

JAMES. What about that woman he was mixed up with? I saw someone uncommonly like her outside as we came in.

COKESON. *That!* Well, I can't keep anything from you. He has met her.

JAMES. Is she with her husband?

COKESON. No.

JAMES. Falder living with her, I suppose?

COKESON. [*Desperately trying to retain the new-found jollity*] I don't know that of my own knowledge. 'Tisn't my business.

JAMES. It's *our* business, if we're going to engage him, Cokeson.

COKESON. [*Reluctantly*] I ought to tell you, perhaps. I've had the party here this morning.

JAMES. I thought so. [*To* WALTER.] No, my dear boy, it won't do. Too shady altogether!

COKESON. The two things together make it very awkward for you —I see that.

WALTER. [*Tentatively*] I don't quite know what we have to do with his private life.

JAMES. No, no! He must make a clean sheet of it, or he can't come here.

WALTER. Poor devil?

COKESON. Will you have him in? [*And as* JAMES *nods.*] I think I can get him to see reason.

JAMES. [*Grimly*] You can leave that to me, Cokeson.

WALTER. [*To* JAMES, *in a low voice, while* COKESON *is summoning* FALDER] His whole future may depend on what we do, dad.

[FALDER *comes in. He has pulled himself together, and presents a steady front.*

JAMES. Now look here, Falder. My son and I want to give you another chance; but there are two things I must say to you. In the first place : It's no good coming here as a victim. If you've any notion that you've been unjustly treated—get rid of it. You can't play fast and loose with morality and hope to go scot-free. If society didn't take care of itself, nobody would—the sooner you realize that the better.

FALDER. Yes, sir ; but—may I say something ?

JAMES. Well ?

FALDER. I had a lot of time to think it over in prison.   [*He stops.*

COKESON. [*Encouraging him*] I'm sure you did.

FALDER. There were all sorts there.   And what I mean, sir, is, that if we'd been treated differently the first time, and put under somebody that could look after us a bit, and not put in prison, not a quarter of us would ever have got there.

JAMES. [*Shaking his head*] I'm afraid I've very grave doubts of that, Falder.

FALDER. [*With a gleam of malice*] Yes, sir, so I found.

JAMES. My good fellow, don't forget that you began it.

FALDER. I never wanted to do wrong.

JAMES. Perhaps not.   But you did.

FALDER. [*With all the bitterness of his past suffering*] It's knocked me out of time.   [*Pulling himself up.*] That is, I mean, I'm not what I was.

JAMES. This isn't encouraging for us, Falder.

COKESON. He's putting it awkwardly, Mr. James.

FALDER. [*Throwing over his caution from the intensity of his feeling*] I mean it, Mr. Cokeson.

JAMES. Now, lay aside all those thoughts, Falder, and look to the future.

FALDER. [*Almost eagerly*] Yes, sir, but you don't understand what prison is.   It's here it gets you.   [*He grips his chest.*

COKESON. [*In a whisper to James*] I told you he wanted nourishment.

WALTER. Yes, but, my dear fellow, that'll pass away.   Time's merciful.

FALDER. [*With his face twitching*] I hope so, sir.

JAMES. [*Much more gently*] Now, my boy, what you've got to do is to put all the past behind you and build yourself up a steady reputation. And that brings me to the second thing. This woman you were mixed up with—you must give us your word, you know, to have done with that.   There's no chance of your keeping straight if you're going to begin your future with such a relationship.

FALDER. [*Looking from one to the other with a hunted expression*] But, sir . . . but, sir . . . it's the one thing I looked forward to all that time. And she too . . . I couldn't find her before last night.

[*During this and what follows* COKESON *becomes more and more uneasy.*

JAMES. This is painful, Falder. But you must see for yourself that it's impossible for a firm like this to close its eyes to everything. Give us this proof of your resolve to keep straight, and you can come back—not otherwise.

FALDER. [*After staring at* JAMES, *suddenly stiffens himself*] I couldn't give her up. I couldn't! Oh, sir! I'm all she's got to look to. And I'm sure she's all I've got.

JAMES. I'm very sorry, Falder, but I must be firm. It's for the benefit of you both in the long run. No good can come of this connection. It was the cause of all your disaster.

FALDER. But, sir, it means—having gone through all that—getting broken up—my nerves are in an awful state—for nothing. I did it for her.

JAMES. Come! If she's anything of a woman she'll see it for herself. She won't want to drag you down further. If there were a prospect of your being able to marry her—it might be another thing.

FALDER. It's not my fault, sir, that she couldn't get rid of him— she would have if she could. That's been the whole trouble from the beginning. [*Looking suddenly at* WALTER.] . . . If anybody would help her! It's only money wanted now, I'm sure.

COKESON. [*Breaking in, as* WALTER *hesitates, and is about to speak.*] I don't think we need consider that—it's rather far-fetched.

FALDER. [*To* WALTER, *appealing*] He must have given her full cause since; she could prove that he drove her to leave him.

WALTER. I'm inclined to do what you say, Falder, if it can be managed.

FALDER. Oh, sir! [*He goes to the window and looks down into the street.*

COKESON. [*Hurriedly*] You don't take me, Mr. Walter. I have my reasons.

FALDER. [*From the window*] She's down there, sir. Will you see her? I can beckon to her from here.

[WALTER *hesitates, and looks from* COKESON *to* JAMES.

JAMES. [*With a sharp nod*] Yes, let her come.

[FALDER *beckons from the window.*

COKESON. [*In a low fluster to* JAMES *and* WALTER] No, Mr. James. She's not been quite what she ought to ha' been, while this young man's been away. She's lost her chance. We can't consult how to swindle the Law.

[FALDER *has come from the window. The three men look at him in a sort of awed silence.*

FALDER. [*With instinctive apprehension of some change—looking from one to the other*] There's been nothing between us, sir, to prevent it. . . . What I said at the trial was true. And last night we only just sat in the Park. [SWEEDLE *comes in from the outer office.*

COKESON. What is it?

SWEEDLE. Mrs. Honeywill.   [*There is silence.*

JAMES. Show her in.

> [RUTH *comes slowly in, and stands stoically with* FALDER *on one side and the three men on the other. No one speaks.* COKESON *turns to his table, bending over his papers as though the burden of the situation were forcing him back into his accustomed groove.*

JAMES. [*Sharply*] Shut the door there. [SWEEDLE *shuts the door.*] We've asked you to come up because there are certain facts to be faced in this matter. I understand you have only just met Falder again.

RUTH. Yes—only yesterday.

JAMES. He's told us about himself, and we're very sorry for him. I've promised to take him back here if he'll make a fresh start. [*Looking steadily at* RUTH.] This is a matter that requires courage, ma'am.

> [*Ruth, who is looking at* FALDER, *begins to twist her hands in front of her as though prescient of disaster.*

FALDER. Mr. Walter How is good enough to say that he'll help us to get you a divorce.

> [RUTH *flashes a startled glance at* JAMES *and* WALTER.

JAMES. I don't think that's practicable, Falder.

FALDER. But, sir—— !

JAMES. [*Steadily*] Now, Mrs. Honeywill. You're fond of him.

RUTH. Yes, sir; I love him.   [*She looks miserably at* FALDER.

JAMES. Then you don't want to stand in his way, do you?

RUTH. [*In a faint voice*] I could take care of him.

JAMES. The best way you can take care of him will be to give him up.

FALDER. Nothing shall make me give you up. You can get a divorce. There's been nothing between us, has there?

RUTH. [*Mournfully shaking her head—without looking at him*] No.

FALDER. We'll keep apart till it's over, sir; if you'll only help us—we promise.

JAMES. [*To* RUTH] You see the thing plainly, don't you? You see what I mean?

RUTH. [*Just above a whisper*] Yes.

COKESON. [*To himself*] There's a dear woman.

JAMES. The situation is impossible.

RUTH. Must I, sir?

JAMES. [*Forcing himself to look at her*] I put it to you, ma'am. His future is in your hands.

RUTH. [*Miserably*] I want to do the best for him.

JAMES. [*A little huskily*] That's right, that's right!

FALDER. I don't understand. You're not going to give me up

—after all this ?   There's something——   [*Starting forward to* JAMES.] Sir, I swear solemnly there's been nothing between us.

JAMES. I believe you, Falder.   Come, my lad, be as plucky as she is.

FALDER. Just now you were going to help us. [*He stares at* RUTH, *who is standing absolutely still; his face and hands twitch and quiver as the truth dawns on him.*] What is it ?   You've not been——

WALTER. Father !

JAMES. [*Hurriedly*] There, there !   That'll do, that'll do !   I'll give you your chance, Falder.   Don't let me know what you do with yourselves, that's all.

FALDER. [*As if he has not heard*] Ruth ?

     [RUTH *looks at him; and* FALDER *covers his face with his hands. There is silence.*

COKESON. [*Suddenly*] There's someone out there.   [*To* RUTH.] Go in here.   You'll feel better by yourself for a minute.

     [*He points to the clerks' room and moves towards the outer office.* FALDER *does not move.* RUTH *puts out her hand timidly. He shrinks back from the touch. She turns and goes miserably into the clerks' room. With a brusque movement he follows, seizing her by the shoulder just inside the doorway.* COKESON *shuts the door.*

JAMES. [*Pointing to the outer office*] Get rid of that, whoever it is.

SWEEDLE. [*Opening the office door, in a scared voice*] Detective-Sergeant Wister.   [*The detective enters, and closes the door behind him.*

WISTER. Sorry to disturb you, sir.   A clerk you had here, two years and a half ago.   I arrested him in this room.

JAMES. What about him ?

WISTER. I thought perhaps I might get his whereabouts from you.

     [*There is an awkward silence.*

COKESON. [*Pleasantly, coming to the rescue*] We're not responsible for his movements ; you know that.

JAMES. What do you want with him ?

WISTER. He's failed to report himself lately.

WALTER. Has he to keep in touch with the police then ?

WISTER. We're bound to know his whereabouts.   I dare say we shouldn't interfere, sir, but we've just heard there's a serious matter of obtaining employment with a forged reference.   What with the two things together—we must have him.

     [*Again there is silence.* WALTER *and* COKESON *steal glances at* JAMES, *who stands staring steadily at the detective.*

COKESON. [*Expansively*] We're very busy at the moment.   If you could make it convenient to call again we might be able to tell you then.

JAMES. [*Decisively*] I'm a servant of the Law, but I dislike peaching.

In fact, I can't do such a thing.   If you want him you must find him without us.

> [*As he speaks his eye falls on* FALDER'S *cap, still lying on the table, and his face contracts.*

WISTER. [*Noting the gesture—quietly*] Very good, sir.   I ought to warn you that sheltering——

JAMES. I shelter no one.   But you mustn't come here and ask questions which it's not my business to answer.

WISTER. [*Dryly*] I won't trouble you further then, gentlemen.

COKESON. I'm sorry we couldn't give you the information.   You quite understand, don't you ?   Good-morning !

> [WISTER *turns to go, but instead of going to the door of the outer office he goes to the door of the clerks' room.*

COKESON. The other door . . . the other door !

> [WISTER *opens the clerks' door.* RUTH'S *voice is heard :* " Oh, do ! " *and* FALDER'S : " I can't ! "   *There is a little pause ; then, with sharp fright,* RUTH *says :* " Who's that ? " WISTER *has gone in.*
>
> > [*The three men look aghast at the door.*

WISTER. [*From within*] Keep back, please !

> [*He comes swiftly out with his arm twisted in* FALDER'S.   *The latter gives a white, staring look at the three men.*

WALTER. Let him go this time, for God's sake !

WISTER. I couldn't take the responsibility, sir.

FALDER. [*With a queer, desperate laugh*] Good !

> [*Flinging a look back at* RUTH, *he throws up his head, and goes out through the outer office, half dragging* WISTER *after him.*

WALTER. [*With despair*] That finishes him.   It'll go on for ever now.

> [SWEEDLE *can be seen staring through the outer door.   There are sounds of footsteps descending the stone stairs ; suddenly a dull thud, a faint " My God ! " in* WISTER'S *voice.*

JAMES. What's that !

> [SWEEDLE *dashes forward.   The door swings to behind him.   There is dead silence.*

WALTER. [*Starting forward to the inner room*] The woman—she's fainting !

> [*He and* COKESON *support the fainting* RUTH *from the doorway of the clerks' room.*

COKESON. [*Distracted*] Here, my dear !   There, there !

WALTER. Have you any brandy ?

COKESON. I've got sherry.

WALTER. Get it, then.   Quick !

> [*He places* RUTH *in a chair—which* JAMES *has dragged forward.*

COKESON. [*With sherry*] Here! It's good strong sherry.

[*They try to force the sherry between her lips.*

[*There is the sound of feet, and they stop to listen.*

[*The outer door is reopened—*WISTER *and* SWEEDLE *are seen carrying some burden.*

JAMES. [*Hurrying forward*] What is it?

[*They lay the burden down in the outer office, out of sight, and all but* RUTH *cluster round it, speaking in hushed voices.*

WISTER. He jumped—neck's broken.

WALTER. Good God!

WISTER. He must have been mad to think he could give me the slip like that. And what was it—just a few months!

WALTER. [*Bitterly*] Was that all?

JAMES. What a desperate thing! [*Then, in a voice unlike his own.*] Run for a doctor—you! [SWEEDLE *rushes from the outer office.*] An ambulance!

[WISTER *goes out. On* RUTH'S *face an expression of fear and horror has been seen growing, as if she dared not turn towards the voices. She now rises and steals towards them.*

WALTER. [*Turning suddenly*] Look!

[*The three men shrink back out of her way.* RUTH *drops on her knees by the body.*

RUTH. [*In a whisper*] What is it? He's not breathing. [*She crouches over him.*] My dear! My pretty!

[*In the outer office doorway the figures of men are seen standing.*

RUTH. [*Leaping to her feet*] No, no! No, no! He's dead!

[*The figures of the men shrink back.*

COKESON. [*Stealing forward. In a hoarse voice*] There, there, poor dear woman! [*At the sound behind her* RUTH *faces round at him.*

COKESON. No one'll touch him now! Never again! He's safe with gentle Jesus!

[RUTH *stands as though turned to stone in the doorway staring at* COKESON, *who, bending humbly before her, holds out his hand as one would to a lost dog.*

The curtain falls.

THE FUGITIVE

" With a hey-ho chivy—
Hark-forrard, Hark-forrard, tantivy ! "

CAST OF THE FIRST PRODUCTION AT THE ROYAL COURT THEATRE, SEPTEMBER 16, 1913

GEORGE DEDMOND.	*Mr. Claude King*
CLARE	*Miss Irene Rooke*
GENERAL SIR CHARLES DEDMOND, K.C.B.	*Mr. Nigel Playfair*
LADY DEDMOND	*Miss Alma Murray*
REGINALD HUNTINGDON	*Mr. Hylton Allen*
EDWARD FULLARTON	*Mr. Leslie Rea*
MRS. FULLARTON	*Miss Estelle Winwood*
PAYNTER	*Mr. Frank Macrae*
BURNEY.	*Miss Doris Bateman*
TWISDEN	*Mr. J. H. Roberts*
HAYWOOD	*Mr. Charles Groves*
MALISE	*Mr. Milton Rosmer*
MRS. MILER	*Mrs. A. B. Tapping*
PORTER.	*Mr. Eric Barber*
A MESSENGER BOY	

CHARACTERS IN ACT FOUR

A YOUNG MAN	*Mr. Vincent Clive*
ARNAUD	*Mr. Clarence Derwent*
MR. VARLEY	*Mr. Charles Groves*
A LANGUID LORD	*Mr. J. H. Roberts*
HIS COMPANION	*Miss More-Dunphie*
A BLOND GENTLEMAN	*Mr. Leslie Rea*
TWO LADIES WITH LARGE HATS . .	*Misses Bateman and Newcombe*

ACT I

The scene is the pretty drawing-room of a flat. There are two doors, one open into the hall, the other shut and curtained. Through a large bay window, the curtains of which are not yet drawn, the towers of West-minster can be seen darkening in a summer sunset ; a grand piano stands across one corner. The man-servant PAYNTER, *clean-shaven and dis-creet, is arranging two tables for Bridge.*

BURNEY, *the maid, a girl with one of those flowery Botticellian faces only met with in England, comes in through the curtained door, which she leaves open, disclosing the glimpse of a white wall.* PAYNTER *looks up at her ; she shakes her head with an expression of concern.*

PAYNTER. Where's she gone ?

BURNEY. Just walks about, I fancy.

PAYNTER. She and the Governor don't hit it ! One of these days she'll flit—you'll see. I like her—she's a lady ; but these thorough-bred 'uns—it's their skin and their mouths. They'll go till they drop if they like the job, and if they don't, it's nothing but jib—jib—jib. How was it down there before she married him ?

BURNEY. Oh ! Quiet, of course.

PAYNTER. Country homes—I know 'em. What's her father the old Rector like ?

BURNEY. Oh ! very steady old man. The mother dead long before I took the place.

PAYNTER. Not a penny, I suppose ?

BURNEY. [*Shaking her head*] No ; and seven of them.

PAYNTER. [*At sound of the hall door*] The Governor !

[BURNEY *withdraws through the curtained door.*

[GEORGE DEDMOND *enters from the hall. He is in evening dress, opera hat, and overcoat ; his face is broad, comely, glossily shaved, but with neat moustaches. His eyes, clear, small, and blue-grey, have little speculation. His hair is well brushed.*

GEORGE. [*Handing* PAYNTER *his coat and hat*] Look here, Paynter ! When I send up from the Club for my dress things, always put in a black waistcoat as well.

PAYNTER. I asked the mistress, sir.

GEORGE. In future—see ?

277

PAYNTER. Yes, sir. [*Signing towards the window.*] Shall I leave the sunset, sir ?

[*But* GEORGE *has crossed to the curtained door ; he opens it and says :* " Clare ! " *Receiving no answer, he goes in.* PAYNTER *switches up the electric light. His face, turned towards the curtained door, is apprehensive.*

GEORGE. [*Re-entering*] Where's Mrs. Dedmond ?

PAYNTER. I hardly know, sir.

GEORGE. Dined in ?

PAYNTER. She had a mere nothing at seven, sir.

GEORGE. Has she gone out, since ?

PAYNTER. Yes, sir—that is, yes. The—er—mistress was not dressed at all. A little matter of fresh air, I think, sir.

GEORGE. What time did my mother say they'd be here for Bridge ?

PAYNTER. Sir Charles and Lady Dedmond were coming at half-past nine ; and Captain Huntingdon, too—Mr. and Mrs. Fullarton might be a bit late, sir.

GEORGE. It's that now. Your mistress said nothing ?

PAYNTER. Not to me, sir.

GEORGE. Send Burney.

PAYNTER. Very good, sir. [*He withdraws.*

[GEORGE *stares gloomily at the card tables.* BURNEY *comes in from the hall.*

GEORGE. Did your mistress say anything before she went out ?

BURNEY. Yes, sir.

GEORGE. Well ?

BURNEY. I don't think she meant it, sir.

GEORGE. I don't want to know what you don't think, I want the fact.

BURNEY. Yes, sir. The mistress said : " I hope it'll be a pleasant evening, Burney ! "

GEORGE. Oh !—Thanks.

BURNEY. I've put out the mistress's things, sir.

GEORGE. Ah !

BURNEY. Thank you, sir. [*She withdraws.*

GEORGE. Damn !

[*He again goes to the curtained door, and passes through.* PAYNTER, *coming in from the hall, announces :* " General Sir Charles and Lady Dedmond." SIR CHARLES *is an upright, well-groomed, grey-moustached, red-faced man of sixty-seven, with a keen eye for molehills, and none at all for mountains.* LADY DEDMOND *has a firm, thin face, full of capability and decision, not without kindliness ; and faintly weathered, as if she had faced many situations in many parts of the world. She is fifty-five.* [PAYNTER *withdraws.*

SIR CHARLES. Hullo! Where are they? H'm!

[*As he speaks* GEORGE *re-enters.*]

LADY DEDMOND. [*Kissing her son*] Well, George. Where's Clare?

GEORGE. Afraid she's late.

LADY DEDMOND. Are we early?

GEORGE. As a matter of fact, she's not in.

LADY DEDMOND. Oh?

SIR CHARLES. H'm! Not—not had a rumpus?

GEORGE. Not particularly. [*With the first real sign of feeling.*] What I can't stand is being made a fool of before other people. Ordinary friction one can put up with. But that——!

SIR CHARLES. Gone out on purpose? What!

LADY DEDMOND. What was the trouble?

GEORGE. I told her this morning you were coming in to Bridge. Appears she'd asked that fellow Malise, for music.

LADY DEDMOND. Without letting you know?

GEORGE. I believe she did tell me.

LADY DEDMOND. But surely——

GEORGE. I don't want to discuss it. There's never anything in particular. We're all anyhow, as you know.

LADY DEDMOND. I see. [*She looks shrewdly at her son.*] My dear, I should be rather careful about him, I think.

SIR CHARLES. Who's that?

LADY DEDMOND. That Mr. Malise.

SIR CHARLES. Oh! That chap!

GEORGE. Clare isn't that sort.

LADY DEDMOND. I know. But she catches up notions very easily. I think it's a great pity you ever came across him.

SIR CHARLES. Where did you pick him up?

GEORGE. Italy—this Spring—some place or other where they couldn't speak English.

SIR CHARLES. Um! That's the worst of travellin'.

LADY DEDMOND. I think you ought to have dropped him. These literary people—— [*Quietly.*] From exchanging ideas to something else, isn't very far, George.

SIR CHARLES. We'll make him play Bridge. Do him good, if he's that sort of fellow.

LADY DEDMOND. Is anyone else coming?

GEORGE. Reggie Huntingdon, and the Fullartons.

LADY DEDMOND. [*Softly*] You know, my dear boy, I've been meaning to speak to you for a long time. It *is* such a pity you and Clare—— What is it?

GEORGE. God knows! I try, and I believe she does.

SIR CHARLES. It's distressin' for us, you know, my dear fellow —distressin'.

LADY DEDMOND. I know it's been going on for a long time.

GEORGE. Oh! leave it alone, mother.

LADY DEDMOND. But, George, I'm afraid this man has brought it to a point—put ideas into her head.

GEORGE. You can't dislike him more than I do. But there's nothing one can object to.

LADY DEDMOND. Could Reggie Huntingdon do anything, now he's home? Brothers sometimes——

GEORGE. I can't bear my affairs being messed about with.

LADY DEDMOND. Well! it would be better for you and Clare to be supposed to be out together, than for her to be out alone. Go quietly into the dining-room and wait for her.

SIR CHARLES. Good! Leave your mother to make up something. She'll do it!   [*A bell sounds.*

LADY DEDMOND. That may be he. Quick!

[GEORGE *goes out into the hall, leaving the door open in his haste.*
LADY DEDMOND, *following, calls* " Paynter!" PAYNTER *enters.*

LADY DEDMOND. Don't say anything about your master and mistress being out. I'll explain.

PAYNTER. The master, my lady?

LADY DEDMOND. Yes, I know. But you needn't say so. Do you understand?

PAYNTER. [*In polite dudgeon*] Just so, my lady.   [*He goes out.*

SIR CHARLES. By Jove! That fellow smells a rat!

LADY DEDMOND. Be careful, Charles!

SIR CHARLES. I should think so.

LADY DEDMOND. I shall simply say they're dining out, and that we're not to wait Bridge for them.

SIR CHARLES. [*Listening*] He's having a palaver with that man of George's.

[PAYNTER, *reappearing, announces :* " Captain Huntingdon."
SIR CHARLES *and* LADY DEDMOND *turn to him with relief.*

LADY DEDMOND. Ah! It's you, Reginald!

HUNTINGDON. [*A tall, fair soldier, of thirty*] How d'you do? How are you, sir? What's the matter with their man?

SIR CHARLES. What!

HUNTINGDON. I was going into the dining-room to get rid of my cigar ; and he said : " Not in there, sir. The master's there, but my instructions are to the effect that he's not."

SIR CHARLES. I knew that fellow——

LADY DEDMOND. The fact is, Reginald, Clare's out, and George is waiting for her. It's so important people shouldn't——

HUNTINGDON. Rather !

[*They draw together, as people do, discussing the misfortunes of members of their families.*

LADY DEDMOND. It's getting serious, Reginald. I don't know what's to become of them. You don't think the Rector—you don't think your father would speak to Clare?

HUNTINGDON. Afraid the governor's hardly well enough. He takes anything of that sort to heart so—especially Clare.

SIR CHARLES. Can't you put in a word yourself?

HUNTINGDON. Don't know where the mischief lies.

SIR CHARLES. I'm sure George doesn't gallop her on the road. Very steady-goin' fellow, old George.

HUNTINGDON. Oh, yes; George is all right, sir.

LADY DEDMOND. They ought to have had children.

HUNTINGDON. Expect they're pretty glad now they haven't. I really don't know what to say, ma'am.

SIR CHARLES. Saving your presence, you know, Reginald, I've often noticed parsons' daughters grow up queer. Get too much morality and rice puddin'.

LADY DEDMOND. [*With a clear look*] Charles!

SIR CHARLES. What was she like when you were kids?

HUNTINGDON. Oh, all right. Could be rather a little devil, of course, when her monkey was up.

SIR CHARLES. I'm fond of her. Nothing she wants that she hasn't got, is there?

HUNTINGDON. Never heard her say so.

SIR CHARLES. [*Dimly*] I don't know whether old George is a bit too matter-of-fact for her. H'm?   [*A short silence.*

LADY DEDMOND. There's a Mr. Malise coming here to-night. I forget if you know him.

HUNTINGDON. Yes. Rather a thorough-bred mongrel.

LADY DEDMOND. He's literary. [*With hesitation.*] You—you don't think he—puts—er—ideas into her head?

HUNTINGDON. I asked Greyman, the novelist, about him; seems he's a bit of an Ishmaelite, even among those fellows. Can't see Clare——

LADY DEDMOND. No. Only, the great thing is that she shouldn't be encouraged. Listen!—It *is* her—coming in. I can hear their voices. Gone to her room. What a blessing that man isn't here yet! [*The door bell rings.*] Tt! There he is, I expect.

SIR CHARLES. What are we goin' to say?

HUNTINGDON. Say they're dining out, and we're not to wait Bridge for them.

SIR CHARLES. Good!

> [*The door is opened, and* PAYNTER *announces* "Mr. Kenneth
> Malise." MALISE *enters. He is a tall man, about thirty-
> five, with a strongly-marked, dark, irregular, ironic face, and
> eyes which seem to have needles in their pupils. His thick
> hair is rather untidy, and his dress clothes not too new.*

10

LADY DEDMOND. How do you do? My son and daughter-in-law are so very sorry. They'll be here directly.

[MALISE *bows with a queer, curly smile.*

SIR CHARLES. [*Shaking hands*] How d'you do, sir?

HUNTINGDON. We've met, I think.

[*He gives* MALISE *that peculiar smiling stare, which seems to warn the person bowed to of the sort of person he is.* MALISE'S *eyes sparkle.*

LADY DEDMOND. Clare will be so grieved. One of those invitations——

MALISE. On the spur of the moment.

SIR CHARLES. You play Bridge, sir?

MALISE. Afraid not!

SIR CHARLES. Don't mean that? Then we shall have to wait for 'em.

LADY DEDMOND. I forget, Mr. Malise—you write, don't you?

MALISE. Such is my weakness.

LADY DEDMOND. Delightful profession.

SIR CHARLES. Doesn't tie you! What!

MALISE. Only by the head.

SIR CHARLES. I'm always thinkin' of writin' my experiences.

MALISE. Indeed!   [*There is the sound of a door banged.*

SIR CHARLES. [*Hastily*] You smoke, Mr. Malise?

MALISE. Too much.

SIR CHARLES. Ah! Must smoke when you think a lot.

MALISE. Or think when you smoke a lot.

SIR CHARLES. [*Genially*] Don't know that I find that.

LADY DEDMOND. [*With her clear look at him*] Charles!

[*The door is opened.* CLARE DEDMOND *in a cream-coloured evening frock comes in from the hall, followed by* GEORGE. *She is rather pale, of middle height, with a beautiful figure, wavy brown hair, full, smiling lips, and large grey mesmeric eyes, one of those women all vibration, iced over with a trained stoicism of voice and manner.*

LADY DEDMOND. Well, my dear!

SIR CHARLES. Ah! George. Good dinner?

GEORGE. [*Giving his hand to* MALISE] How are you? Clare! Mr. Malise!

CLARE. [*Smiling—in a clear voice with the faintest possible lisp*] Yes, we met on the door-mat.   [*Pause.*

SIR CHARLES. Deuce you did!   [*An awkward pause.*

LADY DEDMOND. [*Acidly*] Mr. Malise doesn't play Bridge, it appears. Afraid we shall be rather in the way of music.

SIR CHARLES. What! Aren't we goin' to get a game?

[PAYNTER *has entered with a tray.*

GEORGE. Paynter! Take that table into the dining-room.

PAYNTER. [*Putting down the tray on a table behind the door*] Yes, sir.

MALISE. Let me give you a hand.

[PAYNTER *and* MALISE *carry one of the Bridge tables out,* GEORGE *making a half-hearted attempt to relieve* MALISE.

SIR CHARLES. Very fine sunset!

[*Quite softly* CLARE *begins to laugh. All look at her first with surprise, then with offence, then almost with horror.* GEORGE *is about to go up to her, but* HUNTINGDON *heads him off.*

HUNTINGDON. Bring the tray along, old man.

[GEORGE *takes up the tray, stops to look at* CLARE, *then allows* HUNTINGDON *to shepherd him out.*

LADY DEDMOND. [*Without looking at* CLARE] Well, if we're going to play, Charles?   [*She jerks his sleeve.*

SIR CHARLES. What?   [*He marches out.*

LADY DEDMOND. [*Meeting* MALISE *in the doorway*] Now you will be able to have your music.   [*She follows the* GENERAL *out.*

[CLARE *stands perfectly still, with her eyes closed.*

MALISE. Delicious!

CLARE. [*In her level, clipped voice*] Perfectly beastly of me! I'm so sorry. I simply can't help running amok to-night.

MALISE. Never apologize for being fey. It's much too rare.

CLARE. On the door-mat! And they'd whitewashed me so beautifully! Poor dears! I wonder if I ought——

[*She looks towards the door.*

MALISE. Don't spoil it!

CLARE. I'd been walking up and down the Embankment for about three hours. One does get desperate sometimes.

MALISE. Thank God for that!

CLARE. Only makes it worse afterwards. It seems so frightful to them, too.

MALISE. [*Softly and suddenly, but with a difficulty in finding the right words*] Blessed be the respectable! May they dream of—me! And blessed be all men of the world! May they perish of a surfeit of—good form!

CLARE. I like that. Oh, won't there be a row! [*With a faint movement of her shoulders.*] And the usual reconciliation.

MALISE. Mrs. Dedmond, there's a whole world outside yours. Why don't you spread your wings?

CLARE. My dear father's a saint, and he's getting old and frail; and I've got a sister engaged; and three little sisters to whom I'm supposed to set a good example. Then, I've no money, and I can't do anything for a living, except serve in a shop. I shouldn't be free, either; so what's the good? Besides, I oughtn't to have married if I wasn't going to be happy. You see, I'm not a bit misunderstood or ill-treated. It's only——

MALISE. Prison. Break out!

CLARE. [*Turning to the window*] Did you see the sunset? That white cloud trying to fly up?

[*She holds up her bare arms, with a motion of flight.*

MALISE. [*Admiring her*] Ah-h-h! [*Then, as she drops her arms suddenly.*] Play me something.

CLARE. [*Going to the piano*] I'm awfully grateful to you. You don't make me feel just an attractive female. I wanted somebody like that. [*Letting her hands rest on the notes.*] All the same, I'm glad not to be ugly.

MALISE. Thank God for beauty!

PAYNTER. [*Opening the door*] Mr. and Mrs. Fullarton.

MALISE. Who are *they*?

CLARE. [*Rising*] She's my chief pal. He was in the Navy.

[*She goes forward.* MRS. FULLARTON *is a rather tall woma ,
with dark hair and a quick eye. He, one of those clean-shaven
naval men of good presence who have retired from the sea, but
not from their susceptibility.*

MRS. FULLARTON. [*Kissing* CLARE, *and taking in both* MALISE *and
her husband's look at* CLARE] We've only come for a minute.

CLARE. They're playing Bridge in the dining-room. Mr. Malise doesn't play. Mr. Malise—Mrs. Fullarton, Mr. Fullarton.

[*They greet.*

FULLARTON. Most awfully jolly dress, Mrs. Dedmond.

MRS. FULLARTON. Yes, lovely, Clare. [FULLARTON *abases eyes
which mechanically readjust themselves.*] We can't stay for Bridge, my dear; I just wanted to see you a minute, that's all. [*Seeing* HUNTING-
DON *coming in, she speaks in a low voice to her husband.*] Edward, I want to speak to Clare. How d'you do, Captain Huntingdon?

MALISE. I'll say good night.

[*He shakes hands with* CLARE, *bows to* MRS. FULLARTON, *and
makes his way out.* HUNTINGDON *and* FULLARTON *fore-
gather in the doorway.*

MRS. FULLARTON. How *are* things, Clare? [CLARE *just moves her
shoulders.*] Have you done what I suggested? Your room?

CLARE. No.

MRS. FULLARTON. Why not?

CLARE. I don't want to torture him. If I strike—I'll go clean. I expect I *shall* strike.

MRS. FULLARTON. My dear! You'll have the whole world against you.

CLARE. Even you won't back me, Dolly?

MRS. FULLARTON. Of course I'll back you, all that's possible, but I can't invent things.

CLARE. You wouldn't let me come to you for a bit, till I could find my feet?

[MRS. FULLARTON, *taken aback, cannot refrain from her glance at* FULLARTON *automatically gazing at* CLARE *while he talks with* HUNTINGDON.

MRS. FULLARTON. Of course—the only thing is that——

CLARE. [*With a faint smile*] It's all right, Dolly. I'm not coming.

MRS. FULLARTON. Oh! don't do anything desperate, Clare—you are so desperate sometimes. You ought to make terms—not tracks.

CLARE. Haggle? [*She shakes her head.*] What have I got to make terms with? What he still wants is just what I hate giving.

MRS. FULLARTON. But, Clare——

CLARE. No, Dolly; even you don't understand. All day and every day—just as far apart as we can be—and still—Jolly, isn't it? If you've got a soul at all.

MRS. FULLARTON. It's awful, really.

CLARE. I suppose there are lots of women who feel as I do, and go on with it; only, you see, I happen to have something in me that —comes to an end. Can't endure beyond a certain time, ever.

[*She has taken a flower from her dress, and suddenly tears it to bits. It is the only sign of emotion she has given.*

MRS. FULLARTON. [*Watching*] Look here, my child; this won't do. You must get a rest. Can't Reggie take you with him to India for a bit?

CLARE. [*Shaking her head*] Reggie lives on his pay.

MRS. FULLARTON. [*With one of her quick looks*] That was Mr. Malise then?

FULLARTON. [*Coming towards them*] I say, Mrs. Dedmond, you wouldn't sing me that little song you sang the other night, [*He hums*] "If I might be the falling bee and kiss thee all the day." Remember?

MRS. FULLARTON. "The falling *dew*, Edward. We simply must go, Clare. Good-night. [*She kisses her.*

FULLARTON. [*Taking half-cover between his wife and* CLARE] It suits you down to the ground—that dress.

CLARE. Good-night.

[HUNTINGDON *sees them out. Left alone,* CLARE *clenches her hands, moves swiftly across to the window, and stands looking out.*

HUNTINGDON. [*Returning*] Look here, Clare!

CLARE. Well, Reggie?

HUNTINGDON. This is working up for a mess, old girl. You can't do this kind of thing with impunity. No man'll put up with it. If you've got anything against George, better tell me. [CLARE *shakes her head.*] You ought to know I should stick by you. What is it? Come?

CLARE. Get married, and find out after a year that she's the wrong person; so wrong that you can't exchange a single real thought; that your blood runs cold when she kisses you—then you'll know.

HUNTINGDON. My dear old girl, I don't want to be a brute; but it's a bit difficult to believe in that, except in novels.

CLARE. Yes, incredible, when you haven't tried.

HUNTINGDON. I mean, you—you chose him yourself. No one forced you to marry him.

CLARE. It does seem monstrous, doesn't it?

HUNTINGDON. My dear child, do give us a reason.

CLARE. Look! [*She points out at the night and the darkening towers.*] If George saw that for the first time he'd just say, "Ah, Westminster! Clock Tower! Can you see the time by it?" As if one cared where or what it was—beautiful like that! Apply that to every—every—everything.

HUNTINGDON. [*Staring*] George may be a bit prosaic. But my dear old girl, if that's all——

CLARE. It's not all—it's nothing. I can't explain, Reggie—it's not reason, at all; it's—it's like being underground in a damp cell; it's like knowing you'll never get out. Nothing coming—never anything coming again—never anything.

HUNTINGDON. [*Moved and puzzled*] My dear old thing; you mustn't get into fantods like this. If it's like that, don't think about it.

CLARE. When every day and every night!—Oh! I know it's my fault for having married him, but that doesn't help.

HUNTINGDON. Look here! It's not as if George wasn't quite a decent chap. And it's no use blinking things; you *are* absolutely dependent on him. At home they've got every bit as much as they can do to keep going.

CLARE. I know.

HUNTINGDON. And you've got to think of the girls. Any trouble would be very beastly for them. And the poor old Governor would feel it awfully.

CLARE. If I didn't know all that, Reggie, I should have gone home long ago.

HUNTINGDON. Well, what's to be done? If my pay would run to it—but it simply won't.

CLARE. Thanks, old boy, of course not.

HUNTINGDON. Can't you try to see George's side of it a bit?

CLARE. I *do*. Oh! don't let's talk about it.

HUNTINGDON. Well, my child, there's just one thing—you won't go sailing near the wind, will you? I mean, there are fellows always on the look-out.

CLARE. "That chap Malise, you'd better avoid him!" Why?

HUNTINGDON. Well! I don't know him. He may be all right, but he's not our sort. And you're too pretty to go on the tack of the

New Woman and that kind of thing—haven't been brought up
to it.

CLARE. British home-made summer goods, light and attractive
—don't wear long.   [*At the sound of voices in the hall.*] They seem to
be going, Reggie.   [HUNTINGDON *looks at her vexed, unhappy.*

HUNTINGDON. Don't head for trouble, old girl. Take a pull.
Bless you ! Good-night.

> [CLARE *kisses him, and when he has gone turns away from the door,
> holding herself in, refusing to give rein to some outburst of
> emotion.   Suddenly she sits down at the untouched Bridge table,
> leaning her bare elbows on it and her chin on her hands, quite
> calm.   GEORGE is coming in.   PAYNTER follows him.*

CLARE. Nothing more wanted, thank you, Paynter.   You can go
home, and the maids can go to bed.

PAYNTER. We are much obliged, ma'am.

CLARE. I ran over a dog, and had to get it seen to.

PAYNTER. Naturally, ma'am !

CLARE. Good-night.

PAYNTER. I couldn't get you a little anything, ma'am ?

CLARE. No, thank you.

PAYNTER. No, ma'am. Good-night, ma'am.   [*He withdraws.*

GEORGE. You needn't have gone out of your way to tell a lie that
wouldn't deceive a guinea-pig.   [*Going up to her.*] Pleased with yourself to-night ? [CLARE *shakes her head.*] Before that fellow Malise;
as if our own people weren't enough !

CLARE. Is it worth while to rag me ?   I know I've behaved badly,
but I couldn't help it, really !

GEORGE. Couldn't help behaving like a shop-girl ?   My God !
You were brought up as well as I was.

CLARE. Alas !

GEORGE. To let everybody see that we don't get on—there's only
one word for it—Disgusting !

CLARE. I know.

GEORGE. Then why do you do it ?   I've always kept *my* end up.
Why in heaven's name do you behave in this crazy way ?

CLARE. I'm sorry.

GEORGE. [*With intense feeling*] You like making a fool of me !

CLARE. No—   Really !   Only—I must break out sometimes.

GEORGE. There are things one does not do.

CLARE. I came in because I was sorry.

GEORGE. And at once began to do it again !   It seems to me you
delight in rows.

CLARE. You'd miss your—reconciliations.

GEORGE. For God's sake, Clare, drop cynicism !

CLARE. And truth ?

GEORGE. You are my wife, I suppose.

CLARE. And they twain shall be one—spirit.

GEORGE. Don't talk wild nonsense !   [*There is silence.*

CLARE. [*Softly*] I *don't* give satisfaction.   Please give me notice !

GEORGE. Pish !

CLARE. Five years, and four of them like this ! I'm sure we've served our time.   Don't you really think we might get on better together—if I went away ?

GEORGE. I've told you I won't stand a separation for no real reason, and have your name bandied about all over London.   I have some primitive sense of honour.

CLARE. You mean *your* name, don't you ?

GEORGE. Look here.   Did that fellow Malise put all this into your head ?

CLARE. No ; my own evil nature.

GEORGE. I wish the deuce we'd never met him.   Comes of picking up people you know nothing of.   I distrust him—and his looks— and his infernal satiric way.   He can't even dress decently.   He's not—good form.

CLARE. [*With a touch of rapture*] Ah-h !

GEORGE. Why do you let him come ?   What d'you find interesting in him ?

CLARE. A mind.

GEORGE. Deuced funny one !   To have a mind—as you call it— it's not necessary to talk about Art and Literature.

CLARE. We don't.

GEORGE. Then what do you talk about—your minds ? [CLARE *looks at him.*] Will you answer a straight question ?   Is he falling in love with you ?

CLARE. You had better ask him.

GEORGE. I tell you plainly, as a man of the world, I don't believe in the guide, philosopher and friend business.

CLARE. Thank you.

[*A silence.*   CLARE *suddenly clasps her hands behind her head.*

CLARE. Let me go !   You'd be much happier with any other woman.

GEORGE. Clare !

CLARE. I believe—I'm sure I could earn my living.   Quite serious.

GEORGE. Are you mad ?

CLARE. It has been done.

GEORGE. It will never be done by you—understand that !

CLARE. It really is time we parted.   I'd go clean out of your life. I don't want your support unless I'm giving you something for your money.

GEORGE. Once for all, I don't mean to allow you to make fools of us both.

CLARE. But if we are already! Look at us. We go on, and on. We're a spectacle!

GEORGE. That's not my opinion; nor the opinion of anyone, so long as you behave yourself.

CLARE. That is—behave as you think right.

GEORGE. Clare, you're pretty riling.

CLARE. I don't want to be horrid. But I am in earnest this time.

GEORGE. So am I.   [CLARE *turns to the curtained door*.

GEORGE. Look here! I'm sorry. God knows I don't want to be a brute. I know you're not happy.

CLARE. And you—are you happy?

GEORGE. I don't say I am. But why can't we be?

CLARE. I see no reason, except that you are you, and I am I.

GEORGE. We can try.

CLARE. I *have*—haven't you?

GEORGE. We used——

CLARE. I wonder!

GEORGE. You know we did.

CLARE. Too long ago—if ever.

GEORGE. [*Coming closer*] I—still——

CLARE. [*Making a barrier of her hand*] You know that's only cupboard love.

GEORGE. We've got to face the facts.

CLARE. I thought I was.

GEORGE. The facts are that we're married—for better or worse, and certain things are expected of us. It's suicide for you, and folly for me, in my position to ignore that. You have all you can reasonably want; and I don't—don't wish for any change. If you could bring anything against me—if I drank, or knocked about town, or expected too much of you. I'm not unreasonable in any way, that I can see.

CLARE. Well, I think we've talked enough.

                          [*She again moves towards the curtained door*.

GEORGE. Look here, Clare; you don't mean you're expecting me to put up with the position of a man who's neither married nor unmarried! That's simple purgatory. You ought to know.

CLARE. Yes. I haven't yet, have I?

GEORGE. Don't go like that! Do you suppose we're the only couple who've found things aren't what they thought, and have to put up with each other and make the best of it.

CLARE. Not by thousands.

GEORGE. Well, why do you imagine they do it?

CLARE. I don't know.

GEORGE. From a common sense of decency.

CLARE. Very!

10*

GEORGE. By Jove! You can be the most maddening thing in all the world! [*Taking up a pack of cards, he lets them fall with a long slithering flutter.*] After behaving as you have this evening, you might try to make some amends, I should think.

[CLARE *moves her head from side to side, as if in sight of something she could not avoid. He puts his hand on her arm.*

CLARE. No, no—no!

GEORGE. [*Dropping his hand*] Can't you make it up?

CLARE. I don't feel very Christian.

[*She opens the door, passes through, and closes it behind her.* GEORGE *steps quickly towards it, stops, and turns back into the room. He goes to the window and stands looking out; shuts it with a bang, and again contemplates the door. Moving forward, he rests his hand on the deserted card-table, clutching its edge, and muttering. Then he crosses to the door into the hall and switches off the light. He opens the door to go out, then stands again irresolute in the darkness and heaves a heavy sigh. Suddenly he mutters: "No!" crosses resolutely back to the curtained door, and opens it. In the gleam of light* CLARE *is standing, unhooking a necklet. He goes in, shutting the door behind him with a thud.*

The curtain falls.

ACT II

*The scene is a large, whitewashed, disordered room, whose outer door opens
on to a corridor and stairway. Doors on either side lead to other rooms.
On the walls are unframed reproductions of fine pictures, secured with
tintacks. An old wine-coloured armchair of low and comfortable
appearance, near the centre of the room, is surrounded by a litter of
manuscripts, books, ink, pens and newspapers, as though someone had
already been up to his neck in labour, though by a grandfather's clock it is
only eleven. On a smallish table close by, are sheets of paper, cigarette
ends, and two claret bottles. There are many books on shelves, and on the
floor an overflowing pile, whereon rests a soft hat, and a black knobby
stick. MALISE sits in his armchair, garbed in trousers, dressing-gown,
and slippers, unshaved and uncollared, writing. He pauses, smiles,
lights a cigarette, and tries the rhythm of the last sentence, holding up a
sheet of quarto MS.*

MALISE. " Not a word, not a whisper of Liberty from all those
excellent frock-coated gentlemen—not a sign, not a grimace. Only
the monumental silence of their profound deference before triumphant
Tyranny."

> [*While he speaks, a substantial woman, a little over middle-age, in
> old dark clothes and a black straw hat, enters from the corridor.
> She goes to a cupboard, brings out from it an apron and a Bissell
> broom. Her movements are slow and imperturbable, as if she
> had much time before her. Her face is broad and dark, with
> Chinese eyebrows.*

MALISE. Wait, Mrs. Miler !
MRS. MILER. I'm gettin' be'ind'and, sir.

> [*She comes and stands before him. MALISE writes.*

MRS. MILER. There's a man 'angin' about below.

> [MALISE *looks up ; seeing that she has roused his attention, she stops.
> But as soon as he is about to write again, goes on.*

MRS. MILER. I see him first yesterday afternoon. I'd just been
out to get meself a pennyworth o' soda, an' as I come in I passed 'im
on the second floor, lookin' at me with an air of suspicion. I thought
to meself at the time, I thought : You're a 'andy sort of 'ang-dog
man.

MALISE. Well ?
MRS. MILER. Well—peekin' down through the balusters, I see 'im

291

lookin' at a photograft. That's a funny place, I thinks, to look at pictures—it's so dark there, ye 'ave to use yer eyesight. So I giv' a scrape with me 'eel [*She illustrates*], an' he pops it in his pocket, and puts up 'is 'and to knock at number three. I goes down an' I says : " You know there's no one lives there, don't yer ? " " Ah ! " 'e says with an air of innercence, " I wants the name of Smithers." " Oh ! " I says, " try round the corner, number ten." " Ah ! " 'e says, tactful, " much obliged." " Yes," I says, " you'll find 'im in at this time o' day. Good evenin' ! " And I thinks to meself [*She closes one eye*] Rats ! There's a good many corners hereabouts.

MALISE. [*With detached appreciation*] Very good, Mrs. Miler.

MRS. MILER. So this mornin', there 'e was again on the first floor with 'is 'and raised, pretendin' to knock at number two. " Oh ! you're still lookin' for 'im ? " I says, lettin' him see I was 'is grand-mother. " Ah ! " 'e says, affable, " you misdirected me ; it's here I've got my business." " That's lucky," I says, " cos nobody lives there neither. Good mornin' ! " And I come straight up. If you want to see 'im at work you've only to go downstairs, 'e'll be on the ground floor by now, pretendin' to knock at number one. Wonderful resource !

MALISE. What's he like, this gentleman ?

MRS. MILER. Just like the men you see on the front page o' the daily papers. Nasty, smooth-lookin' feller, with one o' them billycock hats you can't abide.

MALISE. Isn't he a dun ?

MRS. MILER. *They* don't be'ave like that ; *you* ought to know, sir. He's after no good. [*Then, after a little pause.*] Ain't he to be put a stop to ? If I took me time I could get 'im, innercent-like, with a jug o' water.   [MALISE, *smiling, shakes his head.*]

MALISE. You can get on now ; I'm going to shave.

[*He looks at the clock, and passes out into the inner room. MRS. MILER gazes round her, pins up her skirt, sits down in the arm-chair, takes off her hat and puts it on the table, and slowly rolls up her sleeves ; then with her hands on her knees she rests. There is a soft knock on the door. She gets up leisurely and moves flat-footed towards it. The door being opened CLARE is revealed.*]

CLARE. Is Mr. Malise in ?

MRS. MILER. Yes. But 'e's dressin'.

CLARE. Oh.

MRS. MILER. Won't take 'im long. What name ?

CLARE. Would you say—a lady.

MRS. MILER. It's against the rules. But if you'll sit down a moment I'll see what I can do. [*She brings forward a chair and rubs it with her apron. Then goes to the door of the inner room and speaks through it.*] A lady to see you. [*Returning she removes some cigarette ends.*] This is my hour. I shan't make much dust. [*Noting* CLARE's *eyebrows raised at the debris round the armchair.*] I'm particular about not disturbin' things.

CLARE. I'm sure you are.

MRS. MILER. He likes 'is 'abits regular.

[*Making a perfunctory pass with the Bissell broom, she runs it to the cupboard, comes back to the table, takes up a bottle and holds it to the light ; finding it empty, she turns it upside down and drops it into the wastepaper-basket ; then, holding up the other bottle, and finding it not empty, she corks it and drops it into the fold of her skirt.*

MRS. MILER. He takes his claret fresh-opened—not like these 'ere bawgwars.

CLARE. [*Rising*] I think I'll come back later.

MRS. MILER. Mr. Malise is not in my confidence. We keep each other to ourselves. Perhaps you'd like to read the paper ; he has it fresh every mornin'—the *Westminster*.

[*She plucks that journal from out of the armchair and hands it to* CLARE, *who sits down again unhappily to brood.* MRS. MILER *makes a pass or two with a very dirty duster, then stands still. No longer hearing sounds,* CLARE *looks up.*

MRS. MILER. I wouldn't interrupt yer with my workin', but 'e likes things clean. [*At a sound from the inner room.*] That's 'im ; 'e's cut 'isself ! I'll just take 'im the tobaccer !

[*She lifts a green paper screw of tobacco from the debris round the armchair and taps on the door. It opens.* CLARE *moves restlessly across the room.*

MRS. MILER. [*Speaking into the room*] The tobaccer. The lady's waitin'.

[CLARE *has stopped before a reproduction of T tian's picture " Sacred and Profane Love."* MRS. MILER *stands regarding her with a Chinese smile.* MALISE *enters, a thread of tobacco still hanging to his cheek.*

MALISE. [*Taking* MRS. MILER's *hat off the table and handing it to her*] Do the other room.   [*Enigmatically she goes.*

MALISE. Jolly of you to come. Can I do anything ?

CLARE. I want advice—badly.

MALISE. What ! Spreading your wings ?

CLARE. Yes.

MALISE. Ah ! Proud to have given you *that* advice. When ?

CLARE. The morning after you gave it me . . .

MALISE. Well ?

CLARE. I went down to my people. I knew it would hurt my Dad frightfully, but somehow I thought I could make him see. No good. He was awfully sweet, only—he couldn't.

MALISE. [*Softly*] We English love liberty in those who don't belong to us. Yes.

CLARE. It was horrible. There were the children—and my old nurse. I could never live at home now. They'd think I was—— Impossible—utterly! I'd made up my mind to go back to my owner—— And then—he came down himself. I couldn't stand it. To be hauled back and begin all over again ; I simply couldn't. I watched for a chance ; and ran to the station, and came up to an hotel.

MALISE. Bravo !

CLARE. I don't know—no pluck this morning ! You see, I've got to earn my living—no money ; only a few things I can sell. All yesterday I was walking about, looking at the women. How does anyone ever get a chance ?

MALISE. Sooner than you should hurt his dignity by working, your husband would pension you off.

CLARE. If I don't go back to him I couldn't take it.

MALISE. Good !

CLARE. I've thought of nursing, but it's a long training, and I do so hate watching pain. The fact is, I'm pretty hopeless ; can't even do art work. I came to ask you about the stage.

MALISE. Have you ever acted ? [CLARE *shakes her head.*] You mightn't think so, but I've heard there's a prejudice in favour of training. There's Chorus—I don't recommend it. How about your brother ?

CLARE. My brother's got nothing to spare, and he wants to get married ; and he's going back to India in September. The only friend I should care to bother is Mrs. Fullarton, and she's—got a husband.

MALISE. I remember the gentleman.

CLARE. Besides, I should be besieged day and night to go back. I must lie doggo somehow.

MALISE. It makes my blood boil to think of women like you. God help all ladies without money.

CLARE. I expect I shall have to go back.

MALISE. No, no ! We shall find something. Keep your soul alive at all costs. What ! let him hang on to you till you're nothing but—emptiness and ache, till you lose even the power to ache. Sit in his drawing-room, pay calls, play Bridge, go out with him to dinners, return to—duty ; and feel less and less, and be less and less, and so grow old and—die !   [*The bell rings.*

MALISE. [*Looking at the door in doubt*] By the way—he'd no means of tracing you ?   [*She shakes her head.*
                                                               [*The bell rings again.*

MALISE. Was there a man on the stairs as you came up ?

CLARE. Yes. Why ?

MALISE. He's begun to haunt them, I'm told.

CLARE. Oh! But that would mean they thought I—oh! no!

MALISE. Confidence in *me* is not excessive.

CLARE. Spying!

MALISE. Will you go in there for a minute? Or shall we let them ring—or—what? It may not be anything, of course.

CLARE. I'm not going to hide.   [*The bell rings a third time.*

MALISE. [*Opening the door of the inner room*] Mrs. Miler, just see who it is ; and then go, for the present.

[MRS. MILER *comes out with her hat on, passes enigmatically to the door, and opens it. A man's voice says :* " Mr. Malise ? Would you give him these cards ? "

MRS. MILER. [*Re-entering*] The cards.

MALISE. Mr. Robert Twisden. Sir Charles and Lady Dedmond.

[*He looks at* CLARE.

CLARE. [*Her face scornful and unmoved*] Let them come.

MALISE. [*To* MRS. MILER] Show them in!

[TWISDEN *enters—a clean-shaved, shrewd-looking man, with a fighting underlip, followed by* SIR CHARLES *and* LADY DEDMOND. MRS. MILER *goes.   There are no greetings.*

TWISDEN. Mr. Malise? How do you do, Mrs. Dedmond? Had the pleasure of meeting you at your wedding. [CLARE *inclines her head.*] I am Mr. George Dedmond's solicitor, sir. I wonder if you would be so very kind as to let us have a few words with Mrs. Dedmond alone?

[*At a nod from* CLARE, MALISE *passes into the inner room, and shuts the door.   A silence.*

SIR CHARLES. [*Suddenly*] What!

LADY DEDMOND. Mr. Twisden, will you——?

TWISDEN. [*Uneasy*] Mrs. Dedmond—I must apologize, but you— you hardly gave us an alternative, did you? [*He pauses for an answer, and, not getting one, goes on.*] Your disappearance has given your husband great anxiety. Really, my dear madam, you must forgive us for this —attempt to get into communication.

CLARE. Why did you spy *here* ?

SIR CHARLES. No, no! Nobody's spied on you. What!

TWISDEN. I'm afraid the answer is that we appear to have been justified. [*At the expression on* CLARE's *face he goes on hastily.*] Now, Mrs. Dedmond, I'm a lawyer and I know that appearances are misleading. Don't think I'm unfriendly ; I wish you well. [CLARE *raises her eyes.   Moved by that look, which is exactly as if she had said : " I have no friends," he hurries on.*] What we want to say to you is this : Don't let this split go on! Don't commit yourself to what you'll bitterly regret. Just tell us what's the matter. I'm sure it can be put straight,

CLARE. I have nothing against my husband—it was quite unreasonable to leave him.

TWISDEN. Come, that's good.

CLARE. Unfortunately, there's something stronger than reason.

TWISDEN. I don't know it, Mrs. Dedmond.

CLARE. No?

TWISDEN. [*Disconcerted*] Are you—you oughtn't to take a step without advice, in your position.

CLARE. Nor with it?

TWISDEN. [*Approaching her*] Come, now; isn't there anything you feel you'd like to say—that might help to put matters straight?

CLARE. I don't think so, thank you.

LADY DEDMOND. You must see, Clare, that——

TWISDEN. In your position, Mrs. Dedmond—a beautiful young woman without money. I'm quite blunt. This is a hard world. Should be awfully sorry if anything goes wrong.

CLARE. And if I go back?

TWISDEN. Of two evils, if it be so—choose the least!

CLARE. I am twenty-six; he is thirty-two. We can't reasonably expect to die for fifty years.

LADY DEDMOND. That's morbid, Clare.

TWISDEN. What's open to you if you don't go back? Come, what's your position? Neither fish, flesh, nor fowl; fair game for everybody. Believe me, Mrs. Dedmond, for a pretty woman to strike, as it appears you're doing, simply because the spirit of her marriage has taken flight, is madness. You must know that no one pays attention to anything but facts. If now—excuse me—you—you had a lover, [*His eyes travel round the room and again rest on her*] you would, at all events, have some ground under your feet, some sort of protection, but [*He pauses*] as you have not—you've none.

CLARE. Except what I make myself.

SIR CHARLES. Good God!

TWISDEN. Yes! Mrs. Dedmond! There's the bedrock difficulty. As you haven't money, you should never have been pretty. You're up against the world, and you'll get no mercy from it. We lawyers see too much of that. I'm putting it brutally, as a man of the world.

CLARE. Thank you. Do you think you quite grasp the alternative?

TWISDEN. [*Taken aback*] But, my dear young lady, there are two sides to every contract. After all, your husband's fulfilled his.

CLARE. So have I up till now. I shan't ask anything from him—nothing—do you understand?

LADY DEDMOND. But, my dear, you must live.

TWISDEN. Have you ever done any sort of work?

CLARE. Not yet.

TWISDEN. Any conception of the competition nowadays?

CLARE. I can try.   [TWISDEN, *looking at her, shrugs his shoulders.*

CLARE. [*Her composure a little broken by that look*] It's real to me—this—you see!

SIR CHARLES. But, my dear girl, what the devil's to become of George?

CLARE. He can do what he likes—it's nothing to me.

TWISDEN. Mrs. Dedmond, I say without hesitation you've no notion of what you're faced with, brought up to a sheltered life as you've been. Do realize that you stand at the parting of the ways, and one leads into the wilderness.

CLARE. Which?

TWISDEN. [*Glancing at the door through which* MALISE *has gone*] Of course, if you want to play at wild asses there are plenty who will help you.

SIR CHARLES. By Gad! Yes!

CLARE. I only want to breathe.

TWISDEN. Mrs. Dedmond, go back! You can now. It will be too late soon. There are lots of wolves about.

[*Again he looks at the door.*

CLARE. But not where you think. You say I need advice. I came here for it.

TWISDEN. [*With a curiously expressive shrug*] In that case I don't know that I can usefully stay.   [*He goes to the outer door.*

CLARE. Please don't have me followed when I leave here. Please!

LADY DEDMOND. George is outside, Clare.

CLARE. I don't wish to see him. By what right have you come here? [*She goes to the door through which* MALISE *has passed, opens it, and says*] Please come in, Mr. Malise.   [MALISE *enters.*

TWISDEN. I am sorry. [*Glancing at* MALISE, *he inclines his head.*] I am sorry. Good morning.   [*He goes.*

LADY DEDMOND. Mr. Malise, I'm sure, will see——

CLARE. Mr. Malise will stay here, please, in his own room.

[MALISE *bows.*

SIR CHARLES. My dear girl, 'pon my soul, you know, I can't grasp your line of thought at all!

CLARE. No?

LADY DEDMOND. George is most willing to take up things just as they were before you left.

CLARE. Ah!

LADY DEDMOND. Quite frankly—what is it you want?

CLARE. To be left alone. Quite frankly, he made a mistake to have me spied on.

LADY DEDMOND. But, my good girl, if you'd let us know where you were, like a reasonable being. You can't possibly be left to yourself without money or position of any kind.   Heaven knows what you'd be driven to !   [*She looks at* MALISE.

MALISE. [*Softly*] Delicious.

SIR CHARLES. You will be good enough to repeat that out loud, sir.

LADY DEDMOND. Charles !   Clare, you must know this is all a fit of spleen ; your duty and your interest—marriage is sacred, Clare.

CLARE. Marriage !   *My* marriage has become the—the reconciliation—of two animals—one of them unwilling.   That's all the sanctity there is about it.

SIR CHARLES. What !

LADY DEDMOND. You ought to be horribly ashamed.

CLARE. Of the fact—I am.

LADY DEDMOND. [*Darting a glance at* MALISE] If we are to talk this out, it must be in private.

MALISE. [*To* CLARE] Do you wish me to go ?

CLARE. No.

LADY DEDMOND. [*At* MALISE] I should have thought ordinary decent feeling—— Good heavens, girl ! Can't you see that you're being played with ?

CLARE. If you insinuate anything against Mr. Malise, you lie.

LADY DEDMOND. If you *will* do these things—come to a man's rooms——

CLARE. I came to Mr. Malise because he's the only person I know with imagination enough to see what my position is ; I came to him a quarter of an hour ago, for the first time, for definite advice, and you instantly suspect him.   That is disgusting.

LADY DEDMOND. [*Frigidly*] Is this the natural place for me to find my son's wife ?

CLARE. His woman.

LADY DEDMOND. Will you listen to Reginald ?

CLARE. I have.

LADY DEDMOND. Haven't you any religious sense at all, Clare ?

CLARE. None, if it's religion to live as we do.

LADY DEDMOND. It's terrible—this state of mind ! It's really terrible !

[CLARE *breaks into the soft laugh of the other evening.   As if galvanized by the sound,* SIR CHARLES *comes to life out of the transfixed bewilderment with which he has been listening.*

SIR CHARLES. For God's sake don't laugh like that.   [CLARE *stops.*

LADY DEDMOND. [*With real feeling*] For the sake of the simple right, Clare !

CLARE. Right ?   Whatever else is right—*our* life is not. [*She puts her hand on her heart.*] I swear before God that I've tried and tried. I swear before God that if I believed we could ever again love each

other only a little tiny bit, I'd go back. I swear before God that I
don't want to hurt anybody.

LADY DEDMOND. But you are hurting everybody. Do—do be
reasonable !

CLARE. [*Losing control*] Can't you see that I'm fighting for all my
life to come—not to be buried alive—not to be slowly smothered.
Look at me ! I'm not wax—I'm flesh and blood. And you want to
prison me for ever—body and soul.   [*They stare at her.*

SIR CHARLES. [*Suddenly*] By Jove ! I don't know, I don't know !
What !

LADY DEDMOND. [*To* MALISE] If you have any decency left, sir, you
will allow my son, at all events, to speak to his wife alone. [*Beckoning
to her husband.*] We'll wait below.

SIR CHARLES. I—I want to speak. [*To* CLARE.] My dear, if you
feel like this, I can only say as a—as a gentleman——

LADY DEDMOND. Charles !

SIR CHARLES. Let me alone ! I can only say that—damme, I don't
know that I can say anything !

[*He looks at her very grieved, then turns and marches out, followed by*
LADY DEDMOND, *whose voice is heard without, answered by
his :* " What ! " *In the doorway, as they pass,* GEORGE *is
standing ; he comes in.*

GEORGE. [*Going up to* CLARE, *who has recovered all her self-control*]
Will you come outside and speak to me ?

CLARE. No.

[GEORGE *glances at* MALISE, *who is leaning against the wall with
folded arms.*

GEORGE. [*In a low voice*] Clare !

CLARE. Well !

GEORGE. You try me pretty high, don't you, forcing me to come
here, and speak before this fellow ? Most men would think the
worst, finding you like this.

CLARE. You need not have come—or thought at all.

GEORGE. Did you imagine I was going to let you vanish without
an effort——

CLARE. To save me ?

GEORGE. For God's sake be just ! I've come here to say certain
things. If you force me to say them before him—on your head be it !
Will you appoint somewhere else ?

CLARE. No.

GEORGE. Why not ?

CLARE. I know all those " certain things." " You must come back.
It is your duty. You have no money. Your friends won't help you.
You can't earn your living. You are making a scandal." You might
even say for the moment : " Your room shall be respected."

GEORGE. Well, it's true and you've no answer.

CLARE. Oh! [*Suddenly.*] Our life's a lie. It's stupid; it's disgusting. I'm tired of it! Please leave me alone!

GEORGE. You rather miss the point, I'm afraid. I didn't come here to tell you what you know perfectly well when you're sane. I came here to say this: Anyone in her senses could see the game your friend here is playing. It wouldn't take a baby in. If you think that a gentleman like that [*His stare travels round the dishevelled room till it rests on* MALISE] champions a pretty woman for nothing, you make a fairly bad mistake.

CLARE. Take care.

[*But* MALISE, *after one convulsive movement of his hands, has again become rigid.*

GEORGE. I don't pretend to be subtle or that kind of thing; but I have ordinary common sense. I don't attempt to be superior to plain facts——

CLARE. [*Under her breath*] Facts!

GEORGE. Oh! for goodness' sake drop that hifalutin' tone. It doesn't suit you. Look here! If you like to go abroad with one of your young sisters until the autumn, I'll let the flat and go to the Club.

CLARE. Put the fire out with a penny hose. [*Slowly.*] I am not coming back to you, George. The farce is over.

GEORGE. [*Taken aback for a moment by the finality of her tone, suddenly fronts* MALISE] Then there *is* something between you and this fellow.

MALISE. [*Dangerously, but without moving*] I beg your pardon!

CLARE. There—is—nothing.

GEORGE. [*Looking from one to the other*] At all events, I won't— I won't see a woman who once—— [CLARE *makes a sudden effacing movement with her hands.*] I won't see her go to certain ruin without lifting a finger.

CLARE. That is noble.

GEORGE. [*With intensity*] I don't know that you deserve anything of me. But on my honour, as a gentleman, I came here this morning for your sake, to warn you of what you're doing. [*He turns suddenly on* MALISE.] And I tell this precious friend of yours plainly what I think of him, and that I'm not going to play into his hands.

[MALISE, *without stirring from the wall, looks at* CLARE, *and his lips move.*

CLARE. [*Shakes her head at him—then to* GEORGE] Will you go, please?

GEORGE. I will go when you do.

MALISE. A man of the world should know better than that.

GEORGE. Are you coming?

MALISE. That is inconceivable.

GEORGE. I'm not speaking to you, sir.

MALISE. You are right. Your words and mine will never kiss each other.

GEORGE. Will you come ?   [CLARE *shakes her head.*

GEORGE. [*With fury*] D'you mean to stay in this pigsty with that rhapsodical swine ?

MALISE. [*Transformed*] By God, if you don't go, I'll kill you.

GEORGE. [*As suddenly calm*] That remains to be seen.

MALISE. [*With most deadly quietness*] Yes, I will *kill* you.

> [*He goes stealthily along the wall, takes up from where it lies on the pile of books the great black knobby stick, and stealthily approaches* GEORGE, *his face quite fiendish.*

CLARE. [*With a swift movement, grasping the stick*] Please.

> [MALISE *resigns the stick, and the two men, perfectly still, glare at each other.* CLARE, *letting the stick fall, puts her foot on it. Then slowly she takes off her hat and lays it on the table.*

CLARE. *Now* will you go !   [*There is silence.*

GEORGE. [*Staring at her hat*] You mad little fool ! Understand this ; if you've not returned home by three o'clock I'll divorce you, and you may roll in the gutter with this high-souled friend of yours. And mind this, you sir—I won't spare you—by God ! Your pocket shall suffer. That's the only thing that touches fellows like you.

> [*Turning, he goes out, and slams the door.* CLARE *and* MALISE *remain face to face. Her lips have begun to quiver.*

CLARE. Horrible !

> [*She turns away, shuddering, and sits down on the edge of the arm-chair, covering her eyes with the backs of her hands.* MALISE *picks up the stick, and fingers it lovingly. Then putting it down, he moves so that he can see her face. She is sitting quite still, staring straight before her.*

MALISE. Nothing could be better.

CLARE. I don't know what to do !   I don't know what to do !

MALISE. Thank the stars for your good fortune.

CLARE. He means to have revenge on you !   And it's all my fault.

MALISE. Let him. Let him go for his divorce. Get rid of him. Have done with him—somehow.

> [*She gets up and stands with face averted. Then swiftly turning to him.*

CLARE. If I must bring you harm—let me pay you back !   I can't bear it otherwise !   Make some use of me, if you don't mind !

MALISE. My God ! [*She puts up her face to be kissed, shutting her eyes.*

MALISE. You poor——

> [*He clasps and kisses her, then, drawing back, looks in her face. She has not moved, her eyes are still closed ; but she is shivering ; her lips are tightly pressed together ; her hands twitching.*

MALISE. [*Very quietly*] No, no! This is not the house of a
" gentleman."

CLARE. [*Letting her head fall, and almost in a whisper*] I'm sorry.

MALISE. I understand.

CLARE. I don't feel. And without—I can't, can't.

MALISE. [*Bitterly*] Quite right. You've had enough of *that*.

[*There is a long silence. Without looking at him she takes up her hat,
and puts it on.*

MALISE. Not going? [CLARE *nods.*

MALISE. You don't trust me?

CLARE. I *do* ! But I can't take when I'm not giving.

MALISE. I beg—I beg you! What does it matter? Use me!
Get free somehow.

CLARE. Mr. Malise, I know what I ought to be to you, if I let you
in for all this. I know what you want—or will want. Of course—
why not?

MALISE. I give you my solemn word——

CLARE. No! if I can't be *that* to you—it's not real. And I *can't*.
It isn't to be manufactured, is it?

MALISE. It is not.

CLARE. To make use of you in such a way! No.

[*She moves towards the door.*

MALISE. *Where* are you going?

[CLARE *does not answer. She is breathing rapidly. There is a
change in her, a sort of excitement beneath her calmness.*

MALISE. Not back to *him* ? [CLARE *shakes her head.*] Thank God!
But where? To your people again?

CLARE. No.

MALISE. Nothing—desperate?

CLARE. Oh! no.

MALISE. Then what—tell me—come!

CLARE. I don't know. Women manage somehow.

MALISE. But *you*—poor dainty thing!

CLARE. It's all right! Don't be unhappy! Please!

MALISE. [*Seizing her arm*] D'you imagine they'll let you off, out
there—you with your face? Come, trust me—trust me! You must!

CLARE. [*Holding out her hand*] Good-bye!

MALISE. [*Not taking that hand*] This great damned world, and—
you! Listen! [*The sound of the traffic far down below is audible in the
stillness.*] Into that *!* alone—helpless—without money. The men
who work with you; the men you make friends of—d'you think
they'll let you be? The men in the streets, staring at you, stopping
you—pudgy, bull-necked brutes; devils with hard eyes; senile
swine; and the " chivalrous " men, like me, who don't mean you
harm, but can't help seeing you're made for love! Or suppose you

don't take covert but struggle on in the open. Society! The respectable! The pious! Even those who love you! Will they let you be? Hue and cry! The hunt was joined the moment you broke away! It will never let up! Covert to covert—till they've run you down, and you're back in the cart, and God pity you!

CLARE. Well, I'll die running!

MALISE. No, no! Let me shelter you! Let me!

CLARE. [*Shaking her head and smiling*] I'm going to seek my fortune. Wish me luck!

MALISE. I *can't* let you go.

CLARE. You *must.*

[*He looks into her face; then, realizing that she means it, suddenly bends down to her fingers, and puts his lips to them.*

MALISE. Good luck then! Good luck!

[*He releases her hand. Just touching his bent head with her other hand, CLARE turns and goes. MALISE remains with bowed head, listening to the sound of her receding footsteps. They die away. He raises himself, and strikes out into the air with his clenched fist.*

The curtain falls.

ACT III

SCENE I

MALISE'S *sitting-room.   An afternoon, three months later.   On the table are an open bottle of claret, his hat, and some tea-things.   Down in the hearth is a kettle on a lighted spirit-stand.   Near the door stands* HAYWOOD, *a short, round-faced man, with a tobacco-coloured moustache ;* MALISE, *by the table, is contemplating a piece of blue paper.*

HAYWOOD. Sorry to press an old customer, sir, but a year and an 'alf without any return on your money——

MALISE. Your tobacco is too good, Mr. Haywood.   I wish I could see my way to smoking another.

HAYWOOD. Well, sir—that's a funny remedy.

[*With a knock on the half-opened door, a* BOY *appears.*

MALISE. Yes.   What is it ?

BOY. Your copy for *The Watchfire*, please, sir.

MALISE. [*Motioning him out*] Yes.   Wait !

[*The* BOY *withdraws.* MALISE *goes up to the pile of books, turns them over, and takes up some volumes.*

MALISE. This is a very fine unexpurgated translation of Boccaccio's " Decameron," Mr. Haywood—illustrated.   I should say you would get more than the amount of your bill for them.

HAYWOOD. [*Shaking his head*] Them books worth three pound seven !

MALISE. It's scarce, and highly improper.   Will you take them in discharge ?

HAYWOOD. [*Torn between emotions*] Well, I 'ardly know what to say——   No, sir, I don't think I'd like to 'ave to do with that.

MALISE. You could read them first, you know ?

HAYWOOD. [*Dubiously*] I've got my wife at 'ome.

MALISE. You could both read them.

HAYWOOD. [*Brought to his bearings*] No, sir, I couldn't.

MALISE. Very well ; I'll sell them myself, and you shall have the result.

HAYWOOD. Well, thank you, sir.   I'm sure I didn't want to trouble you.

MALISE. Not at all, Mr. Haywood.   It's for me to apologize.

HAYWOOD. So long as I give satisfaction.

MALISE. [*Holding the door for him*] Certainly.   Good evening.

HAYWOOD. Good evenin', sir ; no offence, I hope.

MALISE. On the contrary.

[*Doubtfully* HAYWOOD *goes.   And* MALISE *stands scratching his head ; then slipping the bill into one of the volumes to remind him, he replaces them at the top of the pile.   The* BOY *again advances into the doorway.*

MALISE. Yes, now for you.

[*He goes to the table and takes some sheets of MS. from an old portfolio.   But the door is again timidly pushed open, and* HAYWOOD *reappears.*

MALISE. Yes, Mr. Haywood ?

HAYWOOD. About that little matter, sir.   If—if it's any convenience to you—I've—thought of a place where I could——

MALISE. Read them ?   You'll enjoy them thoroughly.

HAYWOOD. No, sir, no !   Where I can dispose of them.

MALISE. [*Holding out the volumes*] It might be as well. [HAYWOOD *takes the books gingerly.*]   I congratulate you, Mr. Haywood ; it's a classic.

HAYWOOD. Oh, indeed—yes, sir.   In the event of there being any——

MALISE. Anything over ?   Carry it to my credit.   Your bill——
[*He hands over the blue paper.*]   Send me the receipt.   Good evening !

[HAYWOOD, *nonplussed, and trying to hide the books in an evening paper, fumbles out :* " Good evenin', sir ! " *and departs.*
MALISE *again takes up the sheets of MS. and cons a sentence over to himself, gazing blankly at the stolid* BOY.

MALISE. " Man of the world—good form your god !   Poor buttoned-up philosopher " [*the* BOY *shifts his feet*] " inbred to the point of cretinism, and founded to the bone on fear of ridicule [*the* BOY *breathes heavily*]—you are the slave of facts ! "
[*There is a knock on the door.*

MALISE. Who is it ?

[*The door is pushed open, and* REGINALD HUNTINGDON *stands there.*

HUNTINGDON. I apologize, sir ; can I come in a minute ?
[MALISE *bows with ironical hostility.*

HUNTINGDON. I don't know if you remember me—Clare Dedmond's brother.

MALISE. I remember you.
[*He motions to the stolid* BOY *to go outside again.*

HUNTINGDON. I've come to you, sir, as a gentleman——

MALISE. Some mistake.   There is one, I believe, on the first floor.

HUNTINGDON. It's about my sister.

MALISE. D——n you !   Don't you know that I've been shadowed these last three months ?   Ask your detectives for any information you want.

HUNTINGDON. We know that you haven't seen her, or even known where she is.

MALISE. Indeed! You've found that out? Brilliant!

HUNTINGDON. We know it from my sister.

MALISE. Oh! So you've tracked her down?

HUNTINGDON. Mrs. Fullarton came across her yesterday in one of those big shops—selling gloves.

MALISE. Mrs. Fullarton—the lady with the husband. Well! you've got her. Clap her back into prison.

HUNTINGDON. We have not got her. She left at once, and we don't know where she's gone.

MALISE. Bravo!

HUNTINGDON. [*Taking hold of his bit*] Look here, Mr. Malise, in a way I share your feeling, but I'm fond of my sister, and it's damnable to have to go back to India knowing she must be all adrift, without protection, going through God knows what! Mrs. Fullarton says she's looking awfully pale and down.

MALISE. [*Struggling between resentment and sympathy*] Why do you come to me?

HUNTINGDON. We thought——

MALISE. *Who?*

HUNTINGDON. My—my father and myself.

MALISE. Go on.

HUNTINGDON. We thought there was just a chance that, having lost that job, she might come to you again for advice. If she does, it would be really generous of you if you'd put my father in touch with her. He's getting old, and he feels this very much. [*He hands* MALISE *a card.*] This is his address.

MALISE. [*Twisting the card*] Let there be no mistake, sir; I do nothing that will help give her back to her husband. She's out to save her soul alive, and I don't join the hue and cry that's after her. On the contrary—if I had the power. If your father wants to shelter her, that's another matter. But she'd her own ideas about that.

HUNTINGDON. Perhaps you don't realize how unfit my sister is for rough and tumble. She's not one of this new sort of woman. She's always been looked after, and had things done for her. Pluck she's got, but that's all, and she's bound to come to grief.

MALISE. Very likely—the first birds do. But if she drops half-way it's better than if she'd never flown. Your sister, sir, is trying the wings of her spirit, out of the old slave market. For women as for men, there's more than one kind of dishonour, Captain Huntingdon, and worse things than being dead, as you may know in your profession.

HUNTINGDON. Admitted—but——

MALISE. We each have our own views as to what they are. But

they all come to—death of our spirits, for the sake of our carcasses. Anything more ?

HUNTINGDON. My leave's up.   I sail to-morrow.   If you do see my sister I trust you to give her my love and say I begged she would see my father.

MALISE. If I have the chance—yes.

[*He makes a gesture of salute, to which* HUNTINGDON *responds. Then the latter turns and goes out.*

MALISE. Poor fugitive !   Where are you running now ?

[*He stands at the window, through which the evening sunlight is powdering the room with smoky gold.   The stolid* BOY *has again come in.   MALISE stares at him, then goes back to the table, takes up the MS., and booms it at him ; he receives the charge, breathing hard.*

MALISE. " Man of the world—product of a material age ; incapable of perceiving reality in motions of the spirit ; having ' no use,' as you would say, for ' sentimental nonsense ' ; accustomed to believe yourself the national spine—your position is unassailable.   You will remain the idol of the country—arbiter of law, parson in mufti, darling of the playwright and the novelist—God bless you !—while waters lap these shores."

[*He places the sheets of MS. in an envelope, and hands them to the* BOY.

MALISE. You're going straight back to *The Watchfire* ?

BOY. [*Stolidly*] Yes, sir.

MALISE. [*Staring at him*] You're a masterpiece.   D'you know that ?

BOY. No, sir.

MALISE. Get out, then.

[*He lifts the portfolio from the table, and takes it into the inner room.   The* BOY, *putting his thumb stolidly to his nose, turns to go.   In the doorway he shies violently at the figure of* CLARE, *standing there in a dark-coloured dress, skids past her and goes.   CLARE comes into the gleam of sunlight, her white face alive with emotion or excitement.   She looks round her, smiles, sighs ; goes swiftly to the door, closes it, and comes back to the table.   There she stands, fingering the papers on the table, smoothing* MALISE'S *hat—wistfully, eagerly, waiting.*

MALISE. [*Returning*] You !

CLARE. [*With a faint smile*] Not very glorious, is it ?

[*He goes towards her, and checks himself, then slews the armchair round.*

MALISE. Come !   Sit down, sit down ! [CLARE, *heaving a long sigh, sinks down into the chair.*] Tea's nearly ready.

[*He places a cushion for her, and prepares tea ; she looks up at him softly, but as he finishes and turns to her, she drops that glance.*

CLARE. Do you think me an awful coward for coming ? [*She has taken a little plain cigarette case from her dress.*] Would you mind if I smoked ?

[MALISE *shakes his head, then draws back from her again, as if afraid to be too close.   And again, unseen, she looks at him.*

MALISE. So you've lost your job ?

CLARE. How did you—— ?

MALISE. Your brother.   You only just missed him. [CLARE *starts up.*] They had an idea you'd come.   He's sailing to-morrow—he wants you to see your father.

CLARE. Is father ill ?

MALISE. Anxious about you.

CLARE. I've written to him every week. [*Excited.*] They're still hunting me !

MALISE. [*Touching her shoulder gently*] It's all right—all right.

[*She sinks again into the chair, and again he withdraws.   And once more she gives him that soft eager look, and once more averts it as he turns to her.*

CLARE. My nerves have gone funny lately.   It's being always on one's guard, and stuffy air, and feeling people look and talk about you, and dislike your being there.

MALISE. Yes ; that wants pluck.

CLARE. [*Shaking her head*] I curl up all the time.   The only thing I know for certain is, that I shall never go back to him.   The more I've hated what I've been doing, the more sure I've been.   I might come to anything—but not that.

MALISE. Had a very bad time ?

CLARE. [*Nodding*] I'm spoilt.   It's a curse to be a lady when you have to earn your living.   It's not really been so hard, I suppose ; I've been selling things, and living about twice as well as most shop girls.

MALISE. Were they decent to you ?

CLARE. Lots of the girls are really nice.   But somehow they don't want me, can't help thinking I've got airs or something ; and in here [*She touches her breast*] I don't want them !

MALISE. I know.

CLARE. Mrs. Fullarton and I used to belong to a society for helping reduced gentlewomen to get work.   I know now what they want ; enough money *not* to work—that's all ! [*Suddenly looking up at him.*] Don't think me worse than I am—please !   It's working *under* people ; it's *having* to do it, being driven.   I *have* tried, I've not been altogether a coward, really !   But every morning getting there the same time ; every day the same stale " dinner," as they call it ; every evening the same " Good evening, Miss Clare," " Good evening, Miss Simpson," " Good evening, Miss Hart," " Good evening, Miss Clare."   And the same walk home, or the same bus ; and the same men that you mustn't look at, for fear they'll follow you. [*She rises.*] Oh ! and the feeling—always, always—that there's no sun, or life, or hope, or anything.   It was just like being ill, the way I've wanted to ride and dance and get out into the country. [*Her excitement dies away into the old clipped composure, and she sits down again.*] Don't think too badly of me—it really is pretty ghastly !

MALISE. [*Gruffly*] H'm !   Why a shop ?

CLARE.   References.   I didn't want to tell more lies than I could help ; a married woman on strike can't tell the truth, you know. And I can't typewrite or do shorthand yet.   And chorus—I thought —*you* wouldn't like.

MALISE. I ?   What have I——? [*He checks himself.*] Have men been brutes ?

CLARE. [*Stealing a look at him*] One followed me a lot.   He caught hold of my arm one evening.   I just took this out [*She draws out her hatpin and holds it like a dagger, her lip drawn back as the lips of a dog going to bite*] and said : " Will you leave me alone, please ? " And he did.   It was rather nice.   And there was one quite decent little man in the shop—I was sorry for *him*—such a humble little man !

MALISE.   Poor devil—it's hard not to wish for the moon.

[*At the tone of his voice* CLARE *looks up at him ; his face is turned away.*

CLARE. [*Softly*] How have *you* been ?   Working very hard ?

MALISE.   As hard as God will let me.

CLARE. [*Stealing another look*] Have you any typewriting I could do ?   I could learn, and I've still got a brooch I could sell.   Which is the best kind ?

MALISE.   I had a catalogue of them somewhere.

[*He goes into the inner room.   The moment he is gone,* CLARE *stands up, her hands pressed to her cheeks as if she felt them flaming. Then, with hands clasped, she stands waiting.   He comes back with the old portfolio.*

MALISE.   Can you typewrite where you are ?

CLARE.   I have to find a new room anyway.   I'm changing—to be safe. [*She takes a luggage ticket from her glove.*] I took my things to Charing Cross—only a bag and one trunk. [*Then, with that queer expression on her face which prefaces her desperations.*] You don't want me now, I suppose.

MALISE.   What ?

CLARE. [*Hardly above a whisper*] Because—if you still wanted me— I do—now.

MALISE. [*Staring hard into her face that is quivering and smiling*] You mean it ?   You *do* ?   You care——?

CLARE. I've thought of you—so much ! But only—if you're sure.

[*He clasps her and kisses her closed eyes ; and so they stand for a moment, till the sound of a latchkey in the door sends them apart.*

MALISE. It's the housekeeper. Give me that ticket ; I'll send for your things.

[*Obediently she gives him the ticket, smiles, and goes quietly into the inner room.* MRS. MILER *has entered ; her face, more Chinese then ever, shows no sign of having seen.*

MALISE. That lady will stay here, Mrs. Miler. Kindly go with this ticket to the cloak-room at Charing Cross station, and bring back her luggage in a cab. Have you money ?

MRS. MILER. 'Arf a crown. [*She takes the ticket—then impassively.*] In case you don't know—there's two o' them men about the stairs now.

[*The moment she is gone* MALISE *makes a gesture of maniacal fury. He steals on tiptoe to the outer door, and listens. Then, placing his hand on the knob, he turns it without noise, and wrenches back the door. Transfigured in the last sunlight streaming down the corridor are two men, close together, listening and consulting secretly. They start back.*

MALISE. [*With strange, almost noiseless ferocity*] You've run her to earth ; you're job's done. Kennel up, hounds !

[*And in their faces he slams the door.*

The curtain falls.

SCENE II

The same, early on a winter afternoon, three months later. The room has now a certain daintiness. There are curtains over the doors, a couch under the window, all the books are arranged on shelves. In small vases, over the fireplace, are a few violets and chrysanthemums. MALISE *sits huddled in his armchair drawn close to the fire, paper on knee, pen in hand. He looks rather grey and drawn, and round his chair is the usual litter. At the table, now nearer to the window,* CLARE *sits working a typewriter. She finishes a line, puts sheets of paper together, makes a note on a card—adds some figures, and marks the total.*

CLARE. Kenneth, when this is paid, I shall have made two pound seventeen in the three months, and saved you about three pounds. One hundred and seventeen shillings at tenpence a thousand is one hundred and forty thousand words at fourteen hundred words an hour. It's only just over an hour a day. *Can't* you get me more ?

[MALISE *lifts the hand that holds his pen and lets it fall again.* CLARE *puts the cover on the typewriter, and straps it.*

CLARE. I'm quite packed. Shall I pack for you? [*He nods.*] Can't we have more than three days at the sea? [*He shakes his head. Going up to him.*] You *did* sleep last night?

MALISE. Yes, I slept.

CLARE. Bad head? [MALISE *nods.*] By this time the day after to-morrow the case will be heard and done with. You're not worrying for me? Except for my poor old Dad, *I* don't care a bit.

[MALISE *heaves himself out of the chair, and begins pacing up and down.*

CLARE. Kenneth, do you understand why he doesn't claim damages, after what he said that day—here? [*Looking suddenly at him.*] It *is* true that he doesn't?

MALISE. It is not.

CLARE. But you told me yourself——

MALISE. I lied.

CLARE. Why?

MALISE. [*Shrugging*] No use lying any longer—you'd know it to-morrow.

CLARE. How much am I valued at?

MALISE. Two thousand. [*Grimly.*] He'll settle it on you. [*He laughs.*] Masterly! By one stroke, destroys his enemy, avenges his " honour," and gilds his name with generosity!

CLARE. Will you *have* to pay?

MALISE. Stones yield no blood.

CLARE. Can't you borrow?

MALISE. I couldn't even get the costs.

CLARE. Will they make you bankrupt, then? [MALISE *nods.*] But that doesn't mean that you won't have your *income*, does it? [MALISE *laughs.*] What is your income, Kenneth? [*He is silent.*] A hundred and fifty from *The Watchfire*, I know. What else?

MALISE. Out of five books I have made the sum of forty pounds.

CLARE. What else? Tell me.

MALISE. Fifty to a hundred pounds a year. Leave me to gnaw my way out, child.

[CLARE *stands looking at him in distress, then goes quickly into the room behind her.* MALISE *takes up his paper and pen. The paper is quite blank.*

MALISE. [*Feeling his head*] Full of smoke.

[*He drops paper and pen, and crossing to the room on the left goes in.* CLARE *re-enters with a small leather box. She puts it down on her typing table as* MALISE *returns followed by* MRS. MILER, *wearing her hat, and carrying his overcoat.*

MRS. MILER. Put your coat on. It's a bitter wind.

[*He puts on the coat.*

CLARE. Where are you going?

MALISE. To *The Watchfire*.

[*The door closes behind him, and* MRS. MILER *goes up to* CLARE
holding out a little blue bottle with a red label, nearly full.

MRS. MILER. You know he's takin' this [*She makes a little motion
towards her mouth*] to make 'im sleep ?

CLARE. [*Reading the label*] Where was it ?

MRS. MILER. In the bathroom chest o' drawers, where 'e keeps 'is
odds and ends. I was lookin' for 'is garters.

CLARE. Give it to me !

MRS. MILER. He took it once before. He must get his sleep.

CLARE. Give it to me !

[MRS. MILER *resigns it,* CLARE *takes the cork out, smells, then
tastes it from her finger.* MRS. MILER, *twisting her apron in
her hands, speaks.*

MRS. MILER. I've 'ad it on my mind a long time to speak to yer.
Your comin' 'ere's not done 'im a bit o' good.

CLARE. Don't !

MRS. MILER. I don't want to, but what with the worry o' this 'ere
divorce suit, an' you bein' a lady an' 'im havin' to be so careful of yer,
and tryin' to save, not smokin' all day like 'e used, an' not gettin' 'is
two bottles of claret regular ; an' losing his sleep, an' takin' that stuff
for it ; and now this 'ere last business. I've seen 'im sometimes
holdin' 'is 'ead as if it was comin' off. [*Seeing* CLARE *wince, she goes on
with a sort of compassion in her Chinese face.*] I can see yer fond of him ;
an' I've nothin' against yer—you don't trouble me a bit ; but I've been
with 'im eight years—we're used to each other, and I can't bear to see
'im not 'imself, really I can't.

[*She gives a sudden sniff. Then her emotion passes, leaving her as
Chinese as ever.*

CLARE. This last business—what do you mean by that ?

MRS. MILER. If 'e a'nt told yer, I don't know that I've any
call to.

CLARE. Please.

MRS. MILER. [*Her hands twisting very fast*] Well, it's to do with this
'ere *Watchfire*. One of the men that sees to the writin' of it—
'e's an old friend of Mr. Malise, 'e come 'ere this mornin' when you
was out. I was doin' my work in there [*She points to the room on the
right*] an' the door open, so I 'eard 'em. Now you've 'ung them
curtains, you can't 'elp it.

CLARE. Yes ?

MRS. MILER. It's about your divorce case. This 'ere *Watchfire*,
ye see, belongs to some fellers that won't 'ave their men gettin' into the
papers. So this 'ere friend of Mr. Malise—very nice 'e spoke about
it—" If it comes into Court," 'e says, " you'll 'ave to go," 'e says.
" These beggars, these dogs, these logs," 'e says, " they'll 'oof you

out," 'e says.   An' I could tell by the sound of his voice, 'e meant it—
proper upset 'e was.   So that's that !

CLARE.   It's inhuman !

MRS. MILER.   That's what I thinks ; but it don't 'elp, do it ?   'Tain't
the circulation," 'e says, " it's the principle," 'e says ; and then 'e
starts in swearin' horrible.   'E's a very nice man.   And Mr. Malise,
'e says :   " Well, that about does for me ! " 'e says.

CLARE.   Thank you, Mrs. Miler—I'm glad to know.

MRS. MILER.   Yes ; I don't know as I ought to 'ave told you.
[*Desperately uncomfortable.*] You see, I don't take notice of Mr. Malise,
but I know 'im very well.   'E's a good-'earted gentleman, very funny,
that'll do things to help others, and what's more, keep on doin' 'em,
when they hurt 'im ; very obstinate 'e is.   Now, when you first come
'ere, three months ago, I says to meself : " He'll enjoy this 'ere for a
bit, but she's too much of a lady for 'im."   What 'e wants about 'im
permanent is a woman that thinks an' talks about all them things he
talks about.   And sometimes I fancy 'e don't want nothin' permanent
about 'im at all.

CLARE.   Don't !

MRS. MILER.   [*With another sudden sniff*] Gawd knows I don't want
to upset ye.   You're situated very 'ard ; an' women's got no business
to 'urt one another—that's what I thinks.

CLARE.   Will you go out and do something for me ? [MRS. MILER
nods.   CLARE *takes up the sheaf of papers and from the leather box a note
and an emerald pendant.*] Take this with the note to that address—it's
quite close.   He'll give you thirty pounds for it.   Please pay these
bills and bring me back the receipts, and what's over.

MRS. MILER.   [*Taking the pendant and note*] It's a pretty thing.

CLARE.   Yes.   It was my mother's.

MRS. MILER.   It's a pity to part with it ; ain't you got another ?

CLARE.   Nothing more, Mrs. Miler, not even a wedding ring.

MRS. MILER.   [*Without expression*] You make my 'eart ache sometimes.

[*She wraps pendant and note into her handkerchief and goes out to the
door.*

MRS. MILER.   [*From the door*] There'a lady and gentleman out here.
Mrs. Fuller—wants *you*, not Mr. Malise.

CLARE.   Mrs. Fullarton ? [MRS. MILER *nods.*] Ask them to come in.

[MRS. MILER *opens the door wide, says* " Come in," *and goes.*
MRS. FULLARTON *is accompanied not by* FULLARTON, *but by
the lawyer,* TWISDEN.   *They come in.*

MRS. FULLARTON.   Clare ! My dear ! How are you after all this time ?

CLARE.   [*Her eyes fixed on* TWISDEN] Yes ?

MRS. FULLARTON.   [*Disconcerted by the strange greeting*] I brought
Mr. Twisden to tell you something.   May I stay ?

II

CLARE. Yes. [*She points to the chair at the same table:* MRS. FULLARTON *sits down.*] Now !   [TWISDEN *comes forward.*

TWISDEN. As you're not defending this case, Mrs. Dedmond, there is nobody but yourself for me to apply to.

CLARE. Please tell me quickly, what you've come for.

TWISDEN. [*Bowing slightly*] I am instructed by Mr. Dedmond to say that if you will leave your present companion and undertake not to see him again, he will withdraw the suit and settle three hundred a year on you. [*At* CLARE'S *movement of abhorrence.*] Don't misunderstand me, please—it is not—it could hardly be, a request that you should go back. Mr. Dedmond is *not* prepared to receive you again.   The proposal— forgive my saying so—remarkably Quixotic—is made to save the scandal to his family and your own.   It binds you to nothing but the abandonment of your present companion, with certain conditions of the same nature as to the future.   In other words, it assures you a position—so long as you live quietly by yourself.

CLARE. I see.   Will you please thank Mr. Dedmond, and say that I refuse ?

MRS. FULLARTON. Clare, Clare ! For God's sake don't be desperate.
                              [CLARE, *deathly still, just looks at her.*

TWISDEN. Mrs. Dedmond, I am bound to put the position to you in its naked brutality.   You know there's a claim for damages ?

CLARE. I have just learnt it.

TWISDEN. You realize what the result of this suit must be : You will be left dependent on an undischarged bankrupt.   To put it another way, you'll be a stone round the neck of a drowning man.

CLARE. You are cowards.

MRS. FULLARTON. Clare, Clare ! [*To* TWISDEN.] She doesn't mean it ; *please* be patient.

CLARE. I *do* mean it.   You ruin him because of me.   You get him down, and kick him to intimidate me.

MRS. FULLARTON. My dear girl ! Mr. Twisden is not personally concerned.   How can you ?

CLARE. If I were dying, and it would save me, I wouldn't take a penny from my husband.

TWISDEN. Nothing could be more bitter than those words.   Do you really wish me to take them back to him ?

CLARE. Yes.   [*She turns from them to the fire.*

MRS. FULLARTON. [*In a low voice to* TWISDEN] Please leave me alone with her ; don't say anything to Mr. Dedmond yet.

TWISDEN. Mrs. Dedmond, I told you once that I wished you well. Though you have called me a coward, I still do that.   For God's sake, think—before it's too late.

CLARE. [*Putting out her hand blindly*] I'm sorry I called you a coward. It's the whole thing, I meant.

TWISDEN. Never mind that.   Think !

[*With the curious little movement of one who sees something he does not like to see, he goes.* CLARE *is leaning her forehead against the mantelshelf, seemingly unconscious that she is not alone.* MRS. FULLARTON *approaches quietly till she can see* CLARE'S *face.*

MRS. FULLARTON. My dear sweet thing, don't be cross with *me !* [CLARE *turns from her. It is all the time as if she were trying to get away from words and people to something going on within herself.*] How can I help wanting to see you saved from all this ghastliness ?

CLARE. Please don't, Dolly !   Let me be !

MRS. FULLARTON. I must speak, Clare !   I do think you're hard on George.   It's generous of him to offer to withdraw the suit— considering.   You do owe it to us to try and spare your father and your sisters and—and all of us who care for you.

CLARE. [*Facing her*] You say George is generous !   If he wanted to be that he'd never have claimed those damages.   It's revenge he wants—I heard him here.   You think I've done him an injury.   So I did—when I married him.   I don't know what I shall come to, Dolly, but I shan't fall so low as to take money from him.   That's as certain as that I shall die.

MRS. FULLARTON. Do you know, Clare, I think it's awful about you ! You're too fine, and not fine enough, to put up with things ; you're too sensitive to take help, and you're not strong enough to do without it. It's simply tragic.   At any rate, you might go home to your people.

CLARE. After *this !*

MRS. FULLARTON. To us, then ?

CLARE. " If I could be the falling bee, and kiss thee all the day ! " No, Dolly !

[MRS. FULLARTON *turns from her ashamed and baffled, but her quick eyes take in the room, trying to seize on some new point of attack.*

MRS. FULLARTON. You can't be—you aren't—happy, *here ?*

CLARE. Aren't I ?

MRS. FULLARTON. Oh ! Clare ! Save yourself—and all of us !

CLARE. [*Very still*] You see, I love him.

MRS. FULLARTON. You used to say you'd never love ; did not want it—would never want it.

CLARE. Did I ?   How funny !

MRS. FULLARTON. Oh ! my dear !   Don't look like that, or you'll make me cry.

CLARE. One doesn't always know the future, does one ? [*Desperately.*] I love him !   I love him !

MRS. FULLARTON. [*Suddenly*] If you love him, what will it be like for you, knowing you've ruined him ?

CLARE. Go away !   Go away !

MRS. FULLARTON. Love !—you said !

CLARE. [*Quivering at that stab—suddenly*] I must—I will keep him. He's all I've got.

MRS. FULLARTON. Can you—*can* you keep him?

CLARE. Go!

MRS. FULLARTON. I'm going. But, men are hard to keep, even when you've not been the ruin of them. You know whether the love this man gives you is really love. If not—God help you! [*She turns at the door, and says mournfully.*] Good-bye, my child! If you can——

[*Then goes.* CLARE, *almost in a whisper, repeats the words:* "Love! you said!" *At the sound of a latchkey she runs as if to escape into the bedroom, but changes her mind and stands blotted against the curtain of the door.* MALISE *enters. For a moment he does not see her standing there against the curtain that is much the same colour as her dress. His face is that of a man in the grip of a rage that he feels to be impotent. Then, seeing her, he pulls himself together, walks to his armchair, and sits down there in his hat and coat.*

CLARE. Well? *The Watchfire?* You may as well tell me.

MALISE. Nothing to tell you, child.

[*At that touch of tenderness she goes up to his chair and kneels down beside it. Mechanically* MALISE *takes off his hat.*

CLARE. Then you are to lose that, too? [MALISE *stares at her.*] I know about it—never mind how.

MALISE. Sanctimonious dogs!

CLARE. [*Very low*] There are other things to be got, aren't there?

MALISE. Thick as blackberries. I just go out and cry, "Malise, unsuccessful author, too honest journalist, freethinker, co-respondent, bankrupt," and they tumble!

CLARE. [*Quietly*] Kenneth, do you care for me? [MALISE *stares at her.*] Am I nothing to you but just prettiness?

MALISE. Now, now! This isn't the time to brood! Rouse up and fight.

CLARE. Yes.

MALISE. We're not going to let them down us, are we? [*She rubs her cheek against his hand, that still rests on her shoulder.*] Life on sufferance, breath at the pleasure of the enemy! And some day in the fullness of his mercy to be made a present of the right to eat and drink and breathe again. [*His gesture sums up the rage within him.*] Fine! [*He puts his hat on and rises.*] That's the last groan they get from me.

CLARE. Are you going out again? [*He nods.*] Where?

MALISE. Blackberrying! Our train's not till six.

[*He goes into the bedroom.* CLARE *gets up and stands by the fire, looking round in a dazed way. She puts her hand up and mechanically gathers together the violets in the little vase. Suddenly she twists them to a button-hole, and sinks down into*

*the armchair, which he must pass.   There she sits, the violets
in her hand.   MALISE comes out and crosses towards the outer
door.   She puts the violets up to him.   He stares at them,
shrugs his shoulders, and passes on.   For just a moment
CLARE sits motionless.*

CLARE. [*Quietly*] Give me a kiss !

[*He turns and kisses her.   But his lips, after that kiss, have the
furtive bitterness one sees on the lips of those who have done what
does not suit their mood.   He goes out.   She is left motionless
by the armchair, her throat working.   Then, feverishly, she goes
to the little table, seizes a sheet of paper, and writes.   Looking
up suddenly she sees that MRS. MILER has let herself in with
her latchkey.*

MRS. MILER. I've settled the baker, the milk, the washin' an' the
groceries—this 'ere's what's left.

[*She counts down a five-pound note, four sovereigns, and two shillings
on to the little table.   CLARE folds the letter into an envelope,
then takes up the five-pound note and puts it into her dress.*

CLARE. [*Pointing to the money on the table*] Take your wages ;   and
give him this when he comes in.   I'm going away.

MRS. MILER. Without him ?   When'll you be comin' back ?

CLARE. [*Rising*] I shan't be coming back. [*Gazing at* MRS. MILER's
hands, which are plaiting at her dress.] I'm leaving Mr. Malise, and shan't
see him again.   And the suit against us will be withdrawn—the divorce
suit—you understand ?

MRS. MILER. [*Her face all broken up*] I never meant to say anything
to yer.

CLARE. It's not you.   I can see for myself.   Don't make it harder ;
help me.   Get a cab.

MRS. MILER. [*Disturbed to the heart*] The porter's outside, cleanin'
the landin' winder.

CLARE. Tell him to come for my trunk.   It is packed.

[*She goes into the bedroom.*

MRS. MILER. [*Opening the door—desolately*] Come 'ere !

[*The* PORTER *appears in shirt-sleeves at the door.*

MRS. MILER. The lady wants a cab.   Wait and carry 'er trunk down.

[*CLARE comes from the bedroom in her hat and coat.*

MRS. MILER. [*To the* PORTER] Now.

[*They go into the bedroom to get the trunk.   CLARE picks up from
the floor the bunch of violets, her fingers play with it as if they
did not quite know what it was ;   and she stands by the armchair
very still, while MRS. MILER and the PORTER pass her with
trunk and bag.   And even after the PORTER has shouldered the
trunk outside, and marched away, and MRS. MILER has come
back into the room, CLARE still stands there.*

MRS. MILER. [*Pointing to the typewriter*] D'you want this 'ere, too?

CLARE. Yes.

[MRS. MILER *carries it out. Then, from the doorway, gazing at* CLARE *taking her last look, she sobs, suddenly. At sound of that sob* CLARE *throws up her head.*

CLARE. Don't! It's all right. Good-bye!

[*She walks out and away, not looking back.* MRS. MILER *chokes her sobbing into the black stuff of her thick old jacket.*

The curtain falls.

ACT IV

Supper-time in a small room at " The Gascony " on Derby Day. Through the windows of a broad corridor, out of which the door opens, is seen the dark blue of a summer night. The walls are of apricot-gold ; the carpets, curtains, lamp-shades, and gilded chairs, of red ; the wood-work and screens white ; the palms in gilded tubs. A doorway that has no door leads to another small room. One little table behind a screen, and one little table in the open, are set for two persons each. On a service table, above which hangs a speaking-tube, are some dishes of hors d'œuvres, a basket of peaches, two bottles of champagne in ice-pails, and a small barrel of oysters in a gilded tub. ARNAUD, the waiter, slim, dark, quick, his face seamed with a soft, quiet irony, is opening oysters and listening to the robust joy of a distant supper-party, where a man is playing the last bars of : " Do ye ken John Peel " on a horn. As the sound dies away, he murmurs : " Trés joli ! " and opens another oyster. Two Ladies with bare shoulders and large hats pass down the corridor. Their talk is faintly wafted in : " Well, I never like Derby night ! The boys do get so bobbish ! " " That horn—vulgar, I call it ! " ARNAUD'S eyebrows rise, the corners of his mouth droop. A Lady with bare shoulders, and crimson roses in her hair, comes along the corridor, and stops for a second at the window, for a man to join her. They come through into the room. ARNAUD has sprung to attention, but with : " Let's go in here, shall we ? " they pass through into the further room. The MANAGER, a gentleman with neat moustaches, and buttoned into a frock-coat, has appeared, brisk, noiseless, his eyes everywhere ; he inspects the peaches.

MANAGER. Four shillin' apiece to-night, see ?

ARNAUD. Yes, Sare.

> [*From the inner room a young man and his partner have come in. She is dark, almost Spanish-looking ; he fair, languid, pale, clean-shaved, slackly smiling, with half-closed eyes—one of those who are bred and dissipated to the point of having lost all save the capacity for hiding their emotions. He speaks in a :*

LANGUID VOICE. Awful row they're kickin' up in there, Mr. Varley. A fellow with a horn.

MANAGER. [*Blandly*] Gaddesdon Hunt, my lord—always have their supper with us, Derby night. Quiet corner here, my lord. Arnaud !

> [*ARNAUD is already at the table, between screen and palm. And, there ensconced, the couple take their seats. Seeing them safely*

319

landed, the MANAGER, *brisk and noiseless, moves away. In the corridor a lady in black, with a cloak falling open, seems uncertain whether to come in. She advances into the doorway. It is* CLARE.

ARNAUD. [*Pointing to the other table as he flies with dishes*] Nice table, Madame.

[CLARE *moves to the corner of it. An artist in observation of his clients,* ARNAUD *takes in her face—very pale under her wavy, simply-dressed hair; shadowy beneath the eyes; not powdered; her lips not reddened; without a single ornament; takes in her black dress, finely cut, her arms and neck beautifully white, and at her breast three gardenias. And as he nears her, she lifts her eyes. It is very much the look of something lost, appealing for guidance.*

ARNAUD. Madame is waiting for someone? [*She shakes her head.*] Then Madame will be veree well here—veree well. I take Madame's cloak?

[*He takes the cloak gently and lays it on the back of the chair fronting the room, that she may put it round her when she wishes. She sits down.*

LANGUID VOICE. [*From the corner*] Waiter!

ARNAUD. Milord!

LANGUID VOICE. The Roederer.

ARNAUD. At once, milord.

[CLARE *sits tracing a pattern with her finger on the cloth, her eyes lowered. Once she raises them, and follows* ARNAUD's *dark rapid figure.*

ARNAUD. [*Returning*] Madame feels the 'eat? [*He scans her with increased curiosity.*] You wish something, Madame?

CLARE. [*Again giving him that look*] *Must* I order?

ARNAUD. Non, Madame, it is not necessary. A glass of water. [*He pours it out.*] I have not the pleasure of knowing Madame's face.

CLARE. [*Faintly smiling*] No.

ARNAUD. Madame will find it veree good 'ere, veree quiet.

LANGUID VOICE. Waiter!

ARNAUD. Pardon!   [*He goes.*

[*The bare-necked ladies with large hats again pass down the corridor outside, and again their voices are wafted in:* "Tottie! Not she! Oh! my goodness, she has got a pride on her!" "Bobbie'll never stick it!" "Look here, dear——" *Galvanized by those sounds,* CLARE *has caught her cloak and half-risen; they die away and she subsides.*

ARNAUD. [*Back at her table, with a quaint shrug towards the corridor*] It is not rowdy here, Madame, as a rule—not as in some places. To-night a little noise. Madame is fond of flowers? [*He whisks out and returns almost at once with a bowl of carnations from some table in the next room.*] These smell good !

CLARE. You are very kind.

ARNAUD. [*With courtesy*] Not at all, Madame ; a pleasure.

[*He bows.*

[*A young man, tall, thin, hard, straight, with close-cropped, sandyish hair and moustache, a face tanned very red, and one of those small, long, lean heads that only grow in Britain ; clad in a thin dark overcoat thrown open, an opera hat pushed back, a white waistcoat round his lean middle, he comes in from the corridor. He looks round, glances at CLARE, passes her table towards the further room, stops in the doorway, and looks back at her. Her eyes have just been lifted, and are at once cast down again. The young man wavers, catches ARNAUD's eye, jerks his head to summon him, and passes into the further room. ARNAUD takes up the vase that has been superseded, and follows him out. And CLARE sits alone in silence, broken by the murmurs of the languid lord and his partner, behind the screen. She is breathing as if she had been running hard. She lifts her eyes. The tall young man, divested of hat and coat, is standing by her table, holding out his hand with a sort of bashful hardiness.*

YOUNG MAN. How d'you do ? Didn't recognize you at first. So sorry—awfully rude of me.

[CLARE's *eyes seem to fly from him, to appeal to him, to resign herself all at once. Something in the* YOUNG MAN *responds. He drops his hand.*

CLARE. [*Faintly*] How d'you do ?

YOUNG MAN. [*Stammering*] You—you been down there to-day ?

CLARE. Where ?

YOUNG MAN. [*With a smile*] The Derby. What ? Don't you generally go down ? [*He touches the other chair.*] May I ?

CLARE. [*Almost in a whisper*] Yes.

[*As he sits down,* ARNAUD *returns and stands before them.*

ARNAUD. The plovers' eggs veree good to-night, Sare. Veree good, Madame. A peach or two, after. Veree good peaches. The Roederer, Sare—not bad at all. Madame likes it *frappé,* but not too cold—yes ?   [*He is away again to his service-table.*

YOUNG MAN. [*Burying his face in the carnations*] I say—these are jolly, aren't they ? They do you pretty well here.

CLARE. Do they ?

YOUNG MAN. You've never been here ? [CLARE *shakes her head.*] By Jove ! I thought I didn't know your face. [CLARE *looks full at him. Again something moves in the* YOUNG MAN, *and he stammers.*] I mean—not———

CLARE. It doesn't matter.

11*

YOUNG MAN. [*Respectfully*] Of course, if I—if you were waiting for anybody, or anything—I——   [*He half rises.*

CLARE. It's all right, thank you.

[*The* YOUNG MAN *sits down again, uncomfortable, nonplussed. There is silence, broken by the inaudible words of the languid lord, and the distant merriment of the supper party.* ARNAUD *brings the plovers' eggs.*

YOUNG MAN. The wine, quick.

ARNAUD. At once, Sare.

YOUNG MAN. [*Abruptly*] Don't you ever go racing, then?

CLARE. No.   [ARNAUD *pours out champagne.*

YOUNG MAN. I remember awfully well my first day. It was pretty thick—lost every blessed bob, and my watch and chain, playin' three cards on the way home.

CLARE. Everything has a beginning, hasn't it?

         [*She drinks. The* YOUNG MAN *stares at her.*

YOUNG MAN. [*Floundering in these waters deeper than he had bargained for*] I say—about things having beginnings—did you mean anything?

         [CLARE *nods.*

YOUNG MAN. What! D'you mean it's really the first——?

         [CLARE *nods. The champagne has flicked her courage.*

YOUNG MAN. By George! [*He leans back.*] I've often wondered.

ARNAUD. [*Again filling the glasses*] Monsieur finds——

YOUNG MAN. [*Abruptly*] It's all right.

[*He drains his glass, then sits bolt upright. Chivalry and the camaraderie of class have begun to stir in him.*

YOUNG MAN. Of course I can see that you're not—I mean, that you're a—a lady. [CLARE *smiles.*] And I say, you know—if you have to—because you're in a hole—I should feel a cad. Let me lend you——?

CLARE. [*Holding up her glass*] Le vin est tiré, il faut le boire!

[*She drinks. The French words, which he does not too well understand, completing his conviction that she is a lady, he remains quite silent, frowning. As* CLARE *held up her glass, two gentlemen have entered. The first is blond, of good height and a comely insolence. His crisp, fair hair, and fair brushed-up moustache are just going grey; an eyeglass is fixed in one of two eyes that lord it over every woman they see; his face is broad, and coloured with air and wine. His companion is a tall, thin, dark bird of the night, with sly, roving eyes, and hollow cheeks. They stand looking round, then pass into the further room; but in passing, they have stared unreservedly at* CLARE.

YOUNG MAN. [*Seeing her wince*] Look here! I'm afraid you must feel me rather a brute, you know.

CLARE. No, I don't; really.

YOUNG MAN. Are you absolute stoney? [CLARE *nods*.] But [*Looking at her frock and cloak*] you're so awfully well——

CLARE. I had the sense to keep them.

YOUNG MAN. [*More and more disturbed*] I say, you know—I wish you'd let me lend you something. I had quite a good day down there.

CLARE. [*Again tracing her pattern on the cloth—then looking up at him full*] I can't take, for nothing.

YOUNG MAN. By Jove! I don't know—really, I don't—this makes me feel pretty rotten. I mean, it's your being a lady.

CLARE. [*Smiling*] That's not your fault, is it? You see, I've been beaten all along the line. And I really don't care what happens to me. [*She has that peculiar fey look on her face now.*] I really don't; except that I don't take charity. It's lucky for me it's you, and not some——

[*The supper party is getting still more boisterous, and there comes a long view holloa, and a blast of the horn.*]

YOUNG MAN. But I say, what about your people? You must have people of some sort.

[*He is fast becoming fascinated, for her cheeks have begun to flush and her eyes to shine.*]

CLARE. Oh, yes; I've had people, and a husband, and—everything—— And here I am! Queer, isn't it? [*She touches her glass.*] This is going to my head! Do you mind? I sha'n't sing songs and get up and dance, and I won't cry, I promise you!

YOUNG MAN. [*Between fascination and chivalry*] By George! One simply can't believe in this happening to a lady——

CLARE. Have you got sisters? [*Breaking into her soft laughter.*] *My* brother's in India. I sha'n't meet *him*, anyway.

YOUNG MAN. No, but—I say—are you really quite cut off from everybody? [CLARE *nods*.] Something rather awful must have happened?

[*She smiles. The two gentlemen have returned. The blond one is again staring fixedly at CLARE. This time she looks back at him, flaming; and, with a little laugh, he passes with his friend into the corridor.*]

CLARE. Who are those two?

YOUNG MAN. Don't know—not been much about town yet. I'm just back from India myself. You said your brother was there; what's his regiment!

CLARE. [*Shaking her head*] You're not going to find out my name. I haven't got one—nothing.

[*She leans her bare elbows on the table, and her face on her hands.*]

CLARE. First of June! This day last year I broke covert—I've been running ever since.

YOUNG MAN. I don't understand a bit. You—must have had a— a—some one——

[*But there is such a change in her face, such rigidity of her whole body, that he stops and averts his eyes. When he looks again she is drinking. She puts the glass down, and gives a little laugh.*

YOUNG MAN. [*With a sort of awe*] Anyway it must have been like riding at a pretty stiff fence, for you to come here to-night.

CLARE. Yes. What's the other side?

[*The* YOUNG MAN *puts out his hand and touches her arm. It is meant for sympathy, but she takes it for attraction.*

CLARE. [*Shaking her head*] Not yet—please! I'm enjoying this. May I have a cigarette? [*He takes out his case, and gives her one.*

CLARE. [*Letting the smoke slowly forth*] Yes, I'm enjoying it. Had a pretty poor time lately; not enough to eat, sometimes.

YOUNG MAN. Not really! How damnable! I say—do have something more substantial.

[CLARE *gives a sudden gasp, as if going off into hysterical laughter, but she stifles it, and shakes her head.*

YOUNG MAN. A peach? [ARNAUD *brings peaches to the table.*

CLARE. [*Smiling*] Thank you. [*He fills their glasses and retreats.*

CLARE. [*Raising her glass*] Eat and drink, for to-morrow we— Listen!

[*From the supper party comes the sound of an abortive chorus:* " With a hey-ho, chivy, hark-forrard, hark-forrard, tantivy ! " *Jarring out into a discordant whoop, it sinks.*

CLARE. " This day a stag must die." Jolly old song!

YOUNG MAN. Rowdy lot! [*Suddenly.*] I say—I admire your pluck.

CLARE. [*Shaking her head*] Haven't kept my end up. Lots of women do ! You see : I'm too fine, and not fine enough ! My best friend said that. Too fine, and not fine enough. [*She laughs.*] I couldn't be a saint and martyr, and I wouldn't be a soulless doll. Neither one thing nor the other—that's the tragedy.

YOUNG MAN. You must have had awful luck !

CLARE. I *did* try. [*Fiercely.*] But what's the good—when there's nothing before you ?—Do I look ill !

YOUNG MAN. No ; simply awfully pretty.

CLARE. [*With a laugh*] A man once said to me : " As you haven't money, you should never have been pretty ! " But, you see, it is some good. If I hadn't been, I couldn't have risked coming here, could I ? Don't you think it was rather sporting of me to buy these. [*She touches the gardenias*] with the last shilling over from my cab fare ?

YOUNG MAN. Did you really ? D——d sporting !

CLARE. It's no use doing things by halves, is it ? I'm—in for it

—wish me luck! [*She drinks, and puts her glass down with a smile.*] In for it—deep! [*She flings up her hands above her smiling face.*] Down, down, till they're just above water, and then—down, down, down, and—all over! Are you sorry now you came and spoke to me?

YOUNG MAN. By Jove, no! it may be caddish, but I'm not.

CLARE. Thank God for beauty! I hope I shall die pretty! Do you think I shall *do* well?

YOUNG MAN. I say—*don't* talk like that!

CLARE. I want to know. *Do* you?

YOUNG MAN. Well, then—yes, I do.

CLARE. That's splendid. Those poor women in the streets would give their eyes, wouldn't they?—that have to go up and down, up and down! Do you think I—shall——

[*The* YOUNG MAN *half-rising, puts his hand on her arm.*

YOUNG MAN. I think you're getting much too excited. You look all—Won't you eat your peach? [*She shakes her head.*] Do! Have something else, then—some grapes, or something?

CLARE. No, thanks.   [*She has become quite calm again.*

YOUNG MAN. Well, then, what d'you think? It's awfully hot in here, isn't it? Wouldn't it be jollier drivin'? Shall we—shall we make a move?

CLARE. Yes.

[*The* YOUNG MAN *turns to look for the waiter, but* ARNAUD *is not in the room. He gets up.*

YOUNG MAN. [*Feverishly*] D——n that waiter! Wait half a minute, if you don't mind, while I pay the bill.

[*As he goes out into the corridor, the two gentlemen reappear.* CLARE *is sitting motionless, looking straight before her.*

DARK ONE. A fiver you don't get her to!

BLOND ONE. Done!

[*He advances to her table with his inimitable insolence, and taking the cigar from his mouth, bends his stare on her, and says: "Charmed to see you lookin' so well! Will you have supper with me here to-morrow night?" Startled out of her reverie,* CLARE *looks up. She sees those eyes, she sees beyond him the eyes of his companion—sly, malevolent, amused —watching; and she just sits gazing, without a word. At that regard, so clear, the Blond One does not wince. But rather suddenly he says: "That's arranged then. Half-past eleven. So good of you. Good night!" He replaces his cigar, and strolls back to his companion, and in a low voice says: "Pay up!" Then at a languid "Hullo, Charles!" they turn to greet the two in their nook behind the screen.* CLARE *has not moved, nor changed the direction of her gaze. Suddenly she thrusts her hand into the pocket of the cloak that hangs behind her, and brings out the little blue bottle which, six months ago, she took from* MALISE. *She pulls out the cork and pours the whole contents into her champagne. She lifts the glass, holds it before her—smiling, as if to call a toast, then puts it to her lips and drinks. Still smiling, she sets the empty glass down, and lays the gardenia flowers against her face. Slowly she droops back in her chair, the drowsy smile still on her lips ; the gardenias drop into her lap ; her arms relax, her head falls forward on her breast. And the voices behind the screen talk on, and the sounds of joy from the supper party wax and wane.*

[*The waiter,* ARNAUD, *returning from the corridor, passes to his service-table with a tall, be-ribboned basket of fruit. Putting it down, he goes towards the table behind the screen, and sees. He runs up to* CLARE.

ARNAUD. Madame ! Madame ! [*He listens for her breathing ; then suddenly catching sight of the little bottle, smells at it.*] Bon Dieu !

[*At that queer sound they come from behind the screen—all four, and look. The dark night-bird says :* " Hallo ; fainted ! " ARNAUD *holds out the bottle.*

LANGUID LORD. [*Taking it, and smelling*] Good God !

[*The woman bends over* CLARE, *and lifts her hands ;* ARNAUD *rushes to his service-table, and speaks into his tube :*

ARNAUD. The boss. Quick ! [*Looking up he sees the* YOUNG MAN, *returning.*] Monsieur, elle a fui ! Elle est morte !

LANGUID LORD. [*To the* YOUNG MAN *standing there aghast*] What's this ? Friend of yours ?

YOUNG MAN. My God ! She was a lady. That's all I know about her.

LANGUID LORD. A lady !

[*The blond and dark gentlemen have slipped from the room ; and out of the supper party's distant laughter comes suddenly a long, shrill :* " Gone away ! " *And the sound of the horn playing the seven last notes of the old song :* " This day a stag must die ! " *From the last note of all the sound flies up to an octave higher, sweet and thin, like a spirit passing, till it is drowned once more in laughter. The* YOUNG MAN *has covered his eyes with his hands ;* ARNAUD *is crossing himself fervently ; the* LANGUID LORD *stands gazing, with one of the dropped gardenias twisted in his fingers ; and the woman, bending over* CLARE, *kisses her forehead.*

The curtain falls.

THE PIGEON

CAST OF THE FIRST PRODUCTION BY MESSRS. J. E. VEDRENNE AND DENNIS EADIE, AT THE ROYALTY THEATRE, LONDON, ON JANUARY 30, 1912

CHRISTOPHER WELLWYN	Mr. Whitford Kane
ANN	Miss Gladys Cooper
FERRAND	Mr. Dennis Eadie
TIMSON	Mr. Wilfred Shine
MRS. MEGAN	Miss Margaret Morris
MEGAN	Mr. Stanley Logan
CANON BERTLEY	Mr. Hubert Harben
PROFESSOR CALWAY	Mr. Frank Vernon
SIR THOMAS HOXTON	Mr. Frederick Lloyd
POLICE CONSTABLE	Mr. Arthur B. Murray
FIRST HUMBLE-MAN	Mr. W. Lemmon Warde
SECOND HUMBLE-MAN	Mr. F. B. J. Sharp
THIRD HUMBLE-MAN	Mr. Arthur Bowyer
A LOAFER	Mr. Arthur Baxendell

ACT I

It is the night of Christmas Eve, the scene is a Studio flush with the street, having a skylight darkened by a fall of snow. There is no one in the room, the walls of which are whitewashed, above a floor of bare dark boards. A fire is cheerfully burning. On a model's platform stands an easel and canvas. There are busts and pictures; a screen, a little stool, two armchairs, and a long old-fashioned settle under the window. A door in one wall leads to the house, a door in the opposite wall to the model's dressing-room, and the street door is in the centre of the wall between. On a low table a Russian samovar is hissing, and beside it on a tray stands a teapot, with glasses, lemon, sugar, and a decanter of rum. Through a huge uncurtained window close to the street door the snowy lamplit street can be seen, and beyond it the river and a night of stars.

The sound of a latchkey turned in the lock of the street door, and ANN WELL-WYN *enters, a girl of seventeen, with hair tied in a ribbon and covered by a scarf. Leaving the door open, she turns up the electric light and goes to the fire. She throws off her scarf and long red cloak. She is dressed in a high evening frock of some soft white material. Her movements are quick and substantial. Her face, full of no nonsense, is decided and sincere, with deep-set eyes, and a capable, well-shaped forehead. Shredding off her gloves she warms her hands.*

In the doorway appear the figures of two men. The first is rather short and slight, with a soft short beard, bright soft eyes, and a crumply face. Under his squash hat his hair is rather plentiful and rather grey. He wears an old brown ulster and woollen gloves, and is puffing at a hand-made cigarette. He is ANN'S *father,* WELLWYN, *the artist. His companion is a well-wrapped clergyman of medium height and stoutish build, with a pleasant, rosy face, rather shining eyes, and rather chubby clean-shaped lips; in appearance, indeed, a grown-up boy. He is the Vicar of the parish—*CANON BERTLEY.

BERTLEY. My dear Wellwyn, the whole question of reform is full of difficulty. When you have two men like Professor Calway and Sir Thomas Hoxton taking diametrically opposite points of view, as we've seen to-night, I confess, I——

WELLWYN. Come in, Vicar, and have some grog.

BERTLEY. Not to-night, thanks! Christmas to-morrow! Great temptation, though, this room! Good-night, Wellwyn; good-night, Ann!

ANN. [*Coming from the fire towards the tea-table.*] Good-night, Canon Bertley.

[*He goes out, and* WELLWYN, *shutting the door after him, approaches the fire.*

ANN. [*Sitting on the little stool, with her back to the fire, and making tea*] Daddy!

WELLWYN. My dear?

ANN. You say you liked Professor Calway's lecture. Is it going to do you any good, that's the question?

WELLWYN. I—I hope so, Ann.

ANN. I took you on purpose. Your charity's getting simply awful. Those two this morning cleared out all my housekeeping money.

WELLWYN. Um! Um! I quite understand your feeling.

ANN. They both had your card, so I couldn't refuse—didn't know what you'd said to them. Why don't you make it a rule never to give your card to anyone except really decent people, and—picture dealers, of course.

WELLWYN. My dear, I have—often.

ANN. Then why don't you keep it? It's a frightful habit. You *are* naughty, Daddy. One of these days you'll get yourself into most fearful complications.

WELLWYN. My dear, when they—when they look at you?

ANN. You know the house wants all sorts of things. Why do you speak to them at all?

WELLWYN. I don't—they speak to me.

[*He takes off his ulster and hangs it over the back of an armchair.*

ANN. They see you coming. Anybody can see *you* coming, Daddy. That's why you ought to be so careful. I shall make you wear a hard hat. Those squashy hats of yours are hopelessly inefficient.

WELLWYN. [*Gazing at his hat*] Calway wears one.

ANN. As if anyone would beg of Professor Calway.

WELLWYN. Well—perhaps not. You know, Ann, I admire that fellow. Wonderful power of—of—theory! How a man can be so absolutely tidy in his mind! It's most exciting.

ANN. Has anyone begged of you to-day?

WELLWYN. [*Doubtfully*] No—no.

ANN. [*After a long, severe look*] Will you have rum in your tea?

WELLWYN. [*Crestfallen*] Yes, my dear—a good deal.

ANN. [*Pouring out the rum, and handing him the glass*] Well, who was it?

WELLWYN. He didn't beg of me. [*Losing himself in recollection.*] Interesting old creature, Ann—real type. Old cabman.

ANN. Where?

WELLWYN. Just on the Embankment.

ANN. Of course! Daddy, you know the Embankment ones are *always* rotters.

WELLWYN. Yes, my dear; but this wasn't.

ANN. Did you give him your card?

WELLWYN. I—I—don't——

ANN *Did* you, Daddy?

WELLWYN. I'm rather afraid I may have!

ANN. May have! It's simply immoral.

WELLWYN. Well, the old fellow was so awfully human, Ann. Besides, I didn't give him any money—hadn't got any.

ANN. Look here, Daddy! Did you ever ask anybody for anything? You know you never did, you'd starve first. So would anybody decent. Then, why won't you see that people who beg are rotters?

WELLWYN. But, my dear, we're not all the same. They wouldn't do it if it wasn't natural to them. One likes to be friendly. What's the use of being alive if one isn't?

ANN. Daddy, you're hopeless.

WELLWYN. But, look here, Ann, the whole thing's so jolly complicated. According to Calway, we're to give the State all we can spare, to make the undeserving deserving. He's a Professor; he ought to know. But old Hoxton's always dinning it into me that we ought to support private organizations for helping the deserving, and damn the undeserving. Well, that's just the opposite. And he's a J.P. Tremendous experience. And the Vicar seems to be for a little bit of both. Well, what the devil——? My trouble is, whichever I'm with, he always converts me. [*Ruefully.*] And there's no fun in any of them.

ANN. [*Rising*] Oh! Daddy, you are so—don't you know that you're the despair of all social reformers? [*She envelops him.*] There's a tear in the left knee of your trousers. You're not to wear them again.

WELLWYN. Am I likely to?

ANN. I shouldn't be a bit surprised if it isn't your only pair. D'you know what I live in terror of?

[WELLWYN *gives her a queer and apprehensive look.*

ANN. That you'll take them off some day, and give them away in the street. Have you got any money? [*She feels in his coat, and he in his trousers—they find nothing.*] Do you know that your pockets are one enormous hole?

WELLWYN. No!

ANN. Spiritually.

WELLWYN. Oh! Ah! H'm!

ANN. [*Severely*] Now, look here, Daddy! [*She takes him by his lappels.*] Don't imagine that it isn't the most disgusting luxury on your part to go on giving away things as you do ! You know what you really are, I suppose—a sickly sentimentalist !

WELLWYN. [*Breaking away from her, disturbed*] It isn't sentiment. It's simply that they seem to me so—so—jolly. If I'm to give up feeling sort of—nice in here [*he touches his chest*] about people—it doesn't matter *who* they are—then I don't know what I'm to do. I shall have to sit with my head in a bag.

ANN. I think you ought to.

WELLWYN. I suppose they see I like them—then they tell me things. After that, of course you can't help doing what you can.

ANN. Well, if you *will* love them up !

WELLWYN. My dear, I don't want to. It isn't *them* especially— why, I feel it even with old Calway sometimes. It's only Providence that he doesn't want anything of me—except to make me like himself —confound him !

ANN. [*Moving towards the door into the house—impressively*] What you don't see is that other people aren't a bit like *you*.

WELLWYN. Well, thank God !

ANN. It's so old-fashioned too ! I'm going to bed—I just leave you to your conscience.

WELLWYN. Oh !

ANN. [*Opening the door—severely*] Good-night—[*with a certain weakening*] you old—Daddy.   [*She jumps at him, gives him a hug, and goes out.*

> [WELLWYN *stands perfectly still. He first gazes up at the skylight, then down at the floor. Slowly he begins to shake his head, and mutter, as he moves towards the fire.*

WELLWYN. Bad lot. . . . Low type—no backbone, no stability !

> [*There comes a fluttering knock on the outer door. As the sound slowly enters his consciousness, he begins to wince, as though he knew, but would not admit its significance. Then he sits down, covering his ears. The knocking does not cease.* WELLWYN *drops first one, then both hands, rises, and begins to sidle towards the door. The knocking becomes louder.*

WELLWYN. Ah, dear ! Tt ! Tt ! Tt !

> [*After a look in the direction of* ANN's *disappearance, he opens the street door a very little way. By the light of the lamp there can be seen a young girl in dark clothes, huddled in a shawl to which the snow is clinging. She has on her arm a basket covered with a bit of sacking.*

WELLWYN. I can't, you know ; it's impossible.

> [*The girl says nothing, but looks at him with dark eyes.*

WELLWYN. [*Wincing*] Let's see—I don't know you—do I ?

> [*The girl, speaking in a soft hoarse voice, with a faint accent of reproach :* " Mrs. Megan—you give me this——" *She holds out a dirty visiting card.*

WELLWYN. [*Recoiling from the card*] Oh! Did I? Ah! When?

MRS. MEGAN. You 'ad some vi'lets off of me larst spring. You give me 'arf a crown. [*A smile tries to visit her face.*]

WELLWYN. [*Looking stealthily round*] Ah! Well, come in—just for a minute—it's very cold—and tell us what it is.

[*She comes in stolidly, a sphinx-like figure, with her pretty tragic little face.*

WELLWYN. I don't remember you. [*Looking closer.*] Yes, I do. Only—you weren't the same—were you?

MRS. MEGAN. [*Dully*] I seen trouble since.

WELLWYN. Trouble! Have some tea?

[*He looks anxiously at the door into the house, then goes quickly to the table, and pours out a glass of tea, putting rum into it.*

WELLWYN. [*Handing her the tea*] Keeps the cold out! Drink it off!

[MRS. MEGAN *drinks it off, chokes a little, and almost immediately seems to get a size larger.* WELLWYN *watches her with his head held on one side, and a smile broadening on his face.*

WELLWYN. Cure for all evils, um?

MRS. MEGAN. It warms you. [*She smiles.*]

WELLWYN. [*Smiling back, and catching himself out*] Well! You know, I oughtn't.

MRS. MEGAN. [*Conscious of the disruption of his personality, and withdrawing into her tragic abyss*] I wouldn't 'a come, but you told me if I wanted an 'and——

WELLWYN. [*Gradually losing himself in his own nature*] Let me see— corner of Flight Street, wasn't it?

MRS. MEGAN. [*With faint eagerness*] Yes, sir, an' I told you about me vi'lets—it was a luvly spring day.

WELLWYN. Beautiful! Beautiful! Birds singing, and the trees, &c.! We had quite a talk. You had a baby with you.

MRS. MEGAN. Yes. I got married since then.

WELLWYN. Oh! Ah! Yes! [*Cheerfully.*] And how's the baby?

MRS. MEGAN. [*Turning to stone*] I lost her.

WELLWYN. Oh! poor—Um!

MRS. MEGAN. [*Impassive*] You said something abaht makin' a picture of me. [*With faint eagerness.*] So I thought I might come, in case you'd forgotten.

WELLWYN. [*Looking at her intently*] Things going badly?

MRS. MEGAN. [*Stripping the sacking off her basket*] I keep 'em covered up, but the cold gets to 'em. Thruppence—that's all I've took.

WELLWYN. Ho! Tt! Tt! [*He looks into the basket.*] Christmas, too!

MRS. MEGAN. They're dead.

WELLWYN. [*Drawing in his breath*] Got a *good* husband?

MRS. MEGAN. He plays cards.

WELLWYN. Oh, Lord! And what are you doing out—with a cold like that? [*He taps his chest.*

MRS. MEGAN. We was sold up this morning—he's gone off with 'is mates. Haven't took enough yet for a night's lodgin'.

WELLWYN. [*Correcting a spasmodic dive into his pockets*] But who buys *flowers* at this time of night?

[MRS. MEGAN *looks at him, and faintly smiles.*

WELLWYN. [*Rumpling his hair*] Saints above us! Here! Come to the fire!

[*She follows him to the fire. He shuts the street door.*

WELLWYN. Are your feet wet? [*She nods.*] Well, sit down here, and take them off. That's right.

[*She sits on the stool. And after a slow look up at him, which has in it a deeper knowledge than belongs of right to her years, begins taking off her shoes and stockings.* WELLWYN *goes to the door into the house, opens it, and listens with a sort of stealthy casualness. He returns whistling, but not out loud. The girl has finished taking off her stockings, and turned her bare toes to the flames. She shuffles them back under her skirt.*

WELLWYN. How old are you, my child?

MRS. MEGAN. Nineteen, come Candlemas.

WELLWYN. And what's your name?

MRS. MEGAN. Guinevere.

WELLWYN. What? Welsh?

MRS. MEGAN. Yes—from Battersea.

WELLWYN. And your husband?

MRS. MEGAN. No. Irish, 'e is. Notting Dale, 'e comes from.

WELLWYN. Roman Catholic?

MRS. MEGAN. Yes. My 'usband's an atheist as well.

WELLWYN. I see. [*Abstractedly.*] How jolly! And how old is he—this young man of yours?

MRS. MEGAN. 'E'll be twenty soon.

WELLWYN. Babes in the wood! Does he treat you badly?

MRS. MEGAN. No.

WELLWYN. Nor drink?

MRS. MEGAN. No. He's not a bad one. Only he gets playin' cards—then 'e'll fly the kite.

WELLWYN. I see. And when he's not flying it, what does he do?

MRS. MEGAN. [*Touching her basket*] Same as me. Other jobs tires 'im.

WELLWYN. That's very nice! [*He checks himself.*] Well, what am I to do with you?

MRS. MEGAN. Of course, I could get me night's lodging if I like to do—the same as some of them.

WELLWYN. No! no! Never, my child! Never!

MRS. MEGAN. It's easy that way.

WELLWYN. Heavens! But your husband! Um?

MRS. MEGAN. [*With stoical vindictiveness*] He's after one I know of.

WELLWYN. Tt! What a pickle!

MRS. MEGAN. I'll 'ave to walk about the streets.

WELLWYN. [*To himself*] Now how can I?

[MRS. MEGAN *looks up and smiles at him, as if she had already discovered that he is peculiar.*

WELLWYN. You see, the fact is, I mustn't give you anything—because—well, for one thing I haven't got it. There are other reasons, but that's the—real one. But, now, there's a little room where my models dress. I wonder if you could sleep there. Come, and see.

[*The Girl gets up lingeringly, loth to leave the warmth. She takes up her wet stockings.*

MRS. MEGAN. Shall I put them on again?

WELLWYN. No, no; there's a nice warm pair of slippers. [*Seeing the steam rising from her.*] Why, you're wet all over. Here, wait a little!

[*He crosses to the door into the house, and after stealthily listening, steps through. The Girl, like a cat, steals back to the warmth of the fire.* WELLWYN *returns with a candle, a canary-coloured bath-gown, and two blankets.*

WELLWYN. Now then! [*He precedes her towards the door of the model's room.*] Hsssh! [*He opens the door and holds up the candle to show her the room.*] Will it do? There's a couch. You'll find some washing things. Make yourself quite at home. See!

[*The Girl, perfectly dumb, passes through with her basket—and her shoes and stockings.* WELLWYN *hands her the candle, blankets, and bath gown.*

WELLWYN. Have a good sleep, child! Forget that you're alive! [*He closes the door, mournfully.*] Done it again! [*He goes to the table, cuts a large slice of cake, knocks on the door, and hands it in.*] Chow-chow! [*Then, as he walks away, he sights the opposite door.*] Well—damn it, what could I have done? Not a farthing on me! [*He goes to the street door to shut it, but first opens it wide to confirm himself in his hospitality.*] Night like this!

[*A sputter of snow is blown in his face. A voice says : "Monsieur, pardon!"* WELLWYN *recoils spasmodically. A figure moves from the lamp-post to the doorway. He is seen to be young and to have ragged clothes. He speaks again :* "You do not remember me, Monsieur? My name is Ferrand—it was in Paris, in the Champs-Elysées—by the fountain. . . . When you came to the door, Monsieur

—I am not made of iron. . . . Tenez, here is your card—I have never lost it." *He holds out to* WELLWYN *an old and dirty visiting card. As inch by inch he has advanced into the doorway, the light from within falls on him, a tall gaunt young pagan with fair hair and reddish golden stubble of beard, a long ironical nose a little to one side, and large, grey, rather prominent eyes. There is a certain grace in his figure and movements ; his clothes are nearly dropping off him.*

WELLWYN. [*Yielding to a pleasant memory*] Ah ! yes. By the fountain. I was sitting there, and you came and ate a roll, and drank the water.

FERRAND. [*With faint eagerness*] My breakfast. I was in poverty—veree bad off. You gave me ten francs. I thought I had a little the right [WELLWYN *makes a movement of disconcertion*], seeing you said that if I came to England——

WELLWYN. Um ! And so you've come !

FERRAND. It was time that I consolidated my fortunes, Monsieur.

WELLWYN. And you—have——   [*He stops embarrassed.*

FERRAND. [*Shrugging his ragged shoulders*] One is not yet Rothschild.

WELLWYN. [*Sympathetically*] No. [*Yielding to memory.*] We talked philosophy.

FERRAND. I have not yet changed my opinion. We other vagabonds, we are exploited by the bourgeois. This is always my idea, Monsieur.

WELLWYN. Yes—not quite the general view, perhaps ! Well—[*Heartily.*] Come in ! Very glad to see you again.

FERRAND. [*Brushing his arm over his eyes*] Pardon, Monsieur—your goodness—I am a little weak.

> [*He opens his coat, and shows a belt drawn very tight over his ragged shirt.*

I tighten him one hole for each meal, during two days now. That gives you courage.

WELLWYN. [*With cooing sounds, pouring out tea, and adding rum*] Have some of this. It'll buck you up.   [*He watches the young man drink.*

FERRAND. [*Becoming a size larger*] Sometimes I think that I will never succeed to dominate my life, Monsieur—though I have no vices, except that I guard always the aspiration to achieve success. But I will not roll myself under the machine of existence to gain a nothing every day. I must find with what to fly a little.

WELLWYN. [*Delicately*] Yes ; yes—I remember, you found it difficult to stay long in any particular—yes.

FERRAND. [*Proudly*] In one little corner ? No—Monsieur—never ! That is not in my character. I must see life.

WELLWYN. Quite, quite ! Have some cake ?   [*He cuts cake.*

FERRAND. In your country they say you cannot eat the cake and have it. But one must always try, Monsieur; one must never be content. [*Refusing the cake.*] *Grand merci*, but for the moment I have no stomach—I have lost my stomach now for two days. If I could smoke, Monsieur!   [*He makes the gesture of smoking.*

WELLWYN. Rather! [*Handing his tobacco pouch.*] Roll yourself one.

FERRAND. [*Rapidly rolling a cigarette*] If I had not found you, Monsieur—I would have been a little hole in the river to-night—I was so discouraged. [*He inhales and puffs a long luxurious whiff of smoke. Very bitterly.*] Life! [*He disperses the puff of smoke with his finger, and stares before him.*] And to think that in a few minutes HE will be born! Monsieur! [*He gazes intently at* WELLWYN.] The world would reproach you for your goodness to me.

WELLWYN. [*Looking uneasily at the door into the house*] You think so? Ah!

FERRAND. Monsieur, if HE Himself were on earth now, there would be a little heap of gentlemen writing to the journals every day to call Him sloppee sentimentalist! And what is veree funny, these gentlemen they would all be most strong Christians. [*He regards* WELLWYN *deeply.*] But that will not trouble you, Monsieur; I saw well from the first that you are no Christian. You have so kind a face.

WELLWYN. Oh! Indeed!

FERRAND. You have not enough the Pharisee in your character. You do not judge, and you are judged.

[*He stretches his limbs as if in pain.*

WELLWYN. Are you in pain?

FERRAND. I 'ave a little the rheumatism.

WELLWYN. Wet through, of course! [*Glancing towards the house.*] Wait a bit! I wonder if you'd like these trousers; they've—er— they're not quite——

[*He passes through the door into the house.* FERRAND *stands at the fire, with his limbs spread as it were to embrace it, smoking with abandonment.* WELLWYN *returns stealthily, dressed in a Jaeger dressing-gown, and bearing a pair of drawers, his trousers, a pair of slippers, and a sweater.*

WELLWYN. [*Speaking in a low voice, for the door is still open*] Can you make these do for the moment?

FERRAND. *Je vous remercie, Monsieur.* [*Pointing to the screen.*] May I retire?

WELLWYN. Yes, yes.

[FERRAND *goes behind the screen.* WELLWYN *closes the door into the house, then goes to the window to draw the curtains. He suddenly recoils and stands petrified with doubt.*

WELLWYN. Good Lord!

[*There is the sound of tapping on glass. Against the window-pane is pressed the face of a man.* WELLWYN *motions to him to go*

away. He does not go, but continues tapping. WELLWYN
*opens the door. There enters a square old man, with a red,
pendulous-jawed, shaking face under a snow-besprinkled bowler
hat. He is holding out a visiting card with tremulous hand.*

WELLWYN. Who's that? Who are you?

TIMSON. [*In a thick, hoarse, shaking voice*] 'Appy to see you, sir;
we 'ad a talk this morning. Timson—I give you me name. You
invited of me, if ye remember.

WELLWYN. It's a little late, really.

TIMSON. Well, ye see, I never expected to 'ave to call on yer. I
was 'itched up all right when I spoke to yer this mornin', but bein'
Christmas, things 'ave took a turn with me to-day. [*He speaks with
increasing thickness.*] I'm reg'lar disgusted—not got the price of a bed
abaht me. Thought you wouldn't like me to be delicate—not at
my age.

WELLWYN. [*With a mechanical and distracted dive of his hands into
his pockets*] The fact is, it so happens I haven't a copper on me.

TIMSON. [*Evidently taking this for professional refusal*] Wouldn't arsk
you if I could 'elp it. 'Ad to do with 'orses all me life. It's this 'ere
cold I'm frightened of. I'm afraid I'll go to sleep.

WELLWYN. Well, really, I——

TIMSON. To be froze to death—I mean—it's awkward.

WELLWYN. [*Puzzled and unhappy*] Well—come in a moment, and
let's—think it out. Have some tea!

> [*He pours out the remains of the tea, and finding there is not very
> much, adds rum rather liberally.* TIMSON, *who walks a little
> wide at the knees, steadying his gait, has followed.*

TIMSON. [*Receiving the drink*] Yer 'ealth. 'Ere's—soberiety! [*He
applies the drink to his lips with shaking hand. Agreeably surprised.*]
Blimey! Thish yer tea's foreign, ain't it?

FERRAND. [*Reappearing from behind the screen in his new clothes, of which
the trousers stop too soon*] With a needle, Monsieur, I would soon have
with what to make face against the world.

WELLWYN. Too short! Ah! [*He goes to the dais on which stands
ANN's work-basket, and takes from it a needle and cotton.*]

> [*While he is so engaged* FERRAND *is sizing up old* TIMSON, *as one
> dog will another. The old man, glass in hand, seems to have
> lapsed into coma.*

FERRAND. [*Indicating* TIMSON] Monsieur!

> [*He makes the gesture of one drinking, and shakes his head.*

WELLWYN. [*Handing him the needle and cotton*] Um! Afraid so!

> [*They approach* TIMSON, *who takes no notice.*

FERRAND. [*Gently*] It is an old cabby, is it not, Monsieur? *Ceux
sont tous des buveurs.*

WELLWYN. [*Concerned at the old man's stupefaction*] Now, my old friend, sit down a moment. [*They manœuvre* TIMSON *to the settle.*] Will you smoke?

TIMSON. [*In a drowsy voice*] Thank 'ee—smoke pipe of 'baccer. Old 'orse—standin' abaht in th' cold.   [*He relapses into coma.*

FERRAND. [*With a click of his tongue*] Il est parti.

WELLWYN. [*Doubtfully*] He hasn't really left a horse outside, do you think?

FERRAND. *Non, non, Monsieur*—no 'orse. He is dreaming. I know very well that state of him—that catches you sometimes. It is the warmth sudden on the stomach. He will speak no more sense to-night. At the most, drink, and fly a little in his past.

WELLWYN. Poor old buffer!

FERRAND. Touching, is it not, Monsieur? There are many brave gents among the old cabbies—they have philosophy—that comes from 'orses, and from sitting still.

WELLWYN. [*Touching* TIMSON'S *shoulder*] Drenched!

FERRAND. That will do 'im no 'arm, Monsieur—no 'arm at all. He is well wet inside, remember—it is Christmas to-morrow. Put him a rug, if you will; he will soon steam.

[WELLWYN *takes up* ANN'S *long red cloak, and wraps it round the old man.*

TIMSON. [*Faintly roused*] Tha's right. Put—the rug on th' old 'orse.   [*He makes a strange noise, and works his head and tongue.*

WELLWYN. [*Alarmed*] What's the matter with him?

FERRAND. It is nothing, Monsieur; for the moment he thinks 'imself a 'orse. *Il joue " cache-cache,"* 'ide and seek, with what you call —'is bitt.

WELLWYN. But what's to be done with him? One can't turn him out in this state.

FERRAND. If you wish to leave him 'ere, Monsieur, have no fear. I charge myself with him.

WELLWYN. Oh! [*Dubiously.*] You—er—I really don't know, I —hadn't contemplated—You think you could manage if I—if I went to bed?

FERRAND. But certainly, Monsieur.

WELLWYN. [*Still dubiously*] You—you're sure you've everything you want?

FERRAND. [*Bowing*] *Mais oui, Monsieur.*

WELLWYN. I don't know what I can do by staying.

FERRAND. There is nothing you can do, Monsieur. Have confidence in me.

WELLWYN. Well—keep the fire up quietly—very quietly. You'd better take this coat of mine, too. You'll find it precious cold, I expect, about three o'clock.   [*He hands* FERRAND *his ulster.*

FERRAND. [*Taking it*] I shall sleep in praying for you, Monsieur.

WELLWYN. Ah! Yes! Thanks! Well—good-night! By the way, I shall be down rather early. Have to think of my household a bit, you know.

FERRAND. *Très bien, Monsieur.* I comprehend. One must well be regular in this life.

WELLWYN. [*With a start*] Lord! [*He looks at the door of the model's room.*] I'd forgotten——

FERRAND. Can I undertake anything, Monsieur?

WELLWYN. No, no! [*He goes to the electric light switch by the outer door.*] You won't want this, will you?

FERRAND. *Merci, Monsieur.* [WELLWYN *switches off the light.*]

FERRAND. *Bon soir, Monsieur!*

WELLWYN. The devil! Er—good-night!

[*He hesitates, rumples his hair, and passes rather suddenly away.*

FERRAND. [*To himself*] Poor pigeon! [*Looking long at old* TIMSON.] *Espèce de type anglais!*

[*He sits down in the firelight, curls up a foot on his knee, and taking out a knife, rips the stitching of a turned-up end of trouser, pinches the cloth double, and puts in the preliminary stitch of a new hem—all with the swiftness of one well-accustomed. Then, as if hearing a sound behind him, he gets up quickly and slips behind the screen.* MRS. MEGAN, *attracted by the cessation of voices, has opened the door, and is creeping from the model's room towards the fire. She has almost reached it before she takes in the torpid crimson figure of old* TIMSON. *She halts and puts her hand to her chest—a queer figure in the firelight, garbed in the canary-coloured bath-gown and rabbit's-wool slippers, her black matted hair straggling down on her neck. Having quite digested the fact that the old man is in a sort of stupor,* MRS. MEGAN *goes close to the fire, and sits on the little stool, smiling sideways at old* TIMSON. FERRAND, *coming quietly up behind, examines her from above, drooping his long nose as if inquiring with it as to her condition in life; then he steps back a yard or two.*

FERRAND. [*Gently*] Pardon, Ma'moiselle.

MRS. MEGAN. [*Springing to her feet*] Oh!

FERRAND. All right, all right! We are brave gents!

TIMSON. [*Faintly roused*] 'Old up, there!

FERRAND. Trust in me, Ma'moiselle!

[MRS. MEGAN *responds by drawing away.*

FERRAND. [*Gently*] We must be good comrades. This asylum —it is better than a doss-'ouse.

[*He pushes the stool over towards her, and seats himself. Somewhat reassured,* MRS. MEGAN *again sits down.*

MRS. MEGAN. You frightened me.

TIMSON. [*Unexpectedly—in a drowsy tone*] Purple foreigners !

FERRAND. Pay no attention, Ma'moiselle.   He is a philosopher.

MRS. MEGAN. Oh ! I thought 'e was boozed.

[*They both look at* TIMSON.

FERRAND. It is the same—veree 'armless.

MRS. MEGAN. What's that he's got on 'im !

FERRAND. It is a coronation robe.   Have no fear, Ma'moiselle.
Veree docile potentate.

MRS. MEGAN. I wouldn't be afraid of him.   [*Challenging* FERRAND.
I'm afraid o' *you.*

FERRAND. It is because you do not know me, Ma'moiselle.   You
are wrong, it is always the unknown you should love.

MRS. MEGAN. I don't like the way you—speaks to me.

FERRAND. Ah ! You are a Princess in disguise ?

MRS. MEGAN. No fear !

FERRAND. No ?   What is it then you do to make face against the
necessities of life ?   A living ?

MRS. MEGAN. Sells flowers.

FERRAND. [*Rolling his eyes*] It is not a career.

MRS. MEGAN. [*With a touch of devilry*] You don't know what I do.

FERRAND. Ma'moiselle, whatever you do is charming.

[MRS. MEGAN *looks at him, and slowly smiles.*

MRS. MEGAN. You're a foreigner.

FERRAND. It is true.

MRS. MEGAN. What do *you* do for a livin' ?

FERRAND. I am an interpreter.

MRS. MEGAN. You ain't very busy, are you ?

FERRAND. [*With dignity*] At present I am resting.

MRS. MEGAN. [*Looking at him and smiling*] How did you and 'im
come here ?

FERRAND. Ma'moiselle, we would ask you the same question.

MRS. MEGAN. The gentleman let me.   'E's funny.

FERRAND. *C'est un ange !* [*At* MRS. MEGAN's *blank stare he in-
terprets.*] An angel !

MRS. MEGAN. Me luck's out—that's why I come.

FERRAND. [*Rising*] Ah ! Ma'moiselle ! Luck !   There is the little
God who dominates us all.   Look at this old ! [*He points to* TIMSON.]
He is finished.   In his day that old would be doing good business.
He could afford himself—[*He makes a sign of drinking.*] Then come
the motor cars.   All goes—he has nothing left, only 'is 'abits of a
cocher !   Luck !

TIMSON. [*With a vague gesture—drowsily*] Kick the foreign beggars
out.

FERRAND. A real Englishman. . . . And look at me !   My father
was merchant of ostrich feathers in Brussels.   If I had been content

to go in his business, I would 'ave been rich.   But I was born to roll—
" rolling stone "—to voyage is stronger than myself.   Luck ! . . .
And you, Ma'moiselle, shall I tell your fortune ?   [*He looks in her face.*]
You were born for *la joie de vivre*—to drink the wines of life.   *Et vous
voilà !*   Luck !

> [*Though she does not in the least understand what he has said, her
> expression changes to a sort of glee.*

FERRAND. Yes.   You were born loving pleasure.   Is it not ?
You see, you cannot say, No.   All of us, we have our fates.   Give
me your hand.   [*He kneels down and takes her hand.*]   In each of us there
is that against which we cannot struggle.   Yes, yes !

> [*He holds her hand, and turns it over between his own.*   MRS. MEGAN
> *remains stolid, half-fascinated, half-reluctant.*

TIMSON. [*Flickering into consciousness*] Be'ave yourselves !   Yer
crimson canary birds !

> [MRS. MEGAN *would withdraw her hand, but cannot.*

FERRAND. Pay no attention, Ma'moiselle.   He is a Puritan.

> [TIMSON *relapses into comatosity, upsetting his glass, which falls
> with a crash.*

MRS. MEGAN. Let go my hand, please !

FERRAND. [*Relinquishing it, and staring into the fire gravely*] There is
one thing I have never done—'urt a woman—that is hardly in my
character.   [*Then, drawing a little closer, he looks into her face.*] Tell me,
Ma'moiselle, what is it you think of all day long ?

MRS. MEGAN. I dunno—lots, I thinks of.

FERRAND. Shall I tell you ?   [*Her eyes remain fixed on his, the strangeness of him preventing her from telling him to " get along." He goes on in
his ironic voice.*] It is of the streets—the lights—the faces—it is of all
which moves, and is warm—it is of colour—it is [*he brings his face
quite close to hers*] of Love.   That is for you what the road is for me.
That is for you what the rum is for that old—[*He jerks his thumb
back at* TIMSON.   *Then bending swiftly forward to the girl.*] See !   I kiss
you—Ah !

> [*He draws her forward off the stool.   There is a little struggle,
> then she resigns her lips.   The little stool, overturned, falls
> with a clatter.   They spring up, and move apart.   The door
> opens and* ANN *enters from the house in a blue dressing-gown,
> with her hair loose, and a candle held high above her head.
> Taking in the strange half-circle round the stove, she recoils.
> Then, standing her ground, calls in a voice sharpened by
> fright : " Daddy—Daddy ! "*

TIMSON. [*Stirring uneasily, and struggling to his feet*] All ri——— !
I'm comin' !

FERRAND. Have no fear, Madame !

> [*In the silence that follows, a clock begins loudly striking twelve.*

> ANN *remains, as if carved in stone, her eyes fastened on the*
> *strangers.   There is the sound of someone falling downstairs,*
> *and* WELLWYN *appears, also holding a candle above his head.*

ANN. Look !

WELLWYN. Yes, yes, my dear !   It—it happened.

ANN. [*With a sort of groan*] Oh !   Daddy !

> [*In the renewed silence, the church clock ceases to chime.*

FERRAND. [*Softly, in his ironic voice*] HE is come, Monsieur !   'Appy
Christmas !   Bon Noël !

> [*There is a sudden chime of bells.   The stage is blotted dark.*

The curtain falls

ACT II

It is four o'clock in the afternoon of New Year's Day. On the raised dais
MRS. MEGAN *is standing, in her rags, with bare feet and ankles, her
dark hair as if blown about, her lips parted, holding out a dishevelled
bunch of violets. Before his easel,* WELLWYN *is painting her. Behind
him, at a table between the cupboard and the door to the model's room,*
TIMSON *is washing brushes, with the movements of one employed upon
relief works. The samovar is hissing on the table by the stove, the tea
things are set out.*

WELLWYN. Open your mouth.   [MRS. MEGAN *opens her mouth*
ANN. [*In hat and coat, entering from the house*] Daddy !
        [WELLWYN *goes to her ; and, released from restraint,* MRS. MEGAN
            looks round at TIMSON *and grimaces.*
WELLWYN. Well, my dear ?   [*They speak in low voices.*
ANN. [*Holding out a note*] This note from Canon Bertley. He's
going to bring her husband here this afternoon.
                            [*She looks at* MRS. MEGAN.
WELLWYN. Oh !   [*He also looks at* MRS. MEGAN.
ANN. And I met Sir Thomas Hoxton at church this morning, and
spoke to him about Timson.
WELLWYN. Um !
        [*They look at* TIMSON. *Then* ANN *goes back to the door, and*
            WELLWYN *follows her.*
ANN [*Turning*] I'm going round now, Daddy, to ask Professor
Calway what we're to do with that Ferrand.
WELLWYN. Oh ! One each ! I wonder if they'll like it.
ANN. They'll have to lump it.   [*She goes out into the house.*
WELLWYN. [*Back at his easel*] You can shut your mouth now.
        [MRS. MEGAN *shuts her mouth, but opens it immediately to smile.*
WELLWYN. [*Spasmodically*] Ah ! Now that's what I want. [*He
dabs furiously at the canvas. Then standing back, runs his hands through his
hair and turns a painter's glance towards the skylight.*] Dash ! Light's
gone ! Off you get, child—don't tempt me !
        [MRS. MEGAN *descends. Passing towards the door of the model's
            room she stops, and stealthily looks at the picture.*
TIMSON. Ah ! Would yer !
WELLWYN. [*Wheeling round*] Want to have a look ? Well—come on !
        [*He takes her by the arm, and they stand before the canvas. After
            a stolid moment, she giggles.*

344

WELLWYN. Oh! You think so?

MRS. MEGAN. [*Who has lost her hoarseness*] It's not like my picture that I had on the pier.

WELLWYN. No—it wouldn't be.

MRS. MEGAN. [*Timidly*] If I had an 'at on, I'd look better.

WELLWYN. With feathers?

MRS. MEGAN. Yes.

WELLWYN. Well, you can't! I don't like hats, and I don't like feathers.

> [MRS. MEGAN *timidly tugs his sleeve.* TIMSON, *screened as he thinks by the picture, has drawn from his bulky pocket a bottle and is taking a stealthy swig.*

WELLWYN. [*To* MRS. MEGAN, *affecting not to notice*] How much do I owe you?

MRS. MEGAN. [*A little surprised*] You paid me for to-day—all 'cept a penny.

WELLWYN. Well! Here it is. [*He gives her a coin.*] Go and get your feet on!

MRS. MEGAN. You've give me 'arf a crown.

WELLWYN. Cut away now!

> [MRS. MEGAN, *smiling at the coin, goes towards the model's room. She looks back at* WELLWYN, *as if to draw his eyes to her, but he is gazing at the picture; then, catching old* TIMSON's *sour glance, she grimaces at him, kicking up her feet with a little squeal. But when* WELLWYN *turns to the sound, she is demurely passing through the doorway.*

TIMSON. [*In his voice of dubious sobriety*] I've finished these yer brushes, sir. It's not a man's work. I've been thinkin' if you'd keep an 'orse, I could give yer satisfaction.

WELLWYN. Would the horse, Timson?

TIMSON. [*Looking him up and down*] I knows of one that would just suit yer. Reel 'orse, you'd like 'im.

WELLWYN. [*Shaking his head*] Afraid not, Timson! Awfully sorry, though, to have nothing better for you than this, at present.

TIMSON. [*Faintly waving the brushes*] Of course, if you can't afford it, I don't press you—it's only that I feel I'm not doing meself justice. [*Confidentially.*] There's just one thing, sir; I can't bear to see a gen'leman imposed on. That foreigner—'e's not the sort to 'ave about the place. Talk? Oh! ah! But 'e'll never do any good with 'imself. He's a alien.

WELLWYN. Terrible misfortune to a fellow, Timson.

TIMSON. Don't you believe it, sir; it's his *fault*. I says to the young lady yesterday: Miss Ann, your father's a gen'leman [*with a sudden accent of hoarse sincerity*], and so you are—I don't mind sayin' it—*but*, I said, he's too easy-goin'.

WELLWYN. Indeed !

TIMSON. Well, see that girl now ! [*He shakes his head.*] I never did believe in goin' behind a person's back—I'm an Englishman— but [*lowering his voice*] she's a bad hat, sir. Why, look at the street she comes from !

WELLWYN. Oh ! you know it ?

TIMSON. Lived there meself larst three years. See the difference a few days' corn's made in her. She's that saucy you can't touch 'er head.

WELLWYN. Is there any necessity, Timson ?

TIMSON. Artful too. Full o' vice, I call 'er. Where's 'er 'usband ?

WELLWYN. [*Gravely*] Come, Timson ! You wouldn't like *her* to——

TIMSON. [*With dignity, so that the bottle in his pocket is plainly visible*] I'm a man as always beared inspection.

WELLWYN. [*With a well-directed smile*] So I see.

TIMSON. [*Curving himself round the bottle*] It's not for me to say nothing—but I can tell a gen'leman as quick as ever I can tell an 'orse.

WELLWYN. [*Painting*] I find it safest to assume that every man is a gentleman, and every woman a lady. Saves no end of self-contempt. Give me the little brush.

TIMSON. [*Handing him the brush—after a considerable introspective pause*] Would yer like me to stay and wash it for yer again ? [*With great resolution*]. I will—I'll do it for you—never grudged workin' for a gen'leman.

WELLWYN. [*With sincerity*] Thank you, Timson—very good of you, I'm sure. [*He hands him back the brush.*] Just lend us a hand with this. [*Assisted by* TIMSON *he pushes back the dais.*] Let's see ! What do I owe you ?

TIMSON. [*Reluctantly*] It so 'appens, you advanced me to-day's yesterday.

WELLWYN. Then I suppose you want to-morrow's ?

TIMSON. Well, I 'ad to spend it, lookin' for a permanent job. When you've got to do with 'orses, you can't neglect the publics, or you might as well be dead.

WELLWYN. Quite so !

TIMSON. It mounts up in the course o' the year.

WELLWYN. It would. [*Passing him a coin.*] This is for an exceptional purpose—Timson—see ? Not——

TIMSON. [*Touching his forehead*] Certainly, sir. I quite understand. I'm not that sort, as I think I've proved to yer, comin' here regular day after day, all the week. There's one thing, I ought to warn you perhaps—I might 'ave to give this job up any day.

[*He makes a faint demonstration with the little brush, then puts it, absent-mindedly, into his pocket.*

WELLWYN. [*Gravely*] I'd never stand in the way of your bettering yourself, Timson. And, by the way, my daughter spoke to a friend about you to-day. I think something may come of it.

TIMSON. Oh! Oh! She did! Well, it might do me a bit o' good. [*He makes for the outer door, but stops.*] That foreigner! 'E sticks in my gizzard. It's not as if there wasn't plenty o' pigeons for 'im to pluck in 'is own Gawd-forsaken country. Reg-lar jay, that's what I calls 'im. I could tell yer something——

> [*He has opened the door, and suddenly sees that* FERRAND *himself is standing there. Sticking out his lower lip,* TIMSON *gives a roll of his jaw and lurches forth into the street. Owing to a slight miscalculation, his face and raised arms are plainly visible through the window, as he fortifies himself from his bottle against the cold.* FERRAND, *having closed the door, stands with his thumb acting as pointer towards this spectacle. He is now remarkably dressed in an artist's squashy green hat, a frock coat too small for him, a bright blue tie of knitted silk, the grey trousers that were torn, well-worn brown boots, and a tan waistcoat.*

WELLWYN. What luck to-day?

FERRAND. [*With a shrug.*] Again I have beaten all London, Monsieur—not one bite. [*Contemplating himself.*] I think perhaps that, for the bourgeoisie, there is a little too much colour in my costume.

WELLWYN. [*Contemplating him*] Let's see—I believe I've an old top hat somewhere.

FERRAND. Ah! Monsieur, *merci*, but *that* I could not. It is scarcely in my character.

WELLWYN. True!

FERRAND. I have been to merchants of wine, of *tabac*, to hotels, to Leicester Square. I have been to a—Society for spreading Christian knowledge—I thought there I would have a chance perhaps as interpreter. *Toujours même chose*—we regret, we have no situation for you—same thing everywhere. It seems there is nothing doing in this town.

WELLWYN. I've noticed, there never is.

FERRAND. I was thinking, Monsieur, that in aviation there might be a career for me—but it seems one must be trained.

WELLWYN. Afraid so, Ferrand.

FERRAND. [*Approaching the picture*] Ah! You are always working at this. You will have something of very good there, Monsieur. You wish to fix the type of wild savage existing ever amongst our high civilization. *C'est très chic, ça!* [WELLWYN *manifests the quiet delight of an English artist actually understood.*] In the figures of these good citizens, to whom she offers her flower, you would give the idea of all the cage doors open to catch and make tame the wild bird, that will surely die within. *Très gentil!* Believe me, Monsieur, you have there the greatest comedy of life! How anxious are the tame birds to do the wild birds good. [*His voice changes.*] For the wild birds it is not funny. There is in some human souls, Monsieur, what cannot be made tame.

WELLWYN. I believe you, Ferrand.

[*The face of a young man appears at the window, unseen. Suddenly* ANN *opens the door leading to the house.*

ANN. Daddy—I want you.

WELLWYN. [*To* FERRAND] Excuse me a minute!

[*He goes to his daughter, and they pass out.*

[FERRAND *remains at the picture.* MRS. MEGAN *dressed in some of* ANN'S *discarded garments, has come out of the model's room. She steals up behind* FERRAND *like a cat, reaches an arm up, and curls it round his mouth. He turns, and tries to seize her; she disingenuously slips away. He follows. The chase circles the tea table. He catches her, lifts her up, swings round with her, so that her feet fly out; kisses her bent-back face, and sets her down. She stands there smiling. The face at the window darkens.*

FERRAND. La Valse!

[*He takes her with both hands by the waist, she puts her hands against his shoulders to push him off—and suddenly they are whirling. As they whirl, they bob together once or twice, and kiss. Then, with a warning motion towards the door, she wrenches herself free, and stops beside the picture, trying desperately to appear demure.* WELLWYN *and* ANN *have entered. The face has vanished.*

FERRAND. [*Pointing to the picture*] One does not comprehend all this, Monsieur, without well studying. I was in train to interpret for Ma'moiselle the chiaroscuro.

WELLWYN. [*With a queer look*] Don't take it *too* seriously, Ferrand.

FERRAND. It is a masterpiece.

WELLWYN. My daughter's just spoken to a friend, Professor Calway. He'd like to meet you. Could you come back a little later?

FERRAND. Certainly, Ma'moiselle. That will be an opening for me, I trust.   [*He goes to the street door.*

ANN. [*Paying no attention to him*] Mrs. Megan, will you too come back in half an hour?

FERRAND. *Très bien*, Ma'moiselle! I will see that she does. We will take a little promenade together. That will do us good.

[*He motions towards the door;* MRS. MEGAN, *all eyes, follows him out.*

ANN. Oh! Daddy, they *are* rotters. Couldn't you *see* they were having the most high jinks?

WELLWYN. [*At his picture*] I seemed to have noticed something.

ANN. [*Preparing for tea*] They were kissing.

WELLWYN. Tt! Tt!

ANN. They're hopeless, all three—especially her. Wish I hadn't given her my clothes now.

WELLWYN. [*Absorbed*] Something of wild-savage.

ANN. Thank goodness it's the Vicar's business to see that married people live together in his parish.

WELLWYN. Oh! [*Dubiously.*] The Megans are Roman Catholic-Atheists, Ann.

ANN. [*With heat*] Then they're all the more bound.

     [WELLWYN *gives a sudden and alarmed whistle.*

ANN. What's the matter?

WELLWYN. Didn't you say you spoke to Sir Thomas, too? Suppose he comes in while the Professor's here. They're cat and dog.

ANN. [*Blankly*] Oh! [*As* WELLWYN *strikes a match.*] The samovar *is* lighted. [*Taking up the nearly empty decanter of rum and going to the cupboard.*] It's all right. He won't.

WELLWYN. We'll hope not.   [*He turns back to his picture.*

ANN. [*At the cupboard*] Daddy!

WELLWYN. Hi!

ANN. There were *three* bottles.

WELLWYN. Oh!

ANN. Well! Now there aren't any.

WELLWYN. [*Abstracted*] That'll be Timson.

ANN. [*With real horror*] But it's awful!

WELLWYN. It is, my dear.

ANN. In seven days. To say nothing of the stealing.

WELLWYN. [*Vexed*] I blame myself—very much. Ought to have kept it locked up.

ANN. You ought to keep *him* locked up!

     [*There is heard a mild but authoritative knock.*

WELLWYN. Here's the Vicar!

ANN. What are you going to do about the rum?

WELLWYN. [*Opening the door to* CANON BERTLEY] Come in, Vicar! Happy New Year!

BERTLEY. Same to you! Ah! Ann! I've got into touch with her young husband—he's coming round.

ANN. [*Still a little out of her place*] Thank Go—— Moses!

BERTLEY. [*Faintly surprised*] From what I hear he's not really a bad youth. Afraid he bets on horses. The great thing, Wellwyn, with those poor fellows is to put your finger on the weak spot.

ANN. [*To herself—gloomily*] *That's* not difficult. What would you do, Canon Bertley, with a man who's been drinking father's rum?

BERTLEY. Remove the temptation, of course.

WELLWYN. He's done that.

BERTLEY. Ah! Then— [WELLWYN *and* ANN *hang on his words.*] then I should—er——

ANN. [*Abruptly*] Remove *him.*

BERTLEY. Before I say that, Ann, I must certainly see the individual.

WELLWYN. [*Pointing to the window*] There he is !

[*In the failing light* TIMSON'S *face is indeed to be seen pressed against the window pane.*

ANN. Daddy, I do wish you'd have thick glass put. It's so disgusting to be spied at ! [WELLWYN *going quickly to the door, has opened it.*] What do you want ?

[TIMSON *enters with dignity.   He is fuddled.*

TIMSON. [*Slowly*] Arskin' yer pardon—thought it me duty to come back—found thish yer little brishel on me.

[*He produces the little paint brush.*

ANN. [*In a deadly voice*] Nothing else ?

[TIMSON *accords her a glassy stare.*

WELLWYN. [*Taking the brush hastily*] That'll do, Timson, thanks !

TIMSON. As I am 'ere, can I do anything for yer ?

ANN. Yes, you can sweep out that little room. [*She points to the model's room.*] There's a broom in there.

TIMSON. [*Disagreeably surprised*] Certainly ;   never make bones about a little extra—never 'ave in all me life.   Do it at onsh, I will. [*He moves across to the model's room at that peculiar broad gait so perfectly adjusted to his habits.*] You quite understand me—couldn't bear to 'ave anything on me that wasn't mine. [*He passes out.*]

ANN. Old fraud !

WELLWYN. " In " and " on."   Mark my words, he'll restore the—bottles.

BERTLEY. But, my dear Wellwyn, that *is* stealing.

WELLWYN. We all have our discrepancies, Vicar.

ANN. Daddy ! Discrepancies !

WELLWYN. Well, Ann, my theory is that as regards solids Timson's an Individualist, but as regards liquids he's a Socialist . . . or vice versa, according to taste.

BERTLEY. No, no, we mustn't joke about it. [*Gravely.*] I do think he should be spoken to.

WELLWYN. Yes, but not by me.

BERTLEY. Surely you're the proper person.

WELLWYN. [*Shaking his head*] It was my rum, Vicar. Look so personal.   [*There sound a number of little tat-tat knocks.*

WELLWYN. Isn't that the Professor's knock ?

[*While Ann sits down to make tea, he goes to the door and opens it. There, dressed in an ulster, stands a thin, clean-shaved man, with a little hollow sucked into either cheek, who, taking off*

*a grey squash hat, discloses a majestically bald forehead, which
completely dominates all that comes below it.*

WELLWYN. Come in, Professor! So awfully good of you! You
know Canon Bertley, I think?

CALWAY. Ah! How d'you do?

WELLWYN. Your opinion will be invaluable, Professor.

ANN. Tea, Professor Calway?

                    [They have assembled round the tea table.

CALWAY. Thank you; no tea; milk.

WELLWYN. Rum?   *[He pours rum into* CALWAY's *milk.*

CALWAY. A little—thanks! [*Turning to* ANN.] You were going to
show me someone you're trying to rescue, or something, I think.

ANN. Oh! Yes. He'll be here directly—simply perfect rotter.

CALWAY. [*Smiling*] Really! Ah! I think you said he was a
congenital?

WELLWYN. [*With great interest*] What!

ANN. [*Low*] Daddy! [*To* CALWAY.] Yes; I—I think that's what
you call him.

CALWAY. Not old?

ANN. No; and quite healthy—a vagabond.

CALWAY. [*Sipping*] I see! Yes. Is it, do you think, chronic
unemployment with a vagrant tendency? Or would it be nearer the
mark to say: Vagrancy——

WELLWYN. Pure! Oh! pure! Professor. Awfully human.

CALWAY. [*With a smile of knowledge*] Quite! And—er——

ANN. [*Breaking in*] Before he comes, there's another——

BERTLEY. [*Blandly*] Yes, when you came in, we were discussing
what should be done with a man who drinks rum— [CALWAY
pauses in the act of drinking] that doesn't belong to him.

CALWAY. Really! Dipsomaniac?

BERTLEY. Well—perhaps you could tell us—drink certainly changing thine to mine. The Professor could see him, Wellwyn?

ANN. [*Rising*] Yes, do come and look at him, Professor Calway.
He's in there. [*She points towards the model's room.*]

                       *[*CALWAY *smiles deprecatingly.*

ANN. No, *really;* we needn't open the door. You can see him
through the glass. He's more than half——

CALWAY. Well, I hardly——

ANN. Oh! Do! Come on, Professor Calway! We *must* know
what to do with him. [CALWAY *rises.*] You can stand on a chair.
It's all science.

     [*She draws* CALWAY *to the model's room, which is lighted by a glass
         panel in the top of the high door.* CANON BERTLEY *also rises
         and stands watching.* WELLWYN *hovers, torn between respect
         for science and dislike of espionage.*

ANN. [*Drawing up a chair*] Come on !

CALWAY. Do you seriously wish me to ?

ANN. Rather !   It's quite safe ; he can't see you.

CALWAY. But he might come out.

> [ANN *puts her back against the door*. CALWAY *mounts the chair dubiously, and raises his head cautiously, bending it more and more downwards.*

ANN. Well ?

CALWAY. He appears to be—sitting on the floor.

WELLWYN. Yes, that's all right !   [BERTLEY *covers his lips.*

CALWAY. [*To* Ann—*descending*] By the look of his face, as far as one can see it, I should say there was a leaning towards mania.   I know the treatment.

> [*There come three loud knocks on the door.* WELLWYN *and* ANN *exchange a glance of consternation.*

ANN. Who's that ?

WELLWYN. It sounds like Sir Thomas.

CALWAY. Sir Thomas Hoxton ?

WELLWYN. [*Nodding*] Awfully sorry, Professor.   You see, we——

CALWAY. Not at all.   Only, I must decline to be involved in argument with him, please.

BERTLEY. He has experience.   We might get his opinion, don't you think ?

CALWAY. On a point of reform ?   A J.P. !

BERTLEY. [*Deprecating*] My dear sir—we needn't take it.

> [*The three knocks resound with extraordinary fury.*

ANN. You'd better open the door, Daddy.

> [WELLWYN *opens the door.* SIR THOMAS HOXTON *is disclosed in a fur overcoat and top hat.   His square, well-coloured face is remarkable for a massive jaw, dominating all that comes above it.   His voice is resolute.*

HOXTON. Afraid I didn't make myself heard.

WELLWYN. So good of you to come, Sir Thomas.   Canon Bertley ! [*They greet.*] Professor Calway you know, I think.

HOXTON. [*Ominously*] I do.   [*They almost greet.   An awkward pause.*]

ANN. [*Blurting it out*] That old cabman I told you of's been drinking father's rum.

BERTLEY. We were just discussing what's to be done with him, Sir Thomas.   One wants to do the very best, of course.   The question of reform is always delicate.

CALWAY. I beg your pardon.   There *is* no question here.

HOXTON. [*Abruptly*] Oh !   Is he in the house ?

ANN. In there.

HOXTON. Works for you, eh ?

WELLWYN. Er—yes.

HOXTON. Let's have a look at him !   [*An embarrassed pause.*

BERTLEY. Well—the fact is, Sir Thomas——

CALWAY. When last under observation——

ANN. He was sitting on the floor.

WELLWYN. I don't want the old fellow to feel he's being made a show of. Disgusting to be spied at, Ann.

ANN. You can't, Daddy ! He's drunk.

HOXTON. Never mind, Miss Wellwyn. Hundreds of these fellows before me in my time. [*At* CALWAY.] The only thing is a sharp lesson !

CALWAY. I disagree. I've seen the man ; what he requires is steady control, and the Dobbins treatment.

        [WELLWYN *approaches them with fearful interest.*

HOXTON. Not a bit of it ! He wants one for his knob ! Brace 'em up ! It's the only thing.

BERTLEY. Personally, I think that if he were spoken to seriously——

CALWAY. I cannot walk arm in arm with a crab.

HOXTON. [*Approaching* CALWAY] I beg your pardon ?

CALWAY. [*Moving back a little*] You're moving backwards, Sir Thomas. I've told you before, convinced reactionaryism, in these days——   [*There comes a single knock on the street door.*

BERTLEY. [*Looking at his watch*] D'you know, I'm rather afraid this may be our young husband, Wellwyn. I told him half-past four.

WELLWYN. Oh ! Ah ! Yes. [*Going towards the two reformers.*] Shall we go into the house, Professor, and settle the question quietly while the Vicar sees a young man ?

CALWAY. [*Pale with uncompleted statement, and gravitating insensibly in the direction indicated*] The merest sense of continuity—a simple instinct for order——

HOXTON. [*Following*] The only way to get order, sir, is to bring the disorderly up with a round turn. [CALWAY *turns to him in the doorway.*] You people without practical experience——

CALWAY. If you'll listen to me a minute.

HOXTON. I can show you in a mo——   [*They vanish through the door.*

WELLWYN. I was afraid of it.

BERTLEY. The two points of view. Pleasant to see such keenness. I may want you, Wellwyn. And Ann perhaps had better not be present.

WELLWYN. [*Relieved*] Quite so ! My dear !

    [ANN *goes reluctantly.* WELLWYN *opens the street door. The lamp outside has just been lighted, and, by its gleam, is seen the figure of* RORY MEGAN, *thin, pale, youthful.* ANN *turning at the door into the house gives him a long, inquisitive look, then goes.*

WELLWYN. Is that Megan ?

    12*

MEGAN. Yus.

WELLWYN. Come in.

[MEGAN *comes in.* *There follows an awkward silence, during which* WELLWYN *turns up the light, then goes to the tea table and pours out a glass of tea and rum.*

BERTLEY. [*Kindly*] Now, my boy, how is it that you and your wife are living apart like this ?

MEGAN. I dunno.

BERTLEY. Well, if *you* don't, none of us are very likely to, are we ?

MEGAN. That's what I thought, as I was comin' along.

WELLWYN. [*Twinkling*] Have some tea, Megan ? [*Handing him the glass.*] What d'you think of her picture ? 'Tisn't quite finished.

MEGAN. [*After scrutiny*] I seen her look like it—once.

WELLWYN. Good ! When was that ?

MEGAN. [*Stoically*] When she 'ad the measles. [*He drinks.*

WELLWYN. [*Ruminating*] I see—yes. I quite see—feverish !

BERTLEY. My dear Wellwyn, let me—— [*To* MEGAN.] Now, I hope you're willing to come together again, and to maintain her ?

MEGAN. If she'll maintain me.

BERTLEY. Oh ! but—— I see, you mean you're in the same line of business ?

MEGAN. Yus.

BERTLEY. And lean on each other. Quite so !

MEGAN. I leans on 'er mostly—with 'er looks.

BERTLEY. Indeed ! Very interesting—that !

MEGAN. Yus. Sometimes she'll take 'arf a crown off of a toff.

[*He looks at* WELLWYN.

WELLWYN. [*Twinkling*] I apologize to you, Megan.

MEGAN. [*With a faint smile*] I could do with a bit more of it.

BERTLEY. [*Dubiously*] Yes ! Yes ! Now, my boy, I've heard you bet on horses.

MEGAN. No, I don't.

BERTLEY. Play cards, then ? Come ! Don't be afraid to acknowledge it.

MEGAN. When I'm 'ard up—yus.

BERTLEY. But don't you know, that's ruination ?

MEGAN. Depends. Sometimes I wins a lot.

BERTLEY. You know that's not at all what I mean. Come, promise me to give it up.

MEGAN. I dunno abaht that.

BERTLEY. Now, there's a good fellow. Make a big effort and throw the habit off !

MEGAN. Comes over me—same as it might over you.

BERTLEY. Over me ! How do you mean, my boy ?

MEGAN. [*With a look up*] To tork!

  [WELLWYN, *turning to the picture, makes a funny little noise.*

BERTLEY. [*Maintaining his good humour*] A hit! But you forget, you know, to talk's my business. It's not yours to gamble.

MEGAN. You try sellin' flowers. If that ain't a—gamble——

BERTLEY. I'm afraid we're wandering a little from the point. Husband and wife should be together. You were brought up to that. Your father and mother——

MEGAN. Never was.

WELLWYN. [*Turning from the picture*] The question is, Megan: Will you take your wife home? She's a good little soul.

MEGAN. She never let me know it.

    [*There is a feeble knock on the door.*

WELLWYN. Well, now, come. Here she is!

  [*He points to the door, and stands regarding* MEGAN *with his friendly smile.*

MEGAN. [*With a gleam of responsiveness*] I might, perhaps, to please you, sir.

BERTLEY. [*Appropriating the gesture*] Capital, I thought we should get on in time.

MEGAN. Yus.

  [WELLWYN *opens the door.* MRS. MEGAN *and* FERRAND *are revealed. They are about to enter, but catching sight of* MEGAN, *hesitate.*

BERTLEY. Come in! Come in!

  [MRS. MEGAN *enters stolidly.* FERRAND, *following, stands apart with an air of extreme detachment.* MEGAN, *after a quick glance at them both, remains unmoved. No one has noticed that the door of the model's room has been opened, and that the unsteady figure of old* TIMSON *is standing there.*

BERTLEY. [*A little awkward in the presence of* FERRAND—*to the* MEGANS] This begins a new chapter. We won't improve the occasion. No need.

  [MEGAN, *turning towards his wife, makes her a gesture as if to say:* "Here! let's get out of this!"

BERTLEY. Yes, yes, you'll like to get home at once—I know.

    [*He holds up his hand mechanically.*

TIMSON. I forbids the banns.

BERTLEY. [*Startled*] Gracious!

TIMSON. [*Extremely unsteady*] Just cause and impejiment. There 'e stands. [*He points to* FERRAND.] The crimson foreigner! The mockin' jay!

WELLWYN. Timson!

TIMSON. You're a gen'leman—I'm aweer o' that—but I must speak the truth—[*he waves his hand*] an' shame the devil!

BERTLEY. Is this the rum——?

TIMSON. [*Struck by the word*] I'm a teetotaller.

WELLWYN. Timson, Timson!

TIMSON. Seein' as there's ladies present, I won't be conspicuous. [*Moving away, and making for the door, he strikes against the dais, and mounts upon it.*] But what I do say, is: He's no better than 'er and she's worse.

BERTLEY. This is distressing.

FERRAND. [*Calmly*] On my honour, Monsieur!   [TIMSON *growls*.

WELLWYN. Now, now, Timson!

TIMSON. That's all right. You're a gen'leman, an' I'm a gen'leman, but he ain't, an' she ain't.

WELLWYN. We shall not believe you.

BERTLEY. No, no; we shall not believe you.

TIMSON. [*Heavily*] Very well, you doubts my word. Will it make any difference, Guv'nor, if I speaks the truth?

BERTLEY. No, certainly not—that is—of course, it will.

TIMSON. Well, then, I see 'em plainer than I see [*pointing at* BERTLEY] the two of you.

WELLWYN. Be quiet, Timson!

BERTLEY. Not even her husband believes you.

MEGAN. [*Suddenly*] Don't I!

WELLWYN. Come, Megan, you can see the old fellow's in Paradise.

BERTLEY. Do you credit such a—such an object?

[*He points at* TIMSON, *who seems falling asleep.*

MEGAN. Naow!   [*Unseen by anybody,* ANN *has returned.*

BERTLEY. Well, then, my boy?

MEGAN. I seen 'em meself.

BERTLEY. Gracious! But just now you were willing——

MEGAN. [*Sardonically*] There wasn't nothing against me honour, then. Now you've took it away between you, comin' aht with it like this. I don't want no more of 'er, and I'll want a good deal more of 'im; as e'll soon find.

[*He jerks his chin at* FERRAND, *turns slowly on his heel, and goes out into the street.*

[*There follows a profound silence.*

ANN. What did I say, Daddy? Utter! All three.

[*Suddenly alive to her presence, they all turn.*

TIMSON. [*Waking up and looking round him*] Well, p'raps I'd better go.

[*Assisted by* WELLWYN *he lurches gingerly off the dais towards the door, which* WELLWYN *holds open for him.*

TIMSON. [*Mechanically*] Where to, sir?

[*Receiving no answer he passes out, touching his hat; and the door is closed.*

WELLWYN. Ann !   [ANN *goes back whence she came.*
   [BERTLEY, *steadily regarding* MRS. MEGAN, *who has put her arm
     up in front of her face, beckons to* FERRAND, *and the young man
     comes gravely forward.*

BERTLEY. Young people, this is very dreadful. [MRS. MEGAN
lowers her arm a little, and looks at him over it.] Very sad !

MRS. MEGAN. [*Dropping her arm*] Megan's no better than what I am.

BERTLEY. Come, come ! Here's your home broken up ! [MRS.
MEGAN *smiles. Shaking his head gravely.*] Surely—surely—you mustn't
smile. [MRS. MEGAN *becomes tragic.*] That's better. Now, what is
to be done ?

FERRAND. Believe me, Monsieur, I greatly regret.

BERTLEY. I'm glad to hear it.

FERRAND. If I had foreseen this disaster.

BERTLEY. Is that your only reason for regret ?

FERRAND. [*With a little bow*] Any reason that you wish, Monsieur.
I will do my possible.

MRS. MEGAN. I could get an unfurnished room if [*she slides her
eyes round at* WELLWYN] I 'ad the money to furnish it.

BERTLEY. But suppose I can induce your husband to forgive you,
and take you back ?

MRS. MEGAN. [*Shaking her head*] 'E'd 'it me.

BERTLEY. I said to forgive.

MRS. MEGAN. That wouldn't make no difference. [*With a flash
at* BERTLEY.] An' I ain't forgiven him !

BERTLEY. That is sinful.

MRS. MEGAN. *I'm* a Catholic.

BERTLEY. My good child, what difference does that make ?

FERRAND. Monsieur, if I might interpret for her.
                  [BERTLEY *silences him with a gesture.*

MRS. MEGAN. [*Sliding her eyes towards* WELLWYN] If I 'ad the money
to buy some fresh stock.

BERTLEY. Yes ; yes ; never mind the money. What I want to
find in you both, is repentance.

MRS. MEGAN. [*With a flash up at him*] I can't get me livin' off of
repentin'.

BERTLEY. Now, now ! Never say what you know to be wrong.

FERRAND. Monsieur, her soul is very simple.

BERTLEY. [*Severely*] I do not know, sir, that we shall get any great
assistance from your views. In fact, one thing is clear to me, she
must discontinue your acquaintanceship at once.

FERRAND. Certainly, Monsieur. We have no serious intentions.

BERTLEY. All the more shame to you, then !

FERRAND. Monsieur, I see perfectly your point of view. It is very
natural.   [*He bows and is silent.*

Mrs. Megan. I don't want *'im* hurt 'cos o' me. Megan'll get his mates to belt him—bein' foreign like he is.

Bertley. Yes, never mind that. It's *you* I'm thinking of.

Mrs. Megan. I'd sooner they'd hit *me*.

Wellwyn. [*Suddenly*] Well said, my child !

Mrs. Megan. 'Twasn't his fault.

Ferrand. [*Without irony—to* Wellwyn] I cannot accept that Monsieur. The blame—it is all mine.

Ann. [*Entering suddenly from the house*] Daddy, they're having an awful—— !

> [*The voices of* Professor Calway *and* Sir Thomas Hoxton *are distinctly heard.*

Calway. The question is a much wider one, Sir Thomas.

Hoxton. As wide as you like, you'll never——

> [Wellwyn *pushes* Ann *back into the house and closes the door behind her. The voices are still faintly heard arguing on the threshold.*

Bertley. Let me go in here a minute, Wellwyn. I must finish speaking to her. [*He motions* Mrs. Megan *towards the model's room.*] We can't leave the matter thus.

Ferrand. [*Suavely*] Do you desire my company, Monsieur ?

> [Bertley, *with a prohibitive gesture of his hand, shepherds the reluctant* Mrs. Megan *into the model's room.*

Wellwyn. [*Sorrowfully*] You shouldn't have done this, Ferrand. It wasn't the square thing.

Ferrand. [*With dignity*] Monsieur, I feel that I am in the wrong. It was stronger than me.

> [*As he speaks,* Sir Thomas Hoxton *and* Professor Calway *enter from the house. In the dim light, and the full cry of argument, they do not notice the figures at the fire.* Sir Thomas Hoxton *leads towards the street door.*

Hoxton. No, sir, I repeat, if the country once commits itself to your views of reform, it's as good as doomed.

Calway. I seem to have heard that before, Sir Thomas. And let me say at once that your hitty-missy cart-load of bricks *régime*——

Hoxton. Is a deuced sight better, sir, than your grandmotherly methods. What the old fellow wants is a shock ! With all this socialistic molly-coddling, you're losing sight of the individual.

Calway. [*Swiftly*] You, sir, with your " devil take the hindmost," have never even seen him.

> [Sir Thomas Hoxton, *throwing back a gesture of disgust, steps out into the night, and falls heavily.* Professor Calway, *hastening to his rescue, falls more heavily still.*

> [Timson, *momentarily roused from slumber on the doorstep, sits up.*

Hoxton. [*Struggling to his knees*] Damnation !

CALWAY. [*Sitting*] How simultaneous!

       [WELLWYN and FERRAND *approach hastily.*

FERRAND. [*Pointing to* TIMSON] Monsieur, it was true, it seems. They had lost sight of the individual.

    [*A* Policeman *has appeared under the street lamp. He picks up*
      HOXTON'S *hat.*

CONSTABLE. Anything wrong, sir?

HOXTON. [*Recovering his feet*] Wrong? Great Scott! Constable! Why do you let things lie about in the street like this? Look here, Wellwyn!   [*They all scrutinize* TIMSON.

WELLWYN. It's only the old fellow whose reform you were discussing.

HOXTON. How did he come here?

CONSTABLE. Drunk, sir. [*Ascertaining* TIMSON *to be in the street.*] Just off the premises, by good luck. Come along, father.

TIMSON. [*Assisted to his feet—drowsily*] Cert'nly, by no means; take my arm.

    [*They move from the doorway.* HOXTON *and* CALWAY *re-enter,*
      and go towards the fire.

ANN. [*Entering from the house*] What's happened?

CALWAY. Might we have a brush?

HOXTON. [*Testily*] Let it dry!

    [*He moves to the fire and stands before it.* PROFESSOR CALWAY
      following stands a little behind him. ANN *returning begins*
      to brush the Professor's sleeve.

WELLWYN. [*Turning from the door, where he has stood looking after the receding* TIMSON] Poor old Timson!

FERRAND. [*Softly*] Must be philosopher, Monsieur! They will but run him in a little.

    [*From the model's room* MRS. MEGAN *has come out, shepherded by*
      CANON BERTLEY.

BERTLEY. Let's see, your Christian name is——?

MRS. MEGAN. Guinevere.

BERTLEY. Oh! Ah! Ah! Ann, take Gui—— take our little friend into the study a minute; I am going to put her into service. We shall make a new woman of her, yet.

ANN. [*Handing* CANON BERTLEY *the brush, and turning to* MRS. MEGAN] Come on!

    [*She leads into the house, and* MRS. MEGAN *follows stolidly.*

BERTLEY. [*Brushing* CALWAY'S *back*] Have you fallen?

CALWAY. Yes.

BERTLEY. Dear me! How was that?

HOXTON. That old ruffian drunk on the doorstep. Hope they'll give him a sharp dose! These rag-tags!

    [*He looks round, and his angry eyes light by chance on* FERRAND.

FERRAND. [*With his eyes on* HOXTON—*softly*] Monsieur, something tells me it is time I took the road again.

WELLWYN. [*Fumbling out a sovereign*] Take this, then!

FERRAND. [*Refusing the coin*] Non, Monsieur. To abuse 'ospitality is not in my character.

BERTLEY. We must not despair of anyone.

HOXTON. Who talked of despairing? Treat him, as I say, and you'll see!

CALWAY. The interest of the State——

HOXTON. The interest of the individual citizen, sir——

BERTLEY. Come! A little of both, a little of both!

> [*They resume their brushing.*

FERRAND. You are now debarrassed of us three, Monsieur. I leave you instead—these sirs. [*He points.*] *Au revoir, Monsieur!* [*Motioning towards the fire.*] 'Appy New Year!

> [*He slips quietly out.* WELLWYN, *turning, contemplates the three reformers. They are all now brushing away, scratching each other's backs, and gravely hissing. As he approaches them, they speak with a certain unanimity.*

HOXTON. My theory——!

CALWAY. My theory——!

BERTLEY. My theory——!

> [*They stop surprised.* WELLWYN *makes a gesture of discomfort, as they speak again with still more unanimity.*

HOXTON. My——!

CALWAY. My——!

BERTLEY. My——!   [*They stop in greater surprise.*

> *The stage is blotted dark.*

The curtain falls.

362   THE PIGEON   ACT III

WELLWYN. Oh!

ACT III

*It is the first of April—a white spring day of gleams and driving showers.
The street door of* WELLWYN'S *studio stands wide open, and, past it,
in the street, the wind is whirling bits of straw and paper bags. Through
the door can be seen the butt end of a stationary furniture van with its
flap let down. To this van three humble men in shirt sleeves and
aprons are carrying out the contents of the studio. The hissing samovar,
the tea-pot, the sugar, and the nearly empty decanter of rum stand on
the low round table in the fast-being-gutted room.* WELLWYN, *in his
ulster and soft hat, is squatting on the little stool in front of the blazing
fire, staring into it, and smoking a hand-made cigarette. He has a
moulting air. Behind him the humble men pass, embracing busts and
other articles of vertu.*

CHIEF H'MAN. [*Stopping, and standing in the attitude of expectation*]
We've about pinched this little lot, sir.   Shall we take the—reservoir?
                                        [*He indicates the samovar.*
WELLWYN. Ah! [*Abstractedly feeling in his pockets, and finding
coins.*] Thanks—thanks—heavy work, I'm afraid.

H'MAN. [*Receiving the coins—a little surprised and a good deal pleased*]
Thank'ee, sir.   Much obliged, I'm sure.   We'll 'ave to come back
for this. [*He gives the dais a vigorous push with his foot.*] Not a fixture,
as I understand.   Perhaps you'd like us to leave these 'ere for a bit.
                                        [*He indicates the tea things.*

WELLWYN. Ah! do.

      [*The humble-men go out.   There is the sound of horses being started,
      and the butt end of the van disappears.* WELLWYN *stays on
      the stool, smoking and brooding over the fire.   The open doorway
      is darkened by a figure.* CANON BERTLEY *is standing there.*

BERTLEY. Wellwyn! [WELLWYN *turns and rises.*] It's ages since I
saw you.   No idea you were moving.   This is very dreadful.

WELLWYN. Yes, Ann found this—too exposed.   That tall house in
Flight Street—we're going there.   Seventh floor.

BERTLEY. Lift?   [WELLWYN *shakes his head.*

BERTLEY. Dear me!   No lift?   Fine view, no doubt. [WELLWYN
nods.] You'll be greatly missed.

WELLWYN. So Ann thinks.   Vicar, what's become of that little
flower-seller I was painting at Christmas?   You took her into service.

BERTLEY. Not we—exactly!   Some dear friends of ours.   Painful
subject!

WELLWYN. Oh!

BERTLEY. Yes.   She got the footman into trouble.

WELLWYN. Did she, now?

BERTLEY. Disappointing.   I consulted with Calway, and he advised me to try a certain institution.   We got her safely in—excellent place; but, d'you know, she broke out three weeks ago.   And since—I've heard—[*he holds his hands up*] hopeless, I'm afraid—quite!

WELLWYN. I *thought* I saw her last night.   You can't tell me her address, I suppose?

BERTLEY. [*Shaking his head*] The husband, too, has quite passed out of my ken.   He betted on horses, you remember.   I'm sometimes tempted to believe there's nothing for some of these poor folk but to pray for death.

> [ANN *has entered from the house.   Her hair hangs from under a knitted cap.   She wears a white wool jersey, and a loose silk scarf.*

BERTLEY. Ah! Ann.   I was telling your father of that poor little Mrs. Megan.

ANN. Is she dead?

BERTLEY. Worse I fear.   By the way—what became of her accomplice?

ANN. We haven't seen him since.   [*She looks searchingly at* WELL- WYN.] At least—have *you*—Daddy?

WELLWYN. [*Rather hurt*] No, my dear; I have not.

BERTLEY. And the—old gentleman who drank the rum?

ANN. He got fourteen days.   It was the fifth time.

BERTLEY. Dear me!

ANN. When he came out he got more drunk than ever.   Rather a score for Professor Calway, wasn't it?

BERTLEY. I remember.   He and Sir Thomas took a kindly interest in the old fellow.

ANN. Yes, they fell over him.   The Professor got him into an Institution.

BERTLEY. Indeed!

ANN. He was perfectly sober all the time he was there.

WELLWYN. My dear, they only allow them milk.

ANN. Well, anyway, he was reformed.

WELLWYN. Ye—yes!

ANN. [*Terribly*] Daddy!   You've been seeing him!

WELLWYN. [*With dignity*] My dear, I have not.

ANN. How do you know, then?

WELLWYN. Came across Sir Thomas on the Embankment yester- day; told me old Timson had been had up again for sitting down in front of a brewer's dray.

ANN. Why?

WELLWYN. Well, you see, as soon as he came out of the what d'you call 'em, he got drunk for a week, and it left him in low spirits.

BERTLEY. Do you mean he deliberately sat down, with the intention —of—er ?

WELLWYN. Said he was tired of life, but they didn't believe him.

ANN. Rather a score for Sir Thomas ! I suppose he'd told the Professor ? What did *he* say ?

WELLWYN. Well, the Professor said [*with a quick glance at* BERTLEY] he felt there was nothing for some of these poor devils but a lethal chamber.

BERTLEY. [*Shocked*] Did he really !

[*He has not yet caught* WELLWYN'*s glance.*

WELLWYN. And Sir Thomas agreed. Historic occasion. And you, Vicar—H'm !   [BERTLEY *winces.*

ANN. [*To herself*] Well, there isn't.

BERTLEY. And yet ! Some good in the old fellow, no doubt, if one could put one's finger on it. [*Preparing to go.*] You'll let us know, then, when you're settled. What was the address ? [WELLWYN *takes out and hands him a card.*] Ah ! yes. Good-bye, Ann. Good-bye, WELLWYN. [*The wind blows his hat along the street.*] What a wind !   [*He goes, pursuing.*

ANN. [*Who has eyed the card askance*] Daddy, have you told those other two where we're going ?

WELLWYN. Which other two, my dear ?

ANN. The Professor and Sir Thomas.

WELLWYN. Well, Ann, naturally I——

ANN. [*Jumping on to the dais with disgust*] Oh, dear ! When I'm trying to get you away from all this atmosphere. I don't so much mind the Vicar knowing, because he's got a weak heart——

[*She jumps off again.*

WELLWYN. [*To himself*] Seventh floor ! I felt there was something.

ANN. [*Preparing to go*] I'm going round now. But you must stay here till the van comes back. And don't forget you tipped the men after the first load.

WELLWYN. Oh ! yes, yes. [*Uneasily.*] Good sorts they look, those fellows !

ANN. [*Scrutinizing him*] What have you done ?

WELLWYN. Nothing, my dear, really—— !

ANN. What ?

WELLWYN. I—I rather think I may have tipped them twice.

ANN. [*Dryly*] Daddy ! If it *is* the first of April, it's not necessary to make a fool of *oneself*. That's the last time you ever do these ridiculous things. [WELLWYN *eyes her askance.*] I'm going to see that you spend your money on yourself. You needn't look at me like that ! I *mean* to. As soon as I've got you away from here, and all—these——

WELLWYN. Don't rub it in, Ann!

ANN. [*Giving him a sudden hug—then going to the door—with a sort of triumph*] Deeds, not words, Daddy!

> [*She goes out, and the wind catching her scarf blows it out beneath her firm young chin.* WELLWYN, *returning to the fire, stands brooding, and gazing at his extinct cigarette.*

WELLWYN. [*To himself*] Bad lot—low type! No method! No theory!

> [*In the open doorway appear* FERRAND *and* MRS. MEGAN. *They stand, unseen, looking at him.* FERRAND *is more ragged, if possible, than on Christmas Eve. His chin and cheeks are clothed in a reddish-golden beard.* MRS. MEGAN'S *dress is not so woe-begone, but her face is white, her eyes dark-circled. They whisper. She slips back into the shadow of the doorway.* WELLWYN *turns at the sound, and stares at* FERRAND *in amazement.*

FERRAND. [*Advancing*] Enchanted to see you, Monsieur. [*He looks round the empty room.*] You are leaving?

WELLWYN. [*Nodding—then taking the young man's hand*] How goes it?

FERRAND. [*Displaying himself, simply*] As you see, Monsieur. I have done of my best. It still flies from me.

WELLWYN. [*Sadly—as if against his will*] Ferrand, it will always fly.

> [*The young foreigner shivers suddenly from head to foot; then controls himself with a great effort.*

FERRAND. Don't say that, Monsieur. It is too much the echo of my heart.

WELLWYN. Forgive me! I didn't mean to pain you.

FERRAND. [*Drawing nearer the fire*] That old cabby, Monsieur, you remember—they tell me, he nearly succeeded to gain happiness the other day.   [WELLWYN *nods.*

FERRAND. And those sirs, so interested in him, with their theories? He has worn them out? [WELLWYN *nods.*] That goes without saying. And now they wish for him the lethal chamber.

WELLWYN. [*Startled*] How did you know that?   [*There is silence.*

FERRAND. [*Staring into the fire*] Monsieur, while I was on the road this time I fell ill of a fever. It seemed to me in my illness that I saw the truth—how I was wasting in this world—I would never be good for anyone—nor anyone for me—all would go by, and I never of it—fame, and fortune, and peace, even the necessities of life, ever mocking me.

> [*He draws closer to the fire, spreading his fingers to the flame. And while he is speaking, through the doorway* MRS. MEGAN *creeps in to listen.*

FERRAND. [*Speaking on into the fire*] And I saw, Monsieur, so plain,

that I should be vagabond all my days, and my days short, I dying in
the end the death of a dog. I saw it all in my fever—clear as that
flame—there was nothing for us others, but the herb of death.
[WELLWYN *takes his arm and presses it.*] And so, Monsieur, I *wished* to
die. I told no one of my fever. I lay out on the ground—it was
veree cold. But they would not let me die on the roads of their
parishes—they took me to an Institution. Monsieur, I looked in
their eyes while I lay there, and I saw more clear than the blue heaven
that they thought it best that I should die, although they would not
let me. Then, Monsieur, naturally my spirit rose, and I said : " So
much the worse for you. I will live a little more." One is made
like that ! Life is sweet, Monsieur.

WELLWYN. Yes, Ferrand ; Life is sweet.

FERRAND. That little girl you had here, Monsieur—[WELLWYN
nods.] In her, too, there is something of wild-savage. She must have
joy of life. I have seen her since I came back. She has embraced
the life of joy. It is not quite the same thing. [*He lowers his voice.*]
She is lost, Monsieur, as a stone that sinks in water. I can see, if she
cannot. [*As* WELLWYN *makes a movement of distress.*] Oh ! I am not
to blame for that, Monsieur. It had well begun before I knew her.

WELLWYN. Yes, yes—I was afraid of it, at the time.

[MRS. MEGAN *turns silently, and slips away.*

FERRAND. I do my best for her, Monsieur, but look at me ! Besides,
I am not good for her—it is not good for simple souls to be with those
who see things clear. For the great part of mankind, to see anything
—is fatal.

WELLWYN. Even for you, it seems.

FERRAND. No, Monsieur. To be so near to death has done me
good ; I shall not lack courage any more till the wind blows on my
grave. Since I saw you, Monsieur, I have been in three Institutions.
They are palaces. One may eat upon the floor—though it is true—
for Kings—they eat too much of skilly there. One little thing they
lack—those palaces. It is understanding of the 'uman heart. In
them tame birds pluck wild birds naked.

WELLWYN. They mean well.

FERRAND. Ah ! Monsieur, I am loafer, waster—what you like—
for all that [*bitterly*] poverty is my only crime. If I were rich, should
I not be simply veree original, 'ighly respected, with soul above
commerce, travelling to see the world ? And that young girl, would
she not be " that charming ladee," " veree *chic*, you know ! " And
the old Tims——good old-fashioned gentleman—drinking his liquor
well. *Eh ! bien*—what are we now ? Dark beasts, despised by all.
That is life, Monsieur.   [*He stares into the fire.*

WELLWYN. We're our own enemies, Ferrand. I can afford it—
you can't. Quite true !

FERRAND. [*Earnestly*] Monsieur, do you know this? You are the sole being that can do us good—we hopeless ones.

WELLWYN. [*Shaking his head*] Not a bit of it; I'm hopeless too.

FERRAND. [*Eagerly*] Monsieur, it is just that. You *understand*. When we are with you we feel something—here—[*He touches his heart.*] If I had one prayer to make, it would be, Good God, give me to understand! Those sirs, with their theories, they can clean our skins and chain our 'abits—that soothes for them the æsthetic sense; it gives them, too, their good little importance. But our spirits they cannot touch, for they nevare understand. Without that, Monsieur, all is dry as a parched skin of orange.

WELLWYN. Don't be so bitter. Think of all the work they do!

FERRAND. Monsieur, of their industry I say nothing. They do a good work while they attend with their theories to the sick and the tame old, and the good unfortunate deserving. Above all to the little children. But, Monsieur, when all is done, there are always us hopeless ones. What can they do with me, Monsieur, with that girl, or with that old man? Ah! Monsieur, we, too, 'ave our qualities, we others—it wants your courage to undertake a career like mine, or like that young girl's. We wild ones—we know a thousand times more of life than ever will those sirs. They waste their time trying to make rooks white. Be kind to us if you will, or let us alone like Mees Ann, but do not try to change our skins. Leave us to live, or leave us to die when we like in the free air. If you do not wish of us, you have but to shut your pockets and your doors— we shall die the faster.

WELLWYN. [*With agitation*] But that, you know—we can't do— now can we?

FERRAND. If you cannot, how is it our fault? The harm we do to others—is it so much? If I am criminal, dangerous—shut me up! I would not pity myself—nevare. But we in whom something moves —like that flame, Monsieur, that *cannot* keep still—we others— we are not many—that must have motion in our lives, do not let them make us prisoners, with their theories, because we are not like them— it is life itself they would enclose! [*He draws up his tattered figure, then bending over the fire again.*] I ask your pardon; I am talking. If I could smoke, Monsieur!

[WELLWYN *hands him a tobacco pouch; and he rolls a cigarette with his yellow-stained fingers.*]

FERRAND. The good God made me so that I would rather walk a whole month of nights, hungry, with the stars, than sit one single day making round business on an office stool! It is not to my advantage. I cannot help it that I am a vagabond. What would you have? It is stronger than me. [*He looks suddenly at* WELLWYN.] Monsieur, I say to you things I have never said.

WELLWYN. [*Quietly*] Go on, go on.   [*There is silence.*

FERRAND. [*Suddenly*] Monsieur! Are you really English? The English are so civilized.

WELLWYN. And am I not?

FERRAND. You treat me like a brother.

[WELLWYN *has turned towards the street door at a sound of feet, and the clamour of voices.*

TIMSON. [*From the street*] Take her in 'ere. I knows 'im.

[*Through the open doorway come a* POLICE CONSTABLE *and a* LOAFER, *bearing between them the limp, white-faced form of* MRS. MEGAN, *hatless and with drowned hair, enveloped in the policeman's waterproof. Some curious persons bring up the rear, jostling in the doorway, among whom is* TIMSON, *carrying in his hands the policeman's dripping waterproof leg pieces.*

FERRAND. [*Starting forward*] Monsieur, it is that little girl!

WELLWYN. What's happened? Constable! What's happened?

[*The* CONSTABLE *and* LOAFER *have laid the body down on the dais; with* WELLWYN *and* FERRAND *they stand bending over her.*

CONSTABLE. 'Tempted sooicide, sir; but she hadn't been in the water 'arf a minute when I got hold of her. [*He bends lower.*] Can't understand her collapsin' like this.

WELLWYN. [*Feeling her heart*] I don't feel anything.

FERRAND. [*In a voice sharpened by emotion*] Let me try, Monsieur.

CONSTABLE. [*Touching his arm*] You keep off, my lad.

WELLWYN. No, constable—let him. He's her friend.

CONSTABLE. [*Releasing* FERRAND—*to the* LOAFER] Here, you! Cut off for a doctor—sharp now! [*He pushes back the curious persons.*] Now then, stand away there, please—we can't have you round the body. Keep back—Clear out, now!

[*He slowly moves them back, and at last shepherds them through the door and shuts it on them,* TIMSON *being last.*

FERRAND. The rum!

[WELLWYN *fetches the decanter. With the little there is left* FERRAND *chafes the girl's hands and forehead, and pours some between her lips. But there is no response from the inert body.*

FERRAND. Her soul is still away, Monsieur!

[WELLWYN, *seizing the decanter, pours into it tea and boiling water.*

CONSTABLE. It's never drownin', sir—her head was hardly under; I was on to her like knife.

FERRAND. [*Rubbing her feet*] She has not yet her philosophy, Monsieur; at the beginning they often try. If she is dead! [*In a voice of awed rapture.*] What fortune!

CONSTABLE. [*With puzzled sadness*] True enough, sir—that! We'd just begun to know 'er. If she 'as been taken—her best friends couldn't wish 'er better.

WELLWYN. [*Applying the decanter to her lips*] Poor little thing!
I'll try this hot tea.

FERRAND. [*Whispering*] *La mort—le grand ami !*

WELLWYN. Look! Look at her! She's coming round!

> [*A faint tremor passes over* MRS. MEGAN'S *body. He again
> applies the hot drink to her mouth. She stirs and gulps.*

CONSTABLE. [*With intense relief*] That's brave! Good lass! She'll
pick up now, sir.

> [*Then, seeing that* TIMSON *and the curious persons have again opened
> the door, he drives them out, and stands with his back against
> it.* MRS. MEGAN *comes to herself.*

WELLWYN. [*Sitting on the dais and supporting her—as if to a child*]
There you are, my dear. There, there—better now! That's right.
Drink a little more of this tea. [MRS. MEGAN *drinks from the decanter.*

FERRAND. [*Rising*] Bring her to the fire, Monsieur.

> [*They take her to the fire and seat her on the little stool. From
> the moment of her restored animation* FERRAND *has resumed his
> air of cynical detachment, and now stands apart with arms
> folded, watching.*

WELLWYN. Feeling better, my child?

MRS. MEGAN. Yes.

WELLWYN. That's good. That's good. Now, how was it? Um?

MRS. MEGAN. I dunno. [*She shivers.*] I was standin' here just now
when you was talkin', and when I heard 'im, it cam' over me to do it
—like.

WELLWYN. Ah, yes, *I* know.

MRS. MEGAN. I didn't seem no good to meself nor anyone. But
when I got in the water, I didn't want to any more. It was cold in
there.

WELLWYN. Have you been having such a bad time of it?

MRS. MEGAN. Yes. And listenin' to him upset me. [*She signs
with her head at* FERRAND.] I feel better now I've been in the water.
> [*She smiles, and shivers.*

WELLWYN. There, there! Shivery? Like to walk up and down
a little? [*They begin walking together up and down.*

WELLWYN. Beastly when your head goes under?

MRS. MEGAN. Yes. It frightened me. I thought I wouldn't come
up again.

WELLWYN. I know—sort of world without end, wasn't it? What
did you think of, um?

MRS. MEGAN. I wished I 'adn't jumped—an' I thought of my baby
—that died—and—[*in a rather surprised voice*] and I thought of d-dancin'.
> [*Her mouth quivers, her face puckers, she gives a choke and a little sob.*

WELLWYN. [*Stopping and stroking her*] There, there—there!
> [*For a moment her face is buried in his sleeve, then she recovers herself.*

MRS. MEGAN. Then 'e got hold o' me, an' pulled me out.

WELLWYN. Ah! what a comfort—um?

MRS. MEGAN. Yes. The water got into me mouth. [*They walk again.*] I wouldn't have gone to do it but for *him.* [*She looks towards* FERRAND.] His talk made me feel all funny, as if people wanted me to.

WELLWYN. My dear child! Don't think such things! As if anyone would——!

MRS. MEGAN. [*Stolidly*] I thought they did. They used to look at me so sometimes, where I was before I ran away—I couldn't stop there, you know.

WELLWYN. Too cooped-up?

MRS. MEGAN. Yes. No life at all, it wasn't—not after sellin' flowers. I'd rather be doin' what I am.

WELLWYN. Ah! Well—it's all over, now! How d'you feel—eh? Better?

MRS. MEGAN. Yes. I feels all right now.

[*She sits up again on the little stool before the fire.*

WELLWYN. No shivers, and no aches; quite comfy?

MRS. MEGAN. Yes.

WELLWYN. That's a blessing. All well now, Constable—thank you!

CONSTABLE. [*Who has remained discreetly apart at the door—cordially*] First rate, sir! That's capital! [*He approaches and scrutinizes* MRS. MEGAN.] Right as rain, eh, my girl?

MRS. MEGAN. [*Shrinking a little*] Yes.

CONSTABLE. That's fine. Then I think perhaps, for 'er sake, sir, the sooner we move on and get her a change o' clothin', the better.

WELLWYN. Oh! don't bother about that—I'll send round for my daughter—we'll manage for her here.

CONSTABLE. Very kind of you, I'm sure, sir. But [*with embarrassment*] she seems all right. She'll get every attention at the station.

WELLWYN. But I assure you, we don't mind at all; we'll take the greatest care of her.

CONSTABLE. [*Still more embarrassed*] Well, sir, of course, I'm thinkin' of—— I'm afraid I can't depart from the usual course.

WELLWYN. [*Sharply*] What! But—oh! No! No! That'll be all right, Constable! That'll be all right! I assure you.

CONSTABLE. [*With more decision*] I'll have to charge her, sir.

WELLWYN. Good God! You don't mean to say the poor little thing has got to be——

CONSTABLE. [*Consulting with him*] Well, sir, we can't get over the facts, can we? There it is! You know what sooicide amounts to, —it's an awkward job.

WELLWYN. [*Calming himself with an effort*] But look here, Constable, as a reasonable man—— This poor wretched little girl—*you* know what that life means better than anyone! Why! It's to her credit to try and jump out of it! [*The* CONSTABLE *shakes his head.*

WELLWYN. You said yourself her best friends couldn't wish her better! [*Dropping his voice still more.*] Everybody feels it! The Vicar was here a few minutes ago saying the very same thing—the Vicar, Constable! [*The* CONSTABLE *shakes his head.*] Ah! now look here, I know something of her. Nothing can be done with her. We all admit it. Don't you see? Well, then, hang it—you needn't go and make fools of us all by——

FERRAND. Monsieur, it is the first of April.

CONSTABLE. [*With a sharp glance at him*] Can't neglect me duty, sir; that's impossible.

WELLWYN. Look here! She—slipped. She's been telling me. Come, Constable, there's a good fellow. May be the making of her, this.

CONSTABLE. I quite appreciate your good 'eart, sir, an' you make it very 'ard for me—but, come now! I put it to you as a gentleman, would you go back on yer duty if you was me?

[WELLWYN *raises his hat, and plunges his fingers through and through his hair.*

WELLWYN. Well! God in heaven! Of all the d——d topsy-turvy——! Not a soul in the world wants her alive—and now she's to be prosecuted for trying to be where everyone wishes her.

CONSTABLE. Come, sir, come! Be a man!

[*Throughout all this* MRS. MEGAN *has sat stolidly before the fire, but as* FERRAND *suddenly steps forward she looks up at him.*

FERRAND. Do not grieve, Monsieur! This will give her courage. There is nothing that gives more courage than to see the irony of things. [*He touches* MRS. MEGAN'S *shoulder.*] Go, my child; it will do you good. [MRS. MEGAN *rises, and looks at him dazedly.*

CONSTABLE. [*Coming forward, and taking her by the hand*] That's my good lass. Come along! We won't hurt you.

MRS. MEGAN. I don't want to go. They'll stare at me.

CONSTABLE. [*Comforting*] Not they! I'll see to that.

WELLWYN. [*Very upset*] Take her in a cab, Constable, if you must —for God's sake! [*He pulls out a shilling.*] Here!

CONSTABLE. [*Taking the shilling*] I will, sir, certainly. Don't think I want to——

WELLWYN. No, no, I know. You're a good sort.

CONSTABLE. [*Comfortable*] Don't you take on, sir! It's her first try; they won't be hard on 'er. Like as not only bind 'er over in her own recogs. not to do it again. Come, my dear.

MRS. MEGAN. [*Trying to free herself from the policeman's cloak*] I want to take this off. It looks so funny.

[*As she speaks the door is opened by* ANN; *behind whom is dimly seen the form of old* TIMSON, *still heading the curious persons.*

ANN. [*Looking from one to the other in amaze*] What is it? What's happened? Daddy?

FERRAND. [*Out of the silence*] It is nothing, Ma'moiselle! She has failed to drown herself. They run her in a little.

WELLWYN. Lend her your jacket, my dear; she'll catch her death.

[ANN, *feeling* MRS. MEGAN's *arm, strips off her jacket, and helps her into it without a word.*

CONSTABLE. [*Donning his cloak*] Thank you, Miss—very good of you, I'm sure.

MRS. MEGAN. [*Mazed*] It's warm!

[*She gives them all a lost half-smiling look, and passes with the* CONSTABLE *through the doorway.*

FERRAND. That makes the third of us, Monsieur. We are not in luck. To wish us dead, it seems, is easier than to let us die.

[*He looks at* ANN, *who is standing with her eyes fixed on her father.* WELLWYN *has taken from his pocket a visiting card.*

WELLWYN. [*To* FERRAND] Here quick; take this, run after her! When they've done with her tell her to come to us.

FERRAND. [*Taking the card, and reading the address*] " No. 7, Haven House, Flight Street!" Rely on me, Monsieur—I will bring her myself to call on you. *Au revoir, mon bon Monsieur!*

[*He bends over* WELLWYN's *hand; then, with a bow to* ANN, *goes out; his tattered figure can be seen through the window, passing in the wind.* WELLWYN *turns back to the fire. The figure of* TIMSON *advances into the doorway, no longer holding in either hand a waterproof leg-piece.*

TIMSON. [*In a croaky voice*] Sir!

WELLWYN. What—you, Timson?

TIMSON. On me larst legs, sir. 'Ere! You can see 'em for yourself! Shawn't trouble yer long.

WELLWYN. [*After a long and desperate stare*] Not now—Timson—not now! Take this! [*He takes out another card, and hands it to* TIMSON] Some other time.

TIMSON. [*Taking the card*] Yer new address! You *are* a gen'leman.

[*He lurches slowly away.*

[ANN *shuts the street door and sets her back against it. The rumble of the approaching van is heard outside. It ceases.*

ANN. [*In a fateful voice*] Daddy! [*They stare at each other.*] Do you know what you've done? Given your card to those six rotters.

WELLWYN. [*With a blank stare*] Six?

ANN. [*Staring round the naked room*] What was the good of this?

WELLWYN [*Following her eyes—very gravely*] Ann. It is stronger than me.

[*Without a word* ANN *opens the door, and walks straight out. With a heavy sigh,* WELLWYN *sinks down on the little stool before the fire. The three humble-men come in.*

CHIEF HUMBLE-MAN. [*In an attitude of expectation*] This is the larst of it, sir.

WELLWYN. Oh! Ah! yes!

> [*He gives them money ; then something seems to strike him, and he exhibits certain signs of vexation. Suddenly he recovers, looks from one to the other, and then at the tea things. A faint smile comes on his face.*

WELLWYN. You can finish the decanter.   [*He goes out in haste.*

CHIEF HUMBLE-MAN. [*Clinking the coins*] Third time of arskin'! April fool! Not 'arf! Good old pigeon!

SECOND HUMBLE-MAN. 'Uman being, *I* call 'im.

CHIEF HUMBLE-MAN. [*Taking the three glasses from the last packing-case, and pouring very equally into them*] That's right. Tell you wot, I'd never 'a touched this unless 'e'd told me to, I wouldn't—not with 'im.

SECOND HUMBLE-MAN. Ditto to that! This is a bit of orl right! [*Raising his glass.*] Good luck!

THIRD HUMBLE-MAN. Same 'ere!

> [*Simultaneously they place their lips smartly against the liquor, and at once let fall their faces and their glasses.*]

CHIEF HUMBLE-MAN. [*With great solemnity*] Crikey! Bill! *Tea!* . . . 'E's *got* us!   [*The stage is blotted dark.*

The curtain falls.

THE MOB

CAST OF THE ORIGINAL PRODUCTION AT THE GAIETY THEATRE, MANCHESTER, MARCH 30, 1914

STEPHEN MORE	Milton Rosmer
KATHERINE	Irene Rooke
OLIVE	Phyllis Bourke
THE DEAN OF STOUR	Leonard Mudie
GENERAL SIR JOHN JULIAN	Herbert Lomas
CAPTAIN HUBERT JULIAN	William Home
HELEN	Hilda Bruce Potter
EDWARD MENDIP	D. Lewin Mannering
ALAN STEEL	Eric Barber
JAMES HOME	Archibald McClean
CHARLES SHELDER	Percy Foster
MARK WACE	Napier Barry
WILLIAM BANNING	Charles Bibby
NURSE WREFORD	Mrs. A. B. Tapping
WREFORD	Cecil Calvert
HIS SWEETHEART	Hilda Davies
THE FOOTMAN HENRY	Basil Holmes
A DOORKEEPER	Alfred Russell
A STUDENT	Ellis Dee
A GIRL	Muriel Pope

ACT I

*It is half-past nine of a July evening. In a dining-room lighted by sconces,
and apparelled in wall-paper, carpet, and curtains of deep vivid blue, the
large French windows between two columns are open on to a wide terrace,
beyond which are seen trees in darkness, and distant shapes of lighted
houses. On one side is a bay window, over which curtains are partly
drawn. Opposite to this window is a door leading into the hall. At an
oval rosewood table, set with silver, flowers, fruit, and wine, six people
are seated after dinner. Back to the bay window is* STEPHEN MORE,
*the host, a man of forty, with a fine-cut face, a rather charming smile, and
the eyes of an idealist ; to his right,* SIR JOHN JULIAN, *an old soldier,
with thin brown features, and grey moustaches ; to* SIR JOHN'S *right, his
brother, the* DEAN OF STOUR, *a tall, dark, ascetic-looking Churchman ;
to his right* KATHERINE *is leaning forward, her elbows on the table, and
her chin on her hands, staring across at her husband ; to her right sits*
EDWARD MENDIP, *a pale man of forty-five, very bald, with a fine forehead, and on his clear-cut lips a smile that shows his teeth ; between him
and* MORE *is* HELEN JULIAN, *a pretty dark-haired young woman,
absorbed in thoughts of her own. The voices are tuned to the pitch of
heated discussion, as the curtain rises.*

THE DEAN. I disagree with you, Stephen ; absolutely, entirely
disagree.

MORE. I can't help it.

MENDIP. Remember a certain war, Stephen ! Were your chivalrous
notions any good then ? And, what was winked at in an obscure
young Member is anathema for an Under Secretary of State. You
can't afford——

MORE. To follow my conscience ? That's new, Mendip.

MENDIP. Idealism can be out of place, my friend.

THE DEAN. The Government is dealing here with a wild lawless
race, on whom I must say I think sentiment is rather wasted.

MORE. God made them, Dean.

MENDIP. I have my doubts.

THE DEAN. They have proved themselves faithless. We have the
right to chastise.

MORE. If I hit a little man in the eye, and he hits me back, have I
the right to *chastise* him ?

SIR JOHN. We didn't begin this business.

375

More. What! With our missionaries and our trading?

The Dean. It is news indeed that the work of civilization may be justifiably met by murder. Have you forgotten Glaive and Morlinson?

Sir John. Yes. And that poor fellow Groome and his wife?

More. They went into a wild country, against the feeling of the tribes, on their own business. What has the nation to do with the mishaps of gamblers?

Sir John. We can't stand by and see our own flesh and blood ill-treated!

The Dean. Does our rule bring blessing—or does it not, Stephen?

More. Sometimes; but with all my soul I deny the fantastic superstition that our rule can benefit a people like this, a nation of one race, as different from ourselves as dark from light—in colour, religion, every mortal thing. We can only pervert their natural instincts.

The Dean. That to me is an unintelligible point of view.

Mendip. Go into that philosophy of yours a little deeper, Stephen —it spells stagnation. There are no fixed stars on this earth. Nations *can't* let each other alone.

More. Big ones could let little ones alone.

Mendip. If they could there'd be no big ones. My dear fellow, we know little nations are your hobby, but surely office should have toned you down.

Sir John. I've served my country fifty years, and I say she is not in the wrong.

More. I hope to serve her fifty, Sir John, and I say she is.

Mendip. There are moments when such things can't be said, More.

More. They'll be said by me to-night, Mendip.

Mendip. In the House?   [More *nods*.

Katherine. Stephen!

Mendip. Mrs. More, you mustn't let him. It's madness.

More. [*Rising*] You can tell people that to-morrow, Mendip. Give it a leader in *The Parthenon*.

Mendip. Political lunacy! No man in your position has a right to fly out like this at the eleventh hour.

More. I've made no secret of my feelings all along. I'm against this war, and against the annexation we all know it will lead to.

Mendip. My dear fellow! Don't be so Quixotic! We shall have war within the next twenty-four hours, and nothing you can do will stop it.

Helen. Oh! No!

Mendip. I'm afraid so, Mrs. Hubert.

Sir John. Not a doubt of it, Helen.

Mendip. [*To* More] And you mean to charge the windmill?

                                                          [More *nods*.

Mendip. *C'est magnifique!*

MORE. I'm not out for advertisement.

MENDIP. You will get it !

MORE. Must speak the truth sometimes, even at that risk.

SIR JOHN. It is not the truth.

MENDIP. The greater the truth the greater the libel, and the greater the resentment of the person libelled.

THE DEAN. [*Trying to bring matters to a blander level*] My dear Stephen, even if you were right—which I deny—about the initial merits, there surely comes a point where the individual conscience must resign itself to the country's feeling. This has become a question of national honour.

SIR JOHN. Well said, James !

MORE. Nations are bad judges of their honour, Dean.

THE DEAN. I shall not follow you there.

MORE. No. It's an awkward word.

KATHERINE. [*Stopping* THE DEAN] Uncle James ! Please !

                                   [MORE *looks at her intently.*

SIR JOHN. So you're going to put yourself at the head of the cranks, ruin your career, and make me ashamed that you're my son-in-law ?

MORE. Is a man only to hold beliefs when they're popular ? *You've* stood up to be shot at often enough, Sir John.

SIR JOHN. Never by my country ! Your speech will be in all the foreign press—trust 'em for seizing on anything against us. A show-up before other countries—— !

MORE. You admit the show-up ?

SIR JOHN. I do not, sir.

THE DEAN. The position has become impossible. The state of things out there must be put an end to once for all. Come, Katherine, back us up !

MORE. My country, right or wrong ! Guilty—still my country !

MENDIP. That begs the question.

                     [KATHERINE *rises.* THE DEAN, *too, stands up.*

THE DEAN. [*In a low voice*] Quem Deus vult perdere—— !

SIR JOHN. Unpatriotic !

MORE. I'll have no truck with tyranny.

KATHERINE. Father doesn't admit tyranny. Nor do any of us, Stephen.   [HUBERT JULIAN, *a tall soldier-like man, has come in.*

HELEN. Hubert !

       [*She gets up and goes to him, and they talk together near the door.*

SIR JOHN. What in God's name is your idea ? We've forborne long enough, in all conscience.

MORE. Sir John, we great Powers have got to change our ways in dealing with weaker nations. The very dogs can give us lessons— watch a big dog with a little one.

13

MENDIP. No, no, these things are not so simple as all that.

MORE. There's no reason in the world, Mendip, why the rules of chivalry should not apply to nations at least as well as to—dogs.

MENDIP. My dear friend, are you to become that hapless kind of outcast, a champion of lost causes ?

MORE. This cause is not lost.

MENDIP. Right or wrong, as lost as ever was cause in all this world. There was never a time when the word " patriotism " stirred mob sentiment as it does now.   'Ware " Mob," Stephen—'ware, " Mob ! "

MORE. Because general sentiment's against me, I—a public man— am to deny my faith ?   The point is not whether I'm right or wrong, Mendip, but whether I'm to sneak out of my conviction because it's unpopular.

THE DEAN. I'm afraid I must go. [*To* KATHERINE.] Good night, my dear !   Ah !   Hubert !   [*He greets* HUBERT.] Mr. Mendip, I go your way.   Can I drop you ?

MENDIP. Thank you.   Good night, Mrs. More.   Stop him !   It's perdition.

> [*He and* THE DEAN *go out.*   KATHERINE *puts her arm in* HELEN'S, *and takes her out of the room.*   HUBERT *remains standing by the door.*

SIR JOHN. I knew your views were extreme in many ways, Stephen, but I never thought the husband of my daughter would be a Peace-at-any-price man !

MORE. I am not !   But I prefer to fight some one my own size !

SIR JOHN. Well !   I can only hope to God you'll come to your senses before you commit the folly of this speech.   I must get back to the War Office.   Good night, Hubert.

HUBERT. Good night, Father.

> [SIR JOHN *goes out.*   HUBERT *stands motionless, dejected.*

HUBERT. We've got our orders.

MORE. What ?   When d'you sail ?

HUBERT. At once.

MORE. Poor Helen !

HUBERT. Not married a year ; pretty bad luck ! [MORE *touches his arm in sympathy.*] Well !   We've got to put feelings in our pockets. Look here, Stephen—don't make that speech !   Think of Katherine —with the Dad at the War Office, and me going out, and Ralph and old George out there already !   You can't trust your tongue when you're hot about a thing.

MORE. I must speak, Hubert.

HUBERT. No, no !   Bottle yourself up for to-night.   The next few hours'll see it begin. [MORE *turns from him.*] If you don't care whether you mess up your own career—don't tear Katherine in two !

MORE. You're not shirking *your* duty because of *your* wife.

HUBERT. Well! You're riding for a fall, and a godless mucker it'll be. This'll be no picnic. We shall get some nasty knocks out there. Wait and see the feeling here when we've had a force or two cut up in those mountains. It's awful country. Those fellows have got modern arms, and are jolly good fighters. Do drop it, Stephen!

MORE. Must risk something, sometimes, Hubert—even in my profession! [*As he speaks,* KATHERINE *comes in.*

HUBERT. But it's hopeless, my dear chap—absolutely.

[MORE *turns to the window,* HUBERT *to his sister—then with a gesture towards* MORE, *as though to leave the matter to her, he goes out.*

KATHERINE. Stephen! Are you really going to speak? [*He nods.*] I ask you not.

MORE. You know my feeling.

KATHERINE. But it's our own country. We can't stand apart from it. You won't stop anything—only make people hate you. I can't bear that.

MORE. I tell you, Kit, someone must raise a voice. Two or three reverses—certain to come—and the whole country will go wild. And one more little nation will cease to live.

KATHERINE. If you believe in your country, you must believe that the more land and power she has, the better for the world.

MORE. Is that your faith?

KATHERINE. Yes.

MORE. I respect it; I even understand it; but—I can't hold it.

KATHERINE. But, Stephen, your speech will be a rallying cry to all the cranks, and everyone who has a spite against the country. They'll make you their figurehead. [MORE *smiles.*] They *will*. Your chance of the Cabinet will go—you may even have to resign your seat.

MORE. Dogs will bark. These things soon blow over.

KATHERINE. No, no! If you once begin a thing, you always go on; and what earthly good?

MORE. History won't say: "And this they did without a single protest from their public men!"

KATHERINE. There are plenty who——

MORE. Poets?

KATHERINE. Do you remember that day on our honeymoon, going up Ben Lawers? You were lying on your face in the heather; you said it was like kissing a loved woman. There was a lark singing— you said that was the voice of one's worship. The hills were very blue; that's why we had blue here, because it was the best dress of our country. You *do* love her.

MORE. Love Her!

KATHERINE. You'd have done this for me—then.

MORE. Would you have asked me—then, Kit?

KATHERINE. Yes. The country's *our* country! Oh! Stephen, think what it'll be like for me—with Hubert and the other boys out there. And poor Helen and father! I beg you not to make this speech.

MORE. Kit! This isn't fair. Do you want me to feel myself a cur?

KATHERINE. [*Breathless*] I—I—almost feel you'll be a cur to do it. [*She looks at him, frightened by her own words. Then, as the footman* HENRY *has come in to clear the table—very low.*] I ask you not!

[*He does not answer, and she goes out.*

MORE. [*To the servant*] Later please, Henry, later!

[*The servant retires.* MORE *still stands looking down at the dining-table ; then putting his hand to his throat, as if to free it from the grip of his collar, he pours out a glass of water, and drinks it off. In the street, outside the bay window, two street musicians, a harp and a violin, have taken up their stand, and after some twangs and scrapes, break into music.* MORE *goes towards the sound, and draws aside one curtain. After a moment, he returns to the table, and takes up the notes of the speech. He is in an agony of indecision.*

MORE. A cur!

[*He seems about to tear his notes across. Then, changing his mind, turns them over and over, muttering. His voice gradually grows louder, till he is declaiming to the empty room the peroration of his speech.*

MORE. " . . . We have arrogated to our land the title Champion of Freedom, Foe of Oppression. Is that indeed a bygone glory? Is it not worth some sacrifice of our pettier dignity, to avoid laying another stone upon its grave ; to avoid placing before the searchlight eyes of History the spectacle of yet one more piece of national cynicism? We are about to force our will and our dominion on a race that has always been free, that loves its country, and its independence, as much as ever we love ours. I cannot sit silent to-night and see this begin. As we are tender of our own land, so we should be of the lands of others. I love my country. It is because I love my country that I raise my voice. Warlike in spirit these people may be—but they have no chance against ourselves. And war on such, however agreeable to the blind moment, is odious to the future. The great heart of mankind ever beats in sense and sympathy with the weaker. It is against this great heart of mankind that we are going. In the name of Justice and Civilization we pursue this policy ; but by Justice we shall hereafter be judged, and by Civilization—condemned.

[*While he is speaking, a little figure has flown along the terrace outside, in the direction of the music, but has stopped at the sound of his voice, and stands in the open window, listening—a dark-haired,*

dark-eyed child, in a blue dressing-gown caught up in her hand.
The street musicians, having reached the end of a tune, are silent.
[*In the intensity of* MORE's *feeling, a wine-glass, gripped too strongly,*
breaks and falls in pieces on to a finger-bowl. The child starts
forward into the room.

MORE. Olive !

OLIVE. Who were you speaking to, Daddy ?

MORE. [*Staring at her*] The wind, sweetheart !

OLIVE. There isn't any !

MORE. What blew *you* down, then ?

OLIVE. [*Mysteriously*] The music. Did the wind break the wine-glass, or did it come in two in your hand ?

MORE. Now, my sprite ! Upstairs again, before Nurse catches you. Fly ! Fly !

OLIVE. Oh ! no, Daddy ! [*With confidential fervour.*] It feels like things to-night !

MORE. You're right there !

OLIVE. [*Pulling him down to her, and whispering*] I *must* get back again in secret. H'sh !

[*She suddenly runs and wraps herself into one of the curtains of the bay*
window. A young man enters, with a note in his hand.

MORE. Hallo, Steel ! [*The street musicians have again begun to play.*

STEEL. From Sir John—by special messenger from the War Office.

MORE. [*Reading the note*] " The ball is opened."

[*He stands brooding over the note and* STEEL *looks at him anxiously.*
He is a dark, sallow, thin-faced young man, with the eyes of one
who can attach himself to people, and suffer with them.

STEEL. I'm glad it's begun, sir. It would have been an awful pity to have made that speech.

MORE. You too, Steel !

STEEL. I mean, if it's actually started——

MORE. [*Tearing the note across*] Yes. Keep that to yourself.

STEEL. Do you want me any more ?

[MORE *takes from his breast pocket some papers, and pitches them*
down on the bureau.

MORE. Answer these.

STEEL. [*Going to the bureau*] Fetherby was simply sickening. [*He*
begins to write. Struggle has begun again in MORE.] Not the faintest recognition that there are two sides to it.

[MORE *gives him a quick look, goes quietly to the dining-table and*
picks up his sheaf of notes. Hiding them with his sleeve, he
goes back to the window, where he again stands hesitating.

STEEL. Chief gem : [*Imitating*] " We must show Impudence at last that Dignity is not asleep ! "

MORE. [*Moving out on to the terrace*] Nice quiet night !

STEEL. This to the Cottage Hospital—shall I say you will preside ?

MORE. No.

[STEEL *writes ; then looking up and seeing that* MORE *is no longer there, he goes to the window, looks to right and left, returns to the bureau, and is about to sit down again when a thought seems to strike him with consternation. He goes again to the window. Then snatching up his hat, he passes hurriedly out along the terrace. As he vanishes,* KATHERINE *comes in from the hall. After looking out on to the terrace she goes to the bay window ; stands there listening ; then comes restlessly back into the room.* OLIVE, *creeping quietly from behind the curtain, clasps her round the waist.*

KATHERINE. O my darling ! How you startled me ! What *are* you doing down here, you wicked little sinner !

OLIVE. I explained all that to Daddy. We needn't go into it again, need we ?

KATHERINE. Where *is* Daddy ?

OLIVE. Gone.

KATHERINE. When ?

OLIVE. Oh ! only just, and Mr. Steel went after him like a rabbit. [*The music stops.*] They haven't been paid, you know.

KATHERINE. Now, go up at once. I can't think how you got down here.

OLIVE. I can. [*Wheedling.*] If you pay them, Mummy, they're sure to play another.

KATHERINE. Well, give them that ! One more only.

[*She gives* OLIVE *a coin, who runs with it to the bay window, opens the side casement, and calls to the musicians.*

OLIVE. Catch, please ! And would you play just one more ?

[*She returns from the window, and seeing her mother lost in thought, rubs herself against her.*

OLIVE. Have you got an ache ?

KATHERINE. Right through me, darling !

OLIVE. Oh !   [*The musicians strike up a dance.*

OLIVE. Oh ! Mummy ! I must just dance !

[*She kicks off her little blue shoes, and begins dancing. While she is capering* HUBERT *comes in from the hall. He stands watching his little niece for a minute, and* KATHERINE *looks at him.*

HUBERT. Stephen gone !

KATHERINE. Yes—stop, Olive !

OLIVE. Are you good at my sort of dancing, Uncle !

HUBERT. Yes, chick—awfully !

KATHERINE. Now, Olive !

[*The musicians have suddenly broken off in the middle of a bar. From the street comes the noise of distant shouting.*

OLIVE. Listen, Uncle! Isn't it a particular noise?

[HUBERT *and* KATHERINE *listen with all their might, and* OLIVE *stares at their faces.* HUBERT *goes to the window. The sound comes nearer. The shouted words are faintly heard :* " Pyper— war—our force crosses frontier—sharp fightin'—pyper."

KATHERINE. [*Breathless*] Yes! It is.

[*The street cry is heard again in two distant voices coming from different directions :* " War—pyper—sharp fightin' on the frontier—pyper."

KATHERINE. Shut out those ghouls!

[*As* HUBERT *closes the window,* NURSE WREFORD *comes in from the hall. She is an elderly woman endowed with a motherly grimness. She fixes* OLIVE *with her eye, then suddenly becomes conscious of the street cry.*

NURSE. Oh! don't say it's begun.

[HUBERT *comes from the window.*

NURSE. Is the regiment to go, Mr. Hubert?

HUBERT. Yes, Nanny.

NURSE. Oh, dear! My boy!

KATHERINE. [*Signing to where* OLIVE *stands with wide eyes*] Nurse!

HUBERT. I'll look after him, Nurse.

NURSE. And him keepin' company. And you not married a year. Ah! Mr. Hubert, now do 'ee take care ; you and him's both so rash.

HUBERT. Not I, Nurse!

[NURSE *looks long into his face, then lifts her finger, and beckons* OLIVE.

OLIVE. [*Perceiving new sensations before her, goes quietly*] Good-night, Uncle! Nanny, d'you know why I was obliged to come down? [*In a fervent whisper.*] It's a secret! [*As she passes with* NURSE *out into the hall, her voice is heard saying,* " Do tell me all about the war."]

HUBERT. [*Smothering emotion under a blunt manner*] We sail on Friday, Kit. Be good to Helen, old girl.

KATHERINE. Oh! I wish——! Why—can't—women—fight?

HUBERT. Yes, it's bad for you, with Stephen taking it like this. But he'll come round now it's once begun.

[KATHERINE *shakes her head, then goes suddenly up to him, and throws her arms round his neck. It is as if all the feeling pent up in her were finding vent in this hug.*

[*The door from the hall is opened, and* SIR JOHN'S *voice is heard outside :* " All right, I'll find her."

KATHERINE. Father!   [SIR JOHN *comes in.*

SIR JOHN. Stephen get my note? I sent it over the moment I got to the War Office.

KATHERINE. I expect so. [*Seeing the torn note on the table.*] Yes.

SIR JOHN. They're shouting the news now. Thank God, I stopped that crazy speech of his in time.

KATHERINE. Have you stopped it ?

SIR JOHN. What ! He wouldn't be such a sublime donkey ?

KATHERINE. I think that is just what he might be. [*Going to the window.*] We shall know soon.

[SIR JOHN, *after staring at her, goes up to* HUBERT.

SIR JOHN. Keep a good heart, my boy. The country's first.

[*They exchange a hand-squeeze.*

[KATHERINE *backs away from the window.* STEEL *has appeared there from the terrace, breathless from running.*

STEEL. Mr. More back ?

KATHERINE. No. Has he spoken ?

STEEL. Yes.

KATHERINE. Against ?

STEEL. Yes.

SIR JOHN. What ? After !

[SIR JOHN *stands rigid, then turns and marches straight out into the hall. At a sign from* KATHERINE, HUBERT *follows him.*

KATHERINE. Yes, Mr. Steel ?

STEEL. [*Still breathless and agitated*] We were here—he slipped away from me somehow. He must have gone straight down to the House. I ran over, but when I got in under the Gallery he was speaking already. They expected something—I never heard it so still there. He gripped them from the first word—deadly—every syllable. He got some of those fellows. But all the time, under the silence you could feel a—sort of—of—current going round. And then Sherratt—I think it was—began it, and you saw the anger rising in them ; but he kept them down—his quietness ! The feeling ! I've never seen anything like it there. Then there was a whisper all over the House that fighting had begun. And the whole thing broke out—a regular riot —as if they could have killed him. Someone tried to drag him down by the coat-tails, but he shook him off, and went on. Then he stopped dead and walked out, and the noise dropped like a stone. The whole thing didn't last five minutes. It *was* fine, Mrs. More ; like—like lava ; he was the only cool person there. I wouldn't have missed it for anything—it was grand !

[MORE *has appeared on the terrace, behind* STEEL.

KATHERINE. Good night, Mr. Steel.

STEEL. [*Startled*] Oh !—Good night !

[*He goes out into the hall.* KATHERINE *picks up* OLIVE'S *shoes, and stands clasping them to her breast.* MORE *comes in.*

KATHERINE. You've cleared your conscience, then ! I didn't think you'd hurt me so.

[MORE *does not answer, still living in the scene he has gone through, and* KATHERINE *goes a little nearer to him.*

KATHERINE. I'm with the country, heart and soul, Stephen.   I warn you.

[*While they stand in silence, facing each other, the footman*, HENRY, *enters from the hall.*

FOOTMAN. These notes, sir, from the House of Commons.

KATHERINE. [*Taking them*] You can have the room directly.

[*The* FOOTMAN *goes out.*

MORE. Open them !

[KATHERINE *opens one after the other, and lets them fall on the table.*

MORE. Well ?

KATHERINE. What you might expect.   Three of your best friends. It's begun.

MORE. 'Ware Mob ! [*He gives a laugh.*] I must write to the Chief.

[KATHERINE *makes an impulsive movement towards him ; then quietly goes to the bureau, sits down and takes up a pen.*

KATHERINE. Let me make the rough draft. [*She waits.*] Yes ?

MORE. [*Dictating*]

" July 15th.

" DEAR SIR CHARLES,—After my speech to-night, embodying my most unalterable convictions [KATHERINE *turns and looks up at him, but he is staring straight before him, and with a little movement of despair she goes on writing*] I have no alternative but to place the resignation of my Under-Secretaryship in your hands.   My view, my faith in this matter may be wrong—but I am surely right to keep the flag of my faith flying.   I imagine I need not enlarge on the reasons——"

The curtain falls.

13*

ACT II

Before noon a few days later. The open windows of the dining-room let in the sunlight. On the table a number of newspapers are littered. HELEN is sitting there, staring straight before her. A newspaper boy runs by outside calling out his wares. At the sound she gets up and goes out on to the terrace. HUBERT enters from the hall. He goes at once to the terrace, and draws HELEN into the room.

HELEN. Is it true—what they're shouting?

HUBERT. Yes. Worse than we thought. They got our men all crumpled up in the Pass—guns helpless. Ghastly beginning.

HELEN. Oh, Hubert!

HUBERT. My dearest girl!

> [HELEN *puts her face up to his. He kisses her. Then she turns quickly into the bay window. The door from the hall has been opened, and the footman,* HENRY, *comes in, preceding* WREFORD *and his sweetheart.*

HENRY. Just wait here, will you, while I let Mrs. More know. [*Catching sight of* HUBERT.] Beg pardon, sir!

HUBERT. All right, Henry. [*Off-hand.*] Ah! Wreford! [*The* FOOTMAN *withdraws.*] So you've brought her round. That's good! My sister'll look after her—don't you worry! Got everything packed? Three o'clock sharp.

WREFORD. [*A broad-faced soldier, dressed in khaki with a certain look of dry humour, now dimmed—speaking with a West Country burr*] That's right, zurr; all's ready.

> [HELEN *has come out of the window, and is quietly looking at* WREFORD *and the girl standing there so awkwardly.*

HELEN. [*Quietly*] Take care of him, Wreford.

HUBERT. We'll take care of each other, won't we, Wreford?

HELEN. How long have you been engaged?

THE GIRL. [*A pretty, indeterminate young woman*] Six months.
> [*She sobs suddenly.*

HELEN. Ah! He'll soon be safe back.

WREFORD. I'll owe 'em for this. [*In a low voice to her.*] Don't 'ee now! Don't 'ee!

HELEN. No! Don't cry, please!

> [*She stands struggling with her own lips, then goes out on to the terrace,* HUBERT *following.* WREFORD *and his girl remain where they were, strange and awkward, she muffling her sobs.*

WREFORD. Don't 'ee go on like that, Nance ; I'll 'ave to take you 'ome. That's silly, now we've a-come. I might be dead and buried by the fuss you're makin'. You've a-drove the lady away. See !

[*She regains control of herself as the door is opened and* KATHERINE *appears, accompanied by* OLIVE, *who regards* WREFORD *with awe and curiosity, and by* NURSE, *whose eyes are red, but whose manner is composed.*

KATHERINE. My brother told me ; so glad you've brought her.

WREFORD. Ye-as, M'. She feels me goin', a bit.

KATHERINE. Yes, yes ! Still, it's for the country, isn't it ?

THE GIRL. That's what Wreford keeps tellin' me. He've got to go—so it's no use upsettin' 'im. And of course I keep tellin' him I shall be all right.

NURSE. [*Whose eyes never leave her son's face*] And so you will.

THE GIRL. Wreford thought it 'd comfort him to know you were interested in me. 'E's so 'ot-headed I'm sure somethin' 'll come to 'im.

KATHERINE. We've all got someone going. Are you coming to the docks ? We must send them off in good spirits, you know.

OLIVE. Perhaps he'll get a medal.

KATHERINE. Olive !

NURSE. You wouldn't like for him to be hanging back, one of them anti-patriot, stop-the-war ones.

KATHERINE. [*Quickly*] Let me see—I have your address. [*Holding out her hand to* WREFORD.] We'll look after her.

OLIVE. [*In a loud whisper*] Shall I lend him my toffee ?

KATHERINE. If you like, dear. [*To* WREFORD.] Now take care of my brother and yourself, and we'll take care of her.

WREFORD. Ye-as, M'.

[*He then looks rather wretchedly at his girl, as if the interview had not done so much for him as he had hoped. She drops a little curtsey.* WREFORD *salutes.*

OLIVE. [*Who has taken from the bureau a packet, places it in his hand*] It's very nourishing !

WREFORD. Thank you, Miss.

[*Then, nudging each other, and entangled in their feelings and the conventions, they pass out shepherded by* NURSE.

KATHERINE. Poor things !

OLIVE. What is an anti-patriot, stop-the-war one, Mummy !

KATHERINE. [*Taking up a newspaper*] Just a stupid name, dear— don't chatter !

OLIVE. But tell me just one weeny thing !

KATHERINE. Well ?

OLIVE. Is Daddy one ?

KATHERINE. Olive ! How much do you know about this war ?

OLIVE. They won't obey us properly. So we have to beat them, and take away their country. We *shall*, shan't we ?

KATHERINE. Yes. But Daddy doesn't want us to ; he doesn't think it fair, and he's been saying so. People are very angry with him.

OLIVE. Why isn't it fair ?   I suppose we're littler than them.

KATHERINE. No.

OLIVE. Oh ! in history we always are. And we always win. That's why I like history. Which are *you* for, Mummy—us or them ?

KATHERINE. Us.

OLIVE. Then I shall have to be. It's a pity we're not on the same side as Daddy. [KATHERINE *shudders*.] Will they hurt him for not taking our side ?

KATHERINE. I expect they will, Olive.

OLIVE. Then we shall have to be extra nice to him.

KATHERINE. If we can.

OLIVE. *I* can ; I feel like it.

> [HELEN *and* HUBERT *have returned along the terrace. Seeing* KATHERINE *and the child*, HELEN *passes on, but* HUBERT *comes in at the French window.*

OLIVE. [*Catching sight of him—softly*] Is Uncle Hubert going to the front to-day ?   [KATHERINE *nods*.] But not grandfather ?

KATHERINE. No, dear.

OLIVE. That's lucky for *them*, isn't it ?

> [HUBERT *comes in. The presence of the child gives him self-control.*

HUBERT. Well, old girl, it's good-bye. [*To* OLIVE.] What shall I bring you back, chick ?

OLIVE. Are there shops at the front ?   I thought it was dangerous.

HUBERT. Not a bit.

OLIVE. [*Disillusioned*] Oh !

KATHERINE. Now, darling, give Uncle a good hug.

> [*Under cover of* OLIVE's *hug*, KATHERINE *repairs her courage.*

KATHERINE. The Dad and I'll be with you all in spirit. Good-bye, old boy !

> [*They do not dare to kiss, and* HUBERT *goes out very stiff and straight, in the doorway passing* STEEL, *of whom he takes no notice.* STEEL *hesitates, and would go away.*

KATHERINE. Come in, Mr. Steel.

STEEL. The deputation from Toulmin ought to be here, Mrs. More. It's twelve.

OLIVE. [*Having made a little ball of newspaper—slyly*] Mr. Steel, catch !   [*She throws, and* STEEL *catches it in silence.*

KATHERINE. Go upstairs, won't you, darling ?

OLIVE. Mayn't I read in the window, Mummy ?   Then I shall see if any soldiers pass.

KATHERINE. No.   You can go out on the terrace a little, and then you must go up.   [OLIVE *goes reluctantly out on to the terrace.*

STEEL. Awful news this morning of that Pass! And have you seen these? [*Reading from the newspaper.*] "We will have no truck with the jargon of the degenerate who vilifies his country at such a moment. The Member for Toulmin has earned for himself the contempt of all virile patriots." [*He takes up a second journal.*] "There is a certain type of public man who, even at his own expense, cannot resist the itch to advertise himself. We would, at moments of national crisis, muzzle such persons, as we muzzle dogs that we suspect of incipient rabies. . . ." They're in full cry after him!

KATHERINE. I mind much more all the creatures who are always flinging mud at the country making him their hero suddenly! You know what's in his mind?

STEEL. Oh! We *must* get him to give up that idea of lecturing everywhere against the war, Mrs. More; we simply must.

KATHERINE. [*Listening*] The deputation's come. Go and fetch him, Mr. Steel. He'll be in his room, at the House.

[STEEL *goes out, and* KATHERINE *stands at bay. In a moment he opens the door again, to usher in the deputation; then retires. The four gentlemen have entered as if conscious of grave issues. The first and most picturesque is* JAMES HOME, *a thin, tall, grey-bearded man, with plentiful hair, contradictious eyebrows, and the half-shy, half-bold manners, alternately rude and over-polite, of one not accustomed to Society, yet secretly much taken with himself. He is dressed in rough tweeds, with a red silk tie slung through a ring, and is closely followed by* MARK WACE, *a waxy, round-faced man of middle-age, with sleek dark hair, traces of whisker, and a smooth way of continually rubbing his hands together, as if selling something to an esteemed customer. He is rather stout, wears dark clothes, with a large gold chain. Following him comes* CHARLES SHELDER, *a lawyer, of fifty, with a bald egg-shaped head, and gold pince-nez. He has little side whiskers, a leathery, yellowish skin, a rather kind but watchful and dubious face, and when he speaks seems to have a plum in his mouth, which arises from the pre-ponderance of his shaven upper lip. Last of the deputation comes* WILLIAM BANNING, *an energetic-looking, square-shouldered, self-made countryman, between fifty and sixty, with grey moustaches, ruddy face, and lively brown eyes.*

KATHERINE. How do you do, Mr. Home?

HOME. [*Bowing rather extravagantly over her hand, as if to show his independence of women's influence*] Mrs. More! We hardly expected—— This is an honour.

WACE. How do you do, Ma'am?

KATHERINE. And you, Mr. Wace?

WACE. Thank you, Ma'am, well indeed!

SHELDER. How d'you do, Mrs. More?

KATHERINE. Very well, thank you, Mr. Shelder.

BANNING. [*Speaking with a rather broad country accent*] This is but a poor occasion, Ma'am.

KATHERINE. Yes, Mr. Banning. Do sit down, gentlemen.

> [*Seeing that they will not settle down while she is standing, she sits at the table. They gradually take their seats. Each member of the deputation in his own way is severely hanging back from any mention of the subject in hand; and* KATHERINE *as intent on drawing them to it.*

KATHERINE. My husband will be here in two minutes. He's only over at the House.

SHELDER [*Who is of higher standing and education than the others*] Charming position—this, Mrs. More! So near the—er—Centre of —Gravity—um?

KATHERINE. I read the account of your second meeting at Toulmin.

BANNING. It's bad, Mrs. More—bad. There's no disguising it. That speech was moon-summer madness—Ah! it *was!* Take a lot of explaining away. Why did you let him, now? Why did you? Not your views, I'm sure!

> [*He looks at her, but for answer she only compresses her lips.*

BANNING. I tell you what hit me—what's hit the whole constituency —and that's his knowing we were over the frontier, fighting already, when he made it.

KATHERINE. What difference does it make if he did know?

HOME. Hitting below the belt—I should have thought—you'll pardon me!

BANNING. Till war's begun, Mrs. More, you're entitled to say what you like, no doubt—but after! That's going against your country. Ah! his speech was strong, you know—his speech was strong.

KATHERINE. He had made up his mind to speak. It was just an accident the news coming then.   [*A silence.*

BANNING. Well, that's true, I suppose. What we really want is to make sure he won't break out again.

HOME. Very high-minded, his views, of course—but, some consideration for the common herd. You'll pardon me!

SHELDER. We've come with the friendliest feelings, Mrs. More— but, you know, it won't do, this sort of thing!

WACE. We shall be able to smooth him down. Oh! surely.

BANNING. We'd be best perhaps not to mention about his knowing that fighting had begun.

> [*As he speaks,* MORE *enters through the French windows. They all rise.*

MORE. Good morning, gentlemen.

[*He comes down to the table, but does not offer to shake hands.*

BANNING. Well, Mr. More? You've made a woeful mistake, sir; I tell you to your face.

MORE. As everybody else does, Banning. Sit down again, please.

[*They gradually resume their seats, and* MORE *sits in* KATHERINE'S *chair. She alone remains standing leaning against the corner of the bay window, watching their faces.*

BANNING. You've seen the morning's telegrams? I tell you, Mr. More—another reverse like that, and the flood will sweep you clean away. And I'll not blame it. It's only flesh and blood.

MORE. Allow for the flesh and blood in *me*, too, please, When I spoke the other night it was not without a certain feeling here.

[*He touches his heart.*

BANNING. But your attitude's so sudden—you'd not been going that length when you were down with us in May.

MORE. Do me the justice to remember that even then I was against our policy. It cost me three weeks' hard struggle to make up my mind to that speech. One comes slowly to these things, Banning.

SHELDER. Case of conscience?

MORE. Such things have happened, Shelder, even in politics.

SHELDER. You see, our ideals are naturally low—how different from yours!   [MORE *smiles.*

[KATHERINE, *who has drawn near her husband, moves back again, as if relieved at this gleam of geniality.* WACE *rubs his hands.*

BANNING. There's one thing you forget, sir. We send you to Parliament, representing us; but you couldn't find six men in the whole constituency that would have bidden you to make that speech.

MORE. I'm sorry; but I can't help my convictions, Banning.

SHELDER. What was it the prophet was without in his own country?

BANNING. Ah! but we're not funning, Mr. More; I've never known feeling run so high. The sentiment of both meetings was dead against you. We've had showers of letters to headquarters. Some from very good men—very warm friends of yours.

SHELDER. Come now! It's not too late. Let's go back and tell them you won't do it again.

MORE. Muzzling order?

BANNING. [*Bluntly*] That's about it.

MORE. Give up my principles to save my Parliamentary skin. Then, indeed, they might call me a degenerate!

[*He touches the newspapers on the table.*

[KATHERINE *makes an abrupt and painful movement, then remains as still as before, leaning against the corner of the window-seat.*

BANNING. Well, well! I know. But we don't ask you to take your words back—we only want discretion in the future.

MORE. Conspiracy of silence! And have it said that a mob of newspapers have hounded me to it.

BANNING. They won't say that of *you*.

SHELDER. My dear More, aren't you rather dropping to our level? With your principles you ought not to care two straws what people say.

MORE. But I do. I can't betray the dignity and courage of public men. If popular opinion is to control the utterances of her politicians, then good-bye indeed to this country!

BANNING. Come now! I won't say that your views weren't sound enough before the fighting began. I've never liked our policy out there. But our blood's being spilled; and that makes all the difference. I don't suppose they'd want me exactly, but I'd be ready to go myself. We'd all of us be ready. And we can't have the man that represents us talking wild, until we've licked these fellows. That's it in a nutshell.

MORE. I understand your feeling, Banning. I tender you my resignation. I can't and won't hold on where I'm not wanted.

BANNING. No, no, no! Don't do that! [*His accent broader and broader.*] You've 'ad your say, and there it is. Coom now! You've been our Member nine years, in rain and shine.

SHELDER. We want to keep you, More. Come! Give us your promise—that's a good man!

MORE. I don't make cheap promises. You ask too much.

[*There is silence, and they all look at* MORE.

SHELDER. There are very excellent reasons for the Government's policy.

MORE. There are always excellent reasons for having your way with the weak.

SHELDER. My dear More, how you can get up any enthusiasm for those cattle-lifting ruffians?

MORE. Better lift cattle than lift freedom.

SHELDER. Well, all we'll ask is that you shouldn't go about the country saying so.

MORE. But that is just what I must do.

[*Again they all look at* MORE *in consternation.*

HOME. Not down our way, you'll pardon me.

WACE. Really—really, sir——

SHELDER. The time of crusades is past, More.

MORE. Is it?

BANNING. Ah! no, but we don't want to part with you, Mr. More. It's a bitter thing, this, after three elections. Look at the 'uman side of it! To speak ill of your country when there's been a disaster like this terrible business in the Pass. There's your own wife. I see her

brother's regiment's to start this very afternoon. Come now—how
must she feel ?

[MORE *breaks away to the bay window. The* DEPUTATION *exchange
        glances.*

MORE. [*Turning*] To try to muzzle me like this—is going too far.

BANNING. We just want to put you out of temptation.

MORE. I've held my seat with you in all weathers for nine years.
You've all been bricks to me. My heart's in my work, Banning ;
I'm not eager to undergo political eclipse at forty.

SHELDER. Just so—we don't want to see you in that quandary.

BANNING. It'd be no friendliness to give you a wrong impression
of the state of feeling. Silence—till the bitterness is overpast ; there's
naught else for it, Mr. More, while you feel as you do. That tongue
of yours ! Come ! You owe us something. You're a big man ;
it's the big view you ought to take.

MORE. I am trying to.

HOME. And what precisely is your view—you'll pardon my asking.

MORE. [*Turning on him*] Mr. Home—a great country such as ours
—is trustee for the highest sentiments of mankind. Do these few
outrages justify us in stealing the freedom of this little people ?

BANNING. Steal their freedom ! That's rather running before the
hounds.

MORE. Ah, Banning ! now we come to it. In your hearts you're
none of you for that—neither by force nor fraud. And yet you all
know that we've gone in there to stay, as we've gone into other lands
—as all we big Powers go into other lands, when they're little and
weak. The Prime Minister's words the other night were these :
" If we are forced to spend this blood and money now, we must
never again be forced." What does that mean but swallowing this
country ?

SHELDER. Well, and quite frankly, it'd be no bad thing.

HOME. We don't want their wretched country—we're forced.

MORE. We are *not* forced.

SHELDER. My dear More, what is civilization but the logical,
inevitable swallowing up of the lower by the higher types of man ?
And what else will it be here ?

MORE. We shall not agree there, Shelder ; and we might argue it
all day. But the point is, not whether you or I are right—the point
is : What is a man who holds a faith with all his heart to do ? Please
tell me.   [*There is a silence.*

BANNING. [*Simply*] I was just thinkin' of those poor fellows in the
Pass.

MORE. I can see them, as well as you, Banning. But, imagine !
Up in our own country—the Black Valley—twelve hundred foreign
devils dead and dying—the crows busy over them—in our own

country, our own valley—ours—ours—violated. Would you care about " the poor fellows " in *that* Pass ?—Invading, stealing dogs ! Kill them—kill them ! You would, and I would, too !

> [*The passion of those words touches and grips as no arguments could ; and they are silent.*

MORE. Well ! What's the difference out there ? I'm not so inhuman as not to want to see this disaster in the Pass wiped out. But once that's done, in spite of my affection for you ; my ambitions, and they're not few ; [*Very low*] in spite of my own wife's feeling, I must be free to raise my voice against this war.

BANNING. [*Speaking slowly, consulting the others, as it were, with his eyes*] Mr. More, there's no man I respect more than yourself. I can't tell what they'll say down there when we go back ; but I, for one, don't feel it in me to take a hand in pressing you farther against your faith.

SHELDER. We don't deny that—that you have a case of sorts.

WACE. No—surely.

SHELDER. A man should be free, I suppose, to hold his own opinions.

MORE. Thank you, Shelder.

BANNING. Well ! well ! We must take you as you are ; but it's a rare pity ; there'll be a lot of trouble——

> [*His eyes light on* HOME, *who is leaning forward with hand raised to his ear, listening. Very faint, from far in the distance, there is heard a skirling sound. All become conscious of it, all listen.*

HOME. [*Suddenly*] Bagpipes !

> [*The figure of* OLIVE *flies past the window, out on the terrace.* KATHERINE *turns, as if to follow her.*

SHELDER. Highlanders !   [*He rises.*

> [KATHERINE *goes quickly out on to the terrace. One by one they all follow to the window. One by one go out on to the terrace, till* MORE *is left alone. He turns to the bay window. The music is swelling, coming nearer.* MORE *leaves the window —his face distorted by the strife of his emotions. He paces the room, taking, in some sort, the rhythm of the march.*
>
> [*Slowly the music dies away in the distance to a drum-tap and the tramp of a company.* MORE *stops at the table, covering his eyes with his hands.*
>
> [*The* DEPUTATION *troop back across the terrace, and come in at the French windows. Their faces and manners have quite changed.* KATHERINE *follows them as far as the window.*

HOME. [*In a strange, almost threatening voice*] It won't do, Mr. More. Give us your word to hold your peace !

SHELDER. Come ! More.

WACE. Yes, indeed—indeed!

BANNING. We must have it.

MORE. [*Without lifting his head*] I—I——

[*The drum-tap of a regiment marching is heard.*

BANNING. Can you hear that go by, man—when your country's just been struck?

[*Now comes the scuffle and mutter of a following crowd.*

MORE. I give you——

[*Then, sharp and clear above all other sounds, the words:* " Give the beggars hell, boys!" "Wipe your feet on their dirty country!" "Don't leave 'em a gory acre!" *And a burst of hoarse cheering.*

MORE. [*Flinging up his head*] That's reality! By Heaven! No!

KATHERINE. Oh!

SHELDER. In that case, we'll go.

BANNING. You mean it? You lose us, then! [MORE *bows.*

HOME. Good riddance. [*Venomously—his eyes darting between* MORE *and* KATHERINE.] Go and stump the country! Find out what they think of you! You'll pardon me!

[*One by one, without a word, only* BANNING *looking back, they pass out into the hall.* MORE *sits down at the table before the pile of newspapers.* KATHERINE, *in the window, never moves.* OLIVE *comes along the terrace, to her mother.*

OLIVE. They *were* nice ones! Such a lot of dirty people following, and some quite clean, mummy. [*Conscious from her mother's face that something is very wrong, she looks at her father, and then steals up to his side.*] Uncle Hubert's gone, Daddy; and Auntie Helen's crying. And—look at Mummy! [MORE *raises his head and looks.*

OLIVE. Do be on our side! Do.

[*She rubs her cheek against his. Feeling that he does not rub his cheek against hers,* OLIVE *stands away, and looks from him to her mother in wonder.*

The curtain falls.

ACT III

SCENE I

A cobble-stoned alley, without pavement, behind a suburban theatre. The tall, blind, dingy-yellowish wall of the building is plastered with the tattered remnants of old entertainment bills, and the words: " To Let," and with several torn, and one still virgin placard, containing this announcement : " Stop-the-War Meeting, October 1st. Addresses by STEPHEN MORE, ESQ., *and others." The alley is plentifully strewn with refuse and scraps of paper. Three stone steps, inset, lead to the stage door. It is a dark night, and a street lamp close to the wall throws all the light there is. A faint, confused murmur, as of distant hooting is heard. Suddenly a boy comes running, then two rough girls hurry past in the direction of the sound ; and the alley is again deserted. The stage door opens, and a doorkeeper, poking his head out, looks up and down. He withdraws, but in a second reappears, preceding three black-coated gentlemen.*

DOORKEEPER. It's all clear. You can get away down here, gentlemen. Keep to the left, then sharp to the right, round the corner.

THE THREE. [*Dusting themselves, and settling their ties*] Thanks, very much ! Thanks !

FIRST BLACK-COATED GENTLEMAN. Where's More ? Isn't he coming ?   [*They are joined by a fourth black-coated* GENTLEMAN.

FOURTH BLACK-COATED GENTLEMAN. Just behind. [*To the* DOORKEEPER.] Thanks.

> [*They hurry away. The* DOORKEEPER *retires. Another boy runs past. Then the door opens again.* STEEL *and* MORE *come out.*

> [MORE *stands hesitating on the steps ; then turns as if to go back.*

STEEL. Come along, sir, come !

MORE. It sticks in my gizzard, Steel.

STEEL. [*Running his arm through* MORE'S, *and almost dragging him down the steps*] You owe it to the theatre people. [MORE *still hesitates.*] We might be penned in there another hour ; you told Mrs. More half-past ten ; it'll only make her anxious. And she hasn't seen you for six weeks.

MORE. All right ; don't dislocate my arm.

> [*They move down the steps, and away to the left, as a boy comes running down the alley. Sighting* MORE, *he stops dead, spins round,*

and crying shrilly : " 'Ere 'e is !   That's 'im !   'Ere 'e is ! " *he bolts back in the direction whence he came.*

STEEL. Quick, sir, quick !

MORE. That is the end of the limit, as the foreign ambassador remarked.

STEEL. [*Pulling him back towards the door*] Well ! come inside again, anyway !

> [*A number of men and boys, and a few young girls, are trooping quickly from the left. A motley crew, out for excitement ; loafers, artisans, navvies ; girls rough, or dubious. All in the mood of hunters, and having tasted blood. They gather round the steps displaying the momentary irresolution and curiosity that follows on a new development of any chase.* MORE, *on the bottom step, turns and eyes them.*

A GIRL. [*At the edge*] Which is 'im !   The old 'un or the young ?

> [MORE *turns, and mounts the remaining steps.*

TALL YOUTH. [*With lank black hair under a bowler hat*] You blasted traitor !

> [MORE *faces round at the volley of jeering that follows ; the chorus of booing swells, then gradually dies, as if they realized that they were spoiling their own sport.*

A ROUGH GIRL. Don't frighten the poor feller !

> [*A girl beside her utters a shrill laugh.*

STEEL. [*Tugging at* MORE'S *arm*] Come along, sir.

MORE. [*Shaking his arm free—to the crowd*] Well, what do you want ?

A VOICE. Speech.

MORE. Indeed ! That's new.

ROUGH VOICE. [*At the back of the crowd*] Look at his white liver. You can see it in his face.

A BIG NAVVY. [*In front*] Shut it !   Give 'im a chanst !

TALL YOUTH. Silence for the blasted traitor ?

> [*A youth plays the concertina ; there is laughter, then an abrupt silence.*

MORE. You shall have it in a nut-shell !

A SHOPBOY. [*Flinging a walnut-shell which strikes* MORE *on the shoulder*] Here y'are !

MORE. Go home, and think ! If foreigners invaded *us*, wouldn't you be fighting tooth and nail like those tribesmen, out there ?

TALL YOUTH. Treacherous dogs !   Why don't they come out in the open ?

MORE. They fight the best way they can.

> [*A burst of hooting is led by a soldier in khaki on the outskirts.*

MORE. My friend there in khaki led that hooting. I've never said a word against our soldiers. It's the Government I condemn for putting them to this, and the Press for hounding on the Government, and all of you for being led by the nose to do what none of you would do, left to yourselves.

[*The* TALL YOUTH *leads a somewhat unspontaneous burst of execration.*]
MORE. I say not one of you would go for a weaker man.
VOICES IN THE CROWD :
   ROUGH VOICE. Tork sense !
   GIRL'S VOICE. He's gittin' at you !
   TALL YOUTH'S VOICE. Shiny skunk !
  A NAVVY. [*Suddenly shouldering forward*] Look 'ere, Mister ! Don't you come gaffin' to those who've got mates out there, or it'll be the worse for you—you go 'ome !
  COCKNEY VOICE. And git your wife to put cotton-wool in yer ears.

[*A spurt of laughter.*]
  A FRIENDLY VOICE. [*From the outskirts*] Shame ! there ! Bravo, More ! Keep it up !   [*A scuffle drowns this cry.*]
  MORE. [*With vehemence*] Stop that ! Stop that ! You—— !
  TALL YOUTH. Traitor !
  AN ARTISAN. Who black-legged ?
  MIDDLE-AGED MAN. Ought to be shot—backin' his country's enemies !
  MORE. Those tribesmen are defending their homes.
  TWO VOICES. Hear ! hear !   [*They are hustled into silence.*]
  TALL YOUTH. Wind-bag !
  MORE. [*With sudden passion*] Defending their homes ! Not mobbing unarmed men !   [STEEL *again pulls at his arm.*]
  ROUGH. Shut it, or we'll do you in !
  MORE. [*Recovering his coolness*] Ah ! Do me in, by all means ! You'd deal such a blow at cowardly mobs as wouldn't be forgotten in your time.
  STEEL. For God's sake, sir !
  MORE. [*Shaking off his touch*] Well !

[*There is an ugly rush, checked by the fall of the foremost figures, thrown too suddenly against the bottom step. The crowd recoils.*]
[*There is a momentary lull, and* MORE *stares steadily down at them.*]
  COCKNEY VOICE. Don't 'e speak well ! What eloquence.

[*Two or three nutshells and a piece of orange-peel strike* MORE *across the face. He takes no notice.*]
  ROUGH VOICE. That's it ! Give 'im some encouragement.

[*The jeering laughter is changed to anger by the contemptuous smile on* MORE'S *face.*]
  A TALL YOUTH. Traitor !
  A VOICE. Don't stand there like a stuck pig.
  A ROUGH. Let's 'ave 'im dahn off that !

[*Under cover of the applause that greets this, he strikes* MORE *across the legs with a belt.* STEEL *starts forward.* MORE, *flinging*]

*out his arms, turns his back, and resumes his tranquil staring
at the crowd, in whom the sense of being foiled by this silence is
fast turning to rage.*

THE CROWD. Speak up, or get down ! Get off ! Get away, there
—or we'll make you ! Go on ! [MORE *remains immovable.*

A YOUTH. [*In a lull of disconcertion*] I'll make 'im speak ! See !

[*He darts forward and spits, defiling* MORE's *hand.* MORE *jerks it
up as if it had been stung, then stands as still as ever. A spurt
of laughter dies into a shiver of repugnance at the action. The
shame is fanned again to fury by the sight of* MORE's *scornful face.*

TALL YOUTH. [*Out of murmuring*] Shift ! or you'll get it !

A VOICE. Enough of your ugly mug !

A ROUGH. Give 'im one !

[*Two flung stones strike* MORE. *He staggers and nearly falls, then
rights himself.*

A GIRL's VOICE. Shame !

FRIENDLY VOICE. Bravo, More ! Stick to it !

A ROUGH. Give 'im another !

A VOICE. No !

A GIRL's VOICE. Let 'im alone ! Come on, Billy, this ain't no fun !

[*Still looking up at* MORE, *the whole crowd falls into an uneasy
silence, broken only by the shuffling of feet. Then the* BIG
NAVVY *in the front rank turns and elbows his way out to the
edge of the crowd.*

THE NAVVY. Let 'im be !

[*With half-sullen and half-shamefaced acquiescence the crowd breaks
up and drifts back whence it came, till the alley is nearly empty.*

MORE. [*As if coming to, out of a trance—wiping his hand and dusting his
coat*] Well, Steel !

[*And followed by* STEEL, *he descends the steps and moves away. Two
policemen pass glancing up at the broken glass. One of them
stops and makes a note.*

The curtain falls.

SCENE II

The window-end of KATHERINE's *bedroom, panelled in cream-coloured wood.
The light from four candles is falling on* KATHERINE, *who is sitting
before the silver mirror of an old oak dressing-table, brushing her hair.
A door, on the left, stands ajar. An oak chair against the wall close to
a recessed window is all the other furniture. Through this window the
blue night is seen, where a mist is rolled out flat amongst trees, so that
only dark clumps of boughs show here and there, beneath a moonlit sky.*

As the curtain rises, KATHERINE, *with brush arrested, is listening. She begins again brushing her hair, then stops, and taking a packet of letters from a drawer of her dressing-table, reads. Through the just-open door behind her comes the voice of* OLIVE.

OLIVE. Mummy ! I'm awake !

    [*But* KATHERINE *goes on reading ; and* OLIVE *steals into the room in her nightgown.*

OLIVE. [*At* KATHERINE'S *elbow—examining her watch on its stand*] It's fourteen minutes to eleven.

KATHERINE. Olive, Olive !

OLIVE. I just wanted to see the time. I never can go to sleep if I try—it's quite helpless, you know. Is there a victory yet ? [KATHERINE *shakes her head.*] Oh ! I prayed extra special for one in the evening papers. [*Straying round her mother.*] Hasn't Daddy come ?

KATHERINE. Not yet.

OLIVE. Are you waiting for him ? [*Burying her face in her mother's hair.*] Your hair *is* nice, Mummy. It's particular to-night.

    [KATHERINE *lets fall her brush, and looks at her almost in alarm.*

OLIVE. How long has Daddy been away ?

KATHERINE. Six weeks.

OLIVE. It seems about a hundred years, doesn't it ? Has he been making speeches all the time ?

KATHERINE. Yes.

OLIVE. To-night, too ?

KATHERINE. Yes.

OLIVE. The night that man was here whose head's too bald for anything—oh ! Mummy, you know—the one who cleans his teeth so termendously—I heard Daddy making a speech to the wind. It broke a wine-glass. His speeches must be good ones, mustn't they !

KATHERINE. Very.

OLIVE. It felt funny ; you couldn't see any wind, you know.

KATHERINE. Talking to the wind is an expression, Olive.

OLIVE. Does Daddy often ?

KATHERINE. Yes, nowadays.

OLIVE. What does it mean ?

KATHERINE. Speaking to people who won't listen.

OLIVE. What do they do, then ?

KATHERINE. Just a few people go to hear him, and then a great crowd comes and breaks in ; or they wait for him outside, and throw things, and hoot.

OLIVE. Poor Daddy ! Is it people on our side, who throw things ?

KATHERINE. Yes, but only rough people.

OLIVE. Why does he go on doing it ? I shouldn't.

KATHERINE. He thinks it his duty.

OLIVE. To your neighbour, or only to God ?

KATHERINE. To both.

OLIVE. Oh! Are those his letters?

KATHERINE. Yes.

OLIVE. [*Reading from the letter*] " My dear Heart." Does he always call you his dear heart, Mummy? It's rather jolly, isn't it? " I shall be home about half-past ten to-morrow night. For a few hours the fires of p-u-r-g-a-t-o-r-y will cease to burn——" What are the fires of p-u-r-g-a-t-o-r-y!

KATHERINE. [*Putting away the letters*] Come, Olive!

OLIVE. But what are they?

KATHERINE. Daddy means that he's been very unhappy.

OLIVE. Have you, too?

KATHERINE. Yes.

OLIVE. [*Cheerfully*] So have I. May I open the window?

KATHERINE. No; you'll let the mist in.

OLIVE. Isn't it a funny mist—all flat!

KATHERINE. Now, come along, frog!

OLIVE. [*Making time*] Mummy, when is Uncle Hubert coming back?

KATHERINE. We don't know, dear.

OLIVE. I suppose Aunty Helen'll stay with us till he does.

KATHERINE. Yes.

OLIVE. That's something, isn't it?

KATHERINE. [*Picking her up*] Now then!

OLIVE. [*Deliciously limp*] Had I better put in the duty to your neighbour—if there isn't a victory soon? [*As they pass through the door.*] You're tickling under my knee! [*Little gurgles of pleasure follow. Then silence. Then a drowsy voice.*] I must keep awake for Daddy.

> [KATHERINE *comes back. She is about to leave the door a little open, when she hears a knock on the other door. It is opened a few inches, and* NURSE'S *voice says:* " Can I come in, Ma'am? "
> [*The* NURSE *comes in.*

KATHERINE. [*Shutting* OLIVE'S *door, and going up to her*] What is it, Nurse?

NURSE. [*Speaking in a low voice*] I've been meaning to—I'll never do it in the daytime. I'm giving you notice.

KATHERINE. Nurse! *You too!*

> [*She looks towards* OLIVE'S *room with dismay. The* NURSE *smudges a slow tear away from her cheek.*

NURSE. I want to go right away at once.

KATHERINE. Leave Olive! That *is* the sins of the fathers with a vengeance.

NURSE. I've had another letter from my son. No, Miss Katherine, while the master goes on upholdin' these murderin' outlandish creatures, I can't live in this house, not now he's coming back.

KATHERINE. But, Nurse——!

NURSE. It's not like them [*With an ineffable gesture*] downstairs, because I'm frightened of the mob, or of the window's bein' broke again, or mind what the boys in the street say. I should think not—no! It's my heart. I'm sore night and day thinkin' of my son, and him lying out there at night without a rag of dry clothing, and water that the bullocks won't drink, and maggots in the meat; and every day one of his friends laid out stark and cold, and one day—'imself perhaps. If anything were to 'appen to him, I'd never forgive meself—here. Ah! Miss Katherine, I wonder how you bear it—bad news comin' every day—And Sir John's face so sad—And all the time the master speaking against us, as it might be Jonah 'imself.

KATHERINE. But, Nurse, how *can* you leave us, *you*?

NURSE. [*Smudging at her cheeks*] There's that tells me it's encouragin' something to happen, if I stay here; and Mr. More coming back to-night. You can't serve God and Mammon, the Bible says.

KATHERINE. Don't you know what it's costing him?

NURSE. Ah! Cost him his seat, and his reputation; and more than that it'll cost him, to go against the country.

KATHERINE. He's following his conscience.

NURSE. And others must follow theirs, too. No, Miss Katherine, for you to let him—you, with your three brothers out there, and your father fair wasting away with grief. Sufferin' too as you've been these three months past. What'll you feel if anything happens to my three young gentlemen out there, to my dear Mr. Hubert that I nursed myself, when your precious mother couldn't. What would she have said—with you in the camp of his enemies.

KATHERINE. Nurse, Nurse!

NURSE. In my paper they say he's encouraging these heathens and makin' the foreigners talk about us; and every day longer the war lasts, there's our blood on this house.

KATHERINE. [*Turning away*] Nurse, I can't—I won't listen.

NURSE. [*Looking at her intently*] Ah! You'll move him to leave off! I see your heart, my dear. But if you don't, then go I must!

[*She nods her head gravely, goes to the door of* OLIVE'S *room, opens it gently, stands looking for a moment, then with the words :* " My Lamb ! " *she goes in noiselessly and closes the door.*

[KATHERINE *turns back to her glass, puts back her hair, and smooths her lips and eyes. The door from the corridor is opened, and* HELEN'S *voice says :* " Kit ! You're not in bed ? "

KATHERINE. No.

[HELEN *too is in a wrapper, with a piece of lace thrown over her head. Her face is scared and miserable, and she runs into* KATHERINE'S *arms.*

KATHERINE. My dear, what is it?

HELEN. I've seen—a vision!

KATHERINE. Hssh ! You'll wake Olive !

HELEN. [*Staring before her*] I'd just fallen asleep, and I saw a plain that seemed to run into the sky—like—that fog. And on it there were—dark things. One grew into a body without a head, and a gun by its side. And one was a man sitting huddled up, nursing a wounded leg. He had the face of Hubert's servant, Wreford. And then I saw —Hubert. His face was all dark and thin ; and he had—a wound, an awful wound here. [*She touches her breast.*] The blood was running from it, and he kept trying to stop it—oh ! Kit—by kissing it. [*She pauses, stifled by emotion.*] Then I heard Wreford laugh, and say vultures didn't touch live bodies. And there came a voice, from somewhere, calling out : " Oh ! God ! I'm dying ! " And Wreford began to swear at it, and I heard Hubert say : " Don't, Wreford ; let the poor fellow be ! " But the voice went on and on, moaning and crying out : " I'll lie here all night dying—and then I'll die ! " And Wreford dragged himself along the ground ; his face all devilish, like a man who's going to kill.

KATHERINE. My dear ! How ghastly !

HELEN. Still that voice went on, and I saw Wreford take up the dead man's gun. Then Hubert got upon his feet, and went tottering along, so feebly, so dreadfully—but before he could reach and stop him, Wreford fired at the man who was crying. And Hubert called out : " You brute ! " and fell right down. And when Wreford saw him lying there, he began to moan and sob, but Hubert never stirred. Then it all got black again—and I could see a dark woman-thing creeping, first to the man without a head ; then to Wreford ; then to Hubert, and it touched him, and sprang away. And it cried out : " A—ai—ah ! " [*Pointing out at the mist.*] Look ! Out there ! The dark things !

KATHERINE. [*Putting her arms round her*] Yes, dear, yes ! You must have been looking at the mist.

HELEN. [*Strangely calm*] He's dead !

KATHERINE. It was only a dream.

HELEN. You didn't hear that cry. [*She listens.*] That's Stephen. For-give me, Kit ; I oughtn't to have upset you, but I couldn't help coming.

> [*She goes out.* KATHERINE, *into whom her emotion seems to have passed, turns feverishly to the window, throws it open and leans out.* MORE *comes in.*

MORE. Kit !

> [*Catching sight of her figure in the window, he goes quickly to her.*

KATHERINE. Ah.   [*She has mastered her emotion.*

MORE. Let me look at you !

> [*He draws her from the window to the candlelight, and looks long at her.*

MORE. What have you done to your hair ?

KATHERINE. Nothing.

More. It's wonderful to-night.

          [*He takes it greedily and buries his face in it.*

Katherine. [*Drawing her hair away*] Well ?

More. At last !

Katherine. [*Pointing to* Olive's *room*] Hssh ?

More. How is she ?

Katherine. All right.

More. And you ?   [Katherine *shrugs her shoulders.*

More. Six weeks !

Katherine. Why have you come ?

More. Why !

Katherine. You begin again the day after to-morrow. Was it worth while ?

More. Kit !

Katherine. It makes it harder for me, that's all.

More. [*Staring at her*] What's come to you ?

Katherine. Six weeks is a long time to sit and read about your meetings.

More. Put that away to-night. [*He touches her.*] This is what travellers feel when they come out of the desert to—water.

Katherine. [*Suddenly noticing the cut on his forehead*] Your forehead ! It's cut.

More. It's nothing.

Katherine. Oh !   Let me bathe it !

More. No, dear !   It's all right.

Katherine. [*Turning away*] Helen has just been telling me a dream she's had of Hubert's death.

More. Poor child !

Katherine. Dream bad dreams, and wait, and hide oneself—there's been nothing else to do.   Nothing, Stephen—nothing !

More. Hide ?   Because of me ?   [Katherine *nods.*

More. [*With a movement of distress*] I see.   I thought from your letters you were coming to feel—— Kit !   You look so lovely !

        [*Suddenly he sees that she is crying, and goes quickly to her.*

More. My dear, don't cry !   God knows I don't want to make things worse for you.   I'll go away.

      [*She draws away from him a little, and after looking long at her, he sits down at the dressing-table and begins turning over the brushes and articles of toilet, trying to find words.*

More. Never look forward.   After the time I've had—I thought—to-night—it would be summer—I thought it would be you—and everything !

      [*While he is speaking* Katherine *has stolen closer.   She suddenly drops on her knees by his side and wraps his hand in her hair. He turns and clasps her.*

MORE. Kit!

KATHERINE. Ah! yes. But—to-morrow it begins again. Oh! Stephen! How long—how long am I to be torn in two? [*Drawing back in his arms.*] I can't—can't bear it.

MORE. My darling!

KATHERINE. Give it up! For my sake! Give it up! [*Pressing closer to him.*] It shall be me—and everything——

MORE. God!

KATHERINE. It *shall* be—if—if——

MORE. [*Aghast*] You're not making terms? Bargaining? For God's sake, Kit!

KATHERINE. For God's sake, Stephen!

MORE. You!—of all people—you!

KATHERINE. Stephen!

[*For a moment* MORE *yields utterly, then shrinks back.*

MORE. A bargain! It's selling my soul!

[*He struggles out of her arms, gets up, and stands without speaking, staring at her, and wiping the sweat from his forehead. KATHERINE remains some seconds on her knees, gazing up at him, not realizing. Then her head droops; she too gets up and stands apart, with her wrapper drawn close round her. It is as if a cold and deadly shame had come to them both. Quite suddenly MORE turns, and, without looking back, feebly makes his way out of the room. When he is gone KATHERINE drops on her knees and remains there motionless, huddled in her chair.*

The curtain falls.

ACT IV

It is between lights, the following day, in the dining-room of More's *house. The windows are closed, but curtains are not drawn.* Steel *is seated at the bureau, writing a letter from* More's *dictation.*

Steel. [*Reading over the letter*] "No doubt we shall have trouble. But, if the town authorities at the last minute forbid the use of the hall, we'll hold the meeting in the open. Let bills be got out, and an audience will collect in any case."

More. They will.

Steel. "Yours truly"; I've signed for you. [More *nods.*

Steel. [*Blotting and enveloping the letter*] You know the servants have all given notice—except Henry.

More. Poor Henry!

Steel. It's partly nerves, of course—the windows have been broken twice—but it's partly——

More. Patriotism. Quite! they'll do the next smashing themselves. That reminds me—to-morrow *you* begin holiday, Steel.

Steel. Oh, no!

More. My dear fellow—yes. Last night ended your sulphur cure. Truly sorry ever to have let you in for it.

Steel. Someone must do the work. You're half dead as it is.

More. There's lots of kick in me.

Steel. Give it up, sir. The odds are too great. It isn't worth it.

More. To fight to a finish; knowing you must be beaten—is anything better worth it?

Steel. Well, then, I'm not going.

More. This is my private hell, Steel; you don't roast in it any longer. Believe me, it's a great comfort to hurt no one but yourself.

Steel. I *can't* leave you, sir.

More. My dear boy, you're a brick—but we've got off by a miracle so far, and I can't have the responsibility of you any longer. Hand me over that correspondence about to-morrow's meeting.

[Steel *takes some papers from his pocket, but does not hand them.*

More. Come! [*He stretches out his hand for the papers.* As Steel *still draws back he says more sharply.*] Give them to me, Steel! [Steel *hands them over.*] Now, that ends it, d'you see?

[*They stand looking at each other; then* Steel, *very much upset,*

406

turns and goes out of the room. MORE, *who has watched him with a sorry smile, puts the papers into a dispatch-case. As he is closing the bureau, the footman* HENRY *enters, announcing:* "Mr. Mendip, sir." MENDIP *comes in, and the* FOOTMAN *withdraws.* MORE *turns to his visitor, but does not hold out his hand.*

MENDIP. [*Taking* MORE's *hand*] Give me credit for a little philosophy, my friend. Mrs. More told me you'd be back to-day. Have you heard?

MORE. What?

MENDIP. There's been a victory.

MORE. Thank God!

MENDIP. Ah! So you actually are flesh and blood.

MORE. Yes!

MENDIP. Take off the martyr's shirt, Stephen. You're only flouting human nature.

MORE. So—even you defend the mob!

MENDIP. My dear fellow, you're up against the strongest common instinct in the world. What do you expect? That the man in the street should be a Quixote? That his love of country should express itself in philosophic altruism? What on earth do you expect? Men are very simple creatures; and Mob is just conglomerate essence of simple men.

MORE. Conglomerate *excrescence*. Mud of street and market-place gathered in a torrent—This blind howling "patriotism"—what each man feels in here? [*He touches his breast.*] No!

MENDIP. You think men go beyond instinct—they don't. All they know is that something's hurting that image of themselves that they call country. They just feel something big and religious, and go it blind.

MORE. This used to be the country of free speech. It used to be the country where a man was expected to hold to his faith.

MENDIP. There are limits to human nature, Stephen.

MORE. Let no man stand to his guns in face of popular attack. Still your advice, is it?

MENDIP. My advice is: Get out of town at once. The torrent you speak of will be let loose the moment this news is out. Come, my dear fellow, don't stay here!

MORE. Thanks! I'll see that Katherine and Olive go.

MENDIP. Go with them! If your cause is lost, that's no reason why *you* should be.

MORE. There's the comfort of not running away. And—I want comfort.

MENDIP. This is bad, Stephen; bad, foolish—foolish! Well! I'm going to the House. This way?

MORE. Down the steps, and through the gate. Good-bye!

[KATHERINE *has come in followed by* NURSE, *hatted and cloaked,*
with a small bag in her hand. KATHERINE *takes from the*
bureau a cheque which she hands to the NURSE. MORE *comes*
in from the terrace.

MORE. You're wise to go, Nurse.

NURSE. You've treated my poor dear badly, sir. Where's your
heart?

MORE. In full use.

NURSE. On those heathens. Don't your own hearth and home
come first? Your wife that was born in time of war, with her own
father fighting, and her grandfather killed for his country. A bitter
thing, to have the windows of her house broken, and be pointed at
by the boys in the street.

[MORE *stands silent under this attack, looking at his wife.*

KATHERINE. Nurse!

NURSE. It's unnatural, sir—what you're doing! To think more
of those savages than of your own wife! Look at her! Did you
ever see her look like that? Take care, sir, before it's too late!

MORE. Enough, please!

[NURSE *stands for a moment, doubtful; looks long at* KATHERINE;
then goes.

MORE. [*Quietly*] There has been a victory.   [*He goes out.*

[KATHERINE *is breathing fast, listening to the distant hum and stir*
rising in the street. She runs to the window as the footman,
HENRY, *entering, says:* " Sir John Julian, ma'am! " SIR
JOHN *comes in, a newspaper in his hand.*

KATHERINE. At last! A victory!

SIR JOHN. Thank God!   [*He hands her the paper.*

KATHERINE. Oh, Dad.

[*She tears the paper open, and feverishly reads.*

KATHERINE. At last!

[*The distant hum in the street is rising steadily. But* SIR JOHN,
after the one exultant moment when he handed her the paper,
stares dumbly at the floor.

KATHERINE. [*Suddenly conscious of his gravity*] Father!

SIR JOHN. There is other news.

KATHERINE. One of the boys! Hubert? [SIR JOHN *bows his head.*

KATHERINE. Killed?   [SIR JOHN *again bows his head.*

KATHERINE. The dream. [*She covers her face.*] Poor Helen!

[*They stand for a few seconds silent, then* SIR JOHN *raises his head,*
and putting up a hand, touches her wet cheek.

SIR JOHN. [*Huskily*] Whom the gods love——

KATHERINE. Hubert!

SIR JOHN. And hulks like me go on living!

KATHERINE. Dear Dad!

SIR JOHN. But we shall drive the ruffians now! We shall break them. Stephen back?

KATHERINE. Last night.

SIR JOHN. Has he finished his blasphemous speech-making at last? [KATHERINE *shakes her head.*] Not?

[*Then, seeing that* KATHERINE *is quivering with emotion, he strokes her hand.*

SIR JOHN. My dear! Death is in many houses!

KATHERINE. I must go to Helen. Tell Stephen, Father. I can't.

SIR JOHN. If you wish, child.

[*She goes out, leaving* SIR JOHN *to his grave, puzzled grief; and in a few seconds* MORE *comes in.*

MORE. Yes, Sir John. You wanted me?

SIR JOHN. Hubert is killed.

MORE. Hubert!

SIR JOHN. By these—whom you uphold. Katherine asked me to let you know. She's gone to Helen. I understand you only came back last night from your—— No word I can use would give what I feel about that. I don't know how things stand now between you and Katherine; but I tell you this, Stephen; you've tried her these last two months beyond what any woman ought to bear!

[MORE *makes a gesture of pain.*

SIR JOHN. When you chose your course——

MORE. Chose!

SIR JOHN. You placed yourself in opposition to every feeling in her. You knew this might come. It may come again with another of my sons——

MORE. I would willingly change places with any one of them.

SIR JOHN. Yes—I can believe in your unhappiness. I cannot conceive of greater misery than to be arrayed against your country. If I could have Hubert back, I would not have him at such a price—no, nor all my sons. *Pro patriâ mori*—— My boy, at all events, is happy!

MORE. Yes!

SIR JOHN. Yet you can go on doing what you are! What devil of pride has got into you, Stephen?

MORE. Do you imagine I think myself better than the humblest private fighting out there? Not for a minute.

SIR JOHN. I don't understand you. I always thought you devoted to Katherine.

MORE. Sir John, you believe that country comes before wife and child?

SIR JOHN. I do.

MORE. So do I.

SIR JOHN. [*Bewildered*] Whatever my country does or leaves

14

undone, I no more presume to judge her than I presume to judge my God. [*With all the exaltation of the suffering he has undergone for her.*] My country !

MORE. I would give all I have—for that creed.

SIR JOHN. [*Puzzled*] Stephen, I've never looked on you as a crank ; I always believed you sane and honest. But this is—visionary mania.

MORE. Vision of what might be.

SIR JOHN. Why can't you be content with what the grandest nation—the grandest men on earth have found good enough for them ? I've known them, I've seen what they could suffer, for our country.

MORE. Sir John, imagine what the last two months have been to me ! To see people turn away in the street—old friends pass me as if I were a wall ! To dread the post ! To go to bed every night with the sound of hooting in my ears ! To know that my name is never referred to without contempt——

SIR JOHN. You have your new friends. Plenty of them, I understand.

MORE. Does that make up for being spat at as I was last night ? Your battles are fool's play to it.

[*The stir and rustle of the crowd in the street grows louder.* SIR JOHN *turns his head towards it.*

SIR JOHN. You've heard there's been a victory. Do you carry your unnatural feeling so far as to be sorry for that ? [MORE *shakes his head.*] That's something ! For God's sake, Stephen, stop before it's gone past mending. Don't ruin your life with Katherine. Hubert was her favourite brother. You are backing those who killed him. Think what that means to her ! Drop this—mad Quixotism—idealism —whatever you call it. Take Katherine away. Leave the country till the thing's over—this country of yours that you're opposing, and—and—traducing. Take her away ! Come ! What good are you doing ? What earthly good ? Come, my boy ! Before you're utterly undone.

MORE. Sir John ! Our men are dying out there for the faith that's in them ! I believe my faith the higher, the better for mankind—— Am I to slink away ? Since I began this campaign I've found hundreds who've thanked me for taking this stand. They look on me now as their leader. Am I to desert them ? When you led your forlorn hope—did you ask yourself what good you were doing, or whether you'd come through alive ? It's my forlorn hope not to betray those who are following me ; and not to help let die a fire—a fire that's sacred—not only now in this country, but in all countries, for all time.

SIR JOHN. [*After a long stare*] I give you credit for believing what you say. But let me tell you whatever that fire you talk of—I'm too old-fashioned to grasp—one fire you *are* letting die—your wife's love. By God ! This crew of your new friends, this crew of cranks and jays, if they can make up to you for the loss of her love—of your career, of all those who used to like and respect you—so much the better for you. But if you find yourself bankrupt of affection—alone as the last man on earth; if this business ends in your utter ruin and destruction—as it must—I shall not pity—I cannot pity you. Good night!

[*He marches to the door, opens it, and goes out.* MORE *is left standing perfectly still. The stir and murmur of the street is growing all the time, and slowly forces itself on his consciousness. He goes to the bay window and looks out; then rings the bell. It is not answered, and after turning up the lights, he rings again.* KATHERINE *comes in. She is wearing a black hat, and black outdoor coat. She speaks coldly without looking up.*]

KATHERINE. You rang!

MORE. For them to shut this room up.

KATHERINE. The servants have gone out. They're afraid of the house being set on fire.

MORE. I see.

KATHERINE. They have not your ideals to sustain them. [MORE *winces.*] I am going with Helen and Olive to Father's.

MORE. [*Trying to take in the exact sense of her words*] Good! You prefer that to an hotel? [KATHERINE *nods. Gently.*] Will you let me say, Kit, how terribly I feel for you—Hubert's——

KATHERINE. Don't! I ought to have made what I meant plainer. I am not coming back.

MORE. Not——? Not while the house——

KATHERINE. Not—at all.

MORE. Kit!

KATHERINE. I warned you from the first. You've gone too far!

MORE. [*Terribly moved*] Do you understand what this means? After ten years—and all—our love!

KATHERINE. *Was* it love? How could you ever have loved one so unheroic as myself!

MORE. This is madness, Kit—Kit!

KATHERINE. Last night I was ready. You couldn't. If you couldn't then, you never can. You are very exalted, Stephen. I don't like living,—I won't live, with one whose equal I am not. This has been coming ever since you made that speech. I told you that night what the end would be.

MORE. [*Trying to put his arms round her*] Don't be so terribly cruel!

KATHERINE. No! Let's have the truth! People so wide apart don't love! Let me go!

MORE. In God's name, how can I help the difference in our faiths!

KATHERINE. Last night you used the word—bargain. Quite right. I meant to buy you. I meant to kill your faith. You showed me what I was doing. I don't like to be shown up as a driver of bargains, Stephen.

MORE. God knows—I never meant——

KATHERINE. If I'm not yours in spirit—I don't choose to be your —mistress.

[MORE, *as if lashed by a whip, has thrown up his hands in an attitude of defence.*

KATHERINE. Yes, that's cruel ! It shows the heights you live on. I won't drag you down.

MORE. For God's sake, put your pride away, and *see !* I'm fighting for the faith that's in me. What else can a man do ? What else ? Ah ! Kit ! Do see !

KATHERINE. I'm strangled here ! Doing nothing—sitting silent —when my brothers are fighting, and being killed. I shall try to go out nursing. Helen will come with me. I have my faith, too ; my poor common love of country. I can't stay here with you. I spent last night on the floor—thinking—and I know !

MORE. And Olive ?

KATHERINE. I shall leave her at Father's, with Nurse ; unless you forbid me to take her. You can.

MORE. [*Icily*] That I shall not do—you know very well. You are free to go, and to take her.

KATHERINE. [*Very low*] Thank you ! [*Suddenly, she turns to him, and draws his eyes on her. Without a sound, she puts her whole strength into that look.*] Stephen ! Give it up ! Come down to me !

[*The festive sounds from the street grow louder. There can be heard the blowing of whistles, and bladders, and all the sounds of joy.*

MORE. And drown in—*that ?*

[KATHERINE *turns swiftly to the door. There she stands and again looks at him. Her face is mysterious, from the conflicting currents of her emotions.*

MORE. So—you're going ?

KATHERINE. [*In a whisper*] Yes.

[*She bends her head, opens the door, and goes.* MORE *starts forward as if to follow her, but* OLIVE *has appeared in the doorway. She has on a straight little white coat and a round white cap.*

OLIVE. Aren't you coming with us, Daddy ? [MORE *shakes his head.*

OLIVE. Why not ?

MORE. Never mind, my dicky bird.

OLIVE. The motor'll have to go very slow. There are such a lot of people in the street. Are you staying to stop them setting the house on fire ? [MORE *nods.*] May I stay a little, too ? [MORE *shakes his head.*] Why ?

MORE. [*Putting his hand on her head*] Go along, my pretty !

OLIVE. Oh ! love me up, Daddy !   [MORE *takes and loves her up.*

OLIVE. Oo-o!

MORE. Trot, my soul!

[*She goes, looks back at him, turns suddenly and vanishes.*

[MORE *follows her to the door, but stops there. Then, as full
realization begins to dawn on him, he runs to the bay window,
craning his head to catch sight of the front door. There is
the sound of a vehicle starting, and the continual hooting of its
horn as it makes its way among the crowd. He turns from the
window.*

MORE. Alone as the last man on earth!

[*Suddenly a voice rises clear out of the hurly-burly in the street.*

VOICE. There 'e is! That's 'im! More! Traitor! More!

[*A shower of nutshells, orange-peel, and harmless missiles begins
to rattle against the glass of the window. Many voices take
up the groaning:* "More! Traitor! Blackleg! More!"
*And through the window can be seen waving flags and lighted
Chinese lanterns swinging high on long bamboos. The din of
execration swells.* MORE *stands unheeding, still gazing after
the cab. Then, with a sharp crack, a flung stone crashes
through one of the panes. It is followed by a hoarse shout of
laughter, and a hearty groan. A second stone crashes through
the glass.* MORE *turns for a moment, with a contemptuous
look, towards the street, and the flare of the Chinese lanterns
lights up his face. Then, as if forgetting all about the din
outside, he moves back into the room, looks round him, and
lets his head droop. The din rises louder and louder; a third
stone crashes through.* MORE *raises his head again, and,
clasping his hands, looks straight before him. The footman,*
HENRY, *entering, hastens to the French windows.*

MORE. Ah! Henry, I thought you'd gone.

FOOTMAN. I came back, sir.

MORE. Good fellow!

FOOTMAN. They're trying to force the terrace gate, sir. They've
no business coming on to private property—no matter what!

[*In the surging entrance of the mob the footman,* HENRY, *who shows
fight, is overwhelmed, hustled out into the crowd on the terrace,
and no more seen. The* MOB *is a mixed crowd of revellers of
both sexes, medical students, clerks, shopmen and girls, and a
Boy Scout or two. Many have exchanged hats—some wear
masks, or false noses, some carry feathers or tin whistles.
Some with bamboos and Chinese lanterns, swing them up
outside on the terrace. The medley of noises is very great.
Such ring-leaders as exist in the confusion are a* GROUP OF
STUDENTS, *the chief of whom, conspicuous because unadorned,
is an athletic hatless young man with a projecting under-jaw*

*and heavy coal-black moustache, who seems with the swing of
his huge arms and shoulders to sway the currents of motion.
When the first surge of noise and movement subsides, he calls
out:* "To him, boys! Chair the hero!" THE
STUDENTS *rush at the impassive* MORE, *swing him roughly
on to their shoulders and bear him round the room. When
they have twice circled the table to the music of their confused
singing, groans and whistling,* THE CHIEF OF THE STUDENTS
calls out: "Put him down!" *Obediently they set him down
on the table which has been forced into the bay window, and
stand gaping up at him.*

CHIEF STUDENT. Speech! Speech!

[*The noise ebbs, and* MORE *looks round him.*

CHIEF STUDENT. Now then, you, sir.

MORE. [*In a quiet voice*] Very well. You are here by the law that
governs the action of all mobs—the law of Force. By that law, you
can do what you like to this body of mine.

A VOICE. And we will, too.

MORE. I don't doubt it. But before that, I've a word to say.

A VOICE. You've always that.

[ANOTHER VOICE *raises a donkey's braying.*

MORE. You—Mob—are the most contemptible thing under the
sun. When you walk the street—God goes in.

CHIEF STUDENT. Be careful, you—sir.

VOICES. Down him! Down with the beggar!

MORE. [*Above the murmurs*] My fine friends, I'm not afraid of you.
You've forced your way into my house, and you've asked me to
speak. Put up with the truth for once! [*His words rush out.*] You
are the thing that pelts the weak; kicks women; howls down free
speech. This to-day, and that to-morrow. Brain—you have none.
Spirit—not the ghost of it! If you're not meanness, there's no such
thing. If you're not cowardice, there is no cowardice. [*Above the
growing fierceness of the hubbub.*] Patriotism—there are two kinds—that
of our soldiers, and this of mine. You have neither!

CHIEF STUDENT. [*Checking a dangerous rush*] Hold on! Hold on!
[*To* MORE.] Swear to utter no more blasphemy against your country:
Swear it!

CROWD. Ah! Ay! Ah!

MORE. My country is not yours. Mine is that great country which
shall never take toll from the weakness of others. [*Above the groaning.*] Ah! you can break my head and my windows; but don't think
that you can break my faith. You could never break or shake it, if
you were a million to one.

[*A girl with dark eyes and hair all wild, leaps out from the crowd
and shakes her fist at him.*

GIRL. You're friends with them that killed my lad! [MORE *smiles down at her, and she swiftly plucks the knife from the belt of a Boy Scout beside her.*] Smile, you—cur!

> [*A violent rush and heave from behind flings* MORE *forward on to the steel. He reels, staggers back, and falls down amongst the crowd. A scream, a sway, a rush, a hubbub of cries. The* CHIEF STUDENT *shouts above the riot:* " Steady! " *Another:* " My God! He's got it! "*

CHIEF STUDENT. Give him air!

> [*The crowd falls back, and two* STUDENTS, *bending over* MORE, *lift his arms and head, but they fall like lead. Desperately they test him for life.*

CHIEF STUDENT. By the lord, it's over!

> [*Then begins a scared swaying out towards the window. Someone turns out the lights, and in the darkness the crowd fast melts away. The body of* MORE *lies in the gleam from a single Chinese lantern. Muttering the words:* " Poor devil! He kept his end up anyway! " *the* CHIEF STUDENT *picks from the floor a little abandoned Union Jack and lays it on* MORE'S *breast. Then he, too, turns, and rushes out.*

> [*And the body of* MORE *lies in the streak of light; and the noises in the street continue to rise.*

The curtain falls, but rises again almost at once.

AFTERMATH

A late Spring dawn is just breaking. Against trees in leaf and blossom, with the houses of a London Square beyond, suffused by the spreading glow, is seen a dark life-size statue on a granite pedestal. In front is the broad, dust-dim pavement. The light grows till the central words around the pedestal can be clearly read :

ERECTED
To the Memory
of
STEPHEN MORE
" Faithful to his ideal "

High above, the face of MORE *looks straight before him with a faint smile. On one shoulder, and on his bare head, two sparrows have perched, and from the gardens, behind, come the twittering and singing of birds.*

The curtain falls.

A BIT O' LOVE

14*

CAST OF THE ORIGINAL PRODUCTION AT THE
KINGSWAY THEATRE, MAY 25, 1915

MICHAEL STRANGWAY	*Mr. William Armstrong*
BEATRICE STRANGWAY	*Miss Madge McIntosh*
MRS. BRADMERE	*Miss Edith Barwell*
JIM BERE	*Mr. Wilfred E. Shine*
JACK CREMER	*Mr. Frank Randell*
MRS. BURLACOMBE	*Miss Alice Mansfield*
BURLACOMBE	*Mr. Frank Cremlin*
TRUSTAFORD	*Mr. Percy Marmont*
JARLAND	*Mr. William Dexter*
CLYST	*Mr. Lawrence Hanray*
FREMAN	*Mr. Bryan G. Powley*
GODLEIGH	*Mr. Charles R. Stone*
SOL POTTER	*Mr. Harvey Adams*
MORSE	*Mr. Arthur C. Rose*
BOBBIE JARLAND	*Mr. Osmund Willson*
MERCY JARLAND	*Miss Estelle Winwood*
TIBBY JARLAND	*Miss Blanche Fingleston*
IVY BURLACOMBE	*Miss Edith Smith*
CONNIE TRUSTAFORD . . .	*Miss Doris Lloyd*
GLADYS FREMAN	*Miss Eileen Thorndike*

ACT I

*It is Ascension Day in a village of the West. In the low panelled hall
sitting-room of the* BURLACOMBES' *farmhouse on the village green,*
MICHAEL STRANGWAY, *a clerical collar round his throat and a dark
Norfolk jacket on his back, is playing the flute before a very large framed
photograph of a woman, which is the only picture on the walls. His age
is about thirty-five; his figure thin and very upright and his clean-shorn
face thin, upright, narrow, with long and rather pointed ears; his dark
hair is brushed in a coxcomb off his forehead. A faint smile hovers
about his lips that Nature has made rather full and he has made thin,
as though keeping a hard secret; but his bright grey eyes, dark round
the rim, look out and upwards almost as if he were being crucified. There
is something about the whole of him that makes him seem not quite
present. A gentle creature, burnt within.*

*A low, broad window above a window-seat forms the background to his
figure; and through its lattice panes are seen the outer gate and yew-trees
of a churchyard and the porch of a church, bathed in May sunlight. The
front door at right angles to the window-seat, leads to the village green,
and a door on the left into the house.*

It is the third movement of Veracini's violin sonata that STRANGWAY
*plays. His back is turned to the door into the house, and he does not
hear when it is opened, and* IVY BURLACOMBE, *the farmer's daughter,
a girl of fourteen, small and quiet as a mouse, comes in, a prayer-book
in one hand, and in the other a glass of water, with wild orchis and a
bit of deep pink hawthorn. She sits down on the window-seat, and
having opened her book, sniffs at the flowers. Coming to the end of the
movement* STRANGWAY *stops, and looking up at the face on the wall,
heaves a long sigh.*

IVY [*From the seat*] I picked these for yü, Mr. Strangway.

STRANGWAY. [*Turning with a start*] Ah! Ivy. Thank you. [*He
puts his flute down on a chair against the far wall.*] Where are the
others?

> [*As he speaks,* GLADYS FREMAN, *a dark gipsyish girl, and* CONNIE
> TRUSTAFORD, *a fair, stolid, blue-eyed Saxon, both about sixteen,
> come in through the front door, behind which they have evidently
> been listening. They too have prayer-books in their hands.
> They sidle past* IVY, *and also sit down under the window.*

GLADYS. Mercy's comin', Mr. Strangway.

STRANGWAY. Good morning, Gladys; good morning, Connie.

[*He turns to a book-case on a table against the far wall, and taking out a book, finds his place in it. While he stands thus with his back to the girls,* MERCY JARLAND *comes in from the green. She also is about sixteen, with fair hair and china-blue eyes. She glides in quickly, hiding something behind her, and sits down on the seat next the door. And at once there is a whispering.*]

STRANGWAY. [*Turning to them*] Good morning, Mercy.

MERCY. Good morning, Mr. Strangway.

STRANGWAY. Now, yesterday I was telling you what our Lord's coming meant to the world. I want you to understand that before He came there wasn't really love, as we know it. I don't mean to say that there weren't many good people; but there wasn't love for the sake of loving. D'you think you understand what I mean?

[MERCY *fidgets.* GLADYS'S *eyes are following a fly.*]

IVY. Yes, Mr. Strangway.

STRANGWAY. It isn't enough to love people because they're good to you, or because in some way or other you're going to get something by it. We have to love because we love loving. That's the great thing—without that we're nothing but pagans.

GLADYS. Please, what is pagans?

STRANGWAY. That's what the first Christians called the people who lived in the villages and were not yet Christians, Gladys.

MERCY. We live in a village, but we're Christians.

STRANGWAY. [*With a smile*] Yes, Mercy; and what is a Christian?

[MERCY *kicks a foot sideways against her neighbour, frowns over her china-blue eyes, is silent; then, as his question passes on, makes a quick little face, wriggles, and looks behind her.*]

STRANGWAY. Ivy?

IVY. 'Tis a man—whü—whü——

STRANGWAY. Yes?—Connie?

CONNIE. [*Who speaks rather thickly, as if she had a permanent slight cold*] Please, Mr. Strangway, 'tis a man whü goes to church.

GLADYS. He 'as to be baptized—and confirmed; and—and—buried.

IVY. 'Tis a man whü—whü's güde and——

GLADYS. He don't drink, an' he don't beat his horses, an' he don't hit back.

MERCY. [*Whispering*] 'Tisn't your turn. [*To* STRANGWAY.] 'Tis a man like us.

IVY. I know what Mrs. Strangway said it was, cause I asked her once, before she went away.

STRANGWAY. [*Startled*] Yes?

IVY. She said it was a man whü forgave everything.

STRANGWAY. Ah!

> [*The note of a cuckoo comes travelling. The girls are gazing at* STRANGWAY, *who seems to have gone off into a dream. They begin to fidget and whisper.*

CONNIE. Please, Mr. Strangway, father says if yü hit a man and he don't hit yü back, he's no güde at all.

MERCY. When Tommy Morse wouldn't fight, us pinched him—he did squeal! [*She giggles.*] Made me laugh!

STRANGWAY. Did I ever tell you about St. Francis of Assisi?

IVY. [*Clasping her hands*] No.

STRANGWAY. Well, *he* was the best Christian, I think, that ever lived—simply full of love and joy.

IVY. I expect he's dead.

STRANGWAY. About seven hundred years, Ivy.

IVY. [*Softly*] Oh!

STRANGWAY. Everything to him was brother or sister—the sun and the moon, and all that was poor and weak and sad, and animals and birds, so that they even used to follow him about.

MERCY. I know! He had crumbs in his pocket.

STRANGWAY. No; he had love in his eyes.

IVY. 'Tis like about Orpheus, that yü told us.

STRANGWAY. Ah! But St. Francis was a Christian, and Orpheus was a pagan!

IVY. Oh!

STRANGWAY. Orpheus drew everything after him with music; St. Francis by love.

IVY. Perhaps it was the same, really.

STRANGWAY. [*Looking at his flute*] Perhaps it was, Ivy.

GLADYS. Did 'e 'ave a flute like yü?

IVY. The flowers smell sweeter when they 'ear music; they dü.

> [*She holds up the glass of flowers.*

STRANGWAY. [*Touching one of the orchis*] What's the name of this one?

> [*The girls cluster, save* MERCY, *who is taking a stealthy interest in what she has behind her.*

CONNIE. We call it a cuckoo, Mr. Strangway.

GLADYS. 'Tis awful common down by the streams. We've got one medder where 'tis so thick almost as the goldie cups.

STRANGWAY. Odd! I've never noticed it.

IVY. Please, Mr. Strangway, yü don't notice when yü're walkin'; yü go along like this. [*She holds up her face as one looking at the sky.*

STRANGWAY. Bad as that, Ivy?

IVY. Mrs. Strangway often used to pick it last spring.

STRANGWAY. Did she? Did she?

> [*He has gone off again into a kind of dream.*

MERCY. I like being confirmed.

STRANGWAY. Ah! Yes. Now—— What's that behind you, Mercy?

MERCY. [*Engagingly producing a cage a little bigger than a mouse-trap, containing a skylark*] My skylark.

STRANGWAY. What!

MERCY. It can fly; but we're goin' to clip its wings. Bobbie caught it.

STRANGWAY. How long ago?

MERCY. [*Conscious of impending disaster*] Yesterday.

STRANGWAY. [*White hot*] Give me the cage.

MERCY. [*Puckering*] I want my skylark. [*As he steps up to her and takes the cage—thoroughly alarmed.*] I gave Bobby thrippence for it!

STRANGWAY. [*Producing a sixpence*] There!

MERCY. [*Throwing it down—passionately*] I want my skylark!

STRANGWAY. God made this poor bird for the sky and the grass. And you put it in *that*! Never cage any wild thing! Never!

MERCY. [*Faint and sullen*] I want my skylark.

STRANGWAY. [*Taking the cage to the door*] No! [*He holds up the cage and opens it.*] Off you go, poor thing! [*The bird flies out and away.*
[*The girls watch with round eyes the fling up of his arm, and the freed bird flying away.*

IVY. I'm glad!

[MERCY *kicks her viciously and sobs.* STRANGWAY *comes from the door, looks at* MERCY *sobbing, and suddenly clasps his head. The girls watch him with a queer mixture of wonder, alarm, and disapproval.*

GLADYS. [*Whispering*] Don't cry, Mercy. Bobbie'll soon catch yü another.

[STRANGWAY *has dropped his hands, and is looking again at* MERCY. IVY *sits with hands clasped, gazing at* STRANGWAY. MERCY *continues her artificial sobbing.*

STRANGWAY. [*Quietly*] The class is over for to-day.

[*He goes up to* MERCY, *and holds out his hand. She does not take it, and runs out knuckling her eyes.* STRANGWAY *turns on his heel and goes into the house.*

CONNIE. 'Twasn't his bird.

IVY. Skylarks belong to the sky. Mr. Strangway said so.

GLADYS. Not when they'm caught, they don't.

IVY. They dü.

CONNIE. 'Twas her bird.

IVY. He gave her sixpence for it.

GLADYS. She didn't take it.

CONNIE. There it is on the ground.

Ivy. She might have.

GLADYS. He'll p'raps take my squirrel, tü.

Ivy. The bird sang—I 'eard it !   Right up in the sky.   It wouldn't have sanged if it weren't glad.

GLADYS. Well, Mercy cried.

Ivy. I don't care.

GLADYS. 'Tis a shame !   And I know something.   Mrs. Strangway's at Durford.

CONNIE. She's—never !

GLADYS. I saw her yesterday.   An' if she's there she ought to be here.   I told mother, an' she said : " Yü mind yer business."   An' when she goes in to market to-morrow she'm goin' to see.   An' if she's really there, mother says, 'tis a fine tü-dü an' a praaper scandal. So *I* know a lot more'n yü dü.   [Ivy *stares at her.*

CONNIE. Mrs. Strangway told mother she was goin' to France for the winter because her mother was ill.

GLADYS. 'Tisn't winter now—Ascension Day.   I saw her comin' out o' Dr. Desart's house.   I know 'twas her because she had on a blue dress an' a proud lüke.   Mother says the doctor come over here tü often before Mrs. Strangway went away, just afore Christmas. They was old sweethearts before she married Mr. Strangway.   [*To* Ivy.] 'Twas yüre mother told mother that.

                          [Ivy *gazes at them more and more wide-eyed.*

CONNIE. Father says if Mrs. Bradmere an' the old Rector knew about the doctor, they wouldn't 'ave Mr. Strangway 'ere for curate any longer ;   because mother says it takes more'n a year for a güde wife to leave her 'usband, an' 'e so fond of her.   But 'tisn't no business of ours, father says.

GLADYS. Mother says so tü.   She's praaper set against gossip. She'll know all about it to-morrow after market.

Ivy. [*Stamping her foot*] I don't want to 'ear nothin' at all ; I don't, an' I won't.   [*A rather shame-faced silence falls on the girls.*

GLADYS. [*In a quick whisper*] 'Ere's Mrs. Burlacombe.

     [*There enters from the house a stout motherly woman with a round
           grey eye and very red cheeks.*

MRS. BURLACOMBE. Ivy, take Mr. Strangway his ink, or we'll never 'ave no sermon to-night.   He'm in his thinkin' box, but 'tis not a bit o' yüse 'im thinkin' without 'is ink.   [*She hands her daughter an inkpot and blotting-pad.*]   Ivy *takes them and goes out.*   Whatever's this ?   [*She picks up the little bird-cage.*

GLADYS. 'Tis Mercy Jarland's.   Mr. Strangway let her skylark go.

MRS. BURLACOMBE. Aw !   Did 'e now ?   Serve 'er right, bringin' an 'eathen bird to confirmation class.

CONNIE. I'll take it to her.

Mrs. Burlacombe. No. Yü leave it there, an' let Mr. Strangway dü what 'e likes with it. Bringin' a bird like that! Well, I never!

[*The girls, perceiving that they have lighted on stony soil, look at each other and slide towards the door.*

Mrs. Burlacombe. Yes, yü just be off, an' think on what yü've been told in class, an' be'ave like Christians, that's güde maids. An' don't yü come no more in the avenin's dancin' them 'eathen dances in my barn, naighther, till after yü'm confirmed—'tisn't right. I've told Ivy I won't 'ave it.

Connie. Mr. Strangway don't mind—he likes us to; 'twas Mrs. Strangway began teachin' us. He's goin' to give a prize.

Mrs. Burlacombe. Yü just dü what I tell yü an' never mind Mr. Strangway—he'm tü kind to everyone. D'yü think I don't know how gells oughter be'ave before confirmation? Yü be'ave like I did! Now, goo ahn! Shoo!

[*She hustles them out, rather as she might hustle her chickens, and begins tidying the room. There comes a wandering figure to the open window. It is that of a man of about thirty-five, of feeble gait, leaning the weight of all one side of him on a stick. His dark face, with black hair, one lock of which has gone white, was evidently once that of an ardent man. Now it is slack, weakly smiling, and the brown eyes are lost, and seem always to be asking something to which there is no answer.*

Mrs. Burlacombe. [*With that forced cheerfulness always assumed in the face of too great misfortune*] Well, Jim! better? [*At the faint brightening of the smile.*] That's right! Yü'm gettin' on bravely. Want Parson?

Jim. [*Nodding and smiling, and speaking slowly*] I want to tell 'un about my cat.   [*His face loses its smile.*

Mrs. Burlacombe. Why! what's she been düin' then? Mr. Strangway's busy. Won't I dü?

Jim. [*Shaking his head*] No. I want to tell *him*.

Mrs. Burlacombe. Whatever she been düin'? Havin' kittens?

Jim. No. She'm lost.

Mrs. Burlacombe. Dearie me! Aw! she'm not lost. Cats be like maids; they must get out a bit.

Jim. She'm lost. Maybe he'll know where she'll be.

Mrs. Burlacombe. Well, well. I'll go an' find 'im.

Jim. He's a güde man. He's very güde.

Mrs. Burlacombe. That's certain zure.

Strangway. [*Entering from the house*] Mrs. Burlacombe, I can't think where I've put my book on St. Francis—the large, squarish pale-blue one?

Mrs. Burlacombe. Aw! there now! I knü there was somethin' on me mind. Miss Willis she came in yesterday afternüne when yü

was out, to borrow it. Oh! yes—I said—I'm zure Mr. Strangway'll lend it 'ee. Now think o' that!

STRANGWAY. Of course, Mrs. Burlacombe; very glad she's got it.

MRS. BURLACOMBE. Aw! but that's not all. When I tuk it up
there come out a whole flutter o' little bits o' paper wi' little rhymes on
'em, same as I see yü writin'. Aw! my güdeness! I says to meself,
Mr. Strangway widn' want no one seein' them.

STRANGWAY. Dear me! No; certainly not!

MRS. BURLACOMBE. An' so I putt 'em in your secretary.

STRANGWAY. My—ah! Yes. Thank you; yes.

MRS. BURLACOMBE. But I'll goo over an' get the büke for yü.
'Twon't take me 'alf a minit.

          [*She goes out on to the green.* JIM BERE *has come in.*

STRANGWAY [*Gently*] Well, Jim?

JIM, My cat's lost.

STRANGWAY. Lost?

JIM. Day before yesterday. She'm not come back. They've
shot 'er, I think; or she'm caught in one o' they rabbit-traps.

STRANGWAY. Oh! no; my dear fellow, she'll come back. I'll
speak to Sir Herbert's keepers.

JIM. Yes, zurr. I feel lonesome without 'er.

STRANGWAY. [*With a faint smile—more to himself than to* JIM] Lonesome! Yes! That's bad, Jim! That's bad!

JIM. I miss 'er when I sits thar in the avenin'.

STRANGWAY. The evenings—— They're the worst—and when
the blackbirds sing in the morning.

JIM. She used to lie on my bed, ye know, zurr. [STRANGWAY
turns his face away, contracted with pain.] She'm like a Christian.

STRANGWAY. The beasts are.

JIM. There's plenty folk ain't 'alf as Christian as 'er be.

STRANGWAY. Well, dear Jim, I'll do my very best. And any time
you're lonely, come up, and I'll play the flute to you.

JIM. [*Wriggling slightly*] No, zurr. Thank 'ee, zurr.

STRANGWAY. What—don't you like music?

JIM. Ye-es, zurr. [*A figure passes the window. Seeing it he says with
his slow smile :* "'Ere's Mrs. Bradmere, comin' from the Rectory."
With queer malice] She don't like cats. But she'm a cat 'erself, I think.

STRANGWAY. [*With his smile*] Jim!

JIM. She'm always tellin' me I'm lükin' better. I'm not better,
zurr.

STRANGWAY. That's her kindness.

JIM. I don't think it is. 'Tis laziness, an' 'avin' 'er own way.
She'm very fond of 'er own way.

      [*A knock on the door cuts off his speech. Following closely on the
          knock, as though no doors were licensed to be closed against*

*her, a grey-haired lady enters; a capable, brown-faced woman
of seventy, whose every tone and movement exhale authority.
With a nod and a " good morning " to* STRANGWAY *she turns
at once to* JIM BERE.

MRS. BRADMERE. Ah! Jim; you're looking better.

[JIM BERE *shakes his head.*

MRS. BRADMERE. Oh! yes, you are. Getting on splendidly.
And now, I just want to speak to Mr. Strangway.

[JIM BERE *touches his forelock, and slowly, leaning on his stick, goes
out.*

MRS. BRADMERE. [*Waiting for the door to close*] You know how that
came on him? Caught the girl he was engaged to, one night, with
another man, the rage broke something here. [*She touches her forehead.*] Four years ago.

STRANGWAY. Poor fellow!

MRS. BRADMERE. [*Looking at him sharply*] Is your wife back?

STRANGWAY. [*Starting*] No.

MRS. BRADMERE. By the way, poor Mrs. Cremer—is she any better?

STRANGWAY. No; going fast. Wonderful—so patient.

MRS. BRADMERE. [*With gruff sympathy*] Um! Yes. They know
how to die! [*With another sharp look at him.*] D'you expect your wife
soon?

STRANGWAY. I—I—hope so.

MRS. BRADMERE. So do I. The sooner the better.

STRANGWAY. [*Shrinking*] I trust the Rector's not suffering so much
this morning?

MRS. BRADMERE. Thank you! His foot's very bad.

[*As she speaks* MRS. BURLACOMBE *returns with a large pale-blue
book in her hand.*

MRS. BURLACOMBE. Good day, m'm! [*Taking the book across to*
STRANGWAY.] Miss Willis, she says she'm very sorry, zurr.

STRANGWAY. She was very welcome, Mrs. Burlacombe. [*To* MRS.
BRADMERE.] Forgive me—my sermon. [*He goes into the house.*

[*The two women gaze after him. Then, at once, as it were, draw
into themselves, as if preparing for an encounter, and yet seem
to expand as if losing the need for restraint.*

MRS. BRADMERE. [*Abruptly*] He misses his wife very much, I'm
afraid.

MRS. BURLACOMBE. Ah! Don't he? Poor dear man; he keeps a
terrible tight 'and over 'imself, but 'tis suthin' cruel the way he walks
about at night. He'm just like a cow when it's calf's weaned. 'T'as
gone to me 'eart truly to see 'im these months past. T'other day when
I went up to dü his rüme, I yeard a noise like this [*she sniffs*]; an'
ther' 'e was at the wardrobe, snuffin' at 'er things. I did never think
a man cud care for a woman so much as that.

MRS. BRADMERE. H'm!

MRS. BURLACOMBE. 'Tis funny rest—an' 'e comin' 'ere for quiet after that tearin' great London parish! 'E'm terrible absent-minded tü—don't take no interest in 'is füde. Yesterday, goin' on for one o'clock, 'e says to me, " I expect 'tis nearly breakfast-time, Mrs. Burlacombe! " 'E'd 'ad it twice already!

MRS. BRADMERE. Twice! Nonsense!

MRS. BURLACOMBE. Zurely! I give 'im a nummit afore 'e gets up; an' 'e 'as 'is brekjus reg'lar at nine. Must feed un up. He'm on 'is feet all day, goin' to zee folk that widden want to zee an angel, they'm that busy; an' when 'e comes in 'e'll play 'is flute there. He'm wastin' away for want of 'is wife. That's what 'tis. An' 'im so sweet-spoken, tü, 'tes a pleasure to year 'im—— Never says a word!

MRS. BRADMERE. Yes, that's the kind of man who gets treated badly. I'm afraid she's not worthy of him, Mrs. Burlacombe.

MRS. BURLACOMBE. [Plaiting her apron] 'Tesn't for me to zay that. She'm a very pleasant lady.

MRS. BRADMERE. Too pleasant. What's this story about her being seen in Durford?

MRS. BURLACOMBE. Aw! I dü never year no gossip, m'm.

MRS. BRADMERE. [Dryly] Of course not! But you see the Rector wishes to know.

MRS. BURLACOMBE. [Flustered] Well—folk will talk! But, as says to Burlacombe—" 'Tes paltry," I says; and they only married eighteen months, and Mr. Strangway so devoted-like. 'Tes nothing but love, with 'im.

MRS. BRADMERE. Come!

MRS. BURLACOMBE. There's puzzivantin' folk as'll set an' gossip the feathers off an angel. But I dü never listen.

MRS. BRADMERE. Now then, Mrs. Burlacombe!

MRS. BURLACOMBE. Well, they dü say as how Dr. Desart over to Durford and Mrs. Strangway was sweethearts afore she wer' married.

MRS. BRADMERE. I knew that. Who was it saw her coming out of Dr. Desart's house yesterday?

MRS. BURLACOMBE. In a manner of spakin' 'tes Mrs. Freman that says 'er Gladys seen her.

MRS. BRADMERE. That child's got an eye like a hawk.

MRS. BURLACOMBE. 'Tes wonderful how things dü spread. 'Tesn't as if us gossiped. Dü seem to grow-like in the naight.

MRS. BRADMERE. [To herself] I never liked her. That Riviera excuse, Mrs. Burlacombe—— Very convenient things, sick mothers. Mr. Strangway doesn't know?

MRS. BURLACOMBE. The Lord forbid! 'Twid send un crazy, I think. For all he'm so moony an' gentle-like, I think he'm a terrible passionate man inside.   He've a-got a saint in 'im, for zure ; but 'tes only 'alf-baked, in a manner of spakin'.

MRS. BRADMERE. I shall go and see Mrs. Freman.   There's been too much of this gossip all the winter.

MRS. BURLACOMBE. 'Tes unfortunate-like 'tes the Fremans.   Freman he'm a gipsy sort of a feller ; and he've never forgiven Mr. Strangway for spakin' to 'im about the way he trates 'is 'orses.

MRS. BRADMERE. Ah ! I'm afraid Mr. Strangway's not too discreet when his feelings are touched.

MRS. BURLACOMBE. 'E've a-got an 'eart so big as the full müne. But 'tes no yüse expectin' tü much o' this world.   'Tes a funny place, after that.

MRS. BRADMERE. Yes, Mrs. Burlacombe ; and I shall give some of these good people a rare rap over the knuckles for their want of charity.   For all they look as if butter wouldn't melt in their mouths, they're an un-Christian lot. [*Looking very directly at* MRS. BURLA-COMBE.] It's lucky we've some hold over the village.   I'm not going to have scandal.   I shall speak to Sir Herbert, and he and the Rector will take steps.

MRS. BURLACOMBE. [*With covert malice*] Aw ! I dü hope 'twon't upset the Rector, an' 'is füte so poptious !

MRS. BRADMERE. [*Grimly*] His foot'll be sound enough to come down sharp.   By the way, will you send me a duck up to the Rectory ?

MRS. BURLACOMBE. [*Glad to get away*] Zurely, m'm ; at once. I've some luv'ly fat birds. [*She goes into the house.*

MRS. BRADMERE. Old puss-cat !

> [*She turns to go, and in the doorway encounters a very little, red-cheeked girl in a peacock-blue cap, and pink frock, who curtsies stolidly.*

MRS. BRADMERE. Well, Tibby Jarland, what do you want here ? Always sucking something, aren't you ?

> [*Getting no reply from* TIBBY JARLAND, *she passes out.* TIBBY *comes in, looks round, takes a large sweet out of her mouth, contemplates it, and puts it back again.   Then, in a perfunctory and very stolid fashion, she looks about the floor, as if she had been told to find something.   While she is finding nothing and sucking her sweet, her sister* MERCY *comes in furtively, still frowning and vindictive.*

MERCY. What ! Haven't you found it, Tibby ?   Get along with 'ee, then !

> [*She accelerates the stolid* TIBBY'S *departure with a smack, searches under the seat, finds and picks up the deserted sixpence.   Then very quickly she goes to the door.   But it is opened before she reaches it, and, finding herself caught, she slips behind the chintz*

*window-curtain. A woman has entered, who is clearly the
original of the large photograph. She is not strictly pretty,
but there is charm in her pale, resolute face, with its mocking
lips, flexible brows, and greenish eyes, whose lids, square
above them, have short, dark lashes. She is dressed in blue,
and her fair hair is coiled up under a cap and motor-veil. She
comes in swiftly, and closes the door behind her; becomes irresolute; then, suddenly deciding, moves towards the door into
the house. MERCY slips from behind her curtain to make off,
but at that moment the door into the house is opened, and she
has at once to slip back again into covert. It is IVY who has
appeared.*

IVY. [*Amazed*] Oh! Mrs. Strangway!

[*Evidently disconcerted by this appearance, BEATRICE STRANGWAY
pulls herself together and confronts the child with a smile.*

BEATRICE. Well, Ivy—you've grown! You didn't expect me,
did you?

IVY. No, Mrs. Strangway; but I hoped yü'd be comin' soon.

BEATRICE. Ah! Yes. Is Mr. Strangway in?

IVY. [*Hypnotized by those faintly smiling lips*] Yes—oh, yes! He's
writin' his sermon in the little room. He *will* be glad!

BEATRICE. [*Going a little closer, and never taking her eyes off the child*]
Yes. Now, Ivy, will you do something for me?

IVY. [*Fluttering*] Oh, yes, Mrs. Strangway.

BEATRICE. Quite sure?

IVY. Oh, yes!

BEATRICE. Are you old enough to keep a secret?

IVY. [*Nodding*] I'm fourteen now.

BEATRICE. Well, then—I don't want anybody but Mr. Strangway
to know I've been here; nobody, not even your mother. D'you
understand?

IVY. [*Troubled*] No. Only, I *can* keep a secret.

BEATRICE. Mind, if anybody hears, it will hurt—Mr. Strangway.

IVY. Oh! I wouldn't—hurt—him. *Must* yü go away again?
[*Trembling towards her.*] I wish yü were goin' to stay. And perhaps
someone *has* seen yü—They——

BEATRICE. [*Hastily*] No, no one. I came motoring; like this.
[*She moves her veil to show how it can conceal her face.*] And I came straight
down the little lane, and through the barn, across the yard.

IVY. [*Timidly*] People dü see a lot.

BEATRICE. [*Still with that hovering smile*] I know, but—— Now, go
and tell him quickly and quietly.

IVY. [*Stopping at the door*] Mother's pluckin' a duck. Only, please,
Mrs. Strangway, if she comes in even after yü've gone, she'll know,
because—because yü always have that particular nice scent.

BEATRICE. Thank you, my child. I'll see to that.

[IVY *looks at her as if she would speak again, then turns suddenly, and goes out.* BEATRICE'S *face darkens; she shivers. Taking out a little cigarette-case, she lights a cigarette, and watches the puffs of smoke wreathe about her and die away. The frightened* MERCY *peers out, spying for a chance to escape. Then from the house* STRANGWAY *comes in. All his dreaminess is gone.*

STRANGWAY. Thank God! [*He stops at the look on her face.*] I don't understand, though. I thought you were still out there.

BEATRICE. [*Letting her cigarette fall, and putting her foot on it*] No.

STRANGWAY. You're staying? Oh! Beatrice; come! We'll get away from here at once—as far, as far—anywhere you like. Oh! my darling—only come! If you knew——

BEATRICE. It's no good, Michael; I've tried and tried.

STRANGWAY. Not! Then, why——? Beatrice! You said, when you were right away—I've waited——

BEATRICE. I know. It's cruel—it's horrible. But I told you not to hope, Michael. I've done my best. All these months at Mentone, I've been wondering why I ever let you marry me—when that feeling wasn't dead!

STRANGWAY. You can't have come back just to leave me again?

BEATRICE. When you let me go out there with mother I thought —I *did* think I would be able; and I *had* begun—and then—spring came!

STRANGWAY. Spring came here too! Never so—aching! Beatrice, can't you?

BEATRICE. I've something to say.

STRANGWAY. No! No! No!

BEATRICE. You see—I've—fallen.

STRANGWAY. Ah! [*In a voice sharpened by pain.*] Why, in the name of mercy, come here to tell me that? Was *he* out there, then?

[*She shakes her head.*

BEATRICE. I came straight back to him.

STRANGWAY. To Durford?

BEATRICE. To the Crossway Hotel, miles out—in my own name. They don't know me there. I told you not to hope, Michael. I've done my best; I swear it.

STRANGWAY. My God!

BEATRICE. It was your God that brought us to live near *him!*

STRANGWAY. Why have you come to me like this?

BEATRICE. To know what you're going to do. Are you going to divorce me? We're in your power. Don't divorce me—— Doctor and patient—you must know—it ruins him. He'll lose everything. He'd be disqualified, and he hasn't a penny without his work.

STRANGWAY. Why should I spare him?

BEATRICE. Michael, I came to beg. It's hard.

STRANGWAY. No ; don't beg ! I can't stand it.

BEATRICE. [*Recovering her pride*] What are you going to do, then ? Keep us apart by the threat of a divorce ? Starve us and prison us ? Cage me up here with you ? I'm not brute enough to ruin him.

STRANGWAY. Heaven !

BEATRICE. I never really stopped loving him.   I never loved you, Michael.

STRANGWAY. [*Stunned*] Is that true ? [BEATRICE *bends her head.*] Never loved me ? Not—that night—on the river—not—— ?

BEATRICE. [*Under her breath*] No.

STRANGWAY. Were you lying to me, then ? Kissing me, and— hating me ?

BEATRICE. One doesn't hate men like you ; but it wasn't love.

STRANGWAY. Why did you tell me it was ?

BEATRICE. Yes.   That was the worst thing I've ever done.

STRANGWAY. Do you think I would have married you ?   I would have burned first !   I never dreamed you didn't.   I swear it.

BEATRICE. [*Very low*] Forget it !

STRANGWAY. Did *he* try to get you away from me ? [BEATRICE *gives him a swift look.*] Tell me the truth !

BEATRICE. No.   It was—I—alone.   But—he loves me.

STRANGWAY. One does not easily know love, it seems.

[*But her smile, faint, mysterious, pitying, is enough, and he turns away from her.*

BEATRICE. It was cruel to come, I know.   For me, too.   But I couldn't write.   I had to know.

STRANGWAY. Never loved me ?   *Never* loved me ?   That night at Tregaron ? [*At the look on her face.*] You might have told me before you went away !   Why keep me all these——

BEATRICE. I meant to forget him again.   I did mean to.   I thought I could get back to what I was, when I married you ; but, you see, what a girl can do, a woman that's been married—can't.

STRANGWAY. Then it was I—my kisses that——! [*He laughs.*] How did you stand them ? [*His eyes dart at her face.*] Imagination helped you, perhaps !

BEATRICE. Michael, don't, don't !   And—oh ! don't make a public thing of it !   You needn't be afraid I shall have too good a time ! [*He stays quite still and silent, and that which is writhing in him makes his face so strange that* BEATRICE *stands aghast.   At last she goes stumbling on in speech.*] If ever you want to marry someone else—then, of course —that's only fair, ruin or not.   But till then—till then—— He's leaving Durford, going to Brighton.   No one need know.   And you —this isn't the only parish in the world.

STRANGWAY. [*Quietly*] You ask me to help you live in secret with another man?

BEATRICE. I ask for mercy.

STRANGWAY. [*As to himself*] What am I to do?

BEATRICE. What you feel in the bottom of your heart.

STRANGWAY. You ask me to help you live in sin?

BEATRICE. To let me go out of your life. You've only to do— nothing.   [*He goes, slowly, close to her.*

STRANGWAY. I want you. Come back to me! Beatrice, come back!

BEATRICE. It would be torture, now.

STRANGWAY. [*Writhing*] Oh!

BEATRICE. Whatever's in your heart—do!

STRANGWAY. You'd come back to me sooner than ruin *him*? Would you?

BEATRICE. I can't bring him harm.

STRANGWAY. [*Turning away*] God!—if there be one—help me! [*He stands leaning his forehead against the window. Suddenly his glance falls on the little bird-cage, still lying on the window-seat.*] Never cage any wild thing! [*He gives a laugh that is half a sob; then, turning to the door, says in a low voice*]: Go! Go please, quickly! Do what you will. I won't hurt you—can't—— But—go!   [*He opens the door.*

BEATRICE. [*Greatly moved*] Thank you!

[*She passes him with her head down, and goes out quickly.* STRANG- way *stands unconsciously tearing at the little bird-cage. And while he tears at it he utters a moaning sound. The terrified* MERCY, *peering from behind the curtain, and watching her chance, slips to the still open door; but in her haste and fright she knocks against it, and* STRANGWAY *sees her. Before he can stop her she has fled out on to the green and away.*

[*While he stands there, paralysed, the door from the house is opened, and* MRS. BURLACOMBE *approaches him in a queer, hushed way.*

MRS. BURLACOMBE. [*Her eyes mechanically fixed on the twisted bird-cage in his hands*] 'Tis poor Sue Cremer, zurr, I didn't 'ardly think she'd last thrü the mornin'. An' zure enough she'm passed away. [*Seeing that he has not taken in her words.*] Mr. Strangway—yü'm feelin' giddy?

STRANGWAY. No, no! What was it? You said——

MRS. BURLACOMBE. 'Tes Jack Cremer. His wife's gone. 'E'm in a terrible way. 'Tes only yü, 'e ses, can dü 'im any güde. He'm in the kitchen.

STRANGWAY. Cremer? Yes! Of course. Let him——

MRS. BURLACOMBE. [*Still staring at the twisted cage*] Yü ain't wantin' that—'tes all twizzled. [*She takes it from him.*] Sure yü'm not feelin' yer 'ead?

STRANGWAY. [*With a resolute effort*] No!

MRS. BURLACOMBE. [*Doubtfully*] I'll send 'im in, then. [*She goes.*
 [*When she is gone,* STRANGWAY *passes his handkerchief across his forehead, and his lips move fast. He is standing motionless when* CREMER, *a big man in labourer's clothes, with a thick, broad face, and tragic, faithful eyes, comes in, and stands a little in from the closed door, quite dumb.*

STRANGWAY. [*After a moment's silence—going up to him and laying a hand on his shoulder*] Jack! Don't give way. If we give way—we're done.

CREMER. Yes, zurr. [*A quiver passes over his face.*

STRANGWAY. She didn't. Your wife was a brave woman. A dear woman.

CREMER. I never thought to lüse 'er. She never told me 'ow bad she was, afore she tuk to 'er bed. 'Tis a dreadful thing to lüse a wife, zurr.

STRANGWAY. [*Tightening his lips, that tremble*] Yes. But don't give way. Bear up, Jack!

CREMER. Seems funny 'er goin' blue-bell time, an' the sun shinin' so warm. I picked up an 'orse-shü yesterday. I can't never 'ave 'er back, zurr. [*His face quivers again.*

STRANGWAY. Some day you'll join her. Think! Some lose their wives for ever.

CREMER. I don't believe as there's a future life, zurr. I think we goo to sleep like the beasts.

STRANGWAY. We're told otherwise. But come here! [*Drawing him to the window.*] Look! Listen! To sleep in that! Even if we do, it won't be so bad, Jack, will it?

CREMER. She wer' a güde wife to me—no man cüdn't 'ave no better wife.

STRANGWAY. [*Putting his hand out*] Take hold—hard—harder! I want yours as much as you want mine. Pray for me, Jack, and I'll pray for you. And we won't give way, will we?

CREMER. [*To whom the strangeness of these words has given some relief*] No, zurr; thank 'ee, zurr. 'Tes no güde, I expect. Only, I'll miss 'er. Thank 'ee, zurr; kindly.

 [*He lifts his hand to his head, turns, and uncertainly goes out to the kitchen. And* STRANGWAY *stays where he is, not knowing what to do. Then blindly he takes up his flute, and hatless, hurries out into the air.*

The curtain falls.

ACT II

SCENE I

About seven o'clock in the taproom of the village inn. The bar, with the appurtenances thereof, stretches across one end, and opposite is the porch door on to the green. The wall between is nearly all window, with leaded panes, one wide-open casement whereof lets in the last of the sunlight. A narrow bench runs under this broad window. And this is all the furniture, save three spittoons.

GODLEIGH, *the innkeeper, a smallish man with thick ruffled hair, a loquacious nose,* and apple-red cheeks above a reddish-brown moustache, is reading the paper. To him enters* TIBBY JARLAND *with a shilling in her mouth.*

GODLEIGH. Well, Tibby Jarland, what've yü come for, then? Glass o' beer?

[TIBBY *takes the shilling from her mouth and smiles stolidly.*

GODLEIGH. [*Twinkling*] I shid zay glass o' 'arf an' 'arf's about yüre form. [TIBBY *smiles more broadly.*] Yü'm a praaper masterpiece. Well! 'Ave sister Mercy borrowed yüre tongue? [TIBBY *shakes her head.*] Aw, she 'aven't. Well, maid?

TIBBY. Father wants six clay pipes, please.

GODLEIGH. 'E dü, dü 'ee? Yü tell yüre father 'e can't 'ave more'n one, not this avenin'. And 'ere 'tis. Hand up yüre shillin'.

[TIBBY *reaches up her hand, parts with the shilling, and receives a long clay pipe and eleven pennies. In order to secure the coins in her pinafore she places the clay pipe in her mouth. While she is still thus engaged,* MRS. BRADMERE *enters the porch and comes in.* TIBBY *curtsies stolidly.*

MRS. BRADMERE. Gracious, child! What are you doing here? And what have you got in your mouth? Who is it? Tibby Jarland? [TIBBY *curtsies again.*] Take that thing out. And tell your father from me that if I ever see you at the inn again I shall tread on his toes hard. Godleigh, you know the law about children?

GODLEIGH. [*Cocking his eye, and not at all abashed*] Surely, m'm. But she will come. Go away, my dear.

[TIBBY, *never taking her eyes off* MRS. BRADMERE, *or the pipe from her mouth, has backed stolidly to the door, and vanished.*

MRS. BRADMERE. [*Eyeing* GODLEIGH] Now, Godleigh, I've come to talk to you. Half the scandal that goes about the village begins

434

here. [*She holds up her finger to check expostulation.*] No, no—it's no good. You know the value of scandal to your business far too well.

GODLEIGH. Wi' all respect, m'm, I knows the vally of it to yourn, tü.

MRS. BRADMERE. What do you mean by that?

GODLEIGH. If there weren't no Rector's lady there widden' be no notice taken o' scandal; an' if there weren't no notice taken, twidden be scandal, to my thinkin'.

MRS. BRADMERE. [*Winking out a grim little smile*] Very well! You've given me your views. Now for mine. There's a piece of scandal going about that's got to be stopped, Godleigh. You turn the tap of it off here, or we'll turn your tap off. You know me. See?

GODLEIGH. I shouldn't never presume, m'm, to know a lady.

MRS. BRADMERE. The Rector's quite determined, so is Sir Herbert. Ordinary scandal's bad enough, but this touches the Church. While Mr. Strangway remains curate here, there must be no talk about him and his affairs.

GODLEIGH. [*Cocking his eye*] I was just thinkin' how to dü it, m'm. 'Twid be a brave notion to putt the men in chokey, and slit the women's tongues-like, same as they dü in outlandish places, as I'm told.

MRS. BRADMERE. Don't talk nonsense, Godleigh; and mind what I say, because I mean it.

GODLEIGH. Make yüre mind aisy, m'm—there'll be no scandal-monkeyin' here wi' my permission.

[MRS. BRADMERE *gives him a keen stare, but seeing him perfectly grave, nods her head with approval.*

MRS. BRADMERE. Good! You know what's being said, of course?

GODLEIGH. [*With respectful gravity*] Yü'll pardon me, m'm, but ef an' in case yü was goin' to tell me, there's a rüle in this 'ouse : " No scandal 'ere ! "

MRS. BRADMERE. [*Twinkling grimly*] You're too smart by half, my man.

GODLEIGH. Aw fegs, no, m'm—child in yüre 'ands.

MRS. BRADMERE. I wouldn't trust you a yard. Once more, Godleigh! This is a Christian village, and we mean it to remain so. You look out for yourself.

[*The door opens to admit the farmers* TRUSTAFORD *and* BURLACOMBE. *They doff their hats to* MRS. BRADMERE, *who, after one more sharp look at* GODLEIGH, *moves towards the door.*

MRS. BRADMERE. Evening, Mr. Trustaford. [*To* BURLACOMBE.] Burlacombe, tell your wife that duck she sent up was in hard training.

[*With one of her grim winks, and a nod, she goes.*

TRUSTAFORD. [*Replacing a hat which is black, hard, and not very new, on his long head, above a long face, clean-shaved but for little whiskers.*]

What's the old grey mare want, then? [*With a horse-laugh.*] 'Er's lükin' awful wise!

GODLEIGH. [*Enigmatically*] Ah!

TRUSTAFORD. [*Sitting on the bench close to the bar*] Drop o' whisky, an' potash.

BURLACOMBE. [*A taciturn, slim, yellowish man, in a worn soft hat*] What's nüse, Godleigh? Drop o' cider.

GODLEIGH. Nüse? There's never no nüse in this 'ouse. Aw, no! Not wi' my permission. [*In imitation.*] This is a Christian village.

TRUSTAFORD. Thought the old grey mare seemed mighty busy. [*To* BURLACOMBE.] 'Tes rather quare about the curate's wife a-comin' motorin' this mornin'. Passed me wi' her face all smothered up in a veil, goggles an' all. Haw, haw!

BURLACOMBE. Aye!

TRUSTAFORD. Off again she was in 'alf an hour. 'Er didn't give poor old curate much of a chance, after six months.

GODLEIGH. Havin' an engagement elsewhere—— No scandal, please, gentlemen.

BURLACOMBE. [*Acidly*] Never asked to see my missis. Passed me in the yard like a stone.

TRUSTAFORD. 'Tes a little bit rümoursome lately about 'er doctor.

GODLEIGH. Ah! he's the favourite. But 'tes a dead secret, Mr. Trustaford. Don't yü never repate it—there's not a cat don't know it already!

[BURLACOMBE *frowns, and* TRUSTAFORD *utters his laugh. The door is opened and* FREMAN, *a dark gipsyish man in the dress of a farmer, comes in.*

GODLEIGH. Don't yü never tell Will Freman what 'e told me!

FREMAN. Avenin'!

TRUSTAFORD. Avenin', Will; what's yüre glass o' trouble?

FREMAN. Drop o' cider, clove, an' dash o' gin. There's blood in the sky to-night.

BURLACOMBE. Ah! We'll 'ave fine weather now, with the full o' the müne.

FREMAN. Dust o' wind an' a drop or tü, virst, I reckon. 'Eard t' nüse about curate an' 'is wife?

GODLEIGH. No, indeed; an' don't yü tell us. We'm Christians 'ere in this village.

FREMAN. 'Tain't no very Christian nüse, neither. He's sent 'er off to th' doctor. " Go an' live with un," 'e says; " my blessin' on ye." If 'er'd a-been mine, I'd 'a tuk the whip to 'er. Tam Jarland's maid, she yeard it all. Christian, indeed! That's brave Christianity! " Goo an' live with un! " 'e told 'er.

BURLACOMBE. No, no; that's not sense—a man to say that. I'll not 'ear that against a man that bides in my 'ouse.

FREMAN. 'Tes sure, I tell 'ee. The maid was hid-up, scared-like, behind the curtain. At it they went, and parson 'e says : " Go," 'e says, " I won't kape 'ee from 'im," 'e says, " an' I won't divorce 'ee' as yü don't wish it ! " They was 'is words, same as Jarland's maid told my maid, an' my maid told my missis. If that's parson's talk, 'tes funny work goin' to church.

TRUSTAFORD. [*Brooding*] 'Tes wonderful quare, zurely.

FREMAN. Tam Jarland's fair mad wi' curate for makin' free wi' his maid's skylark. Parson or no parson, 'e've no call to meddle wi' other people's praperty. He cam' pokin' 'is nose into my affairs. I told un I knew a sight more 'bout 'orses than 'e ever would !

TRUSTAFORD. He'm a bit crazy 'bout bastes an' birds.

[*They have been so absorbed that they have not noticed the entrance of* CLYST, *a youth with tousled hair, and a bright, quick, Celtic eye, who stands listening, with a bit of paper in his hands.*

CLYST. Ah ! he'm that zurely, Mr. Trustaford.   [*He chuckles.*

GODLEIGH. Now, Tim Clyst, if an' in case yü've a-got some scandal on yer tongue, don't yü never unship it here. Yü go up to Rectory where 'twill be more relished-like.

CLYST. [*Waving the paper*] Will y' give me a drink for thic, Mr. Godleigh ? 'Tes rale funny. Aw ! 'tes somethin' swate. Bütiful readin'. Poetry. Rale spice. Yü've a luv'ly voice for readin', Mr. Godleigh.

GODLEIGH. [*All ears and twinkle*] Aw, what is it then ?

CLYST. Ah ! Yü want t'know tü much.

[*Putting the paper in his pocket.*

[*While he is speaking,* JIM BERE *has entered quietly, with his feeble step and smile, and sits down.*

CLYST. [*Kindly*] Hallo, Jim ! Cat come 'ome ?

JIM BERE. No.

[*All nod, and speak to him kindly. And* JIM BERE *smiles at them, and his eyes ask of them the question, to which there is no answer. And after that he sits motionless and silent, and they talk as if he were not there.*

GODLEIGH. What's all this, now—no scandal in my 'ouse !

CLYST. 'Tes awful peculiar—like a drame. Mr. Burlacombe 'e don't like to hear tell about drames. A guess a won't tell 'ee, arter that.

FREMAN. Out wi' it, Tim.

CLYST. 'Tes powerful thirsty to-day, Mr. Godleigh.

GODLEIGH. [*Drawing him some cider*] Yü're all wild cat's talk, Tim ; yü've a-got no tale at all.

CLYST. [*Moving for the cider*] Aw, indade !

GODLEIGH. No tale, no cider !

CLYST. Did ye ever year tell of Orphus ?

TRUSTAFORD. What? The old vet.: up to Drayleigh?

CLYST. Fegs, no; Orphus that lived in th' old time, an' drawed the bastes after un wi' his music, same as curate was tellin' the maids.

FREMAN. I've 'eard as a gipsy over to Yellacott could dü that wi' 'is viddle.

CLYST. 'Twas no gipsy I see'd this arternüne; 'twas Orphus, down to Mr. Burlacombe's long medder; settin' there all dark on a stone among the dimsy-white flowers an' the cowflops, wi' a bird upon 'is 'ead, playin' his whistle to the ponies.

FREMAN. [*Excitedly*] Yü did never zee a man wi' a bird on 'is 'ead.

CLYST. Didn' I?

FREMAN. What sort o' bird, then? Yü tell me that.

TRUSTAFORD. Praaper old barndoor cock. Haw, haw!

GODLEIGH. [*Soothingly*] 'Tes a vairy-tale; us mustn't be tü partic'lar.

BURLACOMBE. In my long medder? Where were yü, then, Tim Clyst?

CLYST. Passin' down the lane on my bike. Wonderful sorrowful-fine music 'e played. The ponies they did come round 'e—yü cud zee the tears runnin' down their chakes; 'twas powerful sad. 'E 'adn't no 'at on.

FREMAN. [*Jeering*] No; 'e 'ad a bird on 'is 'ead.

CLYST. [*With a silencing grin*] He went on playin' an' playin'. The ponies they never müved. An' all the dimsy-white flowers they waved and waved, an' the wind it went over 'em. Gav' me a funny feelin'.

GODLEIGH. Clyst, yü take the cherry bun!

CLYST. Where's that cider, Mr. Godleigh?

GODLEIGH. [*Bending over the cider*] Yü've a-'ad tü much already, Tim.

[*The door is opened, and* TAM JARLAND *appears. He walks rather unsteadily; a man with a heavy jowl, and sullen, strange, epileptic-looking eyes.*

CLYST. [*Pointing to* JARLAND] 'Tis Tam Jarland there 'as the cargo aboard.

JARLAND. Avenin', all! [*To* GODLEIGH.] Pint o' beer. [*To* JIM BERE.] Avenin', Jim. [JIM BERE *looks at him and smiles.*

GODLEIGH. [*Serving him after a moment's hesitation*] 'Ere y'are, Tam. [*To* CLYST, *who has taken out his paper again.*] Where'd yü get thiccy paper?

CLYST. [*Putting down his cider-mug empty*] Yüre tongue dü watter, don't it, Mr. Godleigh? [*Holding out his mug.*] No zider, no poetry. 'Tis amazin' sorrowful; Shakespeare over again. "The boy stüde on the burnin' deck."

FREMAN. Yü and yer yap !

CLYST. Ah ! Yü wait a bit. When I come back down t'lane again, Orphus 'e was vanished away ; there was naught in the field but the ponies, an' a praaper old magpie, a-top o' the hedge. I zee somethin' white in the beak o' the fowl, so I giv' a " Whisht," an' 'e drops it smart, an' off 'e go. I gets over bank an' picks un up, and here't be.

[*He holds out his mug.*

BURLACOMBE. [*Tartly*] Here, give 'im 'is cider. Rade it yureself, ye young teasewings.

[*CLYST, having secured his cider, drinks it off. Holding up the paper to the light, he makes as if to begin, then slides his eye round, tantalizing.*

CLYST. 'Tes a pity I bain't dressed in a white gown, an' flowers in me 'air.

FREMAN. Read it, or we'll 'ave yü out o' this.

CLYST. Aw, don't 'ee shake my nerve, now !

[*He begins reading with mock heroism, in his soft, high, burring voice Thus, in his rustic accent, go the lines :*

God lighted the zun in 'eaven far,
Lighted the virefly an' the ztar.
My 'eart 'E lighted not !

God lighted the vields fur lambs to play,
Lighted the bright strames, 'an the may.
My 'eart 'E lighted not !

God lighted the müne, the Arab's way,
He lights to-morrer, an' to-day.
My 'eart 'E 'ath vorgot !

[*When he has finished, there is silence. Then* TRUSTAFORD, *scratching his head, speaks :*

TRUSTAFORD. 'Tes amazin' funny stuff.

FREMAN. [*Looking over* CLYST'S *shoulder*] Be danged ! 'Tes the curate's 'andwritin'. 'Twas curate wi' the ponies, after that.

CLYST. Fancy, now ! Aw, Will Freman, an't yü bright !

FREMAN. But 'e 'adn't no bird on 'is 'ead.

CLYST. Ya-as, 'e 'ad.

JARLAND. [*In a dull, threatening voice*] 'E 'ad my maid's bird, this arter-nüne. 'Ead or no, and parson or no, I'll gie 'im one for that.

FREMAN. Ah ! And 'e meddled wi' my 'orses.

TRUSTAFORD. I'm thinkin' 'twas an old cuckoo bird 'e 'ad on 'is 'ead. Haw, haw !

GODLEIGH. " His 'eart *she* 'ath vorgot ! "

FREMAN. 'E's a fine one to be tachin' our maids convirmation.

GODLEIGH. Would ye 'ave it the old Rector then ? Wi' 'is gouty shoe ? Rackon the maids wid rather 'twas curate ; eh, Mr. Burlacombe ?

BURLACOMBE. [*Abruptly*] Curate's a güde man.

JARLAND. [*With the comatose ferocity of drink*] I'll be even wi' un.

FREMAN. [*Excitedly*] Tell 'ee one thing—'tes not a proper man o' God to 'ave about, wi' 'is lüse goin's on. Out vrom 'ere he oughter go.

BURLACOMBE. You med go further an' fare worse.

FREMAN. What's 'e düin', then, lettin' 'is wife run off ?

TRUSTAFORD. [*Scratching his head*] If an' in case 'e can't kape 'er, 'tes a funny way o' düin' things not to divorce 'er, after that. If a parson's not to dü the Christian thing, whü is, then ?

BURLACOMBE. 'Tes a bit immoral-like to pass over a thing like that. 'Tes funny if women's goin's on's to be encouraged.

FREMAN. Act of a coward, I zay.

BURLACOMBE. The curate ain't no coward.

FREMAN. He bides in yüre house ; 'tes natural for yü to stand up for un ; I'll wager *Mrs.* Burlacombe don't, though. My missis was fair shocked. " Will," she says, " if yü ever make vur to let me go like that, I widden never stay wi' yü," she says.

TRUSTAFORD. 'Tes settin' a bad example, for zure.

BURLACOMBE. 'Tes all very aisy talkin' ; what shüde 'e dü, then ?

FREMAN. [*Excitedly*] Go over to Durford and say to that doctor : " Yü come about my missis, an' zee what I'll dü to 'ee." An' take 'er 'ome an' zee she don't misbe'ave again.

CLYST. 'E can't take 'er ef 'er don' want t'come—I've 'eard lawyer, that lodged wi' us, say that.

FREMAN. All right then, 'e ought to 'ave the law of 'er and 'er doctor ; an' zee 'er goin's on don't prosper ; 'e'd get damages, tü. But this way 'tes a nice example he'm settin' folks. Parson indade ! My missis an' the maids they won't goo near the church to-night, an' I wager no one else won't neither.

JARLAND. [*Lurching with his pewter up to* GODLEIGH] The beggar ! I'll be even wi' un.

GODLEIGH. [*Looking at him in doubt*] 'Tes the last, then, Tam.

[*Having received his beer,* JARLAND *stands, leaning against the bar, drinking.*

BURLACOMBE. [*Suddenly*] I don' goo with what curate's düin'—'tes tü soft 'earted ; he'm a müney kind o' man altogether, wi' 'is flute an' 'is poetry ; but he've a-lodged in my 'ouse this year an' more, and always 'ad an 'elpin' 'and for everyone. I've got a likin' for him an' there's an end of it.

JARLAND. The coward!

TRUSTAFORD. I don't trouble nothin' about that, Tam Jarland. [*Turning to* BURLACOMBE.] What gits me is 'e don't seem to 'ave no zense o' what's his own praperty.

JARLAND. Take other folk's property fast enough! [*He saws the air with his empty pewter. The others have all turned to him, drawn by the fascination that a man in liquor has for his fellow-men. The bell for church has begun to ring, the sun is down, and it is getting dusk.*] He wants one on his crop, an' one in 'is belly; 'e wants a man to take an' gie un a güde hidin'—zame as he oughter give 'is fly-be-night of a wife. [STRANGWAY *in his dark clothes has entered, and stands by the door, his lips compressed to a colourless line, his thin, darkish face grey-white.*] Zame as a *man* wid ha' gi'en the doctor, for takin' what isn't his'n.

[*All but* JARLAND *have seen* STRANGWAY. *He steps forward,* JARLAND *sees him now; his jaw drops a little, and he is silent.*

STRANGWAY. I came for a little brandy, Mr. Godleigh—feeling rather faint. Afraid I mightn't get through the service.

GODLEIGH. [*With professional composure*] Martell's Three Star, zurr, or 'Ennessy's?

STRANGWAY. [*Looking at* JARLAND] Thank you; I believe I can do without, now. [*He turns to go.*

[*In the deadly silence,* GODLEIGH *touches the arm of* JARLAND, *who, leaning against the bar with the pewter in his hand, is staring with his strange lowering eyes straight at* STRANGWAY.

JARLAND. [*Galvanized by the touch into drunken rage*] Lave me be— I'll talk to un—parson or no. I'll tache un to meddle wi' my maid's bird. I'll tache un to kape 'is thievin' 'ands to 'imself.

[STRANGWAY *turns again.*

CLYST. Be quiet, Tam.

JARLAND. [*Never loosing* STRANGWAY *with his eyes—like a bull-dog who sees red*] That's for one chake; zee un turn t'other, the white-livered büty! Whü lets another man 'ave 'is wife, an' never the sperit to go vor un!

BURLACOMBE. Shame, Jarland; quiet, man!

[*They are all looking at* STRANGWAY, *who, under* JARLAND'S *drunken insults is standing rigid, with his eyes closed, and his hands hard clenched. The church bell has stopped slow ringing, and begun its five minutes' hurrying note.*

TRUSTAFORD. [*Rising, and trying to hook his arm into* JARLAND'S] Come away, Tam; yü've a-'ad tü much, man.

JARLAND. [*Shaking him off*] Zee, 'e daresn't touch me; I might 'it un in the vace an' 'e darsen't; 'e's afraid—like 'e was o' the doctor.

[*He raises the pewter as though to fling it, but it is seized by* GODLEIGH *from behind, and falls clattering to the floor.* STRANGWAY *has not moved.*

JARLAND. [*Shaking his fist almost in his face*] Lüke at un, lüke at un ! A man wi' a slut for a wife——

> [*As he utters the word " wife " STRANGWAY seizes the outstretched fist, and with a ju-jitsu movement, draws him into his clutch, helpless. And as they sway and struggle in the open window, with the false strength of fury he forces JARLAND through. There is a crash of broken glass from outside. At the sound STRANGWAY comes to himself. A look of agony passes over his face. His eyes light on JIM BERE, who has suddenly risen, and stands feebly clapping his hands. STRANGWAY rushes out.*
> [*Excitedly gathering at the window, they all speak at once.*

CLYST. Tam's hatchin' of yüre cucumbers, Mr. Godleigh.

TRUSTAFORD. 'E did crash ; haw, haw !

FREMAN. 'Twas a brave throw, zürely. Whü wid a' thought it ?

CLYST. Tam's crawlin' out. [*Leaning through window.*] Hallo, Tam— 'ow's t' base, old man ?

FREMAN. [*Excitedly*] They'm all comin' up from churchyard to zee.

TRUSTAFORD. Tam dü lüke wonderful aztonished ; haw, haw ! Poor old Tam !

CLYST. Can yü zee curate ? Rackon 'e'm gone into church. Aw, yes ; gettin' a bit dimsy—sarvice time. [*A moment's hush.*

TRUSTAFORD. Well, I'm jiggered. In 'alf an hour he'm got to prache.

GODLEIGH. 'Tes a Christian village, boys.

> [*Feebly, quietly, JIM BERE laughs. There is silence ; but the bell is heard still ringing.*

The curtain falls.

SCENE II

The same—in daylight dying fast. A lamp is burning on the bar. A chair has been placed in the centre of the room, facing the bench under the window, on which are seated from right to left, GODLEIGH, SOL POTTER the village shopman, TRUSTAFORD, BURLACOMBE, FREMAN, JIM BERE, and MORSE the blacksmith. CLYST is squatting on a stool by the bar, and at the other end JARLAND, sobered and lowering, leans against the lintel of the porch leading to the door, round which are gathered five or six sturdy fellows, dumb as fishes. No one sits in the chair. In the unnatural silence that reigns, the distant sound of the wheezy church organ and voices singing can be heard.

TRUSTAFORD. [*After a prolonged clearing of his throat*] What I mean to zay is that 'tes no yüse, not a bit o' yüse in the world, not düin' of things properly. If an' in case we'm to carry a resolution disapprovin' o' curate, it must all be done so as no one can't zay nothin'.

SOL POTTER. That's what I zay, Mr. Trustaford; ef so be as 'tis to be a village meetin', then it must be all done proper.

FREMAN. That's right, Sol Potter. I purpose Mr. Sol Potter into the chair. Whü seconds that?

[*A Silence. Voices from among the dumb-as-fishes :* " I dü."

CLYST. [*Excitedly*] Yü can't putt that to the meetin'. Only a chairman can putt it to the meetin'. I purpose that Mr. Burlacombe —bein' as how he's chairman o' the Parish Council—take the chair.

FREMAN. Ef so be as I can't putt it, yü can't putt that neither.

TRUSTAFORD. 'Tes not a bit o' yüse; us can't 'ave no meetin' without a chairman.

GODLEIGH. Us can't 'ave no chairman without a meetin' to elect un, that's züre.   [*A silence.*

MORSE. [*Heavily*] To my way o' thinkin', Mr. Godleigh speaks zense; us must 'ave a meetin' before us can 'ave a chairman.

CLYST. Then what we got to dü's to elect a meetin'.

BURLACOMBE. [*Sourly*] Yü'll not find no procedure for that.

[*Voices from among the dumb-as-fishes :* " Mr. Burlacombe 'e oughter know."

SOL POTTER. [*Scratching his head—with heavy solemnity*] 'Tes my belief there's no other way to dü, but to elect a chairman to call a meetin'; an' then for that meetin' to elect a chairman.

CLYST. I purpose Mr. Burlacombe as chairman to call a meetin'.

FREMAN. I purpose Sol Potter.

GODLEIGH. Can't 'ave tü propositions together before a meetin'; that's apple-pie züre vur zurtain.

[*Voice from among the dumb-as-fishes :* " There ain't no meetin' yet, Sol Potter says."

TRUSTAFORD. Us must get the rights of it zettled some'ow. 'Tes like the darned old chicken an' the egg—meetin' or chairman—which come virst?

SOL POTTER. [*Conciliating*] To my thinkin' there shid be another way o' düin' it, to get round it like with a circumbendibus. 'Tall comes from takin' different vüse, in a manner o' spakin'.

FREMAN. Yü goo an' zet in that chair.

SOL POTTER. [*With a glance at* BURLACOMBE—*modestly*] I shid'n never like fur to dü that, with Mr. Burlacombe zettin' there.

BURLACOMBE. [*Rising*] 'Tes all darned fülishness.

[*Amidst an uneasy shufflement of feet he moves to the door and goes out into the darkness.*

CLYST. [*Seeing his candidate thus depart*] Rackon curate's pretty well thrü by now, I'm going to zee. [*As he passes* JARLAND.] 'Ow's ta base, old man?   [*He goes out.*

[*One of the dumb-as-fishes moves from the door and fills the space left on the bench by* BURLACOMBE'S *departure.*

JARLAND. Darn all this puzzivantin' ! [*To* SOL POTTER.] Goo an' zet in that chair.

SOL POTTER. [*Rising and going to the chair ; there he stands, changing from one to the other of his short broad feet and sweating from modesty and worth*] 'Tes my düty now, gentlemen, to call a meetin' of the parishioners of this parish. I beg therefore to declare that this is a meetin' in accordance with my duty as chairman of this meetin' which elected me chairman to call this meetin'. And I purceed to vacate the chair so that this meetin' may now purceed to elect a chairman.

[*He gets up from the chair, and wiping the sweat from his brow, goes back to his seat.*

FREMAN. Mr. Chairman, I rise on a point of order.

GODLEIGH. There ain't no chairman.

FREMAN. I don't give a darn for that. I rise on a point of order.

GODLEIGH. 'Tes a chairman that decides points of order. 'Tes certain yü can't rise on no points whatever till there's a chairman.

TRUSTAFORD. 'Tes no yüse yüre risin', not the least bit in the world, till there's someone to zet yü down again. Haw, haw !

[*Voice from the dumb-as-fishes :* " Mr. Trustaford 'e's right."

FREMAN. What I zay is the chairman ought never to 'ave vacated the chair till I'd risen on my point of order. I purpose that he goo and zet down again.

GODLEIGH. Yü can't purpose that to this meetin' ; yü can only purpose that to the old meetin' that's not zettin' any longer.

FREMAN. [*Excitedly*] I don' care what old meetin' 'tis that's zettin'. I purpose that Sol Potter goo an' zet in that chair again, while I rise on my point of order.

TRUSTAFORD. [*Scratching his head*] 'Tesn't regular—but I guess yü've got to goo, Sol, or us shan't 'ave no peace.

[SOL POTTER, *still wiping his brow, goes back to the chair.*

MORSE. [*Stolidly—to* FREMAN] Zet down, Will Freman.

[*He pulls at him with a blacksmith's arm.*

FREMAN. [*Remaining erect with an effort*] I'm not a-goin' to zet down till I've arisen.

JARLAND. Now then, there 'e is in the chair. What's yüre point of order ?

FREMAN. [*Darting his eyes here and there, and flinging his hand up to his gipsy-like head*] 'Twas—'twas—— Darned ef y'aven't putt it clean out o' my 'ead.

JARLAND. We can't wait for yüre points of order. Come out o' that chair, Sol Potter.

[SOL POTTER *rises and is about to vacate the chair.*

FREMAN. I know ! There ought to 'a been minutes taken. Yü can't 'ave no meetin' without minutes. When us comes to electin' a chairman o' the next meetin', 'e won't 'ave no minutes to read.

SOL POTTER. 'Twas only to putt down that I was elected chairman to elect a meetin' to elect a chairman to preside over a meetin' to pass a resolution dalin' wi' the curate. That's aisy set down, that is.

FREMAN. [*Mollified*] We'll 'ave that zet down, then, while we're electin' the chairman o' the next meetin'.   [*A silence.*

TRUSTAFORD. Well, then, seein' this is the praaper old meetin' for carryin' the resolution about the curate, I purpose Mr. Sol Potter take the chair.   •

FREMAN. I purpose Mr. Trustaford. I 'aven't a-got nothin' against Sol Potter, but seein' that he elected the meetin' that's to elect 'im, it might be said that 'e was electin' of himself in a manner of spakin'. Us don't want that said.

MORSE. [*Amid meditative grunts from the dumb-as-fishes*] There's some-at in that. One o' they tü purposals must be putt to the meetin'.

FREMAN. Second must be putt virst, fur züre.

TRUSTAFORD. I dunno as I wants to zet in that chair. To hiss the curate, 'tis a ticklish sort of a job after that. Vurst comes afore second, Will Freman.

FREMAN. Second is amendment to virst. 'Tes the amendments is put virst.

TRUSTAFORD. 'Ow's that, Mr. Godleigh? I'm not particular eggzac'ly to a dilly zort of a point like that.

SOL POTTER. [*Scratching his head*] 'Tes a very nice point, fur züre.

GODLEIGH. 'Tes undoubtedly for the chairman to decide.

        [*Voice from the dumb-as-fishes :* " But there ain't no chairman yet."

JARLAND. Sol Potter's chairman.

FREMAN. No, 'e ain't.

MORSE. Yes, 'e is—'e's chairman till this second old meetin' gets on the go.

FREMAN. I deny that. What dü yü say, Mr. Trustaford?

TRUSTAFORD. I can't 'ardly tell. It dü zeem a darned long-sufferin' sort of a business altogether.   [*A silence.*

MORSE. [*Slowly*] Tell 'ee what 'tis, us shan't dü no güde like this.

GODLEIGH. 'Tes for Mr. Freman or Mr. Trustaford, one or t'other to withdraw their motions.

TRUSTAFORD. [*After a pause, with cautious generosity*] I've no objections to withdrawin' mine, if Will Freman'll withdraw his'n.

FREMAN. I won't never be be'indhand. If Mr. Trustaford withdraws, I withdraws mine.

MORSE. [*With relief*] That's zensible. Putt the motion to the meetin'.

SOL POTTER. There ain't no motion left to putt.

                        [*Silence of consternation.*
                [*In the confusion* JIM BERE *is seen to stand up.*

GODLEIGH. Jim Bere to spake. Silence for Jim !

VOICES. Aye ! Silence for Jim !

SOL POTTER. Well, Jim ?

JIM. [*Smiling and slow*] Nothin' düin'.

TRUSTAFORD. Bravo, Jim ! Yü'm right. Best zense yet !

> [*Applause from the dumb-as-fishes. With his smile brightening,*
> JIM *resumes his seat.*

SOL POTTER. [*Wiping his brow*] Dü seem to me, gentlemen, seein'
as we'm got into a bit of a tangle in a manner of spakin', 'twid be the
most zimplest and vairest way to begin all over vrom the beginnin',
so's t'ave it all vair an' square for everyone.

> [*In the uproar of "* Aye *" and "* No,*" it is noticed that* TIBBY
> JARLAND *is standing in front of her father with her finger, for
> want of something better, in her mouth.*

TIBBY. [*In her stolid voice*] Please, sister Mercy says, curate 'ave got
to " Lastly." [JARLAND *picks her up, and there is silence.*] An' please
to come quick.

JARLAND. Come on, mates ; quietly now !

> [*He goes out, and all begin to follow him.*

MORSE. [*Slowest, save for* SOL POTTER] 'Tes rare lucky us was all
agreed to hiss the curate afore us began the botherin' old meetin', or
us widn' 'ardly 'ave 'ad time to settle what to dü.

SOL POTTER. [*Scratching his head*] Aye, 'tes rare lucky, but I dunno if
'tes altogether reg'lar.

> *The curtain falls.*

SCENE III

*The village green before the churchyard and the yew-trees at the gate. Into
the pitch dark under the yews, light comes out through the half-open
church door. Figures are lurking, or moving stealthily—people waiting
and listening to the sound of a voice speaking in the church words that are
inaudible. Excited whispering and faint giggles come from the deepest
yew-tree shade, made ghostly by the white faces and the frocks of young
girls continually flitting up and back in the blackness. A girl's figure
comes flying out from the porch, down the path of light, and joins the
stealthy group.*

WHISPERING VOICE OF MERCY. Where's 'e got to now, Gladys ?

WHISPERING VOICE OF GLADYS. 'E've just finished.

VOICE OF CONNIE. Whü pushed t'door open ?

VOICE OF GLADYS. Tim Clyst—I giv' it a little push, meself.

VOICE OF CONNIE. Oh !

VOICE OF GLADYS. Tim Clyst's gone in !

ANOTHER VOICE. O-o-o-h!

VOICE OF MERCY. Whü else is there, tü?

VOICE OF GLADYS. Ivy's there, an' old Mrs. Potter, an' tü o' the maids from th'Hall; that's all as ever.

VOICE OF CONNIE. Not the old grey mare?

VOICE OF GLADYS. No. She ain't ther'. 'Twill just be th'ymn now, an' the Blessin'. Tibby gone for 'em?

VOICE OF MERCY. Yes.

VOICE OF CONNIE. Mr. Burlacombe's gone in home, I saw 'im pass by just now—'e don' like it. Father don't like it neither.

VOICE OF MERCY. Mr. Strangway shouln' 'ave taken my skylark, an' thrown father out o' winder. 'Tis goin' to be awful fun! Oh!

[*She jumps up and down in the darkness. And a voice from far in the shadow says: " Hsssh! Quiet, yü maids! " The voice has ceased speaking in the church. There is a moment's dead silence. The voice speaks again; then from the wheezy little organ come the first faint chords of a hymn.*

GLADYS. " Nearer, my God, to Thee! "

VOICE OF MERCY. 'Twill be funny, with no one 'ardly singin'.

[*The sound of the old hymn sung by just six voices comes out to them rather sweet and clear.*

GLADYS. [*Softly*] 'Tis pretty, tü. Why! They're only singin' one verse!

[*A moment's silence, and the voice speaks, uplifted, pronouncing the Blessing: " The peace of God——" As the last words die away, dark figures from the inn approach over the grass, till quite a crowd seems standing there without a word spoken. Then from out the church porch come the congregation. TIM CLYST first, hastily lost among the waiting figures in the dark; old Mrs. Potter, a half-blind old lady groping her way and perceiving nothing out of the ordinary; the two maids from the Hall, self-conscious and scared, scuttling along. Last, IVY BURLACOMBE quickly, and starting back at the dim, half-hidden crowd.*

VOICE OF GLADYS. [*Whispering*] Ivy! Here, quick!

[*Ivy sways, darts off towards the voice, and is lost in the shadow.*

VOICE OF FREMAN. [*Low*] Wait, boys, till I give signal.

[*Two or three squirks and giggles; TIM CLYST's voice: " Ya-as! Don't 'ee tread on my toe! " A soft, frightened " O-o-h! " from a girl. Some quick, excited whisperings: " Lüke! " " Zee there! " " He's comin'! " And then a perfectly dead silence. The figure of STRANGWAY is seen in his dark clothes, passing from the vestry to the church porch. He stands plainly visible in the lighted porch, locking the door, then steps forward. Just as he reaches the edge of the porch, a low hiss breaks the silence.*

It swells very gradually into a long, hissing groan. STRANGWAY
stands motionless, his hand over his eyes, staring into the dark-
ness. A girl's figure can be seen to break out of the darkness
and rush away. When at last the groaning has died into sheer
expectancy, STRANGWAY *drops his hand.*

STRANGWAY. [*In a low voice*] Yes! I'm glad. Is Jarland there?

FREMAN. He's 'ere—no thanks to yü! Hsss!

                 [*The hiss breaks out again, then dies away.*

JARLAND'S VOICE. [*Threatening*] Try if yü can dü it again.

STRANGWAY. No, Jarland, no! I ask you to forgive me. Humbly!

               [*A hesitating silence, broken by muttering.*

CLYST'S VOICE. Bravo!

A VOICE. That's vair!

A VOICE. 'E's afraid o' the sack—that's what 'tis.

A VOICE. [*Groaning*] 'E's a praaper coward.

A VOICE. Whü funked the doctor?

CLYST'S VOICE. Shame on 'ee, therr!

STRANGWAY. You're right—all of you! I'm not fit!

    [*An uneasy and excited muttering and whispering dies away into*
      renewed silence.

STRANGWAY. What I did to Tam Jarland is not the real cause of what
you're doing, is it? I understand. But don't be troubled. It's
all over. I'm going—you'll get someone better. Forgive me,
Jarland. I can't see your face—it's very dark.

FREMAN'S VOICE. [*Mocking*] Wait for the full müne.

GODLEIGH. [*Very low*] "My 'eart 'E lighted not!"

STRANGWAY. [*Starting at the sound of his own words thus mysteriously
given him out of the darkness*] Whoever found that, please tear it up!
[*After a moment's silence.*] Many of you have been very kind to me.
You won't see me again—— Good-bye, all!

    [*He stands for a second motionless, then moves resolutely down into*
      the darkness so peopled with shadows.

UNCERTAIN VOICES AS HE PASSES. Good-bye, zurr? Good luck,
zurr!   [*He has gone.*

CLYST'S VOICE. Three cheers for Mr. Strangway!

    [*And a queer, strangled cheer, with groans still threading it, arises.*

The curtain falls.

ACT III

SCENE I

In the Burlacombes' *hall sitting-room the curtains are drawn, a lamp burns, and the door stands open.* Burlacombe *and his wife are hovering there, listening to the sound of mingled cheers and groaning.*

Mrs. Burlacombe. Aw! my güdeness—what a thing t'appen! I'd süner 'a lost all me ducks. [*She makes towards the inner door.*] I can't never face 'im.

Burlacombe. 'E can't expect nothin' else, if 'e act like that.

Mrs. Burlacombe. 'Tes only düin' as 'e'd be done by.

Burlacombe. Aw! Yü can't go on forgivin' 'ere, an' forgivin' there. 'Tesn't nat'ral.

Mrs. Burlacombe. 'Tes the mischief 'e'm a parson. 'Tes 'im bein' a lamb o' God—or 'twidden be so quare for 'im to be forgivin'.

Burlacombe. Yü goo an' make un a güde 'ot drink.

Mrs. Burlacombe. Poor soul! What'll 'e dü now, I wonder? [*Under her breath.*] 'E's comin'!

[*She goes hurriedly.* Burlacombe, *with a startled look back, wavers and makes to follow her, but stops undecided in the inner doorway.* Strangway *comes in from the darkness. He turns to the window and drops overcoat and hat and the church key on the window-seat, looking about him as men do when too hard driven, and never fixing his eyes long enough on anything to see it.* Burlacombe, *closing the door into the house, advances a step. At the sound* Strangway *faces round.*

Burlacombe. I wanted for yü to know, zurr, that me an' mine 'adn't nothin' to dü wi' that darned fülishness, just now.

Strangway. [*With a ghost of a smile*] Thank you, Burlacombe. It doesn't matter. It doesn't matter a bit.

Burlacombe. I 'ope yü won't take no notice of it. Like a lot o' silly bees they get. [*After an uneasy pause.*] Yü'll excuse me spakin' of this mornin', an' what 'appened. 'Tes a brave pity it cam' on yü so sudden-like before yü 'ad time to think. 'Tes a sort o' thing a man shüde zet an' chew upon. Certainly 'tes not a bit o' yüse goin' against human nature. Ef yü don't stand up for yüreself there's no one else not goin' to. 'Tes yüre not 'avin' done that 'as made 'em so rampageous. [*Stealing another look at* Strangway.] Yü'll excuse me, zurr,

15*   449

spakin' of it, but 'tes amazin' sad to zee a man let go his own, without a word o' darin'.   'Tes as ef e' 'ad no passions-like.

STRANGWAY. Look at me, Burlacombe.

[BURLACOMBE *looks up, trying hard to keep his eyes on* STRANG-WAY'S, *that seem to burn in his thin face.*

STRANGWAY. Do I look like that?   Please, please!   [*He touches his breast.*] I've too much here.   Please!

BURLACOMBE. [*With a sort of startled respect*] Well, zurr, 'tes not for me to zay nothin', certainly.

[*He turns and after a slow look back at* STRANGWAY *goes out.*

STRANGWAY. [*To himself*] Passions!   No passions!   Ha!

[*The outer door is opened and* IVY BURLACOMBE *appears, and, seeing him, stops. Then, coming softly towards him, she speaks timidly.*

IVY. Oh! Mr. Strangway, Mrs. Bradmere's comin' from the Rectory. I ran an' told 'em.   Oh! 'twas awful.

[STRANGWAY *starts, stares at her, and turning on his heel, goes into the house. IVY's face is all puckered, as if she were on the point of tears. There is a gentle scratching at the door, which has not been quite closed.*

VOICE OF GLADYS. [*Whispering*] Ivy! Come on!

IVY. I won't.

VOICE OF MERCY. Yü must. Us can't dü without yü.

IVY. [*Going to the door*] I don't want to.

VOICE OF GLADYS. "Naughty maid, she won't come out." Ah! dü 'ee!

VOICE OF CONNIE. Tim Clyst an' Bobbie's comin'; us'll only be six anyway. Us can't dance "figure of eight" without yü.

IVY. [*Stamping her foot*] I don't want to dance at all! I don't.

MERCY. Aw! She's temper.   Yü can bang on tambourine, then!

GLADYS. [*Running in*] Quick, Ivy! Here's the old grey mare comin' down the green.   Quick.

[*With whispering and scuffling, gurgling and squeaking, the reluctant* IVY's *hand is caught and she is jerked away. In their haste they have left the door open behind them.*

VOICE OF MRS. BRADMERE. [*Outside*] Who's that?

[*She knocks loudly, and rings a bell; then, without waiting, comes in through the open door.*

[*Noting the overcoat and hat on the window-sill, she moves across to ring the bell. But as she does so,* MRS. BURLACOMBE, *followed by* BURLACOMBE, *comes in from the house.*

MRS. BRADMERE. This disgraceful business! Where's Mr. Strangway! I see he's in.

MRS. BURLACOMBE. Yes, m'm, he'm in—but—but Burlacombe dü zay he'm terrible upzet.

Mrs. Bradmere. I should think so.   I must see him—at once.

Mrs. Burlacombe. I doubt bed's the best place for 'un, an' a güde 'ot drink.   Burlacombe zays he'm like a man standin' on the edge of a cliff, and the laste tipsy o' wind might throw 'un over.

Mrs. Bradmere. [To Burlacombe] You've seen him, then?

Burlacombe. Yeas; an' I don't like the lüke of un—not a little bit, I don't.

Mrs. Burlacombe. [Almost to herself] Poor soul; 'e've a-'ad tü much to try 'un this yer long time past.   I've a-seen 'tis sperrit comin' thrü 'is body, as yü might zay.   He's torn to bits, that's what 'tis.

Burlacombe. 'Twas a praaper cowardly thing to hiss a man when he's down.   But 'twas natural tü, in a manner of spakin'.   But 'tesn't that troublin' 'im.   'Tes in here [touching his forehead], along of his wife, to my thinkin'.   They zay 'e've a-known about 'er afore she went away.   Think of what 'e've 'ad to kape in all this time.   'Tes enough to drive a man silly after that.   I've a-locked my gun up.   I see a man lüke like that once before—an' sure enough e' was dead in the mornin' !

Mrs. Bradmere. Nonsense, Burlacombe !   [To Mrs. Burlacombe.] Go an tell him I want to see him—must see him.   [Mrs. Burlacombe goes into the house.]   And look here, Burlacombe ; if we catch anyone, man or woman, talking of this outside the village, it'll be the end of their tenancy, whoever they may be.   Let them all know that.   I'm glad he threw that drunken fellow out of the window, though it was a little——

Burlacombe. Aye !   The nüspapers would be praaper glad of that, for a tiddy bit o' nüse.

Mrs. Bradmere. My goodness !   Yes !   The men are all up at the inn.   Go and tell them what I said—it's not to get about.   Go at once, Burlacombe.

Burlacombe. Must be a turrable job for 'im, everyone's knowin' about 'is wife like this.   He'm a proud man tü, I think.   'Tes a funny business altogether !

Mrs. Bradmere. Horrible !   Poor fellow !   Now, come !   Do your best, Burlacombe !

[Burlacombe touches his forelock and goes.   Mrs. Bradmere stands quite still, thinking.   Then going to the photograph, she stares up at it.

Mrs. Bradmere. You baggage !

[Strangway has come in noiselessly, and is standing just behind her. She turns, and sees him.   There is something so still, so startlingly still in his figure and white face, that she cannot for the moment find her voice.

Mrs. Bradmere. [At last] This is most distressing.   I'm deeply sorry.   [Then, as he does not answer, she goes a step closer.]   I'm an old woman; and old women must take liberties, you know, or they couldn't get on at all. Come now! Let's try and talk it over calmly and see if we can't put things right.

STRANGWAY. You were very good to come; but I would rather not.

MRS. BRADMERE. I know you're in as grievous trouble as a man can be.

STRANGWAY. Yes.

MRS. BRADMERE. [*With a little sound of sympathy*] What are you—thirty-five? I'm sixty-eight if I'm a day, old enough to be your mother. I can feel what you must have been through all these months, I can indeed. But you know you've gone the wrong way to work. We aren't angels down here below! And a son of the Church can't act as if for himself alone. The eyes of everyone are on him.

STRANGWAY. [*Taking the church key from the window-sill*] Take this, please.

MRS. BRADMERE. No, no, no! Jarland deserved all he got. You had great provocation——

STRANGWAY. It's not Jarland. [*Holding out the key.*] Please take it to the Rector. I beg his forgiveness. [*Touching his breast.*] There's too much I can't speak of—can't make plain. Take it to him, please.

MRS. BRADMERE. Mr. Strangway—I don't accept this. I am sure my husband—the Church—will never accept——

STRANGWAY. Take it!

MRS. BRADMERE. [*Almost unconsciously taking it*] Mind! We don't accept it. You must come and talk to the Rector to-morrow. You're overwrought. You'll see it all in another light, then.

STRANGWAY. [*With a strange smile*] Perhaps. [*Lifting the blind.*] Beautiful night! Couldn't be more beautiful!

MRS. BRADMERE. [*Startled—softly*] Don't turn away from those who want to help you! I'm a grumpy old woman, but I can feel for you. Don't try and keep it all back, like this! A woman would cry, and it would all seem clearer at once. Now won't you let me——?

STRANGWAY. No one can help, thank you.

MRS. BRADMERE. Come! Things haven't gone beyond mending, really, if you'll face them. [*Pointing to the photograph.*] You know what I mean. We dare not foster immorality.

STRANGWAY. [*Quivering as at a jabbed nerve*] Don't speak of that!

MRS. BRADMERE. But think what you've done, Mr. Strangway! If you can't take your wife back, surely you must divorce her. You can never help her to go on like this in secret sin.

STRANGWAY. Torture her—one way or the other?

MRS. BRADMERE. No, no; I want you to do as the Church—as all Christian society would wish. Come! You can't let this go on. My dear man, do your duty at all costs?

STRANGWAY. Break her heart!

MRS. BRADMERE. Then you love that woman—more than God!

STRANGWAY. [*His face quivering*] Love!

MRS. BRADMERE. They told me—— Yes, and I can see you're in a bad way. Come, pull yourself together! You can't defend what you're doing.

STRANGWAY. I do not try.

MRS. BRADMERE. I *must* get you to see! My father was a clergyman; I'm married to one; I've two sons in the Church. I know what I'm talking about. It's a priest's business to guide the people's lives.

STRANGWAY. [*Very low*] But not mine! No more!

MRS. BRADMERE. [*Looking at him shrewdly*] There's something very queer about you to-night. You ought to see a doctor.

STRANGWAY. [*A smile coming and going on his lips*] If I am not better soon——

MRS. BRADMERE. I know it must be terrible to feel that everybody—— [*A convulsive shiver passes over* STRANGWAY, *and he shrinks against the door.*] But come! Live it down! [*With anger growing at his silence.*] Live it down, man! You can't desert your post—and let these villagers do what they like with us? Do you realize that you're letting a woman, who has treated you abominably—yes, abominably—go scot-free, to live comfortably with another man? What an example!

STRANGWAY. Will you, please, not speak of that!

MRS. BRADMERE. I must! This great Church of ours is based on the rightful condemnation of wrong-doing. There are times when forgiveness is a sin, Michael Strangway. You must keep the whip hand. You must fight!

STRANGWAY. Fight! [*Touching his heart.*] My fight is *here*. Have *you* ever been in hell? For months and months—burned and longed; hoped against hope; killed a man in thought day by day? Never rested, for love and hate? I—condemn! I—judge! No! It's rest I have to find—somewhere—somehow—rest! And how—how can I find rest?

MRS. BRADMERE. [*Who has listened to his outburst in a sort of coma*] You are a strange man! One of these days you'll go off your head if you don't take care.

STRANGWAY. [*Smiling*] One of these days the flowers will grow out of me; and I shall sleep.

[MRS. BRADMERE *stares at his smiling face a long moment in silence, then with a little sound, half sniff, half snort, she goes to the door. There she halts.*

MRS. BRADMERE. And you mean to let all this go on—— Your wife——

STRANGWAY. Go! Please go!

MRS. BRADMERE. Men like you have been buried at cross-roads before now! Take care! God punishes!

STRANGWAY. Is there a God?

MRS. BRADMERE. Ah! [*With finality.*] You must see a doctor.

[*Seeing that the look on his face does not change, she opens the door, and hurries away into the moonlight.*

[STRANGWAY *crosses the room to where his wife's picture hangs, and stands before it, his hands grasping the frame. Then he takes it from the wall, and lays it face upwards on the window-seat.*

STRANGWAY. [*To himself*] Gone! What is there, now?

[*The sound of an owl's hooting is floating in, and of voices from the green outside the inn.*

STRANGWAY. [*To himself*] Gone! Taken faith—hope—life!

[JIM BERE *comes wandering into the open doorway.*

JIM BERE. Güde avenin', zurr.

[*At his slow gait, with his feeble smile, he comes in, and standing by the window-seat beside the long dark coat that still lies there, he looks down at* STRANGWAY *with his lost eyes.*

JIM. Yü threw un out of winder. I cud 'ave, once, I cud. [STRANGWAY *neither moves nor speaks; and* JIM BERE *goes on with his unimaginably slow speech.*] They'm laughin' at yü, zurr. An' so I come to tell 'ee how to dü. 'Twas full müne—when I caught 'em, him an' my girl. I caught 'em. [*With a strange and awful flash of fire.*] I did; an' I tuk un [*he takes up* STRANGWAY's *coat and grips it with his trembling hands, as a man grips another's neck*] like that—I tuk un.

[*As the coat falls, like a body out of which the breath has been squeezed,* STRANGWAY, *rising, catches it.*

STRANGWAY. [*Gripping the coat*] And he fell!

[*He lets the coat fall on the floor, and puts his foot on it. Then, staggering back, he leans against the window.*

JIM. Yü see, I loved 'er—I did. [*The lost look comes back to his eyes.*] Then somethin'—I dunno—and—and—— [*He lifts his hand and passes it up and down his side.*] 'Twas like this for ever.

[*They gaze at each other in silence.*

JIM. [*At last*] I come to tell yü. They'm all laughin' at yü. But yü'm strong—yü go over to Durford to that doctor man, an' take un like I did. [*He tries again to make the sign of squeezing a man's neck.*] They can't laugh at yü no more, then. Tha's what I come to tell yü. Tha's the way for a Christian man to dü. Güde naight, zurr. I come to tell ee.

[STRANGWAY *motions to him in silence. And, very slowly,* JIM BERE *passes out.*

[*The voices of men coming down the green are heard.*

VOICES. Güde naight, Tam.   Güde naight, old Jim !

VOICES. Güde naight, Mr. Trustaford.   'Tes a wonderful fine müne.

VOICE OF TRUSTAFORD. Ah !   'Tes a brave müne for th' poor old curate !

VOICE. " My 'eart 'E lighted not ! "

[TRUSTAFORD'S *laugh, and the rattling, fainter and fainter, of wheels.*
A spasm seizes on STRANGWAY'S *face, as he stands there by the open door ; his hand grips his throat ; he looks from side to side, as if seeking a way of escape.*

The curtain falls.

SCENE II

The BURLACOMBES' *high and nearly empty barn.   A lantern is hung by a rope that lifts the bales of straw, to a long ladder leaning against a rafter.   This gives all the light there is, save for a slender track of moonlight, slanting in from the end, where the two great doors are not quite closed.   On a rude bench in front of a few remaining, stacked, square-cut bundles of last year's hay, sits* TIBBY JARLAND, *a bit of apple in her mouth, sleepily beating on a tambourine.   With stockinged feet* GLADYS, IVY, CONNIE, *and* MERCY, TIM CLYST, *and* BOBBIE JARLAND, *a boy of fifteen, are dancing a truncated " Figure of Eight " ; and their shadows are dancing alongside on the walls.   Shoes and some apples have been thrown down close to the side door through which they have come in.   Now and then* IVY, *the smallest and best of the dancers, ejaculates words of direction, and one of the youths grunts or breathes loudly out of the confusion of his mind.   Save for this and the dumb beat and jingle of the sleepy tambourine, there is no sound.   The dance comes to its end, but the drowsy* TIBBY *goes on beating.*

MERCY. That'll dü, Tibby ; we're finished.   Ate yüre apple.
                                        [*The stolid* TIBBY *eats her apple.*

CLYST. [*In his teasing, excitable voice*] Yü maids don't dance 'alf's well as us dü.   Bobby 'e's a great dancer.   'E dance vine.   I'm a güde dancer, meself.

GLADYS. A'n't yü conceited just ?

CLYST. Aw !   Ah !   Yü'll give me kiss for that. [*He chases, but cannot catch that slippery white figure.*] Can't she glimmer !

MERCY. Gladys !   Up ladder !

CLYST. Yü go up ladder ; I'll catch 'ee then.   Naw, yü maids, don't yü give her succour.   That's not vair.
                                        [*Catching hold of* MERCY, *who gives a little squeal.*

CONNIE. Mercy, don't ! Mrs. Burlacombe'll hear. Ivy, go an'
peek. [IVY *goes to the side door and peers through.*
CLYST. [*Abandoning the chase and picking up an apple—they all have
the joyous irresponsibility that attends forbidden doings*] Ya-as, this is a
güde apple. Lüke at Tibby !
[TIBBY, *overcome by drowsiness, has fallen back into the hay, asleep.*
GLADYS, *leaning against the hay, breaks into humming :*

" There cam' three dükes a-ridin', a-ridin', a-ridin',
There cam' three dükes a ridin'
With a ransy-tansy tay ! "

CLYST. Us 'as got on vine ; us'll get prize for our dancin'.
CONNIE. There won't be no prize if Mr. Strangway goes away.
Tes funny 'twas Mrs. Strangway started us.
IVY. [*From the door*] 'Twas wicked to hiss him. [*A moment's hush.*
CLYST. 'Twasn't I.
BOBBIE. I never did.
GLADYS. Oh ! Bobbie, yü did ! Yü blew in my ear.
CLYST. 'Twas the praaper old wind in the trees. Did make a brave
noise, zurely.
MERCY. 'E shuldn't 'a let my skylark go.
CLYST. [*Out of sheer contradictoriness*] Ya-as, 'e shüde, then. What
dü yü want with th' birds of the air ? They'm no güde to yü.
IVY. [*Mournfully*] And now he's goin' away.
CLYST. Ya-as ; 'tes a pity. He's the best man I ever seen since
I was comin' from my mother. He's a güde man. He'm got a zad
face, sure enough, though !
IVY. Güde folk always 'ave zad faces.
CLYST. I knü a güde man—'e sold pigs—very güde man ; 'e 'ad
a büdiful bright vace like the müne. [*Touching his stomach.*] I was
sad, meself, once. 'Twas a funny scrabblin'-like feelin'.
GLADYS. If 'e go away, whü's goin' to finish us for confirmation ?
CONNIE. The Rector and the old grey mare.
MERCY. I don' want no more finishin' ; I'm confirmed enough.
CLYST. Ya-as ; yü'm a büty.
GLADYS. Suppose we all went an' asked 'im not to go ?
IVY. 'Twouldn't be no güde.
CONNIE. Where's 'e goin' ?
MERCY. He'll go to London, of course.
IVY. He's so gentle ; I think 'e'll go to an island, where there's
nothin' but birds and beasts and flowers.
CLYST. Aye ! He'm awful fond o' the dumb things.
IVY. They're kind and peaceful ; that's why.
CLYST. Aw ! Yü see tü praaper old tom cats ; they'm not tü
peaceful, after that, nor kind naighther.

BOBBIE. [*Surprisingly*] If 'e's sad, per'aps 'e'll go to 'Eaven.

IVY. Oh! not yet, Bobbie. He's tü young.

CLYST. [*Following his own thoughts*] Ya-as. 'Tes a funny place, tü, nowadays, judgin' from the papers.

GLADYS. Wonder if there's dancin' in 'Eaven?

IVY. There's beasts, and flowers, and waters, and trees—'e told us.

CLYST. Naw! There's no dumb things in 'Eaven. Jim Bere 'e says there is! 'E thinks 'is old cat's there.

IVY. Yes. [*Dreamily.*] There's stars, an' owls, an' a man playin' on the flute. Where 'tes güde, there must be music.

CLYST. Old brass band, shuldn' wonder, like Salvation Army.

IVY. [*Putting up her hands to an imaginary pipe*] No; 'tis a boy that goes so; an' all the dumb things an' all the people goo after 'im—like this.

[*She marches slowly, playing her imaginary pipe, and one by one they all fall in behind her, padding round the barn in their stockinged feet. Passing the big doors, IVY throws them open.*]
An' 'tes all like that in 'Eaven.

[*She stands there gazing out, still playing on her imaginary pipe. And they all stand a moment silent, staring into the moonlight.*]

CLYST. 'Tes a glory-be full müne to-night!

IVY. A goldie-cup—a big one. An' millions o' little goldie-cups on the floor of 'Eaven.

MERCY. Oh! Bother 'Eaven! Let's dance "Clapperclaws"! Wake up, Tibby!

GLADYS. Clapperclaws, clapperclaws! Come on, Bobbie—make circle!

CLYST. Clapperclaws! I dance that one fine.

IVY. [*Taking the tambourine*] See, Tibby; like this.

[*She hums and beats gently, then restores the tambourine to the sleepy TIBBY, who, waking, has placed a piece of apple in her mouth.*]

CONNIE. 'Tes awful difficult, this one.

IVY. [*Illustrating*] No; yü just jump, an' clap yüre 'ands. Lovely, lovely!

CLYST. Like ringin' bells! Come ahn!

[*TIBBY begins her drowsy beating, IVY hums the tune; they dance, and their shadows dance again upon the walls. When she has beaten but a few moments on the tambourine, TIBBY is overcome once more by sleep and falls back again into her nest of hay, with her little shoed feet just visible over the edge of the bench. IVY catches up the tambourine, and to her beating and humming the dancers dance on.*]

[*Suddenly GLADYS stops like a wild animal surprised, and cranes her neck towards the side door.*]

CONNIE [*Whispering*] What is it?

GLADYS. [*Whispering*] I hear—someone—comin' across the yard.

[*She leads a noiseless scamper towards the shoes.* BOBBIE JARLAND *shins up the ladder and seizes the lantern.* IVY *drops the tambourine. They all fly to the big doors, and vanish into the moonlight, pulling the doors nearly to again after them.*

[*There is the sound of scrabbling at the latch of the side door, and* STRANGWAY *comes into the nearly dark barn. Out in the night the owl is still hooting. He closes the door, and that sound is lost. Like a man walking in his sleep, he goes up to the ladder, takes the rope in his hand, and makes a noose. He can be heard breathing, and in the darkness the motions of his hands are dimly seen, freeing his throat and putting the noose round his neck. He stands swaying to and fro at the foot of the ladder; then, with a sigh, sets his foot on it to mount. One of the big doors creaks and opens in the wind, letting in a broad path of moonlight.*

[STRANGWAY *stops; freeing his neck from the noose, he walks quickly up the track of moonlight, whitened from head to foot, to close the doors.*

[*The sound of his boots on the bare floor has awakened* TIBBY JARLAND. *Struggling out of her hay nest she stands staring at his whitened figure, and bursts suddenly into a wail.*

TIBBY. O-oh! Mercy! Where are yü? I'm frightened! I'm frightened! O-oooo!

STRANGWAY. [*Turning—startled*] Who's that? Who is it?

TIBBY. O-oh! A ghosty! Oo-ooo!

STRANGWAY. [*Going to her quickly*] It's me, Tibby—Tib—only me!

TIBBY. I see'd a ghosty.

STRANGWAY. [*Taking her up*] No, no, my bird, you didn't! It was me.

TIBBY. [*Burying her face against him*] I'm frighted. It was a big one. [*She gives tongue again.*] O-o-oh!

STRANGWAY. There, there! It's nothing but me. Look!

TIBBY. No.   [*She peeps out all the same.*

STRANGWAY. See! It's the moonlight made me all white. See! You're a brave girl now?

TIBBY. [*Cautiously*] I want my apple.

[*She points towards her nest.* STRANGWAY *carries her there, picks up an apple, and gives it her.* TIBBY *takes a bite.*

TIBBY. I want my tambouline.

STRANGWAY. [*Giving her the tambourine, and carrying her back into the track of moonlight*] Now we're both ghosties? Isn't it funny?

TIBBY. [*Doubtfully*] Yes.

STRANGWAY. See ! The moon's laughing at us ! See ? Laugh then !

[TIBBY, *tambourine in one hand and apple in the other, smiles stolidly. He sets her down on the ladder, and stands, holding her level with him.*

TIBBY. [*Solemnly*] I'se still frightened.

STRANGWAY. No ! Full moon, Tibby ! Shall we wish for it ?

TIBBY. Full müne.

STRANGWAY. Moon ! We're wishing for you. Moon, moon !

TIBBY. Müne, we're wishin' for yü !

STRANGWAY. What do you wish it to be ?

TIBBY. Bright new shillin' !

STRANGWAY. A face.

TIBBY. Shillin', a shillin' !

STRANGWAY. [*Taking out a shilling and spinning it so that it falls into her pinafore*] See ! Your wish comes true.

TIBBY. Oh ! [*Putting the shilling in her mouth.*] Müne's still there !

STRANGWAY. Wish for *me*, Tibby !

TIBBY. Müne, I'm wishin' for yü !

STRANGWAY. Not yet !

TIBBY. Shall I shake my tambouline ?

STRANGWAY. Yes, shake your tambouline.

TIBBY. [*Shaking her tambourine*] Müne, I'm shakin' at yü.

[STRANGWAY *lays his hand suddenly on the rope, and swings it up on to the beam.*

TIBBY. What d'yü dü that for ?

STRANGWAY. To put it out of reach. It's better——

TIBBY. Why is it better ?   [*She stares up at him.*

STRANGWAY. Come along, Tibby ! [*He carries her to the big doors, and sets her down.*] See ! All asleep ! The birds, and the fields, and the moon !

TIBBY. Müne, müne, we're wishing for yü !

STRANGWAY. Send her your love, and say good-night.

TIBBY. [*Blowing a kiss*] Good-night, müne !

[*From the barn roof a little white dove's feather comes floating down in the wind.* TIBBY *follows it with her hand, catches it, and holds it up to him.*

TIBBY. [*Chuckling*] Lüke. The müne's sent a bit o' love !

STRANGWAY. [*Taking the feather*] Thank you, Tibby ! I want that bit o' love. [*Very faint, comes the sound of music.*] Listen !

TIBBY. It's Miss Willis, playin' on the pianny !

STRANGWAY. No ; it's Love ; walking and talking in the world.

TIBBY. [*Dubiously*] Is it ?

STRANGWAY. [*Pointing*] See ! Everything coming out to listen ! See them, Tibby ! All the little things with pointed ears, children,

and birds, and flowers, and bunnies; and the bright rocks, and—
men! Hear their hearts beating! And the wind listening!

TIBBY. I can't hear—nor I can't see!

STRANGWAY. Beyond—— [*To himself.*] They are—they must
be; I swear they are! [*Then, catching sight of* TIBBY'S *amazed eyes.*]
And now say good-bye to me.

TIBBY. Where yü goin'?

STRANGWAY. I don't know, Tibby.

VOICE OF MERCY. [*Distant and cautious*] Tibby! Tibby! Where
are yü?

STRANGWAY. Mercy calling; run to her!

[TIBBY *starts off, turns back and lifts her face. He bends to kiss
her, and flinging her arms round his neck, she gives him a good
hug. Then, knuckling the sleep out of her eyes, she runs.*

[STRANGWAY *stands, uncertain. There is a sound of heavy footsteps;
a man clears his throat, close by.*

STRANGWAY. Who's that?

CREMER. Jack Cremer. [*The big man's figure appears out of the shadow
of the barn.*] That yü, zurr?

STRANGWAY. Yes, Jack. How goes it?

CREMER. 'Tes empty, zurr. But I'll get on some'ow.

STRANGWAY. You put me to shame.

CREMER. No, zurr. I'd be killin' meself, if I didn' feel I must
stick it, like yü zaid. [*They stand gazing at each other in the moonlight.*

STRANGWAY. [*Very low*] I honour you.

CREMER. What's that? [*Then, as* STRANGWAY *does not answer.*]
I'll just be walkin'. I won't be goin' 'ome, to-night. 'Tes the full
müne—lucky.

STRANGWAY. [*Suddenly*] Wait for me at the cross-roads, Jack.
I'll come with you. Will you have me, brother?

CREMER. Sure!

STRANGWAY. Wait, then.

CREMER. Aye, zurr.

[*With his heavy tread* CREMER *passes on. And* STRANGWAY
*leans against the lintel of the door, looking at the moon, that,
quite full and golden, hangs not far above the straight horizon,
where the trees stand small, in a row.*

STRANGWAY. [*Lifting his hand in the gesture of prayer*] God, of the
moon and the sun; of joy and beauty, of loneliness and sorrow—
Give me strength to go on, till I love every living thing!

[*He moves away, following* JACK CREMER.
[*The full moon shines; the owl hoots; and someone is shaking*
TIBBY'S *tambourine.*

The curtain falls.

THE FOUNDATIONS

CAST OF THE ORIGINAL PRODUCTION AT THE ROYALTY
THEATRE, JUNE, 1917

LORD WILLIAM DROMONDY, M.P . .	*Mr. Dawson Milward*
POULDER, *his butler*	*Mr. Sidney Paxton*
JAMES, *first footman*	*Mr. Stephen T. Ewart*
HENRY, *second footman*	*Mr. Allan Jeayes*
THOMAS, *third footman*	*Mr. William Lawrence*
CHARLES, *fourth footman*	*Mr. Robert Lawlor*
THE PRESS	*Mr. Lawrence Hanray*
LEMMY, *a plumber*	*Mr. Dennis Eadie*
LADY WILLIAM DROMONDY . . .	*Miss Lydia Bilbrooke*
MISS STOKES	*Miss Gertrude Sterroll*
OLD MRS. LEMMY	*Miss Esme Hubbard*
LITTLE ANNE	*Miss Babs Farren*
LITTLE AIDA	*Miss Dinka Starace*

ACT I

Lord William Dromondy's *mansion in Park Lane. Eight o'clock of the evening.* Little Anne Dromondy *and the large footman,* James, *gaunt and grim, discovered in the wine cellar, by light of gas.* James, *in plush breeches, is selecting wine.*

L. Anne. James, are you really James?

James. No, my proper name's John.

L. Anne. Oh! [*A pause.*] And is Charles's an improper name, too?

James. His proper name's Mark.

L. Anne. Then is Thomas Matthew?

James. Miss Anne, stand clear o' that bin. You'll put your foot through one o' those 'ock bottles.

L. Anne. No, but, James—Henry might be Luke, really?

James. Now shut it, Miss Anne!

L. Anne. Who gave you those names? Not your godfathers and godmothers?

James. Poulder. Butlers think they're the Almighty. [*Gloomily.*] But his name's Bartholomew.

L. Anne. Bartholomew Poulder? It's rather jolly.

James. It's hidjeous.

L. Anne. Which do you like to be called—John or James?

James. I don't give a darn.

L. Anne. What is a darn?

James. 'Tain't in the dictionary.

L. Anne. Do you like my name? Anne Dromondy? It's old, you know. But it's funny, isn't it?

James. [*Indifferently*] It'll pass.

L. Anne. How many bottles have you got to pick out?

James. Thirty-four.

L. Anne. Are they all for the dinner, or for the people who come in to the Anti-Sweating Meeting afterwards?

James. All for the dinner. They give the Sweated—tea.

L. Anne. All for the dinner! They'll drink too much, won't they?

James. We've got to be on the safe side.

L. Anne. Will it be safer if they drink too much?

[James *pauses in the act of dusting a bottle to look at her, as if suspecting irony.*]

463

[*Sniffing*] Isn't the smell delicious here—like the taste of cherries when they've gone bad—[*she sniffs again*] and mushrooms ; and boot blacking——

JAMES. That's the escape of gas.

L. ANNE. Has the plumber's man been ?

JAMES. Yes.

L. ANNE. Which one ?

JAMES. Little blighter I've never seen before.

L. ANNE. What is a little blighter ?   Can *I* see ?

JAMES. He's just gone.

L. ANNE. [*Straying*] Oh ! . . . James, are these really the foundations ?

JAMES. You might 'arf say so.   There's a lot under a woppin' big house like this ; you can't hardly get to the bottom of it.

L. ANNE. Everything's built on something, isn't it ?   And what's *that* built on ?

JAMES. Ask another.

L. ANNE. If you wanted to blow it up, though, you'd have to begin from here, wouldn't you ?

JAMES. Who'd want to blow it up ?

L. ANNE. It *would* make a mess in Park Lane.

JAMES. I've seen a lot bigger messes than this'd make, out in the war.

L. ANNE. Oh ! but that's years ago !   Was it like this in the trenches, James ?

JAMES. [*Grimly*] Ah ! 'Cept that you couldn't lay your 'and on a bottle o' port when you wanted one.

L. ANNE. Do you, when you want it, here ?

JAMES. [*On guard*] I only suggest it's possible.

L. ANNE. Perhaps Poulder does.

JAMES. [*Icily*] I say nothin' about that.

L. ANNE. Oh ! Do say something !

JAMES. I'm ashamed of you, Miss Anne, pumpin' me !

L. ANNE. [*Reproachfully*] I'm not pumpin' !   I only want to make Poulder jump when I ask him.

JAMES. [*Grinning*] Try it on your own responsibility, then ; don't bring me in !

L. ANNE. [*Switching off*] James, do you think there's going to be a bloody revolution ?

JAMES. [*Shocked*] I shouldn't use that word, at your age.

L. ANNE. Why not ?   Daddy used it this morning to Mother. [*Imitating.*] " The country's in an awful state, darling ; there's going to be a bloody revolution, and we shall all be blown sky-high." Do you like Daddy ?

JAMES. [*Taken aback*] Like Lord William ?   What do you think ? We chaps would ha' done anything for him out there in the war.

L. ANNE. He never says that—he always says he'd have done anything for you !

JAMES. Well—that's the same thing.

L. ANNE. It isn't—it's the opposite. What is class hatred, James ?

JAMES. [*Wisely*] Ah ! A lot o' people thought when the war was over there'd be no more o' that. [*He sniggers.*] Used to amuse me to read in the papers about the wonderful unity that was comin'. I could ha' told 'em different.

L. ANNE. Why should people hate ? *I* like everybody.

JAMES. You know such a lot o' people, don't you ?

L. ANNE. Well, Daddy likes everybody, and Mother likes everybody, except the people who don't like Daddy. I bar Miss Stokes, of course ; but then, who wouldn't ?

JAMES. [*With a touch of philosophy*] That's right—we all bars them that tries to get something out of us.

L. ANNE. Who do *you* bar, James ?

JAMES. Well—[*Enjoying the luxury of thought.*]—Speaking generally, I bar everybody that looks down their noses at me. Out there in the trenches, there'd come a shell, and orf'd go some orficer's head, an' I'd think : That might ha' been me—we're all equal in the sight o' the stars. But when I got home again among the torfs, I says to meself : Out there, ye know, *you* filled a hole as well as me ; but here you've put it on again, with mufti.

L. ANNE. James, are your breeches made of mufti ?

JAMES. [*Contemplating his legs with a certain contempt*] Ah ! Footmen were to ha' been off ; but Lord William was scared we wouldn't get jobs in the rush. We're on his conscience, and it's on *my* conscience that I've been on his long enough—so, now I've saved a bit, I'm goin' to take meself orf it.

L. ANNE. Oh ! Are you going ? Where ?

JAMES. [*Assembling the last bottles*] Out o' Blighty !

L. ANNE. Is a little blighter a little Englishman ?

JAMES. [*Embarrassed*] Well—'e can be.

L. ANNE. [*Musing*] James—we're quite safe down here, aren't we, in a revolution ? Only, we wouldn't have fun. Which would you rather—be safe, or have fun ?

JAMES. [*Grimly*] Well, I had my bit o' fun in the war.

L. ANNE. *I* like fun that happens when you're not looking.

JAMES. Do you ? You'd ha' been just suited.

L. ANNE. James, is there a future life ? Miss Stokes says so.

JAMES. It's a belief, in the middle classes.

L. ANNE. What are the middle classes ?

JAMES. Anything from two 'undred a year to super-tax.

L. ANNE. Mother says they're terrible. Is Miss Stokes middle class ?

JAMES. Yes.

L. ANNE. Then I expect they *are* terrible. She's awfully virtuous, though, isn't she ?

JAMES. 'Tisn't so much the bein' virtuous, as the lookin' it, that's awful.

L. ANNE. Are all the middle classes virtuous ? Is Poulder ?

JAMES. [*Dubiously*] Well. . . . Ask him !

L. ANNE. Yes, I will. Look !

[*From an empty bin on the ground level she picks up a lighted taper, burnt almost to the end.*

JAMES. [*Contemplating it*] Careless !

L. ANNE. Oh ! And look ! [*She points to a rounded metal object lying in the bin, close to where the taper was.*] It's a bomb !

[*She is about to pick it up when* JAMES *takes her by the waist and puts her aside.*

JAMES. [*Sternly*] You stand back there ! I don't like the look o' that !

L. ANNE. [*With intense interest*] Is it really a bomb ? What fun !

JAMES. Go and fetch Poulder while I keep an eye on it.

L. ANNE. [*On tiptoe of excitement*] If only I can make him jump ! Oh, James ! we needn't put the light out, need we ?

JAMES. No. Clear off and get him, and don't you come back.

L. ANNE. Oh ! but I must ! I found it !

JAMES. Cut along.

L. ANNE. Shall we bring a bucket ?

JAMES. Yes. [ANNE *flies off.*]

[*Gazing at the object.*] Near go ! Thought I'd seen enough o' them to last my time. That little gas blighter ! He looked a rum 'un, too—one o' these 'ere Bolshies.

[*In the presence of this grim object the habits of the past are too much for him. He sits on the ground, leaning against one of the bottle baskets, keeping his eyes on the bomb, his large, lean gorgeous body spread, one elbow on his plush knee. Taking out an empty pipe, he places it mechanically, bowl down, between his lips. There enter, behind him, as from a communication trench,* POULDER, *in swallow-tails, with* LITTLE ANNE *behind him.*

L. ANNE. [*Peering round him—ecstatic*] Hurrah ! Not gone off yet ! It can't—can it—while James is sitting on it ?

POULDER. [*Very broad and stout, with square shoulders, a large ruddy face, and a small mouth*] No noise, Miss. James !

JAMES. Hallo !

POULDER. What's all this ?

JAMES. Bomb !

POULDER. Miss Anne, off you go, and don't you——

L. ANNE. Come back again! I know!   [*She flies.*

JAMES. [*Extending his hand with the pipe in it*] See!

POULDER. [*Severely*] You've been at it again! Look here, you're
not in the trenches now. Get up! What are your breeches goin'
to be like? You might break a bottle any moment!

JAMES. [*Rising with a jerk to a sort of "Attention!"*] Look here,
you starched antiquity, you and I and that bomb are here in the
sight of the stars. If you don't look out I'll stamp on it and blow us
all to glory! Drop your civilian swank!

POULDER. [*Seeing red*] Ho! Because you had the privilege of
fightin' for your country, you still think you can put it on, do you?
Take up your wine! 'Pon my word, you fellers have got no nerve
left!

> [JAMES *makes a sudden swoop, lifts the bomb and poises it in both
> hands.* POULDER *recoils against a bin and gazes at the object.*

JAMES. Put up your hands!

POULDER. I defy you to make me ridiculous.

JAMES. [*Fiercely*] Up with 'em!

> [POULDER'S *hands go up in an uncontrollable spasm, which he subdues
> almost instantly, pulling them down again.*

JAMES. Very good.   [*He lowers the bomb.*

POULDER. [*Surprised*] *I* never lifted 'em.

JAMES. You'd have made a first-class Boche, Poulder. Take the
bomb yourself; you're in charge of this section.

POULDER. [*Pouting*] It's no part of my duty to carry menial objects;
if you're afraid of it I'll send 'Enry.

JAMES. Afraid! You 'Op o' me thumb!

> [*From the "communication trench" appears* LITTLE ANNE, *followed
> by a thin, sharp, sallow-faced man of thirty-five or so, and
> another* FOOTMAN, *carrying a wine-cooler*.

L. ANNE. I've brought the bucket, and the Press.

PRESS. [*In front of* POULDER'S *round eyes and mouth*] Ah, major domo,
I was just taking the names of the Anti-Sweating dinner. [*He catches
sight of the bomb in* JAMES'S *hand.*] By George! What A 1 irony!
[*He brings out a note-book and writes.*] "Highest class dining to relieve
distress of lowest class—bombed by same!" Tipping!

> [*He rubs his hands.*

POULDER. [*Drawing himself up*] Sir? *This* is present! [*He indicates* ANNE *with the flat of his hand.*]

L. ANNE. I found the bomb.

PRESS. [*Absorbed*] By Jove! This *is* a piece of luck!   [*He writes.*

POULDER. [*Observing him*] This won't do—it won't do at all!

PRESS. [*Writing—absorbed*] "Beginning of the British Revolution!"

POULDER. [*To* JAMES] Put it in the cooler. 'Enry, 'old up the
cooler. Gently! Miss Anne, get be'ind the Press.

JAMES. [*Grimly—holding the bomb above the cooler*] It won't be the Press that'll stop Miss Anne goin' to 'Eaven if one o' this sort goes off. Look out ! I'm goin' to drop it.

[ALL *recoil.* HENRY *puts the cooler down and backs away.*

L. ANNE. [*Dancing forward*] Oh ! Let me see ! I missed all the war, you know !　　　　　　　[JAMES *lowers the bomb into the cooler.*

POULDER. [*Regaining courage—to* THE PRESS, *who is scribbling in his note-book*] If you mention this before the police lay their hands on it, it'll be contempt o' Court.

PRESS. [*Struck*] I say, major domo, don't call in the police ! That's the last resort. Let me do the Sherlocking for you. Who's been down here ?

L. ANNE. The plumber's man about the gas—a little blighter we'd never seen before.

JAMES. Lives close by, in Royal Court Mews—No. 3. I had a word with him before he came down. Lemmy his name is.

PRESS. " Lemmy ! " [*Noting the address.*] Right-o !

L. ANNE. Oh ! Do let me come with you !

POULDER. [*Barring the way*] I've got to lay it all before Lord William.

PRESS. Ah ! What's he like ?

POULDER. [*With dignity*] A gentleman, sir.

PRESS. Then he won't want the police in.

POULDER. *Nor* the Press, if I may go so far as to say so.

PRESS. One to you ! But I defy you to keep this from the Press, major domo. This is the most significant thing that has happened in our time. Guy Fawkes is nothing to it. The foundations of Society reeling ! By George, it's a second Bethlehem ! [*He writes.*

POULDER. [*To* JAMES] Take up your wine and follow me. 'Enry, bring the cooler. Miss Anne, precede us. [*To* THE PRESS.] You defy me ? Very well ; I'm goin' to lock you up here.

PRESS. [*Uneasy*] I say—this is medieval. [*He attempts to pass.*

POULDER. [*Barring the way*] Not so ! James, put him up in that empty 'ock bin. We can't have dinner disturbed in any way.

JAMES. [*Putting his hands on* THE PRESS'S *shoulders*] Look here— go quiet ! I've had a grudge against you yellow newspaper boys ever since the war—frothin' up your daily hate, an' makin' the Huns desperate. You nearly took my life five hundred times out there. If you squeal, I'm goin' to take yours once—and that'll be enough.

PRESS. That's awfully unjust. I'm not yellow !

JAMES. Well, you look it. Hup !

PRESS. Little Lady Anne, haven't you any authority with these fellows ?

L. ANNE. [*Resisting* POULDER'S *pressure*] I won't go ! I simply *must* see James put him up !

PRESS. Now, I warn you all plainly—there'll be a leader on this.

        [*He tries to bolt, but is seized by* JAMES.

JAMES. [*Ironically*] Ho !

PRESS. My paper has the biggest influence——

JAMES. That's the one ! Git up in that 'ock bin, and mind your feet among the claret.

PRESS. This is an outrage on the Press.

JAMES. Then it'll wipe out one by the Press on the Public—an' leave just a million over ! Hup !

POULDER. 'Enry, give 'im an 'and.

        [THE PRESS *mounts, assisted by* JAMES *and* HENRY.

L. ANNE. [*Ecstatic*] It's lovely !

POULDER. [*Nervously*] Mind the '87 ! Mind !

JAMES. Mind your feet in Mr. Poulder's favourite wine !

    [A WOMAN'S *voice is heard, as from the depths of a cave, calling* " Anne ! Anne !"

L. ANNE. [*Aghast*] Miss Stokes—I must hide !

    [*She gets behind* POULDER. *The three Servants achieve dignified positions in front of the bins. The voice comes nearer.* THE PRESS *sits dangling his feet, grinning.* MISS STOKES *appears. She is a woman of forty-five and terribly good manners. Her greyish hair is rolled back off her forehead. She is in a high evening dress, and in the dim light radiates a startled composure.*

MISS S. Poulder, where is Miss Anne ?

        [ANNE *lays hold of the backs of his legs.*

POULDER. [*Wincing*] I am not in a position to inform you, Miss.

MISS S. They told me she was down here. And what is all this about a bomb ?

POULDER. [*Lifting his hand in a calming manner*] The crisis is past ; we have it in ice, Miss. 'Enry, show Miss Stokes !

        [HENRY *indicates the cooler.*

MISS S. Good gracious ! Does Lord William know ?

POULDER. Not at present, Miss.

MISS S. But he ought to, at once.

POULDER. We 'ave 'ad complications.

MISS S. [*Catching sight of the legs of* THE PRESS] Dear me ! What *are* those ?

JAMES. [*Gloomily*] The complications.

        [MISS STOKES *puts up her glasses and stares at them.*

PRESS. [*Cheerfully*] Miss Stokes, would you kindly tell Lord William I'm here from the Press, and would like to speak to him ?

MISS S. But—er—why are you up there ?

JAMES. 'E got up out o' remorse, Miss.

MISS S. What *do* you mean, James ?

PRESS. [*Warmly*] Miss Stokes, I appeal to you. Is it fair to attribute responsibility to an unsigned journalist for what he has to say?

JAMES. [*Sepulchrally*] Yes, when you've got 'im in a nice dark place.

MISS S. James, be more respectful! We owe the Press a very great debt.

JAMES. I'm goin' to pay it, Miss.

MISS S. [*At a loss*] Poulder, this is really most——

POULDER. I'm bound to keep the Press out of temptation, Miss, till I've laid it all before Lord William. 'Enry, take up the cooler. James, watch 'im till we get clear, then bring on the rest of the wine and lock up. Now, Miss.

MISS S. But where *is* Anne?

PRESS. Miss Stokes, as a lady——!

MISS S. I shall go and fetch Lord William!

POULDER. We will all go, Miss.

L. ANNE. [*Rushing out from behind his legs*] No—me!

[*She eludes* MISS STOKES *and vanishes, followed by that distracted but still well-mannered lady.*

POULDER. [*Looking at his watch*] 'Enry, leave the cooler, and take up the wine; tell Thomas to lay it out; get the champagne into ice, and 'ave Charles 'andy in the 'all in case some literary bounder comes punctual. [HENRY *takes up the wine and goes.*

PRESS. [*Above his head*] I say, let me down. This is a bit un-dignified, you know. My paper's a great organ.

POULDER. [*After a moment's hesitation*] Well—take 'im down, James; he'll do some mischief among the bottles.

JAMES. 'Op off your base, and trust to me.

[THE PRESS *slides off the bin's edge, is received by* JAMES, *and not landed gently.*

POULDER. [*Contemplating him*] The incident's closed; no ill-feeling, I hope?

PRESS. No-o.

POULDER. That's right. [*Clearing his throat.*] While we're waitin' for Lord William—if you're interested in wine—[*Philosophically*] you can read the history of the times in this cellar. Take 'ock. [*He points to a bin.*] Not a bottle gone. German product, of course. Now, that 'ock is 'avin' the time of its life—maturin' grandly; got a wonderful chance. About the time we're bringin' ourselves to drink it, we shall be havin' the next great war. With luck that 'ock may lie there another quarter of a century, and a sweet pretty wine it'll be. I only hope I may be here to drink it. Ah! [*He shakes his head*]—but look at claret! Times are hard on claret. We're givin' it an awful doin'. Now, there's a Ponty Canny [*He points to a bin*]—if we weren't so 'opelessly allied with France, that wine

would have a reasonable future. As it is—none! We drink it up
and up; not more than sixty dozen left. And where's its equal to
come from for a dinner wine—ah! I ask you? On the other hand,
port is steady; made in a little country, all but the cobwebs and the
old boot flavour; guaranteed by the British Navy ; we may 'ope for
the best with port. Do you drink it?

PRESS. When I get the chance.

POULDER. Ah! [*Clears his throat.*] I've often wanted to ask :
What do they pay you—if it's not indelicate?

                                 [THE PRESS *shrugs his shoulders.*]
Can you do it at the money?   [THE PRESS *shakes his head.*]
Still—it's an easy life! I've regretted sometimes that I didn't have
a shot at it myself; influencin' other people without disclosin' your
identity—something very attractive about that. [*Lowering his voice.*]
Between man and man, now—what do you think of the situation of
the country—these processions of the unemployed—the Red Flag an'
the Marsillaisy in the streets—all this talk about an upheaval?

PRESS. Well, speaking as a Socialist——

POULDER. [*Astounded*] Why, I thought your paper was Tory!

PRESS. So it is. That's nothing!

POULDER. [*Open-mouthed*] Dear me! [*Pointing to the bomb.*] So you
really think there's something in this?

JAMES. [*Sepulchrally*] 'Igh explosive.

PRESS. [*Taking out his note-book*] Too much, anyway, to let it drop.

                        [*A pleasant voice calls* " Poulder! Hallo! "]

POULDER. [*Forming a trumpet with his hand*] Me Lord!

    [*As* LORD WILLIAM *appears,* JAMES, *overcome by reminiscences,*
      salutes, and is mechanically answered. LORD WILLIAM *has*
      " *charm.*" *His hair and moustache are crisp and just beginning*
      to grizzle. His bearing is free, easy, and only faintly armoured.
      He will go far to meet you any day. He is in full evening dress.

LORD W. [*Cheerfully*] I say, Poulder, what have you and James been
doing to the Press? Liberty of the Press—it isn't what it was, but
there is a limit. Where is he?

    [*He turns to* JAMES *between whom and himself there is still the*
      freemasonry of the trenches.

JAMES. [*Pointing to* POULDER] Be'ind the parapet, me Lord.

    [THE PRESS *moves out from where he has involuntarily been screened*
      by POULDER, *who looks at* JAMES *severely.* LORD WILLIAM
      hides a smile.

PRESS. Very glad to meet you, Lord William. My presence down
here is quite involuntary.

LORD W. [*With a charming smile*] I know. The Press has to put
its—er—to go to the bottom of everything. Where's this bomb,
Poulder? Ah!   [*He looks into the wine cooler.*

PRESS. [*Taking out his note-book*] Could I have a word with you on the crisis, before dinner, Lord William ?

LORD W. It's time you and James were up, Poulder. [*Indicating the cooler.*] Look after this ; tell Lady William I'll be there in a minute.

POULDER. Very good, me Lord.

[*He goes, followed by* JAMES *carrying the cooler.*
[*As* THE PRESS *turns to look after them*, LORD WILLIAM *catches sight of his back.*

LORD W. I must apologize, sir.   Can I brush you ?

PRESS. [*Dusting himself*] Thanks ; it's only behind. [*He opens his note-book.*] Now, Lord William, if you'd kindly outline your views on the national situation ; after such a narrow escape from death, I feel they might have a moral effect.   My paper, as you know, is concerned with the deeper aspect of things.   By the way, what do you value your house and collection at ?

LORD W. [*Twisting his little moustache*] Really—I can't !   Really !

PRESS. Might I say a quarter of a million—lifted in two seconds and a half—hundred thousand to the second.   It brings it home, you know.

LORD W. No, no ; dash it !   No !

PRESS. [*Disappointed*] I see—not draw attention to your property in the present excited state of public feeling ?   Well, suppose we approach it from the view-point of the Anti-Sweating dinner.   I have the list of guests—very weighty !

LORD W. Taken some lifting—wouldn't they ?

PRESS. [*Seriously*] May I say that you designed the dinner to soften the tension, at this crisis ?   You saw that case, I suppose, this morning, of the woman dying of starvation in Bethnal Green ?

LORD W. [*Desperately*] Yes—yes !   I've been horribly affected.   I always knew this slump would come after the war, sooner or later.

PRESS. [*Writing*] " . . . had predicted slump."

LORD W. You see, I've been an Anti-Sweating man for years, and I thought if only we could come together now . . .

PRESS. [*Nodding*] I see—I see !   Get Society interested in the Sweated, through the dinner.   I have the menu here. [*He produces it.*]

LORD W. Good God, man—more than that !   I want to show the people that we stand side by side with them, as we did in the trenches. The whole thing's too jolly awful.   I lie awake over it.

[*He walks up and down.*

PRESS. [*Scribbling*] One moment, please.   I'll just get that down— " Too jolly awful—lies awake over it.   Was wearing a white waistcoat with pearl buttons." [*At a sign of resentment from his victim.*] I want the human touch, Lord William—it's everything in my paper.   What do you say about this attempt to bomb you ?

LORD W. Well, in a way I think it's d——d natural.

PRESS. [*Scribbling*] " Lord William thought it d——d natural."

LORD W. [*Overhearing*] No, no ; don't put that down. What I mean is, I should like to get hold of those fellows that are singing the Marseillaise about the streets—fellows that have been in the war—real sports they are, you know—thorough good chaps at bottom—and say to them : " Have a feeling heart, boys ; put yourself in my position." I don't believe a bit they'd want to bomb me then.

[*He walks up and down.*

PRESS. [*Scribbling and muttering*] " The idea of brotherhood——" D'you mind my saying that ? Word brotherhood—always effective —always—— [*He writes.*

LORD W. [*Bewildered*] " Brotherhood ! " Well, it's pure accident that I'm here and they're there. All the same, I can't pretend to be starving. Can't go out into Hyde Park and stand on a tub, can I ? But if I could only show them what I feel—they're such good chaps —poor devils.

PRESS. I quite appreciate ! [*He writes.*] " Camel and needle's eye." You were at Eton and Oxford ? Your constituency I know. Clubs ? But I can get all that. Is it your view that Christianity is on the up-grade, Lord William ?

LORD W. [*Dubious*] What d'you mean by Christianity—loving-kindness and that ? Of course I think that dogma's got the knock.

[*He walks.*

PRESS. [*Writing*] " Lord William thought dogma had got the knock." I should like you just to develop your definition of Christianity. " Loving-kindness "—strikes rather a new note.

LORD W. *New ?* What about the Sermon on the Mount ?

PRESS. [*Writing*] " Refers to Sermon on Mount." I take it you don't belong to any Church, Lord William ?

LORD W. [*Exasperated*] Well, really—I've been baptized and that sort of thing. But look here——

PRESS. Oh ! you can trust me—I shan't say anything that you'll regret. Now, do you consider that a religious revival would help to quiet the country ?

LORD W. Well, I think it would be a deuced good thing if everybody were a bit more kind.

PRESS. Ah ! [*Musing.*] I feel that your views are strikingly original, Lord William. If you could just open out on them a little more ? How far would you apply kindness in practice ?

LORD W. *Can* you apply it in theory ?

PRESS. I believe it is done. But would you allow yourself to be blown up with impunity ?

LORD W. Well, that's a bit extreme. But I quite sympathize with this chap. Imagine yourself in his shoes. He sees a huge house, all

16

these bottles, us swilling them down; perhaps he's got a starving wife, or consumptive kids.

PRESS. [*Writing and murmuring*] Um-m! "Kids."

LORD W. He thinks: "But for the grace of God, there swill I. Why should that blighter have everything and I nothing?" and all that.

PRESS. [*Writing*] "And all that." [*Eagerly.*] Yes?

LORD W. And gradually—you see—this contrast—becomes an obsession with him. "There's got to be an example made," he thinks; and—er—he makes it, don't you know?

PRESS. [*Writing*] Ye-es? And—when you're the example?

LORD W. Well, you feel a bit blue, of course. But my point is that you quite see it.

PRESS. From the other world. Do you believe in a future life, Lord William? The public took a lot of interest in the question, if you remember, at the time of the war. It might revive at any moment, if there's to be a revolution.

LORD W. The wish is always father to the thought, isn't it?

PRESS. Yes! But—er—doesn't the question of a future life rather bear on your point about kindness? If there isn't one—why be kind?

LORD W. Well, I should say one oughtn't to be kind for any motive—that's self-interest; but just because one feels it, don't you know.

PRESS. [*Writing vigorously*] That's very new—very new!

LORD W. [*Simply*] You chaps are wonderful.

PRESS. [*Doubtfully*] You mean we're—we're——

LORD W. No, really. You have such a d——d hard time. It must be perfectly beastly to interview fellows like me.

PRESS. Oh! Not at all, Lord William. Not at all. I assure you compared with a literary man, it's—it's almost heavenly.

LORD W. You must have a wonderful knowledge of things.

PRESS. [*Bridling a little*] Well—I shouldn't say that.

LORD W. I don't see how you can avoid it. You turn your hands to everything.

PRESS. [*Modestly*] Well—yes, yes.

LORD W. I say: Is there really going to be a revolution, or are you making it up, you Press?

PRESS. We don't know. We never know whether we come before the event, or it comes before us.

LORD W. That's very deep—very deep. D'you mind lending me your note-book a moment. I'd like to stick that down. All right, I'll use the other end. [THE PRESS *hands it hypnotically.*

LORD W. [*Jotting*] Thanks awfully. Now what's your real opinion of the situation?

Press. As a man or a Press man?

Lord W. Is there any difference?

Press. Is there any connection?

Lord W. Well, as a man.

Press. As a man, I think it's rotten.

Lord W. [*Jotting*] " Rotten." And as a pressman?

Press. [*Smiling*] Prime.

Lord W. What! Like a Stilton cheese. Ha, ha!

[*He is about to write.*

Press. My stunt, Lord William. *You* said that.

[*He jots it on his cuff.*

Lord W. But look here! Would you say that a strong press movement would help to quiet the country?

Press. Well, as you ask me, Lord William, I'll tell you. No newspapers for a month would do the trick.

Lord W. [*Jotting*] By Jove! That's brilliant.

Press. Yes, but I should starve. [*He suddenly looks up, and his eyes, like gimlets, bore their way into* Lord William's *pleasant, troubled face.*] Lord William, you could do me a real kindness. Authorize me to go and interview the fellow who left the bomb here; I've got his address. I promise you to do it most discreetly. Fact is—well— I'm in low water. Since the war we simply can't get sensation enough for the new taste. Now, if I could have an article headed : " Bombed and Bomber "—sort of double interview, you know, it'd very likely set me on my legs again. [*Very earnestly.*] Look!

[*He holds out his frayed wristbands.*

Lord W. [*Grasping his hand*] My dear chap, certainly. Go and interview this blighter, and then bring him round here. You can do that for *me*. I'd very much like to see him, as a matter of fact.

Press. Thanks awfully; I shall never forget it. Oh! might I have my note-book?   [Lord William *hands it back*.

Lord W. And look here, if there's anything—when a fellow's fortunate and another's not——

[*He puts his hand into his breast pocket.*

Press. Oh, thank you! But you see, I shall have to write you up a bit, Lord William. The old aristocracy—you know what the public still expects; if you were to lend me money, you might feel——

Lord W. By Jove! Never should have dreamt——

Press. No! But it wouldn't do. Have you a photograph of yourself?

Lord W. Not on me.

Press. Pity! By the way, has it occurred to you that there may be another bomb on the premises?

LORD W. Phew! I'll have a look.

[*He looks at his watch, and begins hurriedly searching the bins, bending down and going on his knees. THE PRESS reverses the note-book again and sketches him.*

PRESS. [*To himself*] Ah! That'll do. "Lord William examines the foundations of his house."

[*A voice calls "Bill!" THE PRESS snaps the note-book to, and looks up. There, where the "communication trench" runs in, stands a tall and elegant woman in the extreme of evening dress.*

[*With presence of mind.*] Lady William? You'll find Lord William— Oh! Have you a photograph of him?

LADY W. Not on me.

PRESS. [*Eyeing her*] Er—no—I suppose not—no. Excuse me!

[*He sidles past her and is gone.*

LADY W. [*With lifted eyebrows*] Bill!

LORD W. [*Emerging, dusting his knees*] Hallo, Nell! I was just making sure there wasn't another bomb.

LADY W. Yes; that's why I came down. Who was that person?

LORD W. Press.

LADY W. He looked awfully yellow. I hope you haven't been giving yourself away.

LORD W. [*Dubiously*] Well, I don't know. They're like corkscrews.

LADY W. What did he ask you?

LORD W. What didn't he?

LADY W. Well, what did you tell him?

LORD W. That I'd been baptized—but he promised not to put it down.

LADY W. Bill, you are absurd.   [*She gives a light little laugh.*

LORD W. I don't remember anything else, except that it was quite natural we should be bombed, don't you know.

LADY W. Why, what harm have we done?

LORD W. Been born, my dear. [*Suddenly serious.*] I say, Nell, how am I to tell what this fellow felt when he left that bomb here?

LADY W. Why do you want to?

LORD W. Out there one used to know what one's men felt.

LADY W. [*Staring*] My dear boy, I really don't think you ought to see the Press; it always upsets you.

LORD W. Well! Why should you and I be going to eat ourselves silly to improve the condition of the sweated, when——

LADY W. [*Calmly*] When they're going to "improve" ours, if we don't look out. We've got to get in first, Bill.

LORD W. [*Gloomily*] I know. It's all fear. That's it! Here we are, and here we shall stay—as if there'd never been a war.

LADY W. Well, thank heaven there's no "front" to a revolution.

You and I can go to glory together this time.   Compact!   Anything that's on, I'm to share in.

LORD W. Well, in reason.

LADY W. No, in rhyme too.

LORD W. I say, your dress!

LADY W. Yes, Poulder tried to stop me, but I wasn't going to have you blown up without me.

LORD W. You duck.   You do look stunning.   Give us a kiss!

LADY W. [*Starting back*] Oh, Bill!   Don't touch me—your hands!

LORD W. Never mind, my mouth's clean.

   [*They stand about a yard apart, and bending their faces towards each other, kiss on the lips.*

L. ANNE. [*Appearing suddenly from the " communication trench," and tip-toeing silently between them.*] Oh, Mum!   You and Daddy *are* wasting time!   Dinner's ready, you know!

The curtain falls.

ACT II

The single room of old MRS. LEMMY, *in a small grey house in Bethnal Green, the room of one cumbered by little save age, and the crockery debris of the past. A bed, a cupboard, a coloured portrait of Queen Victoria, and—of all things—a fiddle, hanging on the wall. By the side of old* MRS. LEMMY *in her chair is a pile of corduroy trousers, her day's sweated sewing, and a small table. She sits with her back to the window, through which, in the last of the light, the opposite side of the little grey street is visible under the evening sky, where hangs one white cloud shaped like a horned beast. She is still sewing, and her lips move. Being old, and lonely, she has that habit of talking to herself, distressing to those who cannot overhear. From the smack of her tongue she was once a West Country cottage woman; from the look of her creased, parchmenty face, she was once a pretty girl with black eyes, in which there is still much vitality. The door is opened with difficulty and a little girl enters, carrying a pile of unfinished corduroy trousers nearly as large as herself. She puts them down against the wall, and advances. She is eleven or twelve years old; large-eyed, dark-haired, and sallow. Half a woman of this and half of another world, except when, as now, she is as irresponsible a bit of life as a little flowering weed growing out of a wall. She stands looking at* MRS. LEMMY *with dancing eyes.*

L. AIDA. I've brought yer to-morrer's trahsers. Y'nt yer finished wiv to-dy's ? I want to tyke 'em.

MRS. L. No, me dear. Drat this last one—me old fengers !

L. AIDA. I learnt some poytry to-dy—I did.

MRS. L. Well, I never !

L. AIDA. [*Reciting with unction*]

> " Little lamb who myde thee ?
> Dost thou know who myde thee,
> Gyve thee life and byde thee feed
> By the stream and o'er the mead ;
> Gyve thee clothing of delight,
> Softest clothing, woolly, bright ;
> Gyve thee such a tender voice,
> Myking all the vyles rejoice.
>> Little lamb who myde thee ?
>> Dost thou know who myde thee ? "

MRS. L. Tes wonderful what things they tache yu nowadays.

L. AIDA. When I grow up I'm goin' to 'ave a revolver an' shoot the people that steals my jools.

MRS. L. Deary-me, wherever du yu get yure notions?

L. AIDA. An' I'm goin' to ride on an 'orse be'ind a man; an' I'm goin' to ryce trynes in my motor car.

MRS. L. [*Dryly*] Ah! Yu'um gwine to be very busy, that's sartin. Can you sew?

L. AIDA. [*With a smile*] Nao.

MRS. L. Don' they tache yu that, there?

L. AIDA. [*Blending contempt and a lingering curiosity*] Nao.

MRS. L. Tes wonderful genteel.

L. Aida. I can sing, though.

MRS. L. Let's 'ear yu, then.

L. AIDA. [*Shaking her head*] I can ply the pianner. I can ply a tune.

MRS. L. Whose pianner?

L. AIDA. Mrs. Brahn's when she's gone aht.

MRS. L. Well, yu are gettin' edjucation! Du they tache yu to love yure neighbours?

L. AIDA. [*Ineffably*] Nao. [*Straying to the window.*] Mrs. Lemmy, what's the moon?

MRS. L. The mune? Us yused to zay 'twas made o' crame cheese.

L. AIDA. I can see it.

MRS. L. Ah! Don' yu never go wishin' for it, me dear.

L. AIDA. I daon't.

MRS. L. Folks as wish for the mune never du no gude.

L. AIDA. [*Craning out, brilliant*] I'm goin' dahn in the street. I'll come back for yer trahsers.

MRS. L. Well, go yu, then, an' get a breath o' fresh air in yure chakes. I'll sune 'a feneshed.

L. AIDA. [*Solemnly*] I'm goin' to be a dancer, I am.

[*She rushes suddenly to the door, pulls it open, and is gone.*

MRS. L. [*Looking after her, and talking to herself*] Ah! 'Er've a-got all 'er troubles before 'er! "Little lamb, 'u made 'ee?" [*Cackling.*] 'Tes a funny world, tu!   [*She sings to herself.*]

"There is a green 'ill far away
        Without a city wall,
Where our dear Lord was crucified,
        'U died to save us all."

[*The door is opened, and* LEMMY *comes in; a little man with a stubble of dark moustache and spiky dark hair; large, peculiar eyes he has, and a look of laying his ears back, a look of doubting, of perversity with laughter up the sleeve, that grows on those who have to do with gas and water. He shuts the door.*

Mrs. L. Well, Bob, I 'aven't a-seen yu this tu weeks.

[LEMMY *comes up to his mother, and sits down on a stool, sets a tool-bag between his knees, and speaks in a cockney voice.*

LEMMY. Well, old lydy o' leisure! Wot would y' 'ave for supper, if yer could choose—salmon wivaht the tin, an' tipsy cyke?

Mrs. L. [*Shaking her head and smiling blandly*] That's showy. Toad in the 'ole I'd 'ave—and a glass o' port wine.

LEMMY. Providential. [*He opens a tool-bag.*] Wot d'yer think I've got yer?

Mrs. L. I 'ope yu've a-got yureself a job, my son!

LEMMY. [*With his peculiar smile*] Yus, or I couldn't 'ave afforded yer this. [*He takes out a bottle.*] Not 'arf! This'll put the blood into yer. Pork wine—once in the cellars of the gryte. We'll drink the ryyal family in this. [*He apostrophizes the portrait of Queen Victoria.*

Mrs. L. Ah! She was a praaper gude queen. I see 'er once, when 'er was bein' burried.

LEMMY. Ryalties—I got nothin' to sy agynst 'em in this country. But the *Styte* 'as got to 'ave its pipes seen to. The 'ole show's goin' up pop. Yer'll wyke up one o' these dyes, old lydy, and find yerself on the roof, wiv nuffin' between yer an' the grahnd.

Mrs. L. I can't tell what yu'm talkin' about.

LEMMY. We're goin' to 'ave a triumpherat in this country—Liberty, Equality, Fraternity; an' if yer arsk me, they won't be in power six months before they've cut each other's throats. But I don't care— I want to see the blood flow! [*Dispassionately.*] I don' care 'oose blood it is. I want to see it flow!

Mrs. L. [*Indulgently*] Yu'm a funny boy, that's sartin.

LEMMY. [*Carving at the cork with a knife*] This 'ere cork is like Sasiety —rotten; it's old—old an' moulderin'. [*He holds up a bit of cork on the point of the knife.*] Crumblin' under the wax, it is. In goes the screw an' out comes the cork [*With unction*]—an' the blood flows. [*Tipping the bottle, he lets a drop fall into the middle of his hand, and licks it up. Gazing with queer and doubting commiseration at his mother.*] Well, old dear, wot shall we 'ave it aht of—the gold loving-cup, or—what? 'Ave yer supper fust, though, or it'll go to yer 'ead! [*He goes to the cupboard and takes out a dish in which a little bread is sopped in a little milk.*] Cold pap! 'Ow can yer? 'Yn't yer got a kipper in the 'ouse?

Mrs. L. [*Admiring the bottle*] Port wine! 'Tis a brave treat! I'll 'ave it out of the " Present from Margitt," Bob. I tuk 'ee therr by excursion when yu was six months. Yu 'ad a shrimp an' it choked yu praaperly. Yu was always a squeamy little feller. I can't never think 'ow yu managed in the war-time, makin' they shells.

[LEMMY, *who has brought to the table two mugs and blown the dust out of them, fills them with port, and hands one to his mother, who is eating her bread and milk.*

LEMMY. Ah! Nothin' worried me, 'cept the want o' soap.

MRS. L. [*Cackling gently*] So it du still, then! Luke at yure face. Yu never was a clean boy, like Jim.

[*She puts out a thin finger and touches his cheek, whereon is a black smudge.*

LEMMY. [*Scrubbing his cheek with his sleeve*] All right! Y'see, I come stryte 'ere, to get rid o' this.   [*He drinks.*

MRS. L. [*Eating her bread and milk*] 'Tes a pity yu'm not got a wife to see't yu wash yureself.

LEMMY. [*Goggling*] Wife! Not me—I daon't want ter myke no food for pahder. Wot oh!—they said, time o' the war—ye're fightin' for yer children's 'eritage. Well, wot's the 'eritage like, now we've got it? Empty as a shell before yer put the 'igh explosive in. Wot's it like? [*Warming to his theme.*] Like a prophecy in the pypers—not a bit more substantial.

MRS. L. [*Slightly hypnotized*] How 'e du talk! The gas goes to yure 'ead, I think!

LEMMY. I did the gas to-dy in the cellars of an 'ouse where the wine was mountains 'igh. A regiment couldn't 'a drunk it. Marble pillars in the 'all, butler broad as an observytion balloon, an' four conscientious khaki footmen. When the guns was roarin' the talk was all for no more o' them glorious weeds—style an' luxury was orf. See wot it is naow. You've got a bare crust in the cupboard 'ere, I works from 'and to mouth in a glutted market—an' there they stand abaht agyne in their britches in the 'ouses o' the gryte. I was reg'lar overcome by it. I left a thing in that cellar—I left a thing. . . . It'll be a bit ork'ard for me to-morrer.   [*Drinks from his mug.*

MRS. L. [*Placidly, feeling the warmth of the little she has drunk*] What thing?

LEMMY. Wot thing? Old lydy, ye're like a winkle afore yer opens 'er—I never see anything so peaceful. 'Ow d'yer manage it?

MRS. L. Settin' 'ere and thenkin'.

LEMMY. Wot abaht?

MRS. L. We-el—Money, an' the works o' God.

LEMMY. Ah! So yer give *me* a thought sometimes.

MRS. L. [*Lifting her mug*] Yu ought never to ha' spent yure money on this, Bob!

LEMMY. I thought that meself.

MRS. L. Last time I 'ad a glass o' port wine was the day yure brother Jim went to Ameriky. [*Smacking her lips.*] For a teetotal drink, it du warm 'ee!

LEMMY. [*Raising his mug*] Well, 'ere's to the British revolution! 'Ere's to the conflygrytion in the sky!

MRS. L. [*Comfortably*] So as it kape up therr, 'twon't du no 'arm.

[LEMMY *goes to the window and unhooks his fiddle; he stands with*

16*

*it halfway to his shoulder. Suddenly he opens the window and
leans out. A confused murmur of voices is heard, and a snatch
of the Marseillaise, sung by a girl. Then the shuffling tramp
of feet, and figures are passing in the street.*

LEMMY. [*Turning—excited*] Wot'd I tell yer, old lydy? There it is
—there it is!

MRS. L. [*Placidly*] What is?

LEMMY. The revolution. [*He cranes out.*] They've got it on a
barrer. Cheerio?

VOICE. [*Answering*] Cheerio!

LEMMY. [*Leaning out*] I sy—you 'yn't tykin' the body, are yer?

VOICE. Nao.

LEMMY. Did she die o' starvytion—O.K.?

VOICE. She bloomin' well did; I know 'er brother.

LEMMY. Ah! That'll do us a bit o' good!

VOICE. Cheerio!

LEMMY. So long!

VOICE. So long!

　　　[*The girl's voice is heard again in the distance singing the Marseillaise.
　　　　The door is flung open and* LITTLE AIDA *comes running in
　　　　again.*

LEMMY. 'Allo, little Aida!

L. AIDA. 'Allo, I been follerin' the corfin. It's better than an
'orse dahn!

MRS. L. What coffin?

L. AIDA. Why, 'er's wot died o' starvytion up the street. They're
goin' to tyke it to 'Yde Pawk, and 'oller.

MRS. L. Well, never yu mind wot they'm goin' to du. Yu wait
an' take my trousers like a gude gell.

　　　[*She puts her mug aside and takes up her unfinished pair of trousers.
　　　　But the wine has entered her fingers, and strength to push the
　　　　needle through is lacking.*

LEMMY. [*Tuning his fiddle*] Wot'll yer 'ave, little Aida? "Dead
March in Saul" or "When the fields was white wiv dysies"?

L. AIDA. [*With a hop and a brilliant smile*] Aoh yus! "When the
fields——"

MRS. L. [*With a gesture of despair*] Deary me! I 'aven't a-got the
strength!

LEMMY. Leave 'em alone, old dear! No one'll be goin' aht wivaht
trahsers to-night 'cos yer leaves that one undone. Little Aida, fold
'em up!

LITTLE AIDA *methodically folds the five finished pairs of trousers into a
　　　pile.* LEMMY *begins playing. A smile comes on the face
　　　of* MRS. LEMMY, *who is rubbing her fingers.* LITTLE AIDA,
　　　trousers over arm, goes and stares at LEMMY *playing.*

LEMMY. [*Stopping*] Little Aida, one o' vese dyes yer'll myke an actress.   I can see it in yer fyce !

[LITTLE AIDA *looks at him wide-eyed.*

MRS. L. Don' 'ee putt things into 'er 'ead, Bob !

LEMMY. 'Tyn't 'er 'ead, old lydy—it's lower.   She wants feedin'— feed 'er an' she'll rise.   [*He strikes into the " Machichi."*] Look at 'er naow.   I tell yer there's a fortune in 'er.

[LITTLE AIDA *has put out her tongue.*

MRS. L. I'd suner there was a gude 'eart in 'er than any fortune.

L. AIDA. [*Hugging her pile of trousers*] It's thirteen pence three farthin's I've got to bring yer, an' a penny aht for me, mykes twelve three farthin's.   [*With the same little hop and sudden smile.*] I'm goin' to ride back on a bus, I am.

LEMMY. Well, you myke the most of it up there ; it's the nearest you'll ever git to 'eaven.

MRS. L. Don' yu discourage 'er, Bob ; she'm a gude little thing, an't yu, dear ?

L. AIDA. [*Simply*] Yus.

LEMMY. Not 'arf ! Wot c'her do wiv yesterdy's penny ?

L. AIDA. Movies.

LEMMY. An' the dy before ?

L. AIDA. Movies.

LEMMY. Wot'd I tell yer, old lydy—she's got vicious tystes, she'll finish in the theayter yet.   Tyke my tip, little Aida ; you put every penny into yer foundytions, yer'll get on the boards quicker that wy.

MRS. L. Don' yu pay no 'eed to his talk.

L. AIDA. I daon't.

LEMMY. Would yer like a sip aht o' my mug ?

L. AIDA. [*Brilliant*] Yus.

MRS. L. Not at yure age, me dear, though it is teetotal.

[LITTLE AIDA *puts her head on one side, like a dog trying to under-
     stand.*

LEMMY. Well, 'ave one o' my gum-drops.   [*Holds out a paper.*]

[LITTLE AIDA, *brilliant, takes a flat, dark substance from it, and
     puts it in her mouth.*]

Give me a kiss, an' I'll give yer a penny.

[LITTLE AIDA *shakes her head, and leans out of window.*]

Muvver, she daon't know the valyer of money.

MRS. L. Never mind, 'im, me dear.

L. AIDA. [*Sucking the gum-drop—with difficulty*] There's a taxi-cab at the corner.

[LITTLE AIDA *runs to the door.   A figure stands in the doorway ;
     she skids round him and out.*   THE PRESS *comes in.*

LEMMY. [*Dubiously*] Wot—oh !

PRESS. Mr. Lemmy ?

LEMMY. The syme.

PRESS. I'm from the Press.

LEMMY. Blimy.

PRESS. They told me at your place you were very likely here.

LEMMY. Yus—I left Downin' Street a bit early to-dy !

[He twangs the fiddle-strings pompously.

PRESS. [*Taking out his note-book and writing*] "Fiddles while Rome is burning !" Mr. Lemmy, it's my business at this very critical time to find out what the nation's thinking. Now, as a representative working man——

LEMMY. That's me.

PRESS. You can help me. What are your views ?

LEMMY. [*Putting down fiddle*] Voos ? Sit dahn !

*[*THE PRESS *sits on the stool which* LEMMY *has vacated.*]
The Press—my Muvver. Seventy-seven. She's a wonder ; 'yn't yer, old dear ?

PRESS. Very happy to make your acquaintance, Ma'am. [*He writes.*] "Mrs. Lemmy, one of the veterans of industry——" By the way, I've just passed a lot of people following a coffin.

LEMMY. Centre o' the cyclone—cyse o' starvytion ; you 'ad 'er in the pyper this mornin'.

PRESS. Ah, yes ! Tragic occurrence. [*Looking at the trousers.*] Hub of the Sweated Industries just here. I especially want to get at the heart——

MRS. L. 'Twasn't the 'eart, 'twas the stomach.

PRESS. [*Writing*] "Mrs. Lemmy goes straight to the point."

LEMMY. Mister, is it my voos or Muvver's yer want ?

PRESS. Both.

LEMMY. 'Cos if yer get Muvver's, yer won't 'ave time for mine. I tell yer stryte [*Confidentially*] she's got a glawss o' port wine in 'er. Naow, mind yer, I'm not anxious to be intervooed. On the other 'and, anyfink I might 'ave to sy of valyer—— There is a clawss o' politician that 'as nuffin' to sy—— Aoh ! an' daon't 'e sy it just ! I dunno wot pyper yer represent——

PRESS. [*Smiling*] Well, Mr. Lemmy, it has the biggest influ——

LEMMY. They all 'as that ; dylies, weeklies, evenin's, Sundyes ; but it's of no consequence—my voos are open and above-board. Naow, wot shall we begin abaht ?

PRESS. Yourself, if you please. And I'd like you to know at once that my paper wants the human note, the real heart-beat of things.

LEMMY. I see ; sensytion ! Well, 'ere am I—a fust-clawss plumber's assistant—in a job to-dy an' out to-morrer. There's a 'eart-beat in that, I tell yer. 'Oo knows wot the morrer 'as for me !

PRESS. [*Writing*] "The great human issue—Mr. Lemmy touches it at once."

LEMMY. I sy—keep my nyme aht o' this—I don' go in fer self-advertisement.

PRESS. [*Writing*] " True working-man—modest as usual."

LEMMY. I daon't want to embarrass the Gover'-ment. They're so ticklish ever since they got the 'abit, war-time, o' mindin' wot people said.

PRESS. Right-o !

LEMMY. For instance, suppose there's goin' to be a revolution——

[THE PRESS *writes with energy.*]

'Ow does it touch me ? Like this : I my go up—I cawn't come dahn ; no more can Muvver.

MRS. L. [*Surprisingly*] Us all goes down into the grave.

PRESS. " Mrs. Lemmy interjects the deeper note."

LEMMY. Naow, the gryte—they can come dahn, but they cawn't go up ! See ! Put two an' two together, an' that's 'ow it touches me. [*He utters a throaty laugh.*] 'Ave yer got that ?

PRESS. [*Quizzical*] Not go up ? What about bombs, Mr. Lemmy ?

LEMMY. [*Dubious*] Wot abaht 'em ? I s'pose ye're on the comic pypers ? 'Ave yer noticed wot a weakness they 'ave for the 'orrible ?

PRESS. [*Writing*] " A grim humour peeped out here and there through the earnestness of his talk."   [*He sketches* LEMMY's *profile.*

LEMMY. We 'ad an explosion in my factory time o' the war, that would just ha' done for you comics. [*He meditates.*] Lord ! They *was* after it too,—they an' the Sundyes ; but the Censor did 'em. Strike me, I could tell yer things !

PRESS. That's what I want, Mr. Lemmy ; tell me things !

LEMMY. [*Musing*] It's a funny world, 'yn't it ? 'Ow we did blow each other up ! [*Getting up to admire.*] I sy, I shall be syfe there. That won't betry me anonymiety. Why ! I looks like the Prime Minister !

PRESS. [*Rather hurt*] You were going to tell me things.

LEMMY. Yus, an' they'll be the troof, too.

PRESS. I hope so ; we don't——

LEMMY. Wot oh !

PRESS. [*A little confused*] We always try to verify——

LEMMY. Yer leave it at tryin', daon't yer ? Never mind, ye're a gryte institootion. Blimy, yer do have jokes wiv it, spinnin' rahnd on yer own tyles, denyin' to-dy wot ye're goin' to print to-morrer. Ah, well ! Ye're like all of us below the line o' comfort—live dyngerously—every dy yer last. That's wy I'm interested in the future.

PRESS. Well now—the future. [*Writing.*] " He prophesies."

LEMMY. It's syfer, 'yn't it ? [*He winks.*] No one never looks back on prophesies. I remembers an editor—spring o' 1915—stykin' 'is reputytion the war'd be over in the follerin' October. Increased 'is circulytion abaht 'arf a million by it. 1917—an' war still on—'ad 'is readers gone back on 'im ? Nao ! They was increasin' like rabbits.

Prophesy wot people want to believe, an' ye're syfe. Naow, I'll styke my reputytion on somethin', you tyke it dahn word for word. This country's goin' to the dawgs—— Naow, 'ere's the sensytion—unless we gets a new religion.

PRESS. Ah! Now for it—yes?

LEMMY. In one word: "Kindness." Daon't mistyke me, nao sickly sentiment and nao patronizin'. Me as kind to the millionaire as im to me. [*Fills his mug and drinks.*

PRESS. [*Struck*] That's queer! Kindness! [*Writing.*] "Extremes meet. Bombed and bomber breathing the same music."

LEMMY. But 'ere's the interestin' pynt. Can it be done wivaht blood?

PRESS. [*Writing*] "He doubts."

LEMMY. No daht wotever. It cawn't! Blood—and—kindness! Spill the blood o' them that aren't kind—an' there ye are!

PRESS. But pardon me, how are you to tell?

LEMMY. Blimy, they leaps to the heye!

PRESS. [*Laying down his note-book*] I say, let me talk to you as man to man for a moment.

LEMMY. Orl right. Give it a rest!

PRESS. Your sentiments are familiar to me. I've got a friend on the Press who's very keen on Christ and kindness; and wants to strangle the last king with the—hamstrings of the last priest.

LEMMY. [*Greatly intrigued*] Not 'arf! Does 'e?

PRESS. Yes. But have you thought it out? Because he hasn't.

LEMMY. The difficulty is—where to stop.

PRESS. Where to begin.

LEMMY. Lawd! I could begin almost anywhere. Why, every month abaht, there's a cove turns me aht of a job 'cos I daon't do just wot 'e likes. *They'd* 'ave to go. I tell yer stryte—the Temple wants cleanin' up.

PRESS. Ye-es. If I wrote what I thought, I should get the sack as quick as you. D'you say that justifies me in shedding the blood of my bosses?

LEMMY. The yaller Press 'as got no blood—'as it? You shed their ile an' vinegar—that's wot you've got to do. Stryte—do yer believe in the noble mission o' the Press?

PRESS. [*Enigmatically*] Mr. Lemmy, I'm a Pressman.

LEMMY. [*Goggling*] I see. Not much! [*Gently jogging his mother's elbow.*] Wyke up, old lydy!

[*For* MRS. LEMMY, *who has been sipping placidly at her port, is nodding. The evening has drawn in.* LEMMY *strikes a match on his trousers and lights a candle.*]

Blood an' kindness—that's what's wanted—'specially blood! The 'istory o' me an' my family'll show yer that. Tyke my bruvver Fred

—crushed by burycrats. Tyke Muvver 'erself. Talk o' the wrongs
o' the people ! I tell yer the foundytions is rotten. [*He empties the
bottle into his mother's mug.*] Daon't mind the mud at the bottom, old
lydy—it's all strengthenin' ! You tell the Press, Muvver. She can
talk abaht the pawst.

PRESS. [*Taking up his note-book, and becoming again his professional self*]
Yes, Mrs. Lemmy ? " Age and Youth—Past and Present——"

MRS. L. Were yu talkin' about Fred ? [*The port has warmed her veins,
the colour in her eyes and cheeks has deepened.*] My son Fred was always a
gude boy—never did nothin' before 'e married. I can see Fred [*She
bends forward a little in her chair, looking straight before her*] comin' in wi'
a pheasant 'e'd found—terrible 'e was at findin' pheasants. When
father died, an' yu was comin', Bob, Fred 'e said to me : " Don't yu
never cry, Mother, I'll look after 'ee." An, so 'e did, till 'e married
that day six months an' tuke to the drink in sorrer. 'E wasn't never the
same boy again—not Fred. An' now 'e's in That. I can see poor
Fred——

      [*She slowly wipes a tear out of the corner of an eye with the back of
        her finger.*

PRESS. [*Puzzled*] In—That ?

LEMMY. [*Sotto voce*] Come orf it ! Prison ! 'S wot she calls it.

MRS. L. [*Cheerful*] They say life's a vale o' sorrows. Well, so
'tes, but don' du to let yureself thenk so.

PRESS. And so you came to London, Mrs. Lemmy ?

MRS. L. Same year as father died. With the four o' them—that's
my son Fred, an' my son Jim, an' my son Tom, an' Alice. Bob there,
'e was born in London—an' a praaper time I 'ad of et.

PRESS. [*Writing*] " Her heroic struggles with poverty——"

MRS. L. Worked in a laundry, I did, at fifteen shellins' a week, an'
brought 'em all up on et till Alice 'ad the gallopin' consumption. I
can see poor Alice wi' the little red spots in 'er cheeks—an' I not
knowin' wot to du wi' her—but I always kept up their buryin' money.
Funerals is very dear ; Mr. Lemmy was six pound ten.

PRESS. " High price of Mr. Lemmy."

MRS. L. I've a-got the money for when my time come ; never touch
et, no matter 'ow things are. Better a little goin' short here below,
an' enter the kingdom of 'eaven independent.

PRESS. [*Writing*] " Death before dishonour—heroine of the slums.
Dickens—Betty Higden."

MRS. L. No, sir. Mary Lemmy. I've seen a-many die, I 'ave ;
an' not one grievin'. I often says to meself : [*With a little laugh.*]
" Me dear, when yu go, yu go 'appy. Don' yu never fret about that,"
I says. An' so I will ; I'll go 'appy.

      [*She stays quite still a moment, and behind her LEMMY draws one
        finger across his face.*]

[*Smiling.*] " Yure old fengers'll 'ave a rest.   Think o' that ! " I says.
" 'Twill be a brave change."   I can see myself lyin' there an' duin'
nothin'.   [*Again a pause, while* MRS. LEMMY *sees herself doing nothing.*

LEMMY. Tell abaht Jim, old lydy.

MRS. L. My son Jim 'ad a family o' seven in six years.   " I don'
know, 'ow 'tes, Mother," 'e used to say to me ; " they just sim to
come ! "   That was Jim—never knu from day to day what was
comin'.   " Therr's another of 'em dead," 'e used to say, " 'tes funny,
tu."   " Well," I used to say to 'im ; " no wonder, poor little things,
livin' in they model dwellin's.   Therr's no air for 'em," I used to say.
" Well," 'e used to say, " what can I du, Mother ?   Can't afford to
live in Park Lane."   An' 'e tuke an' went to Ameriky. [*Her voice for
the first time is truly doleful.*] An' never came back.   Fine feller.   So
that's my four sons—One's dead, an' one's in—That, an' one's in
Ameriky, an' Bob 'ere, poor boy, 'e always was a talker.

       [LEMMY *who has re-seated himself in the window and taken up his
                fiddle, twangs the strings.*

PRESS. And now a few words about your work, Mrs. Lemmy ?

MRS. L. Well, I sews.

PRESS. [*Writing*] " Sews."   Yes ?

MRS. L. [*Holding up her unfinished pair of trousers*] I putt in the
button'oles, I stretches the flies, I lines the crutch, I putt on this
bindin', [*She holds up the calico that binds the top*] I sews on the buttons,
I presses the seams—Tuppence three farthin's the pair.

PRESS. Twopence three farthings a pair !   Worse than a penny a
line !

MRS. L. In a gude day I gets thru four pairs, but they'm gettin'
plaguey 'ard for my old fengers.

PRESS. [*Writing*] " A monumental figure, on whose labour is built
the mighty edifice of our industrialism."

LEMMY. I sy—that's good.   Yer'll keep that, won't yer ?

MRS. L. I find me own cotton, tuppence three farthin's, and other
expension is a penny three farthin's.

PRESS. And are you an exception, Mrs. Lemmy ?

MRS. L. What's that ?

LEMMY. Wot price the uvvers, old lydy ?   Is there a lot of yer
sewin' yer fingers orf at tuppence 'ypenny the pair ?

MRS. L. I can't tell yu that.   I never sees nothin' in 'ere.   I pays a
penny to that little gell to bring me a dozen pair an' fetch 'em back.
Poor little thing, she'm 'ardly strong enough to carry 'em.   Feel !
They'm very 'eavy !

PRESS. On the conscience of Society !

LEMMY. I sy—put that dahn, won't yer ?

PRESS. Have things changed much since the war, Mrs. Lemmy ?

MRS. L. Cotton's a lot dearer.

Press. All round, I mean.

Mrs. L. Aw! Yu don't never get no change, not in my profession. [*She oscillates the trousers.*] I've a-been in trousers fifteen year; ever since I got tu old for laundry.

Press. [*Writing*] " For fifteen years sewn trousers." What would a good week be, Mrs. Lemmy?

Mrs. L. 'Tes a very gude week, five shellin's.

Lemmy. [*From the window*] Bloomin' millionairess, Muvver. She's lookin' forward to 'eaven, where vey don't wear no trahsers.

Mrs. L. [*With spirit*] 'Tidn' for me to zay whether they du. An' 'tes on'y when I'm a bit low-sperrity-like as I wants to go therr. What I am a-lukin' forward to, though, 'tes a day in the country. I've not a-had one since before the war. A kind lady brought me in that bit of 'eather; 'tes wonderful sweet stuff when the 'oney's in et. When I was a little gell I used to zet in the 'eather gatherin' the whorts, an' me little mouth all black wi' eatin' them. 'Twas in the 'eather I used to zet, Sundays, courtin'. All flesh is grass—an' 'tesn't no bad thing—grass.

Press. [*Writing*] " The old paganism of the country." What is your view of life, Mrs. Lemmy?

Lemmy. [*Suddenly*] Wot is 'er voo of life? Shall I tell yer mine? Life's a disease—a blinkin' oak-apple! Daon't myke no mistyke. An' 'uman life's a yumourous disease; that's all the difference. Why —wot else can it be? See the bloomin' promise an' the blighted performance—different as a 'eadline to the noos inside. But yer couldn't myke Muvver see vat—not if yer talked to 'er for a week. Muvver still believes in fings. She's a country gell; at a 'undred and fifty she'll be a country gal, won't yer, old lydy?

Mrs. L. Well, 'tesn't never been 'ome to me in London. I lived in the country forty year—I did my lovin' there; I burried father therr. Therr bain't nothin' in life, yu know, but a bit o' lovin'— all said an' done; bit o' lovin', with the wind, an' the stars out.

Lemmy. [*In a loud apologetic whisper*] She 'yn't often like this. I told yer she'd got a glawss o' port in 'er.

Mrs. L. 'Tes a brave pleasure, is lovin'. I likes to zee et in young folk. I likes to zee 'em kissin'; shows the 'eart in 'em. 'Tes the 'eart makes the world go round; 'tesn't nothin' else, in my opinion.

Press. [*Writing*] " —sings the swan song of the heart."

Mrs. L. [*Overhearing*] No, I *never* yeard a swan sing—never! But I tell 'ee what I 'ave 'eard; the gells singin' in th' orchard 'angin' up the clothes to dry, an' the cuckoos callin' back to 'em. [*Smiling.*] There's a-many songs in the country—the 'eart is free-like in th' country!

Lemmy. [*Sotto voce*] Gi' me the Strand at ar' past nine.

Press. [*Writing*] " Town and country——"

Mrs. L. 'Tidn't like that in London ; one day's jest like another. Not but what therr's a 'eap o' kind-'eartedness 'ere.

Lemmy. [*Gloomily*] Kind-'eartedness ! I daon't fink ! " Boys an' gals come out to play." [*He plays the old tune on his fiddle.*

Mrs. L. [*Singing*] " Boys an' gells come out to play, The mune is shinin' bright as day." [*She laughs.*] I used to sing like a lark when I was a gell. [Little Aida *enters.*

L. Aida. There's 'undreds follerin' the corfin. 'Yn't you goin', Mr. Lemmy—it's dahn your wy !

Lemmy. [*Dubiously*] Well yus—I s'pose they'll miss me.

L. Aida. Aoh ! Tyke me !

Press. What's this ?

Lemmy. The revolution in 'Yde Pawk.

Press. [*Struck*] In Hyde Park ? The very thing. I'll take you down. My taxi's waiting.

L. Aida. Yus ; it's breathin' 'ard, at the corner.

Press. [*Looking at his watch*] Ah ! and Mrs. Lemmy. There's an Anti-Sweating Meeting going on at a house in Park Lane. We can get there in twenty minutes if we shove along. I want you to tell them about the trouser-making. You'll be a sensation !

Lemmy. [*To himself*] Sensytion ! 'E cawn't keep orf it !

Mrs. L. Anti-Sweat. Poor fellers ! I 'ad one come to see me before the war, an' they'm still goin' on ? Wonderful, an't it ?

Press. Come, Mrs. Lemmy ; drive in a taxi, beautiful moonlit night ; and they'll give you a splendid cup of tea.

Mrs. L. [*Unmoved*] Ah ! I cudn't never du without my tea. There's not an avenin' but I thinks to meself : Now, me dear, yu've a-got one more to fennish, an' then yu'll 'ave yure cup o' tea. Thank you for callin', all the same.

Lemmy. Better siccumb to the temptytion, old lydy ; joyride wiv the Press ; marble floors, pillars o' gold ; conscientious footmen ; lovely lydies ; scuppers runnin' tea ! An' the revolution goin' on across the wy. 'Eaven's nuffink to Pawk Lyne.

Press. Come along, Mrs. Lemmy !

Mrs. L. [*Seraphically*] Thank yu. I'm a-feelin' very comfortable. 'Tes wonderful what a drop o' wine'll du for the stomach.

Press. A taxi-ride !

Mrs. L. [*Placidly*] Ah ! I know 'em. They'm very busy things.

Lemmy. Muvver shuns notority. [*Sotto voce to* The Press.] But you watch me ! I'll rouse 'er.

[*He takes up his fiddle and sits on the window-seat. Above the little houses on the opposite side of the street, the moon has risen in the dark blue sky, so that the cloud shaped like a beast seems leaping over it. Lemmy plays the first notes of the Marseillaise. A black cat on the window-sill outside, looks in, hunching its back.* LITTLE AIDA *barks at her.* MRS. LEMMY *struggles to her feet, sweeping the empty dish and spoon to the floor in the effort.*]

The dish ran awy wiv the spoon !   That's right, old lydy !

[*He stops playing.*

MRS. L. [*Smiling, and moving her hands*] I like a bit o' music.   It du that muve 'ee.

PRESS. Bravo, Mrs. Lemmy.   Come on !

LEMMY. Come on, old dear !   We'll be in time for the revolution yet.

MRS. L. 'Tes 'earin' the Old 'Undred again !

LEMMY. [*To* THE PRESS] She 'yn't been aht these two years. [*To his mother, who has put up her hands to her head.*] Nao, never mind yer 'at. [*To* THE PRESS.] She 'yn't got none ! [*Aloud.*] No West-End lydy wears anyfink at all in the evenin' !

MRS. L. 'Ow'm I lukin', Bob ?

LEMMY. Fust-clawss ; yer've got a colour fit to toast by.   We'll show 'em yer've got a kick in yer. [*He takes her arm.*] Little Aida, ketch 'old o' the sensytions.   [*He indicates the trousers.*

[THE PRESS *takes* MRS. LEMMY'S *other arm.*

MRS. L. [*With an excited little laugh*] Quite like a gell !

[*And, smiling between her son and* THE PRESS, *she passes out.* LITTLE AIDA, *with a fling of her heels and a wave of the trousers, follows.*

The curtain falls.

ACT III

An octagon ante-room off the hall at LORD WILLIAM DROMONDY'S. *A shining room lighted by gold candelabra, with gold-curtained pillars, through which the shining hall and a little of the grand stairway are visible. A small table with a gold-coloured cloth occupies the very centre of the room, which has a polished parquet floor and high white walls. Gold-coloured doors on the left. Opposite these doors a window with gold-coloured curtains looks out on Park Lane.* LADY WILLIAM *is standing restlessly between the double doors and the arch which leads to the hall.* JAMES *is stationary by the double doors, from behind which come sounds of speech and applause.*

POULDER. [*Entering from the hall*] His Grace the Duke of Exeter, my lady.

    [HIS GRACE *enters. He is old, and youthful, with a high colour and a short rough white beard.* LADY WILLIAM *advances to meet him.* POULDER *stands by.*

LADY W. Oh! Father, you *are* late!

HIS G. Awful crowd in the streets, Nell. They've got a coffin—Couldn't get by.

LADY W. A coffin? Whose?

HIS G. The Government's I should think—no flowers, by request. I say, have I got to speak?

LADY W. Oh! no, dear.

HIS G. H'm! That's unlucky. I've got it here. [*He looks down his cuff.*] Found something I said in 1914—just have done.

LADY W. Oh! If you've got it—James, ask Lord William to come to me for a moment. [JAMES *vanishes through the door. To* THE DUKE.] Go in, Grand-dad; they'll be so awfully pleased to see you. I'll tell Bill.

HIS G. Where's Anne?

LADY W. In bed, of course.

HIS G. I got her this—rather nice!

    [*He has taken from his breast-pocket one of those street toy-men that jump head over heels on your hand; he puts it through its paces.*

LADY W. [*Much interested*] Oh! no, but how sweet! She'll simply love it.

POULDER. If I might suggest to Your Grace to take it in and operate it. It's sweated, Your Grace. They—er—make them in those places.

His G. By Jove! D'you know the price, Poulder?

POULDER. [*Interrogatively*] A penny, is it? Something paltry, Your Grace!

His G. Where's that woman who knows everything; Miss Munday?

LADY W. Oh! She'll be in there, somewhere.

> [His GRACE *moves on, and passes through the doors. The sound of applause is heard.*]

POULDER. [*Discreetly*] Would you care to see the bomb, my lady?

LADY W. Of course—first quiet moment.

POULDER. I'll bring it up, and have a watch put on it here, my lady.

> [LORD WILLIAM *comes through the double doors, followed by* JAMES. POULDER *retires.*]

LORD W. Can't you come, Nell?

LADY W. Oh! Bill, your Dad wants to speak.

LORD W. The deuce he does—that's bad.

LADY W. Yes, of course, but you *must* let him; he's found something he said in 1914.

LORD W. I knew it. That's what they'll say. Standing stock still, while hell's on the jump around us.

LADY W. Never mind that; it'll please him; and he's got a lovely little sweated toy that turns head over heels at one penny.

LORD W. H'm! Well, come on.

LADY W. No, I must wait for stragglers. There's sure to be an editor in a hurry.

POULDER. [*Announcing*] Mis-ter Gold-rum!

LADY W. [*Sotto voce*] And there he is! [*She advances to meet a thin, straggling man in eyeglasses, who is smiling absently.*] How good of you!

MR. G. Thanks awfully. I just—er—and then I'm afraid I must— er—— Things look very—— Thanks—thanks so much.

> [*He straggles through the doors, and is enclosed by* JAMES.]

POULDER. Miss Mun-day.

LADY W. There! I thought she was in—— She really is the most unexpected woman! How do you do? How awfully sweet of you!

MISS M. [*An elderly female schoolboy*] How do you do? There's a spiffing crowd. I believe things are really going Bolshy. How do you do, Lord William? Have you got any of our people to show? I told one or two, in case—they do so simply love an outing.

JAMES. There are three old chips in the lobby, my Lord.

LORD. W. What? Oh! I say! Bring them in at once. Why— they're the hub of the whole thing.

JAMES. [*Going*] Very good, my Lord.

LADY W. I *am* sorry. I'd no notion; and they're such dears always.

Miss M. I *must* tell you what one of them said to me. I'd told him not to use such bad language to his wife. " Don't you worry, Ma ! " he said, " I expect you can do a bit of that yourself ! "

Lady W. How awfully nice ! It's *so* like them.

Miss M. Yes. They're wonderful.

Lord W. I say, why do we always call them *they* ?

Lady W. [*Puzzled*] Well, why not ?

Lord W. *They* !

Miss M. [*Struck*] Quite right, Lord William ! *Quite* right ! Another species. They ! I must remember that. *They* !

[*She passes on.*

Lady W. [*About to follow*] Well, I don't see ; aren't they ?

Lord W. Never mind, old girl ; follow on. *They'll* come in with me.

[Miss Munday *and* Lady William *pass through the double doors.*

Poulder. [*Announcing*] Some sweated workers, my Lord.

[*There enter a tall, thin, oldish woman ; a short, thin, very lame man, her husband ; and a stoutish middle-aged woman with a rolling eye and gait, all very poorly dressed, with lined and heated faces.*

Lord W. [*Shaking hands*] How d'you do ! Delighted to see you all. It's awfully good of you to have come.

Lame M. Mr. and Mrs. Tomson. We 'ad some trouble to find it. You see, I've never been in these parts. We 'ad to come in the oven ; and the bus-bloke put us dahn wrong. Are you the proprietor ?

Lord W. [*Modestly*] Yes, I—er——

Lame M. You've got a nice plyce. I says to the missis, I says : " 'E's got a nice plyce 'ere," I says ; " there's room to turn rahnd."

Lord W. Yes—shall we—— ?

Lame M. An' Mrs. Annaway she says : " Shouldn't mind livin' 'ere meself," she says ; " but it must cost 'im a tidy penny," she says.

Lord W. It does—it does ; much too tidy. Shall we—— ?

Mrs. Ann. [*Rolling her eye*] I'm very pleased to 'ave come. I've often said to 'em : " Any time you want me," I've said, " I'd be pleased to come."

Lord W. Not so pleased as we are to see you.

Mrs. Ann. I'm sure you're very kind.

James. [*From the double doors, through which he has received a message*] Wanted for your speech, my Lord.

Lord W. Oh ! God ! Poulder, bring these ladies and gentleman in, and put them where everybody can—where they can see everybody, don't you know. [*He goes out hurriedly through the double doors.*

Lame M. Is 'e a lord ?

Poulder. He is. Follow me.

[*He moves towards the doors,* The Three Workers *follow.*

MRS. ANN. [*Stopping before* JAMES] You 'yn't one, I suppose ?

[JAMES *stirs no muscle.*

POULDER. Now, please. [*He opens the doors. The voice of* LORD WILLIAM *speaking is heard.*] Pass in.

[THE THREE WORKERS *pass in,* POULDER *and* JAMES *follow them. The doors are not closed, and through this aperture comes the voice of* LORD WILLIAM, *punctuated and supported by decorous applause.*

[LITTLE ANNE *runs in, and listens at the window to the confused and distant murmurs of a crowd.*

VOICE OF LORD W. We propose to move for a further advance in the chain-making and—er—er—match-box industries.   [*Applause.*]

[LITTLE ANNE *runs across to the door, to listen.*]

[*On rising voice.*] I would conclude with some general remarks. Ladies and gentlemen, the great natural, but—er—artificial expansion which trade experienced the first years after the war has—er—collapsed. These are hard times.   We who are fortunate feel more than ever—er—responsible—[*He stammers, loses the thread of his thoughts.— Applause*]—er—responsible—[*The thread still eludes him*]—er——

L. ANNE. [*Poignantly*] Oh, Daddy !

LORD W. [*Desperately*] In fact—er—you know how—er—responsible we feel.

L. ANNE. Hooray !   [*Applause.*

[*There float in through the windows the hoarse and distant sounds of the Marseillaise, as sung by London voices.*

LORD W. There is a feeling in the air—that I for one should say deliberately was—er—a feeling in the air—er—a feeling in the air——

L. ANNE. [*Agonized*] Oh, Daddy !   Stop !

[JAMES *enters, and closes the door behind him.*

JAMES. Look here !   'Ave I got to report you to Miss Stokes ?

L. ANNE. No-o-o !

JAMES. Well, I'm goin' to.

L. ANNE. Oh, James, be a friend to me !   I've seen nothing yet.

JAMES. No ; but you've eaten a good bit, on the stairs.   What price that Peach Melba ?

L. ANNE. I can't go to bed till I've digested it—can I ?   There's such a lovely crowd in the street !

JAMES. Lovely ?   Ho !

L. ANNE. [*Wheedling*] James, you couldn't tell Miss Stokes !   It isn't *in* you, is it ?

JAMES. [*Grinning*] That's right.

L. ANNE. So—I'll just get under here. [*She gets under the table.*] Do I show ?

JAMES. [*Stooping*] Not 'arf !   [POULDER *enters from the hall.*

POULDER. What are you doin' there ?

James. [*Between him and the table—raising himself*] 'Thinkin'.

[Poulder *purses his mouth to repress his feelings.*

Poulder. My orders are to fetch the bomb up here for Lady William to inspect. Take care no more writers stray in.

James. How shall I know 'em?

Poulder. Well—either very bald or very hairy.

James. Right-o!   [*He goes.*

[Poulder, *with his back to the table, busies himself with the set of his collar.*

Poulder. [*Addressing an imaginary audience—in a low but important voice*] The—ah—situation is seerious. It is up to us of the—ah—leisured classes——

[*The face of* Little Anne *is poked out close to his legs, and tilts upwards in wonder towards the bow of his waistcoat.*]

to—ah—keep the people down. The olla polloi are clamourin'——

[Miss Stokes *appears from the hall, between the pillars.*

Miss S. Poulder!

Poulder. [*Making a* volte face *towards the table*] Miss?

Miss S. Where is Anne?

Poulder. [*Vexed at the disturbance of his speech*] Excuse me, Miss—to keep track of Miss Anne is fortunately no part of my dooties.

Miss S. She really is naughty.

Poulder. She is. If she was mine, I'd spank her.

[*The smiling face of* Little Anne *becomes visible again close to his legs.*

Miss S. Not a nice word.

Poulder. No; but a pleasant haction. Miss Anne's the limit. In fact, Lord and Lady William are much too kind-'earted all round. Take these sweated workers; that class o' people are quite 'opeless. Treatin' them as your equals, shakin' 'ands with 'em, givin' 'em tea—it only puffs 'em out. Leave it to the Church, I say.

Miss S. The Church is too busy, Poulder.

Poulder. Ah! That "Purity an' Future o' the Race Campaign." I'll tell you what I think's the danger o' that, Miss. So much purity that there won't be a future race. [*Expanding.*] Purity of 'eart's an excellent thing, no doubt, but there's a want of nature about it. Same with this Anti-Sweating. Unless you're anxious to come down, you must not put the lower classes up.

Miss S. I don't agree with you at all, Poulder.

Poulder. Ah! You want it both ways, Miss. I should imagine you're a Liberal.

Miss S. [*Horrified*] Oh, no! I certainly am not.

Poulder. Well, I judged from your takin' cocoa. Funny thing that, about cocoa—how it still runs through the Liberal Party! It's virtuous, I suppose. Wine, beer, tea, coffee—all of 'em vices. But cocoa—you might drink a gallon a day and annoy no one but yourself ! There's a lot o' deep things in life, Miss !

MISS S. Quite so.   But I must find Anne.   [*She recedes.*

POULDER. [*Suavely*] Well, I wish you every success ; and I hope you'll spank her.   This modern education—there's no fruitiness in it.

L. ANNE. [*From under the table*] Poulder, are you virtuous ?

POULDER. [*Jumping*] Good Ged !

L. ANNE. D'you mind my asking ?   I promised James I would.

POULDER. Miss Anne, come out !

[*The four footmen appear in the hall,* HENRY *carrying the wine cooler.*

JAMES. Form fours—by your right—quick march !

[*They enter, marching down right of table.*]

Right incline—Mark time !   Left turn !   'Alt !   'Enry, set the bomb ! Stand easy !

[HENRY *places the wine cooler on the table and covers it with a blue embroidered Chinese mat, which has occupied the centre of the tablecloth.*

POULDER. Ah !   You *will* 'ave your game !   Thomas, take the door there !   James, the 'all !   Admit titles an' bishops.   No literary or Labour people.   Charles and 'Enry, 'op it and 'ang about !

[CHARLES *and* HENRY *go out, the other two move to their stations.*
[POULDER *stands by the table looking at the covered bomb. The hoarse and distant sounds of the Marseillaise float in again from Park Lane.*]

[*Moved by some deep feeling.*] And this house an 'orspital in the war ! I ask you—what was the good of all our sacrifices for the country ? No town 'ouse for four seasons—rustygettin' in the shires, not a soul but two boys under me.   Lord William at the front, Lady William at the back.   And all for this !   [*He points sadly at the cooler.*] It comes of meddlin' on the Continent.   I had my prognostications at the time. [*To* JAMES.] You remember my sayin' to you just before you joined up : " Mark my words—we shall see eight per cent. for our money before this is over ! "

JAMES. [*Sepulchrally*] I see the eight per cent., but not the money.

POULDER. Hark at that !

[*The sounds of the Marseillaise grow louder.   He shakes his head.*]

I'd read the Riot Act.   They'll be lootin' this house next !

JAMES. We'll put up a fight over your body : " Bartholomew Poulder, faithful unto death ! "   Have you insured your life ?

POULDER. Against a revolution ?

JAMES. Act o' God !   Why not ?

POULDER. It's not an act o' God.

JAMES. It is ; and I sympathize with it.

POULDER. You—what?

JAMES. I do—only—hands off the gov'nor.

POULDER. Oh! Reely! Well, that's something. I'm glad to see you stand behind *him*, at all events.

JAMES. *I* stand in front of 'im when the scrap begins!

POULDER. Do you insinuate that *my* heart's not in the right place?

JAMES. Well, look at it! It's been creepin' down ever since I knew you. Talk of your sacrifices in the war—they put you on your honour, and you got stout on it. Rations—not 'arf!

POULDER. [*Staring at him*] For independence, I've never seen your equal, James. You might be an Australian!

JAMES. [*Suavely*] Keep a civil tongue, or I'll throw you to the crowd! [*He comes forward to the table.*] Shall I tell you why I favour the gov'nor? Because, with all his pomp, he's a gentleman, as much as I am. Never asks you to do what he wouldn't do himself. What's more, he never comes it over you. If you get drunk, or—well, you understand me, Poulder—he'll just say: " Yes, yes; I know, James! " till he makes you feel he's done it himself. [*Sinking his voice mysteriously.*] I've had experience with him, in the war and out. Why! he didn't even hate the Huns, not as he ought. I tell you he's no Christian.

POULDER. Well, for irreverence——!

JAMES. [*Obstinately*] And he'll never be. He's got too soft a heart.

L. ANNE. [*Beneath the table—shrilly*] Hurrah!

POULDER. [*Jumping*] Come out, Miss Anne!

JAMES. Let 'er alone!

POULDER. In there, under the bomb?

JAMES. [*Contemptuously*] Silly ass! You should *take* 'em lying down!

POULDER. Look here, James! I can't go on in this revolutionary spirit; either you or I resign.

JAMES. Crisis in the Cabinet!

POULDER. I give you your marchin' orders.

JAMES. [*Ineffably*] What's that you give me?

POULDER. Thomas, remove James!   [THOMAS *grins.*

L. ANNE. [*Who, with open mouth, has crept out to see the fun*] Oh! *Do* remove James, Thomas!

POULDER. Go on, Thomas!

> [THOMAS *takes one step towards* JAMES, *who lays a hand on the Chinese mat covering the bomb.*

JAMES. [*Grimly*] If I lose control of meself——

L. ANNE. [*Clapping her hands*] Oh! James! Do lose control! Then I shall see it go off!

JAMES. [*To* POULDER] Well, I'll merely empty the pail over you!

POULDER. This is not becomin'!   [*He walks out into the hall.*

JAMES. Another strategic victory! What a Boche he'd have made. As you were, Tommy!

[THOMAS *returns to the door. The sound of prolonged applause comes from within.*]

That's a bishop.

L. ANNE. Why?

JAMES. By the way he's drawin'. It's the fine fightin' spirit in 'em. They were the backbone o' the war. I see there's a bit o' the old stuff left in you, Tommy.

L. ANNE. [*Scrutinizing the widely-grinning* THOMAS] Where? Is it in his mouth?

JAMES. You've still got a sense of your superiors. Didn't you notice how you moved to Poulder's orders, me boy; an' when he was gone, to mine?

L. ANNE. [*To* THOMAS] March!

[*The grinning* THOMAS *remains immovable.*]

He doesn't, James!

JAMES. Look here, Miss Anne—your lights ought to be out before ten. Close in, Tommy!   [*He and* THOMAS *move towards her.*

L. ANNE. [*Dodging*] Oh, no! Oh, no! Look!

[*The footmen stop and turn. There between the pillars stands* LITTLE AIDA *with the trousers, her face brilliant with surprise.*

JAMES. Good Lord! What's this?

[*Seeing* LITTLE ANNE, LITTLE AIDA *approaches, fascinated, and the two children sniff at each other as it were like two little dogs walking round and round.*

L. ANNE. [*Suddenly*] My name's Anne; what's yours?

L. AIDA. Aida.

L. ANNE. Are you lost?

L. AIDA. Nao.

L. ANNE. Are those trousers?

L. AIDA. Yus.

L. ANNE. Whose?

L. AIDA. Mrs. Lemmy's.

L. ANNE. Does she wear them?   [LITTLE AIDA *smiles brilliantly.*

L. AIDA. Nao. She sews 'em.

L. ANNE. [*Touching the trousers*] They *are* hard. James's are much softer; aren't they, James? [JAMES *deigns no reply.*] What shall we do? Would you like to see my bedroom?

L. AIDA. [*With a hop*] Aoh, yus!

JAMES. No.

L. ANNE. Why not?

JAMES. Have some sense of what's fittin'.

L. ANNE. Why isn't it fittin'? [*To* LITTLE AIDA.] Do you like me?

L. AIDA. Yus-s.

L. ANNE. So do I.   Come on !   [*She takes* LITTLE AIDA'S *hand.*

JAMES. [*Between the pillars*] Tommy, ketch 'em !

[THOMAS *retains them by the skirts.*

L. ANNE. [*Feigning indifference*] All right, then !   [*To* LITTLE AIDA.] Have you ever seen a bomb ?

L. AIDA. Nao.

L. ANNE. [*Going to the table and lifting a corner of the cover*] Look !

L. AIDA. [*Looking*] What's it for ?

L. ANNE. To blow up this house.

L. AIDA. I daon't fink !

L. ANNE. Why not ?

L. AIDA. It's a beautiful big 'ouse.

L. ANNE. That's why.   Isn't it, James ?

L. AIDA. You give the fing to me ; I'll blow up our 'ouse—it's an ugly little 'ouse.

L. ANNE. [*Struck*] Let's all blow up our own ; then we can start fair.   Daddy would like that.

L. AIDA. Yus.   [*Suddenly brilliant.*] I've 'ad a ride in a taxi, an' we're goin' 'ome in it agyne !

L. ANNE. Were you sick ?

L. AIDA. [*Brilliant*] Nao.

L. ANNE. I was, when I first went in one, but I was quite young then.   James, could you get her a Pêche Melba ? There was *one*.

JAMES. No.

L. ANNE. Have you seen the revolution ?

L. AIDA. Wot's that ?

L. ANNE. It's made of people.

L. AIDA. I've seen the corfin, it's myde o' wood.

L. ANNE. Do you hate the rich ?

L. AIDA. [*Ineffably*] Nao.   I hates the poor.

L. ANNE. Why ?

L. AIDA. 'Cos they 'yn't got nuffin'.

L. ANNE. I love the poor.   They're such dears.

L. AIDA. [*Shaking her head with a broad smile*] Nao.

L. ANNE. Why not ?

L. AIDA. I'd tyke and lose the lot, I would.

L. ANNE. Where ?

L. AIDA. In the water.

L. ANNE. Like puppies ?

L. AIDA. Yus.

L. ANNE. Why ?

L. AIDA. Then I'd be shut of 'em.

L. ANNE. [*Puzzled*] Oh !

[*The voice of* THE PRESS *is heard in the hall :* " Where's the little girl ? "

JAMES. That's you. Come 'ere !

[*He puts a hand behind* LITTLE AIDA's *back and propels her towards the hall.* THE PRESS *enters with old* MRS. LEMMY.

PRESS. Oh ! Here she is, major domo. I'm going to take this old lady to the meeting ; they want her on the platform. Look after our friend, Mr. Lemmy here ; Lord William wants to see him presently.

L. ANNE. [*In an awed whisper*] James, it's the little blighter !

[*She dives again under the table.* LEMMY *enters.*

LEMMY. 'Ere ! 'Arf a mo' ! Yer said yer'd drop me at my plyce. Well, I tell yer candid—this 'yn't my plyce !

PRESS. That's all right, Mr. Lemmy. [*He grins.*] They'll make you wonderfully comfortable, won't you, major domo ?

[*He passes on through the room, to the door ushering old* MRS. LEMMY *and* LITTLE AIDA.

[POULDER *blocks* LEMMY's *way, with* CHARLES *and* HENRY *behind him.*

POULDER. James, watch it ; I'll report.

[*He moves away, following* THE PRESS *through the door.* JAMES *between table and window.* THOMAS *has gone to the door.* HENRY *and* CHARLES *remain at the entrances to the hall.* LEMMY *looks dubiously around, his cockney assurance gradually returns.*

LEMMY. I think I knows the gas 'ere. This is where I came to-dy, 'yn't it ? Excuse my hesitytion—these little 'ouses *is* so much the syme !

JAMES. [*Gloomily*] They are !

LEMMY. [*Looking at the four immovable footmen, till he concentrates on* JAMES] Ah ! I 'ad a word wiv you, 'adn't I ? You're the four conscientious ones wot's wyin' on your gov'nor's chest. 'Twas *you* I spoke to, wasn't it ? [*His eyes travel over them again.*] Ye're so monotonous. Well, ye're busy now, I see. I won't wyste yer time.

[*He turns towards the hall, but* CHARLES *and* HENRY *bar the way in silence.*]

[*Skidding a little, and regarding the four immovables once more.*] I never see such pytient men ? Compared wiv yer, mountains is restless !

[*He goes to the table.* JAMES *watches him.* ANNE *barks from underneath.*]

[*Skidding again.*] Why ! There's a dawg under there. [*Noting the grin on* THOMAS's *face.*] Glad it amooses yer. Yer want it, doan't yer, wiv a fyce like that ? Is this a ply wivaht words ? 'Ave I got into the movies by mistyke ? Turn aht, an' let's 'ave six penn'orth o' darkness.

L. ANNE. [*From beneath the table*] No, no ! Not dark !

LEMMY. [*Musingly*] The dawg talks anyway. Come aht, Fido !

[LITTLE ANNE *emerges, and regards him with burning curiosity.*]

I sy : Is this the lytest fashion o' receivin' guests ?

L. ANNE. Mother always wants people to feel at home. What shall we do? Would you like to hear the speeches? Thomas, open the door a little, do!

JAMES. 'Umour 'er a couple o' inches, Tommy!

[THOMAS *draws the door back stealthily an inch or so.*

L. ANNE. [*After applying her eye—in a loud whisper*] There's the old lady. Daddy's looking at her trousers. Listen!

[*For* MRS. LEMMY'S *voice is floating faintly through:* " I putt in the buttonholes, I stretches the flies; I 'ems the bottoms; I lines the crutch; I putt on this bindin'; I sews on the buttons; I presses the seams—Tuppence three farthin's the pair."

LEMMY. [*In a hoarse whisper*] That's it, old lydy: give it 'em!

L. ANNE. Listen!

VOICE OF LORD W. We are indebted to our friends the Press for giving us the pleasure—er—pleasure of hearing from her own lips —the pleasure——

L. ANNE. Oh! Daddy! [THOMAS *abruptly closes the doors.*

LEMMY. [*To* ANNE] Now yer've done it. See wot comes o' bein' impytient. We was just gettin' to the marrer.

L. ANNE. What can we do for you now?

LEMMY. [*Pointing to* ANNE, *and addressing* JAMES] Wot is this one, anywy?

JAMES. [*Sepulchrally*] Daughter o' the house.

LEMMY. Is she insured agynst 'er own curiosity?

L. ANNE. Why!

LEMMY. As I daon't believe in a life beyond the gryve, I might be tempted to send yer there.

L. ANNE. What is the gryve?

LEMMY. Where little gells goes to.

L. ANNE. Oh, *when?*

LEMMY. [*Pretending to look at a watch, which is not there*] Well, I dunno if I've got time to finish yer this minute. Sy to-morrer at 'arf-past.

L. ANNE. Half-past what?

LEMMY. [*Despairingly*] 'Arf-past wot!

[*The sound of applause is heard.*

JAMES. That's 'is Grace. 'E's gettin' wickets, too.

[POULDER *entering from the door.*

POULDER. Lord William is slippin' in.

[*He makes a cabalistic sign with his head.* JAMES *crosses to the door.* LEMMY *looks dubiously at* POULDER.

LEMMY. [*Suddenly—as to himself*] Wot oh! I am the portly one!

POULDER. [*Severely*] Any such allusion aggeravates your offence.

LEMMY. Oh, ah! Look 'ere, it was a corked bottle. Now, tyke

care, tyke care, 'aughty! Daon't curl yer lip! I shall myke a clean breast o' my betryal when the time comes!

[*There is a slight movement of the door.* ANNE *makes a dive towards the table but is arrested by* POULDER *grasping her waistband.* LORD WILLIAM *slips in, followed by* THE PRESS, *on whom* JAMES *and* THOMAS *close the door too soon.*

HALF OF THE PRESS. [*Indignantly*] Look out!

JAMES. Do you want him in or out, me Lord?

LEMMY. I sy, you've divided the Press; 'e was unanimous.

[*The* FOOTMEN *let* THE PRESS *through.*

LORD W. [*To* THE PRESS] I'm so sorry.

LEMMY. Would yer like me to see to 'is gas?

LORD W. So you're my friend of the cellars?

LEMMY. [*Uneasy*] I daon't deny it.

[POULDER *begins removing* LITTLE ANNE.

L. ANNE. Let me stay, Daddy; I haven't seen anything yet! If I go, I shall only have to come down again when they loot the house. Listen!

[*The hoarse strains of the Marseillaise are again heard from the distance.*

LORD W. [*Blandly*] Take her up, Poulder!

L. ANNE. Well, I'm coming down again—and next time I shan't have any clothes on, you know.

[*They vanish between the pillars.* LORD WILLIAM *makes a sign of dismissal.* The FOOTMEN *file out.*

LEMMY. [*Admiringly*] Luv'ly pyces!

LORD W. [*Pleasantly*] Now then; let's have our talk, Mr.——

LEMMY. Lemmy.

PRESS. [*Who has slipped his note-book out*] " Bombed and Bomber face to face——"

LEMMY. [*Uneasy*] I didn't come 'ere agyne on me own, yer know. The Press betryed me.

LORD. W. Is that old lady your mother?

LEMMY. The syme. I tell yer stryte, it was for 'er I took that old bottle o' port. It *was* orful old.

LORD W. Ah! Port! Probably the '63. Hope you both enjoyed it.

LEMMY. So far—yus. Muvver'll suffer a bit to-morrer, I expect.

LORD W. I should like to do something for your mother, if you'll allow me.

LEMMY. Oh! I'll allow yer. But I dunno wot she'll sy.

LORD W. I can see she's a fine independent old lady! But suppose you were to pay her ten bob a week, and keep my name out of it?

LEMMY. Well, that's one wy o' *you* doin' somefink, 'yn't it?

LORD W. I giving you the money, of course.

PRESS. [*Writing*] "Lord William, with kingly generosity——"

LEMMY. [*Drawing attention to* THE PRESS *with his thumb*] I sy—I daon't mind, meself—if you daon't——

LORD W. He won't write anything to annoy me.

PRESS. This is the big thing, Lord William; it'll get the public bang in the throat.

LEMMY. [*Confidentially*] Bit dyngerous, yn't it?—trustin' the Press? Their right 'ands never knows wot their left 'ands is writin'. [*To* THE PRESS.] Yn't that true, speakin' as a man?

PRESS. Mr. Lemmy, even the Press is capable of gratitude.

LEMMY. Is it? I should ha' thought it was too important for a little thing like that. [*To* LORD WILLIAM.] But ye're quite right; we couldn't do wivaht the Press—there wouldn't be no distress, no corfin, no revolution—cos' nobody'd know nuffin' abaht it. Why! There wouldn't be no life at all on Earf in these dyes, wivaht the Press! It's them wot says: "Let there be Light—an' there is Light."

LORD W. Umm! That's rather a new thought to me.

[*Writes on his cuff.*

LEMMY. But abaht Muvver, I'll tell yer 'ow we can arrynge. You send 'er the ten bob a week wivaht syin' anyfink, an' she'll fink it comes from Gawd or the Gover'ment—yer cawn't tell one from t'other in Befnal Green.

LORD W. All right; we'll do that.

LEMMY. Will yer reely? I'd like to shyke yer 'and.

[LORD WILLIAM *puts out his hand, which* LEMMY *grasps.*

PRESS. [*Writing*] "The heart-beat of humanity was in that grasp between the son of toil and the son of leisure."

LEMMY. [*Already ashamed of his emotion*] 'Ere, 'arf a mo'! Which is which? Daon't forget I'm aht o' work; Lord William, if that's 'is nyme, is workin' 'ard at 'is Anti-Sweats! Wish I could get a job like vat—jist suit me!

LORD W. That hits hard, Mr. Lemmy!

LEMMY. Daon't worry! Yer cawn't 'elp bein' born in the purple!

LORD W. Ah! Tell me, what would you do in my place?

LEMMY. Why—as the nobleman said in 'is well-known wy: "Sit in me Club winder an' watch it ryne on the dam people!" That's if I was a average nobleman! If I was a bit more noble, I might be tempted to come the kind-'earted on twenty thou' a year. Some prefers yachts, or ryce 'orses. But philanthropy on the 'ole is syfer, in these dyes.

LORD W. So you think one takes to it as a sort of insurance, Mr. Lemmy? Is that quite fair?

LEMMY. Well, we've all got a weakness towards bein' kind, somewhere abaht us. But the moment wealf comes in, we 'yn't wot I

call single-'earted. If yer went into the foundytions of your wealf
—would yer feel like 'avin' any? It all comes from uvver people's
'ard, unpleasant lybour—it's all built on Muvver as yer might sy.
An' if yer daon't get rid o' some of it in bein' kind—yer daon't feel
syfe nor comfy.

Lord W. [*Twisting his moustache*] Your philosophy is very pessimistic.

Lemmy. Well, *I* calls meself an optimist; I sees the worst of
everyfink. Never disappynted, can afford to 'ave me smile under
the blackest sky. When deaf is squeezin' of me windpipe, I shall
'ave a laugh in it! Fact is, if yer've 'ad to do wiv gas an' water pipes,
yer can fyce anyfing. [*The distant Marseillaise blares up.*] 'Ark at the
revolution!

Lord W. [*Rather desperately*] I know—hunger and all the rest of
it! And here am I, a rich man, and don't know what the deuce
to do.

Lemmy. Well, I'll tell yer. Throw yer cellars open, an' while the
populyce is gettin' drunk sell all yer 'ave an' go an' live in Ireland;
they've got the millennium chronic over there.

> [Lord William *utters a short, vexed laugh, and begins to walk
> about.*]

That's speakin' as a practical man. Speakin' as a synt—" Bruvvers,
all I 'ave is yours. To-morrer I'm goin' dahn to the Lybour Exchynge
to git put on the wytin' list, syme as you!"

Lord W. But, d—— it, man, there we should be, all together!
Would that help?

Lemmy. Nao; but it'd syve a lot o' blood.

> [Lord William *stops abruptly, and looks first at* Lemmy, *then
> at the cooler, still covered with the Chinese mat.*]

Yer thought the Englishman could be taught to shed blood wiv
syfety. Not 'im! Once yer git 'im into an 'abit, yer cawn't git 'im
out of it agyne. 'E'll go on sheddin' blood mechanical—Conservative by nyture. An' 'e won't myke nuffin' o' yours. Not even the
Press wiv 'is 'oneyed words'll sty 'is 'and.

Lord. W. And what do you suggest we could have done, to avoid
trouble?

Lemmy. [*Warming to his theme*] I'll tell yer. If all you wealfy
nobs wiv kepitel 'ad come it kind from the start after the war yer'd
never 'a been 'earin' the Marseillaisy naow. Lord! 'Ow you did
talk abaht Unity and a noo spirit in the Country. Noo spirit! Why,
soon as ever there was no dynger from outside, yer stawted to myke
it inside, wiv an iron 'and. Naow, *you've* been in the war an' it's
given yer a feelin' 'eart; but most of the nobs wiv kepitel was too old
or too important to fight. *They* weren't born agyne. So naow that
bad times is come, we're 'owlin' for their blood.

17

LORD W. I quite agree; I quite agree. I've often said much the same thing.

LEMMY. Voice cryin' in the wilderness—I daon't sy *we* was yngels —there was faults on bofe sides. [*He looks at* THE PRESS.] The Press could ha' helped yer a lot. Shall I tell yer wot the Press did? "It's vital," said the Press, "that the country should be united, or it will never recover." Nao strikes, nao 'uman nature, nao nuffink. Kepitel an' Lybour like the Siamese twins. And, fust dispute that come along, the Press orfs wiv its coat an' goes at it bald-'eaded. An' wot abaht since? Sich a riot o' nymes called, in Press and Pawlyement—Unpatriotic an' outrygeous demands o' lybour. Bloodsuckin' tyranny o' Kepitel; thieves an' dawgs an' 'owlin' Jackybines —gents throwin' books at each other; all the resources of edjucytion exhausted! If I'd been Prime Minister I'd 'ave 'ad the Press's gas cut 'orf at the meter. Puffect liberty of course, nao Censorship; just sy wot yer like—an' never be 'eard of no more.

[*Turning suddenly to* THE PRESS, *who has been scribbling in pace with this harangue, and now has developed a touch of writer's cramp.*]

Why! 'Is 'and's out o' breath! Fink o' vet!

LORD W. Great tribute to your eloquence, Mr. Lemmy!

[*A sudden stir of applause and scraping of chairs is heard; the meeting is evidently breaking up.* LADY WILLIAM *comes in, followed by* MRS. LEMMY *with her trousers, and* LITTLE AIDA. LEMMY *stares fixedly at this sudden radiant apparition. His gaze becomes as that of a rabbit regarding a snake. And suddenly he puts up his hand and wipes his brow.*

[LADY WILLIAM, *going to the table, lifts one end of the Chinese mat, and looks at* LEMMY. *Then she turns to* LORD WILLIAM.

LADY W. Bill!

LEMMY [*To his mother—in a hoarse whisper*] She calls 'im Bill. 'Ow! 'Yn't she IT!

LADY W. [*Apart*] Have you spoken to him?

[LORD WILLIAM *shakes his head.*]

Not? What have you been saying, then?

LORD W. Nothing, he's talked all the time.

LADY W. [*Very low*] What a little caution!

LORD W. Steady, old girl! He's got his eye on you!

[LADY WILLIAM *looks at* LEMMY, *whose eyes are still fixed on her.*

LADY W. [*With resolution*] Well, *I'm* going to tackle him.

[*She moves towards* LEMMY, *who again wipes his brow, and wrings out his hand.*

MRS. LEMMY. Don't 'ee du that, Bob. Yu must forgive 'im, ma'am; it's 'is admiration. 'E was always one for the ladies, and he'm not used to seein' so much of 'em.

LADY W. Don't you think you owe us an explanation?

MRS. L. Speak up, Bob.   [*But* LEMMY *only shifts his feet.*]
My gudeness! 'E've a-lost 'is tongue. I never knu that 'appen to
'e before.

LORD W. [*Trying to break the embarrassment*] No ill-feeling, you
know, Lemmy.   [*But* LEMMY *still only rolls his eyes.*

LADY W. Don't you think it was rather—inconsiderate of you?

LEMMY. Muvver, tyke me aht, I'm feelin' fynte!

> [*Spurts of the Marseillaise and the mutter of the crowd have been
> coming nearer; and suddenly a knocking is heard.* POULDER
> *and* JAMES *appear between the pillars.*

POULDER. The populace, me Lord!

LADY W. What!

LORD W. Where've you put 'em, Poulder?

POULDER. They've put theirselves in the portico, me Lord.

LORD W. [*Suddenly wiping his brow*] Phew! I say, this is awful,
Nell! Two speeches in one evening. Nothing else for it, I suppose.
Open the window, Poulder!

POULDER. [*Crossing to the window*] We are prepared for any sacrifice
me Lord.   [*He opens the window.*

PRESS. [*Writing furiously*] "Lady William stood like a statue at
bay."

LORD W. Got one of those lozenges on you, Nell?
          [*But* LADY WILLIAM *has almost nothing on her.*

LEMMY. [*Producing a paper from his pocket*] 'Ave one o' my gum
drops?   [*He passes it to* LORD WILLIAM.

LORD W. [*Unable to refuse, takes a large flat gum drop from the paper,
and looks at it in embarrassment*] Ah! thanks! Thanks awfully!

> [LEMMY *turns to* LITTLE AIDA, *and puts a gum drop in her mouth.
> A burst of murmurs from the crowd.*

JAMES. [*Towering above the wine cooler*] If they get saucy, me Lord,
I can always give 'em their own back.

LORD W. Steady, James; steady!

> [*He puts the gum drop absently in his mouth, and turns up to the
> open window.*

VOICE. [*Outside*] 'Ere they are—the bally plutocrats.
          [*Voices in chorus:* " Bread! Bread!"

LORD W. Poulder, go and tell the chef to send out anything there
is in the house—nicely, as if it came from nowhere in particular.

POULDER. Very good, me Lord. [*Sotto voce.*] Any wine? If I
might suggest—German—'ock?

LORD W. What you like.

POULDER. Very good, me Lord.   [*He goes.*

LORD W. I say, dash it, Nell, my teeth are stuck!
          [*He works his finger in his mouth.*

LADY W. Take it out, darling.

LORD W. [*Taking out the gum drop and looking at it*] What the deuce did I put it in for?

PRESS. [*Writing*] "With inimitable coolness Lord William prepared to address the crowd."   [*Voices in chorus:* "Bread! Bread!"]

LORD W. Stand by to prompt, old girl. Now for it. This ghastly gum drop!

> [LADY WILLIAM *takes it from his agitated hand, and flips it through the window.*

VOICE. Dahn with the aristo——   [*Chokes.*

LADY W. Oh! Bill—oh! It's gone into a mouth!

LORD W. Good God!

VOICE. Wot's this? Throwin' things? Mind aht, or we'll smash yer winders!

> [*As the voices in chorus chant:* "Bread! Bread!" LITTLE ANNE, *night-gowned, darts in from the hall. She is followed by* MISS STOKES. *They stand listening.*

LORD W. [*To the Crowd*] My friends, you've come to the wrong shop. There's nobody in London more sympathetic with you.

> [*The crowd laughs hoarsely.*

[*Whispering.*] Look out, old girl; they can see your shoulders.

> [LADY WILLIAM *moves back a step.*]

If I were a speaker, I could make you feel——

VOICE. Look at his white weskit! Blood-suckers—fattened on the people!   [JAMES *dives his hand at the wine cooler.*

LORD W. I've always said the Government ought to take immediate steps——

VOICE. To shoot us dahn.

LORD W. Not a bit. To relieve the—er——

LADY W. [*Prompting*] Distress.

LORD W. Distress, and ensure—er—ensure——

LADY W. [*Prompting*] Quiet.

LORD W. [*To her*] No, no. To ensure—ensure——

L. ANNE. [*Agonized*] Oh, Daddy!

VOICE. 'E wants to syve 'is dirty great 'ouse.

LORD W. [*Roused*] D—— if I do!

> [*Rude and hoarse laughter from the crowd.*

JAMES. [*With fury*] Me Lord, let me blow 'em to glory!

> [*He raises the cooler and advances towards the window.*

LORD W. [*Turning sharply on him*] Drop it, James; drop it!

PRESS. [*Jumping*] No, no; don't drop it!

> [JAMES *retires crestfallen to the table, where he replaces the cooler.*

LORD W. [*Catching hold of his bit*] Look here, I must have fought alongside some of you fellows in the war. Weren't we jolly well like brothers?

A Voice. Not so much bloomin' "Kamerad"; hand over yer 'ouse.

Lord W. I was born with this beastly great house, and money, and goodness knows what other entanglements—a wife and family——

Voice. Born with a wife and family!   [*Jeers and laughter*.

Lord W. I feel we're all in the same boat, and I want to pull my weight. If you can show me the way, I'll take it fast enough.

A Deep Voice. Step dahn then, an' we'll step up.

Another Voice. 'Ear, 'ear!   [*A fierce little cheer*.

Lord W. [*To* Lady William—*in despair*] By George! I can't get in anywhere!

Lady W. [*Calmly*] Then shut the window, Bill.

Lemmy. [*Who has been moving towards them slowly*] Lemme sy a word to 'em.

[*All stare at him.* Lemmy *approaches the window, followed by* Little Aida. Poulder *re-enters with the three other footmen*.]

[*At the window.*] Cheerio! Cockies!

[*The silence of surprise falls on the crowd.*]

I'm one of yer. Gas an' water I am. Got more grievances an' out of employment than any of yer. I want to see their blood flow, syme as you.

Press. [*Writing*] "Born orator—ready cockney wit—saves situation."

Lemmy. Wot I sy is: Dahn wiv the country, dahn wiv everyfing. Begin agyne from the foundytions. [*Nodding his head back at the room.*] But we've got to keep one or two o' these 'ere under glawss, to show our future generytions. An' this one is 'armless. His pipes is sahnd, 'is 'eart is good; 'is 'ead is *not* strong. 'Is 'ouse will myke a charmin' palace o' varieties where our children can come an' see 'ow they did it in the good old dyes. Yer never see sich waxworks as 'is butler and 'is four conscientious khaki footmen. Why—wot d'yer think 'e 'as 'em for—fear they might be out-o'-works like you an' me. Nao! Keep this one; 'e's a Flower. 'Arf a mo'! I'll show yer my Muvver. Come 'ere, old lydy; and bring yer trahsers. [Mrs. Lemmy *comes forward to the window.*] Tell abaht yer speech to the meetin'.

Mrs. Lemmy. [*Bridling*] Oh dear! Well, I cam' in with me trousers, an' they putt me up on the pedestory at once, so I tole 'em. [*Holding up the trousers.*] "I putt in the button'oles, I stretches the flies; I lines the crutch; I putt on this bindin', I presses the seams —Tuppence three farthin's a pair."   [*A groan from the crowd.*

Lemmy. [*Showing her off*] Seventy-seven! Wot's 'er income? Twelve bob a week; seven from the Gover'ment, an' five from the sweat of 'er brow. Look at 'er! 'Yn't she a tight old dear to keep it goin'! No workus for 'er, nao fear! The gryve rather!

[*Murmurs from the crowd, at whom* Mrs. Lemmy *is blandly smiling.*]

You cawn't git below 'er—impossible! She's the foundytions of
the country—an' rocky yn't the word for 'em. Worked 'ard all 'er
life, brought up a family and buried 'em on it. Twelve bob a week,
an' seven when 'er fingers goes, which is very near. Well, naow,
this torf 'ere comes to me an' says: " I'd like to do somefin' for yer
muvver. 'Ow's ten bob a week? " 'e says. Naobody arst 'im—
quite on 'is own. That's the sort 'e is. [*Sinking his voice confidentially.*] Sorft. You bring yer muvvers 'ere, 'e'll do the syme for
them. I giv yer the 'int.

VOICE. [*From the crowd*] What's 'is nyme?

LEMMY. They calls 'im Bill.

VOICE. Bill what?

L. ANNE. Dromondy.

LADY W. Anne!

LEMMY. Dromedary 'is nyme is.

VOICE. [*From the crowd.*] Three cheers for Bill Dromedary.

LEMMY. I sy, there's veal an' 'am, an' pork wine at the back for
them as wants it; I 'eard the word passed. An' look 'ere, if yer want
a flag for the revolution, tyke muvver's trahsers an' tie 'em to the
corfin. Yer cawn't 'ave no more inspirin' banner. Ketch! [*He
throws the trousers out.*] Give Bill a double-barrel fust, to show there's
no ill-feelin'. 'Ip, 'ip!

> [*The crowd cheers, then slowly passes away, singing its hoarse version
> of the Marseillaise, till all that is heard is a faint murmuring
> and a distant barrel-organ playing the same tune.*

PRESS. [*Writing*] " And far up in the clear summer air the larks
were singing."

LORD W. [*Passing his hand over his hair, and blinking his eyes*] James!
Ready?

JAMES. Me Lord!

ANNE. Daddy!

LADY W. [*Taking his arm*] Bill! It's all right, old man—all right!

LORD W. [*Blinking*] Those infernal larks! Thought we were on
the Somme again! Ah! Mr. Lemmy, [*Still rather dreamy*] no end
obliged to you; you're so decent. Now, why did you want to blow
us up before dinner?

LEMMY. Blow yer up? [*Passing his hand over his hair in travesty.*]
" Is it a dream? Then wykin' would be pyne."

MRS. LEMMY. Bo-ob! Not so saucy, my boy!

LEMMY. Blow yer up? Wot abaht it?

LADY W. [*Indicating the bomb*] This, Mr. Lemmy!

> [LEMMY *looks at it, and his eyes roll and goggle.*

LORD W. Come, all's forgiven! But why did you?

LEMMY. Orl right! I'm goin' to tyke it awy; it'd a-been a bit
ork-ard for me. I'll want it to-morrer.

LORD. W. What !   To leave somewhere else ?

LEMMY. Yus, of course !

LORD W. No, no ; dash it !   Tell us—what's it filled with ?

LEMMY. Filled wiv ? Nuffin'.   Wot did yer expect ? Toof-pahder ? It's got a bit o' my lead soldered on to it.   That's why it's 'eavy !

LORD W. But what *is* it ?

LEMMY. Wot is it ?   [*His eyes are fearfully fixed on* LADY WILLIAM.] I fought everybody knew 'em.

LADY W. Mr. Lemmy, you must clear this up, please.

LEMMY. [*To* LORD WILLIAM, *with his eyes still fixed on* LADY WILLIAM —*mysteriously*] Wiv lydies present ?   'Adn't I better tell the Press ?

LORD W. All right ; tell someone—anyone !

> [LEMMY *goes down to* THE PRESS, *who is reading over his last note. Everyone watches and listens with the utmost discretion, while he whispers into the ear of* THE PRESS, *who shakes his head violently.*

PRESS. No, no ; it's too horrible.   It destroys my whole——

LEMMY. Well, I tell yer it is.   [*Whispers again violently.*

PRESS. No, no ; I can't have it.   All my article !   All my article ! It can't be—no !

LEMMY. I never see sich an obstinate thick-head !   Yer 'yn't worvy of yer tryde.

> [*He whispers still more violently and makes cabalistic signs.*
> [LADY WILLIAM *lifts the bomb from the cooler into the sight of all.* LORD WILLIAM, *seeing it for the first time in full light, bends double in silent laughter and whispers to his wife.* LADY WILLIAM *drops the bomb and gives way too.   Hearing the sound,* LEMMY *turns, and his goggling eyes pass them all in review.* LORD *and* LADY WILLIAM *in fits of laughter,* LITTLE ANNE *stamping her feet, for* MISS STOKES, *red, but composed, has her hands placed firmly over her pupil's eyes and ears ;* LITTLE AIDA *smiling brilliantly,* MRS. LEMMY *blandly in sympathy, neither knowing why ; the* FOUR FOOTMEN *in a row, smothering little explosions.* POULDER *extremely grave and red,* THE PRESS *perfectly haggard, gnawing at his nails.*

LEMMY. [*Turning to* THE PRESS] Blimy !   It amooses 'em, all but the genteel ones.   Cheer oh ! Press ! Yer can always myke somefin' out o' nuffin' ?   It's not the fust thing as 'as existed in yer imaginytion only.

PRESS. No, d—— it ; I'll keep it a bomb !

LEMMY. [*Soothingly*] Ah ! Keep the sensytion.   Wot's the troof compared wiv that ?   Come on, Muvver !   Come on, Little Aida ! Time we was goin' dahn to 'Earf !

> [*He goes up to the table, and still skidding a little at* LADY WILLIAM, *takes the late bomb from the cooler, placing it under his arm.*

MRS. LEMMY. Gude naight, sir; gude naight, ma'am; thank yu for my cup o' tea, an' all yure kindness.

[*She shakes hands with* LORD *and* LADY WILLIAM, *drops the curtsey of her youth before* MR. POULDER, *and goes out followed by* LITTLE AIDA, *who is looking back at* LITTLE ANNE.

LEMMY. [*Turning suddenly*] Aoh! An' jist one fing! Next time yer build an 'ouse, daon't forget—it's the foundytions as bears the wyte.

[*With a wink that gives way to a last fascinated look at* LADY WILLIAM, *he passes out. All gaze after them, except* THE PRESS, *who is tragically consulting his spiflicated notes.*

L. ANNE. [*Breaking away from* MISS STOKES *and rushing forward*] Oh! Mum! what *was* it?

The curtain falls.

THE SKIN GAME

CHARACTERS

HILLCRIST, *a country gentleman*
AMY, *his wife*
JILL, *his daughter*
DAWKER, *his agent*
HORNBLOWER, *a man newly-rich*
CHARLES, *his elder son*
CHLOE, *wife to Charles*
ROLF, *his younger son*
FELLOWS, *Hillcrist's butler*
ANNA, *Chloe's maid*
THE JACKMANS, *man and wife*
    AN AUCTIONEER
    A SOLICITOR
    TWO STRANGERS

ACT I

HILLCRIST's *study. A pleasant room, with books in calf bindings, and signs that the* HILLCRISTS *have travelled, such as a large photograph of the Taj Mahal, of Table Mountain, and the Pyramids of Egypt. A large bureau [stage Right], devoted to the business of a country estate. Two foxes' masks. Flowers in bowls. Deep armchairs. A large French window open [at Back], with a lovely view of a slight rise of fields and trees in August sunlight. A fine stone fireplace [stage Left]. A door [Left]. A door opposite [Right]. General colour effect—stone, and cigar-leaf brown, with spots of bright colour.*

HILLCRIST *sits in a swivel chair at the bureau, busy with papers. He has gout, and his left foot is encased accordingly. He is a thin, dried-up man of about fifty-five, with a rather refined, rather kindly, and rather cranky countenance. Close to him stands his very upstanding nineteen-year-old daughter* JILL, *with clubbed hair round a pretty, manly face.*

JILL. You know, Dodo, it's all pretty good rot in these days.

HILLCRIST. Cads are cads, Jill, even in these days.

JILL. What is a cad?

HILLCRIST. A self-assertive fellow, without a sense of other people.

JILL. Well, Old Hornblower I'll give you.

HILLCRIST. I wouldn't take him.

JILL. Well, you've got him. Now, Charlie—Chearlie—I say—the importance of not being Charlie——

HILLCRIST. Good heavens! do you know their Christian names?

JILL. My dear father, they've been here seven years.

HILLCRIST. In old days we only knew their Christian names from their tombstones.

JILL. Charlie Hornblower isn't really half a bad sport.

HILLCRIST. About a quarter of a bad sport—I've always thought out hunting.

JILL. [*Pulling his hair*] Now, his wife—Chloe——

HILLCRIST. [*Whimsical*] Gad! your mother'd have a fit if she knew you called her Chloe.

JILL. It's a ripping name.

HILLCRIST. Chloe! H'm! I had a spaniel once——

JILL. Dodo, you're narrow. Buck up, old darling, it won't do. Chloe has seen life, I'm pretty sure; *that's* attractive, anyway. No, mother's not in the room; don't turn your uneasy eyes.

515

HILLCRIST. Really, my dear, you are getting——

JILL. The limit.   Now, Rolf——

HILLCRIST. What's Rolf?   Another dog?

JILL. Rolf Hornblower's a topper; he really is a nice boy.

HILLCRIST. [*With a sharp look*] Oh! He's a nice boy?

JILL. Yes, darling.   You know what a nice boy is, don't you?

HILLCRIST. Not in these days.

JILL. Well, I'll tell you.   In the first place, he's not amorous——

HILLCRIST. What!   Well, that's some comfort.

JILL. Just a jolly good companion.

HILLCRIST. To whom?

JILL. Well, to anyone—me.

HILLCRIST. Where?

JILL. Anywhere.   You don't suppose I confine myself to the home paddocks, do you?   I'm naturally rangey, Father.

HILLCRIST. [*Ironically*] You don't say so!

JILL. In the second place, he doesn't like discipline.

HILLCRIST. Jupiter!   He does seem attractive.

JILL. In the third place, he bars his father.

HILLCRIST. Is that essential to nice *girls* too?

JILL [*With a twirl of his hair*] Fish not!   Fourthly, he's got ideas.

HILLCRIST. I knew it!

JILL. For instance, he thinks—as I do——

HILLCRIST. Ah!   *Good* ideas.

JILL. [*Pulling gently*] Careful!   He thinks old people run the show too much.   He says they oughtn't to, because they're so damtouchy. Are you damtouchy, darling?

HILLCRIST. Well, I'm——!   I don't know about touchy.

JILL. He says there'll be no world fit to live in till we get rid of the old.   We must make them climb a tall tree, and shake them off it.

HILLCRIST. [*Dryly*] Oh!   he says that!

JILL. Otherwise, with the way they stand on each other's rights, they'll spoil the garden for the young.

HILLCRIST. Does his father agree?

JILL. Oh!   Rolf doesn't talk to *him*, his mouth's too large.   Have you ever seen it, Dodo?

HILLCRIST. Of course.

JILL. It's considerable, isn't it?   Now yours is—reticent, darling.

[*Rumpling his hair.*

HILLCRIST. It won't be in a minute.   Do you realize that I've got gout?

JILL. Poor ducky!   How long have we been here, Dodo?

HILLCRIST. Since Elizabeth, anyway.

JILL. [*Looking at his foot*] It has its drawbacks.   D'you think

Hornblower had a father? I believe he was spontaneous. But, Dodo, why all this—this *attitude* to the Hornblowers?

[*She purses her lips and makes a gesture as of pushing persons away.*

HILLCRIST. Because they're pushing.

JILL. That's only because we *are*, as mother would say, and they're *not*—yet. But why not let them be?

HILLCRIST. You can't.

JILL. *Why?*

HILLCRIST. It takes generations to learn to live and let live, Jill. People like that take an ell when you give them an inch.

JILL. But if you gave them the ell, they wouldn't want the inch. Why should it all be such a skin game?

HILLCRIST. Skin game? Where *do* you get your lingo?

JILL. Keep to the point, Dodo.

HILLCRIST. Well, Jill, all life's a struggle between people at different stages of development, in different positions, with different amounts of social influence and property. And the only thing is to have rules of the game and keep them. New people like the Hornblowers haven't learnt those rules; *their* only rule is to get all they can.

JILL. Darling, don't prose. They're not half as bad as you think.

HILLCRIST. Well, when I sold Hornblower Longmeadow and the cottages, I certainly found him all right. All the same, he's got the cloven hoof. [*Warming up.*] His influence in Deepwater is thoroughly bad; those potteries of his are demoralizing—the whole atmosphere of the place is changing. It was a thousand pities he ever came here and discovered that clay. He's brought in the modern cut-throat spirit.

JILL. Cut *our* throat spirit, you mean. What's your definition of a gentleman, Dodo?

HILLCRIST. [*Uneasily*] Can't describe—only feel it.

JILL. Oh! Try!

HILLCRIST. Well—er—I suppose you might say—a man who keeps his form and doesn't let life scupper him out of his standards.

JILL. But suppose his standards are low?

HILLCRIST. [*With some earnestness*] I assume, of course, that he's honest and tolerant, gentle to the weak, and not self-seeking.

JILL. Ah! self-seeking? But aren't we all, Dodo? *I* am.

HILLCRIST. [*With a smile*] You!

JILL. [*Scornfully*] Oh! yes—too young to know.

HILLCRIST. Nobody knows till they're under pretty heavy fire, Jill.

JILL. Except, of course, mother.

HILLCRIST. How do you mean—mother?

JILL. Mother reminds me of England according to herself—always right whatever she does.

HILLCRIST. Ye-es. Your mother *is* perhaps—the perfect woman——

JILL. That's what I was saying. Now, no one could call *you* perfect, Dodo. Besides, you've got gout.

HILLCRIST. Yes ; and I want Fellows. Ring that bell.

JILL. [*Crossing to the bell*] Shall I tell you *my* definition of a gentleman ? A man who gives the Hornblower his due. [*She rings the bell.*] And I think mother ought to call on them. Rolf says old Hornblower resents it fearfully that she's never made a sign to Chloe the three years she's been here.

HILLCRIST. I don't interfere with your mother in such matters. She may go and call on the devil himself if she likes.

JILL. I know you're ever so much better than she is.

HILLCRIST. That's respectful.

JILL. You do keep your prejudices out of your phiz. But mother literally looks down her nose. And she never forgives an " h." They'd get the " hell " from her if they took the " hinch."

HILLCRIST. Jill—your language !

JILL. Don't slime out of it, Dodo. I say, mother ought to call on the Hornblowers.   [*No answer.*] Well ?

HILLCRIST. My dear, I always let people have the last word. It makes them—feel funny. Ugh ! My foot !

[*Enter* FELLOWS, *Left.*]
Fellows, send into the village and get another bottle of this stuff.

JILL. I'll go, darling.

[*She blows him a kiss, and goes out at the window.*
HILLCRIST. And tell cook I've got to go on slops. This foot's worse.

FELLOWS. [*Sympathetic*] Indeed, sir.

HILLCRIST. My third go this year, Fellows.

FELLOWS. Very annoying, sir.

HILLCRIST. Ye—es. Ever had it ?

FELLOWS. I fancy I have had a twinge, sir.

HILLCRIST. [*Brightening*] Have you ? Where ?

FELLOWS. In my cork wrist, sir.

HILLCRIST. Your what ?

FELLOWS. The wrist I draw corks with.

HILLCRIST. [*With a cackle*] You'd have had more than a twinge if you'd lived with my father. H'm !

FELLOWS. Excuse me, sir—Vichy water corks, in my experience, are worse than any wine.

HILLCRIST. [*Ironically*] Ah ! The country's not what it was, is it, Fellows ?

FELLOWS. Getting very new, sir.

HILLCRIST. [*Feelingly*] You're right. Has Dawker come?

FELLOWS. Not yet, sir. The Jackmans would like to see you, sir.

HILLCRIST. What about?

FELLOWS. I don't know, sir.

HILLCRIST. Well, show them in.

FELLOWS. [*Going*] Yes, sir.

> [HILLCRIST *turns his swivel chair round. The* JACKMANS *come in. He, a big fellow about fifty, in a labourer's dress, with eyes which have more in them than his tongue can express; she, a little woman with a worn face, a bright, quick glance, and a tongue to match.*

HILLCRIST. Good morning, Mrs. Jackman! Morning, Jackman! Haven't seen you for a long time.   What can I do?

> [*He draws in foot, and breath, with a sharp hiss.*

JACKMAN. [*In a down-hearted voice*] We've had notice to quit, sir.

HILLCRIST. [*With emphasis*] What!

JACKMAN. Got to be out this week.

MRS. J. Yes, sir, indeed.

HILLCRIST. Well, but when I sold Longmeadow and the cottages, it was on the express understanding that there was to be no disturbance of tenancies.

MRS. J. Yes, sir; but we've all got to go. Mrs. 'Arvey, and the Drews, an' us, and there isn't another cottage to be had anywhere in Deepwater.

HILLCRIST. I know; I want one for my cowman. This won't do at all.   Where do you get it from?

JACKMAN. Mr. 'Ornblower, 'imself, sir. Just an hour ago. He come round and said: " I'm sorry; I want the cottages, and you've got to clear."

MRS. J. [*Bitterly*] He's no gentleman, sir; he put it so brisk. We been there thirty years, and now we don't know what to do. So I hope you'll excuse us coming round, sir.

HILLCRIST. I should think so, indeed! H'm! [*He rises and limps across to the fireplace on his stick.   To himself.*] The cloven hoof. By George! this is a breach of faith. I'll write to him, Jackman. Confound it! I'd certainly never have sold if I'd known he was going to do this.

MRS. J. No, sir, I'm sure, sir. They do say it's to do with the potteries. He wants the cottages for his workmen.

HILLCRIST. [*Sharply*] That's all very well, but he shouldn't have led me to suppose that he would make no change.

JACKMAN. [*Heavily*] They talk about his havin' bought the Centry to put up more chimneys there, and that's why he wants the cottages.

HILLCRIST. The Centry! Impossible!

MRS. J. Yes, sir; it's such a pretty spot—looks beautiful from here. [*She looks out through the window.*] Loveliest spot in all Deepwater, I always say. And your father owned it, and his father before 'im. It's a pity they ever sold it, sir, beggin' your pardon.

HILLCRIST. The Centry!   [*He rings the bell.*

MRS. J. [*Who has brightened up*] I'm glad you're goin' to stop it, sir. It does put us about. We don't know where to go. I said to Mr. Hornblower, I said, " I'm sure Mr. Hillcrist would never 'ave turned us out." An' 'e said : " Mr. Hillcrist be —— " beggin' your pardon, sir. " Make no mistake," 'e said, " you must go, missis." He don't even know our name ; an' to come it like this over us ! He's a dreadful new man, I think, with his overridin' notions. And sich a heavy-footed man, to look at. [*With a sort of indulgent contempt.*] But he's from the North, they say.   [FELLOWS *has entered, Left.*

HILLCRIST. Ask Mrs. Hillcrist if she'll come.

FELLOWS. Very good, sir.

HILLCRIST. Is Dawker here ?

FELLOWS. Not yet, sir.

HILLCRIST. I want to see him at once.   [FELLOWS *retires.*

JACKMAN. Mr. Hornblower said he was comin' on to see you, sir. So we thought we'd step along first.

HILLCRIST. Quite right, Jackman.

MRS. J. I said to Jackman : " Mr. Hillcrist'll stand up for us, I know. He's a gentleman," I said. " This man," I said, " don't care for the neighbourhood, or the people ; he don't care for anything so long as he makes his money, and has his importance. You can't expect it, I suppose," I said ; [*Bitterly*] " havin' got rich so sudden." The gentry don't do things like that.

HILLCRIST. [*Abstracted*] Quite, Mrs. Jackman, quite ! [*To himself.*] The Centry ! No !

[MRS. HILLCRIST *enters. A well-dressed woman, with a firm, clear-cut face.*]

Oh ! Amy ! Mr. and Mrs. Jackman turned out of their cottage, and Mrs. Harvey, and the Drews. When I sold to Hornblower, I stipulated that they shouldn't be.

MRS. J. Our week's up on Saturday, ma'am, and I'm sure I don't know where we shall turn, because of course Jackman must be near his work, and I shall lose me washin' if we have to go far.

HILLCRIST. [*With decision*] You leave it to me, Mrs. Jackman. Good morning ! Morning, Jackman ! Sorry I can't move with this gout.

MRS. J. [*For them both*] I'm sure we're very sorry, sir. Good morning, sir. Good morning, ma'am ; and thank you kindly.

[*They go out.*

HILLCRIST. Turning people out that have been there thirty years. I won't have it. It's a breach of faith.

MRS. H. Do you suppose this Hornblower will care two straws about that, Jack ?

HILLCRIST. He must, when it's put to him, if he's got any decent feeling.

MRS. H. He hasn't.

HILLCRIST. [*Suddenly*] The Jackmans talk of his having bought the Centry to put up more chimneys.

MRS. H. Never ! [*At the window, looking out.*] Impossible ! It would ruin the place utterly, besides cutting us off from the Duke's. Oh, no ! Miss Mullins would never sell behind our backs.

HILLCRIST. Anyway I must stop his turning these people out.

MRS. H. [*With a little smile, almost contemptuous*] You might have known he'd do something of the sort. You will imagine people are like yourself, Jack. You always ought to make Dawker have things in black and white.

HILLCRIST. I said quite distinctly : " Of course you won't want to disturb the tenancies ; there's a great shortage of cottages." Hornblower told me as distinctly that he wouldn't. What more do you want ?

MRS. H. A man like that thinks of nothing but the short cut to his own way. [*Looking out of the window towards the rise.*] If he buys the Centry and puts up chimneys, we simply couldn't stop here.

HILLCRIST. My father would turn in his grave.

MRS. H. It would have been more useful if he'd not dipped the estate, and sold the Centry. This Hornblower hates us ; he thinks we turn up our noses at him.

HILLCRIST. As we do, Amy.

MRS. H. Who wouldn't ?   A man without traditions, who believes in nothing but money and push.

HILLCRIST. Suppose he won't budge, can we do anything for the Jackmans ?

MRS. H. There are the two rooms Beaver used to have, over the stables.   [FELLOWS *enters.*

FELLOWS. Mr. Dawker, sir.

[DAWKER *is a short, square, rather red-faced terrier of a man, in riding clothes and gaiters.*

HILLCRIST. Ah ! Dawker, I've got gout again.

DAWKER. Very sorry, sir.   How de do, ma'am ?

HILLCRIST. Did you meet the Jackmans ?

DAWKER. Yeh.

[*He hardly ever quite finishes a word, seeming to snap off their tails.*

HILLCRIST. Then you heard ?

DAWKER. [*Nodding*] Smart man, Hornblower ; never lets grass grow.

HILLCRIST. Smart ?

DAWKER. [*Grinning*] Don't do to underrate your neighbours.

MRS. H. A cad—I call him.

DAWKER. That's it, ma'am—got all the advantage.

HILLCRIST. Heard anything about the Centry, Dawker?

DAWKER. Hornblower wants to buy.

HILLCRIST. Miss Mullins would never sell, would she?

DAWKER. She wants to.

HILLCRIST. The deuce she does!

DAWKER. He won't stick at the price either.

MRS. H. What's it worth, Dawker?

DAWKER. Depends on what you want it for.

MRS. H. He wants it for spite; we want it for sentiment.

DAWKER. [*Grinning*] Worth what you like to give, then; but he's a rich man.

MRS. H. Intolerable!

DAWKER. [*To* HILLCRIST] Give me your figure, sir. I'll try the old lady before he gets at her.

HILLCRIST. [*Pondering*] I don't want to buy, unless there's nothing else for it. I should have to raise the money on the estate; it won't stand much more. I can't believe the fellow would be such a barbarian. Chimneys within three hundred yards, right in front of this house! It's a nightmare.

MRS. H. You'd much better let Dawker make sure, Jack.

HILLCRIST. [*Uncomfortable*] Jackman says Hornblower's coming round to see me. I shall put it to him.

DAWKER. Make him keener than ever. Better get in first.

HILLCRIST. Ape his methods!—Ugh! Confound this gout! [*He gets back to his chair with difficulty.*] Look here, Dawker, I wanted to see you about gates——

FELLOWS. [*Entering*] Mr. Hornblower.

[HORNBLOWER *enters—a man of medium height, thoroughly broadened, blown out, as it were, by success. He has thick, coarse dark hair, just grizzled, very bushy eyebrows, a wide mouth. He wears quite ordinary clothes, as if that department were in charge of someone who knew about such things. He has a small rose in his buttonhole, and carries a Homburg hat, which one suspects will look too small on his head.*]

HORNBLOWER. Good morning! good morning! How are ye, Dawker? Fine morning! Lovely weather!

[*His voice has a curious blend in its tone of brass and oil, and an accent not quite Scotch nor quite North country.*]

Haven't seen ye for a long time, Hillcrist.

HILLCRIST. [*Who has risen*] Not since I sold you Longmeadow and those cottages, I believe.

HORNBLOWER. Dear me, now! that's what I came about.

HILLCRIST. [*Subsiding again into his chair*] Forgive me ! Won't you sit down ?

HORNBLOWER. [*Not sitting*] Have ye got gout ? That's unfortunate. I never get it. I've no disposition that way. Had no ancestors, you see. Just me own drinkin' to answer for.

HILLCRIST. You're lucky.

HORNBLOWER. I wonder if Mrs. Hillcrist thinks that ! Am I lucky to have no past, ma'am ? Just the future ?

MRS. H. You're sure you have the future, Mr. Hornblower ?

HORNBLOWER. [*With a laugh*] That's your aristocratic rapier-thrust. You aristocrats are very hard people underneath your manners. Ye love to lay a body out. But I've got the future all right.

HILLCRIST. [*Meaningly*] I've had the Jackmans here, Mr. Hornblower.

HORNBLOWER. Who are they—man with the little spitfire wife ?

HILLCRIST. They're very excellent, good people, and they've been in that cottage quietly thirty years.

HORNBLOWER. [*Throwing out his forefinger—a favourite gesture*] Ah ! ye've wanted me to stir ye up a bit. Deepwater needs a bit o' go put into it. There's generally some go where I am. I daresay you wish there'd been no " come."   [*He laughs.*

MRS. H. We certainly like people to keep their word, Mr. Hornblower.

HILLCRIST. Amy !

HORNBLOWER. Never mind, Hillcrist ; takes more than that to upset me.

> [MRS. HILLCRIST *exchanges a look with* DAWKER, *who slips out unobserved.*

HILLCRIST. You promised me, you know, not to change the tenancies.

HORNBLOWER. Well, I've come to tell ye that I have. I wasn't expecting to have the need when I bought. Thought the Duke would sell me a bit down there ; but devil a bit he will ; and now I must have those cottages for my workmen. I've got important works, ye know.

HILLCRIST. [*Getting heated*] The Jackmans have their importance too, sir. Their heart's in that cottage.

HORNBLOWER. Have a sense of proportion, man. My works supply thousands of people, and *my* heart's in *them*. What's more, they make my fortune. I've got ambitions—I'm a serious man. Suppose I were to consider this and that, and every little potty objection—where should I get to ?—nowhere !

HILLCRIST. All the same, this sort of thing isn't done, you know.

HORNBLOWER. Not by you because ye've got no need to do it. Here ye are, quite content on what your fathers made for ye. Ye've no ambitions ; and ye want other people to have none. How d'ye think your fathers got your land ?

HILLCRIST. [*Who has risen*] Not by breaking their word.

HORNBLOWER. [*Throwing out his finger*] Don't ye believe it. They got it by breaking their word and turnin' out Jackmans, if that's their name, all over the place.

MRS. H. That's an insult, Mr. Hornblower.

HORNBLOWER. No ; it's a repartee. If ye think so much of these Jackmans, build them a cottage yourselves ; ye've got the space.

HILLCRIST. That's beside the point. You promised me, and I sold on that understanding.

HORNBLOWER. And I bought on the understandin' that I'd get some more land from the Duke.

HILLCRIST. That's nothing to do with me.

HORNBLOWER. Ye'll find it has ; because I'm going to have those cottages.

HILLCRIST. Well, I call it simply—[*He checks himself.*]

HORNBLOWER. Look here, Hillcrist, ye've not had occasion to understand men like me. I've got the guts, and I've got the money, and I don't sit still on it. I'm going ahead because I believe in meself. I've no use for sentiment and that sort of thing. Forty of your Jackmans aren't worth me little finger.

HILLCRIST. [*Angry*] Of all the blatant things I ever heard said !——

HORNBLOWER. Well, as we're speaking plainly, I've been thinkin' Ye want the village run your old-fashioned way, and I want it run mine. I fancy there's not room for the two of us here.

MRS. H. When are you going ?

HORNBLOWER. Never fear, *I'm* not going.

HILLCRIST. Look here, Mr. Hornblower—this infernal gout makes me irritable—puts me at a disadvantage. But I should be glad if you'd kindly explain yourself.

HORNBLOWER. [*With a great smile*] Ca' canny ; I'm fra' the North.

HILLCRIST. I'm told you wish to buy the Centry and put more of your chimneys up there, regardless of the fact [*He points through the window*] that it would utterly ruin the house we've had for generations, and all our pleasure here.

HORNBLOWER. How the man talks ! Why ! Ye'd think he owned the sky, because his fathers built him a house with a pretty view, where he's nothing to do but live. It's sheer want of something to do that gives ye your fine sentiments, Hillcrist.

HILLCRIST. Have the goodness not to charge me with idleness. Dawker—where is he ?—[*He shows the bureau.*] When you do the drudgery of your works as thoroughly as I do that of my estate—— Is it true about the Centry ?

HORNBLOWER. Gospel true. If ye want to know, my son Chearlie is buyin' it this very minute.

MRS. H. [*Turning with a start*] What do you say ?

HORNBLOWER. Ay, he's with the old lady ; she wants to sell, an' she'll get her price, whatever it is.

HILLCRIST. [*With deep anger*] If that isn't a skin game, Mr. Hornblower, I don't know what is.

HORNBLOWER. Ah ! Ye've got a very nice expression there. " Skin game ! " Well, bad words break no bones, an' they're wonderful for hardenin' the heart. If it wasn't for a lady's presence, I could give ye a specimen or two.

MRS. H. Oh ! Mr. Hornblower, that need not stop you, I'm sure.

HORNBLOWER. Well, and I don't know that it need. Ye're an obstruction—the like of you—ye're in my path. And anyone in my path doesn't stay there long ; or, if he does, he stays there on my terms. And my terms are chimneys in the Centry where I need 'em. It'll do ye a power of good, too, to know that ye're not almighty.

HILLCRIST. And that's being neighbourly !

HORNBLOWER. And how have ye tried bein' neighbourly to me ? If I haven't a wife, I've got a daughter-in-law. Have ye called on her, ma'am ? I'm new, and ye're an old family. Ye don't like me, ye think I'm a pushin' man. I go to chapel, an' ye don't like that. I make things and I sell them, and ye don't like that. I buy land, and ye don't like that. It threatens the view from your windies. Well, I don't like you, and I'm not goin' to put up with your attitude. Ye've had things your own way too long, and now ye're not going to have them any longer.

HILLCRIST. Will you hold to your word over those cottages ?

HORNBLOWER. I'm goin' to have the cottages. I need them, and more besides, now I'm to put up me new works.

HILLCRIST. That's a declaration of war.

HORNBLOWER. Ye never said a truer word. It's one or the other of us, and I rather think it's goin' to be me. I'm the risin' and you're the settin' sun, as the poet says.

HILLCRIST. [*Touching the bell*] We shall see if you can ride rough-shod like this. We used to have decent ways of going about things here. You want to change all that. Well, we shall do our damnedest to stop you. [*To* FELLOWS *at the door.*] Are the Jackmans still in the house ? Ask them to be good enough to come in.

HORNBLOWER. [*With the first sign of uneasiness*] I've seen these people. I've nothing more to say to them. I told 'em I'd give 'em five pounds to cover their moving.

HILLCRIST. It doesn't occur to you that people, however humble, like to have some say in their own fate ?

HORNBLOWER. I never had any say in mine till I had the brass, and nobody ever will. It's all hypocrisy. You country folk are fair awful hypocrites. Ye talk about good form and all that sort o' thing. It's just the comfortable doctrine of the man in the saddle ; sentimental varnish. Ye're every bit as hard as I am, underneath.

MRS. H. [*Who has been standing very still all this time*] You flatter us.

HORNBLOWER. Not at all. God helps those who 'elp themselves— that's at the bottom of all religion. I'm goin' to help meself, and God's going to help me.

MRS. H. I admire your knowledge.

HILLCRIST. We are in the right, and God helps——

HORNBLOWER. Don't ye believe it ; ye 'aven't got the energy.

MRS. H. Nor perhaps the conceit.

HORNBLOWER. [*Throwing out his forefinger*] No, no ; 'tisn't conceit to believe in yourself when ye've got reason to.

[*The* JACKMANS *have entered.*]

HILLCRIST. I'm very sorry, Mrs. Jackman, but I just wanted you to realize that I've done my best with this gentleman.

MRS. J. [*Doubtfully*] Yes, sir. I thought if you spoke for us, he'd feel different-like.

HORNBLOWER. One cottage is the same as another, missis. I made ye a fair offer of five pounds for the moving.

JACKMAN. [*Slowly*] We wouldn't take fifty to go out of that 'ouse. We brought up three children there, an' buried two from it.

MRS. J. [*To* MRS. HILLCRIST] We're attached to it like, ma'am.

HILLCRIST. [*To* HORNBLOWER] How would you like being turned out of a place you were fond of ?

HORNBLOWER. Not a bit. But little considerations have to give way to big ones. Now, missis, I'll make it ten pounds, and I'll send a wagon to shift your things. If that isn't fair—— ! Ye'd better accept, I shan't keep it open.

[*The* JACKMANS *look at each other ; their faces show deep anger— and the question they ask each other is which will speak*.]

MRS. J. We won't take it ; eh, George ?

JACKMAN. Not a farden. We come there when we was married.

HORNBLOWER. [*Throwing out his finger*] Ye're very improvident folk.

HILLCRIST. Don't lecture them, Mr. Hornblower ; they come out of this miles above you.

HORNBLOWER. [*Angry*] Well, I *was* going to give ye another week, but ye'll go out next Saturday ; and take care ye're not late, or your things'll be put out—in the rain.

MRS. H. [*To* MRS. JACKMAN] We'll send down for your things, and you can come to us for the time being.

[MRS. JACKMAN *drops a curtsey ; her eyes stab* HORNBLOWER.]

JACKMAN. [*Heavily, clenching his fists*] You're no gentleman ! Don't put temptation in my way, that's all.

HILLCRIST. [*In a low voice*] Jackman !

HORNBLOWER. [*Triumphantly*] Ye hear that ? That's your protégé ! Keep out o' *my* way, me man, or I'll put the police on to ye for utterin' threats.

HILLCRIST. You'd better go now, Jackman.

[*The* JACKMANS *move to the door.*

MRS. J. [*Turning*] Maybe you'll repent it some day, sir.

[*They go out,* MRS. HILLCRIST *following.*

HORNBLOWER. We—ell, I'm sorry they're such unreasonable folk. I never met people with less notion of which side their bread was buttered.

HILLCRIST. And I never met anyone so pachydermatous.

HORNBLOWER. What's that, in Heaven's name ? Ye needn' wrap it up in long words now your good lady's gone.

HILLCRIST. [*With dignity*] I'm not going in for a slanging match. I resent your conduct much too deeply.

HORNBLOWER. Look here, Hillcrist, I don't object to you personally ; ye seem to me a poor creature that's bound to get left with your gout and your dignity ; but of course ye can make yourself very disagreeable before ye're done. Now I want to be the movin' spirit here. I'm full of plans. I'm goin' to stand for Parliament ; I'm goin' to make this a prosperous place. I'm a good-natured man if you'll treat me as such. Now, you take me on as a neighbour and all that, and I'll manage without chimneys on the Centry. Is it a bargain ?

[*He holds out his hand.*

HILLCRIST. [*Ignoring it*] I thought you said you didn't keep your word when it suited you to break it ?

HORNBLOWER. Now, don't get on the high horse. You and me could be very good friends ; but I can be a very nasty enemy. The chimneys will not look nice from that windie, ye know.

HILLCRIST. [*Deeply angry*] Mr. Hornblower, if you think I'll take your hand after this Jackman business, you're greatly mistaken. You are proposing that I shall stand in with you while you tyrannize over the neighbourhood. Please realize that unless you leave those tenancies undisturbed as you said you would, we don't know each other.

HORNBLOWER. Well, that won't trouble me much. Now, ye'd better think it over ; ye've got gout and that makes ye hasty. I tell ye again : I'm not the man to make an enemy of. Unless ye're friendly, sure as I stand here I'll ruin the look of your place.

[*The toot of a car is heard.*]

There's my car. I sent Chearlie and his wife in it to buy the Centry. And make no mistake—he's got it in his pocket. It's your last chance, Hillcrist, I'm not averse to you as a man ; I think ye're the best of the fossils round here ; at least, I think ye can do me the most harm socially. Come now !   [*He holds out his hand again.*

HILLCRIST. Not if you'd bought the Centry ten times over. Your ways are not mine, and I'll have nothing to do with you.

HORNBLOWER. [*Very angry*] Really! Is that so? Very well. Now ye're goin' to learn something, an' it's time ye did. D'ye realize that I'm very nearly round ye? [*He draws a circle slowly in the air.*] I'm at Uphill, the works are here, here's Longmeadow, here's the Centry that I've just bought, there's only the Common left to give ye touch with the world. Now between you and the Common there's the high road. I come out on the high road here to your north, and I shall come out on it there to your west. When I've got me new works up on the Centry, I shall be makin' a trolley track between the works up to the road at both ends, so my goods will be running right round ye. How'll ye like that for a country place?

[*For answer* HILLCRIST, *who is angry beyond the power of speech, walks, forgetting to use his stick, up to the French window. While he stands there, with his back to* HORNBLOWER, *the door L. is flung open, and* JILL *enters, preceding* CHARLES, *his wife* CHLOE, *and* ROLF. CHARLES *is a goodish-looking, moustached young man of about twenty-eight, with a white rim to the collar of his waistcoat, and spats. He has his hand behind* CHLOE'S *back, as if to prevent her turning tail. She is rather a handsome young woman, with dark eyes, full red lips, and a suspicion of powder, a little under-dressed for the country.* ROLF, *who brings up the rear, is about twenty, with an open face and stiffish butter-coloured hair.* JILL *runs over to her father at the window. She has a bottle.*

JILL. [*Sotto voce*] Look, Dodo, I've brought the lot! Isn't it a treat, dear Papa? And here's the stuff. Hallo!

[*The exclamation is induced by the apprehension that there has been a row.* HILLCRIST *gives a stiff little bow, remaining where he is in the window.* JILL *stays close to him, staring from one to the other, then blocks him off and engages him in conversation.* CHARLES *has gone up to his father, who has remained maliciously still, where he delivered his last speech.* CHLOE *and* ROLF *stand awkwardly waiting between the fireplace and the door.*

HORNBLOWER. Well, Chearlie?

CHARLES. Not got it.

HORNBLOWER. Not!

CHARLES. I'd practically got her to say she'd sell at three thousand five hundred, when that fellow Dawker turned up.

HORNBLOWER. That bull-terrier of a chap! Why, he was *here* a while ago. Oh—ho! So that's it!

CHARLES. I heard him gallop up. He came straight for the old lady, and got her away. What he said I don't know; but she came back looking wiser than an owl ; said she'd think it over, thought she had other views.

HORNBLOWER. Did ye tell her she might have her price ?

CHARLES. Practically I did.

HORNBLOWER. Well ?

CHARLES. She thought it would be fairer to put it up to auction. There were other inquiries.   Oh !   She's a leery old bird—reminds me of one of those pictures of Fate, don't you know.

HORNBLOWER. Auction !   Well, if it's not gone we'll get it yet. That damned little Dawker !   I've had a row with Hillcrist.

CHARLES. I thought so.

[*They are turning cautiously to look at* HILLCRIST, *when* JILL *steps forward.*

JILL. [*Flushed and determined*] That's not a bit sporting of you, Mr. Hornblower.   [*At her words* ROLF *comes forward too.*

HORNBLOWER. Ye should hear both sides before ye say that, missy.

JILL. There isn't another side to turning out the Jackmans after you'd promised.

HORNBLOWER. Oh ! dear me, yes.   They don't matter a row of gingerbread to the schemes I've got for betterin' this neighbourhood.

JILL. I *had* been standing up for you ; now I won't.

HORNBLOWER. Dear, dear !   What'll become of me ?

JILL. I won't say anything about the other thing because I think it's beneath dignity to notice it.   But to turn poor people out of their cottages is a shame.

HORNBLOWER. Hoity me !

ROLF. [*Suddenly*] You haven't been doing that, father ?

CHARLES. Shut up, Rolf !

HORNBLOWER. [*Turning on* ROLF] Ha !   Here's a league o' youth ! My young whipper-snapper, keep your mouth shut and leave it to your elders to know what's right.

[*Under the weight of this rejoinder* ROLF *stands biting his lips.   Then he throws his head up.*

ROLF. I hate it !

HORNBLOWER. [*With real venom*] Oh !   Ye hate it ?   Ye can get out of my house, then.

JILL. Free speech, Mr. Hornblower ; don't be violent.

HORNBLOWER. Ye're right, young lady.   Ye can stay in my house, Rolf, and learn manners.   Come, Chearlie !

JILL. [*Quite softly*] Mr. Hornblower !

HILLCRIST. [*From the window*] Jill !

JILL. [*Impatiently*] Well, what's the good of it ?   Life's too short for rows, and too jolly !

ROLF. Bravo !

HORNBLOWER. [*Who has shown a sign of weakening*] Now, look here !

I will not have revolt in my family. Ye'll just have to learn that a man who's worked as I have, who's risen as I have, and who knows the world, is the proper judge of what's right and wrong. I'll answer to God for me actions, and not to you young people.

JILL. Poor God !

HORNBLOWER. [*Genuinely shocked*] Ye blasphemous young thing ! [*To* ROLF.] And ye're just as bad, ye young freethinker. I won't have it.

HILLCRIST. [*Who has come down, Right*] Jill, I wish you would kindly not talk.

JILL. I can't help it.

CHARLES. [*Putting his arm through* HORNBLOWER'S] Come along, father ! Deeds, not words.

HORNBLOWER. Ay ! Deeds !

[MRS. HILLCRIST *and* DAWKER *have entered by the French window.*

MRS. H. Quite right ! [*They all turn and look at her.*

HORNBLOWER. Ah ! So ye put your dog on to it. [*He throws out his finger at* DAWKER.] Very smart, that—I give ye credit.

MRS. H. [*Pointing to* CHLOE, *who has stood by herself, forgotten and uncomfortable throughout the scene*] May I ask who this lady is ?

[CHLOE *turns round startled, and her vanity bag slips down her dress to the floor.*

HORNBLOWER. No, ma'am, ye may not, for ye know perfectly well.

JILL. I brought her in, mother. [*She moves to* CHLOE'S *side.*

MRS. H. Will you take her out again, then.

HILLCRIST. Amy, have the goodness to remember——

MRS. H. That this is my house so far as ladies are concerned.

JILL. Mother !

[*She looks astonished at* CHLOE, *who, about to speak, does not, passing her eyes, with a queer, half-scared expression, from* MRS. HILLCRIST *to* DAWKER.]

[*To* CHLOE.] I'm awfully sorry. Come on !

[*They go out, Left.* ROLF *hurries after them.*

CHARLES. You've insulted my wife. Why ? What do you mean by it ? [MRS. HILLCRIST *simply smiles.*

HILLCRIST. I apologize. I regret extremely. There is no reason why the ladies of your family or of mine should be involved in our quarrel. For Heaven's sake, let's fight like gentlemen.

HORNBLOWER. Catchwords—sneers ! No ; we'll play what ye call a skin game, Hillcrist, without gloves on ; we won't spare each other. Ye look out for yourselves, for, begod, after this morning I mean business. And as for you, Dawker, ye sly dog, ye think yourself very clever ; but I'll have the Centry yet. Come, Chearlie.

[*They go out, passing* JILL, *who is coming in again, in the doorway.*

HILLCRIST. Well, Dawker ?

DAWKER. [*Grinning*] Safe for the moment. The old lady'll put it up to auction. Couldn't get her to budge from that. Says she don't want to be unneighbourly to either. But, if you ask me, it's money she smells !

JILL [*Advancing*] Now, mother !

MRS. H. Well ?

JILL. Why did you insult her ?

MRS. H. I think I only asked you to take her out.

JILL. Why ? Even if she is Old Combustion's daughter-in-law ?

MRS. H. My dear Jill, allow me to judge the sort of acquaintances I wish to make.   [*She looks at* DAWKER.

JILL. She's all right. Lots of women powder and touch up their lips nowadays. I think she's rather a good sort ; she was awfully upset.

MRS. H. Too upset.

JILL. Oh ! don't be so mysterious, mother. If you know something, do spit it out !

MRS. H. Do you wish me to—er—" spit it out," Jack ?

HILLCRIST. Dawker, if you don't mind——

    [DAWKER, *with a nod, passes away out of the French window.*] Jill, be respectful, and don't talk like a bargee.

JILL. It's no good, Dodo. It made me ashamed. It's just as—as caddish to insult people who haven't said a word, in your own house, as it is to be—old Hornblower.

MRS. H. You don't know what you're talking about.

HILLCRIST. What's the matter with young Mrs. Hornblower ?

MRS. H. Excuse me, I shall keep my thoughts to myself at present.

    [*She looks coldly at* JILL, *and goes out through the French window.*

HILLCRIST. You've thoroughly upset your mother, Jill.

JILL. It's something Dawker's told her ; I saw them. I don't like Dawker, father, he's so common.

HILLCRIST. My dear, we can't all be uncommon. He's got lots of go. You must apologize to your mother.

JILL. [*Shaking her clubbed hair*] They'll make you do things you don't approve of, Dodo, if you don't look out. Mother's fearfully bitter when she gets her knife in. If old Hornblower's disgusting, it's no reason we should be.

HILLCRIST. So you think I'm capable—that's nice, Jill !

JILL. No, no, darling ! I only want to warn you solemnly that mother'll tell you you're fighting fair, no matter what she and Dawker do.

HILLCRIST. [*Smiling*] Jill, I don't think I ever saw you so serious.

JILL. No. Because—[*She swallows a lump in her throat.*] Well—I was just beginning to enjoy myself ; and now—everything's going to be bitter and beastly, with mother in that mood. That horrible old man ! Oh, Dodo ! Don't let them make *you* horrid ! You're such a darling.   How's your gout, ducky ?

HILLCRIST. Better ; lot better.

JILL. There, you see !   That shows !   It's going to be half interesting for you, but not for—us.

HILLCRIST. Look here, Jill—is there anything between you and young what's-his-name—Rolf ?

JILL. [*Biting her lip*] No.   But—now it's *all* spoiled.

HILLCRIST. You can't expect me to regret that.

JILL. I don't mean any tosh about love's young dream ; but I do like being friends.   I want to *enjoy* things, Dodo, and you can't do that when everybody's on the hate.   You're going to wallow in it, and so shall I—oh ! I know I shall !—we shall all wallow, and think of nothing but " one for his nob."

HILLCRIST. Aren't you fond of your home ?

JILL. Of course.   I love it.

HILLCRIST. Well, you won't be able to live in it unless we stop that ruffian.   Chimneys and smoke, the trees cut down, piles of pots. Every kind of abomination.   There ! [*He points.*] Imagine ! [*He points through the French window, as if he could see those chimneys rising and marring the beauty of the fields.*] I was born here, and my father, and his, and his, and his.   They loved those fields, and those old trees.   And this barbarian, with his " improvement " schemes, forsooth !   I learned to ride in the Centry meadows—prettiest spring meadows in the world ; I've climbed every tree there.   Why my father ever sold—— !   But who could have imagined this ?   And come at a bad moment, when money's scarce.

JILL. [*Cuddling his arm*] Dodo !

HILLCRIST. Yes.   But you don't love the place as I do, Jill.   You youngsters don't love anything, I sometimes think.

JILL. I do, Dodo, I do !

HILLCRIST. You've got it all before you.   But you may live your life and never find anything so good and so beautiful as this old home. I'm not going to have it spoiled without a fight.

> [*Conscious of having betrayed sentiment, he walks out at the French window, passing away to the Right.* JILL, *following to the window, looks.   Then throwing back her head, she clasps her hands behind it.*]

JILL. Oh—oh—oh !

> [*A voice behind her says,* " Jill ! "   *She turns and starts back, leaning against the Right lintel of the window.* ROLF *appears outside the window from Left.*]

Who goes there ?

ROLF. [*Buttressed against the Left lintel*] Enemy—after Chloe's bag.

JILL. Pass, enemy !   And all's ill !

> [ROLF *passes through the window, and retrieves the vanity bag from*

the floor where CHLOE *dropped it, then again takes his stand against the Left lintel of the French window.*

ROLF. It's not going to make any difference, is it?

JILL. You know it is.

ROLF. Sins of the fathers.

JILL. Unto the third and fourth generation. What sin has *my* father committed?

ROLF. None, in a way; only, I've often told you I don't see why you should treat us as outsiders. We don't like it.

JILL. Well, you shouldn't be, then; I mean, *he* shouldn't be.

ROLF. Father's just as human as your father; he's wrapped up in us, and all his " getting on " is for us. Would you like to be treated as your mother treated Chloe? Your mother's set the stroke for the other big-wigs about here; nobody calls on Chloe. And why not? Why not? I think it's contemptible to bar people just because they're *new*, as you call it, and have to make their position instead of having it left them.

JILL. It's *not* because they're new, it's because—if your father behaved like a gentleman, he'd be treated like one.

ROLF. Would he? I don't believe it. My father's a very able man; he thinks he's entitled to have influence here. Well, everybody tries to keep him down. Oh! yes, they do. That makes him mad and more determined than ever to get his way. You ought to be just, Jill.

JILL. I *am* just.

ROLF. No, you're not. Besides, what's it got to do with Charlie and Chloe? Chloe's particularly harmless. It's pretty sickening for her. Father didn't expect people to call until Charlie married, but since——

JILL. I think it's all very petty.

ROLF. It *is*—a dog-in-the-manger business; I did think *you* were above it.

JILL. How would you like to have your home spoiled?

ROLF. I'm not going to argue. Only things don't stand still. Homes aren't any more proof against change than anything else.

JILL. All right! You come and try and take ours.

ROLF. We don't want to take your home.

JILL. Like the Jackmans'?

ROLF. All right. I see you're hopelessly prejudiced.

[*He turns to go.*

JILL. [*Just as he is vanishing—softly*] Enemy?

ROLF. [*Turning*] Yes, enemy.

JILL. Before the battle—let's shake hands.

[*They move from the lintels and grasp each other's hands in the centre of the French window.*

The curtain falls.

ACT II

SCENE I

A billiard room in a provincial hotel, where things are bought and sold. The scene is set well forward, and is not very broad; it represents the auctioneer's end of the room, having, rather to stage Left, a narrow table with two chairs facing the audience, where the auctioneer will sit and stand. The table, which is set forward to the footlights, is littered with green-covered particulars of sale. The audience are in effect public and bidders. There is a door on the Left, level with the table. Along the back wall, behind the table, are two raised benches with two steps up to them, such as billiard rooms often have, divided by a door in the middle of a wall, which is panelled in oak. Late September sunlight is coming from a skylight (not visible) on to these seats. The stage is empty when the curtain goes up, but DAWKER *and* MRS. HILLCRIST *are just entering through the door at the back.*

DAWKER. Be out of their way here, ma'am. See old Hornblower with Chearlie?   [*He points down to the audience.*

MRS. H. It begins at three, doesn't it?

DAWKER. They won't be over punctual; there's only the Centry selling. There's young Mrs. Hornblower with the other boy— [*Pointing*] over at the entrance. I've got that chap I told you of down from town.

MRS. H. Ah! make sure quite of her, Dawker. Any mistake would be fatal.

DAWKER. [*Nodding*] That's right, ma'am. Lot of people—always spare time to watch an auction—ever remark that? The Duke's agent's here; shouldn't be surprised if he chipped in.

MRS. H. Where did you leave my husband?

DAWKER. With Miss Jill, in the courtyard. He's coming to you. In case I miss him, tell him when I reach his limit to blow his nose if he wants me to go on; when he blows it a second time, I'll stop for good. Hope we shan't get to that. Old Hornblower doesn't throw his money away.

MRS. H. What limit did you settle?

DAWKER. Six thousand!

MRS. H. That's a fearful price. Well, good luck to you, Dawker!

534

DAWKER. Good luck, ma'am.   I'll go and see to that little matter
of Mrs. Chloe.   Never fear, we'll do them in somehow.

[*He winks, lays his finger on the side of his nose, and goes out at the door.*

[MRS. HILLCRIST *mounts the two steps, sits down Right of the door,
and puts up a pair of long-handled glasses.   Through the door
behind her come* CHLOE *and* ROLF.   *She makes a sign for him
to go, and shuts the door.*

CHLOE. [*At the foot of the steps—in the gangway—in a slightly common
accent*] Mrs. Hillcrist !

MRS. H. [*Not quite starting*] I beg your pardon ?

CHLOE. [*Again*] Mrs. Hillcrist——

MRS. H. Well ?

CHLOE. I never did you any harm.

MRS. H. Did I ever say you did ?

CHLOE. No ; but you act as if I had.

MRS. H. I'm not aware that I've acted at all—as yet.   You are
nothing to me, except as one of your family.

CHLOE. 'Tisn't I that wants to spoil your home.

MRS. H. Stop them then.   I see your husband down there with
his father.

CHLOE. I—I have tried.

MRS. H. [*Looking at her*] Oh !   I suppose such men don't pay
attention to what women ask them.

CHLOE. [*With a flash of spirit*] I'm fond of my husband.   I——

MRS. H. [*Looking at her steadily*] I don't quite know why you spoke
to me.

CHLOE. [*With a sort of pathetic sullenness*] I only thought perhaps
you'd like to treat me as a human being.

MRS. H. Really, if you don't mind, I should like to be left alone just
now.

CHLOE. [*Unhappily acquiescent*] Certainly !   I'll go to the other end.

[*She moves to the Left, mounts the steps and sits down.*

[ROLF, *looking in through the door, and seeing where she is, joins her.*
MRS. HILLCRIST *re-settles herself a little further in on the
Right.*

ROLF. [*Bending over to* CHLOE, *after a glance at* MRS. HILLCRIST] Are
you all right ?

CHLOE. It's awfully hot.   [*She fans herself with the particulars of sale.*

ROLF. There's Dawker.   I hate that chap !

CHLOE. Where ?

ROLF. Down there ; see ?

[*He points down to stage Right of the room.*

CHLOE. [*Drawing back in her seat with a little gasp*] Oh !

ROLF. [*Not noticing*] Who's that next him, looking up
here ?

CHLOE. I don't know.

[*She has raised her auction programme suddenly, and sits fanning herself, carefully screening her face.*

ROLF. [*Looking at her*] Don't you feel well ? Shall I get you some water ? [*He gets up at her nod.*

[*As he reaches the door,* HILLCRIST *and* JILL *come in.* HILLCRIST *passes him abstractedly with a nod, and sits down beside his wife.*

JILL. [*To* ROLF] Come to see us turned out ?

ROLF. [*Emphatically*] No. I'm looking after Chloe ; she's not well.

JILL. [*Glancing at her*] Sorry. She needn't have come, I suppose ?

[ROLF *deigns no answer, and goes out.*

[JILL *glances at* CHLOE, *then at her parents talking in low voices, and sits down next her father, who makes room for her.*

MRS. H. Can Dawker see you there, Jack ? [HILLCRIST *nods.*] What's the time ?

HILLCRIST. Three minutes to three.

JILL. Don't you feel beastly all down the backs of your legs, Dodo ?

HILLCRIST. Yes.

JILL. Do you, mother ?

MRS. H. No.

JILL. A wagon of old Hornblower's pots passed while we were in the yard. It's an omen.

MRS. H. Don't be foolish, Jill.

JILL. Look at the old brute ! Dodo, hold my hand.

MRS. H. Make sure you've got a handkerchief, Jack.

HILLCRIST. I can't go beyond the six thousand ; I shall have to raise every penny on mortgage as it is. The estate simply won't stand more, Amy.

[*He feels in his breast pocket, and pulls up the edge of his handkerchief.*

JILL. Oh ! Look ! There's Miss Mullins, at the back ; just come in. Isn't she a spidery old chip ?

MRS. H. Come to gloat. Really, I think her not accepting your offer is disgusting. Her impartiality is all humbug.

HILLCRIST. Can't blame her for getting what she can—it's human nature. Phew ! I used to feel like this before a *vivâ voce*. Who's that next to Dawker ?

JILL. What a fish !

MRS. H. [*To herself*] Ah ! yes.

[*Her eyes slide round at* CHLOE, *sitting motionless and rather sunk in her seat, slowly fanning herself with the particulars of the sale.*]

Jack, go and offer her my smelling salts.

HILLCRIST. [*Taking the salts*] Thank God for a human touch !

MRS. H. [*Taken aback*] Oh ! I——

JILL. [*With a quick look at her mother, snatching the salts*] I will.

> [*She goes over to* CHLOE *with the salts.*]

Have a sniff; you look awfully white.

CHLOE. [*Looking up, startled*] Oh! no, thanks. I'm all right.

JILL. No, do! You must.   [CHLOE *takes them.*

JILL. D'you mind letting me see that a minute?

> [*She takes the particulars of the sale and studies it, but* CHLOE *has buried the lower part of her face in her hand and the smelling salts bottle.*]

Beastly hot, isn't it? You'd better keep that.

CHLOE. [*Her dark eyes wandering and uneasy*] Rolf's getting me some water.

JILL. Why do you stay? You didn't want to come, did you?

> [CHLOE *shakes her head.*]

All right! Here's your water.

> [*She hands back the particulars and slides over to her seat, passing* ROLF *in the gangway, with her chin well up.*

> [MRS. HILLCRIST, *who has watched* CHLOE *and* JILL *and* DAWKER *and his friend, makes an inquiring movement with her hand, but gets a disappointing answer.*

JILL. What's the time, Dodo?

HILLCRIST. [*Looking at his watch*] Three minutes past.

JILL [*Sighing*] Oh, hell!

HILLCRIST. Jill!

JILL. Sorry, Dodo. I was only thinking. Look! Here he is! Phew!—isn't he——?

MRS. H. 'Sh!

> [*The* AUCTIONEER *comes in Left and goes to the table. He is a square, short, brown-faced, common-looking man, with clipped grey hair fitting him like a cap, and a clipped grey moustache. His lids come down over his quick eyes, till he can see you very sharply, and you can hardly see that he can see you. He can break into a smile at any moment, which has no connection with him, as it were. By a certain hurt look, however, when bidding is slow, he discloses that he is not merely an auctioneer, but has in him elements of the human being. He can wink with anyone, and is dressed in a snuff-brown suit, with a perfectly unbuttoned waistcoat, a low, turned-down collar, and small black and white sailor-knot tie. While he is settling his papers, the* HILL-CRISTS *settle themselves tensely.* CHLOE *has drunk her water and leaned back again, with the smelling salts to her nose.* ROLF *leans forward in the seat beside her, looking sideways at* JILL. *A* SOLICITOR, *with a grey beard, has joined the* AUCTIONEER *at his table.*

AUCTIONEER. [*Tapping the table*] Sorry to disappoint you, gentlemen,

18

but I've only one property to offer you to-day, No. 1, The Centry, Deepwater. The second on the particulars has been withdrawn. The third—that's Bidcot, desirable freehold mansion and farmlands in the Parish of Kenway—we shall have to deal with next week. I shall be happy to sell it you then without reservation. [*He looks again through the particulars in his hand, giving the audience time to readjust themselves to his statements.*] Now, gen'lemen, as I say, I've only the one property to sell. Freehold No. 1—all that very desirable corn and stock-rearing and parklike residential land known as the Centry, Deepwater, unique property—an A 1 chance to an A 1 audience. [*With his smile.*] Ought to make the price of the three we thought we had. Now you won't mind listening to the conditions of sale ; Mr. Blinkard'll read 'em, and they won't wirry you, they're very short.

> [*He sits down and gives two little taps on the table.*
> [*The* SOLICITOR *rises and reads the conditions of sale in a voice which no one practically can hear. Just as he begins to read these conditions of sale,* CHARLES HORNBLOWER *enters at back. He stands a moment, glancing round at the* HILL-CRISTS *and twirling his moustache, then moves along to his wife and touches her.*

CHARLES. Chloe, aren't you well ?

> [*In the start which she gives, her face is fully revealed to the audience.*

CHARLES. Come along, out of the way of these people.

> [*He jerks his head towards the* HILLCRISTS. CHLOE *gives a swift look down to the stage Right of the audience.*

CHLOE. No ; I'm all right ; it's hotter there.

CHARLES. [*To* ROLF] Well, look after her—I must go back.

> [ROLF *nods.* CHARLES *slides back to the door, with a glance at the* HILLCRISTS, *of whom* MRS. HILLCRIST *has been watching like a lynx. He goes out, just as the* SOLICITOR, *finishing, sits down.*

AUCTIONEER. [*Rising and tapping*] Now, gen'lemen, it's not often a piece of land like this comes into the market. What's that ? [*To a friend in front of him.*] No better land in Deepwater—that's right, Mr. Spicer. I know the village well, and a charming place it is ; perfect locality, to be sure. Now I don't want to wirry you by singing the praises of this property ; there it is—well-watered, nicely timbered —no reservation of the timber, gen'lemen—no tenancy to hold you up ; free to do what you like with it to-morrow. You've got a jewel of a site there, too ; perfect position for a house. It lies between the Duke's and Squire Hillcrist's—an emerald isle. [*With his smile.*] No allusion to Ireland, gen'lemen—perfect peace in the Centry. Nothing like it in the county—a gen'leman's site, and you don't get that offered you every day. [*He looks down towards* HORNBLOWER,

stage Left.] Carries the mineral rights, and as you know, perhaps, there's the very valuable Deepwater clay there. What am I to start it at ? Can I say three thousand ? Well, anything you like to give me. I'm not particular. Come now, you've got more time than me, I expect. Two hundred acres of first-rate grazin' and cornland, with a site for a residence unequalled in the county ; and all the possibilities ? Well, what shall I say ?   [*Bid from* SPICER.]
Two thousand ? [*With his smile.*] That won't hurt you, Mr. Spicer. Why, it's worth that to overlook the Duke. For two thousand ?
                                   [*Bid from* HORNBLOWER, *stage Left.*]
And five. Thank you, sir. Two thousand five hundred bid.
                                          [*To a friend just below him.*]
Come, Mr. Sandy, don't scratch your head over it.
                                     [*Bid from* DAWKER, *stage Right.*]
And five. Three thousand bid for this desirable property. Why, you'd think it wasn't desirable. Come along, gen'lemen. A little spirit.   [*A slight pause.*

JILL. Why can't I *see* the bids, Dodo ?

HILLCRIST. The last was Dawker's.

AUCTIONEER. For three thousand. [HORNBLOWER.] Three thousand five hundred ? May I say four ? [*A bid from the centre.*] No, I'm not particular ; I'll take hundreds. Three thousand six hundred bid. [HORNBLOWER.] And seven. Three thousand seven hundred, and——   [*He pauses, quartering the audience.*

JILL. Who was that, Dodo ?

HILLCRIST. Hornblower. It's the Duke in the centre.

AUCTIONEER. Come, gen'lemen, don't keep me all day. Four thousand may I say ? [DAWKER.] Thank you. We're beginning. And one ? [*A bid from the centre.*] Four thousand one hundred. [HORNBLOWER.] Four thousand two hundred. May I have yours, sir ? [*To* DAWKER.] And three. Four thousand three hundred bid. No such site in the county, gen'lemen. I'm going to sell this land for what it's worth. You can't bid too much for me. [*He smiles.*] [HORNBLOWER.] Four thousand five hundred bid. [*Bid from the centre.*] And six. [DAWKER.] And seven. [HORNBLOWER.] And eight. Nine, may I say ? [*But the centre has dried up.*] [DAWKER.] And nine. [HORNBLOWER.] Five thousand. Five thousand bid. That's better ; there's some spirit in it. For five thousand.
                              [*He pauses while he speaks to the* SOLICITOR.

HILLCRIST. It's a duel now.

AUCTIONEER. Now, gen'lemen, I'm not going to give this property away. Five thousand bid. [DAWKER.] And one. [HORNBLOWER.] And two. [DAWKER.] And three. Five thousand three hundred bid. And five, did you say, sir ? [HORNBLOWER.] Five thousand five hundred bid.   [*He looks at his particulars.*

JILL. [*Rather agonized*] Enemy, Dodo.

AUCTIONEER. This chance may never come again.

> "How you'll regret it
> If you don't get it,"

as the poet says. May I say five thousand six hundred, sir ? [DAWKER.] Five thousand six hundred bid. [HORNBLOWER.] And seven. [DAWKER.] And eight. For five thousand eight hundred pounds. We're gettin' on, but we haven't got the value yet.

> [*A slight pause, while he wipes his brow at the success of his own efforts.*

JILL. Us, Dodo ?

> [HILLCRIST *nods.* JILL *looks over at* ROLF, *whose face is grimly set.* CHLOE *has never moved.* MRS. HILLCRIST *whispers to her husband.*

AUCTIONEER. Five thousand eight hundred bid. For five thousand eight hundred. Come along, gen'lemen, come along. We're not beaten. Thank you, sir. [HORNBLOWER.] Five thousand nine hundred. And——? [DAWKER.] Six thousand. Six thousand bid. Six thousand bid. For six thousand ! The Centry—most desirable spot in the county—going for the low price of six thousand.

HILLCRIST. [*Muttering*] Low ! Heavens !

AUCTIONEER. Any advance on six thousand ? Come, gen'lemen, we haven't dried up ? A little spirit. Six thousand ? For six thousand ? For six thousand pounds ? Very well, I'm selling. For six thousand once—[*He taps.*] For six thousand twice—[*He taps.*]

JILL. [*Low*] Oh ! we've got it !

AUCTIONEER. And one, sir ? [HORNBLOWER.] Six thousand one hundred bid.

> [*The* SOLICITOR *touches his arm and says something, to which the* AUCTIONEER *responds with a nod.*

MRS. H. Blow your nose, Jack.   [HILLCRIST *blows his nose.*

AUCTIONEER. For six thousand one hundred. [DAWKER.] And two. Thank you. [HORNBLOWER.] And three. For six thousand three hundred. [DAWKER.] And four. For six thousand four hundred pounds. This coveted property. For six thousand four hundred pounds. Why, it's giving it away, gen'lemen.   [*A pause.*

MRS. H. Giving !

AUCTIONEER. Six thousand four hundred bid. [HORNBLOWER.] And five. [DAWKER.] And six. [HORNBLOWER.] And seven. [DAWKER.] And eight.

> [*A pause, during which, through the door Left, someone beckons to the* SOLICITOR, *who rises and confers.*

HILLCRIST. [*Muttering*] I've done if that doesn't get it.

AUCTIONEER. For six thousand eight hundred. For six thousand eight hundred—once—[*He taps*] twice—[*He taps.*] For the last time. This dominating site. [HORNBLOWER.] And nine. Thank you. For six thousand nine hundred.

> [HILLCRIST *has taken out his handkerchief.*

JILL. Oh! Dodo!

MRS. H. [*Quivering*] Don't give in!

AUCTIONEER. Seven thousand may I say? [DAWKER.] Seven thousand.

MRS. H. [*Whispers*] Keep it down; don't show him.

AUCTIONEER. For seven thousand—going for seven thousand—once—[*Taps*] twice—[*Taps.*] [HORNBLOWER.] And one. Thank you, sir.

> [HILLCRIST *blows his nose.* JILL, *with a choke, leans back in her seat and folds her arms tightly on her chest.* MRS. HILLCRIST *passes her handkerchief over her lips, sitting perfectly still.* HILLCRIST *too is motionless.*

> [*The* AUCTIONEER *has paused, and is talking to the* SOLICITOR, *who has returned to his seat.*

MRS. H. Oh! Jack.

JILL. Stick it, Dodo; stick it!

AUCTIONEER. Now, gen'lemen, I have a bid of seven thousand one hundred for the Centry. And I'm instructed to sell if I can't get more. It's a fair price, but not a big price. [*To his friend* MR. SPICER.] A thumpin' price? [*With his smile.*] Well, you're a judge of thumpin', I admit. Now, who'll give me seven thousand two hundred? What, no one? Well, I can't make you, gen'lemen. For seven thousand one hundred. Once—[*Taps.*] Twice—[*Taps.*]

> [JILL *utters a little groan.*

HILLCRIST. [*Suddenly, in a queer voice*] Two.

AUCTIONEER. [*Turning with surprise and looking up to receive* HILL-CRIST'S *nod*] Thank *you*, sir. And two. Seven thousand two hundred. [*He screws himself round so as to command both* HILLCRIST *and* HORN-BLOWER.] May I have yours, sir? [HORNBLOWER.] And three. [HILLCRIST.] And four. Seven thousand four hundred. For seven thousand four hundred. [HORNBLOWER.] Five. [HILLCRIST.] Six For seven thousand six hundred. [*A pause.*] Well, gen'lemen, this is better, but a record property shid fetch a record price. The possi-bilities are enormous. [HORNBLOWER.] Eight thousand did you say, sir? Eight thousand. Going for eight thousand pounds. [HILLCRIST.] And one. [HORNBLOWER.] And two. [HILLCRIST.] And three. [HORNBLOWER.] And four. [HILLCRIST.] And five. For eight thousand five hundred. A wonderful property for eight thousand five hundred.   [*He wipes his brow.*

JILL. [*Whispering*] Oh, Dodo!

MRS. H. That's enough, Jack, we must stop some time.

AUCTIONEER. For eight thousand five hundred. Once—[*Taps.*] Twice—[*Taps.*] [HORNBLOWER.] Six hundred. [HILLCRIST.] Seven. May I have yours, sir ? [HORNBLOWER.] Eight.

HILLCRIST. Nine thousand.

> [MRS. HILLCRIST *looks at him, biting her lips, but he is quite absorbed.*

AUCTIONEER. Nine thousand for this astounding property. Why, the Duke would pay that if he realized he'd be overlooked. Now, sir ? [*To* HORNBLOWER. *No response.*] Just a little raise on that. [*No response.*] For nine thousand. The Centry, Deepwater, for nine thousand. Once—[*Taps.*] Twice—[*Taps.*]

JILL. [*Under her breath*] Ours !

A VOICE. [*From far back in the centre.*] And five hundred.

AUCTIONEER. [*Surprised and throwing out his arms towards the voice*] And five hundred. For nine thousand five hundred. May I have yours, sir ? [*He looks at* HORNBLOWER. *No response.*]

> [*The* SOLICITOR *speaks to him.*

MRS. H. [*Whispering*] It must be the Duke again.

HILLCRIST. [*Passing his hand over his brow*] That's stopped him, any way.

AUCTIONEER. [*Looking at* HILLCRIST] For nine thousand five hundred ?   [HILLCRIST *shakes his head.* Once more. The Centry, Deepwater, for nine thousand five hundred. Once—[*Taps.*] Twice—[*Taps.*] [*He pauses and looks again at* HORNBLOWER *and* HILLCRIST.] For the last time—at nine thousand five hundred. [*Taps.*] [*With a look towards the bidder.*] Mr. Smalley. Well ! [*With great satisfaction.*] That's that ! No more to-day, gen'lemen.

> [*The* AUCTIONEER *and* SOLICITOR *busy themselves. The room begins to empty.*

MRS. H. Smalley ? Smalley ? *Is* that the Duke's agent ? Jack !

HILLCRIST. [*Coming out of a sort of coma, after the excitement he has been going through*] What ! What !

JILL. Oh, Dodo ! How splendidly you stuck it !

HILLCRIST. Phew ! What a squeak ! I was clean out of my depth. A mercy the Duke chipped in again.

MRS. H. [*Looking at* ROLF *and* CHLOE, *who are standing up as if about to go*] Take care ; they can hear you. Find Dawker, Jack.

> [*Below, the* AUCTIONEER *and* SOLICITOR *take up their papers, and move out Left.*

> [HILLCRIST *stretches himself, standing up, as if to throw off the strain. The door behind is opened, and* HORNBLOWER *appears.*

HORNBLOWER. Ye ran me up a' pretty price. Ye bid very pluckily, Hillcrist. But ye didn't quite get my measure.

HILLCRIST. Oh ! It was *my* nine thousand the Duke capped. Thank God, the Centry's gone to a gentleman !

HORNBLOWER. The Duke ? [*He laughs.*] No, the Centry's not gone to a gentleman, nor to a fool. It's gone to me.

HILLCRIST. What !

HORNBLOWER. I'm sorry for ye ; ye're not fit to manage these things. Well, it's a monstrous price, and I've had to pay it because of your obstinacy. I shan't forget that when I come to build.

HILLCRIST. D'you mean to say that bid was for you ?

HORNBLOWER. Of course I do. I told ye I was a bad man to be up against. Perhaps ye'll believe me now.

HILLCRIST. A dastardly trick !

HORNBLOWER. [*With venom*] What did ye call it—a skin game ? Remember we're playin' a skin game, Hillcrist.

HILLCRIST. [*Clenching his fists*] If we were younger men——

HORNBLOWER. Ay ! 'Twouldn't look pretty for us to be at fisti-cuffs. We'll leave the fightin' to the young ones. [*He glances at* ROLF *and* JILL ; *suddenly throwing out his finger at* ROLF.] No makin' up to that young woman ! I've watched ye. And as for you, missy, you leave my boy alone.

JILL. [*With suppressed passion*] Dodo, may I spit in his eye or something ?

HILLCRIST. Sit down.

[JILL *sits down.   He stands between her and* HORNBLOWER.] You've won this round, sir, by a foul blow. We shall see whether you can take any advantage of it. I believe the law can stop you ruining my property.

HORNBLOWER. Make your mind easy ; it can't. I've got ye in a noose, and I'm goin' to hang ye.

MRS. H. [*Suddenly*] Mr. Hornblower, as you fight foul—so shall we.

HILLCRIST. Amy !

MRS. H. [*Paying no attention*] And it will not be foul play towards you and yours. You are outside the pale.

HORNBLOWER. That's just where I am, outside *your* pale all round ye. Ye're not long for Deepwater, ma'am. Make you dispositions to go ; ye'll be out in six months, I prophesy. And good riddance to the neighbourhood.   [*They are all down on the level now.*

CHLOE. [*Suddenly coming closer to* MRS. HILLCRIST] Here are your salts, thank you. Father, can't you——?

HORNBLOWER. [*Surprised*] Can't I what !

CHLOE. Can't you come to an arrangement ?

MRS. H. Just so, Mr. Hornblower. Can't you ?

HORNBLOWER. [*Looking from one to the other*] As we're speakin' out, ma'am, it's your behaviour to my daughter-in-law—who's as good as you—and better, to my thinking—that's more than half the reason why I've bought this property. Ye've fair got my dander up. Now it's no use to bandy words. It's very forgivin' of ye, Chloe, but come along !

MRS. H. Quite seriously, Mr. Hornblower, you had better come to an arrangement.

HORNBLOWER. Mrs. Hillcrist, ladies should keep to their own business.

MRS. H. I will.

HILLCRIST. Amy, do leave it to us men. You young man [*he speaks to* ROLF] do you support your father's trick this afternoon ?

[JILL *looks round at* ROLF, *who tries to speak, when* HORNBLOWER *breaks in.*

HORNBLOWER. *My* trick ? And what d'ye call it, to try and put me own son against me ?

JILL. [*To* ROLF] Well ?

ROLF. I don't, but——

HORNBLOWER. Trick ? Ye young cub, be quiet. Mr. Hillcrist had an agent bid for him—I had an agent bid for me. Only his agent bid at the beginnin', an' mine bid at the end. What's the trick in that ?   [*He laughs.*

HILLCRIST. Hopeless ; we're in different worlds.

HORNBLOWER. I wish to God we were ! Come you, Chloe. And you, Rolf, you follow. In six months I'll have those chimneys up, and me lorries runnin' round ye.

MRS. H. Mr. Hornblower, if you build——

HORNBLOWER. [*Looking at* MRS. HILLCRIST] Ye know—it's laughable. Ye make me pay nine thousand five hundred for a bit o' land not worth four; and ye think I'm not to get back on ye. I'm goin' on with as little consideration as if ye were a family of blackbeetles. Good afternoon !

ROLF. Father !

JILL. Oh, Dodo ! He's obscene.

HILLCRIST. Mr. Hornblower, my compliments.

[HORNBLOWER, *with a stare at* HILLCRIST'S *half-smiling face, takes* CHLOE'S *arm, and half drags her towards the door on the Left. But there, in the opened doorway, are standing* DAWKER *and a* STRANGER. *They move just out of the way of the exit, looking at* CHLOE, *who sways and very nearly falls.*

HORNBLOWER. Why ! Chloe ! What's the matter ?

CHLOE. I don't know ; I'm not well to-day.

[*She pulls herself together with a great effort.*

MRS. H. [*Who has exchanged a nod with* DAWKER *and the* STRANGER] Mr. Hornblower, you build at your peril. I warn you.

HORNBLOWER. [*Turning round to speak*] Ye think yourself very cool and very smart. But I doubt this is the first time ye've been up against realities. Now, I've been up against them all my life. Don't talk to me, ma'am, about peril and that sort of nonsense ; it makes no impression. Your husband called me pachydermatous. I don't know Greek, and Latin, and all that, but I've looked it out in the dictionary, and I find it means thick-skinned. And I'm none the worse for that when I have to deal with folk like you. Good afternoon.

[*He draws* CHLOE *forward, and they pass through the door followed quickly by* ROLF.

MRS. H. Thank you, Dawker.

[*She moves up to* DAWKER *and the* STRANGER, *Left, and they talk*.

JILL. Dodo ! It's awful !

HILLCRIST. Well, there's nothing for it now but to smile and pay up. Poor old home ! It shall be his wash-pot. Over the Centry will he cast his shoe. By Gad, Jill, I could cry !

JILL. [*Pointing*] Look ! Chloe's sitting down. She nearly fainted just now. It's something to do with Dawker, Dodo, and that man with him. Look at mother ! Ask them ?

HILLCRIST. Dawker !

[DAWKER *comes to him, followed by* MRS. HILLCRIST.]
What's the mystery about young Mrs. Hornblower ?

DAWKER. No mystery.

HILLCRIST. Well, what is it ?

MRS. H. You'd better not ask.

HILLCRIST. I wish to know.

MRS. H. Jill, go out and wait for us.

JILL. Nonsense, mother.

MRS. H. It's not for a girl to hear.

JILL. Bosh ! I read the papers every day.

DAWKER. It's nothin' worse than you get there, anyway.

MRS. H. Do you wish your daughter——

JILL. It's ridiculous, Dodo ; you'd think I was mother at my age.

MRS. H. I was not so proud of my knowledge.

JILL. No, but you had it, dear.

HILLCRIST. What is it—what is it ? Come over here, Dawker.

[DAWKER *goes to him, Right, and speaks in a low voice*.]
What !   [*Again* DAWKER *speaks in a low voice*.]
Good God !

MRS. H. Exactly !

JILL. Poor thing—whatever it is !

MRS. H. Poor thing ?

JILL. What went before, mother ?

MRS. H. It's what's coming after that matters, luckily.

HILLCRIST. How do you know this ?

DAWKER. My friend here [*He points to the* STRANGER] was one of the agents.

18*

HILLCRIST. It's shocking. I'm sorry I heard it.

MRS. H. I told you not to.

HILLCRIST. Ask your friend to come here.

[DAWKER *beckons, and the* STRANGER *joins the group.*]
Are you sure of what you've said, sir ?

STRANGER. Perfectly. I remember her quite well ; her name then
was——

HILLCRIST. I don't want to know, thank you. I'm truly sorry.
I wouldn't wish the knowledge of that about his womenfolk to my
worst enemy. This mustn't be spoken of. [JILL *hugs his arm.*

MRS. H. It will not be if Mr. Hornblower is wise. If he is not
wise, it must be spoken of.

HILLCRIST. I say no, Amy. I won't have it. It's a dirty weapon.
Who touches pitch shall be defiled.

MRS. H. Well, what weapons does he use against us ? Don't be
quixotic. For all we can tell, they know it quite well already, and if
they don't they ought to. Anyway, to know this is our salvation,
and we must use it.

JILL. [*Sotto voce*] Pitch ! Dodo ! Pitch !

DAWKER. The threat's enough ! J.P.—Chapel—Future member
for the constituency——

HILLCRIST. [*A little more doubtfully*] To use a piece of knowledge
about a woman—it's repugnant. I—I won't do it.

MRS. H. If you had a son tricked into marrying such a woman,
would you wish to remain ignorant of it ?

HILLCRIST. [*Struck*] I don't know—I don't know.

MRS. H. At least you'd like to be in a position to help him, if you
thought it necessary ?

HILLCRIST. Well—that—perhaps.

MRS. H. Then you agree that Mr. Hornblower at least should be
told. What he does with the knowledge is not our affair.

HILLCRIST. [*Half to the* STRANGER *and half to* DAWKER] Do you
realize that an imputation of that kind may be ground for a criminal
libel action ?

STRANGER. Quite. But there's no shadow of doubt ; not the
faintest. You saw her just now ?

HILLCRIST. I did. [*Revolting again.*] No ; I don't like it.

[DAWKER *has drawn the* STRANGER *a step or two away, and they
talk together.*

MRS. H. [*In a low voice*] And the ruin of our home ? You're
betraying your fathers, Jack.

HILLCRIST. I can't bear bringing a woman into it.

MRS. H. We don't. If anyone brings her in, it will be Hornblower
himself.

HILLCRIST. We use her secret as a lever.

MRS. H. I tell you quite plainly : I will only consent to holding my tongue about her, if you agree to Hornblower being told. It's a scandal to have a woman like that in the neighbourhood.

JILL. Mother means that, father.

HILLCRIST. Jill, keep quiet.   This is a very bitter position.   I can't tell what to do.

MRS. H. You must use this knowledge.   You owe it to me—to us all.   You'll see that when you've thought it over.

JILL. [*Softly*] Pitch, Dodo, pitch !

MRS. H. [*Furiously*] Jill, be quiet !

HILLCRIST. I was brought up never to hurt a woman.   I can't do it, Amy—I can't do it.   I should never feel like a gentleman again.

MRS. H. [*Coldly*] Oh ! Very well.

HILLCRIST. What d'you mean by that ?

MRS. H. I shall use the knowledge in my own way.

HILLCRIST. [*Staring at her*] You would—against my wishes ?

MRS. H. I consider it my duty.

HILLCRIST. If I agree to Hornblower being told——

MRS. H. That's all I want.

HILLCRIST. It's the utmost I'll consent to, Amy ; and don't let's have any humbug about its being morally necessary. We do it to save our skins.

MRS. H. I don't know what you mean by humbug ?

JILL. He means humbug, mother.

HILLCRIST. It must stop at old Hornblower.   Do you quite understand ?

MRS. H. Quite.

JILL. Will it stop ?

MRS. H. Jill, if you can't keep your impertinence to yourself——

HILLCRIST. Jill, come with me.   [*He turns towards door, Back.*

JILL. I'm sorry, mother.   Only it *is* a skin game, isn't it ?

MRS. H. You pride yourself on plain speech, Jill.   I pride myself on plain thought.   You will thank me afterwards that I can see realities.   I know we are better people than these Hornblowers.   Here we are going to stay, and they—are not.

JILL. [*Looking at her with a sort of unwilling admiration*] Mother, you're wonderful !

HILLCRIST. Jill !

JILL. Coming, Dodo.

[*She turns and runs to the door.   They go out.*   MRS. HILLCRIST, *with a long sigh, draws herself up, fine and proud.*

MRS. H. Dawker !   [*He comes to her.*]
I shall send him a note to-night, and word it so that he will be bound to come and see us to-morrow morning.   Will you be in the study just before eleven o'clock, with this gentleman ?

DAWKER. [*Nodding*] We're going to wire for his partner. I'll bring him too. Can't make too sure.

[*She goes firmly up the steps and out.*]

DAWKER. [*To the* STRANGER, *with a wink*] The Squire's squeamish —too much of a gentleman. But he don't count. The grey mare's all right. You wire to Henry. I'm off to our solicitors. We'll make that old rhinoceros sell us back the Centry at a decent price. These Hornblowers—[*Laying his finger on his nose.*] We've got 'em !

The curtain falls.

SCENE II

CHLOE'S *boudoir at half-past seven the same evening. A pretty room. No pictures on the walls, but two mirrors. A screen and a luxurious couch on the fireplace side, stage Left. A door rather Right of Centre Back, opening inwards. A French window, Right forward. A writing table, Right Back. Electric light burning.*

CHLOE, *in a tea-gown, is standing by the forward end of the sofa, very still, and very pale. Her lips are parted, and her large eyes stare straight before them as if seeing ghosts. The door is opened noiselessly and a* WOMAN'S *face is seen. It peers at* CHLOE, *vanishes, and the door is closed.* CHLOE *raises her hands, covers her eyes with them, drops them with a quick gesture, and looks round her. A knock. With a swift movement she slides on to the sofa, and lies prostrate, with eyes closed.*

CHLOE. [*Feebly*] Come in !

[*Her* MAID *enters ; a trim, contained figure of uncertain years, in a black dress, with the face which was peering in.*]

Yes, Anna ?

ANNA. Aren't you going in to dinner, ma'am ?

CHLOE. [*With closed eyes*] No.

ANNA. Will you take anything here, ma'am ?

CHLOE. I'd like a biscuit and a glass of champagne.

[*The* MAID, *who is standing between sofa and door, smiles.* CHLOE, *with a swift look, catches the smile.*]

Why do you smile ?

ANNA. Was I, ma'am ?

CHLOE. You know you were. [*Fiercely.*] Are you paid to smile at me ?

ANNA. [*Immovable*] No, ma'am. Would you like some eau-de-Cologne on your forehead ?

CHLOE. Yes.—No.—What's the good ? [*Clasping her forehead.*] My headache won't go.

ANNA. To keep lying down's the best thing for it.

CHLOE. I have been—hours.

ANNA. [*With the smile*] Yes, ma'am.

CHLOE. [*Gathering herself up on the sofa*] Anna! Why do you do it?

ANNA. Do what, ma'am?

CHLOE. Spy on me.

ANNA. I—never! I——!

CHLOE. To spy! You're a fool, too. What is there to spy on?

ANNA. Nothing, ma'am. Of course, if you're not satisfied with me, I must give notice. Only—if I were spying, I should expect to have notice given me. I've been accustomed to ladies who wouldn't stand such a thing for a minute.

CHLOE. [*Intently*] Well, you'll take a month's wages and go to-morrow. And that's all, now. [ANNA *inclines her head and goes out.*
      [CHLOE, *with a sort of moan, turns over and buries her face in the cushion.*

CHLOE. [*Sitting up*] If I could see that man—if only—or Dawker——
      [*She springs up and goes to the door, but hesitates, and comes back to the head of the sofa, as* ROLF *comes in. During this scene the door is again opened stealthily, an inch or two.*

ROLF. How's the head?

CHLOE. Beastly, thanks. I'm not going in to dinner.

ROLF. Is there anything I can do for you?

CHLOE. No, dear boy. [*Suddenly looking at him.*] You don't want this quarrel with the Hillcrists to go on, do you, Rolf?

ROLF. No; I hate it.

CHLOE. Well, I think I *might* be able to stop it. Will you slip round to Dawker's—it's not five minutes—and ask him to come and see me.

ROLF. Father and Charlie wouldn't——

CHLOE. I know. But if he comes to the window here while you're at dinner, I'll let him in, and out, and nobody'd know.

ROLF. [*Astonished*] Yes, but what—I mean how——

CHLOE. Don't ask me. It's worth the shot—that's all. [*Looking at her wrist-watch.*] To this window at eight o'clock exactly. First long window on the terrace, tell him.

ROLF. It's nothing Charlie would mind?

CHLOE. No; only I can't tell him—he and father are so mad about it all.

ROLF. If there's a real chance——

CHLOE. [*Going to the window and opening it*] This way, Rolf. If you don't come back I shall know he's coming. Put your watch by mine. [*Looking at his watch.*] It's a minute fast, see!

ROLF. Look here, Chloe——

CHLOE. Don't wait ; go on.

[*She almost pushes him out through the window, closes it after him, draws the curtains again, stands a minute, thinking hard ; goes to the bell and rings it ; then, crossing to the writing-table, Right Back, she takes out a chemist's prescription.*

[ANNA *comes in.*

CHLOE. I don't want that champagne. Take this to the chemist and get him to make up some of these cachets quick, and bring them back yourself.

ANNA. Yes, ma'am ; but you have some.

CHLOE. They're too old ; I've taken two—the strength's out of them. Quick, please ; I can't stand this head.

ANNA. [*Taking the prescription—with her smile*] Yes, ma'am. It'll take some time—you don't want me ?

CHLOE. No ; I want the cachets.   [ANNA *goes out.*

[CHLOE *looks at her wrist-watch, goes to the writing-table, which is old-fashioned, with a secret drawer, looks round her, dives at the secret drawer, takes out a roll of notes and a tissue paper parcel. She counts the notes :* " Three hundred." *Slips them into her breast and unwraps the little parcel. It contains pearls. She slips them too into her dress, looks round startled, replaces the drawer, and regains her place on the sofa, lying prostrate as the door opens, and* HORNBLOWER *comes in. She does not open her eyes, and he stands looking at her a moment before speaking.*

HORNBLOWER. [*Almost softly*] How are ye feelin', Chloe ?

CHLOE. Awful head !

HORNBLOWER. Can ye attend a moment ? I've had a note from that woman.   [CHLOE *sits up.*

HORNBLOWER. [*Reading*] " I have something of the utmost import-ance to tell you in regard to your daughter-in-law. I shall be waiting to see you at eleven o'clock to-morrow morning. The matter is so utterly vital to the happiness of all your family, that I cannot imagine you will fail to come." Now, what's the meaning of it ? Is it sheer impudence, or lunacy, or what ?

CHLOE. I don't know.

HORNBLOWER. [*Not unkindly*] Chloe, if there's anything—ye'd better tell me. Forewarned's forearmed.

CHLOE. There's nothing ; unless it's—[*With a quick look at him.*] —Unless it's that my father was a—a bankrupt.

HORNBLOWER. Hech ! Many a man's been that. Ye've never told us much about your family.

CHLOE. I wasn't very proud of him.

HORNBLOWER. Well, ye're not responsible for your father. If

that's all, it's a relief. The bitter snobs ! I'll remember it in the account I've got with them.

CHLOE. Father, don't say anything to Charlie ; it'll only worry him for nothing.

HORNBLOWER. Na, no, I'll not. If *I* went bankrupt, it'd upset Chearlie, I've not a doubt. [*He laughs. Looking at her shrewdly.*] There's nothing else, before I answer her ? [CHLOE *shakes her head.*] Ye're sure ?

CHLOE. [*With an effort*] She may invent things, of course.

HORNBLOWER. [*Lost in his feud feeling*] Ah ! but there's such a thing as the laws o' slander. If they play pranks, I'll have them up for it.

CHLOE. [*Timidly*] Couldn't you stop this quarrel, father ? You said it was on my account. But *I* don't want to know them. And they do love their old home. I like the girl. You don't really need to build just there, do you ? Couldn't you stop it ? Do !

HORNBLOWER. Stop it ? Now I've bought ? Na, no ! The snobs defied me, and I'm going to show them. I hate the lot of them, and I hate that little Dawker worst of all.

CHLOE. He's only their agent.

HORNBLOWER. He's a part of the whole dog-in-the-manger system that stands in my way. Ye're a woman, and ye don't understand these things. Ye wouldn't believe the struggle I've had to make my money and get my position. These county folk talk soft sawder, but to get anything from them's like gettin' butter out of a dog's mouth. If they could drive me out of here by fair means or foul, would they hesitate a moment ? Not they ! See what they've made me pay ; and look at this letter. Selfish, mean lot o' hypocrites !

CHLOE. But they didn't begin the quarrel.

HORNBLOWER. Not openly ; but underneath they did—that's their way. They began it by thwartin' me here and there and everywhere, just because I've come into me own a bit later than they did. I gave 'em their chance, and they wouldn't take it. Well, I'll show 'em what a man like me can do when he sets his mind to it. I'll not leave much skin on them.

> [*In the intensity of his feeling he has lost sight of her face, alive with a sort of agony of doubt, whether to plead with him further, or what to do. Then, with a swift glance at her wrist-watch, she falls back on the sofa and closes her eyes.*]

It'll give me a power of enjoyment seein' me chimneys go up in front of their windies. That was a bonnie thought—that last bid o' mine. He'd got that roused up, I believe he never would a' stopped. [*Looking at her.*] I forgot your head. Well, well, ye'll be best lyin' quiet.   [*The gong sounds.*]

Shall we send ye something in from dinner ?

CHLOE. No ; I'll try to sleep. Please tell them I don't want to be disturbed.

HORNBLOWER. All right. I'll just answer this note.

[*He sits down at her writing-table.*

[CHLOE *starts up from the sofa feverishly, looking at her watch, at the window, at her watch ; then softly crosses to the window and opens it.*

HORNBLOWER. [*Finishing*] Listen ! [*He turns round towards the sofa.*] Hallo ! Where are ye ?

CHLOE. [*At the window*] It's so hot.

HORNBLOWER. Here's what I've said :

" MADAM,—You can tell me nothing of my daughter-in-law which can affect the happiness of my family. I regard your note as an impertinence, and I shall not be with you at eleven o'clock to-morrow morning.

" Yours truly——"

CHLOE. [*With a suffering movement of her head*] Oh !—Well !——

[*The gong is touched a second time.*

HORNBLOWER. [*Crossing to the door*] Lie ye down, and get a sleep. I'll tell them not to disturb ye ; and I hope ye'll be all right to-morrow. Good-night, Chloe.

CHLOE. Good-night. [*He goes out.*

[*After a feverish turn or two,* CHLOE *returns to the open window and waits there, half screened by the curtains. The door is opened inch by inch, and* ANNA's *head peers round. Seeing where* CHLOE *is, she slips in and passes behind the screen, Left. Suddenly* CHLOE *backs in from the window.*

CHLOE. [*In a low voice*] Come in. [*She darts to the door and locks it.*

[DAWKER *has come in through the window and stands regarding her with a half smile.*

DAWKER. Well, young woman, what do you want of me ?

[*In the presence of this man of her own class, there comes a distinct change in* CHLOE's *voice and manner ; a sort of frank common- ness, adapted to the man she is dealing with, but she keeps her voice low.*

CHLOE. You're making a mistake, you know.

DAWKER. [*With a broad grin*] No. I've got a memory for faces.

CHLOE. I say you are.

DAWKER. [*Turning to go*] If that's all, you needn't 'ave troubled me to come.

CHLOE. No. Don't go ! [*With a faint smile.*] You *are* playing a game with me. Aren't you ashamed ? What harm have I done you ? Do you call this cricket ?

DAWKER. No, my girl—business.

CHLOE. [*Bitterly*] What have I to do with this quarrel ?   I couldn't help their falling out.

DAWKER. That's your misfortune.

CHLOE. [*Clasping her hands*] You're a cruel fellow if you can spoil a woman's life who never did you an ounce of harm.

DAWKER. So they *don't* know about you. That's all right.   Now, look here, I serve my employer.   But I'm flesh and blood too, and I always give as good as I get.   I hate this family of yours.   There's no name too bad for 'em to call me this last month, and no looks too black to give me.   I tell you frankly, I hate 'em.

CHLOE. There's good in them same as in you.

DAWKER. [*With a grin*] There's no good Hornblower but a dead Hornblower.

CHLOE. But—but I'm *not* one.

DAWKER. You'll be the mother of some, I shouldn't wonder.

CHLOE. [*Stretching out her hand—pathetically*] Oh ! leave me alone, do ! I'm happy here.   Be a sport !   Be a sport !

DAWKER. [*Disconcerted for a second*] You can't get at me, so don't try it on.

CHLOE. I had such a bad time in old days.

[DAWKER *shakes his head ; his grin has disappeared and his face is like wood.*

CHLOE. [*Panting*] Ah ! do ! You might ! You've been fond of some woman, I suppose. Think of her !

DAWKER. [*Decisively*] It won't do, Mrs. Chloe. You're a pawn in the game, and I'm going to use you.

CHLOE. [*Despairingly*] What is it to you ? [*With a sudden touch of the tigress.*] Look here ! Don't you make an enemy of me. I haven't dragged through hell for nothing. Women like me can bite, I tell you.

DAWKER. That's better. I'd rather have a woman threaten than whine, any day. Threaten away ! You'll let 'em know that you met me in the Promenade one night. Of course you'll let 'em know that, won't you ?—or that——

CHLOE. Be quiet ! Oh ! Be quiet ! [*Taking from her bosom the notes and the pearls.*] Look ! There's my savings—there's all I've got ! The pearls'll fetch nearly a thousand. [*Holding it out to him.*] Take it, and drop me out—won't you ? Won't you ?

DAWKER. [*Passing his tongue over his lips—with a hard little laugh*] You mistake your man, missis. I'm a plain dog, if you like, but I'm faithful, and I hold fast. Don't try those games on me.

CHLOE. [*Losing control*] You're a beast !—a beast ! a cruel, cowardly beast ! And how dare you bribe that woman here to spy on me ? Oh ! yes, you do ; you know you do. If you drove me mad, you wouldn't care. You beast !

DAWKER. Now, don't carry on! That won't help you.

CHLOE. What d'you call it—to dog a woman down like this, just because you happen to have a quarrel with a man?

DAWKER. Who made the quarrel? Not me, missis. *You* ought to know that in a row it's the weak and helpless—we won't say the innocent—that get it in the neck. That can't be helped.

CHLOE. [*Regarding him intently*] I hope your mother or your sister, if you've got any, may go through what I'm going through ever since you got on my track. I hope they'll know what fear means. I hope they'll love and find out that it's hanging on a thread, and—and—— Oh! you coward, you persecuting coward! Call yourself a man!

DAWKER. [*With his grin*] Ah! You look quite pretty like that. By George! you're a handsome woman when you're roused.

[CHLOE'S *passion fades out as quickly as it blazed up. She sinks down on the sofa, shudders, looks here and there, and then for a moment up at him.*

CHLOE. Is there *anything* you'll take, not to spoil my life? [*Clasping her hands on her breast; under her breath.*] Me?

DAWKER. [*Wiping his brow*] By God! That's an offer. [*He recoils towards the window.*] You—you touched me there. Look here! I've got to use you and I'm going to use you, but I'll do my best to let you down as easy as I can. No, I don't want anything you can give me—that is—— [*He wipes his brow again.*] I'd like it—but I won't take it. [CHLOE *buries her face in her hands.*] There! Keep your pecker up; don't cry. Good-night!

[*He goes through the window.*

CHLOE. [*Springing up*] Ugh! Rat in a trap! Rat——!

[*She stands listening; flies to the door, unlocks it, and, going back to the sofa, lies down and closes her eyes.* CHARLES *comes in very quietly and stands over her, looking to see if she is asleep. She opens her eyes.*

CHARLES. Well, Clo! Had a sleep, old girl?

CHLOE. Ye—es.

CHARLES. [*Sitting on the arm of the sofa and caressing her*] Feel better, dear?

CHLOE. Yes, better, Charlie.

CHARLES. That's right. Would you like some soup?

CHLOE. [*With a shudder*] No.

CHARLES. I say—what gives you these heads? You've been very on and off all this last month.

CHLOE. I don't know. Except that—except that I *am* going to have a child, Charlie.

CHARLES. After all! By Jove! Sure?

CHLOE. [*Nodding*] Are you glad?

CHARLES. Well—I suppose I am. The guv'nor will be mighty pleased, anyway.

CHLOE. Don't tell him—yet.

CHARLES. All right! [*Bending over and drawing her to him.*] My poor girl, I'm so sorry you're seedy. Give us a kiss.

            [CHLOE *puts up her face and kisses him passionately.*]
I say, you're like fire. You're not feverish?

CHLOE. [*With a laugh*] It's a wonder if I'm not. Charlie, are you happy with me?

CHARLES. What do you think?

CHLOE. [*Leaning against him*] You wouldn't easily believe things against me, would you?

CHARLES. What! Thinking of those Hillcrists? What the hell that woman means by her attitude towards you—— When I saw her there to-day, I had all my work cut out not to go up and give her a bit of my mind.

CHLOE. [*Watching him stealthily*] It's not good for me, now I'm like this. It's upsetting me, Charlie.

CHARLES. Yes; and we won't forget. We'll make 'em pay for it.

CHLOE. It's wretched in a little place like this. I say, must you go on spoiling their home!

CHARLES. The woman cuts you and insults you. That's enough for me.

CHLOE. [*Timidly*] Let her. *I* don't care; I can't bear feeling enemies about, Charlie, I—get nervous—I——

CHARLES. My dear girl! What is it? [*He looks at her intently.*

CHLOE. I suppose it's—being like this. [*Suddenly.*] But, Charlie, do stop it for my sake. Do, do!

CHARLES. [*Patting her arm*] Come, come; I say Chloe! You're making mountains. See things in proportion. Father's paid nine thousand five hundred to get the better of those people, and you want him to chuck it away to save a woman who's insulted you. That's not sense, and it's not business. Have some pride.

CHLOE. [*Breathless*] I've got no pride, Charlie. I want to be quiet—that's all.

CHARLES. Well, if the row gets on your nerves, I can take you to the sea. But you ought to enjoy a fight with people like that.

CHLOE. [*With calculated bitterness*] No, it's nothing, of course—what *I* want.

CHARLES. Hallo! Hallo! You *are* on the jump!

CHLOE. If you want me to be a good wife to you, make father stop it.

CHARLES. [*Standing up*] Now, look here, Chloe, what's behind this?

CHLOE. [*Faintly*] Behind?

CHARLES. You're carrying on as if—as if you were really scared!

We've *got* these people. We'll have them out of Deepwater in six months. It's absolute ruination to their beastly old house; we'll put the chimneys on the very edge, not three hundred yards off, and our smoke'll be drifting over them half the time. You won't have this confounded stuck-up woman here much longer. And then we can really go ahead and take our proper place. So long as she's here, we shall never do that. We've only to drive on now as fast as we can.

CHLOE. [*With a gesture*] I see.

CHARLES. [*Again looking at her*] If you go on like this, you know, I shall begin to think there's something you——

CHLOE. [*Softly*] Charlie !   [*He comes to her.*]
Love me !

CHARLES. [*Embracing her*] There, old girl ! I know women are funny at these times. You want a good night, that's all.

CHLOE. You haven't finished dinner, have you ? Go back, and I'll go to bed quite soon. Charlie, don't stop loving me.

CHARLES. Stop ? Not much.

[*While he is again embracing her,* ANNA *steals from behind the screen to the door, opens it noiselessly, and passes through, but it clicks as she shuts it.*

CHLOE. [*Starting violently*] Oh——h !

CHARLES. What is it ? What is it ? You are nervy, my dear.

CHLOE. [*Looking round with a little laugh*] I don't know. Go on, Charlie. I'll be all right when this head's gone.

CHARLES. [*Stroking her forehead and looking at her doubtfully*] You go to bed ; I won't be late coming up.

[*He turns and goes, blowing a kiss from the doorway. When he is gone,* CHLOE *gets up and stands in precisely the attitude in which she stood at the beginning of the Act, thinking, and thinking. And the door is opened, and the face of the* MAID *peers round at her.*

The curtain falls.

ACT III

SCENE I

MORNING

HILLCRIST's *study next morning.*

[JILL, *coming from Left, looks in at the open French window.*

JILL. [*Speaking to* ROLF, *invisible*] Come in here. There's no one.
[*She goes in.* ROLF *joins her, coming from the garden.*

ROLF. Jill, I just wanted to say—Need we? [JILL *nods.*]
Seeing you yesterday—it did seem rotten.

JILL. *We* didn't begin it.

ROLF. No; but you don't understand. If you'd made yourself, as father has——

JILL. I hope I should be sorry.

ROLF. [*Reproachfully*] That isn't like you. Really he can't help thinking he's a public benefactor.

JILL. And we can't help thinking he's a pig. Sorry!

ROLF. If the survival of the fittest is right——

JILL. He may be fitter, but he's not going to survive.

ROLF. [*Distracted*] It looks like it though.

JILL. Is that all you came to say?

ROLF. No. Suppose we joined, couldn't we stop it?

JILL. I don't feel like joining.

ROLF. We *did* shake hands.

JILL. One can't fight and not grow bitter.

ROLF. *I* don't feel bitter.

JILL. Wait; you'll feel it soon enough.

ROLF. Why? [*Attentively.*] About Chloe? I do think your mother's manner to her is——

JILL. Well?

ROLF. Snobbish. [JILL *laughs.*]
She may not be your class; and that's just why it's snobbish.

JILL. I think you'd better shut up.

ROLF. What my father said was true; your mother's rudeness to her that day she came here, has made both him and Charlie ever so much more bitter. [JILL *whistles the Habanera from* "*Carmen.*"]
Staring at her, rather angrily] Is it a whistling matter?

JILL. No.

557

ROLF. I suppose you want me to go ?

JILL. Yes.

ROLF. All right.   Aren't we ever going to be friends again ?

JILL. [*Looking steadily at him*] I don't expect so.

ROLF. That's very—horrible.

JILL. Lots of horrible things in the world.

ROLF. It's our business to make them fewer, Jill.

JILL. [*Fiercely*] Don't be moral.

ROLF. [*Hurt*] That's the last thing I want to be.   I only want to be friendly.

JILL. Better be real first.

ROLF. From the big point of view——

JILL. There isn't any.   We're all out for our own.   And why not ?

ROLF. By jove, you have got——

JILL. Cynical ?   Your father's motto—" Every man for himself." That's the winner—hands down.   Good-bye !

ROLF. Jill ! Jill !

JILL. [*Putting her hands behind her back, hums*] :

> " If auld acquaintance be forgot
>   And days of auld lang syne——"

ROLF. Don't !

> [*With a pained gesture he goes out towards Left, through the French window.*
> [*JILL, who has broken off the song, stands with her hands clenched and her lips quivering.*]   [FELLOWS *enters Left.*

FELLOWS. Mr. Dawker, Miss, and two gentlemen.

JILL. Let the three gentlemen in, and me out.

>   [*She passes him and goes out Left.*
> [*And immediately* DAWKER *and the* TWO STRANGERS *come in.*

FELLOWS. I'll inform Mrs. Hillcrist, sir.   The Squire is on his rounds.   [*He goes out Left.*

> [*The* THREE MEN *gather in a discreet knot at the big bureau, having glanced at the two doors and the open French window.*

DAWKER. Now this may come into Court, you know.   If there's a screw loose anywhere, better mention it.   [*To* SECOND STRANGER.] You knew her personally ?

SECOND S. What do you think ?   I don't take girls on trust for that sort of job.   She came to us highly recommended, too ; and did her work very well.   It was a double stunt—to make sure— wasn't it, George ?

FIRST S. Yes ; we paid her for the two visits.

SECOND S. I should know her in a minute ; striking looking girl ; had something in her face.   Daresay she'd seen hard times.

FIRST S. We don't want publicity.

DAWKER. Not likely. The threat'll do it; but the stakes are heavy—and the man's a slogger; we must be able to push it home. If you can both swear to her, it'll do the trick.

SECOND S. And about—I mean, we're losing time, you know, coming down here.

DAWKER. [*With a nod at* FIRST STRANGER] George here knows me. That'll be all right. I'll guarantee it well worth your while.

SECOND S. I don't want to do the girl harm, if she's married.

DAWKER. No, no; nobody wants to hurt *her*. We just want a cinch on this fellow till he squeals.

[*They separate a little as* MRS. HILLCRIST *enters from Right.*]

DAWKER. Good morning, ma'am. My friend's partner. Hornblower coming?

MRS. H. At eleven. I had to send up a second note, Dawker.

DAWKER. Squire not in?

MRS. H. I haven't told him.

DAWKER. [*Nodding*] Our friends might go in here [*Pointing Right*] and we can use 'em as we want 'em.

MRS. H. [*To the* STRANGERS] Will you make yourselves comfortable?

[*She holds the door open, and they pass her into the room, Right.*]

DAWKER. [*Showing document*] I've had this drawn and engrossed. Pretty sharp work. Conveys the Centry, *and* Longmeadow, to the Squire at four thousand five hundred. Now, ma'am, suppose Hornblower puts his hand to that, he'll have been done in the eye, and six thousand all told out o' pocket. You'll have a very nasty neighbour here.

MRS. H. But we shall still have the power to disclose that secret at any time.

DAWKER. Yeh! But things might happen here you could never bring home to him. You can't trust a man like that. He isn't goin' to forgive *me*, I know.

MRS. H. [*Regarding him keenly*] But if he signs, we couldn't honourably——

DAWKER. No, ma'am, *you* couldn't; and I'm sure *I* don't want to do that girl a hurt. I just mention it because, of course, you can't guarantee that it doesn't get out.

MRS. H. Not absolutely, I suppose.

[*A look passes between them, which neither of them has quite sanctioned.*]

There's his car. It always seems to make more noise than any other.

DAWKER. He'll kick and flounder—but you leave him to ask what you want, ma'am; don't mention this. [*He puts the deed back into his pocket.*] The Centry's no mortal good to him if he's not going to put up works ; I should say he'd be glad to save what he can.

[MRS. HILLCRIST *inclines her head.* FELLOWS *enters Left.*

FELLOWS. [*Apologetically*] Mr. Hornblower, ma'am ; by appointment, he says.

MRS. H. Quite right, Fellows.

[HORNBLOWER *comes in, and* FELLOWS *goes out.*

HORNBLOWER. [*Without salutation*] I've come to ask ye point blank what ye mean by writing me these letters. [*He takes out two letters.*] And we'll discuss it in the presence of nobody, if ye please.

MRS. H. Mr. Dawker knows all that I know, and more.

HORNBLOWER. Does he ? Very well ! Your second note says that my daughter-in-law has lied to me. Well, I've brought her, and what ye've got to say—if it's not just a trick to see me again— ye'll say to her face.   [*He takes a step towards the window.*

MRS. H. Mr. Hornblower, you had better decide that after hearing what it is—we shall be quite ready to repeat it in her presence ; but we want to do as little harm as possible.

HORNBLOWER. [*Stopping*] Oh ! ye do ! Well, what lies have ye been hearin' ? Or what have ye made up ? You and Mr. Dawker ? Of course ye know there's a law of libel and slander. I'm not the man to stop at that.

MRS. H. [*Calmly*] Are you familiar with the law of divorce, Mr. Hornblower ?

HORNBLOWER. [*Taken aback*] No, I'm not. That is——

MRS. H. Well, you know that misconduct is required. And I suppose you've heard that cases are arranged.

HORNBLOWER. I know it's all very shocking—what about it ?

MRS. H. When cases are arranged, Mr. Hornblower, the man who is to be divorced often visits an hotel with a strange woman. I am extremely sorry to say that your daughter-in-law, before her marriage, was in the habit of being employed as such a woman.

HORNBLOWER. Ye dreadful creature !

DAWKER. [*Quickly*] All proved, up to the hilt !

HORNBLOWER. I don't believe a word of it. Ye're lyin' to save your skins. How dare ye tell me such monstrosities ? Dawker, I'll have ye in a criminal court.

DAWKER. Rats ! You saw a gent with me yesterday ? Well, *he's* employed her.

HORNBLOWER. A put-up job ! Conspiracy !

MRS. H. Go and get your daughter-in-law.

HORNBLOWER. [*With the first sensation of being in a net*] It's a foul shame—a lying slander !

MRS. H. If so, it's easily disproved. Go and fetch her.

HORNBLOWER. [*Seeing them unmoved*] I will. I don't believe a word of it.

MRS. H. I hope you are right.

[HORNBLOWER *goes out by the French window.* DAWKER *slips to the door Right, opens it, and speaks to those within.* MRS. HILLCRIST *stands moistening her lips, and passing her handkerchief over them.* HORNBLOWER *returns, preceding* CHLOE, *strung up to hardness and defiance.*

HORNBLOWER. Now then, let's have this impudent story torn to rags.

CHLOE. What story?

HORNBLOWER. That you, my dear, were a woman—it's too shockin' —I don't know how to tell ye——

CHLOE. Go on!

HORNBLOWER. Were a woman that went with men, to get them their divorce.

CHLOE. Who says that?

HORNBLOWER. That lady [*sneering*] there, and her bull-terrier here.

CHLOE. [*Facing* MRS. HILLCRIST] That's a charitable thing to say, isn't it?

MRS. H. Is it true?

CHLOE. No.

HORNBLOWER. [*Furiously*] There! I'll have ye both on your knees to her!

DAWKER. [*Opening the door Right*] Come in.

[*The* FIRST STRANGER *comes in.* CHLOE, *with a visible effort, turns to face him.*

FIRST S. How do you do, Mrs. Vane?

CHLOE. I don't know you.

FIRST S. Your memory is bad, ma'am. You knew me yesterday well enough. One day is not a long time, nor are three years.

CHLOE. Who *are* you?

FIRST S. Come, ma'am, come! The Custer case.

CHLOE. I don't know you, I say. [*To* MRS. HILLCRIST.] How can you be so vile?

FIRST S. Let me refresh your memory, ma'am. [*Producing a notebook.*] Just on three years ago: "Oct. 3. To fee and expenses Mrs. Vane with Mr. C——, Hotel Beaulieu, Twenty pounds. Oct. 10, Do., Twenty pounds." [*To* HORNBLOWER.] Would you like to glance at this book, sir? You'll see they're genuine entries.

[HORNBLOWER *makes a motion to do so, but checks himself and looks at* CHLOE.

CHLOE. [*Hysterically*] It's all lies—lies!

FIRST S. Come, ma'am, we wish you no harm.

CHLOE. Take me away.   I won't be treated like this.

MRS. H. [*In a low voice*] Confess.

CHLOE. Lies!

HORNBLOWER. Were ye ever called Vane?

CHLOE. No, never.

> [*She makes a movement towards the window, but* DAWKER *is in the way, and she halts.*

FIRST S. [*Opening the door Right*] Henry.

> [*The* SECOND STRANGER *comes in quickly. At sight of him* CHLOE *throws up her hands, gasps, breaks down stage Left, and stands covering her face with her hands. It is so complete a confession that* HORNBLOWER *stands staggered; and, taking out a coloured handkerchief, wipes his brow.*

DAWKER. Are you convinced?

HORNBLOWER. Take those men away.

DAWKER. If you're not satisfied, we can get other evidence; plenty.

HORNBLOWER. [*Looking at* CHLOE] That's enough.   Take them out.   Leave me alone with her.   [DAWKER *takes them out Right.*

> [MRS. HILLCRIST *passes* HORNBLOWER *and goes out at the window.*
> HORNBLOWER *moves down a step or two towards* CHLOE.

HORNBLOWER. My God!

CHLOE. [*With an outburst*] Don't tell Charlie!   Don't tell Charlie!

HORNBLOWER. Chearlie!   So that was your manner of life!

> [CHLOE *utters a moaning sound.*]

So that's what ye got out of by marryin' into my family!   Shame on ye, ye Godless thing!

CHLOE. Don't tell Charlie!

HORNBLOWER. And that's all ye can say for the wreck ye've wrought. My family, my works, my future!   How dared ye!

CHLOE. If you'd been me———!

HORNBLOWER. An' these Hillcrists.   The skin game of it!

CHLOE. [*Breathless*] Father!

HORNBLOWER. Don't call me that, woman!

CHLOE. [*Desperate*] I'm going to have a child.

HORNBLOWER. God!   Ye are!

CHLOE. Your grandchild.   For the sake of it, do what these people want; and don't tell anyone———   *Don't tell Charlie!*

HORNBLOWER. [*Again wiping his forehead*] A secret between us.   I don't know that I can keep it.   It's horrible.   Poor Chearlie!

CHLOE. [*Suddenly fierce*] You must keep it, you shall!   I won't have him told.   Don't make me desperate!   I can be—I didn't live that life for nothing.

HORNBLOWER. [*Staring at her revealed in a new light*] Ay; ye look a strange, wild woman, as I see ye.   And we thought the world of ye!

CHLOE. I love Charlie; I'm faithful to him. I can't live without him. You'll never forgive me, I know; but Charlie———!

[*Stretching out her hands.*

[HORNBLOWER *makes a bewildered gesture with his large hands.*

HORNBLOWER. I'm all at sea here. Go out to the car and wait for me. [CHLOE *passes him and goes out, Left.*]

[*Muttering to himself.*] So I'm down! Me enemies put their heels upon me head! Ah! but we'll see yet!

[*He goes up to the window and beckons towards the Right.*]

[MRS. HILLCRIST *comes in.*]

What d'ye want for this secret?

MRS. H. Nothing.

HORNBLOWER. Indeed! Wonderful!—the trouble ye've taken for —nothing.

MRS. H. If you harm us we shall harm you. Any use whatever of the Centry———

HORNBLOWER. For which ye made me pay nine thousand five hundred pounds.

MRS. H. We will buy it from you.

HORNBLOWER. At what price?

MRS. H. The Centry at the price Miss Mullins would have taken at first, and Longmeadow at the price you gave us—four thousand five hundred altogether.

HORNBLOWER. A fine price, and me six thousand out of pocket. Na, no! I'll keep it and hold it over ye. Ye daren't tell this secret so long as I've got it.

MRS. H. No, Mr. Hornblower. On second thoughts, you *must* sell. You broke your word over the Jackmans. We can't trust you. We would rather have our place here ruined at once, than leave you the power to ruin it as and when you like. You will sell us the Centry and Longmeadow now, or you know what will happen.

HORNBLOWER. [*Writhing*] I'll not. It's blackmail.

MRS. H. Very well then! Go your own way and we'll go ours. There is no witness to this conversation.

HORNBLOWER. [*Venomously*] By heaven, ye're a clever woman. Will ye swear by Almighty God that you and your family, and that agent of yours, won't breathe a word of this shockin' thing to mortal soul.

MRS. H. Yes, if you sell.

HORNBLOWER. Where's Dawker?

MRS. H. [*Going to the door, Right*] Mr. Dawker!

[DAWKER *comes in.*

HORNBLOWER. I suppose ye've got your iniquity ready.

[DAWKER *grins and produces the document.*]

It's mighty near conspiracy, this. Have ye got a Testament?

Mrs. H. My word will be enough, Mr. Hornblower.

Hornblower. Ye'll pardon me—I can't make it solemn enough for you.

Mrs. H. Very well; here is a Bible.

[*She takes a small Bible from the bookshelf.*

Dawker. [*Spreading document on bureau*] This is a short conveyance of the Centry and Longmeadow—recites sale to you by Miss Mullins of the first, John Hillcrist of the second, and whereas you have agreed for the sale to said John Hillcrist, for the sum of four thousand five hundred pounds, in consideration of the said sum, receipt whereof, you hereby acknowledge you do convey all that, etc. Sign here. I'll witness.

Hornblower. [*To* Mrs. Hillcrist] Take that Book in your hand, and swear first. I swear by Almighty God never to breathe a word of what I know concerning Chloe Hornblower to any living soul.

Mrs. H. No, Mr. Hornblower; you will please sign first. *We* are not in the habit of breaking our words.

[Hornblower, *after a furious look at them, seizes a pen, runs his eye again over the deed, and signs,* Dawker *witnessing.*]

To that oath, Mr. Hornblower, we shall add the words, " So long as the Hornblower family do us no harm."

Hornblower. [*With a snarl*] Take it in your hands, both of ye, and together swear.

Mrs. H. [*Taking the Book*] I swear that I will breathe no word of what I know concerning Chloe Hornblower to any living soul, so long as the Hornblower family do us no harm.

Dawker. I swear that too.

Mrs. H. I engage for my husband.

Hornblower. Where are those two fellows?

Dawker. Gone. It's no business of theirs.

Hornblower. It's no business of any of ye what has happened to a woman in the past. Ye know that. Good-day!

[*He gives them a deadly look, and goes out, Left, followed by* Dawker.

Mrs. H. [*With her hand on the Deed*] Safe!

[Hillcrist *enters at the French window, followed by* Jill.]
[*Holding up the Deed.*] Look! He's just gone! I told you it was only necessary to use the threat. He caved in and signed this; we are sworn to say nothing. We've beaten him.

[Hillcrist *studies the Deed.*

Jill. [*Awed*] We saw Chloe in the car. How did she take it, mother?

Mrs. H. Denied, then broke down when she saw our witnesses. I'm glad you were not here, Jack.

Jill. [*Suddenly*] I shall go and see her.

Mrs. H. Jill, you will *not*; you don't know what she's done.

JILL. I shall.   She must be in an awful state.

HILLCRIST. My dear, you can do her no good.

JILL. I think I can, Dodo.

MRS. H. You don't understand human nature.   We're enemies for life with those people.   You're a little donkey if you think anything else.

JILL. I'm going, all the same.

MRS. H. Jack, forbid her.

HILLCRIST. [*Lifting an eyebrow*] Jill, be reasonable.

JILL. Suppose I'd taken a knock like that, Dodo, I'd be glad of friendliness from someone.

MRS. H. You never *could* take a knock like *that*.

JILL. You don't know what you can do till you try, mother.

HILLCRIST. Let her go, Amy.   I'm sorry for that young woman.

MRS. H. You'd be sorry for a man who picked your pocket, I believe.

HILLCRIST. I certainly should !   Deuced little he'd get out of it, when I've paid for the Centry.

MRS. H. [*Bitterly*] Much gratitude I get for saving you both our home !

JILL. [*Disarmed*] Oh ! Mother, we *are* grateful.   Dodo, show your gratitude.

HILLCRIST. Well, my dear, it's an intense relief.   I'm not good at showing my feelings, as you know.   What d'you want me to do ? Stand on one leg and crow ?

JILL. *Yes*, Dodo, yes !   Mother, hold him while I—[*Suddenly she stops, and all the fun goes out of her.*] No !   I can't—I can't help thinking of *her*.

          The curtain falls for a minute.

SCENE II

EVENING

When it rises again, the room is empty and dark, save for moonlight coming in through the French window, which is open.

The figure of CHLOE, *in a black cloak, appears outside in the moonlight ; she peers in, moves past, comes back, hesitatingly enters.   The cloak, fallen back, reveals a white evening dress ; and that magpie figure stands poised watchfully in the dim light, then flaps unhappily Left and Right, as if she could not keep still.   Suddenly she stands listening.*

ROLF'S VOICE. [*Outside*] Chloe !   Chloe !   [*He appears.*

CHLOE. [*Going to the window*] What are you doing here?

ROLF. What are *you*? I only followed you.

CHLOE. Go away!

ROLF. What's the matter? Tell me!

CHLOE. Go away, and don't say anything. Oh! The roses! [*She has put her nose into some roses in a bowl on a big stand close to the window.*] Don't they smell lovely?

ROLF. What did Jill want this afternoon?

CHLOE. I'll tell you nothing. Go away!

ROLF. I don't like leaving you here in this state.

CHLOE. What state? I'm all right. Wait for me down in the drive, if you want to.

[ROLF *starts to go, stops, looks at her, and does go.*
[CHLOE, *with a little moaning sound, flutters again, magpie-like, up and down, then stands by the window listening. Voices are heard, Left. She darts out of the window and away to the Right, as* HILLCRIST *and* JILL *come in. They have turned up the electric light, and come down in front of the fireplace, where* HILLCRIST *sits in an armchair, and* JILL *on the arm of it. They are in undress evening attire.*

HILLCRIST. Now, tell me.

JILL. There isn't much, Dodo. I was in an awful funk for fear I should meet any of the others, and of course I did meet Rolf, but I told him some lie, and he took me to her room—boudoir, they call it —isn't boudoir a " dug-out " word?

HILLCRIST. [*Meditatively*] The sulking room. Well?

JILL. She was sitting like this. [*She buries her chin in her hands, with her elbows on her knees.*] And she said in a sort of fierce way: " What do you want? " And I said: " I'm awfully sorry, but I thought you might like it."

HILLCRIST. Well?

JILL. She looked at me hard, and said: " I suppose you know all about it." And I said: " Only vaguely," because of course I don't. And she said: " Well, it was decent of you to come." Dodo, she looks like a lost soul. What has she done?

HILLCRIST. She committed her real crime when she married young Hornblower without telling him. She came out of a certain world to do it.

JILL. Oh! [*Staring in front of her.*] Is it very awful in that world, Dodo?

HILLCRIST. [*Uneasy*] I don't know, Jill. Some can stand it, I suppose; some can't. I don't know which sort she is.

JILL. One thing I'm sure of: she's awfully fond of Chearlie.

HILLCRIST. That's bad; that's very bad.

JILL. And she's frightened, horribly. I think she's desperate.

HILLCRIST. Women like that are pretty tough, Jill; don't judge her too much by your own feelings.

JILL. No; only—— Oh! it was beastly; and of course I dried up.

HILLCRIST. [*Feelingly*] H'm! One always does. But perhaps it was as well; you'd have been blundering in a dark passage.

JILL. I just said: "Father and I feel awfully sorry; if there's anything we can do——"

HILLCRIST. That was risky, Jill.

JILL. [*Disconsolately*] I had to say something. I'm glad I went, anyway. I feel more human.

HILLCRIST. We *had* to fight for our home. I should have felt like a traitor if I hadn't.

JILL. I'm not *enjoying* home to-night, Dodo.

HILLCRIST. I never could hate properly; it's a confounded nuisance.

JILL. Mother's fearfully bucked, and Dawker's simply oozing triumph. I *don't* trust him, Dodo; he's too—not pugilistic—the other one with a pug—naceous.

HILLCRIST. He is rather.

JILL. I'm sure he wouldn't care tuppence if Chloe committed suicide.

HILLCRIST. [*Rising uneasily*] Nonsense! Nonsense!

JILL. I wonder if mother would.

HILLCRIST. [*Turning his face towards the window*] What's that? I thought I heard—[*Louder.*] Is there anybody out there?

        [*No answer.   Jill springs up and runs to the window.*

JILL. You! [*She dives through to the Right, and returns, holding* CHLOE'S *hand and drawing her forward.*] Come in! It's only us! [*To* HILLCRIST.] Dodo!

HILLCRIST. [*Flustered, but making a show of courtesy*] Good evening! Won't you sit down?

JILL. Sit down; you're all shaky.

    [*She makes* CHLOE *sit down in the armchair, out of which they have risen, then locks the door, and closing the windows, draws the curtains hastily over them.*

HILLCRIST. [*Awkward and expectant*] Can I do anything for you?

CHLOE. I couldn't bear it—he's coming to ask you——

HILLCRIST. Who?

CHLOE. My husband. [*She draws in her breath with a long shudder, then seems to seize her courage in her hands.*] I've got to be quick. He keeps on asking—he knows there's something.

HILLCRIST. Make your mind easy. We shan't tell him.

CHLOE. [*Appealing*] Oh! that's not enough. Can't you tell him something to put him back to thinking it's all right? I've done him such a wrong. I didn't realize till after—I thought meeting him was just a piece of wonderful good luck, after what I'd been through. I'm not such a bad lot—not really.

> [*She stops from the over-quivering of her lips.*]
>
> [JILL, *standing beside the chair, strokes her shoulder.* HILLCRIST *stands very still, painfully biting at a finger.*]

You see, my father went bankrupt, and I was in a shop till——

HILLCRIST. [*Soothingly, and to prevent disclosures*] Yes, yes ; yes, yes.

CHLOE. I never gave a man away or did anything I was ashamed of—at least—I mean, I had to make my living in all sorts of ways, and then I met Charlie. [*Again she stopped from the quivering of her lips.*

JILL. It's all right.

CHLOE. He thought I was respectable, and that was such a relief, you can't think, so—so I let him.

JILL. Dodo ! It's awful !

HILLCRIST. It is !

CHLOE. And after I married him, you see, I fell in love. If I had before, perhaps I wouldn't have dared—only, I don't know—you never know, do you ? When there's a straw going, you catch at it.

JILL. Of course you do.

CHLOE. And now, you see, I'm going to have a child.

JILL. [*Aghast*] Oh ! *Are* you ?

HILLCRIST. Good God !

CHLOE. [*Dully*] I've been on hot bricks all this month, ever since —that day here. I knew it was in the wind. What gets in the wind never gets out. [*She rises and throws out her arms.*] Never ! It just blows here and there, [*Desolately*] and then blows home. [*Her voice changes to resentment.*] But I've paid for being a fool—'tisn't fun, that sort of life, I can tell you.   I'm not ashamed and repentant, and all that. If it wasn't for him ; I'm afraid he'll never forgive me ; it's such a disgrace for him—and then, to have his child ! Being fond of him, I feel it much worse than anything I ever felt, and that's saying a good bit.   It is.

JILL. [*Energetically*] Look here !   He simply mustn't find out.

CHLOE. That's it ; but it's started, and he's bound to keep on because he knows there's something. A man isn't going to be satisfied when there's something he suspects about his wife. Charlie wouldn't—never. He's clever, and he's jealous ; and he's coming here.   [*She stops, and looks round wildly, listening.*

JILL. Dodo, what can we say to put him clean off the scent ?

HILLCRIST. Anything in reason.

CHLOE. [*Catching at this straw*] You will !   You see, I don't know what I'll do. I've got soft, being looked after—he does love me. And if he throws me off, I'll go under—that's all.

HILLCRIST. Have you any suggestion ?

CHLOE. [*Eagerly*] The only thing is to tell him something positive, something he'll believe, that's not *too* bad—like my having been a lady clerk with those people who came here, and having been dismissed on suspicion of taking money. I could get him to believe that wasn't true.

JILL. Yes; and it isn't—that's splendid! You'd be able to put such conviction into it. Don't you think so, Dodo?

HILLCRIST. Anything I can. I'm deeply sorry.

CHLOE. Thank you. And don't say I've been here, will you? He's very suspicious. You see, he knows that his father has re-sold that land to you; that's what he can't make out—that, and my coming here this morning; he knows something's being kept from him; and he noticed that man with Dawker yesterday. And my maid's been spying on me. It's in the air. He puts two and two together. But I've told him there's nothing he need worry about; nothing that's true.

HILLCRIST. What a coil!

CHLOE. I'm very honest and careful about money. So he won't believe that about me, and the old man wants to keep it from Charlie, I know.

HILLCRIST. That does seem the best way out.

CHLOE. [*With a touch of defiance*] I'm a true wife to him.

JILL. Of course we know that.

HILLCRIST. It's all unspeakably sad. Deception's horribly against the grain—but——

CHLOE. [*Eagerly*] When I deceived him, I'd have deceived God Himself—I was so desperate. You've never been right down in the mud. You can't understand what I've been through.

HILLCRIST. Yes, yes. I daresay I'd have done the same. I should be the last to judge—— [CHLOE *covers her eyes with her hands.*] There, there! Cheer up! [*He puts his hand on her arm.*

JILL. [*To herself*] Darling Dodo!

CHLOE. [*Starting*] There's somebody at the door. I must go; I must go. [*She runs to the window and slips through the curtains.*
[*The handle of the door is again turned.*

JILL. [*Dismayed*] Oh! It's locked—I forgot.
[*She springs to the door, unlocks and opens it, while* HILLCRIST *goes to the bureau and sits down.*]
It's all right, Fellows; I was only saying something rather important.

FELLOWS. [*Coming in a step or two and closing the door behind him*] Certainly, Miss. Mr. Charles 'Ornblower is in the hall. Wants to see you, sir, or Mrs. Hillcrist.

JILL. What a bore! Can you see him, Dodo?

HILLCRIST. Er—yes. I suppose so. Show him in here, Fellows.
[*As* FELLOWS *goes out*, JILL *runs to the window, but has no time to do more than adjust the curtains and spring over to stand by her*

father, before CHARLES *comes in. Though in evening clothes, he is white and dishevelled for so spruce a young man.*

CHARLES. Is my wife here ?

HILLCRIST. No, sir.

CHARLES. Has she been ?

HILLCRIST. This morning, I believe, Jill ?

JILL. Yes, she came this morning.

CHARLES. [*Staring at her*] I know that—*now*, I mean ?

JILL. No.   [HILLCRIST *shakes his head.*

CHARLES. Tell me what was said this morning.

HILLCRIST. I was not here this morning.

CHARLES. Don't try to put me off. I know too much. [*To* JILL.] You.

JILL. Shall I, Dodo ?

HILLCRIST. No ; I will. Won't you sit down ?

CHARLES. No. Go on.

HILLCRIST. [*Moistening his lips*] It appears, Mr. Hornblower, that my agent, Mr. Dawker——

[CHARLES, *who is breathing hard, utters a sound of anger.*
—that my agent happens to know a firm, who in old days employed your wife. I should greatly prefer not to say any more, especially as we don't believe the story.

JILL. No ; we don't.

CHARLES. Go on !

HILLCRIST. [*Getting up*] Come ! If I were you, I should refuse to listen to anything against my wife.

CHARLES. Go on, I tell you.

HILLCRIST. You insist ! Well, they say there was some question about the accounts, and your wife left them under a cloud. As I told you, we don't believe it.

CHARLES. [*Passionately*] Liars !   [*He makes a rush for the door.*

HILLCRIST. [*Starting*] What did you say ?

JILL. [*Catching his arm*] Dodo ! [*Sotto voce.*] We are, you know.

CHARLES. [*Turning back to them*] Why do you tell me that lie ? When I've just had the truth out of that little scoundrel ! My wife's been here ; she put you up to it.

[*The face of* CHLOE *is seen transfixed between the curtains, parted by her hands.*]

She—she put you up to it. Liar that she is—a living lie. For three years a living lie.

[HILLCRIST, *whose face alone is turned towards the curtains, sees that listening face. His hand goes up from uncontrollable emotion.*]

And hasn't now the pluck to tell me. I've done with her. I won't own a child by such a woman.

[*With a little sighing sound* CHLOE *drops the curtain and vanishes.*

HILLCRIST. For God's sake, man, think of what you're saying. She's in great distress.

CHARLES. And what am I ?

JILL. She loves you, you know.

CHARLES. Pretty love ! That scoundrel Dawker told me—told me—— Horrible ! Horrible !

HILLCRIST. I deeply regret that our quarrel should have brought this about.

CHARLES. [*With intense bitterness*] Yes, you've smashed my life.

[*Unseen by them*, MRS. HILLCRIST *has entered and stands by the door, Left.*

MRS. H. Would you have wished to live on in ignorance ?

[*They all turn to look at her.*

CHARLES. [*With a writhing movement*] I don't know. But—*you*—*you* did it.

MRS. H. You shouldn't have attacked us.

CHARLES. What did we do to you—compared with this ?

MRS. H. All you could.

HILLCRIST. Enough, enough ! What can we do to help you ?

CHARLES. Tell me where my wife is.

[JILL *draws the curtains apart—the window is open—*JILL *looks out. They wait in silence.*

JILL. We don't know.

CHARLES. Then she *was* here ?

HILLCRIST. Yes, sir ; and she heard you.

CHARLES. All the better if she did. She knows how I feel.

HILLCRIST. Brace up ; be gentle with her.

CHARLES. Gentle ? A woman who—who——

HILLCRIST. A most unhappy creature. Come !

CHARLES. Damn your sympathy !

[*He goes out into the moonlight, passing away Left.*

JILL. Dodo, we ought to look for her ; I'm awfully afraid.

HILLCRIST. I saw her there—listening. With child ! Who knows where things end when they once begin ? To the gravel pit, Jill ; I'll go to the pond. No, we'll go together. [*They go out.*

[MRS. HILLCRIST *comes down to the fireplace, rings the bell and stands there, thinking.* FELLOWS *enters.*

MRS. H. I want someone to go down to Mr. Dawker's.

FELLOWS. Mr. Dawker is here, ma'am, waitin' to see you.

MRS. H. Ask him to come in. Oh ! and, Fellows, you can tell the Jackmans that they can go back to their cottage.

FELLOWS. Very good, ma'am. [*He goes out.*

[MRS. HILLCRIST *searches at the bureau, finds and takes out the deed.* DAWKER *comes in ; he has the appearance of a man whose temper has been badly ruffled.*

Mrs. H. Charles Hornblower—how did it happen?

DAWKER. He came to me. I said I knew nothing. He wouldn't take it; went for me, abused me up hill and down dale; said he knew everything, and then he began to threaten me. Well, I lost my temper, and I told him.

Mrs. H. That's very serious, Dawker, after our promise. My husband is most upset.

DAWKER. [*Sullenly*] It's not my fault, ma'am; he shouldn't have threatened and goaded me on. Besides, it's got out that there's a scandal; common talk in the village—not the facts, but quite enough to cook their goose here. They'll have to go. Better have done with it, anyway, than have enemies at your door.

Mrs. H. Perhaps; but—— Oh! Dawker, take charge of this. [*She hands him the deed.*] These people are desperate—and—I'm not sure of my husband when his feelings are worked on.

[*The sound of a car stopping.*

DAWKER. [*At the window, looking to the Left*] Hornblower's, I think. Yes, he's getting out.

Mrs. H. [*Bracing herself*] You'd better wait, then.

DAWKER. He mustn't give me any of his sauce; I've had enough.

[*The door is opened and* HORNBLOWER *enters, pressing so on the heels of* FELLOWS *that the announcement of his name is lost.*

HORNBLOWER. Give me that deed! Ye got it out of me by false pretences and treachery. Ye swore that nothing should be heard of this. Why! me own servants know!

Mrs. H. That has nothing to do with us. Your son came and wrenched the knowledge out of Mr. Dawker by abuse and threats; that is all. You will kindly behave yourself here, or I shall ask that you be shown out.

HORNBLOWER. Give me that deed, I say! [*He suddenly turns on* DAWKER.] Ye little ruffian, I see it in your pocket.

[*The end indeed is projecting from* DAWKER'S *breast pocket.*

DAWKER. [*Seeing red*] Now, look 'ere, 'Ornblower, I stood a deal from your son, and I'll stand no more.

HORNBLOWER. [*To* Mrs. HILLCRIST] I'll ruin your place yet! [*To* DAWKER.] Ye give me that deed, or I'll throttle you.

[*He closes on* DAWKER, *and makes a snatch at the deed.* DAWKER *springs at him, and the two stand swaying, trying for a grip at each other's throats.* Mrs. HILLCRIST *tries to cross and reach the bell, but is shut off by their swaying struggle.*

[*Suddenly* ROLF *appears in the window, looks wildly at the struggle, and seizes* DAWKER'S *hands, which have reached* HORN-BLOWER'S *throat.* JILL, *who is following, rushes up to him and clutches his arm.*

JILL. Rolf! All of you! Stop! Look!

[DAWKER'S *hand relaxes, and he is swung round.* HORNBLOWER *staggers and recovers himself, gasping for breath. All turn to the window, outside which in the moonlight* HILLCRIST *and* CHARLES HORNBLOWER *have* CHLOE'S *motionless body in their arms.*]

In the gravel pit. She's just breathing; that's all.

MRS. H. Bring her in. The brandy, Jill!

HORNBLOWER. No. Take her to the car. Stand back, young woman! I want no help from any of ye. Rolf—Chearlie—take her up.   [*They lift and bear her away, Left.* JILL *follows.*]

Hillcrist, ye've got me beaten and disgraced hereabouts, ye've destroyed my son's married life, and ye've killed my grandchild. I'm not staying in this cursed spot, but if ever I can do you or yours a hurt, I will.

DAWKER. [*Muttering*] That's right. Squeal and threaten. You began it.

HILLCRIST. Dawker, have the goodness! Hornblower, in the presence of what may be death, with all my heart I'm sorry.

HORNBLOWER. Ye hypocrite!

[*He passes them with a certain dignity, and goes out at the window, following to his car.*

[HILLCRIST, *who has stood for a moment stock-still, goes slowly forward and sits in his swivel chair.*

MRS. H. Dawker, please tell Fellows to telephone to Dr. Robinson to go round to the Hornblowers *at once.*

[DAWKER, *fingering the deed, and with a noise that sounds like* " The cur ! " *goes out, Left.*]

[*At the fireplace.*] Jack! Do you blame me?

HILLCRIST. [*Motionless*] No.

MRS. H. Or Dawker? He's done his best.

HILLCRIST. No.

MRS. H. [*Approaching*] What is it?

HILLCRIST. Hypocrite!   [JILL *comes running in at the window.*

JILL. Dodo, she's moved; she's spoken. It may not be so bad.

HILLCRIST. Thank God for that !   [FELLOWS *enters, Left.*

FELLOWS. The Jackmans, ma'am.

HILLCRIST. Who? What's this?

[*The* JACKMANS *have entered, standing close to the door.*

MRS. J. We're so glad we can go back, sir—ma'am, we just wanted to thank you.   [*There is a silence, they see that they are not welcome.*]

Thank you kindly, sir. Good-night, ma'am.   [*They shuffle out.*

HILLCRIST. I'd forgotten their existence. [*He gets up.*] What is it that gets loose when you begin a fight, and makes you what you think you're not? What blinding evil! Begin as you may, it ends in this—skin game! Skin game!

JILL. [*Rushing to him*] It's not you, Dodo; it's not you, beloved Dodo.

HILLCRIST. It is me. For I am, or should be, master in this house.

MRS. H. I don't understand.

HILLCRIST. When we began this fight, we had clean hands—are they clean now? What's gentility worth if it can't stand fire?

The curtain falls.

A FAMILY MAN

CAST OF ORIGINAL PRODUCTION AT THE COMEDY THEATRE, LONDON, IN MAY, 1921

JOHN BUILDER	*Norman M'Kinnel*
JULIA	*Mary Barton*
ATHENE	*Sibell Archdale*
MAUD	*Agatha Kentish*
RALPH BUILDER	*Arthur Burne*
GUY HERRINGHAME	*Francis Lister*
ANNIE	*Olive Walter*
CAMILLE	*Auriol Lee*
TOPPING	*D. A. Clarke Smith*
THE MAYOR	*Laurence Hanray*
HARRIS	*Eric Lugg*
FRANCIS CHANTREY	*John Howell*
MOON	*Eugene Leaby*
MARTIN	*Julian D'Albie*
A JOURNALIST	*Reginald Bach*

ACT I

SCENE I

Th study of JOHN BUILDER *in the provincial town of Breconridge.   A panelled room wherein nothing is ever studied, except perhaps* BUILDER'S *face in the mirror over the fireplace.   It is, however, comfortable, and has large leather chairs and a writing table in the centre, on which is a type-writer, and many papers.   At the back is a large window with French outside shutters, overlooking the street, for the house is an old one, built in an age when the homes of doctors, lawyers and so forth were part of a provincial town, and not yet suburban.   There are two or three fine old prints on the walls, Right and Left; and a fine old fireplace, Left, with a fender on which one can sit.   A door, Left back, leads into the dining-room, and a door, Right forward, into the hall.*

JOHN BUILDER *is sitting in his after-breakfast chair before the fire with " The Times " in his hands.   He has breakfasted well, and is in that condition of first-pipe serenity in which the affairs of the nation seem almost bearable.   He is a tallish, square, personable man of forty-seven, with a well-coloured, jowly, fullish face, marked under the eyes, which have very small pupils and a good deal of light in them.   His bearing has force and importance, as of a man accustomed to rising and ownerships, sure in his opinions, and not lacking in geniality when things go his way.   Essentially a Midlander.   His wife, a woman of forty-one, of ivory tint, with a thin, trim figure and a face so strangely composed as to be almost like a mask (essentially from Jersey) is putting a nib into a pen-holder, and filling an inkpot at the writing-table.*

As the curtain rises CAMILLE *enters with a rather broken-down cardboard box containing flowers.   She is a young woman with a good figure, a pale face, the warm brown eyes and complete poise of a Frenchwoman.   She takes the box to* MRS. BUILDER.

MRS. BUILDER. The blue vase, please, Camille.

> [CAMILLE *fetches a vase.*   MRS. BUILDER *puts the flowers into the vase.*   CAMILLE *gathers up the debris; and with a glance at* BUILDER *goes out.*

BUILDER. Glorious October!   I ought to have a damned good day's shooting with Chantrey to-morrow.

MRS. BUILDER. [*Arranging the flowers*] Aren't you going to the office this morning?

19*   577

BUILDER. Well, no, I was going to take a couple of days off. If you feel at the top of your form, take a rest—then you go on feeling at the top. [*He looks at her, as if calculating.*] What do you say to looking up Athene ?

MRS. BUILDER. [*Palpably astonished*] Athene ? But you said you'd done with her ?

BUILDER. [*Smiling*] Six weeks ago ; but, dash it, one can't have done with one's own daughter. That's the weakness of an Englishman ; he can't keep up his resentments. In a town like this it doesn't do to have her living by herself. One of these days it'll get out we've had a row. That wouldn't do me any good.

MRS. BUILDER. I see.

BUILDER. Besides, I miss her. Maud's so self-absorbed. It makes a big hole in the family, Julia. You've got her address, haven't you ?

MRS. BUILDER. Yes. [*Very still.*] But do you think it's dignified, John ?

BUILDER. [*Genially*] Oh, hang dignity ! I rather pride myself on knowing when to stand on my dignity and when to sit on it. If she's still crazy about Art, she can live at home, and go out to study.

MRS. BUILDER. Her craze was for liberty.

BUILDER. A few weeks' discomfort soon cures that. She can't live on her pittance. She'll have found that out by now. Get your things on and come with me at twelve o'clock.

MRS. BUILDER. I think you'll regret it. She'll refuse.

BUILDER. Not if I'm nice to her. A child could play with me to-day. Shall I tell you a secret, Julia ?

MRS. BUILDER. It would be pleasant for a change.

BUILDER. The Mayor's coming round at eleven, and I know perfectly well what he's coming for.

MRS. BUILDER. Well ?

BUILDER. I'm to be nominated for Mayor next month. Harris tipped me the wink at the last Council meeting. Not so bad at fortyseven—h'm ? I can make a thundering good Mayor. I can do things for this town that nobody else can.

MRS. BUILDER. Now I understand about Athene.

BUILDER [*Good-humouredly*] Well, it's partly that. But [*more seriously*] it's more the feeling I get that I'm not doing my duty by her. Goodness knows whom she may be picking up with ! Artists are a loose lot. And young people in these days are the limit. I quite believe in moving with the times, but one's either born a Conservative, or one isn't. So you be ready at twelve, see. By the way, that French maid of yours, Julia——

MRS. BUILDER. What about her ?

BUILDER. Is she—er—is she all right ? We don't want any trouble with Topping.

MRS. BUILDER. There will be none with—Topping.

[*She opens the door Left.*

BUILDER. I don't know; she strikes me as—very French.

[MRS. BUILDER *smiles and passes out.*

[BUILDER *fills his second pipe. He is just taking up the paper again when the door from the hall is opened, and the manservant* TOPPING, *dried, dark, sub-humorous, in a black cut-away, announces :*

TOPPING. The Mayor, sir, and Mr. Harris !

[THE MAYOR *of Breconridge enters. He is clean-shaven, red-faced, light-eyed, about sixty, shrewd, poll-parroty, naturally jovial, dressed with the indefinable wrongness of a burgher ; he is followed by his Secretary* HARRIS, *a man all eyes and cleverness.*

[TOPPING *retires.*

BUILDER. [*Rising*] Hallo, Mayor ! What brings you so early ? Glad to see you. Morning, Harris !

MAYOR. Morning, Builder, morning.

HARRIS. Good morning, sir.

BUILDER. Sit down—sit down ! Have a cigar !

[*The* MAYOR *takes a cigar,* HARRIS *a cigarette from his own case.*

BUILDER. Well, Mayor, what's gone wrong with the works ?

[*He and* HARRIS *exchange a look.*

MAYOR. [*With his first puff*] After you left the Council the other day, Builder, we came to a decision.

BUILDER. Deuce you did ! Shall I agree with it ?

MAYOR. We shall see. We want to nominate you for Mayor. You willin' to stand ?

BUILDER. [*Stolid*] That requires consideration.

MAYOR. The only alternative is Chantrey ; but he's a light weight, and rather too much County. What's your objection ?

BUILDER. It's a bit unexpected, Mayor. [*Looks at* HARRIS.] Am I the right man ? Following you, you know. I'm shooting with Chantrey to-morrow. What does he feel about it ?

MAYOR. What do you say, 'Arris ?

HARRIS. Mr. Chantrey's a public school and University man, sir; he's not what I call ambitious.

BUILDER. Nor am I, Harris.

HARRIS. No, sir ; of course you've a high sense of duty. Mr. Chantrey's rather dilettante.

MAYOR. We want a solid man.

BUILDER. I'm very busy, you know, Mayor.

MAYOR. But you've got all the qualifications—big business, family man, live in the town, church-goer, experience on the Council and the Bench. Better say " yes," Builder.

BUILDER. It's a lot of extra work. I don't take things up lightly.

MAYOR. Dangerous times, these. Authority questioned all over the place. We want a man that feels his responsibilities, and we think we've got him in you.

BUILDER. Very good of you, Mayor. I don't know, I'm sure. I must think of the good of the town.

HARRIS. I shouldn't worry about that, sir.

MAYOR. The name John Builder carries weight. You're looked up to as a man who can manage his own affairs. Madam and the young ladies well?

BUILDER. First-rate.

MAYOR. [*Rises*] That's right. Well, if you'd like to talk it over with Chantrey to-morrow. With all this extremism, we want a man of principle and common sense.

HARRIS. We want a man that'll grasp the nettle, sir—and that's you.

BUILDER. H'm! I've got a temper, you know.

MAYOR. [*Chuckling*] We do—we do! You'll say " yes," I see. No false modesty! Come along, 'Arris, we must go.

BUILDER. Well, Mayor, I'll think it over, and let you have an answer. You know my faults, and you know my qualities, such as they are. I'm just a plain Englishman.

MAYOR. We don't want anything better than that. I always say the great point about an Englishman is that he's got bottom; you may knock him off his pins, but you find him on 'em again, before you can say " Jack Robinson." He may have his moments of aberration, but he's a sticker. Morning, Builder, morning! Hope you'll say " yes."

> [*He shakes hands and goes out, followed by* HARRIS.
> [*When the door is closed* BUILDER *stands a moment quite still with a gratified smile on his face; then turns and scrutinizes himself in the glass over the hearth. While he is doing so the door from the dining-room is opened quietly and* CAMILLE *comes in.* BUILDER, *suddenly seeing her reflected in the mirror, turns.*

BUILDER. What is it, Camille?

CAMILLE. Madame send me for a letter she say you have, Monsieur, from the dyer and cleaner, with a bill.

BUILDER. [*Feeling in his pockets*] Yes—no. It's on the table.

> [CAMILLE *goes to the writing-table and looks.*

That blue thing.

CAMILLE. [*Taking it up*] Non, Monsieur, this is from the gas.

BUILDER. Oh! Ah!

> [*He moves up to the table and turns over papers.* CAMILLE *stands motionless close by with her eyes fixed on him.*]

Here it is! [*He looks up, sees her looking at him, drops his own gaze, and hands her the letter. Their hands touch. Putting his hands in his pockets.*] What made you come to England?

CAMILLE. [*Demure*] It is better pay, Monsieur, and [*With a smile*] the English are so amiable.

BUILDER. Deuce they are !   They haven't got that reputation.

CAMILLE. Oh ! I admire Englishmen.   They are so strong and kind.

BUILDER. [*Bluffly flattered*] H'm !   We've no manners.

CAMILLE. The Frenchman is more polite, but not in the 'eart.

BUILDER. Yes.   I suppose we're pretty sound at heart.

CAMILLE. And the Englishman have his life in the family—the Frenchman have his life outside.

BUILDER. [*With discomfort*] H'm !

CAMILLE. [*With a look*] Too mooch in the family—like a rabbit in a 'utch.

BUILDER. Oh !   So that's your view of us !

[*His eyes rest on her, attracted but resentful.*

CAMILLE. Pardon, Monsieur, my tongue run away with me.

BUILDER. [*Half conscious of being led on*] Are you from Paris ?

CAMILLE. [*Clasping her hands*] Yes.   What a town for pleasure—Paris !

BUILDER. I suppose so.   Loose place, Paris.

CAMILLE. Loose ?   What is that, Monsieur ?

BUILDER. The opposite of strict.

CAMILLE. Strict !   Oh !   certainly we like life, we other French. It is not like England.   I take this to Madame, Monsieur. [*She turns as if to go.*] Excuse me.

BUILDER. I thought you Frenchwomen all married young.

CAMILLE. I 'ave been married ; my 'usband did die—*en Afrique.*

BUILDER. You wear no ring.

CAMILLE. [*Smiling*] I prefare to be mademoiselle, Monsieur.

BUILDER. [*Dubiously*] Well, it's all the same to us. [*He takes a letter up from the table.*] You might take this to Mrs. Builder too.

[*Again their fingers touch, and there is a suspicion of encounter between their eyes.*   [CAMILLE *goes out.*

BUILDER. [*Turning to his chair*] Don't know about that woman—she's a tantalizer.

[*He compresses his lips, and is settling back into his chair, when the door from the hall is opened and his daughter* MAUD *comes in ; a pretty girl, rather pale, with fine eyes.   Though her face has a determined cast her manner at this moment is by no means decisive.   She has a letter in her hand, and advances rather as if she were stalking her father, who, after a "* Hallo, Maud ! *" has begun to read his paper.*

MAUD. [*Getting as far as the table*] Father.

BUILDER. [*Not lowering the paper*] Well ?   I know that tone.   What do *you* want—money ?

MAUD. I always want money, of course ; but—but——

BUILDER. [*Pulling out a note—abstractedly*] Here's five pounds for you [MAUD, *advancing, takes it, then seems to find what she has come for more on her chest than ever.*

BUILDER. [*Unconscious*] Will you take a letter for me?

    [MAUD *sits down Left of table and prepares to take down the letter.* [*Dictating.*] " Dear Mr. Mayor,—Referring to your call this morning, I have—er—given the matter very careful consideration, and though somewhat reluctant——"

MAUD. Are you really reluctant, father?

BUILDER. Go on—" To assume greater responsibilities, I feel it my duty to come forward in accordance with your wish. The—er—honour is one of which I hardly feel myself worthy, but you may rest assured——"

MAUD. Worthy. But you do, you know.

BUILDER. Look here! Are you trying to get a rise out of me?—because you won't succeed this morning.

MAUD. I thought you were trying to get one out of me.

BUILDER. Well, how would *you* express it?

MAUD. " I know I'm the best man for the place, and so do you——"

BUILDER. The disrespect of you young people is something extraordinary. And that reminds me : where do you go every evening now after tea?

MAUD. I—I don't know.

BUILDER. Come now, that won't do—you're never in the house from six to seven.

MAUD. Well! It has to do with my education.

BUILDER. Why, you finished that two years ago!

MAUD. Well, call it a hobby, if you like, then, father.

    [*She takes up the letter she brought in and seems on the point of broaching it.*

BUILDER. Hobby? Well, what is it?

MAUD. I don't want to irritate you, father.

BUILDER. You can't irritate me more than by having secrets. See what they led to in your sister's case. And, by the way, I'm going to put an end to that this morning. You'll be glad to have her back, won't you?

MAUD. [*Startled*] What!

BUILDER. Your mother and I are going round to Athene at twelve o'clock. I shall make it up with her. She must come back here.

MAUD. [*Aghast, but hiding it*] Oh! It's—it's no good, father. She won't.

BUILDER. We shall see that. I've quite got over my tantrum, and I expect she has.

MAUD. [*Earnestly*] Father! I do really assure you she won't; it's only wasting your time, and making you eat humble pie.

BUILDER. Well, I can eat a good deal this morning. It's all nonsense! A family's a family.

MAUD. [*More and more disturbed, but hiding it*] Father, if I were you, I wouldn't—really! It's not—dignified.

BUILDER. You can leave me to judge of that. It's not dignified for the Mayor of this town to have an unmarried daughter as young as Athene living by herself away from home. This idea that she's on a visit won't wash any longer. Now finish that letter—"worthy, but you may rest assured that I shall do my best to sustain the—er—dignity of the office."   [MAUD *types desperately.*] Got that? "And—er—preserve the tradition so worthily——" No—"so staunchly"—er—er——

MAUD. Upheld.

BUILDER. Ah! "—upheld by yourself.—Faithfully yours."

MAUD. [*Finishing*] Father, you thought Athene went off in a huff. It wasn't that a bit. She always meant to go. She just got you into a rage to make it easier. She *hated* living at *home*.

BUILDER. Nonsense! Why on earth should she?

MAUD. Well, she did! And so do—— [*Checking herself.*] And so you see it'll only make you ridiculous to go.

BUILDER. [*Rises*] Now what's behind this, Maud?

MAUD. Behind—— Oh! nothing!

BUILDER. The fact is, you girls have been spoiled, and you enjoy twisting my tail; but you can't make me roar this morning. I'm too pleased with things. You'll see, it'll be all right with Athene.

MAUD. [*Very suddenly*] Father!

BUILDER. [*Grimly humorous*] Well! Get it off your chest. What's that letter about?

MAUD. [*Failing again and crumpling the letter behind her back*] Oh! nothing.

BUILDER. Everything's nothing this morning. Do you know what sort of people Athene associates with now—I suppose you see her?

MAUD. Sometimes.

BUILDER. Well?

MAUD. Nobody much. There isn't anybody here to associate with. It's all hopelessly behind the times.

BUILDER. Oh! you think so! That's the inflammatory fiction you pick up. I tell you what, young woman—the sooner you and your sister get rid of your silly notions about not living at home, and making your own way, the sooner you'll both get married and make it. Men don't like the new spirit in women—they may say they do, but they don't.

MAUD. *You* don't father, I know.

BUILDER. Well, I'm very ordinary. If you keep your eyes open, you'll soon see that.

MAUD. Men don't like freedom for anybody but themselves.

BUILDER. That's not the way to put it. [*Tapping out his pipe.*] Women in your class have never had to face realities.

MAUD. No, but we want to.

BUILDER. [*Good-humouredly*] Well, I'll bet you what you like, Athene's dose of reality will have cured her.

MAUD. And I'll bet you—— No, I won't!

BUILDER. You'd better not. Athene will come home, and only too glad to do it. Ring for Topping and order the car at twelve.

> [*As he opens the door to pass out,* MAUD *starts forward, but checks herself.*

MAUD. [*Looking at her watch*] Half-past eleven! Good heavens!
> [*She goes to the bell and rings. Then goes back to the table, and writes an address on a bit of paper.* [TOPPING *enters Right.*

TOPPING. Did you ring, Miss?

MAUD. [*With the paper*] Yes. Look here, Topping! Can you manage—on your bicycle—now at once? I want to send a message to Miss Athene—awfully important. It's just this: "Look out! Father is coming." [*Holding out the paper.*] Here's her address. You must get there and away again by twelve. Father and mother want the car then to go there. Order it before you go. It won't take you twenty minutes on your bicycle. It's down by the river near the ferry. But you mustn't be seen by them either going or coming.

TOPPING. If I should fall into their hands, Miss, shall I eat the despatch?

MAUD. Rather! You're a brick, Topping. Hurry up!

TOPPING. Nothing more precise, Miss?

MAUD. M—m—— No.

TOPPING. Very good, Miss Maud. [*Conning the address.*] "Briary Studio, River Road. Look out! Father is coming!" I'll go out the back way. Any answer?

MAUD. No.   [TOPPING *nods his head and goes out.*

MAUD. [*To herself*] Well, it's all I can do.

> [*She stands, considering, as the curtain falls.*

SCENE II

The Studio, to which are attached living rooms, might be rented at eighty pounds a year—some painting and gear indeed, but an air of life rather than of work. Things strewn about. Bare walls, a sloping skylight, no windows; no fireplace visible; a bedroom door, stage Right; a kitchen door, stage Left. A door, Centre back, into the street. The door knocker is going.

From the kitchen door, Left, comes the very young person, ANNIE, *in blotting-*

paper blue linen, with a white Dutch cap.   She is pretty, her cheeks rosy, and her forehead puckered.   She opens the street door.   Standing outside is TOPPING.   *He steps in a pace or two.*

TOPPING. Miss Builder live here ?

ANNIE. Oh ! no, sir ; Mrs. Herringhame.

TOPPING. Mrs. Herringhame !   Oh ! young lady with dark hair and large expressive eyes ?

ANNIE. Oh ! yes, sir.

TOPPING. With an " A.B." on her linen ?   [*Moves to table.*

ANNIE. Yes, sir.

TOPPING. And " Athene Builder " on her drawings ?

ANNIE. [*Looking at one*] Yes, sir.

TOPPING. Let's see. [*He examines the drawing.*] Mrs. Herringhame, you said ?

ANNIE. Oh ! yes, sir.

TOPPING. Wot oh !

ANNIE. Did you want anything, sir ?

TOPPING. Drop the " sir," my dear ; I'm the Builders' man. Mr. Herringhame in ?

ANNIE. Oh ! no, sir.

TOPPING. Take a message. I can't wait. From Miss Maud Builder. " Look out ! Father is coming." Now, whichever of 'em comes in first—that's the message, and don't you forget it.

ANNIE. Oh ! no, sir.

TOPPING. So they're married ?

ANNIE. Oh ! I don't know, sir.

TOPPING. I see. Well, it ain't known to Builder, J.P., either. That's why there's a message. See ?

ANNIE. Oh ! yes, sir.

TOPPING. Keep your head. I must hop it. From Miss Maud Builder. " Look out ! Father is coming."

[*He nods, turns and goes, pulling the door to behind him.* ANNIE *stands " baff " for a moment.*

ANNIE. Ah !

[*She goes across to the bedroom on the Right, and soon returns with a suit of pyjamas, a toothbrush, a pair of slippers and a case of razors, which she puts on the table, and disappears into the kitchen. She reappears with a bread pan, which she deposits in the centre of the room ; then crosses again to the bedroom, and once more reappears with a clothes brush, two hair brushes, and a Norfolk jacket. As she stuffs all these into the bread pan and bears it back into the kitchen, there is the sound of a car driving up and stopping.* ANNIE *reappears at the kitchen door just as the knocker sounds.*

ANNIE. Vexin' and provokin'! [*Knocker again. She opens the door.*]
Oh! [MR. *and* MRS. BUILDER *enter.*

BUILDER. Mr. and Mrs. Builder. My daughter in?

ANNIE. [*Confounded*] Oh! sir, no, sir.

BUILDER. My good girl, not "Oh! sir, no, sir." Simply: No,
sir. See?

ANNIE. Oh! sir, yes, sir.

BUILDER. Where is she?

ANNIE. Oh! sir, I don't know, sir.

BUILDER. [*Fixing her as though he suspected her of banter*] Will she be
back soon?

ANNIE. No, sir.

BUILDER. How do you know?

ANNIE. I d-don't, sir.

BUILDER. Then why do you say so? [*About to mutter* "She's an
idiot!" *he looks at her blushing face and panting figure, pats her on the
shoulder and says*] Never mind; don't be nervous.

ANNIE. Oh! yes, sir. Is that all, please, sir?

MRS. BUILDER. [*With a side look at her husband and a faint smile*] Yes;
you can go.

ANNIE. Thank you, ma'am.

[*She turns and hurries out into the kitchen, Left.* BUILDER *gazes
after her, and* MRS. BUILDER *gazes at* BUILDER *with her faint
smile.*

BUILDER. [*After the girl is gone*] Quaint and Dutch—pretty little
figure! [*Staring round.*] H'm! Extraordinary girls are! Fancy
Athene preferring this to home. What?

MRS. BUILDER. I didn't say anything.

BUILDER. [*Placing a chair for his wife, and sitting down himself*] Well,
we must wait, I suppose. Confound that Nixon legacy! If Athene
hadn't had that potty little legacy left her, she couldn't have done this.
Well, I daresay it's all spent by now. I made a mistake to lose my
temper with her.

MRS. BUILDER. Isn't it always a mistake to lose one's
temper?

BUILDER. That's very nice and placid; sort of thing you women
who live sheltered lives can say. I often wonder if you women
realize the strain on a business man.

MRS. BUILDER. [*In her softly ironical voice*] It seems a shame to add
the strain of family life.

BUILDER. You've always been so passive. When I want a thing
I've got to have it.

MRS. BUILDER. I've noticed that.

BUILDER. [*With a short laugh*] Odd if you hadn't, in twenty-three
years. [*Touching a canvas standing against the chair with his toe.*] Art!

Just a pretext.   We shall be having Maud wanting to cut loose next.
She's very restive.   Still, I oughtn't to have had that scene with
Athene.   I ought to have put quiet pressure.   [MRS. BUILDER *smiles*.

BUILDER. What are you smiling at ?

[MRS. BUILDER *shrugs her shoulders*.]
Look at this—— Cigarettes ! [*He examines the brand on the box*.]
Strong, very—and not good ! [*He opens the door*.] Kitchen ! [*He shuts
it, crosses, and opens the door, Right*.] Bedroom !

MRS. BUILDER. [*To his disappearing form*] Do you think you ought,
John ?

[*He has disappeared, and she ends with an expressive movement of
   her hands, a long sigh, and a closing of her eyes.* BUILDER'S
   peremptory voice is heard : " Julia !"]
What now ?   [*She follows into the bedroom.*

[*The maid* ANNIE *puts her head out of the kitchen door ; she comes
   out a step as if to fly ; then, at* BUILDER'S *voice, shrinks back
   into the kitchen.*

[BUILDER, *reappearing with a razor strop in one hand and a shaving-
   brush in the other, is followed by* MRS. BUILDER.

BUILDER. Explain these !   My God !   Where's that girl ?

MRS. BUILDER. John !   Don't ! [*Getting between him and the kitchen
door*.] It's not dignified.

BUILDER. I don't care a damn.

MRS. BUILDER. John, you mustn't.   Athene has the tiny beginning
of a moustache, you know.

BUILDER. What !   I shall stay and clear this up if I have to
wait a week.   Men who let their daughters——— !   This age is the
limit.

[*He makes a vicious movement with the strop, as though laying it
   across someone's back.*

MRS. BUILDER. She would never stand that.   Even wives object,
nowadays.

BUILDER. [*Grimly*] The war's upset everything.   Women are
utterly out of hand.   Why the deuce doesn't she come ?

MRS. BUILDER. Suppose you leave me here to see her.

BUILDER. [*Ominously*] This is my job.

MRS. BUILDER. I think it's more mine.

BUILDER. Don't stand there opposing everything I say !   I'll go
and have another look—— [*He is going towards the bedroom when the
sound of a latchkey in the outer door arrests him. He puts the strop and
brush behind his back, and adds in a low voice*] Here she is !

[MRS. BUILDER *has approached him, and they have both turned
   towards the opening door.* GUY HERRINGHAME *comes in.
   They are a little out of his line of sight, and he has shut the door
   before he sees them. When he does, his mouth falls open, and*

his hand on to the knob of the door. He is a comely young man
in Harris tweeds. Moreover, he is smoking. He would speak
if he could, but his surprise is too excessive.

BUILDER. Well, sir ?

GUY. [*Recovering a little*] I was about to say the same to you, sir.

BUILDER. [*Very red from repression*] These rooms are not yours,
are they ?

GUY. Nor yours, sir.

BUILDER. May I ask if you know whose they are ?

GUY. My sister's.

BUILDER. Your—you——!

MRS. BUILDER. John !

BUILDER. Will you kindly tell me why your sister signs her drawings
by the name of my daughter, Athene Builder—and has a photograph
of my wife hanging there ?

> [*The* YOUNG MAN *looks at* MRS. BUILDER *and winces, but recovers*
> *himself.*

GUY. [*Boldly*] As a matter of fact this *is* my sister's studio ; she's
in France—and has a friend staying here.

BUILDER. Oh ! And you have a key ?

GUY. My sister's.

BUILDER. Does your sister shave ?

GUY. I—I don't think so.

BUILDER. No. Then perhaps you'll tell me what these mean ?

> [*He takes out the strop and shaving-stick.*

GUY. Oh ! Ah ! Those things ?

BUILDER. Yes. Now then ?

GUY. [*Addressing* MRS. BUILDER] Need we go into this in your
presence, ma'am ? It seems rather delicate.

BUILDER. What explanation have you got ?

GUY. Well, you see——

BUILDER. No lies ; out with it !

GUY. [*With decision*] I prefer to say nothing.

BUILDER. What's your name ?

GUY. Guy Herringhame.

BUILDER. Do you live here ?   [GUY *makes no sign.*

MRS. BUILDER. [*To* GUY] I think you had better go.

BUILDER. Julia, *will* you leave me to manage this ?

MRS. BUILDER. [*To* GUY] When do you expect my daughter in ?

GUY. Now—directly.

MRS. BUILDER. [*Quietly*] Are you married to her ?

GUY. Yes. That is—no-o ; not altogether, I mean.

BUILDER. What's that ? Say that again !

GUY. [*Folding his arms*] I'm not going to say another word.

BUILDER. I am.

MRS. BUILDER. John—please!

BUILDER. Don't put your oar in! I've had wonderful patience so far. [*He puts his boot through a drawing.*] Art! This is what comes of it! Are *you* an artist?

GUY. No; a flying man. The truth is——

BUILDER. I don't want to hear *you* speak the truth. I'll wait for my daughter.

GUY. If you do, I hope you'll be so very good as to be gentle. If you get angry I might too, and that would be awfully ugly.

BUILDER. Well, I'm damned!

GUY. I quite understand that, sir. But, as a man of the world, I hope you'll take a pull before she comes, if you mean to stay.

BUILDER. *If* we mean to stay! That's good!

GUY. Will you have a cigarette?

BUILDER. I—I can't express——

GUY. [*Soothingly*] Don't try, sir. [*He jerks up his chin, listening.*] I think that's her. [*Goes to the door.*] Yes. Now, please! [*He opens the door.*] Your father and mother, Athene.

[ATHENE *enters. She is flushed and graceful. Twenty-two, with a short upper lip, a straight nose, dark hair, and glowing eyes. She wears bright colours, and has a slow, musical voice, with a slight lisp.*

ATHENE. Oh! How are you, mother dear? This is rather a surprise. Father always keeps his word, so I certainly didn't expect *him*.   [*She looks steadfastly at* BUILDER, *but does not approach.*

BUILDER. [*Controlling himself with an effort*] Now, Athene, what's this?

ATHENE. What's what?

BUILDER. [*The strop held out*] Are you married to this—this——?

ATHENE. [*Quietly*] To all intents and purposes.

BUILDER. In law?

ATHENE. No.

BUILDER. My God! You—you——!

ATHENE. Father, don't call names, please.

BUILDER. Why aren't you married to him?

ATHENE. Do you want a lot of reasons, or the real one?

BUILDER. This is maddening!   [*Goes up stage.*

ATHENE. Mother dear, will you go into the other room with Guy?
          [*She points to the door Right.*

BUILDER. Why?

ATHENE. Because I would rather she didn't hear the reason.

GUY. [*To* ATHENE, *sotto voce*] He's not safe.

ATHENE. Oh! yes; go on.

[GUY *follows* MRS. BUILDER, *and after hesitation at the door they go out into the bedroom.*

BUILDER. Now then !

ATHENE. Well, father, if you want to know the real reason, it's—you.

BUILDER. What on earth do you mean ?

ATHENE. Guy wants to marry me. In fact, we—— But I had such a scunner of marriage from watching you at home, that I——

BUILDER. Don't be impudent ! My patience is at breaking-point, I warn you.

ATHENE. I'm perfectly serious, father. I tell you, we meant to marry, but so far I haven't been able to bring myself to it. You never noticed how we children have watched you.

BUILDER. Me ?

ATHENE. Yes. You and mother, and other things ; all sorts of things——

BUILDER. [Taking out a handkerchief and wiping his brow] I really think you're mad.

ATHENE. I'm sure you must, dear.

BUILDER. Don't " dear " me ! What have you noticed ? D'you mean I'm not a good husband and father ?

ATHENE. Look at mother. I suppose you can't, now ; you're too used to her.

BUILDER. Of course I'm used to her. What else is marrying for ?

ATHENE. That ; and the production of such as me. And it isn't good enough, father. You shouldn't have set us such a perfect example.

BUILDER. You're talking the most arrant nonsense I ever heard. [He lifts his hands.] I've a good mind to shake it out of you.

ATHENE. Shall I call Guy ?   [He drops his hands.] Confess that being a good husband and father has tried you terribly. It has us, you know.

BUILDER. [Taking refuge in sarcasm] When you've quite done being funny, perhaps you'll tell me why you've behaved like a common street flapper.

ATHENE. [Simply] I couldn't bear to think of Guy as a family man. That's all—absolutely. It's not his fault ; he's been awfully anxious to be one.

BUILDER. You've disgraced us, then ; that's what it comes to.

ATHENE. I don't want to be unkind, but you've brought it on yourself.

BUILDER. [Genuinely distracted] I can't even get a glimmer of what you mean. I've never been anything but firm. Impatient, perhaps. I'm not an angel ; no ordinary healthy man is. I've never grudged you girls any comfort, or pleasure.

ATHENE. Except wills of our own.

BUILDER. What do you want with wills of your own till you're married ?

ATHENE. You forget mother !

BUILDER. What about her ?

ATHENE. She's very married. Has she a will of her own ?

BUILDER. [Sullenly] She's learnt to know when I'm in the right.

ATHENE. I don't ever mean to learn to know when Guy's in the right. Mother's forty-one, and twenty-three years of that she's been your wife. It's a long time, father. Don't you ever look at her face ?

BUILDER. [Troubled in a remote way] Rubbish !

ATHENE. I didn't want my face to get like that.

BUILDER. With such views about marriage, what business had you to go near a man ? Come, now !

ATHENE. Because I fell in love.

BUILDER. Love leads to marriage—and to nothing else, but the streets. What an example to your sister !

ATHENE. You don't know Maud any more than you knew me. She's got a will of her own, too, I can tell you.

BUILDER. Now, look here, Athene. It's always been my way to face accomplished facts. What's done can't be undone ; but it can be remedied. You must marry this young—— at once, before it gets out. He's behaved like a ruffian : but, by your own confession, you've behaved worse. You've been bitten by this modern disease, this—this utter lack of common decency. There's an eternal order in certain things, and marriage is one of them ; in fact, it's the chief. Come, now. Give me a promise, and I'll try my utmost to forget the whole thing.

ATHENE. When we quarrelled, father, you said you didn't care what became of me.

BUILDER. I was angry.

ATHENE. So you are now.

BUILDER. Come, Athene, don't be childish ! Promise me !

ATHENE. [With a little shudder] No ! We were on the edge of it. But now I've seen you again—— Poor mother !

BUILDER. [Very angry] This is simply blasphemous. What do you mean by harping on your mother ? If you think that—that—she doesn't—that she isn't——

ATHENE. Now, father !

BUILDER. I'm damned if I'll sit down under this injustice. Your mother is—is pretty irritating, I can tell you. She—she—— Everything suppressed. And—and no—blood in her !

ATHENE. I knew it !

BUILDER. [Aware that he has confirmed some thought in her that he had no intention of confirming] What's that ?

ATHENE. Don't you ever look at your own face, father? When you shave, for instance.

BUILDER. Of course I do.

ATHENE. It isn't satisfied, is it?

BUILDER. I don't know what on earth you mean.

ATHENE. You can't help it, but you'd be ever so much happier if you were a Mohammedan, and two or three, instead of one, had—had learned to know when you were in the right.

BUILDER. 'Pon my soul! This is outrageous!

ATHENE. Truth often is.

BUILDER. Will you be quiet?

ATHENE. I don't ever want to feel sorry for Guy in that way.

BUILDER. I think you're the most immodest—— I'm ashamed that you're my daughter. If your mother had ever carried on as you are now——

ATHENE. Would you have been firm with her?

BUILDER. [*Really sick at heart at this unwonted mockery which meets him at every turn*] Be quiet, you——!

ATHENE. Has mother never turned?

BUILDER. You're an unnatural girl! Go your own way to hell!

ATHENE. I am not coming back *home*, father.

BUILDER. [*Wrenching open the door, Right*] Julia! Come! We can't stay here.   [MRS. BUILDER *comes forth, followed by* GUY.] As for you, sir, if you start by allowing a woman to impose her crazy ideas about marriage on you, all I can say is—I despise you. [*He crosses to the outer door, followed by his wife. To* ATHENE.] I've done with *you* !   [*He goes out.*

           [MRS. BUILDER, *who has so far seemed to accompany him, shuts the door quickly and remains in the studio. She stands there with that faint smile on her face, looking at the two young people.*

ATHENE. Awfully sorry, mother; but don't you see what a scunner father's given me?

MRS. BUILDER. My dear, all men are not alike.

GUY. I've always told her that, ma'am.

ATHENE. [*Softly*] Oh! mother, I'm so sorry for you.

           [*The handle of the door is rattled, a fist is beaten on it.* [*She stamps, and covers her ears.*] Disgusting!

GUY. Shall I——?

MRS. BUILDER. [*Shaking her head*] I'm going in a moment. [*To* ATHENE.] You owe it to me, Athene.

ATHENE. Oh! if somebody would give him a lesson!

                               [BUILDER'S *voice :* " Julia ! "]

Have you ever tried, mother?

           [MRS. BUILDER *looks at the* YOUNG MAN, *who turns away out of hearing.*

MRS. BUILDER. Athene, you're mistaken. I've always stood up to him in my own way.

ATHENE. Oh! but, mother—listen!

[*The beating and rattling have recommenced, and the voice :* "Are you coming ?"]

[*Passionately.*] And that's family life! Father was all right before he married, I expect. And now it's like this. How you survive——!

MRS. BUILDER. He's only in a passion, my dear.

ATHENE. It's wicked.

MRS. BUILDER. It doesn't work otherwise, Athene.

[*A single loud bang on the door.*

ATHENE. If he beats on that door again, I shall scream.

[MRS. BUILDER *smiles, shakes her head, and turns to the door.*

MRS. BUILDER. Now, my dear, you're going to be sensible, to please me. It's really best. If *I* say so, it must be. It's all comedy, Athene.

ATHENE. Tragedy!

GUY. [*Turning to them*] Look here! Shall I shift him?

[MRS. BUILDER *shakes her head and opens the door.* BUILDER *stands there, a furious figure.*

BUILDER. Will you come, and leave that baggage and her cad?

[MRS. BUILDER *steps quickly out and the door is closed.* GUY *makes an angry movement towards it.*

ATHENE. Guy!

GUY. [*Turning to her*] That puts the top hat on. So persuasive! [*He takes out of his pocket a wedding ring, and a marriage licence.*] Well! What's to be done with these pretty things, now?

ATHENE. Burn them!

GUY. [*Slowly*] Not quite. You can't imagine I should ever be like that, Athene?

ATHENE. Marriage does wonders.

GUY. Thanks.

ATHENE. Oh! Guy, don't be horrid. I feel awfully bad.

GUY. Well, what do you think I feel? "Cad!"

[*They turn to see* ANNIE *in hat and coat, with a suit-case in her hand, coming from the door Left.*

ANNIE. Oh! ma'am, please, Miss, I want to go home.

GUY. [*Exasperated*] She wants to go home—she wants to go home!

ATHENE. Guy! All right, Annie.

ANNIE. Oh! thank you, Miss.   [*She moves across in front of them.*

ATHENE. [*Suddenly*] Annie!   [ANNIE *stops and turns to her.*] What are you afraid of?

ANNIE. [*With comparative boldness*] I—I might catch it, Miss.

ATHENE. From your people?

ANNIE. Oh! no, Miss; from you. You see, I've got a young man that wants to marry me. And if I don't let him, I might get into trouble meself.

ATHENE. What sort of father and mother have you got, Annie?

ANNIE. I never thought, Miss. And of course I don't want to begin.

ATHENE. D'you mean you've never noticed how they treat each other?

ANNIE. I don't think they do, Miss.

ATHENE. Exactly.

ANNIE. They haven't time. Father's an engine driver.

GUY. And what's your young man, Annie?

ANNIE. [*Embarrassed*] Somethin' like you, sir. But very respectable.

ATHENE. And suppose you marry him, and he treats you like a piece of furniture?

ANNIE. I—I could treat him the same, Miss.

ATHENE. Don't you believe that, Annie!

ANNIE. He's very mild.

ATHENE. That's because he wants you. You wait till he doesn't.

[ANNIE *looks at* GUY.

GUY. Don't you believe her, Annie; if he's decent——

ANNIE. Oh! yes, sir.

ATHENE. [*Suppressing a smile*] Of course—but the point is, Annie, that marriage makes all the difference.

ANNIE. Yes, Miss; that's what I thought.

ATHENE. You don't see. What I mean is that when once he's sure of you, he may change completely.

ANNIE. [*Slowly, looking at her thumb*] Oh! I don't—think—he'll hammer me, Miss. Of course, I know you can't tell till you've found out.

ATHENE. Well, I've no right to influence you.

ANNIE. Oh! no, Miss; that's what I've been thinking.

GUY. You're quite right, Annie—this is no place for you.

ANNIE. You see, we can't be married, sir, till he gets his rise. So it'll be a continual temptation to me.

ATHENE. Well, all right, Annie. I hope you'll never regret it.

ANNIE. Oh! no, Miss.

GUY. I say, Annie, don't go away thinking evil of us; we didn't realize you knew we weren't married.

ATHENE. We certainly did not.

ANNIE. Oh! I didn't think it right to take notice.

GUY. We beg your pardon.

ANNIE. Oh! no, sir. Only, seein' Mr. and Mrs. Builder so upset, brought it 'ome like. And father *can* be 'andy with a strap.

ATHENE. There you are !   *Force majeure !*

ANNIE. Oh ! yes, Miss.

ATHENE. Well, good-bye, Annie.   What are you going to say to your people ?

ANNIE. Oh ! I shan't say I've been livin' in a family that wasn't a family, Miss.   It wouldn't do no good.

ATHENE. Well, here are your wages.

ANNIE. Oh ! I'm puttin' you out, Miss.   [*She takes the money.*

ATHENE. Nonsense, Annie.   And here's your fare home.

ANNIE. Oh ! thank you, Miss.   I'm very sorry.   Of course if you was to change your mind——   [*She stops, embarrassed.*

ATHENE. I don't think——

GUY. [*Abruptly*] Good-bye, Annie.   Here's five bob for the movies.

ANNIE. Oh ! good-bye, sir, and thank you.   I was goin' there now with my young man.   He's just round the corner.

GUY. Be very careful of him.

ANNIE. Oh ! yes, sir, I will.   Good-bye, sir.   Good-bye, Miss.
          [*She goes.*

GUY. So *her* father has a firm hand too.   But it takes *her* back to the nest.   How's that, Athene ?

ATHENE. [*Playing with a leathern button on his coat*] If you'd watched it ever since you could watch anything, seen it kill out all——   It's having power that does it.   I know father's got awfully good points.

GUY. Well, they don't stick out.

ATHENE. He works fearfully hard ; he's upright, and plucky. He's not stingy.   But he's smothered his animal nature—and that's done it.   I don't want to see you smother anything, Guy.

GUY. [*Gloomily*] I suppose one never knows what one's got under the lid.   If he hadn't come here to-day——   [*He spins the wedding ring.*] He certainly gives one pause.   Used he to whack you ?

ATHENE. Yes.

GUY. Brute !

ATHENE. With the best intentions.   You see, he's a Town Councillor, and a magistrate.   I suppose they *have* to be "*firm.*"   Maud and I sneaked in once to listen to him.   There was a woman who came for protection from her husband.   If he'd known we were there, he'd have had a fit.

GUY. Did he give her the protection ?

ATHENE. Yes ; he gave her back to the husband.   Wasn't it— English ?

GUY. [*With a grunt*] Hang it !   We're not all like that.

ATHENE. [*Twisting his button*] I think it's really a sense of property so deep that they don't know they've got it.   Father can *talk* about freedom like a—politician.

GUY. [*Fitting the wedding ring on her finger*] Well! Let's see how it looks, anyway.

ATHENE. Don't play with fire, Guy.

GUY. There's something in atavism, darling; there really is. I like it—I do. [*A knock on the door.*

ATHENE. That sounds like Annie again. Just see.

GUY. [*Opening the door*] It is. Come in, Annie. What's wrong now?

ANNIE. [*Entering in confusion*] Oh! sir, please, sir—I've told my young man.

ATHENE. Well, what does he say?

ANNIE. 'E was 'orrified, Miss.

GUY. The deuce he was! At our conduct?

ANNIE. Oh! no, sir—at mine.

ATHENE. But you did your best; you left us.

ANNIE. Oh! yes, Miss; that's why 'e's horrified.

GUY. Good for your young man.

ANNIE. [*Flattered*] Yes, sir. 'E said I 'ad no strength of mind.

ATHENE. So you want to come back?

ANNIE. Oh! yes, Miss.

ATHENE. All right.

GUY. But what about catching it?

ANNIE. Oh, sir, 'e said there was nothing like Epsom salts.

GUY. He's a wag, your young man.

ANNIE. He was in the Army, sir.

GUY. You said he was respectable.

ANNIE. Oh! yes, sir; but not so respectable as that.

ATHENE. Well, Annie, get your things off, and lay lunch.

ANNIE. Oh! yes, Miss.

[*She makes a little curtsey and passes through into the kitchen.*

GUY. Strength of mind! Have a little, Athene—won't you?

[*He holds out the marriage licence before her.*

ATHENE. I don't know—I don't know! If—it turned out——

GUY. It won't. Come on. Must take chances in this life.

ATHENE. [*Looking up into his face*] Guy, promise me—solemnly that you'll never let me stand in your way, or stand in mine!

GUY. Right! That's a bargain. [*They embrace.*

[ATHENE *quivers towards him. They embrace fervently as* ANNIE *enters with the bread pan. They spring apart.*

ANNIE. Oh!

GUY. It's all right, Annie. There's only one more day's infection before you. We're to be married to-morrow morning.

ANNIE. Oh! yes, sir. Won't Mr. Builder be pleased?

GUY. H'm! That's not exactly our reason.

ANNIE. [*Right*] Oh! no, sir. Of course you can't be a family without, can you?

GUY. What have you got in that thing?

     [ANNIE *is moving across with the bread pan. She halts at the bedroom door.*

ANNIE. Oh! please, ma'am, I was to give you a message—very important—from Miss Maud Builder: "Look out! Father is coming!"   [*She goes out.*

The curtain falls.

ACT II

Builder's *study.* *At the table,* Maud *has just put a sheet of paper into a typewriter. She sits facing the audience, with her hands stretched over the keys.*

Maud. [*To herself*] I must get that expression.

[*Her face assumes a furtive, listening look. Then she gets up, whisks to the mirror over the fireplace, scrutinizes the expression in it, and going back to the table, sits down again with hands outstretched above the keys, and an accentuation of the expression. The door up Left is opened, and* Topping *appears. He looks at* Maud, *who just turns her eyes.*

Topping. Lunch has been ready some time, Miss Maud.

Maud. I don't want any lunch. Did you give it?

Topping. Miss Athene was out. I gave the message to a young party. She looked a bit green, Miss. I hope nothing'll go wrong with the works. Shall I keep lunch back?

Maud. If something's gone wrong, they won't have any appetite, Topping.

Topping. If you think I might risk it, Miss, I'd like to slip round to my dentist. [*He lays a finger on his cheek.*

Maud. [*Smiling*] Oh! What race is being run this afternoon, then, Topping?

Topping. [*Twinkling, and shifting his finger to the side of his nose*] Well, I don't suppose you've 'eard of it, Miss; but as a matter of fact it's the Cesarwitch.

Maud. Got anything on?

Topping. Only my shirt, Miss.

Maud. Is it a good thing, then?

Topping. I've seen worse roll up. [*With a touch of enthusiasm.*] Dark horse, Miss Maud, at twenty to one.

Maud. Put me ten bob on, Topping. I want all the money I can get, just now.

Topping. You're not the first, Miss.

Maud. I say, Topping, do you know anything about the film?

Topping. [*Nodding*] Rather a speciality of mine, Miss.

Maud. Well, just stand there, and give me your opinion of this.

[Topping *moves down Left.*

[*She crouches over the typewriter, lets her hands play on the keys;*

598

> *stops; assumes that listening, furtive look; listens again, and*
> *lets her head go slowly round, preceded by her eyes; breaks it*
> *off, and says:*

What should you say I was?

TOPPING. Guilty, Miss.

MAUD. [*With triumph*] There! Then you think I've got it?

TOPPING. Well, of course, I couldn't say just what sort of a crime you'd committed, but I should think pretty 'ot stuff.

MAUD. Yes; I've got them here.   [*She pats her chest.*

TOPPING. Really, Miss.

MAUD. Yes. There's just one point, Topping; it's psychological.

TOPPING. Indeed, Miss?

MAUD. Should I naturally put my hand on them; or would there be a reaction quick enough to stop me? You see, I'm alone—and the point is whether the fear of being seen would stop me although I knew I couldn't be seen. It's rather subtle.

TOPPING. I think there'd be a rehaction, Miss.

MAUD. So do I. To touch them [*She clasps her chest*] is a bit obvious, isn't it?

TOPPING. If the haudience knows you've got 'em there.

MAUD. Oh! yes, it's seen me put them. Look here, I'll show you that too.

> [*She opens an imaginary drawer, takes out some bits of sealing-wax,*
> *and with every circumstance of stealth in face and hands, conceals*
> *them in her bosom.*]

All right?

TOPPING. [*Nodding*] Fine, Miss. You *have* got a film face. What *are* they, if I may ask?

MAUD. [*Reproducing the sealing-wax*] The Fanshawe diamonds. There's just one thing here too, Topping. In real life, which should I naturally do—put them in here [*She touches her chest*] or in my bag?

TOPPING. [*Touching his waistcoat—earnestly*] Well! To put 'em in *here*, Miss, I should say is more—more pishchological.

MAUD. [*Subduing her lips*] Yes; but——

TOPPING. You see, then you've got 'em on you.

MAUD. But that's just the point. Shouldn't I naturally think: Safer in my bag; then I can pretend somebody put them there. You see, nobody could put them on me.

TOPPING. Well, I should say that depends on your character. Of course I don't know what your character is.

MAUD. No; that's the beastly part of it—the author doesn't, either. It's all left to me.

TOPPING. In that case, I should please myself, Miss. To put 'em in 'ere's warmer.

MAUD. Yes, I think you're right. It's more human.

TOPPING. I didn't know you 'ad a taste this way, Miss Maud.

MAUD. More than a taste, Topping—a talent.

TOPPING. Well, in my belief, we all have a vice about us some-where. But if I were you, Miss, I wouldn't touch bettin', not with this other on you. You might get to feel a bit crowded.

MAUD. Well, then, only put the ten bob on if you're *sure* he's going to win. You can post the money on after me. I'll send you an address, Topping, because I shan't be here.

TOPPING. [*Disturbed*] What! You're not going, too, Miss Maud?

MAUD. To seek my fortune.

TOPPING. Oh! Hang it all, Miss, think of what you'll leave behind. Miss Athene's leavin' home has made it pretty steep, but this'll touch bottom—this will.

MAUD. Yes; I expect you'll find it rather difficult for a bit when I'm gone. Miss Baldini, you know. I've been studying with her. She's got me this chance with the movie people. I'm going on trial as the guilty typist in " The Heartache of Miranda."

TOPPING. [*Surprised out of politeness*] Well, I never! That does sound like 'em! Are you goin' to tell the guv'nor, Miss?

[MAUD *nods.*]

In that case, I think I'll be gettin' off to my dentist before the band plays.

MAUD. All right, Topping; hope you won't lose a tooth.

TOPPING. [*With a grin*] It's on the knees of the gods, Miss, as they say in the headlines.   [*He goes.* MAUD *stretches herself and listens.*

MAUD. I believe that's them. Shivery funky. [*She runs off up Left.*

BUILDER. [*Entering from the hall and crossing to the fireplace*] Monstrous! Really monstrous!

[CAMILLE *enters from the hall. She has a little collecting book in her hand.*

BUILDER. Well, Camille?

CAMILLE. A sistare from the Sacred 'Eart, Monsieur—her little book for the orphan children.

BUILDER. I can't be bothered—*What is it?*

CAMILLE. Orphan, Monsieur.

BUILDER. H'm! Well! [*Feeling in his breast pocket.*] Give her that.

[*He hands her a five-pound note.*

CAMILLE. I am sure she will be veree grateful for the poor little beggars. Madame says she will not be coming to lunch, Monsieur.

BUILDER. *I* don't want any, either. Tell Topping I'll have some coffee.

CAMILLE. Topping has gone to the dentist, Monsieur; 'e 'as the toothache.

BUILDER. Toothache—poor devil! H'm! I'm expecting my brother, but I don't know that I can see him.

CAMILLE. No, Monsieur?

BUILDER. Ask your mistress to come here.

[*He looks up, and catching her eye, looks away.*

CAMILLE. Yes, Monsieur.

[*As she turns he looks swiftly at her, sweeping her up and down. She turns her head and catches his glance, which is swiftly dropped.*]

Will Monsieur not 'ave anything to eat?

BUILDER. [*Shaking his head—abruptly*] No.   Bring the coffee!

CAMILLE. Is Monsieur not well?

BUILDER. Yes—quite well.

CAMILLE. [*Sweetening her eyes*] A cutlet soubise?   No?

BUILDER. [*With a faint response in his eyes, instantly subdued*] Nothing! nothing!

CAMILLE. And Madame nothing too—Tt! Tt!

[*With her hand on the door she looks back, again catches his eyes in an engagement instantly broken off, and goes out.*

BUILDER. [*Stock-still, and staring at the door*] That girl's a continual irritation to me!   She's dangerous!   What a life!   I believe that girl—— [*The door Left is opened and* MRS. BUILDER *comes in.*

BUILDER. There's some coffee coming; do your head good.   Look here, Julia.   I'm sorry I beat on that door.   I apologize.   I was in a towering passion.   I wish I didn't get into these rages.   But—dash it all——!   I couldn't walk away and leave you there.

MRS. BUILDER. Why not?

BUILDER. You keep everything to yourself, so; I never have any notion what you're thinking.   What *did* you say to her?

MRS. BUILDER. Told her it would never work.

BUILDER. Well, that's something.   She's crazy.   D'you suppose she was telling the truth about that young blackguard wanting to marry her?

MRS. BUILDER. I'm sure of it.

BUILDER. When you think of how she's been brought up.   You would have thought that religion alone——

MRS. BUILDER. The girls haven't *wanted* to go to church for years. They've always said they didn't see why they should go to keep up your position.   I don't know if you remember that you once caned them for running off on a Sunday morning.

BUILDER. Well?

MRS. BUILDER. They've never had any religion since.

BUILDER. H'm!   [*He takes a short turn up the room.*]   What's to be done about Athene?

MRS. BUILDER. You said you had done *with* her.

BUILDER. You know I didn't mean that.   I might just as well have said I'd done with you!   Apply your wits, Julia!   At any moment

20

this thing may come out. In a little town like this you can keep nothing dark. How can I take this nomination for Mayor?

Mrs. Builder. Perhaps Ralph could help.

Builder. What? His daughters have never done anything disgraceful, and his wife's a pattern.

Mrs. Builder. Yes; Ralph isn't at all a family man.

Builder. [*Staring at her*] I do wish you wouldn't turn things upside down in that ironical way. It isn't—English.

Mrs. Builder. I can't help having been born in Jersey.

Builder. No; I suppose it's in your blood. The French——

[*He stops short.*

Mrs. Builder. Yes?

Builder. Very irritating sometimes to a plain Englishman—that's all.

Mrs. Builder. Shall I get rid of Camille?

Builder. [*Staring at her, then dropping his glance*] Camille? What's she got to do with it?

Mrs. Builder. I thought perhaps you found *her* irritating.

Builder. Why should I?

[CAMILLE *comes in from the dining-room with the coffee.*]
Put it there. I want some brandy, please.

Camille. I bring it, Monsieur.

[*She goes back demurely into the dining-room.*

Builder. Topping's got toothache, poor chap! [*Pouring out the coffee.*] Can't you suggest any way of making Athene see reason? Think of the example! Maud will be kicking over next. I shan't be able to hold my head up here.

Mrs. Builder. I'm afraid I can't do that for you.

Builder. [*Exasperated*] Look here, Julia! That wretched girl said something to me about our life together. What—what's the matter with that?

Mrs. Builder. It is irritating.

Builder. Be explicit.

Mrs. Builder. We have lived together twenty-three years, John. No talk will change such things.

Builder. Is it a question of money? You can always have more. You know that. [Mrs. Builder *smiles.*] Oh! don't smile like that; it makes me feel quite sick!

[CAMILLE *enters with a decanter and little glasses, from the dining-room.*

Camille. The brandy, sir. Monsieur Ralph Builder has just come.

Mrs. Builder. Ask him in, Camille.

Camille. Yes, Madame. [*She goes through the doorway into the hall.*

[Mrs. Builder, *following towards the door, meets* Ralph Builder, *a man rather older than* Builder *and of opposite build and manner. He has a pleasant, whimsical face and grizzled hair.*

MRS. BUILDER. John wants to consult you, Ralph.

RALPH. That's very gratifying.

[*She passes him and goes out, leaving the two brothers eyeing one another.*]

About the Welsh contract?

BUILDER. No.   Fact is, Ralph, something very horrible's happened.

RALPH. Athene gone and got married?

BUILDER. No.   It's—it's that she's gone and—and not got married.

[RALPH *utters a sympathetic whistle.*]

Jolly, isn't it?

RALPH. To whom?

BUILDER. A young flying bounder.

RALPH. And why?

BUILDER. Some crazy rubbish about family life, of all things.

RALPH. Athene's a most interesting girl.   All these young people are so queer and delightful.

BUILDER. By George, Ralph, you may thank your stars you haven't got a delightful daughter.   Yours are good, decent girls.

RALPH. Athene's tremendously good and decent, John.   I'd bet any money she's doing this on the highest principles.

BUILDER. Behaving like a——

RALPH. Don't say what you'll regret, old man!   Athene always took things seriously—bless her!

BUILDER. Julia thinks you might help.   You never seem to have any domestic troubles.

RALPH. No-o.   I don't think we do.

BUILDER. How d'you account for it?

RALPH. I must ask at home.

BUILDER. Dash it!   You must know!

RALPH. We're all fond of each other.

BUILDER. Well, I'm fond of my girls too; I suppose I'm not amiable enough.   H'm?

RALPH. Well, old man, you do get blood to the head.   But what's Athene's point, exactly?

BUILDER. Family life isn't idyllic, so she thinks she and the young man oughtn't to have one.

RALPH. I see.   Home experience?

BUILDER. Hang it all, a family's a family!   There must be a head.

RALPH. But no tail, old chap.

BUILDER. You don't let your women folk do just as they like?

RALPH. Always.

BUILDER. What happens if one of your girls wants to do an improper thing?   [RALPH *shrugs his shoulders.*]   You don't stop her?

RALPH. Do you?

BUILDER. I try to.

RALPH. Exactly. And she does it. I don't and she doesn't.

BUILDER. [*With a short laugh*] Good Lord! I suppose you'd have me eat humble pie and tell Athene she can go on living in sin and offending society, and have my blessing to round it off.

RALPH. I think if you did she'd probably marry him.

BUILDER. You've never tested your theory, I'll bet.

RALPH. Not yet.

BUILDER. There you are.

RALPH. The *suaviter in modo* pays, John. The times are not what they were.

BUILDER. Look here! I want to get to the bottom of this. Do you tell me I'm any stricter than nine out of ten men?

RALPH. Only in practice.

BUILDER. [*Puzzled*] How do you mean?

RALPH. Well, you profess the principles of liberty, but you practise the principles of government.

BUILDER. H'm! [*Taking up the decanter.*] Have some?

RALPH. No, thank you. [BUILDER *fills and raises his glass.*

CAMILLE. [*Entering*] Madame left her coffee.

[*She comes forward, holds out a cup for* BUILDER *to pour into, takes it and goes out.* BUILDER'S *glass remains suspended. He drinks the brandy off as she shuts the door.*

BUILDER. Life isn't all roses, Ralph.

RALPH. Sorry old man.

BUILDER. I sometimes think I try myself too high. Well, about that Welsh contract?

RALPH. Let's take it.

BUILDER. If you'll attend to it. Frankly, I'm too upset.

[*As they go towards the door into the hall,* MAUD *comes in from the dining-room, in hat and coat.*

RALPH. [*Catching sight of her*] Hallo! All well in your cosmogony, Maud?

MAUD. What is a cosmogony, Uncle?

RALPH. My dear, I—I don't know.

[*He goes out, followed by* BUILDER. MAUD *goes quickly to the table, sits down and rests her elbows on it, her chin on her hands, looking at the door.*

BUILDER. [*Re-entering*] Well, Maud! You'd have won your bet!

MAUD. Oh! father, I—I've got some news for you.

BUILDER. [*Staring at her*] News—what?

MAUD. I'm awfully sorry, but I—I've got a job.

BUILDER. Now, don't go saying you're going in for Art, too, because I won't have it.

MAUD. Art? Oh! no! It's the—— [*With a jerk*] the Movies.

[BUILDER, *who has taken up a pipe to fill, puts it down.*

BUILDER. [*Impressively*] I'm not in a joking mood.

MAUD. I'm not joking, father.

BUILDER. Then what are you talking about?

MAUD. You see, I—I've got a film face, and——

BUILDER. You've what? [*Going up to his daughter, he takes hold of her chin.*] Don't talk nonsense! Your sister has just tried me to the limit.

MAUD. [*Removing his hand from her chin*] Don't oppose it, father, please! I've always wanted to earn my own living.

BUILDER. Living! Living!

MAUD. [*Gathering determination*] You can't stop me, father, because I shan't need support. I've got quite good terms.

BUILDER. [*Almost choking, but mastering himself*] Do you mean to say you've gone as far as that?

MAUD. Yes. It's all settled.

BUILDER. Who put you up to this?

MAUD. No one. I've been meaning to, ever so long. I'm twenty-one, you know.

BUILDER. A film face! Good God! Now, look here! I will not have a daughter of mine mixed up with the stage. I've spent goodness knows what on your education—both of you.

MAUD. I don't want to be ungrateful; but I—I can't go on living at home.

BUILDER. You can't——! Why? You've every indulgence.

MAUD. [*Clearly and coldly*] I can remember occasions when your indulgence hurt, father. [*She wriggles her shoulders and back.*] We never forgot or forgave that.

BUILDER. [*Uneasily*] That! You were just kids.

MAUD. Perhaps you'd like to begin again?

BUILDER. Don't twist my tail, Maud. I had the most painful scene with Athene this morning. Now come! Give up this silly notion! It's really too childish!

MAUD. [*Looking at him curiously*] I've heard you say ever so many times that no man was any good who couldn't make his own way, father. Well, women are the same as men, now. It's the law of the country. I only want to make my own way.

BUILDER. [*Trying to subdue his anger*] Now, Maud, don't be foolish. Consider my position here—a Town Councillor, a Magistrate, and Mayor next year. With one daughter living with a man she isn't married to——

MAUD. [*With lively interest*] Oh! So you did catch them out?

BUILDER. D'you mean to say you knew?

MAUD. Of course.

BUILDER. My God! I thought we were a Christian family.

MAUD. Oh! father.

BUILDER. Don't sneer at Christianity!

MAUD. There's only one thing wrong with Christians—they aren't!

[BUILDER *seizes her by the shoulders and shakes her vigorously. When he drops her shoulders, she gets up, gives him a vicious look, and suddenly stamps her foot on his toe with all her might.*

BUILDER. [*With a yowl of pain*] You little devil!

MAUD. [*Who has put the table between them*] I won't stand being shaken.

BUILDER. [*Staring at her across the table*] You've got my temper up and you'll take the consequences. I'll make you toe the line.

MAUD. If you knew what a Prussian expression you've got!

[BUILDER *passes his hand across his face uneasily, as if to wipe something off.*]

No! It's too deep!

BUILDER. Are you my daughter or are you not?

MAUD. I certainly never wanted to be. I've always disliked you, father, ever since I was so high. I've seen through you. Do you remember when you used to come into the nursery because Jenny was pretty? You think we didn't notice that, but we did. And in the schoolroom—Miss Tipton. And d'you remember knocking our heads together? No, you don't; but we do. And——

BUILDER. You disrespectful monkey! Will you be quiet?

MAUD. No; you've got to hear things. You don't really love anybody but yourself, father. What's good for you has to be good for everybody. I've often heard you talk about independence, but it's a limited company and you've got all the shares.

BUILDER. Rot; only people who can support themselves have a right to independence.

MAUD. That's why you don't want me to support myself.

BUILDER. You can't! Film, indeed! You'd be in the gutter in a year. Athene's got her pittance, but you—you've got nothing.

MAUD. Except my face.

BUILDER. It's the face that brings women to ruin, my girl.

MAUD. Well, when I'm there I won't come to you to rescue me.

BUILDER. Now, mind—if you leave my house, I've done with you.

MAUD. I'd rather scrub floors now, than stay.

BUILDER. [*Almost pathetically*] Well, I'm damned! Look here, Maud—all this has been temper. You got my monkey up. I'm sorry I shook you; you've had your revenge on my toes. Now, come! Don't make things worse for me than they are. You've all the liberty you can reasonably want till you marry.

MAUD. He can't see it—he absolutely can't!

BUILDER. See what?

MAUD. That I want to live a life of my own.

[*He edges nearer to her, and she edges to keep her distance.*

BUILDER. I don't know what's bitten you.

MAUD. The microbe of freedom; it's in the air.

BUILDER. Yes, and there it'll stay—that's the first sensible word you've uttered. Now, come! Take your hat off, and let's be friends !   [MAUD *looks at him and slowly takes off her hat.*

BUILDER. [*Relaxing his attitude, with a sigh of relief*] That's right !
                                                    [*Crosses to fireplace.*

MAUD. [*Springing to the door leading to the hall*] Good-bye, father !

BUILDER. [*Following her*] Monkey !

[*At the sound of a bolt shot,* BUILDER *goes up to the window. There is a fumbling at the door, and* CAMILLE *appears.*

BUILDER. What's the matter with that door ?

CAMILLE. It was bolted, Monsieur.

BUILDER. Who bolted it ?

CAMILLE. [*Shrugging her shoulders*] I can't tell, Monsieur.
                          [*She collects the cups, and halts close to him.*]
[*Softly.*] Monsieur is not 'appy.

BUILDER. [*Surprised*] What ? No ! Who'd be happy in a household like mine ?

CAMILLE. But so strong a man—I wish *I* was a strong man, not a weak woman.

BUILDER. [*Regarding her with reluctant admiration*] Why, what's the matter with *you* ?

CAMILLE. Will Monsieur have another glass of brandy before I take it ?

BUILDER. No !   Yes—I will.

[*She pours it out, and he drinks it, hands her the glass and sits down suddenly in an armchair.* CAMILLE *puts the glass on a tray, and looks for a box of matches from the mantelshelf.*

CAMILLE. A light, Monsieur ?

BUILDER. Please.

CAMILLE. [*She trips over his feet and sinks on to his knee*] Oh ! Monsieur !   [BUILDER *flames up and catches her in his arms.*]
Oh ! Monsieur !

BUILDER. You little devil !

[*She suddenly kisses him, and he returns the kiss. While they are engaged in this entrancing occupation,* MRS. BUILDER *opens the door from the hall, watches unseen for a few seconds, and quietly goes out again.*

BUILDER. [*Pushing her back from him, whether at the sound of the door or of a still small voice*] What am I doing ?

CAMILLE. Kissing.

BUILDER. I—I forgot myself.   [*They rise.*

CAMILLE. It was na-ice.

BUILDER. I didn't mean to.   You go away—go away !

CAMILLE. Oh ! Monsieur, that spoil it.

BUILDER. [*Regarding her fixedly*] It's my opinion you're a temptation of the devil. You know you sat down on purpose.

CAMILLE. Well, perhaps.

BUILDER. What business had you to? I'm a family man.

CAMILLE. Yes. What a pity! But does it matter?

BUILDER. [*Much beset*] Look here, you know! This won't do! It won't do! I—I've got my reputation to think of!

CAMILLE. So 'ave I! But there is lots of time to think of it in between.

BUILDER. I knew you were dangerous. I always knew it.

CAMILLE. What a thing to say of a little woman!

BUILDER. We're not in Paris.

CAMILLE. [*Clasping her hands*] Oh! 'Ow I wish we was!

BUILDER. Look here—I can't stand this; you've got to go. Out with you! I've always kept a firm hand on myself, and I'm not going to——

CAMILLE. But I admire you so!

BUILDER. Suppose my wife had come in?

CAMILLE. Oh! Don't suppose any such a disagreeable thing! If you were not so strict, you would feel much 'appier.

BUILDER. [*Staring at her*] You're a temptress!

CAMILLE. I lofe pleasure, and I don't get any. And you 'ave such a duty, you don't get any sport. Well, I am 'ere!

[*She stretches herself, and* BUILDER *utters a deep sound.*]

BUILDER. [*On the edge of succumbing*] It's all against my—I won't do it! It's—it's wrong!

CAMILLE. Oh! La, la!

BUILDER. [*Suddenly revolting*] No! If you thought it a sin—I might. But you don't; you're nothing but a—a little heathen.

CAMILLE. Why should it be better if I thought it a sin?

BUILDER. Then—then I should know where I was. As it is——

CAMILLE. The English 'ave no idea of pleasure. They make it all so coarse and virtuou‹

BUILDER. Now, out y‹ go before I——! Go on!

[*He goes over to t‹ door and opens it. His wife is outside in a hat and coat. S‹ comes in.*]

[*Stammering.*] Oh! He‹ you are—I wanted you.

[CAMILLE, *takin‹ up the tray, goes out Left, swinging her hips a very little.*

BUILDER. Going out?

MRS. BUILDER. Obviously.

BUILDER. Where?

MRS. BUILDER. I don't know at present.

BUILDER. I wanted to talk to you about—Maud.

MRS. BUILDER. It must wait.

BUILDER. She's—she's actually gone and——

MRS. BUILDER. I must tell you that I happened to look in a minute ago.

BUILDER. [*In absolute dismay*] You! You what?

MRS. BUILDER. Yes. I will put no obstacle in the way of your pleasures.

BUILDER. [*Aghast*] Put no obstacle? What do you mean? Julia, how can you say a thing like that? Why, I've only just——

MRS. BUILDER. Don't! I saw.

BUILDER. The girl *fell* on my knees. Julia, she did. She's—she's a little devil. I—I resisted her. I give you my word there's been nothing beyond a kiss, under great provocation. I—I apologize.

MRS. BUILDER. [*Bows her head*] Thank you! I quite understand. But you must forgive my feeling it impossible to remain a wet blanket any longer.

BUILDER. What! Because of a little thing like that—all over in two minutes, and I doing my utmost.

MRS. BUILDER. My dear John, the fact that you had to do your utmost is quite enough. I feel continually humiliated in your house, and I want to leave it—quite quietly, without fuss of any kind.

BUILDER. But—my God! Julia, this is awful—it's absurd! How can you? I'm your husband. Really—your saying you don't mind what I do—it's not right; it's immoral!

MRS. BUILDER. I'm afraid you don't see what goes on in those who live with you. So, I'll just go. Don't bother!

BUILDER. Now, look here, Julia, you can't mean this seriously. You can't! Think of my position! You've never set yourself up against me before.

MRS. BUILDER. But I do now.

BUILDER. [*After staring at her*] I've given you no real reason. I'll send the girl away. You ought to thank me for resisting a temptation that most men would have yielded to. After twenty-three years of married life, to kick up like this—you ought to be ashamed of yourself.

MRS. BUILDER. I'm sure you must think so.

BUILDER. Oh! for heaven's sake don't be sarcastic! You're my wife, and there's an end of it; you've no legal excuse. Don't be absurd!

MRS. BUILDER. Good-bye!

BUILDER. D'you realize that you're encouraging me to go wrong? That's a pretty thing for a wife to do. You ought to keep your husband straight.

MRS. BUILDER. How beautifully put!

BUILDER. [*Almost pathetically*] Don't rile me, Julia! I've had an awful day. First Athene—then Maud—then that girl—and now you! All at once like this? Like a swarm of bees about one's head. [*Pleading.*] Come, now, Julia, don't be so—so impracticable! You'll

20*

make us the laughing-stock of the whole town. A man in my position, and can't keep his own family; it's preposterous!

MRS. BUILDER. Your own family have lives and thoughts and feelings of their own.

BUILDER. Oh! This damned Woman's business! I knew how it would be when we gave you the vote. You and I are married, and our daughters are our daughters. Come, Julia. Where's your common-sense? After twenty-three years! You know I can't do without you!

MRS. BUILDER. You could—quite easily. You can tell people what you like.

BUILDER. My God! I never heard anything so immoral in all my life from the mother of two grown-up girls. No wonder they've turned out as they have! What is it you want, for goodness' sake!

MRS. BUILDER. We just want to be away from you, that's all. I assure you it's best. When you've shown some consideration for our feelings and some real sign that we exist apart from you—we could be friends again—perhaps—I don't know.

BUILDER. Friends! Good heavens! With one's own wife and daughters! [*With great earnestness.*] Now, look here, Julia, you haven't lived with me all this time without knowing that I'm a man of strong passions; I've been a faithful husband to you—yes, I have. And that means resisting all sorts of temptations you know nothing of. If you withdraw from my society I won't answer for the consequences. In fact, I can't have you withdrawing. I'm not going to see myself going to the devil and losing the good opinion of everybody round me. A bargain's a bargain. And until I've broken my side of it, and I tell you I haven't—you've no business to break yours. That's flat. So now, put all that out of your head.

MRS. BUILDER. No.

BUILDER. [*Intently*] D'you realize that I've supported you in luxury and comfort?

MRS. BUILDER. I think I've earned it.

BUILDER. And how do you propose to live? *I* shan't give you a penny. Come, Julia, don't be such an idiot! Fancy letting a kiss which no man could have helped, upset you like this!

MRS. BUILDER. The Camille, and the last straw!

BUILDER. [*Sharply*] I won't have it. So now you know.

[*But* MRS. BUILDER *has very swiftly gone.*]
Julia, I tell you—— [*The outer door is heard being closed.*] Damnation! I will not have it! They're all mad! Here—where's my hat?

[*He looks distractedly round him, wrenches open the door, and a moment later the street door is heard to shut with a bang.*

The curtain falls.

ACT III

SCENE I

Ten o'clock the following morning, in the study of the Mayor of Breconridge, a panelled room with no window visible, a door Left back and a door Right forward. The entire back wall is furnished with books from floor to ceiling; the other walls are panelled and bare. Before the fireplace, Left, are two armchairs, and other chairs are against the walls. On the Right is a writing-bureau at right angles to the footlights, with a chair behind it. At its back corner stands HARRIS, *telephoning.*

HARRIS. What—[*Pause.*] Well, it's infernally awkward, Sergeant. . . . The Mayor's in a regular stew. . . . [*Listens.*] New constable? I should think so! Young fool! Look here, Martin, the only thing to do is to hear the charge *here* at once. I've sent for Mr. Chantrey; he's on his way. Bring Mr. Builder and the witnesses round sharp. See? And, I say, for God's sake keep it dark. Don't let the Press get on to it. Why you didn't let him go home——! Black eye! The constable? Well, serve him right. Blundering young ass! I mean, it's undermining all authority. . . . Well, you oughtn't—at least, I . . . Damn it all!—it's a nine days' wonder if it gets out——! All right! As soon as you can. [*He hangs up the receiver, puts a second chair behind the bureau, and other chairs facing it.*] [*To himself.*] Here's a mess! Johnny Builder, of all men! What price Mayors! [*The telephone rings.*] Hallo? . . . Poaching charge? Well, bring him too; only, I say, keep him back till the other's over. By the way, Mr. Chantrey's going shooting. He'll want to get off by eleven. What? . . . Righto!

[*As he hangs up the receiver the* MAYOR *enters. He looks worried, and is still dressed with the indefinable wrongness of a burgher.*

MAYOR. Well, 'Arris?

HARRIS. They'll be over in five minutes, Mr. Mayor.

MAYOR. Mr. Chantrey?

HARRIS. On his way, sir.

MAYOR. I've had some awkward things to deal with in my time, 'Arris, but this is just about the [*Sniffs*] limit.

HARRIS. Most uncomfortable, sir; most uncomfortable!

MAYOR. Put a book on the chair, 'Arris; I like to sit 'igh.

[HARRIS *puts a volume of Encyclopædia on the Mayor's chair behind the bureau.*]

611

[*Deeply.*] Our fellow-magistrate! A family man! In my shoes next year. I suppose he won't be, now. You can't keep these things dark.

HARRIS. I've warned Martin, sir, to use the utmost discretion. Here's Mr. Chantrey.

> [*By the door Left, a pleasant and comely gentleman has entered, dressed with indefinable rightness in shooting clothes.*

MAYOR. Ah, Chantrey!

CHANTREY. How de do, Mr. Mayor? [*Nodding to* HARRIS.] This is extraordinarily unpleasant.   [*The* MAYOR *nods.*] What on earth's he been doing?

HARRIS. Assaulting one of his own daughters with a stick; and resisting the police.

CHANTREY. [*With a low whistle*] Daughter! Charity begins at home!

HARRIS. There's a black eye.

MAYOR. Whose?

HARRIS. The constable's.

CHANTREY. How did the police come into it?

HARRIS. I don't know, sir. The worst of it is he's been at the police station since four o'clock yesterday. The Superintendent's away, and Martin never will take responsibility.

CHANTREY. By George! he will be mad. John Builder's a choleric fellow.

MAYOR. [*Nodding*] He is. 'Ot temper, and an 'igh sense of duty.

HARRIS. There's one other charge, Mr. Mayor—poaching. I told them to keep that back till after.

CHANTREY. Oh, well, we'll make short work of that. I want to get off by eleven, Harris. I shall be late for the first drive anyway. John Builder! I say, Mayor—but for the grace of God, there go we!

MAYOR. Harris, go out and bring them in yourself; don't let the servants——   [HARRIS *goes out Left.*

> [*The* MAYOR *takes the upper chair behind the bureau, sitting rather higher because of the book than* CHANTREY, *who takes the lower. Now that they are in the seats of justice, a sort of reticence falls on them, as if they were afraid of giving away their attitudes of mind to some unseen presence.*

MAYOR. [*Suddenly*] H'm!

CHANTREY. Touch of frost. Birds ought to come well to the guns —no wind. I like these October days.

MAYOR. I think I 'ear them. H'm.

> [CHANTREY *drops his eyeglass and puts on a pair of " grandfather " spectacles. The* MAYOR *clears his throat and takes up a pen. They neither of them look up as the door is opened and a little procession files in. First* HARRIS; *then* RALPH

> BUILDER, ATHENE, HERRINGHAME, MAUD, MRS. BUILDER,
> SERGEANT MARTIN, *carrying a heavy Malacca cane with a*
> *silver knob*; JOHN BUILDER *and the* CONSTABLE MOON,
> *a young man with one black eye. No funeral was ever attended*
> *by mutes so solemn and dejected. They stand in a sort of row.*

MAYOR. [*Without looking up*] Sit down, ladies; sit down.

> [HARRIS *and* HERRINGHAME *succeed in placing the three women in*
> *chairs.* RALPH BUILDER *also sits.* HERRINGHAME *stands*
> *behind.* JOHN BUILDER *remains standing between the* TWO
> POLICEMEN. *His face is unshaved and menacing, but he stands*
> *erect staring straight at the* MAYOR. HARRIS *goes to the side*
> *of the bureau, Back, to take down the evidence.*

MAYOR. Charges!

SERGEANT. John Builder, of The Cornerways, Breconridge, Con-
tractor and Justice of the Peace, charged with assaulting his daughter
Maud Builder by striking her with a stick in the presence of Con-
stable Moon and two other persons; also with resisting Constable
Moon in the execution of his duty, and injuring his eye. Constable
Moon!

MOON. [*Stepping forward—one, two—like an automaton, and saluting*]
In River Road yesterday afternoon, Your Worship, about three-
thirty p.m., I was attracted by a young woman callin' "Constable"
outside a courtyard. On hearing the words "Follow me, quick,"
I followed her to a painter's studio inside the courtyard, where I
found three persons in the act of disagreement. No sooner 'ad I
appeared than the defendant, who was engaged in draggin' a woman
towards the door, turns to the young woman who accompanied me,
with violence. "You dare, father," she says; whereupon he hit
her twice with the stick the same which is produced, in the presence
of myself and the two other persons, which I'm given to understand
is his wife and other daughter.

MAYOR. Yes; never mind what you're given to understand.

MOON. No, sir. The party struck turns to me and says, "Come
in. I give this man in charge for assault." I moves accordingly with
the words: "I saw you. Come along with me." The defendant
turns to me sharp and says: "You stupid lout—I'm a magistrate."
"Come off it," I says to the best of my recollection. "You struck
this woman in my presence," I says, "and you come along!" We
were then at close quarters. The defendant gave me a push with the
words "Get out, you idiot!" "Not at all," I replies, and took 'old
of his arm. A struggle ensues, in the course of which I receives
the black eye which I herewith produce.

> [*He touches his eye with awful solemnity.*
> [*The* MAYOR *clears his throat;* CHANTREY'S *eyes goggle;* HARRIS
> *bends over and writes rapidly.*]

During the struggle, Your Worship, a young man has appeared on the scene, and at the instigation of the young woman, the same who was assaulted, assists me in securing the prisoner, whose language and resistance was violent in the extreme. We placed him in a cab which we found outside, and I conveyed him to the station.

CHANTREY. What was his—er—conduct in the—er—cab?

MOON. He sat quiet.

CHANTREY. That seems——

MOON. Seein' I had his further arm twisted behind him.

MAYOR. [*Looking at* BUILDER] Any questions to ask him?

[BUILDER *makes not the faintest sign, and the* MAYOR *drops his glance.*

MAYOR. Sergeant?

[MOON *steps back two paces, and the* SERGEANT *steps two paces forward.*

SERGEANT. At ten minutes to four, Your Worship, yesterday afternoon, Constable Moon brought the defendant to the station in a four-wheeled cab. On his recounting the circumstances of the assault, they were taken down and read over to the defendant with the usual warning. The defendant said nothing. In view of the double assault and the condition of the constable's eye, and in the absence of the Superintendent, I thought it my duty to retain the defendant for the night.

MAYOR. The defendant said nothing?

SERGEANT. He 'as not opened his lips to my knowledge, Your Worship, from that hour to this.

MAYOR. Any questions to ask the Sergeant?

[BUILDER *continues to stare at the* MAYOR *without a word.*

MAYOR. Very well!

[*The* MAYOR *and* CHANTREY *now consult each other inaudibly, and the* MAYOR *nods.*

MAYOR. Miss Maud Builder, will you tell us what you know of this—er—occurrence?

MAUD. [*Rising; with eyes turning here and there*] Must I?

MAYOR. I'm afraid you must.

MAUD. [*After a look at her father, who never turns his eyes from the* MAYOR'S *face*] I—I wish to withdraw the charge of striking me, please. I—I never meant to make it. I was in a temper—I saw red.

MAYOR. I see. A—a domestic disagreement. Very well, that charge is withdrawn. You do not appear to have been hurt, and that seems to me quite proper. Now, tell me what you know of the assault on the constable. Is his account correct?

MAUD. [*Timidly*] Ye-yes. Only——

MAYOR. Yes? Tell us the truth.

MAUD. [*Resolutely*] Only, I don't think my father hit the constable. I think the stick did that.

MAYOR. Oh, the stick?   But—er—the stick was in 'is 'and, wasn't it?

MAUD. Yes; but I mean, my father saw red, and the constable saw red, and the stick flew up between them and hit him in the eye.

CHANTREY. And then he saw black?

MAYOR. [*With corrective severity*] But did 'e 'it 'im with the stick?

MAUD. No-no.   I don't think he did.

MAYOR. Then who supplied the—er—momentum?

MAUD. I think there was a struggle for the cane, and it flew up.

MAYOR. Hand up the cane.

> [*The* SERGEANT *hands up the cane.   The* MAYOR *and* CHANTREY *examine it.*

MAYOR. Which end—do you suggest—inflicted this injury?

MAUD. Oh! the knob end, sir.

MAYOR. What do you say to that, constable?

MOON. [*Stepping the mechanical two paces*] I don't deny there was a struggle, Your Worship, but it's my impression I was 'it.

CHANTREY. Of course you were hit; we can see that. But with the cane or with the fist?

MOON. [*A little flurried*] I—I—with the fist, sir.

MAYOR. Be careful.   Will you swear to that?

MOON. [*With that sudden uncertainty which comes over the most honest in such circumstances*] Not—not so to speak in black and white, Your Worship; but that was my idea at the time.

MAYOR. You won't swear to it?

MOON. I'll swear he called me an idiot and a lout; the words made a deep impression on me.

CHANTREY. [*To himself*] *Mort aux vaches!*

MAYOR. Eh?   That'll do, constable; stand back.   Now, who else saw the struggle?   Mrs. Builder.   You're not obliged to say anything unless you like.   That's your privilege as his wife.

> [*While he is speaking the door has been opened, and* HARRIS *has gone swiftly to it, spoken to someone and returned.   He leans forward to the* MAYOR.]

Eh?   Wait a minute.   Mrs. Builder, do you wish to give evidence?

MRS. BUILDER. [*Rising*] No, Mr. Mayor.   [MRS. BUILDER *sits*.

MAYOR. Very good.   [*To* HARRIS.] Now then, what is it?

> [HARRIS *says something in a low and concerned voice.   The* MAYOR'S *face lengthens.   He leans to his right and consults* CHANTREY, *who gives a faint and deprecating shrug.   A moment's silence.*

MAYOR. This is an open Court.   The Press have the right to attend if they wish.

> [HARRIS *goes to the door and admits a young man in glasses, of a pleasant C 3 appearance, and indicates to him a chair at the*

back.   At this untimely happening BUILDER's *eyes have moved from side to side, but now he regains his intent and bull-like stare at his fellow-justices.*

MAYOR. [*To Maud*] You can sit down, Miss Builder.

[MAUD *resumes her seat.*]

Miss Athene Builder, you were present, I think?

ATHENE. [*Rising*] Yes, sir.

MAYOR. What do you say to this matter?

ATHENE. I didn't see anything very clearly, but I think my sister's account is correct, sir.

MAYOR. Is it your impression that the cane inflicted the injury?

ATHENE. [*In a low voice*] Yes.

MAYOR. With or without deliberate intent?

ATHENE. Oh! without.   [BUILDER *looks at her.*

MAYOR. But you were not in a position to see very well?

ATHENE. No, sir.

MAYOR. Your sister having withdrawn her charge, we needn't go into that.   Very good!   [*He motions her to sit down.*

[ATHENE, *turning her eyes on her Father's impassive figure, sits.*

MAYOR. Now, there was a young man. [*Pointing to* HERRINGHAME.] Is this the young man?

MOON. Yes, Your Worship.

MAYOR. What's your name?

GUY. Guy Herringhame.

MAYOR. Address?

GUY. Er—the Aerodrome, sir.

MAYOR. Private, I mean?   [*The moment is one of considerable tension.*

GUY. [*With an effort*] At the moment, sir, I haven't one.   I've just left my diggings, and haven't yet got any others.

MAYOR. H'm!   The Aerodrome.   How did you come to be present?

GUY. I—er——

[BUILDER's *eyes go round and rest on him for a moment.*] It's in my sister's studio that Miss Athene Builder is at present working, sir.   I just happened to—to turn up.

MAYOR. Did you appear on the scene, as the constable says, during the struggle?

GUY. Yes, sir.

MAYOR. Did he summon you to his aid?

GUY. Ye——   No, sir.   Miss Maud Builder did that.

MAYOR. What do you say to this blow?

GUY. [*Jerking his chin up a little*] Oh! I saw that clearly.

MAYOR. Well, let us hear.

GUY. The constable's arm struck the cane violently and it flew up and landed him in the eye.

MAYOR. [*With a little grunt*] You are sure of that ?

GUY. Quite sure, sir.

MAYOR. Did you hear any language ?

GUY. Nothing out of the ordinary, sir.   One or two damns and blasts.

MAYOR. You call that ordinary ?

GUY. Well, he's a—magistrate, sir.

> [*The* MAYOR *utters a profound grunt.* CHANTREY *smiles. There is a silence.   Then the* MAYOR *leans over to* CHANTREY *for a short colloquy.*

CHANTREY. Did you witness any particular violence other than a resistance to arrest ?

GUY. No, sir.

MAYOR. [*With a gesture of dismissal*] Very well.   That seems to be the evidence.   Defendant John Builder—what do you say to all this ?

BUILDER. [*In a voice different from any we have heard from him*] Say ! What business had he to touch me, a magistrate ?   I gave my daughter two taps with a cane in a private house, for interfering with me for taking my wife home——

MAYOR. That charge is not pressed, and we can't go into the circumstances.   What do you wish to say about your conduct towards the constable ?

BUILDER. [*In his throat*] Not a damned thing !

MAYOR. [*Embarrassed*] I—I didn't catch.

CHANTREY. Nothing—nothing, he said, Mr. Mayor.

MAYOR. [*Clearing his throat*] I understand, then, that you do not wish to h'offer any explanation ?

BUILDER. I consider myself abominably treated, and I refuse to say another word.

MAYOR. [*Dryly*] Very good.   Miss Maud Builder.

> [MAUD *stands up.*

MAYOR. When you spoke of the defendant seeing red, what exactly did you mean ?

MAUD. I mean that my father was so angry that he didn't know what he was doing.

CHANTREY. Would you say as angry as he—er—is now ?

MAUD. [*With a faint smile*] Oh ! much more angry.

> [RALPH BUILDER *stands up.*

RALPH. Would you allow me to say a word, Mr. Mayor ?

MAYOR. Speaking of your own knowledge, Mr. Builder ?

RALPH. In regard to the state of my brother's mind—yes, Mr. Mayor.   He was undoubtedly under great strain yesterday ; certain circumstances, domestic and otherwise——

MAYOR. You mean that he might have been, as one might say, beside himself ?

RALPH. Exactly, sir.

MAYOR. Had you seen your brother?

RALPH. I had seen him shortly before this unhappy business.

[*The* MAYOR *nods and makes a gesture, so that* MAUD *and* RALPH *sit down; then, leaning over, he confers in a low voice with* CHANTREY. *The rest all sit or stand exactly as if each was the only person in the room, except the* JOURNALIST, *who is writing busily and rather obviously making a sketch of* BUILDER.

MAYOR. Miss Athene Builder.   [ATHENE *stands up.*]

This young man, Mr. Herringhame, I take it, is a friend of the family's?

                                        [*A moment of some tension.*

ATHENE. N-no, Mr. Mayor, not of my father or mother.

CHANTREY. An acquaintance of yours?

ATHENE. Yes.

MAYOR. Very good. [*He clears his throat.*] As the defendant, wrongly, we think, refuses to offer his explanation of this matter, the Bench has to decide on the h'evidence as given. There seems to be some discrepancy as to the blow which the constable undoubtedly received. In view of this, we incline to take the testimony of Mr. ——

                                        [HARRIS *prompts him.*]

Mr. 'Erringhame—as the party least implicated personally in the affair, and most likely to 'ave a cool and impartial view. That evidence is to the effect that the blow was accidental. There is no doubt, however, that the defendant used reprehensible language, and offered some resistance to the constable in the execution of his duty. Evidence 'as been offered that he was in an excited state of mind; and it is possible—I don't say that this is any palliation—but it is possible that he may have thought his position as magistrate made him—er——

CHANTREY. [*Prompting*] Cæsar's wife.

MAYOR. Eh? We think, considering all the circumstances, and the fact that he has spent a night in a cell, that justice will be met by—er—discharging him with a caution.

BUILDER. [*With a deeply muttered*] The devil you do!

        [*Walks out of the room. The* JOURNALIST, *grabbing his pad, starts up and follows. The* BUILDERS *rise and huddle, and, with* HERRINGHAME, *are ushered out by* HARRIS.

MAYOR. [*Pulling out a large handkerchief and wiping his forehead*] My Aunt!

CHANTREY. These new constables, Mayor! I say, Builder'll have to go! Damn the Press, how they nose everything out! The Great Unpaid!—We shall get it again! [*He suddenly goes off into a fit of laughter.*] " Come off it," I says, " to the best of my recollection." Oh! Oh! I shan't hit a bird all day! That poor devil Builder! It's no joke for him. You did it well, Mayor; you did it well. British justice is

safe in your hands.   He blacked the fellow's eye all right.   " Which I
herewith produce."   Oh ! my golly !   It beats the band !

> [*His uncontrollable laughter and the* MAYOR's *rueful appreciation are
> exchanged with lightning rapidity for a preternatural solemnity,
> as the door opens, admitting* SERGEANT MARTIN *and the
> lugubrious object of their next attentions.*

MAYOR. Charges.   [SERGEANT *steps forward to read the charge as*

The curtain falls.

SCENE II

Noon the same day.
BUILDER's *study.* TOPPING *is standing by the open window, looking up and
down the street. A* NEWSPAPER BOY's VOICE *is heard calling the
first edition of his wares. It approaches from the Right.*

TOPPING. Here !
BOY's VOICE. Right, guv'nor ! Johnny Builder up before the
beaks !   [*A paper is pushed up.*
TOPPING. [*Extending a penny*] What's that you're sayin' ? You
take care !
BOY's VOICE. It's all 'ere. Johnny Builder—beatin' his wife !
Dischawged.
TOPPING. Stop it, you young limb !
BOY's VOICE. 'Allo ! What's the matter wiv you ? Why, it's
Johnny Builder's house ! [*Gives a cat-call.*] 'Ere, buy anuvver !
'E'll want to read about 'isself. [*Appealing.*] Buy anuvver, guv'nor !
TOPPING. Move on !   [*He retreats from the window, opening the paper.*
BOY's VOICE. [*Receding*] Payper ! First edition ! J.P. chawged !
Payper !
TOPPING. [*To himself as he reads*] Crimes ! Phew ! That accounts
for them bein' away all night.
                    [*While he is reading,* CAMILLE *enters from the hall.*]
Here ! Have you seen this, Camel—in the Stop Press ?
CAMILLE. No.   [*They read eagerly side by side.*
TOPPING. [*Finishing aloud*] " Tried to prevent her father from forcing
her mother to return home with him, and he struck her for so doing.
She did not press the charge.   The arrested gentleman, who said he
acted under great provocation, was discharged with a caution."
Well, I'm blowed !   He has gone and done it !
CAMILLE. A black eye !
TOPPING. [*Gazing at her*] Have you had any hand in this ? I've
seen you making *your* lovely black eyes at him. You foreigners—
you're a loose lot !

CAMILLE. You are drunk!

TOPPING. Not yet, my dear. [*Reverting to the paper; philosophically.*] Well, this little lot's bust up! The favourites will fall down. Johnny Builder! Who'd have thought it?

CAMILLE. He is an obstinate man.

TOPPING. Ah! He's right up against it now. Comes of not knowin' when to stop bein' firm. If you meet a wall with your 'ead, it's any odds on the wall, Camel. Though, if you listened to some, you wouldn't think it. What'll he do now, I wonder? Any news of the mistress?

CAMILLE. [*Shaking her head*] I have pack her tr-runks.

TOPPING. Why?

CAMILLE. Because she take her jewels yesterday.

TOPPING. Deuce she did! They generally leave 'em. Take back yer gifts! She throws the baubles at 'is 'ead. [*Again staring at her.*] You're a deep one, you know! [*There is the sound of a cab stopping.*] Wonder if that's him! [*He goes towards the hall.*]

[CAMILLE *watchfully shifts towards the dining-room door.* MAUD *enters.*]

MAUD. Is my father back, Topping?

TOPPING. Not yet, Miss.

MAUD. I've come for mother's things.

CAMILLE. They are r-ready.

MAUD. [*Eyeing her*] Topping, get them down, please.

[TOPPING, *after a look at them both, goes out into the hall.*] Very clever of you to have got them ready.

CAMILLE. I am clevare.

MAUD. [*Almost to herself*] Yes—father may, and he may not.

CAMILLE. Look! If you think I am a designing woman, you are mistook. I know when things are too 'ot. I am not sorry to go.

MAUD. Oh! you are going?

CAMILLE. Yes, I am going. How can I stay when there is no lady in the 'ouse?

MAUD. Not even if you're asked to?

CAMILLE. Who will ask me?

MAUD. That we shall see.

CAMILLE. Well, you will see I have an opinion of my own.

MAUD. Oh! yes, you're clear-headed enough.

CAMILLE. I am not arguing. Good morning! [*Exits up Left.*

[MAUD *regards her stolidly as she goes out into the dining-room, then takes up the paper and reads.*

MAUD. Horrible! [*TOPPING re-enters from the hall.*

TOPPING. I've got 'em on the cab, Miss. I didn't put your ten bob on yesterday, because the animal finished last. You can't depend on horses.

MAUD. [*Touching the newspaper*] This is a frightful business, Topping.

TOPPING. Ah! However did it happen, Miss Maud?

MAUD. [*Tapping the newspaper*] It's all true. He came after my mother to Miss Athene's, and I—I couldn't stand it. I did what it says here; and now I'm sorry. Mother's dreadfully upset. You know father as well as anyone, Topping; what do you think he'll do now?

TOPPING. [*Sucking in his cheeks*] Well, you see, Miss, it's like this: Up to now Mr. Builder's always had the respect of everybody——

[MAUD *moves her head impatiently.*]

outside his own house, of course. Well, now he hasn't got it. Pishchologically that's bound to touch him.

MAUD. Of course; but which way? Will he throw up the sponge, or try and stick it out here?

TOPPING. He won't throw up the sponge, Miss; more likely to squeeze it down the back of their necks.

MAUD. He'll be asked to resign, of course.

[*The* NEWSPAPER BOY'S VOICE *is heard again approaching*: " First edition! Great sensation! Local magistrate before the Bench! Pay-per!"]

Oh, dear! I wish I hadn't! But I couldn't see mother being——

TOPPING. Don't you fret, Miss; he'll come through. His jaw's above his brow, as you might say.

MAUD. What?

TOPPING. [*Nodding*] Phreenology, Miss. I rather follow that. When the jaw's big and the brow is small, it's a sign of character. I always think the master might have been a Scotchman, except for his fishionomy.

MAUD. A Scotsman?

TOPPING. So down on anything soft, Miss. Haven't you noticed, whenever one of these 'Umanitarians writes to the papers, there's always a Scotchman after him next morning. Seems to be a fact of 'uman nature, like introducin' rabbits into a new country and then weasels to get rid of 'em. And then something to keep down the weasels. But *I* never can see what could keep down a Scotchman! You seem to reach the hapex there!

MAUD. Miss Athene was married this morning, Topping. We've just come from the Registrar's.

TOPPING. [*Immovably*] Indeed, Miss. I thought perhaps she was about to be.

MAUD. Oh!

TOPPING. Comin' events. I saw the shadder yesterday.

MAUD. Well, it's all right. She's coming on here with my uncle.

[*A cab is heard driving up.*]

That's them, I expect. We all feel awful about father.

TOPPING. Ah! I shouldn't be surprised if he feels awful about you, Miss.

MAUD. [*At the window*] It *is* them.

[TOPPING *goes out into the hall;* ATHENE *and* RALPH *enter Right.*

MAUD. Where's father, Uncle Ralph?

RALPH. With his solicitor.

ATHENE. We left Guy with mother at the studio. She still thinks she ought to come. She keeps on saying she *must*, now father's in a hole.

MAUD. I've got her things on the cab; she ought to be perfectly free to choose.

RALPH. You've got freedom on the brain, Maud.

MAUD. So would you, Uncle Ralph, if you had father about.

RALPH. I'm his partner, my dear.

MAUD. Yes; how *do* you manage him?

RALPH. I've never yet given him in charge.

ATHENE. What *do* you do, Uncle Ralph?

RALPH. Undermine him when I can.

MAUD. And when you can't?

RALPH. Undermine the other fellow. You can't go to those movie people now, Maud. They'd star you as the celebrated Maud Builder who gave her father into custody. Come to us instead, and have perfect freedom, till all this blows over.

MAUD. Oh! what will father be like now?

ATHENE. It's so queer you and he being brothers, Uncle Ralph.

RALPH. There are two sides to every coin, my dear. John's the head—and I'm the tail. He has the sterling qualities. Now, you girls have got to smooth him down, and make up to him. You've tried him pretty high.

MAUD. [*Stubbornly*] I never wanted him for a father, Uncle.

RALPH. They do wonderful things nowadays with inherited trouble. Come, are you going to be nice to him, both of you?

ATHENE. We're going to try.

RALPH. Good! I don't even now understand how it happened.

MAUD. When you went out with Guy, it wasn't three minutes before he came. Mother had just told us about—well, about something beastly. Father wanted us to go, and we agreed to go out for five minutes while he talked to mother. We went, and when we came back he told me to get a cab to take mother home. Poor mother stood there looking like a ghost, and he began hunting and hauling her towards the door. I saw red, and instead of a cab I fetched that policeman. Of course father did black his eye. Guy was splendid.

ATHENE. You gave him the lead.

MAUD. I couldn't help it, seeing father standing there all dumb.

ATHENE. It was awful ! Uncle, why didn't you come back with Guy ?

MAUD. Oh, yes ! why didn't you, Uncle ?

ATHENE. When Maud had gone for the cab, I warned him not to use force. I told him it was against the law, but he only said : " The law be damned ! "

RALPH. Well, it all sounds pretty undignified.

MAUD. Yes ; everybody saw red.

[*They have not seen the door opened from the hall, and* BUILDER *standing there. He is still unshaven, a little sunken in the face, with a glum, glowering expression. He has a document in his hand. He advances a step or two and they see him.*

ATHENE and MAUD. [*Aghast*] Father !

BUILDER. Ralph, oblige me ! See them off the premises !

RALPH. Steady, John !

BUILDER. Go !

MAUD. [*Proudly*] All right ! We thought you might like to know that Athene's married, and that I've given up the movies. Now we'll go.

[BUILDER *turns his back on them, and, sitting down at his writing-table, writes.*

[*After a moment's whispered conversation with their Uncle, the two girls go out.*

[RALPH BUILDER *stands gazing with whimsical commiseration at his brother's back. As* BUILDER *finishes writing, he goes up and puts his hand on his brother's shoulder.*

RALPH. This is an awful jar, old man !

BUILDER. Here's what I've said to that fellow :—

" MR. MAYOR,—You had the effrontery to-day to discharge me *with a caution*—forsooth !—your fellow-magistrate. I've consulted my solicitor as to whether an action will lie for false imprisonment. I'm informed that it won't. I take this opportunity of saying that justice in this town is a travesty. I have no wish to be associated further with you or your fellows ; but you are vastly mistaken if you imagine that I shall resign my position on the Bench or the Town Council.—Yours,   " JOHN BUILDER."

RALPH. I say—keep your sense of humour, old boy.

BUILDER. [*Grimly*] Humour ? I've spent a night in a cell. See this ! [*He holds out the document.*] It disinherits my family.

RALPH. John !

BUILDER. I've done with those two ladies. As to my wife—if she doesn't come back—— ! When I suffer, I make others suffer.

RALPH. Julia's very upset, my dear fellow ; we all are. The girls came here to try and——

BUILDER. [*Rising*] They may go to hell ! If that lousy Mayor thinks I'm done with—he's mistaken ! [*He rings the bell.*] I don't want any soft sawder.   I'm a fighter.

RALPH. [*In a low voice*] The enemy stands within the gate, old chap.

BUILDER. What's that ?

RALPH. Let's boss our own natures before we boss those of other people.   Have a sleep on it, John, before you do anything.

BUILDER. Sleep ?   I hadn't a wink last night.   If you'd passed the night I had——

RALPH. I hadn't many myself.   [TOPPING *enters.*

BUILDER. Take this note to the Mayor with my compliments, and don't bring back an answer.

TOPPING. Very good, sir.   There's a gentleman from the *Comet* in the hall, sir.   Would you see him for a minute, he says.

BUILDER. Tell him to go to——

[*A voice says, "* Mr. Builder ! *"* BUILDER *turns to see the figure of the* JOURNALIST *in the hall doorway.* TOPPING *goes out.*

JOURNALIST. [*Advancing with his card*] Mr. Builder, it's very good of you to see me.   I had the pleasure this morning—I mean—I tried to reach you when you left the Mayor's.   I thought you would probably have your own side of this unfortunate matter.   We shall be glad to give it every prominence.

[TOPPING *has withdrawn, and* RALPH BUILDER, *at the window, stands listening.*

BUILDER. [*Dryly, regarding the* JOURNALIST, *who has spoken in a pleasant and polite voice*] Very good of you !

JOURNALIST. Not at all, sir.   We felt that you would almost certainly have good reasons of your own which would put the matter in quite a different light.

BUILDER. Good reasons ?   I should think so !   I tell you—a very little more of this liberty—licence I call it—and there isn't a man who'll be able to call himself head of a family.

JOURNALIST. [*Encouragingly*] Quite !

BUILDER. If the law thinks it can back up revolt, it's damned well mistaken.   I struck my daughter—I was in a passion, as *you* would have been.

JOURNALIST. [*Encouraging*] I'm sure——

BUILDER. [*Glaring at him*] Well, I don't know that you would ; you look a soft sort ; but any man with any blood in him.

JOURNALIST. Can one ask what she was doing, sir ?   We couldn't get that point quite clear.

BUILDER. Doing ?   I just had my arm round my wife, trying to induce her to come home with me after a little family tiff, and this girl came at me.   I lost my temper, and tapped her with my cane.   And—that policeman brought by my own daughter—a policeman !   If the law is going to enter private houses and abrogate domestic authority, where the hell shall we be ?

JOURNALIST. [*Encouraging*] No, I'm sure—I'm sure !

BUILDER. The maudlin sentimentality in these days is absolutely rotting this country. A man can't be master in his own house, can't require his wife to fulfil her duties, can't attempt to control the conduct of his daughters, without coming up against it and incurring odium. A man can't control his employees ; he can't put his foot down on rebellion anywhere, without a lot of humanitarians and licence-lovers howling at him.

JOURNALIST. Excellent, sir ; excellent !

BUILDER. Excellent ! It's damnable. Here am I—a man who's always tried to do his duty in private life and public—brought up before the Bench—my God ! because I was doing that duty ; with a little too much zeal, perhaps—I'm not an angel !

JOURNALIST. No ! No ! of course.

BUILDER. A proper Englishman never is. But there are no proper Englishmen nowadays. [*He crosses the room in his fervour.*

RALPH. [*Suddenly*] As I look at faces——

BUILDER. [*Absorbed*] What ! I told this young man I wasn't an angel.

JOURNALIST. [*Drawing him on*] Yes, sir ; I quite understand.

BUILDER. If the law thinks it can force me to be one of your weak-kneed sentimentalists who let everybody do what they like——

RALPH. There are a good many who stand on their rights left, John.

BUILDER. [*Absorbed*] What ! How can men stand on their rights left ?

JOURNALIST. I'm afraid you had a painful experience, sir.

BUILDER. Every kind of humiliation. I spent the night in a stinking cell. I haven't eaten since breakfast yesterday. Did they think I was going to eat the muck they shoved in ? And all because in a moment of anger—which I regret, I regret !—I happened to strike my daughter, who was interfering between me and my wife. The thing would be funny if it weren't so disgusting. A man's house used to be sanctuary. What is it now ? With all the world poking their noses in ?

[*He stands before the fire with his head bent, excluding as it were his interviewer and all the world.*

JOURNALIST. [*Preparing to go*] Thank you very much, Mr. Builder. I'm sure I can do you justice. Would you like to see a proof ?

BUILDER. [*Half conscious of him*] What ?

JOURNALIST. Or will you trust me ?

BUILDER. I wouldn't trust you a yard.

JOURNALIST. [*At the door*] Very well, sir ; you shall have a proof, I promise. Good afternoon, and thank you.

BUILDER. Here !

> [*But he is gone, and* BUILDER *is left staring at his brother, on whose face is still that look of whimsical commiseration.*

RALPH. Take a pull, old man ! Have a hot bath and go to bed.

BUILDER. They've chosen to drive me to extremes, now let them take the consequences. I don't care a kick what anybody thinks.

RALPH. [*Sadly*] Well, I won't worry you any more, now.

BUILDER. [*With a nasty laugh*] No ; come again to-morrow !

RALPH. When you've had a sleep. For the sake of the family name, John, don't be hasty.

BUILDER. Shut the stable door ? No, my boy, the horse has gone.

RALPH. Well, well !

> [*With a lingering look at his brother, who has sat down sullenly at the writing-table, he goes out into the hall.*

> [BUILDER *remains staring in front of him. The dining-room door opens, and* CAMILLE'S *head is thrust in. Seeing him, she draws back, but he catches sight of her.*

BUILDER. Here !

> [CAMILLE *comes doubtfully up to the writing-table. Her forehead is puckered as if she were thinking hard.*

BUILDER. [*Looking at her, unsmiling*] So you want to be my mistress, do you ?   [CAMILLE *makes a nervous gesture.*] Well, you shall. Come here.

CAMILLE. [*Not moving*] You f-frighten me.

BUILDER. I've paid a pretty price for you. But you'll make up for it ; you and others.

CAMILLE. [*Starting back*] No ; I don't like you to-day ! No !

BUILDER. Come along ! [*She is just within reach and he seizes her arm.*] All my married life I've put a curb on myself for the sake of respectability. I've been a man of principle, my girl, as you saw yesterday. Well, they don't want that ! [*He draws her close.*] You can sit on my knee now.

CAMILLE. [*Shrinking*] No ; I don't want to, to-day.

BUILDER. But you shall. They've asked for it !

CAMILLE. [*With a supple movement slipping away from him*] They ? What is all that ? I don't want any trouble. No, no ! I am not taking any. [*She moves back towards the door.* BUILDER *utters a sardonic laugh.*] Oh ! you are a dangerous man. No, no ! Not for me ! Good-bye, sare !   [*She turns swiftly and goes out.*

> [BUILDER *again utters his glum laugh. And then, as he sits alone staring before him, perfect silence reigns in the room. Over the window-sill behind him a* BOY'S *face is seen to rise ; it hangs there a moment with a grin spreading on it.*

Boy's Voice. [*Sotto*] Johnny Builder !

             [*As* Builder *turns sharply, it vanishes.*]

'Oo beat 'is wife ?   [Builder *rushes to the window.*

Boy's Voice. [*More distant and a little tentative*] Johnny Builder !

Builder. You little devil ! If I catch you, I'll wring your blasted little neck !

Boy's Voice. [*A little distant*] 'Oo blacked the copper's eye ?

     [Builder, *in an ungovernable passion, seizes a small flower-pot from the sill and flings it with all his force. The sound of a crash.*

Boy's Voice. [*Very distant*] Ya-a-ah ! Missed !

     [Builder *stands leaning out, face injected with blood, shaking his fist.*

       The curtain falls for a few seconds.

SCENE III

Evening the same day.

Builder's *study is dim and neglected-looking ; the window is still open, though it has become night. A street lamp outside shines in, and the end of its rays fall on* Builder *asleep. He is sitting in a high chair at the fireside end of the writing-table, with his elbows on it, and his cheek resting on his hand. He is still unshaven, and his clothes unchanged. A* Boy's *head appears above the level of the window-sill, as if beheaded and fastened there.*

Boy's Voice. [*In a forceful whisper*] Johnny Builder !

     [Builder *stirs uneasily. The* Boy's *head vanishes.* Builder, *raising his other hand, makes a sweep before his face, as if to brush away a mosquito. He wakes. Takes in remembrance, and sits a moment staring gloomily before him. The door from the hall is opened and* Topping *comes in with a long envelope in his hand.*

Topping. [*Approaching*] From the *Comet*, sir. Proof of your interview, sir ; will you please revise, the messenger says ; he wants to take it back at once.

Builder. [*Taking it*] All right. I'll ring.

Topping. Shall I close in, sir ?

Builder. Not now.   [Topping *withdraws.*

     [Builder *turns up a standard lamp on the table, opens the envelope, and begins reading the galley slip. The signs of uneasiness and discomfort grow on him.*

Builder. Did I say that ? Muck ! Muck ! [*He drops the proof, sits a moment moving his head and rubbing one hand uneasily on the surface of the table, then reaches out for the telephone receiver.*] Town, 245. [*Pause.*] The *Comet* ? John Builder. Give me the Editor. [*Pause.*]

That you, Mr. Editor ?   John Builder speaking.   That interview. I've got the proof.   It won't do.   Scrap the whole thing, please.   I don't want to say anything. [*Pause.*]   Yes.   I know I said it all ; I can't help that. [*Pause.*]   No ; I've changed my mind.   Scrap it, please. [*Pause.*]   No, I will not say anything. [*Pause.*]   *You* can say what you dam' well please. [*Pause.*]   I mean it ; if you put a word into my mouth I'll sue you for defamation of character.   It's undignified muck.   I'm tearing it up.   Good night. [*He replaces the receiver, and touches a bell ; then, taking up the galley slip, he tears it viciously across into many pieces, and rams them into the envelope.*]   [TOPPING *enters.*] Here, give this to the messenger—sharp, and tell him to run with it.

TOPPING. [*Whose hand can feel the condition of the contents, with a certain surprise*] Yes, sir.   [*He goes, with a look back from the door.*] The Mayor is here, sir.   I don't know whether you would wish——

[BUILDER, *rising, takes a turn up and down the room.*

BUILDER. Nor do I.   Yes !   I'll see him.

[TOPPING *goes out, and* BUILDER *stands over by the fender, with his head a little down.*

TOPPING. [*Re-entering*] The Mayor, sir.   [*He retires up Left.*

[*The* MAYOR *is overcoated, and carries, of all things, a top hat.   He reaches the centre of the room before he speaks.*

MAYOR. [*Embarrassed*] Well, Builder ?

BUILDER. Well ?

MAYOR. Come !   That caution of mine was quite parliamentary. I 'ad to save face, you know.

BUILDER. And what about my face ?

MAYOR. Well, you—you made it difficult for me.   'Ang it all !   Put yourself into my place !

BUILDER. [*Grimly*] I'd rather put you into mine, as it was last night.

MAYOR. Yes, yes !   I know ; but the Bench has got a name to keep up—must stand well in the people's eyes.   As it is, I sailed very near the wind.   Suppose we had an ordinary person up before us for striking a woman ?

BUILDER. I didn't strike a woman—I struck my daughter.

MAYOR. Well, but she's not a child, you know.   And you did resist the police, if no worse.   Come !   You'd have been the first to maintain British justice.   Shake 'ands !

BUILDER. Is that what you came for ?

MAYOR. [*Taken aback*] Why—yes ; nobody can be more sorry than I——

BUILDER. Eye-wash !   You came to beg me to resign.

MAYOR. Well, it's precious awkward, Builder.   We all feel——

BUILDER. Save your powder, Mayor.   I've slept on it since I wrote you that note.   Take my resignations.

MAYOR. [*In relieved embarrassment*] That's right. We must face your position.

BUILDER. [*With a touch of grim humour*] I never yet met a man who couldn't face another man's position.

MAYOR. After all, what is it ?

BUILDER. Splendid isolation. No wife, no daughters, no Councillorship, no Magistracy, no future—[*With a laugh*] not even a French maid. And why ? Because I tried to exercise a little wholesome family authority. That's the position you're facing, Mayor.

MAYOR. Dear, dear ! You're devilish bitter, Builder. It's unfortunate, this publicity. But it'll all blow over ; and you'll be back where you were. You've a *good* sound practical sense underneath your temper. [*A pause.*] Come, now ! [*A pause.*] Well, I'll say good night, then.

BUILDER. You shall have them in writing to-morrow.

MAYOR. [*With sincerity*] Come ! Shake 'ands.

> [BUILDER, *after a long look, holds out his hand. The two men exchange a grip. The* MAYOR, *turning abruptly, goes out.*
>
> [BUILDER *remains motionless for a minute, then resumes his seat at the side of the writing-table, leaning his head on his hands.*
>
> [*The* BOY'S *head is again seen rising above the level of the window-sill, and another and another follows, till the three, as if decapitated, heads are seen in a row.*

BOYS' VOICES. [*One after another in a whispered crescendo*] Johnny Builder ! Johnny Builder ! Johnny Builder !

> [BUILDER *rises, turns and stares at them. The* THREE HEADS *disappear, and a* BOY'S *voice cries shrilly :* "Johnny Builder ! " BUILDER *moves towards the window ; voices are now crying in various pitches and keys :* "Johnny Builder ! " "Beatey Builder ! " "Beat 'is wife-er ! " "Beatey Builder ! " BUILDER *stands quite motionless, staring, with the street lamp lighting up a queer, rather pitiful defiance on his face. The voices swell. There comes a sudden swish and splash of water, and broken yells of dismay.*

TOPPING'S VOICE. Scat ! you young devils !

> [*The sound of scuffling feet and a long-drawn-out and distant* "Miaou ! "
>
> [BUILDER *stirs, shuts the window, draws the curtains, goes to the armchair before the fireplace and sits down in it.*
>
> [TOPPING *enters with a little tray on which is a steaming jug of fluid, some biscuits and a glass. He comes stealthily up level with the chair.* BUILDER *stirs and looks up at him.*

TOPPING. Excuse me, sir, you must 'ave digested yesterday morning's breakfast by now—must live to eat, sir.

BUILDER. All right. Put it down.

TOPPING. [*Putting the tray down on the table and taking up* BUILDER'S *pipe*] I fair copped those young devils.

BUILDER. You're a good fellow.

TOPPING. [*Filling the pipe*] You'll excuse me, sir ; the Missis—has come back, sir——

[BUILDER *stares at him and* TOPPING *stops. He hands* BUILDER *the filled pipe and a box of matches.*

BUILDER. [*With a shiver*] Light the fire, Topping. I'm chilly.

[*While* TOPPING *lights the fire* BUILDER *puts the pipe in his mouth and applies a match to it.* TOPPING, *having lighted the fire, turns to go, gets as far as half way, then comes back level with the table and regards the silent brooding figure in the chair.*

BUILDER. [*Suddenly*] Give me that paper on the table. No ; the other one—the Will.

[TOPPING *takes up the Will and gives it to him.*

TOPPING. [*With much hesitation*] Excuse me, sir. It's pluck that get's 'em 'ome, sir—begging your pardon.

[BUILDER *has resumed his attitude and does not answer.*]
[*In a voice just touched with feeling.*] Good night, sir.

BUILDER. [*Without turning his head*] Good night.

[TOPPING *has gone.*

[BUILDER *sits drawing at his pipe between the firelight and the light from the standard lamp. He takes the pipe out of his mouth and a quiver passes over his face. With a half angry gesture he rubs the back of his hand across his eyes.*

BUILDER. [*To himself*] Pluck ! Pluck ! [*His lips quiver again. He presses them hard together, puts his pipe back into his mouth, and, taking the Will, thrusts it into the newly-lighted fire and holds it there with a poker.*

[*While he is doing this the door from the hall is opened quietly, and* MRS. BUILDER *enters without his hearing her. She has a work-bag in her hand. She moves slowly to the table, and stands looking at him. Then going up to the curtains she mechanically adjusts them, and still keeping her eyes on* BUILDER, *comes down to the table and pours out his usual glass of whisky toddy.* BUILDER, *who has become conscious of her presence, turns in his chair as she hands it to him. He sits a moment motionless, then takes it from her, and squeezes her hand.* MRS. BUILDER *goes silently to her usual chair below the fire, and taking out some knitting begins to knit.* BUILDER *makes an effort to speak, does not succeed, and sits drawing at his pipe.*

The curtain falls.

LOYALTIES

CAST OF THE ORIGINAL PRODUCTION AT THE ST. MARTIN'S THEATRE, LONDON, MARCH 8, 1922

CHARLES WINSOR	*Edmond Breon*
LADY ADELA	*Dorothy Massingham*
FERDINAND DE LEVIS	*Ernest Milton*
TREISURE	*Gilbert Ritchie*
GENERAL CANYNGE	*Dawson Milward*
MARGARET ORME	*Cathleen Nesbitt*
CAPTAIN RONALD DANCY	*Eric Maturin*
MABEL DANCY	*Meggie Albanesi*
INSPECTOR DEDE	*Griffith Humphreys*
ROBERT	*Clifford Mollison*
A CONSTABLE	*Ian Hunter*
MAJOR COLFORD	*Malcolm Keen*
AUGUSTUS BORRING	*J. H. Roberts*
LORD ST. ERTH	*Ben Field*
A CLUB FOOTMAN	*Ian Hunter*
EDWARD GRAVITER	*Clifford Mollison*
A YOUNG CLERK	*Ian Hunter*
GILMAN	*Ben Field*
JACOB TWISDEN	*J. H. Roberts*
RICARDOS	*Griffith Humphreys*

ACT I

SCENE I

The dressing-room of CHARLES WINSOR, *owner of Meldon Court, near Newmarket; about eleven-thirty at night. The room has pale grey walls, unadorned; the curtains are drawn over a window Back Left Centre. A bed lies along the wall, Left. An open door, Right Back, leads into* LADY ADELA'S *bedroom; a door, Right Forward, into a long corridor, on to which abut rooms in a row, the whole length of the house's left wing.* WINSOR'S *dressing-table, with a light over it, is Stage Right of the curtained window. Pyjamas are laid out on the bed, which is turned back. Slippers are handy, and all the usual gear of a well-appointed bed-dressing-room.* CHARLES WINSOR, *a tall, fair, good-looking man about thirty-eight, is taking off a smoking jacket.*

WINSOR. Hallo! Adela!

V. OF LADY A. [*From her bedroom*] Hallo!

WINSOR. In bed?

V. OF LADY A. No.

> [*She appears in the doorway in under-garment and a wrapper. She, too, is fair, about thirty-five, rather delicious, and suggestive of porcelain.*

WINSOR. Win at Bridge?

LADY A. No fear.

WINSOR. Who did?

LADY A. Lord St. Erith and Ferdy De Levis.

WINSOR. That young man has too much luck—the young bounder won two races to-day; and he's as rich as Crœsus.

LADY A. Oh! Charlie, he did look so exactly as if he'd sold me a carpet when I was paying him.

WINSOR. [*Changing into slippers*] His father did sell carpets, whole-sale, in the City.

LADY A. Really? And you say I haven't intuition! [*With a finger on her lips.*] Morison's in there.

WINSOR. [*Motioning towards the door, which she shuts*] Ronny Dancy took a tenner off him, anyway, before dinner.

LADY A. No! How?

WINSOR. Standing jump on to a bookcase four feet high. De

Levis had to pay up, and sneered at him for making money by parlour tricks.   That young Jew gets himself disliked.

LADY A. Aren't you rather prejudiced?

WINSOR. Not a bit.   I like Jews.   That's not against him—rather the contrary these days.   But he pushes himself.   The General tells me he's deathly keen to get into the Jockey Club.   [*Taking off his tie.*]   It's amusing to see him trying to get round old St. Erth.

LADY A. If Lord St. Erth and General Canynge backed him he'd get in if he *did* sell carpets!

WINSOR. He's got some pretty good horses.   [*Taking off his waist-coat.*]   Ronny Dancy's on his bones again, I'm afraid.   He had a bad day.   When a chap takes to doing parlour stunts for a bet—it's a sure sign.   What made him chuck the Army?

LADY A. He says it's too dull, now there's no fighting.

WINSOR. Well, he can't exist on backing losers.

LADY A. Isn't it just like him to get married now?   He really is the most reckless person.

WINSOR. Yes.   He's a queer chap.   I've always liked him, but I've never quite made him out.   What do you think of his wife?

LADY A. Nice child; awfully gone on him.

WINSOR. Is *he*?

LADY A. Quite indecently—both of them.   [*Nodding towards the wall, Left.*]   They're next door.

WINSOR. Who's beyond them?

LADY A. De Levis;   and Margaret Orme at the end.   Charlie, do you realize that the bathroom out there has to wash those four?

WINSOR. I know.

LADY A. Your grandfather was crazy when he built this wing; six rooms in a row with balconies like an hotel, and only one bath— if we hadn't put ours in.

WINSOR. [*Looking at his watch*] Half-past eleven.   [*Yawns.*]   New-market always makes me sleepy.   You're keeping Morison up.

[LADY ADELA *goes to the door, blowing a kiss.*]

[CHARLES *goes up to his dressing-table and begins to brush his hair, sprinkling on essence.   There is a knock on the corridor door.*]

Come in.

[DE LEVIS *enters, clad in pyjamas and flowered dressing-gown.   He is a dark, good-looking, rather Eastern young man.   His face is long and disturbed.*]

Hallo! De Levis! Anything I can do for you?

DE LEVIS. [*In a voice whose faint exoticism is broken by a vexed excite-ment*] I say, I'm awfully sorry, Winsor, but I thought I'd better tell you at once.   I've just had—er—rather a lot of money stolen.

WINSOR. What!   [*There is something of outrage in his tone and glance, as who should say: " In my house? "*]   How do you mean *stolen*?

DE LEVIS. I put it under my pillow and went to have a bath; when I came back it was gone.

WINSOR. Good Lord! How much?

DE LEVIS. Nearly a thousand—nine hundred and seventy, I think.

WINSOR. Phew! [*Again the faint tone of outrage, that a man should have so much money about him.*

DE LEVIS. I sold my Rosemary filly to-day on the course to Kentman the bookie, and he paid me in notes.

WINSOR. What? That weed Dancy gave you in the Spring?

DE LEVIS. Yes. But I tried her pretty high the other day; and she's in the Cambridgeshire. I was only out of my room a quarter of an hour, and I locked my door.

WINSOR. [*Again outraged*] You *locked*——

DE LEVIS. [*Not seeing the fine shade*] Yes, and had the key here. [*He taps his pocket.*] Look here! [*He holds out a pocket-book.*] It's been stuffed with my shaving papers.

WINSOR. [*Between feeling that such things don't happen, and a sense that he will have to clear it up*] This is damned awkward, De Levis.

DE LEVIS. [*With steel in his voice*] Yes. I should like it back.

WINSOR. Have you got the numbers of the notes?

DE LEVIS. No.

WINSOR. What were they?

DE LEVIS. One hundred, three fifties, and the rest tens and fives.

WINSOR. What d'you want me to do?

DE LEVIS. Unless there's anybody you think——

WINSOR. [*Eyeing him*] Is it likely?

DE LEVIS. Then I think the police ought to see my room. It's a lot of money.

WINSOR. Good Lord! We're not in Town; there'll be nobody nearer than Newmarket at this time of night—four miles.

[*The door from the bedroom is suddenly opened and* LADY ADELA *appears. She has on a lace cap over her finished hair, and the wrapper.*

LADY A. [*Closing the door*] What is it? Are you ill, Mr. De Levis?

WINSOR. Worse; he's had a lot of money stolen. Nearly a thousand pounds.

LADY A. Gracious! Where?

DE LEVIS. From under my pillow, Lady Adela—my door was locked—I was in the bath-room.

LADY A. But how fearfully thrilling!

WINSOR. Thrilling! What's to be done? He wants it back.

LADY A. Of course! [*With sudden realization.*] Oh! But—— Oh! it's quite too unpleasant!

WINSOR. Yes! What am I to do? Fetch the servants out of their rooms? Search the grounds? It'll make the devil of a scandal.

De Levis. Who's next to me?

Lady A. [*Coldly*] Oh! Mr. De Levis!

Winsor. Next to you? The Dancys on this side, and Miss Orme on the other. What's that to do with it?

De Levis. They may have heard something.

Winsor. Let's get them. But Dancy was downstairs when I came up. Get Morison, Adela! No. Look here! When *was* this exactly? Let's have as many alibis as we can.

De Levis. Within the last twenty minutes, certainly.

Winsor. How long has Morison been up with you?

Lady A. I came up at eleven, and rang for her at once.

Winsor. [*Looking at his watch*] Half an hour. Then she's all right. Send her for Margaret and the Dancys—there's nobody else in this wing. No; send her to bed. We don't want gossip. D'you mind going yourself, Adela?

Lady A. Consult General Canynge, Charlie.

Winsor. Right. Could you get him too? D'you really want the police, De Levis?

De Levis. [*Stung by the faint contempt in his tone of voice*] Yes, I do.

Winsor. Then, look here, dear! Slip into my study and telephone to the police at Newmarket. There'll be somebody there; they're sure to have drunks. I'll have Treasure up, and speak to him.

[*He rings the bell.*

[Lady Adela *goes out into her room and closes the door.*

Winsor. Look here, De Levis! This isn't an hotel. It's the sort of thing that doesn't happen in a decent house. Are you sure you're not mistaken, and didn't have them stolen on the course?

De Levis. Absolutely. I counted them just before putting them under my pillow; then I locked the door and had the key here. There's only one door, you know.

Winsor. How was your window?

De Levis. Open.

Winsor. [*Drawing back the curtains of his own window*] You've got a balcony like this. Any sign of a ladder or anything?

De Levis. No.

Winsor. It must have been done from the window, unless someone had a skeleton key. Who knew you'd got that money? Where did Kentman pay you?

De Levis. Just round the corner in the further paddock.

Winsor. Anybody about?

De Levis. Oh, yes!

Winsor. Suspicious?

De Levis. I didn't notice anything.

Winsor. You must have been marked down and followed here.

De Levis. How would they know my room?

WINSOR. Might have got it somehow. [*A knock from the corridor*.] Come in.

> [TREISURE, *the Butler, appears, a silent, grave man of almost supernatural conformity.* DE LEVIS *gives him a quick, hard look, noted and resented by* WINSOR.

TREISURE. [*To* WINSOR] Yes, sir?

WINSOR. Who valets Mr. De Levis?

TREISURE. Robert, sir.

WINSOR. When was he up last?

TREISURE. In the ordinary course of things, about ten o'clock, sir.

WINSOR. When did he go to bed?

TREISURE. I dismissed at eleven.

WINSOR. But did he go?

TREISURE. To the best of my knowledge. Is there anything *I* can do, sir?

WINSOR. [*Disregarding a sign from* DE LEVIS] Look here, Treisure, Mr. De Levis has had a large sum of money taken from his bedroom within the last half-hour.

TREISURE. Indeed, sir!

WINSOR. Robert's quite all right, isn't he?

TREISURE. He is, sir.

DE LEVIS. How do you know? [TREISURE'S *eyes rest on* DE LEVIS.

TREISURE. I am a pretty good judge of character, sir, if you'll excuse me.

WINSOR. Look here, De Levis, eighty or ninety notes must have been pretty bulky. You didn't have them on you at dinner?

DE LEVIS. No.

WINSOR. Where did you put them?

DE LEVIS. In a boot, and the boot in my suit-case, and locked it.

> [TREISURE *smiles faintly*.

WINSOR. [*Again slightly outraged by such precautions in his house*] And you found it locked—and took them from there to put under your pillow?

DE LEVIS. Yes.

WINSOR. Run your mind over things, Treisure—has any stranger been about?

TREISURE. No, sir.

WINSOR. This seems to have happened between 11.15 and 11.30. Is that right? [DE LEVIS *nods*.] Any noise—anything outside—anything suspicious anywhere?

TREISURE. [*Running his mind—very still*] No, sir.

WINSOR. What time did you shut up?

TREISURE. I should say about eleven-fifteen, sir. As soon as Major Colford and Captain Dancy had finished billiards. What was Mr. De Levis doing out of his room, if I may ask, sir?

WINSOR. Having a bath; with his room locked and the key in his pocket.

TREISURE. Thank you, sir.

DE LEVIS. [*Conscious of indefinable suspicion*] Damn it! What do you mean? I *was*.

TREISURE. I beg your pardon, sir.

WINSOR. [*Concealing a smile*] Look here, Treisure, it's infernally awkward for everybody.

TREISURE. It is, sir.

WINSOR. What do you suggest?

TREISURE. The proper thing, sir, I suppose, would be a cordon and a complete search—in our interests.

WINSOR. I entirely refuse to suspect anybody.

TREISURE. But if Mr. De Levis feels otherwise, sir?

DE LEVIS. [*Stammering*] I? All I know is—the money was there, and it's gone.

WINSOR. [*Compunctious*] Quite! It's pretty sickening for you. But so it is for anybody else. However, we must do our best to get it back for you.　　　　　　　　　　　　[*A knock on the door.*

WINSOR. Hallo!

[TREISURE *opens the door, and* GENERAL CANYNGE *enters.*]
Oh! It's you, General. Come in. Adela's told you?

　　　[GENERAL CANYNGE *nods. He is a slim man of about sixty, very
　　　　well preserved, intensely neat and self-contained, and still in
　　　　evening dress. His eyelids droop slightly, but his eyes are keen
　　　　and his expression astute.*

WINSOR. Well, General, what's the first move?

CANYNGE. [*Lifting his eyebrows*] Mr. De Levis presses the matter?

DE LEVIS. [*Flicked again*] Unless you think it's too plebeian of me, General Canynge—a thousand pounds.

CANYNGE. [*Dryly*] Just so! Then we must wait for the police, Winsor. Lady Adela has got through to them. What height are these rooms from the ground, Treisure?

TREISURE. Twenty-three feet from the terrace, sir.

CANYNGE. Any ladders near?

TREISURE. One in the stables, sir, very heavy. No others within three hundred yards.

CANYNGE. Just slip down, and see whether that's been moved.

TREISURE. Very good, General.　　　　　　　　　　　　[*He goes out.*

DE LEVIS. [*Uneasily*] Of course, he—I suppose you——

WINSOR. We do.

CANYNGE. You had better leave this in our hands, De Levis.

DE LEVIS. Certainly; only, the way he——

WINSOR. [*Curtly*] Treisure has been here since he was a boy. I should as soon suspect myself.

DE LEVIS. [*Looking from one to the other—with sudden anger*] You seem to think——! What was I to do? Take it lying down and let whoever it is get clear off? I suppose it's natural to want my money back? [CANYNGE *looks at his nails; WINSOR out of the window.*

WINSOR. [*Turning*] Of course, De Levis!

DE LEVIS. [*Sullenly*] Well, I'll go to my room. When the police come, perhaps you'll let me know. [*He goes out.*

WINSOR. Phew! Did you ever see such a dressing-gown?

[*The door is opened. LADY ADELA and MARGARET ORME come in. The latter is a vivid young lady of about twenty-five in a vivid wrapper; she is smoking a cigarette.*

LADY A. I've told the Dancys—she was in bed. And I got through to Newmarket, Charles, and Inspector Dede is coming like the wind on a motor cycle.

MARGARET. Did he say, "like the wind," Adela? He must have imagination. Isn't this gorgeous? Poor little Ferdy!

WINSOR. [*Vexed*] You might take it seriously, Margaret; it's pretty beastly for us all. What time did *you* come up?

MARGARET. I came up with Adela. Am I suspected, Charles? How thrilling!

WINSOR. Did you hear anything?

MARGARET. Only little Ferdy splashing.

WINSOR. And saw nothing?

MARGARET. Not even that, alas!

LADY A. [*With a finger held up*] Leste! Un peu leste! Oh! Here are the Dancys. Come in, you two!

[*MABEL and RONALD DANCY enter. She is a pretty young woman with bobbed hair, fortunately, for she has just got out of bed, and is in her nightgown and a wrapper. DANCY is in his smoking jacket. He has a pale, determined face with high cheekbones, small, deep-set dark eyes, reddish crisp hair, and looks like a horseman.*

WINSOR. Awfully sorry to disturb you, Mrs. Dancy; but I suppose you and Ronny haven't heard anything. De Levis's room is just beyond Ronny's dressing-room, you know.

MABEL. I've been asleep nearly half an hour, and Ronny's only just come up.

CANYNGE. Did you happen to look out of your window, Mrs. Dancy?

MABEL. Yes. I stood there quite five minutes.

CANYNGE. When?

MABEL. Just about eleven, I should think. It was raining hard then.

CANYNGE. Yes, it's just stopped. You saw nothing?

MABEL. No.

DANCY. What time does he say the money was taken?

WINSOR. Between the quarter and half past. He'd locked his door and had the key with him.

MARGARET. How quaint! Just like an hotel. Does he put his boots out?

LADY A. Don't be so naughty, Meg.

CANYNGE. When exactly did *you* come up, Dancy?

DANCY. About ten minutes ago. I'd only just got into my dressing-room before Lady Adela came. I've been writing letters in the hall since Colford and I finished billiards.

CANYNGE. You weren't up for anything in between?

DANCY. No.

MARGARET. The mystery of the grey room.

DANCY. Oughtn't the grounds to be searched for footmarks?

CANYNGE. That's for the police.

DANCY. The deuce! Are they coming?

CANYNGE. Directly. [*A knock.*] Yes? [TREASURE *enters.*] Well?

TREASURE. The ladder has not been moved, General. There isn't a sign.

WINSOR. All right. Get Robert up, but don't say anything to him. By the way, we're expecting the police.

TREASURE. I trust they will not find a mare's-nest, sir, if I may say so. [*He goes.*]

WINSOR. De Levis has got wrong with Treasure. [*Suddenly.*] But I say, what would any of us have done if *we'd* been in his shoes?

MARGARET. A thousand pounds? I can't even conceive having it.

DANCY. We probably shouldn't have found it out.

LADY A. No—but if we had.

DANCY. Come to you—as he did.

WINSOR. Yes; but there's a way of doing things.

CANYNGE. We shouldn't have wanted the police.

MARGARET. No. That's it. The hotel touch.

LADY A. Poor young man; I think we're rather hard on him.

WINSOR. He sold that weed you gave him, Dancy, to Kentman the bookie, and these were the proceeds.

DANCY. Oh!

WINSOR. He'd tried her high, he said.

DANCY. [*Grimly*] He would.

MABEL. Oh! Ronny, what bad luck!

WINSOR. He must have been followed here. [*At the window.*] After rain like that, there ought to be footmarks.

[*The splutter of a motor cycle is heard.*]

MARGARET. Here's the wind!

WINSOR. What's the move now, General?

CANYNGE. You and I had better see the Inspector in De Levis's room, Winsor. [*To the others.*] If you'll all be handy, in case he wants to put questions for himself.

MARGARET. I hope he'll want me; it's just too thrilling.

DANCY. I hope he won't want me; I'm dog-tired. Come on, Mabel.   [*He puts his arm in his wife's.*

CANYNGE. Just a minute, Charles.

[*He draws close to* WINSOR *as the others are departing to their rooms.*

WINSOR. Yes, General?

CANYNGE. We must be careful with this Inspector fellow. If he pitches hastily on somebody in the house it'll be very disagreeable.

WINSOR. By Jove! It *will*.

CANYNGE. We don't want to rouse any ridiculous suspicion.

WINSOR. Quite. [*A knock.*] Come in!   [TREISURE *enters.*

TREISURE. Inspector Dede, sir.

WINSOR. Show him in.

TREISURE. Robert is in readiness, sir; but I could swear he knows nothing about it.

WINSOR. All right.

[TREISURE *re-opens the door, and says:* "Come in, please." *The* INSPECTOR *enters, blue, formal, moustachioed, with a peaked cap in his hand.*

WINSOR. Good evening, Inspector. Sorry to have brought you out at this time of night.

INSPECTOR. Good evenin', sir. Mr. Winsor? You're the owner here, I think?

WINSOR. Yes. General Canynge.

INSPECTOR. Good evenin', General. I understand, a large sum of money?

WINSOR. Yes. Shall we go straight to the room it was taken from? One of my guests, Mr. De Levis. It's the third room on the left.

CANYNGE. We've not been in there yet, Inspector; in fact, we've done nothing, except to find out that the stable ladder has not been moved. We haven't even searched the grounds.

INSPECTOR. Right, sir; I've brought a man with me. [*They go out.*

The curtain falls.   An interval of a minute.

SCENE II*

The bedroom of DE LEVIS *is the same in shape as* WINSOR'S *dressing-room, except that there is only one door—to the corridor. The furniture, however, is differently arranged; a small four-poster bedstead stands against the wall, Right Back, jutting into the room. A chair, on*

---

* The same set is used for this Scene, with the different arrangement of furniture, as specified.

21*

which DE LEVIS'S *clothes are thrown, stands at its foot. There is a dressing-table against the wall to the left of the open windows, where the curtains are drawn back and a stone balcony is seen. Against the wall to the right of the window is a chest of drawers, and a washstand is against the wall, Left. On a small table to the right of the bed an electric reading lamp is turned up, and there is a light over the dressing-table. The* INSPECTOR *is standing plumb centre looking at the bed, and* DE LEVIS *by the back of the chair at the foot of the bed.* WINSOR *and* CANYNGE *are close to the door, Right Forward.*

INSPECTOR. [*Finishing a note*] Now, sir, if this is the room as you left it for your bath, just show us exactly what you did after takin' the pocket-book from the suit-case. Where was that, by the way?

DE LEVIS. [*Pointing*] Where it is now—under the dressing-table.

[*He comes forward to the front of the chair, opens the pocket-book, goes through the pretence of counting his shaving papers, closes the pocket-book, takes it to the head of the bed and slips it under the pillow. Makes the motion of taking up his pyjamas, crosses below the* INSPECTOR *to the washstand, takes up a bath sponge, crosses to the door, takes out the key, opens the door.*

INSPECTOR. [*Writing*] We now have the room as it was when the theft was committed. Reconstruct accordin' to 'uman nature, gentlemen—assumin' the thief to be in the room, what would he try first?—the clothes, the dressin'-table, the suit-case, the chest of drawers, and last the bed.

[*He moves accordingly, examining the glass on the dressing-table, the surface of the suit-cases, and the handles of the drawers, with a spy-glass for finger-marks.*

CANYNGE. [*Sotto voce to* WINSOR] The order would have been just the other way.

[*The* INSPECTOR *goes on hands and knees and examines the carpet between the window and the bed.*

DE LEVIS. Can I come in again?

INSPECTOR. [*Standing up*] Did you open the window, sir, or was it open when you first came in?

DE LEVIS. I opened it.

INSPECTOR. Drawin' the curtains back first?

DE LEVIS. Yes.

INSPECTOR. [*Sharply*] Are you sure there was nobody in the room already?

DE LEVIS. [*Taken aback*] I don't know. I never thought. I didn't look under the bed, if you mean that.

INSPECTOR. [*Jotting*] Did not look under bed. Did you look under it after the theft?

DE LEVIS. No. I didn't.

INSPECTOR. Ah! Now, what *did* you do after you came back from your bath? Just give us that precisely.

DE LEVIS. Locked the door and left the key in. Put back my sponge, and took off my dressing-gown and put it there. [*He points to the foot-rails of the bed.*] Then I drew the curtains, again.

INSPECTOR. Shutting the window?

DE LEVIS. No. I got into bed, felt for my watch to see the time. My hand struck the pocket-book, and somehow it felt thinner. I took it out, looked into it, and found the notes gone, and these shaving papers instead.

INSPECTOR. Let me have a look at those, sir. [*He applies the spy-glasses.*] And then?

DE LEVIS. I think I just sat on the bed.

INSPECTOR. Thinkin' and cursin' a bit, I suppose. Ye-es?

DE LEVIS. Then I put on my dressing-gown and went straight to Mr. Winsor.

INSPECTOR. Not lockin' the door?

DE LEVIS. No.

INSPECTOR. Exactly. [*With a certain finality.*] Now, sir, what time did you come up?

DE LEVIS. About eleven.

INSPECTOR. Precise, if you can give it me.

DE LEVIS. Well, I *know* it was eleven-fifteen when I put my watch under my pillow, before I went to the bath, and I suppose I'd been about a quarter of an hour undressing. I should say after eleven, if anything.

INSPECTOR. Just undressin'? Didn't look over your bettin' book?

DE LEVIS. No.

INSPECTOR. No prayers or anything?

DE LEVIS. No.

INSPECTOR. Pretty slippy with your undressin' as a rule?

DE LEVIS. Yes. Say five past eleven.

INSPECTOR. Mr. Winsor, what time did the gentleman come to you?

WINSOR. Half-past eleven.

INSPECTOR. How do you fix that, sir?

WINSOR. I'd just looked at the time, and told my wife to send her maid off.

INSPECTOR. Then we've got it fixed between 11.15 and 11.30. [*Jots.*] Now, sir, before we go further I'd like to see your butler and the footman that valets this gentleman.

WINSOR. [*With distaste*] Very well, Inspector; only—my butler has been with us from a boy.

INSPECTOR. Quite so. This is just clearing the ground, sir.

WINSOR. General, d'you mind touching that bell?

[CANYNGE *rings a bell by the bed.*

INSPECTOR. Well, gentlemen, there are four possibilities. Either the thief was here all the tme, waiting under the bed, and slipped out after this gentleman had gone to Mr. Winsor. Or he came in with a key that fits the lock ; and I'll want to see all the keys in the house. Or he came in with a skeleton key and out by the window, probably droppin' from the balcony. Or he came in by the window with a rope or ladder and out the same way. [*Pointing.*] There's a footmark here from a big boot which has been out of doors since it rained.

CANYNGE. Inspector—you—er—walked up to the window when you first came into the room.

INSPECTOR. [*Stiffly*] I had not overlooked that, General.

CANYNGE. Of course. [*A knock on the door relieves a certain tension.*

WINSOR. Come in.

[*The footman* ROBERT, *a fresh-faced young man, enters, followed by* TREISURE.

INSPECTOR. You valet Mr.—Mr. De Levis, I think ?

ROBERT. Yes, sir.

INSPECTOR. At what time did you take his clothes and boots ?

ROBERT. Ten o'clock, sir.

INSPECTOR. [*With a pounce*] Did you happen to look under his bed ?

ROBERT. No, sir.

INSPECTOR. Did you come up again, to bring the clothes back ?

ROBERT. No, sir ; they're still downstairs.

INSPECTOR. Did you come up again for anything ?

ROBERT. No, sir.

INSPECTOR. What time did you go to bed ?

ROBERT. Just after eleven, sir.

INSPECTOR. [*Scrutinizing him*] Now, he careful. Did you go to bed at all ?

ROBERT. No, sir.

INSPECTOR. Then why did you say you did ? There's been a theft here, and anything you say may be used against you.

ROBERT. Yes, sir. I meant, I went to my room.

INSPECTOR. Where is your room ?

ROBERT. On the ground floor, at the other end of the right wing, sir.

WINSOR. It's the extreme end of the house from this, Inspector. He's with the other two footmen.

INSPECTOR. Were you there alone ?

ROBERT. No, sir. Thomas and Frederick was there too.

TREISURE. That's right ; I've seen them.

INSPECTOR. [*Holding up his hand for silence*] Were you out of the room again after you went in ?

ROBERT. No, sir.

INSPECTOR. What were you doing, if you didn't go to bed ?

ROBERT. [*To* WINSOR] Beggin' your pardon, sir, we were playin'
Bridge.

INSPECTOR. Very good.   You can go.   I'll see *them* later on.

ROBERT. Yes, sir.   They'll say the same as me.

[*He goes out, leaving a smile on the face of all except the* INSPECTOR
and DE LEVIS.

INSPECTOR. [*Sharply*] Call him back.

[TREASURE *calls* " Robert," *and the* FOOTMAN *re-enters.*

ROBERT. Yes, sir ?

INSPECTOR. Did you notice anything particular about Mr. De
Levis's clothes ?

ROBERT. Only that they were very good, sir.

INSPECTOR. I mean—anything peculiar ?

ROBERT. [*After reflection*] Yes, sir.

INSPECTOR. Well ?

ROBERT. A pair of his boots this evenin' was reduced to one, sir.

INSPECTOR. What did you make of that ?

ROBERT. I thought he might have thrown the other at a cat or
something.

INSPECTOR. Did you look for it ?

ROBERT. No, sir ; I meant to draw his attention to it in the morning.

INSPECTOR. Very good.

ROBERT. Yes, sir.   [*He goes again.*

INSPECTOR. [*Looking at* DE LEVIS] Well, sir, there's *your* story
corroborated.

DE LEVIS. [*Stiffly*] I don't know why it should need corroboration,
Inspector.

INSPECTOR. In my experience, you can never have too much of
that.   [*To* WINSOR.] I understand there's a lady in the room on this
side [*pointing Left*] and a gentleman on this [*pointing Right*]. Were
they in their rooms ?

WINSOR. Miss Orme was ; Captain Dancy not.

INSPECTOR. Do they know of the affair ?

WINSOR. Yes.

INSPECTOR. Well, I'd just like the keys of their doors for a minute.
My man will get them.

[*He goes to the door, opens it, and speaks to a constable in the corridor.*
[*To* TREASURE.] You can go with him. ·   [TREASURE *goes out.*]
In the meantime I'll just examine the balcony.

[*He goes out on the balcony, followed by* DE LEVIS.

WINSOR. [*To* CANYNGE] Damn De Levis and his money !   It's
deuced invidious, all this, General.

CANYNGE. The Inspector's no earthly.

[*There is a simultaneous re-entry of the* INSPECTOR *from the balcony
and of* TREASURE *and the* CONSTABLE *from the corridor.*

CONSTABLE. [*Handing key*] Room on the left, sir. [*Handing key*.] Room on the right, sir.

[*The* INSPECTOR *tries the keys in the door, watched with tension by the others. The keys fail.*

INSPECTOR. Put them back.

[*Hands keys to* CONSTABLE, *who goes out, followed by* TREISURE.] I'll have to try every key in the house, sir.

WINSOR. Inspector, do you really think it necessary to disturb the whole house and knock up all my guests ? It's most disagreeable, all this, you know. The loss of the money is not such a great matter. Mr. De Levis has a very large income.

CANYNGE. You could get the numbers of the notes from Kentman the bookmaker, Inspector ; he'll probably have the big ones, anyway.

INSPECTOR. [*Shaking his head*] A bookie. I don't suppose he will, sir. It's come and go with them, all the time.

WINSOR. We don't want a Meldon Court scandal, Inspector.

INSPECTOR. Well, Mr. Winsor, I've formed my theory.

[*As he speaks*, DE LEVIS *comes in from the balcony.*] And I don't say to try the keys is necessary to it ; but strictly, I ought to exhaust the possibilities.

WINSOR. What do you say, De Levis ? D'you want everybody in the house knocked up so that their keys can be tried ?

DE LEVIS. [*Whose face, since his return, expresses a curious excitement*] No, I don't.

INSPECTOR. Very well, gentlemen. In my opinion the thief walked in before the door was locked, probably during dinner ; and was under the bed. He escaped by dropping from the balcony—the creeper at that corner [*He points stage Left*] has been violently wrenched. I'll go down now, and examine the grounds, and I'll see you again, sir. [*He makes another entry in his note-book.*] Good night, then, gentlemen !

CANYNGE. Good night !

WINSOR. [*With relief*] I'll come with you, Inspector.

[*He escorts him to the door, and they go out.*

DE LEVIS. [*Suddenly*] General, I know who took them.

CANYNGE. The deuce you do ! Are you following the Inspector's theory ?

DE LEVIS. [*Contemptuously*] That ass ! [*Pulling the shaving papers out of the case.*] No ! The man who put those there was clever and cool enough to wrench that creeper off the balcony, as a blind. Come and look here, General. [*He goes to the window ; the* GENERAL *follows.* DE LEVIS *points stage Right.*] See the rail of my balcony, and the rail of the next ? [*He holds up the cord of his dressing-gown, stretching his arms out.*] I've measured it with this. Just over seven feet, that's all ! If a man can take a standing jump on to a narrow bookcase four feet high and balance there, he'd make nothing of that. And, look here! [*He goes out on the balcony and returns with a bit of broken creeper in his hand, and holds it out into the light.*] Someone's stood on that—the stalk's crushed—the inner corner too, where he'd naturally stand when he took his jump back.

CANYNGE. [*After examining it—stiffly*] That other balcony is young Dancy's, Mr. De Levis; a soldier and a gentleman. This is an extraordinary insinuation.

DE LEVIS. Accusation.

CANYNGE. What!

DE LEVIS. I have intuitions, General; it's in my blood. I see the whole thing. Dancy came up, watched me into the bathroom, tried my door, slipped back into his dressing-room, saw my window was open, took that jump, sneaked the notes, filled the case up with these, wrenched the creeper there [*He points stage Left*] for a blind, jumped back, and slipped downstairs again. It didn't take him four minutes altogether.

CANYNGE. [*Very gravely*] This is outrageous, De Levis. Dancy says he was downstairs all the time. You must either withdraw unreservedly, or I must confront you with him.

DE LEVIS. If he'll return the notes and apologize, I'll do nothing—except cut him in future. He gave me that filly, you know, as a hopeless weed, and he's been pretty sick ever since that he was such a flat as not to see how good she was. Besides, he's hard up, I know.

CANYNGE. [*After a vexed turn up and down the room*] It's mad, sir, to jump to conclusions like this.

DE LEVIS. Not so mad as the conclusion Dancy jumped to when he lighted on my balcony.

CANYNGE. Nobody could have taken this money who did not know you had it.

DE LEVIS. How do you know that he didn't?

CANYNGE. Do you know that he did?

DE LEVIS. I haven't the least doubt of it.

CANYNGE. Without any proof. This is very ugly, De Levis. I must tell Winsor.

DE LEVIS. [*Angrily*] Tell the whole blooming lot. You think I've no feelers, but I've felt the atmosphere here, I can tell you, General. If I were in Dancy's shoes and he in mine, your tone to me would be very different.

CANYNGE. [*Suavely frigid*] I'm not aware of using any tone, as you call it. But this is a private house, Mr. De Levis, and something is due to our host and to the *esprit de corps* that exists among gentlemen.

DE LEVIS. Since when is a thief a gentleman? Thick as thieves —a good motto, isn't it?

CANYNGE. That's enough! [*He goes to the door, but stops before opening it.*] Now, look here ! I have some knowledge of the world. Once an accusation like this passes beyond these walls no one can foresee the consequences. Captain Dancy is a gallant fellow, with a fine record as a soldier ; and only just married. If he's as innocent as —Christ—mud will stick to him, unless the real thief is found. In the old days of swords, either you or he would not have gone out of this room alive. If you persist in this absurd accusation, you will *both* of you go out of this room dead in the eyes of Society : you for bringing it, he for being the object of it.

DE LEVIS. Society ! Do you think I don't know that I'm only tolerated for my money ? Society can't add injury to insult and have my money as well, that's all. If the notes are restored I'll keep my mouth shut ; if they're not, I shan't. I'm certain I'm right. I ask nothing better than to be confronted with Dancy ; but, if you prefer it, deal with him in your own way—for the sake of your *esprit de corps.*

CANYNGE. 'Pon my soul, Mr. De Levis, you go too far.

DE LEVIS. Not so far as I shall go, General Canynge, if those notes aren't given back.   [WINSOR *comes in.*

WINSOR. Well, De Levis, I'm afraid that's all we can do for the present. So very sorry this should have happened in my house.

CANYNGE. [*After a silence*] There's a development, Winsor. Mr. De Levis accuses one of your guests.

WINSOR. What ?

CANYNGE. Of jumping from his balcony to this, taking the notes, and jumping back. I've done my best to dissuade him from indulging the fancy—without success. Dancy must be told.

DE LEVIS. You can deal with Dancy in your own way. All I want is the money back.

CANYNGE. [*Dryly*] Mr. De Levis feels that he is only valued for his money, so that it is essential for him to have it back.

WINSOR. Damn it ! This is monstrous, De Levis. I've known Ronald Dancy since he was a boy.

CANYNGE. You talk about adding injury to insult, De Levis. What do you call such treatment of a man who gave you the mare out of which you made this thousand pounds ?

DE LEVIS. I didn't want the mare ; I took her as a favour.

CANYNGE. With an eye to possibilities, I venture to think—the principle guides a good many transactions.

DE LEVIS. [*As if flicked on a raw spot*] In my race, do you mean ?

CANYNGE. [*Coldly*] I said nothing of the sort.

DE LEVIS. No ; you don't *say* these things, any of you.

CANYNGE. Nor did I think it.

DE LEVIS. Dancy does.

WINSOR. Really, De Levis, if this is the way you repay hospitality——

DE LEVIS. Hospitality that skins my feelings and costs me a thousand pounds !

CANYNGE. Go and get Dancy, Winsor; but don't say anything to him.   [WINSOR *goes out*.

CANYNGE. Perhaps you will kindly control yourself, and leave this to me.

[DE LEVIS *turns to the window and lights a cigarette.* WINSOR *comes back, followed by* DANCY.

CANYNGE. For Winsor's sake, Dancy, we don't want any scandal or fuss about this affair.   We've tried to make the police understand that.   To my mind the whole thing turns on our finding who knew that De Levis had this money.   It's about that we want to consult you.

WINSOR. Kentman paid De Levis round the corner in the further paddock, he says.

[DE LEVIS *turns round from the window, so that he and* DANCY *are staring at each other*.

CANYNGE. Did you hear anything that throws light, Dancy? As it was your filly originally, we thought perhaps you might.

DANCY. I? No.

CANYNGE. Didn't hear of the sale on the course at all?

DANCY. No.

CANYNGE. Then you can't suggest anyone who could have known? Nothing else was taken, you see.

DANCY. De Levis is known to be rolling, as I am known to be stony.

CANYNGE. There are a good many people still rolling, besides Mr. De Levis, but not many people with so large a sum in their pocket-books.

DANCY. He won two races.

DE LEVIS. Do you suggest that I bet in ready money?

DANCY. I don't know how you bet, and I don't care.

CANYNGE. You can't help us, then?

DANCY. No. I can't. Anything else?

[*He looks fixedly at* DE LEVIS.

CANYNGE. [*Putting his hand on* DANCY's *arm*] Nothing else, thank you, Dancy.

[DANCY *goes.*   CANYNGE *puts his hand up to his face.   A moment's silence.*

WINSOR. You see, De Levis? He didn't even know you'd got the money.

DE LEVIS. Very conclusive.

WINSOR. Well! You are—— !

[*There is a knock on the door, and the* INSPECTOR *enters.*

INSPECTOR. I'm just going, gentlemen. The grounds, I'm sorry to say, have yielded nothing. It's a bit of a puzzle.

CANYNGE. You've searched thoroughly?

INSPECTOR. We have, General. I can pick up nothing near the terrace.

WINSOR. [*After a look at* DE LEVIS, *whose face expresses too much*] H'm! You'll take it up from the other end, then, Inspector!

INSPECTOR. Well, we'll see what we can do with the bookmakers about the numbers, sir. Before I go, gentlemen—you've had time to think it over—there's no one you suspect in the house, I suppose?

[DE LEVIS's *face is alive and uncertain.* CANYNGE *is staring at him very fixedly.*

WINSOR. [*Emphatically*] No.

[DE LEVIS *turns and goes out on to the balcony.*

INSPECTOR. If you're coming in to the racing to-morrow, sir, you might give us a call. I'll have seen Kentman by then.

WINSOR. Right you are, Inspector. Good night, and many thanks.

INSPECTOR. You're welcome, sir.   [*He goes out.*

WINSOR. Gosh! I thought that chap [*With a nod towards the balcony*] was going to——! Look here, General, we *must* stop his tongue. Imagine it going the rounds. They may never find the real thief, you know. It's the very devil for Dancy.

CANYNGE. Winsor! Dancy's sleeve was damp.

WINSOR. How d'you mean?

CANYNGE. Quite damp. It's been raining.

[*The two look at each other.*

WINSOR. I—I don't follow——

[*His voice is hesitative and lower, showing that he does.*

CANYNGE. It was coming down hard; a minute out in it would have been enough——   [*He motions with his chin towards the balcony.*

WINSOR. [*Hastily*] He must have been out on his balcony since.

CANYNGE. It stopped before I came up, half an hour ago.

WINSOR. He's been leaning on the wet stone, then.

CANYNGE. With the outside of the *upper* part of the arm?

WINSOR. Against the wall, perhaps. There may be a dozen explanations. [*Very low and with great concentration.*] I entirely and absolutely refuse to believe anything of the sort against Ronald Dancy —in my house. Dash it, General, we must do as we'd be done by. It hits us all—it hits us all. The thing's intolerable.

CANYNGE. I agree. Intolerable. [*Raising his voice.*] Mr. De Levis!

[DE LEVIS *returns into view, in the centre of the open window.*

CANYNGE. [*With cold decision*] Young Dancy was an officer and is a gentleman; this insinuation is pure supposition, and you must not make it. Do you understand me?

DE LEVIS. My tongue is still mine, General, if my money isn't!

CANYNGE. [*Unmoved*] Must not. You're a member of three Clubs, you want to be member of a fourth. No one who makes such an insinuation against a fellow-guest in a country house, except on absolute proof, can do so without complete ostracism. Have we your word to say nothing ?

DE LEVIS. Social blackmail ? H'm !

CANYNGE. Not at all—simple warning. If you consider it necessary in your interests to start this scandal—no matter how, we shall consider it necessary in ours to dissociate ourselves completely from one who so recklessly disregards the unwritten code.

DE LEVIS. Do you think your code applies to me ? Do you, General ?

CANYNGE. To anyone who aspires to be a gentleman, sir.

DE LEVIS. Ah ! But you haven't known *me* since I was a boy.

CANYNGE. Make up your mind.   [*A pause.*

DE LEVIS. I'm not a fool, General. I know perfectly well that you can get me outed.

CANYNGE. [*Icily*] Well ?

DE LEVIS. [*Sullenly*] I'll say nothing about it, unless I get more proof.

CANYNGE. Good ! We have implicit faith in Dancy.

> [*There is a moment's encounter of eyes ; the* GENERAL'S *steady, shrewd, impassive ;* WINSOR'S *angry and defiant ;* DE LEVIS'S *mocking, a little triumphant, malicious. Then* CANYNGE *and* WINSOR *go to the door, and pass out.*

DE LEVIS. [*To himself*] Rats !

The curtain falls.

ACT II

SCENE I

Afternoon, three weeks later, in the card room of a London Club. A fire is burning, Left. A door, Right, leads to the billiard-room. Rather Left of Centre, at a card table, LORD ST. ERTH, *an old John Bull, sits facing the audience ; to his right is* GENERAL CANYNGE, *to his left* AUGUSTUS BORRING, *an essential Clubman, about thirty-five years old, with a very slight and rather becoming stammer or click in his speech. The fourth Bridge player,* CHARLES WINSOR, *stands with his back to the fire.*

BORRING. And the r-rub.

WINSOR. By George ! You do hold cards, Borring.

ST. ERTH. [*Who has lost*] Not a patch on the old whist—this game. Don't know why I play it—never did.

CANYNGE. St. Erth, shall we raise the flag for whist again ?

WINSOR. No go, General. You can't go back on pace. No getting a man to walk when he knows he can fly. The young men won't look at it.

BORRING. Better develop it so that t-two can sit out, General.

ST. ERTH. We ought to have stuck to the old game. Wish I'd gone to Newmarket, Canynge, in spite of the weather.

CANYNGE. [*Looking at his watch*] Let's hear what's won the Cambridgeshire. Ring, won't you, Winsor ?   [WINSOR *rings.*

ST. ERTH. By the way, Canynge, young De Levis was blackballed.

CANYNGE. What !

ST. ERTH. I looked in on my way down.

[CANYNGE *sits very still, and* WINSOR *utters a disturbed sound.*

BORRING. But of c-course he was, General. What did you expect ?

[*A* FOOTMAN *enters.*

FOOTMAN. Yes, my lord ?

ST. ERTH. What won the Cambridgeshire ?

FOOTMAN. Rosemary, my lord. Sherbet second ; Barbizon third. Nine to one the winner.

WINSOR. Thank you. That's all.   [FOOTMAN *goes.*

BORRING. Rosemary ! And De Levis sold her ! But he got a good p-price, I suppose.   [*The other three look at him.*

ST. ERTH. Many a slip between price and pocket, young man.

CANYNGE. Cut! [*They cut.*

BORRING. I say, is that the yarn that's going round about his having had a lot of m-money stolen in a country house? By Jove! He'll be pretty s-sick.

WINSOR. You and I, Borring.

[*He sits down in* CANYNGE'S *chair, and the* GENERAL *takes his place by the fire.*

BORRING. Phew! Won't Dancy be mad! He gave that filly away to save her keep. He was rather pleased to find somebody who'd take her. Kentman must have won a p-pot. She was at thirty-threes a fortnight ago.

ST. ERTH. All the money goes to fellows who don't know a horse from a haystack.

CANYNGE. [*Profoundly*] And care less. Yes! We want men racing to whom a horse means something.

BORRING. I thought the horse m-meant the same to everyone, General—chance to get the b-better of one's neighbour.

CANYNGE. [*With feeling*] The horse is a noble animal, sir, as you'd know if you'd owed your life to them as often as I have.

BORRING. They always try to *take* mine, General. I shall never belong to the noble f-fellowship of the horse.

ST. ERTH. [*Dryly*] Evidently. Deal!

[*As* BORRING *begins to deal the door is opened and* MAJOR COLFORD *appears—a lean and moustached cavalryman.*

BORRING. Hallo, C-Colford.

COLFORD. General!

[*Something in the tone of his voice brings them all to a standstill.*

COLFORD. I want your advice. Young De Levis in there [*He points to the billiard-room from which he has just come*] has started a blasphemous story——

CANYNGE. One moment. Mr. Borring, d'you mind——

COLFORD. It makes no odds, General. Four of us in there heard him. He's saying it was Ronald Dancy robbed him down at Winsor's. The fellow's mad over losing the price of that filly now she's won the Cambridgeshire.

BORRING. [*All ears*] Dancy! Great S-Scott!

COLFORD. Dancy's in the Club. If he hadn't been I'd have taken it on myself to wring the bounder's neck.

[WINSOR *and* BORRING *have risen.* ST. ERTH *alone remains seated.*

CANYNGE. [*After consulting* ST. ERTH *with a look*] Ask De Levis to be good enough to come in here. Borring, you might see that Dancy doesn't leave the Club. We shall want him. Don't say anything to him, and use your tact to keep people off.

[BORRING *goes out, followed by* COLFORD.

WINSOR. Result of hearing he was blackballed—pretty slippy.

CANYNGE. St. Erth, I told you there was good reason when I asked you to back young De Levis. Winsor and I knew of this insinuation ; I wanted to keep his tongue quiet. It's just wild assertion ; to have it bandied about was unfair to Dancy. The duel used to keep people's tongues in order.

ST. ERTH. H'm ! It never settled anything, except who could shoot straightest.

COLFORD. [Reappearing] De Levis says he's nothing to add to what he said to you before, on the subject.

CANYNGE. Kindly tell him that if he wishes to remain a member of this Club he must account to the Committee for such a charge against a fellow-member. Four of us are here, and form a quorum.
[COLFORD goes out again.

ST. ERTH. Did Kentman ever give the police the numbers of those notes, Winsor ?

WINSOR. He only had the numbers of two—the hundred, and one of the fifties.

ST. ERTH. And they haven't traced 'em ?

WINSOR. Not yet.

[As he speaks, DE LEVIS comes in. He is in a highly-coloured, not to say excited state. COLFORD follows him.

DE LEVIS. Well, General Canynge ! It's a little too strong all this—a little too strong. [Under emotion his voice is slightly more exotic.

CANYNGE. [Calmly] It is obvious, Mr. De Levis, that you and Captain Dancy can't both remain members of this Club. We ask you for an explanation before requesting one resignation or the other.

DE LEVIS. You've let me down.

CANYNGE. What !

DE LEVIS. Well, I shall tell people that you and Lord St. Erth backed me up for one Club, and asked me to resign from another.

CANYNGE. It's a matter of indifference to me, sir, what you tell people.

ST. ERTH. [Dryly] You seem a venomous young man.

DE LEVIS. I'll tell you what seems to me venomous, my lord—chasing a man like a pack of hounds because he isn't your breed.

CANYNGE. You appear to have your breed on the brain, sir. Nobody else does, so far as I know.

DE LEVIS. Suppose I had robbed Dancy, would you chase him out for complaining of it ?

COLFORD. My God ! If you repeat that——

CANYNGE. Steady, Colford !

WINSOR. You make this accusation that Dancy stole your money in my house on no proof—no proof ; and you expect Dancy's friends to treat you as if you were a gentleman ! That's too strong, if you like !

DE LEVIS. No proof?   Kentman told me at Newmarket yesterday that Dancy *did* know of the sale.   He told Goole, and Goole says that he himself spoke of it to Dancy.

WINSOR. Well—if he did?

DE LEVIS. Dancy told you he *didn't* know of it in General Canynge's presence, and mine.   [*To* CANYNGE.] You can't deny that, if you want to.

CANYNGE. Choose your expressions more nicely, please !

DE LEVIS. Proof !   Did they find any footmarks in the grounds below that torn creeper ?   Not a sign !   You saw how he can jump ; he won ten pounds from me that same evening betting on what he knew was a certainty.   That's your Dancy—a common sharper !

CANYNGE. [*Nodding towards the billiard-room*] Are those fellows still in there, Colford ?

COLFORD. Yes.

CANYNGE. Then bring Dancy up, will you ?   But don't say anything to him.

COLFORD. [*To* DE LEVIS] You may think yourself damned lucky if he doesn't break your neck.

> [*He goes out.   The three who are left with* DE LEVIS *avert their eyes from him.*

DE LEVIS. [*Smouldering*] I have a memory, and a sting too.   Yes, my lord—since you are good enough to call me venomous.   [*To* CANYNGE.] I quite understand—I'm marked for Coventry now, whatever happens.   Well, I'll take Dancy with me.

ST. ERTH. [*To himself*] This Club has always had a decent, quiet name.

WINSOR. Are you going to retract, and apologize in front of Dancy and the members who heard you ?

DE LEVIS. No fear !

ST. ERTH. You must be a very rich man, sir.   A jury is likely to take the view that money can hardly compensate for an accusation of that sort.   [DE LEVIS *stands silent.*

CANYNGE. Courts of law require proof.

ST. ERTH. He can make it a criminal action.

WINSOR. Unless you stop this at once, you may find yourself in prison.   *If* you can stop it, that is.

ST. ERTH. If I were young Dancy, nothing should induce me.

DE LEVIS. But you didn't steal my money, Lord St. Erth.

ST. ERTH. You're deuced positive, sir.   So far as I could understand it, there were a dozen ways you could have been robbed.   It seems to me you value other men's reputations very lightly.

DE LEVIS. Confront me with Dancy and give me fair play.

WINSOR. [*Aside to* CANYNGE] Is it fair to Dancy not to let him know ?

CANYNGE. Our duty is to the Club now, Winsor. We must have this cleared up. [COLFORD *comes in, followed by* BORRING *and* DANCY.

ST. ERTH. Captain Dancy, a serious accusation has been made against you by this gentleman in the presence of several members of the Club.

DANCY. What is it?

ST. ERTH. That you robbed him of that money at Winsor's.

DANCY. [*Hard and tense*] Indeed! On what grounds is he good enough to say that?

DE LEVIS. [*Tense too*] You gave me that filly to save yourself her keep, and you've been mad about it ever since; you knew from Goole that I had sold her to Kentman and been paid in cash, yet I heard you myself deny that you knew it. You had the next room to me, and you can jump like a cat, as we saw that evening; I found some creepers crushed by a weight on my balcony on that side. When I went to the bath your door was open, and when I came back it was shut.

CANYNGE. That's the first we have heard about the door.

DE LEVIS. I remembered it afterwards.

ST. ERTH. Well, Dancy?

DANCY. [*With intense deliberation*] I'll settle this matter with any weapons, when and where he likes.

ST. ERTH. [*Dryly*] It can't be settled that way—you know very well. You must take it to the Courts, unless he retracts.

DANCY. Will you retract?

DE LEVIS. Why did you tell General Canynge you didn't know Kentman had paid me in cash?

DANCY. Because I didn't.

DE LEVIS. Then Kentman and Goole lied—for no reason?

DANCY. That's nothing to do with me.

DE LEVIS. If you were downstairs all the time, as you say, why was your door first open and then shut?

DANCY. Being downstairs, how should I know? The wind, probably.

DE LEVIS. I should like to hear what your wife says about it.

DANCY. Leave my wife alone, you damned Jew!

ST. ERTH. Captain Dancy!

DE LEVIS. [*White with rage*] Thief!

DANCY. Will you fight?

DE LEVIS. You're very smart—dead men tell no tales. No! Bring your action, and we shall see.

[DANCY *takes a step towards him, but* CANYNGE *and* WINSOR *interpose.*

ST. ERTH. That'll do, Mr. De Levis; we won't keep you. [*He looks round.*] Kindly consider your membership suspended till this matter has been threshed out.

DE LEVIS. [*Tremulous with anger*] Don't trouble yourselves about my membership. I resign it. [*To* DANCY.] You called me a damned Jew. My race was old when you were all savages. I am proud to be a Jew. *Au revoir*, in the Courts.

[*He goes out, and silence follows his departure.*

ST. ERTH. Well, Captain Dancy?

DANCY. If the brute won't fight, what am I to do, sir?

ST. ERTH. We've told you—take action, to clear your name.

DANCY. Colford, you saw me in the hall writing letters after our game.

COLFORD. Certainly I did; you were there when I went to the smoking-room.

CANYNGE. How long after you left the billiard-room?

COLFORD. About five minutes.

DANCY. It's impossible for me to prove that I was there all the time.

CANYNGE. It's for De Levis to prove what he asserts. You heard what he said about Goole?

DANCY. If he told me, I didn't take it in.

ST. ERTH. This concerns the honour of the Club. Are you going to take action?

DANCY. [*Slowly*] That is a very expensive business, Lord St. Erth, and I'm hard up. I must think it over. [*He looks round from face to face.*] Am I to take it that there is a doubt in your minds, gentlemen?

COLFORD. [*Emphatically*] No.

CANYNGE. That's not the question, Dancy. This accusation was overheard by various members, and we represent the Club. If you don't take action, judgment will naturally go by default.

DANCY. I might prefer to look on the whole thing as beneath contempt.

[*He turns and goes out. When he is gone there is an even longer silence than after* DE LEVIS'S *departure.*

ST. ERTH. [*Abruptly*] I don't like it.

WINSOR. I've known him all his life.

COLFORD. You may have my head if he did it, Lord St. Erth. He and I have been in too many holes together. By Gad! My toe itches for that fellow's butt end.

BORRING. I'm sorry; but has he t'taken it in quite the right way? I should have thought—hearing it s-suddenly——

COLFORD. Bosh!

WINSOR. It's perfectly damnable for him.

ST. ERTH. More damnable if he did it, Winsor.

BORRING. The Courts are b-beastly distrustful, don't you know.

COLFORD. His word's good enough for me.

CANYNGE. We're as anxious to believe Dancy as you, Colford, for the honour of the Army and the Club.

WINSOR. Of course, he'll bring a case, when he's thought it over.

ST. ERTH. What are we to do in the meantime?

COLFORD. If Dancy's asked to resign, you may take my resignation too.

BORRING. I thought his wanting to f-fight him a bit screeny.

COLFORD. Wouldn't you have wanted a shot at the brute? A law court? Pah!

WINSOR. Yes. What'll be his position even if he wins?

BORRING. Damages, and a stain on his c-character.

WINSOR. Quite so, unless they find the real thief. People always believe the worst.

COLFORD. [*Glaring at* BORRING] They do.

CANYNGE. There *is* no decent way out of a thing of this sort.

ST. ERTH. No. [*Rising.*] It leaves a bad taste. I'm sorry for young Mrs. Dancy—poor woman!

BORRING. Are you going to play any more?

ST. ERTH. [*Abruptly*] No, sir. Good night to you. Canynge, can I give you a lift?   [*He goes out, followed by* CANYNGE.

BORRING. [*After a slight pause*] Well, I shall go and take the t-temperature of the Club.   [*He goes out.*

COLFORD. Damn that effeminate stammering chap! What can we do for Dancy, Winsor?

WINSOR. Colford! [*A slight pause.*] The General felt his coat sleeve that night, and it was wet.

COLFORD. Well! What proof's that? No, by George! An old school-fellow, a brother officer, and a pal.

WINSOR. If he did do it——

COLFORD. He didn't. But if he did, I'd stick to him, and see him through it, if I could.

[WINSOR *walks over to the fire, stares into it, turns round and stares at* COLFORD, *who is standing motionless.*]

Yes, by God!

The curtain falls.

SCENE II*

Morning of the following day. The DANCY'S *flat. In the sitting-room of this small abode* MABEL DANCY *and* MARGARET ORME *are sitting full face to the audience, on a couch in the centre of the room, in front of the*

* NOTE.—This should be a small set capable of being set quickly within that of the previous scene.

imaginary window.   There is a fireplace, Left, with fire burning; a door below it, Left; and a door on the Right, facing the audience, leads to a corridor and the outer door of the flat, which is visible.   Their voices are heard in rapid exchange; then as the curtain rises, so does MABEL.

MABEL. But it's monstrous !

MARGARET. Of course ! [*She lights a cigarette and hands the case to* MABEL, *who, however, sees nothing but her own thoughts.*] De Levis might just as well have pitched on me, except that I can't jump more than six inches in these skirts.

MABEL. It's wicked ! Yesterday afternoon at the Club, did you say ? Ronny hasn't said a word to me.   Why ?

MARGARET. [*With a long puff of smoke*] Doesn't want you bothered.

MABEL. But— Good heavens !—— Me !

MARGARET. Haven't you found out, Mabel, that he isn't exactly communicative ?   No desperate character is.

MABEL. Ronny ?

MARGARET. Gracious ! Wives *are* at a disadvantage, especially early on. You've never hunted with him, my dear. I have. He takes more sudden decisions than any man I ever knew. He's taking one now, I'll bet.

MABEL. That beast, De Levis !   I was in our room next door all the time.

MARGARET. Was the door into Ronny's dressing-room open ?

MABEL. I don't know ; I—I think it was.

MARGARET. Well, you can say so in court anyway. Not that it matters. Wives are liars by law.

MABEL. [*Staring down at her*] What do you mean—Court ?

MARGARET. My dear, he'll have to bring an action for defamation of character, or whatever they call it.

MABEL. Were they talking of this last night at the Winsors' ?

MARGARET. Well, you know a dinner-table, Mabel—Scandal is heaven-sent at this time of year.

MABEL. It's terrible, such a thing—terrible !

MARGARET. [*Gloomily*] If only Ronny weren't known to be so broke.

MABEL. [*With her hands to her forehead*] I can't realize—I simply can't. If there's a case would it be all right afterwards ?

MARGARET. Do you remember St. Offert—cards ?   No, you wouldn't—you were in high frocks.   Well, St. Offert got damages, but he also got the hoof, underneath. He lives in Ireland. There isn't the slightest connection, so far as I can see, Mabel, between innocence and reputation. Look at me !

MABEL. We'll fight it tooth and nail !

MARGARET. Mabel, you're pure wool, right through ; everybody's sorry for you.

MABEL. It's for *him* they ought——

MARGARET. [*Again handing the cigarette case*] Do smoke, old thing.

                [MABEL *takes a cigarette this time, but does not light it.*]
It isn't altogether simple. General Canynge was there last night.
You don't mind my being beastly frank, do you ?

MABEL. No. I want it.

MARGARET. Well, he's all for *esprit de corps* and that. But he was
awfully silent.

MABEL. I hate half-hearted friends. Loyalty comes before everything.

MARGARET. Ye-es ; but loyalties cut up against each other sometimes, you know.

MABEL. I *must* see Ronny. D'you mind if I go and try to get him
on the telephone ?

MARGARET. Rather not.   [MABEL *goes out by the door Left.*]
Poor kid !

    [*She curls herself into a corner of the sofa, as if trying to get away from
        life. The bell rings. MARGARET stirs, gets up, and goes out
        into the corridor, where she opens the door to LADY ADELA
        WINSOR, whom she precedes into the sitting-room.*]
Enter the second murderer ! D'you know that child knew nothing ?

LADY A. Where is she ?

MARGARET. Telephoning. Adela, if there's going to be an action,
we shall be witnesses. I shall wear black georgette with an écru hat.
Have you ever given evidence ?

LADY A. Never.

MARGARET. It must be too frightfully thrilling.

LADY A. Oh ! Why did I ever ask that wretch De Levis ? I used
to think him pathetic. Meg—did you know—— Ronald Dancy's
coat was wet ? The General happened to feel it.

MARGARET. So that's why he was so silent.

LADY A. Yes ; and after the scene in the Club yesterday he went to
see those bookmakers, and Goole—what a name !—is sure he told
Dancy about the sale.

MARGARET. [*Suddenly*] I don't care. He's my third cousin. Don't
you feel you *couldn't*, Adela ?

LADY A. Couldn't—what ?

MARGARET. Stand for De Levis against one of ourselves ?

LADY A. That's very narrow, Meg.

MARGARET. Oh ! I know lots of splendid Jews, and I rather liked
little Ferdy ; but when it comes to the point——! *They* all stick
together ; why shouldn't we ? It's in the blood. Open your jugular,
and see if you haven't got it.

LADY A. My dear, my great grandmother was a Jewess. I'm proud
of her.

MARGARET. Inoculated. [*Stretching herself.*] Prejudices, Adela—or
are they loyalties—I don't know—criss-cross—we all cut each other's
throats from the best of motives.

LADY A. Oh ! I shall remember that. Delightful ! [*Holding up
a finger.*] You got it from Bergson, Meg. Isn't he wonderful ?

MARGARET. Yes ; have you ever read him ?

LADY A. Well—No. [*Looking at the bedroom door.*] That poor child !
I quite agree. I shall tell everybody it's ridiculous. You don't really
think Ronald Dancy—— ?

MARGARET. I don't know, Adela. There are people who simply
can't live without danger. I'm rather like that myself. They're all
right when they're getting the D.S.O. or shooting man-eaters ; but if
there's no excitement going, they'll make it—out of sheer craving.
I've seen Ronny Dancy do the maddest things for no mortal reason
except the risk. He's had a past, you know.

LADY A. Oh ! Do tell !

MARGARET. He did splendidly in the war, of course, because it
suited him ; but—just before—don't you remember—a very queer
bit of riding ?

LADY A. No.

MARGARET. Most dare-devil thing—but not quite. You must
remember—it was awfully talked about. And then, of course, right
up to his marriage—— [*She lights a cigarette.*]

LADY A. Meg, you're very tantalizing !

MARGARET. A foreign-looking girl—most plummy. Oh ! Ronny's
got charm—this Mabel child doesn't know in the least what she's got
hold of !

LADY A. But they're so fond of each other !

MARGARET. That's the mistake. The General isn't mentioning the
coat, is he ?

LADY A. Oh, no ! It was only to Charles.   [MABEL *returns.*

MARGARET. Did you get him ?

MABEL. No ; he's not at Tattersall's, nor at the Club.

[LADY ADELA *rises and greets her with an air which suggests bereave-
          ment.*

LADY A. Nobody's going to believe this, my dear.

MABEL. [*Looking straight at her*] Nobody who does need come
here, or trouble to speak to *us* again.

LADY A. That's what I was afraid of ; you're going to be defiant.
Now don't ! Just be perfectly natural.

MABEL. So easy, isn't it ? I could kill anybody who believes such
a thing.

MARGARET. You'll want a solicitor, Mabel. Go to old Mr. Jacob
Twisden.

LADY A. Yes ; he's so comforting.

MARGARET. He got my pearls back once—without loss of life. A frightfully good fireside manner. Do get him here, Mabel, and have a heart-to-heart talk, all three of you!

MABEL. [*Suddenly*] Listen! There's Ronny! 　　[DANCY *comes in.*]

DANCY. [*With a smile*] Very good of you to have come.

MARGARET. Yes. We're just going. Oh! Ronny, this is quite too—— 　　　[*But his face dries her up ; and sidling past, she goes.*]

LADY A. Charles sent his—love——

　　　　　　　[*Her voice dwindles on the word, and she, too, goes.*]

DANCY. [*Crossing to his wife*] What have they been saying?

MABEL. Ronny! Why didn't you tell me?

DANCY. I wanted to see De Levis again first.

MABEL. That wretch! How dare he! Darling! [*She suddenly clasps and kisses him. He does not return the kiss, but remains rigid in her arms, so that she draws away and looks at him.*] It's hurt you awfully, I know.

DANCY. Look here, Mabel! Apart from that muck—this is a ghastly tame-cat sort of life. Let's cut it and get out to Nairobi. I can scare up the money for that.

MABEL. [*Aghast*] But how can we? Everybody would say——

DANCY. Let them! We shan't be here.

MABEL. I couldn't bear people to think——

DANCY. I don't care a damn what people think—monkeys and cats. I never could stand their rotten menagerie. Besides, what does it matter how I act; if I bring an action and get damages—if I pound him to a jelly—it's all no good! I can't *prove* it. There'll be plenty of people unconvinced.

MABEL. But they'll find the real thief.

DANCY. [*With a queer little smile*] Will staying here help them to do that?

MABEL. [*In a sort of agony*] Oh! I couldn't—it looks like running away. We *must* stay and fight it!

DANCY. Suppose I didn't get a verdict—you never can tell.

MABEL. But you must—I was there all the time, with the door open.

DANCY. Was it?

MABEL. I'm almost sure.

DANCY. Yes. But you're my wife.

MABEL. [*Bewildered*] Ronny, I don't understand—suppose I'd been accused of stealing pearls!

DANCY. [*Wincing*] I can't.

MABEL. But I might—just as easily. What would you think of me if I ran away from it?

DANCY. I see. [*A pause.*] All right! You shall have a run for your money. I'll go and see old Twisden.

MABEL. Let me come! [DANCY *shakes his head.*] Why not? I can't be happy a moment unless I'm fighting this.

[DANCY *puts out his hand suddenly and grips hers.*

DANCY. You *are* a little brick!

MABEL. [*Pressing his hand to her breast and looking into his face*] Do you know what Margaret called you?

DANCY. No.

MABEL. A desperate character.

DANCY. Ha! I'm not a tame cat, any more than she.

[*The bell rings.* MABEL *goes out to the door and her voice is heard saying coldly:*

MABEL. Will you wait a minute, please? [*Returning.*] It's De Levis—to see you. [*In a low voice.*] Let me see him alone first. Just for a minute! Do!

DANCY. [*After a moment's silence*] Go ahead!

[*He goes out into the bedroom.*

MABEL. [*Going to the door, Right*] Come in.

[DE LEVIS *comes in, and stands embarrassed.*] Yes?

DE LEVIS. [*With a slight bow*] Your husband, Mrs. Dancy?

MABEL. He is in. Why do you want to see him?

DE LEVIS. He came round to my rooms just now, when I was out. He threatened me yesterday. I don't choose him to suppose I'm afraid of him.

MABEL. [*With a great and manifest effort at self-control*] Mr. De Levis, you are robbing my husband of his good name.

DE LEVIS. [*Sincerely*] I admire your trustfulness, Mrs. Dancy.

MABEL. [*Staring at him*] How can you do it? What do you want? What's your motive? You can't possibly believe that my husband is a *thief!*

DE LEVIS. Unfortunately.

MABEL. How dare you? How dare you? Don't you know that I was in our bedroom all the time with the door open? Do you accuse me too?

DE LEVIS. No, Mrs. Dancy.

MABEL. But you do. I must have seen, I must have heard.

DE LEVIS. A wife's memory is not very good when her husband is in danger.

MABEL. In other words, I'm lying.

DE LEVIS. No. Your wish is mother to your thought, that's all.

MABEL. [*After staring again with a sort of horror, turns to get control of herself. Then turning back to him*] Mr. De Levis, I appeal to you as a gentleman to behave to us as you would we should behave to you. Withdraw this wicked charge, and write an apology that Ronald can show.

DE LEVIS. Mrs. Dancy, I am not a gentleman, I am only a—damned Jew. Yesterday I might possibly have withdrawn to spare you. But when my race is insulted I have nothing to say to your husband, but as he wishes to see me, I've come. Please let him know.

MABEL. [*Regarding him again with that look of horror—slowly*] I think what you are doing is too horrible for words.

[DE LEVIS *gives her a slight bow, and as he does so* DANCY *comes quickly in, Left. The two men stand with the length of the sofa between them.* MABEL, *behind the sofa, turns her eyes on her husband, who has a paper in his right hand.*

DE LEVIS. You came to see me.

DANCY. Yes. I want you to sign this.

DE LEVIS. I will sign nothing.

DANCY. Let me read it: "I apologize to Captain Dancy for the reckless and monstrous charge I made against him, and I retract every word of it."

DE LEVIS. Not much!

DANCY. You will sign.

DE LEVIS. I tell you this is useless. I will sign nothing. The charge is true; you wouldn't be playing this game if it weren't. I'm going. You'll hardly try violence in the presence of your wife; and if you try it anywhere else—look out for yourself.

DANCY. Mabel, I want to speak to him alone.

MABEL. No, no!

DE LEVIS. Quite right, Mrs. Dancy. Black and tan swash-buckling will only make things worse for him.

DANCY. So you shelter behind a woman, do you, you skulking cur!

[DE LEVIS *takes a step, with fists clenched and eyes blazing.* DANCY, *too, stands ready to spring—the moment is cut short by* MABEL *going quickly to her husband.*

MABEL. Don't, Ronny. It's undignified! He isn't worth it.

[DANCY *suddenly tears the paper in two, and flings it into the fire.*

DANCY. Get out of here, you swine!

[DE LEVIS *stands a moment irresolute, then, turning to the door, he opens it, stands again for a moment with a smile on his face, then goes.* MABEL *crosses swiftly to the door, and shuts it as the outer door closes. Then she stands quite still looking at her husband—her face expressing a sort of startled suspense.*

DANCY. [*Turning and looking at her*] Well! Do you agree with him?

MABEL. What do you mean?

DANCY. That I wouldn't be playing this game unless——

MABEL. Don't! You hurt me!

DANCY. Yes. You don't know much of me, Mabel.

MABEL. Ronny!

DANCY. What did you say to that swine?

MABEL. [*Her face averted*] That he was robbing *us*. [*Turning to him suddenly.*] Ronny—you—didn't ? I'd rather know.

DANCY. Ha ! I thought that was coming.

MABEL. [*Covering her face*] Oh ! How horrible of me—how horrible !

DANCY. Not at all. The thing looks bad.

MABEL. [*Dropping her hands*] If *I* can't believe in you, who can ? [*Going to him, throwing her arms round him, and looking up into his face.*] Ronny ! If all the world—*I'd* believe in you. You know I would.

DANCY. That's all right, Mabs ! That's all right ! [*His face, above her head, is contorted for a moment, then hardens into a mask.*] Well, what shall we do ?

MABEL. Oh ! Let's go to that lawyer—let's go at once !

DANCY. All right. Get your hat on.

> [MABEL *passes him, and goes into the bedroom, Left.* DANCY, *left alone, stands quite still, staring before him. With a sudden shrug of his shoulders he moves quickly to his hat and takes it up just as* MABEL *returns, ready to go out. He opens the door ; and crossing him, she stops in the doorway, looking up with a clear and trustful gaze as*

The *curtain falls*:

ACT III

SCENE I

Three months later. Old Mr. Jacob Twisden's *Room, at the offices of Twisden and Graviter, in Lincoln's Inn Fields, is spacious, with two large windows at back, a fine old fireplace, Right, a door below it, and two doors, Left. Between the windows is a large table sideways to the window wall, with a chair in the middle on the right-hand side, a chair against the wall, and a client's chair on the left-hand side.*

[Graviter, Twisden's *much younger partner, is standing in front of the right-hand window looking out on to the Fields, where the lamps are being lighted, and a taxi's engine is running down below. He turns his sanguine, shrewd face from the window towards a grandfather clock, between the doors, Left, which is striking "four." The door, Left Forward, is opened.*

Young Clerk. [*Entering*] A Mr. Gilman, sir, to see Mr. Twisden.

Graviter. By appointment?

Young Clerk. No, sir. But important, he says.

Graviter. I'll see him. [*The* Clerk *goes.*

[Graviter *sits right of table. The* Clerk *returns, ushering in an oldish man, who looks what he is, the proprietor of a large modern grocery store. He wears a dark overcoat and carries a pot hat. His gingery-grey moustache and mutton-chop whiskers give him the expression of a cat.*

Graviter. [*Sizing up his social standing*] Mr. Gilman? Yes.

Gilman. [*Doubtfully*] Mr. Jacob Twisden?

Graviter. [*Smiling*] His partner. Graviter my name is.

Gilman. Mr. Twisden's not in, then?

Graviter. No. He's at the Courts. They're just up; he should be in directly. But he'll be busy.

Gilman. Old Mr. Jacob Twisden—I've heard of him.

Graviter. Most people have. [*A pause.*

Gilman. It's this Dancy De Levis case that's keepin' him at the Courts, I suppose? [Graviter *nods.*]
Won't be finished for a day or two? [Graviter *shakes his head.*]
No. Astonishin' the interest taken in it.

Graviter. As you say.

666

GILMAN. The Smart Set, eh ? This Captain Dancy got the D.S.O., didn't he ?   [GRAVITER *nods*.]
Sad to have a thing like that said about you. I thought he gave his evidence well ; and his wife too. Looks as if this De Levis had got some private spite. *Searchy la femme*, I said to Mrs. Gilman only this morning, before I——

GRAVITER. By the way, sir, what is your business ?

GILMAN. Well, my business here—— No, if you'll excuse me, I'd rather wait and see old Mr. Jacob Twisden. It's delicate, and I'd like his experience.

GRAVITER. [*With a shrug*] Very well ; then, perhaps, you'll go in there.   [*He moves towards the door, Left Back*.

GILMAN. Thank you. [*Following*.] You see, I've never been mixed up with the law——

GRAVITER. [*Opening the door*] No ?

GILMAN. And I don't want to begin. When you do, you don't know where you'll stop, do you ? You see, I've only come from a sense of duty ; and—other reasons.

GRAVITER. Not uncommon.

GILMAN. [*Producing card*] This is my card. Gilman's—several branches, but this is the 'ead.

GRAVITER. [*Scrutinizing card*] Exactly.

GILMAN. Grocery—I daresay you know me ; or your wife does. They say old Mr. Jacob Twisden refused a knighthood. If it's not a rude question, why was that ?

GRAVITER. Ask him, sir ; ask him.

GILMAN. I said to my wife at the time, " He's holdin' out for a baronetcy."   [GRAVITER *closes the door with an exasperated smile*.

YOUNG CLERK. [*Opening the door, Left Forward*] Mr. Winsor, sir, and Miss Orme.   [*They enter, and the* CLERK *withdraws*.

GRAVITER. How d'you do, Miss Orme ? How do you do, Winsor ?

WINSOR. Twisden not back, Graviter ?

GRAVITER. Not yet.

WINSOR. Well, they've got through De Levis's witnesses. Sir Frederic was at the very top of his form. It's looking quite well. But I hear they've just subpœnaed Canynge after all. His evidence is to be taken to-morrow.

GRAVITER. Oho !

WINSOR. I said Dancy ought to have called him.

GRAVITER. We considered it. Sir Frederic decided that he could use him better in cross-examination.

WINSOR. Well ! I don't know that. Can I go and see him before he gives evidence to-morrow ?

GRAVITER. I should like to hear Mr. Jacob on that, Winsor. He'll be in directly.

WINSOR. They had Kentman, and Goole, the Inspector, the other bobby, my footman, Dancy's banker, and his tailor.

GRAVITER. Did we shake Kentman or Goole?

WINSOR. Very little. Oh! by the way, the numbers of those two notes were given, and I see they're published in the evening papers. I suppose the police wanted that. I tell you what I find, Graviter— a general feeling that there's something behind it all that doesn't come out.

GRAVITER. The public wants its money's worth—always does in these Society cases; they brew so long beforehand, you see.

WINSOR. They're looking for something lurid.

MARGARET. When I was in the box, I thought they were looking for me. [*Taking out her cigarette case.*] I suppose I mustn't smoke, Mr. Graviter?

GRAVITER. Do!

MARGARET. Won't Mr. Jacob have a fit?

GRAVITER. Yes, but not till you've gone.

MARGARET. Just a whiff. [*She lights a cigarette.*

WINSOR. [*Suddenly*] It's becoming a sort of Dreyfus case—people taking sides quite outside the evidence.

MARGARET. There are more of the chosen in Court every day. Mr. Graviter, have you noticed the two on the jury?

GRAVITER. [*With a smile*] No; I can't say——

MARGARET. Oh! but quite distinctly. Don't you think they ought to have been challenged?

GRAVITER. De Levis might have challenged the other ten, Miss Orme.

MARGARET. Dear me, now! I never thought of that.

[*As she speaks, the door Left Forward is opened and old* MR. JACOB TWISDEN *comes in. He is tallish and narrow, sixty-eight years old, grey, with narrow little whiskers curling round his narrow ears, and a narrow bow ribbon curling round his collar. He wears a long, narrow-tailed coat, and strapped trousers on his narrow legs. His nose and face are narrow, shrewd, and kindly. He has a way of narrowing his shrewd and kindly eyes. His nose is seen to twitch and sniff.*

TWISDEN. Ah! How are you, Charles? How do you do, my dear?

MARGARET. Dear Mr. Jacob, I'm smoking. Isn't it disgusting? But they don't allow it in Court, you know. Such a pity. The Judge might have a hookah. Oh! wouldn't he look sweet—the darling!

TWISDEN. [*With a little, old-fashioned bow*] It does not become everybody as it becomes you, Margaret.

MARGARET. Mr. Jacob, how charming!

[*With a slight grimace she puts out her cigarette.*

GRAVITER. Man called Gilman waiting in there to see you specially.

TWISDEN. Directly. Turn up the light, would you, Graviter?

GRAVITER. [*Turning up the light*] Excuse me.   [*He goes.*

WINSOR. Look here, Mr. Twisden——

TWISDEN. Sit down; sit down, my dear.

[*And he himself sits behind the table, as a cup of tea is brought in to him by the* YOUNG CLERK, *with two Marie biscuits in the saucer.*]

Will you have some, Margaret?

MARGARET. No, dear Mr. Jacob.

TWISDEN. Charles?

WINSOR. No, thanks.   [*The door is closed.*

TWISDEN. [*Dipping a biscuit in the tea*] Now, then?

WINSOR. The General knows something which on the face of it looks rather queer. Now that he's going to be called, oughtn't Dancy to be told of it, so that he may be ready with his explanation, in case it comes out?

TWISDEN. [*Pouring some tea into the saucer*] Without knowing, I can't tell you.

[WINSOR *and* MARGARET *exchange looks, and* TWISDEN *drinks from the saucer.*

MARGARET. Tell him, Charles.

WINSOR. Well! It rained that evening at Meldon. The General happened to put his hand on Dancy's shoulder, and it was damp.

[TWISDEN *puts the saucer down and replaces the cup in it. They both look intently at him.*

TWISDEN. I take it that General Canynge won't say anything he's not compelled to say.

MARGARET. No, of course; but, Mr. Jacob, they might ask; they know it rained. And he is such a George Washington.

TWISDEN. [*Toying with a pair of tortoise-shell glasses*] They didn't ask either of *you*. Still—no harm in your telling Dancy.

WINSOR. I'd rather *you* did it, Margaret.

MARGARET. I daresay.

[*She mechanically takes out her cigarette case, catches the lift of* TWISDEN'S *eyebrows, and puts it back.*

WINSOR. Well, we'll go together. I don't want Mrs. Dancy to hear.

MARGARET. Do tell me, Mr. Jacob; is he going to win?

TWISDEN. I think so, Margaret; I think so.

MARGARET. It'll be too frightful if he doesn't get a verdict, after all this. But I don't know what we shall do when it's over. I've been sitting in that Court all these three days, watching, and it's made me feel there's nothing we like better than seeing people skinned. Well, bye-bye, bless you!   [TWISDEN *rises and pats her hand.*

WINSOR. Half a second, Margaret. Wait for me.

                                   [*She nods and goes out.*]

Mr. Twisden, what do you really think?

TWISDEN. I am Dancy's lawyer, my dear Charles, as well as yours.

WINSOR. Well, can I go and see Canynge?

TWISDEN. Better not.

WINSOR. If they get that out of him, and recall me, am I to say he told me of it at the time?

TWISDEN. You didn't feel the coat yourself? And Dancy wasn't present? Then what Canynge told you is not evidence. *We'll* stop your being asked.

WINSOR. Thank goodness. Good-bye!   [WINSOR *goes out.*

[TWISDEN, *behind his table, motionless, taps his teeth with the eye-glasses in his narrow, well-kept hand. After a long shake of his head and a shrug of his rather high shoulders he sniffs, goes to the window and opens it. Then crossing to the door, Left Back, he throws it open and says:*

TWISDEN. At your service, sir.

[GILMAN *comes forth, nursing his pot hat.*]

Be seated.   [TWISDEN *closes the window behind him, and takes his seat.*

GILMAN. [*Taking the client's chair, to the left of the table*] Mr. Twisden, I believe? My name's Gilman, head of Gilman's Department Stores. You have my card.

TWISDEN. [*Looking at the card*] Yes. What can we do for you?

GILMAN. Well, I've come to you from a sense of duty, sir, and also a feelin' of embarrassment. [*He takes from his breast pocket an evening paper.*] You see, I've been followin' this Dancy case—it's a good deal talked of in Putney—and I read this at half-past two this afternoon. To be precise, at 2.25. [*He rises and hands the paper to* TWISDEN, *and with a thick gloved forefinger indicates a passage.*] When I read these numbers, I 'appened to remember givin' change for a fifty-pound note —don't often 'ave one in, you know—so I went to the cash-box out of curiosity, to see that I 'adn't got it. Well, I 'ad; and here it is. [*He draws out from his breast pocket and lays before* TWISDEN *a fifty-pound bank-note.*] It was brought in to change by a customer of mine three days ago, and he got value for it. Now, that's a stolen note, it seems, and you'd like to know what I did. Mind you, that customer of mine I've known 'im—well—eight or nine years; an Italian he is—wine salesman, and so far's I know, a respectable man—foreign-lookin', but nothin' more. Now, this was at 'alf-past two, and I was at my head branch at Putney, where I live. I want you to mark the time, so as you'll see I 'aven't wasted a minute. I took a cab and I drove straight to my customer's private residence in Putney, where he lives with his daughter—Ricardos his name is, Paolio Ricardos. They tell me there that he's at his business shop in the City. So off I go in the cab again, and there I find him. Well, sir, I showed this paper to him and I produced the note. " Here," I said, " you brought this to me and you got value for it." Well, that man was taken aback. If I'm a judge, Mr. Twisden, he was taken aback, not to speak in a guilty way, but he was, as you might say, flummoxed. "Now," I said to him, "where did you get it—that's the point?" He took his time to answer, and then he said: "Well, Mr. Gilman," he said, "you know me; I am an honourable man. I can't tell you offhand, but I am above the board." He's foreign, you know, in his expressions. "Yes," I said, "that's all very well," I said, "but here I've got a stolen note and you've got the value for it. Now I tell you," I said, "what I'm going to do; I'm going straight with this note to Mr. Jacob Twisden, who's got this Dancy De Levis case in 'and. He's a well-known Society lawyer," I said, "of great experience." "Oh!" he said, "that is what you do?"—funny the way he speaks! "Then I come with you!"—And I've got him in the cab below. I want to tell you everything before he comes up. On the way I tried to get something out of him, but I couldn't—I could *not*. "This is very awkward," I said at last. "It is, Mr. Gilman," was his reply; and he began to talk about his Sicilian claret—a very good wine, mind you; but under the circumstances it seemed to me uncalled for. Have I made it clear to you?

TWISDEN. [*Who has listened with extreme attention*] Perfectly, Mr. Gilman. I'll send down for him. [*He touches a hand-bell.*]
        [*The* YOUNG CLERK *appears at the door, Left Forward.*]
A gentleman in a taxi—waiting. Ask him to be so good as to step up. Oh! and send Mr. Graviter here again.
                              [*The* YOUNG CLERK *goes out.*
GILMAN. As I told you, sir, I've been followin' this case. It's what you might call piquant. And I should be very glad if it came about that this helped Captain Dancy. I take an interest, because, to tell you the truth, [*Confidentially*] I don't like—well, not to put too fine a point upon it—'Ebrews. They work harder; they're more sober; they're honest, and they're everywhere. I've nothing against them, but the fact is—they get *on* so.

TWISDEN. [*Cocking an eye*] A thorn in the flesh, Mr. Gilman.

GILMAN. Well, I prefer my own countrymen, and that's the truth of it.   [*As he speaks,* GRAVITER *comes in by the door Left Forward.*

TWISDEN. [*Pointing to the newspaper and the note*] Mr. Gilman has brought this, of which he is holder for value. His customer, who changed it three days ago, is coming up.

GRAVITER. The fifty-pounder. I see. [*His face is long and reflective.*

YOUNG CLERK. [*Entering*] Mr. Ricardos, sir. [*He goes out.*
        [RICARDOS *is a personable, Italian-looking man in a frock coat, with a dark moustachioed face and dark hair a little grizzled. He looks anxious, and bows.*

TWISDEN. Mr. Ricardos? My name is Jacob Twisden. My

partner. [*Holding up a finger*, *as* RICARDOS *would speak*.]   Mr. Gilman
has told us about this note.   You took it to him, he says, three days
ago ; that is, on Monday, and received cash for it ?

RICARDOS. Yes, sare.

TWISDEN. You were *not* aware that it was stolen ?

RICARDOS. [*With his hand to his breast*] Oh ! no, sare.

TWISDEN. You received it from——?

RICARDOS. A minute, sare ; I would weesh to explain—— [*With
an expressive shrug*] in private.

TWISDEN. [*Nodding*] Mr. Gilman, your conduct has been most
prompt.   You may safely leave the matter in our hands, now.   Kindly
let us retain this note ; and ask for my cashier as you go out and give
him [*He writes*] this.   He will reimburse you.   We will take any
necessary steps ourselves.

GILMAN. [*In slight surprise, with modest pride*] Well, sir, I'm in your
'ands.   I must be guided by you, with your experience.   I'm glad
you think I acted rightly.

TWISDEN. Very rightly, Mr. Gilman—very rightly. [*Rising.*] Good
afternoon !

GILMAN. Good afternoon, sir.   Good afternoon, gentlemen !
[*To* TWISDEN.] I'm sure I'm very 'appy to have made your acquaintance,
sir.   It's a well-known name.

TWISDEN. Thank you.

[GILMAN *retreats, glances at* RICARDOS, *and turns again.*

GILMAN. I suppose there's nothing else I ought to do, in the
interests of the law ?   I'm a careful man.

TWISDEN. If there is, Mr. Gilman, we will let you know.   We have
your address.   You may make your mind easy ; but don't speak of
this.   It might interfere with Justice.

GILMAN. Oh ! I shouldn't dream of it.   I've no wish to be mixed
up in anything conspicuous.   That's not my principle at all.   Good-
day, gentlemen.   [*He goes.*

TWISDEN. [*Seating himself*] Now, sir, will you sit down.

[*But* RICARDOS *does not sit ; he stands looking uneasily across the
table at* GRAVITER.]

You may speak out.

RICARDOS. Well, Mr. Tweesden and sare, this matter is very serious
for me, and very delicate—it concairns my honour.   I am in a great
difficulty.

TWISDEN. When in difficulty—complete frankness, sir.

RICARDOS. It is a family matter, sare, I——

TWISDEN. Let me be frank with *you*. [*Telling his points off on his
fingers.*] We have your admission that you changed this stopped note
for value.   It will be our duty to inform the Bank of England that it
has been traced to you.   You will have to account to them for your

possession of it.   I suggest to you that it will be far better to account frankly to us.

RICARDOS. [*Taking out a handkerchief and quite openly wiping his hands and forehead*] I received this note, sare, with others, from a gentleman, sare, in settlement of a debt of honour, and I know nothing of where he got them.

TWISDEN. H'm! that is very vague.   If that is all you can tell us, I'm afraid——

RICARDOS. Gentlemen, this is very painful for me.   It is my daughter's good name——   [*He again wipes his brow.*

TWISDEN. Come, sir, speak out!

RICARDOS. [*Desperately*] The notes were a settlement to her from this gentleman, of whom she was a great friend.

TWISDEN. [*Suddenly*] I am afraid we must press you for the name of the gentleman.

RICARDOS. Sare, if I give it to you, and it does 'im 'arm, what will my daughter say?   This is a bad matter for me.   He behaved well to her;   and she is attached to him still;   sometimes she is crying yet because she lost him.   And now we betray him perhaps, who knows?   This is very unpleasant for me.   [*Taking up the paper.*] Here it gives the number of another note—a 'undred-pound note.   I 'ave that too.

     [*He takes a note from his breast pocket.*

GRAVITER. How much did he give you in all?

RICARDOS. For my daughter's settlement one thousand pounds. I understand he did not wish to give a cheque because of his marriage. So I did not think anything about it being in notes, you see.

TWISDEN. When did he give you this money?

RICARDOS. The middle of Octobare last.

TWISDEN. [*Suddenly looking up*] Mr. Ricardos, was it Captain Dancy?

RICARDOS. [*Again wiping his forehead*] Gentlemen, I am so fond of my daughter.   I have only the one, and no wife.

TWISDEN. [*With an effort*] Yes, yes; but I must know.

RICARDOS. Sare, if I tell you, will you give me your good word that my daughter shall not hear of it?

TWISDEN. So far as we are able to prevent it—certainly.

RICARDOS. Sare, I trust you.—It was Captain Dancy. [*A long pause.*

GRAVITER. [*Suddenly*] Were you blackmailing him?

TWISDEN. [*Holding up his hand*] My partner means, did you press him for this settlement?

RICARDOS. I did think it my duty to my daughter to ask that he make compensation to her.

TWISDEN. With threats that you would tell his wife?

RICARDOS. [*With a shrug*] Captain Dancy was a man of honour.   He said: " Of course I will do this."   I trusted him.   And a month later I did remind him, and he gave me this money for her.   I do not know

22*

where he got it—I do not know. Gentlemen, I have invested it all on her—every penny—except this note, for which I had the purpose to buy her a necklace. That is the swearéd truth.

TWISDEN. I must keep this note. [*He touches the hundred-pound note.*] You will not speak of this to anyone. *I* may recognize that you were a holder for value received—others might take a different view. Good-day, sir. Graviter, see Mr. Ricardos out, and take his address.

RICARDOS. [*Pressing his hands over the breast of his frock coat—with a sigh*] Gentlemen, I beg you—remember what I said. [*With a roll of his eyes.*] My daughter—I am not happee. Good day.

> [*He turns and goes out slowly, Left Forward, followed by* GRAVITER.

TWISDEN. [*To himself*] Young Dancy ! [*He pins the two notes together and places them in an envelope, then stands motionless except for his eyes and hands, which restlessly express the disturbance within him.*]

> [GRAVITER *returns, carefully shuts the door, and going up to him, hands him* RICARDOS' *card.*]

[*Looking at the card.*] Villa Benvenuto. This will have to be verified, but I'm afraid it's true. That man was not acting.

GRAVITER. What's to be done about Dancy ?

TWISDEN. Can you understand a gentleman—— ?

GRAVITER. I don't know, sir. The war loosened " form " all over the place. I saw plenty of that myself. And some men have no moral sense. From the first I've had doubts.

TWISDEN. We can't go on with the case.

GRAVITER. Phew ! . . . [*A moment's silence.*] Gosh ! It's an awful thing for his wife.

TWISDEN. Yes.

GRAVITER. [*Touching the envelope*] Chance brought this here, sir. That man won't talk—he's too scared.

TWISDEN. Gilman.

GRAVITER. Too respectable. If De Levis got those notes back, and the rest of the money, anonymously ?

TWISDEN. But the case, Graviter ; the case.

GRAVITER. I don't believe this alters what I've been thinking.

TWISDEN. Thought is one thing—knowledge another. There's duty to our profession. Ours is a fine calling. On the good faith of solicitors a very great deal hangs.

> [*He crosses to the hearth as if warmth would help him.*

GRAVITER. It'll let him in for a prosecution. He came to us in confidence.

TWISDEN. Not as against the law.

GRAVITER. No. I suppose not. [*A pause.*] By Jove, I don't like losing this case. I don't like the admission we backed such a wrong 'un.

TWISDEN. Impossible to go on. Apart from ourselves, there's Sir

FREDERIC. We must disclose to him—can't let him go on in the dark. Complete confidence between solicitor and counsel is the essence of professional honour.

GRAVITER. What are you going to do then, sir ?

TWISDEN. See Dancy at once.   Get him on the 'phone.

GRAVITER. [*Taking up the telephone*] Get me Captain Dancy's flat. . . . What ? . . . [*To* TWISDEN.] Mrs. Dancy is here. That's *à propos* with a vengeance.   Are you going to see her, sir ?

TWISDEN. [*After a moment's painful hesitation*] I must.

GRAVITER. [*Telephoning*] Bring Mrs. Dancy up.

[*He turns to the window.*

[MABEL DANCY *is shown in, looking very pale.*   TWISDEN *advances from the fire, and takes her hand.*

MABEL. Major Colford's taken Ronny off in his car for the night. I thought it would do him good.   I said I'd come round in case there was anything you wanted to say before to-morrow.

TWISDEN. [*Taken aback*] Where have they gone ?

MABEL. I don't know, but he'll be home before ten o'clock to-morrow.   Is there anything ?

TWISDEN. Well, I'd like to see him before the Court sits.   Send him on here as soon as he comes.

MABEL. [*With her hand to her forehead*] Oh ! Mr. Twisden, when will it be over ?   My head's getting awful sitting in that Court.

TWISDEN. My dear Mrs. Dancy, there's no need at all for you to come down to-morrow ; take a rest and nurse your head.

MABEL. Really and truly ?

TWISDEN. Yes ; it's the very best thing you can do.

[GRAVITER *turns his head, and looks at them unobserved.*

MABEL. How do you think it's going ?

TWISDEN. It went very well to-day ; very well indeed.

MABEL. You must be awfully fed up with us.

TWISDEN. My dear young lady, that's our business.

[*He takes her hand.*

[MABEL'S *face suddenly quivers.   She draws her hand away, and covers her lips with it.*]

There, there !   You want a day off badly.

MABEL. I'm so tired of——— !   Thank you so much for all you're doing.   Good night !   Good night, Mr. Graviter !

GRAVITER. Good night, Mrs. Dancy.   [MABEL *goes.*

GRAVITER. D'you know, I believe she knows.

TWISDEN. No, no ! She believes in him implicitly. A staunch little woman.   Poor thing !

GRAVITER. Hasn't that shaken you, sir ?   It has me.

TWISDEN. No, no ! I—I can't go on with the case. It's breaking faith.   Get Sir Frederic's chambers.

GRAVITER. [*Telephoning, and getting a reply, looks round at* TWISDEN] Yes?

TWISDEN. Ask if I can come round and see him.

GRAVITER. [*Telephoning*] Can Sir Frederic spare Mr. Twisden a few minutes now if he comes round? [*Receiving reply.*] He's gone down to Brighton for the night.

TWISDEN. H'm! What hotel?

GRAVITER. [*Telephoning*] What's his address? What . . .? [*To* TWISDEN.] The Bedford.

TWISDEN. I'll go down.

GRAVITER. [*Telephoning*] Thank you. All right.   [*He rings off.*

TWISDEN. Just look out the trains down and up early to-morrow.

[GRAVITER *takes up an* A B C, *and* TWISDEN *takes up the* RICARDOS *card.*

TWISDEN. Send to this address in Putney, verify the fact that Ricardos has a daughter, and give me a trunk call to Brighton. Better go yourself, Graviter. If you see her, don't say anything, of course—invent some excuse. [GRAVITER *nods*.] I'll be up in time to see Dancy.

GRAVITER. By George! I feel bad about this.

TWISDEN. Yes. But professional honour comes first. What time is that train?   [*He bends over the* A B C.

The curtain falls.

SCENE II

The same room on the following morning at ten-twenty-five, by the grandfather clock.

[*The* YOUNG CLERK *is ushering in* DANCY, *whose face is perceptibly harder than it was three months ago, like that of a man who has lived under great restraint.*

DANCY. You wanted to see me before the Court sat.

YOUNG CLERK. Yes, sir. Mr. Twisden will see you in one minute. He had to go out of town last night.

[*He prepares to open the waiting-room door.*

DANCY. Were *you* in the war?

YOUNG CLERK. Yes.

DANCY. How can you stick this?

YOUNG CLERK. [*With a smile*] My trouble was to stick that, sir.

DANCY. But you get no excitement from year's end to year's end. It'd drive me mad.

YOUNG CLERK. [*Shyly*] A case like this is pretty exciting. I'd give a lot to see us win it.

DANCY. [*Staring at him*] Why ?   What is it to you ?

YOUNG CLERK. I don't know, sir.   It's—it's like football—you want your side to win. [*He opens the waiting-room door. Expanding.*] You see some rum starts, too, in a lawyer's office in a quiet way.

> [DANCY *enters the waiting-room, and the* YOUNG CLERK, *shutting the door, meets* TWISDEN *as he comes in, Left Forward, and takes from him overcoat, top hat, and a small bag.*

YOUNG CLERK. Captain Dancy's waiting, sir.

> [*He indicates the waiting-room.*

TWISDEN. [*Narrowing his lips*] Very well.   Mr. Graviter gone to the Courts ?

YOUNG CLERK. Yes, sir.

TWISDEN. Did he leave anything for me ?

YOUNG CLERK. On the table, sir.

TWISDEN. [*Taking up an envelope*] Thank you.   [*The* CLERK *goes.*

TWISDEN. [*Opening the envelope and reading*] " All corroborates." H'm ! [*He puts it in his pocket and takes out of an envelope the two notes, lays them on the table, and covers them with a sheet of blotting-paper ; stands a moment preparing himself, then goes to the door of the waiting-room, opens it, and says :*] Now, Captain Dancy.   Sorry to have kept you waiting.

DANCY. [*Entering*] Winsor came to me yesterday about General Canynge's evidence.   Is that what you wanted to speak to me about ?

TWISDEN. No.   It isn't that.

DANCY. [*Looking at his wrist watch*] By me it's just on the half-hour, sir.

TWISDEN. Yes.   I don't want you to go to the Court.

DANCY. Not ?

TWISDEN. I have very serious news for you.

DANCY. [*Wincing and collecting himself*] Oh !

TWISDEN. These two notes. [*He uncovers the notes.*] After the Court rose yesterday we had a man called Ricardos here. [*A pause.*] Is there any need for me to say more ?

DANCY. [*Unflinching*] No.   What now ?

TWISDEN. Our duty is plain ; we could not go on with the case. I have consulted Sir Frederic.   He felt—he felt that he must throw up his brief—and he will do that the moment the Court sits.   Now I want to talk to you about what you're going to do.

DANCY. That's very good of you, considering.

TWISDEN. I don't pretend to understand, but I imagine you may have done this in a moment of reckless bravado, feeling, perhaps, that as you gave the mare to De Levis, the money was by rights as much yours as his.   [*Stopping* DANCY, *who is about to speak, with a gesture.*] To satisfy a debt of honour to this—lady ; and, no doubt, to save your wife from hearing of it from the man, Ricardos.   Is that so ?

DANCY. To the life.

TWISDEN. It was mad, Captain Dancy, mad——! But the question now is : What do you owe to your wife ? She doesn't dream—I suppose ?

DANCY. [*With a twitching face*] No.

TWISDEN. We can't tell what the result of this collapse will be. The police have the theft in hand. They may issue a warrant. The money could be refunded, and the costs paid—somehow that can all be managed. But it may not help. In any case, what end is served by your staying in the country ? You can't save your honour—that's gone. You can't save your wife's peace of mind. If she sticks to you—do you think she will ?

DANCY. Not if she's wise.

TWISDEN. Better go ! There's a war in Morocco.

DANCY. [*With a bitter smile*] Good old Morocco !

TWISDEN. Will you go, then, at once, and leave me to break it to your wife ?

DANCY. I don't know yet.

TWISDEN. You must decide quickly, to catch a boat train. Many a man has made good. You're a fine soldier.

DANCY. There are alternatives.

TWISDEN. Now, go straight from this office. You've a passport, I suppose ; you won't need a *visa* for France, and from there you can find means to slip over. Have you got money on you ? [*Dancy nods.*] We will see what we can do to stop or delay proceedings.

DANCY. It's all damned kind of you. [*With difficulty.*] But I must think of my wife. Give me a few minutes.

TWISDEN. Yes, yes ; go in there and think it out.

> [*He goes to the door, Right, and opens it.* DANCY *passes him and goes out.* TWISDEN *rings a bell and stands waiting.*]

CLERK. [*Entering*] Yes, sir ?

TWISDEN. Tell them to call a taxi.

CLERK. [*Who has a startled look*] Yes, sir. Mr. Graviter has come in, sir, with General Canynge. Are you disengaged ?

TWISDEN. Yes.

> [*The* CLERK *goes out, and almost immediately* GRAVITER *and* CANYNGE *enter.*]

Good morning, General. [*To* GRAVITER.] Well ?

GRAVITER. Sir Frederic got up at once and said that since the publication of the numbers of those notes, information had reached him which forced him to withdraw from the case. Great sensation, of course. I left Bromley in charge. There'll be a formal verdict for the defendant, with costs. Have you told Dancy ?

TWISDEN. Yes. He's in there deciding what he'll do.

CANYNGE. [*Grave and vexed*] This is a dreadful thing, Twisden.

I've been afraid of it all along. A soldier! A gallant fellow, too.
What on earth got into him?

TWISDEN. There's no end to human nature, General.

GRAVITER. You can see queerer things in the papers, any day.

CANYNGE. That poor young wife of his! Winsor gave me a
message for you, Twisden. If money's wanted quickly to save proceedings, draw on him. Is there anything *I* can do?

TWISDEN. I've advised him to go straight off to Morocco.

CANYNGE. I don't know that an asylum isn't the place for him.
He must be off his head at moments. That jump—crazy! He'd
have got a verdict on that alone—if they'd seen those balconies. I
was looking at them when I was down there last Sunday. Daring
thing, Twisden. Very few men, on a dark night—— He risked his
life twice. That's a shrewd fellow—young De Levis. He spotted
Dancy's nature.   [*The* YOUNG CLERK *enters.*

CLERK. The taxi's here, sir. Will you see Major Colford and Miss
Orme?

TWISDEN. Graviter—— No; show them in.

                                          [*The* YOUNG CLERK *goes.*

CANYNGE. Colford's badly cut up.

                         [MARGARET ORME *and* COLFORD *enter.*

COLFORD. [*Striding forward*] There must be some mistake about this,
Mr. Twisden.

TWISDEN. Hssh! Dancy's in there. He's admitted it.

                                  [*Voices are subdued at once.*

COLFORD. What? [*With emotion.*] If it were my own brother, I
couldn't feel it more. But—damn it! What right had that fellow
to chuck up the case—without letting him know, too. I came down
with Dancy this morning, and he knew nothing about it.

TWISDEN. [*Coldly*] That was unfortunately unavoidable.

COLFORD. Guilty or not, you ought to have stuck to him—it's
not playing the game, Mr. Twisden.

TWISDEN. You must allow me to judge where my duty lay, in a
very hard case.

COLFORD. I thought a man was safe with his solicitor.

CANYNGE. Colford, you don't understand professional etiquette.

COLFORD. No, thank God!

TWISDEN. When you have been as long in your profession as I
have been in mine, Major Colford, you will know that duty to your
calling outweighs duty to friend or client.

COLFORD. But I serve the Country.

TWISDEN. And I serve the Law, sir.

CANYNGE. Graviter, give me a sheet of paper. I'll write a letter
for him.

MARGARET. [*Going up to* TWISDEN] Dear Mr. Jacob—pay De Levis.

You know my pearls—put them up the spout again.   Don't let Ronny be——

TWISDEN. Money isn't the point, Margaret.

MARGARET. It's ghastly ! It really is.

COLFORD. I'm going in to shake hands with him.

[*He starts to cross the room.*

TWISDEN. Wait ! We want him to go straight off to Morocco. Don't upset him. [*To* COLFORD *and* MARGARET.] I think you had better go. If, a little later, Margaret, you could go round to Mrs. Dancy——

COLFORD. Poor little Mabel Dancy ! It's perfect hell for her.

[*They have not seen that* DANCY *has opened the door behind them.*

DANCY. It is !   [*They all turn round in consternation.*

COLFORD. [*With a convulsive movement*] Old boy !

DANCY. No good, Colford. [*Gazing round at them.*] Oh ! clear out—I can't stand commiseration ; and let me have some air.

[TWISDEN *motions to* COLFORD *and* MARGARET *to go ; and as he turns to* DANCY, *they go out.* GRAVITER *also moves towards the door. The* GENERAL *sits motionless.* GRAVITER *goes out.*

TWISDEN. Well ?

DANCY. I'm going home, to clear up things with my wife. General Canynge, I don't quite know why I did the damned thing. But I did, and there's an end of it.

CANYNGE. Dancy, for the honour of the Army, avoid further scandal if you can. I've written a letter to a friend of mine in the Spanish War Office. It will get you a job in their war.

[CANYNGE *closes the envelope.*

DANCY. Very good of you. I don't know if I can make use of it.

[CANYNGE *stretches out the letter, which* TWISDEN *hands to* DANCY, *who takes it.* GRAVITER *reopens the door.*

TWISDEN. What is it ?

GRAVITER. De Levis is here.

TWISDEN. De Levis ? Can't see him.

DANCY. Let him in !

[*After a moment's hesitation* TWISDEN *nods, and* GRAVITER *goes out. The three wait in silence with their eyes fixed on the door, the* GENERAL *sitting at the table,* TWISDEN *by his chair,* DANCY *between him and the door Right.* DE LEVIS *comes in and shuts the door. He is advancing towards* TWISDEN *when his eyes fall on* DANCY, *and he stops.*

TWISDEN. You wanted to see me ?

DE LEVIS. [*Moistening his lips*] Yes. I came to say that—that I overheard—I am afraid a warrant is to be issued. I wanted you to realize—it's not *my* doing. It'll give it no support. I'm content. I don't want my money. I don't even want costs. Dancy, do you understand ?

[DANCY *does not answer, but looks at him with nothing alive in his face but his eyes.*

TWISDEN. We are obliged to you, sir.   It was good of you to come.

DE LEVIS. [*With a sort of darting pride*] Don't mistake me. I didn't come because I feel Christian ; I am a Jew. I will take no money—not even that which was stolen. Give it to a charity. I'm proved right. And now I'm done with the damned thing. Good morning !

[*He makes a little bow to* CANYNGE *and* TWISDEN, *and turns to face* DANCY, *who has never moved.   The two stand motionless, looking at each other, then* DE LEVIS *shrugs his shoulders and walks out.   When he is gone there is a silence.*

CANYNGE. [*Suddenly*] You heard what he said, Dancy. You have no time to lose.   [*But* DANCY *does not stir.*

TWISDEN. Captain Dancy ?

[*Slowly, without turning his head, rather like a man in a dream,* DANCY *walks across the room, and goes out.*

The curtain falls.

SCENE III

The DANCYS' *sitting-room, a few minutes later.*

[MABEL DANCY *is sitting alone on the sofa with a newspaper on her lap ; she is only just up, and has a bottle of smelling-salts in her hand.   Two or three other newspapers are dumped on the arm of the sofa.   She topples the one off her lap and takes up another as if she couldn't keep away from them ; drops it in turn, and sits staring before her, sniffing at the salts.   The door, Right, is opened and* DANCY *comes in.*

MABEL. [*Utterly surprised*] Ronny ! Do they want me in Court ?

DANCY. No.

MABEL. What is it, then ? Why are you back ?

DANCY. Spun.

MABEL. [*Blank*] Spun ? What do you mean ? What's spun ?

DANCY. The case. They've found out through those notes.

MABEL. Oh ! [*Staring at his face.*] Who ?

DANCY. Me !

MABEL. [*After a moment of horrified stillness*] Don't, Ronny ! Oh, No ! Don't ! [*She buries her face in the pillows of the sofa.*]

[DANCY *stands looking down at her.*

DANCY. Pity you wouldn't come to Africa three months ago.

MABEL. Why didn't you tell me then? I would have gone.

DANCY. You wanted this case. Well, it's fallen down.

MABEL. Oh! Why didn't I face it? But I couldn't—I *had* to believe.

DANCY. And now you can't. It's the end, Mabel.

MABEL. [*Looking up at him*] No.

[DANCY *goes suddenly on his knees and seizes her hand.*

DANCY. Forgive me!

MABEL. [*Putting her hand on his head*] Yes; oh, yes! I think I've known a long time, really. Only—why? What made you?

DANCY. [*Getting up and speaking in jerks*] It was a crazy thing to do; but, damn it, I was only looting a looter. The money was as much mine as his. A decent chap would have offered me half. You didn't see the brute look at me that night at dinner as much as to say: " You blasted fool! " It made me mad. That wasn't a bad jump —twice over. Nothing in the war took quite such nerve. [*Grimly.*] I rather enjoyed that evening.

MABEL. But—money! To keep it!

DANCY. [*Sullenly*] Yes, but I had a debt to pay.

MABEL. To a woman!

DANCY. A debt of honour—it wouldn't wait.

MABEL. It was—it *was* to a woman. Ronny, don't lie any more.

DANCY. [*Grimly*] Well! I wanted to save your knowing. I'd promised a thousand. I had a letter from her father that morning, threatening to tell you. All the same, if that tyke hadn't jeered at me for parlour tricks!—But what's the good of all this now? [*Sullenly.*] Well—it may cure you of loving me. Get over that, Mab; I never was worth it—and I'm done for!

MABEL. The woman—have you—since——?

DANCY. [*Energetically*] No! You supplanted her. But if you'd known I was leaving a woman for you, you'd never have married me.

[*He walks over to the hearth.*

[MABEL *too gets up. She presses her hands to her forehead, then walks blindly round to behind the sofa and stands looking straight in front of her.*

MABEL. [*Coldly*] What has happened, exactly?

DANCY. Sir Frederic chucked up the case. I've seen Twisden; they want me to run for it to Morocco.

MABEL. To the war there?

DANCY. Yes. There's to be a warrant out.

MABEL. A prosecution? Prison? Oh, go! Don't wait a minute! Go!

DANCY. Blast them!

MABEL. Oh, Ronny! Please! Please! Think what you'll want.

I'll pack. Quick! No! Don't wait to take things. Have you
got money?

DANCY. [*Nodding*] This'll be good-bye, then!

MABEL. [*After a moment's struggle*] Oh! No! No, no! I'll follow
—I'll come out to you there.

DANCY. D'you mean you'll stick to me?

MABEL. Of course I'll stick to you.

    [DANCY *seizes her hand and puts it to his lips. The bell rings.*

MABEL. [*In terror*] Who's that?

        [*The bell rings again. DANCY moves towards the door.*]

No! Let *me!*

    [*She passes him and steals out to the outer door of the flat, where she*
        stands listening. The bell rings again. She looks through
        the slit of the letter-box. While she is gone DANCY stands
        quite still, till she comes back.

MABEL. Through the letter-box—I can see—— It's—it's police.
Oh! God! . . . Ronny! I can't bear it.

DANCY. Heads up, Mab! Don't show the brutes!

MABEL. Whatever happens, I'll go on loving you. If it's prison—
I'll wait. Do you understand? I don't care what you did—I don't
care! I'm just the same. I will be just the same when you come
back to me.

DANCY. [*Slowly*] That's not in human nature.

MABEL. It is. It's in *me.*

DANCY. I've crocked up your life.

MABEL. No, no! Kiss me!

    [*A long kiss, till the bell again startles them apart, and there is a*
        loud knock.

DANCY. They'll break the door in. It's no good—we must open.
Hold them in check a little. I want a minute or two.

MABEL. [*Clasping him*] Ronny! Oh, Ronny! It won't be for
long—I'll be waiting! I'll be waiting—I swear it.

DANCY. Steady, Mab! [*Putting her back from him.*] Now!

    [*He opens the bedroom door, Left, and stands waiting for her to go.*
        Summoning up her courage, she goes to open the outer door.
        A sudden change comes over DANCY's face; from being stony
        it grows almost maniacal.

DANCY. [*Under his breath*] No! No! By God! No!

        [*He goes out into the bedroom, closing the door behind him.*

    [MABEL *has now opened the outer door, and disclosed* INSPECTOR
    DEDE *and the* YOUNG CONSTABLE *who were summoned to*
    Meldon Court on the night of the theft, and have been witnesses
    in the case. Their voices are heard.

MABEL. Yes?

INSPECTOR. Captain Dancy in, madam?

MABEL. I am not quite sure—I don't think so.

INSPECTOR. I wish to speak to him a minute.   Stay here, Grover. Now, madam !

MABEL. Will you come in while I see ?

[*She comes in, followed by the* INSPECTOR.

INSPECTOR. I should think you must be sure, madam.   This is not a big place.

MABEL. He was changing his clothes to go out.   I think he has gone.

INSPECTOR. What's that door ?

MABEL. To our bedroom.

INSPECTOR. [*Moving towards it*] He'll be in there, then.

MABEL. What do you want, Inspector ?

INSPECTOR. [*Melting*] Well, madam, it's no use disguising it.   I'm exceedingly sorry, but I've a warrant for his arrest.

MABEL. Inspector !

INSPECTOR. I'm sure I've every sympathy for you, madam ; but I must carry out my instructions.

MABEL. And break my heart ?

INSPECTOR. Well, madam, we're—we're not allowed to take that into consideration.   The Law's the Law.

MABEL. Are you married ?

INSPECTOR. I am.

MABEL. If you—your wife——

[*The* INSPECTOR *raises his hand, deprecating.*]

[*Speaking low.*] Just half an hour !   Couldn't you ?   It's two lives— two whole lives !   We've only been married four months.   Come back in half an hour.   It's such a little thing—nobody will know. Nobody.   Won't you ?

INSPECTOR. Now, madam—you must know my duty.

MABEL. Inspector, I beseech you—just half an hour.

INSPECTOR. No, no—don't you try to undermine me—I'm sorry for you ; but don't you try it !

[*He tries the handle, then knocks at the door.*

DANCY'S VOICE. One minute !

INSPECTOR. It's locked.   [*Sharply.*] Is there another door to that room ?   Come, now !   [*The bell rings.*]

[*Moving towards the door, Left ; to the* CONSTABLE] Who's that out there ?

CONSTABLE. A lady and gentleman, sir.

INSPECTOR. What lady and——   Stand by, Grover !

DANCY'S VOICE. All right !   You can come in *now*.

[*There is the noise of a lock being turned.   And almost immediately the sound of a pistol shot in the bedroom.   MABEL rushes to the door, tears it open, and disappears within, followed by the*

INSPECTOR, *just as* MARGARET ORME *and* COLFORD *come in from the passage, pursued by the* CONSTABLE. *They, too, all hurry to the bedroom door and disappear for a moment; then* COLFORD *and* MARGARET *reappear, supporting* MABEL, *who faints as they lay her on the sofa.* COLFORD *takes from her hand an envelope, and tears it open.*

COLFORD. It's addressed to *me.*

[*He reads it aloud to* MARGARET *in a low voice.*]

" DEAR COLFORD.—This is the only decent thing I can do. It's too damned unfair to her. It's only another jump. A pistol keeps faith. Look after her, Colford—my love to her, and you."

[MARGARET *gives a sort of choking sob, then, seeing the smelling bottle, she snatches it up, and turns to revive* MABEL.

COLFORD. Leave her ! The longer she's unconscious, the better.

INSPECTOR. [*Re-entering*] This is a very serious business, sir.

COLFORD. [*Sternly*] Yes, Inspector ; you've done for my best friend.

INSPECTOR. I, sir ? He shot himself.

COLFORD. Hara-kiri.

INSPECTOR. Beg pardon ?

COLFORD. [*He points with the letter to* MABEL] For her sake, and his own.

INSPECTOR. [*Putting out his hand*] I'll want that, sir.

COLFORD. [*Grimly*] You shall have it read at the inquest. Till then—it's addressed to me, and I stick to it.

INSPECTOR. Very well, sir. Do you want to have a look at him ?

[COLFORD *passes quickly into the bedroom, followed by the* INSPECTOR. MARGARET *remains kneeling beside* MABEL.

[COLFORD *comes quickly back.* MARGARET *looks up at him. He stands very still.*

COLFORD. Neatly—through the heart.

MARGARET. [*Wildly*] Keeps faith ! We've all done that. It's not enough.

COLFORD. [*Looking down at* MABEL] All right, old boy !

The curtain falls.

WINDOWS

CAST OF THE ORIGINAL PRODUCTION BY LEON M. LION AND J. T. GREIN, AT THE ROYAL COURT THEATRE, LONDON, APRIL 25, 1922

GEOFFREY MARCH	*Herbert Marshall*
JOAN MARCH	*Irene Rooke*
MARY MARCH	*Janet Eccles*
JOHNNY MARCH	*John Howell*
COOK	*Clare Greet*
MR. BLY	*Ernest Thesiger*
FAITH	*Mary Odette*
BLUNTER	*Leslie Banks*
MR. BARNABAS	*C. R. Norris*

ACT I

The MARCHS' *dining-room opens through French windows on one of those gardens which seem infinite, till they are seen to be coterminous with the side walls of the house, and finite at the far end, because only the thick screen of acacias and sumachs prevents another house from being seen. The French and other windows form practically all the outer wall of that dining-room, and between them and the screen of trees lies the difference between the characters of* MR. *and* MRS. MARCH, *with dots and dashes of* MARY *and* JOHNNY *thrown in. For instance, it has been formalized by* MRS. MARCH *but the grass has not been cut by* MR. MARCH, *and daffodils have sprung up there, which* MRS. MARCH *desires for the dining-room, but of which* MR. MARCH *says : " For God's sake, Joan, let them grow." About half therefore are now in a bowl on the breakfast table, and the other half still in the grass, in the compromise essential to lasting domesticity. A hammock under the acacias shows that* MARY *lies there sometimes with her eyes on the gleam of sunlight that comes through ; and a trail in the longish grass, bordered with cigarette ends, proves that* JOHNNY *tramps there with his eyes on the ground or the stars, according. But all this is by the way, because except for a yard or two of gravel terrace outside the windows, it is all painted on the backcloth. The* MARCHES *have been at breakfast, and the round table, covered with blue linen, is thick with remains, seven baskets full. The room is gifted with old oak furniture : there is a door, stage Left, Forward ; a hearth, where a fire is burning, and a high fender on which one can sit, stage Right, Middle ; and in the wall below the fireplace, a service hatch covered with a sliding shutter, for the passage of dishes into the adjoining pantry. Against the wall, stage Left, is an old oak dresser, and a small writing table across the Left Back corner.* MRS. MARCH *still sits behind the coffee pot, making up her daily list on tablets with a little gold pencil fastened to her wrist. She is personable, forty-eight, trim, well-dressed, and more matter-of-fact than seems plausible.* MR. MARCH *is sitting in an armchair, sideways to the windows, smoking his pipe and reading his newspaper, with little explosions to which no one pays any attention, because it is his daily habit. He is a fine-looking man of fifty odd, with red-grey moustaches and hair, both of which stiver partly by nature and partly because his hands often push them up.* MARY *and* JOHNNY *are close to the fireplace, stage Right.* JOHNNY *sits on the fender, smoking a cigarette and warming his back. He is a commonplace-looking young*

*man, with a decided jaw, tall, neat, soulful, who has been in the war
and writes poetry. MARY is less ordinary; you cannot tell exactly
what is the matter with her. She too is tall, a little absent, fair, and
well-looking. She has a small china dog in her hand, taken from the
mantelpiece, and faces the audience. As the curtain rises she is saying
in her soft and pleasant voice : " Well, what is the matter with us
all, Johnny ? "*

JOHNNY. Stuck, as we were in the trenches—like china dogs.
                             [He points to the ornament in her hand.
MR. MARCH. [*Into his newspaper*] *Damn* these people !
MARY. If there isn't an ideal left, Johnny, it's no good pretending
one.
JOHNNY. That's what I'm saying : Bankrupt !
MARY. What do you want ?
MRS. MARCH. [*To herself*] Mutton cutlets. Johnny, will you be
in to lunch ? [JOHNNY *shakes his head.*] Mary ? [MARY *nods.*] Geof ?
MR. MARCH. [*Into his paper*] Swine !
MRS. MARCH. That'll be three. [*To herself.*] Spinach.
JOHNNY. If you'd just missed being killed for three blooming years
for no spiritual result whatever, you'd want something to bite on, Mary.
MRS. MARCH. [*Jotting*] Soap.
JOHNNY. What price the little and weak, now ? Freedom and self-
determination, and all that ?
MARY. Forty to one—no takers.
JOHNNY. It doesn't seem to worry *you*.
MARY. Well, what's the good ?
JOHNNY. Oh, you're a looker-on, Mary.
MR. MARCH. [*To his newspaper*] Of all God-forsaken time-servers !
        [MARY is moved so far as to turn and look over his shoulder a minute.
JOHNNY. Who ?
MARY. Only the Old-Un.
MR. MARCH. This is absolutely Prussian !
MRS. MARCH. Soup, lobster, chicken salad. Go to Mrs. Hunt's.
MR. MARCH. And this fellow hasn't the nous to see that if ever
there were a moment when it would pay us to take risks, and be
generous—My hat ! He ought to be—knighted ! [*Resumes his paper.*
JOHNNY. [*Muttering*] You see, even Dad can't suggest chivalry
without talking of payment for it. That shows how we've sunk.
MARY. [*Contemptuously*] Chivalry ! Pouf ! Chivalry was " off "
even before the war, Johnny. Who wants chivalry ?
JOHNNY. Of all shallow-pated humbug—that sneering at chivalry's
the worst. Civilization—such as we've got—is built on it.
MARY. [*Airily*] Then it's built on sand.
                                 [She sits beside him on the fender.

JOHNNY. Sneering and smartness! Pah!

MARY. [*Roused*] I'll tell you what, Johnny, it's mucking about with chivalry that makes your poetry rotten. [JOHNNY *seizes her arm and twists it.*] Shut up—that hurts. [JOHNNY *twists it more.*] You brute! [JOHNNY *lets her arm go.*

JOHNNY. Ha! So you don't mind taking advantage of the fact that you can cheek me with impunity, because you're weaker. You've given the whole show away, Mary. Abolish chivalry and I'll make you sit up.

MRS. MARCH. What are you two quarrelling about? Will you bring home cigarettes, Johnny—not Bogdogunov's Mamelukes— something more Anglo-American.

JOHNNY. All right! D'you want any more illustrations, Mary?

MARY. Pig! [*She has risen and stands rubbing her arm and recovering her placidity, which is considerable.*

MRS. MARCH. Geof, can you eat preserved peaches?

MR. MARCH. Hell! What a policy! Um?

MRS. MARCH. Can you eat preserved peaches?

MR. MARCH. Yes. [*To his paper.*] Making the country stink in the eyes of the world!

MARY. Nostrils, Dad, nostrils. [MR. MARCH *wriggles, half hearing.*

JOHNNY. [*Muttering*] Shallow idiots! Thinking we can do without chivalry!

MRS. MARCH. I'm doing my best to get a parlourmaid, to-day, Mary, but these breakfast things won't clear themselves.

MARY. I'll clear them, Mother.

MRS. MARCH. Good! [*She gets up. At the door.*] Knitting silk.
[*She goes out.*

JOHNNY. Mother hasn't an ounce of idealism. You might make her see stars, but never in the singular.

MR. MARCH. [*To his paper*] If God doesn't open the earth soon——

MARY. Is there anything special, Dad?

MR. MARCH. This sulphurous government. [*He drops the paper.*] Give me a match, Mary.
[*As soon as the paper is out of his hands he becomes a different— an affable man.*

MARY. [*Giving him a match*] D'you mind writing in here this morning, Dad? Your study hasn't been done. There's nobody but Cook.

MR. MARCH. [*Lighting his pipe*] Anywhere.
[*He slews the armchair towards the fire.*

MARY. I'll get your things, then. [*She goes out.*

JOHNNY. [*Still on the fender*] What do you say, Dad? Is civilization built on chivalry or on self-interest?

MR. MARCH. The question is considerable, Johnny. I should say it was built on contract, and jerry-built at that.

JOHNNY. Yes; but why do we keep contracts when we can break them with advantage and impunity?

MR. MARCH. But do we keep them?

JOHNNY. Well—say we do; otherwise you'll admit there isn't such a thing as civilization at all. But *why* do we keep them? For instance, why don't we make Mary and Mother work for us like Kafir women? We could lick them into it. Why did we give women the vote? Why free slaves; why anything decent for the little and weak?

MR. MARCH. Well, you might say it was convenient for people living in communities.

JOHNNY. I don't think it's convenient at all. I should like to make Mary sweat. Why not jungle law, if there's nothing in chivalry.

MR. MARCH. Chivalry is altruism, Johnny. Of course it's quite a question whether altruism isn't enlightened self-interest!

JOHNNY. Oh! Damn!

[*The lank and shirt-sleeved figure of* MR. BLY, *with a pail of water and cloths, has entered, and stands near the window, Left.*

BLY. Beg pardon, Mr. March; d'you mind me cleanin' the winders here?

MR. MARCH. Not a bit.

JOHNNY. Bankrupt of ideals. That's it!

[MR. BLY *stares at him, and puts his pail down by the window.*
[MARY *has entered with her father's writing materials, which she puts on a stool beside him.*

MARY. Here you are, Dad! I've filled up the ink-pot. Do be careful! Come on, Johnny!

[*She looks curiously at* MR. BLY, *who has begun operations at the bottom of the left-hand window, and goes, followed by* JOHNNY.

MR. MARCH. [*Relighting his pipe and preparing his materials*] What do *you* think of things, Mr. Bly?

BLY. Not much, sir.

MR. MARCH. Ah! [*He looks up at* MR. BLY, *struck by his large philosophical eyes and moth-eaten moustache.*] Nor I.

BLY. I rather thought that, sir, from your writin's.

MR. MARCH. Oh! Do you read?

BLY. I was at sea, once—formed the 'abit.

MR. MARCH. Read any of my novels?

BLY. Not to say all through—I've read some of your articles in the Sunday papers, though. Make you think!

MR. MARCH. *I'm* at sea now—don't see dry land anywhere, Mr. Bly.

BLY. [*With a smile*] That's right.

MR. MARCH. D'you find that the general impression?

BLY. No. People *don't* think. You 'ave to 'ave some cause for thought.

MR. MARCH. Cause enough in the papers.

BLY. It's nearer 'ome with me. I've often thought I'd like a talk with you, sir. But I'm keepin' you.   [*He prepares to swab the pane.*

MR. MARCH. Not at all. I enjoy it. Anything to put off work.

BLY. [*Looking at* MR. MARCH, *then giving a wipe at the window*] What's drink to one is drought to another. I've seen two men take a drink out of the same can—one die of it and the other get off with a pain in his stomach.

MR. MARCH. You've seen a lot, I expect.

BLY. Ah! I've been on the beach in my day. [*He sponges at the window.*] It's given me a way o' lookin' at things that I don't find in other people. Look at the 'Ome Office. *They* got no philosophy.

MR. MARCH. [*Pricking his ears*] What? Have you had dealings with them?

BLY. Over the reprieve that was got up for my daughter. But I'm keepin' you.

          [*He swabs at the window, but always at the same pane, so that he
          does not advance at all.*

MR. MARCH. Reprieve?

BLY. Ah! She was famous at eighteen. The *Sunday Mercury* was full of her, when she was in prison.

MR. MARCH. [*Delicately*] Dear me! I'd no idea.

BLY. She's out now; been out a fortnight. I always say that fame's ephemeral. But she'll never settle to that weavin'. Her head got turned a bit.

MR. MARCH. I'm afraid I'm in the dark, Mr. Bly.

BLY. [*Pausing—dipping his sponge in the pail and then standing with it in his hand*] Why! Don't you remember the Bly case? They sentenced 'er to be 'anged by the neck until she was dead, for smotherin' her baby. She was only eighteen at the time of speakin'.

MR. MARCH. Oh! yes! An inhuman business!

BLY. Ah! The jury recommended 'er to mercy. So they reduced it to Life.

MR. MARCH. Life! Sweet Heaven!

BLY. That's what I said; so they give her two years. I don't hold with the *Sunday Mercury*, but it put *that* over. It's a misfortune to a girl to be good-lookin'.

MR. MARCH. [*Rumpling his hair*] No, no! Dash it all! Beauty's the only thing left worth living for.

BLY. Well, I like to see green grass and a blue sky; but it's a mistake in a 'uman bein'. Look at any young chap that's good-lookin'—'e's doomed to the screen, or hair-dressin'. Same with the girls. My girl went into an 'airdresser's at seventeen and in six months she was in trouble. When I saw 'er with a rope round her neck, as you might say, I said to meself : " Bly," I said, " you're responsible for this— If she 'adn't been good-lookin'—it'd never 'ave 'appened."

[*During this speech* MARY *has come in with a tray, to clear the break-fast, and stands unnoticed at the dining-table, arrested by the curious words of* MR. BLY.

MR. MARCH. Your wife might not have thought that you were wholly the cause, Mr. Bly.

BLY. Ah! My wife. She's passed on. But Faith—that's my girl's name—she never was like 'er mother; there's no 'eredity in 'er on that side.

MR. MARCH. What sort of girl is she ?

BLY. One for colour—likes a bit o' music—likes a dance, and a flower.

MARY. [*Interrupting softly*] Dad, I was going to clear, but I'll come back later.

MR. MARCH. Come here and listen to this ! Here's a story to get your blood up ! How old was the baby, Mr. Bly ?

BLY. Two days—'ardly worth mentionin'. They say she 'ad the 'ighstrikes after—an' when she comes to she says : " I've saved my baby's life." An' that's true enough when you come to think what that sort o' baby goes through as a rule ; dragged up by somebody else's hand, or took away by the Law. What can a workin' girl do with a baby born under the rose, as they call it ? Wonderful the difference money makes when it comes to bein' outside the Law.

MR. MARCH. Right you are, Mr. Bly. God's on the side of the big battalions.

BLY. Ah! Religion ! [*His eyes roll philosophically.*] Did you ever read 'Aigel ?

MR. MARCH. Hegel, or Haekel ?

BLY. Yes ; with an aitch. There's a balance abart 'im that I like. There's no doubt the Christian religion went too far. Turn the other cheek ! What oh ! An' this Anti-Christ, Neesha, what came in with the war—he went too far in the other direction. Neither of 'em practical men. You've got to strike a balance, and foller it.

MR. MARCH. Balance ! Not much balance about us. We just run about and jump Jim Crow.

BLY. [*With a perfunctory wipe*] That's right ; we 'aven't got a faith these days. But what's the use of tellin' the Englishman to act like an angel. He ain't either an angel or a blond beast. He's between the two, an 'ermumphradite. Take my daughter—— If I was a blond beast, I'd turn 'er out to starve ; if I was an angel, I'd starve meself to learn her the piano. I don't do either. Why ? Becos my instincts tells me not.

MR. MARCH. Yes, but my doubt is whether our instincts at this moment of the world's history are leading us up or down.

BLY. What is up and what is down ? Can you answer me that ? Is it up or down to get so soft that you can't take care of yourself ?

MR. MARCH. Down.

BLY. Well, is it up or down to get so 'ard that you can't take care of others ?

MR. MARCH. Down.

BLY. Well, there you are !

MR. MARCH. Then our instincts are taking us down ?

BLY. Nao. They're strikin' a balance, unbeknownst, all the time.

MR. MARCH. You're a philosopher, Mr. Bly.

BLY. [*Modestly*] Well, I do a bit in that line, too. In my opinion Nature made the individual believe he's goin' to live after 'e's dead just to keep 'im livin' while 'e's alive—otherwise he'd 'a died out.

MR. MARCH. Quite a thought—quite a thought !

BLY. But I go one better with Nature. Follow your instincts is my motto.

MR. MARCH. Excuse me, Mr. Bly, I think Nature got hold of that before you.

BLY. [*Slightly chilled*] Well, I'm keepin' you.

MR. MARCH. Not at all. You're a believer in conscience, or the little voice within. When my son was very small, his mother asked him once if he didn't hear a little voice within, telling him what was right. [MR. MARCH *touches his diaphragm.*] And he said : " I often hear little voices in here, but they never *say* anything." [MR. BLY *cannot laugh, but he smiles.*] Mary, Johnny must have been awfully like the Government.

BLY. As a matter of fact, I've got my daughter here—in obeyance.

MR. MARCH. Where ? I didn't catch.

BLY. In the kitchen. Your Cook told me you couldn't get hold of an 'ouse parlour-maid. So I thought it was just a chance—you bein' broad-minded.

MR. MARCH. Oh ! I see. What would your mother say, Mary ?

MARY. Mother would say : " Has she had experience ? "

BLY. I've told you about her experience.

MR. MARCH. Yes, but—as a parlour-maid.

BLY. Well ! She can do hair. [*Observing the smile exchanged between* MR. MARCH *and* MARY.] And she's quite handy with a plate.

MR. MARCH. [*Tentatively*] I'm a little afraid my wife would feel——

BLY. You see, in this weavin' shop—all the girls 'ave 'ad to be in trouble, otherwise they wouldn't take 'em. [*Apologetically towards* MARY.] It's a kind of a disorderly 'ouse without the disorders. Excusin' the young lady's presence.

MARY. Oh ! You needn't mind me, Mr. Bly.

MR. MARCH. And so you want her to come here? H'm!

BLY. Well, I remember when she was a little bit of a thing—no higher than my knee—— [*He holds out his hand.*

MR. MARCH. [*Suddenly moved*] My God! yes. They've all been that. [*To* MARY.] Where's your mother?

MARY. Gone to Mrs. Hunt's. Suppose she's engaged one, Dad?

MR. MARCH. Well, it's only a month's wages.

MARY. [*Softly*] She won't like it.

MR. MARCH. Well, let's see her, Mr. Bly; let's see her, if you don't mind.

BLY. Oh, I don't mind, sir, and she won't neither; she's used to bein' inspected by now. Why! she 'ad her bumps gone over just before she came out!

MR. MARCH. [*Touched on the raw again*] H'm! Too bad! Mary, go and fetch her. [MARY, *with a doubting smile, goes out.*] [*Rising.*] You might give me the details of that trial, Mr. Bly. I'll see if I can't write something that'll make people sit up. *That's* the way to send Youth to hell! How can a child who's had a rope round her neck——!

BLY. [*Who has been fumbling in his pocket, produces some yellow paper-cuttings clipped together*] Here's her references—the whole literature of the case. And here's a letter from the chaplain in one of the prisons sayin' she took a lot of interest in him; a nice young man, I believe. [*He suddenly brushes a tear out of his eye with the back of his hand.*] I never thought I could 'a felt like I did over her bein' in prison. Seemed a crool senseless thing—that pretty girl o' mine. All over a baby that hadn't got used to bein' alive. Tain't as if she'd been follerin' her instincts; why, she missed that baby something crool.

MR. MARCH. Of course, human life—even an infant's——

BLY. I know you've got to 'ave a close time for it. But when you come to think how they take 'uman life in Injia and Ireland, and all those other places, it seems 'ard to come down like a cartload o' bricks on a bit of a girl that's been carried away by a moment's abiration.

MR. MARCH. [*Who is reading the cuttings*] H'm! What hypocrites we are!

BLY. Ah! And 'oo can tell 'oo's the father? She never give us his name. I think the better of 'er for that.

MR. MARCH. Shake hands, Mr. Bly. So do I. [BLY *wipes his hand, and* MR. MARCH *shakes it.*] Loyalty's loyalty—especially when we men benefit by it.

BLY. That's right, sir.

[MARY *has returned with* FAITH BLY, *who stands demure and pretty on the far side of the table, her face an embodiment of the pathetic watchful prison faculty of adapting itself to whatever*

*may be best for its owner at the moment.   At this moment
it is obviously best for her to look at the ground, and yet to take
in the faces of* MR. MARCH *and* MARY *without their taking
her face in.   A moment, for all, of considerable embarrassment.*

MR. MARCH. [*Suddenly*] Well, here we are !

[*The remark attracts* FAITH ; *she raises her eyes to his softly with
a little smile, and drops them again.*]

So you want to be our parlour-maid ?

FAITH. Yes, please.

MR. MARCH. Well, Faith can remove mountains ; but—er—I
don't know if she can clear tables.

BLY. I've been tellin' Mr. March and the young lady what you're
capable of.   Show 'em what you can do with a plate.

[FAITH *takes the tray from the sideboard and begins to clear the
table, mainly by the light of nature.   After a glance,* MR.
MARCH *looks out of the window and drums his fingers on the
uncleaned pane.* MR. BLY *goes on with his cleaning.* MARY, *after
watching from the hearth, goes up and touches her father's arm.*

MARY. [*Between him and* MR. BLY, *who is bending over his bucket,
softly*] You're not watching, Dad.

MR. MARCH. It's too pointed.

MARY. We've got to satisfy mother.

MR. MARCH. I can satisfy her better if I don't look.

MARY. You're right.

[FAITH *has paused a moment and is watching them.   As* MARY
turns, she resumes her operations. MARY *joins, and helps
her finish clearing, while the two men converse.*

BLY. Fine weather, sir, for the time of year.

MR. MARCH. It is.   The trees are growing.

BLY. Ah ! I wouldn't be surprised to see a change of Government
before long.   I've seen 'uge trees in Brazil without any roots—seen
'em come down with a crash.

MR. MARCH. Good image, Mr. Bly.   Hope you're right !

BLY. Well, Governments !   They're all the same—Butter when
they're out of power, and blood when they're in.   And Lord ! 'ow
they do abuse other Governments for doin' the things they do
themselves.   Excuse me, I'll want her dosseer back, sir, when you've
done with it.

MR. MARCH. Yes, yes.   [*He turns, rubbing his hands at the cleared
table.*] Well, that seems all right !   And you can do hair ?

FAITH. Oh ! Yes, I can do hair.

[*Again that little soft look, and smile so carefully adjusted.*

MR. MARCH. That's important, don't you think, Mary ?   [MARY,
accustomed to candour, smiles dubiously.] [*Brightly.*] Ah ! And cleaning
plate ?   What about that ?

23

FAITH. Of course, if I had the opportunity——

MARY. You haven't—so far?

FAITH. Only tin things.

MR. MARCH. [*Feeling a certain awkwardness*] Well, I daresay we can find some for you. Can you—er—be firm on the telephone?

FAITH. Tell them you're engaged when you're not? Oh! yes.

MR. MARCH. Excellent! Let's see, Mary, what else is there?

MARY. Waiting, and house work.

MR. MARCH. Exactly.

FAITH. I'm very quick. I—I'd like to come. [*She looks down.*] I don't care for what I'm doing now. It makes you feel your position.

MARY. Aren't they nice to you?

FAITH. Oh! yes—kind; but— [*She looks up.*] It's against my instincts.

MR. MARCH. Oh! [*Quizzically.*] You've got a disciple, Mr. Bly.

BLY. [*Rolling his eyes at his daughter*] Ah! but you mustn't 'ave instincts here, you know. You've got a chance, and you must come to stay, and do yourself credit.

FAITH. [*Adapting her face*] Yes, I know, I'm very lucky.

MR. MARCH. [*Deprecating thanks and moral precept*] That's all right! Only, Mr. Bly, I can't absolutely answer for Mrs. March. She may think——

MARY. There *is* Mother; I heard the door.

BLY. [*Taking up his pail*] I quite understand, sir; I've been a married man myself. It's very queer the way women look at things. I'll take her away now, and come back presently and do these other winders. You can talk it over by yourselves. But if you do see your way, sir, I shan't forget it in an 'urry. To 'ave the responsibility of her—really, it's dreadful.

[FAITH's *face has grown sullen during this speech, but it clears up in another little soft look at* MR. MARCH, *as she and* MR. BLY *go out.*

MR. MARCH. Well, Mary, have I done it?

MARY. You have, Dad.

MR. MARCH. [*Running his hands through his hair*] Pathetic little figure! Such infernal inhumanity!

MARY. How are you going to put it to mother?

MR. MARCH. Tell her the story, and pitch it strong.

MARY. Mother's not impulsive.

MR. MARCH. We *must* tell her, or she'll think me mad.

MARY. She'll do that, anyway, dear.

MR. MARCH. Here she is! Stand by!

[*He runs his arm through* MARY's, *and they sit on the fender, at bay.* MRS. MARCH *enters, Left.*

MR. MARCH. Well, what luck?

MRS. MARCH. None.

MR. MARCH. [*Unguardedly*] Good!

MRS. MARCH. What?

MR. MARCH. [*Cheerfully*] Well, the fact is, Mary and I have caught one for you; Mr. Bly's daughter——

MRS. MARCH. Are you out of your senses? Don't you know that she's the girl who——

MR. MARCH. That's it. She wants a lift.

MRS. MARCH. Geof!

MR. MARCH. Well, don't we want a maid?

MRS. MARCH. [*Ineffably*] Ridiculous!

MR. MARCH. We tested her, didn't we, Mary?

MRS. MARCH. [*Crossing to the bell, and ringing*] You'll just send for Mr. Bly and get rid of her again.

MR. MARCH. Joan, if we comfortable people can't put ourselves a little out of the way to give a helping hand——

MRS. MARCH. To girls who smother their babies?

MR. MARCH. Joan, I revolt. I won't be a hypocrite and a Pharisee.

MRS. MARCH. Well, for goodness sake let *me* be one.

MARY. [*As the door opens*] Here's Cook!

[COOK *stands—sixty, stout, and comfortable—with a crumpled smile.*

COOK. Did you ring, ma'am?

MR. MARCH. We're in a moral difficulty, Cook, so naturally we come to you.   [COOK *beams.*

MRS. MARCH. [*Impatiently*] Nothing of the sort, Cook; it's a question of common sense.

COOK. Yes, ma'am.

MRS. MARCH. That girl, Faith Bly, wants to come here as parlourmaid. Absurd!

MR. MARCH. You know her story, Cook? I want to give the poor girl a chance. Mrs. March thinks it's *taking* chances. What do you say?

COOK. Of course, it is a risk, sir; but there! you've got to take 'em to get maids nowadays. If it isn't in the past, it's in the future. I daresay I could learn 'er.

MRS. MARCH. It's not her work, Cook, it's her instincts. A girl who smothered a baby that she oughtn't to have had——

MR. MARCH. [*Remonstrant*] If she hadn't had it how could she have smothered it?

COOK. [*Soothingly*] Perhaps she's repented, ma'am.

MRS. MARCH. Of course she's repented. But did you ever know repentance change anybody, Cook?

COOK. [*Smiling*] Well, generally it's a way of gettin' ready for the next.

Mrs. March. Exactly.

Mr. March. If we never get another chance *because* we repent——

Cook. I always think of Master Johnny, ma'am, and my jam; he used to repent so beautiful, dear little feller—such a conscience! I never could bear to lock it away.

Mrs. March. Cook, you're wandering. I'm surprised at your encouraging the idea; I really am. [Cook *plaits her hands*.

Mr. March. Cook's been in the family longer than I have—haven't you, Cook? [Cook *beams*.] She knows much more about a girl like that than we do.

Cook. We had a girl like her, I remember, in your dear mother's time, Mr. Geoffrey.

Mr. March. How did she turn out?

Cook. Oh! She didn't.

Mrs. March. There!

Mr. March. Well, I can't bear behaving like everybody else. Don't you think we might give her a chance, Cook?

Cook. My 'eart says yes, ma'am.

Mr. March. Ha!

Cook. And my 'ead says no, sir.

Mrs. March. Yes!

Mr. March. Strike your balance, Cook.

[Cook *involuntarily draws her joined hands sharply in upon her amplitude.*]

Well? . . . I didn't catch the little voice within.

Cook. Ask Master Johnny, sir; he's been in the war.

Mr. March. [*To* Mary] Get Johnny. [Mary *goes out*.

Mrs. March. What on earth has the war to do with it?

Cook. The things he tells me, ma'am, is too wonderful for words. He's 'ad to do with prisoners and generals, every sort of 'orror.

Mr. March. Cook's quite right. The war destroyed all our ideals and probably created the baby.

Mrs. March. It didn't smother it; or condemn the girl.

Mr. March. [*Running his hands through his hair*] The more I think of that——! [*He turns away*.

Mrs. March. [*Indicating her husband*] You see, Cook, that's the mood in which I have to engage a parlour-maid. What am I to do with your master?

Cook. It's an 'ealthy rage, ma'am.

Mrs. March. I'm tired of being the only sober person in this house.

Cook. [*Reproachfully*] Oh! ma'am, I never touch a drop.

Mrs. March. I didn't mean anything of that sort. But they do break out so.

Cook. Not Master Johnny.

MRS. MARCH. Johnny ! He's the worst of all. His poetry is nothing but one long explosion.

MR. MARCH. [*Coming from the window*] I say : We ought to have faith and jump.

MRS. MARCH. If we do have Faith, we shall jump.

COOK. [*Blankly*] Of course, in the Bible they 'ad faith, and just look what it did to them !

MR. MARCH. I mean faith in human instincts, human nature, Cook.

COOK. [*Scandalized*] Oh ! no, sir, *not* human nature ; I never let that get the upper hand.

MR. MARCH. You talk to Mr. Bly. He's a remarkable man.

COOK. I do, sir, every fortnight when he does the kitchen windows.

MR. MARCH. Well, doesn't he impress you ?

COOK. Ah ! When he's got a drop o' stout in 'im—Oh ! dear !

[*She smiles placidly.*

[JOHNNY *has come in.*

MR. MARCH. Well, Johnny, has Mary told you ?

MRS. MARCH. [*Looking at his face*] Now, my dear boy, don't be hasty and foolish !

JOHNNY. Of course you ought to take her, Mother.

MRS. MARCH. [*Fixing him*] Have you seen her, Johnny ?

JOHNNY. She's in the hall, poor little devil, waiting for her sentence.

MRS. MARCH. There are plenty of other chances, Johnny. Why on earth should we—— ?

JOHNNY. Mother, it's just an instance. When something comes along that takes a bit of doing—— Give it to the other chap !

MR. MARCH. Bravo, Johnny !

MRS. MARCH. [*Dryly*] Let me see, which of us will have to put up with her shortcomings—Johnny or I ?

MARY. She looks quick, Mother.

MRS. MARCH. Girls pick up all sorts of things in prison. We can hardly expect her to be honest. You don't mind that, I suppose ?

JOHNNY. It's a chance to make something decent out of her.

MRS. MARCH. I can't understand this passion for vicarious heroism, Johnny.

JOHNNY. Vicarious !

MRS. MARCH. Well, where do you come in ? You'll make poems about the injustice of the Law. Your father will use her in a novel. She'll wear Mary's blouses, and everybody will be happy—except Cook and me.

MR. MARCH. Hang it all, Joan, you might be the Great Public itself !

MRS. MARCH. I am—get all the kicks and none of the ha'pence.

JOHNNY. We'll all help you.

MRS. MARCH. For Heaven's sake—no, Johnny !

MR. MARCH. Well, make up your mind !

MRS. MARCH. It was made up long ago.

JOHNNY. [*Gloomily*] The more I see of things the more disgusting they seem. I don't see what we're living for. All right. Chuck the girl out, and let's go rooting along with our noses in the dirt.

MR. MARCH. Steady, Johnny !

JOHNNY. Well, Dad, there was one thing anyway we learned out there—— When a chap was in a hole—to pull him out, even at a risk.

MRS. MARCH. There are people who—the moment you pull them out—jump in again.

MARY. We can't tell till we've tried, Mother.

COOK. It's wonderful the difference good food'll make, ma'am.

MRS. MARCH. Well, you're all against me. Have it your own way, and when you regret it—remember me !

MR. MARCH. We will—we will ! That's settled, then. Bring her in and tell her. We'll go on to the terrace.

> [*He goes out through the window, followed by* JOHNNY.

MARY. [*Opening the door*] Come in, please.

> [FAITH *enters and stands beside* COOK, *close to the door.* MARY *goes out.*

MRS. MARCH. [*Matter-of-fact in defeat as in victory*] You want to come to us, I hear.

FAITH. Yes.

MRS. MARCH. And you don't know much ?

FAITH. No.

COOK. [*Softly*] Say ma'am, dearie.

MRS. MARCH. Cook is going to do her best for you. Are you going to do yours for us ?

FAITH. [*With a quick look up*] Yes—ma'am.

MRS. MARCH. Can you begin at once ?

FAITH. Yes.

MRS. MARCH. Well, then, Cook will show you where things are kept, and how to lay the table and that. Your wages will be thirty until we see where we are. Every other Sunday, and Thursday afternoon. What about dresses ?

FAITH. [*Looking at her dress*] I've only got this—I had it before ; of course, it hasn't been worn.

MRS. MARCH. Very neat. But I meant for the house. You've no money, I suppose ?

FAITH. Only one pound thirteen, ma'am.

MRS. MARCH. We shall have to find you some dresses, then. Cook will take you to-morrow to Needham's. You needn't wear a cap unless you like. Well, I hope you'll get on. I'll leave you with Cook now.

[*After one look at the girl, who is standing motionless, she goes out.*

FAITH. [*With a jerk, as if coming out of plaster of Paris*] She's never been in prison !

COOK [*Comfortably*] Well, my dear, we can't all of us go everywhere, 'owever 'ard we try !

[*She is standing back to the dresser, and turns to it, opening the right-hand drawer.*

COOK. Now, 'ere's the wine. The master likes 'is glass. And 'ere's the spirits in the tantalizer—'tisn't ever kept locked, in case Master Johnny should bring a friend in. Have you noticed Master Johnny ? [FAITH *nods.*] Ah ! He's a dear boy ; and wonderful high-principled since he's been in the war. He'll come to me sometimes and say : " Cook, we're all going to the devil ! " They think 'ighly of 'im as a poet. He spoke up for you beautiful.

FAITH. Oh ! He spoke up for me ?

COOK. Well, of course they had to talk you over.

FAITH. I wonder if they think I've got feelings.

COOK. [*Regarding her moody, pretty face*] Why ! We all have feelin's !

FAITH. Not below three hundred a year.

COOK. [*Scandalized*] Dear, dear ! Where were you educated ?

FAITH. I wasn't.

COOK. Tt ! Well—it's wonderful what a change there is in girls since my young days. [*Pulling out a drawer.*] Here's the napkins. You change the master's every day at least because of his moustache ; and the others every two days, but always clean ones Sundays. Did you keep Sundays in *there* ?

FAITH. [*Smiling*] Yes. Longer chapel.

COOK. It'll be a nice change for you, here. They don't go to Church ; they're agnosticals. [*Patting her shoulder.*] How old are you ?

FAITH. Twenty.

COOK. Think of that—and such a life ! Now, dearie, I'm your friend. Let the present bury the past—as the sayin' is. Forget all about yourself, and you'll be a different girl in no time.

FAITH. Do you want to be a different woman ?

[COOK *is taken flat aback by so sudden a revelation of the pharisaism of which she has not been conscious.*

COOK. Well ! You *are* sharp ! [*Opening another dresser drawer.*] Here's the vinegar ! And here's the sweets, and [*rather anxiously*] you mustn't eat them.

FAITH. I wasn't in for theft.

COOK. [*Shocked at such rudimentary exposure of her natural misgivings*] No, no ! But girls have appetites.

FAITH. *They* didn't get much chance where I've been.

COOK. Ah! You must tell me all about it. Did you have adventures?

FAITH. There isn't such a thing in a prison.

COOK. You don't say! Why, in the books they're escapin' all the time. But books is books; I've always said so. How were the men?

FAITH. Never saw a man—only a chaplain.

COOK. Dear, dear! They must be quite fresh to you, then! How long was it?

FAITH. Two years.

COOK. And never a day out? What did you do all the time? Did they learn you anything?

FAITH. Weaving. That's why I hate it.

COOK. Tell me about your poor little baby. I'm sure you meant it for the best.

FAITH. [*Sardonically*] Yes; I was afraid they'd make it a ward in Chancery.

COOK. Oh! dear—what things do come into your head! Why! No one can take a baby from its mother.

FAITH. Except the Law.

COOK. Tt! Tt! Well! Here's the pickled onions. Miss Mary loves 'em! Now then, let me see you lay the cloth.

[*She takes a tablecloth out, hands it to* FAITH, *and while the girl begins to unfold the cloth she crosses to the service shutter.*]

And here's where we pass the dishes through into the pantry.

[*The door is opened, and* MRS. MARCH'S *voice says:* " Cook—a minute! "]

[*Preparing to go.*] Salt-cellars one at each corner—four, and the peppers. [*From the door.*] Now the decanters. Oh! you'll soon get on. [MRS. MARCH: " Cook! "] Yes, ma'am. [*She goes.*

[FAITH, *left alone, stands motionless, biting her pretty lip, her eyes mutinous. Hearing footsteps, she looks up.* MR. BLY, *with his pail and cloths, appears outside.*

BLY. [*Preparing to work, while* FAITH *prepares to set the salt cellars*] So you've got it! You never know your luck. Up to-day and down to-morrow. I'll 'ave a glass over this to-night. What d'you get?

FAITH. Thirty.

BLY. It's not the market price; still, you're not the market article. Now, put a good heart into it and get to know your job; you'll find Cook full o' philosophy if you treat her right—she can make a dumplin' with anybody. But look 'ere; you confine yourself to the ladies!

FAITH. I don't want your advice, father.

BLY. I know parents are out of date; still, I've put up with a lot on your account, so gimme a bit of me own back.

FAITH. I don't know whether I shall like this. I've been shut up so long. I want to see some life.

BLY. Well, that's natural. But I want you to do well. I suppose you'll be comin' 'ome to fetch your things to-night?

FAITH. Yes.

BLY. I'll have a flower for you. What'd you like—daffydils?

FAITH. No; one with a scent to it.

BLY. I'll ask at Mrs. Bean's round the corner. She'll pick 'em out from what's over. Never 'ad much nose for a flower meself. I often thought you'd like a flower when you was in prison.

FAITH. [*A little touched*] Did you? Did you—really?

BLY. Ah! I suppose I've drunk more glasses over your bein' in there than over anything that ever 'appened to me. Why! I couldn't relish the war for it? And I suppose you 'ad none to relish. Well, it's over. So, put an 'eart into it.

FAITH. I'll try.

BLY. " There's compensation for everything "—'Aigel says. At least, if it wasn't 'Aigel it was one o' the others. I'll move on to the study now. Ah! He's got some winders there lookin' right over the country. And a wonderful lot o' books, if you feel inclined for a read one of these days.

COOK'S VOICE. Faith!

[FAITH *sets down the salt-cellar in her hand, puts her tongue out a very little, and goes out into the hall.* MR. BLY *is gathering up his pail and cloths when* MR. MARCH *enters at the window.*

MR. MARCH. So it's fixed up, Mr. Bly.

BLY. [*Raising himself*] I'd like to shake your 'and, sir. [*They shake hands.*] It's a great weight off my mind.

MR. MARCH. It's rather a weight on my wife's, I'm afraid. But we must hope for the best. The country wants rain, but—I doubt if we shall get it with this Government.

BLY. Ah! We want the good old times—when you could depend on the seasons. The further you look back the more dependable the times get; 'ave you noticed that, sir?

MR. MARCH. [*Suddenly*] Suppose they'd hanged your daughter, Mr. Bly. What would you have done?

BLY. Well, to be quite frank, I should 'ave got drunk on it.

MR. MARCH. Public opinion's always in advance of the Law. I think your daughter's a most pathetic little figure.

BLY. Her looks *are* against her. I never found a man that didn't.

MR. MARCH. [*A little disconcerted*] Well, we'll try and give her a good show here.

BLY. [*Taking up his pail*] I'm greatly obliged; she'll appreciate anything you can do for her. [*He moves to the door and pauses there to say*:] Fact is—her winders wants cleanin', she 'ad a dusty time in there.

23*

MR. MARCH. I'm sure she had.

[MR. BLY *passes out, and* MR. MARCH *busies himself in gathering up his writing things preparatory to seeking his study. While he is so engaged* FAITH *comes in. Glancing at him, she resumes her placing of the decanters, as* JOHNNY *enters by the window, and comes down to his father by the hearth.*

JOHNNY. [*Privately*] If you haven't begun your morning, Dad, you might just tell me what you think of these verses.

[*He puts a sheet of notepaper before his father, who takes it and begins to con over the verses thereon, while* JOHNNY *looks carefully at his nails.*

MR. MARCH. Er—I—I like the last line awfully, Johnny.

JOHNNY. [*Gloomily*] What about the other eleven?

MR. MARCH. [*Tentatively*] Well—old man, I—er—think perhaps it'd be stronger if they were out.

JOHNNY. Good God!

[*He takes back the sheet of paper, clutches his brow, and crosses to the door. As he passes* FAITH, *she looks up at him with eyes full of expression.* JOHNNY *catches the look, jibs ever so little, and goes out.*

COOK'S VOICE. [*Through the door, which is still afar*] Faith!

[FAITH *puts the decanters on the table, and goes quickly out.*

MR. MARCH. [*Who has seen this little by-play—to himself—in a voice of dismay*] Oh! oh! I wonder!

The curtain falls.

ACT II

A fortnight later in the MARCH'S *dining-room; a day of violent April showers. Lunch is over and the table littered with remains—twelve baskets full.*

[MR. MARCH *and* MARY *have lingered.* MR. MARCH *is standing by the hearth where a fire is burning, filling a fountain pen.* MARY *sits at the table opposite, pecking at a walnut.*

MR. MARCH. [*Examining his fingers*] What it is to have an inky present! Suffer with me, Mary!

MARY. " Weep ye no more, sad Fountains!
Why need ye flow so fast ? "

MR. MARCH. [*Pocketing his pen*] Coming with me to the British Museum ? I want to have a look at the Assyrian reliefs.

MARY. Dad, have you noticed Johnny ?

MR. MARCH. I have.

MARY. Then only Mother hasn't.

MR. MARCH. I've always found your mother extremely good at seeming not to notice things, Mary.

MARY. Faith! She's got on very fast this fortnight.

MR. MARCH. The glad eye, Mary. I got it that first morning.

MARY. *You*, Dad ?

MR. MARCH. No, no! Johnny got it, and I got him getting it.

MARY. What are you going to do about it ?

MR. MARCH. What *does* one do with a glad eye that belongs to some one else ?

MARY. [*Laughing*] No. But, seriously, Dad, Johnny's not like you and me. Why not speak to Mr. Bly ?

MR. MARCH. Mr. Bly's eyes are not glad.

MARY. Dad! Do be serious! Johnny's capable of anything except a sense of humour.

MR. MARCH. The girl's past makes it impossible to say anything to her.

MARY. Well, I warn you. Johnny's very queer just now; he's in the " lose the world to save your soul " mood. It really is *too* bad of that girl. After all, we did what most people wouldn't.

MR. MARCH. Come! Get your hat on, Mary, or we shan't make the Tube before the next shower.

MARY. [*Going to the door*] Something must be done.

707

MR. MARCH. As you say, something——— Ah ! Mr. Bly !

[MR. BLY, *in precisely the same case as a fortnight ago, with his pail and cloths, is coming in.*

BLY. Afternoon, sir ! Shall I be disturbing you if I do the winders here ?

MR. MARCH. Not at all. [MR. BLY *crosses to the windows.*

MARY. [*Pointing to* MR. BLY'S *back*] Try !

BLY. Showery, sir.

MR. MARCH. Ah !

BLY. Very tryin' for winders. [*Resting.*] My daughter givin' satisfaction, I hope ?

MR. MARCH. [*With difficulty*] Er—in her work, I believe, coming on well. But the question is, Mr. Bly, do—er—any of us ever really give satisfaction except to ourselves ?

BLY. [*Taking it as an invitation to his philosophical vein*] Ah ! that's one as goes to the roots of 'uman nature. There's a lot of disposition in all of us. And what I always say is : One's man's disposition is another man's indisposition.

MR. MARCH. By George ! Just hits the mark.

BLY. [*Filling his sponge*] Question is : How far are you to give rein to your disposition ? When I was in Durban, Natal, I knew a man who had the biggest disposition I ever come across. 'E struck 'is wife, 'e smoked opium, 'e was a liar, 'e gave all the rein 'e could, and yet withal one of the pleasantest men I ever met.

MR. MARCH. Perhaps in giving rein he didn't strike you.

BLY. [*With a big wipe, following his thought*] He said to me once : " Joe," he said, " if I was to hold meself in, I should be a devil." There's where you get it. Policemen, priests, prisoners. Cab'net Ministers, any one who leads an unnatural life, see how it twists 'em. You can't suppress a thing without it's swellin' you up in another place.

MR. MARCH. And the moral of that is——— ?

BLY. Follow your instincts. You see—if I'm not keepin' you— now that we ain't got no faith, as we were sayin' the other day, no Ten Commandments in black an' white—we've just got to be 'uman bein's —raisin' Cain, and havin' feelin' hearts. What's the use of all these lofty ideas that you can't live up to ? Liberty, Fraternity, Equality, Democracy—see what comes o' fightin' for 'em ! 'Ere we are— wipin' out the lot. We thought they was fixed stars ; they was only comets—hot air. No ; trust 'uman nature, I say, and follow your instincts.

MR. MARCH. We were talking of your daughter—I—I———

BLY. There's a case in point. Her instincts was starved goin' on for three years, because, mind you, they kept her hangin' about in prison months before they tried her. I read your article, and I thought to meself after I'd finished : Which would I feel smallest—if I was—

the Judge, the Jury, or the 'Ome Secretary ?   It *was* a treat, that article !
They ought to abolish that in'uman " To be hanged by the neck until
she is dead."   It's my belief they only keep it because it's poetry ; that
and the wigs—they're hard up for a bit of beauty in the Courts of Law.
Excuse my 'and, sir ; I do thank you for that article.

> [*He extends his wiped hand, which* MR. MARCH *shakes with the
> feeling that he is always shaking* MR. BLY'S *hand.*

MR. MARCH. But, apropos of your daughter, Mr. Bly.   I suppose
none of us ever change our natures.

BLY. [*Again responding to the appeal that he senses to his philosophical
vein*] Ah ! but 'oo can see what our natures are ?   Why, I've known
people that could see nothin' but theirselves and their own families,
unless they was drunk.   At my daughter's trial, I see right into the
lawyers, judge and all.   There she was, hub of the whole thing, and
all they could see of her was 'ow far she affected 'em personally—one
tryin' to get 'er guilty, the other tryin' to get 'er off, and the judge
summin' 'er up cold-blooded.

MR. MARCH. But that's what they're paid for, Mr. Bly.

BLY. Ah !   But which of 'em was thinkin : " 'Ere's a little bit o'
warm life on its own.   'Ere's a little dancin' creature.   What's she
feelin', wot's 'er complaint ? "—impersonal-like.   I like to see a man
do a bit of speculatin', with his mind off of 'imself, for once.

MR. MARCH. " The   man   that hath   not   speculation   in   his
soul."

BLY. That's right, sir.   When I see a mangy cat or a dog that's lost,
or a fellow-creature down on his luck, I always try to put meself in his
place.   It's a weakness I've got.

MR. MARCH. [*Warmly*] A deuced good one.   Shake——

> [*He checks himself, but* MR. BLY *has wiped his hand and extended it.*
> [*While the shake is in progress* MARY *returns, and, having seen it to
> a safe conclusion, speaks.*

MARY. Coming, Dad ?

MR. MARCH. Excuse me, Mr. Bly, I must away.

> [*He goes towards the door, and* BLY *dips his sponge.*

MARY. [*In a low voice*] Well ?

MR. MARCH. Mr. Bly is like all the greater men I know—he
can't listen.

MARY. But you were shaking——

MR. MARCH. Yes ; it's a weakness we have—every three minutes.

MARY. [*Bubbling*] Dad—Silly !

MR. MARCH. Very !

> [*As they go out* MR. BLY *pauses in his labours to catch, as it were,
> a philosophical reflection.   He resumes the wiping of a pane,
> while quietly, behind him,* FAITH *comes in with a tray.   She is
> dressed now in lilac-coloured linen, without a cap, and looks*

*prettier than ever. She puts the tray down on the sideboard with
a clap that attracts her father's attention, and stands contemplating the debris on the table.*

BLY. Winders! There they are! Clean, dirty! All sorts—
All round yer! Winders!

FAITH. [*With disgust*] Food!

BLY. Ah! Food and winders! That's life!

FAITH. Eight times a day—four times for them and four times for us.
I hate food!   [*She puts a chocolate into her mouth.*

BLY. 'Ave some philosophy. I might just as well hate me winders.

FAITH. Well!   [*She begins to clear.*

BLY. [*Regarding her*] Look 'ere, my girl! Don't you forget that
there ain't many winders in London out o' which they look as philosophical as these here. Beggars can't be choosers.

FAITH. [*Sullenly*] Oh! Don't go on at me!

BLY. They spoiled your disposition in that place, I'm afraid.

FAITH. Try it, and see what they do with yours.

BLY. Well, I may come to it yet.

FAITH. You'll get no windows to look out of there; a little bit of
a thing with bars to it, and lucky if it's not thick glass. [*Standing still
and gazing past* MR. BLY.] No sun, no trees, no faces—people don't
pass in the sky, not even angels.

BLY. Ah! But you shouldn't brood over it. I knew a man in
Valpiraso that 'ad spent 'arf 'is life in prison—a *jolly* feller; I forget
wha 'e'd done, somethin' bloody. I want to see you like him. Aren't
you happy here?

FAITH. It's right enough, so long as I get out.

BLY. This Mr. March—he's like all these novel-writers—thinks 'e
knows 'uman nature, but of course, 'e don't. Still, I can talk to 'im—
got an open mind, and hates the Gover'ment. That's the two great
things. Mrs. March, so far as I see, 'as got her head screwed on much
tighter.

FAITH. She has.

BLY. What's the young man like? He's a long feller.

FAITH. Johnny? [*With a shrug and a little smile.*] Johnny.

BLY. Well, that gives a very good idea of him. They say 'e's a
poet; does 'e leave 'em about?

FAITH. I've seen one or two.

BLY. What's their tone?

FAITH. All about the condition of the world; and the moon.

BLY. Ah! Depressin'. And the young lady?

                                   [FAITH *shrugs her shoulders.*]
Um—'ts what I thought. *She* 'asn't moved much with the times. She
thinks she 'as, but she 'asn't. Well, they seem a pleasant family.
Leave you to yourself. 'Ow's Cook?

FAITH. Not much company.

BLY. More body than mind? Still, you get out, don't you?

FAITH. [*With a slow smile*] Yes. [*She gives a sudden little twirl, and puts her hands up to her hair before the mirror.*] My afternoon, to-day. It's fine in the streets, after—being in *there*.

BLY. Well! Don't follow your instincts too much, that's all! I must get on to the drawin'-room now. There's a shower comin'. [*Philosophically.*] It's 'ardly worth while to do these winders. You clean 'em, and they're dirty again in no time. It's like life. And people talk o' progress. What a sooperstition! Of course there ain't progress; it's a world-without-end affair. You've got to make up your mind to it, and not be discouraged. All this depression comes from 'avin' 'igh 'opes. 'Ave low 'opes, and you'll be all right.

[*He takes up his pail and cloths and moves out through the windows.*

[FAITH *puts another chocolate into her mouth, and taking up a flower, twirls round with it held to her nose, and looks at herself in the glass over the hearth. She is still looking at herself when she sees in the mirror a reflection of* JOHNNY, *who has come in. Her face grows just a little scared, as if she had caught the eye of a warder peering through the peep-hole of her cell door, then brazens, and slowly sweetens as she turns round to him.*

JOHNNY. Sorry! [*He has a pipe in his hand and wears a Norfolk jacket.*] Fond of flowers?

FAITH. Yes. [*She puts back the flower.*] Ever so!

JOHNNY. Stick to it. Put it in your hair; it'll look jolly. How do you like it here?

FAITH. It's quiet.

JOHNNY. Ha! I wonder if you've got the feeling I have. We've both had hell, you know; I had three years of it out there, and you've had three years of it here. The feeling that you can't catch up; can't live fast enough to get even.   [FAITH *nods.*] Nothing's big enough; nothing's worth while enough—is it?

FAITH. I don't know. I know I'd like to bite.

[*She draws her lips back.*

JOHNNY. Ah! Tell me all about your beastly time; it'll do you good. You and I are different from anybody else in this house. We've lived—they're just vegetated. Come on; tell me!

[FAITH, *who up to now has looked on him as a young male, stares at him for the first time without sex in her eyes.*

FAITH. I can't. We didn't talk in there, you know.

JOHNNY. Were you fond of the chap who——?

FAITH. No. Yes. I suppose I was—once.

JOHNNY. He must have been rather a swine.

FAITH. He's dead.

JOHNNY. Sorry! Oh, sorry!

FAITH. I've forgotten all that.

JOHNNY. Beastly things, babies; and absolutely unnecessary in the present state of the world.

FAITH. [*With a faint smile*] My baby wasn't beastly; but I—I got upset.

JOHNNY. Well, I should think so!

FAITH. My friend in the manicure came and told me about hers when I was lying in the hospital. She couldn't have it with her, so it got neglected and died.

JOHNNY. Um! I believe that's quite common.

FAITH. And she told me about another girl—the Law took her baby from her. And after she was gone, I—got all worked up—— [*She hesitates, then goes swiftly on.*] And I looked at mine; it was asleep just here, quite close. I just put out my arm like that, over its face— quite soft—I didn't hurt it. I didn't really. [*She suddenly swallows, and her lips quiver.*] I didn't feel anything under my arm. And—and a beast of a nurse came on me, and said: "You've smothered your baby, you wretched girl!" I didn't want to kill it—I only wanted to save it from living. And when I looked at it, I went off screaming.

JOHNNY. I nearly screamed when I saved my first German from living. I never felt the same again. They say the human race has got to go on, but I say they've first got to prove that the human race wants to. Would you rather be alive or dead?

FAITH. Alive.

JOHNNY. But would you have in prison?

FAITH. I don't know. You can't tell anything in there. [*With sudden vehemence.*] I wish I had my baby back, though. It was mine; and I—I don't like thinking about it.

JOHNNY. I know. I hate to think about anything I've killed, really. At least, I should—but it's better not to think.

FAITH. I could have killed that judge.

JOHNNY. Did he come the heavy father? That's what I can't stand. When they jaw a chap and hang him afterwards. Or was he one of the joking ones?

FAITH. I've sat in my cell and cried all night—night after night, I have. [*With a little laugh.*] I cried all the softness out of me.

JOHNNY. You never believed they were going to hang you, did you?

FAITH. I didn't care if they did—not then.

JOHNNY. [*With a reflective grunt*] You had a much worse time than I. You were lonely——

FAITH. Have you been in a prison, ever?

JOHNNY. No, thank God!

FAITH. It's awfully clean.

JOHNNY. You bet.

FAITH. And it's stone cold. It turns your heart.

JOHNNY. Ah! Did you ever see a stalactite?

FAITH. What's that?

JOHNNY. In caves. The water drops like tears, and each drop has some sort of salt, and leaves it behind till there's just a long salt petrified drip hanging from the roof.

FAITH. Ah! [*Staring at him.*] I used to stand behind my door. I'd stand there sometimes I don't know how long. I'd listen and listen—the noises are all hollow in a prison. You'd think you'd get used to being shut up, but I never did.   [JOHNNY *utters a deep grunt.*] It's awful the feeling you get here—so tight and chokey. People who are free don't know what it's like to be shut up. If I'd had a proper window even—— When you can see things living, it makes you feel alive.

JOHNNY. [*Catching her arm*] *We*'ll make you feel alive again.

  [FAITH *stares at him; sex comes back to her eyes. She looks down.*] I bet you used to enjoy life, before.

FAITH. [*Clasping her hands*] Oh! yes, I did. And I love getting out now. I've got a fr—— [*She checks herself.*] The streets are beautiful, aren't they? Do you know Orleens Street?

JOHNNY. [*Doubtful*] No-o. . . . Where?

FAITH. At the corner out of the Regent. That's where we had our shop. I liked the hair-dressing. We had fun. Perhaps I've seen you before. Did you ever come in there?

JOHNNY. No.

FAITH. I'd go back there; only they wouldn't take me—I'm too conspicuous now.

JOHNNY. I expect you're well out of that.

FAITH. [*With a sigh*] But I did like it. I felt free. We had an hour off in the middle of the day; you could go where you liked; and then, after hours—I love the streets at night—all lighted. Olga—that's one of the other girls—and I used to walk about for hours. That's life. Fancy! I never saw a street for more than two years. Didn't you miss them in the war?

JOHNNY. I missed grass and trees more—the trees! All burnt, and splintered. Gah!

FAITH. Yes, I like trees too; anything beautiful, you know. I think the parks are lovely—but they might let you pick the flowers. But the lights are best, really—they make you feel happy. And music —I love an organ. There was one used to come and play outside the prison—before I was tried. It sounded so far away and lovely. If I could 'ave met the man that played that organ, I'd have kissed him. D'you think he did it on purpose?

JOHNNY. He would have, if he'd been me.

  [*He says it unconsciously, but* FAITH *is instantly conscious of the implication.*

FAITH. He'd rather have had pennies, though.   It's all earning ; working and earning.   I wish I were like the flowers. [*She twirls the flower in her hand.*] Flowers don't work, and they don't get put in prison.

JOHNNY. [*Putting his arm round her*] Never mind ! Cheer up ! You're only a kid.   You'll have a good time yet.

[FAITH *leans against him, as it were indifferently, clearly expecting him to kiss her, but he doesn't.*

FAITH. When I was a little girl I had a cake covered with sugar.   I ate the sugar all off and then I didn't want the cake—not much.

JOHNNY. [*Suddenly, removing his arm*] Gosh ! If I could write a poem that would show everybody what was in the heart of everybody else——— !

FAITH. It'd be too long for the papers, wouldn't it ?

JOHNNY. It'd be too strong.

FAITH. Besides, you don't know.   [*Her eyelids go up.*

JOHNNY. [*Staring at her*] I could tell what's in you now.

FAITH. What ?

JOHNNY. You feel like a flower that's been picked.

                                    [FAITH's *smile is enigmatic.*

FAITH. [*Suddenly*] Why do you go on about me so ?

JOHNNY. Because you're weak—little and weak. [*Breaking out again.*] Damn it ! We went into the war to save the little and weak ; at least we *said* so ; and look at us now ! The bottom's out of all that. [*Bitterly.*] There isn't a faith or an illusion left. Look here ! I want to help you.

FAITH. [*Surprisingly*] My baby was little and weak.

JOHNNY. You never meant—— You didn't do it for your own advantage.

FAITH. It didn't know it was alive. [*Suddenly.*] D'you think I'm pretty ?

JOHNNY. As pie.

FAITH. Then you'd better keep away, hadn't you ?

JOHNNY. Why ?

FAITH. You might want a bite.

JOHNNY. Oh ! I can trust myself.

FAITH. [*Turning to the window, through which can be seen the darkening of a shower*] It's raining. Father says windows never stay clean.

[*They stand close together, unaware that* COOK *has thrown up the service shutter, to see why the clearing takes so long. Her astounded head and shoulders pass into view just as* FAITH *suddenly puts up her face.* JOHNNY's *lips hesitate, then move towards her forehead. But her face shifts, and they find themselves upon her lips. Once there, the emphasis cannot help but be considerable.* COOK's *mouth falls open.*

COOK. Oh !   [*She closes the shutter, vanishing.*

FAITH. What was that?

JOHNNY. Nothing. [*Breaking away.*] Look here! I didn't mean—
I oughtn't to have—— Please forget it!

FAITH. [*With a little smile*] Didn't you like it?

JOHNNY. Yes—that's just it. I didn't mean to—— It won't do.

FAITH. Why not?

JOHNNY. No, no! It's just the opposite of what—— No, no!

> [*He goes to the door, wrenches it open and goes out.*
> [FAITH, *still with that little half-mocking, half-contented smile,
> resumes the clearing of the table. She is interrupted by the
> entrance through the French windows of* MR. MARCH *and* MARY,
> *struggling with one small wet umbrella.*

MARY. [*Feeling his sleeve*] Go and change, Dad.

MR. MARCH. Women's shoes! We could have made the Tube
but for your shoes.

MARY. It was *your* cold feet, not mine, dear. [*Looking at* FAITH *and
nudging him.*] Now!

> [*She goes towards the door, turns to look at* FAITH *still clearing the
> table, and goes out.*

MR. MARCH. [*In front of the hearth*] Nasty spring weather, Faith.

FAITH. [*Still in the mood of the kiss*] Yes, sir.

MR. MARCH. [*Sotto voce*] "In the spring a young man's fancy."
I—I wanted to say something to you in a friendly way.

> [FAITH *regards him as he struggles on.*]

Because I feel very friendly towards you.

FAITH. Yes.

MR. MARCH. So you won't take what I say in bad part?

FAITH. No.

MR. MARCH. After what you've been through, any man with a sense
of chivalry—— [FAITH *gives a little shrug.*]
Yes, I know—but we don't all support the Government.

FAITH. I don't know anything about the Government.

MR. MARCH. [*Side-tracked on to his hobby*] Ah! I forgot. You saw
no newspapers. But you ought to pick up the threads now. What
paper does Cook take?

FAITH. *Cosy.*

MR. MARCH. *Cosy?* I don't seem—— What are its politics?

FAITH. It hasn't any—only funny bits, and fashions. It's full of
corsets.

MR. MARCH. What does Cook want with corsets?

FAITH. She likes to think she looks like that.

MR. MARCH. By George! Cook an idealist! Let's see!—er—I
was speaking of chivalry. My son, you know—er—my son has
got it.

FAITH. Badly?

MR. MARCH. [*Suddenly alive to the fact that she is playing with him*] I started by being sorry for *you*.

FAITH. Aren't you, any more ?

MR. MARCH. Look here, my child !   [FAITH *looks up at him*.] [*Protectingly*.] We want to do our best for you. Now, don't spoil it by—— Well, you know !

FAITH. [*Suddenly*] Suppose you'd been stuffed away in a hole for years !

MR. MARCH. [*Side-tracked again*] Just what your father said. The more I see of Mr. Bly, the more wise I think him.

FAITH. About other people.

MR. MARCH. What sort of bringing up did he give you ?

[FAITH *smiles wryly and shrugs her shoulders.*

MR. MARCH. H'm ! Here comes the sun again !

FAITH. [*Taking up the flower which is lying on the table*] May I have this flower ?

MR. MARCH. Of course. You can always take what flowers you like—that is—if—er——

FAITH. If Mrs. March isn't about ?

MR. MARCH. *I* meant, if it doesn't spoil the look of the table. We must all be artists in our professions, mustn't we ?

FAITH. My profession was cutting hair. I *would* like to cut yours.

[MR. MARCH'S *hands instinctively go up to it.*

MR. MARCH. You mightn't think it, but I'm talking to you seriously.

FAITH. I was, too.

MR. MARCH. [*Out of his depth*] Well ! I got wet ; I must go and change.

[FAITH *follows him with her eyes as he goes out, and resumes the clearing of the table.*

[*She has paused and is again smelling at the flower when she hears the door, and quickly resumes her work. It is* MRS. MARCH, *who comes in and goes to the writing-table, Left Back, without looking at* FAITH. *She sits there writing a cheque, while* FAITH *goes on clearing.*

MRS. MARCH. [*Suddenly, in an unruffled voice*] I have made your cheque out for four pounds. It's rather more than the fortnight, and a month's notice. There'll be a cab for you in an hour's time. Can you be ready by then ?

FAITH. [*Astonished*] What for—ma'am ?

MRS. MARCH. You don't suit.

FAITH. Why ?

MRS. MARCH. Do you wish for the reason ?

FAITH. [*Breathless*] Yes.

MRS. MARCH. Cook saw you just now.

FAITH. [*Blankly*] Oh ! I didn't mean her to.

MRS. MARCH. Obviously.

FAITH. I—I——

MRS. MARCH. Now go and pack up your things.

FAITH. He asked me to be a friend to him. He said he was lonely here.

MRS. MARCH. Don't be ridiculous. Cook saw you kissing him with p—p——

FAITH. [Quickly] Not with pep.

MRS. MARCH. I was going to say " passion." Now, go quietly.

FAITH. Where am I to go ?

MRS. MARCH. You will have four pounds, and you can get another place.

FAITH. How ?

MRS. MARCH. That's hardly my affair.

FAITH. [Tossing her head] All right !

MRS. MARCH. I'll speak to your father, if he isn't gone.

FAITH. Why do you send me away—just for a kiss ! What's a kiss ?

MRS. MARCH. That will do.

FAITH. [Desperately] He wanted to—to save me.

MRS. MARCH. You know perfectly well people can only save themselves.

FAITH. I don't care for your son ; I've got a young—— [She checks herself.] I—I'll leave your son alone, if he leaves me.

[MRS. MARCH rings the bell on the table.] [Desolately.] Well ? [She moves towards the door. Suddenly holding out the flower.] Mr. March gave me that flower ; would you like it back ?

MRS. MARCH. Don't be absurd ! If you want more money till you get a place, let me know.

FAITH. I won't trouble you.   [She goes out.

[MRS. MARCH goes to the window and drums her fingers on the pane. COOK enters.

MRS. MARCH. Cook, if Mr. Bly's still here, I want to see him. Oh ! And it's three now. Have a cab at four o'clock.

COOK. [Almost tearful] Oh, ma'am—anybody but Master Johnny, and I'd 'ave been a deaf an' dummy. Poor girl ! She's not responsive, I daresay. Suppose I was to speak to Master Johnny ?

MRS. MARCH. No, no, Cook ! Where's Mr. Bly ?

COOK. He's done his windows ; he's just waiting for his money.

MRS. MARCH. Then get him ; and take that tray.

COOK. I remember the master kissin' me when he was a boy. But then he never meant anything ; so different from Master Johnny. Master Johnny takes things to 'eart.

MRS. MARCH. Just so, Cook.

COOK. There's not an ounce of vice in 'im. It's all his goodness, dear little feller.

MRS. MARCH. That's the danger, with a girl like that.

COOK. It's eatin' hearty all of a sudden that's made her poptious. But there, ma'am, try her again. Master Johnny'll be so cut up!

MRS. MARCH. No playing with fire, Cook. We were foolish to let her come.

COOK. Oh! dear, he *will* be angry with me. If you hadn't been in the kitchen and heard me, ma'am, I'd ha' let it pass.

MRS. MARCH. That would have been very wrong of you.

COOK. Ah! But I'd do a lot of wrong things for Master Johnny. There's always someone you'll go wrong for!

MRS. MARCH. Well, get Mr. Bly; and take that tray, there's a good soul.

[COOK *goes out with the tray; and while waiting*, MRS. MARCH *finishes clearing the table. She has not quite finished when* MR. BLY *enters*.

BLY. Your service, ma'am!

MRS. MARCH. [*With embarrassment*] I'm very sorry, Mr. Bly, but circumstances over which I have no control——

BLY. [*With deprecation*] Ah! we all has them. The winders *ought* to be done once a week now the spring's on 'em.

MRS. MARCH. No, no; it's your daughter——

BLY. [*Deeply*] Not been givin' way to 'er instincts, I do trust.

MRS. MARCH. Yes. I've just had to say good-bye to her.

BLY. [*Very blank*] Nothing to do with property, I hope?

MRS. MARCH. No, no! Giddiness with my son. It's impossible; she really must learn.

BLY. Oh! but 'oo's to learn 'er? Couldn't you learn your son instead?

MRS. MARCH. No. My son is very high-minded.

BLY. [*Dubiously*] I see. How am I goin' to get over this? Shall I tell you what I think, ma'am?

MRS. MARCH. I'm afraid it'll be no good.

BLY. That's it. Character's born, not made. You can clean yer winders and clean 'em, but that don't change the colour of the glass. My father would have given her a good hidin', but I shan't. Why not? Because my glass ain't as thick as his. I see through it; I see my girl's temptations, I see what she is—likes a bit o' life, likes a flower, an' a dance. She's a natural morganatic.

MRS. MARCH. A what?

BLY. Nothin'll ever make her regular. Mr. March'll understand how I feel. Poor girl! In the mud again. Well, we must keep smilin'. [*His face is as long as his arm.*] The poor 'ave their troubles, there's no doubt. [*He turns to go.*] There's nothin' can save her but money, so as she can do as she likes. Then she wouldn't want to do it.

MRS. MARCH. I'm very sorry, but there it is.

BLY. And I thought she was goin' to be a success here. Fact is, you can't see anything till it 'appens. There's winders all round, but you can't see. Follow your instincts—it's the only way.

MRS. MARCH. It hasn't helped your daughter.

BLY. I was speakin' philosophic ! Well, I'll go 'ome now, and prepare meself for the worst.

MRS. MARCH. Has Cook given you your money ?

BLY. She 'as.

[*He goes out gloomily and is nearly overthrown in the doorway by the violent entry of* JOHNNY.

JOHNNY. What's this, Mother ?   I won't have it—it's pre-war.

MRS. MARCH. [*Indicating* MR. BLY] Johnny !

[JOHNNY *waves* BLY *out of the room and closes the door.*

JOHNNY. I won't have her go.   She's a pathetic little creature.

MRS. MARCH. [*Unruffled*] She's a minx.

JOHNNY. Mother !

MRS. MARCH. Now, Johnny, be sensible. She's a very pretty girl, and this is my house.

JOHNNY. Of course you think the worst. Trust anyone who wasn't in the war for that !

MRS. MARCH. I don't think either the better or the worse.   Kisses are kisses !

JOHNNY. Mother, you're like the papers—you put in all the vice and leave out all the virtue, and call that human nature. The kiss was an accident that I bitterly regret.

MRS. MARCH. Johnny, how can you ?

JOHNNY. Dash it ! You know what I mean. I regret it with my —my conscience. It shan't occur again.

MRS. MARCH. Till next time.

JOHNNY. Mother, you make me despair. You're so matter-of-fact, you never give one credit for a pure ideal.

MRS. MARCH. I know where ideals lead.

JOHNNY. Where ?

MRS. MARCH. Into the soup. And the purer they are, the hotter the soup.

JOHNNY. And you married father !

MRS. MARCH. I did.

JOHNNY. Well, that girl is not to be chucked out ; I won't have her on my chest.

MRS. MARCH. That's why she's going, Johnny.

JOHNNY. She is not. Look at me !

[MRS. MARCH *looks at him from across the dining-table, for he has marched up to it, till they are staring at each other across the now cleared rosewood.*

MRS. MARCH. How are you going to stop her ?

JOHNNY. Oh, I'll stop her right enough. If I stuck it out in Hell, I can stick it out in Highgate.

MRS. MARCH. Johnny, listen. I've watched this girl; and I don't watch what I want to see—like your father—I watch what *is*. She's not a hard case—yet; but she will be.

JOHNNY. And why? Because all you matter-of-fact people make up your minds to it. What earthly chance has she had?

MRS. MARCH. She's a baggage. There are such things, you know, Johnny.

JOHNNY. She's a little creature who went down in the scrum and has been kicked about ever since.

MRS. MARCH. I'll give her money, if you'll keep her at arm's length.

JOHNNY. I call that revolting. What she wants is the human touch.

MRS. MARCH. I've not a doubt of it.   [JOHNNY *rises in disgust.*] Johnny, what is the use of wrapping the thing up in catchwords? Human touch! A young man like you never saved a girl like her. It's as fantastic as—as Tolstoi's "Resurrection."

JOHNNY. Tolstoi was the most truthful writer that ever lived.

MRS. MARCH. Tolstoi was a Russian—always proving that what isn't, is.

JOHNNY. Russians are charitable, anyway, and see into other people's souls.

MRS. MARCH. That's why they're hopeless.

JOHNNY. Well—for cynicism——

MRS. MARCH. It's at least as important, Johnny, to see into ourselves as into other people. I've been trying to make your father understand that ever since we married. He'd be such a good writer if he did—he wouldn't write at all.

JOHNNY. Father has imagination.

MRS. MARCH. And no business to meddle with practical affairs. You and he always ride in front of the hounds. Do you remember when the war broke out, how angry you were with me because I said we were fighting from a sense of self-preservation? Well, weren't we?

JOHNNY. That's what I'm doing now, anyway.

MRS. MARCH. Saving this girl, to save yourself?

JOHNNY. I must have something decent to do sometimes. There isn't an ideal left.

MRS. MARCH. If you knew how tired I am of the word, Johnny!

JOHNNY. There are thousands who feel like me—that the bottom's out of everything. It sickens me that anything in the least generous should get sat on by all you people who haven't risked your lives.

MRS. MARCH. [*With a smile*] I risked mine when you were born, Johnny. You were always very difficult.

JOHNNY. That girl's been telling me—I can see the whole thing.

MRS. MARCH. The fact that she suffered doesn't alter her nature ; or the danger to you and us.

JOHNNY. There *is* no danger—I told her I didn't mean it.

MRS. MARCH. And she smiled ? Didn't she ?

JOHNNY. I—I don't know.

MRS. MARCH. If you were ordinary, Johnny, it would be the girl's look-out. But you're not, and I'm not going to have you in the trap she'll set for you.

JOHNNY. You think she's a designing minx. I tell you she's got no more design in her than a rabbit. She's just at the mercy of anything.

MRS. MARCH. That's the trap. She'll play on your feelings, and you'll be caught.

JOHNNY. I'm not a baby.

MRS. MARCH. You are—and she'll smother *you*.

JOHNNY. How beastly women are to each other !

MRS. MARCH. We know ourselves, you see. The girl's father realizes perfectly what she is.

JOHNNY. Mr. Bly is a dodderer. And she's got no mother. I'll bet you've never realized the life girls who get outed lead. I've seen them—I saw them in France. It gives one the horrors.

MRS. MARCH. I can imagine it. But no girl gets " outed," as you call it, unless she's predisposed that way.

JOHNNY. That's all you know of the pressure of life.

MRS. MARCH. Excuse me, Johnny. I worked three years among factory girls, and I know how they manage to resist things when they've got stuff in them.

JOHNNY. Yes, I know what you mean by stuff—good hard self-preservative instinct. Why should the wretched girl who hasn't got that be turned down ? She wants protection all the more.

MRS. MARCH. I've offered to help with money till she gets a place.

JOHNNY. And you know she won't take it. She's got that much stuff in her. This place is her only chance. I appeal to you, Mother —please tell her not to go.

MRS. MARCH. I shall not, Johnny.

JOHNNY. [*Turning abruptly*] Then we know where we are.

MRS. MARCH. I know where you'll be before a week's over.

JOHNNY. Where ?

MRS. MARCH. In her arms.

JOHNNY. [*From the door, grimly*] If I am, I'll have the right to be !

MRS. MARCH. Johnny !   [*But he is gone.*

            [MRS. MARCH *follows to call him back, but is met by* MARY.

MARY. So you've tumbled, Mother ?

MRS. MARCH. I should think I have ! Johnny is making an idiot of himself about that girl.

MARY. He's got the best intentions.

MRS. MARCH. It's all your father. What can one expect when your father carries on like a lunatic over his paper every morning ?

MARY. Father must have opinions of his own.

MRS. MARCH. He has only one : Whatever is, is wrong.

MARY. He can't help being intellectual, Mother.

MRS. MARCH. If he would only learn that the value of a sentiment is the amount of sacrifice you are prepared to make for it !

MARY. Yes : I read that in *The Times* yesterday. Father's much safer than Johnny. Johnny isn't safe at all ; he might make a sacrifice any day. What were they doing ?

MRS. MARCH. Cook caught them kissing.

MARY. How truly horrible !   [*As she speaks* MR. MARCH *comes in.*

MR. MARCH. I met Johnny using the most poetic language. What's happened ?

MRS. MARCH. He and that girl. Johnny's talking nonsense about wanting to save her. I've told her to pack up.

MR. MARCH. Isn't that rather coercive, Joan ?

MRS. MARCH. Do you approve of Johnny getting entangled with this girl ?

MR. MARCH. No. I was only saying to Mary——

MRS. MARCH. Oh ! You were !

MR. MARCH. But I can quite see why Johnny——

MRS. MARCH. The Government, I suppose !

MR. MARCH. Certainly.

MRS. MARCH. Well, perhaps you'll get us out of the mess you've got us into.

MR. MARCH. Where's the girl ?

MRS. MARCH. In her room—packing.

MR. MARCH. We must devise means——   [MRS. MARCH *smiles.*] The first thing is to see into them—and find out exactly——

MRS. MARCH. Heavens ! Are you going to have them X-rayed ? They haven't got chest trouble, Geof.

MR. MARCH. They may have heart trouble. It's no good being hasty, Joan.

MRS. MARCH. Oh ! For a man that can't see an inch into human nature, give me a—psychological novelist !

MR. MARCH. [*With dignity*] Mary, go and see where Johnny is.

MARY. Do you want him here !

MR. MARCH. Yes.

MARY. [*Dubiously*] Well—if I can.   [*She goes out.*

[*A silence, during which the* MARCHES *look at each other by thos turns which characterize exasperated domesticity.*

MRS. MARCH. If she doesn't go, Johnny must. Are you going to turn him out?

MR. MARCH. Of course not. We must reason with him.

MRS. MARCH. Reason with young people whose lips were glued together half an hour ago! Why ever did you force me to take his girl?

MR. MARCH. [*Ruefully*] One can't *always* resist a kindly impulse, Joan. What does Mr. Bly say to it?

MRS. MARCH. Mr. Bly? " Follow your instincts "—and then complains of his daughter for following them.

MR. MARCH. The man's a philosopher.

MRS. MARCH. Before we know where we are, we shall be having Johnny married to that girl.

MR. MARCH. Nonsense!

MRS. MARCH. Oh, Geof! Whenever you're faced with reality, you say " Nonsense ! " You know Johnny's got chivalry on the brain. [MARY *comes in.*

MARY. He's at the top of the servants' staircase, outside her room. He's sitting in an armchair, with its back to her door.

MR. MARCH. Good Lord! Direct action?

MARY. He's got his pipe, a pound of chocolate, three volumes of " Monte Cristo," and his old concertina. He says it's better than the trenches.

MR. MARCH. My hat! Johnny's made a joke. This is serious.

MARY. Nobody can get up, and she can't get down. He says he'll stay there till all's blue, and it's no use either of you coming unless another caves in.

MR. MARCH. I wonder if Cook could do anything with him?

MARY. She's tried. He told her to go to hell.

MR. MARCH. I say! And what did Cook—— ?

MARY. She's gone.

MR. MARCH. Tt! tt! This is very awkward.

[COOK *enters through the door which* MARY *has left open.*

MR. MARCH. Ah, Cook! You're back, then? What's to be done?

MRS. MARCH. [*With a laugh*] We must devise means!

COOK. Oh, ma'am, it does remind me so of the tantrums he used to get into, dear little feller! [*Smiles with recollection.*

MRS. MARCH. [*Sharply*] You're not to take him up anything to eat, Cook!

COOK. Oh! But Master Johnny does get so hungry. It'll drive him wild, ma'am. Just a snack now and then!

MRS. MARCH. No, Cook. Mind—that's flat!

COOK. Aren't I to feed Faith, ma'am?

MR. MARCH. Gad! It wants it!

MRS. MARCH. Johnny must come down to earth.

COOK. Ah! I remember how he used to fall down when he wa
little—he *would* go about with his head in the air. But he alway
picked himself up like a little man.

MARY. Listen!

> [*They all listen. The distant sounds of a concertina being playe
> with fury drift in through the open door.*

COOK. Don't it sound 'eavenly!   [*The concertina utters a long wai*

The curtain falls.

ACT III

The MARCH'S dining-room on the same evening at the end of a perfunctory dinner. MRS. MARCH sits at the dining-table with her back to the windows, MARY opposite the hearth, and MR. MARCH with his back to it. JOHNNY is not present. Silence and gloom.

MR. MARCH. We always seem to be eating.

MRS. MARCH. *You've* eaten nothing.

MR. MARCH. [*Pouring himself out a liqueur glass of brandy but not drinking it*] It's humiliating to think we can't exist without.

[*Relapses into gloom.*

MRS. MARCH. Mary, pass him the walnuts.

MARY. I was thinking of taking them up to Johnny.

MR. MARCH. [*Looking at his watch*] He's been there six hours; even he can't live on faith.

MRS. MARCH. If Johnny wants to make a martyr of himself, I can't help it.

MARY. How many days are you going to let him sit up there, Mother ?

MR. MARCH. [*Glancing at* MRS. MARCH] I never in my life knew anything so ridiculous.

MRS. MARCH. Give me a little glass of brandy, Geof.

MR. MARCH. Good ! That's the first step towards seeing reason.

[*He pours brandy into a liqueur glass from the decanter which stands between them. MRS. MARCH puts the brandy to her lips and makes a little face, then swallows it down manfully. MARY gets up with the walnuts and goes. Silence. Gloom.*

MRS. MARCH. Horrid stuff !

MR. MARCH. Haven't you begun to see that your policy's hopeless, Joan ? Come ! Tell the girl she can stay. If we make Johnny *feel* victorious—we can deal with him. It's just personal pride—the curse of this world. Both you and Johnny are as stubborn as mules.

MRS. MARCH. Human nature *is* stubborn, Geof. That's what you easy-going people never see.

[MR. MARCH *gets up, vexed, and goes to the fireplace.*

MR. MARCH. [*Turning*] Well ! This goes further than you think. It involves Johnny's affection and respect for you.

[MRS. MARCH *nervously refills the little brandy glass, and again empties it, with a grimacing shudder.*

725

MR. MARCH. [*Noticing*] That's better ! You'll begin to see thing presently. [MARY *re-enters*

MARY. He's been digging himself in. He's put a screen across the head of the stairs, and got Cook's blankets. He's going to sleep there

MRS. MARCH. Did he take the walnuts ?

MARY. No ; he passed them in to *her*. He says he's on hunge strike. But he's eaten all the chocolate and smoked himself sick He's having the time of his life, Mother.

MR. MARCH. There you are !

MRS. MARCH. Wait till this time to-morrow.

MARY. Cook's been up again. He wouldn't let her pass. She'l have to sleep in the spare room.

MR. MARCH. I say !

MARY. And he's got the books out of her room.

MRS. MARCH. D'you know what they are ? " The Scarlet Pim pernel," " The Wide Wide World," and the Bible.

MARY. Johnny likes romance. [*She crosses to the fire*

MR. MARCH. [*In a low voice*] Are you going to leave him up ther with the girl and that inflammatory literature, all night ? Where' your common sense, Joan ?

[MRS. MARCH *starts up, presses her hand over her brow, and sit*
down again. She is stumped.]

[*With consideration for her defeat.*] Have another tot ! [*He pours it out.*
Let Mary go up with a flag of truce, and ask them both to come dowr for a thorough discussion of the whole thing, on condition that the can go up again if we don't come to terms.

MRS. MARCH. Very well ! I'm quite willing to meet him. I hat quarrelling with Johnny.

MR. MARCH. Good ! I'll go myself. [*He goes out*

MARY. Mother, this isn't a coal strike ; *don't* discuss it for three hours and then at the end ask Johnny and the girl to do precisel what you're asking them to do now !

MRS. MARCH. Why should I ?

MARY. Because it's so usual. Do fix on half-way at once.

MRS. MARCH. There is no half-way.

MARY. Well, for goodness sake think of a plan which will mak you both *look* victorious. That's always done in the end. Why no let her stay, and make Johnny promise only to see her in the presenc of a third party ?

MRS. MARCH. Because she'd see him every day while he was lookin for the third party. She'd help him look for it.

MARY. [*With a gurgle*] Mother, I'd no idea you were so—French

MRS. MARCH. It seems to me you none of you have any idea wha I am.

MARY. Well, do remember that there'll be no publicity to mak

either of you look small.   You can have Peace with Honour, whatever
you decide.   [*Listening.*] There they are !   Now, Mother, don't be
logical !   It's so *feminine.*

[*As the door opens,* MRS. MARCH *nervously fortifies herself with
the third little glass of brandy.   She remains seated.* MARY
is on her right.

[MR. MARCH *leads into the room and stands next his daughter,
then* FAITH *in hat and coat to the left of the table, and* JOHNNY,
*pale but determined, last.   Assembled thus, in a half fan, of
which* MRS. MARCH *is the apex, so to speak, they are all
extremely embarrassed, and no wonder.*

[*Suddenly* MARY *gives a little gurgle.*

JOHNNY. You'd think it funnier if you'd just come out of prison
and were going to be chucked out of your job, on to the world again.

FAITH. I didn't want to come down here.   If I'm to go I want to
go at once.   And if I'm not, it's my evening out, please.

[*She moves towards the door.* JOHNNY *takes her by the shoulders.*

JOHNNY. Stand still, and leave it to me.   [FAITH *looks up at him,
hypnotized by his determination.*]   Now, mother, I've come down at your
request to discuss this ; are you ready to keep her ?   Otherwise up
we go again.

MR. MARCH. That's not the way to go to work, Johnny.   You
mustn't ask people to eat their words raw—like that.

JOHNNY. Well, I've had no dinner, but I'm not going to eat *my*
words, I tell you plainly.

MRS. MARCH. Very well then ; go up again.

MARY. [*Muttering*] Mother—logic.

MR. MARCH. Great Scott !   You two haven't the faintest idea of
how to conduct a parley.   We have—to—er—explore every path
to find a way to peace.

MRS. MARCH. [*To* FAITH] Have you thought of anything to do, if
you leave here ?

FAITH. Yes.

JOHNNY. What !

FAITH. I shan't say.

JOHNNY. Of course, she'll just chuck herself away.

FAITH. No, I won't.   I'll go to a place I know of, where they
don't want references.

JOHNNY. Exactly !

MRS. MARCH. [*To* FAITH] I want to ask you a question.   Since you
came out, is this the first young man who's kissed you ?

[FAITH *has hardly had time to start and manifest what may or may
not be indignation when* MR. MARCH *dashes his hands through
his hair.*

MR. MARCH. Joan, really !

JOHNNY. [*Grimly*] Don't condescend to answer !

MRS. MARCH. I thought we'd met to get at the truth.

MARY. But do they ever ?

FAITH. I *will* go out !

JOHNNY. No ! [*And, as his back is against the door, she can't.*] *I'll* see that you're not insulted any more.

MR. MARCH. Johnny, I know you have the best intentions, but really the proper people to help the young are the old—like——

[FAITH *suddenly turns her eyes on him, and he goes on rather hurriedly.*] —your mother. I'm sure that she and I will be ready to stand by Faith.

FAITH. I don't want charity.

MR. MARCH. No, no ! But I hope——

MRS. MARCH. To devise means.

MR. MARCH. [*Roused*] Of course, if nobody will modify their attitude—Johnny, you ought to be ashamed of yourself, and [*To* MRS. MARCH] so ought you, Joan.

JOHNNY. [*Suddenly*] I'll modify mine. [*To* FAITH.] Come here—close ! [*In a low voice to* FAITH.] Will you give me your word to stay here, if I make them keep you ?

FAITH. Why ?

JOHNNY. To stay here quietly for the next two years ?

FAITH. I don't know.

JOHNNY. I can make them, if you'll promise.

FAITH. You're just in a temper.

JOHNNY. Promise !

[*During this colloquy the* MARCHES *have been so profoundly uneasy that* MRS. MARCH *has poured out another glass of brandy.*]

MR. MARCH. Johnny, the terms of the Armistice didn't include this sort of thing. It was to be all open and above-board.

JOHNNY. Well, if you don't keep her, I shall clear out.

[*At this bombshell* MRS. MARCH *rises.*]

MARY. Don't joke, Johnny ! You'll do yourself an injury.

JOHNNY. And if I go, I go for good.

MR. MARCH. Nonsense, Johnny ! Don't carry a good thing too far !

JOHNNY. I mean it.

MRS. MARCH. What will you live on ?

JOHNNY. Not poetry.

MRS. MARCH. What, then ?

JOHNNY. Emigrate or go into the Police.

MR. MARCH. Good Lord ! [*Going up to his wife—in a low voice.*] Let her stay till Johnny's in his right mind.

FAITH. I don't want to stay.

JOHNNY. You shall !

MARY. Johnny, don't be a lunatic !   [COOK *enters, flustered.*

Cook. Mr. Bly, ma'am, come after his daughter.

Mr. March. He can have her—he can have her!

Cook. Yes, sir. But, you see, he's—— Well, there! He's cheerful.

Mr. March. Let him come and take his daughter away.

[*But* Mr. Bly *has entered behind him. He has a fixed expression, and speaks with a too perfect accuracy.*

Bly. Did your two Cooks tell you I'm here?

Mr. March. If you want your daughter, you can take her.

Johnny. Mr. Bly, get out!

Bly. [*Ignoring him*] I don't want any fuss with your two Cooks. [*Catching sight of* Mrs. March.] I've prepared myself for this.

Mrs. March. So we see.

Bly. I 'ad a bit o' trouble, but I kep' on till I see 'Aigel walkin' at me in the loo-lookin' glass. Then I knew I'd got me balance.

[*They all regard* Mr. Bly *in a fascinated manner.*

Faith. Father! You've been drinking.

Bly. [*Smiling*] What do you think?

Mr. March. We have a certain sympathy with you, Mr. Bly.

Bly. [*Gazing at his daughter*] I don't want that one. I'll take the other.

Mary. Don't repeat yourself, Mr. Bly.

Bly. [*With a flash of muddled insight*] Well! There's two of everybody; two of my daughter; an' two of the 'Ome Secretary; and two—two of Cook—an' I don't want either. [*He waves* Cook *aside, and grasps at a void alongside* Faith.] Come along!

Mr. March. [*Going up to him*] Very well, Mr. Bly! See her home, carefully. Good-night!

Bly. Shake hands!

[*He extends his other hand;* Mr. March *grasps it and turns him round towards the door.*

Mr. March. Now, take her away! Cook, go and open the front door for Mr. Bly and his daughter.

Bly. Too many Cooks!

Mr. March. Now then, Mr. Bly, take her along!

Bly. [*Making no attempt to acquire the real* Faith—*to an apparition which he leads with his right hand*] You're the one that died when my girl was 'ung. Will you go first or shall—I?

[*The apparition does not answer.*

Mary. Don't! It's horrible!

Faith. I *did* die.

Bly. Prepare yourself. Then you'll see what you never saw before.

[*He goes out with his apparition, shepherded by* Mr. March.
[Mrs. March *drinks off her fourth glass of brandy. A peculiar whistle is heard through the open door, and* Faith *starts forward.*

24

JOHNNY. Stand still!

FAITH. I—I must go.

MARY. Johnny—let her!

FAITH. There's a friend waiting for me.

JOHNNY. Let her wait! You're not fit to go out to-night.

MARY. Johnny! Really! You're not the girl's Friendly Society!

JOHNNY. You none of you care a pin's head what becomes of her. Can't you see she's on the edge?

> [*The whistle is heard again, but fainter.*

FAITH. I'm not in prison now.

JOHNNY. [*Taking her by the arm*] All right! I'll come with you.

FAITH. [*Recoiling*] No.   [*Voices are heard in the hall.*

MARY. Who's that with father? Johnny, for goodness' sake don't make us all ridiculous.

> [MR. MARCH'S *voice is heard saying :* " Your friend is in here."
> *He enters, followed by a reluctant young man in a dark suit,
> with dark hair and a pale square face, enlivened by strange, very
> living, dark, bull's eyes.*

MR. MARCH. [*To* FAITH, *who stands shrinking a little*] I came on this—er—friend of yours outside; he's been waiting for you some time, he says.

MRS. MARCH. [*To* FAITH] You can go now.

JOHNNY. [*Suddenly, to the* YOUNG MAN] Who are you?

YOUNG M. Ask another! [*To* FAITH.] Are you ready?

JOHNNY. [*Seeing red*] No, she's not; and you'll just clear out.

MR. MARCH. Johnny!

YOUNG M. What have *you* got to do with her!

JOHNNY. Quit.

YOUNG M. I'll quit with her, and not before. She's my girl.

JOHNNY. *Are* you his girl?

FAITH. Yes.

> [MRS. MARCH *sits down again, and reaching out her left hand,
> mechanically draws to her the glass of brandy which her husband
> had poured out for himself and left undrunk.*

JOHNNY. Then why did you—[*He is going to say :* " Kiss me," *but checks himself*]—let me think you hadn't any friends? Who is this fellow?

YOUNG M. A little more civility, please.

JOHNNY. You look a blackguard, and I believe you are.

MR. MARCH. [*With perfunctory authority*] I really can't have this sort of thing in my house. Johnny, go upstairs; and you two, please go away.

YOUNG M. [*To* JOHNNY] We know the sort of chap *you* are—takin' advantage of workin' girls.

JOHNNY. That's a foul lie. Come into the garden and I'll prove it on your carcase.

YOUNG M. All right !

FAITH. No ; he'll hurt you. He's been in the war.

JOHNNY. [*To the* YOUNG MAN] *You* haven't, I'll bet.

YOUNG M. I didn't come here to be slanged.

JOHNNY. This poor girl is going to have a fair deal, and *you're* not going to give it her. I can see that with half an eye.

YOUNG M. You'll see it with no eyes when I've done with you.

JOHNNY. Come on, then.   [*He goes up to the windows.*

MR. MARCH. For God's sake, Johnny, stop this vulgar brawl !

FAITH. [*Suddenly*] I'm not a " poor girl " and I won't be called one. I don't want any soft words. Why can't you let me be ? [*Pointing to* JOHNNY.] He talks wild. [JOHNNY *clutches the edge of the writing-table.*] Thinks he can " rescue " me. I don't want to be rescued. I—— [*All the feeling of years rises to the surface now that the barrier has broken.*]—I want to be let alone. I've paid for everything I've done—a pound for every shilling's worth. And all because of one minute when I was half crazy. [*Flashing round at* MARY.] Wait till *you've* had a baby you oughtn't to have had, and not a penny in your pocket ! It's money—money—all money !

YOUNG M. Sst ! That'll do !

FAITH. I'll have what I like now, not what you think's good for me.

MR. MARCH. God knows we don't want to——

FAITH. You mean very well, Mr. March, but you're no good.

MR. MARCH. I knew it.

FAITH. You were very kind to me. But you don't see ; nobody *sees.*

YOUNG M. There ! That's enough ! You're gettin' excited. You come away with me.

              [FAITH'S *look at him is like the look of a dog at her master.*

JOHNNY. [*From the background*] I know you're a blackguard—I've seen your sort.

FAITH. [*Firing up*] Don't call him names ! I won't have it. I'll go with whom I choose ! [*Her eyes suddenly fix themselves on the* YOUNG MAN'S *face.*] And I'm going with him !   [COOK *enters.*

MR. MARCH. What now, Cook ?

COOK. A Mr. Barnabas in the hall, sir. From the police.

              [*Everybody starts.* MRS. MARCH *drinks off her fifth little glass of brandy, then sits again.*

MR. MARCH. From the police ?

              [*He goes out, followed by* COOK. *A moment's suspense.*

YOUNG M. Well, I can't wait any longer. I suppose we can go out the back way ?

              [*He draws* FAITH *towards the windows. But* JOHNNY *stands there, barring the way.*

JOHNNY. No, you don't.

FAITH. [*Scared*] Oh! Let me go—let him go!

JOHNNY. *You* may go. [*He takes her arm to pull her to the window.*] He can't.

FAITH. [*Freeing herself*] No—no! Not if he doesn't.

> [JOHNNY *has an evident moment of hesitation, and before it is over* MR. MARCH *comes in again, followed by a man in a neat suit of plain clothes.*]

MR. MARCH. I should like you to say that in front of her.

P. C. MAN. Your service, ma'am. Afraid I'm intruding here. Fact is, I've been waiting for a chance to speak to this young woman quietly. It's rather public here, sir; but if you wish, of course, I'll mention it. [*He waits for some word from someone; no one speaks, so he goes on almost apologetically.*] Well, now, you're in a good place here, and you ought to keep it. You don't want fresh trouble, I'm sure.

FAITH. [*Scared*] What do you want with me?

P. C. MAN. I don't want to frighten you; but we've had word passed that you're associating with the young man there. I observed him to-night again, waiting outside here and whistling.

YOUNG M. What's the matter with whistling?

P. C. MAN. [*Eyeing him*] I should keep quiet if I was you. As *you* know, sir, [*To* MR. MARCH] there's a law nowadays against soo-tenors.

MR. MARCH. Soo——?

JOHNNY. I knew it.

P. C. MAN. [*Deprecating*] I don't want to use any plain English— with ladies present——

YOUNG M. I don't know you. What are you after? Do you dare——?

P. C. MAN. We cut the darin', 'tisn't necessary. We know all about you.

FAITH. It's a lie!

P. C. MAN. There, miss, don't let your feelings——

FAITH. [*To the* YOUNG MAN] It's a lie, isn't it?

YOUNG M. A blankety lie.

MR. MARCH. [*To* BARNABAS] Have you actual proof?

YOUNG M. Proof? It's his job to get chaps into a mess.

P. C. MAN. [*Sharply*] None of your lip, now!

> [*At the new tone in his voice* FAITH *turns and visibly quails, like a dog that has been shown a whip.*]

MR. MARCH. Inexpressibly painful!

YOUNG M. Ah! How would you like to be insulted in front of your girl? If you're a gentleman you'll tell him to leave the house. If he's got a warrant, let him produce it; if he hasn't, let him get out.

P. C. MAN. [*To* MR. MARCH] You'll understand, sir, that my object in speakin' to you to-night was for the good of the girl. Strictly, I've gone a bit out of my way. If my job was to get men into trouble, as he says, I'd only to wait till he's got hold of her. These fellows, you know, are as cunning as lynxes and as impudent as the devil.

YOUNG M. Now, look here, if I get any more of this from you— I—I'll consult a lawyer.

JOHNNY. Fellows like you——

MR. MARCH. Johnny !

P. C. MAN. Your son, sir ?

YOUNG M. Yes ; and wants to be where I am. But my girl knows better ; don't you ? [*He gives* FAITH *a look which has a certain magnetism.*

P. C. MAN. If we could have the Court cleared of ladies, sir, we might speak a little plainer.

MR. MARCH. Joan !

    [*But* MRS. MARCH *does not vary her smiling immobility ;* FAITH
    draws a little nearer to the YOUNG MAN. MARY *turns to*
    the fire.

P. C. MAN. [*With half a smile*] I keep on forgettin' that women are men nowadays. Well !

YOUNG M. When you've quite done joking, we'll go for our walk.

MR. MARCH. [*To* BARNABAS] I think you'd better tell her anything you know.

P. C. MAN. [*Eyeing* FAITH *and the* YOUNG MAN] I'd rather not be more precise, sir, at this stage.

YOUNG M. I should think not ! Police spite ! [*To* FAITH.] *You* know what the Law is, once they get a down on you.

P. C. MAN. [*To* MR. MARCH] It's our business to keep an eye on all this sort of thing, sir, with girls who've just come out.

JOHNNY. [*Deeply*] You've only to look at his face !

YOUNG. M. My face is as good as yours.   [FAITH *lifts her eyes to his.*

P. C. MAN. [*Taking in that look*] Well, there it is ! Sorry I wasted my time and yours, sir !

MR. MARCH. [*Distracted*] My goodness ! Now, Faith, consider ! This is the turning-point. I've told you we'll stand by you.

FAITH. [*Flashing round*] Leave me alone ! I stick to my friends. Leave me alone, and leave him alone ! What is it to you ?

P. C. MAN. [*With sudden resolution*] Now, look here ! This man George Blunter was had up three years ago for livin' on the earnings of a woman called Johnson. He was dismissed with a caution. We got him again last year over a woman called Lee—that time he did——

YOUNG M. Stop it ! That's enough of your lip. I won't put up with this—not for any woman in the world. Not I !

FAITH. [*With a sway towards him*] It's not—— !

YOUNG M. I'm off ! Bong Swore la Companee !

    [*He turns on his heel and walks out unhindered.*

P. C. MAN. [*Deeply*] A bad hat, that; if ever there was one. We'll be having him again before long.

> [*He looks at* FAITH. *They all look at* FAITH. *But her face is so strange, so tremulous, that they all turn their eyes away.*

FAITH. He—he said—he——!

> [*On the verge of an emotional outbreak, she saves herself by an effort. A painful silence.*

P. C. MAN. Well, sir—that's all.   Good evening!

> [*He turns to the door, touching his forehead to* MR. MARCH, *and goes.*
> [*As the door closes,* FAITH *sinks into a chair, and burying her face in her hands, sobs silently.* MRS. MARCH *sits motionless with a faint smile.* JOHNNY *stands at the window biting his nails.* MARY *crosses to* FAITH.

MARY. [*Softly*] Don't.   You weren't really fond of him?

> [FAITH *bends her head.*

MARY. But how could you!   He——!

FAITH. I—I couldn't see inside him.

MARY. Yes; but he looked—couldn't you see he looked——?

FAITH. [*Suddenly flinging up her head*] If you'd been two years without a word, you'd believe anyone that said he liked you.

MARY. Perhaps I should.

FAITH. But I don't want him—he's a liar.   I don't like liars.

MARY. I'm awfully sorry.

FAITH. [*Looking at her*] Yes—you keep off feeling—then you'll be happy!   [*Rising.*] Good-bye!

MARY. Where are you going?

FAITH. To my father.

MARY. With him in that state?

FAITH. *He* won't hurt me.

MARY. You'd better stay.   Mother, she *can* stay, can't she?

> [MRS. MARCH *nods.*

FAITH. No!

MARY. Why not?   We're all sorry.   Do!   You'd better.

FAITH. Father'll come over for my things to-morrow.

MARY. What are you going to do?

FAITH. [*Proudly*] I'll get on.

JOHNNY. [*From the window*] Stop!

> [*All turn and look at him.   He comes down.*]

Will you come to *me*?

> [FAITH *stares at him.* MRS. MARCH *continues to smile faintly.*

MARY. [*With a horrified gesture*] Johnny!

JOHNNY. Will you?   I'll play cricket if you do.

MR. MARCH. [*Under his breath*] Good God!

> [*He stares in suspense at* FAITH, *whose face is a curious blend of fascination and live feeling.*

JOHNNY. Well?

FAITH. [*Softly*] Don't be silly! I've got no call on you. You don't care for me, and I don't for you. No! You go and put your head in ice. [*She turns to the door.*] Good-bye, Mr. March! I'm sorry I've been so much trouble.

MR. MARCH. Not at all, not at all!

FAITH. Oh! Yes, I have. There's nothing to be done with a girl like me.　　　　　　　　　　　　　　　　　　　[*She goes out.*

JOHNNY. [*Taking up the decanter to pour himself out a glass of brandy*] Empty!

COOK. [*Who has entered with a tray*] Yes, my dearie, I'm sure you are.

JOHNNY. [*Staring at his father*] A vision, Dad! Windows of Clubs —men sitting there; and that girl going by with rouge on her cheeks——

COOK. Oh! Master Johnny!

JOHNNY. A blue night—the moon over the Park. And she stops and looks at it.—— What has she wanted—the beautiful—something better than she's got—something that she'll never get!

COOK. Oh! Master Johnny!

> [*She goes up to* JOHNNY *and touches his forehead. He comes to himself and hurries to the door, but suddenly* MRS. MARCH *utters a little feathery laugh. She stands up, swaying slightly. There is something unusual and charming in her appearance, as if formality had dropped from her.*

MRS. MARCH. [*With a sort of delicate slow lack of perfect sobriety*] I see—it—all. You—can't—help—unless—you—love!

> [JOHNNY *stops and looks round at her.*

MR. MARCH. [*Moving a little towards her*] Joan!

MRS. MARCH. She—wants—to—be—loved. It's the way of the world.

MARY. [*Turning*] Mother!

MRS. MARCH. You thought she wanted—to be saved. Silly! She—just—wants—to—be—loved. Quite natural!

MR. MARCH. Joan, what's happened to you?

MRS. MARCH. [*Smiling and nodding*] See—people—as—they—are! Then you won't be—disappointed. Don't—have—ideals! Have— vision—just simple—vision!

MR. MARCH. Your mother's not well.

MRS. MARCH. [*Passing her hand over her forehead*] It's hot in here!

MR. MARCH. Mary!　　　　　　　[MARY *throws open the French windows.*

MRS. MARCH. [*Delightfully*] The room's full of—GAS. Open the windows! Open! And let's—walk—out—into the air!

> [*She turns and walks delicately out through the opened windows;* JOHNNY *and* MARY *follow her. The moonlight and the air flood in.*

COOK. [*Coming to the table and taking up the empty decanter*] My Holy Ma !

MR. MARCH. Is this the Millennium, Cook ?

COOK. Oh ! Master Geoffrey—there isn't a millehennium. There's too much human nature. We must look things in the face.

MR. MARCH. Ah ! Neither up—nor down—but straight in the face ! Quite a thought, Cook ! Quite a thought !

The curtain falls.

THE FOREST

CAST OF THE ORIGINAL PRODUCTION AT THE ST. MARTIN'S THEATRE, ON MARCH 6, 1924

TREGAY	*Mr. Nicholas Hannen*
FARRELL	*Mr. J. H. Roberts*
ADRIAN BASTAPLE	*Mr. Franklyn Dyall*
LORD ELDERLEIGH	*Mr. A. Carlaw Grand*
STANFORTH	*Mr. Campbell Gullan*
POLE REVERS	*Mr. Felix Aylmer*
ROBERT BETON	*Mr. Edward Irwin*
BARON ZIMBOSCH	*Mr. Edward Rigby*
JOHN STROOD	*Mr. Leslie Banks*
SAMWAY	*Mr. William E. Hallman*
HERRICK	*Mr. John Howell*
AMINA	*Miss Hermione Baddeley*
SADIG	*Mr. David Hallam*
CAPTAIN LOCKYER	*Mr. Ian Hunter*
DR. FRANKS	*Mr. H. R. Hignett*
JAMES COLLIE	*Mr. Campbell Gullan*
MAHMOUD	*Mr. Qwashie*
SAMEHDA	*Mr. Felix Aylmer*

ACT I

The sanctum of ADRIAN BASTAPLE, *in the City of London, furnished in the style of the nineties, solid and comfortable—living-room rather than office. On a small table centre is a box of cigars with a little spirit flame (as in tobacconists' shops) alight beside it. A door on the Left leads to an inner sanctuary. A door on the Right to a waiting-room ; a door Back to the room of* FARRELL, BASTAPLE'S *confidential man. There is a telephone on the Right of the room.*

As the curtain rises FARRELL *enters from his room, ushering in* TREGAY.
FARRELL *is perhaps forty-five ; a rather small man with eyes that show a quick brain behind a mild and nervy manner. His face has the habit of little wandering smiles and quick upward looks.* TREGAY *is a bronzed, upstanding man of forty, with a clipped fair beard, fine silky hair, and a face at once sanguine and sardonic.*

TREGAY. Before my time, Mr. Farrell. Perhaps you can tell me what the deuce I've come for ?

FARRELL. Your advantage, Mr. Tregay, I trust ; sit down, sir.
    [*It is noticeable that chairs have been arranged more or less in radiation from a deep armchair with the little table beside it.*

TREGAY. Thought it might have been your chief's, Mr. Farrell ; [*reversing a chair and sitting astride of it*] unless your City of London has changed its spots since I last saw it.

FARRELL. The City ! Oh ! no, sir. It doesn't change.

TREGAY. What's the latest financial circus ? Haven't seen you since that Matabeleland racket, three years ago—in '95. How's Adrian Bastaple ? Successful as ever ?

FARRELL. [*With a nervous look at the sanctuary on the Left*] Oh ! yes, sir—quite !

TREGAY. Well ! Why have I been asked into the lion's den ? 'Um !

FARRELL. [*With again a nervous look*] You've been away a long time, Mr. Tregay. China, was it ?

TREGAY. And Peru. Good places to study finance while the blood flows. You should go yourself and see finance in flower—generally red !

FARRELL. A little hard on finance ; necessary evil, Mr. Tregay, believe me—like—like manure.

TREGAY. Not bad ! [*Pointing to the chairs.*] Before they come, put

739

me wise, as the Yanks say. What's Charles Stanforth doing in this galley? Adrian Bastaple and a Liberal Daily is not a marriage made in heaven. Any offspring so far?

FARRELL. Well, they're—they're expecting delivery to-day, sir.

TREGAY. What a little mongrel it'll be! Who else is coming to the ceremony? [FARRELL *gives him one of his quick looks.*

FARRELL. Er—Lord Elderleigh.

TREGAY. Old Elderleigh of the Bible League? Ye gods! What's the next portent?

FARRELL. Mr. Robert Beton.

TREGAY. [*Absorbed*] Robert Beton? Empire and the Bible! Well, that's all right. Who else?

FARRELL. Mr. Pole Revers.

TREGAY. Foreign Office!

FARRELL. Oh! Not officially. Under the rose, sir.

TREGAY. You bet! Well, the ingredients are all there for some fine tummy upsets. Am I the bicarbonate of soda?

FARRELL. Didn't Mr. Stanforth tell you?

TREGAY. [*Shaking his head*] Just got a message to come here at five.

FARRELL. Perhaps I oughtn't——

TREGAY. Out with it, Mr. Farrell.

FARRELL. Well, sir, your experience of Africa, and your reputation for lost causes——

TREGAY. Adrian Bastaple and a lost cause! Something's got loose!

FARRELL. Oh! no! Mr. Bastaple has quite set his heart——

TREGAY. Then there's money in it?

FARRELL. No, sir, a pure matter of benevolence. [*One of his looks.*

TREGAY. Now I think of it, I *have* seen his name in charity lists.

FARRELL. You have, sir—I see to that.

TREGAY. Ah! No limit to the things you do for him. Proud position, Mr. Farrell. What's the pure benevolence this time?

FARRELL. I'm sure it'll have your sympathy, sir; it's—the slave trade.

TREGAY. What! in the British Empire?

FARRELL. [*With a smile*] Oh! no, sir—oh! no!

TREGAY. Where then?

FARRELL. Congo.

TREGAY. But the Belgians rousted them out a year or two ago.

FARRELL. Well—[*with one of his looks*]—yes. [*The door on the Left is opened.*] Here is Mr. Bastaple. Mr. Tregay, sir.

> [TREGAY *rises from the chair he has been riding, and, reversing it,
> bows to the advancing figure.* ADRIAN BASTAPLE *is a man
> with a thick trunk and rather short neck, iron-grey hair once
> dark, subfusc, rather olive complexion, and heavy-lidded eyes*

*with power in them.   He may be sixty-five, and wears a frock
coat and a dark cravat of the nineties, with a pearl pin.   He
speaks without accent, but with a slight thickness of voice, as
if he were lined with leather.*

BASTAPLE. Mr. Tregay. Pleased to meet you. Farrell, cigars.
Smoke cigars, Mr. Tregay ? [*Taking the box from* FARRELL.] Light up.

TREGAY. [*Taking one and lighting it*] Thank you ! [*Reading the
label, with a quizzical look at Bastaple.*] Divinos !

[FARRELL, *after a look from one to the other, goes back to his room.*

BASTAPLE. When did you get back ?

TREGAY. Yesterday.

BASTAPLE. Interesting time ?

TREGAY. Very.

BASTAPLE. Fine life a war correspondent's.

TREGAY. When you don't live it, Mr. Bastaple.

BASTAPLE. [*With a steady look*] I enjoy your writing, those Boxers
that got messed up at that river—very powerful. Not much light
in China, I think ?

TREGAY. Not much light anywhere.

BASTAPLE. What are you doing now you're back ?

TREGAY. Time to smell Piccadilly, and I shall be at the service of
the angels of light.

FARRELL. [*Entering*] Lord Elderleigh, sir ; Mr. Stanforth.

TREGAY. Talk of—, and you hear——

[LORD ELDERLEIGH *is a white-bearded, pink-faced person, short
and bird-like, with a quick step and turn of the head ;* CHARLES
STANFORTH *a polished looking man between forty and fifty.*

ELDERLEIGH. Mr. Bastaple ?   [*He extends half a hand.*

STANFORTH. Ah ! Tregay. You got my message then. [*He
shakes hands with* TREGAY.] Glad you're back safe and sound.

BASTAPLE. Sit down, gentlemen. Cigars, Farrell.

[*He himself sits in the armchair by the small table.   They all seat
themselves.* LORD ELDERLEIGH *has refused to smoke ;*
STANFORTH *has lighted one of his own cigarettes.*

ELDERLEIGH. I hope we're going to clinch things to-day, Stanforth.
Time's getting on.

FARRELL. [*From the doorway*] Mr. Pole Revers.

[POLE REVERS *is quick, tall, dark, and a bit of a dandy.   He bows
to* BASTAPLE, *nods to* STANFORTH *and* LORD ELDERLEIGH,
stares at TREGAY, *and takes a chair.*

FARRELL. [*From the doorway*] Mr. Robert Beton.

[*He stands watching the company a moment.* BETON *comes in,
filling the eye with his large head on a short body and the breadth
of his forehead.   His eyes have power—epileptic eyes, seeing
visions.   He takes the end chair to the left of* BASTAPLE.

BETON. How do, my lord? How do, Stanforth? Revers, yours.
[FARRELL *goes*.

BASTAPLE. [*Introducing*] Mr. Tregay.

[BETON *leans forward, staring, and makes an amicable movement
of the hand at* TREGAY.

BETON. Ah! Mr. Tregay, glad to meet you. I suggested your
name to Mr. Stanforth. You know a Dr. Franks, I believe?

TREGAY. Franks! Clement Franks? My cousin—Out at
Mombasa.

BETON. Exactly! You know what we're here for?

TREGAY. Limelight on the slave trade, is it?

BETON. Yes. Your cousin suggested you could help to throw it.

STANFORTH. East of the Congo, Tregay. You were out there in
'94, wasn't it?   [TREGAY *nods*.

STANFORTH. Well, since then the Belgians have had two cam-
paigns. But we're convinced the job's only been half done.

ELDERLEIGH. What's that country like, Mr. Tregay?

TREGAY. Forest thick as the city of London, my lord; fever—
cannibals—all the luxuries.

STANFORTH. Quite; but we Liberals feel——

TREGAY. That you want a war-cry.

[STANFORTH *turns on him a stony stare*.

ELDERLEIGH. Mr. Beton, you spoke of having a man; is he ready?

BETON. At Mombasa, waiting for the word "Go." John
Strood.

REVERS. Strood! H'm!

STANFORTH. The man who discovered——?

REVERS. Not too savoury, that, Beton.

BETON. Well, he's right for this business, it's no child's play. Will
the F.O. let him through Uganda? That's what we want to know
from you, Revers.

REVERS. [*To* TREGAY] Where must he start from to get among
the slavers?

TREGAY. Albert Edward Nyanza—south end.

BETON. That's what he says himself.

REVERS. What's said here goes no further? [*He looks for signs
of assent, which are given to him*.] Uganda's still very disturbed, but I
don't think the authorities will hinder a reconnaissance with such
an object. Discretion though, our hands are full.

ELDERLEIGH. Beton, you can—what's that nice expression?—
tip him the wink, eh?   [BETON *nods*.]
Good! Now—ways and means? Our League will venture a
thousand. What will your paper do, Stanforth?

STANFORTH. Two thousand.

ELDERLEIGH. I'm afraid it'll cost more.

BETON. Mr. Tregay? An expedition starting from the Albert Edward covering country between the lakes and the Upper Congo, or Lualaba river, don't they call it?

TREGAY. [*Nodding*] About the size of Spain.

BETON. Well? What do you say?

TREGAY. Ten thousand'll be under the mark before you've done.

ELDERLEIGH. Dear me! Ten thousand! Well, for such a cause——   [*Looking at* BETON.

BETON. Idealism will put up three. What says Finance?

      [*He turns to* BASTAPLE.

BASTAPLE. [*Taking his cigar from his mouth*] I asked you to come here, gentlemen, at Mr. Beton's suggestion. You'll forgive a little frankness. [*During the forthcoming he looks mainly at* TREGAY.] Financiers are never credited with doing anything for nothing. Admit it! We all have our own fish to fry. Lord Elderleigh fries the devil; Mr. Stanforth the Tories.

STANFORTH. Same thing.

BASTAPLE. Mr. Revers fries the virtue of neighbouring States, and Mr. Beton—fries his dreams. That leaves me. Well! I'd like to fry my reputation a little, gentlemen. I'd like a little kudos—I put up—ten thousand.   [*There is a moment's silence.*

TREGAY. [*Taking his cigar from his mouth*] Bra—vo!

ELDERLEIGH. Very generous, sir; very generous indeed. Will you put that in writing for us?

BASTAPLE. Glad to see religion has a sense of business, my lord.

ELDERLEIGH. Grievous experience, Mr. Bastaple. Well, that takes a weight off our minds. We can go ahead, then.

STANFORTH. Do we accept Strood?

REVERS. Properly warned.

BETON. Certainly.

REVERS. Then you want us to cable Mombasa to give them a pass through Uganda to the Albert Edward.

BETON. That's it.

ELDERLEIGH. Would Mr. Tregay go out for us too? There couldn't be a stronger pen to bring things home to the British public.

TREGAY. What do you want brought home, my lord?

ELDERLEIGH. My dear Mr. Tregay, the truth.

TREGAY. Will *your* people pay two thousand, Stanforth, to be told the truth?

STANFORTH. What do you mean?

TREGAY. Suppose the Belgians are doing their best?

STANFORTH. We mustn't fall foul of the Belgians, of course; but this blind eye of theirs towards the slave trade——

TREGAY. Both ways—I see; true Liberalism.

      [*Again* STANFORTH *turns on him a stony stare.*

Beton. [*To* Tregay] Do you know Strood ? [Tregay *nods.*] What d'you think of him ?

Tregay. Drives things through ; but not Stanley's hold on the black man.

Beton. Ah ! But Stanley ! Stanley ! Well, then I can set Strood in motion ? [*He rises, and all follow suit.*] I'll cable him fully, and draw on you, Bastaple ?

[Bastaple *nods, and there is a general break up.*]
Mr. Tregay, your address is—— ?

Tregay. [*Hands him a card ; then advancing—rather low*] Good-bye, Mr. Bastaple. Fine investment !

[Bastaple *stares at him steadily.* Tregay *follows the others out.*
Beton. [*Coming from the door.*] Now then, Bastaple !

[Bastaple *reseats himself at the little table.*]
We've got 'em side-tracked.

Bastaple. Long and expensive way round, Mr. Beton.

Beton. Can't be helped. Our coolie labour scheme is the only thing to make quick development possible in Africa. And it won't stand a dog's chance if the unco' guid aren't already employed elsewhere in bettering their neighbours. They started this anti-slavery racket themselves by God's own mercy ! Old Elderleigh and brisk salvation ; Stanforth and his precious principles. Yes, Bastaple, I've got my dreams. Stanley used to say that central forest of his reminded him of London—the swarm and push, the struggle for mere existence, the frightful riot of vitality without aim or end, but a fight for food and light and air. [*Walking.*] Well, like him, in the early mornings I've watched the swarms of human ants coming in over these bridges—pale, overworked, dwarfed, stoop-shouldered —the ghastly, teeming struggle of it ! [*Standing still.*] By God, Bastaple, it makes you dream, it gives you nightmare. And all those great spaces in South Africa, Canada, Australia, that want populations, white populations, where people can live a man's life, not a louse's ! And fellows like Elderleigh, Stanforth, and their kidney —if we hadn't got this slave-trade red herring to draw across the trail, the hullabaloo they'd raise over my coolie scheme.

Bastaple. When's your General Meeting of South African Concessions ?

Beton. Next July—we've got ten months. Strood will do it for us, if we hurry him. We'll have this anti-slavery campaign in full blast.

Bastaple. Wait till the very morning of the Meeting, then plump Strood's report on the slave trade into the papers. If it's sensational enough, the coolie scheme will go through and not a dog bark.

Beton. That's it, Bastaple, that's it. [*Off in his dreams.*] A real life for hundreds of thousands of these poor struggling devils here, who turn me sick to look at them.

BASTAPLE. [*Watching him*] You will die a great man, Mr. Beton.

BETON. Well, look at this country, Bastaple. "Nothing so ugly in forest nature as the visible selfish rush towards the sky, in a clearing . . . the uproar of the rush, the fierce, heartless jostling and trampling." The life of that forest of Stanley's, Bastaple, is our big city life.   [BASTAPLE *has a little smile on his face.*] Ah! to you that's "all me eye and Betty Martin"; I know, I know. Flim-flam—that about your reputation—eh? Well? Once get coolie labour, and up go the shares of all our companies, with a bound, sir, with a bound.

BASTAPLE. Our friend Tregay?

BETON. What about him?

BASTAPLE. [*Shaking his head*] Mustn't go out. He's got a nose!

BETON. H'm! They seem to want him to.

BASTAPLE. Leave that to me. Do you use a code with Strood?

[BETON *nods.*]

And trust him?

BETON. Certainly.

BASTAPLE. Is he an Empire man?

BETON. Rather!

BASTAPLE. Then code him that he needn't mind treading on the Belgians' toes. The more fuss the better. Nothing like the sins of your neighbours for diverting attention from your own.

BETON. [*With a laugh*] I don't admit sin.

BASTAPLE. Never yet met anyone who did. *I'll* cable Strood credit at Mombasa. If we want speed, we must pay for it. [*He writes. Then looking up.*] Mr. Beton, I find these dreams of yours very interesting. The struggle for existence! So you think we can improve on Nature?

BETON. I remember my boyhood, Bastaple. My father left six of us in Glasgow without a penny, and jungle there as thick as here. I went out with my little billhook and cut a path—we all did. But we suffered. Until I was nigh on forty I did as I was told, and it didn't suit me. Food I got, but light and air—no. Well, I've shot up among the tops, into the sunlight; but I haven't forgotten. I want to save thousands of boys such as I was, want them to have decent lives. What was your boyhood like?

BASTAPLE. [*With a slow puff of smoke*] Never had one.

BETON. Ah! One feels there's a lot behind you. You're a kind of mystery man. Well, I'm going to code that cable. Here's Tregay's address. [*He hands the card.*] I don't thank you; it's as much your interest as mine. Without coolie labour the shares can't rise. Good night!

Bastaple. [*Holding out his hand*] Cigar?

Beton. No, thanks.

> [*He shakes the outstretched hand and goes out, Back.*
>
> [Bastaple *sinks deeper in his chair, with a smile flickering about his lips and his brooding eyes. He strikes a bell on the little table.* Farrell *enters.*

Bastaple. What's my total holding now in all the companies of South African Concessions?

Farrell. Three hundred and fifty-seven thousand shares, sir.

Bastaple. Standing me—in——?

Farrell. Three hundred and twelve thousand pounds.

Bastaple. How many in my name?

Farrell. About a hundred thousand, sir; the rest are in dummies.

Bastaple. I want them *all* in dummies, Farrell, except—twenty thousand. Get that done quietly, before Christmas.

Farrell. Yes, sir.

Bastaple. Baron Zimbosch here yet?

Farrell. In the waiting-room, sir.

Bastaple. [*Nodding*] Ask him in.

Farrell. [*Goes to the door, Right, opens it, and says:*] Will you come in, Baron?

> [Baron Zimbosch *enters; a personable man with a brown beard parted in two and stiffish hair. He wears a frock-coat and carries a top hat.*
>
> [Farrell *shuts the door and retires to his own room.*

Bastaple. Evening, Baron.

Zimbosch. [*In goodish English with a slight accent*] Good evening, Mr. Bastaple.

Bastaple. What news for me?

Zimbosch. [*With a shrug*] Well—for anything precise it is too early in the morning as you say. But Dr. Leyds is active—my hat! He is active!

Bastaple. Well! What of that?

Zimbosch. [*Sinking his voice*] War, Mr. Bastaple, war.

Bastaple. Phew! That's a long jump.

Zimbosch. You think? Dr. Leyds gives Kruger always the impression that Europe is favourable to the Boers. These Hollanders they lead him by the nose. Oom Paul Kruger—they play with that obstinate old man. And they want war, these Hollanders. And Majuba, Mr. Bastaple—the English have never forgotten Majuba—they never will till they wipe the eye. And the Uitlanders—will they get what they want from Paul Kruger? Not much. About this time next year, Mr. Bastaple—war, or I am a Dutchman, as you say.

Bastaple. Old Kruger's too slim. What chance have the Boers, Baron?

ZIMBOSCH. Mr. Bastaple, the Englishman never sees his enemy —he eats too much fog and Yorkshire puddin'—so he is never ready. What Englishman believes he is at war till he 'as been beaten three or four time ? Then he begins to scratch his head and say, " Dear me, there is a war on ? "

BASTAPLE. And how do you Congo people view it ?

ZIMBOSCH. [*With one of his expressive shrugs*] If you lose South Africa, we get what we want from the Boers ; they will 'ave more than they want themselves ; anyway, your 'ands are full for a long time. In both case we stand in velvet, as you call it.

BASTAPLE. Well, Baron, I think you're riding before the hounds, as we say ; but I'm obliged to you. Keep me well informed about Dr. Leyds.

ZIMBOSCH. [*Bowing*] And for our steamers, Mr. Bastaple, you will help our scheme ?

BASTAPLE. I see nothing against it at present, Baron ; on the contrary.

ZIMBOSCH. *Bien !* We shall bring you the figures, then.

BASTAPLE. Cigar ?   [*Rings the bell.*

ZIMBOSCH. Divinos ! Ah ! So excellent ! [*Taking and lighting it.*] Good evening, Mr. Bastaple. Good evening !

[*He is ushered out by* FARRELL.

BASTAPLE. [*Brooding in his chair*] The beggar's right.

[*He rings the bell again.*
[FARRELL *enters.*]

Farrell, take down this letter to Mr. Beton.   [*Dictating.*]

" Dear Mr. Beton,

" Thinking things over, I conceive despatch of the utmost importance. The less time, the less chance of a slip. Please advance your General Meeting of South African Concessions to early June at latest ; and impress on Strood that we *must* have something to go on before the end of May. I hope he is a man who reads between the lines—something adequate, no matter whose toes are trodden on.

" Believe me, dear Mr. Beton,

" Yours faithfully."

[FARRELL *has taken it down in shorthand.*

BASTAPLE. Farrell, *if necessary* buy shares in all the Companies of South African Concessions sufficient to keep prices steady till the General Meeting in June.

FARRELL. My limit, sir ?

BASTAPLE. You may raise my holding to half a million shares— not in my name.

FARRELL. No, sir. As to Press enquiries ?

BASTAPLE. Discourage pessimism and all rumours of serious trouble with the Boers.

FARRELL. [*With his quick look up*] Very good, sir.

[*He is going away when* BASTAPLE *turns in his chair and speaks sharply.*]

BASTAPLE. Farrell!

FARRELL. Sir?

BASTAPLE. What's the general impression of me in the City? After twenty-five years you ought to know.

FARRELL. [*Deprecating*] Well, sir—— [*His eyes in play.*

BASTAPLE. Am I a mystery man?

FARRELL. [*Relieved*] Oh! very much so, sir.

BASTAPLE. In what way?

FARRELL. [*Deprecating*] Well, speculation about your beginnings, sir; curiosity as to your—er—general game. Some think——

BASTAPLE. Yes, Farrell?

FARRELL. Think you're after political power, sir; others that you aim at a peerage. I have heard, sir, that you were a—a Jew and want to buy the Holy Land. But then, I've heard too that you've got a Christian grudge against Rothschilds, and the object of your life is to give them a big knock.

[BASTAPLE *is listening with a smile, and seeing this smile,* FARRELL *is beginning to enjoy himself.*]

Beehive for rumour, sir, the City.

BASTAPLE. What else?

FARRELL. I've heard you called a great man, sir; and I've heard you called—er——

BASTAPLE. Yes?

FARRELL. A great scoundrel, if you don't mind, sir. Mr. Tregay, for instance—named this the lion's den. [*Without animus.*] He didn't call me the jackal, but he wanted to.

BASTAPLE. That reminds me, Tregay musn't go out.

FARRELL. No, sir? Stop him with——?

BASTAPLE. A club, if you can't think of anything softer.

FARRELL. [*With a snigger*] Would a cable from Mombasa—saying he'd be too late?

BASTAPLE. If you can get it.

FARRELL. Oh! I can get it, sir.

BASTAPLE. Good! What else about me?

FARRELL. Well, sir, a whole lot say you're just a gambler on a huge scale. And there's one man got the fixed idea you've a passion for philanthropy. Everything with a bit of romance to it goes in the City of London.

BASTAPLE. And what do *you* think, Farrell?

FARRELL. [*With his look up*] Well, sir—I never think about the—origin of species.

BASTAPLE. Oh! yes, you do. Come along!

FARRELL. [*Taking hold of himself*] Perhaps you wouldn't like, sir——

BASTAPLE. Risk that.

FARRELL. I don't take the romantic view. No, sir. Great gifts, great energy—trained in a hard school, whatever it was.

[*He stops with his quick look up.*

BASTAPLE. Go on, Farrell.

FARRELL. I don't believe you have an object, sir, nor a passion. It's—it's—you couldn't stop yourself—that's all about it. Beg your pardon, sir—it's only a private view ; I never mention it.

BASTAPLE. Romance useful, eh ?

FARRELL. Of course, I've always admired your coolness and resource, and your never being turned by any little—er——

BASTAPLE. Yes, Farrell ?

FARRELL. [*Drying up*] I'm sure, sir, I had no intention of giving an opinion.   [*Edging towards the door.*

BASTAPLE. Come here !

[FARRELL *comes to the table and* BASTAPLE *looks up into his face.*] For a quarter of a century you've deserved my confidence, so far as I know. I hope you always will.

FARRELL. You're very good, sir ; I'm sure I want to—I feel——

BASTAPLE. [*Staring at him a moment*] Thank you, Farrell. Send off this cable to Mombasa. [*He hands the cable to* FARRELL.] And give me the map of Africa.   [FARRELL *is getting the atlas as*

The curtain falls.

ACT II

SCENE I

The scene is the shack of Samway, *the elephant-hunter, on the south shore of the Albert Edward Nyanza. A room divided only by a low wooden partition from a stoep, or low, roofless verandah, seen through the opening at back.*

> [*In long chairs, with drinks and pipes,* Strood *and* Samway *are seated;* Strood *has a map on his lap,* Samway's *left leg is bandaged.*

Samway. [*Lean, brown, bearded*] Well, Mr. Strood, you sure did hustle. No man could have come through from the coast quicker.

Strood. From Beton's cables, Samway, what they're really after is trouble with the Belgians. [*Putting his finger on the map.*] They want that Katanga region coloured red, and so do I.

Samway. All one to me what darned flag flies.

Strood. The slave trade's a stale pretext.

Samway. [*After a shrewd glance, holding up a little leather bag which he has taken out of his pocket*] If you want to stir mud—see this !

> [Strood *stares at him.* Samway *tosses the bag to him, and he undoes it and stares at the contents.*

Samway. Yes, sir—diamonds; not very large, but plenty where those come from. Fetch me over that map.

> [Strood *rises, spreads it on* Samway's *knee, and stands behind him, ready to follow* Samway's *finger.*]

Down here [*putting his finger on the map*] between the Kasai river and the Luembe, there's diamonds—all over that country—and no one knows of them but me and one Belgian. Last I heard of that fellow, he was gettin' busy at Basoko with an expedition to go south. He's after them diamonds. Now, get there first, make a discoverer's claim, and keep some founders' shares for me. How's that for making trouble ?

> [*He looks quizzically up at* Strood, *who has raised himself and is staring before him—a face brown and sanguine, a jaw of iron.*

Strood. [*Shaking his head*] Clean away from instructions, Samway.

Samway. Nothing like diamonds to raise brotherly love. It'd make all the fuss they want sure enough.

750

STROOD. H'm! [*Looking at* SAMWAY'S *leg.*] Why did you go and get your leg chawed up like that?

SAMWAY. [*Pointing to a lion skin*] Ask that guy there.

STROOD. Anyone here who knows that country besides you?

SAMWAY. Not a mother's son.

STROOD. Nyangwe on the Lualaba was my limit. How many weeks from there?

SAMWAY. [*Tracing on map*] Say 350 miles as the crow flies—and I guess the darned fowl flies straighter in Africa than anywhere else; six to seven hundred miles of marching; through Batetela country, too.

STROOD. Mine's too small a caravan for that!

SAMWAY. Yeh! Those Batetela are a worse set of varmints than the Manyema—by golly, they are! They got the poison trick bad. When they hit you you sure die. An' they eat you after.

STROOD. How did *you* get through them, then?

SAMWAY. We—ell! Friend of mine has almighty power in those parts—son of one of those old Zanzibar slavers that the Belgians chawed up in '92; does a bit on his own still.

STROOD. Have you a pull on him?

SAMWAY. Why, yes—this Samehda was in trouble with a lion when we was huntin' there; I took care of the lion, so we kind of made blood-brotherhood. Brought his sister, too, back up here with me, to get her eyes cured—nearly blind, she was—quite a local beauty; she's livin' with Herrick now.

STROOD. What! That naturalist?

SAMWAY. Yeh. Devoted to him; spaniels round him all the time. Strikin' figure, Herrick.

STROOD. Unsociable devil.

SAMWAY. He certainly has mighty little use for anyone, s'long as he can watch his monkeys. [*An idea strikes him.*] See here, Mr. Strood!

STROOD. Well?

SAMWAY. Between the Lualaba and Lake Tanganyika there's a brand of chimpanzee that Herrick's just got to chum with, to finish his book on the Central African monkey. Take him and his girl along; she'll fix her brother for you.

STROOD. On a trip like mine?

SAMWAY. Hard bit o' goods; go all day, and all night too.

STROOD. [*Shaking his head*] Women!

SAMWAY. You won't get hold of Samehda without her. And that belt between the Lualaba river and the Lomami river is the darnedest bit of country God ever spat out—forest and marsh and Batetela cannibals savage as hell.

STROOD. [*Taking another turn or two*] Time, Samway—time! I've got to send them news before the end of May.

SAMWAY. Reach Samehda, and you'll have plenty news of slavery. Kill two birds with one stone, there.

STROOD. Would Herrick go?

SAMWAY. Crazy to meet that chimpanzee.

STROOD. [*Suddenly*] Could you get him here?

SAMWAY. Sure.

> [STROOD *strikes his hands together, and* SADIG, *his Berberine servant, appears from the verandah.*

SAMWAY. Go to Mr. Herrick. Samway wants palaver say.

> [SADIG *goes.*]

Mind! If you let on where you're going, you'll lose your carriers. They're scared to death of them Batetela.

STROOD. [*Nodding*] How long can I reckon on—before that Belgian?

SAMWAY. Why! He'll be all of five months by the road he'll go.

STROOD. By the Lord, Samway, I'll have a try!

SAMWAY. That's great! But pack your halo; you'll have to drive your crowd.

STROOD. Mustn't I tell my white men?

SAMWAY. Not safe. Let 'em think there's nothing beyond your original plan—to hunt up what's left of the slave trade. When are you scheduled to start?

STROOD. Day after to-morrow.

SAMWAY. Well! Forced marches play the devil. I don't hold with beatin' niggers, but take a sjambok; you'll need it.

STROOD. [*Smiling*] This isn't a land for the chicken-livered, Samway.

SAMWAY. Well, there's been travellers here who never raised a hand, but I judge they didn't live long.

STROOD. Where does Herrick hail from?

SAMWAY. New Zealand. Independent as a jack rabbit.

STROOD. Bad man to take, Samway. An expedition like this has to be all of a piece, in the leader's hand.

SAMWAY. Well, it's the girl or nothing; and she won't go without him.

> [*A tall man, lean and dark, with a good deal of hair, a pointed beard and deep, remarkable eyes, has come on to the stoep.*

SAMWAY. Evening, Mr. Herrick!

HERRICK. [*Advancing*] Evening to you. How's the leg?

SAMWAY. It kind of feels complimented when you call it that. Know Mr. Strood?

HERRICK. [*With a slight bow*] Yes.

STROOD. Good evening.

SAMWAY. Mr. Herrick, we was talkin' about that chimpanzee the other evenin'.

HERRICK. Marungensis variety. Well?

SAMWAY. Mr. Strood is goin' into the home of that gentleman.
Thought maybe you'd like to ask him to get you a specimen.   Your
girl comes from there.   You don't talk to her about critters, I guess,
or she might 'a' told you.

HERRICK. I want to see the fellow living, Samway.

STROOD. Like to come with us, Mr. Herrick ?

HERRICK. What ? [*Surprised.*] How long are you to be away ?

STROOD. Seven months or so with luck.

SAMWAY. Take your girl ; she'll be useful there, I tell you.

HERRICK. Amina ?   No.

SAMWAY. [*Quizzically*] You won't be two days out before she'll be
with you.   That's the worst of these half-Arab girls.   Never let 'em
get fond of you or they'll follow you like a dog.

HERRICK. Could I leave her with you, Samway ?

SAMWAY. [*With a secret glance at* STROOD] What'll *she* say to that ?
Call her in.   I judge she'll be around.

HERRICK. Amina !

> [*Instantly the* GIRL *walks in from the stoep.   A fine figure, veiled,
> not very dark in colour, with black eyes fixed on* HERRICK, *quite
> ignoring the other men.*

AMINA. [*She stands just inside the room with her eyes on* HERRICK]
You want me ?

HERRICK. Listen.   I go a journey—six months I leave you with
Mr. Samway.

AMINA. [*After a moment's silence*] No—no !   I come.

SAMWAY. [*Grinning*] What !   Amina !   Won't you stay with me ?

AMINA. No.   Go with Herrick.

> [*She crosses swiftly and puts his hand to her forehead.*

SAMWAY. See that, Mr. Strood ?   You'll have to take her, I reckon.

AMINA. [*With a swift look at the two men, and some instinctive com-
prehension*] Ya, Mist' Strood, take me with Herrick ; I know forest.
Good traveller, Mist' Samway—not ?

SAMWAY. Sure, you are !

HERRICK. Amina, go home.   I come directly.   Hear me ?

AMINA. I cook for you—know good water—make bandage—
mend your clo'es—keep watch.

SAMWAY. Why not, Mr. Herrick ?   She's good on the road ; she
won't trouble you any.

HERRICK. [*Revolted at the thought of being the only man with a woman
in all that crowd*] No.   If she won't stay, I give up the idea.   Good-
night.

> [*He turns from the* GIRL *and goes out on to the stoep and away.*

SAMWAY. [*Sharply*] Amina !

> [AMINA, *who is following* HERRICK, *stops.*]

Here !

AMINA. [*Going to* SAMWAY] Herrick angry.

SAMWAY. See here, my girl! Listen! Mr. Strood wants Herrick to go with him; understand? [AMINA *looks at* STROOD, *who nods.*] And *I* want to send salaam to your brother. Understand? Now, you do what I tell you. You let Herrick go; you stay, be good girl, obedient—let him go. [AMINA *makes a movement of refusal.*] Listen! I send you after him one day behind; you follow; you catch him in five days, not before; too far to send you back. Then he take you with him—see? Herrick's going after a monkey; he wants that monkey good. If he's got to stay here because of you, he'll certainly get mad with you. See?

AMINA. [*Looking deeply at him*] You—true?

SAMWAY. Sure!

AMINA. [*With a suspicious look at* STROOD] Why *he* want take Herrick?

SAMWAY. [*After a look at* STROOD; *to* AMINA] Herrick write all about Mr. Strood—make much noise in white man's country; good for Herrick good for Mr. Strood.

AMINA. [*To* STROOD] Why you not like Herrick?

STROOD. [*Taken aback*] I?

SAMWAY. You don't understand white men yet, Amina; they're not like Arabs. Mr. Strood and Herrick not friends and not enemies —all business. Now, will you do what I say or not?

AMINA. I go home. If Herrick angry at me, then I do what you say—stay behind—come to you, you send me follow. [*She touches her heart.*] You friend to me, Mist' Samway. My brother love you good. So?

SAMWAY. So—it is.

[*She makes a gestue of salute to the two men and goes out.*

SAMWAY. That's fixed it. He'll sure be riled, thinkin' of his chimpanzee. His mouth's waterin' after that critter. Cute, ain't she? These half-caste Arabs are deep. Simple, too. You may bet on— their gratitude; and you may bet on—their revenge.

STROOD. Not much nigger in that girl.

SAMWAY. Half Manyema. Their women are mighty handsome, and light-coloured. The father was pretty pure Arab.

[*From the stoep appears the white-clothed figure of a youngish brown-skinned* MAN.

STROOD. Well, Sadig?

SADIG. Cap'en Lockyer, Docker Franks, Missah Collie here, sah.

STROOD. Mind if I see them, Samway?

SAMWAY. Sure, no. Bring them right in.

[LOCKYER, FRANKS *and* COLLIE *enter from the stoep.* LOCKYER *is in tropical cloth;* FRANKS *and* COLLIE *in Holland drill.* LOCKYER *is soldierly, dry, and brown, with a small, fairish moustache and refined features.* FRANKS *is dark-haired and sallow-faced.* COLLIE, *a biggish man, has a good deal of roughish hair and moustache and rugged features. They greet* SAMWAY.

STROOD. Well, gentlemen, all ready ? How are your men's feet, Captain Lockyer ?

LOCKYER. None too sound, sir. I'd rather have had Bangalas. The Soudanese are bad stragglers, as Barttelot found.

STROOD. Can't make a soldier out of a Bangala under three months. How's your prospector's kit, Collie ?

COLLIE. Ah've known worse, and—ah've known better.

STROOD. Well, if you never commit yourself beyond that, you won't disgrace the north of the Tweed. Through with the vaccinations, Doctor ? [FRANKS *nods.*] Got any of Parke's antidote for poisoned arrows ?

FRANKS. Can't get it.

STROOD. Well, take plenty of ammonium carbonate. We start 4 a.m. sharp, day after to-morrow. I'm going to make long marches till we get to forest. See you keep 'em up to it. Got all the quinine you want, Dr. Franks ? [FRANKS *nods.*] Right ! Look after your men's feet, Lockyer. I want to get to Manyema country quick. It's there we'll begin to find any slaving that's left. Anything to ask friend Samway ?

LOCKYER. Are the Manyema active, Samway ?

SAMWAY. Why ! they take a Bank Holiday now and then, Captain. Don't let your men stray, or they'll end in the frying-pan.

FRANKS [*To* STROOD] Are we going further south or west than Nyangwe ?

STROOD. [*After exchanging a look with* SAMWAY] I don't know, Franks. The Belgians won't love us, so where exactly the job will take us, I can't tell. It's a roving commission.

[*He looks from one to another.*

LOCKYER. That's all right, sir.   [*The others nod.*

STROOD. Mr. Herrick may come with us, in search of a new sort of chimpanzee.

COLLIE. Losh ! Aren't there enough monkeys in the world a'ready ?

SAMWAY. We—ell ! I judge we all want ancestors.

COLLIE. Aye ! That's a morbid curiosity.

LOCKYER. I'd give all mine to know what's won the Leger.

STROOD. Well, gentlemen, stout hearts, prepared for anything, I hope.

COLLIE. I got a christenin' bottle here, Chief.

[*Produces a champagne bottle from his pocket and a corkscrew.*

SAMWAY [*To* SADIG, *who is standing at the back*] Glasses, boy !

SADIG. Missa Herrick come back, sah.

[*He takes the bottle and goes to fetch the glasses.*
[HERRICK *comes in, with the* GIRL *following.*

HERRICK. [*Looking round*] Evening to you !

SAMWAY. Thought it over, Mr. Herrick ?

HERRICK. [*To* STROOD] If you really meant it, I'll come, and thanks for the chance.

STROOD. Glad to have you.

HERRICK. [*To* SAMWAY] She'll stay with you, Samway ; if you'll be kind enough to look after her.

SAMWAY. [*Looking at* AMINA] Sure thing.

STROOD. One word, Mr. Herrick. You understand, of course, thay you'll be under my orders, like these gentlemen. In this sort of trip the leader has to be an autocrat. It's a queer country.

[HERRICK *bows. The* GIRL, *standing with her arm raised, half hiding her face, looks intently at* STROOD. *The glasses have been brought, and handed round.*

SAMWAY. [*Raising his glass*] Gentlemen—safe return ! Luck to you all !

STROOD. Samway—success !   [*He drains his glass.*
[*The* GIRL *stands unmoving, looking from* STROOD *to* HERRICK.
[*Having emptied their glasses,* FRANKS, LOCKYER *and* COLLIE *go out on to the stoep.*

STROOD. [*Following*] A moment, Doctor.

[*He joins them on the stoep, and they pass away, talking. The* GIRL *remains motionless, watching* HERRICK *and listening.*

HERRICK. [*Approaching* SAMWAY] Samway ! Why don't I cotton to Strood ?

SAMWAY. Strood and me have been in one or to mix-ups together, Mr. Herrick.

HERRICK. You know him all the better, then. Well ?

SAMWAY. [*Smiling*] I judge Strood makes Gawd in his own image. Maybe that's the reason ?

HERRICK. Sticks at nothing, you mean ?

SAMWAY. You've gotten a habit of plain words. Well, he gets things done, whether in London City or an African forest.

HERRICK. I see.

SAMWAY. Old man Allah 'll need a full flush to knock Strood out ; he couldn't die to save his life.

HERRICK. Thanks. [*Lowering his voice.*] The girl will be all right with you ?

SAMWAY. So she don't run away. Can't lock her up.

HERRICK. If she can't have *me*, she won't leave *you*. Good-night !

[*He shakes* SAMWAY'S *hand, and beckoning to* AMINA, *goes out. The* GIRL *comes swiftly down to* SAMWAY.

SAMWAY. Well, Amina ?

AMINA. You swear by Allah—I follow Herrick ?

SAMWAY. By Allah !

AMINA. You friend to me—friend to my brother.

[*She leans forward, takes his hand and puts it to her forehead.*

SAMWAY. That's right, Amina.

AMINA. I trust.

[*She rises and goes swiftly out to follow* HERRICK, *just as* STROOD *comes in. He passes her with a stare, and she puts up her arm to cover her face. He stops, and stands looking at her.*

STROOD. Girl—understand ! You obey me just as if you were a man.

AMINA. [*Keeping her arm up*] Obey Herrick.

STROOD. That's just what you don't do, it seems.

AMINA. Obey Herrick when I with him.

STROOD. And no tricks with any other man.

AMINA. [*Dropping her arm. Proudly*] Trick ! I no play trick !

STROOD. All right ! Remember !

AMINA. [*With a flash of eyes and teeth*] Yes, I remember.

[*He passes her. She stands looking intently back at him over her shoulder ; then goes out.*

SAMWAY. Queer critter, that girl. Knife you as soon as look. Don't get wrong with her.

STROOD. So long as she behaves ; but she'll have to toe the line like all the rest. What do you think of my crowd, Samway ? Collie's a rough diamond ; Franks knows his job. What about young Lockyer ?

SAMWAY. English gentleman, I judge.

STROOD. That against him ?

SAMWAY. Well, too many points of honour are liable to get him eaten in a country like that.

STROOD. [*With a laugh*] Now, Samway, write me that letter to the girl's brother ; and tell me every last bit you know about the route— I'm going to get there.   [*He spreads the map, and they pore over it as*

The curtain falls.

SCENE II

Eight weeks later, on the west bank of the Lualaba river. Noon. A large native hut of the better type. Over an opening in the centre of the back wall some matting has been lifted, revealing trodden mud, undergrowth, high trees, and glimpses of river. The hut is of saplings and large leaves of the amoma tree, plastered inside with dried mud ; it has conical roofing.

There is nothing in the hut save white man's kit and mess-tins dumped here and there.

COLLIE, *wrapped in a blanket, lies asleep on the Left. He is recovering from a bout of fever. Centre,* LOCKYER, *with the remnants of soldierly neatness, in shirt and breeches, sits cross-legged on the ground writing up his log. A native pitcher stands on the floor close to him. Some clothes are stretched here and there to dry. A Soudanese* SENTRY, *with rifle, at long invervals crosses and recrosses the opening. Through the opening* FRANKS *enters. He has a growth of dark beard and is thin, stained, and haggard. He comes forward, takes up the pitcher and raises it to drink.*

LOCKYER. Steady on, Franks. It's not been boiled. Here !

[*He hands his water-bottle to* FRANKS, *who drinks.*

FRANKS. Your Soudanee is food for the crocodiles, Lockyer.

LOCKYER. Poor devil !

FRANKS. Ammonium carbonate hardly touches this brand of poison. The two carriers will die too—tetanus supervening.

[*He leans against the wall, Right, in an exhausted attitude, looking down at* LOCKYER.

LOCKYER. How's the chief's fever ?

FRANKS. Passed off. Strong as a bull. Now he's on his legs we shall be off again.

LOCKYER. Got fever yourself, haven't you ?   [FRANKS *nods.*] Collie's temp.'s down. [*Shutting up his log.*] Look here, old man, I'll go on guard. Lie down ; if we're off again, you'll need a spell.

FRANKS. [*Fever mounting in him*] Lockyer, why have we crossed the Lualaba ? Our job was to lie between this river and the Lakes. Eight hellish weeks getting here, and nothing done ! No attempt to find slave trade—no trace of it. Driving—driving these poor wretches on. Six dead. Two more will die. Eight can't carry—can't march even—have to be left here ; at least six more will founder when we start again. All forest in front. Forest again—my God ! [*His voice has risen ;* COLLIE *wakes and sits up.*] What's Strood doing ? Damn him !

LOCKYER. Steady, old son !

COLLIE. Physician, heal thaself ! [*Rising.*] Eh ! but I'm feelin' fine again. Lie down, Franks ; ye've no constitution. I told ye to get out of your wet togs last night.

FRANKS. With three men dying on my hands, and the chief cursing at every man we lose ! He's playing some game we know nothing of. I've felt it all along. We can't go on like this ; the men are skeletons. We *must* rest and feed them up.

COLLIE. If we rest, it's not ourselves we'll be feedin' up. Drums all night. We'll be attacked again directly.

LOCKYER. We gave them a pill yesterday, crossing the river.

COLLIE. Aye, but they're forgetfu' loons in this forest. [*As* FRANKS *crosses to the blankets.*] I'm with the doctor; we want a reason for goin' on the way we are.

FRANKS. They can spare their arrows; we'll all founder in a fortnight, driven on like this. These stinking swamps!

[*He is seized with a violent fit of shivering.* COLLIE *wraps him in a blanket, and almost forces him down against the wall, Left.*

[*The Soudanese* SENTRY *stands to attention in the opening and speaks.*

SENTRY. Chief—come! Captain! [*He grunts, and is silent, at attention.*

[STROOD *enters. The* SENTRY *moves on.* STROOD, *though lined and sallowed, has not lost, like the others, his look of physical strength. He has a revolver in his belt and a cloud on his face.*

STROOD. Gentlemen—no officer on guard! Do you happen to remember we were attacked in crossing yesterday? Whose duty?

LOCKYER. I was just going, sir.

STROOD. "Just going" doesn't do, Captain Lockyer. Where's Herrick? Let *him* take his turn.

LOCKYER. We wanted to ask you, sir——

STROOD. [*Ominously*] Well?

LOCKYER. Why have we crossed the Lualaba? We understood——

STROOD. Thought you were a soldier.

LOCKYER. [*Steadily*] We consider the position pretty desperate, sir. We signed for an expedition between the Lakes and the Lualaba.

STROOD. You signed to be under my leadership for seven months. You have five months to run, Captain Lockyer, and your reputation in the Army at stake.

LOCKYER. I know that, sir. But you've crossed into cannibal country and the men are scared. We may have wholesale desertions.

STROOD. I've only flogged for desertion so far; I'll shoot the next man who tries it on. [*Grimly.*] But there'll be no straggling between this river and the Lomami. Any straggler now is food for cannibals.

FRANKS. And if we *all* recross the river?

STROOD. [*Putting his hand on his revolver*] Dr. Franks?

LOCKYER. [*Quietly*] Franks has fever, sir. But we shall be grateful if you'll tell us the exact purpose for which the whole expedition is risking its life.

COLLIE. Aye, chief; is it a pure pleasure trip?

STROOD. [*Controlling himself*] Gentlemen, I've had to be on the safe side and keep my counsel, or lose my carriers. Well, we're on the safe side now. Our real destination is south, in the Lualaba Kasai.

[*Sensation.*

COLLIE. How's that?

STROOD. Diamonds. No one else knows of them but one Belgian. And we're racing his outfit from Basoko.   [FRANKS *laughs.*

COLLIE. Diamonds! Losh!

Lockyer. We're not after the slave trade, then?

Strood. Certainly. I'm expecting news of it hereabouts. But this other object is just as important.

Lockyer. Frankly, sir, if I'd known this was a commercial expedition, I shouldn't have come.

Strood. Commercial! You've heard of the copper deposits in Katanga? The south-east of the Congo State is a mass of minerals, gentlemen. It should never have been let slip. Samway's shown me the diamonds he found further west. If we can make a discoverer's claim, it should lead to an alteration of the whole frontier, and add one of the richest bits of Africa to the British flag. Is that commercial, Lockyer?

Lockyer. [*Steadily*] How do you mean, sir? A frontier once fixed——

Strood. Frontiers are never fixed.

Lockyer. If it's for the flag——

Collie. It's a bonnie idea.

Strood. Worth a few lives and a few scruples!

Franks. Only twenty-six carriers can march at all—and six of *them* will founder in a day or two. Eight men can't march, and two are dying. What are you going to do with them?

Strood. Put them and you, Dr. Franks, and Mr. Herrick, back across the river to camp until you're fit; then you will take them home the way we came, or to Tanganyika, as you find best. I hope to send news by you of the slave trade.

Franks. Slave trade! It's we're the slavers—driving on these men—— [*He laughs a disordered laugh.*

Lockyer. Franks! . . . With only nine Soudanese, sir, and less than thirty carriers—all in bad shape; it's precious long odds against our getting through. We shall be attacked all the way.

Strood. Why do you think I brought that girl of Herrick's?

Lockyer. Yes, sir, why? She's a sullen little snake.

Strood. Because she's sister to an Arab friend of Samway's, who rules these parts. From him—we shall get safe conduct to the Lomami, and more carriers if we need them.

Lockyer. I see. That sounds good enough.

Strood. Enough said, Lockyer. [*He holds out his hand, which* Lockyer *takes.*] Put Herrick on guard. I'm going to send the girl off now, with Samway's letter.

> [*He looks grimly at* Franks, *huddled in his blanket against the wall, and goes out.*
>
> [Lockyer *takes belt, revolver, and stick, buckles on the belt, and stands looking at* Franks.

Lockyer. Get a sleep, old chap.

> [*He goes out, speaking to the* Sentry *in the entrance.* Collie *begins attending to the gear in the hut.*

FRANKS. [*Huddled on the floor, with knees drawn up*] Good fellow, Lockyer, but a fool, Collie.   The Empire's built with the bones of fools like Lockyer.

COLLIE. [*Close to him*] Na, no !   The Empire's built by men that's got an itch to measure theirsels against the impossible.   Strood's a great man in his way.

FRANKS. Lockyer's worth ten of him.

COLLIE. Doctor, ye're no' just.   There's not a square mile of civilized airth that hasn't had a Strood at work on it.   But for your Stroods we'd all be savages.   England was forest no' so verra long ago.

FRANKS. [*In the tone of one who utters an unimaginable word*] England !

COLLIE. [*Who is bending down*] Doctor, I'm eaten up wi' critters; the hut I slept in last night was fair crawlin' wi' 'em.

[*He contemplates his stringy legs.*

FRANKS. [*Suddenly*] Driving on these poor devils—the skeletons we've made of them ?

COLLIE. [*Humouring*] Well, ye can nurse 'em back home.

FRANKS. They'll never see home ; the forest'll have their bones, and he knows it.

COLLIE. Aweel !   [*Stretching.*] Ah'd give ma conscience for the smell of whisky.

[HERRICK *appears in the opening.   He comes forward, impressively gaunt.*

HERRICK. Got the map ?

COLLIE. Lockyer's told ye, then ?

HERRICK. [*Nodding*] Cat's paws.   [*Looking at the map.*] Franks ! We'll make for the Bambara Hills and Tanganyika when your men can march.   Fever ?

[FRANKS *nods.   He is now shivering violently.*

HERRICK. Pain ?   Across the back ?   Like an injection ?   [*He takes a little case from* FRANKS'S *pocket and prepares to inject.*] Collie, yesterday, crossing the river, I caught a frog with unwebbed toes. He's got long, sharp claws.   Now, doctor——   [*He injects.*

COLLIE. Grand stuff, opium !   [*Pointing on the map.*] Losh !   Those diamonds are a way off !   Heard about your girl ?

HERRICK. I have.

COLLIE. Will she go, d'ye think ?   She's no' friendly to Strood. Ma God, the way she looks at him !   Aye, but it's a misfortune ye don't get on with Strood.   There's a ween o' plans go wrong because o' personalities.

HERRICK. He's a bully.

COLLIE. [*Angrily*] Ah !   you and the doctor !   How would *you* get a caravan across this country ?   Ye'd never get beyond your front door.

25

Herrick [*To* Franks] Any easier?

> [Franks *nods.* *He is getting drowsy from the injection.*

Collie. Ye can't eat pie without cuttin' crust. It's the lives of niggers against the glories of trade and science. I'm thinkin' ye'd be best to go and sit down by the Round Pond, Herrick, and study the chimpanzee in Kensington Gardens—What's the trouble now?

> [*Sounds of commotion without.*]

Another of your men dead, doctor?

> [Franks *half raises himself, but droops again somnolently. The sounds of commotion increase.*

Collie. Aye, well! It's no' a God-fearin' parish this.

> [*He reaches for his revolver.*
> [Herrick *steps towards the door, but stands aside to let* Strood *pass in. He has a sjambok in his hands and looks furious. The Soudanese* Sentry *blocks the entry after him.*

Strood. [*Halting at sight of* Herrick] Do you know anything of this?

Herrick. [*Haughtily*] Of *what?*

Strood. Did you put your girl up to sneaking into my tent?

Herrick. Don't treat me like your black men, Mr. Strood.

Lockyer's Voice. Into the hut!

> [*Four ragged Soudanese* Soldiers *enter with the girl* Amina *between them.* Lockyer *follows. By his direction they open out, and, leaving the* Girl *between* Strood *and* Herrick, *block the entrance. The* Girl *stands quite still, but her eyes move and glitter dangerously.* Strood *has recovered his self-command.*

Strood. Lockyer—Collie—the letter from Samway to this girl's brother is missing from my tent since I was here a few minutes ago. Sadig there? Call him!

> [Lockyer *looks out through the opening and beckons.* Sadig, Strood's *Berberine servant, enters. The* Girl *turns her eyes on him malevolently.*

Strood. Sadig, you saw this girl come out of my tent just now?

Sadig. Yes, sah.

Amina. Not true; you no see me come out!

Sadig. [*With a gesture of solemn affirmation*] Sah—that true. I see her come out.

Strood. With something in her hand?

Sadig. Yes, sah; white thing.

Strood. A letter?

Sadig. Sah—too far away. Can't say.

Amina. You no see me.

Strood. Quiet, you! How did she look—like a thief?

Sadig. Sah—she look this way, that way—[*He mimics what he*

has seen] then see me, and run for Missah Herrick's tent.   I follow. Missah Herrick—he not there.   This girl stand and look at me and curse.   I ask her what she do in my master's tent.   She say she not do noting there, she say.   Sah, I see her coming out.   She bad —she steal something.

STROOD. What did you do then ?

SADIG. Keep watch on her, an' call out big.   Captain Lockyer he come and take her with these boys and send me fetch you, sah.

STROOD. What did she do while you were watching her ?

SADIG. Spit at me—call me dog—she bad woman.

STROOD. Did she try and hide anything ?   Move her hands ?

SADIG. She make her hands like this.   [*He mimics hands on hips.*] She is not a good one.

STROOD. [*To* HERRICK] Did you know of this letter ?

HERRICK. Lockyer told me of it just now.

STROOD. Where ?

HERRICK. In my tent.

STROOD. Was the girl present ?

HERRICK. Yes.

STROOD. Lockyer, go with Sadig ;   search Mr. Herrick's tent thoroughly and come back quick.   [LOCKYER *and* SADIG *go out.*

HERRICK. By what right ?

STROOD. Self-preservation.   If the letter is not found in your tent, it is on this girl.

HERRICK. [*To the* GIRL, *sternly*] Did you steal this letter ?

AMINA. [*With a spaniel's look*] I no steal.   Arab girl not steal. Why I steal letter ?   No good for me.

HERRICK. What made you go into Mr. Strood's tent ?

AMINA. I no go—stand outside.

HERRICK. Why ?

AMINA. I go look in—see whether he got better tent than Herrick.

STROOD. Mr. Collie, go and search between my tent and Mr. Herrick's.   Look well to both sides of a bee-line between.

[COLLIE *goes out.*

HERRICK. Whatever she's done, you'll treat her gently, please.

STROOD. The life of the expedition hangs on this letter.   And by God, I'll have it, if I have to flay her alive.   It's the life of one tricky baggage against all our lives.

HERRICK. You've been making cat's paws of us.

[*But as he speaks,* LOCKYER, SADIG, *and* COLLIE *appear in the entrance.*

STROOD. Well, Captain Lockyer ?

LOCKYER. Not there, sir.

STROOD. Collie !

COLLIE. Not a sign.

STROOD. [*Taking a step forward with the sjambok raised ; to the* GIRL] Now ! Give me that letter.   Quick !

> [*The* GIRL *stands cowering, her eyes alive with hate.   She gives a quick look of supplication at* HERRICK, *who takes a step towards her.*

STROOD. Surround her.   [*The* SOUDANESE *surround her.*] Stand still, Mr. Herrick. [*To the* GIRL.] Will you give me that letter ?

AMINA. I no got letter.

STROOD. Search her !

HERRICK. Stop that !   Leave her to me !

> [*Two* SOUDANESE *bar him off with rifles ; two seize the* GIRL. *A moment's pause.*

STROOD. Strip her !

LOCKYER. [*Suddenly*] Halt !   [*The* SOUDANESE *are still.*] Sorry, sir. Can't do that.

STROOD. [*Furiously*] Captain Lockyer—no damned squeamishness ! It's your life and mine, and every man's here.

LOCKYER. Keep her in custody, sir ; she'll give up the letter presently.

AMINA. [*With a proud and triumphant gesture*] I no got letter.   I eat it !

> [STROOD *lashes at her, but the blow is intercepted by* LOCKYER's *cane, and only falls lightly.*

AMINA. I kill you—one day.

STROOD. [*Recovering his self-possession in the strange way peculiar to him*] Very well !   Captain Lockyer, raise camp.   We march in an hour.   Tell off three of your men to guard this girl, on pain of a flogging if they let her get away.   She will go with us, and be shot if we're attacked.   Sadig, bring me the two natives we took yesterday, and stand by to interpret.   I'll tell them we've got Samehda's sister, and release them to spread the news of it.   [SADIG *goes out.*

COLLIE. Chief, have we a chance, now, to get through at all ?

STROOD. I don't know ; but we're going to try, Collie.   Raise camp.

> [COLLIE *shrugs his shoulders, gathers up the two collected kits of himself and* LOCKYER, *and goes out.*

STROOD. Captain Lockyer, bind her fast and take her away.   You will leave four of your men here with Dr. Franks, in charge of the ten carriers who can't march.

> [LOCKYER *and his* MEN *go out with the* GIRL.]

Dr. Franks, you will take the canoe and recross the river as soon as you can ; you will camp till your men can march ; then make your way back to the Albert Edward, or to Tanganyika, as you find best.   [FRANKS, *who has risen, stares at him without reply.*]

Herrick, I shall keep your wench till we've crossed the Lomami river. No harm will come to her unless we're attacked. She has brought us to this pass, and she must get us out of it. You object to my ways of conducting a caravan; well, you now have an opportunity of judging how far you can get on without them.

[*He goes out, detaching the skin covering of the hut and letting it fall over the opening. There is silence, and but a dim light in the hut.*

HERRICK. [*Crossing to where he can see* FRANKS] Marooned, Doctor.

[FRANKS *breaks into weak laughter.*

FRANKS. Lopped off—the rotten branches! [*He stops with a sharp ejaculation and sinks down on to the blankets.*]

HERRICK. Here! [*He lifts him and prepares to give him another injection.*]

FRANKS. [*Feebly*] Thanks, thanks! [*His mouth is distorted with pain.*]

[HERRICK *makes the injection; a faint smile comes on* FRANKS'S *face. He falls back drowsy.*]

The forest!

The curtain falls.

SCENE III

The curtain has been lowered for a few seconds to indicate the lapse of time. The scene is the same, three days later. Noon.

[*The hut is empty of all gear except a medicine chest. The matting over the doorway is gone.* FRANKS *is feebly going through contents of chest. The fever has left him, but he looks wan and exhausted.* HERRICK *enters, followed by a* SOUDANEE.

HERRICK. Doctor, quinine for this man.

FRANKS. [*Holding up a bottle*] This is all Strood's left me. [*He beckons to the* SOUDANEE, *looks at him searchingly, and gives him a dose.*

[*The* MAN *salutes and goes out.*

HERRICK. He's the best man we've got. . . . Still they don't attack—three days! Odd!

FRANKS. They must be following Strood up.

HERRICK. Practically no food, Franks. Daren't let them forage. Are you up to crossing!

FRANKS. [*Shrugging*] Must be.

HERRICK. Queer thing, colour. Suppose I shall never see that girl again; find I haven't half the feeling for her I'd have for a dog. Got room in that chest for this bottle? My frog; don't want to lose him. Quaint chap, isn't he? [*He holds up the bottled specimen for* FRANKS *to see.*] The variety of creature—the riot of life and death, in this forest !

FRANKS. Remember the carrier's dying wife in Stanley's book : " It's a bad world, master, and you have lost your way in it." We have. How many journeys in that canoe ? Fourteen of us, and the loads ?

HERRICK. Four, I should say. I'll just label this chap.

[FRANKS *goes out.*

[HERRICK *sits down, tears a sheet from his pocket-book and writes :* " Unwebbed frog, with claws. Found on the Lualaba river, Christmas, '98. C. Herrick."

[*As he is attaching the label, the girl* AMINA *comes in ; her garments are torn, but her face and body show no great signs of fatigue. She steals round with the swaying movement peculiar to her, and has clasped his knees before he realizes that she is there.*

AMINA. Amina come back ! Escape—come through forest—back to Herrick. [*Again she embraces his knees, and is about to kiss his feet.*

HERRICK. [*Rising*] Get up. I don't like you to do that. [*Raising her by the shoulder and stroking it.*] Where did you leave them, Amina ?

AMINA. Two marches. [*With a smile that shows her white teeth.*] They not clever—Amina too clever. At night—she burn rope—look ! [*She shows a burnt place on her arm.*

HERRICK. God ! That must have hurt !

AMINA. Five carrier run away—I find two dead of arrow. Soon all killed now or run away. They not go other marches—many. [*Her eyes and teeth gleam.*] Now I guide Herrick home, quick. Amina clever—got letter still. [*She steals her hand into the garment round her waist and brings out the letter.*

HERRICK. You little snake !

AMINA. [*Proudly*] Save it for Herrick ! [*She gives him the letter.*] Herrick safe now.

HERRICK. [*Reading the letter ; grave and puzzled*] Tell me now—what made you steal this letter ?

AMINA. Strood hate Herrick—use letter—then leave Herrick behind, so Batetela kill. Now Batetela kill Strood instead—soon kill.

HERRICK. [*To himself*] Who'd ever understand how their minds work ! Jezebel !

[*The word is Greek to* AMINA, *but his gesture disturbs her.*

AMINA. Save Herrick's life. Herrick use letter—make my brother friend.

HERRICK. [*Alive to the expedition's danger*] Good God ! What am I to do ?

AMINA. Strood soon die—dog !

HERRICK. Listen, Amina ! Strood and I not friends, but I never let Strood, Lockyer, Collie die. Understand ? Never !

AMINA. No. Strood die.   He strike me.

HERRICK. Take me to your brother.   Come, now at once.

AMINA. No! Amina cross river now—take Herrick home.

HERRICK. Very well then—I go to join Strood and Lockyer.

AMINA. Ah, no! Why you care for Strood—he not care for you!

HERRICK. I don't care for Strood ; but white men stick together.

AMINA. He enemy.

HERRICK. Come, now! Do what I tell you.   Guide me to your brother.

AMINA. [*Passionately*] I live two year with Herrick—not want my people now.   Not want forest—want only Herrick.

HERRICK. I swear by Allah, that you live no more with me unless you take me to your brother.

AMINA. If my brother know Strood strike me, he kill him.

HERRICK. You won't tell him.   Come, now!   Come!

AMINA. My brother angry.   Why Strood come in his country? Make bad for my brother's trade.   Send news to white men that my brother catch slave.   Amina know.   She hear talk.   My brother all ready to kill Strood now.   Strood very few men—very weak.

HERRICK. Amina, once for all, take me to your brother, or you never see me again.

AMINA. [*Beating her breast*] Ah, no! I do all for Herrick—burn rope—come all this way alone in forest to save his life.

HERRICK. Save the others too, then!

AMINA. Not Strood—bad man ; leave Herrick and Doctor Frank behind to die.

HERRICK. Will you take me to your brother?

AMINA. [*Impassive ; suddenly*] You angry—I do what you tell.

[FRANKS *has appeared in the opening of the hut.*

FRANKS. The canoe's gone, Herrick.

HERRICK. [*Holding out the letter and pointing with it to the* GIRL] She escaped.   She's got this still.

FRANKS. And Strood?

HERRICK. In mortal danger, all of them!   Her brother's the only chance.   She must take me to him, now—at once.

FRANKS. And we?

HERRICK. Make a raft.   Hang on, Franks ; get across somehow. I'll come back or send a message within three days.   They're in worse straits than we are—far.

FRANKS. [*In a low voice*] Can you trust her?

HERRICK. With myself? Yes. Good-bye, old man. Amina—come!

[*He goes out.   The* GIRL *follows him.* FRANKS *stands aside, watching them go.*

The curtain falls.

ACT III

SCENE I

The tent of LOCKYER *and* COLLIE *in the forest, evening of the following day, four short marches from the Lualaba river. An oil lamp illumines the tent, the front side of which is open. Around is the loom of the forest ; the faint outline of another tent is seen on one side and on the other four* SOUDANESE *are grouped—three squatting, one leaning on his rifle.*

[LOCKYER *and* COLLIE, *in front of the tent, have just finished their scanty meal of bananas and biscuit, and are lighting their pipes —rifles and revolvers close at hand. Now and then drifts up the sound of native drums beaten out in the forest.*

COLLIE. [*Listening*] Those damned drums ! Heh ! but 'tis awfu' like the Salvation Army in Glasgow.

LOCKYER. Salvation ! Rum idea that ! What do you make of it, Collie ?

COLLIE. We—el ! I've known maself verra queer—times. A wee bit more, and I wouldna've been answerable for the consequences. Have ye never felt lik' that ?

LOCKYER. Never !

COLLIE. That's your upbringin'. Ye can always tell an English gentleman—never drunk on anything but liquor.

LOCKYER. Well ! He makes up there.

COLLIE. Wish to God I were drunk now. The girl's escape has fair finished us. We won't last to the Lomami river.

LOCKYER. What distance d'you make it still ?

COLLIE. Forty miles. We've not come thirty these four days, and lost twelve men. And Strood won't turn ; the man's demented.

LOCKYER. [*With a shrug*] Mahmoud !

[*The* SOUDANESE *on foot comes up at the call.*]
Keep on your rounds, there !

[*The* MAN *salutes, and goes on his round to the Right.*]
I've got fever coming on, Collie ; feel so darned talkative.

COLLIE. Aye, that's a sure sign of fever or insanity. Well, I'm no for a sleep meself till I've given Strood me mind. Got a drain of brandy there ?   [LOCKYER *hands him a flask.*

LOCKYER. Collie ! Mutton cutlets with new peas and asparagus, and a pint of iced champagne.

COLLIE. Na! A fresh-run salmon and a gallon o' mountain dew!

LOCKYER. Wonder what sort of a season they're having with the Quorn! What on earth brings us out into places like this? Good Lord! I think we're all mad! This tobacco tastes rotten—always does before fever. My brother's got a horse running in the National next spring—wonder if he'll think of putting me anything on? Wonder if he thinks of me at all? Wonder if anyone thinks of fools like us? Collie! Cold pigeon pie and iced claret-cup, what! Or how about marrow-bones and a bottle of Steinberg Cabinet! Oh, damn! at home I never think of what I eat. If we were Belgians, we'd be talking about women. Ever play cricket?

COLLIE. [*Shaking his head*] Na—golf's ma diversion.

LOCKYER. Rotten game! I say, what do you think death really is?

COLLIE. We'll be no needin' to *think* if Strood won't turn.

LOCKYER. Change of trains—or a black-out, eh!

COLLIE. I'm no' certain. But it canna be worse than this forest.

LOCKYER. Ah! Imagine haunting this forest!

"And I am black, but oh! my soul is white;
    White as an angel is the English child!"

COLLIE. Here! Tak' your temperature. [*Hands him a thermometer.*

LOCKYER. [*Refusing it*] Wonder if the Almighty ever had to keep his wicket up against bowling like this? Almighty? But *if Almighty*, Collie—He can change the attack whenever it doesn't suit Him.

COLLIE. Na! I'm thinkin' the Deity has a manly vocation. Fancy findin' ye'd made this forest! That'd tak' some livin' down.

LOCKYER. It is a corker. But think how we shall look back on it! By George! I can see myself with a long drink looking back.

COLLIE. Aye! Ye've got fever. Tak' some of these.
                        [*Handing him a little bottle of tabloids.*

LOCKYER. [*Swallowing two tabloids*] Married, aren't you, Collie?
                                                    [COLLIE *nods.*]
That's bad. Children?

COLLIE. Two. Bonnie bairns.

LOCKYER. What on earth brought *you* out here?

COLLIE. We—el! Ah've got ambeetions for them.
                        [LOCKYER *bursts into a sort of laughter.*

LOCKYER. Sorry, old man! Only—ambitions here! It's rather —funny—what!

COLLIE. Aye! And I'm goin' to see Strood about it.
          [*He gets up and passes towards the other tent at the back.*

LOCKYER. [*To himself*] Poor old Collie!

[*The sound of the drums rises.* LOCKYER *leans forward over his crossed legs, listening. The drum beats swell.*

25*

Lockyer. Gosh !

[*The* Soudanese, *who have been squatting in talk, rise ; they are joined by* Mahmoud, *and come down to* Lockyer.

Mahmoud. Capt'n Sahib ! Men say no go any more—in morning all run away. This too bad country—bad men—cannibal.

[*The beating of the drums seems to come from every side. The* Soudanese *manifest an attentive alarm.*]

No can go more.

Lockyer. [*Grasping his revolver and rising to his feet*] 'Shun !

[*The* Men *stand half-heartedly at attention.*]

What's this, Mahmoud ? If I tell Strood Sahib, he'll have you shot for mutiny.

Mahmoud. No can shoot all. In morning all go.

Lockyer. Come, Mahmoud—soldiers are not afraid. Obey orders.

Mahmoud. [*Touching his mouth and stomach, imitated by the others*] No can march if not eat. Lockyer Sahib tell men " Right about." Then obey—men march—all go back to river. Lockyer Sahib good —our officer—Strood Sahib——   [*He shakes his head.*

Lockyer. Mahmoud !

Mahmoud. [*Grimly*] Our officer—he lead us—no mutiny then.

Lockyer. You scoundrel ! How dare you ?

Mahmoud. No, Sahib, we not bad—we hungry—got sores—no like die for not'ing. Carrier men run away—leave us—then all die quick—white men too. [*With a salute.*] Lockyer Sahib, save um all.

Lockyer. You are under my orders, Mahmoud ! I am under Strood Sahib's.

Mahmoud. [*Fiercely*] By Allah ! No can go more.

[Lockyer *blows a whistle. There is a stir, and the emaciated forms of* Carriers *gather in the darkness behind the* Soudanese *to the left.* Collie *and* Strood *come hurriedly from the darkness Right, with revolvers in their hands. They are followed by* Sadig.

Strood. What's this, Captain Lockyer ?

Lockyer. The men refuse to march to-morrow.

Strood. Who speaks for them ?

Lockyer. [*Pointing*] Mahmoud—there.

Strood. [*Covering him with his revolver*] Put him under arrest.

Lockyer. [*To* Mahmoud] Ground arms !

[Mahmoud *lays down his rifle and folds his arms with a certain dignity.*

Strood. Now, my man, refuse orders to-morrow morning, and you'll be shot. [*To the* Carriers.] Listen, children. Those who run away—all killed by Batetela.

[*Two of the* Carriers *emerge from among the huddled mass of them. They are poor, emaciated creatures.*

1st CARRIER. Master! No food—got many sores—got fever.
Dis bad caravan. Go back to ribber—cross ribber—some food.

2nd CARRIER. We not engage come in dis country, master; hab
wife—hab children. Soon we fall down—no able carry load. Look,
Master! We not go-ee, go-ees. Look! [*He lifts the rag of his
garment to display his emaciated leg, disfigured by a great sore.*

[LOCKYER *turns his head away.*

STROOD. Listen! [*Pointing to* MAHMOUD.] This man tell you
wrong. No can go back. If go back, Batetela attack, kill every man.
Now, sons, trust me. No one else can save you. Trust me.

[*The* CARRIERS *look at him, beseeching, doubting, trying to see if
he is speaking truth.*

1st CARRIER. [*A Zanzibari*] Master, to-day Khamis die—
[*pointing to 2nd* CARRIER] to-morrow Umari die—[*pointing to another*]
my brother Mabruk he die soon; this too far from our country—
bad forest—bad men—eat enemy.

3rd CARRIER. [MABRUK] Master, two moons we travel—carry
load too fast—all that thick forest not like our country. Sometime
no food—our stomach empty. When we try find food—No!—
White men drive on—drive on. Sometime want little sleep—sit
down—white man come with whip—[*He makes the appropriate
gesture*] We not go-ee go-ees. We men—not dog.

STROOD. Not men. Mabruk—children! The whip saved your
lives. You fools! stray away in that forest, you never come back!
Manyema in that old forest; Batetela in this forest. Keep together,
children, keep on, keep on; if not, death all round to take you,
Mabruk.

3rd CARRIER. Inshallah—death come when it come. Me tired—
me sick——

STROOD. Listen, my son; listen, all! In four days I bring you out
of the forest. Bring you to good country—plenty food—no bad
men—more carriers—plenty more! All this way—a little further,
and we're safe. Courage, men! Trust me! Now go and sleep!
Go and sleep! To-morrow we march quickly!

[*He waves his hand, and the shadowy figures melt away into the
darkness, with murmurs of:* "Inshallah! Inshallah!"

Mahmoud, take up your rifle! Obey orders!

[MAHMOUD *resumes his rifle, and the* FOUR SOUDANESE *retreat
to their picket.*

LOCKYER. Poor devils!

STROOD. [*Turning on him*] Our only chance is carrying on. We're
in mid-stream. The pressure'll get less.

COLLIE. Ye'll never get 'em forrard. There's a limit; and it's
well to know when ye've reached it.

STROOD. No limit to will power, Collie, none!

COLLIE. There's a limit to human strength. Ye're sacrificing the lot of us for no good. Turn back!

STROOD. Never! Never have, never shall. You, Lockyer—a soldier! One spurt and we'll win out. Come!

LOCKYER. If you order me on [*with a shrug*] I'll go.

STROOD. I do. Collie!

[HERRICK's *voice from the darkness :* "Don't shoot! Friends!"

LOCKYER. Herrick!

[*The* THREE MEN *stand alert and waiting. From Left Back appear* HERRICK *and* AMINA, *surrounded by the* SOUDANESE *picket.*

STROOD. Seize that wench!

HERRICK. [*Who looks exhausted*] No. [*He takes the* GIRL *by the arm.*] Drink.

[LOCKYER *hands him a water-bottle, which he passes to the* GIRL *first. She drinks and sinks down, squatting and watching.*

[HERRICK, *after drinking, takes out the letter.*

STROOD. She had it—after all? So much for squeamishness, Captain. Twelve men lost by it!

HERRICK. Do you want this letter delivered now?

STROOD. [*Sardonically*] Do we want to live?

HERRICK. Amina, go—fetch your brother.

[AMINA *stands up. Her eyes seem to stab* STROOD.] Go! call him.

[*As if hypnotized, the* GIRL *sways out to the edge of the clearing and is lost among the trees. The* MEN *stand waiting. Presently a long, shrill, peculiar call is heard—repeated—then answered faintly from the forest. Round the* WHITE MEN *grouped in the light from the tent lantern, and the motionless* SOUDANESE, *the emaciated forms of the* CARRIERS *can be seen dimly to the Left, gathering in the darkness.*

COLLIE. Is she for a bit o' new treachery, d'ye think?

HERRICK. Got any brandy?

[LOCKYER *hands him the flask and some biscuits.*]

[HERRICK *drinks from it and nibbles a biscuit.*] You're surrounded here.

STROOD. [*To* LOCKYER] Take your men and see what she's doing.

HERRICK. Wait! Wait!

[*There is another moment of silent waiting. Then* TWO FIGURES *are seen coming from the darkness, Right Back. The* GIRL *comes first, and after her, imposing, dark, hawk-faced, clad in light garments, her brother, the half-caste Arab,* SAMEHDA. *She leads him up to the group, and the two stand silent and apart.*

HERRICK. Samehda! Salaam!

AMINA. [*To her brother*] Herrick—good.

[HERRICK *advances, holding out the letter. As he does so,* AMINA
says something low and rapid to her brother in their language.

HERRICK. From Samway.

[SAMEHDA *steps forward and takes the letter with a salaam. He
reads it by the light of the oil lantern and then retreats and
stands with his head drawn back, looking from one white man
to another,* AMINA *at his elbow.*

SAMEHDA. Chief man?

[AMINA *points to* STROOD, *and again speaks low and rapidly in
a language the white men do not understand.*

SAMEHDA. [*Making a movement to silence her*] Samway—my brother.
You Strood?   [STROOD *advances, holding out his hand.*

[SAMEHDA *does not take it, but salaams.*

SAMEHDA. Palaver.

[*After a certain hesitation they sit down cross-legged. The* CARRIERS
also squat in the background; only the SOUDANESE *remain
standing, leaning on their rifles.*

SAMEHDA. Belgian man here?

STROOD. No; Englishmen—all.

SAMEHDA. [*With a deep sound*] Belgian my enemy. Belgian kill
many my people—take away my slave. Why you come my country?

STROOD. Samehda, we are no friends of Belgians. We come to
take Belgian country many marches from here. [*Pointing to the south.*]
South—far.

SAMEHDA. [*Pointing to* HERRICK] This man friend of my sister—
Samway say—long time friend?

HERRICK. [*Bowing*] Yes.

SAMEHDA. [*Pointing to* LOCKYER] This man no Belgian?

LOCKYER. English.

SAMEHDA. [*Pointing to* COLLIE] This man?

COLLIE. Scot.

STROOD. Brother of English.

SAMEHDA. [*With a deep sound which may or may not be approval*]
What you come for?

STROOD. I tell you: we pass through your country, go far south,
take away some Belgian country.

SAMEHDA. [*Reserved and ironic*] I born Zanzibar—I know white
men—come from across sea—take country—ivory—slave—all that
belong Arab. Belgian—English—German. And all say: " Serve
Allah! Free slave!" All steal from Arab.

STROOD. Arab stole first from black men, Samehda.

SAMEHDA. Then Arab keep if can; white men take if can. Arab
serve Allah too.

STROOD. Allah made men free, Samehda; Arab make men slaves.

SAMEHDA. White men make slave too—carrier men. If run away —whip, shoot.

STROOD. Hear me, Samehda. Samway is my friend.

SAMEHDA. Samway my brother.

STROOD. Help us to cross your country : we will make you a large present. Come ! Do what Samway asks you.

                    [AMINA *murmurs rapidly in the unknown tongue.*

SAMEHDA. My father chief man. I his son. [*Touching* AMINA.] This one his daughter—daughter of Arab chief man. You—[*He makes the motion of striking.*] Why ?

STROOD. She stole that letter from my tent. Suppose you have a great strong letter, Samehda, a woman steal it—what you do ?

SAMEHDA. No whip for Arab. Arab not black man.

STROOD. [*Pressing him*] She did a very bad thing to steal that letter. That letter is from your brother Samway. He saved your life ; Arab never forget.

SAMEHDA. [*Loftily*] Arab good man.

STROOD. Listen ! You give us carriers—forty. You make all quiet for us. At the Lomami river we give you good present—some rifles—some cloth. Afterward more present—bigger.

SAMEHDA. How much rifle—how many cloth ?

STROOD. Ten pieces of cloth when we reach the Lomami ; after crossing, ten rifles.

SAMEHDA. You give me rifle made in Germany ?

STROOD. Good rifles.

SAMEHDA. No ! You give me ten English rifle now ; then I see.

STROOD. At the river, Samehda.

SAMEHDA. Suppose I no help ?—Batetela very many—very strong. Got poison arrow ; kill all. Take all rifles, then.

STROOD. [*Vigorously*] If we are killed, a great army will avenge us. Remember your father—how the white men came.

SAMEHDA. [*With a smile*] This Belgian country. English soldier no come here. English—Belgian not good friend.

STROOD. Samehda, listen ! I, too, am a chief man in my country —a strong chief. My death will make much noise. My Government will make the Belgians send an army—kill you—take your country.

SAMEHDA. [*Softly*] If you die, no one know. [*With a gesture.*] Forest hide all.

STROOD. You refuse, then ?

SAMEHDA. [*Elusive*] Samway my brother.

STROOD. Well ?

SAMEHDA. You give me ten rifle now

STROOD. [*Rising*] Palaver finish.   I take you both with me to the Lomami river.

               [SAMEHDA *and the* GIRL *spring up.   All are on their feet.*]
No attack, while I have *you.*

               [SAMEHDA'S *glance slides round,* STROOD *lifts his revolver.*]
Stand ! Don't move !

SAMEHDA. [*With dignity*] This *peace* palaver—you no keep word.

STROOD. For our lives—you force me.

       [*While he is speaking the* GIRL *has glided forward, stooping, and
       strikes upward at* STROOD'S *lifted arm, with a little dagger ;
       he drops the revolver, wounded in the wrist, and tries to seize
       her with the other hand ; but she glides past him and away into
       the darkness, pursued by* TWO SOUDANESE *and* SADIG.
       SAMEHDA *has sprung back, drawing a knife.* LOCKYER
       dashes forward to seize him ; there is a swift ham-stringing
       cut and* LOCKYER *stumbles, clinging to the tent-pole for support.
       SAMEHDA *turns and darts away.* COLLIE *rushes in pursuit
       of him ; they disappear in the darkness to the Right.   There
       are two shots, then a long groan, and in wailing, chattering
       confusion the* CARRIERS *disperse into the darkness.*

STROOD. Stop them ! Herrick ! Mahmoud ! Lockyer !—stop
them !   [*He,* HERRICK, *and the* SOUDANESE *dash after them.*

       [LOCKYER *is left clinging to the tent-pole.   One or two more shots
       are heard ; the drum-beats swell furiously.* LOCKYER *tries
       to leave the support of the tent-pole and walk, but sinks to the
       ground.   He sits there, feeling and examining his leg.*

LOCKYER. Ham-strung ! My God !

       [*He crawls back to the tent-pole, takes up his revolver and painfully
       raises himself till he is leaning against the pole, the lantern
       hanging quite close to his face.   To this one lighted spot* STROOD
       and HERRICK *come back.*

STROOD. Lockyer !

LOCKYER. Here !

STROOD. Gone—every rat ! Soudanese too. Not a man left.
Not a man !

LOCKYER. Collie ?

HERRICK. I stumbled over his body.

          [*Savage cries from the forest and the beating of drums.*]
They're on us.

STROOD. Into the bushes, quick ! Stick together.   Come !

HERRICK. Any chance ?

STROOD. Yes ! Yes ! Come on ! We'll slip through them yet.
Come on—both of you.   Stick close to me.

HERRICK. Hurt, Lockyer ?

LOCKYER. Nothing.

STROOD. By compass—due west.   Keep close, now !   Keep close.
      [*He moves to the Left, followed by* HERRICK.
LOCKYER. I'll just put out this light.
      [*He extinguishes the lantern and sinks down under the lee of the tent.
      A moment's empty, dark silence.*
HERRICK. [*Returning ; in a low voice*] Lockyer ! Lockyer !
STROOD'S VOICE. [*From Left*] Come on ! I can hear him—he's
ahead.   [HERRICK *feels the tent-pole and peers about.*]
Come on ! Come on !   [HERRICK *goes.*
      [*Silence but for the sound of the drums.   Then dead silence.*
LOCKYER'S VOICE. [*Low, in the darkness*] Good luck !

                    The curtain falls.

                    SCENE II*

*The forest on the following day—noon.   A fallen trunk, huge and rotten
with viper-like creepers, lies along the Back Centre of the scene leading
up Stage.* HERRICK *lies propped against the log, unconscious.* STROOD
*is bending over him.   He moves a step away, and himself squats down,
staring at* HERRICK.   *He seems to be struggling to form a resolve.
He leans forward and listens for the sound of* HERRICK's *breathing ;
then, at some noise, recoils, every nerve taut, listening to the forest.
Nothing !   He relaxes a moment in physical exhaustion.   Then with
an effort, again forces his mind to the forming of that resolve, fixing his
queer stare on* HERRICK, *still unconscious.   His shoulders shrug
convulsively and he rises.   He has taken two stealthy steps away when*
HERRICK *stirs.* STROOD *stands still, then turns his head.*
HERRICK's *eyes have opened ; they are fixed on his.   The two men
stare at each other without speaking.   A faint smile flickers on*
HERRICK's *face.*
HERRICK. It's all right—go !
STROOD. For water.
HERRICK. [*With the same smile*] For water ?
STROOD. Do you think I was leaving you ?
HERRICK. Yes. Why not ? I've got a shot left. Our souls are
naked here, Strood. Not worth keeping it from me. Shake hands.
STROOD. I meant to go. But damn me if I do. We'll get through
yet. Lie here, I'll find some water. Back—soon !
      [*He goes, treading stealthily away among the trees to the Left.*
      HERRICK, *left alone, mumbles his dry lips with his tongue,
      and leans back against the trunk, the picture of exhaustion,
      with his hand on his revolver.*

* With the tent gone, entirely different lighting, and a fresh backcloth, the
same setting can be used as in the preceding scene.

HERRICK. [*Muttering*] Back—will he ?

> [*The face of* AMINA *is poked out from some bushes on the Right. She steals noiselessly up to* HERRICK'S *side. With her eyes fixed on his face she waits for him to stir.* HERRICK *opens his eyes and sees her.*

HERRICK. You !

AMINA. Batetela track all night.   I follow—kill one fellow in bush there. [*She shows her dagger.*] Come with Amina ! Samehda friend to my friend.   All safe with Amina ! [*Putting his hand to her breast.*] Come !   [HERRICK *continues to stare at her without speaking.*

AMINA. If not quick, too late.   Batetela soon here—find dead fellow — kill Herrick then.   My brother not far — two three mile.

HERRICK. Strood.

AMINA. Quick !

HERRICK. Wait for him.

AMINA. No.   He strike me.   He break word.   Strood dead man.   Batetela all round—all over forest—many—soon find Herrick too.

HERRICK. [*Raising his revolver*] Not alive.

AMINA. [*Embracing his knees*] Ah ! no ! Come ! Herrick safe with Samehda.   Come quick !   Strood leave you here to die.

HERRICK. No.   Gone for water.

AMINA. Strood find water ; he go on.   Strood let all die, if he live.

HERRICK. [*Slowly*] No, I'll wait.

AMINA. If Strood come back, he shoot me.   [HERRICK *rises.*

AMINA. [*Clinging to him, twining round him, trying to draw him away into the bushes*] Come ! Come !

HERRICK. Let go, girl !   I'll wait !

AMINA. [*Recoiling suddenly*] Strood.

> [STROOD *has appeared from the forest, Left.*

HERRICK. [*With triumph, to the* GIRL] See !

> [*The* GIRL *shrinks behind the trunk.*

> [STROOD *lifts his revolver, but the* GIRL, *interposing the trunk, creeps back into cover.*

STROOD. Why didn't you hold her ?   Are they on us ?

HERRICK. She killed a tracker out there.

> [*The sound of drums is heard.*

STROOD. [*Slicing a length of creeper from the tree*] Here ! Tie yourself to me.   Come on !   She'll follow.   We'll get her yet.

> [*They tie the creeper around their waists.*

> [*The almost naked form of a* SAVAGE *emerges from the bushes on the Right.   With a cry, he darts back into the bushes.   Yells follow and the beating of drums.*

STROOD. Back to back, when we must.   Now !   Into the thick.

[*He hastens forward, half dragging* HERRICK *into the forest.   Two dark* FIGURES *glide from the bushes and pass crouching.   Then a splendid* SAVAGE *is seen standing clear, he leaps on to the fallen trunk, and stretches his bow.   There is a shot ; the* SAVAGE *shoots his arrow and leaps forward into the forest.   The stage is empty again ; three more shots are heard, some fierce cries ; then* STROOD, *half dragging, half supporting* HERRICK, *comes back towards the trunk.   Two arrows have pierced* HERRICK's *back, the shafts visible.*

HERRICK. [*Prostrate*] Cut, cut ! I'm done !

[*For answer* STROOD *lifts him.* AMINA *emerges from the bushes, Right, and leaps towards* HERRICK. STROOD, *dropping* HERRICK, *who sinks down dead, levels his revolver and fires.   But the revolver clicks.   It is empty.   He throws it down, and stands quite still, unarmed, exposed, with his eyes fixed on the* GIRL, *who crouches forward towards him.*

STROOD. Well ! . . . Come on if you dare, you forest hell-cat !

[*His face has a kind of exaltation of defiance, as if holding a wild beast at bay with the force of his gaze.   The* GIRL *stands hypnotized.   At a sound from the bushes* STROOD *turns his head for a second.   Quick as thought the* GIRL *springs and drives her dagger into his heart.   With a gasp, he falls against the trunk, dead.   The* GIRL *flings herself down by* HERRICK's *dead body, stroking it and uttering a crooning lament.*

[*A* SAVAGE *steals out of the bushes and stops three paces away, looking down at* STROOD's *half-recumbent body.   A kind of contraction passes over* STROOD's *face.   The* SAVAGE *recoils, raising his spear.* STROOD's *face relaxes in death.   The* SAVAGE *bends forward, regarding the dead white man with a sort of awe.   Drums are being beaten in the forest.   The stage is darkened.*

The curtain falls.

ACT IV

SCENE I

The following June. BASTAPLE'S *outer sanctum in the City of London. Afternoon.*

[BASTAPLE *is seated at his little table.* BARON ZIMBOSCH *in a chair to his right.*

ZIMBOSCH. Since the middle of May, Mr. Bastaple, they have been sitting there at Bloemfontein, Milner and Oom Paul Kruger. Well, it is over—the Conference.

BASTAPLE. What's the result?

ZIMBOSCH. Impasse. The more Kruger ask, the more Milner refuse; the more Milner ask, the more Kruger stick his heel. No one will know for a fortnight; but take it from me, Mr. Bastaple: this is a cert—no agreement.

BASTAPLE. H'm!

ZIMBOSCH. [*Nodding*] War—in the autumn. When the result of this Conference is known—up go the temperatures. A bad attack of war fever—you will see.

BASTAPLE. Quite sure about your news?

ZIMBOSCH. Absolute! Cable this morning; best information from the back stair. You may bottom your dollar on it, Mr. Bastaple. My word—Africans! La! la! But you have a fortnight still before the news is out. Your friend Beton has his General Meeting the day after to-morrow, isn't it? If he gets his coolie labour, you have your chance to get out yet. I admire Robert Beton, he is idealist to his toptoes. *Bon Dieu!* you are all idealists in this country.

[BASTAPLE *smiles.*]

Ah! not you, Mr. Bastaple—not you!

[*The door, Back, is opened, and* FARRELL *appears; he closes and is about to advance when* BASTAPLE *waves him back.*

BASTAPLE. One minute, Farrell. [FARRELL *retires.*

ZIMBOSCH. [*Rising*] Well, I hope I have brought you some useful news this time. You remember how Rothschild won the battle of Waterloo. And they put that lion up in the sky—the British-Belgian lion! My Lord! What a monster! Curious no country has taken a tiger for its pet animal!

779

BASTAPLE. No uplift about a tiger, Baron.

ZIMBOSCH. [*Preparing to go*] And our steamers, Mr. Bastaple? We are looking to you for that loan.

BASTAPLE. You have my word, Baron.

ZIMBOSCH. The word of Adrian Bastaple. [*With a bow.*] Good afternoon then, Mr. Bastaple. You have yet a fortnight.

[*He is moving to the door, Back.*

BASTAPLE. [*Rising and motioning to the door, Right*] This way, Baron.

[*He shows him out, then presses his bell.* FARRELL *enters from his room.*

FARRELL. Mr. Beton is here, sir; but Mr. Stanforth and Lord Elderleigh have not yet come.

BASTAPLE. What are South African Concessions at this afternoon?

FARRELL. Still sagging, sir—fifteen shillings.

BASTAPLE. Back about three-sixteenths all round, um?

FARRELL. Yes, sir. Oh! you saw this, sir, in this morning's paper? [*Reads from cutting.*] " Dr. Clement Franks arrived in London yesterday from Mombasa. He has lately returned from the Congo, where he accompanied Mr. Strood, Captain Lockyer, and Mr. Collie in the expedition of which as yet no news has been received. Dr. Franks was left at the Lualaba river, in command of the men who were unfit to travel further. His mission in London is to communicate with those who promoted this mysterious adventure. He declined to give our representative any further details."

BASTAPLE. Yes, I saw that.

FARRELL. Will you have Mr. Beton in?

BASTAPLE. Yes.

FARRELL. [*Opening the door*] Oh! the others have just come, sir. Will you come in, gentlemen?

[BETON *comes in, followed almost immediately by* STANFORTH *and* LORD ELDERLEIGH.

BETON. Seen that about Franks, Bastaple. I hope to God he'll give us some good news.

ELDERLEIGH. He sent a letter overland to his cousin Mr. Tregay.

BETON. What does he say?

STANFORTH. [*Coldly*] We have come about that.

ELDERLEIGH. I'm afraid we shall have to speak plainly. Mr. Tregay holds the theory that this expedition has been dust in our eyes, Mr. Beton. It appears you are bringing forward a scheme for coolie labour at your meeting the day after to-morrow which is entirely —entirely contrary to our ideals and views. Mr. Tregay has suggested that you and Mr. Bastaple have tried to blind us with this anti-slavery expedition. He calls it a red herring.

BASTAPLE. Mr. Tregay is a picturesque person, my lord.

ELDERLEIGH. That may be. But this coolie scheme is not a

figure of speech, and we—I speak for Nonconformist opinion—are dead against it.

STANFORTH. I speak for Liberalism—dead against it. Africa is for the white man, and we won't have the yellow there, nor that dressed-up slavery, indentured labour.

BETON. Africa will not be for the white man in our time, *without* my coolie labour. I want to see the white man there, and you don't care two straws about it. No, you don't—neither of you. You just want to air your principles, or whatever you call them. Very well; it's a fight.

ELDERLEIGH. I should like to know : was it a red herring ?

BASTAPLE. Really, my lord——

BETON. It was ; I don't care a damn whether you know it or not. I'm too sorry about those poor fellows swallowed up in that forest.

ELDERLEIGH. Stanforth, is there anything to stay for ?

STANFORTH. No, there's everything to go for.

ELDERLEIGH. Then we meet the day after to-morrow at—Philippi. Good afternoon !   [*They go out.*

BETON. This is a bolt from the blue ! We've made a mistake not to have proxies, Bastaple. The cat's out of the bag and might just as well have been out sooner. Well, I shall let myself go at the meeting—they'll get it from the shoulder. " Africa for the white man ! " Bunkum ! It'll take a hundred years that way. I want to see my dreams come true in my lifetime.

BASTAPLE. The market's got wind ; shares are sagging.

BETON. Let 'em ; their future's safe.

BASTAPLE. The Boers, Beton ?

BETON. Oh ! old Kruger will have climbed down all right. If Dr. Franks comes here, let me have the news. I must go to work on this. I shall get it through, yet.

[*He goes out, Back.* BASTAPLE *is left brooding.*

BASTAPLE. [*To himself*] Not he ! [*He takes a sheet of paper and begins figuring.*] A damned bad hole !

[*He crosses over to the telephone, takes up the receiver, but puts it back again. After a turn up and down, he goes to the table, takes a cigar from the box, and is about to light it when*

[FARRELL *enters, Right, from the waiting-room.*

FARRELL. Dr. Franks, sir, in the waiting-room.

BASTAPLE. Oh ! very well !   [FARRELL *retires to his own room.*

[BASTAPLE *replaces the cigar, crosses to the waiting-room, and opens the door.*

BASTAPLE. Dr. Franks ?   Adrian Bastaple.

[FRANKS *comes in. Very sun-dark and thin, with the look of a man who has been through a terrible strain. He is a great contrast to* BASTAPLE.

BASTAPLE. Glad to see you, Dr. Franks. Read of your arrival in this morning's paper. What news ?

FRANKS. [*Taking a long envelope from his pocket*] You had the long cable I sent through your agents at Mombasa ! [BASTAPLE *nods*.] This is my detailed report. But from the time Strood left me at the Lualaba river, I've no news—none. They went on in hostile country —thick forest ahead—savage cannibals ; they were very weak, very ill-provided in every way to resist attack. They must have foundered utterly.

BASTAPLE. But you ?

FRANKS. By a miracle I got through to Tanganyika with six out of the twelve men left with me.

BASTAPLE. [*Impressed by his voice and his look*] You have been through much, I'm afraid.

FRANKS. [*Sombrely*] The forest.

BASTAPLE. And you struck no signs of the slave trade ?

FRANKS. None. You'll find it all here [*handing the report.*]

BASTAPLE. Shortly—what's the story ?

FRANKS. We travelled from the Albert Edward to the Lualaba——

BASTAPLE. One second. [*He goes to the table, takes out and spreads a map.*] Put your finger on the places.

[*They stand side by side behind the table, and* FRANKS *touches the map from time to time.*

FRANKS. From here to here at the utmost speed we could manage in that forest ; forced marches, avoiding native villages, every human being we could.

BASTAPLE. How do you account for that ?

FRANKS. After we'd crossed the Lualaba river—which was never in the programme as we thought—Strood told us : he was not really looking for the slave trade. His objective was down here [*points*] —diamond fields, reported to him by an elephant-hunter called Samway.

BASTAPLE. Diamonds ?

FRANKS. Besides Samway, a Belgian knew of them, he was travelling from Basoko—here—to claim them. Strood was racing him.

BASTAPLE. A wild departure, Dr. Franks.

FRANKS. Strood seemed to think the discovery important to the British Empire ; our lives of no account so long as he got there first.

BASTAPLE. [*Brooding*] You were left here [*he points*], you say ? Why mightn't Strood have got through ?

FRANKS. Imagine the back of night, the bottom of hell, and you'll have some conception of the conditions.

BASTAPLE. Still—you yourself——

FRANKS. I recrossed the river. The country's terrible enough, but not full of hostile cannibals.   If he hadn't perished, some news *must* have filtered through.

BASTAPLE. What about that Belgian expedition ?

FRANKS. It turned back.

BASTAPLE. Ah !

FRANKS. Strood was alone among us in wishing to go on.   [*With a sudden look at* BASTAPLE.] May I ask you a question ?

[BASTABLE *nods*.]

Was he told to embroil us with the Belgians ?

BASTAPLE. He was told to look for the slave trade, Dr. Franks.

FRANKS. Forgive me.   I——

BASTAPLE. [*With a conciliatory wave of his hand ; tracing on the map*] All this country in front of Strood.   What is there ?

FRANKS. Forest, marsh, hostile natives.   Further on, I believe, it's better.

BASTAPLE. No white posts ?

FRANKS. Not south of him.

BASTAPLE. [*His eyes very alive*] I see.   Dr. Franks, we owe you a great debt for what you've been through.   In what way can I serve you ?

FRANKS. Oh ? thank you—none.

BASTAPLE. What are you going to do now ?

FRANKS. See Captain Lockyer's people, and Mr. Collie's.   After that, I don't know.

BASTAPLE. Is any money due to you ?

FRANKS. No ; it was all paid up at Mombasa.   [*Looking suddenly at* BASTAPLE.] I want to forget the whole thing—if I can.

BASTAPLE. I understand : painful—newspaper gossip, and all that.   The less said !

FRANKS. Yes.   But with my report my duty ends.   I can make no promises.

BASTAPLE. Why should you, Dr. Franks ?   Why should you ? [*He rings.*] I shall read your report at once.   [FARRELL *enters*.] Please leave your address.   Many thanks, again.   Good-bye !

FRANKS. Good-bye.   [FARRELL *and* FRANKS *go out*.

•[BASTAPLE, *alone, brings his hands together, presses the palms closely, rubs them ; then stands still.   On his face is the look of a man who suddenly sees his way.   Then, going to the map, he examines it, passing his finger down, as if tracing an imaginary route.   When he raises his head, the expression on his face has changed to one of great determination.   He rings the bell and stands behind the map, waiting.*   [FARRELL *enters*.

FARRELL. Yes, sir ?

BASTAPLE. Farrell, Dr. Franks has been telling me about Strood's expedition.   Follow me.   [*He traces with his finger on the map*.] It seems that when Franks was left behind, here, Strood was making for some diamond fields—there in the Kasai—to secure them for South African Concessions.

FARRELL. [*Startled*] Indeed, sir?

BASTAPLE. Dr. Franks thinks he cannot possibly have reached those diamond fields, and that the whole expedition has foundered. I think—he is unduly pessimistic.

FARRELL. You—you do, sir?

BASTAPLE. I shouldn't be surprised if at any moment we had news —of his having reached them. My instinct is not often wrong. [*As if to himself.*] A new De Beers discovered for South African Concessions——! God-sent! God-sent, Farrell!

FARRELL. [*His mouth opening a little*] Yes, sir.

BASTAPLE. But no use, if it doesn't come within a fortnight. When the Transvaal news is out, Africans will drop to nothing.

FARRELL. Oh! . . . If Strood—how should we be likely to hear, sir?

BASTAPLE. [*Pointing to map*] From the west coast, I imagine—a Portuguese source, probably. [*Turning to* FARRELL.] If coolie labour doesn't go through, Farrell, I am face to face with something like disaster.

FARRELL. [*Gazing intently*] I—I—see, sir. I heard of the opposition; Mr. Stanforth was most sarcastic. But is there *no* chance of coolie labour going through?

BASTAPLE. We must wait for the General Meeting. If it does go through, Strood's success is less material. If it doesn't—and it won't, Farrell, it won't—his success is vital. [*A pause—with sudden emphasis.*] But he's no more a man to fail than I.

FARRELL. N—no, sir.

BASTAPLE. [*Hardening*] Did you ever know my instinct wrong?

FARRELL. N—no, sir.

BASTAPLE. Dr. Franks got through, then why not Strood? We are not all so pessimistic, Farrell.

FARRELL. N—no, sir.

BASTAPLE. What shares are left in my name?

FARRELL. Only the twenty thousand, sir.

BASTAPLE. Good. The rest are to be sold at any price above a pound. [*Putting his finger on a spot in the map.*] Study this map.

[*He crosses to the door and goes through into his inner sanctum.*

[FARRELL *is left gazing at the map with round eyes. He blows out his cheeks and lets them slowly subside.*

FARRELL. [*To himself*] What a man!

The curtain falls.

SCENE II

The same, in the afternoon, four days later.

[FARRELL *is at the telephone.*

FARRELL. No, he's been out of town the last three days. . . . Yes . . . I quite follow—two currents—selling on the coolie failure—buying on this report . . . much the stronger ! . . . I see. What have they touched ? . . . Thirty shillings ! Still upward ? . . . Ah, ha ! Batson ! buy me five thousand for Mr. Bastaple's account ; you've just time before they close. . . . Yes, yes. . . . Exactly . . . Right. [*Cutting off. To himself.*] Buying ! [*He sits, smiling.*] A master stroke.

[*The door, Back, is opened and* BASTAPLE *comes in, top-hatted.* FARRELL *starts up and looks at him eagerly. But his face is like that of a graven image. He passes without a word into his inner sanctum.* FARRELL *is hesitating whether to follow, when he comes back without hat or gloves.*

BASTAPLE. Well, Farrell ?

FARRELL. There's been a very heavy rise all day on this report—buying mostly from the general public. [*With his quick look.*] There's been heavy selling too, sir.   [*A little meaning smile.*

BASTAPLE. Really ?

FARRELL. Yes, sir. The demand is so great, I fully expect all the dummies will be sold before closing time. [*He rubs his hands.*] In fact, I'm waiting for——

BASTAPLE. Did you get my wire ?

FARRELL. Yes, sir, and I've bought you the fifteen thousand, in three hands ; it—it must be well over the City that you're buying. [*Nervously.*] Er—" Another De Beers," that's what——

BASTAPLE. Yes, this report about Strood is almost too good to be true. Where did it come from, Farrell ?

FARRELL. [*With his quick look.*] Portuguese source, sir.

BASTAPLE. As I thought. Mr. Beton been here ?

FARRELL. Yes, sir ; he came the morning after the General Meeting, very upset by the coolie failure. And again this morning about the report of Strood's finding these diamonds. I told him you'd been out of town ever since he was here with Mr. Stanforth and Lord Elderleigh.

BASTAPLE. What did he say to this report about Strood ?

FARRELL. Seemed doubtful, sir—wanted to know what *you* thought. I told him ; I'd just had a wire from you to buy. *That* impressed him. But he said this find wouldn't console him for the smash of his coolie scheme. Only Strood's being safe was a great relief. He

wanted to know if the news had come from Dr. Franks.   I said I
thought not.   Dr. Franks had been here, but he had no news.

BASTAPLE.   I must see Dr. Franks again.   Send for him.

> [*He goes back into his inner sanctum.*

> [FARRELL *stands for a moment looking after him, nervously licking
> his lips.   He has turned to the door, Back, to go out, when it
> is opened and a* CLERK *says :*

CLERK.   Mr. Tregay and Dr. Franks, sir.   [*They come in.*

TREGAY.   Mr. Farrell, can we see your chief ?

FARRELL.   Certainly, sir ?   He was just saying he wanted to see
Dr. Franks.   Will you take a seat ?

> [TREGAY *and* FRANKS *stand over on the Right, and* FARRELL *goes
> into the sanctum.   He returns almost immediately.*

FARRELL.   In a minute, gentlemen.   Will you smoke ?

> [*They will not, and* FARRELL *goes into his room, with a quick look
> round at them.   They are close together and speak in low voices.*

TREGAY.   You've told   no one   else   what   Strood   was   really
after ?

FRANKS.   Not a soul.

TREGAY.   Any proof.

FRANKS.   My word of honour.

TREGAY.   Not legal tender, Clement.

FRANKS.   Isn't a man's word believed in the City ?

TREGAY.   It has been known.

FRANKS.   I must have my name cleared of this, Roger.   In my
report there wasn't a shred of hope that Strood could ever reach
those diamonds.   What am I to say to poor Lockyer's people, and to
Collie's, now ?   What am I to do ?

TREGAY.   Keep your head, my boy.

> [*While he is speaking* BASTAPLE'S *door is opened, and he comes in.*

BASTAPLE.   Good evening, gentlemen.

> [*They turn abruptly.*   TREGAY *reserved, ironic.*   FRANKS *tense
> and quivering.*

I've read your report, Dr. Franks.   Terrible, that forest !   I was
just sending round to you about this news in the papers.

FRANKS.   I came about that.

BASTAPLE.   I thought you unduly pessimistic the other day.

FRANKS.   You believe it ?

TREGAY.   Striking coincidence, Mr. Bastaple.

BASTAPLE.   How do you mean ?

TREGAY.   On Monday my cousin reports Strood's objective ;   on
Thursday comes the news that he has reached it.

BASTAPLE.   You think something let fall by Dr. Franks has inspired
the imagination of some journalist ?

FRANKS.   I've let nothing fall.

BASTAPLE. [*Shrugging his shoulders*] How about Mr. Tregay——?
Walls have ears, Dr. Franks.

FRANKS. [*Drawing a cutting from his pocket*] " On behalf of South
African Concessions ? " How could I have said that ? I've been
away six years—didn't even know there was such a concern.

BASTAPLE. Ever heard of Robert Beton ?

FRANKS. Yes, from Strood.

BASTAPLE. Robert Beton *is* South African Concessions. Beton
picked him for this trip.

FRANKS. [*Flustered*] Yes ; but I—I've never spoken of Beton.

BASTAPLE. Well ! It looks more and more as if the news were true.
We must try and verify it, Dr. Franks.

TREGAY. How about beginning in this office ?

BASTAPLE. The report, you mean ? . . . Hasn't been out of my
personal possession, Mr. Tregay. [*He takes it from his breast pocket.*]
And since I saw Dr. Franks, I've been away from town until an hour
ago.

TREGAY. Walls have ears, Mr. Bastaple.

BASTAPLE. Not these walls, gentlemen, or a good many projects
would have gone agley.

FRANKS. [*Excitedly*] There's a wild buying of shares, they tell me.
See this headline : " Another De Beers."

BASTAPLE. Let's look at that wording. [*Reading the cutting.*]
" Another De Beers is reported to have been discovered on behalf
of South African Concessions, by the explorer John Strood, who
last autumn penetrated the Congo region from the Albert Edward
Nyanza." Been down to the office of that journal ?

FRANKS. Yes, and to others. The only answer I get is that it comes
from a reliable source.

BASTAPLE. The craze for sensation—it *may* be a canard.

TREGAY. If so, how comes it they pitched on Strood's *real* objective !

BASTAPLE. [*Shrugging*] Exactly ! how ?

FRANKS. People are losing and making fortunes on the strength of
this report. I don't believe it ; I want my name cleared of it.

BASTAPLE. What are you going to do, then ?

FRANKS. Disclaim any connection, in the papers, warn people
against the report.

    [FARRELL *appears from his room, with evening papers in his hand.*
        He puts them down on the little table ; then hands BASTAPLE
        a slip of paper, and goes out.

BASTAPLE. [*After a glance at the slip of paper, smiles ; then, curling
it up in his hand, spreads an evening journal*] Let's see if there's anything
fresh about it.   [*Reading to himself.*] Um ! It says here : " From a
Portuguese source." That absolves you, Dr. Franks.

FRANKS. [*Startled*] Portuguese ! If it's true, after all !

BASTAPLE. Why not? I'm buying on the strength of it. Still, send that denial of your responsibility.

TREGAY. At once, Clement, if it's to be in to-morrow's press.

FRANKS. Could I write it quietly in there?
                                        [*He points to the door, Right.*

BASTAPLE. Certainly. You'll find everything.

FRANKS. Thanks.   [*He goes out.*

TREGAY. Might I have a look at that bit of paper in your left hand?

BASTAPLE. [*Involuntarily closing his hand*] I beg your pardon!

TREGAY. This is a ramp, Mr. Bastaple.

BASTAPLE. [*Slowly*] Are you unwell, sir?

TREGAY. Who financed the Strood expedition? You! Why? Because you wanted coolie labour to boost your shares with. Coolie labour fell down two days ago,
                [BASTAPLE *makes a gesture of impatience.*]
and you were in deep—or you'd never have pulled out ten thousand pounds last autumn for a slave-trade story. What then? Shares falling—time pressing; you know why, and so do I. Old Kruger—war coming. And so—you whispered " diamonds," and someone heard you, and——   [*Again* BASTAPLE *makes a movement.*]
Well! Why not? You win instead of losing—someone loses instead of winning. And you have made——? Do show me that bit of paper!

BASTAPLE. This is amusing.

TREGAY. Ah! Then, may I have a look?

BASTAPLE. You may be damned! [*He takes a cigar and lights it from the little flame burning beside his cigar box.*

TREGAY. [*Staring at him*] Self for self and devil take the hindmost—fine motto, Mr. Bastaple.

BASTAPLE. Confound your impudence. What business have you——?

TREGAY. My cousin is not exactly at home in this city of yours, poor devil.

BASTAPLE. You are offensive, sir.

TREGAY. I've seen your sort at work too often, stalking your game, mousing after the oof-bird. The cat force!

BASTAPLE. Romanticism! Ha!
            [*While he speaks,* FRANKS *has returned and stands amazed.*

TREGAY. Clement, there's some plain speaking going on. This rumour's a fake.

BASTAPLE. I have a witness now, sir.

TREGAY. [*Looking at his watch*] The Stock Exchange has closed. If you want to know what he's made out of this, ask him to let you see the bit of paper in his left hand. Let's take it from him!
                                        [*He steps forward.*

BASTAPLE. [*Putting his hand near the flame*] You have the advantage of me, in age and numbers, gentlemen !

[*The word brings* TREGAY *to a standstill.*

FRANKS. You say *he* issued that report ?

TREGAY. Or got it issued.

FRANKS. To make money ! [*With sudden passion.*] By God ! You people who sit here—if I had you in the forest, at the tail of a caravan, covered with sores, with shrunken stomachs, and your ribs sticking out of you ! That'd teach you not to juggle with lives !

BASTAPLE. [*Icily*] Dr. Franks, I judged from your report that your heart is better than your head. Take your romantic friend here away, and ask him quietly on what evidence he bases his fantastic accusation, and he will have to tell you " On none ! " Do you understand me ? None ! Ask him to get you some, if he can. Beating the air is not an occupation for serious men. Go away !

TREGAY. Not so fast ! You went down to the newspapers, Clement. So did I. You got nothing—you don't know the ropes. I do, and I got this. [*He takes a bit of paper from his pocket and reads.*] " John Strood, English explorer for South African Concessions, discovered diamond fields Kasai, Congo Territory, March last, signed Central Press Agency, Lisbon."

FRANKS. But that sounds——   [BASTAPLE *is standing very attentive.*

TREGAY. Too slick, my boy. They gave me this at five o'clock yesterday. I wired off to a friend at Lisbon—and got this answer just before you came to see me. [*Reading.*] " Press Agency Lisbon, no knowledge of message, cannot trace sender." [*He shows it to* FRANKS.] What do you say to that, Mr. Bastaple ?

[BASTAPLE *presses the bell.*]

Cherchez l'homme—Who profits by this report ?

BASTAPLE. Precisely ! . . . Go and make your inquiries on the Stock Exchange. You will find that since this report appeared I have bought fifteen thousand shares and sold none. You two owe your immunity from an action to the fact that Dr. Franks has suffered what he has. [FARRELL *has appeared in the doorway.*] Farrell, show these people out.

TREGAY. Hold on !

[FARRELL *closes the door, and* BASTAPLE, *who is moving towards his inner sanctum, stops.*

Mr. Farrell, you knew of Strood's ultimate destination.

FARRELL. [*Hesitating*] N—no, sir—unless you—you mean——

[*His finger takes the direction of the floor.*

TREGAY. For once I'm not joking in bad taste. After Dr. Franks left last Monday, Mr. Bastaple told you.

FARRELL. [*Looking at* BASTAPLE] Did you, sir ? I—I don't seem——

BASTAPLE. You must remember whether I did or not.

FARRELL. [*Closing up*] Certainly, sir ; you did not.

TREGAY. Mr. Farrell, be careful.

FARRELL. I am naturally careful, sir.

TREGAY. Will you swear he didn't tell you ?

BASTAPLE. This is not a Court of Law.

TREGAY. No ; but you may find yourself in one.

BASTAPLE. And you, sir.

TREGAY. [*To* FARRELL] I say you knew that Strood was after those diamonds in the Kasai. I further say that on Wednesday night, after the General Meeting, when coolie labour was defeated, you wired in cipher to Lisbon instructing your agent there to send this report about Strood. Look at it !   [*He thrusts it before* FARRELL'*s eyes.*

[*While* FARRELL *is reading, all three men are staring hard at him.*
FARRELL *finishes reading and looks up.*

FARRELL. I certainly did not.

TREGAY. Pardon me if I've underrated the astuteness of your methods, but somehow you got that message sent. Look at *this :* "Press Agency Lisbon no knowledge—cannot trace sender." [*He shows* FARRELL *the telegram.*] Bring an action for slander if you didn't rig that report.

FARRELL. You're talking wild, sir.

TREGAY. [*Patting his pocket*] That bit of paper you brought in just now ? What a nice round figure, isn't it ? [*Putting his hand in his pocket, bringing it out as if with the paper in it, and looking at the inside of his hand.*

FARRELL [*After a moment of suspense*] Yes, sir, what *is* the—the amount ?

BASTAPLE. Your bluff called. Ha ! My patience is exhausted. [*Opening the door into his inner sanctum.*] Farrell.

[*He goes out, followed by* FARRELL.

TREGAY. There goes a tiger. But he's right, Clement ; we shall never bring it home to him. *His* pads leave no track.

FRANKS. [*As if to himself*] " It's a bad world, master, and you have lost your way in it." Just to make money !

TREGAY. Your own by tooth and claw, my boy. Forest law. [*He takes* FRANKS'*s arm.*] Come on !

[*The door of the inner sanctum has been reopened, and* FARRELL *stands there.*]

[*Regarding him steadily.*] What about that action, Mr. Farrell ? You've got two witnesses.

FARRELL. I also have a wife and children.   I don't go in for luxuries.

TREGAY. He might pay you better for his dirty work.

FARRELL. [*With heat*] Whet your tongue on me ; but keep it off *him*, please !

TREGAY. By Jove, Mr. Farrell, there's sand in you.   Tell me, isn't he ever ashamed of himself ?

FARRELL. No more than you, sir.

TREGAY. [*With a shrug*] Come along, Clement.

> [*They go out, followed by the gaze of* FARRELL.
> [*As the door is shut,* BASTAPLE *comes from the inner sanctum, still smoking his cigar.   He seats himself and opens a drawer of the little table.*

FARRELL. [*Nervously*] Mr. Tregay——

BASTAPLE. [*Stopping him with a gesture and taking a cheque-book from a drawer, writes*] For you.   On my account with Buenos Aires.   Ten per cent. on [*Uncrisping his left hand to read from the scrap of paper in it*] two hundred and five thousand pounds.

> [*He finishes the cheque and hands it to* FARRELL.

FARRELL. [*Open-mouthed*] Sir !

BASTAPLE. [*Stopping his attempt to speak, with a little motion of his hand*] Increase my charities this year.   Double them.

FARRELL. [*Almost in a whisper*] Yes, sir, with—with pleasure.   Of course—Strood *may* have, sir, mayn't he ?

> [BASTAPLE *turns his face towards him, and slowly smiles.   Unable to bear that sardonic grin,* FARRELL *curls away to the door and goes out.*   BASTAPLE *puts the piece of paper to the little spirit flame and watches it burn.   Then, square to the room, takes his cigar from his mouth and emits a great puff of smoke.   His face has on it a half-smile, and he stretches himself with a sigh of satisfaction, his fingers spreading and crisping unconsciously like the claws of a cat.*

The curtain falls.

OLD ENGLISH

PERSONS OF THE PLAY IN ORDER OF THEIR APPEARANCE

SYLVANUS HEYTHORP, *chairman of " The Island Navigation Company "*
GILBERT FARNEY, *secretary of the same*
BOB PILLIN, *of Pillin and Son, shipowners*
CHARLES VENTNOR, *solicitor*
MR. BROWNBEE, *a creditor of old Heythorp*
FOUR OTHER CREDITORS *of old Heythorp*
ROSAMUND LARNE, *a connection of old Heythorp*
PHYLLIS ⎱ *her children*
JOCK ⎰
JOSEPH PILLIN, *senior partner of Pillin and Son*
ADELA HEYTHORP, *daughter of old Heythorp*
TWO CLERKS *of " The Island Navigation Company "*
TWO DIRECTORS *of " The Island Navigation Company "*
MR. WESTGATE ⎱
MR. WINKLEY ⎰ *shareholders of " The Island Navigation Company "*
MR. BUDGEN ⎱
MR. APPLEBY ⎰
EIGHT OTHER SHAREHOLDERS *of the same*
A REPORTER *of the " Liverpool Press "*
LETTY, *the Larnes' maid-of-all-work*
MELLER, *old Heythorp's body-servant*
MOLLY, *his daughter's Irish housemaid*

ACT I

SCENE I

The Board Room of " The Island Navigation Company, Ltd." in Liverpool, about five in the afternoon. There are doors, Right, to the inner office, and Back, to the outer office. On the walls are photographs, and one or two models of ships. The Board is over, only the Chairman, OLD HEYTHORP, remains, presiding over the deserted battlefield of the brain—a long table still littered with the ink, pens, blotting-paper, and abandoned documents of five persons. He is sitting at the head of the table, with closed eyes, still and heavy as an image. One puffy, feeble hand rests on the arm of his chair. The thick white hair on his massive head, his red folded cheeks, white moustache, and little tuft of white on his chin, glisten in the light from green-shaded lamps. He seems asleep.

> [GILBERT FARNEY, *the Company's Secretary, enters from the outer office, Back, and steps briskly to the table. About thirty-five, he has the bright hues of the optimist in his eyes, cheeks, and lips. He begins silently to gather papers, but stops and looks at his Chairman. " Wonderful old boy ! " he seems saying. Suddenly he sees the Chairman looking at him, and cuts off his regard. OLD HEYTHORP heaves a rumbling sigh.*

HEYTHORP. Have they come, Mr. Farney ?

FARNEY. Yes, sir ; but I wasn't going to wake you.

HEYTHORP. Haven't been asleep. Let 'em wait. Suppose you know what they've come for ?

FARNEY. Did I understand, sir, it was a meeting of your—er—creditors ?

HEYTHORP. You did. Gold mine, Mr. Farney.

FARNEY. Yes, sir. I've heard—in Ecuador, wasn't it ?

HEYTHORP. [*Nodding*] Thirteen years ago. Bought it lock, stock and barrel—half in cash, half in promises. These are the promises. Never been able to pay 'em off. The mine was as empty as their heads. [*Rumbling.*] Well, not bankrupt, yet.

FARNEY. No, indeed, sir. No one could get *you* down. Your speech for our General Meeting to-morrow ? I suppose I'm to word it according to the decision of the Board this afternoon to buy the Pillin ships. That's a big thing, sir.

795

HEYTHORP. Never rest on your oars ; go forward or you go back. *Toujours de l'audace !*

FARNEY. I should like to have that on our writing paper, sir : " The Island Navigation Company—*Toujours de l'audace.*" But I must say I hope freights have touched bottom. Sixty thousand pounds is a lump for a small company like ours to lay out ; there's bound to be some opposition from the shareholders.

HEYTHORP. They'll come to heel.

FARNEY. By the way, sir, young Mr. Pillin is here. He wants to see you for a minute.

HEYTHORP. Bring him in.

> [FARNEY *goes to the door, Back, opens it and says* " Mr. Pillin ! "
>> BOB PILLIN *enters ; a tall young man with round, well-coloured cheeks, round eyes, little moustache, fur coat, spats, diamond pin, and silver-headed Malacca cane.*

BOB PILLIN. How de do, Mr. Heythorp ?

HEYTHORP. How's your father ?

BOB PILLIN. Tha-anks, rather below par, worryin' about our ships. He sent me round to see if you've any news for him. He was comin' himself, only this weather——

HEYTHORP. Your father's got no chest—never had. Tell him from me to drink port—add five years to his life.   [BOB PILLIN *chuckles.*] Beginning to look forward to his shoes, eh ? Dibs and no responsibility.   [BOB PILLIN *stops his own mouth with the head of his cane.*

HEYTHORP. Scratch a poll, Poll !

> [BOB PILLIN *evacuates his mouth, startled.*]
Give you a note for him presently. Help me up, Mr. Farney.

> [FARNEY *heaves and* HEYTHORP *pulls. The old man gets on his feet and passes, unimaginably slow, towards the inner office.*]
You can bring 'em in now.   [*He goes.*

BOB PILLIN. By Jove ! the old boy *is* gettin' a back number. His nickname fits him down to the ground—" Old English ! " He is.

FARNEY. [*Loyal to his Chairman*] He's a wonderful man. It's a treat to see him cross a road—everything has to wait for him.

BOB PILLIN. I say, those chaps in there—what have they come for ?

FARNEY. I wonder, sir. [*Opening the door into the outer office.*] Come in, gentlemen. Will you wait in here, Mr. Pillin ?

> [SIX GENTLEMEN *enter*—CHARLES VENTNOR, *first, encountering* BOB PILLIN *in the doorway.*

VENTNOR. Hallo, Pillin !

BOB PILLIN. Hallo, Ventnor ! How are you ?

VENTNOR. Thanks, bobbish !

BOB PILLIN. Mrs. Ventnor well ?

VENTNOR. So-so.   [*They cross each other and* BOB PILLIN *goes out.*
    [CHARLES VENTNOR *is short, squarely built, with a reddish-brown*
      moustache ; a certain fulvous-foxy look about him. He sits at
      the table. The second gentleman to come in, MR. BROWNBEE,
      is seventy years old, with a pink face and little thin grey whiskers.
      He sits next to VENTNOR. *The other* FOUR GENTLEMEN
      also take seats. FARNEY *goes into the outer office.*

VENTNOR. The old chap's got a nerve, keeping us hanging about
like this.

BROWNBEE. I'm afraid he's very feeble, Mr. Ventnor—very feeble ;
only just gets about.

VENTNOR. He sticks to his Boards all right, Mr. Brownbee.

BROWNBEE. Can't retire, I fear—lives on his fees, they tell me.

VENTNOR. Old guinea-pig !

BROWNBEE. I think one must admire his resolution ; quite a figure
in Liverpool these twenty years—quite.

VENTNOR. [*Sinking his voice*] Awful old rip. Got at least one family
he oughtn't to.

BROWNBEE. Tt, Tt ! Is that so ?

VENTNOR. [*Sinking his voice*] Fact ! Rosamund Larne—the story-
writer—client of mine—she's the widow of a son of his born long
before his marriage. Fine-looking woman she is, too.

BROWNBEE. Ah ! The early Victorians ! Before the influence
of the dear old Queen. Well, times change.

VENTNOR. Um ! Don't know about that. But I do know he
keeps me out of my money. [*Raising his voice.*] If you ask me,
gentlemen, we'd better break the old ship up and salve what we
can.

A CREDITOR. Pretty hard wood, Mr. Ventnor ; real old man-o'-
war teak.

VENTNOR. Well, his autocratic airs don't suit me. I'm for putting
the screw on tight.

BROWNBEE. I think—I think, if you would leave it to me, Mr.
Ventnor. The *suaviter in modo*——

VENTNOR. Will never get me my three hundred.

    [OLD HEYTHORP *has entered. A silence falls. Five of the*
      CREDITORS *rise, but* VENTNOR *continues to sit.* OLD HEY-
      THORP *advances slowly, resumes his seat at the table, and looks*
      round with a defiant twinkle. They all sit. FARNEY *enters*
      from the inner office, bringing a cup of tea which he places befor
      OLD HEYTHORP.

HEYTHORP. [*With a bow*] Excuse me, gentlemen ; had a long
Board. [*He conveys the cup to his mouth and drinks ; his* CREDITORS
*watch in suspense with which is blended a sort of admiration at his accom-
plishment of this difficult feat.* OLD HEYTHORP *puts the cup down, and*

feebly removes some drops from the little white tuft on his chin.] Well! My bankers have given you every information, I hope.

A CREDITOR. [*A Clergyman*] Mr. Heythorp, we've appointed Mr. Brownbee to voice our views. Mr. Brownbee!

BROWNBEE. Mr. Heythorp, we are here to represent about £14,000. When we had the pleasure of meeting you last July, you held out a prospect of some more satisfactory arrangement by Christmas. But we are now in February, and I am bound to say none of us get younger.

HEYTHORP. Don't you? H'm! *I* feel like a boy.

[*The* CREDITORS *shuffle.*

VENTNOR. [*To* BROWNBEE] He's going to put us off again.

BROWNBEE. [*Suavely*] I'm sure we're very glad to hear it—very glad, indeed. U'm! To come to the point, however. We feel, Mr. Heythorp, not unreasonably, I think, that—well—bankruptcy would be the most satisfactory solution. We have waited a long time, and, to be quite frank, we don't see any prospect of improvement; indeed, we fear the opposite.

HEYTHORP. Think I'm going to join the majority, eh?

[*A slight embarrassment among the* CREDITORS.

VENTNOR. Put it that way if you like.

HEYTHORP. My grandfather lived to be a hundred, gentlemen; my father ninety-six—three-bottle men, both of 'em. Only eighty odd myself; blameless life compared with theirs.

BROWNBEE. Indeed, we hope you have many years of this life before you—many.

HEYTHORP. You're getting a thousand a year out of my fees. I'll make it thirteen hundred. Bankrupt me, I shall lose my directorships, and you won't get a rap.

BROWNBEE. [*After a pause, clearing his throat*] We think you should make it at least fifteen hundred, Mr. Heythorp. We fancy you greatly underrate the possibilities of your bankruptcy.

HEYTHORP. I know 'em—you don't. My qualifying shares will fetch about a couple of thousand; my bank'll take most of that. House I live in, and everything in it, bar my togs, my wine, and my cigars, belong to my daughter under a settlement fifteen years old. Got nothing else. Position in a nutshell, gentlemen.

BROWNBEE. We understand your income from your fees and dividends to be some two thousand pounds a year, sir.

HEYTHORP. [*Shaking his head*] Nineteen hundred in a good year. Must eat and drink—must have a man to look after me, not as active as I was. Got people dependent on me. Can't do on less than six hundred. Thirteen hundred a year's all I can give you, gentlemen. No use beating about the bush; take it or leave it.

[*The* CREDITORS *rise to consult.*

VENTNOR. And if we leave it?

HEYTHORP. Kill the goose that lays the golden eggs—that's all.

BROWNBEE. Mr. Heythorp, in consideration of your—er— [*But he stops at the old man's fighting look*] we shall accept your offer of thirteen hundred a year.

HEYTHORP. Ah! Keep the bird alive—sound policy.

BROWNBEE. We certainly don't wish to press too hardly on one who for many years has been a man of mark in Liverpool. In fact, we—excuse me—admire your courage in keeping a stiff lip in spite of your—your—infirmities. [OLD HEYTHORP *bows to him, and he bows to* OLD HEYTHORP.] We feel you will do your best to give us all you can; and we—er—wish you many years of life.

CREDITOR. [*The Clergyman, rising*] I have long felt—not as a man of the world precisely—that Mr. Heythorp would feel his conscience lighter if we could relieve him of——

VENTNOR. Our money.

CREDITOR. [*Slightly disconcerted*] Well, that is perhaps in effect the position. We—er—are, in fact, a thorn in his side, and for his own good he feels no doubt that he would like to have us—er—removed. [*Laughs.*] If, however, the process must be—er—prolonged——

VENTNOR. Get on with it, sir.

CREDITOR. [*Disconcerted*] Exactly! With these few words, I am entirely at one with Mr. Brownbee.

VENTNOR. [*Sotto voce*] Amen!

HEYTHORP. Much obliged to you, gentlemen—very sporting of you. Shall act toward you in the same spirit.

BROWNBEE. Good-day, then, sir. Don't get up, I beg.

CREDITORS. Good-day, sir.

[OLD HEYTHORP *salutes them. They follow on the heels of* MR. BROWNBEE. MR. VENTNOR *has remained behind.*]

VENTNOR. Sorry not to have been able to join the mutual admiration society, Mr. Heythorp. Your debt to me is £300. I think it might be worth your while to consider whether you can't settle that separately. I'm a lawyer, and neither very trustful nor very patient.

HEYTHORP. Go behind their backs, do you? Eh.

[VENTNOR, *very angry, is about to speak, when the door from the outer office is opened, and* FARNEY *enters.*]

VENTNOR. You made a big mistake in saying that, Mr. Heythorp. Good evening!   [*He goes out.*

FARNEY. I beg your pardon, I thought you were alone, sir.

HEYTHORP. That's an ugly dog. What's his name?

FARNEY. Ventnor, sir; a solicitor. There are two ladies to see you, sir.

HEYTHORP. Ladies?

FARNEY. A Mrs. and Miss Larne; there's a boy with them.

HEYTHORP. M'yes ! Well, show 'em in.

[FARNEY *opens the door into the outer office.* ROSAMUND LARNE *enters, preceded by her children,* PHYLLIS *and* JOCK, *who tweaks* FARNEY'S *coat-tail as he passes, then stands seraphic, gazing at the ceiling, while* FARNEY *pursues his way out with dignity.*

PHYLLIS. Jock, you *are* an awful boy ! Guardy, he really is too awful.

[PHYLLIS *is like a day in April, fair and fresh, and seventeen. The boy* JOCK *has a pink seraphic face, and the just breaking voice of fourteen ; he wears Eton jacket and collar, and carries a school cap.*

PHYLLIS. He won't wear his overcoat, and he will wear that frightful cap with his Eton jacket. [JOCK *puts in on dreamily.*] Look ! Isn't he a horror ?

[MRS. LARNE *takes* OLD HEYTHORP'S *puffy hand and presses it to her ample bosom. She is of a fine florid beauty and perhaps thirty-eight.*

MRS. LARNE. Dear old Guardy ! Do forgive us for coming. I had to see you, and I couldn't leave these children outside, you never know what they'll do.

[*While she speaks the boy* JOCK *has quietly pinned his mother's and sister's floating hat-scarves together, and, withdrawing, puts his fingers to his mouth and emits a piercing whistle.* PHYLLIS *rushing to thump him, the two hats fall off, and two hands fly to two heads.*

PHYLLIS. Isn't he a pig ?

[*Advancing on* JOCK, *she hustles him out into the outer office and stands with her back against the door.* MRS. LARNE *adjusts her hat calmly, with her low, full, seductive laugh.*

MRS. LARNE. I really had to come and see you, Guardy ; we haven't had a sight of you for such an age. Phyllis, go and see after Jock, there's a darling.

[PHYLLIS *tosses her head, wrenches open the door and slides out.*] How are you, dear old Guardy !

HEYTHORP. Never better. But I haven't a penny for you.

MRS. LARNE. [*With her laugh*] How naughty of you to think I came for that ! But I am in a terrible fix, Guardy.

HEYTHORP. Never knew you not to be.

MRS. LARNE. Just let me tell you. It'll be some relief. I'm having the most dreadful time. [*She subsides into a chair beside him, with a luxurious sigh.*] Expect to be sold up any moment. We may be on the streets to-morrow. And I daren't tell the children ; they're so happy, poor darlings. I've been obliged to take Jock away from school. And Phyllis has had to stop her piano and dancing ; it's an absolute crisis. But for your three hundred, Guardy, you know I'm entirely dependent on my pen. And those Midland Syndicate people—I've been counting on at least two hundred from them for my new story, and the wretches have refused it. Such a delightful story! [*She prevents a tear from rolling on to her powdered cheek with a tiny handkerchief.*] It *is* hard, Guardy. I worked my brain silly over it.

HEYTHORP. Rats!

MRS. LARNE. Guardy, how can you? [*With a sigh that would rend no heart.*] You couldn't, I suppose, let me have just one little hundred?

HEYTHORP. Not a bob.

[MRS. LARNE *looks round the room, then leans towards him.*

MRS. LARNE. Guardy, you *are* so like my dear Philip.

HEYTHORP. Your dear Philip! You led him a devil of a life, or I'm a Dutchman.

MRS. LARNE. Guardy! [*Her eyes wandering.*] This office looks so rich. I smelt money all the way upstairs. And your lovely house. We went there first, of course.

HEYTHORP. Not my house. My daughter's. She see you?

MRS. LARNE. We saw *someone* in the hall, when the butler was saying you were here at the office.

HEYTHORP. Deuce you did!

MRS. LARNE. *Such* a lovely house! Guardy, just imagine if your grandchildren were thrown out into the street. Even if they don't know it, still you *are* their grandfather. [OLD HEYTHORP *only grins.*] Do come to my rescue this once. You really might do something for them.

[OLD HEYTHORP'S *defiant cynicism gives way to an idea which strikes him.*

HEYTHORP. H'm! Do something for them! Just got an idea. Yes.

MRS. LARNE. Oh! Guardy!

HEYTHORP. Wait a bit. I'll see. Yes! I'll see. Might be able.

MRS. LARNE. How lovely! But, Guardy, not *just* fifty now? [OLD HEYTHORP *shakes his head.*] Well, [*Getting up*] you'll be sorry when we come round one night and sing for pennies under your window. Isn't Phyllis growing a sweet gairl?

[*Throwing clouds of perfume, to judge by the expression of* OLD HEYTHORP'S *nose, she goes out calling* "Phyllis!"

PHYLLIS. [*Entering*] There's *such* a young man in there. He can only just see over his collar. And the way he squints at me—Lawks!

HEYTHORP. Oh! that young pup—I'd clean forgot him. Phyllis! Help me up. [PHYLLIS *tries, and they succeed.*] You a good girl?

PHYLLIS. No, Guardy. Can't be when Jock's at home.

HEYTHORP. [*He pats her cheek*] Mind! Chaps like that little-headed young pup in there—not for you. All the same mould, no drive, no vices—nothing. Thinks himself a spark. Why! at his

26*

age I'd broken my neck, winged a Yankee, been drowned for a bet, and lost my last bob on the Derby.

PHYLLIS. Had you, Guardy ?   How *lovely !*

HEYTHORP. H'm !   Just keep him looking through his dog-collar, while I write a letter.

[*He again pats her cheek and goes out into the inner office.   A piercing whistle is heard through the open door.*

PHYLLIS. [*At the fire—to herself*] There goes Jock ! He's bitten that young man, or something juicy.   [BOB PILLIN *comes in.*

PHYLLIS. Oh ! young man — so you've escaped !   Isn't he a terror ?

BOB PILLIN. [*Who is evidently much struck by her*] He is—er—rather. Er—cold, isn't it ?   [*Approaches fire.*

PHYLLIS. Yes—jolly.

BOB PILLIN. [*Nervously*] I say, I've left my hat ; do you think it's safe ?

PHYLLIS. No, of course it isn't.   I'll get it ?

BOB PILLIN. [*More and more impressed*] No, no ! Please don't go. It doesn't matter a bit.   My name's Pillin—er—Bob.   Are you a relation of " Old English ? "

PHYLLIS. " Old English ! "

BOB PILLIN. What !   Don't you know his nick-name.

PHYLLIS. No ; we call him Guardy.   Isn't he a chook ?

BOB PILLIN. Er—I don't know that I should have called him that— er—exactly.   It's my Dad who's a friend of his, don't you know ?

PHYLLIS. Is your Dad like him ?

BOB PILLIN. *Not much !*

PHYLLIS. What a pity !

BOB PILLIN. Ha ! D'you mind tellin' me your name ?

PHYLLIS. Phyllis.

BOB PILLIN. Rippin' !   We live at the last house in Sefton Park.

PHYLLIS. Oh ! We live at Millicent Villas.   It's a poky little house. We have awful larks though.

BOB PILLIN. Your brother keeps things lively, I expect.

PHYLLIS. Yes.   He goes off all the time like a squib.

[*Sounds are heard from the outer office.*]
That's mother pinching him.   We've never been here before.   We call Guardy the last of the Stoic-uns.

BOB PILLIN. [*Still more struck*] I say—that's awfully good—that's— that's very funny.

[*The outer office door is opened and* MRS. LARNE *appears, holding* JOCK *by the ear, and in her other hand* BOB PILLIN'S *flattened-out top hat.*

MRS. LARNE. Is this your h-h-hat, Mr.—Mr.——— ?

[*Laughter overcomes her.* PHYLLIS *is in convulsions.* JOCK *seraphic.*

BOB PILLIN. [*Taking it*] Er—it—it was.

PHYLLIS. I told you so.

MRS. LARNE. I'm so ashamed. I *thought* he was too quiet. And of course—he—he—was si-itting on it.

BOB PILLIN. [*With a sort of gallantry*] Really! It's—it's—nothing. It doesn't matter a bit.

PHYLLIS. Oh! young man. What a fib! Such a lovely hat!

MRS. LARNE. What *can* we do? You must come and see us, Mr. Billing.

PHYLLIS. Pillin—mother.

BOB PILLIN. Ah! er—yes.

MRS. LARNE. We shall be so pleased if you will.

BOB PILLIN. Thanks. [*Gazing at his hat.*] That'll be jolly!

PHYLLIS. We'll tie Jock up.   [JOCK *rolls his eyes fearfully*.

MRS. LARNE. Yes, you horrible boy! Ah! Here's dear Guardy. I shall tell him.

    [JOCK *simulates terror, as* OLD HEYTHORP *enters from the inner office.*]

Guardy, we must go. Good-bye! [*Lowering her voice.*] Then very soon you *will* do something, won't you? The children are *so* fond of you, Guardy!   [*She presses his hand and swings to the door*.

HEYTHORP. [*To* BOB PILLIN] Go round and tell your father I want to see him—now, at once.

BOB PILLIN. Oh! Thanks awf'ly, sir. I hope you'll cheer the old man up.

HEYTHORP. [*Pointing*] What's that thing?

BOB PILLIN. My—er—hat, sir.

         [PHYLLIS *gives way*, JOCK *simulates terror*.

MRS. LARNE. [*From the door*] Come along, you dreadful children. Mr. Pillin, will you see us to our train?

BOB PILLIN. Delighted! I—I'll just run up to our office—next door. Shan't be a shake.

PHYLLIS. [*To* BOB, *who is staring at his hat*] Oh! put it on. *Do* put it on.

    [BOB PILLIN *puts it on and goes*. PHYLLIS *claps her hands*. MRS. LARNE *and* JOCK *go out*.

PHYLLIS. Good-bye, Guardy dear!

HEYTHORP. Fond of me?

PHYLLIS. Oh! Guardy, I adore you. I wish you'd come and see us oftener.

HEYTHORP. Well! I'll come to-morrow.

PHYLLIS. That'll be *lovely*.   [*She kisses him.*
                                [*She goes out.*

HEYTHORP. [*To himself*] Fresh as April—clean run stock. By George, I'll do it!   [FARNEY *enters from the outer office*.

FARNEY. Miss Heythorp is below, sir, with a carriage to take you home ; she says she'll wait.

HEYTHORP. Deuce she is ! Devil to pay !

FARNEY. And Mr. Joseph Pillin has just come in.

HEYTHORP. [*Sinking into his chair*] Bring him here ! Don't want to be disturbed.

FARNEY. Very good, sir.

[*He waits for* JOSEPH PILLIN *to enter ; then crosses and goes out into the inner office.* JOSEPH PILLIN *is a parchmenty, precise, thin, nervous man, with slight grey whiskering, between seventy and eighty, in a fur coat and top hat.*

JOE PILLIN. [*In his rather quavering voice*] Well, Sylvanus, I had your message.

HEYTHORP. Um, Joe ! Have a cigar ?

[*He puts one in his own mouth, and lights it.*

JOE PILLIN. Cigar ! You know I never smoke them. You've a monstrous constitution, Sylvanus. If I drank port and smoked cigars I should be in my grave in a fortnight. I'm getting old—growing nervous——

HEYTHORP. Always were as scary as an old hen, Joe. Sit down.

JOE PILLIN. Well, my nature's not like yours. About my ships. What news have you ? I'm getting anxious. I want to retire. Freights are very depressed. I don't think they'll recover in my time. I've got my family to think of.

HEYTHORP. Crack on sail and go broke—buck you up like anything.

JOE PILLIN. Now, Sylvanus ! You make a joke of everything. I'm quite serious.

HEYTHORP. Never knew you anything else, Joe.

JOE PILLIN. Hasn't your Board decided to-day ? The sixty thousand I'm asking is a very small price for four good ships.

[OLD HEYTHORP *looks at him deeply, twinkles, and blows a puff of smoke.*]

Well, Sylvanus ?

HEYTHORP. Make it worth my while, Joe, or it won't go through.

JOE PILLIN. Worth your while ? [*Bending forward and lowering his voice.*] How do you mean—a commission ? You could never disclose it.

HEYTHORP. Who wants to ? I'll get you sixty thousand for your ships if you'll give me ten per cent. of it. If you don't—deal's off, Joe—not a brass rap.

JOE PILLIN. But it means coming down six thousand in my price.

HEYTHORP. Well, try elsewhere.

JOE PILLIN. But I have. There's no market at all.

HEYTHORP. Then take my offer.

JOE PILLIN. My dear Sylvanus—that's—that's positively cynical. A commission—it's not legal.

HEYTHORP. Not going to take a penny piece myself. I want you to settle it on some protégées of mine.

JOE PILLIN. [*In agitation*] But it's a breach of trust! I really can't be a party to a breach of trust. Suppose it came out.

HEYTHORP. Won't come out.

JOE PILLIN. Yes, yes, so you say; but you never know.

HEYTHORP. Nothing to prevent your executing a settlement on some third parties. Who's your lawyer?

JOE PILLIN. My lawyer? Scriven's my lawyer.

HEYTHORP. Well! Get him to draw up a deed poll to-morrow morning. Bring it to me here after the general meeting to-morrow afternoon. If the purchase goes through, you sign it; if it doesn't you tear it up. What stock have you got that gives 4 per cent?

JOE PILLIN. Midland Railway.

HEYTHORP. That'll do—you needn't sell, then.

JOE PILLIN. Yes; but who—who are these—these third parties?

HEYTHORP. Woman and her children—must make provision for 'em. [*At* JOE PILLIN'S *expression.*] Afraid of being mixed up with a woman, Joe?

JOE PILLIN. Yes, you may laugh. I *am* afraid of being mixed up with someone else's woman. I don't like it—I don't like it at all. I've not led your life, Sylvanus.

HEYTHORP. Lucky for you—been dead long ago. Tell your lawyer it's an old flame of yours—you old dog.

JOE PILLIN. Yes, there it is at once, you see. I might be subject to blackmail.

HEYTHORP. Tell him to keep your name dark and just pay over the income quarterly.

JOE PILLIN. [*Rising*] I don't like it, Sylvanus—I don't really.

HEYTHORP. Then leave it and be hanged to you! But there'll be no deal, Joe.

JOE PILLIN. Is there no other way?

HEYTHORP. No. Matter must be settled to-morrow. And if I don't pitch it strong to the shareholders, the sale won't go through, that's flat.

JOE PILLIN. It's playing round the law, Sylvanus.

HEYTHORP. No law to prevent you doing what you like with your money. Taking nothing myself—not a mag. You assist the fatherless and widowed—just your line, Joe.

JOE PILLIN. What a fellow you are, Sylvanus! You don't seem capable of taking anything seriously.

HEYTHORP. Care killed the cat. Well?

JOE PILLIN. No, I—I don't think I can do it. Besides, such a sacrifice—six thousand pounds.

HEYTHORP. Very well! Get another bid if you can—freights'll go lower yet.

JOE PILLIN. Oh! do you think so?

HEYTHORP. Sure of it.

JOE PILLIN. Very well, Sylvanus, very well! I suppose I must.

HEYTHORP. Here's the name for your lawyer. Write it down.

[JOE PILLIN *writes*.]

Rosamund Larne—with an " e "—23 Millicent Villas, Liverpool, widow of Philip Larne, late of Dublin, barrister-at-law; income to her, until her children, Phyllis Larne and John Larne, attain the age of twenty-one or marry, then to said Phyllis and said John Larne in equal shares for life, remainder to their children. Got that? Get it drawn to-morrow morning.

JOE PILLIN. [*Raising himself*] It seems to me very irregular—very risky.

HEYTHORP. Go home and drink a bottle of champagne on it. Good-night, Joe. No deed, no deal! I'll trust you.

JOE PILLIN. Well, good-night, Sylvanus, good-night. You always were a dare-devil. [*He quavers to the door of the outer office.*] Good-night.

[*He passes out.*

HEYTHORP. [*To himsel,*] He'll jump. Better than beggary for 'em.

[*He sits back with a smile. Then closes his eyes as if in sleep.*

[*The door back Left is reopened and* ADELA HEYTHORP, *his daughter, comes in; a woman of thirty-two, with dark hair and thin, straight face and figure. She stands just in the room regarding him severely.*

ADELA. You really ought not to be so late, Father. It's most dangerous at this time of year. Are you ready, now?

HEYTHORP. [*Opening his eyes*] No.

ADELA. It's really terrible the way you neglect your health. I've noticed that every time you drink port, you do something dangerous the next day. In weather like this you ought always to get back before dark. And of course you eat much too much. One would think you were forty, instead of over eighty.

HEYTHORP. Not if they saw you.

ADELA. Really, Father, is that your idea of repartee? Who were your visitors?

HEYTHORP. Ladies and a boy.

ADELA. So I saw. They came to the house first. I know their name is Larne, but it conveyed nothing to me.

HEYTHORP. [*With a grin*] My daughter-in-law, and my grand-children; that's all.

ADELA. That isn't a bit funny, either.

HEYTHORP. No, it's gospel truth.

ADELA. Then do you mean to say you were married before you married my mother?

HEYTHORP. No.

ADELA. Not married! I see. I suppose these people are hanging round your neck, then. I begin to understand your difficulties. Are there any more of them?

[OLD HEYTHORP *makes a violent and ineffectual effort to rise.*] You'll hurt yourself. [*Seeing him motionless again.*] I suppose you don't realize that it's not an agreeable discovery. I don't know what to think——

HEYTHORP. Think what you like.

ADELA. Are you coming?

HEYTHORP. No.

ADELA. I can't keep this carriage any longer. You'll be late for dinner.

HEYTHORP. Dine in my own room in future. Tell Meller.

ADELA. I don't see why *you* should lose your temper.

HEYTHORP. Because I can't get up, you think you can stand there and worry me.

ADELA. Well, really, I've come especially to fetch you home, and you call it worrying.

HEYTHORP. Paddle my own canoe, thank you.

[ADELA *turns and goes out.*]
[*To himself.*] Self-righteous cat! [*He makes a slow and considered effort to rise, but fails, and sits motionless. He raps the table with a pen. There is no result. Reaching for an inkpot, he rams it on the table twice.*]

[TWO YOUNG CLERKS *appear at the door, Right.*

HEYTHORP. You young gentlemen had forgotten me.

FIRST CLERK. Mr. Farney said you didn't want to be disturbed, sir.

HEYTHORP. Give me my hat and coat.

SECOND CLERK. Yes, sir.

[*They come, raise him, and help him into hat and coat.*

HEYTHORP. Thank you. That carriage gone?

FIRST CLERK. [*Crossing to window and looking out*] Yes, sir.

HEYTHORP. All right. Tell Mr. Farney to come and see me at noon, about my speech for the General Meeting to-morrow.

FIRST CLERK. Yes, sir.

HEYTHORP. Good-night to you.

CLERKS. Good-night, sir.

[*He passes like a tortoise to the door, Back, opens it feebly, and goes out.*

FIRST CLERK. Poor old Chairman, he's on his last.

SECOND CLERK. Gosh! He's a tough old hulk—he'll go down fighting. [*Raising the window.*] There he goes—slow as a barnacle. He's held the whole street up. Look—under the lamp! [*The* FIRST CLERK *joins him at the window.*] I say—that was a near thing— that cart!

FIRST CLERK. He doesn't give a damn for anything.

SECOND CLERK. He's got his tram all right.

FIRST CLERK. See him raising his hat to that old woman—you'd think he'd got all night before him.

SECOND CLERK. Old school—what !

FIRST CLERK. He's got pluck, and he's got manners. Good " Old English ! "

SECOND CLERK. There they go !   Ting-a-ling !

[*He shuts the window down.*

The curtain is lowered for a minute.

SCENE II

The same, converted to the purposes of the General Meeting. The three chairs back to the fire, on the Right, are those of OLD HEYTHORP *and two fellow-Directors, of whom the first is on his feet.* FARNEY *stands by the Chairman, a little back of him.   Facing them are four rows of five chairs each, with fourteen seated* SHAREHOLDERS.   *At a small table, on the far Left, is a* REPORTER.   OLD HEYTHORP *is finishing his Chairman's speech.*

HEYTHORP. Come to this arrangement with Messrs. Pillin—owners of the four steamships, *Smyrna, Damascus, Tyre and Sidon*— [*His voice is failing*]—vessels in prime condition. . . .

MR. BUDGEN (A SHAREHOLDER). [*From the back*] Excuse me, sir, we can't hear a word down here.

HEYTHORP. With a total freight-carrying capacity of fifteen thousand tons.   [THREE SHAREHOLDERS *rise.*

MR. BUDGEN. We might as well go home.   If the Chairman's got no voice can't somebody read for him ?

[OLD HEYTHORP *takes a sip of water and goes on, a little louder.*

HEYTHORP. At the low inclusive price of £60,000.   Gentlemen, *Vestigia nulla retrorsum.*

SHAREHOLDER. Can't hear a word.

[OLD HEYTHORP *hands his speech to* FARNEY *and sinks into his seat.*

FARNEY. The Chairman has just said, " *Vestigia nulla retrorsum.*"

MR. BUDGEN. Yes, very convincing.

FARNEY. [*Reading*] " Times are bad, but they are touching bottom. I have said freights will go up.   This is the moment for a forward stroke.   With the utmost confidence we recommend your ratification of this purchase, which we believe will soon substantially increase the profits of the Company."

[FARNEY *sits down and glances at* OLD HEYTHORP, *who nods to the* DIRECTOR *on his left.*

DIRECTOR. [*Rising and combing his beard with his fingers*] Before moving the adoption of the Report, we welcome any comment from shareholders.   *[He sits down.*

    [Two SHAREHOLDERS, *one in the second, one in the third row, rise.*
       OLD HEYTHORP *nods at the one in the second row.*

FARNEY. Mr. Brownbee.

MR. BROWNBEE. I should like, if I may be allowed, to congratulate the Board on having piloted our ship so smoothly through the troublous waters of the past year. (" Hear, hear ! ") With our worthy Chairman still at the helm, I have no doubt that, in spite of the still low, I might even say falling barometer, and the—er—unseasonable climacteric, we may rely on weathering the—er—storm. I confess that the present dividend of 4 per cent. is not one which satisfies—er—every aspiration ; (" Hear, hear ! ") but speaking for myself, and I hope for others, [*He looks round*] I recognize that in all the circumstances it is as much as we have the right to expect. (" No, no.") It is very gratifying to have these ample reserves ; and by following the bold, but to my mind prudent, development which the Board proposes to make, we may reasonably, if not sanguinely, expect a more golden future. (" No, no ! ") A shareholder keeps on saying, " No, no " —from that lack of confidence I should like to dissociate myself. Our Chairman, whose strategic wisdom has been proved on many a field, would not so strongly advocate the purchase of these Pillin ships without good reason. He well said " *Vestigia nulla retrorsum.*" I venture to think there can be no better motto for Englishmen. Ahem ! Ahem !   *[He sits down.*

    [*The other* SHAREHOLDER *rises again.* OLD HEYTHORP *nods at him.*

FARNEY. Mr. Westgate.

MR. WESTGATE. [*A breezy fellow*] I want to know much more about this proposition to purchase these ships. I doubt its wisdom ; I very much doubt it. To whom was the proposal first made ?

HEYTHORP. To me, sir.

MR. WESTGATE. The Chairman says to him. Very well ! But what I want to know is why are Pillins sellin', if freights are to go up as the Chairman prophesies.

HEYTHORP. Matter of opinion.

MR. WESTGATE. Quite so. And in my opinion they're goin' lower ; and Pillins are right to sell. If that's so, we're wrong to buy. (" Hear, hear ! ") (" No, no ! ") Pillins are shrewd people.

HEYTHORP. They're rattled.

MR. WESTGATE. Business men ! Rattled ! I wonder what young Mr. Pillin there says to that.

BOB PILLIN. Er, I'm not in—er—a position to—er—state.

MR. WESTGATE. Well, that's not very conclusive. Perhaps you'll say I'm rattled too. [OLD HEYTHORP *nods.*] Well, rattled or not, I think it's a rash purchase in times like these. We're in the trough of the sea.

HEYTHORP. Always buy at the bottom of the market.

MR. WESTGATE. And who's to tell we're there. We're losin' our trade hand over hand. The Germans are buildin' us out o' house and home ; and the Yanks are goin' ahead like the very devil.

HEYTHORP. The Old Country's sound enough.

MR. WESTGATE. Well, I can see no signs of it.

[A SHAREHOLDER *in the front row rises.*

FARNEY. Mr. Winkley.

MR. WINKLEY. [*Lean and cautious*] I agree, sir, with Mr. Westgate. I can see nothing in the present condition of shipping which calls for confidence. We are not a large company, and this proposed purchase will absorb at least two-thirds of our reserves. Beyond the dictum of the Chairman that freights will go up this year, where is the argument in favour of depleting ourselves in this way ? I deprecate the proposal.

HEYTHORP. Any other shareholder anything to say before I put the Report to the meeting ?

MR. BUDGEN. [*Rising*] Yes, sir. Mr. Westgate requires answering.

FARNEY. Name, please ?

SHAREHOLDER. Budgen.

HEYTHORP. Mr. Budgen.

MR. BUDGEN. I don't like this business either. I don't impute anything to anybody, but I don't like the short notice we've 'ad, nor the way the thing's pressed on us. Not only that, but, to say truth, I'm not satisfied to be galloped over in this fashion by one who, whatever he may have been in the past, is now clearly not in his prime.

[*A certain sensation.* OLD HEYTHORP *looks over his shoulder at* FARNEY, *who heaves him up from behind.*

HEYTHORP. [*Voice low*] My best services have been at your disposal nineteen years ; my experience of shipping is a little greater than that of the three gentlemen who spoke last. [*Voice suddenly rises.*] If I'm not in my prime, my brain's solid and my heart's stout. " There is a tide in the affairs of limited companies "—I'm not content to stagnate. If *you* want to stagnate, give your support to these gentlemen, and have done with it. But I repeat, freights will go up before the end of the year. The purchase is sound, more than sound—it's a dam' fine one ; and I stand or fall by it.   [*He sinks back into his seat.*

[*A pause. Then an old pink* GENTLEMAN *in the second row rises.*

FARNEY. Mr. Appleby.

MR. APPLEBY. It has been painful to me—painful—and I have no doubt to others, to hear an attack made on the Chairman. If he is old in body, he is young in mental vigour and courage. I wish we were all as young. We ought to support him, gentlemen ; most certainly we ought to support him.

[OLD HEYTHORP *bows, and* MR. APPLEBY *bows and sits down.*

VENTNOR. [*Rising*] We don't want sentiment interfering with our judgment in this matter. The question is simply : How are our pockets to be affected ? I came here with some misgiving. [*In a rather queer voice.*] I can't say I've lost it ; but on the whole—I say on the whole—I favour the proposition. The ships are undoubtedly very cheap. We've got these reserves, and we might as well use them. [*A pause.*] The Chairman knows his way about.   [*He sits down.*]

HEYTHORP. Any more remarks ? [*Heaved up.*] Very well, I move the adoption of the report and accounts.

MR. BROWNBEE. I second that.

HEYTHORP. Those in favour signify the same in the usual way.

> [*Except* MR. WESTGATE, MR. BUDGEN, *and one other, all hold up their hands.*

HEYTHORP. Contrary ?

> [MR. BUDGEN *and the other hold up their hands.* MR. WESTGATE *does not.*

HEYTHORP. Carried. Only other business, gentlemen, is the election of a director in place of Mr. Popham who retires, and offers himself for re-election. Mr. Popham's not here to-day—indisposed. [*Voice going again.*] Very valuable director. Those in favour of his re-election ?

> [*All hands are held up except* MR. BROWNBEE'S *and* MR. WESTGATE'S.]

Contrary ? [*No hands are held up.*] Carried. All the business, gentlemen.

> [*The meeting breaks up.* BOB PILLIN *is first out of the room.*
> [*The* DIRECTORS *file out into the inner office. The* REPORTER *rises and comes to* FARNEY.

REPORTER. Name of the last speaker but one—Applepie, was it ?

FARNEY. Appleby.

REPORTER. Oh ! Haythorp—with an " a " ?

FARNEY. " E."

REPORTER. Oh ! an " e." He seems an old man. Thank you. Would you like to see a proof ? With an " a " you said—— ?

FARNEY. " E."

REPORTER. Oh ! an " e." Oh ! Good afternoon !

FARNEY. [*To* MR. BROWNBEE, *who is lingering*] Fancy his not knowing how to spell the Chairman's name after all these years ! What does go on inside them ?

MR. BROWNBEE. Indeed, yes. The Press is very peculiar—they seem to have no—no passions. I hope I was useful, Mr. Farney. That fellow Westgate was very unpleasant.

FARNEY. Yes, sir, he wants to come on the Board.

MR. BROWNBEE. [*Who also does*] Ah ! Indeed ! Ah ! I see.

FARNEY. Yes, sir ; always kicks up a fuss—hopes they'll put him on to keep him quiet.

MR. BROWNBEE. Dear, dear ! And will they ?

FARNEY. [*With a smile*] Not while the Chairman lives, sir. He prefers the other way—services rendered.

MR. BROWNBEE. [*Pleased*] Ah-h ! Yes, I'm glad to hear that. Yes. I suppose there isn't a question of another director at the moment ?

FARNEY. I believe not, sir. But, of course, it's always the unexpected that happens.

MR. BROWNBEE. I know, I know. One must be prepared for everything. I thought that—er—well—that possibly *I*—I think the Chairman would favour me—— [*Here he catches sight of* VENTNOR *who has approached.*] But this, perhaps, isn't the moment. On the whole a pleasant meeting. Good afternoon !

> [*He goes,* FARNEY *looking after him with a smile. The room is now empty but for* VENTNOR *and* FARNEY.

VENTNOR. So *he* wants to get on the Board. The old fox ! Can I see the Chairman, Mr. Farney ?

> [*Before* FARNEY *can answer, a* CLERK *announces from the outer office :* " MR. PILLIN, sir ! " JOE PILLIN *enters, nipped and yellow and wrapped to the nose in a fur coat.* FARNEY *goes into the inner office.*

VENTNOR. How de do, Mr. Pillin ? I know your son. So we've bought your ships. Hope they'll do us some good. But I suppose you hope they won't, or you wouldn't have sold. One man's meat——

JOE PILLIN. Mr. Ventnor, I think ? Thank you. Very cold, isn't it ?

FARNEY. [*Returning : to* VENTNOR] Will you wait in here, sir ? The Chairman will see you presently.

> [VENTNOR *goes into the outer office, and* FARNEY *follows him, as* OLD HEYTHORP *comes in.*

JOE PILLIN. [*Quavering*] Ah ! Sylvanus ? Aren't you perished ?

HEYTHORP. What a quavering thread-paper of a chap you are, Joe ! Take off your coat.

JOE PILLIN. I ? I should be lost without my fur. You must have a fire inside you.

HEYTHORP. Sound innards, nothing more.

JOE PILLIN. [*Nervously scrutinizing the closed doors*] So—it's gone through, Sylvanus ? It means a wretched price for me—wretched.

HEYTHORP. You may think yourself damned lucky, Joe. Brought that deed ?

JOE PILLIN. [*Nervously produces a parchment and unfolds it on the little table to show his signature*] Yes. And I've—I've signed it. I don't like it—it's irrevocable. I can't bear irrevocable things. Never could. I consider you stampeded me, Sylvanus—playing on my nerves like that.

HEYTHORP. Your lawyer must think you a sad dog, Joe.

JOE PILLIN. Ah! suppose it comes to the knowledge of my wife at my death!

HEYTHORP. Nothing'll make you shiver then.

JOE PILLIN. Really! That's very bad taste, Sylvanus. Well, you've got your way, you always do. Who is this Mrs. Larne? It seems my son met them here yesterday. I thought at least nobody knew you were connected with them.

HEYTHORP. Mother of my grandchildren under the rose, Joe; and you've provided for 'em—best thing you ever did.

JOE PILLIN. [*Pocketing the deed*] Oh! I'm sorry you told me. It's worse than I thought. It's a clear breach of trust on your part—there's no question; and I'm conniving at it. As soon as the transfer of the ships is signed, I shall get away abroad. This cold's killing me. I wish you'd give me your recipe for keeping warm.

HEYTHORP. Get a new inside, and drink port.

JOE PILLIN. And yet, I suppose, with your full habit, your life hangs by a thread?

HEYTHORP. Stout one, my boy.

JOE PILLIN. Well, good-bye, Sylvanus. You're a Job's comforter. I must be getting home. I don't like it.

HEYTHORP. Then lump it.

[JOE PILLIN *puts on his hat, and goes.* FARNEY *enters.*

FARNEY. Will you see Mr. Ventnor now, sir?

[OLD HEYTHORP *nods.* VENTNOR *enters.*

VENTNOR. Things are looking up with you, Mr. Heythorp.

[OLD HEYTHORP *looks at him deeply without reply.*]

Your creditors put their tails between their legs yesterday, thanks to Mr. Brownbee. And you've carried your purchase through to-day—thanks to me.

HEYTHORP. Come to your point, sir, if you've got one.

VENTNOR. Oh! yes, I've got one. You had your way, Mr. Heythorp, but the meeting to-day might have turned very nasty. You rode roughshod; but, as you saw, I'm not the only one, by a long way, who feels that a Chairman ought to be in full possession of his faculties. If the shareholders to-day had turned you down, where would you have been?

HEYTHORP. In the soup. But they didn't.

VENTNOR. No, they just didn't. But there wasn't much in it. I could have turned the scales against you instead of for. And if they'd thrown you over, your other companies would shelve you too. Your position, Mr. Heythorp, if I may say so, is precarious, in spite of the way you carry it off.

HEYTHORP. Will you come to the point, sir?

VENTNOR. Yes. It's this: Am I to make it more precarious?

HEYTHORP. How?

VENTNOR. By filing a petition for your bankruptcy. That would be quite enough to tip the beam.

HEYTHORP. File away!

VENTNOR. You won't pay me, then?

HEYTHORP. No.

VENTNOR. Is that wise, Mr. Heythorp—is it wise? Take time. Think it over. By the way, you put the case for that purchase very high, didn't you?

HEYTHORP. [*Looking at him steadily*] Not a bit too high. Freights have touched bottom—go up soon.

VENTNOR. D'you know what passed through my mind?

HEYTHORP. Not an idea.

VENTNOR. [*Smiling*] And you won't reconsider your refusal?

HEYTHORP. [*With rising choler*] You heard the sporting way they treated me yesterday. Let 'em down by giving you preference? Not for Joe!

VENTNOR. Mr. Heythorp, you've had your way all your life, I fancy——

HEYTHORP. Wish I had.

VENTNOR. And it's given you the idea that you can always have it. Well, Humpty Dumpty had a great fall—not all the King's horses nor all the King's men—remember the old rhyme?

HEYTHORP. You're good enough to be mysterious, sir.

VENTNOR. Once more, won't you reconsider——?

HEYTHORP. My answer's flat: I'll see you damned first.

VENTNOR. Very good, Mr. Heythorp! Very good indeed! To our next meeting, then. You've not heard the last of this. Good-day.   [*He goes to the door.*

HEYTHORP. Good-day to you!   [VENTNOR *goes out.*

HEYTHORP. [*To himself, rumbling*] That cur smells a rat. [*He moves very slowly to the inner office door and calls.*] Mr. Farney!

                                                        [FARNEY *enters.*

HEYTHORP. Bring me my hat and coat.   [FARNEY *brings them.*] Get me a taxi-cab; tell the driver Millicent Villas; if he doesn't know it, let him ask.

FARNEY. Yes, sir.   [*Helping him on with his coat.*

HEYTHORP. That chap Ventnor. What's his holding?

FARNEY. Nothing to speak of, sir. Ten shares, I believe.

            [*He goes out.* OLD HEYTHORP *slowly puts on his hat.*

The curtain falls.

ACT II

*The Larnes' small drawing-room at Millicent Villas, about three-thirty
the same afternoon. A general effect of subdued disorder and chintz.
A deep-cushioned sofa; a tea table with not only tea-things, but a
liqueur bottle, glasses, and cigarette box on it. Water-colours by Mrs.
Larne on the walls; an untidy bureau, Right. A cheerful fire, Left,
and on the fender before it* PHYLLIS *drying her hair. A garden window,
Right. A door, Back.* MRS. LARNE, *at her bureau in a negligée,
is scribbling furiously and smoking a cigarette.*

> [*Enter* LETTY, *the little maid-of-all-work.*

LETTY. [*Holding out a bill to* MRS. LARNE] Gas, ma'am. And he's
goin' to cut it off to-morrer.

MRS. LARNE. [*With a puff of smoke and a gesture of despair*] That
man's incorrigible!

LETTY. The water's been, again.

MRS. LARNE. [*With dignity*] Next time he comes, I'll see him
myself.

LETTY. Yes, ma'am—he ain't goin' away next time, 'e says, till
you 'ave.

MRS. LARNE. Their impudence!

LETTY. Ah! 'e's a caution. Never knew such a man for not takin'
no for an answer.

MRS. LARNE. [*With her laugh*] He'll take it from me, Letty.

LETTY. Yus, an' turn the water off. What for supper, please?

MRS. LARNE. Oh! something light. Use your wits.

LETTY. The cold bacon?

PHYLLIS. Ugh-h!

MRS. LARNE. [*Dreamily*] Yes! Delicious.

LETTY. There ain't nothin' else.

MRS. LARNE. [*Scribbling*] Exactly. Don't worry me.

LETTY. Laundry's comin' at six.

> [MRS. LARNE *continues to scribble;* PHYLLIS, *drying her hair,
> pays sudden attention.*

PHYLLIS. The laundry, mother. I must have my things back.
I'm down to my last com.

MRS. LARNE. Tt, Tt! It'll be all right. Where's Jock?

LETTY. In the kitchen, ma'am—'e's thinkin'!

MRS. LARNE. Well, don't let him. [*Impressively.*] And mind!

He's not to come in here. I'm expecting Mr. Pillin at half-past. Go and dress, Letty.

LETTY. 'Im with the 'igh collar—same as yesterday?

MRS. LARNE. [*With her laugh*] Gracious! What a way of putting it. [PHYLLIS *sneezes.*

LETTY. Ain't your 'air dry, Miss?

PHYLLIS. No.

LETTY. Will you want tea, ma'am?

MRS. LARNE. [*Scribbling*] Of course!

LETTY. Shan't be able to bile no kettle to-morrer.

MRS. LARNE. Make tea while the gas burns. Run away, you awful little drumstick. I shall never get this article finished.

LETTY. I'll try and sneak one from the basket, miss, when 'er 'ead's turned-like. She won't leave nothin' if she ain't paid this time. [*She goes out.*

PHYLLIS. Mother!

MRS. LARNE. [*Conning*] "She had on black moiré, with teeny tucks and flounces, and a flame-coloured fillet. There was a *je ne sais quoi* in the general effect. Lady Baker, on the other hand——"

PHYLLIS. *Mother!*

MRS. LARNE. What?

PHYLLIS. That young man!

MRS. LARNE. Well, what about him?

PHYLLIS. It's horrible to borrow from people you've only seen once.

MRS. LARNE. Well! you're not going to, I hope.

PHYLLIS. No, but you are.

MRS. LARNE. Will you hold your tongue, you disrespectful gairl!

PHYLLIS. I can't mother. I hate it!

MRS. LARNE. There it is! I slave for you children, I beg for you. I wear myself to the bone——

PHYLLIS. Mother!

MRS. LARNE. [*With a large sigh, and her hand on her ample bosom*] Well, almost—yes, I can feel one rib. I never knew such ingratitude. "Lady Baker, on the other hand, filled the eye"—You've put it all out of my head—what did she fill the eye with? How do you think I'm to keep a roof over us?

PHYLLIS. I don't want a roof kept over me by borrowing.

MRS. LARNE. [*Sarcastically*] Oh! no. Of course not!—"filled the eye with red velvet."—There! I don't know whether it was red velvet or not. I wonder [*musing*] is "red velvet" libellous? I write this stuff—I—I—an artist—It's too hard! [*She wipes her eye with a tiny handkerchief.*

PHYLLIS. [*Going to her*] Mother—don't! I didn't mean—only I do so loathe it. Father *was* a gentleman, wasn't he?

MRS. LARNE. I suppose you mean I'm not a lady? 'Pon my word!

PHYLLIS. Oh! Mother, I *know* you're descended from the Cornish kings. Well, I think we ought to live up to it. Look here, I'll sell my hair.

MRS. LARNE. You'll what! What d'you think you'd look like without your hair?

PHYLLIS. [*Darkly*] Like enough for *that* young man.

MRS. LARNE. I never met a gairl who said such things—never.

PHYLLIS. Well, of course, I know what he's coming for. I won't be a decoy duck, mother. If you borrow from him, I'll steal it from you, and pay it back. I will!

MRS. LARNE. Of all ungrateful little wretches!

[PHYLLIS *rubs her cheek against her mother's.*]
No! Go away!

PHYLLIS. Mum, don't be grumpsy!

[*Her mother has taken out a little mirror, and is looking at herself.* PHYLLIS *takes a peep.*]

PHYLLIS. [*Rubbing her own cheek*] Oh! it's come off on me.

MRS. LARNE. You little cat!   [*The front door-bell is heard to ring.*] Good gracious, there he is! And look at me—look at me! [*She gathers herself up and swims to the door. Her voice is heard in the passage saying:*] Don't open, Letty, till I'm invisible.

[PHYLLIS *takes the little mirror to the window, for the light is failing, and rubs her cheek more vigorously. Through the open door she can hear voices.*]

BOB PILLIN. Er—Mrs. Larne at home?

LETTY. Yes, sir—but she's invisible.

BOB PILLIN. Ha'r! I'm sorry.

LETTY. Miss Phyllis is at 'ome, sir.

BOB PILLIN. Er—her! Wonder if she'd see me?

LETTY. She's been washin' 'er 'air, but it may be dry be now. I'll see.   [LETTY *enters. She is in black with an apron.*]

LETTY. It's '*im*, Miss. Will you see '*im*?

PHYLLIS. Oh! Gefoozlem! In a jiff.

[*She hands* LETTY *the mirror, tears open the window, and disappears into the garden.*]

LETTY. [*At the door*] Come in. She'll see you in a jiff. Oh! and Master Jock's loose, sir.

BOB PILLIN. [*Coming in*] Is he—ah!

[LETTY *takes his cane from him and gives him the little mirror, looks round, takes a towel from the fender, and retires.*]

[BOB PILLIN *is beautifully dressed, with a narrow white piping round his waistcoat, a buttonhole of tuberoses, and his hat still in one hand. He stands uneasily twisting the little mirror, then lifts it and examines his face.*]

PHYLLIS. [*Opening the door*] Oh! Conceited young man! [*Her hair is fluffed out on her shoulders, and the sight of it is almost too much for* BOB PILLIN.]

BOB PILLIN. I say, how topping!

PHYLLIS. [*Shaking her mane*] Lawks! It's awful. Have you come to see mother?

BOB PILLIN. Er-r—yes; I'm glad she's not here, though.

PHYLLIS. Don't be foolish! Sit down! [*She sits on the sofa and taps it; he sits beside her.*] Isn't washing one's head awful?

BOB PILLIN. Er—well! Of course, I haven't much experience.

PHYLLIS. I said head—not hair! [*A pause.*] Why do you know such frightful men?

BOB PILLIN. What! I don't know any frightful men.

PHYLLIS. You know that man who was at Guardy's yesterday—I saw you. He's a horror.

BOB PILLIN. Ventnor—oh! Well, I only just know him. What's the matter with him?

PHYLLIS. He's mother's lawyer. Mother doesn't mind him— but I think he's a beast.

BOB PILLIN. Why? What's he done?

PHYLLIS. It isn't what he's done. It's what he'd like to do. Isn't money horrible?

BOB PILLIN. Well, I don't know, I think money's rather a good thing.

PHYLLIS. Oh! do you? Well, you'd better take care of what you've got then, or you won't have it.

BOB PILLIN. [*Staring at her*] Look here, Miss Larne—er—Phyllis —look here?

PHYLLIS. Well, I'm looking.

BOB PILLIN. Isn't there something on your mind, or—or something?

PHYLLIS. [*Shaking her mane, then looking down*] I wish mother wouldn't —I hate it. Beastly!

BOB PILLIN. Really—I mean—if there's anything you want me to do.

PHYLLIS. Yes, go away before mother comes.

BOB PILLIN. Why?

PHYLLIS. Oh! you know. You've got eyes. Why d'you think you're here?

BOB PILLIN. Really—I don't know.

PHYLLIS. [*Scanning him*] I thought you were an up-to-date young man.

BOB PILLIN. [*Modestly—settling his tie*] Well—er—I've knocked about at bit.

PHYLLIS. It hasn't knocked the bloom off, has it?

BOB PILLIN. [*Taking out his buttonhole*] Ah! I say, do have these!

PHYLLIS. [*Wrinkling her nose*] Not for worlds.

BOB PILLIN. I think you might tell me what's the matter with you.

PHYLLIS. [*Almost fiercely*] Well, I will! Can't you see what a poky street we live in? We're always hard up.

BOB PILLIN. What a beastly shame!

PHYLLIS. Nobody can come here without—disgusting!

[*She turns away from him, almost in tears.*

BOB PILLIN. I say! What is it?

PHYLLIS. Oh! if you can't see, I'm not going to tell you.

BOB PILLIN. Well, I'm damned!

PHYLLIS. [*Glancing through her lashes*] That's better!

BOB PILLIN. Look here! Er—Phyllis! I came here to see *you.*

PHYLLIS. [*Nodding, gravely*] Exactly!

BOB PILLIN. Do you object—really—I wouldn't for the world do anything you don't like.

PHYLLIS. Then you'd better go, or you will. [*She sneezes.*] My hair isn't a bit dry. [*She sits on the fender again before the fire.*] Well! Aren't you going?

BOB PILLIN. You don't really mean it, do you?

[*He breathes with rising emotion.*

PHYLLIS. [*After a pause*] Oh! don't breathe so loud!

BOB PILLIN. [*Indignant*] Breathe! I wasn't breathing.

PHYLLIS. You were.

BOB PILLIN. I wasn't—— Well, I can stand anything from you. You see I've taken the knock.

PHYLLIS. What! Where?

BOB PILLIN. [*Touching his breast pocket*] Here.

PHYLLIS. Oh! Does it hurt?

BOB PILLIN. Yes, awfully. It kept me awake all last night.

PHYLLIS. That's why you look so woolly.

BOB PILLIN. You're making it rather hard for me, aren't you? You see I've seen a good deal of—er—life.

PHYLLIS. Oh! *Do* tell me!

BOB PILLIN. Well, er—no—I think—not.

PHYLLIS. That's mean.

BOB PILLIN. What I meant was that—er—seeing—er—you is so different. I mean it's like—er—going out of a—er—into a—er.

PHYLLIS. [*Softly*] Poor young man!

BOB PILLIN. Look here! What I came to say chiefly was: Will you all come to the theatre with me to-morrow night? I've got a box.

PHYLLIS. [*Jumping up and clapping her hands*] What larks! We jolly well will! That is, if—I say, d'you mind—I *must* just go and see that my white petticoat. [*Stops at the door.*] You see, the laundress is an awful beast. She *will* be paid. [*She runs out.*

[BOB PILLIN *waits ecstatically. It is not* PHYLLIS, *however, who comes back, but* MRS. LARNE, *richly attired, and breathing perfume.*

MRS. LARNE. [*Greeting him*] Ah! Has my naughty gairl been making you comfortable, Mr. Pillin?

BOB PILLIN. Ha'r! Oh! Quite!

MRS. LARNE. Do you really want us to go to the theatre to-morrow. How nice of you! I should have loved it, but—— [*Motioning him to the sofa.*] Come and sit down. We poor Bohemians, my dear young man, you can't conceive how we live from hand to mouth. Just imagine—that poor gairl of mine hasn't anything to go in. D'you know, I simply don't know where to turn. [*With a heavy sigh.*] An artist can't be business-like, and put by for this, that, and the other. And they take such advantage of one. You know those Midland Syndicate people—No, of course you don't — you're one of those rich young men who own ships and things, aren't you?

BOB PILLIN. Well, my father does—as a matter of fact, we've just sold our ships.

MRS. LARNE. How delightful! What a lovely lot of money you must have! [*Absent-mindedly taking his hand and putting it to her head and heart.*] My poor ships are all here and here, and they don't sell—isn't it tragic? And that gairl of mine absolutely adores the theatre. If I only had the price of a dress for her on me, as the dear old cabbies say. Of course *I* should be in rags, myself. And in a box—everybody sees you. Still, you wouldn't mind that. But my lovely gairl —because she is lovely, isn't she?

BOB PILLIN. [*More and more hypnotized*] But I say, you know, if it's only that——

MRS. LARNE. *Only!* If you knew how rich that sounds! I can't bear money—it's in my blood, I suppose. And yet, you know, every day I find it more and more impossible to live without it.

BOB PILLIN. But, Mrs. Larne—look here—you know, I mean—what's money? [*He dives his hands into his breast pocket.*

MRS. LARNE. [*Apparently oblivious*] You see, I never can help paying my debts. It's almost a disease with me; hereditary. [*Watching out of the corner of her eye the slow, mesmerized appearance of a cheque-book.*] My dear young man, whatever's that?

BOB PILLIN. Oh!—er—I thought perhaps—but of course, if you——

MRS. LARNE. If you only knew what it was to see a cheque-book with so many cheques in it! It gives me the most perfect feeling, here. [*She lays her hand on her heart.*

BOB PILLIN. Then won't you let me—er——

[*But during the foregoing* PHYLLIS *has softly opened the door, Back, and appears, pushing* JOCK *before her. He ducks and creeps on hands and feet to the sofa; then raises himself suddenly till his face appears over the top like a full moon between his mother and* BOB PILLIN. BOB PILLIN *drops the cheque-book and his mouth falls open.* MRS. LARNE *clasps her bosom.*

MRS. LARNE. You awful boy! How dare you?

[*She turns and sees* PHYLLIS. BOB PILLIN *also turns, and sheepishly pockets the cheque-book.* PHYLLIS *comes circling round to the fire and stands with her back to it, eyeing them.* MRS. LARNE *has nipped* JOCK *by the ear.*

MRS. LARNE. This boy of mine will be the death of us, Mr. Pillin.

JOCK. I say—that hurts!

MRS. LARNE. [*Smoothly*] I mean it to.

PHYLLIS. [*Meaningly*] Mother, *I* put him up to it.

MRS. LARNE. [*Releasing* JOCK, *and with a gesture of despair*] Well, I give it up. When I'm dead of work and anxiety, you'll both be sorry. [*To* BOB PILLIN.] Are we going to have supper before or after, Mr. Pillin?

BOB PILLIN. Oh!—er—both—don't you think? Er—her!

JOCK. I say, you are a topper! Have some toffee?

[*He holds out a substance.*

PHYLLIS. Look out, young man; it looks exactly like, but it's beeswax.

BOB PILLIN. [*Gazing at it*] Oh! I say!

[JOCK *jabs it promptly into his opened mouth, and flies. He is met at the door, however, by* LETTY.

LETTY. Mr. Aesop.

[OLD HEYTHORP, *slow as fate, in his overcoat, hat in hand, advances into the room, and the boy* JOCK *backs before him, bowing low, as to an idol.* MRS. LARNE *hastens to greet him,* PHYLLIS *too.* BOB PILLIN, *risen, is removing beeswax.*

LETTY. [*Sotto voce*] Kettle's bilin'.

MRS. LARNE. [*Majestically*] Tea, Letty.

[*They settle* OLD HEYTHORP *on the sofa, whence he stares up at* BOB PILLIN, *and gives him a curt nod.*

BOB PILLIN. How are you, sir? Saw you at the meeting.

HEYTHORP. How did *you* come here?

BOB PILLIN. [*Disconcerted*] Oh!—er—just dropped in.

MRS. LARNE. Guardy dear, you *must* try our new liqueur. Jock, get Guardy a glass.

[*The boy* JOCK, *having put a glass to his eye, fills it rapidly.*

MRS. LARNE. You horrible boy! You could see that glass has been used.

JOCK. Oh! sorry, mother. *I'll* get rid of it.

> [*He drinks off the liqueur.*

MRS. LARNE. [*Laughing*] Guardy, what am I to do with him?

> [PHYLLIS, *who has taken* JOCK *by the ear to lead him from the room,
> suddenly drops him with a squeal and clasps her hand to her
> arm. He has run a pin into her.* BOB PILLIN *hastens to her.*

MRS. LARNE. Aren't those children awful? [*Lowering her voice.*]
Jock takes after you terribly, Guardy. Jock, come here. Look at
the shape of his head.

> [*The boy* JOCK *approaches and stands seraphically gazing at* OLD
> HEYTHORP. *He is seized by feigned terror and, falling on
> to the stool before the fire, sits there grinning and cross-legged
> with his eyes fixed on* OLD HEYTHORP.

MRS. LARNE. He has absolutely no reverence. Jock, take Mr.
Pillin and show him your rats. And Phyllis, do hurry up the tea,
there's a dear girl.   [*At the word "Rats"* JOCK *has risen.*

JOCK. Oh! ah! Come on! They only bite if you worry them.
You needn't worry them if you don't like.

> [BOB PILLIN, *seeing that* PHYLLIS *is leaving the room, follows* JOCK
> *out.*

HEYTHORP. Making up to that young pup, are you?

MRS. LARNE. He's such a nice fellow. We like him ever so.
Guardy, I'm sure your coming means good news.

HEYTHORP. Settled six thousand on the children.

MRS. LARNE. Guardy! [*She becomes thoughtful.*] On the children?——

HEYTHORP. Yes. *You* can't blew it, so don't try!

MRS. LARNE. How unkind! As if——!

HEYTHORP. Scriven, the lawyer, will pay you the income till they
come of age or marry. Sixty pounds a quarter. Now! *Ask no
questions—not a word to anyone.*

MRS. LARNE. Of course not! But—quarterly—when will the
first——?

HEYTHORP. Lady Day.

MRS. LARNE. Nearly six weeks? This isn't in place of the three
hundred you give us, Guardy?

HEYTHORP. No—additional.

MRS. LARNE. How sweet of you!

HEYTHORP. Humbug!

MRS. LARNE. Guardy!

HEYTHORP. About young Pillin. She mustn't be grabbed up by
any fool who comes along.

MRS. LARNE. Oh! the dear girl is *much* too young. He's quite
harmless; a nice simple fellow.

HEYTHORP. Drop him! Not a word of this settlement to **anyone.**

MRS. LARNE. N-no, Guardy. But I am so pressed. Couldn't I have twenty-five in advance?

[OLD HEYTHORP *shakes his head; she throws up her hands in despair, but as* LETTY *comes in with the tea, followed by* PHYLLIS, *a thought strikes her.*]

Come and give Guardy tea, Phyllis. I've forgotten something; I must just telephone.

PHYLLIS. Can't I, mother?

MRS. LARNE. No; Guardy wants you. Back in a minute.

[*She goes out behind* LETTY.

PHYLLIS. [*At the tea table*] Tea, Guardy?

[OLD HEYTHORP *shakes his head.*]

D'you mind if I do? I've been washing my hair, it makes you frightfully hungry. [*Uncovering a dish.*] Geewhiz! Crumpets! Guardy, just one crumpet? [OLD HEYTHORP *shakes his head.*] [*Filling her mouth with a crumpet.*] Scrummy! Lucky Jock didn't know. Was our Dad like Jock? Mother's always so mysterious about him. I suppose you knew *his* father well?

[*She sits down beside him on the sofa.*

HEYTHORP. Man about London in my day.

PHYLLIS. Oh! your day must have been jolly. Did you wear peg-top trousers, and Dundrearys, and ride in the Row?

[OLD HEYTHORP *nods.*]

What larks! And I suppose you had lots of adventures with opera dancers and gambling? The young men are all so good now. That young man, for instance, is a perfect stick of goodness.

[OLD HEYTHORP *grunts.*]

You wouldn't know how good he was unless you'd sat next him going through a tunnel. Yesterday, coming home with us, he had his waist squeezed, and he simply sat still. And then, when the tunnel ended, it was Jock, after all, not me. His face was—— Oh! ah! ha, ha! he!

[OLD HEYTHORP *contemplates her charming throat, thrown back in laughter, with a sort of pride in his face.*]

He likes to pretend, of course, that he's fearfully lively. He's going to take us to the theatre to-morrow night, and give us *two* suppers. Won't it be lummy? Only [*With a sigh*] I haven't anything to go in.

[OLD HEYTHORP *begins to fumble in his breast pocket.*

PHYLLIS. Isn't money beastly, Guardy? If one could put out a plate over night and have just enough in the morning to use during the day!

HEYTHORP. [*Fumbling out a note and putting it in her lap*] Little present for you—buy a dress—don't tell your mother.

PHYLLIS. Ten pounds! How *lovely!* You *are* a chook. [*She throws her arms round him, and bobs her lips against his nose. Sitting back and contemplating him.*] To-morrow's Valentine's Day. Guardy, you've got the grand manner. Do tell me about that Yankee. *Where* did you wing him.

HEYTHORP. At Dieppe.

PHYLLIS. No, but where *on* him?

HEYTHORP. Where he couldn't sit down afterwards.

PHYLLIS. Was he turning his back?

HEYTHORP. Side view.

PHYLLIS. Oh! Yes, of course! Why did you fight the duel?

HEYTHORP. Said old England was played out.

PHYLLIS. Fifty years ago? [OLD HEYTHORP *nods.*] But, she's still full of beans, isn't she?

HEYTHORP. And always will be.

PHYLLIS. That's what I think—look at Jock, for instance.

[OLD HEYTHORP *looks at her instead.*] Why d'you look at me like that, Guardy?

HEYTHORP. You're more like your father than Jock. Listen! When you come of age, you'll have a hundred and twenty a year of your own that you can't get rid of. Don't ever be persuaded into doing what you don't want. Don't marry a fool for his money. And remember: your mother's a sieve—no good giving her anything; keep what you'll get for yourself—only a pittance, you'll want it all, every mag.

PHYLLIS. Mother's a darling, really, Guardy.

HEYTHORP. H'm! I daresay. Only one thing in life matters— independence. Lose that, lose everything. Get old like me, you'll find that out. Keep your independence—only value of money. And—that young pup—'ware fools! Help me up!

[PHYLLIS *helps him up and puts his hat on her own head; it comes down right over the ears.*

PHYLLIS. [*Enchanted.*] Oh! Guardy! What a whopper! You *must* have a big head! They're all so small now. I shall marry someone with a head like yours. [*Pensively.*] I do wonder about that young man. I bet he's got the dead rat down his back by now. And isn't it niffy! Jock was keeping it for something special. [*She wrinkles her nose and plants the hat on* OLD HEYTHORP.] Why! It only just goes on. *Must* you go? I do love you to come. [*With a sudden warm impulse*] And I do love you altogether!

[*She trembles up close to him.*

HEYTHORP. [*Patting her cheek*] That's right! Be a good girl. And don't tell your mother what I've been saying. Shall enjoy my dinner to-night.

PHYLLIS. Don't you always? I always think of you having *such* a good dinner. You look like it, you know.

HEYTHORP. Got a daughter.   Mustn't eat, mustn't drink!   Always at me.

PHYLLIS. Oh! yes, we saw her in the distance.   She looked too good for anything.

HEYTHORP. That's the trouble.

PHYLLIS. Is she married?

HEYTHORP. No.

PHYLLIS. Why not?

HEYTHORP. Too holy.

PHYLLIS. [*At the window*] I thought so—Jock's pinned it to his coat behind, and he can't tell [*Fingers pinching her nose*] where it's coming from.   Oh! poor young man!   Oh, well, that's all right!   He's safe for to-day—nobody'll be able to go near him.   They're coming in.   Guardy, would you mind taking him away with you in your cab —you can smoke a cigar, you know.   I'll light it for you. [*She feels in his pockets, finds his cigar case, gives him a cigar and lights it.*] There! It's a good strong cigar. [*At the window.*]   Oh! he's found it out. There it goes, over the wall!   Thank goodness!   Now, look out, smoke! [*She dives for a cigarette from the table and lights it.*] Good-bye, Guardy darling, I'm off.   I know that rat.

[*She sidles to the door as* BOB PILLIN *comes in.*

HEYTHORP. Give you a lift if you're going my way.

BOB PILLIN. [*Looking at* PHYLLIS] Well, sir, I wasn't thinking of——

PHYLLIS. Oh! yes he is.   Guardy; he *is*.

BOB PILLIN. [*Taken aback*] Oh! ah!   Tha-anks, then.

[PHYLLIS *vanishes.*

HEYTHORP. Make the most of your opportunities, I see.

BOB PILLIN. I—I don't know what you mean, sir.   Mrs. Larne is very kind.

HEYTHORP. No doubt.   Don't try and pick the flowers, that's all.

BOB PILLIN. [*With some dignity*] Are you a relative of theirs, sir?

[OLD HEYTHORP *nods.*]

I quite understand what you mean.   But I should like to know what your objection to me is.

HEYTHORP. Milk-and-water masquerading as port wine.

BOB PILLIN. [*Outraged*] Awfully sorry, sir, if you don't think I'm wild enough.   Anything I can do for you in that line—be most happy. I—er—know I'm not in debt, no entanglements, got a decent income, pretty good expectations and that; but I can soon put that all right, if I'm not fit without.

HEYTHORP. [*After a silence during which he puffs sturdily*] Fatter, but no more sand than your father.

[*He leads out, and* BOB PILLIN, *hypnotized by such very plain speech, is following, when* MRS. LARNE *enters.*

27

Mrs. Larne. Oh ! are you going, Guardy ? [Heythorp *nods.*]
And you, Mr. Pillin—we haven't half——

Bob Pillin. Awfully sorry—find I've got to. I'll send you a line
about to-morrow.

> [Mrs. Larne *is almost securing his lappel, when her nose apprehends*
> *something, and she refrains.* Bob Pillin *slides out behind*
> Old Heythorp.

Mrs. Larne. [*To herself*] Dear me ! what a peculiar——! [*She*
wrinkles her nose, then goes to her bureau, sits down, sighs profoundly, and takes
up her pen.] "With red velvet. The gathering was brilliant in th]
extreme." Oh, dear ! What lies the papers do tell ! [Phyllis *enters.*e
Ah ! there you are, you naughty gairl. I've just telephoned to my
lawyer to come round.

Phyllis. That horrid man ! What d'you want him for, mother ?

Mrs. Larne. What do I want him for ? What do I want any man
for ? Money—Money.

Phyllis. I wish Jock hadn't wasted that rat. I'm sure he's a beast.

Mrs. Larne. Now, Phyllis ! I won't have you call him names.
He's very nice for a lawyer. If *he* can't get me some money, we shall
all have to go into the workhouse. I want you to be extra sweet to
him.

Phyllis. Well, I can't.

Mrs. Larne. Then you'd better go upstairs.

Phyllis. I will when he comes. If he pretends to be nice—I know
what it'll mean.

Mrs. Larne. And what is that ?

Phyllis. That you're what he calls " a fine woman." Ugh !
He's a horrid man !

Mrs. Larne. Can I help it if people admire me ?

Phyllis. If course we all admire you. Only *that* sort of man !
I'm sure he never does anything for nothing.

Mrs. Larne. You're getting very knowing. [*With some dignity.*]
As a matter of fact, Guardy gave me some news, and I expect to be
able to—er—use it for our benefit.

Phyllis. Guardy told *me*, too, mother.

Mrs. Larne. Oh ! What ?

Phyllis. That I shall have some money when I come of age, and
that I wasn't to give—— But, Mummy, anything I ever have of
course you'll have half.

Mrs. Larne. [*Putting out her hand*] Darling, I know. But by then
there won't be any Mummy—she'll have wasted away. [*She sighs*
heavily.] Never mind !

> " La vie est brève, un peu d'amour.
> Un peu de rêve, et puis bonjour ! "

I wonder if I could work that in ! [*Takes up her pen.*

PHYLLIS. [*Producing the ten pound note, with a sigh*] Mum! Guardy gave me this to buy a dress. Would you like it?

MRS. LARNE. [*Touched*] Ducky! No! Waste it on those wretched tradesmen? You get yourself a lovely frock.

PHYLLIS. Oh! I said you were a darling!   [*Kisses her nose.*

MRS. LARNE. Listen! I believe that's his cab. Now, Phyllis, this is a crisis, and you must help me.

PHYLLIS. [*Regarding her*] Mother, I believe you love a crisis.

MRS. LARNE. Just open the door a weeny bit.

PHYLLIS. [*Doing so*] Why?

MRS. LARNE. Hssh!

VENTNOR'S *voice without* : Mrs. Larne at home?

MRS. LARNE. [*Under her breath*] It is.

LETTY'S *voice* : Can't say yet, depends on 'oo you are.

VENTNOR'S *voice* : I think she is, young woman.

LETTY'S *voice* : Are you about the water?

MRS. LARNE. [*Under her breath*] That awful little drumstick!

VENTNOR'S *voice* : Mr. Charles Ventnor, say! Give her this card!

LETTY'S *voice* : Just wait outside the door, will yer?

[MRS. LARNE, *throwing up her hands, goes to the door.*

MRS. LARNE. Oh! Is that you, Mr. Ventnor? Do come in.

[VENTNOR *appears, hat in hand.*]

Phyllis, dear, Mr. Ventnor.

[VENTNOR *bows smilingly,* PHYLLIS *nods.*]

That appalling little drumstick of mine has got water on the brain. Such a faithful little soul! We Bohemians, you know, Mr. Ventnor——

VENTNOR. Precisely!

MRS. LARNE. Do sit down. [*He sits on the sofa.*] Tea?—But I'm afraid it's cold. A glass of liqueur—it's really quite nice, and rather original in the afternoon, don't you think? [*Handing him a glass.*] And do smoke; we smoke everywhere. Even that naughty gairl of mine smokes.

VENTNOR. No, thanks. [*Tasting the liqueur.*] Very good tipple, Mrs. Larne. I came at some little inconvenience, so perhaps——

[*He glances at* PHYLLIS.

PHYLLIS. All right!   [*She goes out without a look back.*

MRS. LARNE. [*Sitting down on the sofa beside him*] She's so abrupt, dear child. In my young days——

VENTNOR. [*Gallantly*] Your *young* days, Mrs. Larne. And what are these? But now—what is it?

MRS. LARNE. Well, as you know, my affairs are very embarrassed; but to-day I had some splendid news. A settlement has been made upon us—perfect Godsend, Mr. Ventnor, in the nick of time. Only of course I shan't get any interest from it till Lady Day. And, you see, I simply must have fifty pounds now—so I thought you would be so kind as to advance that on the security of this interest, charging, of course, what you like. It's quite ridiculous, but to-morrow I shall be without gas or coals, and probably have my furniture seized for rates. They are so hasty and unreasonable.

VENTNOR. [*Dubiously*] Settlement?

MRS. LARNE. Yes, I receive the income quarterly till my children are of age.

VENTNOR. How much?

MRS. LARNE. Six thousand pounds.

VENTNOR. Oh! [*Pricking his ears.*] Who made it?

MRS. LARNE. Ah! well—that I'm *not* supposed to tell you.

VENTNOR. Six thousand—— [*To himself.*] Sixty thousand—ten per cent—— !

MRS. LARNE. Oh! no, not six thousand a year—that would be too heavenly; six thousand altogether.

VENTNOR. Quite!

MRS. LARNE. You can verify everything for yourself, of course. The lawyers are Messrs. Scriven.

VENTNOR. Not Crow & Donkin?

MRS. LARNE. No, the name was Scriven. Aren't they lawyers?

VENTNOR. Oh! certainly—very good firm. Very interesting news, Mrs. Larne. I thought Crow & Donkin because—— [*Suddenly looking at her*] they're old Mr. Heythorp's solicitors.

MRS. LARNE. Ah! but you see I promised not to mention any names, except of course the solicitor's. If I didn't mention him, I could hardly expect you to lend me the money, could I?

VENTNOR. Afraid I must ask you to be more frank, Mrs. Larne. Mr. Heythorp *is* your late husband's father?

MRS. LARNE. Why? How *did* you know that?

VENTNOR. When you first came to see me, you spoke of his being behind you—remember? I confess I originally had a—— [*With a look.*] Well! a rather more intimate theory, but that didn't tally with my inquiries in Dublin.

MRS. LARNE. [*Flattering*] What a terrible man!

VENTNOR. Ah! We lawyers, Mrs. Larne, like to know something about our clients. So "Old English" has been to see you this——

MRS. LARNE. What a nose you have!

VENTNOR. Exactly! [*Sniffing.*] Cigar—not long gone!

MRS. LARNE. Wonderful! It's quite like that great criminal—Sherlock Holmes.

VENTNOR. So you want fifty pounds, Mrs. Larne.

MRS. LARNE. Unless you *could* manage to make it a hundred.

VENTNOR. First you've heard of this settlement? Scriven? [*Suddenly.*] Do you know a Mr. Pillin?

MRS. LARNE. Of course, we met him yesterday while you were there! Delightful young man, so cheery.

VENTNOR. [*Slyly*] Very different from his father, isn't he?

MRS. LARNE. Oh! We don't know his father. Do tell me— they're rich people, aren't they?

VENTNOR. Ye-es, warm man, old Pillin. Young Pillin's a lucky fellow—only son.

MRS. LARNE. [*Dreamily*] How right!

VENTNOR. [*Clutching his chest*] I've got it!

MRS. LARNE. Oh! have you? [*Putting out her hand.*] Even if it's only fifty, it'll be my salvation.

VENTNOR. [*With a laugh*] No, no, Mrs. Larne; no, no!

MRS. LARNE. But you said you'd got it.

VENTNOR. I don't carry fifty pounds about with me. [*With a peculiar look at her.*] Unless I know I've got a use for it. I must ask you to give me a little note to Scriven.

MRS. LARNE. Oh! of course.

[*She goes to her bureau and writes at his dictation.*]

VENTNOR. [*Dictating*]

" DEAR SIR,—Will you be so good as to give my lawyer, Mr. Charles Ventnor, details of the settlement of six thousand pounds just made on my children and myself, that he may have record of the matter.— Yours faithfully, etc."

Just pin your card. I'll go and see them first thing to-morrow—know 'em quite well. If it's all right, you shall have the money; and I won't charge you a penny.

MRS. LARNE. Oh! but—how unusual!

VENTNOR. Not at all! Very glad to render you the little service. Hope it won't be the last. [*While she finishes writing and pins her card, he moves down to the fire, rubbing his hands; to himself, softly.*] Got the old rascal! Neat—oh, neat!

MRS. LARNE. [*Finishing*] There! Such a relief! [*Sniffing.*] Dear me! There's that——! [*Sniffing.*] You don't smell a rat, do you?

[VENTNOR *looks round at her, startled.*]

It's my dreadful boy. He keeps them too long sometimes. [*Handing him the letter.*] I suppose you couldn't see Scriven's to-night?

VENTNOR. [*Looking at his watch*] Too late, Mrs. Larne, I'm afraid; but if you'll add a postscript, you shall have the money by special messenger to-morrow.   [MRS. LARNE *writes at his dictation.*]

VENTNOR. " I shall further be glad if you will pay Mr. Ventnor the first fifty pounds of interest when you receive it, in satisfaction of that sum advanced by him." [*Taking the letter again.*] And now I must be off.

MRS. LARNE. [*Rising*] It *was* good of you to come. I feel so different. Could I have just five pounds ?

VENTNOR. [*A little taken aback*] Er—well—Oh ! yes, certainly.

MRS. LARNE. [*Taking the note*] How chivalrous !

VENTNOR. Not a bit, not a bit ! [*He holds her hand impressively, and looks into her eyes.*] You know, my dear Mrs. Larne, I am very much at your service. Your humble admirer——

> [*While, carried away by sudden fervour and general perfume, he presses closer, the door is opened by* PHYLLIS, *who stands there with* BOB PILLIN *behind her.*]

And if you—if you liked, you need have no more money troubles, I assure you.

MRS. LARNE. [*Not yet aware of the door*] But how wonderful !

PHYLLIS. The laundress is here.

MRS. LARNE. Oh ! how provoking. I must just see her. Goodbye, Mr. Ventnor ! [*Seeing* BOB PILLIN.] Why, my dear young man, I thought you'd gone !

PHYLLIS. [*With meaning*] He came back for his *stick*. [*As her mother goes, to* BOB PILLIN *in a low voice, and pointing her chin at* VENTNOR.] That's your friend.

> [*She crosses to the fire, takes* BOB PILLIN'S *cane, and holds it out to him by the end.* BOB PILLIN *takes it ; and suddenly, as if moved by some force outside himself, he stretches it out and taps* VENTNOR, *who is just going through the doorway, on the shoulder. The latter turns sharply.* PHYLLIS *is at the fire glaring at him.* BOB PILLIN *is consulting her eyes.*]

BOB PILLIN. Hold on a minute !

VENTNOR. What's that ?

BOB PILLIN. How's Mrs. Ventnor to-day ?

VENTNOR. [*Sullenly*] Perfectly well.

BOB PILLIN. [*Gazing at* PHYLLIS *and still moved by her face*] It's a bit thick !

VENTNOR. It's what ?

BOB PILLIN. [*More and more moved*] Ye-es. And—er—I want an explanation, don't you know.

VENTNOR. Do you ? Well, you won't get it.

> [BOB PILLIN *stands nonplussed.*

PHYLLIS. [*Low*] Go on !

BOB PILLIN. I have the honour to be—er—be a—a friend here. And, look here, Ventnor, it's—it's not the conduct of a gentleman.

VENTNOR. [*Angrily*] You young——! Mind your own business, will you ?

BOB PILLIN. I'm going to.

PHYLLIS. Good !

BOB PILLIN. And I won't have it. It's not the thing.

VENTNOR. You—you won't have it! *Indeed*! Now I tell you what, you'd better not exasperate me, you [*Glancing angrily from* BOB *to* PHYLLIS] moonstruck young calf!

BOB PILLIN. [*With real resolution*] Phyllis, shall I shift him?

PHYLLIS. Yes.

BOB PILLIN. Clear, Ventnor! And don't come again.

VENTNOR. By George! The impudence! I'll bring the whole pack of cards about your ears, young cock!

BOB PILLIN. Out? [*Advancing on him.*] Going? Once—twice—for the last time——!

VENTNOR. [*Goes, turning in the doorway*] You wait and see which boot the leg is on!   [BOB PILLIN *closes the door.*

BOB PILLIN. Phew! What a scorcher!

PHYLLIS. [*Impulsively giving him her hand*] You've got ever so much more sand than I thought.

BOB PILLIN. [*Humbly*] Might I—I kiss it?

PHYLLIS. All right. It's generally dirty.   [BOB PILLIN *kisses it.* [*Drawing it away.*] Mother hated it. Beastly man—you do understand that mother hated it!

BOB PILLIN. Of course! *Of course!*

PHYLLIS. But you'd better go before she comes.

BOB PILLIN. [*Blankly*] Well, I suppose I must go some time. I couldn't—— [*Approaching her face.*] Could I?

PHYLLIS. No.

BOB PILLIN. Well, I mean to say that—er—I shall dream about it.

PHYLLIS. I don't mind. Ta-ta!

> [*She waves her hand. He backs hypnotized towards the door and vanishes.* PHYLLIS *turns to the fire, with a sneeze, and runs her hands through her hair.*

MRS. LARNE. [*Entering*] Well, that's that! The impudent woman took it nearly all.

PHYLLIS. Has she left my white petticoat, mother, and my——

MRS. LARNE. Everything. [*Sitting at her bureau.*] Have they gone?

PHYLLIS. Um!

MRS. LARNE. [*Considering*] "La vie est brève, un peu d'amour." Life is brief, a little love! Perhaps it *is* a bit cynical for the *Liverpool Pilot.*

The curtain falls.

ACT III

SCENE I

OLD HEYTHORP'S *sanctum in his daughter's house—a cosy room, with oil paintings, deep armchairs, and red curtains.* OLD HEYTHORP, *in a plum-coloured velvet smoking-jacket, is sitting before the log fire, Right, reading the "Morning Post." On a little table, close to him, is a reading lamp, a bell, and a card. A little pink letter has dropped to the floor. There are two doors on the Left—one to the hall, one to his bedroom—and a window at the Back looking over an open space with trees. It is about five in the afternoon.*

> [*The door is opened quietly and* ADELA HEYTHORP *comes in.*

ADELA. Well, father, are you going to keep to that absurd idea of dining here in future—giving twice the trouble?

> [OLD HEYTHORP *looks round at her with the white hairs on his lower lip bristling.*]

I'm going out to-night: I shall have something light early, so it doesn't matter—but I do hope by to-morrow you'll feel more sociable. It *looks* so bad.

> [OLD HEYTHORP *resumes his paper. She takes up the card from the little table. It is large and has a naked Cupid.*

ADELA. Cupid! With nothing on—not even a quiver. [*Reading.*] "To be your Valentine."

> [*She picks up the little pink letter and reads, ironically :*]

"DEAREST GUARDY,—I'm sorry this is such a mangy valentine. I stayed in bed for breakfast because I've got a cold coming, so I asked Jock, and the pig bought this. I'm going to get a scrummy dress this afternoon. I'm frightfully excited about the theatre to-night. It's simply ripping. Just going to have rum and honey for my cold. Good-bye.   "Your PHYLLIS."

So they don't call you grandfather! I'm afraid I feel relieved.

HEYTHORP. [*Very angry*] Be so good as to leave my letters alone!

ADELA. Now, father, please don't get into a rage. [*Smelling at the valentine.*] Patchouli!

HEYTHORP. How I ever had you for a daughter—why I ever put you in the position you are!

832

ADELA. Did my mother know about—this sort of thing ?

HEYTHORP. No.

ADELA. How fortunate !

HEYTHORP. She could have stood it.

ADELA. Is that a sneer or a statement ?

HEYTHORP. Your mother was as hard as wood—just like you.

ADELA. Really, father, they tell me you have the manners of the old school—where do you keep them ?

HEYTHORP. Well, you put my back up.

ADELA. I'm sorry. Are you going to Bath, as Dr. Somers wants.

HEYTHORP. No.

ADELA. Are you going, at least, to stop drinking port ?

HEYTHORP. No ! *Carpe diem*—live while I can.

ADELA. You know that any day you might have apoplexy !

HEYTHORP. Sooner have done with it than turn teetotaller !

ADELA. There's only one word for it—pagan. If you can't think of this life, you might of the next.

HEYTHORP. When they're roasting me, you'll be able to say " I told you so."   [*He rings the bell.*

ADELA. Profanity, as usual !

HEYTHORP. Let me alone, then.

ADELA. As if I could.

    [*As she goes out*, MELLER, *the valet, a discreet, clean-shaven man, comes in.*

MELLER. Would you like a hand up, sir ?

HEYTHORP. No ! Tell cook I shall want a good dinner to-night.

MELLER. I will, sir.

HEYTHORP. And get up a bottle of the '68 port.

MELLER. [*Dubiously*] Yes, sir.

HEYTHORP. Send me Molly.

MELLER. Just come, sir, by hand.

                     [*Hands him a note, and goes out.*

    [OLD HEYTHORP, *after scrutinizing the note, as one does those which suggest the unpleasant, is about to open it, when the housemaid* MOLLY *comes in—a grey-eyed, dark-haired Irish damsel, who stands, pretty to look at, with her hands folded, her head a little to one side, her lips a little parted.*

MOLLY. Yes, sirr ?

HEYTHORP. Want to look at you.

MOLLY. Oh ! I'm not tidy, sirr.   [*Puts her hands to her hair.*

HEYTHORP. Like pretty faces. Can't bear sour ones. Had a valentine ?

MOLLY. No, sirr. Who would send me one, then ?

HEYTHORP. Not got a young man ?

MOLLY. Well, I might. But he's over in my counthry.

27*

HEYTHORP. [*Holding out the valentine*] What do you think of this?

MOLLY. [*Scrutinizing the card reverently*] Indeed, an' ut's pretty, too.

HEYTHORP. Like to keep it?

MOLLY. Oh! if 'tis not takin' ut from you, sirr.

HEYTHORP. [*Fumbling out a coin*] Little present for you.

MOLLY. [*Gasping*] Oh! sirr, a sovereign—ut's too much; 'tis kingly.

HEYTHORP. Going to ask you to do something as a human being.

MOLLY. Shure an' I will do annything you like.

HEYTHORP. Then put your nose in here every now and then—can't get up without a hand—don't like ringing—can't bear feeling dependent. Understand me?

MOLLY. Och! an' I *do*. And you so active in your brain, and such a grand gentleman. 'Tis an honour, ut is. I'll be puttin' me nose in all the time, I will.

HEYTHORP. [*With a little courtly bow*] Much obliged to you.

MOLLY. Would you be afther wantin' annything now, sirr? Could I be pullin' you on your feet, or anny thrifle?

HEYTHORP. No, thank you. You're a good girl.

MOLLY. 'Tis proud ye make me, sirr.

HEYTHORP. Tell me. Have I got bad manners?

MOLLY. Oh! sirr, no. 'Tis lovely manners ye have—the rale old manners.

HEYTHORP. When I was young I was fond of an Irish girl.

MOLLY. An' wouldn't that be the pleasure of her!

HEYTHORP. Blarney! No. I didn't know my luck.

MOLLY. Ah! the luck—'tis a chancey thing.

HEYTHORP. Yes. If you ever get any—stick to it.

MOLLY. I will that. Could I be bringin' you your tay, or a bottle, or annything?

HEYTHORP. No, thank you.   [*She goes out.*

HEYTHORP. [*He fumbles the letter open and reads it; drops his hand, and sits staring before him*] Ruffian!

MELLER. [*Entering*] Mr. Farney, sir.   [*He goes out again.*

FARNEY. Good afternoon, sir. Great change in the weather; quite spring-like. I've brought you the purchase deed to sign for the Company. Pillins' have signed already.

[*He places a document before* OLD HEYTHORP, *and a stylographic pen.*

HEYTHORP. [*After signing*] Best thing the Company ever did, Mr. Farney. Four sound ships for sixty thousand pounds. Conscience clear on that.

FARNEY. [*With enthusiasm*] I should think so, sir. A great stroke of business, I feel.

HEYTHORP. Heard from a shareholder called Ventnor?

FARNEY. No, sir.

HEYTHORP. Well, I have. You may get a letter that'll make you open your eyes. Just write for me, will you?

"*Feb.* 14.

"CHARLES VENTNOR, ESQ.,
    "12, Fawcitt Street, Liverpool.

"SIR,—I have your letter of even date, the contents of which I fail to understand. My solicitors will be informed of it.

"Yours truly——"

[*He signs.*

FARNEY. [*All eyes*] Can *I* do anything for you, sir?

HEYTHORP. Get straight back to the office and drop that on him as you go—impudent ruffian!

FARNEY. Might I ask what he—— ?

HEYTHORP. [*Shaking his head*] My letter'll bring him round here, if I'm not mistaken.

FARNEY. I take this opportunity of saying, sir, how much I've admired the way you got this purchase through, in spite of all the opposition. In fact, sir, in the office we all swear by you.

HEYTHORP. [*With his little bow*] Thank you, Mr. Farney—pleasure to hear that.

FARNEY. The way you rallied your voice for that last speech. Such pluck, sir. I don't know if you ever heard your nickname in Liverpool "Old English?" Personally I think it's a proud one.

HEYTHORP. "Æquam memento," Mr. Farney, "rebus in arduis servare mentem." Pronounce Horace like foreigners now, don't they?

FARNEY. I believe they do, sir. Of course I don't especially object to foreigners.

HEYTHORP. Don't know what they were made for—except to give trouble.

FARNEY. There isn't very much of old England left, as you remember it, I suppose, sir.

HEYTHORP. The breed goes on; it's in the bone.

FARNEY. Yes, sir, but there isn't much meat on it, nowadays.

[*He looks at a picture.*

HEYTHORP. Bought that after the Crimea—hung in my chambers in the Albany, before I married. Never marry, Mr. Farney—lose your independence.

FARNEY. [*With a smile*] Afraid I've lost it, sir. Can't say I ever had much.

HEYTHORP. Only thing in life. Heel on your neck—no matter whose—better dead.

FARNEY. You must have had a good life, sir.

HEYTHORP. Lasted out all my cronies, every man Jack of 'em——

can't call Joe Pillin alive. Careful fellows, too—some. Live a bit longer, I hope. Good day to you. Give that chap my letter.

FARNEY. Good day, sir. I hope you'll live for many years. The ship wouldn't be the same without you.

[OLD HEYTHORP *cuts him off with a nod and movement of his hand, and he goes out.* OLD HEYTHORP *takes up the little pink note, muttering.*

HEYTHORP. Fond of me—worth the risk.

[MELLER *enters with a bunch of hyacinths.*

MELLER. A young lady's brought these, sir. A Miss Larne.

HEYTHORP. Where?

MELLER. In the hall.

HEYTHORP. Tell her to come in.

MELLER. Shall I put them in water, sir? Very partial to water—the 'yacinth.

HEYTHORP. Smell 'em first—the dam teetotallers.

[*He takes a long sniff.*
[*Then* MELLER *takes them out, and* PHYLLIS *comes in.*

PHYLLIS. I've bought my dress, Guardy! It's a oner. I won't kiss you because of my cold. We're going to the *Mikado*. Fancy! I've never seen it. Do you like hyacinths?

HEYTHORP. Favourite scent.

PHYLLIS. Oh! what luck! Somehow I thought you would. This is a jolly room. It's got all your lar-es and penat-es, I suppose?

HEYTHORP. Lārēs et penātēs.

PHYLLIS. Oh! I just read it, you know—in a novel. D'you like novels, Guardy?

HEYTHORP. Never read 'em.

PHYLLIS. Ah! but you've had real adventures of your own. Adventures must be lovely.

HEYTHORP. Not for young ladies.

PHYLLIS. I don't care a bit for mother's stories. There's always a baronet. And they're pretty steep.

HEYTHORP. Steep?

PHYLLIS. Hideously good and strong. You know, Guardy, you can't love anyone who isn't a little bad. *You* never were too good, I'm sure.

HEYTHORP. Human being.

PHYLLIS. That means you had some jolly go's.

HEYTHORP. Come here!

PHYLLIS. My cold, Guardy!

HEYTHORP. Don't catch colds—my age—haven't time. Enjoy yourself, but remember—world's hard; lots of ruffians always on the look-out.

PHYLLIS. I know. There's a man comes to see mother. He makes me squirm. We had rather larks with him, though, yesterday after you'd gone.

HEYTHORP. Oh?

PHYLLIS. Yes, we heard him being insulting to mother, and that young man—Guardy, he's got more sand than you think. You should have heard him say " Out you go !   One, two——" and out he did go. I wish he hadn't, then Bob could have knocked him down.

HEYTHORP. Bob !

PHYLLIS. Well, that's his name. He really had quite a nice glare in his eye.

HEYTHORP. Who is this visitor fellow ?

PHYLLIS. He's mother's lawyer ; Ventnor he's called.

HEYTHORP. The devil he is !

PHYLLIS. Oh yes. You know him, don't you ?

HEYTHORP. I do. So he came to see her yesterday !   What about ?

PHYLLIS. Oh ! money. Guardy, I've been thinking about what you told me. It would be lovely to have money of my own. I think it's perfectly splendid of you, because I know you're not well off.

HEYTHORP. Poor as a church mouse.

PHYLLIS. [*Clasping her hands*] I adore your expressions—they're real old English. Being with you is like being in a boat—it's so breezy. And you've got such a ripping name—Sylvanus. It means made of wood, doesn't it ?

HEYTHORP. Not quite. Name in my family old as the hills. When I go, it goes.

PHYLLIS. [*Clouding*] Don't, Guardy !

HEYTHORP. Can't stop Anno Domini. Never mind !   Stick him up all we can. Give me a kiss.

PHYLLIS. On the top of your head only. My cold's coming back. Rum and honey only last three hours. I'm going to sneak Jock's go when I get in. Do you call that low down ? He's only trying to have a cold.

HEYTHORP. Young rascal !

PHYLLIS. Do you ever have remorse, Guardy ?

HEYTHORP. No.

PHYLLIS. Jock had it once—I never heard such a noise. [*She gurgles.*] You see, he had a pet rabbit, and one day we had it for dinner without knowing.

HEYTHORP. Ate his pet rabbit ?

PHYLLIS. His remorse didn't come from *that* exactly. You see, after we'd eaten it, we found out it wasn't his.

HEYTHORP. Stole it ?

PHYLLIS. Not altogether ; you see it came into the garden after a bit of lettuce he happened to be holding out, so, of course, he kept it. The owner only came round after we'd eaten it, and Jock got a frightful hiding ; it was then he had his remorse. I do hope the pig'll behave to-night. We shall have awful larks, Guardy.

HEYTHORP. Remember ! Bread and butter with independence better than champagne with a fool.

PHYLLIS. Yes. Only somehow I don't think Bob is a fool ; I think he's just been too well brought up. Were you ever in love, Guardy—I mean, really and truly ? [HEYTHORP *nods*.] Did you marry her ? [HEYTHORP *shakes his head*.] Why not ?

HEYTHORP. [*Grimly*] Ask no questions—be told no lies.

PHYLLIS. No. Only—only—you know I *have* got a sort of feeling——

HEYTHORP. Out with it !

PHYLLIS. That—that you're our grandfather.

HEYTHORP. [*After a long stare*] Quite right ! Sorry ?

PHYLLIS. *Rather not !* I think it's awfully jolly. Did she die ? [OLD HEYTHORP *nods*.] Poor Guardy ! [*Cuddling*.] Well, it's all the same now, isn't it ? Here we are ! I suppose your daughter doesn't know ?

HEYTHORP. Told her yesterday. Been praying for me ever since.

PHYLLIS. M'm ! I don't believe in praying for other people. I think it's cheek. Besides, things that are done are done, aren't they ?

HEYTHORP. [*Nodding*] Never look back—doesn't do.

PHYLLIS. [*Switching off*] I do so wonder what you'll think of me in that dress. [*Suddenly*.] I know ! [*To herself*.] Nobby !

[MELLER *enters with the hyacinths*.

MELLER. Mr. Joseph Pillin, sir.

PHYLLIS. [*Awed*] Oh ! Is that Bob's father ?

HEYTHORP. Yes. Run along.

[PHYLLIS *gives him a hasty kiss, and goes towards the door, looking curiously at* JOE PILLIN, *who enters behind his top hat, very pale and grave.*

HEYTHORP. Well, Joe, what a death's-head you look ! Sorry you sold your ships ?

JOE PILLIN. [*After making sure of the door*] Who was that ?

HEYTHORP. My granddaughter.

JOE PILLIN. What ! One of those that I've—— Does she come here ? She's very pretty.

HEYTHORP. Yes. And your son's sweet on her.

JOE PILLIN. Oh, dear ! He picks up with everyone. Sylvanus, I've had a man called Ventnor to see me.

HEYTHORP. H'm ! What do you make of this ?

[*He holds out* VENTNOR'S *letter*.

JOE PILLIN. [*Reading*] " Certain facts having come to my know-ledge, I—" what's that word ?—" deem it my duty to call a special meeting of ' The Island Navigation Company ' to consider circumstances in connection with the purchase of Mr. Joseph Pillin's fleet. And I give you notice that at this meeting your conduct will be called in question.—Charles Ventnor." Ah! There it is! Why did you get me to make that settlement, Sylvanus?

HEYTHORP. Natural affection, Joe.

JOE PILLIN. But that's no excuse for cheating your Company.

HEYTHORP. Didn't—cheated you; they'd agreed to the £60,000 before I saw you.

JOE PILLIN. Well, really, Sylvanus—really—an old friend! But the fact remains. It's a commission—a breach of trust. This man asked me if I knew that Mrs. Larne. What could I say? I d-don't know her. But why did he ask?

HEYTHORP. Her lawyer—smells the rat.

JOE PILLIN. Oh, dear! oh, dear! This'll be the death of me.

[*He sits down, quite crumpled up.*

HEYTHORP. Pull yourself together, Joe. Can't touch *you*; can't upset the purchase, or the settlement. Worst comes to the worst, upset me, that's all.

JOE PILLIN. How you can sit there and look the same as ever! Are you sure they can't touch me?

HEYTHORP. Not they! Keep your pecker up and your mouth shut, and get off abroad.

JOE PILLIN. Yes, yes, I must. I'm very bad. But I don't know, I'm sure, with this hanging over me. What are you thinking of, Sylvanus? You look very funny.

HEYTHORP. [*Coming out of a sort of coma*] Thinking I'll diddle him yet.

JOE PILLIN. How are you going to do it?

HEYTHORP. Bluff the beggar out of it.

JOE PILLIN. But suppose you can't.

HEYTHORP. Buy him off; he's one of my creditors.

JOE PILLIN. You always had such nerve. Do you ever wake up between two and four, and see everything black?

HEYTHORP. Not I! Put a good stiff nightcap on, my boy.

JOE PILLIN. Yes, I sometimes wish I was less temperate. But I couldn't stand it. I'm told your doctor forbids you alcohol.

HEYTHORP. He does.

JOE PILLIN. And yet you drink it. Sylvanus, do you think—if my son is sweet on this young lady, we could—we could give that as a reason for the settlement.

HEYTHORP. [*After a moment's thought, stoutly*] No! Won't have it. She's too good for him.

JOE PILLIN. Really, Sylvanus! I'm sure *I* don't want my son to marry her. I only thought it would make it more natural. We could say they were engaged, and break it off later. It would prevent——

HEYTHORP. No! Won't have her dragged in. Pay my own scot.

JOE PILLIN. But if they hold this meeting and my name gets into the papers——

HEYTHORP. Won't! Leave it to me!

JOE PILLIN. He must be stopped, Sylvanus, he really must. And you—you advise me to get off to-morrow? [OLD HEYTHORP *nods*.] Well, good-bye. I can't forgive you—it was too bad, you know, too bad, altogether. All the same, I wish I had your nerve.

HEYTHORP. Poor shaky chap, you are! All to pieces at the first shot. Buck up, Joe!

[*He holds out his hand and* JOE PILLIN *puts his quavering hand into it.*

JOE PILLIN. You won't let them, Sylvanus? You can't afford it. It would make a terrible scandal. And without the fees from your Boards, you'd be a pauper. You'll find a way; you owe it to me, you know. Well, good-bye! I don't suppose I shall be back till the summer, if I ever come back. [*He quavers out of the room.*

HEYTHORP. [*To himself*] Pauper. Dependent on that holy woman —byword and a beggar—not if I know it!

[MELLER *comes in, draws the curtains, then turns up a lamp on the little table beside* OLD HEYTHORP.

MELLER. Cup of tea, sir? [OLD HEYTHORP *shakes his head.*

HEYTHORP. Have my nap.

MELLER. Excuse me, sir, can I go out this evening, after dinner? Miss Heythorp's going to a ball, sir.

HEYTHORP. Ball!

MELLER. Charity ball, sir, I believe.

HEYTHORP. Ah! it would be!

MELLER. The Mersey Temperance League, I fancy, sir.

HEYTHORP. Good God!

MELLER. Yes, sir. Anything else, sir.

HEYTHORP. Nothing, thank you.

[MELLER, *going to the door, pauses a moment to look at the old man, who, with a rumbling sigh, has taken out a silk handkerchief to put over his head. A bell sounds.*

MELLER. That was the front door, sir. Do you wish to see anybody?

HEYTHORP. Man called Ventnor—no one else.

MELLER. No, sir. [*He goes out.*

[OLD HEYTHORP, *on whom the light from the reading lamp falls brightly, sits back, listening, his eyes very much alive.*

MELLER. [*Re-entering, Left forward*] Mr. Ventnor, sir.

[VENTNOR *comes in, the door is closed, and he stands as if trying to adjust himself, in the dark room, to the pool of light and the richly-coloured old figure in it.*

HEYTHORP. Sorry, can't get up—sit down.

[VENTNOR *draws a chair forward and sits within the radius of the light on the opposite side of the little table where the lamp stands.*

VENTNOR. I got your answer, Mr. Heythorp. [OLD HEYTHORP *nods.*] I think it best to give you a chance to explain your conduct before going further.

HEYTHORP. Your letter's Greek to me.

VENTNOR. I can soon make it into plain English.

HEYTHORP. Sooner the better.

VENTNOR. Well, Mr. Heythorp, the long and the short of the matter is this : Our friend Mr. Pillin paid you a commission of ten per cent. on the sale of his ships.   [OLD HEYTHORP *makes a movement.* Oh ! excuse me ! The money was settled on Mrs. Larne and her children—your grandchildren, you know.

HEYTHORP. Where did you get hold of that cock-and-bull story ?

VENTNOR. It won't do, Mr. Heythorp ! My witnesses are Mrs. Larne, Mr. Pillin himself, and Mr. Scriven. After I left you yesterday, you paid a visit to Mrs. Larne and told her of this settlement ; told her to keep it dark, too. I happen to be her lawyer, and she telephoned to me.   [OLD HEYTHORP *makes a movement.*] Yes—that gets you. The good lady is hard pressed, and she wanted to raise money on it. For that purpose she gave me a note to Scriven. Oh ! you did it very neatly ; but you're dealing with a man of the world, Mr. Heythorp.

HEYTHORP. [*Inaudibly*] With a blackguard.

VENTNOR. Beg pardon ? I didn't get you. [*His voice hardens.*] I had to drag it out of Scriven, but I find, as I surmised, that Mr. Pillin is the settlor. Here's the joke, Mr. Heythorp ; Mrs. Larne doesn't know Mr. Pillin, and Mr. Pillin doesn't know Mrs. Larne. I have it from their own mouths. Amusing, isn't it ? £6,000 is the sum in settlement—10 per cent. on £60,000—a child could put that two and two together.

HEYTHORP. Nothing to me what Joe Pillin does with his money.

VENTNOR. Can you point to any other reason why Mr. Pillin should make this very clandestine sort of settlement on a woman he doesn't know ?

HEYTHORP. [*After a pause*] Could—but won't.

VENTNOR. Easily said. You see, Mr. Heythorp, *you* told Mrs. Larne of this settlement.

HEYTHORP. Think you can tell that rigmarole to a meeting ?

VENTNOR. I not only can, but, if necessary, I will.

HEYTHORP. You'll get the lie direct—no proof.

VENTNOR. Pardon me, I have the note from Mrs. Larne to her lawyer.

HEYTHORP. Nothing to connect her with me.

VENTNOR. Oh! I've not had dealings with Mrs. Larne without careful inquiry. It's well known in Dublin that her late husband was your natural son. I've got written testimony to that.

HEYTHORP. Bring an action against you—make you pay through the nose.

VENTNOR. Bluff—it won't do, Mr. Heythorp, and you know it. I've got you; the merest whiff of dicky-dealing like this will blow you out of your directorships. You've outstayed your welcome as it is. I told you as much yesterday.

HEYTHORP. Yes, you were good enough to sneer at my infirmities.

VENTNOR. [*Angrily*] I spoke the truth. And this business will finish you off.

HEYTHORP. If you're going to call this meeting, what have you come here for—blackmail?

VENTNOR. [*With growing choler*] Oh! you take that tone, do you? Still think you can ride roughshod? Well, you're very much mistaken. I advise you to keep a civil tongue and consider your position.

HEYTHORP. What d'you want?

VENTNOR. I'm not sure this isn't a case for a prosecution.

HEYTHORP. Gammon!

VENTNOR. Neither gammon nor spinach. Now look here! You owe me three hundred pounds; you've owed it me for thirteen years. Either you pay me what you owe me at once, or I call this meeting and make what I know public. You'll very soon find out where you are, and a good thing too, for a more unscrupulous—unscrupulous——

HEYTHORP. [*Very red and swollen, and as if trying to rise*] So—you—you bully me?

VENTNOR. [*Rising*] You'll do no good for yourself by getting into a passion. At your age, and in your condition, I recommend a little prudence. Now just take my terms quietly, or you know what'll happen. I'm not to be intimidated by any of your brass. You've said you won't pay me, and I've said you shall. I'm out to show you who's master.

HEYTHORP. You cowardly, pettifogging attorney, do your damnedest!

VENTNOR. [*Seeing red*] Oho! Bluster it out, do you? You miserable old turkey-cock! You apoplectic old image! I'll have you off your Boards—I'll have you in the gutter. You think in your dotage you can still domineer? Two can play at that game. By George! One foot in bankruptcy, and one foot in the grave—Ha!

    [OLD HEYTHORP *has reached forward for the bell.* VENTNOR *removes it from his reach, and the old man sinks back. Somewhat relaxed by this assertion of his dominance,* VENTNOR *stands looking at the old man, who is lying back breathing hard.*

VENTNOR. Ah! that's shown you. Well, it's never too late to learn. For once you've come up against someone a leetle bit too much for you. Haven't you now? Better cry "Peccavi" and have done with it. [*Putting down the bell on the far edge of the table, he looks again at the old man, then takes a turn up and down, and again stops and looks at him.*] You shouldn't have called me names. You're an old man, and I don't want to be too hard on you. I'm only showing you that you can't play God Almighty any longer. You've had your own way for too many years. And now you can't have it, see—that's all.   [OLD HEYTHORP *moves forward in his chair again.*] Now, don't get into a passion again, calm yourself.

[*The old man is very still.*]
That's better. I see you'll come round. For, mind you, this is your last chance. I'm a man of my word; and what I say, I do. Now then, are you going to pay me, and look pleasant?

[OLD HEYTHORP, *by a violent and unsuspected effort, jerks himself
    forward and reaches the bell. As it rings* VENTNOR *makes a
    grab at it too late.*

VENTNOR. [*Angrily*] You're going to ruin, then?

[MELLER *has appeared.*
HEYTHORP. Show this hound out!

VENTNOR. [*Clenching his fists; then as* MELLER *moves towards him*] That's it, is it? Very well, Mr. Heythorp! Ah! *Very* well!

[*Carefully shepherded by* MELLER, *he goes out.*

[OLD HEYTHORP *sits slightly rocking his body from side to side;
    he puts his hand to his throat as if it had been worried.* MELLER
    comes back.

MELLER. [*Close*] Hope he hasn't hurt you, sir?

HEYTHORP. No! Open the window—get the smell of the fellow out. Lost my temper—mistake. Pull me up!

[MELLER, *who has drawn back the curtains and opened the window,
    disclosing the shapes of dark trees and the grape-bloom sky of
    a mild, moist night, now pulls him up.*]
That's better. [*He takes a long breath.*] Get me a hot bath before dinner, and put some pine stuff into it. Evening clothes.

MELLER. Really, sir?

HEYTHORP. Why not?

MELLER. No, indeed, sir.

HEYTHORP. Get up a bottle of the Perrier Jouet. What's the menu?

MELLER. Germane soup, sir; filly de sole; sweetbread; cutlet soubees; rum souffly.

HEYTHORP. H'm! Tell her to get me an oyster, and put on a savoury.

MELLER. Yes, sir. Excuse me, sir, but did that—er—fellow—threaten you?

HEYTHORP. Bullied me.

MELLER. Could I do anything about it ?   I'm pretty handy with the gloves.   [*He puts up his fists.*

HEYTHORP. No.   Trifle.   Give me an appetite.

MELLER. Yes, sir.   Then what time shall I turn the bath in ?

[OLD HEYTHORP *returns to his chair and lowers himself into it.*

HEYTHORP. Seven o'clock.   Have my nap now.

MELLER. Yes, sir.   [*He closes the window and draws the curtains.*] Shall I turn out the light, sir ?

[OLD HEYTHORP *nods.*   MELLER *turns the lamp out, leaving only firelight, then goes out.*

HEYTHORP. [*Murmuring*] Cooked my own goose !   H'm !

[*He settles himself for a sleep.*

The curtain falls for a minute.

SCENE II

The scene is the same, about three hours later.   OLD HEYTHORP, *in evening dress, is finishing dinner, his napkin tucked in low down on his dress shirt.   He is just lifting a large empty champagne glass to a napkined champagne bottle in* MELLER's *hand.*

HEYTHORP. Fill up.

MELLER. [*Remonstrative*] These are the special glasses, sir, only four to the bottle.

HEYTHORP. Fill up !   Buzz the bottle, before the sweet.

[MELLER *fills the glass, emptying the bottle.*   OLD HEYTHORP *drinks.*]

Good wine.

MELLER. I frapped it just a little, sir.

HEYTHORP. [*Attacking the soufflé before him*] Old fur coat in the wardrobe, no use for it—take it for yourself.

MELLER. Thank you, sir.

HEYTHORP. Only get moth.

MELLER. It's got it, sir.

HEYTHORP. M'm !   Afraid I've worried you a lot.

MELLER. Oh !   no, sir—not more than reason.

HEYTHORP. Very sorry—can't help it—find that when you get like me.

MELLER. I've always admired your pluck, sir ; keeping the flag flyin'.

HEYTHORP. [*Bowing*] Much obliged to you.

[OLD HEYTHORP *finishes the soufflé and sips brown sherry.*

MELLER. [*Touching the bell*] Cook's done a cheese remmyquin, sir.

HEYTHORP. Give her my compliments—capital dinner.

[*The maid* MOLLY *comes in with the " remmyquin," and gives it to* MELLER.

HEYTHORP. Have my port with it.

MELLER. [*Serving the ramequin*] Excuse me, sir, but after a bottle of champagne—are you sure you ought ?

HEYTHORP. [*Digging into the ramequin*] No, but I'm going to.

MELLER. It's very hot, sir.   Shall I take it out of the case ?

HEYTHORP. Touch of cayenne.

MELLER. Yes, sir.   About the port—would you mind if I asked Miss Heythorp ?

HEYTHORP. [*With fork arrested*] If you do you can leave my service.

MELLER. Well, sir, I don't accept the responsibility.

HEYTHORP. Who asked you to ?   Not a baby.

MELLER. No, sir.

HEYTHORP. Well, get it then !

[MELLER, *after a look, shrugs his shoulders and goes to the improvised sideboard for the port.   He pours it out gingerly, while* OLD HEYTHORP *finishes the savoury.*

HEYTHORP. Fill !   [*He drinks the glass savorously.*] Help me up. [*He is helped up and into his chair.*] Put the decanter there.

[MOLLY *enters with a tray, on which are coffee and cigars.*

MELLER. [*Taking it from her—softly*] Gov'nor's goin' for the gloves to-night.   Sherry—champagne—port.   Simply can't hold him in.

MOLLY. [*As softly*] Poor old gentleman, let um have his pleasure. Shure he's only got his dinner.

[*He prepares the coffee, and she goes out.*

MELLER. Shall I cut your cigar, sir ?

HEYTHORP. Um !   What's that squealing ?

MELLER. [*Listening*] I think it's Miss Heythorp singing, sir.

HEYTHORP. Cat.   [*Finishing his third glass of port.*] Ever hear Jenny Lind—eh—Swedish nightingale ?

MELLER. Beg your pardon, sir.

HEYTHORP. No, weren't born.   Mario—Grisi—old Lablache— great days of opera, those.

MELLER. I'm sure, sir.

HEYTHORP. Theatre too—old Kemble, Power, Little Robson—once saw Edmund Kean.

MELLER. Indeed, sir !   Would that be a relation of the present Edmund Keen ?

HEYTHORP. Who's he ?

MELLER. On the Halls, sir, the great ventrilóquist.

HEYTHORP. No actors now.   Saw Hermit win his Derby.

MELLER. [*Interested*] Did you, indeed, sir ?   Was he the equal of Pretty Polly, do you think ?

HEYTHORP. Don't know the lady.

MELLER. [*With a touch of pity*] No, sir, you don't keep up with it, I suppose.

HEYTHORP. All four-in-hands then, tandems, gigs—drove my own cab—tiger behind.

MELLER. Those were little boys, weren't they, sir?

HEYTHORP. Little rascals in boots—blue liveries—tight as a drum. Cremorne—Star and Garter. Wet sheet and a flowing tide. Great days.

MELLER. Your cigar, sir?

HEYTHORP. [*Drinking off his coffee and taking his cigar, which* MELLER *lights*] All gone! [*Following the first puff of smoke, with a feeble wave of his cigar.*] Smoke! Statesmen then—roast beef. Stout oak! Old Pam!

MELLER. Beg pardon, sir?

HEYTHORP. Get me the old brandy.

MELLER. [*Aghast*] Brandy, sir! I really daren't.

HEYTHORP. Bunkum!

MELLER. You'll forgive me, sir; but if Miss Heythorp heard——

HEYTHORP. Are you my servant, or hers?

MELLER. Yours, sir. But the doctor's orders were positive.

HEYTHORP. Damn the doctor! Get the brandy—mother's milk.

[MELLER *wavers to the sideboard, and brings the bottle.*

HEYTHORP. Large glass—want to swing it round, get the aroma.

[MELLER *fetches a goblet and puts it and the bottle on the little table by the hand-bell, removing the port decanter, glass, and coffee cup.*

HEYTHORP. Pour it out.   [MELLER *pours out a little brandy.*

MELLER. You said I might go out, sir, but perhaps I'd better stay.

HEYTHORP. Why? [*With a grin.*] Where I dines I sleeps. Ever hear of Jorrocks?

MELLER. No, sir.

HEYTHORP. Good Lord!

MELLER. Yes, sir. Of course, Molly will be handy, sir, if you want anything.

[*He goes to the door, stands a moment, looking at the old man blowing rings from his cigar: throws up his hands suddenly, and goes out.*

[*Old* HEYTHORP *very slowly and with a feeble hand takes up the glass and sits revolving it before his nose.*

HEYTHORP. [*To himself*] Send in my resignations to-morrow—not give that cur a chance.

[*He is drinking the brandy as the door is opened and* ADELA HEY-THORP *comes in. She is in a white cloak, with one hand and arm in a long white glove and the other glove dangling from it. She has reached him before he sees her.*

ADELA. Father! Meller let out you're drinking brandy after champagne and port. That's absolute poison. It'll kill you.

[OLD HEYTHORP *thrusts out his tufted lower lip and reaches for the bottle.*]

Oh! no. If you behave like a baby, you must be treated like one.

[*She seizes the bottle and puts it back on the sideboard.*

HEYTHORP. [*With his hand to his throat, as if he felt again the sensation of the afternoon*] So—you bully me—too—to-night!

ADELA. Well, really, father! One would think you had no self-control at all. I don't know whether I ought to go out.

[OLD HEYTHORP'S *passion seems to yield before a thought. His face slowly assumes a sort of grin, in which there is a dash of cunning.*

HEYTHORP. Perfectly well. Why not?

ADELA. If it weren't for Temperance I wouldn't. And I tell you, plainly: If you go on like this, I won't have liquor in the house. Good-night!   [*She turns and goes rustling away.*

[*The old man sits listening. There is the sound of a door shut and of a carriage moving from the door.*

HEYTHORP. [*To himself*] Gone! Not so fast, my lady! Not under your heel till to-morrow. [*He makes an effort to get up, but cannot, and sits a moment breathing hard; then, stretching out his hand, he rings the bell.*] Last night to call my soul my own.

[*After a moment the girl* MOLLY *comes in, and stands regarding him.*

MOLLY. What would you be wantin', sirr?

HEYTHORP. Good girl. Help me up.

[MOLLY *takes his hands and pulls, but cannot raise him. He looks rather helplessly from side to side.*

MOLLY. Oh! Ut's me that's not strong enough. Would I get Cook?

[OLD HEYTHORP *shakes his head. He puts his hands on the arms of the chair, and shifts his body towards the edge of the chair, then holds out his hands.*

HEYTHORP. Now!

[*The girl pulls and this time slowly raises him. He stands very still and flushed.*

MOLLY. Sure, it's you have the big heart; it's never bate you are.

HEYTHORP. Thank you. That'll do. Want you again—ring.

MOLLY. Yes, sirr. I'll be up all the time. It's the great unhookin' there'll be when the misthress comes home from her ball.   [*She goes.*

[*He does not move till she has gone. Then a smile comes on his face, and he goes across to the sideboard. Throughout the scene he retains his dignity.*

HEYTHORP. [*Muttering*] Bully me—will she! [*He reaches up and takes the brandy bottle and a sherry glass. With infinite difficulty he pours into it, and slowly, slowly drinks it down; then, grasping the bottle to his chest, he moves across back to his chair, and sinks into it, with the bottle still clasped. For a few seconds he remains like that: then seems to realize that the attitude does not become a gentleman. Now begins his last struggle. The bottle is clasped in his arms; but his hands, with which he must place it on the table, have lost all feeling. Again he struggles, and succeeds in shifting his body in the chair towards the table which nearly overlaps the arm. He rests, breathing stertorously. Inch by inch he edges the base of the bottle till it touches the table; then rests again. With a groan and a supreme effort he screws his trunk over towards the table, and the bottle stands.]* Done it! *[His lips relax in a smile.]* What's this? Red? *[His body sags back in the chair, he sits motionless, and slowly his eyes close.]* To-morrow! *[There is a sound of suffering, and the word "To-morrow," repeated in a whispering sigh, dies into silence.]*

The stage is darkened for twenty seconds, to represent the lapse of two hours.

SCENE III

The same. The door from the hall is opened and MELLER *enters. He moves two or three steps, looking at* OLD HEYTHORP *still recumbent in his chair.* PHYLLIS *has come into the doorway.*

MELLER. *[Turning back towards her, in a low voice]* Half-past eleven, Miss. Afraid it's too late for you to see him. He's asleep.

PHYLLIS. *[Low]* I won't wake him, unless he happens to. But I did want to show him my dress! *[She has on a cloak over a dress of white tulle, her first low-cut frock; a bunch of lilies of the valley is at her breast.*

MELLER. As a fact, Miss, it wouldn't matter if you did wake him. He's got to go to bed.

*[*BOB PILLIN *has moved into the doorway and stands close to* PHYLLIS; MELLER *passes them and goes out.*

PHYLLIS. *[Under her breath]* Bob, hold my cloak!

*[*BOB PILLIN *reverently removes the cloak, which catches.* Oh! you duffy! Is it clear!

BOB PILLIN. *[Under his breath]* Not quite. It's a pin. I'm so afraid of hurting you.

PHYLLIS. Oh! Gefoozlem! Let it rip! Ouch!

BOB PILLIN. *[Cloak in hand]* My God! Did I—— ?

PHYLLIS. *[Mending him with a smile]* All serene! *[She steals into the lamp glow.]* Guardy! My dress, Guardy!

[No answer. She stands twiddling the bunch of lilies; BOB PILLIN *closes up.*

PHYLLIS. [*Whispering*] He *is* fast and deep, isn't he ? [*Holding up the flowers.*] I'll put it in his buttonhole. When he wakes, won't he jump ? [*She steals close, bends, and slips the flowers into the buttonhole. Then kisses the tip of her finger, and blows the kiss at him.*] Good-night, Guardy, dear ; bless you ! [*She skips back, twirls round, reluctant to go without being seen, and blows another kiss.*] I do wish he'd wake ! He'll be sorry he didn't see my dress.

> [*At the disappointed whisper* BOB PILLIN *walks up to the old man, and bends. Suddenly he stands up and looks back at* PHYLLIS.

PHYLLIS. Is he awake ?

BOB PILLIN. [*In a queer voice*] No.

PHYLLIS. I *must* just try again.

BOB PILLIN. No. [*He moves as she comes near, and very decisively places his hands on her shoulders.*] No. Not fair. Come along. [*She looks up at him, intrigued by the firmness of his voice and touch.*]

PHYLLIS. [*Wilfully*] I *will* wake him !

> [*As she speaks, he just turns her round, and pushes her before him quietly and slowly off into the hall.*

PHYLLIS. [*Under her breath, mockingly, to the air before her*] Oo-oh ! Aren't we strong !

> [*There is a little laugh from her, outside. Then the sound of a closing door, and of a carriage driving away.*

> [MELLER *comes hastening into the room and goes quickly up to the chair.*

MELLER. Sir ! [*Louder.*] Sir ! [*He touches the shoulder, then shakes it slightly.*] Bed-time, sir !

> [*He bends down, listens ; stands up abruptly and beckons to* MOLLY *in the doorway. The girl comes quickly.*

MELLER. [*Sharply*] That gentleman's right. He's not breathing. Feel his forehead !   [*The girl, feeling it, draws her hand away sharply.*

MOLLY. Oh ! Ut's cold as ice. Oh ! no ! Shure, an' he's niver—— !

MELLER. [*With his hand on the old man's pulse, in an awed voice*] Gone !

MOLLY. Mother o' Jasus ! The grand old fightin' gintleman ! The great old sinner he was !

The curtain falls.

THE SHOW

PRODUCED AT THE ST. MARTIN'S THEATRE,
JULY 1st, 1925

CAST

ANNE MORECOMBE . . .	*Miss Molly Kerr*
A MAID	*Miss Eileen Sharp*
A DETECTIVE	*Mr. Leslie Banks*
A DIVISIONAL SURGEON . .	*Mr. Marcus Barron*
A CONSTABLE (ACT I) . .	*Mr. Bryan Powley*
A COOK	*Miss Una O'Connor*
DAISY ODIHAM . . .	*Miss Hermione Baddeley*
A REPORTER	*Mr. Clifford Mollison*
COLONEL ROLAND . . .	*Mr. Felix Aylmer*
GEOFFREY DARREL . . .	*Mr. Ian Hunter*
AN EDITOR	*Mr. Aubrey Mather*
A SECRETARY	*Miss Ethne Honan*
A NEWS EDITOR . . .	*Mr. Eliot Makeham*
LADY MORECOMBE . . .	*Miss Haidee Wright*
MR. ODIHAM	*Mr. Ben Field*
A CORONER'S CLERK . .	*Mr. Lawrence Baskcomb*
A LADY	*Miss Mary Forbes*
AN OFFICER OF THE AIR MINISTRY	*Mr. Eliot Makeham*
THREE LADIES	*Mesdames Una O'Connor, Vane, and Valerie Taylor*
A CONSTABLE (ACT III) . .	*Mr. Aubrey Mather*
LIEUT. OSWALD, R.N . .	*Mr. Robert Harris*
FOREMAN OF THE JURY . .	*Mr. Bryan Powley*
THE CORONER'S JURY . .	*Messrs. Robert Drysdale, A. G. Poulton, Marcus Barron, Carleton Hobbs, Ivor Barnard, Ian O. Will, and Malcolm Rignold*
PRESS ASSOCIATION REPORTER .	*Mr. Vere Bennett*

Produced by BASIL DEAN.

ACT I

*It is ten o'clock on a March morning.   The study of a house in Kensington is
empty and curtained, but narrow streaks of daylight come in between the
window-curtains of the two windows, Back.   A low-backed armchair
is drawn up to the fireplace, Right.   There is a door below the fireplace,
and another opposite to it, Left.   A bureau stands over on the left.   On
it is a telephone.   On a stool by the armchair is a tray with a decanter
of brandy, a syphon, and a glass.   The room is tastefully enough
apparelled, and there is a bookcase between the windows.   A small
model of a flying-machine stands on the top of it.*

> [*The door on the right is opened, and* ANNE MORECOMBE *comes in ;
> about twenty-five years old, dark, very pale, with an excellent
> figure and a reticent beauty.   She turns up the light, stands
> gazing at the armchair, shudders, passes swiftly across the room,
> locks the door, Left, and takes up the receiver of the telephone.*

ANNE. Chelsea 0012. . . . Is that—is that you, Geof ?—Anne
speaking. [*Her voice is low, quick and tense.*] An awful thing's happened.
Colin has shot himself. . . . Yes . . . through the heart . . . last
night. . . . When I got in from you, I found him here in the study in
—his—armchair—dead.   The doctor said about two hours. . . .
Yes, the police came. . . . No, no doubt—no.   The pistol was still
in his hand—his own. . . . Us. . . . No, no !   He didn't know—I'm
sure not.   And if he had, he wouldn't have cared.   You know he
wouldn't. . . . No !   I can't conceive—I don't know anything of
his affairs—no more than he knew of mine——

> [*She hears a sound, swiftly replaces the receiver, swiftly unlocks the
> door, and recrosses to the door, Right, just as the door Left is
> opened and a* MAID *enters, saying :*

MAID. This is the room, sir.

> [*Two* MEN *enter.   One is a Detective in plain clothes with a valise,
> the other a Divisional Surgeon of Police.*

DETECTIVE. Mrs. Morecombe ?

ANNE. Yes.

DETECTIVE. I'm Detective-Inspector Flayne from Scotland Yard.
The Superintendent sent me round.   The Divisional Surgeon, ma'am.
He was away last night.   I'd like him to see the body before it's
removed.

ANNE. This way.

DETECTIVE. One moment. This is the chair ? Nothing's been touched since the police were here last night ?

ANNE. No. Not since they took him upstairs.

DETECTIVE. [*Referring to a note, sitting down in the chair, head forward, right hand on lap*] Is that right, ma'am ?

ANNE. [*In a whisper*] Yes.

DETECTIVE. [*Touching his own chest*] The clothes were undone here, I believe ?

ANNE. Yes.

DETECTIVE. [*Nodding to the surgeon, and rising*] The Superintendent tells me they went carefully through everything in this room last night. I have the Major's papers here. [*Lifts the valise.*] Is there anything upstairs, ma'am, I ought to have ?

ANNE. I don't think so. He kept everything here.

DETECTIVE. We'll just go up, if you'll kindly take us. Excuse me, you were down here to—— ?

ANNE. I was telephoning.

DETECTIVE. I see. If you'll take the doctor up, I'll come in a minute.

[ANNE *goes out, followed by the* SURGEON, *who has eyed her keenly.*]

[*The* DETECTIVE *draws the curtains of one window fully back, and looks out, then round the room. The telephone bell rings. He takes up the receiver and listens.*]

DETECTIVE. Who's speaking ? [*There is instant cessation as if he had been cut off.*] Um ! Wrong number, or was mine the wrong voice ? [*He replaces the receiver ; stands a moment considering, then goes to the door, Left, and opens it.*] Simpson ?   [A CONSTABLE *in uniform appears.*] You were on duty last night, this beat ?

CONSTABLE. Yes, sir.

DETECTIVE. You didn't hear this shot ? [*Referring to his notes.*] The doctor puts his death at about nine, I see.

CONSTABLE. No, sir, I didn't.

DETECTIVE. See anybody come out of this house ?

CONSTABLE. No, sir. I saw the lady come in.

DETECTIVE. What time ?

CONSTABLE. Half-past ten, sir, I should say

DETECTIVE. [*Referring to his notes*] Alone ?

CONSTABLE. Yes, sir.

DETECTIVE. How did you come to notice her ?

CONSTABLE. I know her pretty well. She parted from a gentleman half-way up the street, round the corner.

DETECTIVE. Oh ! Do you know him ?

CONSTABLE. No, sir, I don't know him ; but it's not the first time, by many.

DETECTIVE. Then you'd know him if you saw him? [*Receiving a nod.*] What's he like?

CONSTABLE. Tallish young man with a soft hat.

> [DETECTIVE, *after a moment's reflection, goes to the telephone and looks at the number on it.*

DETECTIVE. [*Taking up receiver*] Exchange. This house has just been rung up and the call was cut off somehow. . . . Oh! They're still waiting—just put me back. . . . Hallo! What number is that? . . . Chelsea 0012. Thank you! [*He replaces the receiver and jots the number down. To the* CONSTABLE.] Take my card, and this number, find out to what name and address it belongs, and bring it back to me at once. Send that maid in here.

CONSTABLE. Yes, sir.   [*He goes out.*

> [*The* DETECTIVE *crosses the room, takes up the glass by its base and examines the rim for finger-marks. The* MAID *comes in.*

MAID. Yes, sir?

DETECTIVE. Ah! you. Name?

MAID. Ellen Frost.

DETECTIVE. No one's touched this, of course?

MAID. Oh, no!

DETECTIVE. When did Major Morecombe come in last night?

MAID. About eight, sir.

DETECTIVE. How d'you know?

MAID. I saw him coming from the gate. He called down that he'd had dinner.

DETECTIVE. Oh! What sort of voice?

MAID. Just his usual, sir.

DETECTIVE. Did you bring him this brandy?

MAID. Yes. He rang for it about half-past eight. He was finishing a letter—he gave it to me to post at once.

DETECTIVE. A letter? Who to?

MAID. I didn't notice, sir. I just went out with it and dropped it in the box, and brought up the brandy. Then he was sitting in that chair.

DETECTIVE. How did he look?

MAID. Very quiet-like—had his head on his hand—like this.

> [*Places her hand to her forehead.*

DETECTIVE. Said nothing?

MAID. No, sir.

DETECTIVE. How much brandy should you say he drank?

MAID. [*Scrutinizing decanter*] A good deal, sir.

DETECTIVE. Half a tumbler?

MAID. About that, I should think.

DETECTIVE. [*Taking a revolver from the valise*] Do you know this?

MAID. [*Wincing*] Yes, I think so. He used to keep it in the bureau drawer.

DETECTIVE. You didn't see it when you brought the brandy up ?

MAID. No, sir.

DETECTIVE. Did you see him again alive ?

MAID. [*Upset*] No, sir.

DETECTIVE. Did you hear the shot ?

MAID. Well, sir, I did seem to hear a sound when the gramophone was singing " Butter me 'eart, Charlie." I don't know If you know it, it's rather a loud song.

DETECTIVE. Where were you ?

MAID. In the kitchen—[*Pointing Stage Left*]—that's in the basement, below the drawing-room. It was just before our supper.

DETECTIVE. What time ?

MAID. About nine it would be.

DETECTIVE. But what you heard didn't bring you up ?

MAID. Well, I didn't rightly think it was in the house at all like.

DETECTIVE. How long have you been here ?

MAID. Ever since they were married and come to this house, sir. Four years now.

DETECTIVE. [*Referring to his notes*] They didn't sleep in the same room, I see.

MAID. No, sir.

DETECTIVE. How long's that been going on ?

MAID. It must be—a year, or fifteen months, about, that the Major's been on the top floor.

DETECTIVE. They weren't on terms, then ? [*The* MAID *hesitates.*] Better be quite frank.

MAID. There was never any words, sir.

DETECTIVE. Come ! Were they living together ? You know what I mean.

MAID. No, sir, they weren't ; at least as far as I know.

DETECTIVE. And hadn't been, for a long time ?

MAID. No.

DETECTIVE. They went out separately a good deal ?

MAID. Yes.

DETECTIVE. Mrs. Morecombe was out last night ?

MAID. Yes ; I let her in at half-past ten.

DETECTIVE. I see. The Major a violent man ?

MAID. Oh ! no, sir. Very depressed at times.

DETECTIVE. How d'you mean ?

MAID. I hardly know. He seemed to come to an end, like.

DETECTIVE. Hold his head in his hands—that sort of thing ?

MAID. Yes.

DETECTIVE. Distinguished flying man in the war, I believe ?

MAID. Oh! yes, sir. He was a hero.

DETECTIVE. H'm! There were others. Did he get many letters?

MAID. I don't know what you'd call many—six or seven a day, perhaps.

DETECTIVE. Any money pressure that you know of, eh?

MAID. Oh! no, sir; I'm sure there wasn't.

DETECTIVE. What makes you sure?

MAID. Well, I've never heard money mentioned, 'ardly.

DETECTIVE. Not much talk between them at all, eh?

MAID. No, that's true. Still, you know what money is. If there's money trouble, you're bound to hear of it.

DETECTIVE. That's right. Which did you like best—the Major or Mrs. Morecombe?

MAID. Oh! well, sir, I like them both very much. The poor Major.

DETECTIVE. Ah! Sad thing—very! So you like Mrs. Morecombe, too?

MAID. I *do.*

DETECTIVE. What's her family?

MAID. I think there's only her father, old Colonel Roland.

DETECTIVE. Still in the Service?

MAID. Oh! no; he's too old—near seventy, I should think.

DETECTIVE. No brothers?

MAID. No, sir. She was an only child, I believe.

DETECTIVE. [*Suddenly*] Some reason for the Major and her being estranged. What was it?

MAID. I couldn't tell you, really.

DETECTIVE. How d'you mean—couldn't?

MAID. Well, I don't know.

DETECTIVE. Come! A love affair, eh?

MAID. [*Flustered*] Really, I can't tell you—I've never seen anything.

DETECTIVE. Yes, but straws show the way the wind blows.

MAID. [*Suddenly resolute*] I never saw any straws.

DETECTIVE. [*With a sharp look*] I see. Knows, but won't tell.

MAID. [*Flustered again*] No, sir, really; and it wasn't my business.

DETECTIVE. It's your business to tell what you know. We've got to find out why this happened; and you've got to help us. Come along with it! Here we have two young people who haven't lived together for fifteen months, you say. Well, that means that one or other of them, or both, was friendly with someone else. Now doesn't it?

MAID. [*Stubbornly*] Not knowing, I can't say.

DETECTIVE. Very well. Who came here calling? While I go upstairs, sit down and write the names down, and mind you don't leave any out.

28

MAID. No, sir.   [*He goes out by the door, Right.*
    [*She sits down at the bureau : and, sucking a pencil, writes down name
    after name, as they occur to her. The door Left is thrown open,
    and the* COOK, *an older woman, appears.*
COOK. Here's a young woman—I can't keep her out.
    [DAISY ODIHAM *passes her and comes in : pretty, soft, distracted.
    The* MAID *has started up, the* COOK *hangs, as it were, in the
    doorway.*
DAISY. [*Quite abandoned to emotion—not a very educated voice*] It's not true
—it's not true, is it ? Say it's not true ! Not dead—I mean ; not *dead ?*
MAID. [*Affected*] Yes, it's true enough.
DAISY. Oh, God ! Oh, God !
    [*She sinks down in the chair, burying her forehead against the bureau
    and rocking her body. The* COOK *crosses to the brandy, pours
    out some and brings it to her.*
COOK. Here, drink some of this. Who are you, my dear ?
                        [*The* GIRL, *after repulsing it, drinks.*
DAISY. [*Throwing up her head*] What's it matter who I am ? I'm
nobody—Oh, God ! [*Suddenly.*] Didn't he leave a word for me ?
Not a word ? Nothing ?
MAID. I don't know ; I'll ask them if you'll tell me your name.
DAISY. Oh ! no ; what does it matter—if he's dead ? Leave me
alone. I'm going.
COOK. You're not going to do anything rash ?
DAISY. [*Still wild*] Rash ? I couldn't see him, could I ?
MAID. Mrs. Morecombe's up there, with the police.
DAISY. Oh ! I'm going—I'm going ! [*Suddenly calmer—almost
hard.*] It's all right—thank you.
    [*She puts aside the* COOK's *hand and walks out, with the back of her
    hand over her face ; the* MAIDS *staring after her.*
COOK. Poor thing ! [*Coming in a little.*] I say—d'you think she's the
skeleton in the cupboard ?
MAID. [*Still much upset*] And they worrying me with their questions !
What am I to say to them now ?
COOK. That girl ought to be follered. She might throw herself
in the river.
    [*Suddenly they see that a* YOUNG MAN *is standing in the doorway,
    a nice-looking young newspaper reporter.*
REPORTER. It's all right. She *is* being followed. Don't be
alarmed. She left the front door open, so I came in to tell you that
my friend won't lose sight of her. [*Looking at their hostile faces.*] I'm
afraid I'm giving you trouble. [*He goes close to the* MAID *and tries to
place a note in her hand.*] So sorry !
MAID. [*Rejecting the note*] No ; I don't know who you are or what
business you've got here.

REPORTER. [*With an engaging smile*] Oh! of course, if you feel like that. But it's quite all right. I'm from *The Evening Sun.*

COOK. Oh! That's the one that's " Bright and Early "—ain't it? What does it want here?

REPORTER. Well, you can imagine—this is tremendously interesting to the public. Major Morecombe was a real war hero; everybody remembers that flight of his into Germany. So this is the room? That the chair? [*He crosses.*] No blood, I see.

[*He is swiftly touring the room.*

MAID. Excuse me, I think I'll tell the Inspector you're here, and you can ask him any questions you want. [*To* COOK, *sotto voce.*] Watch it!   [*She goes out, Right.*

REPORTER. [*To* COOK] I say, before they come—*you* know all the ins and outs. Do tell me your theory?

COOK. [*Dryly*] Not me. I don't want none of your questions—this is a private house.

REPORTER. [*Hurt*] It's not idle curiosity. Men like Major More-combe can't shoot themselves without intriguing the public.

COOK. Well, I don't hold with the papers. If I put my head under the gas, I can do very well without any fuss.

REPORTER. But you'd get it.

COOK. Well, I'm not goin' to oblige, yet, nor 'elp you make a show of the poor Major neither. Let him rest in peace.

REPORTER. Unfortunately, it's my job not to.

COOK. Then I'd get another if I was you.

REPORTER. Easily said, I'm afraid.

[*He stands dignified and still as the* DETECTIVE *enters. The* COOK, *who is close to the door, Left, lingers.*

REPORTER. [*Handing a card to the* DETECTIVE] Can you give me any information?

DETECTIVE. None at present. There'll be an inquest.

REPORTER. Can I say anything?

DETECTIVE. [*With a faint smile*] You may say " the police have the matter in hand."

[*The* CONSTABLE *enters, and goes up to the* DETECTIVE.

CONSTABLE. Name and address of that number, sir.

DETECTIVE. Thank you.   [*The* REPORTER *has pricked his ears.*

REPORTER. Any development, Inspector?

DETECTIVE. No; and not likely to be, so long as you take up my time.

REPORTER. Sorry, Inspector. Then I'll say good-bye for the present.

DETECTIVE. I should.

COOK. Shall I show him out?   [*The* DETECTIVE *nods.*

REPORTER. [*With a smile*] Coldly received. Good morning.

[*He goes out, Left, followed by the* COOK.

DETECTIVE. Confound these fellers—like flies, the way they buzz round a carcase. [*Consulting the bit of paper given him.*] You'll come with me and identify this gentleman, Simpson.

CONSTABLE. Very good, sir.

[*He goes out at a nod from the* DETECTIVE.

[*The* DETECTIVE *goes over to the bureau and takes up the list of names the* MAID *has written down. He compares it with the name given him by the* CONSTABLE, *and rings the bell. The* MAID *enters.*

DETECTIVE. These all you can think of?

MAID. No, sir. I was interrupted. There might be a few others.

DETECTIVE. [*With a sharp look, showing her the paper given him by the* CONSTABLE] Doesn't that gentleman come here?

MAID. [*Disconcerted*] He—he has been, sir; but not for a long time now.

DETECTIVE. Friend of Mrs. Morecombe. Come—the truth!

MAID. I—I think so, sir.

DETECTIVE. Friend of the Major's, too? [*The* MAID *hesitates.*] You needn't answer, that's quite enough. There was a row over him —some time back?

MAID. No, sir—at least, I never——

DETECTIVE. How do you account for his ceasing to come, then?

MAID. I'm sure I don't know; perhaps he's got other things to do.

DETECTIVE. How long since he came?

MAID. About a year, I think.

DETECTIVE. Exactly; and the Major went upstairs fifteen months ago. Now, about that letter you posted. You *can't* remember who it was to?

MAID. No, sir; I never read the address.

DETECTIVE. Sure? There's nothing to be ashamed of.

MAID. I'm not ashamed, because I didn't read it.

DETECTIVE. Well now—keep my questions to yourself—see?

MAID. [*With quivering lips*] Y-yes, sir.

DETECTIVE. [*As the* SURGEON *and* ANNE *come in*] You can go now.

[*The* MAID *goes, Left.*

SURGEON. I must be going on, Inspector. The barrel was carefully adjusted and resting against the bare skin; death instantaneous. Quite satisfied with Dr. Mackay's report; nothing to indicate he's got the time wrong. So far as one can judge as yet, and from what this lady says, he was quite a healthy subject. Good day, madam.

DETECTIVE. The inquest will be the day after to-morrow, sir. I'll be taking [*Lowering his voice*] the body round to the mortuary before lunch.

SURGEON. Quite. Good morning. [*He goes out, Left.*

DETECTIVE. Sit down, madam—you must be worn out. I just

want to ask you a question or two. [ANNE *remains standing.*] Now, can you tell me why this happened ?

ANNE. [*With a quick little negative movement*] No, I can't. I can't.

DETECTIVE. Both the doctors seem agreed there was no disease. What do you say to that ?

ANNE. Oh ! None, I'm sure.

DETECTIVE. And no money troubles ?

ANNE. No.

DETECTIVE. Comfortably off, eh ?

ANNE. Yes, both of us.

DETECTIVE. Now, ma'am—we have to know everything—why were you and the Major on distant terms ?

ANNE. We weren't on bad terms at all.

DETECTIVE. Were you husband and wife ?

ANNE. Not in one sense.

DETECTIVE. Excuse me, there must have been some reason for that.

ANNE. Only that we agreed not to be, some time ago.

DETECTIVE. Did that suggestion emanate from you or from your husband ?

ANNE. From—from him first.

DETECTIVE. Oh ! from him ! And you didn't object ?

ANNE. No.

DETECTIVE. Now you see, the question is : Why did the Major take his life ? The Coroner'll want to know how to direct the Jury. Was it insanity, or was there a good reason ?

ANNE. What does it matter ? Nothing will bring him back.

DETECTIVE. Well, that's a way of looking at it, but it's not customary. A violent death like this has to be gone into. When exactly did you agree to go your own ways ?

ANNE. The Christmas before last.

DETECTIVE. Fifteen months. And you won't give me a reason ?

ANNE. You must excuse me.

DETECTIVE. [*Dryly*] Very well, ma'am. It would be better for you to be frank, but please yourself. Am I to take it that you know of nothing that should make your husband take his life ?

ANNE. No—unless——

DETECTIVE. [*Intrigued*] Yes ?

ANNE. Unless it was in a fit of black depression. He was very moody.

DETECTIVE. [*Disappointed*] Oh ! Come ! Had he ever threatened to ?

ANNE. Not to me.

DETECTIVE. It really is a pity, ma'am, that you can't give me a better reason. It simply means we've got to look for one.

ANNE. I don't know anything about my husband's private affairs.

DETECTIVE. But you know your own, ma'am.

ANNE. [*After a pause*] What do you mean ?

DETECTIVE. Most of us have them.

ANNE. It sounded insulting.

DETECTIVE. [*A little harder*] You came in at ten-thirty, I believe, last night ?

ANNE. Yes.

DETECTIVE. What time had you gone out ?

ANNE. At six o'clock.

DETECTIVE. And between those hours ?

ANNE. [*After a pause*] No, Inspector, I object to being asked questions that have no bearing on this.　　　　[*She points to the armchair.*]

DETECTIVE. Madam, reservations in a case of this sort have the worst construction placed on them ; and rightly.

ANNE. I can't help that.

DETECTIVE. [*Looking at her with a sort of admiration*] Was your husband in last evening when you went out ?

ANNE. No.　He went out just before me.

DETECTIVE. Perhaps you can tell me at least if he knew where you were going ?

ANNE. He didn't.

DETECTIVE. How can you tell that ?

ANNE. I'm sure.

DETECTIVE. Would he have minded if he had known ?

ANNE. I—I don't think so.

DETECTIVE. I'm suggesting, you know, that he did happen to know, and that this [*Pointing to the chair*] was the result.

ANNE. No—oh ! no.

DETECTIVE. Well, ma'am, you're making it all very mysterious. We shall have to know where you were last night.

ANNE. [*Twisting her hands*] I tell you that where I was has no bearing on this.　If you persist, it won't help you.

DETECTIVE. I should consult your father, if I were you, ma'am, and follow his advice.　I'll be seeing you again before long. [*He looks at the bit of paper given him by the* CONSTABLE, *encloses it in his notebook, snaps that to, and goes towards the door, Left.*] For the present, madam.

[*He goes out.*

[ANNE, *left alone, twists her hands, clasps them on her breast, and looks restlessly about her.　She springs towards the telephone, but stops and shakes her head.　Then she rings the bell.　The* MAID *enters.*

ANNE. Has that man gone, Ellen ?

MAID. Yes, ma'am. [*Looking at her.*] They don't seem to have an idea of privacy. [*After a glance.*] He wanted to know who comes here. I had to write down all I could think of——　[*A little pause, and* ANNE *makes a movement with her hands*] in the last six months.

ANNE. [*Relieved*] Oh! yes; of course.

MAID. [*About to go, and turning*] Please, while you was upstairs—there was a—a young man too—from the Press. [*A bell rings.*] The front door, ma'am. You won't wish to see people, I suppose.

ANNE. Only my father—I'm expecting him.

[*The* MAID *goes out and returns immediately.*

MAID. It *is* Colonel Roland, ma'am.

[COLONEL ROLAND *follows her in and the* MAID *goes out. He is tall, grey, slightly bowed, Irish by birth, with a look as of a kindly Bengal tiger in his highly-coloured face. He goes straight up to his daughter and puts his hands on her shoulders.*

COL. ROLAND. My poor girl! This is a dreadful thing.

ANNE. [*Dully*] Yes, dad.

COL. ROLAND. Why, in the name of the Saints——?

ANNE. I don't know.

COL. ROLAND. Surely, my child——

ANNE. I don't, dad.

COL. ROLAND. To take his own life—with his record!

[*He looks at her searchingly; puzzled.*

ANNE. [*After a little pause*] I've never bothered you, dad, with our affairs, but Colin and I had been strangers for a long time.

COL. ROLAND. Strangers? How's that, Anne?

ANNE. The whole thing was a mistake, I'm afraid.

COL. ROLAND. [*Disturbed*] Well, well, I won't ask you any questions now. It hasn't been your fault, I know.

ANNE. Nor his.

COL. ROLAND. I'm glad to hear that; I liked Colin—I liked um. He was a fine fellow—for a flyin' man. Have the police been?

ANNE. Yes; and the Press.

COL. ROLAND. Confound them—they'll make a show of it, if they can. What do the police say?

ANNE. Only that they have to know everything for the inquest. They've taken all his papers.

COL. ROLAND. What's in them, Anne?

ANNE. I tell you, dad, I know no more of Colin than he knew of me.

COL. ROLAND. Of you? What should there be to know of you, my child?

ANNE. [*Lowering her head—suddenly*] Father, I don't know what's coming of this. But you must believe there was an absolute compact between us to go our own ways. If it hadn't been for you, we might have thought of a divorce; but I knew you'd hate it so.

COL. ROLAND. Divorce! Indeed, I would! Well, the poor fellow's gone! In his prime! Well—well! [*The* MAID *enters.*

MAID. Excuse me, ma'am. This young man again—from the newspaper.

Col. Roland. Tell um to go to ———! No. I'll tell um myself. [*He follows the* Maid *to the door, where he meets the* Reporter *coming in.*] Now then, sir, what is it you want?

Reporter. [*To* Anne] Mrs. Morecombe?

Col. Roland. Will you be good enough to understand that my daughter has just suffered a bereavement? This sort of intrusion is unwelcome.

Reporter. Colonel Roland, I believe? I'm extremely sorry, sir. It's very distasteful to me, too. But the Public——

Col. Roland. Damn the Public!

Anne. What is it you want to know?

Reporter. If you *could* tell me anything—about the Major's health for instance; or whether his new aeroplane design had been refused. He was such a distinguished man. Any news——

Anne. My husband's health was good; and I don't think he had even offered any design lately.

Reporter. [*Nervously*] Well, thank you, very much. Of course, that adds to the mystery, doesn't it?

Col. Roland. I'd be glad if you'd tell your paper, sir, to keep its nose out of people's private affairs.

Reporter. [*Pleasantly*] When you say private, you forget the inquest, don't you?

Col. Roland. I presume the inquest will be a decent quiet affair.

Reporter. Oh! do you, sir? I wonder!

Anne. Are you married?

Reporter. Yes.

Anne. If she committed suicide, would you like persons coming to ask you about her?

Reporter. Oh! But surely—a paper isn't an ordinary——

Col. Roland. No! It's a devilish sight worse.

Reporter. [*Ruefully*] Well, sir, really, we *have* to take notice when things like this happen. What do you suppose we're for?

Col. Roland. Good day to you.

> [*The* Reporter *hesitates a moment, then, with a murmured "*Good
> morning—so sorry!*" goes out.*

Anne. [*With a sudden breakdown of her composure, burying her face against her father's chest*] Oh! dad—it's horrible!

Col. Roland. There, there, my child! Don't think about it! Go and lie down. You must be half dead. I'll come back after lunch.

Anne. Yes, I *will* lie down. Good-bye, dad!

Col. Roland. [*Kissing her forehead*] Good-bye, my dear; bless you! Get a good sleep. [*He goes out.*

Anne. [*Stands a moment, considering, then goes to the telephone*] Give me Chelsea 0012. . . . [*A pause.*] Haven't you got that number? [*Pause.*] Ring them again, please. . . . [*Pause.*] No answer?

MAID. [*Entering*] You said you wouldn't see anyone, ma'am. But——

ANNE. Who is it ?

MAID. Mr. Darrel, ma'am.

ANNE. Oh ! [*Replacing the receiver, she stares hard at the* MAID, *who exhibits signs of confusion.*] I'll see him.

[*She clasps her hands. The* MAID *goes out, and returns ushering in* GEOFFREY DARREL, *a tall young man, very constrained, who the moment she has gone, darts forward to* ANNE *and kisses her.*

DARREL. My darling !

ANNE. Geof ! How could you come here ? You mustn't. I'd just rung you up again. We simply can't see each other till this is all over.

DARREL. It's awful for you—this ! I had to come. I couldn't stick it.

ANNE. Did you meet my father going away ?

DARREL. No—nobody.

ANNE. You mustn't stay. The Police—the Press. They want to find his motive. They'll drag up everything they can for the inquest.

DARREL. They don't know about us ?

ANNE. They suspect *something*. I'm terrified, for father's sake.

DARREL. My child, it's Nemesis. We ought to have gone off long ago.

ANNE. Oh ! Geof, I know ; I was wrong—I was wrong. Why didn't I face telling father ? But he's so old-fashioned, and a Catholic never——

DARREL. Thank Heaven you're free now !

ANNE. Last night—— [*Shuddering and pointing to the chair.*] I'd seen him at tea-time—he seemed just as usual. And yet, he must have known then what he was going to do. He looked——! Things came back.

DARREL. [*Jealously*] Anne !

ANNE. No, no ! Only it seemed so brutal. I was all warm coming from you. And he was so white and cold. The last thing I said to you—and he was dead when I said it.   [*Her lips quiver.*

DARREL. Don't, darling, don't !

ANNE. But *why—why* ? It's an utter mystery. If I thought it was because of us—but I'm sure—I'm sure it wasn't. I'm sure he never knew. Besides, I feel certain he had someone. Geof, you mustn't stay ! Quick ! Think ! What's best ?

DARREL. Abroad. Couldn't we go now ? *Must* you be at the inquest ?

ANNE. Of course ! I found him. Geof, suppose it comes out about us ?

DARREL. [*Suddenly—low*] Listen ! The bell !

28*

ANNE. [*Breathless*] Oh !   [*She moves to the door.*

[*The* MAID *comes in and stands staring at* DARREL.

MAID. [*Low*] It's the Detective again, ma'am.

ANNE. I can't see anyone just now.

MAID. Shall I say you're asleep, ma'am ? I don't think anything else'd stop him.

ANNE. Ask him to come again at twelve.

[*But as the* MAID *opens the door to go, the* DETECTIVE *enters, and shuts the door on her.*

DETECTIVE. Excuse me, madam. Mr. Geoffrey Darrel, I believe ?

DARREL. [*Startled*] Yes.

DETECTIVE. [*Showing* DARREL *his card*] I've been round to your rooms, sir. About this death of Major Morecombe—if you'll kindly answer a question or two.

DARREL. I ?

DETECTIVE. Where did you spend last evening ?

DARREL. At home. Why ?

DETECTIVE. Didn't go out ?

DARREL. I went out soon after ten for a bit.

DETECTIVE. Exactly ! You parted from Mrs. Morecombe close here about ten-twenty ?

DARREL. What ? How do you mean ?

DETECTIVE. Now, sir, don't prevaricate, please. The Constable on this beat saw you taking leave of her at that time. Was she with you at your rooms ?

DARREL. What right have you to ask these questions ?

DETECTIVE. I happen to be in charge of this case, sir.

DARREL. I've nothing on earth to do with this suicide, and I can't answer you.

DETECTIVE. It's known to us that you've often left this lady close to her house at night. You were with her last evening, and she telephoned to you this morning. It's further known that you used to be a caller here, and ceased to be a year ago. Now, sir, you received a letter from Major Morecombe this morning. . . .

DARREL. I did not.

DETECTIVE. Excuse me !

DARREL. I tell you I did *not*.

DETECTIVE. He wrote and posted one just before he committed suicide, and we want it.

DARREL. I give you my word of honour I received no such letter.

DETECTIVE. If you did not receive this letter, it will go far to show that your friendship with Mrs. Morecombe was not the cause of the Major's suicide. Do you mind emptying your pockets ? Now, sir, sensibly. If you haven't got it, it can't do you any harm.

[DARREL *empties his pockets. The* DETECTIVE *glances at the letters.*]

As a matter of form, sir. [*He runs his hands skilfully over* DARREL.]
Very good! I took the Constable round to your place, and he
identified you by a photograph.

DARREL. What! You broke in?

DETECTIVE. [*With a smile*] You see, I didn't know when I'd get
you, and I've no time to waste.

DARREL. This is an outrage!

DETECTIVE. Well, not exactly, sir; no. There's just one thing I
brought away that I'd like you to open for me. [*He goes to the door
and calls :*] Simpson!

      [*The* CONSTABLE *appears with a locked japanned box.*

DARREL. This is abominable!

DETECTIVE. [*Taking the box—to* CONSTABLE] This *is* the gentleman?

CONSTABLE. Yes, sir.

DETECTIVE. That'll do, then!   [*The* CONSTABLE *goes out.*

DARREL. Give me that box.

DETECTIVE. Yes, sir; I want you to open it.

DARREL. I shall do nothing of the sort.

DETECTIVE. Then I must force the lock.

DARREL .[*At his wits' end*] Look here, this is a horrible business for
everyone. Surely you don't want to make it worse? I've given you
my solemn word.

DETECTIVE. A gentleman will always give that, sir, to save a lady.
Kindly unlock it.   [*Holds out the box.*

DARREL. My friendship for Mrs. Morecombe has nothing to do
with this suicide. Major Morecombe didn't know of it; if he had,
he wouldn't have cared—they were quite apart.

DETECTIVE. Exactly; and if you'll excuse me, I think you're the
reason of that.

DARREL. I am *not*.

DETECTIVE. Then what is?

DARREL. I don't know.

DETECTIVE. In my opinion, the letter I want will tell us.

DARREL. [*Passionately*] I have had no letter.

DETECTIVE. We shall see that.

DARREL. [*Seizing the box*] Shall we?

  [*But as he speaks* ANNE *comes from where she has been standing,
   motionless.*

ANNE. [*Very calmly to the* DETECTIVE] That's enough. You are
quite right. We are lovers. *The* DETECTIVE *makes her a little bow.*]
But you'll serve no purpose by making that public; you'll only cause
my father great sorrow. Isn't it all painful enough without?

DETECTIVE. [*Uncomfortable*] That's as may be, ma'am. But a
matter like this has to be cleared up.

ANNE. Why?

DETECTIVE. The law takes no account of privacy when a thing like this happens.

DARREL. The law ! It's got no guts.

DETECTIVE. Very sensibly said, sir. Kindly open this box.

DARREL. It contains nothing but private letters from this lady to me.

DETECTIVE. Well, we'll just confirm that.

ANNE. Open it, Geof.

DETECTIVE. That's right, ma'am ; in view of your admission, there's every chance we shan't need them. They shall be kept under seal, and returned.

[DARREL, *taking a key from his watch-chain, opens the little box.
The* DETECTIVE *takes out a packet of letters. From the first
he takes a dried flower and puts it carefully back into the box.
The* TWO LOVERS *have unconsciously clasped hands, watching
the* DETECTIVE *rapidly turning over letter after letter to see
that they are all in the same handwriting.*

DETECTIVE. All correct, sir. You'd like to seal them up yourself, no doubt.

[DARREL *has wrenched his hand from* ANNE'S, *and covered his eyes.
She goes to the bureau and taking a large envelope hands it to the*
DETECTIVE, *who puts the letters in and closes it.*

DARREL. Why do you take them, if you're not going to use them ?

DETECTIVE. Well, sir, we shan't use them unless Mrs. Morecombe contradicts the statement she made just now. To have them will remove that temptation. You shall have them back, sir, just as they are, if you'll put your seal on them.

[*He lays the envelope on the bureau.* DARREL *seals it.*

DARREL. Will you let me attend the inquest instead of her ?

DETECTIVE. [*Placing the envelope in his breast pocket*] Out of the question, sir. [*Points to the chair.*] She found the body.

DARREL. The whole thing's inhuman.

DETECTIVE. Well, sir, there it is. . . . Off the carpet, and you never know where you'll land. But you can trust me.

DARREL. Will you give me your card, please ?

[*The* DETECTIVE *hands him a card, and the little box, empty of all
except the flower.*

DETECTIVE. You persist in saying you got no letter from Major Morecombe this morning, sir ?

DARREL. Yes.

DETECTIVE. Well, I hope we shall get hold of it. [*Looking at his
face intently.*] And I sincerely trust we shan't need——

[ANNE *moves a step, looking at him.*]
[*With a gesture of discomfort.*] My duty, ma'am.

[*He goes out. The door is shut.*
[*The* TWO LOVERS *stand side by side without a word.*

DARREL. [*Suddenly*] What could I have done?

ANNE. [*Taking his hand*] Nothing, Geof. Don't look like that. It's just fatality. I must tell father now. How horrible for him, how horrible! He'll never understand!

DARREL. Wait, darling. There's always a chance. This letter——

ANNE. He gave one to Ellen to post, it seems, just before——

DARREL. You say he had someone?

ANNE. But who? We never asked each other anything. That was agreed. The letter may have been to his mother, of course.

[*There is a knock. The door is opened by the* REPORTER.

REPORTER. Could I speak to you again for just one minute, Mrs. Morecombe? I'm afraid I must seem very intrusive——

ANNE. Yes. [*The* REPORTER *stands embarrassed, looking from one to the other.*] Well?

REPORTER. It's just this. Did you know that a young woman came to your house this morning, in a state of great distress?

ANNE. A young——! [*She and* DARREL *exchange a glance.*] No.

REPORTER. Perhaps it may throw some light—— [*He has noted their glance, and looks from one to the other.*] Luckily I had a friend, who followed her.

ANNE. [*Suddenly*] Are you going to drag another wretched woman into this?

REPORTER. [*Nonplussed*] Well, you see, she was in such a state.

ANNE. Do you want to make it worse?

REPORTER. No, indeed! Only, of course—— Then you *can't* tell me anything about her?

ANNE. I know nothing of her.

REPORTER. Thank you very much. That simplifies things, anyway. I wanted to be sure. I'm very much obliged to you. Good morning.

ANNE. [*Suddenly*] My husband has a mother, to whom he was a hero.

REPORTER. Oh! Could you give me her address?

ANNE. She's in the country. She must be broken-hearted. She adored him. Don't you realize?

REPORTER. Yes, indeed. It's a terrible drama.

DARREL. [*Grimly*] Perhaps you'd like to ask why *I'm* here?

REPORTER. Oh! no, thank you. I can—er—imagine.

[*He goes out.*

DARREL. My God!   [ANNE *is standing motionless.*

The curtain falls.

ACT II

SCENE I

The Editor's room, at the offices of " The Evening Sun," on the following morning. The room, moderately snug, is longish and narrow, the windows at the back have a view of Fleet Street. Right, Forward, there is a door. A large bureau stands between the windows. Left, is a fireplace.

> [*The* EDITOR *is sitting at the bureau with his back to the fireplace. He is about fifty, short, with an involuted and ironical face and quick eyes. He is dictating to his secretary, a fresh-faced girl.*

EDITOR. " The object is good, of course ; but in order to strike a note with the public, a much bigger name is required." Umm ! it's a pity—the really valuable names are in prison. Whom do you suggest, Miss Price ? [*Checking her at the first movement of her lips.*] No, no ! *Not* a novelist—the public are fed up with novelists. Isn't there a cleric ?

SECRETARY. Well, of course, there's——

EDITOR. Oh ! Not him ! These humanitarian stunts depend on a touch of novelty. How about a judge. Well—it doesn't press. I want to see the News Editor.

SECRETARY. Yes, Mr. Eagles ; he's waiting. [*Goes to the door and says :*] Will you come in, Mr. Kenting ?

> [*The* NEWS EDITOR *enters : he is of a brisk, rather sandy type, with a short-clipped moustache, and a pipe in his hand.*

EDITOR. Morning, Kenting. [*He takes up a copy of yesterday's issue.*] That'll do, Miss Price. [*She goes out, with a pile of finished letters.* Look here ! Who passed this paragraph on the Morecombe suicide —about a young woman calling at the house in a state of distress ?

NEWS ED. I did.

EDITOR. I don't like it.

NEWS ED. What's wrong ?

EDITOR. Suggestive.

NEWS ED. *He* can't bring a libel action—poor chap.

EDITOR. No ; but we shall have the police round about it.

NEWS ED. Well, it's all to our credit ; they wouldn't have got hold of it without.

EDITOR. Yes ; but this thing is *sub judice*.

NEWS ED. Not yet.

EDITOR. That's all very well, Kenting, but you can't be too careful. Who was the reporter ?

NEWS ED. Young Forman's on it. He's a very decent chap— there's no name given. I've got to get news. This Morecombe suicide is bound to make a stir. He bombed farther into Germany than any flying man we had.

EDITOR. Exactly ! But this is going to hurt his people.

NEWS ED. Well ! Forman says the police are running *Mrs.* Morecombe's private life.

EDITOR. Oh ! When's the inquest ?

NEWS ED. To-morrow.   [*The* SECRETARY *enters with a card.*

EDITOR. [*After glancing at it, makes a face, and hands it to* KENTING] Here we are, you see.

NEWS ED. [*Reading*] *Lady* Morecombe. Who's that—his mother ?

EDITOR. Show her in, Miss Price. This is up to you, Kenting.

> [*They stand at attention.* LADY MORECOMBE *is a little grey-haired lady in black, wiry and of a Highland type. The contrast between her little figure and the tall form of* COLONEL ROLAND, *who accompanies her, is striking.*

LADY M. Give me that paper, Colonel Roland. [*Taking a newspaper from* COLONEL ROLAND'S *hand.*] Are you the editor ?

EDITOR. Yes.

LADY M. [*With intense suppressed feeling*] Why do you put this about my son ?

EDITOR. We were just discussing that, Lady Morecombe. This is the news editor, Mr. Kenting.

LADY M. Is it you who are responsible ?

NEWS ED. I passed it. What do you object to, ma'am ? It's a fact.

LADY M. " A young woman in great distress " ! It suggests— suggests—— ! I was in the country when I had this awful news. I come up ; and this is the first thing I see.

NEWS ED. It's quite vague—no name—might be anyone.

LADY M. Don't you know people better than that ? The worst construction, of course, will be put.

NEWS ED. Very sorry if it hurts you, Lady Morecombe ; but you don't realize, I'm afraid, that an inquest makes everything public. We're merely helping to get at the truth as quickly as possible.

LADY M. The truth ? What is that to you ?

EDITOR. Immense subject, that, Lady Morecombe. The Press is the chief safeguard against injustice of all sorts. Secret inquiries are to no one's interest in the long run.

LADY M. [*With passion*] That is cant. You want to sell your paper.

And because of that, my son, who can't defend himself, is to be blackened—his affairs hawked about on the street.

EDITOR. [*With a sort of dignity*] It's hardly as simple as that. We do want to sell our paper, of course. A Press that doesn't pay its way, can't live. But if there's a villain in the piece, it's the Public, Lady Morecombe—not us.

LADY M. Will you contradict this paragraph!

EDITOR. I appreciate your feelings, but I assure you it would serve no purpose. The inquest will bring out every circumstance, and more, that concerns your son's death.

LADY M. But for your meddling, this would never have been known.

EDITOR. [*Subtly*] You admit it, then?

LADY M. I admit nothing against my son; he was a hero.

EDITOR. Quite! But don't you want to know the reason of his suicide?

LADY M. It is known to God.

EDITOR. Ah! I'm afraid He will keep it to Himself. If no one else is to know, the blame may be wrongly assigned. I am told, for instance, that the police believe it to be due to Mrs. Morecombe's conduct.

COL. ROLAND. What?

EDITOR. I beg your pardon.

COL. ROLAND. That lady is my daughter, sir. Be good enough to explain yourself. [*The* EDITOR *looks at the* NEWS EDITOR.

NEWS ED. You'll find that the police are following a clue in that direction.

COL. ROLAND. What devil's gossip's this? Speak out!

NEWS ED. Entirely in confidence—that is the line they're going on. Our reporter——

COL. ROLAND. Ah! What d'you mean by sending people to meddle with private affairs?

NEWS ED. [*Angrily*] That's not the way to——

EDITOR. One moment, Kenting. [*He sounds a bell.*] Forman, you said? [KENTING *nods sullenly. The* SECRETARY *has appeared.*

EDITOR. Miss Price, if Mr. Forman's in, ask him to come here.
[*She goes.*

EDITOR. Now, excuse me, all this is very human, but we should be glad of civility. It's often very difficult to decide between private susceptibilities and our duty to the Public.

COL. ROLAND. What concern is it of the Public? What business have you to feed their confounded curiosity? Thank God, there's a law of libel!

NEWS ED. Yes; but it won't lie against the police. *We* haven't said anything about your daughter.

EDITOR. This shows you, Lady Morecombe, how important it is that everything should be known, if the real truth is to come out.

[*Before* LADY MORECOMBE *can answer, the* REPORTER *enters.*

EDITOR. Mr. Forman, I understand you have the Morecombe case in hand. Here are Major Morecombe's mother and Mrs. Morecombe's father.

REPORTER. Yes, sir.   [*He bows.*

COL. ROLAND. What have you been saying about my daughter?

REPORTER. [*Uneasy*] Well, sir, after I saw you, I had a question to put to Mrs. Morecombe about the young woman who came there yesterday morning——

LADY M. [*Breaking in*] It's you, then, who are responsible for this calumny on my son?

REPORTER. [*With a glance at* KENTING] Really, I simply carry out my orders.

COL. ROLAND. What did you tell your chief about my daughter?

REPORTER. Merely what I gathered from my own observation. There's nothing about that in the paper.

LADY M. Why did you invent that lie about this woman?

REPORTER. [*Angry*] Lie! She was Major Morecombe's mistress, by her own account.

LADY M. [*Mastering herself again*] If she was, what has that to do with his death?

NEWS ED. That, I take it, will be for the Jury.

LADY M. Will you give me her address, please?

REPORTER. [*To the* EDITOR] Am I to give it, sir?

EDITOR. Yes.

REPORTER. Miss Odiham, 48, Burdells Buildings, Fulham.

LADY M. [*Writing it down*] Are you coming, Colonel Roland?

COL. ROLAND. Just a moment. [*To* EDITOR.] Do I understand, sir, that your paper will make no further allusion to this death except to report the inquest?

EDITOR. [*After a moment's pause*] To give you that assurance would be to admit my paper in the wrong, which I am far from doing. I must be guided by events.

LADY M. It's ghoulish—ghoulish!   [*She turns and goes out.*

COL. ROLAND. You had better give me that assurance.

EDITOR. No, sir. The Press is not to be abused and hectored in this manner.

COL. ROLAND. Very well. I shall go straight to my lawyers.

[*He follows* LADY MORECOMBE *out.*

EDITOR. This'll never do. If they get hold of the girl and spirit her away, we shan't be able to substantiate our paragraph. We must keep the whip hand. Mr. Forman, cut off at once and get her away yourself.

REPORTER. If I can, sir. [*He goes out.*

EDITOR. What a little tigress ! And that old Irish-Indian !

NEWS ED. Peppery devil !

EDITOR. They seem to think one *wants* to hurt their feelings.

[*The* SECRETARY *enters.*

SECRETARY. Detective-Inspector Flayne, from Scotland Yard, wishes to see you, Mr. Eagles.

EDITOR. [*Groans*] What did I tell you, Kenting ? Bring him in.

[*The* DETECTIVE *enters. He looks from one to the other.*

DETECTIVE. I've called about your paragraph on the Morecombe suicide, sir.

EDITOR. Yes ?

DETECTIVE. What's this about a girl ?

EDITOR. Well, Inspector, we have some news that you haven't, as yet.

DETECTIVE. Excuse my saying so, but this is entirely a matter for the police. We don't want any interference. If you wish to give me your information, you can ; otherwise I'm afraid we shall have to get an attachment for contempt.

EDITOR. I don't think you can. The matter's not yet *sub judice.*

DETECTIVE. [*Dryly*] We shall see that.

EDITOR. We have our duty to the Public as well as to you, Inspector. This is a mysterious business, and Morecombe was the best-known flying man we had, far and away.

DETECTIVE. Am I to have that young woman's name and address ?

EDITOR. Well, we want to give you every assistance. But I think we're entitled to a little kudos, Inspector.

DETECTIVE. Now, sir. Hindering the law——

EDITOR. Helping. In return for this information—favoured nation terms in regard to anything you give out to the Press—eh ?

DETECTIVE. All right. That's understood.

EDITOR. Give him the address, Kenting.

NEWS ED. Daisy Odiham, 48, Burdells Buildings, Fulham.

DETECTIVE. [*Entering it in his notebook*] Thank you. Good morning.

[*He goes out.*

NEWS ED. [*Again looking at his watch*] If Forman's smart, all our friends will find the bird flown. What then ?

EDITOR. We'll see. I'm just a little fed up, Kenting. The Press gets all the blame for the natural instincts of mankind. I don't care what they say, curiosity is the greatest thing in the world ; I'm quite keen myself to know why Morecombe committed suicide. I suppose he *did ?*

NEWS ED. Yes. No improving on that.

EDITOR. [*Following out his own line of thought*] Someone's got to stand up for the man in the street. Why shouldn't he know ? News—

so long as it's true.   I'm not going to be dictated to by those people.
Go ahead as if they didn't exist.   Ordinary discretion and decency,
of course.   We'll produce the girl if the police want her.   But it
does them no harm to know that we're more spry than they are.
That's all now, Kenting.   Send in Miss Price again, will you?

> [*As the* NEWS EDITOR *turns to go out, he reseats himself and turns
> over some papers.*

The curtain falls.

SCENE II

A little later, the same morning.
*The Morecombes' Study, still curtained, with daylight coming through the
curtains in narrow streaks.*

> [*As the curtain goes up, the* MAID *enters, turning up the light and
> showing in* MR. ODIHAM *and his* DAUGHTER. *The girl is
> drooping, and seems to have been crying. Her father is a short
> man of the house-painter type, with all the oddity and reserved
> judgments of the cockney workman.*

MAID. Mrs. Morecombe's at lunch.   What name shall I tell her?
ODIHAM. Odiham. [*He pronounces it Oddium.*] And make it
special, if it's all the same to you.

> [*The* MAID *goes out. The* TWO *stand disconsolate.*

DAISY. [*Suddenly*] Oh! daddy, I can't bear to see her!
ODIHAM. Come now, Daisy; she won't eat you.   If they'd done
with each other, as you keep tellin' me——
DAISY. Oh! They had—they had!
ODIHAM. Perk up, then, and let's put the hat on it.   It's the only
way to stop these noospaper chaps.   [*He takes a folded paper out of
his side pocket.* ANNE *enters.*]
ANNE. Yes?   You wanted to see me?   [*The* GIRL *gasps.*
ODIHAM. That's right, ma'am.   You're keepin' well, I 'ope?
[*Smoothing his trousers.*] P'r'aps I oughtn't to 'a brought my daughter
'ere, but fact is—when you can't get out of a thing, you've got to face
it.
ANNE. [*Looking intently at the* GIRL] I see.
ODIHAM. Did you notice this in yesterday's *Evenin'*, ma'am?
ANNE. [*Taking the newspaper*] Yes.
ODIHAM. I get it every day with my supper.   Of course, when I
read it last night, I'd no idea it was my daughter.   I just 'appened to
show it to 'er an' that fetched it all out of 'er sudden—about 'er and
your 'usband, ma'am.   First I knew of it, an' that's the truth.   And of
course as to what you know, I can't tell.

ANNE. Nothing.

ODIHAM. Dear, dear! Well, I always say—When you once begin to tell the truth, it don't do to stop sudden. There's no denyin' the liaison, it seems. Of course 'er mother was Irish, an' brought 'er up too strict. And bein' in a restaurant, she's liable to admiration. But I never dreamed of 'er 'avin' a private life, and I can only ask you to look over it.

ANNE. [*Coldly*] There's no need.

ODIHAM. You see, this noospaper 'ints that "the girl in distress," as they call 'er 'ere, is the cause of the catastrofe. And, of course, she tells me she ain't. Daisy, tell the lady about what you told me about when you saw the Major last.

ANNE. Yes, tell me.

DAISY. [*Choking a little, but mastering her voice*] Oh, madam, I—I saw him the evening before—he—he—— He took me down to Richmond. Madam, I'm *sure* I'm not the cause of—of what happened. He was just as nice as ever he could be, and I—I didn't give him any —trouble, ever. We never—never had any words. [*She covers her face ; recovering with a brusque movement.*] I was too fond of him. I *adored* him. I wouldn't ever have given him any trouble.

ANNE. [*Quietly*] You came here yesterday morning, didn't you?

DAISY. I was crazy ; and as I went away a man followed me. He told me he'd have to tell the police if I didn't give him the truth. I lost my head, and I don't know what I said. And then they go and put this in the paper. There was no call for anything to come out about me. Oh! if I've done him a mischief! I wouldn't have hurt him for the world! [*She masters herself with difficulty.*

ODIHAM. [*With heat*] Ah! You don't know where to have these noospaper fellers, they're all over it. There's another after 'er now— wants 'er to go away an' 'ide 'erself. I said to him : "What game is this? She's got nothin' to do with this tradegy." But 'e kept on, till I thought to meself : "I got to stop this, some'ow. The only way is to go to 'eadquarters." I didn't like to bring her 'ere, but I 'ave. And, what's more, I believe 'e's followed us.

ANNE. I'm sure he has.

ODIHAM. He'd better watch it. My girl may 'ave done wrong, but she's a good girl, and I stand by her. From what she says, she ain't accessory to the fact, and if you'd just tell this feller the reason of your 'usband's havin' done what he did, ma'am—and stop 'em gluin' their noses to the shop winder.

ANNE. I don't know the reason.

ODIHAM. [*Blank*] Aow! "Veiled in mystery." I thought, as the paper said that, you'd be *sure* to know reely. [*Scratching his head.*] Well, some'ow it's got to be stopped. 'Er name ain't mentioned yet.

ANNE. My father, and my husband's mother have gone down to

the office of this newspaper ; but I'm afraid it's too late.   The police
will have seen this paragraph, and follow it up, I suppose.

ODIHAM. [*With anger*] Call that English !   It's a terrible thing for
my girl, if they're goin' to make 'er public.

ANNE. It's terrible for us all, Mr.——

ODIHAM. Oddium.

ANNE. [*To the* GIRL] Did you get a letter from Major Morecombe
this morning ?

DAISY. No.   And he never said good-bye special when I left him
on Sunday.   I can't hardly believe he's gone.

ANNE. Can you think of *any* reason ?

DAISY. [*Shaking her head*] No !   Only sometimes he'd be silent
suddenly, and look——

ANNE. Yes.

ODIHAM. Savin' your presence, ma'am, I don't think a man's the
right to leave everybody like this gapin' for news of why ; I don't
reely.

ANNE. It seems he wrote a letter, but to whom we don't know ;
it might throw light if we could trace it.

ODIHAM. Ah ! well—it's a warnin' against 'avin' a private life.

[*The* MAID *enters.*

MAID. That young man from the newspaper wants to see this
—gentleman again.

ODIHAM. Ah ! I thought he'd bob up.

ANNE. Do you wish to see him, Mr. Odiham ?

ODIHAM. [*Shifting from foot to foot*] Reely, ma'am, it's so noo to
me—all this.   Would you advise me to ?

ANNE. Perhaps you'd better.   Ask him to come in, Ellen.

[ELLEN *opens the door, and the* REPORTER *enters.*

REPORTER. [*To* ANNE] How do you do, ma'am ?   Please forgive
me—but my paper is so anxious to minimize any consequences of
that paragraph.

ODIHAM. [*Sullenly*] You should 'a thought o' that before.   What
call 'ad you ?   I've always read your paper and enjoyed it.

REPORTER. Exactly, Mr. Odiham.

ODIHAM. [*Agape*] 'Ow's that ?

REPORTER. If you didn't enjoy cases like this, we shouldn't put
them in, you know.

ODIHAM. Aow !

REPORTER. But you've changed your mind, I hope.   Do let me
see that Miss Odiham goes into the country quietly till the inquest's
over.   That's the only way to keep her out of it all.

ODIHAM. And what about her job ?

REPORTER. She could be indisposed.   We pay all expenses.

ODIHAM. What do you say, Daisy ?

DAISY. Oh! Yes, yes.

REPORTER. Come along, then, at once. We'll send your things down after you this afternoon.

ODIHAM. [*With sudden distrust*] 'Ow am I to know you're on the square?

REPORTER. [*With a disarming gesture, very simply and nicely*] Mr. Odiham, anyone can see that your daughter is very—sad. I really am quite a decent chap.

ANNE. You can trust him.

REPORTER. Thank you.

> [*But as he speaks, the door, Left, is opened, and* LADY MORE-COMBE *and* COLONEL ROLAND *come in and stand, taking in the situation.*

LADY M. Is this the young woman?

ANNE. Yes.

LADY M. [*To the* GIRL] We have been to your address.

ANNE. They came here to see if anything could be done.

LADY M. [*To the* REPORTER] And you?

REPORTER. I was told to try and prevent things going further, Lady Morecombe.

LADY M. [*Advancing—to the* GIRL] Is it true, as this man says, that you were my son's—— ?

DAISY. [*Very low*] Yes.

LADY M. Is it true that he did this because of you?

DAISY. [*Louder*] No.

LADY M. [*To the* REPORTER, *who is about to speak*] You hear that? Leave us, please.

REPORTER. I regret——

LADY M. Regret what sells your paper? Never!

REPORTER. Forgive me, that's very unfair. I hate this sort of thing as much as you, but I can't help the public taste. Ask Mr. Odiham, ask anybody! [*He goes out, Left.*

COL. ROLAND. [*Crossing the room*] Anne, I want to speak to you.

> [*He takes her arm and they go out, Right.*

LADY M. Did you take my son away from his wife?

DAISY. No! Oh, no!

LADY M. What are you?

ODIHAM. I'd be obliged if you wouldn't tease 'er, ma'am. She's 'ad a great shock.

LADY M. So have I.

ODIHAM. Excuse me, that ought to give you a fellow-feelin'.

DAISY. I'd have done anything for him.

LADY M. [*More softly*] I am an old woman, in great grief. I only want the truth, so as to know how best to serve my son's memory.

DAISY. Tell me what to do, and I'll do it, if I can.

ODIHAM. We're all in the same cart, I think.

LADY M. You're right. Will you deny your relationship to my son ?

ODIHAM. [*Scratching his head*] Perjury ? That's awk !

LADY M. Is it known to anyone except that newspaper man ?

DAISY. Not of my telling.

ODIHAM. You can't keep them sort of things dark if the police get after it. To be irregular's one thing ; but to swear you ain't if you are, is askin' for trouble.

LADY M. How long had you known my son ?

DAISY. Nearly a year.

LADY M. Had you an allowance from him ?

DAISY. Never. It was for love.

LADY M. Will you go quietly away by yourself at once ?

DAISY. Oh ! yes.

[*But as she speaks,* COLONEL ROLAND *returns by the door Right. He is extremely grave.*

LADY M. [*To him*] She will go away at once.

COL. ROLAND. Impossible.

LADY M. Why ?

[*He shakes his head.* LADY MORECOMBE, *after staring at him, speaks to the* ODIHAMS.]

Will you wait a minute or two in the dining-room opposite.

[*The* ODIHAMS *go out, Left.*]

Why not, Colonel Roland ?

COL. ROLAND. Anne.

LADY M. Unfaithful ?——

COL. ROLAND. Colin and Anne went their own ways. But Colin had this girl ; Anne's conduct could have had no bearing on his death. If the police know the whole, they will see that.

LADY M. You mean to give them this girl's name ? [COLONEL ROLAND *nods.*] It's treachery to the dead.

COL. ROLAND. I can't have Anne disgraced.

LADY M. Does she *want* Colin's name blackened ?

COL. ROLAND. No. But Anne's all I've got. To have her tarred and feathered before my eyes !

LADY M. And I ? [*With emotion.*] Isn't it enough that my boy is dead ?   [*She places her hand on the door just as the* MAID *comes in.*

MAID. The detective, my lady. Shall I tell the mistress ?

LADY M. [*In alarm*] *Where* ?

MAID. In the hall, my lady.

LADY M. And those people ?

MAID. In the dining-room.

LADY M. Has he seen them ?

MAID. I don't think so, my lady.

LADY M. Bring him in here at once!   [*The* MAID *goes.*]
Colonel Roland! You won't tell him—you can't!

    [COLONEL ROLAND *throws his head back and stands very still.
The* DETECTIVE *comes in briskly.*

DETECTIVE. Lady Morecombe? Your service. Colonel Roland,
I believe? I've come to see your daughter, sir.

COL. ROLAND. I'll fetch her.   [*He goes out, Right.*

DETECTIVE. Sad business, my lady. Can you tell me of anything
that bears on it?

LADY M. Nothing.

DETECTIVE. You had no letter from your son?

LADY M. No.

DETECTIVE. Are you staying here?

LADY M. Yes.

DETECTIVE. Possibly you'd like to withdraw; it must all be very
trying.

LADY M. No, thank you. I'll stay.

DETECTIVE. As you wish, my lady. But it may be a bit painful
for you.

LADY M. I am used to pain.

DETECTIVE. [*As* ANNE *and her* FATHER *come in, Right*] Excuse me,
Major Morecombe never had shell-shock, had he?

LADY M. No; but he went through every horror in the
war.

DETECTIVE. [*Soberly*] We all did that. [*Turning to* ANNE.] I've
received information, Mrs. Morecombe, that a young woman called
here the morning after the event, in great distress. I have her address,
but before I see her, I'd like to ask you what you know about the
matter. [*From his central position he loses no gesture, neither the assenting
movement of* COLONEL ROLAND'S *head, nor* LADY MORECOMBE'S *intense
rigidity, nor* ANNE'S *compressed lips.*]

ANNE. Nothing.

DETECTIVE. Not aware of any reason why she should have
come?

ANNE. No.

DETECTIVE. Never saw her? [*Again he misses nothing—neither*
COLONEL ROLAND'S *jerked-up hand, nor* LADY MORECOMBE'S *quick turn
and look at* ANNE, *nor the droop of* ANNE'S *eyes, raised again as she speaks.*]

ANNE. No.

DETECTIVE. This is a delicate matter, but I'd like a frank answer
from someone. No knowledge of any intimacy between Major
Morecombe and this young woman? [*To* ANNE.] Madam?

ANNE. No.

DETECTIVE. [*To* LADY MORECOMBE] My lady?

LADY M. No.

DETECTIVE. [*To* COLONEL ROLAND] You, sir?

[*There is a moment of suspense—a tiny shake of* ANNE'S *head, a movement of* LADY MORECOMBE'S *hands.*

COL. ROLAND. [*After a long breath, with eyes almost closed*] No.

[*A moment's silence.*

DETECTIVE. In that case, as they're in the dining-room, I'll have her and her father in. [*He watches the sensation.*] Kindly send for her, madam.

[ANNE *moves to the bell by the fireplace.* COLONEL ROLAND *takes a long breath of relief.*

LADY M. Leave my son alone!

DETECTIVE. [*Quietly*] My lady!

[LADY MORECOMBE, *clasping her little thin hands together, sways slightly; then sinks down on to the chair at the bureau.*

[*The* MAID *enters, Left.*

ANNE. Ask Mr. and Miss Odiham to come in.

[*The* MAID *goes out.*

DETECTIVE. I quite understand your reluctance, but, you'll excuse me—we want the truth.

[ODIHAM *and his* DAUGHTER *come in from the Hall. The* DETECTIVE *looks shrewdly at the girl, and beckons her up to him.*

DETECTIVE. I'm the detective in charge of this matter. Your name is Daisy Odiham, of 48, Burdells Buildings?

DAISY. Yes.

[*Her* FATHER *closes up to her;* COLONEL ROLAND *is at the fireplace;* ANNE *by the armchair.*

DETECTIVE. You came here yesterday morning?

[DAISY, *whose eyes move restlessly, is silent.*] Answer, please.

DAISY. Yes.

DETECTIVE. Why?

DAISY. I was upset.

DETECTIVE. By what?

ODIHAM. [*Stepping forward*] What d'you want to worry my girl for? She knows nothin' o' this.

DETECTIVE. We shall see. [*To* DAISY.] You heard of this death —what was it to you?

DAISY. It's cruel!   [*She suddenly covers her face.*

ODIHAM. What do you call this? I tell you she knows nothing of why the Major shot hisself.

DETECTIVE. She'll have to answer on oath to-morrow in the box, unless she answers me now. [*To* DAISY.] Come! What was the Major's death to you?

DAISY. [*Freeing her face and flinging out the word*] The world!

DETECTIVE. You mean *he* was the world?

DAISY. Yes.

DETECTIVE. And you to him?

LADY M. [*Sharply*] Only my son could answer that.

DETECTIVE. [*Staring steadily at* DAISY] She knows what I mean. Were you?

DAISY. [*Stony of a sudden*] No.

> [*The gestures of surprise from* ANNE *and* COLONEL ROLAND, LADY MORECOMBE'S *relief, and* ODIHAM'S *uneasiness—the* DETECTIVE *marks them all.*

DETECTIVE. When did you see the Major last?

DAISY. The day before he——

DETECTIVE. Where?

DAISY. At Richmond.

DETECTIVE. Now come—speak the truth—you were on terms with him?

DAISY. No.

DETECTIVE. [*With a faint smile*] And yet he was the world to you. What are you?

DAISY. [*Sullenly*] Waitress.

DETECTIVE. Respectable profession. You were pursuing this gentleman, then?

DAISY. I loved him.

DETECTIVE. With no result?

DAISY. I won't be questioned any more.

DETECTIVE. [*Soothingly*] Now, now!

> [ODIHAM *edges closer to his daughter and pulls her sleeve.*]

Ah! *You* understand that it's no good telling lies to the Law. Your daughter was the Major's—— Come, it's only fair to everyone, out with it!

ODIHAM. Can't you see she's 'ighsterical?

DETECTIVE. [*To* DAISY] Give me the letter you had from Major Morecombe yesterday morning.

DAISY. I never had one.

DETECTIVE. What? When it gave you the news that brought you round here?

DAISY. It's a lie! I read it in the paper.

DETECTIVE. [*For the first time sharply*] Don't speak to me like that, my girl. Just answer my questions, and give me that letter.

DAISY. Oh! Won't somebody help me?

COL. ROLAND. [*With a step forward*] Leave the wretched girl alone! [*In a tone of old days.*] Do you hear me, Inspector?

DETECTIVE. Yes, sir; but we're not in the Army now. And, excuse my saying so, it's not to your interest, or to your daughter's, that she should refuse to answer me.

LADY M. [*Rising*] She *has* answered you. What she has said she will repeat on oath. She admired my son—many did—she loved him, if you like. And—that—is—all. [*She says this with such incision and finality that the* DETECTIVE *is for the moment thoroughly taken aback.*]

DETECTIVE. Tell me why your son committed suicide, and I will leave it at that, my lady.

LADY M. I *cannot ;* but you will leave it at that, all the same.

DETECTIVE. [*Recovering himself*] Now, this is all very natural, no doubt, but it gets us no further. [*To the* GIRL.] I'll give you a last chance. If you aren't frank, I shall start inquiring, and you best know how that'll suit you.

DAISY. [*With sudden passion*] I won't tell you a thing—not a thing —not if ever so ! I won't say a word to hurt him !

ODIHAM. [*Warningly*] Daisy !

DAISY. Well, I won't. He's dead.

[LADY MORECOMBE *puts her little thin hand on the girl's arm and gives it a squeeze.*

DETECTIVE. [*Impassively*] That's the Law defied, if ever I heard it.

COL. ROLAND. " De mortuis nil nisi bonum," Sergeant.

DETECTIVE. Precisely, Colonel ; I know the saying. But it's my business to put the case up to the Coroner with every circumstance that'll throw light on this death. [*He crosses to the door, opens it and says.*] Simpson, ask that reporter to come in.

ODIHAM. Why, this is the ruddy Inquisition ! Come along, Daisy !

DETECTIVE. [*Calmly*] You can go, but your daughter can't.

[*As he speaks, the* REPORTER *comes in. The* DETECTIVE *stands with his back to the door.*

DETECTIVE. Kindly repeat to me what you said just now when I questioned you in the street.

[*The* REPORTER, *who is pivoting, and trying to take in the sense of the situation, fronts the* DETECTIVE.

REPORTER. But why, Inspector ? It's painful, and perfectly well known to everyone here.

LADY M. Haven't *you* finished mischief-making ?

DETECTIVE. Just repeat it. Was this girl Major Morecombe's mistress ?

REPORTER. [*Resentful of* LADY MORECOMBE'S *words*] She told our representative so yesterday.

DETECTIVE. [*To the* GIRL] Do you still deny it ?

[DAISY *has closed her eyes and sways.*

ANNE. [*Crossing swiftly*] She's going to faint.

LADY M. [*Sharply*] Girl, don't faint ! [*The* GIRL *reopens her eyes.*

DETECTIVE. And you still say you had no letter ?

DAISY. [*In a dead voice*] I had no letter.

DETECTIVE. [*To* ODIHAM] You can take her away now. [*To the* REPORTER.] You can go too. But mind ! Anyone who plays tricks with her before the inquest will be up against it.   Unless I'm given that letter, she'll have to go into the box.

ODIHAM. Well, you are a blanky bloke.

DETECTIVE. Thank you.

[*The* ODIHAMS *go out,* ODIHAM *half carrying his daughter.   The* REPORTER *stands uncertain, but at a sharp motion of the* DETECTIVE'S *chin, he too goes.*

DETECTIVE. She had that letter right enough.   [*Turning sharply to* ANNE.] Unless *you* can tell me who had it now, ma'am.   You've all had time to think things over.

ANNE. Mr. Darrel received no letter.

DETECTIVE. Well, I've made every inquiry about the Major's affairs. There's nothing wrong anywhere.   Bank balance good, no recent sale of securities ; no debts to speak of.   No monetary complications of any sort ; no ill-health ; and five years since the war.   [*To* LADY MORECOMBE.] Nothing wrong in your family, my lady ?

LADY M. No.

DETECTIVE. So I should say.   His father was the great ironmaster, I believe ?

LADY M. Yes.

DETECTIVE. Nothing wrong there ?

LADY M. I know of nothing.

DETECTIVE. That's how it is, then.   We're driven on to private life.   [*To* ANNE.] Yours, madam, or his.   I don't know how far you've confided in your father ?

ANNE. Entirely.

DETECTIVE. I'm glad of that.   Well, the day before his death the Major takes this girl to Richmond.   And the evening of his death you spend with another gentleman.   That's the case [*With a sharp glance at* LADY MORECOMBE *and* ANNE] apart from the letter.

ANNE. Have you inquired for it ?

DETECTIVE. [*Dryly*] I should say so.   Posted in a pillar-box—sorted and sent out at eleven p.m. by people dying for a sleep—that's a letter that only gets traced on the film, ma'am.

COL. ROLAND. Anne, go.

[ANNE *looks at him, and goes out, Right.   The* DETECTIVE *eyes the tall figure to his right, the tiny figure to his left.*

COL. ROLAND. Now, Inspector, you were a soldier—use your reason.

DETECTIVE. Never allowed one in the Army, sir.

COL. ROLAND. Try it for a change.   My son-in-law had this girl, and my daughter's behaviour can have had nothing to do with his death.

LADY M. This poor foolish girl was utterly devoted.   She cannot have been the cause.

COL. ROLAND. Neither of them can be.   Come, Inspector !

DETECTIVE. You expect me to go up with this case, after two clear days, without a single fact that has any bearing whatever on this suicide of a well-known man ?   All I can say is, if I stood for that, neither the Coroner nor the Public would.

COL. ROLAND. But why drag in what has no bearing ?

DETECTIVE. It's not for me to say what has bearing and what hasn't.   You know nothing of inquests, perhaps.   The Coroner will ask : When and where did this death take place ; by whose hand ; if by his own, what was the state of mind at the time ?   It's his state of mind I have to show to the best of my ability ; and these are the only facts I have knowledge of that can have affected him.

LADY M. And will knowing his state of mind console *me* ?   What will help me, Inspector, is that no one shall think lightly of my son now he's dead.

DETECTIVE. [*With a shrug*] The custom's what it is, my lady. There's a feeling a man shouldn't take his life while he's got his wits.

LADY M. Do these facts of yours point to sound or to unsound mind ?

DETECTIVE. That's very clever, my lady.

LADY M. Clever !   I've lost my only son.   It's like losing my sight.   Clever !

DETECTIVE. [*Stubbornly*] I'm sorry.   But——

COL. ROLAND. By the Lord, Inspector, I should have thought you more of a man !

DETECTIVE. [*Dryly*] Man enough to do my duty, Colonel.

COL. ROLAND. Duty !   Wantonly to make a show of this !   You see what it means to Lady Morecombe !   As for me—I can't tell you what my daughter is to me—to watch her disgraced !   One's only daughter pilloried in the papers !   The Public all agog !   Those women who come and gloat !   I'm told there's never a death or a divorce where there isn't a pack o' women in furs and feathers.   And this is far worse than a divorce.   There was the poor fellow lying dead—when she came in from her . . .

LADY M. Colonel Roland has served the country all his life ; he's been wounded three times.   And my son was gallantry itself !   Do you want to smirch his memory before everybody ?

DETECTIVE. [*Moved*] I'm sure I've every feeling for you both, my lady.   These things come very hard on families.   But aren't you making too much of it ?   A little private life in these days—what is it ?

LADY M. [*Like a little statue of dignity*] We don't belong to these days.   We ought to have been dead.   Enough !   Colonel Roland, he means to do it ; nothing we can say will stop him !

DETECTIVE. [*Quickly*] The Law, my lady, not me.   Get me that letter, and it may turn out different.

LADY M. In our belief, neither had the letter.

DETECTIVE. [*Shrugging his shoulders*] Take my word for it, one of them had. Well, we've the best part of a day to get it still. Good morning!

> [*The* DETECTIVE *bows first to one and then to the other; but neither makes a sign. He makes a vexed movement of his head and goes out. There is a moment's silence.*

COL. ROLAND. Has the girl got it?

LADY M. No; I'm sure she was speaking the truth.

COL. ROLAND. Anne is positive.

LADY M. We're in a net. Colonel Roland, haven't you influence enough to stop this?

COL. ROLAND. I? I'm nobody. On the shelf. I'll try my lawyers, but for the life of me I don't see what they can do.

LADY M. Try! Try everything! Forgive me for what I said!

COL. ROLAND. I know—I know! My poor friend!

> [*He takes her hand and puts it to his lips, passes on and goes out into the hall.*

> [LADY MORECOMBE, *left alone, moves restlessly. Hearing the outer door close, she goes to the window, slightly draws back the curtain, and watches his departure, then stands gazing at the armchair, with her hand to her forehead.*

> [ANNE *comes in from Right. She has on a hat and carries a dressing-bag. Seeing her,* LADY MORECOMBE *drops her hand, and reins back from the chair.*

ANNE. I'm going to my father's. You will like to be alone here.

LADY M. I can leave, instead.

ANNE. No. It's Colin's house.   [*She is moving on.*

LADY M. Wait! Was it your doing that you were apart?

ANNE. No.

LADY M. You loved each other when you married.

ANNE. We thought so.

LADY M. Were you the first to be unfaithful?

ANNE. It was not I who broke off our life together.

LADY M. Were there scenes between you?

ANNE. Never.

LADY M. Anne! Are you keeping anything back?

ANNE. Nothing.

LADY M. Do you love this other man?

ANNE. With all my heart.

LADY M. Did Colin love this girl?

ANNE. I can't tell you.

LADY M. Nobody can tell me anything. Oh! God! [*Suddenly.*] I suppose you are glad that he is gone?

ANNE. [*Wincing*] That's not fair. You know it's not!

LADY M. The heart is never fair.   But you have none, perhaps.
ANNE. I have told you.

> [*There is a long look between them, then* ANNE *passes on and out into the hall.*

> [*At the closing of the door,* LADY MORECOMBE *moves and turns out the light.   A streak of sunlight from where the curtain was left by her half drawn falls across the armchair.   She moves into it, standing behind the chair, as if looking down on someone seated there.   Slowly her hands go out as if taking a head between them.   She bends and presses her lips to the head that she does not hold.   There is the sound of a kiss, and very low the word :* " Colin ! "

The curtain falls.

ACT III

Just before eleven o'clock the following day.
A waiting-room at the Coroner's Court, rather small, and furnished like a
railway station waiting-room, but fresher-looking, having walls of
green distemper, with a dado. A narrow oblong table stands parallel
to a long seat along the wall, Left. There are some chairs against the
right-hand wall, which turns at a right angle, forward, forming an alcove
in which, facing the audience, is the wide open doorway leading to lobby,
public entrance, and Court.

> [*Seated on the long seat are* Mr. Odiham *and his* Daughter,
> *and a little way from them, the maid* Ellen. *At the top of*
> *the table, in a chair, sits* Lady Morecombe, *very still and*
> *alone. In the alcove and lobby is a bustle of figures, the pivot*
> *of which is the* Coroner's Clerk, *a moustachioed man in a gown.*

Coroner's C. Only those interested in the case.

Lady. [*With aigrette*] Oh! but we're very interested. Can't you find us seats?

Coroner's C. Witnesses?

Lady. [*With aigrette, pushing forward a younger lady*] Not exactly, but my friend is a great friend of Mrs. Morecombe.

Coroner's C. You can go and try, but the Court's full.

Lady. [*With aigrette*] What a bore! Come along, Ursula! We must get in.

Reporter. [*Forman, showing his card*] Press.

Coroner's C. All right—room at the table, I think.

> [*The* Reporter *stands a moment looking at the* Odihams; *sud-*
> *denly he sees* Lady Morecombe *beckoning with her black-*
> *gloved hand. He goes to her, standing Right of table.*

Lady M. [*Pointing to a paper on the table before her*] Did you put that headline?

Reporter. I've nothing to do with headlines. Excuse me, I have to get my seat.

> [*He moves quickly back, and encounters* Colonel Roland *and*
> Anne, *coming in.*

Col. Roland. [*In a low voice*] Hell take your paper, sir!

Reporter. [*With a little involuntary skip*] Quite! Quite!

> [*He goes out through the throng.*

> [Colonel Roland *and* Anne *stand by the table, Right Forward.*
> *He makes a motion of the hand to* Mr. Odiham, *and bows to*
> Lady Morecombe.

888

MAN. [*With* THREE LADIES, *at the door*] I'm from the Air Ministry —could you manage to get us in ?

CORONER'S C. [*Glancing at the card*] I'll see, sir. . . . Now then, please, only witnesses in this room. [*He shepherds out figures by the door, then turns to those in the body of the room.*] All witnesses ?

COL. ROLAND. I'm with my daughter—Mrs. Morecombe.

CORONER'S C. Oh ! Very good. [*To* LADY MORECOMBE.] And you, madam ?

LADY M. My son——

CORONER'S C. Indeed ! [*Respectfully.*] Ahem ! I don't know if you wish to—er—view the proceedings, madam ? If so, I shall be happy to have a chair put for you.

LADY M. [*Standing up*] Yes. I will come.

CORONER'S C. [*Leading*] This way then, madam.

LADY M. [*Avoiding* ANNE, *but looking up into* COLONEL ROLAND'S *face*] Nothing, I suppose ? [*He shakes his head.*] Courage ?

> [COLONEL ROLAND *nods, and she goes out, following the* CLERK.
> [*The room is now empty, but for the* ODIHAMS, *the* MAID, ANNE, COLONEL ROLAND, *and a* CONSTABLE *standing in the open doorway.* FIGURES *are still bustling outside in the entrance lobby.*

COL. ROLAND. Sit down, my dear.

> [ANNE *sits Right of the table, and idly reaches for the paper, turning it over blankly as one does at the dentist's.* COLONEL ROLAND *stands grasping the back of her chair, gnawing his moustache. The* DETECTIVE *appears in the doorway with a bit of paper in his hand. He moves quickly in a little and takes in the* FIVE FIGURES, *of whom* ODIHAM *alone notices him—with a muttered* " The blanky blank ! " *Then, moving back, he speaks to the* CONSTABLE.

DETECTIVE. [*In a low voice*] The three women—see they don't flit. I've got the officer, and the two doctors ; that's the lot. [*The* CONSTABLE *nods.*] Right, then ! I'll come for them. [*He goes.*

ANNE. [*Suddenly turning*] Don't come with me, dad—*please !*

COL. ROLAND. Let you go alone, child ? Impossible !

ANNE. Please, *please !* Father ! I can't bear it, if you're there.

COL. ROLAND. My dear, I must see they treat you——

ANNE. I shall be all right, dad—really I shall. It'll be a thousand times worse if you come. Please !

> [*She takes one of his buttons and twists it.*

COL. ROLAND. [*Muttering*] Those harpies and cats—those writing monkeys—feasting on it !

ANNE. So long as *you* don't see, I shan't care.

COL. ROLAND. D'you think I'll not be seeing, if I stay here ? I'll see every bit of it, as plain as your face.

ANNE. Nothing's so bad as it seems beforehand. [*With a smile.*] Really and truly, I shall be all right.

> [COLONEL ROLAND *turns abruptly away, marches up, down, and puts his hand on her shoulder.*

COL. ROLAND. So be it, then. I'll stay here, and God help me.

CONSTABLE. [*Moving in a step from the door*] The Coroner's taken his seat, ladies.   [*They look at him in silence.   He moves back.*

ODIHAM. Time 'e took something. Hangin' about! You'd think it was a ruddy first night—this! [*To the* MAID.] I say, come down 'ere.

> [*The* MAID *moves down beside the* GIRL.   ANNE *and the* COLONEL *watch silently.*

ODIHAM. She's not opened 'er mouth all mornin'. However's she goin' through with this? 'Ave you got a smellin' salt about yer?

> [*The* MAID *shakes her head.*

ANNE. [*Going across*] Take one of these.

ODIHAM. Thank you, ma'am. A sniff in time saves nine.

> [ANNE *breaks an ammonia capsule and waves it before* DAISY'S *face.*

ODIHAM. Rouse up, Daisy. Sniff!

> [*The* GIRL *sniffs apathetically.   ANNE *moves back.*

ODIHAM. [*To the* MAID] I never seen 'er like this in all me life. I say, would you kindly look after 'er in there? Reely I'm afraid to trust meself. I might come it unpleasant. I'll be 'andy 'ere when she comes back.

CONSTABLE. [*Taking a step*] Won't be three minutes now. The Jury 'ave gone to view the body.

DAISY. [*Starting up*] Oh! God!

> [*There is a perfectly dead silence. The* CONSTABLE, *an oldish, wary fellow, stares; the others are motionless, with their eyes on the* GIRL. *She sinks back into her seat, and sits as before.* ODIHAM *fans her with his hat. The* DETECTIVE *appears in the doorway, carefully out of sight of his victims, and signs to the* CONSTABLE.

CONSTABLE. Now, please, ladies.

ANNE. [*Advancing towards* DAISY] Ellen! [*The* MAID *takes the* GIRL'S *arm. To* ODIHAM.] We'll look after her, Mr. Odiham. [*Taking the* GIRL'S *hand—firmly.*] Come! We must see it through!

> [*The* GIRL *rises and goes between them like a sleep-walker. The* CONSTABLE *closes them in as they pass through the door. The* TWO MEN *stand as if at " Attention."*

COL. ROLAND. [*To himself*] I've seen men shot, but their eyes were bandaged.   [*He continues to stand unmoving.*

> [ODIHAM *shuffles to the table, takes up the paper, goes back with it to his seat, sits down with it on his knee, rubs his hand across his eyes, gives a sort of gulp, and says:*

ODIHAM. This Chelsea lot's pretty 'ot stuff. Wouldn't say but what they'll win this afternoon.

  [*The* COLONEL *starts, then moves, and sits on the table, facing* ODIHAM.

COL. ROLAND. Ah! They'll be a good team, I suppose.

  [*A short silence. They listen. Then* ODIHAM *takes out a pipe.*

ODIHAM. D'you think I could 'ave a smoke, Colonel?

COL. ROLAND. I shouldn't think so.

ODIHAM. Well, I must chance it. Can't stand it 'ere without. [*Filling his pipe.*] Your daughter's a rare-plucked one, Colonel, if you'll excuse the liberty.

COL. ROLAND. Women are braver than men—no doubt of it.

ODIHAM. And yet they'll run from a mouse. You should see my girl with a black-beetle! Abrams on the sprint is nothing to 'er! [*Stops. With a jerk.*] I think this Labour's come to stay, Colonel; but p'r'aps you're not a politician.

COL. ROLAND. Not since I cut my wisdom teeth.

ODIHAM. Ah! Public life! It's a put-up job.

  [*The* COLONEL'S *head goes round as if he heard a sound.* ODIHAM, *too, stays, pipe in hand, as if listening. They relax.*

ODIHAM. [*Holding up the paper*] Did you see these 'eadlines? "The Mysterious Suicide," "England's Greatest Flying Man." "Sensational Developments Expected." That's what's filled the 'ouse to-day. They're turnin' away money.

COL. ROLAND. Damn them!

ODIHAM. Everything's a show nowadays. If you get two sparrers scrappin' you'll have a ring round 'em in no time. T'other day I read about an American journalist who missed the show when that man an' wife—you remember—went over Niagara Falls on a niceberg. There they was—slowly driftin' towards it for an 'our an' a 'alf; thousands watchin', and nobody could save 'em. Then a bloke thought of hangin' ropes down from the bridge; the man caught 'old of one all right, but the woman missed 'ers; so the man dropped 'is again and over they went together. The journalist said it was the greatest tradegy of 'is life that 'e 'adn't seen it.

COL. ROLAND. The beauty!

ODIHAM. Well, you can't say but what we do like to see other people put through it. What would you 'ave done, Colonel, with a show like that before yer very eyes?

COL. ROLAND. Run like a hare.

ODIHAM. [*Shaking his head*] Nao! Not when it come to the point. You'd 'a stood watchin' like the others, till your eyes dropped out. It's human nature to want to see all there is.

COL. ROLAND. I never would go to a bull-fight.

ODIHAM. [*Meditatively*] And yet you must 'ave seen a lot of blood in your time. [*Pause, while they listen.*] Excuse me, but 'ave you a match ? [*The* COLONEL *produces a box of matches.*] Thank you.

　　　　　　　　　　　　　　　　　[ODIHAM *lights his pipe and blows a puff or two.*

COL. ROLAND. What's that ?　　　　　　　　　　　　　　[*They listen.*

ODIHAM. I fancy it was a car. Some of them cars make very 'uman noises.

COL. ROLAND. Torturing women !

ODIHAM. [*Puffing*] Colonel, what made the Major do it ? D'you think there was *another* woman in it ?

COL. ROLAND. [*Making an impatient movement*] Do you take him for a Mormon ?

ODIHAM. Well, there must ha' been 'ot stuff somewhere, to make him bust the boiler like that.

COL. ROLAND. God only knows why a man takes his own life !

ODIHAM. Ah ! 'E 'as to know a lot.

CONSTABLE. [*Moving from the door*] No smoking in there, please.

　　　　　　[ODIHAM *removes his pipe and lays it on the seat. The* CONSTABLE
　　　　　　moves back.

ODIHAM. The Law wants plumbin', don't it ? 'Tain't 'uman. [*They listen. Suddenly.*] Well, I can't stick it 'ere without a smoke. [*He rises.*] I think I'll go and 'ang about outside, Colonel.

　　　　　　[COLONEL ROLAND *nods.* ODIHAM *passes him, goes out, and is
　　　　　　seen speaking to the* CONSTABLE *in the lobby. The* COLONEL
　　　　　　*sits down at the table with his back to the alcove, resting his head
　　　　　　on his hands.*

CONSTABLE. [*Close to the door, speaking to a newcomer*] Whom do you want, sir ?　　　　　　　[*The newcomer comes in—he is seen to be* DARREL.

DARREL. Mrs. Morecombe.

CONSTABLE. The widow ? She's in Court now, but she'll be down before long, I daresay. If you'll wait in here ? Perhaps I could get a word for you of whether she's been taken yet. [*He receives a coin.*] I'll do it, sir.

DARREL. Thank you.

　　　　　　[*He comes in ; strung up to the last pitch of intensity, he walks,
　　　　　　unseeing, across to the long seat, picking up from it the paper,
　　　　　　dropping it again, and passing up, Back, to the head of the table,
　　　　　　where he stands looking towards the alcove.* COLONEL ROLAND
　　　　　　has remained motionless, with his head on his hands. DARREL
　　　　　　*becomes conscious of him, amd involuntarily covers the lower part
　　　　　　of his face with his hand.*

CONSTABLE. [*Reappearing*] They've just got through with her, sir.

COL. ROLAND. [*Coming out of his stillness*] With whom ?

CONSTABLE. The widow, sir. As she found the body, they took her first. [*To* DARREL.] Sometimes witnesses comes out, and sometimes they stays—you can't tell.

> [*The* COLONEL *stares at him without replying. The* CONSTABLE *steps back into the lobby ; the* COLONEL, *turning, becomes half-conscious of who* DARREL *is, gets up and moves a step or two towards him.*]

DARREL. [*Answering his look*] Yes—I am. Colonel Roland, I suppose ?

COL. ROLAND. [*Drawing himself up*] You have much to answer for.

DARREL. If it hadn't been for you, sir, we should have gone off long ago.

COL. ROLAND. Do you suppose that I should wish an affair to be clandestine ?

DARREL. No ; but Anne——

COL. ROLAND. Why didn't you have the manliness to insist ?

DARREL. [*Hotly*] I see no manliness in forcing the woman you love. She couldn't bear to hurt you.

COL. ROLAND. Then you should have waited till I was out of the way.

DARREL. Yes, sir ; but we are in love.

COL. ROLAND. That's no excuse for dishonour.

DARREL. Morecombe and she were quite estranged before I knew her.

COL. ROLAND. Is that true ?

DARREL. Absolutely.

COL. ROLAND. Um ! What are you going to do now ?

DARREL. Marry her—take her abroad at once. I'd have cut off my hand to save her *that*—— [*He jerks his head towards the door.*] How long has she been there ?

COL. ROLAND. One can die many deaths in ten minutes.

CONSTABLE. [*From lobby*] There's a gentleman for you in there, madam.

DARREL. Anne !

> [ANNE *comes in. She has fixed red spots in her cheeks. She moves to the end of the table and sits down facing the audience, with her back to the two men.* DARREL *has moved quickly down Left of the table,* COLONEL ROLAND *to the back of her chair.*]

DARREL. Anne ! Darling !

> [ANNE *just shakes her head and does not answer, her lips quiver ; her expression is that of one who has been through, without giving way, something too much for her nerves. She sits without movement, staring before her.*]

COL. ROLAND. Shall we go, my dear ?   [*No sound.*]

DARREL. Anne ! Speak !

ANNE. [*Shakes her head*] I—may—be wanted—again.

> [*She shivers, then controls herself.*]

COL. ROLAND. By the Lord—it's too much!

[DARREL *sinks on one knee and kisses her hand. No movement. He gets up abruptly and stands interrogating the* COLONEL.

COL. ROLAND. Water, Anne?

ANNE. Nothing.

[DARREL *makes another impulsive movement, but the* COLONEL *beckons him, and they move up to the head of the table.*

COL. ROLAND. [*In a low voice*] Let her be! I saw a woman on the North-West Frontier once—— Um! There's more than one kind of outrage. The nerves want time.

CONSTABLE'S VOICE. [*At the door*] You won't find room, sir.

LIEUT. OSWALD'S VOICE. [*Outside*] But I tell you I've got something for the Coroner.

CONSTABLE. Step in here, then. [*Stepping in, followed by the speaker— a man about thirty, of a naval cut.*] Well, sir, what is it; and I'll see what I can do for you.

[*He receives nothing but a card.* DARREL *and the* COLONEL *have moved back, watching* ANNE.

CONSTABLE. [*After reading the card*] Lieutenant Oswald, His Majesty's Ship *Zéus*. [*Salutes.*

OSWALD. I got this letter at Portsmouth, Constable, only this morning. The Coroner ought to have it at once. I've been on manœuvres—this is the first I've heard of this business. My poor old pal! [*Holding out an envelope.*

CONSTABLE. [*Scrutinizing envelope*] From the deceased?

OSWALD. Yes.

CONSTABLE. I'll get the Sergeant in charge, sir.

OSWALD. [*Suddenly perceiving* ANNE, *who has turned and is staring at him*] Mrs. Morecombe! I'm so sor—— [*Breaking off at the look on her face.*] I—I'm frightfully cut up.

ANNE. [*Bitterly*] The letter?

OSWALD. Only just reached me.

ANNE. Too late.

OSWALD. What——

[*The* DETECTIVE *has entered, followed by the* CONSTABLE.

DETECTIVE. [*Brusquely*] Now, sir, what's this? You've got a letter?

[OSWALD *hands the letter. The* DETECTIVE *compares the handwriting on the envelope with that of other letters, then opens it and reads swiftly.*

DETECTIVE. My God! Come with me, sir!

[*He leads out, and* OSWALD *follows.*
[*The* CONSTABLE *goes back to his place in the doorway.*

DARREL. Who was that?

COL. ROLAND. Morecombe's best man.

[ANNE *has turned to the table, and is sitting with her forehead on her hand.*]

Speak to her now !

[*He moves up the room and stands with his back turned.* DARREL *goes to the front end of the table and bends over her.*

DARREL. Anne !

ANNE. Who minds being skinned ?   Do I show ?   Am I bleeding ?
Their eyes !   [*Stir in the lobby.*

CONSTABLE. [*Moving in*] The Sergeant's sent down to say you won't
be required further, ma'am.   [*Moves out.*

DARREL. Come, Anne, come—out of this !

ANNE. [*Turning up her face with closed eyes*] Put my mask on, Geof—
it's slipped !

DARREL. [*Touching her face*] Darling !

[*He takes her arm and leads her out.*

COL. ROLAND. [*Spinning round and coming quickly down*] Begad, I'd
like um at the end of a pistol !   [*He levels his hand as if to fire.*

CONSTABLE. Beg pardon, sir ?

COL. ROLAND. [*Conscious of the comic*] Not you, my man.

CONSTABLE. Anything I can get you, sir ?

COL. ROLAND. Yes—human nature with its mouth open.

[*He goes out.*

[*The* CONSTABLE'S *mouth opens ; rolling his eyes, he looks round the
empty room as if for damage done, adjusts a chair, takes up the
paper, folds it ; crosses to the far side and comes on* ODIHAM'S
*pipe, takes it up rather as if he were arresting somebody, holds it
out, looks at it, examining it as if it were a piece of evidence, then
places it in his side pocket and buttons it up.   Then, with a
final look round, he takes the paper and returns towards the door.*

ODIHAM'S VOICE. [*Outside*] Take her out in the air.   Shan't be a
tick ; I left my pipe.

[*He comes in and crosses to the long bench.   The* CONSTABLE *regards
him with an unmoved face.*

ODIHAM. [*Puzzled*] 'Ere's where I left it. [*To the* CONSTABLE.]
Seen a pipe ?

CONSTABLE. What sort o' pipe ?

ODIHAM. Briar—bit gone in the stem.

CONSTABLE. Any marks on it ?

ODIHAM. Marks ?   What d'you think ?   Tattooed on the left
forearm ?   Just a pipe.

CONSTABLE. [*Producing pipe*] This the article ?

ODIHAM. That's it !

CONSTABLE. By rights I ought to hand it in at Scotland Yard.

[*He seems to weigh the pipe.*

ODIHAM. Aoh! I shouldn't like you to be wastin' your time over me. [*Holding out a bob*] 'Ow's that?

CONSTABLE. [*Taking the bob*] A pipe's a man's friend.

ODIHAM. [*Taking the pipe*] Ah! about the only one 'e 'as. 'Ave you got a light?

> [*The* CONSTABLE *hands him a box of matches and* ODIHAM *lights his pipe.*]

Well, you 'aven't too cheery a job among the bodies—So long!

> [*The* CONSTABLE'S *mouth opens, but* ODIHAM *has hurried out.*
> [*The* CONSTABLE *puts the bob away and steps out into the lobby. His voice is heard.*

CONSTABLE. Now then, make way for the Jury, there! In here, gentlemen. You'll find all in order for considering your verdict. In here.

> [*He comes back into the doorway. And the* JURY *pass him one by one; eight decent men fresh from a painful scene, and divided in expression between relief and responsibility. The* FOREMAN, *a veterinary surgeon's assistant, has a letter in his hand.*

CONSTABLE. [*Moving in after them*] Got everything you want, gentlemen?

FOREMAN. Yes, thank you.

> [*The* CONSTABLE *goes out and closes the door.*

We might as well sit down while we're thinking it over.

> [FOUR JURYMEN *sit on the long seat, Left;* THREE *on chairs to Right of table. The* FOREMAN *sits at the head of the table.*

FOREMAN. Well, gentlemen, we're clear, I suppose, that deceased came by his death on Monday night last between eight and nine o'clock, in his own house at Kensington? [*There is a general assent.*] That's agreed then. Now, did he take his own life? That's the second question we have to answer.

2ND JURYMAN. [*Next on Left of* FOREMAN—*a grey-headed man in a small way of business*] Can't be a doubt about that, after the letter, and what the doctors said. [*Pause.*

FOREMAN. Anyone who has a doubt, give it a voice please.

[*No voice.*]

We're agreed, then. He took his own life. Now, what was his state of mind when he took it? That's the third question before us.

3RD JURYMAN. [*Second on Right of* FOREMAN—*a goggle-eyed commercial traveller*] Ah! It'll take a bit of answerin', in my opinion. I'd like that letter read again, Mr. Foreman. It's a painful letter, and I'd like it read again.

FOREMAN. Very well! It's addressed to Lieutenant Oswald, H.M.S. *Zéus*.

5TH JURYMAN [*Right front chair, a working jeweller, rather æsthetic*] Zeus —it's ancient Greek.

6TH JURYMAN. [*Left, at the front end of the seat—a self-owning barber and hard little nut*] Let's 'ave it in plain English.

FOREMAN. *Zéus*, Portsmouth. And it's headed from his own house : " 17, Southern Place, Kensington. March 23rd "—the fatal Monday —" 8.15 p.m." He put it precise, you see. This is the letter :—

" My dear old Pal,

"I write to you as my oldest and best friend. I am going off the deep end in a few minutes."

4TH JURYMAN. [*Right, next* FOREMAN—*a chemist*] One moment, Mr. Foreman. Speaking as a chemist : " Off the deep end " is an expression I've heard used, but never in that particular connection.

6TH JURYMAN. Speakin' as an 'airdresser, it means losin' your 'air.

FOREMAN. It can't mean anything here but what he was going to do.

3RD JURYMAN. That's right. Go on.

FOREMAN. [*Resuming*] " Off the deep end in a few minutes. Neither you nor anyone else, not even my mother, or Anne in the days before we split, have known that I have twice been clean off my chump. It was that, you know, which really botched up my life with Anne. She wanted children and I daren't, and couldn't tell her why. I simply couldn't tell anybody. The first time was soon after the war. I was up in Scotland fishing—a very remote place : for three days it was all darkness. I had only a gillie with me, and I swore him to silence. The second time was just before we definitely split—I was away in Belgium over that A.B.Z. parachute design of mine. For two days I wandered about, out of my wits, and came to myself in a wood. My dear old man, I don't suppose you can realize what it means to be at the mercy of a thing like that, to have the feeling of its coming on me— slowly, slowly creeping on me again. And not to know whether next time won't be the last." [*The* FOREMAN *coughs.*] " I go about in " —here's a word I can't read—" fer "—no—ah !—" terror "—that's it, " terror. I've known for days that it's coming on me again now. I can't stick it, old man. Better for myself and everybody that I should clear out. Good-bye, and God bless you. Comfort my poor mother.   Your old Pal,

COLIN MORECOMBE."

[*The* FOREMAN's *voice has been distinctly husky during the reading of the last words, and an audible sniff has been heard from the* 3RD JURYMAN. *In fact, all the* JURYMEN *have shown signs of discomfort, except the youngest, almost a boy, and the* 6TH JURYMAN, *who have listened unmoved.*

5TH JURYMAN. It's a dreadfully sad letter.

6TH JURYMAN. The question is, is it a sane letter ? The Coroner 'ad a word to say on that. But it struck me that gentleman was thinkin' more of 'imself than of deceased.

29*

7TH JURYMAN. [*On the Left, second from front—a bright-haired green-grocer*] You can't honestly say there's a word in it you or I couldn't have written. He's got everything exact, even to the split with his wife.

6TH JURYMAN. Ah! We needn't think about *that* lady.

3RD JURYMAN. No better than she should be, I should say.

5TH JURYMAN. Well, there was his own affair with the girl.

2ND JURYMAN. Pity they brought that in, in my opinion. The Coroner was right to stop that evidence, when he got the letter. After all, the poor fellow's gone.

6TH JURYMAN. Ah! I rather think that 'tec put his foot in his mouth, there.

4TH JURYMAN. Saved a faint, anyway, stopping her evidence—never saw a girl so white ; and I've had some in my shop.

FOREMAN. We must keep to the point—his sanity.

6TH JURYMAN. He was sane enough when he took the girl to Richmond, anyway.

5TH JURYMAN. The day before—you can't count that.

7TH JURYMAN. The letter was the last thing he did ; we needn't go further back than that.

FOREMAN. To my mind, gentlemen, the important words are the " slowly creeping on me again." As a Vet, I can tell you that a dog knows when he's going mad. And you may take it from me that as soon as he knows it, you've got to destroy him—practically he's mad already. Is a *man* still sane when he feels insanity creeping on him ? That's the *real* question.

6TH JURYMAN. If he was insane when he wrote that letter, we're all as mad as 'atters.

7TH JURYMAN. There it is, you see : the Coroner warned us not to bring him in of unsound mind unless we truly felt he was.

6TH JURYMAN. Ah! that gentleman—*full* of his own position ! Did he pay any attention to that question I asked him ? Not 'e !

3RD JURYMAN. [*Suddenly*] Hero in the war ! I remember that flight of 'is perfectly. And there he lies—poor feller !

5TH JURYMAN. I'm thinking of his family.

6TH JURYMAN. We're not concerned with the widder in this case ; *she* 'as 'er consolations.

5TH JURYMAN. His mother hasn't.

6TH JURYMAN. Ah! That was the little one in black.

FOREMAN. There's always someone to be hurt. Well, gentlemen, it must be one thing or the other. [*A silence.*

7TH JURYMAN. I can't see a madman using the words " off his chump."

3RD JURYMAN. Why not ? It's a very 'andy expression.

7TH JURYMAN. I think if a man was mad, he wouldn't use slang.

2ND JURYMAN. Some men'd use slang in their graves. [*To his neighbour—the boy,* 8TH JURYMAN.] What do *you* say ?

8TH JURYMAN. [*Startled*] I ?   Oh !   Mad.

4TH JURYMAN. Mr. Foreman, I'd like to say a word for the Coroner. I thought him very fair ; and on the whole I should say he was against Insanity.

6TH JURYMAN. Too many insane verdicts lately ; that's what's the matter with him.   We'll vote independent of that gentleman.

FOREMAN. Very well !   I'll take a vote. . . . Those in favour of unsound mind hold up their hands.

[*His own, and those of the* 2ND, 3RD, 5TH *and* 8TH JURYMEN *are held up.*]

Contrary ?

[*Those of the* 7TH *and* 4TH *are held up.   The* 6TH *does not hold up his at all.*

6TH JURYMAN. I thought so ; not agreed—we want a little more discussion.   They've brought us away from our businesses—let 'em wait for us.

7TH JURYMAN. Honestly, I don't see how he could have written that letter if he'd been insane at the time of writing.

4TH JURYMAN. I really think, gentlemen, we should follow the Coroner, with his experience.

6TH JURYMAN. Well, I don't.

5TH JURYMAN. [*Heatedly*] Then why didn't you hold up your hand ?

6TH JURYMAN. Wait and see !

FOREMAN. [*Calming them*] Now, gentlemen, please.   If you'd like to have *my* views.   I've been on a Coroner's Jury before.   In my opinion there's *always* a doubt in these cases, and it does no harm to anyone to give the benefit of it to the deceased.   That's human nature, and human nature's the best guide, after all.   Who can tell to a tick when a man's over the edge ?   I don't see what they want to ask the question for at all.   Where and when did a man die ?   Did he die by his own hand ?   Yes.   But what was his state of mind ?   No. Sound or unsound, he's dead.   In this case he tells us himself he was mad, or on the point of it.   The benefit o' the doubt, gentlemen.

4TH JURYMAN. Mr. Foreman, I think you're right after all.

2ND JURYMAN. Certainly he is.   It's common sense.   Speaking from the business point of view : am I going to do a deal with a man who writes a letter like that ?   Course I'm not.   That's the plain test.

7TH JURYMAN. Well, if you put it that way—I'm sure I don't want to be inhuman.

6TH JURYMAN. He was as sane as you or me when he wrote that letter.

FOREMAN. Do I understand that you follow the Coroner, after all, sir ?

6TH JURYMAN. Not much !   Unsound mind, every time.

FOREMAN. We're agreed, then.   The deceased took his own life, in his own house, between eight and nine in the evening, on Monday last, when of unsound mind.   Shall we offer an expression of sympathy with his family?

6TH JURYMAN. Not the widder—confine it to his mother.

FOREMAN. Well, perhaps that'll meet the case better. [*General assent.*] Come along then, gentlemen.   We'll go back and give it them.

[*They file out.*

[*The* CONSTABLE *comes in, looking over the room as if for another pipe.*   LADY MORECOMBE *comes in.*

LADY M. Officer!

CONSTABLE. Madam!

LADY M. Can I see the reporters before they go?

CONSTABLE. I'm afraid it's not in the book, madam, for any witness——

LADY M. I was not a witness.

CONSTABLE. Ah! I remember—you're the deceased's mother.   I don't know, I'm sure, madam.   It's not in my department.

[*He stands stock.*

LADY M. I know that. [*She puts a note into his hand.*] I only want you to get me the first who comes down.

CONSTABLE. Well, I see no reason, ma'am, why you shouldn't see the Press, as one private person to another.

LADY M. Then please——!

CONSTABLE. I will, ma'am; very glad to do you the service.

[*He goes out.*

[LADY MORECOMBE *moves to the end of the table and stands trembling, working her lips. The* CONSTABLE *returns, followed by the* REPORTER, FORMAN.

CONSTABLE. This is the first down, madam.   Lady wants to see you, sir.

[*He withdraws.   The* REPORTER *moves towards* LADY MORECOMBE.

REPORTER. Yes, Lady Morecombe?   Excuse me, I'm in a hurry.

LADY M. I've been rude to you, I'm afraid.   Please forgive me.

REPORTER. Oh! Our backs are broad, thank you.

LADY M. As a human being in distress, I beg you: please don't put that girl into your report!

REPORTER. [*Affected*] Lady Morecombe, I—I must hand it in; but I'll gladly ask them not to mention her.   I daresay they won't; her evidence didn't matter, as it turned out.   You left before the verdict. It's " Unsound mind," if that's any consolation to you.

CONSTABLE. [*Appearing*] Here's another for you, madam.   Press Association.

2ND REPORTER. [*From just within the doorway*] What is it?

LADY M. My son's name, sir.   The girl——

2ND REPORTER. Oh! That's all right, ma'am. The Coroner's just said she mustn't be mentioned.

REPORTER. Thank the Lord! I'm *so* glad, Lady Morecombe!

[LADY MORECOMBE *hides her face, overcome for the first time. The* 2ND REPORTER, *with a sound of sympathy, follows the first out.*

[LADY MORECOMBE *has turned to the wall,* Left, *weeping silently behind her handkerchief.* THREE LADIES *and the* MAN *from the Air Ministry have come into the alcove.*

THE MAN. Well, the show's over. I've sent for the car.

1ST LADY. I'd no idea it'd be so frightfully interesting, John.

2ND LADY. I've always wanted to see a case.

3RD LADY. Never was so thrilled in my life as when that girl——

2ND LADY. Oh! The wife's evidence was much the most exciting——

1ST LADY. She was rather wonderful, I thought. It must have been a nasty jar to have to——

3RD LADY. There's nothing like real life, after all. Beats the theatre hollow. Only it was *much* too short.

THE MAN. Of course the verdict was tosh. A man isn't insane when he knows what he's doing.

1ST LADY. But I thought Juries always said " Insane " as a matter of course ?

3RD LADY. Wasn't the Coroner amusin' ? So professional !

2ND LADY. Well, poor man, what else *could* he be ?

THE MAN. Morecombe's a real loss.

3RD LADY. It *was* a piece of luck the letter only coming like that— all the drama was in seeing the witnesses——

THE MAN. Pretty rough on his wife, and that girl !

2ND LADY. Oh! well, bad luck, of course. Still, *that* was the really exciting part.

1ST LADY. Thanks awfully, John, for bringing us down. It was *too* thrilling !

THE MAN. Hsssh !

[*A sudden silence comes over them ; they have become aware of the black figure of* LADY MORECOMBE *standing close by, looking at them.*

3RD LADY. Er—— The car *must* be there by now !

[*Like a bunch of frightened poultry they fluster through the doorway and are lost in the throng outside.*

LADY M. [*To herself—very low*] The Show is over.

The curtain falls.

THE FIRST AND THE LAST

PERSONS OF THE PLAY

KEITH DARRANT, K.C.
LARRY DARRANT, *his brother.*
WANDA.

SCENE I.	KEITH'S *Study.*
SCENE II.	WANDA'S *Room.*
SCENE III.	*The Same.*

Between SCENE I. and SCENE II.—Thirty hours.
Between SCENE II. and SCENE III.—Two months.

SCENE I

It is six o'clock of a November evening, in KEITH DARRANT'S *study. A large, dark-curtained room where the light from a single reading-lamp falling on Turkey carpet, on books beside a large armchair, on the deep blue-and-gold coffee service, makes a sort of oasis before a log fire. In red Turkish slippers and an old brown velvet coat,* KEITH DARRANT *sits asleep. He has a dark, clean-cut, clean-shaven face, dark grizzling hair, dark twisting eyebrows.*

The curtained door away out in the dim part of the room behind him is opened so softly that he does not wake. LARRY DARRANT *enters and stands half lost in the curtain over the door. A thin figure, with a worn, high cheekboned face, deep-sunk blue eyes and wavy hair all ruffled—a face which still has a certain beauty. He moves inwards along the wall, stands still again and utters a gasping sigh.* KEITH *stirs in his chair.*

KEITH. Who's there?

LARRY. [*In a stifled voice*] Only I—Larry.

KEITH. [*Half-waked*] Come in! I was asleep.

    [*He does not turn his head, staring sleepily at the fire. The sound of* LARRY'S *breathing can be heard.*]

[*Turning his head a little.*] Well, Larry, what is it?

    [LARRY *comes skirting along the wall, as if craving its support, outside the radius of the light.*]

[*Staring.*] Are you ill?

                        [LARRY *stands still again and heaves a deep sigh.*

KEITH. [*Rising, with his back to the fire, and staring at his brother*] What is it, man? [*Then with a brutality born of nerves suddenly ruffled.*] Have you committed a murder that you stand there like a fish?

LARRY. [*In a whisper*] Yes, Keith.

KEITH. [*With vigorous disgust*] By Jove! Drunk again! [*In a voice changed by sudden apprehension.*] What do you mean by coming here in this state? I told you—— If you weren't my brother——! Come here, where I can see you! What's the matter with you, Larry?

    [*With a lurch* LARRY *leaves the shelter of the wall and sinks into a chair in the circle of light.*

LARRY. It's true.

    [KEITH *steps quickly forward and stares down into his brother's eyes, where is a horrified wonder, as if they would never again get on terms with his face.*

905

KEITH. [*Angry, bewildered—in a low voice*] What in God's name is this nonsense?

> [*He goes quickly over to the door and draws the curtain aside, to see that it is shut, then comes back to* LARRY, *who is huddling over the fire.*]

Come, Larry! Pull yourself together and drop exaggeration! What on earth do you mean?

LARRY. [*In a shrill outburst*] It's true, I tell you; I've killed a man.

KEITH. [*Bracing himself; coldly*] Be quiet!

> [LARRY *lifts his hands and wrings them.*]

[*Utterly taken aback.*] Why come here and tell *me* this?

LARRY. Whom *should* I tell, Keith? I came to ask what I'm to do—give myself up, or what?

KEITH. When—when—what——?

LARRY. Last night.

KEITH. Good God! How? Where? You'd better tell me quietly from the beginning. Here, drink this coffee; it'll clear your head.

> [*He pours out and hands him a cup of coffee.* LARRY *drinks it off.*

LARRY. My head! Yes! It's like this, Keith—there's a girl——

KEITH. Women! Always women, with you! Well?

LARRY. A Polish girl. She—her father died over here when she was sixteen, and left her all alone. There was a mongrel living in the same house who married her—or pretended to. She's very pretty, Keith. He left her with a baby coming. She lost it, and nearly starved. Then another fellow took her on, and she lived with him two years, till that brute turned up again and made her go back to him. He used to beat her black and blue. He'd left her again when I met her. She was taking anybody then. [*He stops, passes his hand over his lips, looks up at* KEITH, *and goes on defiantly.*] I never met a sweeter woman, or a truer, that I swear. Woman! She's only twenty now! When I went to her last night, that devil had found her out again. He came for me—a bullying, great, hulking brute. Look! [*He touches a dark mark on his forehead.*] I took his ugly throat, and when I let go—— [*He stops and his hands drop.*

KEITH. Yes?

LARRY. [*In a smothered voice*] Dead, Keith. I never knew till afterwards that she was hanging on to him—to h-help me.

> [*Again he wrings his hands.*

KEITH. [*In a hard, dry voice*] What did you do then?

LARRY. We—we sat by it a long time.

KEITH. Well?

LARRY. Then I carried it on my back down the street, round a corner, to an archway.

KEITH. How far?

LARRY. About fifty yards.

KEITH. Was—did anyone see ?

LARRY. No.

KEITH. What time ?

LARRY. Three in the morning

KEITH. And then ?

LARRY. Went back to her.

KEITH. Why—in heaven's name ?

LARRY. She was lonely and afraid.   So was I, Keith.

KEITH. Where is this place ?

LARRY. Forty-two Borrow Square, Soho.

KEITH. And the archway ?

LARRY. Corner of Glove Lane.

KEITH. Good God !   Why, I saw it in the paper this morning.
They were talking of it in the Courts !   [*He snatches the evening paper
from his armchair, and runs it over and reads.*]   Here it is again.   " Body
of a man was found this morning under an archway in Glove Lane.
From marks about the throat grave suspicion of foul play are enter-
tained.   The body had apparently been robbed."   My God !   [*Suddenly he turns.*]   You saw this in the paper and dreamed it.   D'you
understand, Larry ?—you dreamed it.

LARRY. [*Wistfully*]   If only I had, Keith.

　　　[KEITH *makes a movement of his hands almost like his brother's.*

KEITH. Did you take anything from the—body ?

LARRY. [*Drawing an envelope from his pocket*]   This dropped out while
we were struggling.

KEITH. [*Snatching it and reading*]   " Patrick Walenn "—Was that
his name ?—" Simon's Hotel, Farrier Street, London."   [*Stooping
he puts it in the fire.*]   No !—that makes me——   [*He bends to pluck
it out, stays his hand, and stamps it suddenly further in with his foot.*]   What
in God's name made you come here and tell *me* ?   Don't you know
I'm—I'm within an ace of a Judgeship ?

LARRY. [*Simply*]   Yes.   You *must* know what I ought to do.   I
didn't mean to kill him, Keith.   I love the girl—I love her.   What
shall I do ?

KEITH. Love !

LARRY. [*In a flash*]   Love !—That swinish brute !   A million
creatures die every day, and not one of them deserves death as he did.
But—but I feel it here.   [*Touching his heart.*]   Such an awful clutch,
Keith.   Help me if you can, old man.   I may be no good, but I've
never hurt a fly if I could help it.   [*He buries his face in his hands.*

KEITH. Steady, Larry !   Let's think it out.   You weren't seen,
you say ?

LARRY. It's a dark place, and dead night.

KEITH. When did you leave the girl again ?

LARRY. About seven.

KEITH. Where did you go?

LARRY. To my rooms.

KEITH. Fitzroy Street?

LARRY. Yes.

KEITH. What have you done since?

LARRY. Sat there—thinking.

KEITH. Not been out?

LARRY. No.

KEITH. Not seen the girl?   [LARRY *shakes his head.*]
Will she give you away?

LARRY. Never.

KEITH. Or herself—hysteria?

LARRY. No.

KEITH. Who knows of your relations with her?

LARRY. No one.

KEITH. No one?

LARRY. I don't know who should, Keith.

KEITH. Did anyone see you go in last night, when you first went
to her?

LARRY. No.   She lives on the ground floor.   I've got keys.

KEITH. Give them to me.

     [LARRY *takes two keys from his pocket and hands them to his brother.*

LARRY. [*Rising*] I can't be cut off from her!

KEITH. What!   A girl like that?

LARRY. [*With a flash*] Yes, a girl like that.

KEITH. [*Moving his hand to put down all emotion*] What else have
you that connects you with her?

LARRY. Nothing.

KEITH. In your rooms?   [LARRY *shakes his head.*]
Photographs?   Letters?

LARRY. No.

KEITH. Sure?

LARRY. Nothing.

KEITH. No one saw you going back to her?

                              [LARRY *shakes his head.*]
Nor leave in the morning?   You can't be certain.

LARRY. I am.

KEITH. You were fortunate.   Sit down again, man.   I must think.

     [*He turns to the fire and leans his elbows on the mantelpiece and his
          head on his hands.   LARRY sits down again obediently.*

KEITH. It's all too unlikely.   It's monstrous!

LARRY. [*Sighing it out*] Yes.

KEITH. This Walenn—was it his first reappearance after an
absence?

LARRY. Yes.

KEITH. How did he find out where she was ?

LARRY. I don't know.

KEITH. [*Brutally*] How drunk were you ?

LARRY. I was not drunk.

KEITH. How much had you drunk, then ?

LARRY. A little claret—nothing !

KEITH. You say you didn't mean to kill him.

LARRY. God knows.

KEITH. That's something.

LARRY. He hit me.   [*He holds up his hands.*] I didn't know I was so strong.

KEITH. She was hanging on to him, you say ?—That's ugly.

LARRY. She was scared for me.

KEITH. D'you mean she—loves you ?

LARRY. [*Simply*] Yes, Keith.

KEITH. [*Brutally*] Can a woman like that love ?

LARRY. [*Flashing out*] By God, you are a stony devil ! Why not ?

KEITH. [*Dryly*] I'm trying to get at truth. If you want me to help, I must know everything. What makes you think she's fond of you ?

LARRY. [*With a crazy laugh*] Oh, you lawyer ! Were you never in a woman's arms ?

KEITH. I'm talking of *love*.

LARRY. [*Fiercely*] So am I. I tell you she's devoted. Did you ever pick up a lost dog ? Well, she has the lost dog's love for me. And I for her ; we picked each other up. I've never felt for another woman what I feel for her—she's been the saving of me !

KEITH. [*With a shrug*] What made you choose that archway ?

LARRY. It was the first dark place.

KEITH. Did his face look as if he'd been strangled ?

LARRY. Don't !

KEITH. Did it ?   [LARRY *bows his head.*]
Very disfigured ?

LARRY. Yes.

KEITH. Did you look to see if his clothes were marked ?

LARRY. No.

KEITH. Why not ?

LARRY. [*In an outburst*] I'm not made of iron, like you. Why not ? If you had done it——!

KEITH. [*Holding up his hand*] You say he was disfigured. Would he be recognizable ?

LARRY. [*Wearily*] I don't know.

KEITH. When she lived with him last—where was that ?

LARRY. In Pimlico, I think.

KEITH. Not Soho?   [LARRY *shakes his head.*]
How long has she been at this Soho place?

LARRY. Nearly a year.

KEITH. Living this life?

LARRY. Till she met me.

KEITH. Till she met you?   And you believe——?

LARRY. [*Starting up*] Keith!

KEITH. [*Again raising his hand*] Always in the same rooms?

LARRY. [*Subsiding*] Yes.

KEITH. What was *he*?   A professional bully?   [LARRY *nods.*]
Spending most of his time abroad, I suppose.

LARRY. I think so.

KEITH. Can you say if he was known to the police?

LARRY. I've never heard.

> [KEITH *turns away and walks up and down; then, stopping at*
> LARRY'S *chair, he speaks.*

KEITH. Now listen, Larry.   When you leave here, go straight
home, and stay there till I give you leave to go out again.   Promise.

LARRY. I promise.

KEITH. Is your promise worth anything?

LARRY. [*With one of his flashes*] "Unstable as water, he shall not
excel!"

KEITH. Exactly.   But if I'm to help you, you must do as I say.
I must have time to think this out.   Have you got money?

LARRY. Very little.

KEITH. [*Grimly*] Half-quarter day—yes, your quarter's always spent
by then.   If you're to get away—never mind, I can manage the money.

LARRY. [*Humbly*] You're very good, Keith; you've always been
very good to me—I don't know why.

KEITH. [*Sardonically*] Privilege of a brother.   As it happens, I'm
thinking of myself and our family.   You can't indulge yourself in
killing without bringing ruin.   My God!   I suppose you realize
that you've made me an accessory after the fact—me, King's Counsel
—sworn to the service of the Law, who, in a year or two, will have
the trying of cases like yours!   By heaven, Larry, you've surpassed
yourself!

LARRY. [*Bringing out a little box*] I'd better have done with it.

KEITH. You fool!   Give that to me.

LARRY. [*With a strange smile*] No.   [*He holds up a tabloid between
finger and thumb.*] White magic, Keith!   Just one—and they may do
what they like to you, and you won't know it.   Snap your fingers
at all the tortures.   It's a great comfort!   Have one to keep by you?

KEITH. Come, Larry!   Hand it over.

LARRY. [*Replacing the box*] Not quite!   You've never killed a
man, you see.   [*He gives that crazy laugh.*] D'you remember that

hammer when we were boys and you riled me, up in the long room ?
I had luck then. I had luck in Naples once. I nearly killed a driver
for beating his poor brute of a horse. But now——! My God !

> [*He covers his face.*
> [KEITH *touched, goes up and lays a hand on his shoulder.*

KEITH. Come, Larry ! Courage !   [LARRY *looks up at him.*

LARRY. All right, Keith ; I'll try.

KEITH. Don't go out. Don't drink. Don't talk. Pull yourself
together !

LARRY. [*Moving towards the door*] Don't keep me longer than you
can help, Keith.

KEITH. No, no. Courage !

> [LARRY *reaches the door, turns as if to say something—finds no
>   words, and goes.*]

[*To the fire.*] Courage ! My God ! *I* shall need it !

The curtain falls.

SCENE II

About eleven o'clock the following night in WANDA'S *room on the ground
      floor in Soho. In the light from one close-shaded electric bulb the room
      is but dimly visible. A dying fire burns on the left. A curtained
      window in the centre of the back wall. A door on the right. The
      furniture is plush-covered and commonplace, with a kind of shabby
      smartness. A couch, without back or arms, stands aslant, between
      window and fire.*

On this WANDA *is sitting, her knees drawn up under her, staring at the
      embers. She has on only her nightgown and a wrapper over it ; her
      bare feet are thrust into slippers. Her hands are crossed and pressed
      over her breast. She starts and looks up, listening. Her eyes are
      candid and startled, her face alabaster pale, and its pale brown hair,
      short and square-cut, curls towards her bare neck. The startled dark
      eyes and the faint rose of her lips are like colour-staining on a white
      mask.*

*Footsteps as of a policeman, very measured, pass on the pavement outside,
      and die away. She gets up and steals to the window, draws one curtain
      aside so that a chink of the night is seen. She opens the curtain wider,
      till the shape of a bare, witch-like tree becomes visible in the open space
      of the little Square on the far side of the road. The footsteps are heard
      once more coming nearer.* WANDA *closes the curtains and cranes back.
      They pass and die again. She moves away and stands looking down
      at the floor between the door and couch, as though seeing something there ;*

*shudders; covers her eyes; goes back to the couch and sits down again
just as before, to stare at the embers. Again she is startled by noise
of the outer door being opened. She springs up, runs and turns out
the light by a switch close to the door. By the dim glimmer of the fire
she can just be seen standing by the dark window-curtains, listening.
There comes the sound of subdued knocking on her door. She stands in
breathless terror. The knocking is repeated. The sound of a latchkey in the door is heard. Her terror leaves her. The door opens;
a man enters in a dark fur overcoat.*

WANDA. [*In a voice of breathless relief, with a rather foreign accent*]
Oh! it's you, Larry! Why did you knock? I was so frightened.
Come in! [*She crosses quickly, and flings her arms round his neck. Re-
coiling—in a terror-stricken whisper.*] Oh! Who is it?

KEITH. [*In a smothered voice*] A friend of Larry's. Don't be
frightened.

[*She has recoiled again to the window; and when he finds the switch
and turns the light up, she is seen standing there holding her dark
wrapper up to her throat, so that her face has an uncanny look
of being detached from the body.*]

[*Gently.*] You needn't be afraid. I haven't come to do you harm—
quite the contrary. [*Holding up the keys.*] Larry wouldn't have given
me these, would he, if he hadn't trusted me?

[WANDA *does not move, staring like a spirit startled out of the flesh.*]
[*After looking round him.*] I'm sorry to have startled you.

WANDA. [*In a whisper*] Who are you, please?

KEITH. Larry's brother.

[WANDA, *with a sigh of utter relief, steals forward to the couch
and sinks down. KEITH goes up to her.*]

He's told me.

WANDA. [*Clasping her hands round her knees*] Yes?

KEITH. An awful business!

WANDA. Yes; oh, yes! Awful—it is awful!

KEITH. [*Staring round him again*] In this room?

WANDA. Just where you are standing. I see him now, always
falling.

KEITH. [*Moved by the gentle despair in her voice*] You look very young.
What's your name?

WANDA. Wanda.

KEITH. Are you fond of Larry?

WANDA. I would die for him!   [*A moment's silence.*

KEITH. I—I've come to see what you can do to save him.

WANDA. [*Wistfully*] You would not deceive me. You are really
his brother?

KEITH. I swear it.

WANDA. [*Clasping her hands*] If I *can* save him! Won't you sit down?

KEITH. [*Drawing up a chair and sitting*] This man, your—your husband, before he came here the night before last—how long since you saw him?

WANDA. Eighteen month.

KEITH. Does anyone about here know you are his wife?

WANDA. No. I came here to live a bad life. Nobody know me. I am quite alone.

KEITH. They've discovered who he was—you know that?

WANDA. No; I have not dared to go out.

KEITH. Well, they have; and they'll look for anyone connected with him, of course.

WANDA. He never let people think I was married to him. I don't know if I was—really. We went to an office and signed our names; but he was a wicked man. He treated many, I think, like me.

KEITH. Did my brother ever see him before?

WANDA. Never! And that man first went for him.

KEITH. Yes. I saw the mark. Have you a servant?

WANDA. No. A woman come at nine in the morning for an hour.

KEITH. Does she know Larry?

WANDA. No. He is always gone.

KEITH. Friends—acquaintances?

WANDA. No; I am verree quiet. Since I know your brother, I see no one, sare.

KEITH. [*Sharply*] Do you mean that?

WANDA. Oh, yes! I love him. Nobody come here but him for a long time now.

KEITH. How long?

WANDA. Five month.

KEITH. So you have not been out since——?

[WANDA *shakes her head.*]

What have you been doing?

WANDA. [*Simply*] Crying. [*Pressing her hands to her breast.*] He is in danger because of me. I am so afraid for him.

KEITH. [*Checking her emotion*] Look at me.   [*She looks at him.*] If the worst comes, and this man is traced to you, can you trust yourself not to give Larry away?

WANDA. [*Rising and pointing to the fire*] Look! I have burned all the things he have given me—even his picture. Now I have nothing from him.

KEITH. [*Who has risen too*] Good! One more question. Do the police know you—because—of your life?

[*She looks at him intently, and shakes her head.*]

You know where Larry lives?

WANDA. Yes.

KEITH. You mustn't go there, and he mustn't come to you.

[*She bows her head ; then suddenly comes close to him.*

WANDA. Please do not take him from me altogether. I will be so careful. I will not do anything to hurt him. But if I cannot see him sometimes, I shall die. Please do not take him from me.

[*She catches his hand and presses it desperately between her own.*

KEITH. Leave that to me. I'm going to do all I can.

WANDA. [*Looking up into his face*] But you will be kind ?

[*Suddenly she bends and kisses his hand.* KEITH *draws his hand away, and she recoils a little humbly, looking up at him again. Suddenly she stands rigid, listening.*]

[*In a whisper.*] Listen ! Someone—out there !

[*She darts past him and turns out the light. There is a knock on the door. They are now close together between door and window.*

[*Whispering*] Oh ! Who is it ?

KEITH. [*Under his breath*] You said no one comes but Larry.

WANDA. Yes, and you have his keys. Oh ! if it is Larry ! I must open !

[KEITH *shrinks back against the wall.* WANDA *goes to the door.*]

[*Opening the door an inch.*] Yes ? Please ? Who ?

[*A thin streak of light from a bull's-eye lantern outside plays over the wall. A Policeman's voice says :* " All right, Miss. Your outer door's open. You ought to keep it shut after dark, you know."

WANDA. Thank you, sir.

[*The sound of retreating footsteps, of the outer door closing.* WANDA *shuts the door.*]

A policeman !

KEITH. [*Moving from the wall*] Curse ! I must have left that door. [*Suddenly—turning up the light.*] You told me they didn't know you.

WANDA. [*Sighing*] I did not think they did, sir. It is so long I was not out in the town ; not since I had Larry.

[KEITH *gives her an intent look, then crosses to the fire. He stands there a moment, looking down, then turns to the girl, who has crept back to the couch.*

KEITH. [*Half to himself*] After your life, who can believe—— ? Look here ! You drifted together and you'll drift apart, you know. Better for him to get away and make a clean cut of it.

WANDA. [*Uttering a little moaning sound*] Oh, sir ! May I not love, because I have been bad ? I was only sixteen when that man spoiled me. If you knew——

KEITH. I'm thinking of Larry. With you, his danger is much greater. There's a good chance as things are going. You may

wreck it. And for what? Just a few months more of—well—
you know.

WANDA. [*Standing at the head of the couch and touching her eyes with
her hands*] Oh, sir! Look! It *is* true. He is my life. Don't take
him away from me.

KEITH. [*Moved and restless*] You must know what Larry is. He'll
never stick to you.

WANDA. [*Simply*] He will, sir.

KEITH. [*Energetically*] The last man on earth to stick to anything!
But for the sake of a whim he'll risk his life and the honour of all his
family. I know him.

WANDA. No, no, you do not. It is *I* who know him.

KEITH. Now, now! At any moment they may find out your
connection with that man. So long as Larry goes on with you, he's
tied to this murder, don't you see?

WANDA. [*Coming close to him*] But he love me. Oh, sir! he love
me!

KEITH. Larry has loved dozens of women.

WANDA. Yes, but——   [*Her face quivers.*

KEITH. [*Brusquely*] Don't cry! If I give you money, will you
disappear, for his sake!

WANDA. [*With a moan*] It will be in the water, then. There will
be no cruel men there.

KEITH. Ah! First Larry, then you! Come now. It's better
for you both. A few months, and you'll forget you ever met.

WANDA. [*Looking wildly up*] I will go if Larry say I must. But not
to live. No! [*Simply.*] I could not, sir. [KEITH, *moved, is silent.*]
I could not live without Larry. What is left for a girl like me—when
she once love? It is finish.

KEITH. I don't want you to go back to that life.

WANDA. No; you do not care what I do. Why should you?
I tell you I will go if Larry say I must.

KEITH. That's not enough. You know that. You must take it
out of his hands. He will never give up his present for the sake of
his future. If you're as fond of him as you say, you'll help to save him.

WANDA. [*Below her breath*] Yes! Oh, yes! But do not keep him
long from me—I beg! [*She sinks to the floor and clasps his knees.*

KEITH. Well, well! Get up. [*There is a tap on the window-pane.*]
Listen!   [*A faint, peculiar whistle.*

WANDA. [*Springing up*] Larry! Oh, thank God!
      [*She runs to the door, opens it, and goes out to bring him in.* KEITH
            stands waiting, facing the open doorway.
                  [LARRY *entering with* WANDA *just behind him.*

LARRY. Keith!

KEITH. [*Grimly*] So much for your promise not to go out!

LARRY. I've been waiting in for you all day.   I couldn't stand it any longer.

KEITH. Exactly !

LARRY. Well, what's the sentence, brother ?   " Transportation for life and then to be fined forty pounds " ?

KEITH. So you can joke, can you ?

LARRY. Must.

KEITH. A boat leaves for the Argentine the day after to-morrow ; you must go by it.

LARRY. [*Putting his arms round* WANDA, *who is standing motionless with her eyes fixed on him*] Together, Keith ?

KEITH. You can't go together.   I'll send her by the next boat.

LARRY. Swear ?

KEITH. Yes.   You're lucky—they're on a false scent.

LARRY. What !

KEITH. You haven't seen it ?

LARRY. I've seen nothing, not even a paper.

KEITH. They've taken up a vagabond who robbed the body.   He pawned a snake-shaped ring, and they identified this Walenn by it. I've been down and seen him charged myself.

LARRY. With murder ?

WANDA. [*Faintly*] Larry !

KEITH. He's in no danger.   They always get the wrong man first. It'll do him no harm to be locked up a bit—hyena like that.   Better in prison, anyway, than sleeping out under archways in this weather.

LARRY. What was he like, Keith ?

KEITH. A little yellow, ragged, lame, unshaven scarecrow of a chap.   They were fools to think he could have had the strength.

LARRY. What ! [*In an awed voice.*] Why, I saw him—after I left you last night.

KEITH. You ?   Where ?

LARRY. By the archway.

KEITH. You went back there ?

LARRY. It draws you, Keith.

KEITH. You're mad, I think.

LARRY. I talked to him, and he said, " Thank you for this little chat. It's worth more than money when you're down."   Little grey man like a shaggy animal.   And a newspaper boy came up and said : " That's right, guv'nors !   'Ere's where they found the body—very spot.   They 'yn't got 'im yet."

[*He laughs ; and the terrified girl presses herself against him.*] An innocent man ?

KEITH. *He's* in no danger, I tell you.   He could never have strangled—— Why, he hadn't the strength of a kitten.   Now, Larry ! I'll take your berth to-morrow.   Here's money.   [*He brings out a pile of notes and puts them on the couch.*] You can make a new life of it out there together presently, in the sun.

LARRY. [*In a whisper*] In the sun!   " A cup of wine and thou." [*Suddenly.*] How *can* I, Keith?   I must see how it goes with that poor devil.

KEITH. Bosh!   Dismiss it from your mind; there's not nearly enough evidence.

LARRY. Not?

KEITH. No.   You've got your chance.   Take it like a man.

LARRY. [*With a strange smile—to the girl*] Shall we, Wanda?

WANDA. Oh, Larry!

LARRY. [*Picking the notes up from the couch*] Take them back, Keith.

KEITH. What!   I tell you no jury would convict; and if they did, no judge would hang.   A ghoul who can rob a dead body, ought to be in prison.   He did worse than you.

LARRY. It won't do, Keith.   I must see it out.

KEITH. Don't be a fool!

LARRY. I've still got some kind of honour.   If I clear out before I know, I shall have none—nor peace.   Take them, Keith, or I'll put them in the fire.

KEITH. [*Taking back the notes; bitterly*] I suppose I may ask you not to be entirely oblivious of our name.   Or is that unworthy of your honour?

LARRY. [*Hanging his head*] I'm awfully sorry, Keith; awfully sorry, old man.

KEITH. [*Sternly*] You owe it to me—to our name—to our dead mother—to do nothing anyway till we see what happens.

LARRY. I know.   I'll do nothing without you, Keith.

KEITH. [*Taking up his hat*] Can I trust you?

[*He stares hard at his brother.*

LARRY. You can trust me.

KEITH. Swear?

LARRY. I swear.

KEITH. Remember, *nothing !*   Good night!

LARRY. Good night!   [KEITH *goes.*

[LARRY *sits down on the couch and stares at the fire.   The girl steals up and slips her arms about him.*

LARRY. An innocent man!

WANDA. Oh, Larry!   But so are you.   What did we want—to kill that man?   Never!   Oh! kiss me!

[LARRY *turns his face.   She kisses his lips.*

I have suffered so—not seein' you.   Don't leave me again—don't! Stay here.   Isn't it good to be together?—Oh! Poor Larry! How tired you look!—Stay with me.   I am so frightened all alone.   So frightened they will take you from me.

LARRY. Poor child !

WANDA. No, no ! Don't look like that !

LARRY. You're shivering.

WANDA. I will make up the fire. Love me, Larry ! I want to forget.

LARRY. The poorest little wretch on God's earth—locked up— for me ! A little wild animal, locked up. There he goes, up and down, up and down—in his cage—don't you see him ?—looking for a place to gnaw his way through—little grey rat.

[*He gets up and roams about.*

WANDA. No, no ! I can't bear it ! Don't frighten me more !

[*He comes back and takes her in his arms.*

LARRY. There, there ! [*He kisses her closed eyes.*

WANDA. [*Without moving*] If we could sleep a little—wouldn't it be nice ?

LARRY. Sleep ?

WANDA. [*Raising herself*] Promise to stay with me—to stay here for good, Larry. I will cook for you ; I will make you so comfortable. They will find him innocent. And then—Oh, Larry !—in the sun— right away—far from this horrible country. How lovely ! [*Trying to get him to look at her.*] Larry !

LARRY. [*With a movement to free himself*] To the edge of the world —and—over !

WANDA. No, no ! No, no ! You don't want me to die, Larry, do you ? I shall if you leave me. Let us be happy ! Love me !

LARRY. [*With a laugh*] Ah ! Let's be happy and shut out the sight of him. Who cares ? Millions suffer for no mortal reason. Let's be strong, like Keith. No ! I won't leave you, Wanda. Let's forget everything except ourselves. [*Suddenly.*] There he goes—up and down !

WANDA. [*Moaning*] No, no ! See ! I will pray to the Virgin. She will pity us !

[*She falls on her knees and clasps her hands, praying. Her lips move.* LARRY *stands motionless, with arms crossed, and on his face are yearning and mockery, love and despair.*

LARRY. [*Whispering*] Pray for us ! Bravo ! Pray away !

[*Suddenly the girl stretches out her arms and lifts her face with a look of ecstasy.*]

What ?

WANDA. She is smiling ! We shall be happy soon.

LARRY. [*Bending down over her*] Poor child ! When we die, Wanda, let's go together. We should keep each other warm out in the dark,

WANDA. [*Raising her hands to his face*] Yes ! oh, yes ! If you die I could not—I could not go on living !

The curtain falls.

SCENE III

Two Months Later

WANDA'S *room.   Daylight is just beginning to fail of a January afternoon.
The table is laid for supper, with decanters of wine.*

> [WANDA *is standing at the window looking out at the wintry trees
> of the Square beyond the pavement.   A newspaper* BOY'S *voice
> is heard coming nearer.*

VOICE. Pyper !   Glove Lyne murder !   Trial and verdict !   [*Receding.*] Verdict !   Pyper !

> [WANDA *throws up the window as if to call to him, checks herself,
> closes it and runs to the door.   She opens it, but recoils into the
> room.   KEITH is standing there.   He comes in.*

KEITH. Where is Larry ?

WANDA. He went to the trial.   I could not keep him from it.
The trial—Oh ! what has happened, sir ?

KEITH. [*Savagely*] Guilty !   Sentence of death !   Fools !—idiots !

WANDA. Of death !   [*For a moment she seems about to swoon.*

KEITH. Girl !   Girl !   It may all depend on you.   Larry's still
living here ?

WANDA. Yes.

KEITH. I must wait for him.

WANDA. Will you sit down, please ?

KEITH. [*Shaking his head*] Are you ready to go away at any time ?

WANDA. Yes, yes ; always I am ready.

KEITH. And he ?

WANDA. Yes—but now !   What will he do ?   That poor man !

KEITH. A graveyard thief—a ghoul !

WANDA. Perhaps he was hungry.   I have been hungry : you do
things then that you would not.   Larry has thought of him in prison
so much all these weeks.   Oh ! what shall we do now ?

KEITH. Listen !   Help me.   Don't let Larry out of your sight.
I must see how things go.   They'll never hang this wretch.   [*He
grips her arms.*] Now, we must stop Larry from giving himself up.
He's fool enough.   D'you understand ?

WANDA. Yes.   But why has he not come in ?   Oh ! If he have,
already !

KEITH. [*Letting go her arms*] My God !   If the police come—find
me here—— [*He moves to the door.*] No, he wouldn't—without
seeing you first.   He's sure to come.   Watch him like a lynx.   Don't
let him go without you.

WANDA. [*Clasping her hands on her breast*] I will try, sir.

KEITH. Listen !   [*A key is heard in the lock.*]
It's he ! [LARRY *enters. He is holding a great bunch of pink lilies and white narcissus. His face tells nothing.* KEITH *looks from him to the girl, who stands motionless.*

LARRY. Keith ! So you've seen ?

KEITH. The thing can't stand. I'll stop it somehow. But you must give me time, Larry.

LARRY. [*Calmly*] Still looking after your honour, Keith ?

KEITH. [*Grimly*] Think my reasons what you like.

WANDA. [*Softly*] Larry !   [LARRY *puts his arm round her.*

LARRY. Sorry, old man.

KEITH. This man can and shall get off. I want your solemn promise that you won't give yourself up, nor even go out till I've seen you again.

LARRY. I give it.

KEITH. [*Looking from one to the other*] By the memory of our mother, swear that.

LARRY. [*With a smile*] I swear.

KEITH. I have your oath—both of you—both of you. I'm going at once to see what can be done.

LARRY. [*Softly*] Good luck, brother.   [KEITH *goes out.*

WANDA. [*Putting her hands on* LARRY's *breast*] What does it mean ?

LARRY. Supper, child—I've had nothing all day. Put these lilies in water. [*She takes the lilies and obediently puts them into a vase.*
            LARRY *pours wine into a deep-coloured glass and drinks it off.*]
We've had a good time, Wanda. Best time I ever had, these last two months ; and nothing but the bill to pay.

WANDA. [*Clasping him desperately*] Oh, Larry ! Larry !

LARRY. [*Holding her away to look at her*] Take off those things and put on a bridal garment.

WANDA. Promise me—wherever you go, I go too. Promise ! Larry, you think I haven't seen, all these weeks. But I have seen everything ; all in your heart, always. You cannot hide from me. I knew—I knew ! Oh, if we might go away into the sun ! Oh ! Larry—couldn't we ? [*She searches his eyes with hers—then shuddering.*] Well ! If it must be dark—I don't care, if I may go in your arms. In prison we could not be together. I am ready. Only love me first. Don't let me cry before I go. Oh ! Larry, will there be much pain ?

LARRY. [*In a choked voice*] No pain, my pretty.

WANDA. [*With a little sigh*] It is a pity.

LARRY. If you had seen him, as I have, all day, being tortured. Wanda, we shall be out of it. [*The wine mounting to his head.*] We shall be free in the dark ; free of their cursed inhumanities. I hate this world—I loathe it ! I hate its God-forsaken savagery ; its pride and smugness ! Keith's world—all righteous will-power and success.

We're no good here, you and I—we were cast out at birth—soft, will-less—better dead. No fear, Keith! I'm staying indoors. [*He pours wine into two glasses.*] Drink it up!

[*Obediently* WANDA *drinks, and he also.*]
Now go and make yourself beautiful.

WANDA. [*Seizing him in her arms*] Oh, Larry!

LARRY. [*Touching her face and hair*] Hanged by the neck until he's dead—for what I did.

[WANDA *takes a long look at his face, slips her arms from him, and goes out through the curtains below the fireplace.*

[LARRY *feels in his pocket, brings out the little box, opens it, fingers the white tabloids.*

LARRY. Two each—after food. [*He laughs and puts back the box.*] Oh! my girl!

[*The sound of a piano playing a faint festive tune is heard afar off. He mutters, staring at the fire.*]
Flames—flame, and flicker—ashes.

"No more, no more, the moon is dead,
And all the people in it."

[*He sits on the couch with a piece of paper on his knees, adding a few words with a stylo pen to what is already written.*

[*The girl, in a silk wrapper, coming back through the curtains, watches him.*

LARRY. [*Looking up*] It's all here—I've confessed. [*Reading.*] " Please bury us together.

" LAURENCE DARRANT.

" *January* 28*th, about six p.m.*"
They'll find us in the morning.   Come and have supper, my dear love.

[*The girl creeps forward.   He rises, puts his arm round her, and with her arm twined round him, smiling into each other's faces, they go to the table and sit down.*

[*The curtain falls for a few seconds to indicate the passage of three hours.   When it rises again, the lovers are lying on the couch, in each other's arms, the lilies strewn about them.   The girl's bare arm is round LARRY'S neck.   Her eyes are closed; his are open and sightless.   There is no light but fire-light.*

[*A knocking on the door and the sound of a key turned in the lock. KEITH enters.   He stands a moment bewildered by the half-light, then calls sharply : " Larry ! " and turns up the light. Seeing the forms on the couch, he recoils a moment.   Then, glancing at the table and empty decanters, goes up to the couch.*

KEITH. [*Muttering*] Asleep !   Drunk !   Ugh !

[*Suddenly he bends, touches* LARRY, *and springs back.*]
What ! [*He bends again, shakes him and calls.*] Larry ! Larry !

[*Then, motionless, he stares down at his brother's open, sightless eyes.*

30

Suddenly he wets his finger and holds it to the girl's lips, then to LARRY'S.]

Larry !

[*He bends and listens at their hearts ; catches sight of the little box lying between them and takes it up.*]

My God !

[*Then, raising himself, he closes his brother's eyes, and as he does so, catches sight of a paper pinned to the couch ; detaches it and reads :*

" I, Laurence Darrant, about to die by my own hand, confess that I——"

[*He reads on silently, in horror ; finishes, letting the paper drop, and recoils from the couch on to a chair at the dishevelled supper table. Aghast, he sits there. Suddenly he mutters :*

If I leave that there—my name—my whole future !—

[*He springs up, takes up the paper again, and again reads.*]

My God ! It's ruin !

[*He makes as if to tear it across, stops, and looks down at those two ; covers his eyes with his hand ; drops the paper and rushes to the door. But he stops there and comes back, magnetized, as it were, by that paper. He takes it up once more and thrusts it into his pocket.*

[*The footsteps of a Policeman pass, slow and regular, outside. His face crisps and quivers ; he stands listening till they die away. Then he snatches the paper from his pocket, and goes past the foot of the couch to the fire.*]

All my—— No ! Let him hang !

[*He thrusts the paper into the fire, stamps it down with his foot, watches it writhe and blacken. Then suddenly clutching his head, he turns to the bodies on the couch. Panting and like a man demented, he recoils past the head of the couch, and rushing to the window, draws the curtains and throws the window up for air. Out in the darkness rises the witch-like skeleton tree, where a dark shape seems hanging. KEITH starts back.*]

What's that ? What—— !

[*He shuts the window and draws the dark curtains across it again.*]

Fool ! Nothing !

[*Clenching his fists, he draws himself up, steadying himself with all his might. Then slowly he moves to the door, stands a second like a carved figure, his face hard as stone.*

[*Deliberately he turns out the light, opens the door, and goes.*

[*The still bodies lie there before the fire which is licking at the last blackened wafer.*

The curtain falls.

THE LITTLE MAN

CHARACTERS

THE LITTLE MAN.
THE AMERICAN.
THE ENGLISHMAN.
THE ENGLISHWOMAN.
THE GERMAN.
THE DUTCH BOY.

THE MOTHER.
THE BABY
THE WAITER
THE STATION OFFICIAL
THE POLICEMAN
THE PORTER

SCENE I

Afternoon, on the departure platform of an Austrian railway station. At several little tables outside the buffet persons are taking refreshment, served by a pale young WAITER. *On a seat against the wall of the buffet a* WOMAN *of lowly station is sitting beside two large bundles, on one of which she has placed her* BABY, *swathed in a black shawl.*

WAITER. [*Approaching a table whereat sit an English traveller and his wife*] Two coffee?

ENGLISHMAN. [*Paying*] Thanks. [*To his wife, in an Oxford voice.*] Sugar?

ENGLISHWOMAN. [*In a Cambridge voice*] One.

AMERICAN TRAVELLER. [*With field-glasses and a pocket camera— from another table*] Waiter, I'd like to have you get my eggs. I've been sitting here quite a while.

WAITER. Yes, sare.

GERMAN TRAVELLER. Kellner, bezahlen! [*His voice is, like his moustache, stiff and brushed up at the ends. His figure also is stiff and his hair a little grey; clearly once, if not now, a colonel.*]

WAITER. Komm' gleich!

> [*The* BABY *on the bundle wails. The* MOTHER *takes it up to soothe it. A young, red-cheeked* DUTCHMAN *at the fourth table stops eating and laughs.*]

AMERICAN. My eggs! Get a wiggle on you!

WAITER. Yes, sare.   [*He rapidly recedes.*

> [*A* LITTLE MAN *in a soft hat is seen to the right of tables. He stands a moment looking after the hurrying* WAITER, *then seats himself at the fifth table.*

ENGLISHMAN. [*Looking at his watch*] Ten minutes more.

ENGLISHWOMAN. Bother!

AMERICAN. [*Addressing them*] 'Pears as if they'd a prejudice against eggs here, anyway.   [*The* ENGLISH *look at him, but do not speak.*

GERMAN. [*In creditable English*] In these places man can get nothing.

> [*The* WAITER *comes flying back with a compote for the* DUTCH YOUTH, *who pays.*

GERMAN. Kellner, bezahlen!

WAITER. Eine Krone sechzig.   [*The* GERMAN *pays.*

AMERICAN. [*Rising, and taking out his watch—blandly*] See here. If I don't get my eggs before this watch ticks twenty, there'll be another waiter in heaven.

WAITER. [*Flying*] Komm' gleich !

AMERICAN. [*Seeking sympathy*] I'm gettin' kind of mad !

[*The* ENGLISHMAN *halves his newspaper and hands the advertisement half to his wife. The* BABY *wails. The* MOTHER *rocks it. The* DUTCH YOUTH *stops eating and laughs. The* GERMAN *lights a cigarette. The* LITTLE MAN *sits motionless, nursing his hat. The* WAITER *comes flying back with the eggs and places them before the* AMERICAN.

AMERICAN. [*Putting away his watch*] Good ! I don't like trouble. How much ?

[*He pays and eats. The* WAITER *stands a moment at the edge of the platform and passes his hand across his brow. The* LITTLE MAN *eyes him and speaks gently.*

LITTLE MAN. Herr Ober !   [*The* WAITER *turns.*] Might I have a glass of beer ?

WAITER. Yes, sare.

LITTLE MAN. Thank you very much.   [*The* WAITER *goes.*

AMERICAN. [*Pausing in the deglutition of his eggs—affably*] Pardon me, sir ; I'd like to have you tell me why you called that little bit of a feller " Herr Ober." Reckon you would know what that means ? Mr. Head Waiter.

LITTLE MAN. Yes, yes.

AMERICAN. I smile.

LITTLE MAN. Oughtn't I to call him that ?

GERMAN. [*Abruptly*] Nein—Kellner.

AMERICAN. Why, yes ! Just " waiter."

[*The* ENGLISHWOMAN *looks round her paper for a second. The* DUTCH YOUTH *stops eating and laughs. The* LITTLE MAN *gazes from face to face and nurses his hat.*

LITTLE MAN. I didn't want to hurt his feelings.

GERMAN. Gott !

AMERICAN. In my country we're very democratic—but that's quite a proposition.

ENGLISHMAN. [*Handling coffee-pot, to his wife*] More ?

ENGLISHWOMAN. No, thanks.

GERMAN. [*Abruptly*] These fellows—if you treat them in this manner, at once they take liberties. You see, you will not get your beer.

[*As he speaks the* WAITER *returns, bringing the* LITTLE MAN'S *beer, then retires.*

AMERICAN. That 'pears to be one up to democracy. [*To the* LITTLE MAN.] I judge you go in for brotherhood ?

LITTLE MAN. [*Startled*] Oh, no !

AMERICAN. I take considerable stock in Leo Tolstoi myself. Grand man—grand-souled apparatus. But I guess you've got to pinch those waiters some to make 'em skip. [*To the* ENGLISH, *who have carelessly looked his way for a moment.*]   You'll appreciate that, the way he acted about my eggs.

> [*The* ENGLISH *make faint motions with their chins and avert their eyes.*]

[*To the* WAITER, *who is standing at the door of the buffet.*] Waiter! Flash of beer—jump, now !

WAITER. Komm' gleich !

GERMAN. Cigarren !

WAITER. Schön !   [*He disappears.*

AMERICAN. [*Affably—to the* LITTLE MAN] Now, if I don't get that flash of beer quicker'n you got yours, I shall admire.

GERMAN. [*Abruptly*] Tolstoi is   nothing—nichts !   No   good ! Ha ?

AMERICAN. [*Relishing the approach of argument*] Well, that is a matter of temperament.   Now, I'm all for equality.   See that poor woman there—very humble woman—there she sits among us with her baby. Perhaps you'd like to locate her somewhere else ?

GERMAN. [*Shrugging*] Tolstoi is sentimentalisch.   Nietzsche is the true philosopher, the only one.

AMERICAN. Well, that's quite in the prospectus—very stimulating party—old Nietch—virgin mind.   But give me Leo ! [*He turns to the red-cheeked* YOUTH.] What do you opine, sir ?   I guess by your labels you'll be Dutch.   Do they read Tolstoi in your country ?

> [*The* DUTCH YOUTH *laughs.*

AMERICAN. That is a very luminous answer.

GERMAN. Tolstoi is nothing.   Man should himself express.   He must push—he must be strong.

AMERICAN. That is so.   In America we believe in virility ; we like a man to expand.   But we believe in brotherhood too.   We draw the line at niggers ; but we aspire.   Social barriers and distinctions we've not much use for.

ENGLISHMAN. Do you feel a draught ?

ENGLISHWOMAN. [*With a shiver of her shoulder toward the* AMERICAN] I do—rather.

GERMAN. Wait !   You are a young people.

AMERICAN. That is so ; there are no flies on us. [*To the* LITTLE MAN, *who has been gazing eagerly from face to face.*] Say !   I'd like to have you give us your sentiments in relation to the duty of man.

> [*The* LITTLE MAN *fidgets, and is about to open his mouth.*

AMERICAN. For example—is it your opinion that we should kill off the weak and diseased, and all that can't jump around ?

GERMAN. [*Nodding*] Ja, ja !   That is coming.

LITTLE MAN. [*Looking from face to face*] They might be me.

> [*The* DUTCH YOUTH *laughs.*

AMERICAN. [*Reproving him with a look*] That's true humility.   'Tisn't grammar.   Now, here's a proposition that brings it nearer the bone : Would you step out of your way to help them when it was liable to bring you trouble ?

GERMAN. Nein, nein !   That is stupid.

LITTLE MAN. [*Eager but wistful*] I'm afraid not.   Of course one wants to——   There was St. Francis d'Assisi and St. Julien l'Hospitalier, and——

AMERICAN. Very lofty dispositions.   Guess they died of them. [*He rises.*] Shake hands, sir—my name is—[*He hands a card.*] I am an ice-machine maker.   [*He shakes the* LITTLE MAN'S *hand.*] I like your sentiments—I feel kind of brotherly.   [*Catching sight of the* WAITER *appearing in the doorway.*] Waiter, where to h—ll is that flash of beer ?

GERMAN. Cigarren !

WAITER. Komm' gleich !   [*He vanishes.*

ENGLISHMAN. [*Consulting watch*] Train's late.

ENGLISHWOMAN. Really ! Nuisance !

[*A station* POLICEMAN, *very square and uniformed, passes and repasses.*

AMERICAN. [*Resuming his seat—to the* GERMAN] Now, we don't have so much of that in America.   Guess we feel more to trust in human nature.

GERMAN. Ah ! ha ! you will bresently find there is nothing in him but self.

LITTLE MAN. [*Wistfully*] Don't you believe in human nature ?

AMERICAN. Very stimulating question.   [*He looks round for opinions.*
                                                    [*The* DUTCH YOUTH *laughs.*

ENGLISHMAN. [*Holding out his half of the paper to his wife*] Swap !
                                                    [*His wife swaps.*

GERMAN. In human nature I believe so far as I can see him—no more.

AMERICAN. Now that 'pears to me kind o' blasphemy.   I believe in heroism.   I opine there's not one of us settin' around here that's not a hero—give him the occasion.

LITTLE MAN. Oh ! Do you believe that ?

AMERICAN. Well ! I judge a hero is just a person that'll help another at the expense of himself.   Take that poor woman there.   Well, now, she's a heroine, I guess.   She would die for her baby any old time.

GERMAN. Animals will die for their babies.   That is nothing.

AMERICAN. I carry it further.   I postulate we would all die for that baby if a locomotive was to trundle up right here and try to handle it.   [*To the* GERMAN.] I guess *you* don't know how good you are.   [*As the* GERMAN *is twisting up the ends of his moustache—to the* ENGLISHWOMAN.] I should like to have you express an opinion, ma'am.

ENGLISHWOMAN. I beg your pardon.

AMERICAN. The English are very humanitarian; they have a very high sense of duty. So have the Germans, so have the Americans. [*To the* DUTCH YOUTH.] I judge even in your little country they have that. This is an epoch of equality and high-toned ideals. [*To the* LITTLE MAN.] What is *your* nationality, sir?

LITTLE MAN. I'm afraid I'm nothing particular. My father was half-English and half-American, and my mother half-German and half-Dutch.

AMERICAN. My! That's a bit streaky, any old way. [*The* POLICE-MAN *passes again.*] Now, I don't believe we've much use any more for those gentlemen in buttons. We've grown kind of mild—we don't think of self as we used to do.

> [*The* WAITER *has appeared in the doorway.*

GERMAN. [*In a voice of thunder*] Cigarren! Donnerwetter!

AMERICAN. [*Shaking his fist at the vanishing* WAITER] That flash of beer!

WAITER. Komm' gleich!

AMERICAN. A little more, and he will join George Washington! I was about to remark when he intruded: In this year of grace 1913 the kingdom of Christ is quite a going concern. We are mighty near to universal brotherhood. The colonel here [*He indicates the* GERMAN] is a man of blood and iron, but give him an oppor-tunity to be magnanimous, and he'll be right there. Oh, sir! yep!

> [*The* GERMAN, *with a profound mixture of pleasure and cynicism, brushes up the ends of his moustache.*

LITTLE MAN. I wonder. One wants to, but somehow——

> [*He shakes his head.*

AMERICAN. You seem kind of skeery about that. You've had experience, maybe. I'm an optimist—I think we're bound to make the devil hum in the near future. I opine we shall occasion a good deal of trouble to that old party. There's about to be a holocaust of selfish interests. The colonel there with old-man Nietch—he won't know himself. There's going to be a very sacred opportunity.

> [*As he speaks, the voice of a* RAILWAY OFFICIAL *is heard in the distance calling out in German. It approaches, and the words become audible.*

GERMAN. [*Startled*] Der Teufel!

> [*He gets up, and seizes the bag beside him.*
> [*The* STATION OFFICIAL *has appeared; he stands for a moment casting his commands at the seated group. The* DUTCH YOUTH *also rises, and takes his coat and hat. The* OFFICIAL *turns on his heel and retires, still issuing directions.*

ENGLISHMAN. What does he say?

30*

GERMAN. Our drain has come in, de oder platform; only one minute we haf.   [ALL *have risen in a fluster.*

AMERICAN. Now, that's very provoking. I won't get that flash of beer.

[*There is a general scurry to gather coats and hats and wraps, during which the lowly* WOMAN *is seen making desperate attempts to deal with her* BABY *and the two large bundles. Quite defeated, she suddenly puts all down, wrings her hands, and cries out:* "Herr Jesu! Hilfe!" *The flying procession turn their heads at that strange cry.*

AMERICAN. What's that? Help?   [*He continues to run.*

[*The* LITTLE MAN *spins round, rushes back, picks up* BABY *and bundle on which it was seated.*

LITTLE MAN. Come along, good woman, come along!

[*The* WOMAN *picks up the other bundle and they run.*

[*The* WAITER, *appearing in the doorway with the bottle of beer, watches with his tired smile.*

The curtain falls.

SCENE II

A second-class compartment of a corridor carriage, in motion. In it are seated the ENGLISHMAN *and his* WIFE, *opposite each other at the corridor end, she with her face to the engine, he with his back. Both are somewhat protected from the rest of the travellers by newspapers. Next to her sits the* GERMAN, *and opposite him sits the* AMERICAN; *next the* AMERICAN *in one window corner is seated the* DUTCH YOUTH; *the other window corner is taken by the* GERMAN'S *bag. The silence is only broken by the slight rushing noise of the train's progression and the crackling of the English newspapers.*

AMERICAN. [*Turning to the* DUTCH YOUTH] Guess I'd like that window raised; it's kind of chilly after that old run they gave us.

[*The* DUTCH YOUTH *laughs, and goes through the motions of raising the window. The* ENGLISH *regard the operation with uneasy irritation. The* GERMAN *opens his bag, which reposes on the corner seat next him, and takes out a book.*

AMERICAN. The Germans are great readers. Very stimulating practice. I read most anything myself!

[*The* GERMAN *holds up the book so that the title may be read.*]
"Don Quixote"—fine book. We Americans take considerable stock in old man Quixote. Bit of a wild-cat—but we don't laugh at him.

GERMAN. He is dead. Dead as a sheep. A good thing, too.

AMERICAN. In America we have still quite an amount of chivalry.

GERMAN. Chivalry is nothing—sentimentalisch. In modern days —no good.   A man must push, he must pull.

AMERICAN. So you say.   But I judge your form of chivalry is sacrifice to the state.   We allow more freedom to the individual soul. Where there's something little and weak, we feel it kind of noble to give up to it.   That way we feel elevated.

[*As he speaks there is seen in the corridor doorway the* LITTLE MAN, *with the* WOMAN'S BABY *still on his arm and the bundle held in the other hand. He peers in anxiously. The* ENGLISH, *acutely conscious, try to dissociate themselves from his presence with their papers. The* DUTCH YOUTH *laughs.*

GERMAN. Ach!   So!

AMERICAN. Dear me!

LITTLE MAN. Is there room?   I can't find a seat.

AMERICAN. Why, yes!   There's a seat for one.

LITTLE MAN. [*Depositing bundle outside, and heaving* BABY] May I?

AMERICAN. Come right in!

[*The* GERMAN *sulkily moves his bag. The* LITTLE MAN *comes in and seats himself gingerly.*

AMERICAN. Where's the mother?

LITTLE MAN. [*Ruefully*] Afraid she got left behind.

[*The* DUTCH YOUTH *laughs. The* ENGLISH *unconsciously emerge from their newspapers.*

AMERICAN. My!   That   would   appear   to   be   quite   a   domestic incident.

[*The* ENGLISHMAN *suddenly utters a profound* " Ha, Ha!" *and disappears behind his paper. And that paper and the one opposite are seen to shake, and little squirls and squeaks emerge.*

GERMAN. And you haf got her bundle, and her baby.   Ha!

[*He cackles dryly.*

AMERICAN. [*Gravely*] I smile.   I guess Providence has played it pretty low down on you.   It's sure acted real mean.

[*The* BABY *wails, and the* LITTLE MAN *jigs it with a sort of gentle desperation, looking apologetically from face to face. His wistful glance renews the fire of merriment wherever it alights. The* AMERICAN *alone preserves a gravity which seems incapable of being broken.*

AMERICAN. Maybe you'd better get off right smart and restore that baby.   There's nothing can act madder than a mother.

LITTLE MAN. Poor thing, yes!   What she must be suffering!

[*A gale of laughter shakes the carriage. The* ENGLISH *for a moment drop their papers, the better to indulge. The* LITTLE MAN *smiles a wintry smile.*

AMERICAN. [*In a lull*] How did it eventuate?

LITTLE MAN. We got there just as the train was going to start; and I jumped, thinking I could help her up.   But it moved too quickly, and—and left her.   [*The gale of laughter blows up again.*

AMERICAN. Guess I'd have thrown the baby out to her.

LITTLE MAN. I was afraid the poor little thing might break.

   [*The* BABY *wails; the* LITTLE MAN *heaves it; the gale of laughter blows.*

AMERICAN. [*Gravely*] It's highly entertaining—not for the baby. What kind of an old baby is it, anyway ? [*He sniffs.*] I judge it's a bit —niffy.

LITTLE MAN. Afraid I've hardly looked at it yet.

AMERICAN. Which end up is it ?

LITTLE MAN. Oh ! I think the right end.   Yes, yes, it is.

AMERICAN. Well, that's something.   Maybe you should hold it out of window a bit.   Very excitable things, babies !

ENGLISHWOMAN. [*Galvanized*] No, no !

ENGLISHMAN. [*Touching her knee*] My dear !

AMERICAN. You are right, ma'am.   I opine there's a draught out there.   This baby is precious.   We've all of us got stock in this baby in a manner of speaking.   This is a little bit of universal brotherhood. Is it a woman baby ?

LITTLE MAN. I—I can only see the top of its head.

AMERICAN. You can't always tell from that.   It looks kind of over-wrapped up.   Maybe it had better be unbound.

GERMAN. Nein, nein, nein !

AMERICAN. I think you are very likely right, colonel.   It might be a pity to unbind that baby.   I guess the lady should be consulted in this matter.

ENGLISHWOMAN. Yes, yes, of course—I——

ENGLISHMAN. [*Touching her*] Let it be !   Little beggar seems all right.

AMERICAN. That would seem only known to Providence at this moment.   I judge it might be due to humanity to look at its face.

LITTLE MAN. [*Gladly*] It's sucking my finger.   There, there—nice little thing—there !

AMERICAN. I would surmise in your leisure moments you have created babies, sir ?

LITTLE MAN. Oh ! no—indeed, no.

AMERICAN. Dear me !—That is a loss. [*Addressing himself to the carriage at large.*] I think we may esteem ourselves fortunate to have this little stranger right here with us.   Demonstrates what a hold the little and weak have upon us nowadays.   The colonel here—a man of blood and iron—there he sits quite ca'm next door to it. [*He sniffs.*] Now, this baby is ruther chastening—that is a sign of grace, in the colonel—that is true heroism.

LITTLE MAN. [*Faintly*] I—I can see its face a little now.

[*All bend forward.*

AMERICAN. What sort of physiognomy has it, anyway?

LITTLE MAN. [*Still faintly*] I don't see anything but—but spots.

GERMAN. Oh! Ha! Pfui!   [*The* DUTCH YOUTH *laughs.*

AMERICAN. I am told that is not uncommon amongst babies. Perhaps we could have you inform us, ma'am.

ENGLISHWOMAN. Yes, of course—only—what sort of——

LITTLE MAN. They seem all over its—[*At the slight recoil of everyone.*] I feel sure it's—it's quite a good baby underneath.

AMERICAN. That will be ruther difficult to come at. I'm just a bit sensitive. I've very little use for affections of the epidermis.

GERMAN. Pfui!

[*He has edged away as far as he can get, and is lighting a big cigar.*

[*The* DUTCH YOUTH *draws his legs back.*

AMERICAN. [*Also taking out a cigar*] I guess it would be well to fumigate this carriage. Does it suffer, do you think?

LITTLE MAN. [*Peering*] Really, I don't—I'm not sure—I know so little about babies. I think it would have a nice expression—if—if it showed.

AMERICAN. Is it kind of boiled looking?

LITTLE MAN. Yes—yes, it is.

AMERICAN. [*Looking gravely round*] I judge this baby has the measles.

[*The* GERMAN *screws himself spasmodically against the arm of the* ENGLISHWOMAN's *seat.*

ENGLISHWOMAN. Poor little thing! Shall I——?   [*She half rises.*

ENGLISHMAN. [*Touching her*] No, no—— Dash it!

AMERICAN. I honour your emotion, ma'am. It does credit to us all. But I sympathize with your husband too. The measles is a very important pestilence in connection with a grown woman.

LITTLE MAN. It likes my finger awfully. Really, it's rather a sweet baby.

AMERICAN. [*Sniffing*] Well, that would appear to be quite a question. About them spots, now? Are they rosy?

LITTLE MAN. No-o; they're dark, almost black.

GERMAN. Gott! Typhus!

[*He bounds up on to the arm of the* ENGLISHWOMAN's *seat.*

AMERICAN. Typhus! That's quite an indisposition!

[*The* DUTCH YOUTH *rises suddenly, and bolts out into the corridor. He is followed by the* GERMAN, *puffing clouds of smoke. The* ENGLISH *and* AMERICAN *sit a moment longer without speaking. The* ENGLISHWOMAN's *face is turned with a curious expression —half pity, half fear—towards the* LITTLE MAN. *Then the* ENGLISHMAN *gets up.*

ENGLISHMAN. Bit stuffy for you here, dear, isn't it?

[*He puts his arm though hers, raises her, and almost pushes her through the doorway. She goes, still looking back.*

AMERICAN. [*Gravely*] There's nothing I admire more'n courage. Guess I'll go and smoke in the corridor.

[*As he goes out the* LITTLE MAN *looks very wistfully after him. Screwing up his mouth and nose, he holds the* BABY *away from him and wavers ; then rising, he puts it on the seat opposite and goes through the motions of letting down the window. Having done so, he looks at the* BABY, *who has begun to wail. Suddenly he raises his hands and clasps them, like a child praying. Since, however, the* BABY *does not stop wailing, he hovers over it in indecision ; then, picking it up, sits down again to dandle it with his face turned toward the open window. Finding that it still wails, he begins to sing to it in a cracked little voice. It is charmed at once. While he is singing, the* AMERICAN *appears in the corridor. Letting down the passage window, he stands there in the doorway with the draught blowing his hair and the smoke of his cigar all about him. The* LITTLE MAN *stops singing and shifts the shawl higher to protect the* BABY's *head from the draught.*

AMERICAN. [*Gravely*] This is the most sublime spectacle I have ever envisaged. There ought to be a record of this.

[*The* LITTLE MAN *looks at him, wondering.*]

You are typical, sir, of the sentiments of modern Christianity. You illustrate the deepest feelings in the heart of every man.

[*The* LITTLE MAN *rises with the* BABY *and a movement of approach.*]

Guess I'm wanted in the dining-car.   [*He vanishes.*

[*The* LITTLE MAN *sits down again, but back to the engine, away from the draught, and looks out of the window, patiently jogging the* BABY *on his knee.*

The curtain falls.

SCENE III

An arrival platform. The LITTLE MAN, *with the* BABY *and the bundle, is standing disconsolate, while travellers pass and luggage is being carried by. A* STATION OFFICIAL, *accompanied by a* POLICEMAN, *appears from a doorway, behind him.*

OFFICIAL. [*Consulting telegram in his hand*] Das ist der Herr.

[*They advance to the* LITTLE MAN.

OFFICIAL. Sie haben einen Buben gestohlen?

LITTLE MAN. I only speak English and American.

OFFICIAL. Dies ist nicht Ihr Bube ?   [*He touches the* BABY.

LITTLE MAN. [*Shaking his head*] Take care—it's ill.

[*The man does not understand.*]

Ill—the baby——

OFFICIAL. [*Shaking his head*] Verstehe nicht. Dis is nod your baby? No?

LITTLE MAN. [*Shaking his head violently*] No, it is not.   No.

OFFICIAL. [*Tapping the telegram*] Gut !   You are 'rested.

[*He signs to the* POLICEMAN, *who takes the* LITTLE MAN'S *arm.*

LITTLE MAN. Why ?   I don't want the poor baby.

OFFICIAL. [*Lifting the bundle*] Dies ist nicht Ihr Gepäck—pag ?

LITTLE MAN. No.

OFFICIAL. Gut.   You are 'rested.

LITTLE MAN. I only took it for the poor woman.   I'm not a thief —I'm—I'm——

OFFICIAL. [*Shaking head*] Verstehe nicht.

[*The* LITTLE MAN *tries to tear his hair.   The disturbed* BABY *wails.*

LITTLE MAN. [*Dandling it as best he can*] There, there—poor, poor !

OFFICIAL. Halt still !   You are 'rested.   It is all right.

LITTLE MAN. Where is the mother ?

OFFICIAL. She comm by next drain.   Das telegram say : Halt einen Herrn mit schwarzem Buben und schwarzem Gepack.   'Rest gentleman mit black baby und black—pag.

[*The* LITTLE MAN *turns up his eyes to heaven.*

OFFICIAL. Komm mit us.

[*They take the* LITTLE MAN *toward the door from which they have come.   A voice stops them.*

AMERICAN. [*Speaking from as far away as may be*] Just a moment !

[*The* OFFICIAL *stops ; the* LITTLE MAN *also stops and sits down on a bench against the wall.   The* POLICEMAN *stands stolidly beside him.   The* AMERICAN *approaches a step or two, beckoning ; the* OFFICIAL *goes up to him.*

AMERICAN. Guess you've got an angel from heaven there ?   What's the gentleman in buttons for ?

OFFICIAL. Was ist das ?

AMERICAN. Is there anybody here that can understand American ?

OFFICIAL. Verstehe nicht.

AMERICAN. Well, just watch my gestures.   I was saying [*He points to the* LITTLE MAN, *then makes gestures of flying*] you have an angel from heaven there.   You have there a man in whom Gawd [*He points upward*] takes quite an amount of stock.   You have no call to arrest him. [*He makes the gesture of arrest.*] No, sir.   Providence has acted pretty mean, loading off that baby on him. [*He makes the motion of dandling.*] The little man has a heart of gold.

[*He points to his heart, and takes out a gold coin.*

OFFICIAL. [*Thinking he is about to be bribed*] Aber, das ist *zu* viel !

AMERICAN. Now, don't rattle me ! [*Pointing to the* LITTLE MAN.] Man [*Pointing to his heart*] Herz [*Pointing to the coin*] von Gold. This is a flower of the field—he don't want no gentleman in buttons to pluck him up.

[*A little crowd is gathering, including the* TWO ENGLISH, *the* GERMAN, *and the* DUTCH YOUTH.

OFFICIAL. Verstehe absolut nichts. [*He taps the telegram.*] Ich muss mein duty do.

AMERICAN. But I'm telling you. This is a white man. This is probably the whitest man on Gawd's earth.

OFFICIAL. Das macht nichts—gut or no gut, I muss mein duty do.

[*He turns to go towards the* LITTLE MAN.

AMERICAN. Oh ! Very well, arrest him ; do your duty. This baby has typhus. [*At the word " typhus " the* OFFICIAL *stops.*

AMERICAN. [*Making gestures*] First-class typhus, black typhus, schwarzen typhus. Now you have it. I'm kind o' sorry for you and the gentleman in buttons. Do your duty !

OFFICIAL. Typhus ? Der Bub'—die baby hat typhus ?

AMERICAN. I'm telling you.

OFFICIAL. Gott im Himmel !

AMERICAN. [*Spotting the* GERMAN *in the little throng*] Here's a gentleman will corroborate me.

OFFICIAL. [*Much disturbed, and signing to the* POLICEMAN *to stand clear*] Typhus ! Aber das ist grässlich !

AMERICAN. I kind o' thought you'd feel like that.

OFFICIAL. Die Sanitätsmachine ! Gleich !

[*A* PORTER *goes to get it. From either side the broken half-moon of persons stand gazing at the* LITTLE MAN, *who sits unhappily dandling the* BABY *in the centre.*

OFFICIAL. [*Raising his hands*] Was zu thun?

AMERICAN. Guess you'd better isolate the baby.

[*A silence, during which the* LITTLE MAN *is heard faintly whistling and clucking to the* BABY.

OFFICIAL. [*Referring once more to his telegram*] " 'Rest gentleman mit black baby." [*Shaking his head.*] Wir must de gentleman hold. [*To the* GERMAN.] Bitte, mein Herr, sagen Sie ihm, den Buben zu niedersetzen.

[*He makes the gesture of deposit.*

GERMAN. [*To the* LITTLE MAN] He say : Put down the baby.

[*The* LITTLE MAN *shakes his head, and continues to dandle the* BABY.

OFFICIAL. You must. [*The* LITTLE MAN *glowers in silence.*

ENGLISHMAN. [*In background—muttering*] Good man !

GERMAN. His spirit ever denies.

OFFICIAL. [*Again making his gesture*] Aber er muss !

                [*The* LITTLE MAN *makes a face at him.*]

Sag' Ihm : Instantly put down baby, and komm' mit us.

                        [*The* BABY *wails.*

LITTLE MAN. Leave the poor ill baby here alone ? Be—be—be d ——d to you !

AMERICAN. [*Jumping on to a trunk—with enthusiasm*] Bully !

    [*The* ENGLISH *clap their hands ; the* DUTCH YOUTH *laughs. The* OFFICIAL *is muttering, greatly incensed.*

AMERICAN. What does that body-snatcher say ?

GERMAN. He say this man use the baby to save himself from arrest. Very smart—he say.

AMERICAN. I judge you do him an injustice. [*Showing off the* LITTLE MAN *with a sweep of his arm.*] This is a white man. He's got a black baby, and he won't leave it in the lurch. Guess we would all act noble, that way, give us the chance.

    [*The* LITTLE MAN *rises, holding out the* BABY, *and advances a step or two. The half-moon at once gives, increasing its size ; the* AMERICAN *climbs on to a higher trunk. The* LITTLE MAN *retires and again sits down.*

AMERICAN. [*Addressing the* OFFICIAL] Guess you'd better go out of business and wait for the mother.

OFFICIAL. [*Stamping his foot*] Die Mutter sall 'rested be for taking out baby mit typhus. Ha ! [*To the* LITTLE MAN.] Put ze baby down !

                      [*The* LITTLE MAN *smiles.*]

Do you 'ear ?

AMERICAN. [*Addressing the* OFFICIAL] Now, see here. 'Pears to me you don't suspicion just how beautiful this is. Here we have a man giving his life for that old baby that's got no claim on him. This is not a baby of his own making. No, sir, this is a very Christ-like proposition in the gentleman.

OFFICIAL. Put ze baby down, or ich will gommand someone it to do.

AMERICAN. That will be very interesting to watch.

OFFICIAL. [*To* POLICEMAN] Dake it vrom him.

                [*The* POLICEMAN *mutters, but does not.*

AMERICAN. [*To the* GERMAN] Guess I lost that.

GERMAN. He say he is not his officier.

AMERICAN. That just tickles me to death.

OFFICIAL. [*Looking round*] Vill nobody dake ze Bub' ?

ENGLISHWOMAN. [*Moving a step—faintly*] Yes—I——

ENGLISHMAN. [*Grasping her arm*] By Jove ! Will you !

OFFICIAL. [*Gathering himself for a great effort to take the* BABY, *and advancing two steps*] Zen I gommand you—— [*He stops and his voice dies away.*] Zit dere !

AMERICAN. My! That's wonderful. What a man this is! What a sublime sense of duty!

[*The* DUTCH YOUTH *laughs. The* OFFICIAL *turns on him, but as he does so the* MOTHER *of the* BABY *is seen hurrying.*

MOTHER. Ach! Ach! Mei' Bubi!

[*Her face is illumined; she is about to rush to the* LITTLE MAN.

OFFICIAL. [*To the* POLICEMAN] Nimm die Frau!

[*The* POLICEMAN *catches hold of the* WOMAN.

OFFICIAL. [*To the frightened woman*] Warum haben Sie einen Buben mit Typhus mit ausgebracht?

AMERICAN. [*Eagerly, from his perch*] What was that? I don't want to miss any.

GERMAN. He say: Why did you a baby with typhus with you bring out?

AMERICAN. Well, that's quite a question.

[*He takes out the field-glasses slung around him and adjusts them on the* BABY.

MOTHER. [*Bewildered*] Mei' Bubi—Typhus—aber Typhus? [*She shakes her head violently.*] Nein, nein, nein! Typhus!

OFFICIAL. Er hat Typhus.

MOTHER. [*Shaking her head*] Nein, nein, nein!

AMERICAN. [*Looking through his glasses*] Guess she's kind of right! I judge the typhus is where the baby's slobbered on the shawl, and it's come off on him.   [*The* DUTCH YOUTH *laughs.*

OFFICIAL. [*Turning on him furiously*] Er hat typhus.

AMERICAN. Now, that's where you slop over. Come right here.

[*The* OFFICIAL *mounts, and looks through the glasses.*

AMERICAN. [*To the* LITTLE MAN] Skin out the baby's leg. If we don't locate spots on that, it'll be good enough for me.

[*The* LITTLE MAN *fumbles out the* BABY'S *little white foot.*

MOTHER. Mei' Bubi!   [*She tries to break away.*

AMERICAN. White as a banana. [*To the* OFFICIAL—*affably.*] Guess you've made kind of a fool of us with your old typhus.

OFFICIAL. Lass die Frau!

[*The* POLICEMAN *lets her go, and she rushes to her* BABY.

MOTHER. Mei' Bubi!

[*The* BABY, *exchanging the warmth of the* LITTLE MAN *for the momentary chill of its* MOTHER, *wails.*

OFFICIAL. [*Descending and beckoning to the* POLICEMAN] Sie wollen den Herrn accusiren? [*The* POLICEMAN *takes the* LITTLE MAN'S *arm.*

AMERICAN. What's that? They goin' to pinch him after all?

[*The* MOTHER, *still hugging her* BABY, *who has stopped crying, gazes at the* LITTLE MAN, *who sits dazedly looking up. Suddenly she drops on her knees, and with her free hand lifts his booted foot and kisses it.*

AMERICAN. [*Waving his hat*] Ra! Ra! [*He descends swiftly, goes up to the* LITTLE MAN, *whose arm the* POLICEMAN *has dropped, and takes his hand.*] Brother, I am proud to know you. This is one of the greatest moments I have ever experienced. [*Displaying the* LITTLE MAN *to the assembled company.*] I think I sense the situation when I say that we all esteem it an honour to breathe the rather inferior atmosphere of this station here along with our little friend. I guess we shall all go home and treasure the memory of his face as the whitest thing in our museum of recollections. And perhaps this good woman will also go home and wash the face of our little brother here. I am inspired with a new faith in mankind. Ladies and gentlemen, I wish to present to you a sure-enough saint—only wants a halo, to be transfigured. [*To the* LITTLE MAN.] Stand right up.

> [*The* LITTLE MAN *stands up bewildered. They come about him. The* OFFICIAL *bows to him, the* POLICEMAN *salutes him. The* DUTCH YOUTH *shakes his head and laughs. The* GERMAN *draws himself up very straight, and bows quickly twice. The* ENGLISHMAN *and his* WIFE *approach at least two steps, then, thinking better of it, turn to each other and recede. The* MOTHER *kisses his hand. The* PORTER *returning with the Sanitäts-machine, turns it on from behind, and its pinkish shower, goldened by a ray of sunlight, falls around the* LITTLE MAN'S *head, transfiguring it as he stands with eyes upraised to see whence the portent comes.*

AMERICAN. [*Rushing forward and dropping on his knees*] Hold on just a minute! Guess I'll take a snapshot of the miracle. [*He adjusts his pocket camera.*] This ought to look bully!

The curtain falls.

HALL-MARKED

CHARACTERS

HERSELF	THE DOCTOR
LADY ELLA	THE CABMAN
THE SQUIRE	THE MAID
MAUD	HANNIBAL *and*
THE RECTOR	EDWARD

HALL-MARKED

The scene is the sitting-room and verandah of HER *bungalow.*

The room is pleasant, and along the back, where the verandah runs, it seems all window, both French and casement. There is a door right and a door left. The day is bright ; the time morning.

HERSELF, *dripping wet, comes running along the verandah, through the French window, with a wet Scotch terrier in her arms. She vanishes through the door left. A little pause, and* LADY ELLA *comes running, dry, thin, refined, and agitated. She halts where the tracks of water cease at the door left. A little pause, and* MAUD *comes running, fairly dry, stolid, breathless, and dragging a bull-dog, wet, breathless, and stout, by the crutch end of her en-tout-cas.*

LADY ELLA. Don't bring Hannibal in till I know where she's put Edward.

MAUD. [*Brutally, to* HANNIBAL] Bad dog ; Bad dog !

[HANNIBAL *snuffles.*

LADY ELLA. Maud, do take him out ! Tie him up. Here ! [*She takes out a lace handkerchief.*] No—something stronger ! Poor darling Edward ! [*To* HANNIBAL.] You are a bad dog ! [HANNIBAL *snuffles.*

MAUD. Edward began it, Ella. [*To* HANNIBAL.] Bad dog ! Bad dog ! [HANNIBAL *snuffles.*

LADY ELLA. Tie him up outside. Here, take my scarf. Where *is* my poor treasure ? [*She removes her scarf.*] Catch ! His ear's torn ; I saw it.

MAUD. [*Taking the scarf, to* HANNIBAL] Now ! [HANNIBAL *snuffles.*] [*She ties the scarf to his collar.*] He smells horrible. Bad dog—getting into *ponds* to fight !

LADY ELLA. Tie him up, Maud. I *must* try in here.

[*Their husbands,* THE SQUIRE *and* THE RECTOR, *come hastening along the verandah.*

MAUD. [*To* THE RECTOR] Smell him, Bertie ! [*To* THE SQUIRE.] You *might* have that pond drained, Squire !

[*She takes* HANNIBAL *out, and ties him to the verandah.* THE SQUIRE *and* RECTOR *come in.* LADY ELLA *is knocking on the door left.*

HER VOICE. All right ! I've bound him up !

LADY ELLA. May I come in ?

HER VOICE. Just a second ! I've got nothing on.

[LADY ELLA *recoils.* THE SQUIRE *and* RECTOR *make an involuntary movement of approach.*

943

LADY ELLA. Oh! There you are!

THE RECTOR. [*Doubtfully*] I was just going to wade in——

LADY ELLA. Hannibal would have killed him, if she hadn't rushed in.

THE SQUIRE. Done him good, little beast!

LADY ELLA. Why didn't *you* go in, Tommy?

THE SQUIRE. Well, I *would*—only she——

LADY ELLA. I can't think how she got Edward out of Hannibal's awful mouth!

MAUD. [*Without—to* HANNIBAL, *who is snuffling on the verandah and straining at the scarf*] Bad dog!

LADY ELLA. We must simply thank her tremendously! I shall never forget the way she ran in, with her skirts up to her waist!

THE SQUIRE. By Jove! No. It was topping.

LADY ELLA. Her clothes must be ruined. That pond—ugh! [*She wrinkles her nose.*] Tommy, *do* have it drained.

THE RECTOR. [*Dreamily*] I don't remember her face in church.

THE SQUIRE. Ah! Yes. Who is she? Pretty woman!

LADY ELLA. I must get the Vet. to Edward. [*To* THE SQUIRE.] Tommy, do exert yourself! [MAUD *re-enters.*

THE SQUIRE. All right! [*Exerting himself.*] Here's a bell!

HER VOICE. [*Through the door*] The bleeding's stopped. [*They listen.*] Shall I send him in to you?

LADY ELLA. Oh, please! Poor darling!

[LADY ELLA *prepares to receive* EDWARD. THE SQUIRE *and* RECTOR *stand transfixed. The door opens, and a bare arm gently pushes* EDWARD *forth. He is bandaged with a smooth towel. There is a snuffle—*HANNIBAL *has broken the scarf, outside.*

LADY ELLA. [*Aghast*] Look! Hannibal's loose! Maud—Tommy [*To* THE RECTOR.] You!

[*The* THREE *rush to prevent* HANNIBAL *from re-entering.*

LADY ELLA. [*To* EDWARD] Yes, I know—you'd like to! You *shall* bite him when it's safe. Oh! my darling, you *do*—— [*She sniffs.*] [MAUD *and* THE SQUIRE *re-enter.*] Have you tied him properly this time?

MAUD. With Bertie's braces.

LADY ELLA. Oh! but—

MAUD. It's all right; they're almost leather.

[THE RECTOR *re-enters, with a slight look of insecurity.*

LADY ELLA. Rector, are you sure it's safe?

THE RECTOR. [*Hitching at his trousers*] No, indeed, Lady Ella—I——

LADY ELLA. Tommy, do lend a hand!

THE SQUIRE. All right, Ella; all right! He doesn't mean what you mean!

LADY ELLA. [*Transferring* EDWARD *to* THE SQUIRE] Hold him, Tommy. He's sure to smell out Hannibal!

THE SQUIRE. [*Taking* EDWARD *by the collar, and holding his own nose*] Jove! Clever if he can smell anything but himself. Phew! She ought to have the Victoria Cross for goin' in that pond.

[*The door opens, and* HERSELF *appears; a fine, frank, handsome woman, in a man's orange-coloured motor-coat, hastily thrown on over the substrata of costume.*

SHE. So very sorry—had to have a bath, and change, of course!

LADY ELLA. We're so awfully grateful to you. It was splendid.

MAUD. Quite.

THE RECTOR. [*Rather holding himself together*] Heroic! I was just myself about to——

THE SQUIRE. [*Restraining* EDWARD] Little beast *will* fight—must apologize—you were too quick for me——

[*He looks up at her. She is smiling, and regarding the wounded dog, her head benevolently on one side.*

SHE. Poor dears! They thought they were so safe in that nice pond!

LADY ELLA. Is he very badly torn?

SHE. Rather nasty. There ought to be a stitch or two put in his ear.

LADY ELLA. I thought so. Tommy, do——

THE SQUIRE. All right. Am I to let him go?

LADY ELLA. No.

MAUD. The fly's outside. Bertie, run and tell Jarvis to drive in for the Vet.

THE RECTOR. [*Gentle and embarrassed*] Run? Well, Maud—I——

SHE. The doctor would sew it up. My maid can go round.

[HANNIBAL *appears at the open casement with the broken braces dangling from his collar.*

LADY ELLA. Look! Catch him! Rector!

MAUD. Bertie! Catch him!

[THE RECTOR *seizes* HANNIBAL, *but is seen to be in difficulties with his garments.* HERSELF, *who has gone out left, returns, with a leather strop in one hand and a pair of braces in the other.*

SHE. Take this strop—he can't break that. And would these be any good to you?

[SHE *hands the braces to* MAUD *and goes out on to the verandah and hastily away.* MAUD, *transferring the braces to the* RECTOR, *goes out, draws* HANNIBAL *from the casement window, and secures him with the strop.* THE RECTOR *sits suddenly with the braces in his hands. There is a moment's peace.*

LADY ELLA. Splendid, isn't she? I do admire her.

THE SQUIRE. She's all there.

THE RECTOR. [*Feelingly*] Most kind.

[*He looks ruefully at the braces and at* LADY ELLA. *A silence.*
MAUD *reappears at the door and stands gazing at the braces.*

THE SQUIRE. [*Suddenly*] Eh?

MAUD. Yes.

THE SQUIRE. [*Looking at his wife*] Ah!

LADY ELLA. [*Absorbed in* EDWARD] Poor darling!

THE SQUIRE. [*Bluntly*] Ella, the Rector wants to get up!

THE RECTOR. [*Gently*] Perhaps—just for a moment——

LADY ELLA. Oh!   [*She turns to the wall.*

[*The* RECTOR, *screened by his* WIFE, *retires on to the verandah
to adjust his garments.*

THE SQUIRE. [*Meditating*] So she's married!

LADY ELLA. [*Absorbed in* EDWARD] Why?

THE SQUIRE. Braces.

LADY ELLA. Oh! Yes. We ought to ask them to dinner, Tommy.

THE SQUIRE. Ah! Yes. Wonder who they are?

[THE RECTOR *and* MAUD *reappear.*

THE RECTOR. Really very good of her to lend her husband's——
I was—er—quite——

MAUD. That'll do, Bertie.

[THEY *see* HER *returning along the verandah, followed by a sandy,
red-faced gentleman in leather leggings, with a needle and cotton
in his hand.*

HERSELF. Caught the doctor just starting. So lucky!

LADY ELLA. Oh! Thank goodness!

DOCTOR. How do, Lady Ella? How do, Squire?—how do,
Rector? [*To* MAUD.] How de do! This the beastie? I see.
Quite! Who'll hold him for me?

LADY ELLA. Oh! I!

HERSELF. D'you know, I *think* I'd better. It's so dreadful when
it's your own, isn't it? Shall we go in here, doctor? Come along,
pretty boy!   [*She takes* EDWARD, *and they pass into the room, Left.*

LADY ELLA. I dreaded it. She *is* splendid!

THE SQUIRE. Dogs take to her. That's a sure sign.

THE RECTOR. Little things—one can always tell.

THE SQUIRE. Something very attractive about her—what! Fine
build of woman.

MAUD. I shall get hold of her for parish work.

THE RECTOR. Ah! Excellent—excellent! Do!

THE SQUIRE. Wonder if her husband shoots? She seems quite—
er—quite——

LADY ELLA. [*Watching the door*] Quite! Altogether charming;
one of the nicest faces I ever saw.   [THE DOCTOR *comes out alone.*
Oh! Doctor—have you?—is it—— ?

DOCTOR. Right as rain! She held him like an angel—he just licked her, and never made a sound.

LADY ELLA. Poor darling! Can I—— [*She signs toward the door.*

DOCTOR. Better leave 'em a minute. She's moppin' 'im off. [*He wrinkles his nose.*] Wonderful clever hands!

THE SQUIRE. I say—who *is* she?

DOCTOR. [*Looking from face to face with a dubious and rather quizzical expression*] Who? Well—there you have me! All I know is she's a first-rate nurse—been helpin' me with a case in Ditch Lane. Nice woman, too—thorough good sort! Quite an acquisition here. H'm! [*Again that quizzical glance.*] Excuse me hurryin' off—very late. Good-bye, Rector. Good-bye, Lady Ella. Good-bye!

[*He goes—a silence.*

THE SQUIRE. H'm! I suppose we ought to be a bit careful.

[*JARVIS, flyman of the old school, has appeared on the verandah.*

JARVIS. [*To THE RECTOR*] Beg pardon, sir. Is the little dog all right?

MAUD. Yes.

JARVIS. [*Touching his hat*] Seein' you've missed your train, m'm, shall I wait, and take you 'ome again?

MAUD. No.

JARVIS. Cert'nly, m'm. [*He touches his hat with a circular gesture, and is about to withdraw.*]

LADY ELLA. Oh, Jarvis—what's the name of the people here?

JARVIS. Challenger's the name I've driven 'em in, my lady.

THE SQUIRE. Challenger? Sounds like a hound. What's he like?

JARVIS. [*Scratching his head*] Wears a soft 'at, sir.

THE SQUIRE. H'm! Ah!

JARVIS. Very nice gentleman, very nice lady. 'Elped me with my old mare when she 'ad the 'ighsteria last week—couldn't 'a' been kinder if they'd 'a' been angels from 'eaven. Wonderful fond o' dumb animals, the two of 'em. I don't pay no attention to gossip, meself.

MAUD. Gossip? What gossip?

JARVIS. [*Backing*] Did I make use of the word, m'm? You'll excuse me, I'm sure. There's always talk where there's newcomers. I takes people as I finds 'em.

THE RECTOR. Yes, yes, Jarvis—quite—quite right.

JARVIS. Yes, sir. I've—I've got a 'abit that way at my time o' life.

MAUD. [*Sharply*] How long have they been here, Jarvis?

JARVIS. Well—er—a matter of three weeks, m'm.

[*A slight involuntary stir.*]

[*Apologetic.*] Of course, in my profession I can't afford to take notice of whether there's the trifle of a ring between 'em, as the sayin' is. 'Tisn't 'ardly my business like.   [*A silence.*

LADY ELLA. [*Suddenly*] Er—thank you, Jarvis; you needn't wait.

JARVIS. No, m'lady! Your service, sir—service, m'm.

                              [*He goes. A silence.*

THE SQUIRE. [*Drawing a little closer*] Three weeks? I say—er—wasn't there a book?

THE RECTOR. [*Abstracted*] Three weeks—— I certainly haven't seen them in church.

MAUD. A *trifle* of a ring!

LADY ELLA. [*Impulsively*] Oh, bother! I'm sure she's all right. And if she isn't, I don't care. She's been much too splendid.

THE SQUIRE. Must think of the village. Didn't quite like the doctor's way of puttin' us off.

LADY ELLA. The poor darling owes his life to her.

THE SQUIRE. H'm! Dash it! Yes! Can't forget the way she ran into that stinkin' pond.

MAUD. *Had* she a wedding-ring on?

                    [*They look at each other, but no one knows.*

LADY ELLA. Well, *I'm* not going to be ungrateful!

THE SQUIRE. It'd be dashed awkward—mustn't take a false step, Ella.

THE RECTOR. And I've got his braces!

                              [*He puts his hand to his waist.*

MAUD. [*Warningly*] Bertie!

THE SQUIRE. That's all right, Rector—we're goin' to be perfectly polite, and—and—thank her, and all that.

LADY ELLA. We can *see* she's a good sort. What *does* it matter?

MAUD. My dear Ella! "What does it matter!" We've *got to know.*

THE RECTOR. We *do* want light.

THE SQUIRE. I'll ring the bell.   [*He rings.*

                    [*They look at each other aghast.*

LADY ELLA. What did you ring for, Tommy?

THE SQUIRE. [*Flabbergasted*] God knows!

MAUD. Somebody'll come.

THE SQUIRE. Rector—you—you've got to——

MAUD. Yes, Bertie.

THE RECTOR. Dear me! But—er—what—er—— How?

THE SQUIRE. [*Deeply—to himself*] The whole thing's damn delicate.

     [*The door right is opened and a* MAID *appears. She is a determined-looking female. They face her in silence.*

THE RECTOR. Er—er—your master is not in?

THE MAID. No. 'E's gone up to London.

THE RECTOR. Er—*Mr. Challenger,* I think?

THE MAID. Yes.

THE RECTOR. Yes! Er—quite so!

THE MAID. [*Eyeing them*] D'you want—Mrs. Challenger?

THE RECTOR. Ah! Not precisely——

THE SQUIRE. [*To him in a low, determined voice*] Go on.

THE RECTOR. [*Desperately*] I asked because there was a—a—Mr. Challenger I used to know in the 'nineties, and I thought—you wouldn't happen to know how long they've been married? My friend marr——

THE MAID. Three weeks.

THE RECTOR. Quite so—quite so! I shall hope it will turn out to be—— Er—thank you—Ha!

LADY ELLA. Our dog has been fighting with the Rector's, and Mrs. Challenger rescued him; she's bathing his ear. We're waiting to thank her. You needn't——

THE MAID. [*Eyeing them*] No. [*She turns and goes out.*

THE SQUIRE. Phew! What a gorgon! I say, Rector, did you really know a Challenger in the 'nineties?

THE RECTOR. [*Wiping his brow*] No.

THE SQUIRE. Ha! Jolly good!

LADY ELLA. Well, you see!—it's all right.

THE RECTOR. Yes, indeed. A great relief!

LADY ELLA. [*Moving to the door*] I must go in now.

THE SQUIRE. Hold on! You goin' to ask 'em to—to—anything?

LADY ELLA. Yes.

MAUD. I shouldn't.

LADY ELLA. Why not? We all like the look of her.

THE RECTOR. I think we should punish ourselves for entertaining that uncharitable thought.

LADY ELLA. Yes. It's horrible not having the courage to take people as they are.

THE SQUIRE. As they are? H'm! How *can* you till you know?

LADY ELLA. Trust our instincts, of course.

THE SQUIRE. And supposing she'd turned out not married—eh?

LADY ELLA. She'd still be *herself*, wouldn't she?

MAUD. Ella!

THE SQUIRE. H'm! Don't know about that.

LADY ELLA. Of course she would, Tommy.

THE RECTOR. [*His hand stealing to his waist*] Well! It's a great weight off my——!

LADY ELLA. There's the poor darling snuffling. I must go in.

[*She knocks on the door. It is opened, and* EDWARD *comes out briskly, with a neat little white pointed ear-cap on one ear.*

LADY ELLA. Precious!

[*SHE HERSELF comes out, now properly dressed in flax-blue linen.*

LADY ELLA. How perfectly sweet of you to make him that !

SHE. He's such a dear.   And the other poor dog ?

MAUD. Quite safe, thanks to your strop.

[HANNIBAL *appears at the window, with the broken strop dangling.*
Following her gaze, they turn and see him.

MAUD. Oh ! There, he's broken it.   Bertie !

SHE. Let me !   [*She seizes* HANNIBAL.

THE SQUIRE. We're really most tremendously obliged to you.
Afraid we've been an awful nuisance.

SHE. Not a bit.   I love dogs.

THE SQUIRE. Hope to make the acquaintance of Mr.—— of your
husband.

LADY ELLA. [*To* EDWARD, *who is straining*] Gently, darling !
Tommy, take him.   [THE SQUIRE *does so.*

MAUD. [*Approaching* HANNIBAL] Is he behaving ?

[*She stops short, and her face suddenly shoots forward at* HER
hands that are holding HANNIBAL'*s neck.*

SHE. Oh ! yes—he's a love.

MAUD. [*Regaining her upright position, and pursing her lips ; in a*
peculiar voice] Bertie, take Hannibal.   [THE RECTOR *takes him.*

LADY ELLA. [*Producing a card*] I can't be too grateful for all you've
done for my poor darling.   This is where we live.   Do come—and
see——

[MAUD, *whose eyes have never left those hands, tweaks* LADY ELLA'*s*
dress.

LADY ELLA. That is—I'm—I——

[HERSELF *looks at* LADY ELLA *in surprise.*

THE SQUIRE. I don't know if your husband shoots, but if——

[MAUD, *catching his eye, taps the third finger of her left hand.*]
—er—he—does—er—er——

[HERSELF *looks at* THE SQUIRE *surprised.*

MAUD. [*Turning to her husband, repeats the gesture with the low and*
simple word] Look !

THE RECTOR. [*With round eyes, severely*] Hannibal !

[*He lifts him bodily and carries him away.*

MAUD. Don't squeeze him, Bertie !

[*She follows through the French window.*

THE SQUIRE. [*Abruptly—of the unoffending* EDWARD] That dog'll
be forgettin' himself in a minute.

[*He picks up* EDWARD *and takes him out.*   LADY ELLA *is left*
staring.

LADY ELLA. [*At last*] You mustn't think, I—— You mustn't
think, we—— Oh ! I *must* just see they don't let Edward get at
Hannibal.   [*She skims away.*

[HERSELF *is left staring after* LADY ELLA, *in surprise.*

SHE. What is the matter with them?   [*The door is opened.*

THE MAID. [*Entering and holding out a wedding-ring—severely*] You left this, m'm, in the bathroom.

SHE. [*Looking, startled, at her finger*] Oh! [*Taking it.*] I hadn't missed it. Thank you, Martha.   [THE MAID *goes.*

  [*A hand, slipping in at the casement window, softly lays a pair of braces on the window-sill.* SHE *looks at the braces, then at the ring.* HER *lip curls.*

SHE. [*Murmuring deeply*] Ah!

The curtain falls

DEFEAT

A TINY DRAMA

CHARACTERS

THE OFFICER   THE GIRL

DEFEAT

DURING THE GREAT WAR. EVENING.

*An empty room. The curtains drawn and gas turned low. The furniture
and walls give a colour-impression as of greens and beetroot. There is
a prevalence of plush. A fireplace on the Left, a sofa, a small table ;
the curtained window is at the back. On the table, in a common pot,
stands a little plant of maidenhair fern, fresh and green.*

*Enter from the door on the Right, a GIRL and a YOUNG OFFICER in khaki.
The GIRL wears a discreet dark dress, hat, and veil, and stained yellow
gloves. The YOUNG OFFICER is tall, with a fresh open face, and
kindly eager blue eyes ; he is a little lame. The GIRL, who is evidently
at home, moves towards the gas jet to turn it up, then changes her mind,
and going to the curtains, draws them apart and throws up the window.
Bright moonlight comes flooding in. Outside are seen the trees of a
little Square. She stands gazing out, suddenly turns inward with a
shiver.*

YOUNG OFF. I say ; what's the matter ?   You were crying when
I spoke to you.

GIRL. [*With a movement of recovery*] Oh ! nothing. The beautiful
evening—that's all.

YOUNG OFF. [*Looking at her*] Cheer up !

GIRL. [*Taking off hat and veil ; her hair is yellowish and crinkly*] Cheer
up !   You are not lonelee, like me.

YOUNG OFF. [*Limping to the window—doubtfully*] I say, how did you
—how did you get into this ?   Isn't it an awfully hopeless sort of life ?

GIRL. Yees, it ees.   You haf been wounded ?

YOUNG OFF. Just out of hospital to-day.

GIRL. The horrible war—all the misery is because of the war.
When will it end ?

YOUNG OFF. [*Leaning against the window-sill, looking at her attentively*]
I say, what nationality are you ?

GIRL. [*With a quick look and away*] Rooshian.

YOUNG OFF. Really !   I never met a Russian girl. [*The GIRL
gives him another quick look.*] I say, is it as bad as they make out ?

GIRL. [*Slipping her hand through his arm*] Not when I haf anyone as
ni-ice as you ; I never haf had, though. [*She smiles, and her smile,
like her speech, is slow and confiding.*] You stopped because I was sad,
others stop because I am gay.   I am not fond of men at all.   When
you know—you are not fond of them.

YOUNG OFF. Well, you hardly know them at their best, do you? You should see them in the trenches. By George! They're simply splendid—officers and men, every blessed soul. There's never been anything like it—just one long bit of jolly fine self-sacrifice; it's perfectly amazing.

GIRL. [*Turning her blue-grey eyes on him*] I expect you are not the last at that. You see in them what you haf in yourself, I think.

YOUNG OFF. Oh, not a bit; you're quite out! I assure you when we made the attack where I got wounded there wasn't a single man in my regiment who wasn't an absolute hero. The way they went in—never thinking of themselves—it was simply ripping.

GIRL. [*In a queer voice*] It is the same too, perhaps, with—the enemy.

YOUNG OFF. Oh, yes! I know that.

GIRL. Ah! You are not a mean man. How I hate mean men!

YOUNG OFF. Oh! they're not mean really—they simply don't understand.

GIRL. Oh! You are a babee—a good babee—aren't you?

[*The* YOUNG OFFICER *doesn't like this, and frowns. The* GIRL *looks a little scared.*

GIRL. [*Clingingly*] But I li-ke you for it. It is so good to find a ni-ice man.

YOUNG OFF. [*Abruptly*] About being lonely? Haven't you any Russian friends?

GIRL. [*Blankly*] Rooshian? No. [*Quickly.*] The town is so beeg. Were you at the concert before you spoke to me?

YOUNG OFF. Yes.

GIRL. I too. I lofe music.

YOUNG OFF. I suppose all Russians do.

GIRL. [*With another quick look at him*] I go there always when I haf the money.

YOUNG OFF. What! Are you as badly on the rocks at that?

GIRL. Well, I haf just one shilling now.

[*She laughs bitterly. The laugh upsets him; he sits on the window-sill, and leans forward towards her.*

YOUNG OFF. I say, what's your name?

GIRL. May. Well, I call myself that. It is no good asking yours.

YOUNG OFF. [*With a laugh*] You're a distrustful little soul, aren't you?

GIRL. I haf reason to be, don't you think?

YOUNG OFF. Yes. I suppose you're bound to think us all brutes.

GIRL. [*Sitting on a chair close to the window where the moonlight falls on one powdered cheek*] Well, I haf a lot of reasons to be afraid all my time. I am dreadfully nervous now; I am not trusding anybody. I suppose you haf been killing lots of Germans?

YOUNG OFF. We never know, unless it happens to be hand to hand; I haven't come in for that yet.

GIRL. But you would be very glad if you had killed some.

YOUNG OFF. Oh, glad? I don't think so. We're all in the same boat, so far as that's concerned. We're not glad to kill each other—not most of us. We do our job—that's all.

GIRL. Oh! It is frightful. I expect I haf my brothers killed.

YOUNG OFF. Don't you get any news ever?

GIRL. News? No, indeed, no news of anybody in my country. I might not haf a country; all that I ever knew is gone; fader, moder, sisters, broders, all; never any more I shall see them, I suppose, now. The war it breaks and breaks, it breaks hearts. [*She gives a little snarl.*] Do you know what I was thinking when you came up to me? I was thinking of my native town, and the river in the moonlight. If I could see it again I would be glad. Were you ever homeseeck?

YOUNG OFF. Yes, I have been—in the trenches. But one's ashamed —with all the others.

GIRL. Ah! Yees! Yees! You are all comrades there. What is it like for me here, do you think, where everybody hates and despises me, and would catch me and put me in prison, perhaps.
[*Her breast heaves.*

YOUNG OFF. [*Leaning forward and patting her knee*] Sorry—sorry.

GIRL. [*In a smothered voice*] You are the first who has been kind to me for so long! I will tell you the truth—I am not Rooshian at all —I am German.

YOUNG OFF. [*Staring*] My dear girl, who cares? We aren't fighting against women.

GIRL. [*Peering at him*] Another man said that to me. But he was thinkin' of his fun. You are a veree ni-ice boy; I am so glad I met you. You see the good in people, don't you? That is the first thing in the world—because—there is really not much good in people, you know.

YOUNG OFF. [*Smiling*] You are a dreadful little cynic! But of course you are!

GIRL. Cyneec? How long do you think I would live if I was not a cyneec! I should drown myself to-morrow. Perhaps there are good people, but, you see, I don't know them.

YOUNG OFF. I know lots.

GIRL. [*Leaning towards him*] Well now—see, ni-ice boy—you haf never been in a hole, haf you?

YOUNG OFF. I suppose not a real hole.

GIRL. No, I should think not, with your face. Well, suppose I am still a good girl, as I was once, you know; and you took me to your mother and your sisters and you said: "Here is a little German girl that has no work, and no money, and no friends." They will say: "Oh! how sad! A German girl!" And they will go and wash their hands. [*The* OFFICER *is silent, staring at her.*

GIRL. You see.

YOUNG OFF. [*Muttering*] I'm sure there *are* people.

GIRL. No. They would not take a German, even if she was good. Besides, I don't want to be good any more—I am not a humbug; I have learned to be bad. Aren't you going to kees me, ni-ice boy?

[*She puts her face close to his. Her eyes trouble him; he draws back.*

YOUNG OFF. Don't. I'd rather not, if you don't mind. [*She looks at him fixedly, with a curious inquiring stare.*] It's stupid. I don't know—but you see, out there, and in hospital, life's different. It's —it's—it isn't mean, you know. Don't come too close.

GIRL. Oh! You are fun—[*She stops.*] Eesn't it light? No Zeps to-night. When they burn—what a 'orrible death! And all the people cheer. It is natural. Do you hate us veree much?

YOUNG OFF. [*Turning sharply*] Hate? I don't know.

GIRL. I don't hate even the English—I despise them. I despise my people too; even more, because they began this war. Oh! I know that. I despise all the peoples. Why haf they made the world so miserable—why haf they killed all our lives—hundreds and thousands and millions of lives—all for noting? They haf made a bad world—everybody hating, and looking for the worst everywhere. They haf made me bad, I know. I believe no more in anything. What is there to believe in? Is there a God? No! Once I was teaching little English children their prayers—isn't that funnee? I was reading to them about Christ and love. I believed all those things. Now I believe noting at all—no one who is not a fool or a liar can believe. I would like to work in a 'ospital; I would like to go and 'elp poor boys like you. Because I am a German they would throw me out a 'undred times, even if I was good. It is the same in Germany, in France, in Russia, everywhere. But do you think I will believe in Love and Christ and God and all that—— Not I! I think we are animals—that's all! Oh, yes! you fancy it is because my life has spoiled me. It is not that at all—that is not the worst thing in life. The men I take are not ni-ice, like you, but it's their nature; and—they help me to live, which is something for me, anyway. No, it is the men who think themselves great and good and make the war with their talk and their hate, killing us all—killing all the boys like you, and keeping poor people in prison, and telling us to go on hating; and all these dreadful cold-blood creatures who write in the papers —the same in my country—just the same; it is because of all of them that I think we are only animals.

[*The* YOUNG OFFICER *gets up, acutely miserable. She follows him with her eyes.*

GIRL. Don't mind me talkin', ni-ice boy. I don't know anyone to talk to. If you don't like it, I can be quiet as a mouse.

Young Off. Oh, go on! Talk away; I'm not obliged to believe you, and I don't.

[*She, too, is on her feet now, leaning against the wall; her dark dress and white face just touched by the slanting moonlight. Her voice comes again slow and soft and bitter.*

Girl. Well, look here, ni-ice boy, what sort of world is it, where millions are being tortured, for no fault of theirs, at all? A beautiful world, isn't it? 'Umbog! Silly rot, as you boys call it. You say it is all "Comrades" and braveness out there at the front, and people don't think of themselves. Well, I don't think of myself veree much. What does it matter? I am lost now, anyway. But I think of my people at 'ome; how they suffer and grieve. I think of all the poor people there, and here, who lose those they love, and all the poor prisoners. Am I not to think of them? And if I do, how am I to believe it a beautiful world, ni-ice boy?

[*He stands very still, staring at her.*

Girl. Look here! We haf one life each, and soon it is over. Well, *I* think that is lucky.

Young Off. No! There's more than that.

Girl. [*Softly*] Ah! *You* think the war is fought for the future; you are giving your lives for a better world, aren't you?

Young Off. We must fight till we win.

Girl. Till you win. My people think that too. All the peoples think that if they win the world will be better. But it will not, you know; it will be much worse, anyway.

[*He turns away from her, and catches up his cap. Her voice follows him.*

Girl. I don't care which win. I don't care if my country is beaten. I despise them all—animals—animals. Ah! Don't go, ni-ice boy; I will be quiet now.

[*He has taken some notes from his tunic pocket; he puts them on the table and goes up to her.*

Young Off. Good-night.

Girl. [*Plaintively*] Are you really going? Don't you like me enough?

Young Off. Yes, I like you.

Girl. It is because I am German, then?

Young Off. No.

Girl. Then why won't you stay?

Young Off. [*With a shrug*] If you must know—because you upset me.

Girl. Won't you kees me once?

[*He bends, puts his lips to her forehead. But as he takes them away she throws her head back, presses her mouth to his, and clings to him.*

YOUNG OFF. [*Sitting down suddenly*] Don't! I don't want to feel a brute.

GIRL. [*Laughing*] You are a funny boy; but you are veree good. Talk to me a little, then. No one talks to me. Tell me, haf you seen many German prisoners?

YOUNG OFF. [*Sighing*] A good many.

GIRL. Any from the Rhine?

YOUNG OFF. Yes, I think so.

GIRL. Were they veree sad?

YOUNG OFF. Some were; some were quite *glad* to be taken.

GIRL. Did you ever see the Rhine? It will be wonderful to-night. The moonlight will be the same there, and in Rooshia too, and France, everywhere; and the trees will look the same as here, and people will meet under them and make love just as here. Oh! isn't it stupid, the war? As if it were not good to be alive!

YOUNG OFF. You can't tell how good it is to be alive till you're facing death. You don't live till then. And when a whole lot of you feel like that—and are ready to give their lives for each other, it's worth all the rest of life put together.

[*He stops, ashamed of such sentiment before this girl, who believes in nothing.*

GIRL. [*Softly*] How were you wounded, ni-ice boy?

YOUNG OFF. Attacking across open ground; four machine bullets got me at one go off.

GIRL. Weren't you veree frightened when they ordered you to attack? [*He shakes his head and laughs.*

YOUNG OFF. It was great. We did laugh that morning. They got me much too soon, though—a swindle.

GIRL. [*Staring at him*] You laughed?

YOUNG OFF. Yes. And what do you think was the first thing I was conscious of next morning? My old Colonel bending over me and giving me a squeeze of lemon. If you knew my Colonel you'd still believe in things. There *is* something, you know, behind all this evil. After all, you can only die once, and, if it's for your country —all the better!

[*Her face, in the moonlight, with intent eyes touched up with black, has a most strange, other-world look.*

GIRL. No; I believe in nothing, not even in my country. My heart is dead.

YOUNG OFF. Yes; you think so, but it isn't, you know, or you wouldn't have been crying when I met you.

GIRL. If it were not dead, do you think I could live my life—walking the streets every night, pretending to like strange men; never hearing a kind word; never talking, for fear I will be known for a German? Soon I shall take to drinking; then I shall be "Kaput" veree quick.

You see, I am practical; I see things clear. To-night I am a little emotional; the moon is funny, you know. But I live for myself only, now. I don't care for anything or anybody.

YOUNG OFF. All the same, just now you were pitying your folk at home, and prisoners and that.

GIRL. Yees; because they suffer. Those who suffer are like me —I pity myself, that's all; I am different from your English women. I see what I am doing; I do not let my mind become a turnip just because I am no longer moral.

YOUNG OFF. Nor your heart either, for all you say.

GIRL. Ni-ice boy, you are veree obstinate. But all that about love is 'umbog. We love ourselves, noting more.

[*At that intense soft bitterness in her voice, he gets up, feeling stifled, and stands at the window. A newspaper boy some way off is calling his wares. The* GIRL'S *fingers slip between his own, and stay unmoving. He looks round into her face. In spite of make-up it has a queer, unholy, touching beauty.*

YOUNG OFF. [*With an outburst*] No; we don't only love ourselves; there *is* more. I can't explain, but there's something great; there's kindness—and—and——

[*The shouting of newspaper boys grows louder, and their cries, passionately vehement, clash into each other and obscure each word. His head goes up to listen; her hand tightens within his arm —she too is listening. The cries come nearer, hoarser, more shrill and clamorous; the empty moonlight outside seems suddenly crowded with figures, footsteps, voices, and a fierce distant cheering.* "Great victory—great victory! Official! British! 'Eavy Defeat of the 'Uns! Many thousand prisoners! 'Eavy Defeat!" It speeds by, intoxicating, filling him with a fearful joy; he leans far out, waving his cap and cheering like a madman; the night seems to flutter and vibrate and answer. He turns to rush down into the street, strikes against something soft, and recoils. The* GIRL *stands with hands clenched, and face convulsed, panting. All confused with the desire to do something, he stoops to kiss her hand. She snatches away her fingers, sweeps up the notes he has put down, and holds them out to him.*

GIRL. Take them—I will not haf your English money—take them.

[*Suddenly she tears them across, twice, thrice, lets the bits flutter to the floor, and turns her back on him. He stands looking at her leaning against the plush-covered table, her head down, a dark figure in a dark room, with the moonlight sharpening her outline. Hardly a moment he stays, then makes for the door. When he is gone, she still stands there, her chin on her breast, with the sound in her ears of cheering, of hurrying feet, and voices*

31*

crying: " *'Eavy Defeat!* " *stands, in the centre of a pattern made by the fragments of the torn-up notes, staring out into the moonlight, seeing not this hated room and the hated Square outside, but a German orchard, and herself, a little girl, plucking apples, a big dog beside her ; and a hundred other pictures, such as the drowning see. Then she sinks down on the floor, lays her forehead on the dusty carpet, and presses her body to it. Mechanically, she sweeps together the scattered fragments of notes, assembling them with the dust into a little pile, as of fallen leaves, and dabbling in it with her fingers, while the tears run down her cheeks.*

GIRL. Defeat! Der Vaterland! Defeat! . . . One shillin'!

[*Then suddenly, in the moonlight, she sits up, and begins to sing with all her might:* " *Die Wacht am Rhein.*" *And outside men pass, singing:* " *Rule, Britannia!* "

The curtain falls.

THE SUN

CHARACTERS

THE GIRL
THE MAN
THE SOLDIER

THE SUN

A Girl sits crouched over her knees on a stile close to a river. A Man with a silver badge stands beside her, clutching the worn top plank. The Girl's level brows are drawn together ; her eyes see her memories. The Man's eyes see The Girl ; he has a dark, twisted face. The bright sun shines ; the quiet river flows ; the Cuckoo is calling ; the mayflower is in bloom along the hedge that ends in the stile on the towing-path.

The Girl. God knows what 'e'll say, Jim.

The Man. Let 'im. 'E's come too late, that's all.

The Girl. He couldn't come before. I'm frightened. 'E was fond o' me.

The Man. And aren't I fond of you ?

The Girl. I ought to 'a waited, Jim ; with 'im in the fightin'.

The Man. [*Passionately*] And what about me ? Aren't I been in the fightin'—earned all I could get ?

The Girl. [*Touching him*] Ah !

The Man. Did you——? [*He cannot speak the words.*

The Girl. Not like you, Jim—not like you.

The Man. Have a spirit, then.

The Girl. I promised him.

The Man. One man's luck's another's poison.

The Girl. I ought to 'a waited. I never thought he'd come back from the fightin'.

The Man. [*Grimly*] Maybe 'e'd better not 'ave.

The Girl. [*Looking back along the tow-path*] What'll he be like, I wonder ?

The Man. [*Gripping her shoulder*] Daisy, don't you never go back on me, or I should kill you, and 'im too.

[*The Girl looks at him, shivers, and puts her lips to his.*

The Girl. I never could.

The Man. Will you run for it ? 'E'd never find us.

[*The Girl shakes her head.*

The Man. [*Dully*] What's the good o' stayin' ? The world's wide.

The Girl. I'd rather have it off me mind, with him home.

The Man. [*Clenching his hands*] It's temptin' Providence.

The Girl. What's the time, Jim ?

965

THE MAN. [*Glancing at the sun*] 'Alf past four.

THE GIRL. [*Looking along the towing-path*] He said four o'clock. Jim, you better go.

THE MAN. Not *I*. I've not got the wind up. I've seen as much of hell as he has, any day. What like is he?

THE GIRL. [*Dully*] I dunno, just. I've not seen him these three years. I dunno no more, since I've known you.

THE MAN. Big or little chap?

THE GIRL. 'Bout your size. Oh! Jim, go along!

THE MAN. No fear! What's a blighter like that to old Fritz's shells? We didn't shift when they was comin'. If you'll go, I'll go; not else. [*Again she shakes her head.*

THE GIRL. Jim, do you love me true?

[*For answer* THE MAN *takes her avidly in his arms.*] I ain't ashamed—I ain't ashamed. If 'e could see me 'eart.

THE MAN. Daisy! If I'd known you out there, I never could 'a stuck it. They'd 'a got me for a deserter. That's how I love you!

THE GIRL. Jim, don't lift your hand to 'im! Promise!

THE MAN. That's according.

THE GIRL. Promise!

THE MAN. If 'e keeps quiet, I won't. But I'm not accountable— not always, I tell you straight—not since I've been through that.

THE GIRL. [*With a shiver*] Nor p'raps he isn't.

THE MAN. Like as not. It takes the lynch pins out, I tell you.

THE GIRL. God 'elp us!

THE MAN. [*Grimly*] Ah! We said that a bit too often. What we want we take, now; there's no one else to give it us, and there's no fear'll stop us; we seen the bottom of things.

THE GIRL. P'raps he'll say that too.

THE MAN. Then it'll be 'im or me.

THE GIRL. I'm frightened.

THE MAN. [*Tenderly*] No, Daisy, no! The river's handy. One more or less. 'E shan't 'arm you; nor me neither.

[*He takes out a knife.*

THE GIRL. [*Seizing his hand*] Oh, no! Give it to me, Jim.

THE MAN. [*Smiling*] No fear! [*He puts it away.*] Shan't 'ave no need for it like as not. All right, little Daisy; you can't be expected to see things like what we do. What's life, anyway? I've seen a thousand lives taken in five minutes. I've seen dead men on the wires like flies on a flypaper. I've been as good as dead meself a hundred times. I've killed a dozen men. It's nothin'. He's safe, if 'e don't get my blood up. If he does, nobody's safe; not 'im, nor anybody else; not even you. I'm speakin' sober.

THE GIRL. [*Softly*] Jim, you won't go fightin' in the sun, with the birds all callin'?

THE MAN. That depends on 'im. I'm not lookin' for it. Daisy, I love you. I love your hair. I love your eyes. I love you.

THE GIRL. And I love you, Jim. I don't want nothin' more than you in all the world.

THE MAN. Amen to that, my dear. Kiss me close!

[*The sound of a voice singing breaks in on their embrace.* THE GIRL *starts from his arms, and looks behind her along the towing-path.* THE MAN *draws back against the hedge, fingering his side, where the knife is hidden. The song comes nearer :*

" I'll be right there to-night,
Where the fields are snowy white ;
Banjos ringing, darkies singing—
All the world seems bright ! "

THE GIRL. It's him !

THE MAN. Don't get the wind up, Daisy. I'm here !

[*The singing stops. A man's voice says :* " Christ ! It's Daisy ; it's little Daisy 'erself ! " THE GIRL *stands rigid. The figure of a soldier appears on the other side of the stile. His cap is tucked into his belt, his hair is bright in the sunshine ; he is lean, wasted, brown, and laughing.*

SOLDIER. Daisy ! Daisy ! Hallo, old pretty girl !

[THE GIRL *does not move, barring the way, as it were.*

THE GIRL. Hallo, Jack ! [*Softly.*] I got things to tell you !

SOLDIER. What sort o' things, this lovely day ? Why, I got things that'd take me years to tell. Have you missed me, Daisy ?

THE GIRL. You been so long.

SOLDIER. So I 'ave. My Gawd ! It's a way they 'ave in the Army. I said when I got out of it I'd laugh. Like as the sun itself I used to think of you, Daisy, when the crumps was comin' over, and the wind was up. D'you remember that last night in the wood ? " Come back and marry me quick, Jack." Well, here I am—got me pass to heaven. No more fightin', no more drillin', no more sleepin' rough. We can get married now, Daisy. We can live soft an' 'appy. Give us a kiss, my dear.

THE GIRL. [*Drawing back*] No.

SOLDIER. [*Blankly*] Why not ?

[THE MAN, *with a swift movement, steps along the hedge to* THE GIRL'S *side.*

THE MAN. That's why, soldier.

SOLDIER. [*Leaping over the stile*] 'Oo are you, Pompey? The sun don't shine in your inside, do it? 'Oo is he, Daisy?

THE GIRL. My man.

SOLDIER. Your—man! Lummy! "Taffy was a Welshman, Taffy was a thief!" Well, mate! So you've been through it, too. I'm laughin' this mornin' as luck will 'ave it. Ah! I can see your knife.

THE MAN. [*Who has half drawn his knife*] Don't laugh at *me*, I tell you.

SOLDIER. Not at you, not at you. [*He looks from one to the other.*] I'm laughin' at things in general. Where did *you* get it, mate?

THE MAN. [*Watchfully*] Through the lung.

SOLDIER. Think o' that! An' I never was touched. Four years an' never was touched. An' so you've come an' took my girl! Nothin' doin'! Ha! [*Again he looks from one to the other—then away.*] Well! The world's before me! [*He laughs.*] I'll give you Daisy for a lung protector.

THE MAN. [*Fiercely*] You won't. I've took her.

SOLDIER. That's all right, then. You keep 'er. I've got a laugh in me you can't put out, black as you look! Good-bye, little Daisy!

[THE GIRL *makes a movement towards him.*

THE MAN. Don't touch 'im!

[THE GIRL *stands hesitating, and suddenly bursts into tears.*

SOLDIER. Look 'ere, mate; shake 'ands! I don't want to see a girl cry, this day of all, with the sun shinin'. I seen too much of sorrer. You and me've been at the back of it. We've 'ad our whack. Shake!

THE MAN. Who are you kiddin'? *You* never loved 'er!

SOLDIER. [*After a long moment's pause*] Oh! I thought I did.

THE MAN. I'll fight you for her. [*He drops his knife.*

SOLDIER. [*Slowly*] Mate, you done your bit, an' I done mine. It's took us two ways, seemin'ly.

THE GIRL. [*Pleading*] Jim!

THE MAN. [*With clenched fists*] I don't want 'is charity. I only want what I can take.

SOLDIER. Daisy, which of us will you 'ave?

THE GIRL. [*Covering her face*] Oh! *Him!*

SOLDIER. You see, mate! Put your 'ands down. There's nothin' for it but a laugh. You an' me know that. Laugh, mate!

THE MAN. You blarsted——!

[THE GIRL *springs to him and stops his mouth.*

SOLDIER. It's no use, mate. I can't do it. I said I'd laugh to-day, and laugh I will. I've come through that, an' all the stink of it; I've come through sorrer. Never again! Cheerio, mate! The sun's a-shinin'! [*He turns away.*

THE GIRL. Jack, don't think too 'ard of me!

SOLDIER. [*Looking back*] No fear, my dear! Enjoy your fancy!
So long! Gawd bless you both!

> [*He sings, and goes along the path, and the song:*

> " I'll be right there to-night,
>   Where the fields are snowy white;
>   Banjos ringing, darkies singing—
>   All the world seems bright!"

fades away.

THE MAN. 'E's mad.

THE GIRL. [*Looking down the path with her hands clasped*] The sun
has touched 'im, Jim!

The curtain falls.

PUNCH AND GO

" Orpheus with his lute made trees
And the mountain tops that freeze . . ."

PERSONS OF THE PLAY

JAMES G. FRUST, *the boss*
E. BLEWITT VANE, *the producer*
MR. FORESON, *the stage manager*
" ELECTRICS," *the electrician*
" PROPS," *the property man*
HERBERT, *the call boy*

OF THE PLAY WITHIN THE PLAY

GUY TOONE, *the professor.*
VANESSA HELLGROVE, *the wife*
GEORGE FLEETWAY, *Orpheus*
MAUDE HOPKINS, *the faun*

SCENE : The Stage of a Theatre.

Action continuous, though the curtain is momentarily lowered according to that action.

PUNCH AND GO

*The scene is the stage of the theatre set for the dress rehearsal of the little
play : " Orpheus with his Lute." The curtain is up and the audience,
though present, is not supposed to be. The set scene represents the end
section of a room, with wide French windows, Back Centre, fully opened
on to an apple orchard in bloom. The Back Wall, with these French
windows, is set only about ten feet from the footlights, and the rest of
the stage is orchard. What is visible of the room would indicate the
study of a writing man of culture.* In the wall, Stage Left, is a curtained opening, across which the curtain is half drawn. Stage Right
of the French windows is a large armchair turned rather towards the
window, with a book-rest attached, on which is a volume of the " Encyclopædia Britannica," while on a stool alongside are writing materials such as
a man requires when he writes with a pad on his knees. On a little
table close by is a reading-lamp with a dark green shade. A crude light
from the floats makes the stage stare ; the only person on it is* MR.
FORESON, *the stage manager, who is standing in the centre looking
upwards as if waiting for someone to speak. He is a short, broad
man, rather blank, and fatal. From the back of the auditorium, or
from an empty box, whichever is most convenient, the producer,* MR.
BLEWITT VANE, *a man of about thirty-four, with his hair brushed
back, speaks.*

VANE. Mr. Foreson ?

FORESON. Sir ?

VANE. We'll do that lighting again.

[FORESON *walks straight off the stage into the wings Right. A pause.*]
Mr. Foreson ! [*Crescendo.*] Mr. Foreson.

[FORESON *walks on again from Right and shades his eyes.*

VANE. For Goodness' sake, stand by ! We'll do that lighting again.
Check your floats.

FORESON. [*Speaking up into the prompt wings*] Electrics !

VOICE OF ELECTRICS. Hallo !

FORESON. Give it us again. Check your floats.

[*The floats go down, and there is a sudden blinding glare of blue lights,
in which* FORESON *looks particularly ghastly.*

---

* NOTE.—If found advantageous for scenic purposes, this section of room can
be changed to a broad verandah or porch with pillars supporting its roof,

VANE. Great Scott! What the blazes! Mr. Foreson!

[FORESON *walks straight out into the wings Left. Crescendo.*]

Mr. Foreson!

FORESON. [*Reappearing*] Sir?

VANE. Tell Miller to come down.

FORESON. Electrics! Mr. Blewitt Vane wants to speak to you. Come down!

VANE. Tell Herbert to sit in that chair.

[FORESON *walks straight out into the Right wings.*]

Mr. Foreson!

FORESON. [*Reappearing*] Sir?

VANE. Don't go off the stage. [FORESON *mutters.*]

[ELECTRICS *appears from the wings, stage Left. He is a dark, thin-faced man with rather spiky hair.*]

ELECTRICS. Yes, Mr. Vane?

VANE. Look!

ELECTRICS. That's what I'd got marked, Mr. Vane.

VANE. Once for all, what I want is the orchard in full moonlight, *and the room dark* except for the reading-lamp. Cut off your front battens.

[ELECTRICS *withdraws Left.* FORESON *walks off the stage into the Right wings.*]

Mr. Foreson!

FORESON. [*Reappearing*] Sir?

VANE. See this marked right. Now, come on with it! I want to get some beauty into this!

[*While he is speaking,* HERBERT, *the call boy, appears from the wings Right, a mercurial youth of about sixteen with a wide mouth.*]

FORESON. [*Māliciously*] Here you are, then, Mr. Vane. Herbert, sit in that chair.

[HERBERT *sits in the armchair, with an air of perfect peace.*

VANE. Now! [*All the lights go out. In a wail.*] Great Scott!

[*A throaty chuckle from* FORESON *in the darkness. The light dances up, flickers, shifts, grows steady, falling on the orchard outside. The reading lamp darts alight and a piercing little glare from it strikes into the auditorium away from* HERBERT.]

[*In a terrible voice.*] Mr. Foreson.

FORESON. Sir?

VANE. Look—at—that—shade!

[FORESON *mutters, walks up to it and turns it round so that the light shines on* HERBERT'S *legs.*]

On his face, on his face! [FORESON *turns the light accordingly.*

FORESON. Is that what you want, Mr. Vane?

VANE. Now, mark that!

FORESON. [*Up into wings Right*] Electrics !

ELECTRICS. Hallo !

FORESON. Mark that !   [*The blue suddenly becomes amber.*

VANE. My God !

  [*The blue returns. All is steady.* HERBERT *is seen diverting himself with an imaginary cigar.*

Mr. Foreson.

FORESON. Sir ?

VANE. Ask him if he's got that ?

FORESON. Have you got that ?

ELECTRICS. Yes.

VANE. Now pass to the change. Take your floats off altogether.

FORESON. [*Calling up*] Floats out.   [*They go out.*

VANE. Cut off that lamp. [*The lamp goes out.*] Put a little amber in your back batten. Mark that ! Now pass to the end. Mr. Foreson !

FORESON. Sir ?

VANE. Black out !

FORESON. [*Calling up*] Black out !   [*The lights go out.*

VANE. Give us your first lighting—lamp on. And then the two changes. Quick as you can. Put some pep into it. Mr. Foreson !

FORESON. Sir ?

VANE. Stand for me where Miss Hellgrove comes in.

    [FORESON *crosses to the window.*]

No, no !—by the curtain.

  [FORESON *takes his stand by the curtain ; and suddenly the three lighting effects are rendered quickly and with miraculous exactness.*]

Good ! Leave it at that. We'll begin. Mr. Foreson, send up to Mr. Frust.

  [*He moves from the auditorium and ascends on to the stage, by some steps stage Right.*

FORESON. Herb ! Call the boss, and tell beginners to stand by. Sharp, now !

    [HERBERT *gets out of the chair, and goes off Right.*
    [FORESON *is going off Left as* VANE *mounts the stage.*

VANE. Mr. Foreson.

FORESON. [*Reappearing*] Sir ?

VANE. I want " Props."

FORESON. [*In a stentorian voice*] " Props ! "

  [*A rather moth-eaten man appears through the French windows.*

VANE. Is that boulder firm ?

PROPS. [*Going to where, in front of the back-cloth, and apparently among its apple trees, lies the counterfeitment of a mossy boulder ; he puts his foot on it*] If you don't put too much weight on it, sir.

VANE. It won't creak ?

PROPS. Nao.   [*He mounts on it, and a dolorous creaking arises.*

VANE. Make that right.   Let me see that lute.

[PROPS *produces a property lute.*

[*While they scrutinize it, a broad man with broad leathery clean-shaven face and small mouth, occupied by the butt end of a cigar, has come on to the stage from stage Left, and stands waiting to be noticed.*

PROPS. [*Attracted by the scent of the cigar*] The Boss, sir.

VANE. [*Turning to* " PROPS "] That'll do, then.

[" PROPS " *goes out through the French windows.*

VANE. [*To* FRUST] Now, sir, we're all ready for rehearsal of " Orpheus with his Lute.

FRUST. [*In a Cosmopolitan voice*] " Orphoos with his loot ! " That his loot, Mr. Vane ?   Why didn't he pinch something more precious ?   Has this high-brow curtain-raiser of yours got any " pep " in it ?

VANE. It has charm.

FRUST. I'd thought of " Pop goes the Weasel " with little Miggs.   We kind of want a cock-tail before " Louisa Loses," Mr. Vane.

VANE. Well, sir, you'll see.

FRUST. This your lighting ?   It's a bit on the spiritool side.   I've left my glasses.   Guess I'll sit in the front row.   Ha'f a minute. Who plays this Orphoos ?

VANE. George Fleetway.

FRUST. Has he got punch ?

VANE. It's a very small part.

FRUST. Who are the others ?

VANE. Guy Toone plays the Professor ; Vanessa Hellgrove his wife ; Maude Hopkins the faun.

FRUST. H'm ! Names don't draw.

VANE. They're not expensive, any of them.   Miss Hellgrove's a find, I think.

FRUST. Pretty ?

VANE. Quite.

FRUST. Arty ?

VANE. [*Doubtfully*] No.   [*With resolution.*] Look here, Mr. Frust, it's no use your expecting another " Pop goes the Weasel."

FRUST. We-ell, if it's got punch and go, that'll be enough for me. Let's get *to* it !

[*He extinguishes his cigar and descends the steps and sits in the centre of the front row of the stalls.*

VANE. Mr. Foreson ?

FORESON. [*Appearing through curtain, Right*] Sir !

VANE. Beginners. Take your curtain down.

[*He descends the steps and seats himself next to* FRUST. *The curtain goes down.*

[*A woman's voice is heard singing very beautifully Sullivan's song:* " Orpheus with his lute, with his lute made trees and the mountain tops that freeze," *etc.*

FRUST. Some voice! [*The curtain rises.*

[*In the armchair the* PROFESSOR *is yawning, tall, thin, abstracted, and slightly grizzled in the hair. He has a pad of paper on his knee, ink on the stool to his right and the Encyclopædia volume on the stand to his left—barricaded in fact by the article he is writing. He is reading a page over to himself, but the words are drowned in the sound of the song his wife is singing in the next room, partly screened off by the curtain. She finishes, and stops. His voice can then be heard conning the words of his article.*

PROF. " Orpheus symbolized the voice of Beauty, the call of life, luring us mortals with his song back from the graves we dig for ourselves. Probably the ancients realized this neither more nor less than we moderns. Mankind has not changed. The civilized being still hides the faun and the dryad within its broadcloth and its silk. And yet——" [*He stops, with a dried-up air—rather impatiently.*] Go on, my dear! It helps the atmosphere.

[*The voice of his wife begins again, gets as far as " made them sing " and stops dead, just as the* PROFESSOR'S *pen is beginning to scratch. And suddenly, drawing the curtain further aside,*

[SHE *appears. Much younger than the* PROFESSOR, *pale, very pretty, of a Botticellian type in face, figure, and in her clinging cream-coloured frock. She gazes at her abstracted husband; then swiftly moves to the lintel of the open window, and stands looking out.*

THE WIFE. God! What beauty!

PROF. [*Looking up*] Umm?

THE WIFE. I said: God! What beauty!

PROF. Aha!

THE WIFE. [*Looking at him*] Do you know that I have to repeat everything to you nowadays?

PROF. What!

THE WIFE. That I have to repeat——

PROF. Yes; I heard. I'm sorry. I get absorbed.

THE WIFE. In all but me.

PROF. [*Startled*] My dear, your song was helping me like anything to get the mood. This paper is the very deuce—to balance between the historical and the natural.

THE WIFE. Who wants the natural?

PROF. [*Grumbling*] Ummm! Wish *I* thought that! Modern taste! History may go hang; they're all for tuppence-coloured sentiment nowadays.

THE WIFE. [*As if to herself*] Is the Spring sentiment?

PROF. I beg your pardon, my dear; I didn't catch.

WIFE. [*As if against her will—urged by some pent-up force*] Beauty, beauty!

PROF. That's what I'm trying to say here. The Orpheus legend symbolizes to this day the call of Beauty! [*He takes up his pen, while she continues to stare out at the moonlight. Yawning.*] Dash it! I get so sleepy; I wish you'd tell them to make the after-dinner coffee twice as strong.

WIFE. I will.

PROF. How does this strike you? [*Conning.*] " Many Renaissance pictures, especially those of Botticelli, Francesca and Piero di Cosimo were inspired by such legends as that of Orpheus, and we owe a tiny gem-like Raphael ' Apollo and Marsyas ' to the same Pagan inspiration."

WIFE. We owe it more than that—rebellion against the dry-as-dust.

PROF. Quite! I might develop that : " We owe it our revolt against the academic ; or our disgust at ' big business,' and all the grossness of commercial success. We owe——" [*His voice peters out.*

WIFE. It—love.

PROF. [*Abstracted*] Eh?

WIFE. I said : We owe it love.

PROF. [*Rather startled*] Possibly. But—er—[*With a dry smile*] I mustn't say that here—hardly!

WIFE. [*To herself and the moonlight*] Orpheus with his lute!

PROF. Most people think a lute is a sort of flute. [*Yawning heavily.*] My dear, if you're not going to sing again, d'you mind sitting down? I want to concentrate.

WIFE. I'm going out.

PROF. Mind the dew!

WIFE. The Christian virtues and the dew.

PROF. [*With a little dry laugh*] Not bad! Not bad! The Christian virtues and the dew. [*His hand takes up his pen, his face droops over his paper, while his wife looks at him with a very strange face.*] " How far we can trace the modern resurgence against the Christian virtues to the symbolic figures of Orpheus, Pan, Apollo, and Bacchus might be difficult to estimate, but——"

[*During those words his* WIFE *has passed through the window into the moonlight, and her voice rises, singing as she goes :* " Orpheus with his lute, with his lute made trees . . . ."*]

PROF. [*Suddenly aware of something*] She'll get her throat bad. [*He*

is silent as the voice swells in the distance.] Sounds queer at night—H'm!
[*He is silent—Yawning. The voice dies away. Suddenly his head nods;
he fights his drowsiness; writes a word or two, nods again, and in twenty
seconds is asleep.* [*The Stage is darkened by a black-out.*
[FRUST'S *voice is heard speaking.*

FRUST. What's that girl's name?

VANE. Vanessa Hellgrove.

FRUST. Aha!

[*The stage is lighted up again. Moonlight bright on the orchard;
the room in darkness where the Professor's figure is just visible
sleeping in the chair, and screwed a little more round towards
the window. From behind the mossy boulder a faun-like
figure uncurls itself and peeps over with ears standing up and
elbows leaning on the stone, playing a rustic pipe; and there
are seen two rabbits and a fox sitting up and listening. A
shiver of wind passes, blowing petals from the apple-trees.*

[*The* FAUN *darts his head towards where, from Right, comes slowly
the figure of a Greek youth, holding a lute or lyre which his
fingers strike, lilting out little wandering strains as of wind
whinnying in funnels and odd corners. The* FAUN *darts down
behind the stone, and the youth stands by the boulder playing
his lute. Slowly while he plays the whitened trunk of an
apple-tree is seen to dissolve into the body of a girl with bare
arms and feet, her dark hair unbound, and the face of the* PRO-
FESSOR'S WIFE. *Hypnotized, she slowly sways towards
him, their eyes fixed on each other, till she is quite close. Her
arms go out to him, cling round his neck, and, their lips meet.
But as they meet there comes a gasp and the* PROFESSOR *with
rumpled hair is seen starting from his chair, his hands thrown
up; and at his horrified "Oh!" the stage is darkened with a
black-out.* [*The voice of* FRUST *is heard speaking.*

FRUST. Gee!

[*The stage is lighted up again, as in the opening scene. The* PRO-
FESSOR *is seen in his chair, with spilt sheets of paper round him,
waking from a dream. He shakes himself, pinches his leg,
stares heavily round into the moonlight, rises.*

PROF. Phew! Beastly dream! Boof! H'm!
[*He moves to the window and calls.*]
Blanche! Blanche! [*To himself.*] Made trees—made trees! [*Calling.*]
Blanche!

WIFE'S VOICE. Yes.

PROF. Where are you?

WIFE. [*Appearing by the stone with her hair down*] Here!

PROF. I say—I—I've been asleep—had a dream. Come in. I'll
tell you. [*She comes, and they stand in the window.*

PROF. I dreamed I saw a—faun on that boulder blowing on a pipe. [*He looks nervously at the stone.*] With two damned little rabbits and a fox sitting up and listening. And then from out there came our friend Orpheus playing on his confounded lute, till he actually turned that tree there into *you*. And gradually he—he drew you like a snake till you—er—put your arms round his neck and—er—kissed him. Boof! I woke up. Most unpleasant. Why! Your hair's down!

WIFE. Yes.

PROF. Why?

WIFE. It was no dream. He was bringing me to life.

PROF. What on earth——?

WIFE. Do you suppose I *am* alive? I'm as dead as Eurydice.

PROF. Good heavens, Blanche, what's the matter with you to-night?

WIFE. [*Pointing to the litter of papers*] Why don't we *live*, instead of writing of it? [*She points out into the moonlight.*] What do we get out of life? Money, fame, fashion, talk, learning? Yes. And what good are they? I want to *live*!

PROF. [*Helplessly*] My dear, I really don't know what you mean.

WIFE. [*Pointing out into the moonlight*] Look! Orpheus with his lute, and nobody can see him. Beauty, beauty, beauty—we let it go. [*With sudden passion.*] Beauty, love, the spring. They should be in us, and they're all outside.

PROF. My dear, this is—this is—awful.   [*He tries to embrace her.*

WIFE. [*Avoiding him—in a stilly voice*] Oh! Go on with your writing!

PROF. I'm—I'm upset. I've never known you so—so——

WIFE. Hysterical? Well! It's over. I'll go and sing.

PROF. [*Soothingly*] There, there! I'm sorry, darling; I really am. You're hipped—you're hipped. [*He gives and she accepts a kiss.*] Better? [*He gravitates towards his papers.*] All right, now?

WIFE. [*Standing still and looking at him*] Quite!

PROF. Well, I'll try and finish this to-night; then, to-morrow we might have a jaunt. How about a theatre? There's a thing—they say—called " Chinese Chops," that's been running years.

WIFE. [*Softly to herself as he settles down into his chair*] Oh! God!

> [*While he takes up a sheet of paper and adjusts himself, she stands at the window staring with all her might at the boulder, till from behind it the faun's head and shoulders emerge once more.*

PROF. Very queer the power suggestion has over the mind. Very queer! There's nothing really in animism, you know, except the curious shapes rocks, trees and things take in certain lights—effect they have on our imagination. [*He looks up.*] What's the matter now?

WIFE. [*Startled*] Nothing! Nothing!

[*Her eyes waver to him again, and the* FAUN *vanishes. She turns again to look at the boulder; there is nothing there; a little shiver of wind blows some petals off the trees. She catches one of them, and turning quickly, goes out through the curtain.*

PROF. [*Coming to himself and writing*] "The Orpheus legend is the —er—apotheosis of animism. Can we accept——"

[*His voice is lost in the sound of his* WIFE's *voice beginning again:* "Orpheus with his lute—with his lute made trees——" *It dies in a sob. The* PROFESSOR *looks up startled, as the curtain falls.*

FRUST. Fine! Fine!

VANE. Take up the curtain. Mr. Foreson? [*The curtain goes up.*

FORESON. Sir?

VANE. Everybody on.

[*He and* FRUST *leave their seats and ascend on to the stage, on which are collecting the four Players.*

VANE. Give us some light.

FORESON. Electrics! Turn up your floats!

[*The footlights go up, and the blue goes out; the light is crude as at the beginning.*

FRUST. I'd like to meet Miss Hellgrove. [*She comes forward eagerly and timidly. He grasps her hand.*] Miss Hellgrove, I want to say I thought that fine—fine. [*Her evident emotion and pleasure warm him so that he increases his grasp and commendation.*] Fine. It quite got my soft spots. Emotional. Fine!

MISS H. Oh! Mr. Frust; it means so much to me. Thank you!

FRUST. [*A little balder in the eye, and losing warmth*] Er—fine! [*His eye wanders.*] Where's Mr. Flatway?

VANE. Fleetway. [*Fleetway comes up.*

FRUST. Mr. Fleetway, I want to say I thought your Orphoos very remarkable. Fine.

FLEETWAY. Thank you, sir, indeed—so glad you liked it.

FRUST. [*A little balder in the eye*] There wasn't much to it, but what there was was fine. Mr. Toone.

[*Fleetway melts out and* TOONE *is precipitated.*] Mr. Toone, I was very pleased with your Professor—quite a character-study. [*TOONE bows and murmurs.*] Yes, sir! I thought it fine. [*His eye grows bald.*] Who plays the goat?

MISS HOPK. [*Appearing suddenly between the windows*] I play the faun, Mr. Frust.

FORESON. [*Introducing*] Miss Maude 'Opkins.

FRUST. Miss Hopkins, I guess your fawn was fine.

MISS HOPK. Oh! Thank you, Mr. Frust. How nice of you to say so. I do so enjoy playing him.

FRUST. [*His eye growing bald*] Mr. Foreson, I thought the way you fixed that tree was very cunning ; I certainly did. Got a match ?

> [*He takes a match from* FORESON, *and lighting a very long cigar, walks up stage through the French windows followed by* FORESON, *and examines the apple-tree.*

> [*The two Actors depart, but* MISS HELLGROVE *runs from where she has been lingering, by the curtain, to* VANE, *stage Right.*

MISS H. Oh ! Mr. Vane—do you think ? He seemed quite— Oh ! Mr. Vane, [*Ecstatically*] if only——

VANE. [*Pleased and happy*] Yes, yes. All right—you were splendid. He liked it. He quite——

MISS H. [*Clasping her hand*] How wonderful ! Oh, Mr. Vane, thank you !

> [*She clasps his hands ; but suddenly, seeing that* FRUST *is coming back, flits across to the curtain and vanishes.*

> [*The stage, in the crude light, is empty now save for* FRUST, *who, in the French windows, Centre, is mumbling his cigar ; and* VANE, *stage Right, who is looking up into the wings, stage Left.*

VANE. [*Calling up*] That lighting's just right now, Miller. Got it marked carefully ?

ELECTRICS. Yes, Mr. Vane.

VANE. Good. [*To* FRUST *who is coming down.*] Well, sir ? So glad——

FRUST. Mr. Vane, we got little Miggs on contract ?

VANE. Yes.

FRUST. Well, I liked that little pocket piece fine. But I'm blamed if I know what it's all about.

VANE. [*A little staggered*] Why ! Of course it's a little allegory. The tragedy of civilization—all real feeling for Beauty and Nature kept out, or pent up even in the cultured.

FRUST. Ye-ep. [*Meditatively.*] Little Miggs'd be fine in " Pop goes the Weasel."

VANE. Yes, he'd be all right, but——

FRUST. Get him on the 'phone, and put it into rehearsal right now.

VANE. What ! But this piece—I—I——!

FRUST. Guess we can't take liberties with our public, Mr. Vane. They want pep.

VANE. [*Distressed*] But it'll break that girl's heart. I—really—I can't——

FRUST. Give her the part of the 'tweeny in " Pop goes."

VANE. Mr. Frust, I—I beg. I've taken a lot of trouble with this little play. It's good. It's that girl's chance—and I——

FRUST. We-ell ! I certainly thought she was fine. Now, you phone up Miggs, and get right along with it. I've only one rule, sir ! Give the Public what it wants, and what the Public wants is punch and go.

They've got no use for Beauty, Allegory, all that high-brow racket. I know 'em as I know my hand.

    [*During this speech* MISS HELLGROVE *is seen listening by the French window, in distress, unnoticed by either of them.*

VANE. Mr. Frust, the Public *would* take this, I'm sure they would; I'm convinced of it. You underrate them.

FRUST. Now, see here, Mr. Blewitt Vane, is this my theatre? I tell you, I can't afford luxuries.

VANE. But it—it moved *you*, sir; I saw it. I was watching.

FRUST. [*With unmoved finality*] Mr. Vane, I judge I'm not the average man. Before " Louisa Loses " the Public'll want a stimulant. " Pop goes the Weasel " will suit us fine. So—get right along with it. I'll go get some lunch.

    [*As he vanishes into the wings,* Left, MISS HELLGROVE *covers her face with her hands. A little sob escaping her attracts* VANE'S *attention. He takes a step towards her, but she flies.*

VANE. [*Dashing his hands through his hair till it stands up*] Damnation!

    [FORESON *walks on from the wings,* Right.

FORESON. Sir?

VANE. " Punch and go ! " That *superstition !*

    [FORESON *walks straight out into the wings,* Left.

VANE. Mr. Foreson !

FORESON. [*Reappearing*] Sir?

VANE. This is scrapped. [*With savagery.*] Tell 'em to set the first act of " Louisa Loses," and put some pep into it.

    [*He goes out through the French windows with the wind still in his hair.*

FORESON. [*In the centre of the stage*] Electrics !

ELECTRICS. Hallo !

FORESON. Where's Charlie ?

ELECTRICS. Gone to his dinner.

FORESON. Anybody on the curtain ?

A VOICE. Yes, Mr. Foreson.

FORESON. Put your curtain down.

    [*He stands in the centre of the stage with eyes uplifted*

as the curtain descends.

ESCAPE

CAST OF THE ORIGINAL PRODUCTION AT THE AM-
BASSADORS THEATRE, LONDON, AUGUST 12, 1926
PRODUCED BY LEON M. LION

MATT DENANT	Nicholas Hannen
THE GIRL OF THE TOWN	Ursula Jeans
THE PLAIN CLOTHES MAN	Frank Freeman
THE POLICEMAN	Harold Lester
THE OTHER POLICEMAN	Cyril Hardingham
THE FELLOW CONVICT	Leon M. Lion
THE WARDER	Gerard Clifton
THE OTHER WARDER	Stafford Hilliard
THE SHINGLED LADY	Molly Kerr
THE MAID	Phyllis Konstam
THE OLD GENTLEMAN	Leon M. Lion
THE CAPTAIN	Gerard Clifton
THE SHOPKEEPER	Paul Gill
HIS WIFE	Ethel Manning
HIS SISTER	Ann Codrington
THE MAN IN PLUS FOURS	Stafford Hilliard
HIS WIFE	Phyllis Konstam
THE DARTMOOR CONSTABLE	Frank Freeman
THE LABOURER	Cyril Hardingham
THE OTHER LABOURER	Harold Lester
THE FARMER	Paul Gill
THE LITTLE GIRL	Betty Astell
MISS GRACE	Ann Codrington
MISS DORA	Margaret Halstan
THE PARSON	Austin Trevor
THE BELLRINGER	Stafford Hilliard

PROLOGUE

Hyde Park at night. Summer. The Row with its iron railing, footwalk, seats, trees and bushes behind. A Woman, *or* Girl (*you can't tell*), *is sitting alone, in dim radiance from lamps unseen to Right and Left. Her painted mask is not unattractive, her attitude slack and uneasy. A* Plain Clothes Man *passes Right to Left, glances at her inviting him and increases his pace. By the expression on her face as he approaches and recedes, it is easy for him to see what she is.* Two People *pass without glancing at her at all—they are talking of what* "he said to me" *and* "I said to him." *Then nobody passes, and, powdering her nose, she seems preparing to shift along, when from the Left,* Matt Denant *appears strolling. He is a young man, tallish and athletic, dressed as if he has been racing in hot weather; he has a pair of race glasses and a cigar. The* Girl *shifts forward on her seat as he approaches. He is going by when she looks suddenly up and says in a low voice :* "Good evening!" *He halts, looks at her, gives a little shrug, carries his hand to his hat, and answering,* "Good evening!" *is moving on when she speaks again.*

Girl. Have you a match? [*She is holding out a cigarette; he stops and hands her his cigarette lighter.*]
Girl. [*Fingering the lighter*] Gold?
Matt. Brass.
Girl. Have one? [*Offering her cigarette case.*
Matt. Thanks, I'm smoking. [*He shows her his cigar; resting his foot on the seat and dangling his race glasses*]
Girl. Been racing?
Matt. Goodwood.
Girl. I went to see the Jubilee this year.
Matt. And what did you back?
Girl. Everything that didn't win. It's rotten when you don't back winners.
Matt. Don't you like the horses?
Girl. They look pretty.
Matt. Prettiest things in the world.
Girl. Pretty as women?
Matt. Saving your presence.
Girl. Do you mean that?
Matt. Well, you get a woman once in a way that can arch her neck.

987

GIRL. You don't like women—that's clear.

MATT. Not too much.

GIRL. [*Smiling*] You speak your mind, anyway.

MATT. If you ask me, they've got such a lot of vice about 'em compared with horses.

GIRL. And who puts vice into them?

MATT. I know—you all say men, but d'you believe it?

GIRL. [*With a laugh*] Well, I don't know. Don't men put vice into horses?

MATT. [*Struck*] M'yes! [*Sitting down.*] All the same, there's nothing wilder than a wild horse—I've seen 'em out West.

GIRL. There's nothing *so* wild as a wild woman.

[*A momentary silence while they stare at each other.*

MATT. Women haven't the excuse of horses—they've been tame since Eve gave Adam his tea.

GIRL. Um! Garden of Eden! Must have been something like Hyde Park—there was a prize cop there, anyway.

MATT. D'you come here often?

GIRL. [*Nodding*] Where else *can* one go? They're so particular now.

MATT. They do seem to keep you on the run.

GIRL. What are you—soldier?

MATT. Once upon a time.

GIRL. What now?

MATT. Thinking of being a parson.

GIRL. [*Laughs*] You've got money of your own, then?

MATT. A little.

GIRL. [*With a sigh*] If I had money of my own, d'you know what I'd do?

MATT. Get rid of it.

GIRL. Just what I wouldn't. If ever I got myself dependent on you men again, [*Very grimly*] shut my lights off.

MATT. Not like the lady under laughing gas.

GIRL. What was the matter with her?

MATT. Kept shouting, "I don't want to be a free, independent, economic agent! I want to be loved."

GIRL. She was wrong—No, *sir!* Get my head under a second time? Not much! But we can't save—don't make enough. So; there you are! It's a good bit worse than it used to be, they say——

MATT. The ordinary girl more free and easy now, you mean?

GIRL. [*Grimly*] The *ordinary* girl?

MATT. Well, you don't call yourself ordinary, do you?

[*The GIRL sits quite still and doesn't answer.*

MATT. Sorry! Didn't mean to hurt you.

GIRL. Give me the fellow that does : he doesn't hurt half so much. But you're quite right. [*Bitterly.*] There isn't much excuse for us, now.

MATT. Aren't we getting a bit solemn ?

GIRL. The gay girl—eh ? They say you get used to anything : but I'll tell you—you never get used to playing the canary when you don't feel like it.

MATT. Ah ! I always sympathized with canaries—expected to sing, and so permanently yellow.

GIRL. It was nice of you to sit down and talk.

MATT. Thanks ; it's all secondary education.

[*She slides her hand along to his, with a card.*

GIRL. Here's my address ; you might come and see me now and then.

MATT. [*Twiddling the card—amused and embarrassed*] On verra !

GIRL. What's that ?

MATT. It's an expression of hope.

GIRL. [*Mouth opening*] Ow ! How about now ?

MATT. Thanks—afraid not—due somewhere at ten.

GIRL. Another ?

MATT. No.

GIRL. You don't like me, I believe.

MATT. [*With a shrug*] Oh ! Don't say that. You're original.

GIRL. Original sin.

MATT. There are worse things, I guess.

GIRL. You bet ! There's modest worth. If *that* isn't worse ! Not that this is a pretty life. It's just about as rotten as it can be.

MATT. How did you get into it ?

GIRL. Cut it out ! You all ask that, and you can take it from me you never get told. Well ! I belong to the oldest profession in the world ! That isn't true, either—there's an older.

MATT. Not really.

GIRL. The cop's. Mine wouldn't ever have been a profession but for them.

MATT. Good for you !

GIRL. It isn't good for me. Look in at Bow Street on Monday morning.

MATT. To see 'em shoot the sitting pheasant ?—no, thanks. The Law isn't exactly sporting. Can't be, I suppose, if it's got to keep the course clear.

GIRL. They might wait till one makes oneself a nuisance.

MATT. Ever been run in ?

GIRL. [*With a look, and a decision*] Um ! Not yet ! [*Suddenly.*] What can we do ? If we don't make a sign, who's to know us ?

MATT. That's delightful.

GIRL. Clean streets!—that's the cry. Clean men! That'd be better!

MATT. And then where'd you be?

GIRL. [*Passionately*] Not here!

MATT. [*After staring at her*] Um! The kettle and the pot. What! Give me horses and dogs, all the time.

GIRL. I've got a cat.

MATT. Persian?

GIRL. [*Nodding*] A real beauty. [*Suddenly.*] Wouldn't you like to come and see him?

[*He shakes his head, rises, takes his glasses, and holds out his hand. She is going to take it—then draws her hand back sharply, frowning and biting her lips. He gives a shrug, salutes, and moves on. She catches at his sleeve, misses it, sits a second, then rises and follows. Unseen by her, the* PLAIN CLOTHES MAN *has reappeared, Left. He moves swiftly and grasps her arm just as she is vanishing Right. The* GIRL *gives a little squeal as he draws her back towards the seat. She resists.*

GIRL. Who are *you?*

PLAIN CLOTHES MAN. Plain clothes. [*And, as she still resists, he tries to calm her by a slight twist of the arm.*]

GIRL. You brute—you brute!

PLAIN CLOTHES MAN. Now then—quietly, and you won't get hurt.

GIRL. I wasn't doing anything.

PLAIN CLOTHES MAN. Oh! no, of course not.

GIRL. [*Looking after* MATT] I wasn't, I tell you; and he'll tell you so too! [MATT *has reappeared, Right.*] Won't you? You talked to me of your own accord?

MATT. I did. Who may you be?

PLAIN CLOTHES MAN. [*Showing his card*] This woman accosted you. I've observed her carefully, and not for the first time.

MATT. Well, you've made a blooming error. We had a chat, that's all.

PLAIN CLOTHES MAN. I saw her accost you. I saw her try to detain you—and I've seen her do it before now.

MATT. I don't care what you've seen before now—you can't arrest her for that. You didn't see it this time.

PLAIN CLOTHES MAN. [*Still holding the* GIRL *and looking at* MATT *steadily*] You know perfectly well the woman accosted you—and you'd better keep out of this.

MATT. Let the girl go, then. You're exceeding your duty.

PLAIN CLOTHES MAN. What do you know about my duty? It's my duty to keep the park decent, man or woman. Now then, are you going to clear off?

MATT. No, I'm going to stay on.

PLAIN CLOTHES MAN. All right then, you can follow us to the station.

MATT. Mayn't two people talk! I've made no complaint.

PLAIN CLOTHES MAN. I know this woman, I tell you. Don't interfere with me, or I shall want you too.

MATT. You can have me if you let the girl go.

PLAIN CLOTHES MAN. Now look here, I'm being very patient. But if you don't stop hindering me in the execution of my duty, I'll summon assistance and you'll *both* go to the station.

MATT. Don't lose your hair—I tell you, on my honour, this lady did not annoy me in the least. On the contrary——

PLAIN CLOTHES MAN. She was carrying on her profession here, as she's done before; my orders are to prevent that, and she's going to be charged. This is the third night I've watched her.

GIRL. I've never seen your face before.

PLAIN CLOTHES MAN. No, but I've seen yours—I've given you plenty of rope. That's enough, now——

[*He puts his whistle in his mouth.*

MATT. It's a rotten shame! Drop that girl's arm!

[*He lays his hand on the* PLAIN CLOTHES MAN'S *arm. The* PLAIN CLOTHES MAN *blows his whistle, drops the* GIRL'S *arm and seizes* MATT.

MATT. [*Breaking from him; to the* GIRL] Run for it!

GIRL. Oh! no—don't fight! The police have got it on you all the time. I'll go with him.

MATT. [*With fists up, keeping the* PLAIN CLOTHES MAN *at arm's-length*] Run, I tell you. He'll have his work cut out with me.

[*But the* PLAIN CLOTHES MAN *is spryer than he thinks, runs in and catches him round the body.*

GIRL. Oh! Oh!

MATT. No, you don't!

[*In the violent struggle the* PLAIN CLOTHES MAN'S *bowler hat falls off.* MATT *emerges at arm's-length again, squaring up.*

MATT. Come on, then, if you will have it!

[*The* PLAIN CLOTHES MAN *rushes in. He gets* MATT'S *right straight from the shoulder on the point of the jaw, topples back, and goes down like a log.*

GIRL. Oh! Oh!

MATT. Run, you little idiot; run!

GIRL. [*Aghast*] Oh! he hit his head—on the rail! I heard the crack. See, he don't move!

MATT. Well, of course. I knocked him out. [*He goes a step nearer, looking down.*] The rail—did he—— ?

GIRL. [*Kneeling and feeling the* PLAIN CLOTHES MAN'S *head*] Feel!

MATT. My God! That was a wump. I say!

GIRL. I told you not to fight. What did you want to fight for?

MATT. [*Pulling open the* PLAIN CLOTHES MAN'S *coat, and diving for his heart*] I can't feel it. Curse! Now we can't leave him. [*Feeling for the heart.*] Good God!

GIRL. [*Bending and snatching at his arm*] Quick! Before anybody comes. Across the grass back there. Who'd know?

MATT. [*Listening*] I can't leave the poor devil like this. [*Looking round.*] Take his hat; go and get some water in it from the Serpentine.

[*The* GIRL *picks up the hat and stands undecided.*

GIRL. [*Agonized*] No, no! Come away! It's awful, this! Suppose—suppose he's dead! [*She pulls at him.*

MATT. [*Shaking her off*] Don't be a little fool! Go and get some water. Go on!

[*The* GIRL *wrings her hands, then turns and runs off Left, with the hat.* MATT *continues to kneel, rubbing the* PLAIN CLOTHES MAN'S *temples, feeling his pulse, listening at his heart.*

MATT. I don't see how it's possible! [*With a gesture of despair he resumes his efforts to revive the body. Suddenly he looks up.*]

[TWO POLICEMEN *have come from the Right.*

POLICEMAN. What's this?

MATT. I don't know. I'm a little afraid he——

POLICEMAN. What! Who is he? [*Looking at the face.*] Phew! One of ours! [*Bending, kneeling, putting the back of his hand to the mouth.*] Not a breath! How did this happen?

MATT. [*Pointing to the rail*] He knocked his head on that.

POLICEMAN. Where's his hat?

MATT. It fell off. Someone's gone to get water in it.

POLICEMAN. Who?

MATT. A girl——

POLICEMAN. He blew his whistle. Did you hit him?

MATT. There was a row. He seized me. I smote him on the jaw. He fell back and hit his head on the rail.

POLICEMAN. What was the row about?

MATT. [*Putting his hands to his head*] Oh! God knows! Original sin.

POLICEMAN. [*To the other* POLICEMAN] Mate, stay with him. I'll get an ambulance. [*To* MATT.] And you—come with me!

The curtain falls.

PART I

EPISODE I

More than a year has passed. On the prison farm, Dartmoor, in a heavy fog. The stone wall of the field runs along the back (on the back-cloth) and a stone wall joins it on the Left. MATT DENANT *and a* FELLOW CONVICT *are picking up the potatoes they have dug up earlier. They are but dimly seen in the fog, flinging the potatoes right and left into two baskets between them. They are speaking in low voices.*

MATT. The poor blighter was dead, and I got five years for manslaughter.

FELLOW CONVICT. Cripes! A cop! You were lucky not to swing, mate.

MATT. The girl stood by me like a brick. If she hadn't come forward——

FELLOW CONVICT. Lucky there, too. Most of 'em wouldn't. They're too mortal scared. 'Ow much you got left to do?

MATT. Three years, if I behave like a plaster saint.
[*He stops and straightens himself.*

FELLOW CONVICT. I got four. I say, you're a torf, yn't you?

MATT. Toff! [*With a laugh.*] Item, one Oxford accent; item, one objection to being spoken to like a dog.

FELLOW CONVICT. Hush! [*Jerking his thumb towards the wall, Right.*] Fog don't prevent 'em hearin', blight 'em!

MATT. It's come up mighty sudden. Think it's going to last?

FELLOW CONVICT. After a wet spell—this time o' year, when the wind's gone—yus. They'll be roundin' us up in a minute, you'll see—and 'ome to Blighty. Makes 'em nervous—fog. That's when you get the escapes.

MATT. No one's ever got away from here, they say.

FELLOW CONVICT. There've been a good few tries, though.

MATT. Gosh! I'd like to have one.

FELLOW CONVICT. Don't you do it, mate. You want clothes, you want money, you want a car, to give you a dawg's chance. And then they'd get you. This moor's the 'ell of a place. I say, you must 'ave hit that cop a fair knock!

MATT. Just an ordinary knock-out on the jaw. It wasn't that. He landed the back of his head on the Row rail. [*He resumes potato picking.*] Poor devil! He wasn't married, luckily.

FELLOW CONVICT. Luckily? Well, you never know about *that*.

32*   993

But get 'im off your chest, mate—'e wouldn't sit on mine—no more than an 'Un did in the War.　That's a good fair potato.

[Holding one up.

[The figure of a WARDER *is dimly seen coming along from the Right under the wall.　He stops.*

WARDER. No talking there! When you've finished that row, pick back the next and then stand by to fall in.　[*No answer from the* CONVICTS.] Hear me?　Answer, can't you?

FELLOW CONVICT. Right, sir!

[The WARDER'S *figure is seen moving back.]*

Nice man, ain't he?　Wot'd I tell you?　Early 'ome to tea.

MATT. [*Very low*] Like a dog!　Three more years—like a dog!

FELLOW CONVICT. 'E's all right, reely.　It's the fog.　Fog makes 'em nervous; an' when a man's nervous I've always noticed 'e speaks like that.

MATT. Yes; well, *I* can't get used to it.

FELLOW CONVICT. Too particular, you torfs—get too much corn when you're two-year-olds.

MATT. [*Sharp and low*] *You* know the moor—where's Two Bridges?

FELLOW CONVICT. There—a mile.

MATT. And Tavistock?

FELLOW CONVICT. [*Pointing right back.*] Seven.　Guv'nor—don't do it.　There ain't a chance in a million.　You'll only get pneumonium in this stinkin' wet, and they'll have you into the bargain, sure as eggs—bread and water, cells, and the rest of it.

MATT. I got out of Germany.

FELLOW CONVICT. Out of Germany!　Cripes!　That was none so dusty!

MATT. They've got no dogs here now, have they?

FELLOW CONVICT. Don't fancy they 'ave.　But, Guv'nor, the whole countryside round 'ere's agynst you.　They don't like convicts.　Funny, yn't it?

[They have reached the end of the row, Left, and stop, stooping, with their heads close together.

MATT. Draw me a plan with this stick.

FELLOW CONVICT. Blimy!　[*Marking the earth.*] 'Ere's the main road, and 'ere's the cross road to Tavistock.　'Ere's the Inn at Two Bridges, and 'ere's Post Bridge.　'Ere's Bee Tor Cross, ten to twelve mile.　Chagford up there, Moreton 'Ampstead 'ere.

MATT. What's across the main road from Two Bridges?

FELLOW CONVICT. Moor.　A long bit o' wood about 'ere; then 'Ambledon; then you drops into fields to Widecombe; then up, and more moor to Heytor and Bovey.　[*Pronounce* BUVVY.] There's rail at Bovey or Lustleigh, or Moreton or Tavistock, and much good that'll do you with everybody as eager to see you as if you was the

Prince of Wyles !   Out this way you got Fox Tor Mire—ruddy bad
bog, that !

    [*A moment's silence while* MATT *studies the chart in the soil.*

WARDER'S VOICE. [*Off*] Hurry up with that last row—you two
men !   [*The fog grows thicker.*

MATT. [*Smearing out the chart with his foot*] It's real thick now.
Gosh ! I'll have a shot !

    [*They move back, Right, beginning the last row.*

FELLOW CONVICT. [*Jerking his thumb Left*] There's another blighter
thirty yards out on the wall there.   'E'll shoot.

MATT. I know.   I'm going over that wall in the corner, and then
along under his nose on the near side.   Ten to one he'll be looking
out on the off side in this fog.   If that chap there [*Jerking his head,
Right*] doesn't spot me I'll get by.

FELLOW CONVICT. You're mad, Guv'nor.   They'll shoot at sight.
And if they don' see you—in ten minutes I'll have finished this row,
an' they're bound to know you're gone.   You 'aven't the chance of
a cock-louse.

MATT. All right, friend, don't worry !   A bullet'd be a nice change
for me.   If I don't get one—I'll give 'em a run for their money.

FELLOW CONVICT. Well, if you must go, mate—Strike the
main road and run that way. [*Pointing.*] In this fog they'll 'ave to
take us back before they dare start after you.   You'll find a scrap of
a wood a bit beyond the river on the left side.   Get into it and cover
yourself with leaves till it's dead dark.   Then you'll still be close to
the road and you can myke shift in a stack or something till the morning.   If you go wandering about the moor all night in this fog,
you won't get nowhere, and you'll be done in stiff before dawn.

MATT. Thanks.   Sooner the better, now—Never stop to
look at a fence.   Next time the steam's full on. [*Puts some potatoes
in his pocket.*]   Pommes crus—sauce Dartmoor.   Can one eat these
raw ?   I ate turnips in Germany.

FELLOW CONVICT. Never tried, Guv'nor.   Tyke this.

    [*He holds out a slice of bread.*

MATT. Thanks awfully.   You're a good chap.

FELLOW CONVICT. Wish you luck.   Wish I was comin' too, but
I 'aven't got the pluck, an' that's a fact.

MATT. Now !   Turn your head the other way and keep it there.
Remember me to Blighty.   So long !

    [*He moves three steps away from his fellow convict, pauses a few
       seconds, then suddenly, stooping low, runs to the wall, Left,
       and is over it like a cat.   In the minute of silence that follows,
       one can see the* CONVICT *listening.*

FELLOW CONVICT. [*Counting the seconds to himself, up to twenty, in
an excited murmur*] Gawd !   'E's past that blighter ! [*Listens again.*]

Gawd! 'E's orf! [*With realization of his fellow's escape comes an itch to attempt it himself.*] Shall I 'ave a shoot meself? Shall I? Gawd! I must!

    [*He has just turned to sneak off, when the* WARDER'*s voice is heard off, Right.*

WARDER. You, man, there! Where's your mate?

FELLOW CONVICT. 'Ad a call, sir.   [*He stands still.*

VOICE OF WARDER. [*Nearing*] What d'you mean?

FELLOW CONVICT. Went over to that wall, sir.

WARDER. [*Appearing*] He's not there. Now then! Where is he?

FELLOW CONVICT. No use arstin' me. *I* don' know where he is.

WARDER. Come with me. [*He marches sharply along the wall back, towards the Left. Halting.*] Convict! Out there! Answer! Warder! You, Williams! Anyone passed you? Lost a man here!

VOICE OF SECOND WARDER. No one's passed.

FIRST WARDER. Sharp, then! There's a man gone!

    [SECOND WARDER *appears on the top of the wall.*

SECOND WARDER. He must ha' got past *you*, then.

FIRST WARDER. Curse this fog! Fire a shot for warning. No, don't, or we'll have others running for it. Muster sharp and get off home and report—that's the only thing. [*To* CONVICT.] Here, you! Keep your mouth shut. You know all about it, I bet.

FELLOW CONVICT. Not me, sir. 'E just said 'e 'ad a call to 'ave tea with the Duchess; an' I went on pickin' up, knowin' you was in an 'urry.

FIRST WARDER. Mind your lip! Come on, Williams. March, you!

      They are marching, Right, as the curtain falls.

EPISODE II

Seven hours have passed. The moor in the dark and the fog, close to the main road. Nothing visible.

VOICE OF FIRST WARDER. What the hell's the use of picketing this blighted road—you can see nothing!

VOICE OF SECOND WARDER. I've seen two cops made just here. When a man's out on a night like this, it's human nature to cling to the road.

FIRST WARDER. But he may be anywhere.

SECOND WARDER. If he's travelling at all, he's on a road. You can't make it on the moor in fog as thick as this.

FIRST WARDER. He may have headed for Cornworthy.

SECOND WARDER. They never go that way—too afraid of Fox Tor Mire.

FIRST WARDER. Or Tavistock?

SECOND WARDER. Well, that road's picketed all right.

FIRST WARDER. I'd flog for escapes. They never think of us—out after these blighters nights like this. It's too bad, you know. Got a drain of the stuff?

SECOND WARDER. Here you are. Put it to your mouth by the smell.

FIRST WARDER. If I get this cove, I'll let him know it. 'Tisn't in nature not to feel murderous towards a chap that keeps you out all night in this sort o' muck!   [*He drinks.*

SECOND WARDER. Leave some for me, mate. [*In a whisper.*] What was that? Hark!   [*They listen.*

FIRST WARDER. Don't 'ear nothing.

[*He is about to put the flask to his mouth again.*

SECOND WARDER. Thought I heard a scraping noise. Shall I show a glim?

FIRST WARDER. Better not!   [*They listen.*

SECOND WARDER. There's ponies round here.

FIRST WARDER. This fellow was a toff.

SECOND WARDER. Um! Captain in the War.

FIRST WARDER. Him that killed the 'tec in Hyde Park. He's a sporty beggar. Got blood in him. That's the worst sort when it comes to an escape—they run till they drop.

SECOND WARDER. Man of education—might have had more sense than to run for it. He must know he can't get off.

FIRST WARDER. There's a spirit in some of these higher-class chaps you can't break. D'you know that lawyer in the left wing—embezzlement? That chap gives me the creeps. He's got the self-possession of an image.

SECOND WARDER. I'm sorry for some of these fellows, but I'm damned if I'm ever sorry for a gentleman. They ought to know better than to get themselves here. And, as you say, they've got the devil's brass.

FIRST WARDER. Still—up on the ladder and down with a whump —it hits 'em harder than it does the others.

SECOND WARDER. [*Yawning*] Wish I was in bed! [*Startlingly.*] There it is again! [*They listen.*] It'll be a pony. A warder's life's about the limit. If it wasn't for the missus, I'd sooner sweep streets.

FIRST WARDER. I've got used to it, barring a circus like this. The devil himself couldn't get used to that. It's only fit for the movies.

SECOND WARDER. I believe you. Did you see that picture with Duggie in it? 'Ow'd you think 'e does that roof business? We got some pretty tidy cat burglars, but I don't believe there's one could do what he does.

FIRST WARDER. Well, I'll tell you. I think he has spring heels; and I notice his hands are very blurry in the picture. I believe he holds a rope, and they take that out afterwards, by some process.

SECOND WARDER. Never thought o' that! But when he falls and catches on that ledge?

FIRST WARDER. That's an optical deception. Some of those movie jossers ought to be in prison, the way they deceive the public.

SECOND WARDER. I never saw anything on the screen I liked better than " My Old Dutch " ! That fair got me. I took the missus, and I tell you there wasn't a dry eye about the pair of us.

FIRST WARDER. Charlie knocks *me*. I feel a better man after I've seen 'im. Now, why is that?

SECOND WARDER. 'E's very 'uman. Must make a pot of money.

FIRST WARDER. I'm wet through—give me another drain. [*Gurgling sounds.*] If I catch that chap, you'll 'ave to stop me quick, or I'll manhandle him for sure.

SECOND WARDER. Same here. We'd better toss up which stops the other. Call !

FIRST WARDER. 'Eads.

SECOND WARDER. Which is it? Throw a glim.

[*The* FIRST WARDER *throws from an electric torch the first light of the scene. Their two faces, on the footlight side of the road, are seen close together over the coin.*

SECOND WARDER. Tails—You've lost. [*The glim is dowsed.*] 'Ow do we stand, then? Do I stop you, or do you stop me?

FIRST WARDER. You stop me.

SECOND WARDER. No, I won. That means *I* get the go at him. Lawd Gawd! what a night! Just feel if that rope's all right across the road.

FIRST WARDER. It's taut. Bit too low, though—ought to catch him mid-thigh by rights.

SECOND WARDER. You trust me, old hoss ; if it catches 'im as high as that, he stops and goes off sideways, or turns and runs back. It should catch him just below the knee. Then, ten to one he goes over, and we're on to him before he can get up. He'll be goin' a good bat, remember. You'll find me on 'is 'ead when you come to stoppin' me.

FIRST WARDER. To think we can't even smoke. D'you hold with givin' prisoners tobacco, Williams?

SECOND WARDER. On the whole, I do. It sweetens 'em, and that's better for us. I'd give 'em two pipes a week, and stop 'em if they gave a warder any trouble. I've got one or two fellers I'm quite fond of. I'd be glad for 'em to have a smoke every day. Listen ! [*They listen. In a whisper.*] Footsteps ! They are !

FIRST WARDER. Yes.

SECOND WARDER. [*Still in a whisper*] Look here, mate! Just before he gets to the rope, I'll throw the light into his face, then dowse it sharp. He'll start to run forward and go head foremost. Stand by!   [*They listen.*

FIRST WARDER. He's comin' on! Suppose it isn't him?

SECOND WARDER. Must chance that. I'll throw the light as I say——

[*A moment of utter black tenseness, during which the footsteps are heard clearer and clearer.*]

Now! Stand by!

[*He flashes the light on the figure of* MATT *advancing along the road. The light is dowsed, the* WARDERS *rush forward. Darkness and the sound of a scramble.*

SECOND WARDER'S VOICE. I've got him!

FIRST WARDER'S VOICE. [*Half strangled*] No, you ruddy fool— you've got me!

The curtain falls.

EPISODE III

Thirty-two hours have passed. A bedroom at an Inn on the moor. Dark with streaks of daylight coming in from two curtained windows, back, opening on to a long balcony. Between them a bed juts into the room. Right, forward, a dressing table with chair. Left, back, a washstand. Left, forward, a door opening inwards. At foot of the bed a chair with a woman's undergarments thrown on it. A dressing-gown over the foot-rail of the bed, some slippers on the left side of the bed. A SHINGLED LADY *asleep in the bed. Knocking on the door, Left.*

LADY. [*Sleepily*] Come in!

[*A* MAID *enters with a can of hot water, which she places on the washstand, Left.*

MAID. 'Alf past seven, madam.

LADY. [*Yawning*] What sort of day?

MAID. Foggy still. Taking a bath, madam?

LADY. Yes. Oh! My husband's coming back this evening. I'm to be moved back to the double room.

MAID. Yes, madam; they told me.

[*She has drawn aside the curtains, Left, and now moves round and draws back the curtains, Right.*]

That escaped convict, madam; they haven't got him yet.

LADY. No? How thrilling!

MAID. It's the fog. He's been out nearly two days. They say it's the young man who killed the detective in Hyde Park, that made such a fuss.

LADY. Oh? That Captain Denant! I remember. It might have been worse, then.

MAID. Of course they'll catch him—no one ever gets off.

LADY. Don't they?

MAID. Oh! no, madam! It wouldn't never do.

LADY. I should have thought in fog like this——

MAID. You see, they got to eat and get clothes. That's where they're caught.

LADY. [*Yawning*] This horrible fog!—one can't ride or fish, or even walk. Shall I get up, or shall I——?

MAID. [*Rather coldly*] Just as you please, madam.

LADY. [*With a laugh*] Well, I suppose I'd better.

MAID. I'll turn the bath on.

LADY. Thank you.

[*The* MAID *goes out, and the* LADY, *in her pyjamas, emerges from bed, feels for her slippers, and puts on her dressing-gown. She goes to a window, and looks out. It is a French window, and slightly open on a short hook.*

LADY. Ugh! What a day!

[*Taking sponge and bath towel from the washstand, she goes to the door and out. As soon as the door is shut there is a commotion where the bed touches the wall, and from behind the window curtain* MATT DENANT *cautiously emerges, glances quickly round, and stretches himself. He looks haggard, sodden, and crumpled, and has his boots in his hand.*

MATT. [*Muttering*] A lady! Dash it! I must get out!

[*He goes to the window and looks cautiously out, then recoils, drawing in his breath with a hiss. Then, after once more glancing round the room, he steps to the door.*

LADY'S VOICE. [*Off*] I simply can't take cold baths!

[MATT *flattens himself against the wall, so that he will be behind the door if it is opened. And suddenly it is.*

LADY'S VOICE. [*In doorway*] Let me know when the water's hot, please.

MAID'S VOICE. [*Off*] Yes, madam.

The LADY *re-enters, and passing the door knob from her right hand to her left behind her as she naturally would, closes it without seeing* MATT, *and crosses to the dressing-table, where she sits down and takes up a brush to brush her shingled hair.* MATT *moves quickly to the door, and has his hand on the handle, when his image passes into the mirror. The* LADY *drops the brush, and faces round with an exclamation on her open mouth.*

MATT. Hush! It's quite O.K.

LADY. Who—how—what d'you mean by coming into my room?

[MATT *drops the door handle, turning the key in the lock.*

MATT. [*In a low voice*] Really, I'm most frightfully sorry.

[*Suddenly the fact that he is the escaped convict dawns on her.*

LADY. You're the escaped—— [*She starts up to go to the window and call for help ; but stops at the gestures he makes.*]

MATT. I wonder if you'd mind awfully speaking pianissimo.

LADY. [*Tensely*] What made you come in here ? How did you get in ?

MATT. I've been under the bed for hours. You see, I couldn't tell it was a lady.

LADY. D'you mean my hair ?

MATT. Oh no ! I couldn't see that.

LADY. I didn't snore ?

MATT. No ; but that's not an infallible test of sex. I didn't either, or you'd have heard me.

LADY. D'you mean to say you went to sleep ?

MATT. I'm afraid I did. Of course, if I'd known—— [*A pause.*

LADY. Well, as you're a gentleman, aren't you going ?

MATT. I'd simply love to. But where ?

LADY. Really, I can't tell you.

MATT. Look at me ! What can one do in these togs ?

LADY. D'you expect me to lend you some ?

MATT. Hardly. But I'd be eternally grateful if you'd give me something to eat.

LADY. [*Opening a drawer and taking out some chocolate*] This is pretty cool, you know. I ought to ring and hand you over.

MATT. Yes. But—you look such a sport.

LADY. [*Subtly flattered*] I know who you are. Your name's in the paper. But do you realize my position ?

MATT. Afraid I only realize my own.

LADY. If I don't hand you over, how on earth are you going to get out of here without being seen ?

MATT. Might I have that chocolate ?

LADY. [*Taking it from the dressing-table drawer*] It's only local.

MATT. That won't deter me. I've been forty hours on a piece of bread and two raw potatoes. [*He takes the chocolate, bites some off, and puts the rest in his pocket.*] Would you mind frightfully if I drank some water ?

LADY. Of course not.

[MATT *goes over to the washstand. When his back is turned she springs to action, but instead of going to door or window, rapidly conceals underneath the bedclothes the corsets and underclothes flung on the chair at the foot of the bed, then returns to the dressing-table.* MATT *is drinking deeply.*

MATT. [*Turning*] That's good. Ever had the hunted feeling ? [*She shakes her head.*] Well, don't ! A coursed hare is nothing to it. Oh ! I am so jolly stiff !

LADY. [*Thrilled in spite of herself*] Do you know you're only three miles from the Prison?

MATT. I do. The first night I meant to get near Exeter by morning, and where d'you think I was? A mile from where I started. I'd been ringing. That's what you do in fog. Is that a razor?

LADY. [*On stilts*] My husband's. Why? [*As* MATT *takes it up.*] No! There's a limit, Captain Denant. You can't have a weapon.

MATT. No, of course! But would you mind awfully if I shaved? You see, like this [*Passes his hand over his chin*] I haven't an earthly, even if I could get clothes. There's nothing more attractive than a three days' beard. [*While speaking he has lathered himself without a brush.*] I'm a very quick shaver. It takes me three minutes. I can do it in thirty-two and a half strokes.

LADY. [*Gasping*] Well, I never—It takes me [*hand to her neck*]—that is—I mean—Have you nearly been caught?

MATT. [*Between scraping motions of the razor*] Twice I've been within twenty feet of the hounds——

LADY. Hounds!

MATT. Human! Just out of their jaws. [*Groans.*] D'you know anything so frightful as a shave like this?

LADY. Well, really——

MATT. I mean except, of course, not having it.

LADY. How did you get in here?

MATT. You see, I *did* so want a dry night, so I hid up and waited till every light was out. I tried to get in below, and couldn't; then I made a boss shot at the corner of the balcony and fell on my back—— Did you feel a sort of earthquake? No? I did. When I got over that, I had another shot at a pillar and made it that time. I chose your window because it was open—hooked it up again and slid straight under the bed. I meant to sneak some clothes, and be off before daylight, but I only woke up when the maid came in. [*She indicates a towel; he steeps it in water and wipes his face.*] D'you mind if I put on my boots?   [*He stoops and puts them on.*

LADY. So you actually slept under there?

MATT. Alas! I did.

LADY. Well! It's about the limit.

MATT. Will be if I get clear—no one ever has.

LADY. Tell me, Captain Denant, weren't you at Harcheston with my brother—he used to talk of a Matt Denant, who was an awfully good runner.

MATT. Quite likely. I was at school with an awful lot of brothers. What was his name?

LADY. No. That won't do.

MATT. You're right. Never tell a convict anything he can tell anybody else.

LADY. I really don't see how I can help you.

MATT. Nor do I, worse luck !

LADY. I read your trial.

MATT. [*Standing up*] And you think me a bad lot, of course. [*Bitterly.*] D'you know how I spend most of my time in prison ? Holding imaginary conversations with the respectable.

LADY. [*With a smile*] Respectable ! D'you think you're holding a real one now ?

MATT. I certainly don't. . . . I . . . I beg your pardon. . . . You know what I mean. But I bet most people have put me down a rotter.

LADY. Was all you said true ?

MATT. Gospel.

LADY. I suppose they do hunt those girls rather.

MATT. Yes, but you know, I didn't even really see red. I've been sorry enough for that poor chap.

LADY. Well, Captain Denant, what now ?

MATT. You've been most awfully kind and I don't want to impose on you ; but I shall never get out of here as I am.

LADY. Why not ?

MATT. [*Jerking his head towards the window*] They're too thoughtful. There's a picket out there.

> [*The* LADY *turns to the window and looks out ; then she turns to* MATT *and finds him smiling.*]

Oh ! No, I wasn't scared. One doesn't give one's own kind away.

LADY. I don't know that. Go and try some of those other rooms. Try the couple next door to me.

> [*A knock on the door.* BOTH *stand alert.*

LADY. Yes ?

VOICE OF MAID. [*Off*] The bath water's hot now, madam.

LADY. All right. Thank you. [*Her finger is on her lips.*] D'you think she could hear us ?

MATT. Hope not. [*Going close.*] Thanks most awfully. You don't know how decent it's been after a year in there, to talk to a lady. I won't leave any traces.

LADY. What are you going to do ?

MATT. Wait till he's looking the other way, sneak along the balcony, drop at the end, and bolt for it again.

LADY. Are you still a good runner ?

MATT. Pretty fair, if I wasn't so stiff.

LADY. [*After a long look at him*] No ! Look here ! When I go to my bath I'll make sure there's no one. If I don't come back, slip down the stairs, they're almost opposite. In the hall, hanging, you'll find my husband's old Burberry and fishing basket, rod, and fishing hat ; a long brown Burberry, with stains, and flies in the hat. Put them on and go out of the front door ; the river's down to the left.

Can you fish? [*At his nod.*] You'd better, then. The bathroom's not that side, so I shan't see you. But—whistle " Lady, be good," if you know it.

MATT. Rather! It's the only tune that's got into prison. Well, I can't thank you—you're just a brick! [*He holds out his hand.*

LADY. [*Taking it*] Good luck! [*She passes him to the door.*] Wait a second! [*Getting a flask from drawer.*] Take this. If you see anyone looking at you—drink! Nothing gives one more confidence in a man than to see him drinking.

MATT. Splendid! What are you going to say to your husband?

LADY. Um! Yes! He comes to-night. Well, if he doesn't like it, he'll have to lump it. Oh! And these two pounds. It's all I've got here.

[*She has taken two pounds out of her bag lying on the dressing-table.*

MATT. [*Moved*] By George! I think you're sublime!

LADY. I'm afraid I doubt it.

MATT. If I'm caught, I shall say I pinched everything, of course; and if I get clear, I'll——

LADY. Oh! don't bother about that! Get behind the door now.

[MATT *gets behind the door, and she opens it and goes out. After a moment she returns.*

LADY. All clear!

[*Then, closing the door behind her, she goes.* MATT *takes a look round the room to see that he has not left any trace, and moves softly to the door. His hand is on the handle, when it is opened by the* MAID; *he has just time to shrink behind it while she stands looking curiously round the room, as if for somebody or something.*

LADY'S VOICE. [*Off*] Ellen! D'you mind going and getting me the suit I sent down to dry last night?

MAID. [*Starting*] Yes, madam. [*She goes, closing the door.*

[MATT *has just time for a breath of relief when it is opened again and the* LADY *reappears.*

LADY. [*Seeing him breathless*] This is a bit hectic. [*In a whisper.*] Now! Quick!

[MATT *dives past her. She stands a moment, hustles out her underclothing from under the bedclothes, then drawing the door to, goes to the window, opens it a little wider, and stands there listening. In half a minute the faint strains of " Lady, be good," whistled, are heard.*

LADY. [*Waving a stocking like a hat. Under her breath.*] Gone away!

[*Whistling " Lady, be good," she crosses jauntily towards the door, meeting the* MAID, *who is coming in with the dried suit. Continuing to whistle, she passes her with a roll of the eyes, leaving the* MAID *in three minds as*

The curtain falls.

PART II

EPISODE IV

Seven hours have passed. Dartmeet. An open space of fern and grass above the river and away from trippers.

[MATT, *who has been working along the river all the morning, is squatting with his catch beside him—some eight smallish trout. He is eating the last of his chocolate and drinking diligently from the already empty flask. The more so as an* OLD GENTLEMAN *in Lovat tweeds is straying towards him.* MATT *begins taking his rod to pieces.*

OLD GENTLEMAN. [*Approaching from Left*] Afternoon! Cleared up too well for *you*, I'm afraid.

MATT. Yes, it's a bit bright now.

OLD GENTLEMAN. Best eating in the world, those little brown chaps. Except perhaps the blue trout in the Tirol. " Blaue forellen " with butter and potatoes, and a bottle of Voslauer Goldeck, eh ?

MATT. My Golly, yes !   [*He looks wolfishly at his trout.*

OLD GENTLEMAN. [*Eyeing him askance*] Very foggy this morning. Worst point about the moor, these fogs. Only good for convicts—um ?

MATT. [*Subduing a start*] Escapes, you mean ? But they never get clear, I believe.

OLD GENTLEMAN. No, I'm told ; but they try, you know—they try. I've often wondered what I should do if I blundered into an escaped convict.

MATT. Yes, sir ; bit of a problem.

OLD GENTLEMAN. [*Sitting down on his overcoat*] Between the Law and one's gentlemanly instincts—if it's gentlemanlike to dally with a felon—I wonder !

MATT. [*Warming to the subject*] A chap who tries to escape must be a sportsman, anyway. He takes a pretty long chance.

OLD GENTLEMAN. Yes, I don't envy a man in this country ; we're a law-abiding people. I remember being very much struck with the difference in America last year—vital race, that—sublime disregard of the law themselves, and a strong sense of moral turpitude in others. Been in America ?

MATT. I was out West ranching when the war broke out.

OLD GENTLEMAN. Indeed! Judging by the films, escaping justice is still fashionable there. I think I prefer a more settled country.

MATT. Personally, I've got rather a complex. Escaped from Germany in the war.

OLD GENTLEMAN. Did you? How very interesting!

MATT. If you want to get thin. It's a top-hole cure for adipose. An escape's no picnic.

OLD GENTLEMAN. I imagine not, indeed. Where did you get over the border?

MATT. Holland, after three days and nights on beets and turnips. Do you know the turnip in a state of nature, sir? He's a homely fellow—only beaten by the beet. Beg your pardon, sir, it slipped out. By the way, a convict got off the day before yesterday.

OLD GENTLEMAN. Yes, I saw that—a Captain Matt Denant. I read his case with interest at the time. How did it strike you?

MATT. [On guard] Don't believe I remember it.

OLD GENTLEMAN. What? The Hyde Park case?

MATT. Oh! Ah! yes. There was a girl. In those cases they might wait till you complain.

OLD GENTLEMAN. The detective was undoubtedly doing his duty. And yet, quite a question—Rather dangerous giving the police a discretion on morals. The police are very like ourselves; and—er —most of us haven't got discretion, and the rest haven't got morals. The young man didn't complain, I think. D'you happen to recollect?

MATT. [With an uneasy look] So far as I remember, he said she was an intellectual.

[The OLD GENTLEMAN has taken out a cigar-case and is offering it.

OLD GENTLEMAN. Smoke?

MATT. Thanks very much. I've got into a bad habit of coming out without tobacco. [They bite and light cigars.

OLD GENTLEMAN. I suppose one might run across that convict fellow any moment. It would be a little like meeting an adder. The poor thing only wants to get away from you. And yet, if you don't break its back, ten to one it'll bite a dog. I had two dogs die of snakebite. It's a duty, perhaps—what do you say?

MATT. Probably. But I don't always do mine.

OLD GENTLEMAN. Oh! don't you? I'm so glad of that. Neither do I.

MATT. Do you know that prison? It's a bad style of architecture.

OLD GENTLEMAN. No. The fact is, I've had the misfortune in my time to send a good many people to prison. And in those days I did make a point of seeing a prison now and then. I remember I used to give my Juries a pass to go and see where they sent their fellow-beings. Once I tested whether they went to look round or not, and out of three Juries—no, it was four—how many do you think had had the curiosity?

MATT. None.

OLD GENTLEMAN. Isn't that a little cynical? [*With his sideway bird-like glance.*] No, it was—one. Ha!

MATT. Who'd want to go into a prison? I'd as soon visit the Morgue. The bodies there aren't *living*, anyway.

OLD GENTLEMAN. They tell me prisons are much improved. They've introduced a human feeling.

MATT. Have they? Splendid! What was the date of that?

OLD GENTLEMAN. [*His eyes busy*] They've abolished the arrows, anyway. And I believe they don't shave their heads now. Do you know any convicts?

MATT. [*With a wriggle*] I? No. Only one.

OLD GENTLEMAN. Indeed? And is he interesting?

MATT. The most interesting chap I know.

OLD GENTLEMAN. Ha! Suppose this escaped convict suddenly turned up here. [*Jerking his thumb towards* MATT.] What should you do?

MATT. Run like a hare.

OLD GENTLEMAN. Dear me, yes. I think it would depend on whether anyone was about. Human nature is very—er—sensitive. D'you find this climate bracing? Dartmoor has quite a reputation.

MATT. Overrated—I think.

OLD GENTLEMAN. You know it well?

MATT. No; this is my first visit.

OLD GENTLEMAN. And will you be here long?

MATT. Hope not.

OLD GENTLEMAN. Beautiful spot—Dartmeet!

MATT. I prefer Two Bridges.

[*Putting up his rod and whistling " Lady, be good."*

OLD GENTLEMAN. Ah! What fly have you been using?

MATT. Just a tag.

OLD GENTLEMAN. I've not fished for years. [*As* MATT *suddenly passes his hand over his brow under his hat.*] Anything the matter?

MATT. Afraid I shall have to abandon your excellent cigar. I've enjoyed it, but I'm smoking on a rather empty stomach.

[*He looks ruefully at the unsmoked portion of his cigar, and pitches it away.*

OLD GENTLEMAN. Dear me! Yes. I remember that feeling coming over me once at the Royal Academy banquet—just before I had to make a speech. [*Another of his birdlike glances.*] Tobacco must be one of the great deprivations in prison, I always think. Didn't you find that so in—in—Germany?

MATT. [*Breathing rather fast and completing the dismantlement of his fishing rod*] Oh! we got tobacco now and then.

OLD GENTLEMAN, And empty stomachs too, I'm afraid.

MATT. Yes.

OLD GENTLEMAN. One never ceases to be grateful to those who endured such things. [*Offering his cigar case.*] Will you try again after tea ? These moor teas with cream and jam.

MATT. [*Taking it*] Well, thank you, sir. I shall down him next time.

[MATT *is now ready for departure, for he has been getting increasingly uneasy with this* OLD GENTLEMAN. *He takes up his basket and lays the fish within it.*

OLD GENTLEMAN. Well [*Getting up*] I must be getting on too. It's been very pleasant. I've enjoyed our little talk. At my time of life one doesn't often get new sensations.

MATT. [*Nonplussed*] Good Lord, sir ! Have I given you any ?

OLD GENTLEMAN. Well, I don't remember ever having talked before to a prisoner who'd escaped from—Germany.

MATT. Good-bye, sir.

OLD GENTLEMAN. Good-bye, Captain Denant—[MATT *starts.*] I hope you'll have a pleasant journey, especially as no one seems to have noticed our little chat.

MATT. [*Staring at him*] D'you mind frightfully telling me how you spotted me ?

OLD GENTLEMAN. Not at all ! First, the way you looked at your trout—shall I say—er—wolfishly ? And then—forgive me—your legs.

MATT. [*Drawing up his Burberry and contemplating his legs*] Yes. I hoped you'd think I was a leader of fashion.

OLD GENTLEMAN. And there was another thing—your obvious sympathy with yourself.

MATT. That's a prison habit, sir. You're not allowed to sympathize with other people, for fear of contaminating them. Before I got into quod I don't remember ever feeling sorry for myself. But I doubt if I shall ever again feel sorry for anyone else.

OLD GENTLEMAN. That must be very natural. Well, it's been most interesting, because now you see I know what I should do——

MATT. [*Intently*] Is it indiscreet to ask, sir ?

OLD GENTLEMAN. Well, Captain Denant, this time—I say *this* time —wink the other eye. Good-day to you !

MATT. Good-day, sir. It's most frightfully sporting of you. For the moment I feel quite human.

OLD GENTLEMAN. Do you know, that's been rather the effect on me. Original sin, I suppose. Good-day !

[*He goes off, watching the smoke of his cigar and smiling faintly to himself. On* MATT, *affected by kindness,*

The curtain falls.

EPISODE V

An hour has passed.   On the Moor ; a high spot.

[FOUR TRIPPERS, *two men and two women, disgorged from a Ford
car, are picnicking.   One of the men, about fifty, in blue clothes,
has a Merchant Service look and a concertina ; the other looks
more like a shopkeeper, and is perhaps fifty-five.   His wife
is a stout woman, about forty, of mellow appearance.   The
other woman is the shopkeeper's sister, dried-up and spinsterish.
Their clothes are of a suitable nature—some feathers.   They
are all eating heavily.*

WIFE. Captain, you're a prophet—considerin' what it was when
we left Ashburton.   I call this lovely !   [*Eats.*

CAPTAIN. Takes a bit o' weather to flummox a sailor, ma'am.
                                                             [*Drinks.*

WIFE. " You trust the Captain," I said to Pinkem this morning,
didn't I, father ?   *I* knew, you see ; [*archly*] my corns weren't
shootin'.

SISTER. That's not very nice, Fanny.

WIFE. Why not ?   I'd like to see someone who 'asn't corns, if
the truth was known.   'Ave another of these cut rounds, Dolly, and
cheer up.   Father, don't you eat any more cream—your eyes are
yeller.

SHOPKEEPER. When I first came to Devonshire I could put away
'alf a pound o' cream at a meal.

WIFE. Yes, and it spoiled your temper for life.

SHOPKEEPER. Am I bad-tempered, Dolly ?

SISTER. So-so, James.

SHOPKEEPER. What do you say, Captain !

CAPTAIN. You keep it for your wife, my boy.   Outside the bosom
of your family you're a perfect cherub.

WIFE. Captain, you're an 'opeless Benedick.

CAPTAIN. Bachelor born, ma'am.

WIFE. With a wife in every port, eh ?

SISTER. Oh !   That reely isn't nice, Fanny ; so old-fashioned,
too.

CAPTAIN. Is it, ma'am ?

WIFE. Now, Captain, don't go shockin' Dolly.   Oh !   There's an
insect on my skirt !   I never seen one like it.

SHOPKEEPER. Kill it, then.

WIFE. Why ?

SHOPKEEPER. Always kill what you don't know.

WIFE. [*Flipping it off*] It's only a biddle—poor thing !   Give us a

tune, Captain.   [*The* CAPTAIN *draws a long blast from his concertina.*]
Hallo ! 'Oo's this ?

> [MATT, *in Burberry, with rod and basket, has appeared Left, and
> stands lifting his hat.*

MATT. Afternoon !   Wonder if you could put me right for
Bovey ?

SHOPKEEPER. Bovey ! That's a goodish step—matter of twelve
miles, I should say.

MATT. My Lord !   Not really ?

SHOPKEEPER. You go down the 'ill, through Ponsworthy to
Widecombe, and up the 'ill, turn to the left, and ask again.

MATT. I see.   Will there be anyone to ask ?

SHOPKEEPER. I shouldn't think so.

CAPTAIN. Had any sport, sir ?

MATT. [*Opening the basket*] Eight, rather small.

WIFE. My !   Don't they look nice !   Such good eatin', too.

MATT. Would you like them, ma'am ?

WIFE. [*With affected restraint*] I'm sure it's very good of you.

CAPTAIN. Don't you miss the chance, Mrs. Pinkem ; nothing like
moor trout, with a moor appetite.

SISTER. [*Distantly*] I'm *sure* it's most kind, from a stranger.

WIFE. [*Suddenly*] Well, I don't know, if you're so obliging.   'And
me the *Daily Mail*, father.   I'll wrap 'em up ; and thank you very
much.   I quite appreciate it.

MATT. That's splendid ! [*He hands them.*] Turned out quite nice,
hasn't it ?   Have you come far ?

SHOPKEEPER. From Ashburton—ten mile.

MATT. Heard anything there of the escaped convict ?

SHOPKEEPER. What about it ?   Haven't looked at the paper last
day or two.

WIFE. Another escape !—Oh, my !

MATT. Rather !   He got off in the fog, night before last.

SISTER. I always hate to think of one of those dreadful men at large.
You can't sleep in your bed.

CAPTAIN. Don't you get *too* excited, ma'am.   Think of the choice
'e's got.

WIFE. [*Scanning the paper*] Why ! It's the man that killed the poor
detective in 'Yde Park !   That villain !   It says 'ere they nearly got
him—twice.

> [MATT, *who is eyeing them closely, eyes a loaf even more closely, and
> tries to manœuvre into a position to annex it.*

SHOPKEEPER. I 'ope everybody's helping to catch him.   He must
be a regular desperado.   That was a bad case.   I never believed the
girl.

SISTER. I should think not, indeed !

SHOPKEEPER. Nor the young man neither. They were up to no good there. They tell me those London parks are in a proper state.

CAPTAIN. They ain't a Sunday School, that's certain.

WIFE. Fie, Captain!

SISTER. [*Acidly*] I believe some people quite sympathized with him. Fancy!

MATT. Well, if you won't think it too eccentric, I did, for one.

SHOPKEEPER. You!—Why?

MATT. I thought he had devilish hard luck.

SHOPKEEPER. Ah! there's always a fuss made about the Law. You can't even 'ang a woman for murderin' her 'usband without a lot o' 'ysterical nonsense. Look at that case not long ago—there was a petition as long as your arm.

CAPTAIN. I remember. The young chap was a steward. I don't recall this Hyde Park case.

WIFE. Why! the detective arrested one o' those women this young man had been sittin' with—a gentleman he was too—and if he didn't 'it him an' break 'is 'ead, an' kill 'im, poor man!

CAPTAIN. Then why didn't they string him up?

MATT. The jury found it was a quarrel, not an attempt to evade arrest. Besides, in falling the detective hit his head on the iron railing of the Row, and the doctors said he died of the concussion.

SHOPKEEPER. That didn't ought to have got 'im off. He hit the man. If 'e 'adn't 'it him, 'e wouldn't have fallen.

MATT. Exactly! Brilliant! But if the detective hadn't seized him, he wouldn't have hit him.

SHOPKEEPER. Well! *I'd* 'ave hung 'im.

WIFE. Don't be so bloodthirsty, father!

SHOPKEEPER. Well, I would! Hitting an officer for doing his duty. Sitting with a woman in the Park, too! He only got off because he was quality.

MATT. Don't you think that's a superstition?

[*The* SHOPKEEPER *glares at him, but decides that he is a gentleman, and therefore prejudiced, and only snorts slightly.*

SISTER. Did they punish the woman?

MATT. What for, ma'am?

SISTER. *I'd* keep them shut up; then they wouldn't tempt young men—the 'arpies!

MATT. [*Unexpectedly*] Oh! God!

[*They all stare at him. Then the* SHOPKEEPER *fatuously breaks the silence.*

SHOPKEEPER. Can't say I was ever tempted by a woman.

MATT. No, you've got a Ford car, I see. D'you find them good in this sort of country?

SHOPKEEPER. [*Distantly*] I do, sir.

MATT. Do they get up these hills?

SHOPKEEPER. I should think so. I'd engage to catch any convict with my car.

MATT. Would you? [*A thought strikes him.*] Splendid!

WIFE. Well, I think we ought to be gettin' 'ome. 'And me the teapot, Captain. Now, Dolly! Never mind those bits o' cake and bread—they're no good. Just leave the deebris. I'd like to be in before dark, with a convict loose like this. He might come prowlin' round, pickin' things up.

[MATT *with a secret movement pockets some scraps.*

MATT. Good afternoon! Hope you'll enjoy the trout.

[*He moves away out of the picture.*

WIFE and CAPTAIN. Good afternoon—Good afternoon, sir!

[MATT *salutes and vanishes, Right.*

SISTER. Here, Fanny! Did you see him pocket the scraps?

WIFE. No! Why's he's a gentleman—didn't you hear his sniffy way o' talkin'?

SISTER. I saw him with my own eyes—two bits of cake and a round.

[*Sound of a car being started.*

SHOPKEEPER. I say! [*Jumping up.*] What's 'e doin' with the Ford?

CAPTAIN. Hi, there! You, sir!

SHOPKEEPER. He's got in. Hi!

SISTER. The villain!

ALL. Hi! hi! hi!

[*Sounds of a levanting car, and a halloed* " So long!"

[*The* TWO MEN *run out of the picture.*

WIFE. Well, I——

SISTER. *You!* Taking his fish like that! You might ha' known he was a thief. Why—why—of course! He's the—oh! oh!

WIFE. Dry up, Dolly! 'Ow are we to get 'ome?

[*The* TWO MEN *run back into the picture, breathless.*

SHOPKEEPER. Well, of all the impudent villains!

CAPTAIN. I'm jiggered!

[*He sits down with his hands on his knees and goes off into wheezy laughter.*

SISTER. 'Ow *can* you? 'Ow *can* you, Captain? And we talking about him all the time!

CAPTAIN. [*Stopping*] What! Him!

SISTER. The escaped convict! He hadn't the leggins of a gentleman.

CAPTAIN. What! Did *you* look at his legs, ma'am?

WIFE. It's all your fault, Pinkem; you and Dolly's—callin' 'im names. If you 'adn't called 'im names, he wouldn't 'a stole the car—talkin' of hanging 'im! I could see 'im gettin' heated.

SHOPKEEPER. You called 'im a villain yourself. Well—Bovey—we know where to look for him.

CAPTAIN. A blind, old bean.

SHOPKEEPER. I say 'e will go there.

CAPTAIN. I say 'e won't.

SHOPKEEPER. I say 'e'll see we'll think 'e won't, and put the double cross on us.

CAPTAIN. Well, I say, 'e'll see we'll think 'e's going to put the double cross on us.

WIFE. Oh! My corns!

SISTER. Impudence, givin' us 'is fish!

CAPTAIN. Well, there's nothin' for it but tote the things and walk till we get a lift.

WIFE. Oh! my corns are shootin'. I can't walk.

CAPTAIN. Cheerio, ma'am! Be English.

SHOPKEEPER. English! 'Tisn't *your* car.

CAPTAIN. Don't worry, old sport. 'E'll leave that in a ditch when he gets there.

SHOPKEEPER. There—ye-es—John o' Groats?

CAPTAIN. Come along, ma'am. Lift your corns well up. I'll give you a tune.

[*They have picked up the gear and are trailing off Right, leaving papers strewn about.*

WIFE. Oh! Look! We've left 'is fish.

SISTER. Fish! Infra dig, I call it.   [*She sniffs.*

WIFE. Nonsense, Dolly! Dish of trout like that'll cost five shillings in Ashburton. May as well 'ave the worth of the petrol 'e'll use. Father, pick 'em up.

[*The* SHOPKEEPER *turns back, picks them up in the " Daily Mail," puts the combination to his nose, finds it good and follows the others off as the* CAPTAIN *begins to play his concertina and*

The curtain falls.

EPISODE VI

Half an hour has passed.   An open space with the moor rising from it.

[A MAN *in plus fours and his* WIFE *are returning from a walk.   The* WIFE *has stopped and is moving her foot uneasily.*

WIFE. I've got something in my shoe, Philip.

MAN. What?

WIFE. I've got something in my shoe.

MAN. [*In front, stopping too*] Take it off, then. [*Goes back to her.*] Hold on to me.

WIFE. [*Taking off shoe and shaking it*] It isn't in the shoe—it's inside the stocking.

MAN. You can't sit down here ; the ground's still wet.

WIFE. There—feel !

MAN. Yes, I can feel it.

WIFE. [*Standing on one leg*] Well !   Hold me.

> [*He holds her and she has slipped her stocking off when there is the sound of an approaching car.*

MAN. Look out !   Here's a car !

WIFE. [*Letting her skirt fall and standing on one leg*] Bother !

> [*Sound of the car stopping.*

MAN. Hallo !   He's coming to speak to us.

> [*The* WIFE *bends and slips the shoe on hurriedly, but her dress is short. She holds the stocking behind her.*

MATT. [*Appearing*] Beg your pardon, sir, but can you direct me to Bovey ?

MAN. Afraid we're strangers.   Pity you didn't ask as you came through Widecombe.

MATT. Well, but it's up this hill, anyway, isn't it ?

MAN. Must be, I think.   That's the way to Heytor Rock.

MATT. Oh !   Can you see the promised land from there ?

WIFE. Yes.   You go up the hill and turn to the right, then to the left through a gate.

MATT. And ask again, I suppose. [*Preparing to leave.*] Thanks very much.

MAN. Fine place, the moor, sir.   Splendid air.

MATT. [*Dryly*] Oh !   Splendid.   So dry and clear !

WIFE. [*With a giggle*] Yes, the fog *was* awful yesterday.

MAN. They say Bovey's pretty.

MATT. Yes, I've some Aunts there.   Good place for Aunts.

WIFE. [*Laughing*] What makes a good place for Aunts ?

MATT. Oh !   not too stirring.   Awfully good knitting there, I believe.

MAN. Ha !   That's good.   Ha !

MATT. I must get on, or I shall be late for tea.   So I whizz past Heytor rocks—— ?

WIFE. Yes, and come down on the church.

MATT. Thanks very much.   My Aunts are close there, I know. Good afternoon.

> [*He lifts his hat discreetly and goes, Right.   The* MAN *and* WIFE *gaze after him.*

WIFE. What a nice young man !

MAN. That was good about Aunts.   Ha ! [*Sound of car moving on.*] Now for your stocking !

WIFE. [*Bending down and taking off her shoe*] I should think he was County, wouldn't you ?

MAN. [*Holding her from behind*] Um !   Only " County " would drive such a shockin' bad car.

WIFE. He saw my leg and kept his eyes off it. I thought that was charming of him.

MAN. Fellow-feelin' ; he had some shockin' leg gear on himself.

WIFE. [*Turning stocking inside out*] See, there it is—a beastly little three-cornered bit of grit. Extraordinary how they get in——

MAN. [*Suddenly*] Look out ! Here's a constable on a bike.

[*The* WIFE *drops her skirt and stands balancing again, the stocking in her hand. A very hot* CONSTABLE *appears, wheeling a bicycle.*

CONSTABLE. Zeen convict pass ?

MAN. [*Astonished*] Convict ? No.

CONSTABLE. Zeen anybody ?

MAN. Only a car.

CONSTABLE. What zort of car ?

MAN. Ford, I think.

CONSTABLE. Whu was in it ?

MAN. A man.

CONSTABLE. What zort of man ?

MAN. Oh !—er—a gentleman.

CONSTABLE. How d'yu know ?

MAN. By his voice.

WIFE. He spoke to us.

CONSTABLE. What d'e zay ?

MAN. Asked the way to Bovey.

CONSTABLE. Ha ! What 'ad 'e on ?

MAN. Long Burberry and a hat like mine ; he was quite all right.

CONSTABLE. [*Mopping his face*] Was 'e ? Bovey—yu zay ?

WIFE. Yes, he had some Aunts there—he was going to tea with them.

CONSTABLE. [*Deeply*] Aunts in Bovey ! Did yu direct 'im ?

WIFE. We told him to go by Heytor rocks. Wasn't that right ?

CONSTABLE. Well, yu've directed the escaped convict.

MAN. [*Alarmed*] No, really ! But I tell you——

WIFE. He was quite charming.

CONSTABLE. Was 'e ? 'Ow much start's 'e got ?

MAN. Oh ! not five minutes. Of course, I didn't know—I should never have——

CONSTABLE. [*Muttering and mopping*] This plaguey 'ill !

MAN. Hadn't you better telephone to Bovey ?

CONSTABLE. [*Smartly*] Bovey ! Why d'yu suppose he spoke to 'ee ? Because 'e idn' goin' to Bovey and wants me to think 'e is.

WIFE. But really he was a gentleman.

CONSTABLE. [*Dryly*] Volk 'e stole that car from 'alf an hour gone, don't think so.   [*He mops his face.*

WIFE. I can't believe——

MAN. There were his legs. [*To* CONSTABLE, *whose eyes are on the lady's leg.*] I noticed they looked like nothing at all.

CONSTABLE. Then why didn' yu stop 'im?

MAN. [*Flustered*] I would have, of course, if I'd suspected for a moment.

CONSTABLE. Stop first—suspect arterwards.

MAN. Well, I'm very sorry. If I'd——

CONSTABLE. 'Tes done now. I must get down along sharp and telephone. [*He turns and wheels his bicycle off to the road.*

WIFE. [*On one leg*] I don't see why you need be sorry, Philip. He *was* a gentleman.

MAN. A convict's a convict; you can't play about with the Law.

WIFE. Well, we have, that's one comfort. That constable didn't keep *his* eyes off my leg.

MAN. I suppose you'd have had me get into a row with the police!

WIFE. Don't be silly, Philip! You needn't get angry because your nerves are rattled. No, don't hold me, I can put it on perfectly by myself.

[*She stands wobbling on one leg, and pulls the stocking on.*

MAN. The brass of that chap—talking about his Aunts!

WIFE. You thought it very funny, when he did.

MAN. If I'd known——

WIFE. Oh! Yes, if you'd known—you haven't an ounce of original sin in you. Thank goodness, I have.

MAN. Where? *I've* never——

WIFE. No, I don't keep it for you.

WIFE. Hallo! He's coming back.

WIFE. Who? The constable?

MAN. No—that chap—the convict. [*Sounds of car.*

WIFE. Hooray!

MAN. What do you mean—hooray! What am I to do? This is infernal.

WIFE. [*Maliciously*] Run out and stop him, of course.

MAN. [*On one leg and the other*] He'd run over me. These chaps are desperate.

WIFE. Well, *I* will, then; and warn him of the constable.

MAN. You won't!—Hallo! He's stopping. That's worse. What the devil shall I do now?

[*The* WIFE *laughs. Sounds of car stopping.* MATT *reappears.*

MATT. Awfully sorry, but my car jibbed. There's another way round, isn't there? Through Widecombe, to the right—I saw a road?

MAN. Um! Well—I—er——

WIFE. Yes, but I shouldn't advise you to take it.

MATT. Must, I'm afraid. My car started to back down the hill.

MAN. I'm afraid—er—that I—er—ought to——

WIFE. My husband means that there's a constable in Widecombe.
[*Pointing*.

MATT. Yes. [*Looking back under his hand.*] I see him.

WIFE. So you'd better go on up.

MATT. There are *two* up there, you see.   My car's very sensitive.

WIFE. Oh, dear !

MAN. Joan ! [*Resolutely*.] Now, sir, that constable's been talking to us.   The game's up.   If you don't mind, I'll take that car.   He says it isn't yours.

MATT. [*Stepping back*] You know that's most frightfully true.   But then—it isn't yours either.

MAN. Well, just let's argue it.   I'm afraid you're helpless.

MATT. What do you take me for ?

MAN. Why—er—the escaped convict, if you know what I mean.

MATT. Oh ! Well—even so, I've still got a kick in me.   I see your point of view, of course ; but unfortunately I've got my own.

MAN. After that constable, I simply can't play about with it.

MATT. Look here ! I've got a brain-wave.   Let's all go into Widecombe in the car ?

MAN. Ah ! thanks very much ; I thought you'd be sporting.

MATT. You see, if you're with me, I shall get through Widecombe all right, and I'll drop you just on the far side.

MAN. But——! What ?   No—that won't——

MATT. It's all right.   You take me in custody into Widecombe—you can't help it if I whizz through and shoot you out.   I want to make it easy for you, and I hope you want to make it easy for me.

MAN. Why should I ?   An escaped convict !

MATT. What do you call *yourself* ?

MAN. What ! Just an average man.

MATT. D'you mean to say the average man isn't a sportsman ?

MAN. Yes.   But I've had warning.   I'm up against it.

WIFE. *I'll* come in the car.   If you're with a lady, you'll get through without being spotted.

MATT. Splendid !   Thanks ever so !   Will you get in ?

MAN. Joan !

MATT. Put yourself in my position, sir——

MAN. Look here !   I ought to be knocking you down and sitting on your head, if you know what I mean.

MATT. [*Squaring up*] Well, any little thing you've got to do, please do it quickly.

MAN. Well, I mean—that's very crude.

WIFE. [*Ironically*] Oh ! no, Philip !   Oh, no !

MAN. Well, suppose you let me drive.

MATT. Why should I ?   I stole the car.   Now, madam, shall we start ?

33

WIFE. [*Winding her scarf round her face*] Right-o!

MAN. This is monstrous! Look here, sir, you seem to think——

MATT. I'll tell you what I think—[*Grimly*] I've been in purgatory too long, and I'm going to get out, and you're not going to stop me, if you know what I mean.

MAN. I jolly well am!

WIFE. Philip!

MAN. I'm not going to have it. If you won't surrender, I shall tackle you.

MATT. [*Dangerously*] Oh!   [*He takes a spanner out of his pocket.*

WIFE. [*Stepping between them—to* MATT] D'you know, I think you'd better go on.

MATT. I think so, too. Sorry to be a boor and bring out a thing like this. [*Tapping the spanner.*] But I'm not playing, you see. [*Sombrely.*] The life we live spoils our sense of humour! Good-bye, ma'am, I'm very grateful to *you*.   [*He turns and vanishes.*

MAN. Look here! You're not going like that—I'm damned if you are! Stop!

WIFE. Masterly, Philip! Masterly! [*Sound of a car starting.*] Run! My dear! Run! It's all right. You'll be too late.

MAN. You really *are*——

[*They stand looking at each other as the sound of the car fails slowly, and*

The curtain falls.

EPISODE VII

An hour has passed.

[*In a gravel pit on the edge of the moor are a wheelbarrow, with a pick in it, and* MATT *lying on his face, apparently asleep, waiting for dark.*

[*From Right comes the figure of a* LABOURER. *He is a burly great fellow with a shovel. Seeing the recumbent figure, he stands still, gazing. Then, turning, he goes back whence he came.* MATT, *who has been conscious of this visitor, gathers himself to spring up and rush away. Then he takes a resolution and lies down again in the same attitude, as if asleep. The* LABOURER *returns, followed by another* LABOURER *as big as himself. The* FIRST LABOURER *clears his throat.*

MATT. [*Sitting up with his feet under him*] Well, my men! What's the matter with you?

FIRST LABOURER. Beg pardon, zurr. We'm lukin' for th' escaped convict. We 'ad a zort of a thought as yu med be 'err.

MATT. Did you? That's pretty good! And now you see I'm not, suppose you apologize?

FIRST LABOURER. [*Cautiously*] 'Course, ef we knu 'u'm yu werr——

MATT. Whom do you work for?

FIRST LABOURER. Varmer Brownin'. 'Tes 'is grazin' yere.

MATT. I'll see Farmer Browning. It's funny, but I don't altogether like being taken for an escaped convict.

FIRST LABOURER. Yas, I rackon as 'ow yu'd better zee Maester Browning. George, goo and vind Maester. 'E'm in th' orchard long across.   [*The* SECOND LABOURER *goes off, Left.*

FIRST LABOURER. We'm 'ad nues o' this joker, yu zee. Zeemingly 'e pinched a car and we'm found it just back along in the ditch. 'Tes the zame old car, tu.

MATT. What on earth's the car to do with me.

FIRST LABOURER. A don' zay nothin' 'bout that. Maester'll know when 'e comes.

MATT. I'll go and meet him.   [*He makes as if to rise.*

FIRST LABOURER. No, yu zett therr.

MATT. Now, look here, my friend! Do I talk like a convict?

FIRST LABOURER. Can't zay, never 'eerd none. They'm town folk, I rackon—mos'ly.

MATT. Well, I was bred in the country, like you. What wages do you get here?

[*He pulls the flask out of his pocket, whistling "Lady, be good."*

FIRST LABOURER. Waal, ef yu'm the convict, yu'm a cule customer arter that.

MATT. But why on earth should you *think* I'm the convict? I'm just a fisherman staying at Lustleigh. [*He takes a pull at the empty flask.*] You're making a fool of yourself, you know.

FIRST LABOURER. [*Scratching his head*] Ef so be as yu'm what yu zay yu be, wot d'you goo vur to 'ide yere?

MATT. Hide? I was having a nap out of the wind, before walking home.

FIRST LABOURER. This joker 'ad a fishin'-rod wi' un, tu.

MATT. The convict? Bosh!

FIRST LABOURER. Not zo much bosh, neither.

MATT. Look you, my man, I've had enough of this.

[*He stands up suddenly.*

[*The* LABOURER *steps back and lifts his shovel. But at this moment the* FARMER *and* SECOND LABOURER *step into the picture from Left, accompanied by a* LITTLE GIRL *of thirteen or so, who has been riding.*

FARMER. Now then, now then! That'll du, Jim. Yu there, on my land, kindly give me yure name, and account for yureself. There's a rough customer about, with a fishin'-rod, same as yu.

MATT. Mr. Browning?

FARMER. Ay! that's my name.

MATT. Mine's Matthew. Captain Matthew. I'm staying at the Inn at Lustleigh. There's some very absurd mistake. This good trusty dog thinks he's treed a convict.

FARMER. [*Impressed by* MATT'S *accent and air, and the flask in his hand*] Well, sir, when there's these escapes on the moor, we 'ave to be careful. Miss 'Lizbeth, yu run along.

        [*The* LITTLE GIRL *does not move, but remains spellbound.*] Constable's just been in wi' nues from Widecombe of the car yonder, and the man that pinched it 'ad a long brown coat, a fishin'-rod, and an 'at like yurn.

MATT. If the constable's here still, you'd better take me to him.

FARMER. No, rackon I'll ask 'im to step over 'ere. George, run and fetch constable, he'm down along by thiccy car.

        [*The* SECOND LABOURER *departs, Right, the* FIRST LABOURER
           retires a little to the Right, leaving the FARMER *and* MATT *by*
           themselves on the Left, the FARMER *being on the outside. The*
           LITTLE GIRL *still lurks breathless.*

MATT. Now, Mr. Browning—dash it all!—you ought to know better than this!

FARMER. Oh! I daresay yu'm a gentleman, but so's this convict, seemin'ly. Leastways he'm a captain. Perhaps yu'll tell me the name o' the innkeeper where yu'm stayin' at Lustleigh?

MATT. Has he got a name? I hadn't noticed.

FARMER. No; nor the name of the Inn neither, maybe?

MATT. The Red Lion.

FARMER. Ha!

MATT. Well, it ought to be.

FARMER. And per'aps yu'll show me the clothes yu've got on.

MATT. [*Taking a resolution*] Well, I own up.

LITTLE GIRL. Oh!

FARMER. I thowt yu'd come to it.

MATT. [*Lowering his voice*] Be sporting. Give me a show!

FARMER. Now yu know I can't du that; what's the yuse of askin'?

MATT. Well, I've had forty-eight hours' freedom, and given them a good run. You haven't a cigarette?

FARMER. I don't smoke them things. Jim, got a fag for this gentleman?

        [FIRST LABOURER *brings out a packet of cigarettes which he holds out.*
           MATT *takes one and lights it from a match sheltered in the horny*
           hands of the LABOURER, *who then retires again, Right, with the*
           shovel.

MATT. Thanks very much!   [*He sits on the wheelbarrow.*
        [*There ensues a silence. The* LITTLE GIRL *steals up to* MATT.

LITTLE GIRL. [*Holding out a small book*] Would you mind giving me your autograph?

FARMER. Miss 'Lizabeth!

LITTLE GIRL. Well, I've only just begun—I *have* to ask anybody at all thrilling.

MATT. [*With a grin*] Ink or—blood?

LITTLE GIRL. Oh! that'd be splendid!

MATT. Mine or—yours?

LITTLE GIRL. Oh! I've got a fountain pen. [*Hands it. MATT writes his name.*] Thank you so much.

MATT. [*Handing back the book*] Shake hands on it.

[*The LITTLE GIRL and he shake hands.*] When you're an old woman you'll be able to say you met Murderous Matt.—Mr. Browning, you won't give me a chance?

FARMER. Aid and abet a convict? No, no, Captain!

MATT. Vermin, eh? [*Looking round him.*] Well, you see, I've gone to earth. D'you hold with digging foxes out?

FARMER. I do, the varmints!

MATT. Ah! Well, you may thank your stars you were never in prison.

FARMER. No, an' I 'ope I'll never du nothin' to putt me there.

MATT. Take care you don't have bad luck, that's all.

FARMER. Bad luck? I rackon a man as kills a man can think he's havin' *gude* luck if he don't swing for it.

MATT. [*Sombrely*] I meant the poor beggar no harm.

LITTLE GIRL. Have you really killed a man?

MATT. Not yet.

FARMER. [*Removing the pick from the barrow*] Yu struck the blow, and he died of 't. What's more, so far as I remember, he was duin' his duty, same as I'm duin' mine.

[*He looks intently at MATT, as if warning him not to try another blow.*]

MATT. You needn't be afraid; there's a child here. If there weren't! I hope you'll see that my friend here [*Pointing to the LABOURER*] has the reward for my capture.

FARMER. 'E can 'ave it; I don' want no reward for duin' *my* duty.

MATT. [*Nodding gravely*] That's lucky! I appreciate your excellent intentions, Mr. Browning. Glad to have met you! Good-bye!

[*He leaps from the barrow, and with a twist like a footballer evading a tackle, is past him and away to the Left. The LITTLE GIRL claps her hands.*]

FARMER. [*Astonished*] The varmint! Hi! Jim! Arter 'im!

[*The LABOURER utters a sort of roar and starts running. The FARMER is about to follow.*]

LITTLE GIRL. Oh! Mr. Browning!

FARMER. Well?

LITTLE GIRL. Oh! nothing.

FARMER. Darn!   [*He follows out, running, Left.*

[*The* CONSTABLE *and* SECOND LABOURER *come hurrying from Right.*

CONSTABLE. Gone! Which way, missy?

LITTLE GIRL. [*With distant blankness*] I don't know.

CONSTABLE. Come on, then!

[*He and the* LABOURER *go out, Left, running.*

LITTLE GIRL. Oh! I do hope he gets off! Oh!

[*On the hue and cry*

The curtain falls.

EPISODE VIII

A few minutes have passed.

[*In the parlour of a cottage of gentility are two maiden ladies—*MISS GRACE, *about forty-seven, brewing tea at a little table before the fire, Right, and* MISS DORA, *much younger, still dressed in hunting togs, standing at the open French window, Back.*

MISS DORA. There's such a glow on the Cleave, Grace. Most lovely red. We killed. Everybody was looking out for that escaped convict.

MISS GRACE. Did you see him?

MISS DORA. No, thank goodness. Poor hunted wretch!

MISS GRACE. If you think hunted things are poor, why do you go hunting?

MISS DORA. Foxes hunt and expect to be hunted.

MISS GRACE. So do convicts. Sympathy's wasted on them. Tea, Dora.

MISS DORA. This isn't a common convict. It's that Captain Denant, you remember——

MISS GRACE. Oh!—not likely to forget the row we had about his case! Well! it served him right!

MISS DORA. [*Going to the table and sitting down. Looking steadily at her sister*] For a good woman, Grace, you know—you're awfully hard.

MISS GRACE. Tea-cake, please. I like consistency.

MISS DORA. [*Deeply*] I think you're right.

MISS GRACE. [*Surprised*] How?

MISS DORA. It *is* a shame to hunt a fox—much better to shoot it.

MISS GRACE. There'd soon be no foxes. Don't get *that* bee into your bonnet *here*. What with rabbits, and chained dogs, you've set the farmers by the ears as it is. Wait till we go to Bath. You can have as many bees as you like there.

MISS DORA. I shan't hunt any more.

Miss Grace. Then you're very foolish, if you enjoy it. Will you come over to the Service with me this evening ?

Miss Dora. D'you know what I wish *you'd* say, Grace ? " I shan't go to church any more."

Miss Grace. I wish to God, Dora, you'd give up free thought !

Miss Dora. I wish to God, Grace, you'd give up religion.

Miss Grace. You only hurt the vicar by it.

Miss Dora. [*Shaking her head*] He's too good a sort to mind.

Miss Grace. You're too perverse for anything. I've only to say something and you set your will to the opposite.

Miss Dora. My dear, my will is nothing to yours. I haven't the ego for it.

Miss Grace. [*Coldly*] You mean I'm egoistic ? Thank you.

Miss Dora. Sorry, Grace.

Miss Grace. Will you have another cup ?

Miss Dora. Please.

> [*She is holding out her cup and* Miss Grace *has poured from the teapot, when a Figure comes rushing through the French window. They both drop their hands and stare.* Matt, *panting and distressed, makes a sudden revealing gesture of appeal, and blots himself out behind a window curtain. The hue and cry is heard off. The two ladies are still staring in wild surprise, when the* Farmer *appears at the French window.*

Farmer. Which way d' 'e go ?

Miss Dora. Who ?

Farmer. Convict. Mun cam' over your waal un' round the corner ther'.

Miss Dora. Oh ! Yes. I thought I saw. Across the lawn, and over the wall at the far end, Mr. Browning. Quick !

> [*Behind her the figure and face of* Miss Grace *are expressive.*

Farmer. Gude ! Woi ! Over the waal 'e went. To him, boys ! Chop him before he'm into the spinney.

> [*The hue and cry passes the window, running—the* Two Labourers, *the* Constable, *and* Two Tourist Youths. *The cries die off and leave a charged silence—the* Two Ladies *on their feet.*

Matt. [*Emerging, still breathless, with his hat in his hand. Noting* Miss Dora's *riding kit, he turns to* Miss Grace] Thank you, madam.

Miss Grace. Not me.

Matt. [*Making a bow to* Miss Dora] That was great of you, great !

Miss Dora. Keep back—one of them might see.

> [*She draws the curtains as* Matt *shrinks back.*

Miss Grace. Great ! To tell such a lie ! And for a convict !

Matt. [*Recovering his self-possession*] If you'll forgive my saying so, that makes it greater. To tell a lie for an archbishop wouldn't strain one a bit.

MISS GRACE. Please don't blaspheme.

MISS DORA. [*Pouring out tea*] Will you have a cup of tea, sir?

MISS GRACE. [*In a low voice*] Really, Dora!

MATT. [*Dropping his hat and taking the cup from* MISS DORA] It's too good of you. [*He drinks it straight off and hands it back.*] I'm most awfully sorry for butting in like this; but it was neck or nothing.

MISS GRACE. Then I think it should have been nothing, sir, considering the position you've placed my poor sister in.

MISS DORA. [*Hotly*] Poor sister! Grace, you——!

MATT. When you're hunted all you think of is the next move.

MISS DORA. I'm afraid you're awfully done.

MATT. Thanks, I'm getting my wind back. I feel like kissing the hem of your garment.

MISS DORA. It hasn't got one. Wasn't it rather mad to escape?

MATT. I don't think so. It's shown me how decent people can be.

MISS DORA. Did they ill-treat you?

MATT. Oh! no, the treatment's all right—a trifle monotonous.

MISS DORA. Listen!   [*They listen. Faint shouting.*] Where are you making for?

MATT. No plan. They're no good. It's like a battle—you change 'em before you use 'em.

MISS DORA. I read who you were in the papers.

MATT. Oh! yes. I'm in big print? Thank you most awfully. I'll clear out now.

MISS DORA. No, wait! [*At the curtains.*] I'll be back in a minute.
                                        [*She slips out.*

MISS GRACE. [*Turning round to him*] I suppose you call yourself a gentleman?

MATT. I really don't know. Depends on who I'm with. I might be contradicted.

MISS GRACE. You see the sort of woman my sister is—impulsive, humanitarian. I'm—I'm very fond of her.

MATT. Naturally. She's splendid.

MISS GRACE. If you don't want to involve her——

MISS DORA. [*Reappearing through the curtains*] I think I can hide you.

MISS GRACE. Dora!

MATT. No, no! It's not good enough. I can't let you——

MISS DORA. [*Turning on her sister*] I'm going to, Grace.
                              [*They speak together in rapid tones.*

MISS GRACE. Not in this house.

MISS DORA. It's as much my house as yours. You need have nothing to do with it.

MISS GRACE. [*Drawing her from the window*] At least you haven't broken the law yet. And you're not going to now.

MISS DORA. I can't bear to see a soldier and a gentleman chased by a lot of chawbacons.

MISS GRACE. [*With a glance at* MATT] Dora, you mustn't. It's wrong and it's absurd.

MISS DORA. [*Heated*] Go upstairs. If I have to refer to you, I'll say you've seen nothing. And so can you.

MISS GRACE. [*Her voice rising*] You expect *me* to tell lies?

[MATT, *unseen in the heat of this discussion, makes a motion of despair and slips out of the window.*

MISS DORA. I'm going to hide him, I tell you. Captain—[*Suddenly turning to* MATT, *she sees that he is no longer there.*] Where is he?

[*The* TWO SISTERS *stand silent, blankly gazing about them.*

MISS DORA. Did he go by the door or the window?

MISS GRACE. I don't know.

MISS DORA. Didn't you see him?

MISS GRACE. I did not. [*At the expression on her sister's face.*] I say I did not.

[MISS DORA *looks behind the window curtain, then cautiously out of the window, then recoils before the* CONSTABLE, *who comes in heated and breathless, followed by the* FARMER *and the* FIRST LABOURER, *who stops outside.*

CONSTABLE. Beg pardon, miss. We've lost un. He'm a fair twister. Maybe he doubled back. We'll 'ave a luke over, if an' in case he'm hidin' yere somewhere about. Can we go thru yere?

MISS DORA. He can't be in the house.

[MISS GRACE *stands pursing her lips.*

FARMER. We med 'ave a luke, miss, after that. 'E'm a proper varmint.

[*Without waiting for further permission, the two pass through the room and go out, Left. The* TWO SISTERS *stand looking at each other.*

MISS DORA. I won't have him caught! [*She moves towards the door.*

MISS GRACE. [*Seizing her sister's skirt*] Stop! I tell you!

MISS DORA. Let go!

MISS GRACE. I shall not. You're crazy. What is it to you?

MISS DORA. Let go, Grace!

MISS GRACE. You can't help him without breaking the law.

MISS DORA. Will you let me go, Grace? I shall hit you.

MISS GRACE. Very well. Hit me, then!

[*The* TWO SISTERS *clinch ,and for a moment it looks as if there were to be a physical struggle between them. There are sounds of approach.*

MISS DORA. Let go!

[*They unclinch, and wait for the door to open. Re-enter the* FARMER *and* CONSTABLE.

33*

FARMER. Well, he'm not yere; that's certain for zure.

CONSTABLE. [*Between the two*] You're quite sure, miss, yu saw 'im over that wall?   [*A tense moment.*

MISS DORA. Quite! [MISS GRACE *has drawn her breath in with a hiss.*

FARMER. And not seen un since?

MISS DORA. No.

FARMER. Nor yu, miss?   [MISS DORA *stares at her sister.*

MISS GRACE. [*Throwing up her head, and with a face like a mask*] No.

FARMER. [*Picking up* MATT'S *hat, left by him as he fled*] 'Ere, what's this?

MISS DORA. [*Recovering*] That? An old hat of my brother's that I use sometimes.

FARMER. 'Tis uncommon like the one that varmint was wearin'.

MISS DORA. Is it? Those fishing hats are all the same. [*Taking the hat.*] Have you tried the orchard, Mr. Browning?

FARMER. Ah! we mun try that, but 'tis gettin' powerful dimsy. Come, boys, we mun 'ave a gude old luke. The varmint fuled me bravely. I mun get me own back.

MISS DORA. Try the vicarage!

CONSTABLE. Ah! we'll try that tu.   [*They pass out at the window.*

    [*The* TWO SISTERS *are left silent.* MISS GRACE *suddenly sits down at the table and covers her face with her hand.*

MISS DORA. You told it beautifully, Grace. Thank you!

MISS GRACE. [*Uncovering her face with a fierce gesture*] Thank me for telling a lie!

MISS DORA. I'm sorry.

MISS GRACE. Sorry? You'd make me do it again!

MISS DORA. [*Simply*] I would. [*Looking after the hunt.*] Poor fellow!   [*On the look between them*

       The curtain falls.

EPISODE IX

No time has passed. In the vestry of a village church lighted by an oil lamp, where, at the back, surplices and cassocks are hanging on pegs, a door, Right, leads to the churchyard and an open door, Left, into the church. There is no furniture except a chair or two, and a small table with a jug on it against the wall " up " from the door, Left.

    [*The stage is empty, but almost at once the* PARSON *enters from the church, carrying some overpast Harvest decorations, which he places on the table. He is a slim, grizzle-haired, brown, active, middle-aged man with a good, lined, clean-shaven face, and a black Norfolk jacket; obviously a little " High " in his doctrine. He pours water from a jug into two large vases, humming: " O for the wings—for the wings of a dove !" Then carrying the vases, one in each hand, he goes back into the church. The door on the Right is opened and the hunted, hatless* MATT *slips in, closing the door behind him. He stands taking in the situation, crosses to the open door opposite, spies the* PARSON, *and, recoiling, blots himself out behind a cassock. His face, peeping out, is withdrawn as the* PARSON *returns, this time literally singing: " O for the wings—for the wings of a dove !" Taking off his coat, he prepares to hang it on a peg and take a cassock, and as he reaches the highest note, he lifts the cassock from in front of* MATT *and starts back.*

PARSON. Hullo !

MATT. Sanctuary, sir !

PARSON. What d'you mean ?   Who are you ?

[MATT *opens his Burberry.*]

Oh !   [*That " Oh !" is something more than astonishment ; it has in it an accent of dismay, as if the speaker were confronted by his own soul.*] The escaped convict !   You oughtn't to have come in here.

MATT. Then where, sir ?   In old days the Church——

PARSON. In old days the Church was a thing apart ; now it belongs to the State.   [MATT *makes a move towards the door.*] Wait a minute !   [*He has hung up his coat and put on the cassock, as if to strengthen the priest within him.*] I think I read that you were that Captain Denant who——

MATT. Yes.

PARSON. [*Almost to himself*] Poor fellow !

[MATT *stares at him and there is a silence.*

MATT. Death isn't as much to us who were in the war, as it is to you.

PARSON. I know ; I was there.

MATT. Padre ?

PARSON. [*Nodding*] Where have you come from ?

MATT. House of the two ladies over there.   Left them fighting over me.   Couldn't stand that—not worth it.

PARSON. [*With a little smile*] Yes, Miss Dora wanted to keep you and Miss Grace to throw you out.   H'm ?   And yet Miss Dora doesn't come to church, and Miss Grace does.   Something wrong there ; or is it something right ?   [*He stares at* MATT.] Are they after you ?

MATT. Full cry.

PARSON. Sanctuary ?   If I were a Roman.   Sometimes wish I were.

MATT. More logical.

PARSON. More powerful. This is a situation I've never had to face, Captain Denant.

MATT. Well, sir, I'm just about done. If you could let me rest a bit, that's all I ask.

PARSON. My dear fellow! Sit down! [*He pulls a chair forward.*] I'll lock the door. [*He does so; then, as* MATT *looks up at the window, which is in the fourth wall.*] No, they can't see in. I expect you're very hungry too.

MATT. [*Sitting*] No, thanks—beyond it. You know that feeling, I bet?

PARSON. [*Shaking his head.*] I'm afraid we of the Church lead too regular lives.

MATT. Not at the Front? It was pretty rife *there*.

PARSON. No, I'm ashamed to say—not even there.
                    [*While speaking, he is evidently pondering and torn.*

MATT. [*Suddenly*] Well, Padre, how does it look to you? Giving me up?

PARSON. [*Moved*] Padre! [*He takes a turn and comes to a sudden halt in front of* MATT's *chair.*] As man to man—who am I to give you up? One poor fellow to another! [*Shaking his head.*] I can't help you to escape, but if you want rest, take it.

MATT. [*Suddenly*] Wonder what Christ would have done!

PARSON. [*Gravely*] That, Captain Denant, is the hardest question in the world. Nobody ever knows. You may answer this or that, but nobody ever knows. The more you read those writings, the more you realize that He was incalculable. You see—He was a genius! It makes it hard for us who try to follow Him. [*Gazing at* MATT, *who is sitting forward with his elbows on his knees and his head on his hands.*] Very tired?

MATT. Gosh! I didn't think one could feel so tired. My joints have gone on strike. I was a three-mile runner, too.

PARSON. Were you? Good man!

MATT. It's the strain here. [*Touching his head.*] If they get me and I have to go back! Odd! I didn't feel it half as much when I was escaping from Germany.

PARSON. Did anyone see you come in here?

MATT. Can't have—they'd have been in on my heels.

PARSON. Who's after you?

MATT. Villagers—and a constable.

PARSON. My villagers—and here am I——

MATT. [*Standing up*] By George, yes, Padre! It's too bad. I'll clear out.

PARSON. [*Putting his hand on his shoulder and pressing him back into the chair.*] No, no! Rest while you can. You've asked for sanctuary. I don't know that I've the right to turn you out of here. I

don't know—anyway I can't.   Take your time.   I have a little brandy
here.   Sometimes we get a faint in church.   [*He takes a bottle and a
little glass from the corner cupboard.*]   Drink it down.

MATT. [*Drinking it off.   Pulling out the flask*]   I say—I wonder if
you'd return *this* for me ; it's empty—to that name and address.
[*He takes a tailor-sewn label out of his pocket.*]   I ripped it off this Burberry.   You might say " with unending gratitude."   But please
don't give that name away.

PARSON.   No, no ; I'll see to it.   [*Pockets it.*]   Tell me !   What made
you escape ?

MATT.   Stick a bob-cat in a cage and open the door by mistake ;
and see what happens.   [*Looking at the* PARSON'S *face.*]   Oh !   Yes, I
know what you mean—but I've paid my scot long ago.

PARSON.   Didn't you have a fair trial ?

MATT.   You can't " try " bad luck.

PARSON.   All bad luck ?

MATT.   Well, I oughtn't to have hit him, of course ; original sin,
you know ; but for an ordinary knock-out six weeks is about all you'd
get ; and I got four years more for that Rotten Row rail.   Yes, I
think I was perfectly entitled to have a shot.

PARSON.   If you're quiet in your own mind—that's the only
thing.

MATT.   Well, you needn't worry, Padre.   I shall be caught all
right.

PARSON.   [*With a smile*]   I'm not worrying about that.   Cæsar can
look after himself, he has the habit.   What bothers me is my own
peace of mind.   I don't like the thoughts that keep rising in it.   You
led a company in the war.   And I lead——

MATT.   Your parishioners—um ?

PARSON.   Yes.   [*Nodding*]   When you're gone—shall I be entitled
to have been silent about you without telling *them* that I have been
silent ?   Am I entitled to refrain from helping the Law without
letting *them* know it ?   If I let them know it, can I keep what little
influence I now possess ?   And is it right for a parson to go on where
he has no influence ?   That's my trouble, Captain Denant.

MATT.   I see.   [*With a start.*]   Someone's trying the door.

[*The* PARSON *moves to the door, Right ;* MATT *has started forward.*
PARSON.   [*At the door*]   Who is that ?

VOICE OF BELLRINGER.   Me, zurr.

PARSON.   No, Thomas, I'm busy ; I can't let anyone into the church
now till Service time.   [*He stands listening, then returns, Centre.*]   My
bellringer.

MATT.   [*In a low voice*]   The hospitality of God—I shan't forget,
Padre.   But I don't want to be on your conscience.   I'll flit.   Wish
I had the wings of that dove, though !

PARSON. I have Service at half-past six. There will only be one or two gathered together, I'm afraid. Make a third. You can rest through the Service. No one comes in here.

MATT. You're a trump! But I'd rather go and take my chance again. It's dark now. I don't like to give in. I'll bolt, and be caught in the open. You might give me your blessing.

PARSON. [*Shaking his head*] Not certain enough of myself—not certain enough. It takes a bishop at least to give a blessing.

[*A very loud knocking on the door.*

MATT. Trapped, by George!

[*He springs towards the cassocks and blots himself out.*
[*The* PARSON *has gone again to the door.*

PARSON. [*Rather sharply*] What is that?

VOICE OF CONSTABLE. Open the door, zurr, please!

PARSON. Who is it?

VOICE OF CONSTABLE. Constable, zurr; open, please.

[*The* PARSON, *with a gesture of distress, opens the door. Enter the* CONSTABLE, *the* FARMER, *the* TWO LABOURERS, *and the* BELLRINGER.

PARSON. I told you, Thomas, I could see no one till after Service.

BELLRINGER. Yes, zurr; but Constable 'e thought you ought to know as 'ow I zeed a man enter 'ere a while back.   [*He looks round.*

PARSON. What's all this, Constable?

CONSTABLE. 'Tis th' escaped convict, zurr. We'm after 'e. These tu men yere found 'e down to the old gravel-pit. 'E give 'em the slip, an' we chased un to the ladies' 'ouse yonder, wherr 'e gave us the goo-by again; and Tammas says 'e saw a man come in 'ere as sounds praaperly like the varmint. You ben 'ere long, zurr?

PARSON. An hour, at least.

CONSTABLE. Front door's locked, but I got men in the porch. Be 'ee sure as there's no one in the church?

PARSON. [*Moving towards the church door*] I don't know whether you have the right to search a holy place; but look for yourselves, as quietly as you can, please. [*He stands at the church door to let them pass.*

[*They go, with the exception of the* BELLRINGER, *who has remained by the vestry door. The* PARSON *crosses to him.*]

You can go too, Thomas. I'll stand here.

[*The* BELLRINGER, *with uneasy eyes and motions, crosses under the compulsion of the* PARSON'S *glance.*

PARSON. [*Hardly moving his lips*] Now, quick!

[*But as he speaks, the* FARMER *reappears in the church doorway; the* PARSON *has just time to make a warning gesture,* MATT *just time to blot himself out again.*

PARSON. Well, Browning?

FARMER. 'Eem not therr ; 'tes zo bare's me 'and. 'Eem a proper twisty customer for sure, but we'll get 'e yet.

[*His eyes rest suspiciously on the* PARSON'S *face.*

PARSON. [*With a forced smile*] He got away from you, then, did he ?

FARMER. Aye ! 'E can run an' twist like a rabbit. He'm a desperate foxy chap. What's behind they cassocks ?

PARSON. [*Still with that forced smile*] I'll look, Browning.

[*He moves to the cassocks, and, from the middle, takes a look behind them, but to the Left only. And at this moment they all return from the church and he turns to them.*

CONSTABLE. Thank 'ee, zurr ; 'e'm not yere, Tammas. Yu made a fule of us zeemin'ly.

BELLRINGER. [*Stammering*] I zeed mun come in 'ere , I zeed mun wi' these eyes—I did zurely.

PARSON. [*Looking at his watch*] Service, Thomas. Go and ring the bell. [*To the* CONSTABLE.] I'm afraid I must ask you to go too, please, unless you would all like to stay for Service.

[*A certain length of face becomes apparent.*

CONSTABLE. [*Opening the door and beckoning the* MEN *out*] My juty, zurr, ef yu'll excuse us.

PARSON. That's all right, Constable.

FARMER. [*Suddenly*] Jest a minute, Vicar. Yu'll pardon me askin', but are yo zartun zure as yu'm not zeen this joker ?

PARSON. [*Drawing himself up*] What is it you are asking me ?

FARMER. I'm askin' yu on yure honour as a Christian gentleman, whether or no yu've zeen the escaped convict ?

[*After a moment's intense silence.*

PARSON. I——

MATT. [*Stepping out without the Burberry*] Certainly he's not. Sorry, sir, I was hidden there. [*Holding up his hands.*] I surrender, Constable.

FARMER. Woi ! The varmint ! Got un ! Worry, worry, worry !

PARSON. Be quiet in this place ; and go out—You shame God !

[*Astonished at this outburst, they slink out, leaving* MATT, *Centre, in the grip of the* CONSTABLE. *The* PARSON *is on his Left.*

MATT. [*To the* PARSON] Forgive me, sir ! Oughtn't to have come in here. It wasn't playing cricket.

PARSON. No, no ! That you *have* done—that you *have* done.

MATT. It's one's decent *self* one can't escape.

PARSON. Ah ! that's it ! [*Very low.*] God keep you !

[*He watches the* CONSTABLE *and* MATT *go out. The bell begins to ring, as*

The curtain falls.

EXILED

CAST OF THE ORIGINAL PRODUCTION UNDER MR.
LEON M. LION'S MANAGEMENT AT WYNDHAM'S
THEATRE, LONDON, JUNE 19, 1929.

SIR CHARLES DENBURY, BT	*Lewis Casson*
SIR JOHN MAZER	*Edmund Gwenn*
JOAN MAZER	*Jean Shepeard*
MISS CARD	*Mabel Russell*
MR. EAST	*J. H. Roberts*
HADDON	*Arthur Grenville*
GEORGE	*Douglas Jeffries*
A COMMERCIAL TRAVELLER	*Roger Maxwell*
A JOURNALIST	*Michael Shepley*
MO BENDER	*Aubrey Dexter*
JO TODD	*Pete Warren*
FOSTER	*Julian Andrews*
GOSSETT	*Victor Hilton*
TEBBUTT	*Sydney Benson*
TULLEY	*D. J. Williams*
HODGKIN	*Edward Irwin*
GASCOYNE	*Ernest Ruston*
CLARKE	*Granville Ferrier*
MITCHELL	*Jack Minster*
RICHARD TULLEY	*Campbell Logan*
GOFFER	*Ronald Kerr*
A TRAMP	*Brember Wills*
A WOMAN	*Una O'Connor*

The Play produced by LEON M. LION

ACT I

The billiard-room (at the back of which is the slightly-raised bar) of the "Rose and Nettle" Inn at Bableigh, near Nunchester. The clock points to ten-thirty on the day of the Nunchester Cup. The centre of the stage is occupied by a small billiard-table, end on to the foot-lights. Stage Left is a fireplace burning logs, though it is early May. There are arm-chairs above and below it, and a door leads off behind the arm-chair above into the commercial room. The other side of the room is right-angled by a bay-windowed excrescence, at the lower left-hand corner of which is a French window opening on to the hotel garden. The bar of the Inn extends along the whole of the back wall, except for a door, Right, into the hall, and a door, Left, into the smoking-room. So far as the room of an inn with a bar and a billiard-table in it can have a look of refinement, this room has—the Inn-KEEPER having once served in a good old family.

[Just now he is standing behind the bar, personable—say seventy— a brown-eyed old John Bull, watching his BARMAN mixing sherry and bitters for an obvious COMMERCIAL TRAVELLER, and an unobvious young man who is in fact a JOURNALIST.

C. TRAV. Flyin' Kite. 'Ow'd yer spell it?

BARMAN. K.I.T.E.

C. TRAV. Ow! The gell's nyme?

BARMAN. No. K.*I.*T.E.

C. TRAV. Ow! Not with an i—with an *i*. I see. Flyin' Kite. Good nyme for a ryce-'orse—with their 'abit of fallin' down.

INNKEEPER. Sir Charles never gave an 'orse a bad name.

C. TRAV. What Sir Charles is that, Mr. Innkeeper?

INNKEEPER. Sir Charles Denbury.

C. TRAV. One o' these new knights?

INNKEEPER. [*With a sniff*] Twelfth baronet.

C. TRAV. A Barronight? I see. So she's the goods for the Nunchester Cup.

BARMAN. Ah! they've tried 'er a cert.

C. TRAV. That's not promisin'.

INNKEEPER. Sir Charles never was one to keep a good thing dark.

C. TRAV. Aw! Then he's seen better days, I s'pose?

INNKEEPER. He used to own the land here and the coal under it.

C. Trav. Pore feller! I'd like to see 'im. A man that's goin' bankrupt 'as a peculiar look—too bright.

Innkeeper. When I was coachman at Luxford Hall in Sir Charles's grandfather's day, coal and land were property; now you can't get 'em taken off your hands. D'ye think I can make my farm pay? It's a hobby, that's all it is. Sir Charles has had to sell the house he was brought up in.

C. Trav. To an American? Bit gallin'.

Innkeeper. No. To Sir John Mazer.

C. Trav. Ow! One of our kings of industry.

Innkeeper. Head of the Mazer Company that closed the pits here.

Journalist. Has the last pit been closed long?

Innkeeper. Six months.

Journalist. How about the miners?

Innkeeper. [*Shaking his head*] Sad times here in Bableigh. Men that have been at it all their lives, and their fathers before them. Sad times.

Journalist. Sir Charles is staying here, isn't he? D'you know where he is just now?

Innkeeper. Are you connected with the Press?

Journalist. [*Smiling*] That is my weakness.

Innkeeper. Then I don't.

Journalist. But I've been told to get his views.

C. Trav. Never 'ave a view, you only 'ave to change 'em. Every season I travel a new fashion, and tell people why they gotta take the exact oppo*site* of what I told 'em last season was perfection.

[*While he speaks a gentle-looking person has entered from the French window, Right. He has a pocket camera, which he deposits on the bar.*]

Innkeeper. Well, Mr. East?

Mr. East. [*In a peculiarly soft and apologetic voice, which struggles with his r's*] I'm so sorry, but have you a clinical thermometer?

Innkeeper. What d'you want it for?

Mr. East. My dog. His eyes are very yellow. I should like to take his temperature.

Innkeeper. Is he bad?

Mr. East. I'm afraid so.

Innkeeper. I'll get one.   [*He goes out to the commercial room.*

Journalist. What breed of dog, sir?

Mr. East. A near-poodle?

Barman. If he's got jaundice you won't save 'im.

Mr. East. I shall try my best. He's an old friend.

Journalist. Where is he?

Mr. East. I have him in a little greenhouse outside here.

INNKEEPER. [*Re-entering with thermometer*] Here we are, Mr. East. I'll come with you.

MR. EAST. Thank you so much.

[*They go out through the French window, and can be seen through the window entering a greenhouse.*

C. TRAV. [*Fingering camera*] I got the facsimillar o' that at home.

BARMAN. Here, you got it wrong—facsimile.

C. TRAV. Nao! Think I can't speak me own language? So photography's 'is 'obby? Never 'ad an 'obby meself, too fatiguin'. [*To the* BARMAN] Another little drink for me, Sonny.

[*The* BARMAN *mixes another sherry and bitters.*

BARMAN. He's a professional photographer is Mr. East.

C. TRAV. Seems fond of animals.

JOURNALIST. Curious how much fonder of animals we English are than any other people!

C. TRAV. Ah! It's a bad sign. [*Taking cue.*] Shall we play fifty up?

JOURNALIST. Right. [*Taking cue.*] Why bad?

C. TRAV. Soppy. But I like to see the 'Umanitarians set about each other. An Antivivisectionist and a doctor. You can't 'ave better sport than that.

JOURNALIST. You wouldn't call a doctor humanitarian, would you?

C. TRAV. Well, he's supposed to 'ave a leanin' that way. [*Stringing out of baulk.*] What about this coal crisis?

JOURNALIST. [*Chalking his cue*] The British coal age is passing.

C. TRAV. Why! I read the other day we got enough coal to last five 'undred years, includin' bank 'olidays. [*Plays.*

JOURNALIST. Lots of coal and no profit on it. Evolution——

C. TRAV. [*To the* BARMAN] Are you going to mark, Job?

BARMAN. [*Dryly*] My name's George.

C. TRAV. My mistake. But what a pytient life—a barman's! Mixin' drinks for other fellers. [*He plays.*

[*The* BARMAN *comes from behind the bar, takes the rest and stands by the marking-board on the wall, stage Right.*]

What are you goin' to ask Sir Charles if 'e comes in?

JOURNALIST. [*Playing*] What more can be done for the miners.

C. TRAV. Well! if your paper's Conservative, he'll say: Nothing. If it's Liberal, he'll say: Everything. And if it's Labour, he'll say: Go to 'ell. My turn? I'll trouble you in a minute, Job.

JOURNALIST. [*To* BARMAN] What sort of man is Sir Charles?

BARMAN. Gentleman.

C. TRAV. The word's gone out. Try again!

BARMAN. [*Sulkily*] Well, he's just come back from Africa—photographin' live lions in a state o' nature.

C. TRAV. Wow! Is there any money in that?

[*As he speaks the door from the hall is opened, and a quiet, un-assuming man of middle age and height, in a tweed suit and a soft hat, comes in. He has a very brown, wrinkled face, and humorous mouth. He takes his hat off to the company at large, nods to the* BARMAN, *and crossing to the fireplace, sits down in an arm-chair, saying:* "Lemon juice, please, George."

BARMAN. Right-o, Sir Charles.

[*The* COMMERCIAL TRAVELLER, *after finishing the stroke he is engaged on, winks at the* JOURNALIST *and jerks his thumb towards* SIR CHARLES, *who is filling a pipe.*

C. TRAV. Go in and win.

[*The* JOURNALIST *leans his cue against the table and goes up to* SIR CHARLES.

JOURNALIST. Sir Charles Denbury? Would you be frightfully kind, sir, and give my paper your view of the coal situation here?

SIR CHARLES. [*With a twinkle*] My view! It's unprintable.

JOURNALIST. Of course, sir; but—er—could you tell me what you'd do about it if you were the country?

[*The* BARMAN *brings the decoction.*

SIR CHARLES. Thank you, George. [*Drinking it off.*] I'd rather tell you what will win the Cup. Flying Kite. D'you mind if I go and send a wire?

[*He slips from his chair and goes out into the smoking-room.*

C. TRAV. [*With a chuckle*] No flies on Sir Charles. [*Goggling.*] What you goin' to make him say in your article?

[MR. EAST *has entered from the French window and goes towards the bar.*

MR. EAST. [*To the* BARMAN] Could you give me a cheese sand-wich, and a glass of stout?

JOURNALIST. Dog better?

MR. EAST. He doesn't seem to be in pain. I have sent for the Vet.

C. TRAV. 'Ow's things in the photographin' line, sir?

MR. EAST. Fairly constant if I may say so.

C. TRAV. Ah! It's like drink. Any 'uman weakness gives very steady results.

[MR. EAST *picks up his camera, receives the sandwich and glass of stout, and takes them towards the window.*]

Well, I must go and get my bag and be off. Finish our game some time. [*He goes out into the commercial room.*

JOURNALIST. D'you know this part well?

MR. EAST. [*Sitting at the window*] I am a native of Nunchester.

JOURNALIST. Pretty country round.

MR. EAST. Beautiful.

JOURNALIST. See anything of the miners?

MR. EAST. I have taken portraits of some.   [*He nibbles.*

JOURNALIST. I want to find out their view of the situation.

MR. EAST. Their view is very simple.

JOURNALIST. How?

MR. EAST. [*Very softly*] Just bloody hell.

JOURNALIST. You've heard them?

MR. EAST. Frequently.

JOURNALIST. I don't wonder.   D'you know Sir Charles Denbury?

MR. EAST. I have that privilege.

JOURNALIST. He seems to be left high and dry, too.

MR. EAST. Yes. He has no royalties now, and no land.   His view is very similar.

JOURNALIST. Alas! My editor is too sensitive for simple Anglo-Saxon statements.

MR. EAST. I recently photographed an editor who spoke very vigorously about his own face.   I sometimes think with Shakespeare : " The face is out of drawing, O cursed spite that ever I was born to set it right ! "

JOURNALIST. Are you backing Sir Charles's horse?

MR. EAST. I shall have my little bit on.   May I ask if you believe in the Tote?   When a bookmaker gave me *his* views the other day, his face became an outsize.

JOURNALIST. And his views, too?

MR. EAST. Yes. People are very frank in the photographer's room.   A kind of desperation, I think.

JOURNALIST. Well, Mr. East, I must go and worry Sir Charles again.

[TWO MEN *have entered from the hall and gone up to the bar.   One is short and stout and one is tall and lean ; both are weathered, but more from whisky than from water.*

BARMAN. [*To the stout* MAN] What's yours, Mr. Bender?   Sherry? Ditto, Mr. Todd?

BENDER. This Flyin' Kite—any money goin'?   We're still layin' eights.

MR. EAST. [*From the window*] Might I have a sovereign on, each way?

BENDER. Certainly, Mr. East.   Jo, Mr. East quid each way, eights and twos.

JOURNALIST. [*To* MR. TODD] You might book me the same.

TODD. [*Jerking chin at* BENDER] Gent 'ere, Mo.

BENDER. Eights and twos.   Book it, Jo.

[TODD *takes name and money from* JOURNALIST.]

Now Sir Charles is back in England, I want an 'eart-to-'eart talk with 'im about this Tote. Someone's got to say a word for the poor bookmaker.

JOURNALIST. [*Pricking ears*] You're definitely averse?

BENDER. [*His face a study*] Averse! The English language isn't up to what I think.

JOURNALIST. Oh! have a shot. It's a rich tongue.

BENDER. 'Ard-workin' lot o' men and the bread taken out of their mouths by a bloomin' machine.

TODD. What's *your* complaint?

JOURNALIST. [*A little startled*] Journalism. Oh! I see! Sherry and bitters, please. [*To* BENDER.] Will you have one? Do tell me, what will happen to the bookmakers ruined by the Tote?

[*He puts down a coin for* BENDER's *drink*.

BENDER. What do you say, Jo? Gentleman wants to know what'll 'appen to us.

TODD. We'll just get outed. There'll be no National Fund got up for us.

JOURNALIST. Exactly! What price Evolution?

BENDER. Sir John Mazer's 'orse! 'E's favourite. D'you want to back it?

JOURNALIST. [*Laughing*] No, no! Excuse me—I—I've got a fish to land. [*He goes into the smoking-room*.

BENDER. [*Taking his sherry and bitters*] Thank 'ee, George! Did you read that about beer? Consumption goin' down all the time. And now you've got free tea to contend with. What a state o' things.

BARMAN. [*Deeply*] Ah!

BENDER. George, could you get me a word with Sir Charles? Won't keep 'im five minutes, but it's important.

BARMAN. I'll see. [*He goes into the smoking-room*.

BENDER. *You've* got the only soft job left, Mr. East. They'll never stop people bein' photographed by Act o' Parlyment. *You* know my views on this Tote.

MR. EAST. Yes; when you gave them to me the other day you broke a little blood-vessel.

BENDER. Ah! My nose bled, and no wonder. They'll run 'orses by machinery next; they'll 'ave waxwork jocks; shouldn't be surprised if they 'ave india-rubber grass. There's no 'uman nature left in anything. [*He grimaces*.

MR. EAST. Except the face.

[SIR CHARLES *comes in from the smoking-room*.

SIR CHARLES. What is it, Bender?

BENDER. This Tote, Sir Charles—you know us.

SIR CHARLES. Undoubtedly.

BENDER. Well, can't you say a word for us? Don't we give fair

odds ? Aren't we an honest lot—take us all round? Don't we
work 'ard in all weathers ?

SIR CHARLES. Quite.

BENDER. A blinkin' machine. This Tote don't get rheumatism ;
it's got no lungs, and it's got no guts. Times are 'ard for you too,
Sir Charles. You ought to feel for us. If this Tote comes in, a
lot of us'll be squeezed out.

SIR CHARLES. Don't you worry, Bender, you'll find a way round.
But your custom among the miners looks dicky, poor devils !

BENDER. [*Sententiously*] Ah ! it's a bad day for old England when
the miner can't afford to 'ave his bob on.

SIR CHARLES. Are they backing my mare ? I should like to
do them a turn.

[BENDER *looks somewhat stealthily round the room, and seeing
that* GEORGE *the barman is going out to the commercial room
with some glasses, comes a step closer to* SIR CHARLES.

BENDER. [*Beckoning to* TODD] Come 'ere, Jo.   [TODD *approaches.*]
This Sir John Mazer that owns the favourite.

SIR CHARLES. What about him ?

BENDER. Well ! They were sayin' in the " Red Lion " last night
that 'e sticks at nothin'.

SIR CHARLES. [*With a laugh*] The miners ? They would. He
closed the pits here, you know.

BENDER. Has your mare started for Nunchester, Sir Charles ?

SIR CHARLES. [*Looking at his watch*] Just about.

BENDER. Well, if I was you I should——

SIR CHARLES. Dash it ! This is England, Bender.

BENDER. You never can be too careful with 'orses, even in
England.

SIR CHARLES. [*Going to the telephone*] Give me Luxford sixty.
Hallo ? Foster ? Charles Denbury speaking. Everything all
right ? . . . Good ! . . . Boxing her by the eleven o'clock. Just
starting ? Right ! Take care of her. Good-bye !

BENDER. Jo, what about a prawn and a spot o' the boy before we
start. See you at the Races, Sir Charles.

[*The* TWO BOOKMAKERS *move towards the commercial room, and
go out.*

SIR CHARLES. Gather ye champagne while ye may. Are you on
my mare, Mr. East ?

MR. EAST. I have that pleasure.

SIR CHARLES. Hear what that fellow was saying ?

MR. EAST. I'm afraid so.

SIR CHARLES. Sir John Mazer—a millionaire ! Amusing how
horses breed suspicion ! Any experience of racing ?

MR. EAST. I once went, Sir Charles. A gentleman whom I

did not know was so kind as to back several horses for me—they were all last.

SIR CHARLES. They would be.

MR. EAST. And on my way home I played at three cards.

SIR CHARLES. That's usual, too.

MR. EAST. I had selected the right card, when, unfortunately, they had to leave the train.

SIR CHARLES. With your money?

MR. EAST. And my watch.

SIR CHARLES. Well, we all buy experience. I've had to buy mine in Africa.

MR. EAST. I was wondering—if you go out there again, Sir Charles, whether you could take me?

SIR CHARLES. You!

MR. EAST. I am very fond of animals; and, if I may say so, I can face anything with a camera except old ladies.

SIR CHARLES. It's an idea, Mr. East. Only I've put my last shirt on my mare, and if she wins I shan't need to go out again, thank God.

MR. EAST. I must hope then that she will win. But there is a certain dreariness in civilized photography.

SIR CHARLES. I hate leaving England, myself. You're not serious, are you?

MR. EAST. Quite serious. I think I should be a success with lions. My canary feeds out of my mouth.

SIR CHARLES. [*Going towards the smoking-room, but stopping to say*] These aren't the days to chuck a safe job.

MR. EAST. Safety first is rather boring, Sir Charles.

SIR CHARLES. That's the spirit. All right, then. If I do go, it's a bargain. I'd love to have someone from the old county.

[*He is going out into the smoking-room when* JOAN MAZER, *the pretty, but very modern, daughter of* SIR JOHN MAZER, *comes in from the garden, and halts to look at him. She is followed by* SIR JOHN MAZER'S SECRETARY, *a singularly lady-like person, made up to a certain shortage of her uncertain age.*

JOAN. [*Looking at* MR. EAST, *who is smiling and rubbing his hands—sotto voce*] Looney! Shall we play pills, Miss Card?

MISS CARD. A never have, but A should lake to tray.

[*They take cues.*

JOAN. I'm rotten myself. [*To* BARMAN, *who is bringing in freshly-washed glasses.*] The carburetter's gone phut. D'you mind letting us know when the car's all right—Sir John Mazer's car.

BARMAN. Right, Miss. The shover's comin' in when he's ready.

JOAN. [*To* MISS CARD] Dad'll be pretty sick if this Flying Kite beats Evolution. Are you going to back her, Miss Card?

MISS CARD. A hardly think Sir John would lake me to, Miss Mazer. A think he would prefer me to have ma little bit on his own horse.

JOAN. You *are* a posh secretary. I shall put my skirt on Flying Kite.

MISS CARD. You won't lose too much—he, he!

JOAN. Sir Charles looks a perfect darling. It was providential breaking down; this makes the fourth time I've run across him this week; and I haven't spoken to him yet.

MISS CARD. But how singulah!   [JOAN *plays and misses.*

JOAN. Well, I'm going to break the ice to-day. Your turn, Miss Card.   [MISS CARD *plays.*

MISS CARD. He, he! A've missed.

JOAN. Have a cocktail?

MISS CARD. A should love one.

JOAN. Two dry Martinis, please. [*Playing and missing.*] I do wish Dad would put in a table at Luxford. I cannot play this game. [*To* BARMAN.] You needn't mark. [*Lighting cigarette. To* MR. EAST.] D'you mind if we have a window open?

MR. EAST. Not at all. Fresh air is good even for lunatics, I believe.   [*He opens the window behind him.*

JOAN. I say, I didn't mean you to hear me.

MR. EAST. I was afraid you didn't.

JOAN. Well, we all look potty at times, don't we?

MISS CARD. [*Preparing to play*] A do when A'm playing billiards. [*Misses.*] He, he! A've missed.

[*The ladies take the cocktails from the* BARMAN.

JOAN. [*To* MR. EAST] Do you play pills?

MR. EAST. Only snooker, I fear.

JOAN. How marvellous!

MR. EAST. If I may ask, why?

JOAN. [*Taken aback*] Oh! I don't know. Why is it marvellous, Miss Card?   [*Plays and misses.*

MISS CARD. Snooker! He, he! [*Plays and misses.*] A wondah whay A miss.

BARMAN. [*To* JOAN *playing, and missing even her own ball*] If you cut the cloth, Miss, it's five quid.

JOAN. Not for beginners, surely?

[*The* BARMAN *with a shrug goes into the commercial room.*

MR. EAST. If you were to point your cue rather at the ball than at the cloth——

JOAN. I've tried that; then the cue slips up.

MR. EAST. Perhaps if you placed the thumb more firmly against the joint of the forefinger——

JOAN. What would happen then?

MR. EAST. Then I think you might hit your own ball.

JOAN. That'd be marvellous. I'll try. How's that?

[*Plays and misses.*

MR. EAST. Your ball *has* moved, you see.

JOAN. [*Taking chalk*] I believe it's all done by chalk. Isn't it, Mr.——? [*Chalking cue.*

MR. EAST. East, if I may say so.

JOAN. East? Oh! I say, that last photo you took of my Dad was marvellous, Mr. East. [*Offering chalk.*] Chalk, Miss Card?

MISS CARD. [*Taking chalk*] It was delaightful. The expression of the ayes.

MR. EAST. I was rather worried about that photograph.

JOAN. Oh! but it's got his best bulldog expression, with just that splash of Henry Ford that's so valuable.

MR. EAST. Yes, Sir John is one of the hopes of England.

MISS CARD. [*Who has been chalking her cue*] May one chalk the ball?

MR. EAST. I'm afraid it is not done by the best players.

MISS CARD. Quate! [*Playing.*] He, he! A haven't missed.

JOAN. Do you know Sir Charles Denbury?

MR. EAST. Yes.

JOAN. I wish you'd introduce me. He must simply hate us for having his place.

MR. EAST. He was very attached to it.

JOAN. I suppose he was frightfully hard up. Of course the land's worth nothing; land never is now.

MISS CARD. The farmers are quate extortionate, and always behind with the rent. I fear that land is a whate elephant.

JOAN. Don't you think Sir Charles is very attractive, Mr. East?

MR. EAST. He seems a very nice man.

JOAN. I've absolutely fallen for him—he's so brown and wrinkly. [*Plays and misses.*] Why don't you laugh at us?

MR. EAST. I am not feeling very gay.

JOAN. Why?

MR. EAST. My dog is ill.

JOAN. Oh! I hate animals to be ill.

MR. EAST. "When pain and anguish wring the brow."—Excuse me, I must go to him. [*He goes out by the French window.*

JOAN. [*Looking after him*] That ministering angel wheeze! Don't you hate it, Miss Card?

MISS CARD. No, A rather lake it. A love Tennyson.

JOAN. Let's go and see his poor tike.

MISS CARD. Quate!

[*As they go out through the French window the* COMMERCIAL TRAVELLER *with his sample bag and bowler hat on comes in from the commercial room, followed by the* BARMAN.

C. Trav. Quate! 'Ow culchad! Hairs and grices! Why the 'ell can't she speak the King's English?

[*He crosses to the door into the hall and goes out.*

[*The* Barman, *in possession of the scene, replaces cues and balls. He is retiring behind his bar when* Sir Charles *comes in from the smoking-room, followed by the young* Journalist.

Barman. Some miners want to see you, Sir Charles. They're in the commercial room.

Sir Charles. All right!

[*The* Barman *goes out into the commercial room.*

Journalist. You were just saying about Evolution, Sir Charles?

Sir Charles. There's always someone in its grip. Remember the old cabbies? No, you wouldn't. Now it's miners and farmers; and bookies and landlords for comic relief.

Journalist. And what's the remedy, sir? Are you one of those who put it all on the politician?

Sir Charles. Poor devils, no!

Journalist. But don't you think they might do more, sir?

Sir Charles. If they pulled together, certainly.

Journalist. But isn't it the essence of politics that they shouldn't?

Sir Charles. Looks like it. Labour pulls one way. Big Business pulls another. The Liberals prance and the Tories stick their toes in.

Journalist. Then you think the situation's hopeless?

Sir Charles. Well, the country's getting richer all the time.

Journalist. Yes. That makes it all the harder on the victims, doesn't it?

Sir Charles. Ever noticed a growing plantation—how the trees push up at each other's expense? It's the same with us, camouflage it as you like.

Journalist. But in the present state of affairs—— What would you do, sir, if you had your way?

Sir Charles. Increase agriculture; speed up emigration; abolish the slums.

Journalist. Do you think we shall?

Sir Charles. No. In these circumstances you'll have something to drink?

Journalist. No, thank you, sir. I feel rather upset.

Sir Charles. Brandy's a good restorative. [*To the returning* Barman.] George, two of the old Courvoisier.

[*The* Barman *brings the brandies. He has been followed in by the* Miners, *seven in number, ranging from* Tebbutt, *aged sixty-seven, to* Richard Tulley, *aged twenty-six.* Tebbutt *is a little, old, blue-marked miner with indrawn cheeks, as good a worker as the youngest.* Tulley *is a cheery, sturdy,*

grizzled, square-faced and sensible man of fifty-eight. HODGKIN
*is a bull of a man of fifty-six, with a shock of red hair gone
grey.* GASCOYNE *is lame, with refined eyes and brows, and
a cave-man's jaw; he is forty-eight.* CLARKE *is a tall fine
fellow of thirty-six, with the blue eyes and pink cheeks that
come of perfect health and an opinion of himself.* MITCHELL
is thirty—he looks worried to death. RICHARD TULLEY
is yellow-haired, with a broad, frank face.

SIR CHARLES. [*Raising his glass and tossing off his brandy*] Very glad
to see you all again. What'll you have? George!

[GEORGE *prepares a variety of drinks according to various tastes.*]
What's wrong with your leg, Gascoyne?

GASCOYNE. Bit 'f 'n accident in ta pit, Sir Charles, broke ma leg
in two places.

SIR CHARLES. Bad luck!

GASCOYNE. Well, a pension's soomthing nowadays.

[*The* MEN *are standing along the bar;* SIR CHARLES *is between
them and the fire. The* JOURNALIST *is seated on the arm of
the chair below the fireplace.*

SIR CHARLES. Do you want a tip, my friends?

HODGKIN. Eh, but we're all on Flyin' Kite, Sir Charles. Mo
Bender's got our money. Is she t'flyer they say?

SIR CHARLES. If she doesn't win, Hodgkin, there's nothing in
form; and she's fit to run for her life.

TULLEY. Sir Charles, can'st tell us wha Sir John Mazer closed
ta Blue Pit? Seein' tha've lost tha royalties, they've maybe given
tha t'reasons, now th' art back 'ome.

SIR CHARLES. Well! They showed me the accounts, Tulley. It
hasn't paid for two years. They're dropping money all the
time.

TULLEY. After all t'mooney they spent last year t' bring't oop to
date! It's sooch bad management.

SIR CHARLES. I can't judge of that. They told me there was
nothing for it but to cut their losses.

TEBBUTT. Forty year ah've worked in that pit. 'T'as been a good
pit, and 't'as got plenty life in't yet.

GASCOYNE. They'll never tek oop ta pit again—'twas always wet.
The water's in. 'T's stagnated for good an' all.

MITCHELL. Aye; and so's us stagnated. Without a by your
leave—done for—the lot of us. The managers 'ave got new jobs.
'Tis only us chaps.

[*A shuffle among the others, as if deprecating this note of shrillness.*

TULLEY. Ah! well—the 'ead manager was a good man. I've
noothin' against 'im. He was very oopset when they closed. In
ma opinion th' 'ad too much over'ead.

SIR CHARLES. God may know about that, Tulley. I don't. Coal's in a bad way all round.

[*The* TWO LADIES *come in at the French window and slide round to the window-seat, where they sit listening.* MR. EAST *follows, and stands just inside the French window.*

GASCOYNE. 'Tis in the marketin'—there's too much lost between ta pit'ead an' ta pooblic.

CLARKE. They've no call to shut a pit till they've found us chaaps fresh liveli'ood. 'Tis fair slaughter. That Mazer sticks at noothin'.

HODGKIN. 'E's a 'ard man Mazer. A Coompany 'as no guts.

JOAN. [*Sotto voce*] That's one for my dad.

MISS CARD. Pooah Sir John! His insaide—he, he!

JOURNALIST. [*Suddenly, as it were, coming to life*] It's terrible, I think—the position.

TEBBUTT. [*Out of a somewhat disconcerted silence*] Eh, laad! 'tis that.

JOURNALIST. But now that the Public are roused——

HODGKIN. The Pooblic! Pooblic's all raight, but 't'as got its 'ands full, payin' taxes, an' keeping ta police in order.

JOURNALIST. What will you do?

MITCHELL. Watch our feet coomin' through our boots. What else?   [*Again an uneasy shuffle at this outburst.*

JOURNALIST. [*Agitated*] The Government ought to have looked ahead sooner.

HODGKIN. Eh! but Goovernments are always late with the milk. When t' pig's dead they'll cure it, fast enoof.

SIR CHARLES. Are you out to take jobs if they're found for you?

MITCHELL. If ta worth takkin'. Better be stagnated 't home than stagnated some road Gawd knows where.

HODGKIN. Noon of us oop in years'll ever get jobs again, Sir Charles. Who'll tek an old un? Mebbe they'll send us abroad for slaughter, like t' old 'osses.

SIR CHARLES. My God! That's bitter, Hodgkin.

HODGKIN. I'm not bitter, Sir Charles. Not at all. We're oop against it. The coontry's in a moodle—that's a fact.

SIR CHARLES. Well, she always muddles through in time, Hodgkin, if that's any help.

TEBBUTT. Can't wait long myssen. Sixty-seven ah be. But ah can shift with the yoongest, yet.

SIR CHARLES. I know you can, Tebbutt. Stout fellow!

MITCHELL. The Bolshies'll be busy 'ere before long.

TULLEY. We don't want none o' they chaps.

MITCHELL. There's flesh and blood to be considered.

GASCOYNE. [*Deeply*] Miners father to son, and nowt but weed-stuff now.

SIR CHARLES. Why not the Dominions?

CLARKE. Not for me! The blinkin' things they want to know about a man. Aren't ah good enoof for them?

HODGKIN. They'll never tak' the old uns.

TEBBUTT. Ma grandsoon went to Canady, but 'e's coom back.

SIR CHARLES. Why?

TEBBUTT. 'Ome-sick.

SIR CHARLES. So was I in Africa, Tebbutt, but you learn to put up with it. There's Mr. East here begging me to take him if I have to go again.

HODGKIN. [*Turning*] Mr. East, that picture of mine's fine; the missus says she'd know it in the dark.

MR. EAST. Does she know it in the light, Mr. Hodgkin?

HODGKIN. Ah! That she does, she says you got my Soonday expression to the life.

MR. EAST. [*To the* MINERS *generally*] I wanted to say, as one of the public, I am terribly sorry for your position here. I shall be so happy to take your pictures without charge, if that is any comfort.

TULLEY. Mr. East, shake 'ands. Every man, woman, and child'll coom to thee.

MR. EAST. [*Shaking hands.*] I'm sure of that, Mr. Tulley.

SIR CHARLES. About my mare—I was going to suggest that you should all be a pound on her with me both ways.

JOAN. [*Sotto voce to* MISS CARD] Isn't he marvellous!

MISS CARD. Divane!

HODGKIN. [*With enthusiasm*] Eh! We'll noon of us say no to thaat, Sir Charles; an' I 'ope ta mare doos you joostice.

[BENDER *and* TODD, *followed by the* INNKEEPER, *come in from the commercial room.*

SIR CHARLES. Ah! Bender, all these gentlemen are on a pound with me both ways. Take their names.

[*While* TODD *is noting the names* JOAN *slips round the table.*

JOAN. [*To* BENDER, *taking out notes*] Will you put me on two pounds to win and one for a place, please.

BENDER. Right-o, Missy! Eights and twos. Jo, take 'er name.

TODD. What name?

JOAN. [*With a look at* SIR CHARLES] Joan Mazer.

TODD. [*Staring at her*] Mazer, did you say? Sir John's daughter?

[JOAN *nods.*

SIR CHARLES. [*More unconscious of her than she is of him*] George, drinks all round.

[*The* BARMAN *busies himself. The telephone bell rings, and the* INNKEEPER *attends to it.*

INNKEEPER. Foster to speak to you, Sir Charles.

[SIR CHARLES *goes to the telephone.*

SIR CHARLES. What! . . . *What!* . . .

[*At the first sound there is a pricking of ears, at the second, a dead silence.*

SIR CHARLES. Good God! The ruffian! . . . Do with him? Bring the brute here. . . . Can she walk? . . . Only just? My God! 'Phone the Vet, and lead her gently home. When I've seen this swine I'll be down. Don't let him get away from you. [*He leaves the 'phone and comes down, his face utterly changed.*] Foul play!

JOURNALIST. [*Taking out a note-book*] May I ask——?

SIR CHARLES. No! Put that away. If you stay here, kindly say nothing. [*To* BENDER.] My poor mare's been smashed at with a spanner by a brute of a tramp—she's dead lame.

JOAN. Oh! No!

BENDER. [*Shaking his head*] Eh, Jo? That's bad.

[*There is a growl from the* MINERS.

HODGKIN. Eh! boot that's moocky work—a doomb animal.

SIR CHARLES. The swine'll be here in five minutes.

MR. EAST. I trust the poor creature's leg is not broken?

SIR CHARLES. But for the knee-pad it might well have been.

HODGKIN. 'Ow did it 'appen, Sir Charles?

SIR CHARLES. They were taking her across the station yard to box her when this brute darted out from behind a truck, swung a spanner full force on her off fore, and bolted back to a motor-cycle. Luckily the thing didn't click, and they got him. The mare can hardly put foot to ground. So bang goes the Cup. Sorry, men.

TULLEY. Ma God, Sir Charles, 'tis a shockin' thing.

SIR CHARLES. And who's behind it? This fellow was a tool of course.

BENDER. What did I tell you, Sir Charles?

SIR CHARLES. Oh! That! Nonsense!

MITCHELL. So Mr. Bender knew, did 'e? [*His tone is unpleasant.*

BENDER. [*Sharply*] What's biting *you?*

CLARKE. Fooney thing to know!

MITCHELL. Takin' our mooney on the mare!

SIR CHARLES. Easy, easy! friends! We all know Mo Bender.

BENDER. [*Very angry, to the* MINERS] 'Ere, you! I'll 'ave none o' your money. 'And them their money, Jo, every one. I'll 'ave no man blackenin' my character. 'And the young lady 'er money too, and this young man 'ere. [*He points to the* JOURNALIST.

SIR CHARLES. Steady, Bender! It was all fair betting.

BENDER. Ah! 'twas all fair bettin', but I'll 'ave no man givin' me a black mark. I've a good name, I 'ave.

HODGKIN. Eh, man! but ye didn't tell us what ye telled Sir Charles.

34

BENDER. Why should I gossip to a set o' bl—— [*Catches sight of the* YOUNG WOMEN, *who are hanging on his words, and refrains*] black beetles like you?

MISS CARD. [*Uncontrollably*] He, he!

BENDER. You're gettin' your money back, aren't you?

SIR CHARLES. Very fair, Bender; too fair, I think.   My bet stands.

JOAN. And mine.

BENDER. No; pay the young lady, Jo.   As for those that think a bookmaker's not as honest as the best, I'll show 'em.

TULLEY. Ah never said nowt agen ye, Bender.

GASCOYNE. Nor ah.

RICHARD T. Nor ah.

TEBBUTT. Fair's the word wi' Mo Bender.

BENDER. [*Somewhat mollified*] 'T makes no matter.   I don' want your dollars.   I'll be on the rates meself before long.   Pay 'em off, Jo.   Pay off the blinkin' lot.

> [*While* TODD *is refunding the* MINERS' *stakes, the sound of a car is heard.* SIR CHARLES *crosses, Right, and looks out of the window.*

SIR CHARLES. They're coming!   Haddon, can I see this brute here?   Would you all be good enough to clear into the commercial room for a bit?   Young ladies, d'you mind going into the garden?   Mr. East, you can stay if you like.   [*To the* JOURNALIST, *who is making a sign as if he also would like to stay.*] No; I'd rather you didn't, sir.

> [*In a disappointed way the crowd begins trickling out into the commercial room.*

JOAN. [*To* MISS CARD] Shall we stay?

MISS CARD. I fear it would be rather unladylike.

> [*They go out through the French window.*
>
> [SIR CHARLES *takes his old position, back to the fire.* MR. EAST *his old position, on the window-seat.   Of the rest, the* INN-KEEPER *alone remains, standing behind the bar.   The door from the hall is opened, and* TWO MEN, *a* HEAD GROOM *and a* CHAUFFEUR, *enter with a bearded, wild-looking figure between them, whose hands are tied behind his back.   They bring him to the centre of the far side of the billiard-table, so that he stands facing* SIR CHARLES.

GROOM. Here he is, Sir Charles.

SIR CHARLES. [*Moving from the fire to the edge of the billiard-table, exactly opposite the tramp*] Free his hands.

> [*The* CHAUFFEUR *swings the strap free from the* TRAMP'S *hand.*

GROOM. Terribly sorry, Sir Charles.   The blighter was like greased lightnin'.

SIR CHARLES. All right, Foster. Better get back to the mare. If I want help with this fellow, I've got lots handy. [*To the* CHAUFFEUR.] Stand by, Gossett.

> [*The* HEAD GROOM *salutes and goes out into the hall; the* CHAUFFEUR *comes nearer the* TRAMP.

TRAMP. [*To the immaculate* CHAUFFEUR] Are you lousy?

CHAUFFEUR. [*In sheer surprise*] I? No.

TRAMP. Then don't you touch me.

SIR CHARLES. I am the owner of the mare you lamed.

TRAMP. [*With a start*] You? Wot's your name?

SIR CHARLES. Sir Charles Denbury. [*The* TRAMP *starts again.*] You can ride a motor-cycle, it seems. Not always a tramp, then?

TRAMP. [*Grinning*] 'Ave it your own way.

SIR CHARLES. Who put you up to this?

> [*The* TRAMP *shrugs his dishevelled shoulders.*]

Have you searched him, Gossett?

CHAUFFEUR. [*Rather ruefully*] Yes, Sir Charles. Nothin' on him.

SIR CHARLES. How much were you to get for trying to break the leg of my poor mare?

TRAMP. Poor? She 'as a better life than me, I know.

SIR CHARLES. You sickening brute! The only thing to be said for you is that those who bribed you are ten times worse. I want their blood so badly, that if you tell me who they are, you shall go scot-free.

TRAMP. An' if there ain't none, Guv'nor?

SIR CHARLES. Bosh! Tell me, or go to gaol.

> [*The* TRAMP *turns and is about to dart for the French window, when* MR. EAST *with a swift movement grips his throat from behind with both hands. The* TRAMP *gives an astonished gurgle.*

MR. EAST. [*From behind him*] Incline the head slightly, if you please.

TRAMP. Leggo. I'll stand easy.

SIR CHARLES. Thank you, Mr. East.

> [MR. EAST *places the* TRAMP *where he was and removes his hands.*

TRAMP. [*Turning on him*] You put your 'ands on me!

MR. EAST. I regret the necessity.

TRAMP. I'll have the law of you.

SIR CHARLES. Rats! Was the cycle yours?

TRAMP. [*Grinning*] Not bleedin' likely!

SIR CHARLES. Where did you sleep last night?

TRAMP. In Choke.

SIR CHARLES. Come now! Give me the name of the man who put you up to this.

TRAMP. [*Grinning*] No one put me up to it.

SIR CHARLES. [*Grimly*] Oh! So you haven't got your blood-money yet? Well, it won't come to you for some months.

TRAMP. If I go to quod——

SIR CHARLES. You're going to get the third degree first. What's your name?

TRAMP. We don't 'ave names on the road.

MR. EAST. [*To the* TRAMP] You are an Englishman?

TRAMP. I did my bit in the war, anyway.

MR. EAST. Was it a large bit?

TRAMP. Middlin'.

[*He pulls up a trouser-leg and shows a long scar and no sock.*

MR. EAST. Dear me! that was very near the tibia. Why did you sleep in prison last night?

TRAMP. For tryin' to sleep out of it. A poor beggar without a blasted sixpence, and mayn't sleep under the stars o' Gawd.

MR. EAST. That is poetry, if I may say so. Being a poet, how could you hit that poor mare?

TRAMP. She'll be all right in a month.

MR. EAST. It wasn't very English, was it?

TRAMP. If a man mayn't sleep on English soil, 'e ain't English.

MR. EAST. My sympathies are with you about sleeping out. Especially if one is lousy.

TRAMP. 'Oo says I'm lousy?

MR. EAST. Pardon me, I understood you to imply it.

TRAMP. Your mistake.

MR. EAST. [*Looking at his hands*] Thank you; that is very good news.

SIR CHARLES. [*To the* INNKEEPER] Got a coal-cellar you can lock, Haddon?

INNKEEPER. Yes, Sir Charles.

SIR CHARLES. I may want it for this chap. I'm going to have that name out of him.

TRAMP. [*Turning to the* INNKEEPER] I'll 'ave 'Abeas Corpius against the lot of you. Call this a free country!

MR. EAST. Not very. There is imprisonment even for cruelty to animals.

TRAMP. [*Sullenly*] I just 'it her, same as I'd like to 'it you.

MR. EAST. But *she* couldn't hit you back.

SIR CHARLES. Were you lying when you said you were in the war?

TRAMP. No.

SIR CHARLES. Where, then? If you've got anything in your favour, make the most of it.

TRAMP. I was gassed at Armonteers. I was blown up on the Somme. I was buried at Chatter Teary. I died o' fever in Mespot, an' I was drowned comin' 'ome.

SIR CHARLES. I see. The usual record. Where did you get that scar?

TRAMP. I got it savin' a cat at Ginchy.

SIR CHARLES. Saving what?

TRAMP. A bleedin' cat. She was the mascot for my platoon. An' a bit o' shell ran up my leg like a streak o' lightnin'. That cat lived to 'ave three families.

MR. EAST. Forgive me, but that sounds an heroic action.

TRAMP. Ah! I fished 'er up with an' ook out of a gassed pot-hole.

MR. EAST. Under fire, if I may ask?

TRAMP. Under fire! D'you think the war was a flahr-show?

MR. EAST. No; unfortunately, I was there.

TRAMP. Ah! Thought you'd been taught to speak by a sergeant-major.

MR. EAST. Yes; he was very careful that I should not reply to him in his own language. But if you did that for a cat, how could you hit that poor mare?

TRAMP. There you are—at it again.

SIR CHARLES. What were you before the war?

TRAMP. Motor mechanic.

SIR CHARLES. Why didn't you go back to it?

TRAMP. I did. But I 'ad an 'abit of shiverin'. So I lost that. Ah—and I lost something else—[*his face darkens*] and I took to whisky. Why? Because I was 'appy when I 'ad it inside me, and un'appy when I 'adn't. That's why!

MR. EAST. [*Who has been listening, absorbed*] Go on.

TRAMP. I got to walkin' from town to town lookin' for something regular, but there was a million an' a 'arf out o' work. If all that lot couldn't get a job, what was the use of me tryin'? So I went on the road. I've been on it four years now, an' I don't suppose I'll ever be off it again.

MR. EAST. Sleeping under the stars of God?

TRAMP. Ah! What is it to them where I sleep, s'long as I'm not doin' 'arm? *You* can bring out your five bob and say you're 'avin' a fresh-air cure, or some such classy bunk, an' they lick your boots and put you in the papers. But a poor beggar that 'ain't got the price of a room on 'im——

MR. EAST. True! But for money we should all be in prison.

TRAMP. That's the first sensible word I've 'eard from you.

MR. EAST. Thank you so much.

SIR CHARLES. Come now, give me that name. *Somebody* bribed you.

TRAMP. I wish somebody 'ad.

SIR CHARLES. What on earth, then, made you hit a harmless animal? Had you backed another horse?

TRAMP. I 'adn't backed no 'orse. And what's all this about 'armless animals? You'd shoot a pheasant. 'As 'e done you any 'arm? You'd break 'is leg an' let 'im die a lingerin' death.

SIR CHARLES. Thanks! We won't discuss the ethics of sport.

TRAMP. Nao. And 'ow about this 'ere vividsuction? You'd take an' 'armless dawg an' cut 'im up.

[*The* BARMAN *enters from the commercial room.*

BARMAN. The miners are gettin' impatient, Sir Charles.

SIR CHARLES. They can come in, Haddon.

[*The* INNKEEPER *goes out.*

MR. EAST. If you'll excuse me, I must go to my dog.

SIR CHARLES. Just a moment. George, take Mr. East's place down there.

[*The* BARMAN *comes round the table and stands between the* TRAMP
and the French window, out of which MR. EAST *passes.*]

Stand him against the wall.

[*The* CHAUFFEUR *and* BARMAN *hustle the* TRAMP *till his back
is to the wall, Right.*

[*The* MEN *come in, the* YOUNGER MEN *leading.*]

He won't give me the name of the blackguard who put him up to it. Perhaps you can get it from him.

[*He lights a cigarette and sits down in the arm-chair below the fire.*

[*The* JOURNALIST, *who has followed the* MEN *in, clings uneasily
to the other arm-chair.* TULLEY, TEBBUTT, GASCOYNE
and the INNKEEPER *are behind the bar; the other* FOUR
MEN *in front of it with* CLARKE *nearest, and* HODGKIN
farthest from the TRAMP.

CLARKE. Well, laad, think ye can get away wi' it, do ye? We're all a matter o' twel' poond out o' pocket owin' t' you. That needs compensation—it does.

[*The* TRAMP, *who has shown signs of real uneasiness, slowly regains
his hardihood.*

HODGKIN. Ma God, he's a lousy chaap!

SIR CHARLES. He says he was in the war, if that's in his favour.

CLARKE. Ba Goom, 'tis not. Sh'd know better. Was in t'war myssen.

RICHARD T. Dirty dog to soss an 'orse lik' thaat.

HODGKIN. Mr. Innkeeper, what's for lunch to-day?

INNKEEPER. Beef—chicken.

HODGKIN. 'Ot or cold?

INNKEEPER. Hot.

HODGKIN. Thaat's fine. [*To* RICHARD.] Goo an' fetch ta feathers from ta kitchen, laad. Mitchell, fetch ta boocket o' tar, that's oop against ta fence.

JOURNALIST. I say—this isn't America.

CLARKE. If 'twas, 'e'd 'ave a rope round 'is neck be now.

HODGKIN. 'E'll strip orkard. Laads, we'll toss 'oo's to strip ta lousy chaap.

[*The* FOUR YOUNGER MEN *and* HODGKIN *put coins on the backs of their hands.*]

King George—to strip un.   [*They look at the result.*]

Richard, Mitchell, Clarke.   Richard, off and get ta stoof!

[RICHARD *and* MITCHELL *go out into the commercial room.*

TRAMP. I'll fight the biggest of yer.

CLARKE. Na, laad, na.   You've 'ad your foon, 'tis our turn now.

[MR. EAST *re-enters from the garden, and the faces of the* TWO LADIES *are seen peering in at the open window ; they, too, re-enter by the French window.*

TRAMP. [*To* SIR CHARLES] Are you goin' to sit there and watch 'em lynch me ?   [SIR CHARLES *nods.*

CLARKE. We got families to feed, m'laad ; you've lost us mebbee a coople o' months' livin'.   We're goin' to tell you off all right.

[MITCHELL *and* RICHARD TULLEY *re-enter with the bucket of tar and the feathers, which they place on the bar.*

MR. EAST. [*Starting forward*] Are you really going to tar and feather him ?

HODGKIN. Thaat's right, Mr. East.

MR. EAST. Is it not rather extreme ?

HODGKIN. Roogh joostice.   But 't'll larn un to be a tud.   E'll be a nice soobject for a picture, Mr. East.

SIR CHARLES. [*Rising*] Haddon !

[*The* INNKEEPER *goes down to him.*]

Will one of you take George's place, please.

[MITCHELL *takes the* BARMAN'S *place.*]

Now, Haddon, take George and this gentleman away, and keep away yourself.   I'll see it's not done on your premises.

JOURNALIST. Really, Sir Charles, I do think——

SIR CHARLES. Yes ; go and think in there.

TULLEY. [*Coming forward*] Sir Charles, ah'm not likin' this, myssen.

SIR CHARLES. Suppose you go, too, then, Tulley.   Tebbutt ?

TEBBUTT. Na.   'Twill be a gradely sight.

[*He stands pat against the bar.*

[HADDON *shepherds the* JOURNALIST *out into the smoking-room.* TULLEY, *too, goes out into the commercial room.   The* BARMAN, *who has come round the bottom of the billiard-table, hesitates, looking back longingly.*

SIR CHARLES. No, George.   Off you go !

[*The* BARMAN *goes out into the commercial room.*]

Gossett, somebody take your place—you get off too. I don't want anyone to lose his job over this.

> [RICHARD TULLEY *takes the place of* GOSSETT, *who goes reluctantly out into the hall.*]

Now, Mr. East.

MR. EAST. I should prefer to remain.

SIR CHARLES. Very well. Gascoyne, you'd better go—you might lose your pension.

> [GASCOYNE *hesitates, then limps out into the commercial room. The* TRAMP *has watched these preparations for his execution with a sort of increasing wildness : he now starts forward to the edge of the billiard-table.*]

TRAMP. Call this yuman ?

SIR CHARLES. Extremely. [*Noticing the* LADIES.] Young ladies, do you mind going away ?

JOAN. Oh ! but Sir Charles, it's so thrilling !

SIR CHARLES. Good God !

MISS CARD. Quate !

SIR CHARLES. Well, stand clear of that window, please !

> [*The* LADIES *think better of it, and go out.*]

Now then. We're not bluffing. None of us here have anything at stake. I tried my mare for a certainty so far as there is such a thing. By laming her, you condemned me to exile. You took a nice little sum of money from each of my friends here, to whom it would have been a Godsend. You shall go free if you give me the name of the blackguard who put you up to this. If not—— [*He points to the bucket.*]

TRAMP. [*Sullenly*] I told yer—no one put me up to it.

SIR CHARLES. Then why——?

> [*For answer the* TRAMP *breaks suddenly free and seizes a cue that has been left on the table. Grasping it with both hands, he swings it round his head, backing towards the French window. The* MEN *recoil out of reach of the formidable swing. The* TRAMP *turns suddenly to escape through the French window, and finds* MR. EAST *standing in front of it.*

MR. EAST. I fear I am in your way.

TRAMP. [*Too close to use the cue*] You little barstard !

> [*The* MEN *have closed in on the* TRAMP *again and seized the cue. The* TRAMP *drops it and stands hunched up, covering his face with his arms.*

MR. EAST. [*Locking the French window and putting the key in his pocket. To the* MEN] Might I suggest that you leave him to me for a minute ?

SIR CHARLES. Stand back, my friends.

[*Something in the* TRAMP'S *attitude has impressed everybody. The* MEN *move to the top of the table and stand in a group, talking in low voices.* SIR CHARLES *stands watching.*

MR. EAST. Might I speak to him in private. I shall be happy to be tarred and feathered if I let him escape.

SIR CHARLES. [*To the* MEN] Shall we go out for a bit and stand by?

[*The* MEN *go out into the hall, and* SIR CHARLES *walks into the smoking-room.*

MR. EAST. We are alone, if I may say so.

TRAMP. [*Dropping his arm*] Oh! let a chap be!

MR. EAST. Had you some special trouble that made you run amok?

TRAMP. Ah!

MR. EAST. Will you tell me the nature of it?

TRAMP. No, I won't!

MR. EAST. Has it to do with a woman, then?

TRAMP. Yes.

MR. EAST. Your wife?

TRAMP. 'Ere! What are you—a bleedin' corkscrew? Yes, my wife.

MR. EAST. Something that made you curse your God.

TRAMP. Gawd! What should I do with a Gawd! Let me alone—I'm through.

MR. EAST. [*After gazing at him*] Will you promise to sit here a minute?

[*The* TRAMP *nods, turns up to the window-seat and sits bent in a sort of circle, as you may see a wood-louse curled up to avoid death.* MR. EAST *crosses to the door into the coffee-room.*

MR. EAST. Sir Charles.

[SIR CHARLES *comes out to him and they stand before the fire with their eyes on the* TRAMP.

MR. EAST. Some special trouble in connection with his wife seems to have made him run amok. And if he was really bribed perhaps we should respect him for not squealing.

SIR CHARLES. Um! I always hated seeing a fox broken up. But I don't know if the men will let him go.

MR. EAST. I think I could induce them.

SIR CHARLES. Well! Try!

MR. EAST. [*Goes to the door into the hall*] Will you come in, please?

[*The* FOUR MINERS *come in.*

[*Pointing*] You see him.

[*The* MEN *come down till they can see the hunched-up figure on the window-seat.*]

34*

He is down-and-out, if I may so express it. Sir Charles thought you might like to let him go, having your own misfortunes, and being Englishmen.

[*Uneasy movements among the* MEN, *then* HODGKIN *heaves himself and speaks.*

HODGKIN. That's all right, Mr. East, that's all right. Let the beggar go. We want the chaap that bribed 'im. 'Ere Richard, poot that stoof back.

[*The younger* MEN *move,* RICHARD *and* MITCHELL *take the tar and feathers, and they all clear off into the hall.*]

Sir Charles, I 'ope the mare'll soon be 'andy again. 'Tis roogh loock.

[SIR CHARLES *crosses to him and wrings his hand.*

SIR CHARLES. By George, Hodgkin, I wish to God I could do something for you all ; but we're in the soup together now.

HODGKIN. That's right. Spilt milk—ye can't scoop it oop. [*Turning to* MR. EAST.] Eh ! Mr. East—[*Pointing with his thumb towards the* TRAMP] that fellow—ef you want to photograph a bad dream. Well, good loock to you ; good loock, Sir Charles !

[*He follows the others out.*

SIR CHARLES. What good chaps ! Here ! Let the brute go before I think better of it.   [*He goes up to the fire and stands staring into it.*

[MR. EAST *crosses to the French window, unlocks and opens it, then approaches the* TRAMP.

MR. EAST. [*Touching him on the shoulder*] There is nothing now to detain you.

[*The* TRAMP *looks up, shrugs his unkempt body, then rises. He stands a moment gazing at* MR. EAST. *Then, with a shrug he shuffles to the door and passes out.*

SIR CHARLES. [*Turning from the fire*] This is a queer thing, you know, after what that bookie was saying.

MR. EAST. Sir John Mazer is too rich not to be honest, Sir Charles.

SIR CHARLES. I shall go and see him all the same. The beggar ought to do something for the miners. I must be off to my poor mare now.

MR. EAST. It is a terrible calamity, Sir Charles.

SIR CHARLES. Yes. It's good-bye to England for me. [*Catching sight of* JOAN *in the garden.*] Who's that pretty young vampire ? I'm always seeing her about.

MR. EAST. [*As* JOAN *comes in through the French window*] That is Sir John Mazer's daughter, Sir Charles.

SIR CHARLES. The deuce she is !

JOAN. Forgive my butting in. But our car's in action again— could I give you a lift anywhere to save time ?

SIR CHARLES. [*Dubiously*] Well—thanks, if you could drop me at the Stables.

JOAN. I'd drop you anywhere.   I never knew such frightful luck. You've been too marvellous.

> [SIR CHARLES *bows, and she precedes him into the hall with a bright look back.*

MR. EAST. [*To himself—with his head on one side*] Dear me! The human eye is very powerful! [*Suddenly remembering.*] Oh! My poor dog!

> [*He goes towards the French window as*

The curtain falls.

ACT II

The same morning, a few minutes later, in the study of SIR JOHN MAZER *king of industry, at Luxford Hall, once the seat of* SIR CHARLES DENBURY, *not far from Bableigh. The side walls of the room are lined to within some five feet of the ceiling with books that have a virginal aspect. Along the top of the bookcases are busts of Napoleon, Oliver Cromwell, Abraham Lincoln, and Mussolini. A door down stage, Right, leads into the drawing-room, and a door opposite into the hall. French windows Right and Left in the back wall lead on to a terrace and look over a park. Between them is a bookcase, which supports the bust of Julius Cæsar.*

> [*A table, sumptuously munitioned with papers and books of reference, with a telephone and a bowl of flowers, stands out parallel with the right-hand wall, and at it, back to the wall, sits* SIR JOHN, *a stocky man with a broad, self-made face, and a general look as if he were carved out of rubber, a material, indeed, which first made his fortune. He may be under sixty, and he may not. To him, from the hall, enters his lady-in-waiting,* MISS CARD.

SIR JOHN. Very late, Miss Card, very late !

MISS CARD. Miss Joan and A broke down, Sir John—at Bableigh. Bay the way, Sir John, Flaying Kate is scratched.

SIR JOHN. What's that ? Flying Kite—Denbury's mare ? Why ?

MISS CARD. The pooah deah was injured by a tramp, and they had to scratch her.

SIR JOHN. By Gosh ! That's luck ! I was afraid of that mare, Miss Card. Evolution'll about win now.

MISS CARD. A hope so, Sir John. The Press will be heah very soon now. Am A to telephone for the photographah ?

SIR JOHN. Yes, get that little chap in Nunchester High Street— what's his name—East. I'll sign and seal as soon as they're here.

MISS CARD. We saw Mr. East at the " Rose and Nettle " at Bableigh, Sir John. Shall I send a Ford for him, there ? [SIR JOHN *nods*.] [*Telephoning.*] Bableigh fave fave . . . no . . . not nane fave . . . double fave. . . . Could you get me Mr. East ? Oh ! . . . Mr. East, would you very kandly come at once to Luxford Hall to take a pictchah ? . . . At once. . . . We will send a car to fetch you. . . .

Yes, an interior. . . . No, not mane. . . . Sir John's. . . . Thank
you ; that is very kand of you. The car will be with you in ten
minutes. [*She drops the receiver and takes up a speaking tube.*] Is that
Whate ? Whate, would you kandly order a Ford to go at once to
" The Rose and Nettle " at Bableigh, to fetch Mr. East, the photographah. At once. Thank you. And if the Press comes—it can
be shown in. [*To* SIR JOHN.] Will you have the Rolls-Royce to go
to the races, Sir John ?   [SIR JOHN *nods.*]
Oh ! And, Whate—the Rolls-Royce for the races at one-fifteen.
[*To* SIR JOHN.] May A run through your engagements, Sir John ?

SIR JOHN. Ah ! Shoot !

MISS CARD. It is now eleven-thirty. Saign cheques and telephone
Malayan Rubbah. Eleven-forty : The Press, concerning the Coaline
Process Combane. Eleven-fifty : Affix the seal, and saign—with
pictchahs. Twelve o'clock : See two bulldogs. Twelve-ten :
Consider draft speech for the meeting of National Asphalt and Coal
Tar Corporation. Twelve-twenty : Superintendent of the Casual
Wards. Twelve-thirty : A have nothing for twelve-thirty.

SIR JOHN. Thank God !

MISS CARD. Twelve-forty : Papers in the Pontypool Power Con-
version. Twelve-fifty : Lunch. One-fifteen : To Nunchester races.
Fave——

SIR JOHN. That'll do, Miss Card ; shan't be alive. Give me the
cheques, and get on to Malayan Rubber.

[MISS CARD *places before him a pile of cheques, and takes up the
telephone.*

MISS CARD. A trunk call to London, please. Precaisely. . . .
Trunks : City, O three six nane . . . not fave . . . nane—nane
. . no, not nane nane—six nane.

[*As she hangs up the 'phone* JOAN *enters through the French window.*

JOAN. Heard about Flying Kite, Dad ?   [SIR JOHN *nods.*]
Isn't it perfectly rotten ?

SIR JOHN. [*Signing away*] Hard lines on Denbury !

JOAN. Yes, and he's such a dear. The miners at Bableigh nearly
tarred and feathered that tramp.

SIR JOHN. Serve the scoundrel right !

JOAN. We took Sir Charles to the stables. The mare's quite lame.
I say, Dad, the miners there are awfully on their uppers.

SIR JOHN. [*Signing*] Eh ! What ! Bableigh ! Beast of a pit that—
always was.

JOAN. I've been thinking.

SIR JOHN. Glad to hear it.

JOAN. *You* closed that pit.

SIR JOHN. [*Signing*] Course I closed it ; throwing good money
after bad.

JOAN. But—Dad——

SIR JOHN. Don't worry me, child.   [*Signs on.*

JOAN. If a child mayn't worry its own father——   [*Switching off.*] I'd backed Flying Kite.

SIR JOHN. What d'you do that for, with my horse running ?

JOAN. Because she'd have beaten him.

SIR JOHN. Well, now she won't ; and you've lost your money.

JOAN. No, I haven't.

SIR JOHN. [*With arrested pen*] How ?

JOAN. The bookmaker gave it me back.

SIR JOHN. Why ?

JOAN. He was sensitive.

SIR JOHN. [*With a laugh*] What !   A bookmaker ?   Fear of the Tote must be undermining their constitutions.   A lot of those chaps are marked for slaughter.   Good thing, too.

JOAN. Do you like seeing people ruined, Dad ?

SIR JOHN. What d'you mean ?   Of course I don't.

JOAN. I hate ruin—it's so wintry.   [*The telephone bell rings.*

MISS CARD. Yes ?   Is thet Malayan Rubbah ?   Sir John Mazer will speak to the Managah, please. . . . Is thet the Managah ?   [*Handing telephone to* SIR JOHN.] The Managah, Sir John.

SIR JOHN. ['*Phoning*] Hallo !   Look here !   That fresh issue— how's it going ?   Sticky ? . . . Um. . . . Tell 'em they've dam' well got to put it over, if they want any more business from me. . . . No. . . . I give 'em a week. . . . Oh !   yes, I know—depression. But it's got to be done, Wilkin, let 'em bite on that. . . . Keep me informed.   Good-bye !   [*Hanging up receiver.*] They're all the same —no guts.   [*The speaking tube whistles softly.*

MISS CARD. Yes, Whate. . . . The Press has arraved, Sir John.

SIR JOHN. [*Frowning*] Well, get my " What to Give 'Em " book out, and look up Combinations.

JOAN. Nothing like silk, dear.

SIR JOHN. Don't be a monkey.   Got it, Miss Card ?   [*Takes from* MISS CARD *a slim book.   Opens.   Reads.*] All right ; I've got the hang.

MISS CARD. [*Down the tube*] Show the Press in, Whate.

SIR JOHN. Get out the deed and seal ready for the photograph. Cut along, Joan.   You can't be in this.   [MISS CARD *busies herself.*

JOAN. Why not ?   " Right : Sir John's pretty young daughter."

[*The door from the hall is opened, and the* YOUNG JOURNALIST *enters.   JOAN hovers at the window.*

SIR JOHN. How de do ?

JOURNALIST. This is a great privilege, Sir John.   I understand from the prospectus that this Coaline process is going to save the coal situation.   Might I ask if that is true, or if it's—er—official ?

Sir John. You may grin, but it's both.   I shall want to see what you write.

Journalist. Certainly, Sir John.

Sir John. Well! This Combine will cover ten districts—you can get their names from my secretary here—the Coaline process will be applied at the pit's mouth.

Journalist. How many mouths would that be?

Sir John. Er——

Miss Card. [*As if to herself*] Sixty-fave.

Sir John. [*Severely*] Sixty-six—er—or rather less.

Journalist. Will that mean closing many more pits?

Sir John. Yes.

Journalist. How many?

Miss Card. [*As if to herself*] Twelve.

Sir John. Eleven—er—or rather more.

Journalist. More miners will be thrown out, then?   How many?

Sir John. About—er——

Miss Card. [*As if to herself*] Twenty thousand.

Sir John. Impossible to say exactly.

Journalist. And *their* mouths——

Sir John. Eh?

Journalist. Might I have your views on what ought to be done for them?

Sir John. What! That's for the Government. *We're* only concerned with making the coal industry pay again in this country. We're out to put coal back on an efficient basis.   The essence of Combines [*Stealing a look at his note-book, and not finding the right place*] is—er—er—more power of putting the fear of God into people. Don't *say* that!

Journalist. [*Writing*] A more authoritative position in regard to machinery, workers, middlemen, and consumers?

Sir John. That's what it comes to.

Journalist. Good for Big Business, and bad for everybody else.

Sir John. Eh!—er—Well! Put it nicely.

Journalist. That'll be all right, Sir John.   I'll translate it.   And you are to be Chairman?   [Sir John *nods*.] May I touch on your other activities?

Sir John. Malayan Rubber; National Asphalt, and Coal Tar Corporation; my secretary here can give you the others—so many of the confounded things.   [*A discreet whistle is heard.*

Miss Card. [*Smothering it and speaking into the tube*] Yes, Whate. . . . The photographah is heah, Sir John.

Sir John. Let 'em all come.

Journalist. The life of a king of industry like you, sir, must be pretty strenuous.   Do you ever get a rest?

Sir John. Yes.

Journalist. May I ask when?

Sir John. When I'm being photographed.

[Mr. East *enters from the hall, bearing a camera.*

Sir John. How de do, Mr. East? Got the guillotine, I see.

Mr. East. The process will be swift this morning, Sir John, the light is admirable.

Sir John. [*Putting his hand up to his hair*] Excuse me a minute, then.

[*He crosses and goes into the hall.* Mr. East *greets the* Journalist, *and goes over to pitch his camera.*

Miss Card. A should suggest at most a half-tame exposure.

Joan. Why, Miss Card?

Miss Card. A think Sir John maight go off the deep end this morning—he, he!

[*She gets out the seal. The* Journalist *writes in his note-book, and takes particulars from* Miss Card.

Joan. How's your dog, Mr. East?

Mr. East. The Vet has taken him. He says he can cure him.

Joan. They always say that.

Mr. East. That is true, I'm afraid. Am I to have the pleasure of making a portrait of you, Miss Mazer?

Joan. I hope so.

Mr. East. You like being photographed?

Joan. I adore it.

Mr. East. How frank! So many people adore it who don't say so. Usually they *say* they prefer the dentist.

Joan. Before or after?

Mr. East. Before, *and* sometimes after. I am hoping to photograph lions in future.

Joan. Here!

Mr. East. In Africa.

Joan. Wild lions? That'll be simply marvellous.

Mr. East. The tame lion is somewhat trying.

Joan. Yes, that's what's made him a lion.

Mr. East. I believe wild lions are singularly modest.

Joan. It sounds frightfully sporting, but why are you running wild like this?

Mr. East. I have had one or two misfortunes lately. The other day I was induced to photograph a baby for Balsopp's Bottles.

Joan. But that's not fatal, is it?

Mr. East. Unfortunately they had acquired the signature of a young lady, and they affixed it under my portrait of the baby, with the words, "My baby dotes on Balsopp's Bottles."

Joan. I still don't see the crime.

Mr. East. No? You see, she wasn't married.

JOAN. Oh! That *was* a bit steep.

MR. EAST. And it was a particularly hideous baby.

JOAN. D'you get many thrills like that?

MR. EAST. I have recently had to make a series of pictures for a patent food called Vital. "Richard Bott, at six years old," a singularly wretched-looking child; then "Richard Bott after taking Vital, at six years and three months"; "Richard Bott at six years six months, after the continued use of Vital." I do so wish I could take Richard at seven years, showing the permanent results of Vital.

JOAN. Well, won't you?

MR. EAST. I fear I shall not be allowed to photograph him in his coffin.

MISS CARD. He, he!

MR. EAST. I believe lions have no patent foods.

JOAN. You'll be their first, Mr. East.

MR. EAST. I trust not, for their sakes. I am very tough.

JOAN. Are you going alone?

MR. EAST. No—with Sir Charles Denbury.

JOAN. What! Is he going back there?

MR. EAST. Unfortunately he is ruined.

JOAN. I know; but there are other ways. Why doesn't he marry for instance?

MR. EAST. For that I believe you require a lady.

JOAN. There are lots about.

MR. EAST. Perhaps he does not care for any of them.

JOAN. That wouldn't matter at his age, if she had money and was young.

MR. EAST. Do you know of someone like that?

JOAN. [*Embarrassed by his gaze*] I say! Dad's taking his time, he must be putting some hair on.

MR. EAST. The need does not usually arise till after I have said " Just one more ! " four times.

MISS CARD. [*Having finished with the* JOURNALIST] Will you prefer Sir John to sit or to stand, Mr. East? You will find him more intellectual sitting.

MR. EAST. I shall not want his legs, if I may say so.

SIR JOHN. [*Re-entering*] What's the matter with my legs?

MR. EAST. I have not discovered anything, Sir John. Only, with a king of industry I should prefer to concentrate on the cranium.

JOAN. He's thinking of your feet of clay, dear.

SIR JOHN. [*Sticking out his jaw*] Dash it! I'm not in the police.

MR. EAST. I should like to stress the brain rather than the jaw, Sir John.

JOAN. Sit down and show your bumps, darling.

[SIR JOHN *sits down, taking up sealing-wax.*

Miss Card. [*Handing him the seal*] The seal, Sir John. Do you wish for realism? Shall A laight the candle?

Mr. East. If you could hold that for a minute.

[*Retires under black cloth.*

Sir John. [*Composing his expression*] Sing out when you're ready. How's that, Miss Card?

Miss Card. Psachologically, I think, raight, Sir John. Perhaps a little smale?

Joan. You're frowning, Dad.

Sir John. Good Gad! [*Grins.*] That do?

Mr. East. [*Emerging*] That is a little too hilarious. If I might know on what transaction you are setting the seal, Sir John?

Sir John. Well, it affects about sixty-five thousand people.

Mr. East. Could I get that expression on your face?

[Sir John *modifies his face.*

Mr. East. Thank you. If I may say so, the transaction is now affecting about fifty-two thousand people. I should be sorry to miss out the others.

Journalist. Does the sixty-five thousand include the twenty thousand that'll be thrown out of work, Sir John?

Joan. Yes, you want to throw in a spot of sorrow, Dad.

Sir John. [*Dumping down the seal*] Now, how the deuce am I to— sit—to pose—if—if—Joan, go away! And you, young man, kindly curb your curiosity.

Journalist. I'm very sorry, sir.

[Sir John *takes up the seal again, but he is now scowling heavily.*

Joan. [*Sotto voce*] Good practice for the lions, Mr. East.

Mr. East. [*Greatly embarrassed*] If I might suggest—thinking of something pleasant——

Sir John. Well, what?

Miss Card. Oysters, Sir John. Oh! dear! He, he! it's May.

[Sir John's *expression wobbles.*

Mr. East. Admirable! [*He shoots.*] May I take just *one* more?

Joan. Can't *I* be in this? I could be handing you the seal, Dad.

Miss Card. The Public would love the human touch, Sir John.

Sir John. Damn the Public!

Miss Card. Quate!

Journalist. I thought, sir, it was the Public you wanted to reach. Otherwise, I mean to say, why have a photograph at all?

Joan. If I'm in it they won't be able to confuse you with the Prime Minister receiving the freedom of Peebles, Dad.

Sir John. I don't know where the reverence of the young is. Here, take the seal!

Joan. [*Taking it*] Now, Mr. East?

Mr. East. [*To* Joan] Your head a little to one side, as if wondering what you were doing.

Joan. I see. Whimsical. D'you want Dad whimsical too?

Mr. East. If Sir John were reaching for the seal, with his mind fixed on the state of England. Your eyes straight into the camera, Sir John. It will give you a look of benevolent anxiety. Miss Joan, if you would think of a " Present from Blackpool "—the head a leetle —perfectly still for one second. [*Replaces cap.*] Thank you so much. May I take just *one* more?

Sir John. No.

Joan. Oh! come on, Dad.

Sir John. I will not.

Joan. Then come and take me, Mr. East, on the terrace.

[*A low whistle from the tube.*

Miss Card. Yes, Whate? . . . Sir Charles Denbury, Sir John.

Sir John. Denbury? I don't know what he wants.

Joan. I do.

Sir John. What?

Joan. He said he was coming to ask you to do something for the miners at Bableigh.

Sir John. In that case, I don't want to see him.

Miss Card. Shall A say you are indisposed, Sir John; or shall I merely tell him the truth?

Sir John. The truth? Of course not!

Miss Card. Quate! I will lay to him.

[*Goes towards the door to the hall.*

Joan. You *must* be civil, Dad; after all, we're his Jacobs——

Sir John. His what?

Joan. We supplanted him here. Besides, he's perfectly charming; and he's just had the most monstrous luck.

[Sir Charles *enters from the hall.*

Journalist. [*To* Sir John] If you'll excuse me, sir, I'll be going. [*To* Miss Card.] You'll let me have the photographs.

[*He greets* Sir Charles *in passing, and goes out into the hall.*

Sir John. [*Rising*] How are you, Denbury? Sorry to hear about your mare.

Sir Charles. Thank you. How are you?

Sir John. Overworked—otherwise bobbish.

Sir Charles. [*Nodding to* Mr. East, *who is at the French window, hovering with his camera*] Ah! Mr. East; been practising?

Joan. The lion in his den. Mr. East has great courage, Sir Charles; he's just going to shoot me.   [*Her demeanour is somewhat arch.*

Sir Charles. [*Dryly*] How exciting!

Miss Card. He, he!

Mr. East. If when you have finished your conversation, I might take just one more, Sir John, in case the expression should turn out a little too fierce.

Sir John. Well, well—if you must.

[Mr. East *goes out on to the terrace, followed by* Joan.

Miss Card. [*At the tube*] The maner has brought the bulldogs, Sir John. Shall A detain him?

Sir John. Yes, yes. [*She goes out into the hall.*] Now, Denbury! Sit down, won't you? [Sir Charles *sits.*] You remember this room, I suppose?

Sir Charles. I had thirty-six years of it.

Sir John. I like the place, you know. But I've had to spend the deuce of a lot of money on it, one way and another.

Sir Charles. Yes, I'm afraid we did let it down towards the end.

Sir John. You were—er—you were hard hit.

Sir Charles. Well, I had a grandfather. And then with my father dying three years after him, the double duties finished us off. You've got some pretty useful men of business up there.

[*Pointing at the busts.*

Sir John. [*Presenting Julius Cæsar*] Yes. That one of George Washington's good.

Sir Charles. [*With a smile*] Queer likeness to Julius Cæsar!

Sir John. [*Impervious*] Eh? What's that? About your mare, Denbury? Who put that ruffian up to it?

Sir Charles. [*Looking at him intently*] Couldn't get it out of him. Well, your horse will win now. I should have beaten you—my mare ran a wonderful trial.

Sir John. Shocking luck! Shocking!

Sir Charles. Ye-es. Means exile for me—going back to Africa for keeps. But I came to see you about the miners at Bableigh.

Sir John. [*Defensively*] What about them?

Sir Charles. Eight hundred of 'em, as stranded as myself.

Sir John. [*Impatiently*] If there were eight thousand, I can't help it. That pit was a regular sink. There was nothing for it but to cut it out.

Sir Charles. It's damned hard on those fellows and their families.

Sir John. It's a damned hard world, Denbury.

Sir Charles. Except for the Brass Pots.

Sir John. That's it—they swim because they're hard. This coal business has been tinkered with long enough. We've simply *got* to cut our losses.

Sir Charles. Your losses and their lives.

Sir John. What can I do? There's no getting round it, we must have a paying basis.

Sir Charles. Evolution! It's the devil!

SIR JOHN. Well, what's your remedy? You're not a Socialist.

SIR CHARLES. No; but even Big Business isn't entitled to scrap human beings wholesale.

SIR JOHN. It's the whole hog or nothing, in these times.

SIR CHARLES. [*Shrugging*] You don't mind what people say of you, I take it?

SIR JOHN. Not a kick.

SIR CHARLES. That's lucky. By the way, I passed that tramp just now, turning into your drive. I wondered if he were coming to see you.

SIR JOHN. *Me!*

SIR CHARLES. [*Switching off*] You don't feel you can do anything for those miners, then?

SIR JOHN. [*With a shrug*] It's up to the Government. We can't carry eight hundred families on our backs. Losing our capital's bad enough.

[*As he speaks* JOAN *enters through the open French window. A low whistle comes from the tube.*

SIR JOHN. [*Rising and taking it up*] Yes! . . . All right. Shall you be seeing the Cup, Denbury?

SIR CHARLES. No. You named your horse well, Mazer—Evolution first, the rest nowhere.

SIR JOHN. Let's hope so! Excuse me a minute, I've got to see some bulldogs. Joan, look after Sir Charles.

[*He walks out into the hall.*

[SIR CHARLES *has also risen, and turned towards the young woman, who comes down.*

JOAN. Pretty rotten for you, seeing other people here!

SIR CHARLES. Happily one seldom speaks the truth.

JOAN. If *I'd* lost an old family place, I should never rest until I'd got it back.

SIR CHARLES. What would you try—murder?

JOAN. [*With a quick look*] No—marriage.

SIR CHARLES. I see. Unluckily, the more the money, the shyer I should fight.

JOAN. But that's frightfully unpractical.

SIR CHARLES. We all have our weak points, Miss Mazer.

JOAN. What was this room in your day?

SIR CHARLES. A sort of sanctum.

JOAN. I see; nice and messy.

SIR CHARLES. Every mortal thing.

JOAN. Books.

SIR CHARLES. Yes, but read.

JOAN. [*Nodding*] These are stumers. We had them laid on. Dad *can* read, but he hasn't time.

SIR CHARLES. And you?

JOAN. Oh! I've got time, but I can't read.

SIR CHARLES. Not novels?

JOAN. Novels bore me to tears—except bloods, of course, about the " body " and all that. By the way, did you think me too terrible for wanting to see that tar and feathering?

SIR CHARLES. Oh, no! It seemed very natural. Sensation's the rule of the road now, isn't it?

JOAN. I suppose you don't think much of the modern girl?

SIR CHARLES. [*Politely*] Oh! Well! I don't understand her, of course.

JOAN. You don't *want* to understand her.

SIR CHARLES. Not *very* much, perhaps.

JOAN. That's not fair. You ought. She's a perfectly natural product.

SIR CHARLES. With slight additions?

JOAN. [*Touching her lips and cheeks*] Well! we don't wear bustles, anyway. What don't you understand about us?

SIR CHARLES. What you're after.

JOAN. I'll tell you—it's a great secret—A good time. But I suppose you were brought up to think men should have a good time and women shouldn't.

SIR CHARLES. Hardly so crude as that. No! My suspicion is that we, none of us, get a good time if we're after it.

JOAN. What *would* you go after, then?

SIR CHARLES. You have me—ask a moralist.

JOAN. Aren't you one?

SIR CHARLES. Not much!

JOAN. Oh! I thought that was just the difference between us.

SIR CHARLES. Well, perhaps a belief or two still hangs about my generation.

JOAN. I suppose you're bitter because you're exiled.

SIR CHARLES. [*Good-temperedly*] There's more than one kind of exile, Miss Mazer.

JOAN. Meaning the modern girl—no beliefs, no morals?

SIR CHARLES. [*Shrugging*] That's for you to judge.

JOAN. Look here! When you were a gay young spark I bet you thought you were a devil of a fellow, and were proud of it. Well, when *we* go gay we don't think we're devils of fellows, so we can't be proud of it. And that's all the difference.

SIR CHARLES. Very shrewd, young lady.

JOAN. What's the good of morals and beliefs? What do they lead to? Tell me that! I mean if you want me to go somewhere you must tell me why.   [SIR CHARLES *shrugs his shoulders.*

[*The face of the* TRAMP, *unseen, peers in at the shut French window, and withdraws itself.*

JOAN. No. You're not going to get out of it. If I want a thing, why shouldn't I have it? One can be certain about what one wants, anyway.

SIR CHARLES. Until one's got it.

JOAN. Now, honestly, [*Looking at him intently*] if you saw a thing you really wanted, would you let scruples, or good form, or whatever you call it, stand in the way of your getting it?

SIR CHARLES. Yes, and so would you.

JOAN. Would I? You've been too long in Africa. You simply mustn't go back.

SIR CHARLES. My dear young lady, I have no money, and, consequently, no choice.

JOAN. I say you have. You've only to—— Oh, well! While you're here, would you like to look into the other rooms, and see how beautifully we've spoiled *them*, too.

[*She goes towards the door into the drawing-room.*

SIR CHARLES. [*Following*] Thank you. It may be sentimental, but I should. [*They go out.*

[*The door is scarcely shut when the figure of the* TRAMP *passes the shut French window, looking in; then comes to the open French window, and stands there darkening the sunlight. At this moment* SIR JOHN *comes back into the room from the hall.*

SIR JOHN. Hallo! What the——?

TRAMP. Can I get a word with you, Guv'nor?

SIR JOHN. What d'you mean by coming round here—instead of——?

TRAMP. [*Stepping in*] Well, I put it to you—if I 'adn't come round, should I 'ave got a word with you?

SIR JOHN. No; and you won't now.

TRAMP. Excuse me, Guv'nor, but wot I've got to say is worth your listenin' to.

SIR JOHN. Are you the chap who lamed that mare?

TRAMP. Yes; luckily for you.

SIR JOHN. You confounded blackguard!

TRAMP. 'Ere, Guv'nor, considerin' what you stand to win by what I did——

SIR JOHN. Get out of here!

TRAMP. No, no! You 'aven't got the 'ang of it. You don't know what they're sayin' about you.

SIR JOHN. What the devil do you mean?

TRAMP. Well! You bein' unpopular and ownin' the favourite, there's some goin' about already sayin' it was you put me up to that job.

SIR JOHN. What!

TRAMP. And wot I can't see is why I should trouble to deny it, unless it's made worth my while. Slip me a tenner quiet, an' I'll deny it till I 'aven't a squeak left in me.

SIR JOHN. You impudent ruffian !

TRAMP. It's worth it, Guv'nor—mud sticks. You're not the miners' pet, you know. There's a good few round 'ere wantin' your blood, along o' closin' pits.

SIR JOHN. [*Taking up the tube*] I'm going to have the police called.

TRAMP. Won't do, Guv'nor. This ain't blackmail. I've just come to let you know I'm not goin' out o' my way unless it's made worth my while. What's it to me what they think about you ? The worse they think of you the better I shall like it.

SIR JOHN. What made you lame that mare ?

TRAMP. That's tellin', Guv'nor. You can't do nothin' to me ; so you'd better make the best o' me. You've hit a nasty snag, I tell you.

SIR JOHN. I don't believe a word you're saying. Suspecting *me !* Moonshine !

TRAMP. Well, see for yourself this afternoon. There'll be a lot o' miners at the races. [*He turns to go ; then turning back.*] If you want me, Guv'nor, when you've thought it over, blow your dog whistle. I'll be be'ind those bushes.

[*He turns abruptly and slips out of the window.*

SIR JOHN. [*To himself*] Infernal ruffian ! [*Taking up the tube.*] Hi ! Has Sir Charles Denbury gone ? . . . What ? . . . And Mr. East ? . . . Ask them both to come back here.   [*Enter* MISS CARD.] What is it, Miss Card, what is it ?

MISS CARD. The bulldogs, Sir John.

SIR JOHN. They must stand over.

MISS CARD. [*With an ill-advised and terribly refined facetiousness*] They rather do, don't they ? Quate marvellously bow-legged, pooah darlings ! He, he !

SIR JOHN. Blast the bulldogs !

MISS CARD. [*Frozen*] Quate. Is the maner who brought them to wait ?

SIR JOHN. Yes.

MISS CARD. Is anything the mattah, Sir John ?

SIR JOHN. Yes—no—why ?

MISS CARD. A only thought——

SIR JOHN. Well, don't !

MISS CARD. Quate.   [*She turns to the table and fills his pipe.*

[SIR JOHN *has gone restlessly to the open window, and stands glaring out of it.* SIR CHARLES, *followed by* MR. EAST *and* JOAN, *enter from the hall.*

SIR JOHN. [*Turning abruptly*] Look here, Denbury—about your mare?

SIR CHARLES. Yes?

SIR JOHN. Go away, Joan; and you too, Miss Card.

MISS CARD. Your pipe, Sir John.

[*She hands him the pipe, and a box of matches, then goes.* JOAN *sits down in her father's chair behind the table.*

SIR JOHN. D'you hear me, Joan?

JOAN. [*Unmoving*] Who wouldn't, dear?

SIR CHARLES. What about my mare?

SIR JOHN. Have you heard any gossip?

SIR CHARLES. Ask the miner who brought those dogs here.

SIR JOHN. Why?

SIR CHARLES. It's among the miners that the gossip runs.

SIR JOHN. They'd better be careful. Have *you* heard any gossip, Mr. East?

MR. EAST. Not yet, Sir John; but Nunchester is a cathedral city, if I may say so.

SIR JOHN. Um! [*Turning impatiently to* SIR CHARLES.] Now, Denbury, spit it out!

SIR CHARLES. Very well. It seems the miners in Bableigh are saying that *you* put that tramp up to laming my mare.

JOAN. [*Springing up*] Oh!

SIR CHARLES. Exactly!

[SIR JOHN *is in such a passion that he cannot speak.*] You must remember that you're in bad odour there.

SIR JOHN. The swine! [*Striding across to the tube and blowing into it.*] Bring that miner fellow here.

SIR CHARLES. He's a very good chap, Jo Hodgkin.

SIR JOHN. Is he? The most monstrous—the most outrageous——!

MR. EAST. If I might venture, Sir John——

SIR JOHN. Don't put your oar in.

MR. EAST. I *seem* to have caught a crab.

SIR JOHN. In all my life——

JOAN. [*Sitting again*] Don't get rattled, Dad. As if anybody in their senses——   [SIR JOHN *turns to the window.*

MR. EAST. [*Very softly*] " The heathen rage furiously together, and the people imagine a vain thing."

SIR JOHN. [*Turning*] What's that?

MR. EAST. A psalm, Sir John!

SIR JOHN. Blast!

[*Enter* MISS CARD *followed by* HODGKIN, *who obviously trails the bulldogs.*

MISS CARD. The miner, Sir John.

SIR JOHN. Leave those dogs outside.

MISS CARD. A will take them, pooah darlings.

[She takes the lead and disappears.

HODGKIN. Eh, Mr. East. Ah've told ma Missis about your offer to take a picture of 'er. She's composin' 'er faace already.

SIR JOHN. What have you and your mates been saying about me?

HODGKIN. Ah've said noothin'.

SIR JOHN. Oh! *You've* not, but *they* have. Well, what?

HODGKIN. Ah never tell tales.

SIR JOHN. Sir Charles Denbury says that some of you are going about saying that I procured the laming of his mare. Is that true?

HODGKIN. Ah've 'eard soomthing like it.

SIR JOHN. D'you believe the foul lie?

HODGKIN. If Ah'd believed it, Ah wouldn' want ma dawgs to associate with ye.

SIR JOHN. Is this because I closed your pit?

HODGKIN. Wha! Ye're not joost Bableigh's bonny boy, Sir John.

SIR JOHN. You know perfectly well we were losing money hand over fist.

HODGKIN. That's as mebbe; but when men are stagnated like us, 'tis yuman nature to squint a bit. Try goin' without your Soonday dinner, try seein' yer daughter there in split boots, ye'll not see ta man that cut ta brass off too straight-like.

SIR JOHN. Between that and spreading a foul lie——

HODGKIN. 'Tis your misfortune y'own ta favourite for ta Coop. If your 'orse wins this afternoon, there'll be a proper 'ullabaloo on the coorse.

SIR JOHN. D'you really mean to tell me that your mates can be such blood-blinded fools as to think I'd have truck with a filthy tramp, to lame a horse?

HODGKIN. *[Nodding]* Ah! There's soom of us'll believe anything of a man in your position. Ah'll speak frank—you've been one of the get-rich-quick, Sir John. You're a 'ard man o' business. Now, Sir Charles 'ere—we'd noon of us believe sooch a thing against 'im. Wha? Becos we know 'e can't take care of 'issen. 'Is grandfather was rich when yours was a workin' man like me. An' look where Sir Charles is now—stagnated, an' got to live in Afriky. There's no Noomber One with Sir Charles.

SIR CHARLES. Thank you for nothing, Hodgkin.

HODGKIN. *[At SIR JOHN]* But there's little Sir John Mazer'll stick at in the opinion o' those 'e've a-chucked into the gutter.

SIR JOHN. It's some Bolshy brute among them. How did they get this monstrous notion into their heads? Did that tramp——

HODGKIN. Ye'd find it 'ard to trace a thing lik' thaat. Soomone maybe says: "Well, 'oo stood to win by't?" Anoother says:

"Well, Mazer!" Anoother says: "Ah! that old blue-bottle!"
—if the young lady'll excuse me—"'E'd stick at noothin'." Then
the next man says: "'Ave ye 'eard about Mazer?" An' so't goes
round. Ah do a bit of thinkin', ah can see things oothers can't.
D'ye want to buy ma dawgs, Sir John?

SIR JOHN. I want to buy nothing till I've knocked this on the head.

HODGKIN. 'Twon't be easy. Men's thoughts are their own, an'
so's tha tongues. Think an' talk; they've little else to do in Bableigh.

SIR JOHN. Then I'll treat it with contempt, like the gutter-stuff it
is.

HODGKIN. Ah! but ah woodn't go to the Races.

SIR JOHN. I damned well will!

HODGKIN. [*Ironically*] That's ta stoof to give 'em! Well, ah'll be
takin' ma dawgs back. Coomin', Mr. East? Ah'd like to show 'em
to ye; they'd be the boys to tackle a lion in Afriky.

[*Saluting* SIR CHARLES *but not* SIR JOHN, *he goes out into the hall.*

JOAN. What does it matter, Dad? People are always thinking
the worst of other people. Who cares about a few disgruntled miners?

SIR JOHN. Be quiet! Denbury, you're a man of the world—what
do you say?

SIR CHARLES. Rumour travels at race meetings as it does in an
African forest.

SIR JOHN. Is there any way I can stop it?

SIR CHARLES. I believe the miners' char-a-bancs start from the
"Rose and Nettle" at noon. [*Looks at his watch.*] It's just that now.
You might catch them, you can get there in five minutes.

SIR JOHN. See the brutes?

SIR CHARLES. If that's the way you regard them—no.

SIR JOHN. Well! How would you look on men who believed a
thing like that about you?

SIR CHARLES. If you could get hold of that tramp——

SIR JOHN. He's out there.   [*Pointing.*

SIR CHARLES. What! Have you—seen him?

SIR JOHN. [*Sullenly*] Yes; the barefaced ruffian wants paying to
deny it.

SIR CHARLES. [*Dubiously*] H'm!

SIR JOHN. [*Rounding on him*] By Gad, Denbury, if I thought that
you——

JOAN. [*Quickly*] Dad! What utter nonsense!

SIR CHARLES. [*With a little bow to her*] Thank you, Miss Mazer,
I couldn't have put it better myself.

SIR JOHN. Sorry! I'm—I'm rattled. Suppose they do hoot my
horse.—You know the ropes, whát d'you say?

SIR CHARLES. [*With a shrug*] Those who know you won't believe,
or—will, according to what your dealings with them may have been.

As to the rest : responsible people won't believe it, but it always tickles the groundlings to believe the worst about a rich man.

SIR JOHN. Hell ! It's fantastic.

SIR CHARLES. Get hold of that tramp and see the miners. I'll come too, if you like, to show there's no ill feeling.

JOAN. That's terribly sweet of you.

SIR JOHN. [*Gruffly*] Thanks ! Thanks ! I'll get that brute in.

    [*He takes a dog whistle from his pocket and blows it.*

SIR CHARLES. Take Mr. East, he's a good man in a tight place.

    [*The* TRAMP *has appeared in the window.* SIR CHARLES *turns his back on him.*

TRAMP. Well, Guv'nor ?

SIR JOHN. I'm going to see the miners, and you're coming too.

TRAMP. Cash before delivery, Guv'nor. I'll want the money first.

SIR JOHN. What ! I don't trust you a yard !

TRAMP. Same 'ere, Guv'nor ; and I got a need for that money.

SIR JOHN. Need ? What d'you mean, need ?

TRAMP. It's a private matter, but I don't mind tellin' '*im*. [*Pointing to* MR. EAST] He can do the job for me. I'll want 'im to go to prison.

MR. EAST. If you'll excuse me, I should prefer to commit my own crimes.

TRAMP. Nao, nao ! It's just to pay a fine for a third party.

    [MR. EAST *crosses to him. . . .* JOAN *takes up the speaking tube.*

JOAN. White. . . . The Rolls-Royce at once. And please bring an old Burberry and a cap. [*To* MR. EAST.] The Ford's still out there, Mr. East ; you'll want it if you're going to the prison.

MR. EAST. Thank you, it would be highly suitable.

          [SIR JOHN *crosses, and goes into the hall.*

JOAN. [*To* SIR CHARLES] I wouldn't have missed this for worlds.

SIR CHARLES. Oh! why?

JOAN I simply love seeing fur fly.   [SIR CHARLES *shrugs.*] Is that very cynical ?

SIR CHARLES. Very.

JOAN. Well, *you* needn't worry—you're scratch-proof.

    [MISS CARD *comes in bearing a Burberry and fishing hat. She is followed shortly after by* SIR JOHN.

MISS CARD. [*To the* TRAMP] A think you may lake to put these on.

TRAMP. That's right, miss. I'd be sorry to disgrace a Rolls-Royce.

    [*He puts them on, squashing his own battered cap into a pocket.*

MISS CARD. You will faind the chauffeur with the Rolls at the front door.

MR. EAST. I require ten pounds, Sir John. The object is laudable, if I may say so.

SIR JOHN. Ruffian ! Here you are ! [*Handing* MR. EAST *a ten-pound note*] Take the Ford.

MR. EAST. Thank you! I will do what he wants, and join you at the "Rose and Nettle." Do you mind if I give Mr. Hodgkin's dogs a lift, Sir John?

SIR JOHN. You may give a lift to the devil, if you like.

MISS CARD. He, he!

MR. EAST. [*To the* TRAMP] You trust me with the ten pounds?

TRAMP. Yes, you're a yuman bein'.

MR. EAST. That is a proud distinction, if I may say so.

SIR CHARLES. [*Suddenly turning*] I'm not too damned sure of that.

[MR. EAST *and the* TRAMP *go out by the French window.*

JOAN. [*To* SIR JOHN] You'll take me, Dad?

SIR JOHN. I will not.   [*He goes towards the hall.*

JOAN. [*To his back as he goes out*] I'm afraid you will, dear.

MISS CARD. [*As they are following out*] A very maild animal really, the British bulldog!

The curtain falls.

ACT III

SCENE I

A few minutes later. The scene is again the bar and billiard-room of the "Rose and Nettle" Inn.

> [*The* BARMAN *is at work behind his bar.* JOAN, *followed by the* TRAMP, *enters from the hall. She goes over to the hearth, where she fiddles with a cue which is resting there. The* TRAMP *stands by the billiard-marking machine.*

BARMAN. [*Alarmed*] Excuse me, miss, you're not goin' to play billiards with 'im?

JOAN. [*Laughing and putting down the cue*] No. It's all right. My father'll be here in a minute. He wants to see the miners.

BARMAN. They've gone aboard the char-a-bangs. To get a miner off a char-a-bang's like gettin' toffee off a tooth.

JOAN. Sir Charles is performing the operation. [*To the* TRAMP.] Have you had any breakfast?

TRAMP. No.

JOAN. I say! [*To* BARMAN.] Could you get him a cup of coffee and a sandwich?   [*The* BARMAN *hesitates, then goes.*] Where are you going to sleep to-night?

TRAMP. Under the stars. But don't mention it, lidy.

JOAN. Why not?

TRAMP. There's a predijuce against it.

JOAN. Why, it's the one thing I envy you!

TRAMP. [*Sardonically*] Eggsactly. That's what I say—it's their jealousy.

JOAN. D'you mean they won't let you?

TRAMP. Not if they know it.

JOAN. Why not?

TRAMP. It excites 'em to see a man as poor as that.

JOAN. What a shame!

TRAMP. Quite right, Miss!

> [SIR JOHN *enters from the hall, followed by the* INNKEEPER, *and walks over to the hearth. The* INNKEEPER *advances in front of the bar.* JOAN *sits in the armchair above the hearth.*

SIR JOHN. [*Before the hearth*] D'you get the miners' custom *here?*

INNKEEPER. No. The " Red Lion's " their house.

SIR JOHN. Heard the outrageous rumour they're putting about ?

INNKEEPER. [*Uncomfortably*] Well, Bableigh's a little place, Sir John.

SIR JOHN. You were at Luxford 'All—Hall—once, weren't you ?

INNKEEPER. Yes, and me father before me, and his father. I left when it was sold to you.

SIR JOHN. Um. D'*you* think I've treated the miners here badly ?

INNKEEPER. [*Sturdily*] As you ask me, I do.

SIR JOHN. Oh ! You hold your farm from me.—D'you pay for labour that you don't need ? No ! And even then you don't make your rent, or so you say.

> [*Fortunately for the* INNKEEPER *at this moment the* BARMAN *re-enters with fodder for the* TRAMP, *who takes it and sits on the end of the window-seat, eating.*

BARMAN. They're comin' up the garden.

INNKEEPER. Bring 'em in through the window, George.

> [*The* BARMAN *goes out through the French window.*

SIR JOHN. [*Pursuing his offensive*] You'd like your farm subsidized by the State, perhaps ?

INNKEEPER. No, Sir John, no. I don't hold with Socialism.

SIR JOHN. And yet you blame me when I try to make my concerns pay their own way. Oh ! well—there are lots like you. The country's crammed with them. Shallow-pated—— !

> [SIR CHARLES *has appeared at the French window. The* TRAMP *swigs off his coffee and moves away to the bar, where he stands wolfing his sandwich and edging towards the hearth side.*

JOAN. [*Sotto voce*] Now, Dad, don't go off the deep end ! Think of the House of Lords !

SIR CHARLES. [*To the* MINERS] Shall we come in ?

> [*The troop of* MINERS *comes in. All those, except* HODGKIN, *who were present before, and four others :* GOFFER, *a thin, dry, grey-haired man with a lawyer-like gift of the gab ; a saturnine, moustached fellow ; a pale and emaciated man with a short beard as from illness ; and a young fellow, very red in the face, with his hair sticking up in spikes. All are in their Sunday best for the races. They fill the recess, overflowing almost to the edge of the billiard-table, and stare at* SIR JOHN, *who returns the stare with interest.* SIR CHARLES *crosses below the table to the fireside.*

SIR JOHN. I hear you've been good enough to suggest that I bribed this fellow here to lame Sir Charles Denbury's mare.

> [*There is no answer from the* MINERS.]

So you daren't say it to my face ? Come on ; out with it ! I want to know whom to proceed against for slander.

TULLEY. Best proceed against the lot of us, Sir John—tha'st not left too mooch mooney in Bableigh.

SIR JOHN. It's right down cowardly to spread such a report behind a man's back ; and you'll just dam' well stop it.

JOAN. [*Sotto voce*] Dad, the House of Lords !

GOFFER. Ye can't stop men thinkin'.

SIR JOHN. I can stop them talking, and I will.

MITCHELL. Try it.

SIR JOHN. You know you none of you believe it. Ask this fellow to my face.

GOFFER. What's ta good o' that in a poot-oop job ?

SIR JOHN. You be careful ! [*To the* TRAMP, *who is leaning back against the middle of the bar*] Did I ever speak to you before this morning ?

TRAMP. Yes.

SIR JOHN. What ! Where ?

TRAMP. In the Court yesterday, you give me a night cells for sleepin' out.

SIR JOHN. Oh ! Wish I'd given you ten. Is that the only time ?

TRAMP. Yes.

SIR JOHN. Will you swear that ?

TRAMP. I will.

CLARKE. Will ye swear no brass 'as passed between ye ?

TRAMP. [*With a grin*] I'll swear that too.

MITCHELL. Easy sworn.

SIR CHARLES. [*Quietly*] This is a wild notion, my friends. It wasn't in your heads an hour ago.

TULLEY. Art tha satisfied thissen, Sir Charles ?

SIR CHARLES. Of course I'm satisfied, Tulley.

TULLEY. What Sir Charles says goes for me. 'Twas 'is mare. If Sir Charles is satisfied, that's enoof. [*Murmuring from some of the* MEN.

SIR JOHN. The whole thing is spite, because I closed your pit.

MITCHELL. Ah ! And wha did ye close it ? We never 'ad no reasons given us. Ye chucked us on the scrap'eap wi'out a word.

SIR JOHN. It didn't pay—you know that as well as I do.

GASCOYNE. Ye should have managed better, then. Ye've got wages down, ye've got ta eight-'our day. 'Tis just bad management.

SIR JOHN. Bosh !

GOFFER. That's it. Ye tak' our livin' from us, an' when we open our mouths, ye answer " Bosh ! " I tell ye this : if we think ye've got the right these days to scrap 'undreds of men, women, and children, without so mooch as " By your leave," ye make a big mistake.

SIR JOHN. Now we're getting down to it. I say I have the right. It's the only way to put industry on its legs again.

TULLEY. What's tha say to that, Sir Charles ?

SIR CHARLES. It's the question we're all faced with these days, Tulley, and it's devilish hard to answer.

GASCOYNE. Well, if you'd been in Sir John Mazer's place, would ye 'ave closed ta pit and stagnated one an' all, without givin' us a say in it?

SIR CHARLES. No, I would not. Sooner than that I'd have given you the pit.

CLARKE. Ah! that's talkin'. Given us ta pit. An' wha not? Now ta water's in, 'tis gone for ever. We'd 'a saved ta pit—we would thaat. Ah! and made it pay.

SIR JOHN. [*Grimly*] I'd like to have seen you.

GOFFER. Then wha didn't ye give us the chance?

SIR JOHN. Because I don't believe in Labour running things.

GOFFER. Fact is, ye don't believe in anything but yissen. What's it to you if we've nowt before us?

SIR JOHN. You've got the dole; and you've got the rates.

GOFFER. Ah! An' would we if you and your laikes 'ad your way? Missen 'eard you say the dole was ruinin' the coontry.

SIR JOHN. Well, you've got the Government.

GOFFER. Shall Ah tell thee what Goovernment in England is? 'Tis joost shuttin' ta stable door after t' 'oss is stolen.

SIR CHARLES. [*To* SIR JOHN] We don't seem to be getting on, exactly.

SIR JOHN. Now, look here. I can't help the mess the country's in. I didn't make the war, or alter the whole conditions of industry. If the workman's standard of living is higher here than it is abroad, it's not my doing.

MITCHELL *and* CLARKE. [*Jeering*] Ba Goom! . . . Ye're right there!

SIR JOHN. I'm not responsible for the coal strikes.

MITCHELL *and* GASCOYNE. Lock-outs! . . . Oh! Ma mistaak.

SIR JOHN. [*Boring on*] It's not my fault that there are a million too many people in England. I do my job, and my job is to make what industry I control pay its way; and I say that's the only thing that can do *you* good in the long run.

TULLEY. 'Tis a main long run, Sir John.

SIR JOHN. I'm sorry for you, devilish sorry. But if I said so, you wouldn't believe it.

CLARKE. We know ye too well. Ye just drive on, no matter 'oo you drive over.

SIR JOHN. That's all tommy rot. I'm as human as you.

MITCHELL. Ye don't advertise it, Mister.

GOFFER. Wha! Ye even named your 'orse "Evolution"! The weakest can go to the wall—for you. That's your rule o' the road. Well, coom to the races, and we'll rouse your 'orse for ye. Ma Goom! I'm lookin' forward to thaat.

35

SIR JOHN. [*Very angry*] Are you? Then you'll dashed well have nothing to look forward to. I'll scratch my horse first.

CLARKE. Ba Gosh! That's great. Eh, laads, we've poot the wind oop 'ee.

SIR JOHN. The wind be damned. I'll stop you venting your spite, that's all.   [*Laughter and jeers from the* MINERS.

SIR CHARLES. Must this dog-fight go on? There's a lady present, men.

JOAN. Oh! don't worry about me—it's perfectly thrilling.

TEBBUTT. [*Slowly—he being the oldest, they listen*] When I was a yoong chaap, Sir Charles, I maind your grandfather sayin' : " Tebbutt, ye're as good a man as me. 'Tis queer," he said, " wha Providence made one man a miner and another a bar'net." What a pity he didna keep ta pits an' save all ta trooble.

SIR JOHN. [*Muttering*] Wish the deuce he had, then I shouldn't have lost *my* money trying to keep them open.

CLARKE. Did Providence give *you* yer title?

SIR JOHN. No, I bou—er—earned it. The only men who can help this country to get on her feet again are men who'll look ahead and drive ahead. My father began as a working man; he looked ahead and drove ahead; and so have I; and if you think you're going to be any better off by getting rid of men like me, you're going balmy. [*He has cooled down during* TEBBUTT'S *speech, and adds with a sort of grim humour*] Fact is, you're balmy already.

MITCHELL. Aw! An' ah'll tell ye this : If there's many men like you, there's goin' to be a bloody time in England.

SIR JOHN. There we are! The Bolshy coming out! Try it, my man! Try it, and see!

SIR CHARLES. Steady, steady! We're not in Parliament.

CLARKE. How did this joker [*Pointing to the* TRAMP] come to be ridin' with you in a Rolls-Royce? Tell us thaat.

SIR JOHN. I brought him from my place.

GOFFER. 'As 'e been stayin' with you?

SIR JOHN. [*Exploding*] Oh! Go to hell, the lot of you!

JOAN. [*Suddenly rising from her chair*] Just a second, before you go. Does my Dad look slim? He may be a trifle arbitrary, but does he look like doing the dirty on you?

SIR JOHN. Sit down, Joan.

GOFFER. Let 'im explain 'ow 'e come to 'ave 'is 'and on this fellow then.

TRAMP. [*Stirring suddenly*] See 'ere, fair play! Let me 'ave a fag and I'll tell you the 'ole bloomin' story. [*A fag is handed him by the* BARMAN *from behind the bar ; he lights it and begins his tale, which from the start rivets everyone's attention.*] It's like this : I 'ad larst night in choke for sleepin' out; and yesterday when I was up before the Beaks,

[*Pointing at* SIR JOHN] I see a woman that I used to know once on a time—I see 'er quodded for—for walkin' the stree—, for walkin' abaht—she 'adn't the money to pay 'er fine.   Mazer there, e' quodded 'er—Mazer.   Well, I come out of choke this mornin' thinkin' o' things—   [*His face is darkened*] thinkin' o' things.   I took the road an' I come on a feller—close by 'ere—miner 'e was—an' we fell talkin'.   We talked of 'ow things were 'ere, an' we talked o' Nunchester races ; an' when we was passin' Luxford station, 'e says to me : " They'll be boxin' the 'orses in to-day from Luxford trainin' stables. Funny thing," 'e says, " we got the favourite for the Cup—' Evolution,' what belongs to Sir John Mazer, 'im that shut down the pits 'ere ; but we got Flyin' Kite, too, wot's goin' to beat it ; and won't that old blister Mazer be mad just ?   Shouldn't be surprised," 'e, says, " if somethin' 'appened to Flyin' Kite.   'E'd stick at nothin', Mazer."   Well, we come to the " Red Lion," and 'e stood me a double whisky.   I'd an empty stomach, mind you.   And when I come out I thought to meself : " Mazer !   Why !   that's the beak that quodded me and my—her I told you of ; and she gone consump, if I got eyes.   Mazer !   So 'e owns the favourite, does 'e ?   We'll see about that."   Well, I walked back to the station, and I see an 'orse-box ready.   I asked a bloke, an' 'e said 'twas for Mazer's 'orse. So I waited.   I can't say what was in me mind exactly ; what with the drink and thinkin', I was a bit light-'eaded.   Well !   Presently they brought the 'orse.   Mazer's 'orse !   And—giv' you me word— I see the face of 'er—of 'er as used to be my wife—same as 'twas when Mazer quodded 'er.   I see it clear as I see you ; and I nicked a spanner from a motor-bike and ran and giv' the 'orse's leg a wipe—and made back for the bike.   I can ride a bike with any man, but the blasted thing wouldn't click.   So there I was.   Speakin' in cold blood, I— I'm sorry I 'it the mare—as it turned aht, she was the other one's— not Mazer's at all.   That's where the catch was.   Things was upside down.

SIR CHARLES. My God !

TRAMP. After I left 'ere just now, I 'eard 'em through the winder of the " Red Lion " about suspectin' Mazer.   So I went to see 'im about it.   And that's all.

[*There is a silence when he has finished, broken at last by a deep grunt from* SIR JOHN.

SIR JOHN. Well, you're a beauty !

SIR CHARLES. Why didn't you tell *me* all this just now ?

TRAMP. [*Sullenly*] I 'ad my feelin's.

SIR JOHN. Worse luck for you than we thought, Denbury.   Too bad ! Look here, if my horse wins, I'll give my winnings to the village.

MITCHELL. We don't want your winnin's.

[HODGKIN *enters from the hall.*

TULLEY. Eh, laad! Don't be 'asty. There's others beside yissen. 'Ere's Jo Hodgkin. Wot dost say, Jo?

HODGKIN. Wot's oop?

TULLEY. Sir John Mazer says he'll give 'is winnin's to the village.

HODGKIN. First catch your 'are. But that's the stoof. [*Stretching his hand across the table.*] Shake 'ands, Sir John. [SIR JOHN *hesitates.*

JOAN. That's marvellous, Mr. Hodgkin. [*Softly.*] Don't back through your collar, Dad! Attaboy!

[SIR JOHN *puts out his hand, which is overgrasped by* HODGKIN.

HODGKIN. [*Relishing his position*] We ought to 'ave Mr. East take a picture o' this, Sir John. Should 'ave a record o' the Peace Treaty. [*Letting* SIR JOHN's *mangled hand go with reluctance.*] Well, coom on, laads, time we was startin'. Coop's not roon for every day.

[*As the* MINERS *troop out into the hall, following by the* INNKEEPER *and* BARMAN, MISS CARD *enters from the hall.*

SIR JOHN. Hallo, Miss Card—what's the matter?

MISS CARD. A just walked over, Sir John, to say that the superintendent of the casual wards has come and gone.

SIR JOHN. Why the hell didn't he wait?

MISS CARD. That was precasely the reason.

SIR JOHN. Reason? What? How d'you mean?

MISS CARD. The hell—it was all he said, Sir John.

SIR JOHN. Eh! What? Ha!

MISS CARD. Quate!

SIR JOHN. Did you come over to tell me that?

MISS CARD. A thought perhaps in the circumstances you maight wish to go straight on to the races, Sir John. So A brought your glasses and another hat. [*She displays the two articles.*

SIR JOHN. What's the matter with this hat? [*Waving his trilby.*

MISS CARD. All the best people go racing in bowler hats.

SIR JOHN. Deuce they do! Miss Card, you're priceless.

MISS CARD. Cheap at the prace, Sir John, perhaps, but A shouldn't say praceless—he, he!

SIR JOHN. [*Turning to* SIR CHARLES, *who stands alone by the lower armchair*] Can I take you in, Denbury?

SIR CHARLES. No. Thanks very much.

SIR JOHN. It really is sickening for you.

SIR CHARLES. [*With a wave of his hand*] Good luck to your horse!

SIR JOHN. [*Turning on the* TRAMP, *who has moved over to the window*] You dangerous brute! Wish I'd given you a month. You won't prosecute, Denbury?

SIR CHARLES. [*Shaking his head*] Dog doesn't eat dog.

SIR JOHN. What's that?

[SIR CHARLES *shrugs his shoulders*; SIR JOHN, *after staring at him a moment, takes the hat from* MISS CARD.

Well, well! Let's be one of the best people. Coming, Joan?

[*He goes out into the hall, followed by* MISS CARD.

JOAN. [*Sotto voce*] How terribly Christian of you!

SIR CHARLES. Not at all! Just tribal feeling—one exile to another.

JOAN. You don't mean you're *really* going back to Africa?

SIR CHARLES. Next week as ever is.

JOAN. It's crazy!

SIR CHARLES. In what way, exactly?

JOAN. [*Showing, for her, considerable embarrassment*] Well—I mean, when the place of your fathers and all that—is waiting to drop back into your mouth? I can't very well put it any plainer—can I?

SIR CHARLES. I don't venture to grasp your meaning.

JOAN. Oh! yes, you do! [*Suddenly, and holding her hand out ever so little.*] I'm an only child, you know.

SIR CHARLES. [*Gently*] That is really most extraordinarily nice of you.

JOAN. It isn't. It's brazen. Even I think it's brazen. But if you're going off to Africa——

SIR CHARLES. Alas!

JOAN. [*In a hard voice*] Oh! all right! If you don't know which side your bread's buttered.

SIR CHARLES. You heard Jo Hodgkin's opinion of me.

JOAN. That you can't take care of yourself? I think he got it in once.

SIR CHARLES. [*Smiling*] In that case I'd better not add to my responsibilities, had I?

JOAN. No but you might add to mine.

SIR CHARLES. Sorry, but it wouldn't be decent.

JOAN. Oh! Well, if you like to be a martyr! Good-bye!

[*She goes to the door, hesitates a moment, tosses her head and goes out into the hall.*

[SIR CHARLES, *who has watched her, gives a shrug and a faint whistle. The* TRAMP, *who is over at the French window chewing the butt end of his fag, comes forward a little as if to speak.* SIR CHARLES *stands staring at him.*

TRAMP. Guv'nor——

[SIR CHARLES *deliberately turns his back on him.*]

Why, look 'ere, Guv'nor, you know I never meant to 'urt your 'orse. I'm sorry I 'it 'er—she was a pretty creature.

SIR CHARLES. [*Turning*] Let it go!

[*The* TRAMP *makes a motion with his shoulders, slouches to the French window, hesitates, and goes out.*

[*He has barely disappeared when* MR. EAST, *followed by a* WOMAN, *comes from the commercial room. The* WOMAN *is about thirty-five, hollow-cheeked and hollow-eyed, with the remains of good looks under her indifferent make-up.*

MR. EAST. [*To* SIR CHARLES] I thought our friend was still here, Sir Charles.

SIR CHARLES. Just gone. [*Looking with a certain alarm at the woman*] Shall I—er—um—send him to you?

MR. EAST. If you would be so very good.

[SIR CHARLES *crosses and goes out by the French window. The* WOMAN, *after staring round her, is warming herself at the fire.*

MR. EAST. Are you cold after your drive?

WOMAN. Yes, I'm a bit chilly.

MR. EAST. I trust the two bulldogs did not incommode you in the car?

WOMAN. No; I like dawgs. They're friendly things.

MR. EAST. More friendly, I'm afraid, than human beings.

WOMAN. You're right.

MR. EAST Did you have an unpleasant time in—choke?

WOMAN. I've had worse.

MR. EAST. You owe your release to an intervention of Providence, if I may say so.

WOMAN. Ah! I been wonderin' when you were goin' to start talkin' about salvation.

MR. EAST. I'm afraid salvation is not in my line.

WOMAN. Why? Aren't you a missionary?

MR. EAST. No. A photographer. [*The* WOMAN *stares.*] Photographers are full of original sin.

WOMAN. Don't you pull my leg. I don't feel like I could stand it.

MR. EAST. Believe me, I am not trying to. [*Catching sight of the* TRAMP *in the garden*] Here is an old friend of yours, if I may so express it.

[*He goes out into the hall. The* TRAMP *comes in at the French window, and the* WOMAN *and he stare at each other. Any surprise or emotion is checked by both.*

WOMAN. Why! It's Jack, ain't it? My Gawd! 'Ow are you, Jack?

TRAMP. Thereabouts. Well, 'ere we are again! 'Usband and wife! Heu! 'Ow are you, Milly?

WOMAN. As you see. Fancy seein' you again, Jack! Still in the motor mechanics?

TRAMP. *Nommuch.*

WOMAN. Beard don't suit you, Jack.

TRAMP. Nao. You didn't reckernize me in the Court yesterday, but I got your phiz all right.

WOMAN. [*Defiantly*] It's changed a bit.

TRAMP. Nine years, come July, since I found you gone.

WOMAN. [*Sullenly*] That's right.

TRAMP. Bit of a shock at the time.

WOMAN. Waitin' like that—'twasn't a life.

TRAMP. And 'ow d'you like life now you got it?

WOMAN. Well, there it is. How are *you* keepin', Jack?

TRAMP. [*Laughs*] Oh! I'm the King of Egypt.

WOMAN. You look it. What d'you do with yourself?

TRAMP. On the road.

WOMAN. Any fat in that?

TRAMP. I'm not 'Enry Ford. How d'you come to be in these parts?

WOMAN. Chasin' round after the races. That's my best stunt, now.

TRAMP. [*Staring at her*] Upset me yesterday—seein' you; it fair did.

WOMAN. S'pose you think I'm the world's worst?

TRAMP. Don't think nothin'. Gawd's truth! Given up thinkin' these years past.

WOMAN. No; it don't do to think. [*For a moment they both stand motionless, staring before them. With a jerky laugh.*] It's real funny meetin' you again, Jack. 'Ow's your old mother?

TRAMP. Dead.

WOMAN. I often think o' Tooting. That was a good little time we had together.

TRAMP. Ah!

WOMAN. That crimson war did *us* in.

TRAMP. That's a fact. [*Staring at her.*] *You* don't look too bright, Milly.

WOMAN. Oh! I'm a treat. I say, Jack, where's the barman?— drop o' gin'd do me proud. [*She looks longingly at the bottles.*]

TRAMP. 'Elp yourself, then.

WOMAN. [*With a shudder*] No; don't want no more nights in there.

TRAMP. [*Staring at her again*] Take it all round—is it a life?

WOMAN. [*Mastering her lips with an effort*] It's rock bottom.

TRAMP. And where's the end to it?

WOMAN. I say! Solemn! Short life and a merry one. [*She laughs.*] What about you, if it comes to that?

TRAMP. " The rabbits 'ave 'oles, an' the fowls of the air 'ave their nests, but the son o' man——" knew me Bible when I was a nipper.

WOMAN. Ah! The son o' man cops it fair—an' the daughter o' man too. That's how I see it.

TRAMP. 'Usband an' wife!

WOMAN. Well, I always 'ad a liking for you, Jack.

TRAMP. And showed it proper, eh?

WOMAN. My nature's bad, I suppose. [*She laughs.*

TRAMP. Well, you've struck it rocky, comin' 'ere, not a bob in the village.

WOMAN. Why—what's up?

TRAMP. Pits closed—everybody on their uppers.

WOMAN. I say, Jack, what did that loony, soft-voiced chap pay my fine for?

TRAMP. *I* sent 'im with the money.

WOMAN. You?

TRAMP. Got it off the old blister that quodded us.

WOMAN. You got it off the beak?   Never!

TRAMP. Long story, that.

WOMAN. Got any more rhino, Jack?

TRAMP. Not a bean.

WOMAN. I've the price of two drinks, and when that blighted barman comes back, we'll have 'em.   Oh!   here 'e is!

[*The* BARMAN *has come in from the commercial room.   He looks at the* WOMAN *askance.*

WOMAN. Two double gins, please.

BARMAN. We don't serve drinks to women.

WOMAN. Oh!   You don't.   Why?   'Aven't we got the vote?

BARMAN. Never you mind; and we don't serve 'em to tramps. So if you've quite done, perhaps you'll both go down the road.   The " Red Lion's " the other side.

WOMAN. My Gawd!   If you——

TRAMP. 'Ere, Milly!   Let me—Look 'ere, this lady is my wife.

BARMAN. I don't give a darn if she's your grandmother; you've got to go down the road.   So go on, and go quiet!

TRAMP. 'Aven't we got trouble enough without your lip?   If you weren't in the trenches there, I'd knock your 'ead off.

BARMAN. [*Stolidly*] If you don't go, I'll come over the top and shift you.

WOMAN. Let 'im be, Jack.   I got no kick in me this mornin'.

[*She coughs.*

[TRAMP *stands looking at her.*

TRAMP. [*Suddenly throwing his hands up to his head*] Gawd!   And this is a world!

[*He has not seen* MR. EAST, *who has come in from the hall.*

MR. EAST. George, will you very kindly make me two nice hot drinks with gin and cloves.

BARMAN. [*After hesitation*] It's your responsibility, Mr. East.

[*He begins to prepare the drinks, and then goes out for hot water.*

MR. EAST. I hope you have had a pleasant talk?

TRAMP. Well!   We was tryin' to decide which of us was too good for the other.

MR. EAST. And which is the superior?

TRAMP. Heu! She's got the price o' two drinks, an' I've got the price o' none.

MR. EAST. [*Looking from one to the other*] I only paid five of that ten pounds for the fine. If I might divide the other five between you, and possibly you would not mind my adding five of my own.

[*They say nothing, but they seem suddenly to have become all eyes.*] [*To the* WOMAN.] Would you take these, then?

[*He holds out to her five notes.*

WOMAN. I ask your pardon.   [*She takes the notes.*

MR. EAST. Why?

WOMAN. Takin' you for a missionary.

MR. EAST. Yes, that was too good to be true. [*Turning to the* TRAMP *and handing him five notes.*] And perhaps you would take these before he comes back. I have to take care of my reputation. They might call me looney.   [*The* TRAMP *takes them in silence.*]
Will you shake hands?

[*First the* TRAMP *and then the* WOMAN *having stealthily wiped a hand, shake* MR. EAST'S.

[*The* BARMAN *re-enters with the kettle and pours into the two glasses.*

BARMAN. [*Handing the drinks*] 'Ere you are, Mr. East. Gin and bitters for you?

MR. EAST. [*Taking the two hot drinks and handing one to each*] It will serve, George. [*He watches the outcasts with a smile; then, taking the gin and bitters.*] May I be permitted to drink your healths?

[*He raises the glass.*
[*The* OUTCASTS *also raise their glasses and the three drink.*

TRAMP. [*Putting his glass down*] Well, I'll be gettin' on.

WOMAN. [*Putting her glass down*] Can I come with you a bit, Jack?

TRAMP. Shouldn't be surprised. So long, Mister. You've played the good Samaritan, you 'ave.

MR. EAST. Not at all.

WOMAN. Well, you 'ave. I don't say much, but I feel it.

[*Almost in spite of herself she touches her heart.*

TRAMP. So do I, Mister. So long! Good luck!

MR. EAST. And to you both.

[*The Two move to the French window in single file, hesitate there a moment, look back at* MR. EAST, *say nothing, and go out.*
MR. EAST *stands quite still.*

BARMAN. Mr. East, is it true you're goin' to Africa with Sir Charles?

MR. EAST. Yes, George. Lions will be very restful.

BARMAN. You'll be missed 'ere.

MR. EAST. Thank you. But with so many poor people having nothing to look forward to, it seems almost the first duty of the Englishman to leave England.

35*

BARMAN. Things do look a bit blue. The liquor trade's declinin'. You don't think the old country's goin' to peg out, do you, Mr. East?

MR. EAST. No, George, far from it! England is very tough; but she is rather like a pint pot with a quart of beer trying to remain in it.

BARMAN. Overflowin', ah! When are you goin'?

MR. EAST. Next week, I believe.

BARMAN. Well, if there's anything I can do for you, Mr. East——

MR. EAST. Nothing; unless perhaps you could do something dangerous to me, so that I could exercise my courage.

BARMAN. I could give you another drink.

MR. EAST. That would be capital, if I may say so.

[*On the* BARMAN'S *beginning to mix the drink, and* MR. EAST *smiling and rubbing his hands,* SIR CHARLES *enters.*

BARMAN. [*Bringing drink to* MR. EAST] Anything for you, Sir Charles?

SIR CHARLES. No, thank you, George.

[*The* BARMAN, *with some glasses, goes out into the commercial room.*] Well, Mr. East, Africa's not smiling on me a little bit. The old country's in my very bones.

MR. EAST. [*Looking out of the window*] She is very beautiful this morning.

SIR CHARLES. [*Gazing out of the window*] Yes! Damn!

MR. EAST. Sir Charles, I am afraid that, contrary to my interests, I ought to tell you something.

SIR CHARLES. Oh! What's that?

MR. EAST. Miss Mazer has a crush on you, if I may so express it.

SIR CHARLES. [*With a wry smile*] Yes. That's put the lid on. I prefer bodily exile to spiritual. When can you start, Mr. East?

MR. EAST. I fear that I shall require to arrange for my dog, and buy an extra tooth-brush. After that at any moment.

SIR CHARLES. Shall we go up to-morrow and buy tooth-brushes together? There's a British-India for Mombasa to-day week.

MR. EAST. I am wildly excited, Sir Charles.

SIR CHARLES. Never travelled?

MR. EAST. Once—to Boulogne.

SIR CHARLES. That hardly makes you a master of the art.

MR. EAST. So I found when I volunteered for the South Pole.

SIR CHARLES. Shake hands, Mr. East, you're the salt of England.

[*They shake, and* SIR CHARLES *turns up to the smoking-room.*

MR. EAST. [*Shaking his head*] Only Cerebos, I fear.

[*He goes towards the hall door.*

The curtain falls.

SCENE II

*Ten hours have passed ; it is night.   One light only burns below the dying
fire.*

    [SIR CHARLES, *still in day clothes, is sitting in the armchair above
the hearth, a pipe in his mouth, a glass by his side, a novel on his
knee which he is not reading.   The garden is misty and moonlit.
The* BARMAN *enters the bar and takes some glasses into the
smoking-room, through the opened door of which voices are heard.*

VOICE OF COMMERCIAL TRAVELLER. Well, I got my money.   Did
you back it, Job ?

V. OF BARMAN. Ask Mr. Bender.   You 'ad a bad race, Mr. Bender.
There was a lot of money on Evolution.

V. OF BENDER. Ah !   That old blister 'as the luck o' the world.

V. OF C. TRAV. All the money goes to those 'oo've got it.   That's
the first law of yuman nature.   Cruel 'ard on this Sir Charles, I call it.
                                        [*The voices drop.*

    [SIR CHARLES *rises, and goes across to the window, where he stands
looking out into the moonlit mist.   The* INNKEEPER *puts his
face in at the door, and seeing what seems to be an empty room,
speaks aloud.*

V. OF INNKEEPER. Can't bear to see it !   A Sport like Sir Charles
drove out o' the country.

V. OF BENDER. 'E won't be the last.

V. OF BARMAN. Little Mr. East was saying to me——
      [*Voice dies down, and what he was saying is lost.*

    [SIR CHARLES *throws the window open—the hoot of an owl is heard.*

V. OF C. TRAV. [*Lifting out*] Africa !   Black men and musqueeters ;
and not a drink to the square mile, I'm told.

V. OF INNKEEPER. And to think he'd have won enough to set him
up on the land of his fathers, even if it don't pay.

    [SIR CHARLES *gives himself a shake and puts his pipe into his mouth.
The sound of* MEN'S VOICES *singing in chorus floats in across
the garden, followed by a burst of laughter.*

V. OF C. TRAV. Bit of a beano at the " Red Lion."

V. OF BENDER. They're spendin' Mazer's money before they get
it—just as well ; 'e'll cook 'is balance sheet all right.

V. OF C. TRAV. It's the miners I'm sorry for ; they're a lot more
wonky than Sir Charles, or you, Mr. Bender.

V. OF BARMAN. That's right ; there's no place for 'em any more.

V. OF C. TRAV. George, you'll be losin' your job next.   Terrible
the sobriety there is abaht.   It's lucky we English in'erited the earth,
there yn't much else left for some of us, bar taxes—eh, Mr. 'Addon ?

V. OF INNKEEPER. There's English blood and bone. If the old country'd put her back into it, the whole trouble would mop up like one of these ground mists. That's my opinion.

V. OF C. TRAV. Why can't these politicians drop their Parties an' put their 'eads together. We want a national policy, same as in the war.

[*The sound of a dog howling, very far away, drifts in.* SIR CHARLES *leans back against the sill, crossing his arms on his chest.*]

I 'ate to 'ear a dog 'owl; that's what they call the banshee in Ireland.

V. OF INNKEEPER. [*Severely*] We're not in Ireland. We're in England, and thank God for it.

V. OF C. TRAV. Ah! We're in England, good old England; and ain't she gettin' old?

V. OF INNKEEPER. Not she? She's a two-year-old.

V. OF C. TRAV. [*With vulgar jocularity*] And we love 'er; and we lov 'er!

SIR CHARLES. [*To himself*] That *is* the little trouble.

[*As if in answer, comes the hoot of the owl. The* CHORUS OF MINERS' VOICES *rises; they are singing " John Brown's body," and the tramp of their feet is heard as they march down the street away from the " Red Lion."*]

SIR CHARLES. [*Softly*] But *her* soul goes marching on!

The curtain falls.

THE ROOF

CAST OF THE ORIGINAL PRODUCTION, FIRST PRODUCED
BY MR. BASIL DEAN AT THE VAUDEVILLE THEATRE,
LONDON, ON MONDAY, NOVEMBER 4, 1929

GUSTAVE	*Mr. Horace Hodges*
THE HON. REGGIE FANNING . . .	*Mr. Frank Lawton*
MAJOR MOULTENEY	*Mr. James Fenton*
BAKER	*Mr. David Horne*
BRICE	*Mr. Eric Maturin*
MR. BEETON	*Mr. Ben Field*
MRS. BEETON	*Miss Barbara Gott*
HENRY LENNOX	*Mr. H. O. Nicholson*
EVELYN LENNOX	*Miss Cicely Byrne*
DIANA	*Miss Peggy Simpson*
BRYN	*Miss Ann Casson*
A NURSE	*Miss Lydia Sherwood*
A YOUNG MAN	*Mr. Eric Portman*
A YOUNG WOMAN	*Miss Madeleine Carroll*
FROBA	*Mr. Paul Furness*
TWO POMPIERS	{ *Mr. Phillip Hatfield* { *Mr. Desmond Davis*

A BLACK CAT

SCENE I

GROUND FLOOR

Evening : eleven o'clock.

The dining room of the little hotel, divided from a service room, on the left, by a partition, which ends some six feet from the footlights, and is screened on the dining room side. The audience looks end-on at what passes in both rooms. The service room has a sink and shelves [one over the other] for glasses, bottles, plates, spoons, etc., along the left wall forward, and a chair close to the opening. Owing to its narrowness it is difficult to see what is at the back of this little room. The dining room, which occupies the right hand and centre of the stage, has three small tables, set with white cloths, a glass or two, and salt-cellars, and one table [forward Left Centre] set for a meal, at which a pretty, pleasant-faced NURSE in uniform is sitting half-way through a simple repast. There is a curtained window in the right wall, and the dining room doorway is glass-screened from a corridor at the Back. The walls of the dining room, as indeed of each room throughout the play, are of a pleasant pearl grey with panelling outlined in a deeper shade of the same. A clock points to eleven.

> *[When the curtain rises* GUSTAVE, *the waiter, a man of nearly sixty with an infinitely patient, lined clean-shaven face, and a frequent faint smile, is stroking a black cat. He puts it down, and moves to and from service room to dining room, setting two of the tables with cups and plates for next morning's café.*

NURSE. [*Watching him*] Eleven o'clock! Don't you get awfully tired, Gustave ?

GUSTAVE. [*Inclining his ear towards her, in a patient, caressing voice*] Ye-es, Mees, a leetle tired ; we 'ave no leeft, as you see.

NURSE. Well, *I* shan't want anything more now, thank you.

GUSTAVE. Tt-tt ! [*Concerned*] A leetle fruit-rafraichi—veree cold.

> [*He goes across to the serving room.*

NURSE. No, really. You sit down and rest.

GUSTAVE. [*Wheedling*] Veree nice. I' ave it ready. [*He brings it.*

NURSE. Delicious cooking here.

GUSTAVE. [*Bridling*] We 'ave a pride, Mees.

NURSE. Are you left here all alone at night ?

GUSTAVE. With the night porter, ye-es, Mees.

NURSE. What time do you generally finish?

GUSTAVE. Meednight.　Gentlemen want drinks—a leetle supper some time.

NURSE. [*Looking at clock*] Another hour!　I feel for you, Gustave. I know what feet are!

> [*Sound of men's voices in the corridor. Three men*—REGGIE FANNING, *very young*, BAKER *and* BRICE, *getting on for forty, appear in the doorway. They all appear to have been revelling. The youngest speaks.*

FANNING. I shall go up to the poor, poor Major.

BRICE. Up—up—up—up!

BAKER. Private life for me.

BRICE. We want cocktails, we want cocktails!

GUSTAVE. Three Martinis, Sare?　Veree dry—veree cold.

BAKER. Four, Gustave.　Right!

GUSTAVE. Ye-es, Sare.

> [*He moves to prepare them at the table at the entrance of the service room*; *the* MEN *disperse down the corridor*, FANNING *to the left*; *the other two to the right.*

NURSE. That boy looks nice; pity he should go about like that.

GUSTAVE. In Paree, Mees, everyone a leetle fresh.

NURSE. Yes, and why?　You French are the steadiest people in the world.

GUSTAVE. [*Shaking cocktails*] Paree not France, Mees.　In Paree good wine, good food.　People come, they eat, they drink—suddenly their blood is surprised—it march queecker.

NURSE. [*Smiling*] Excellent, Gustave; I believe you're perfectly right.

GUSTAVE. We 'ave a couple, numero douze—old people, veree comme il faut, veree sage.　I watch them at dinner—at once they get red, their blood march.

NURSE. A Mr. and Mrs. Beeton—real stolid English.　We English do seem stolid in Paris.　Not my poor Mr. Lennox, though—he's very ill, Gustave.

GUSTAVE. Such a nice gentleman—'ave such a nice face.　And 'is leetle girls, so charmeeng, très gentilles.

NURSE. I'm terribly sorry for Mrs. Lennox.　I only hope they get back to England all right.

GUSTAVE. Poor ladee—she' ave a look, always watching. [*Pouring out the cocktails.*] We 'ave a love couple, too—veree different—young mariés, or [*Tolerantly*] perhaps not.

NURSE. Perhaps not?　Why?

GUSTAVE. Veree moch in love.

NURSE. [*Sighing*] It *can* go together, Gustave.

GUSTAVE. In Paree—not always, Mees.　Sometime they come to

see 'ow it work. Sometime they come for a little rest from being
married.

NURSE. Are they English, these two?

GUSTAVE. Ye-es, Mees, 'igh society, as you call eet.

BAKER. [*Appearing in doorway, followed by* BRICE] Gustave, where
those cocktails?

[GUSTAVE *carries them to him on a tray.*]

Right! [*He drinks his off and hands one to* BRICE, *who tosses his off, too.
Then, carrying the other two cocktails, they go off upstairs, rather noisily.*

[*Enter* FROBA, *a young violinist, with a Jugo-Slavian face, a lot of
hair and a somewhat hoarse, semi-Americanized voice.*

FROBA. Say, Waiter, I'm dry. Give me a long, squashy lemon drink.

GUSTAVE. Ye-es, Mister Froba.   [*Begins to squeeze lemons.*

FROBA. Say! Dose men are rader fresh. [*Seats himself at the table
on the right in a line with the* NURSE.] How's de sick gentleman, Nurse?

NURSE. He's not yet got over his journey from Nauheim.

FROBA. What's his trouble? Heart?

NURSE. Yes.

FROBA. Is dat so? Dey admire his books in Amurrica. He's kind
of a big bug dere.   [*The contrast between his speech and his rather spiritual face is intriguing.*

NURSE. In spite of his being English?

FROBA. I guess dat's not his funeral in God's own country.

NURSE. I'm told his novels are delightful.

FROBA. Sure dey are! He's got a soul, dat man. Say Nurse—in
a hundred human beings, how many have got souls?

NURSE. It's difficult to say. [*Smiling.*] So many people keep their
souls locked up.

FROBA. I get you; and take dem walks once a week, but not on
Sundays.

NURSE. It's like the weekly bath of old days.

FROBA. Say, have you noticed dere's more baths, and more cars,
and fewer souls in Amurrica dan anywheres?

NURSE. I've never been in America. But I expect the souls are in
the bottom drawers all right.

FROBA. Well, I'm telling you. I've been in Amurrica ten years.
Dey wash so much, and dey move around so; it dakes quite an
occasion to make dem open de bottom drawer.

NURSE. A little soul goes a long way, Mr. Froba. Just as well to
keep them for Bank Holidays.

FROBA. Well, when I play at my concerts, I look at all dose faces,
and if I see a soul it kind of goes to my head. I make quite a noise
playing to it.

GUSTAVE. [*Bringing him the drink*] Veree long, Sare; veree
cold.

FROBA. Gustave, you're a man and a broder, and you, sure, have a soul.

[BRICE *and* FANNING *enter, chanting as they come Left to the tune of the " Three Blind Mice," they sing :*
  We wants drinks, we want drinks,
  We want 'em cold, we want 'em long—
  Make no mistake we want 'em strong—
  And don't you get the mixing wrong—
  We want drinks.

FANNING. [*Halting at sight of the* NURSE] We beg your pardon. [*To* GUSTAVE.] Could you get us two whiskies and sodas ?

GUSTAVE. Black and White, Sare—veree Scotch, veree strong.

FANNING. [*Weakly*] Ve'y Scotch, ve'y strong ; Mr. Brice, that's a *mot*, if you know what I mean.

GUSTAVE. [*Bringing bottle and syphon to table at the back, bottle in hand*] Say ven, Sare ?

BRICE. Never say ' when,' never say ' when ' !

FANNING. [*To* GUSTAVE] I leave it to you to give me what you think is pup-proper.

GUSTAVE. [*Patiently to* FANNING] One fingare, Sare ?
         [*A bell rings in the service room.*

BRICE. Put it down. We'll fix it.
  [GUSTAVE *marks with his eye the height of the whisky in the bottle and goes out to answer the bell.*
      [*The two attend to the adjustment of their drinks.*

FROBA. [*Who has gone over to the* NURSE] I guess dey've lost de keys of deir bottom drawers.

NURSE. You never know, Mr. Froba. The soul has a way of coming out under pressure.

FROBA. Well, I judge *you* get a chance to see it pressed.
  [*He turns to stare at the young man, who is looking rather fascinated, at the back of the* NURSE'*s head.*

FANNING. [*Half seas over*] I beg your pardon, Nurse, but could you take my temperachure ? I feel so—so hot.

NURSE. [*Turning, startled*] I've no thermometer, here. [*Looking at him, steadily.*] But I can tell you exactly what you want. No more whisky and a good long sleep.

FANNING. [*Grave and considerate*] Oh ! do you think so ? Thank you ve'y much. As a matter of fact, I believe you're pup-perfectly right.

NURSE. [*Getting up*] I'm sure I am. Good-night.
    [*She goes.* FROBA *gets up, too, and follows her out.*
  GUSTAVE *comes back and prepares a tray with caviare, some bread, some olives, and a bottle of Chateau d'Yquem ; and presently goes out with it.*

FANNING. That was ve'y quick diag-diagnosis, Mister Brice. She's a ve'y nice woman, I should think. I like her face, and I like her voice.

BRICE. Ho, ho! Don't you try to get off with that nurse, young man.

FANNING. Mister Brice, you may think you are funny, but you are not.

BRICE. [*Whistling*] Keep it on! Keep it on, my lad!

FANNING. I am not your lad, and I thank God for it.

BRICE. I say! Don't get ratty!

FANNING. You seem to think that I have a low opinion of women, like your own.

BRICE. I should say you've got no opinion of women at all. Never seen one, have you—except your mother and your nurse?

FANNING. I shall be obliged if you will not be insulting.

BRICE. Well, then, [*grinning*] let's hear your adventures with women.

FANNING. No gentleman ever talks about his adventures with women.

BRICE. Not when he's had none.

FANNING. Mr. Brice, please consider yourself a stranger to me.

BRICE. Look here, young man, d'you want some advice? You've been brought up at home, I'm told. You're just ten years below your proper age. When I was your age——

FANNING. I don't care a hoo-hoot what happened when you were my age.

BRICE. That's lucky, because I'm not going to tell you. But if you think that because you've been brought up with cotton-wool in your ears, you can criticize men of the world, you're ruddy well mistaken.

FANNING. [*Finishing his drink and staring at* BRICE *in a prolonged manner*] Mister Brice, I excuse you because you are drunk.

[GUSTAVE *returns*.]

I leave this gentleman, if he can be called a gentleman, in your cus-custody. I am going up.

BRICE. Up—up—up—up! [FANNING *looks at him with inebriated haughtiness and goes out.*] Young pup, pup, pup!

GUSTAVE. [*Quietly*] Excuse, Sare,. Not right to make so young gentlemen drunk.

BRICE. Heh! [*Staring.*] What—what the deuce are you butting in for?

GUSTAVE. No, Sare, A nice young man—not a strong 'ead.

BRICE. Why didn't you refuse to serve him, then, eh?

GUSTAVE. Not my place to refuse, Sare.

BRICE. Nor is it your place to tell me what I ought to do. Darned impudence, Waiter, darned impudence!

GUSTAVE. Ye-es, Sare. But when gentlemen 'ave some drink on board, as you say—not careful. Onlee a boy—a peetee.

BRICE. Look here, my careful friend, are you suggesting that I'm d-drunk myself?

GUSTAVE. Not yet, Sare.

BRICE. Oh! not yet! Well, I'm damned!

GUSTAVE. No, Sare, only a leetle fresh.

BRICE. [*Staring at him*] I shall darned well complain to your Manager.

GUSTAVE. [*With his faint smile*] Manager 'ave gone for the night, Sare. Onlee myself 'ere! To-morrow, not complain—cold feet, Sare. Perhaps not remembare.

BRICE. Don't you bet on that! I've a dashed good memory. [*He finishes his drink and pours out some more whisky.*] Do they pay y' extra for givin' unpleasant advice in this establishment.

GUSTAVE. [*Deprecating*] Veree sorree, Sare—'ave no weesh to offend you.

BRICE. Well, you have. You French think you're everybody, and I—I don't give a kick for the lot of you.

GUSTAVE. [*Ironically*] We are desolate, Monsieur.

[*A bell rings and he looks at the board.*

BRICE. You will be when I've done with you. [*Returning to his first grievance.*] Silly young cuckoo! I'm not his keeper.

GUSTAVE. No, Sare, the Major 'is keeper—veree nice man—veree quiet.

BRICE. Meaning I'm neither. H'm! Didn't you hear that bell?

GUSTAVE. Ye-es, Sare—just attending to see if you 'ave feenished with me.

BRICE. [*Grinning*] Finished with you? Not I. Not by a long chalk. You wait and see.

GUSTAVE. [*With his faint smile*] Yes, Sare, the bull-dogue 'e 'old on.

BRICE. You bet he does. You've got your trouble comin' to you, my friend.

GUSTAVE. Excuse, Sare. I go now. [*He goes to answer the bell.*
[*BRICE, left alone, glares after him, and finishes his whisky.*

BRICE. Old dotard! [*A slow grin spreads over his face.*] I'll make him sit up, up, up!

[*The NURSE enters busily and goes towards the service room, where she looks for something on the shelves. BRICE gets up and goes to the entrance of the service room.*

BRICE. Are you looking for anything? Can I h-help you loo-look?

NURSE. No thanks; I just want some cold consommé. Oh! there it is! [*Takes down a basin of consommé from the top shelf, and begins to prepare a little tray with a cup of it, biscuits, etc.*

BRICE. That old waiter is an of-offensive ass.

NURSE. Oh! Do you think so? *I* think he's a dear. What makes you say he's offensive?

BRICE. Because he gives advice. He's not my grea—great—grandmother. [*Laughs inanely.*] All people are offensive when they give advice. Don't you agree with me?

NURSE. It depends on the people, and the advice.

BRICE. I—I don't say I wouldn't take advice from the Archbishop of Canterbury. But—a waiter! I mean to say— What!

NURSE. Out of the mouths of babes and sucklings——

BRICE. Babes and sucklings! I'm not fond of babes and sucklings. Not I! I don't mind telling you, Nurse, I'm going to give that old waiter a jolly good jog.

NURSE. [*Regarding him steadily*] Don't you think you'd better sleep on it.

BRICE. Not on your life! I've just had an i-idea.

NURSE. [*Sharply*] I should keep it, and have it stuffed.

[*Comes out with the tray, which she deposits for a moment on a table and looks it over carefully to see that she has everything.*

[BRICE *has stepped into the service room and stands looking at the back of it. He suddenly utters a crow.*

NURSE. [*Startled*] Is anything the matter with you?

BRICE. [*Laughing and turning to her*] Take it from me, it's a magnificent idea.   [*Laughs.*

NURSE. Really! I've known so many magnificent ideas asking for soda-water the next morning.   [*She takes up the tray.*

[BRICE *follows her and as she disappears, shouts at the top of his voice:* "We want cocktails, we want cocktails!" *then suddenly covers his lips, saying:* "H'ssh!" *laughs inanely and goes back to the service room, where he disappears in its back recesses.*

While he is engaged there in whatever he is engaged in, the faint sounds from a violin playing a tango steal into the hush. After about a minute BRICE *comes back into the open, snapping his fingers and drunkenly pleased with himself.*

BRICE. That's all right—! I've got back on the old swine. That'll shake 'im up. That'll give him the twice over. Ha, ha, ha! [*He goes to his table and pours himself out some more whisky.*

[GUSTAVE *re-enters.*]

Oh! here you are again! Just in time.

GUSTAVE. Ye-es, Sare.

BRICE. Ha, ha, ha! Ha, ha, ha! Ha, ha, ha!

GUSTAVE. Excuse, Sare.

[*But* BRICE *continues to laugh, and goes out. He can be heard calling inanely,* "Up—up—up—up" *as he mounts the stairs.*

GUSTAVE. [*Measuring the whisky, which is nearly gone*] Oh! Là! Quel sale type! [*He sits down on the chair by the service room.*] Mon Dieu!

Que j' suis fatigué ! [*He sits there with his head on his hands, when suddenly he raises his nose and sniffs.*] Que qu'il ya ? [*He starts up.*] Cré nom de Dieu ! Qu'y a-t-il ! [*He dashes into the service room. The light goes out.*] Oh ! Là, là !

        [*Returning into the dining-room and running to the Entry.*]
Pierre ! Pierre ! Vite ! Vite ! Allez chercher les——!]

The curtain falls.

SCENE II

FIRST FLOOR

The same evening : eleven o'clock.

The Lounge of the little hotel, occupying the whole of the stage. Chairs, settees, and a card table. The window, uncurtained, on the right, looks out on to a little French Square. A wide doorway Back, with curtains looped, to the stairway. A clock points to eleven.

    [MAJOR MOULTENEY, *a shrewd quiet man of fifty, in dinner jacket, is sitting in an armchair finishing a cigar and looking at a copy of " La Vie Parisienne."*

MOULTENEY. [*Yawning*] Oh-h ! Eleven ! Darn it ! [*Cheerful sounds are heard.*] That sounds like him. [*Young FANNING appears.*] [*Looking up.*] Hallo, Reggie ! Where are your boon companions ?

FANNING. [*Making a motion as if hitting a ball with a racquet*] Coming up—up—up——very boon, Major. [*Halting at " La Vie Parisienne."*] " La Vie Parisienne " ! Major ! That is not a pup-proper pup-periodical.

    [*He takes it from the* MAJOR'S *hands. The* MAJOR *grins up at him.*

MOULTENEY. Strikes me, young man, you've been wetting your whistle.

FANNING. Not enough to matter, Major. Whenever I was tempted I thought of you sitting here, and I thought to myself—must set an example to the Major. Besides, Mr. Baker's going to teach me poker.

MOULTENEY. He can teach you, but he's not going to play with you.

FANNING. Why not ?

MOULTENEY. My dear boy, poker's an art—you don't learn it in an evening.

FANNING. But he says it's so simple. He's a very good egg, Major.

MOULTENEY. [*Dryly*] I've no doubt.

FANNING. Brice, his friend, is not quite such a good egg, in my opinion.   [*Sounds of revelry below.*

MOULTENEY. They're noisy beggars, anyway.

FANNING. Noisy but nice, Major.

   [*Dropping " La Vie Parisienne" and moving towards the doorway as the figure of a* YOUNG MAN *in evening dress with a hat and overcoat over his arm, appears in it.*]

Hallo !

YOUNG MAN. [*After a moment's hesitation and a jerky movement as if to cover his face with his hat*] Hallo, Fanning ! You staying here ?

FANNING. Yes, I'm staying here ; are you ?

YOUNG MAN. Perching—off to-morrow. What's brought you to Paris ?

FANNING. Oh ! only getting ready for the jolly old Guards.

YOUNG MAN. Oh ! yes, you're going into the Guards ? Um !

FANNING. Round the world first—aren't we, Major ? Going to shoot big game. This is my m-mentor, Major Moulteney. [*Turns to the* MAJOR.] Major, this is——

YOUNG MAN. How d'you do ? Sorry, I've got to go. Good-night !   [*He slips away abruptly.*

FANNING. That was Tony—— [*Waving his hands slightly.*] Can't remember his other name ! Met him in a country house. Have you noticed, Major, how people leave their surnames about in country-houses. But I remember his profession, he's a polo-playing poet.

MOULTENEY. H'm ! That sounds a new form of trouble.

FANNING. He plays a very good game ; and his poetry's remark-able—I haven't read it. I say—poetry, polo, poker ! Sounds like the whole duty of man. Why don't you teach me poker yourself, Major ?

MOULTENEY. Not in my contract, Reggie. Your mother'd have a fit.

FANNING. Oh ! Mother. She throws a fit if I blow my old nose. You know, the extraordinary thing is, Major, somebody told me : My mother was wild in her youth.

MOULTENEY. Lady Ilfracombe ! [*Shakes his head.*] Not wild, Reggie —no—merely unmanageable.

   [*With sounds of revelry* BAKER *and* BRICE *appear arm-in-arm in the doorway. Each holds a cocktail in the off hand.*

FANNING. Hallo ! Here they are, booner than ever, Major.

BAKER. Reggie, cocktail for you. [*Hands cocktail.*] Major, cock-tail for you. [BRICE *hands the* MAJOR *a cocktail.*] Right ! The old waiter makes 'em well. He's a character.

FANNING. Mr. Baker, you were going to teach me poker.

BAKER. Right ! Brice ? Got some cards ?

BRICE. What d'you take me for—a conjuror ? [*Produces a pack from his pocket.*] So I am. Splendid !

BAKER. [*Taking them*] Right! [*He sits at the card table.*] Now, what games do you know, young man? Old Maid? Beggar-my-Neighbour? Patience?

FANNING. [*With difficulty*] No, I only know Bridge.

BAKER. Well, in poker the great thing is to have a cooler head than the other fellows.

FANNING. I don't know if I have this evening.

BRICE. Hear, hear!

[*He and* FANNING *are standing by the table; the* MAJOR *gets up too, to watch.*

BAKER. And a face you can take off. See! [*His face becomes mask-like with a slightly japing look, then returns to normal.*] Right!

FANNING. That's very interesting!

BAKER. That's for the bluff! When you've bluffed, remember to look as if you hadn't. And when you haven't bluffed, to look as if you had! See?

FANNING. That's terribly interesting. I—I'll practise in a looking-glass. I'll certainly practise in a loo-looking glass.

BAKER. Right! Now for the double cross. Attention!

[*But* FANNING, *who has drunk his cocktail, has a vacant air.*

FANNING. What—what double cross?

BAKER. You're goin' to see. Watch my face!

FANNING. If you'll excuse me, I'd rather not. I'm so thirsty. Could I have a real drink?

BRICE. [*Linking his arm*] We want drinks, we want drinks!

[*He and* FANNING *go out, chanting to the tune of " Three Blind Mice."*

BAKER. Major, that young man is a proposition—— Greener than I ever thought to see a boy again.

MOULTENEY. He's never been away from home—neither school, nor college. Got a mother.

BAKER. Ho! Great mistake, mothers!

MOULTENEY. Great mistake, *his* mother.

BAKER. Well, the French all have mothers, and the boys live at home, but they don't stay green like that. What you going to do about it?

MOULTENEY. [*Shaking his head*] Don't know. Keep him integer vitæ if I can.

BAKER. Scelerisque purus? What! He wanted to get off to-night. Saw a girl for the first time.

MOULTENEY. Thanks for stopping him. He's not at all a bad boy —just an un-blooded pup, that's all.

BAKER. What's your scheme?

MOULTENEY. Get him down to Africa.

BAKER. Shooting and so on. Right!

MOULTENEY. I made a mistake to stop in Paris. I hate Paris, anyway.

BAKER. Take my tip! Let him get properly drunk, Major.

[GUSTAVE, *who is seen without on his way upstairs, pauses.*

GUSTAVE. [*In entrance, thinking himself addressed*] Sare?

BAKER. Not you, Gustave.

GUSTAVE. No, Sare. [*He passes on.*

MOULTENEY. [*With a smile*] Drunk? Why?

BAKER. Next morning. Remember your first drunk? Pleasant?

MOULTENEY. Horrid!

BAKER. First woman—that's different. First gamble—all depends. But first drunk's a cert.

MOULTENEY. The real trouble is that he plays no games.

BAKER. Ah! A boy's got to play games, or he'll take it out in "life." Funny word, "life," Major.

MOULTENEY. Very. In the big sense very fine.

BAKER. Right! Hated bein' in the war, but never regretted it since, and never want it again.

MOULTENEY. No, by George!

BAKER. Once find out that you can stand fire, and you don't want any more fire. What! [*Getting up.*] First-rate cooking here, Major. Funny little hole—very French.

[FANNING *appears, ornamentally inebriated.*

[*Sotto voce.*] Drunk! Right!

MOULTENEY. Reggie, bed for us, I think.

FANNING. [*Cheerful and exhilarated*] Bed! That's just what the nurse said, Major. I asked her to take my temperachure, and she said—she nevah took strange temperachures. At least she practically said that, because she's a nice woman. Mr. Brice and I have had a row about her. I was obliged to leave him in charge of the old waiter. Have you notished the old waiter—he's an early Victorian. Shall we ask him for some nishe drinks? [*Laughs.*

MOULTENEY. No more drinks for you, Reggie.

FANNING. No more drinks? Why? What did we come to Parish for? We haven't even danced. Mister Baker, will you give me the pleasure of a dansh?

MOULTENEY. Sit down, Reggie, and don't play the fool.

FANNING. [*Sitting down and contemplating the* MAJOR *anxiously*] Major, do you sus-suspect me? Mister Baker, how many drinks did we have?

BAKER. Three, I guess.

FANNING. And two makes five. And six—the one I want.

MOULTENEY. And won't get.

FANNING. [*Solemnly*] Major, you and Mister Baker have both been drunk many times.

BAKER. We have, have we Major?

FANNING. Ve'y well. I never have, so that even if I'm drunk now, I'm shtill a lot of holes down.

MOULTENEY. Neither Mr. Baker nor myself are proud of having been drunk.

BAKER. Not too fearfully.

FANNING. I should like to argue that point, Major. I feel that if you had never been drunk, you wouldn't know what it felt like, and that would be a losh to you. You wouldn't be the men you are, would you?

MOULTENEY. Which way are we to take that, Baker?

FANNING. Major, isn't the duty of man to be a man, a whole man, and nothing but a man? But are you nothing but a man if you've never been drunk? Excuse my logic.

MOULTENEY. All puppies eat muck, till they learn better.

FANNING. [*Triumphantly*] Eggsactly! I'm quite 'ware of being a pup-puppy. [*Very earnestly.*] But I want to say that—[*Wanders*] er—er—oh! I know. [*Smiles blandly.*] Mister Baker, I was brought up ve'y strictly, and I want to tell you about it.

BAKER. [*Interested*] Right!

FANNING. I think it may be a lesson to the Major.

MOULTENEY. Oh! you do?

FANNING. Yes. [*Earnestly.*] You see, I've got an inferirority complexsh—if y'know what I mean.

MOULTENEY. Don't be an ass, Reggie.

FANNING. Not at all! I feel I have to wipe out my mothersh apron-shtrings.

BAKER. Very natural!

FANNING. [*Gratefully*] Thank you! Don't misunderstand me— I'm not saying anything against my mother. She's a wonderful woman, Mister Baker—full of good works. I—I'm one of her good works.   [*He smiles pleasantly and goes into a sort of dream.*

BAKER. [*Aside*] He's O.K., Major.

FANNING. [*Coming out of his dream*] Not at all! That's where you make a mistake. Who knows whether I'm O.K?

[*Again goes into his dream.*

BAKER. [*Aside to the* MAJOR] Not as drunk as we thought.

[MOULTENEY *nods.*

FANNING. Who knows—if I don't know; an' what I mean to say is: How am I to know? I've always been so beautifully looked after. Nothing's ever happened to me.

BAKER. [*Sotto voce*] Kid's right.

MOULTENEY. That'll cure itself fast enough, Reggie.

FANNING. [*Shaking his head solemnly*] No, not fast enough—if you'll excuse me—lots of arrears to make up. I d-don't know even whether I'm a cak-coward.

MOULTENEY. Of course you're not.

FANNING. [*Blandly*] Why do you say that?

MOULTENEY. No decently bred chap is.

FANNING. Excuse me, Major tha's not logic, it's an assumption. I don't know if I can take my liquor like a—a sportsman.

BAKER. That's a matter of practice.

[*Shout from below :* " We want cocktails, we want cocktails ! " *is heard.*

FANNING. Mister Baker, you're ve'y sympathetic. But I—I don't even know whether I can lose my money pup-properly.

BAKER. Can you stick to it properly?

FANNING. Excuse me, that isn't part of the education of a sportsman. Then again : I don't know whether I can make love, if you'll forgive my mentioning such a thing.

MOULTENEY. You'll know as soon as ever you need.

FANNING. There speaks my mother. That is my difficulty, Major, if you don't mind my saying so. My mother is always speaking.

[*Enter* GUSTAVE.

GUSTAVE. You want cocktails, Sare !

MOULTENEY. *I* don't.

FANNING. Mushtn't dishappoint him. He—he might die of disappointment.

MOULTENEY. Stop it, Reggie—you've had too much. [*To* GUSTAVE.] No, thanks.

GUSTAVE. No, Sare.   [*He goes.*

FANNING. You see, Major, it isn't so much that I want to be a bad lad, as that I want to know what sort of bad lad I should be.

MOULTENEY. I quite see, old man.

FANNING. I thought you would ; I have a great respect for you, Major.

MOULTENEY. [*Grinning*] When you're squiffy.

FANNING. No, no—not—not only then. Sometimes I have a great respect for you when I'm sober. But sometimes I think you are too conshi-onshi-enshi-us, if you follow me.

MOULTENEY. Quite, Reggie !

FANNING. [*Getting up and taking the* MAJOR's *hand*] Thank you ve'y much, Major. You see, I've got to become a *m-man*, if you know what I mean.

BAKER. That's settled.

[BRICE *appears from the stairs ; his hair is standing up ; he looks rather drunk, and professionally funny, as if he had done something clever. He begins at once to chant :* " We want beds ; we want beds ; " *in which chant* FANNING *automatically joins.*

MOULTENEY. Shut up, Reggie, you'll wake people. If there's a nurse here, there must be somebody ill.

FANNING. [*Stopping*] Oh! I never thought of that—how ve'y inconshiderate of me!

BRICE. We want——

BAKER. [*To* BRICE] Dry up!

BRICE. That old waiter's goin' to get surprise of his life.

[*He laughs inanely.*

FANNING. [*Seriously to the* MAJOR] Do you think I ought to go an' apologize to the nurse, Major?

BRICE. [*Crowing*] Young r-rip!

BAKER. Chuck it, Brice!

FANNING. Mister Brice, I am sorry to say that I cannot consider you a proper person to associate with the Major.

BRICE. You young pup!

MOULTENEY. Kennel up, Reggie! You've had too much and you know it.

FANNING. [*With dignity*] In that case, you will excuse me if I blood Mister Brice's nose.

BRICE. [*Laughing and squaring up*] Try it, my boy!

[*As he speaks,* GUSTAVE *appears between the curtains; his figure is distraught and his hands raised.*

GUSTAVE. Messieurs! Ze 'ouse burn! I send ze porter to call the engines.

MOULTENEY. [*Sharply*] What? What's that?

GUSTAVE. Fire! Beeg fire! It spread! Queeck—come!

[*He turns and runs, followed by the* MAJOR.

[BRICE *collapses into a chair with a drunken laugh that turns into an expression of amazed horror.* FANNING *sways a little, trying to get hold of himself.*

BAKER. Here! Get up! Young Fanning, pull yourself together!

[*The* MAJOR'S *voice is heard shouting up the stairs.*

MAJOR. Baker! Baker! Telephone for the engines. Sharp!

BAKER. Right! [*He goes to the telephone and rapidly calls up the fire station.*] Caserne d'incendie, caserne—de pompiers. Si! Il y a incendie. Si, si! Vite! Il paraît que c'est grave.

[*The* MAJOR'S *voice:* "Water, you fellows! It's caught the stairs!" FANNING *seizes a bottle of water on a table, then puts it down.*

FANNING. That's no good.

BAKER. [*Who has finished telephoning*] Come on, boys, bathroom, cans.

[*He runs out.* FANNING, *with a visible effort, pulls himself together and follows. There is a sound of metal clanging, of water swishing.* BRICE *jumps up and runs out with the hoarse cry:* "We want water!"

[*The stage is empty, and suddenly the light goes out; figures pass dimly in the corridor with cans. The* MAJOR'S *voice is heard:*

MAJOR. Steady, Reggie! Good man! That's the stuff! Baker, pull down those curtains!

BAKER. [*Appearing, dim, in the doorway*] Right!

[*He pulls the curtains down.*

MOULTENEY. [*Appearing in the dim light*] It's burning like hell. We'll try and stop it here. Make a line—pass the cans. You, waiter, go and rouse people, send 'em on the roof! Stand by, Reggie! Good man! Now, line along!

BAKER. Steady, son. Now's the time to show your metal.

[*Swishing of water.*

The curtain falls.

SCENE III

SECOND FLOOR

The same evening: eleven o'clock.

A bedroom with bathroom carved out of it on the Left, and a door below the bathroom into a visible corridor. A bedroom, momentarily filled, as one may say, by the lively forms of two GIRLS *of fourteen and twelve, in pyjamas, pillow-fighting.*

As the curtain rises the skirmish ceases, and the eldest, DIANA, *takes a flying leap on to her bed and plumps down cross-legged.*

DIANA. Pax, Bryn!

BRYN. Pig! You've pulled out three hairs. Look!

[*Holds them out.*

DIANA. We can stick them in again. Mum's got some seccotine. [*Giggles.*] Have you wound your watch?

BRYN. No. [*Putting it to her ear.*] It's stopped, Di.

DIANA. Put it to eleven. It's striking! Hallo! Listen! Open the door, Bryn.

[BRYN *opens the door. The sound of a violin playing a Leclair Tambourin comes in.*

[*Under her breath.*] I say! Isn't it topping?

[*Both listen with all their ears. The player reaches the end, and there is silence.*

BRYN. Shall I go up and ask if he'd like us in to hear him. They love audiences, you know. It's all rot when they pretend they don't.

DIANA. You can't in pys.

BRYN. Why not?

DIANA. [*Flying up and grabbing her.*] We don't know him.

BRYN. He wouldn't mind, Di.

DIANA. No, Bryn, you can't.   Besides, I bet he doesn't wash his head.

BRYN. [*Wide-eyed*] Really?

DIANA. Musicians don't.

BRYN. How d'you know?

DIANA. It takes the gloss off.   That one at Nauheim *never* washed —— I simply know he didn't.

BRYN. This one washes his ears anyway.

DIANA. He hasn't got any.

BRYN. I saw part of *one*.

DIANA. Nobody could see through all that hair.   You do tell whackers, Bryn.

BRYN. [*Looking out of the door*] Here he is, Di, coming down.   I dare you to ask him if he washes his head.

DIANA. Bryn—if you——!

BRYN. [*To* FROBA *passing in the corridor*] Oh! Do come in, my sister wants to ask you something?

DIANA. [*Under her breath*] You little toad!

FROBA. [*Moving into the doorway*] Ye-es?   What is it?

DIANA. [*Recoiling*] Oh! Do you like Paris?

FROBA. Well! I judge it's some town.

DIANA. Yes, we judge that, too.

FROBA. I guess quite some people do.   Is dat all?

DIANA. Y-yes.   Thank you!

FROBA. Heu! Den I'll go get my drink.   Say, you look cunning in dose pajamas.

[*The children make faces as he goes out and away down the corridor.*

BRYN. [*Shutting the door*] You *are* a funk, Di.   [*Going across to the window.*] You see he was quite used to pyjamas.   What can we do now?

DIANA. Yes, I'm not a bit sleepy.

BRYN. I've got a hunch.   Those two old things next door—let's tap like the prisoners in Dad's novel—the one we're not allowed to read.

DIANA. Now, that's what I call sensible.   They're stuffy old things.

BRYN. We must do it properly, Di.   You say over the alphabet and I'll do the tapping.   [*They crouch on the beds against the wall.*] What shall I tap with?

DIANA. I'll get the odol bottle.   [*Gets it from the bathroom.*

BRYN. They always ask each other's names first.

DIANA. Yes, but we know their's—it's Beeton.

BRYN. Let's start with S.O.S. then.

DIANA. It's an awful strain getting the alphabet right every time. Ready?   [*As she says the alphabet over to* S, BRYN *taps.*] Stop! Now for O.   [*Says alphabet to* O. BRYN *taps once too often.*

BRYN. Oh! Di! I over-tapped. They've got P.

DIANA. Well, what begins with S.P. ?

BRYN. Spot! Sport! Spillikins.

DIANA. I know, Starting Price. Only that doesn't seem to lead to anything. We'll have to begin again. Let's try: Are you there? A. [BRYN *taps once.*] Now R. [*Begins alphabet to which* BRYN *taps when a resounding knock on the wall breaks them off. They giggle.*] It sounds as if they didn't like it.

BRYN. I don't expect they were ever in prison. They don't look sports. Shall we try again?

DIANA. It's too risky.

BRYN. Well, we must do something.

DIANA. I tell you what. There are some honeyspooners in the room opposite.

BRYN. How d'you know they're honeyspooners?

DIANA. I watched them at dinner. Their eyes were all swimmy. Disgusting! We might give them a lesson. They're only French.

BRYN. They aren't, if you mean the girl with all that neck.

DIANA. Well! They were speaking French with an awful lot of accent.

BRYN. Only showing off. I heard the man say " damn " in the hall.

DIANA. [*Doubtfully*] Oh! that makes a difference. They might cut up rusty.

BRYN. Well, let's only put on hats and coats and run in as if we thought it was our room.

DIANA. Yes, that's quite natural.

BRYN. Only—the door'll be locked, Di.

DIANA. It mightn't be, yet.

BRYN. Honeyspooners always lock their doors the first minute.

DIANA. How d'you know?

BRYN. Because the moment they get in, he says: " Darling ! " and she says : " Oh ! James ! " and then they begin to kiss. B-beu !

DIANA. Bryn, you're awful !

BRYN. *I* know ! Let's stand outside their door and miaow.

DIANA. That's a scheme !

BRYN. *You* do it, Di. And I'll watch you when they come out.

DIANA. You are a worm.

BRYN. Well, bag's last !

DIANA. We'd better rehearse. You spit best—you do the spitting.

[*They rehearse softly.*]

Safety first ! If we put this screen outside their door we can get back before they see us.

BRYN. All right !   [*They go out on tiptoe.*

DIANA. [*Outside in the lighted corridor*] Begin low, Bryn, and rather rallentando, then we'll work up. Now !

[*The sound of their caterwauling rises, swells a little, and then suddenly with a scuttle they are back. A moment later* MRS. LENNOX *appears in the corridor and enters their room. She is a lady of about forty—pale and anxious-looking.*

BRYN. [*With innocent wide eyes*] Oh ! is that you, Mum ?

MRS. L. What were you doing ?

BRYN. Just practising cats.

MRS. L. Did you put that screen out there ?

DIANA. We thought you wouldn't like us to be seen, Mum.

MRS. L. Di ! you really ought to know better.

DIANA. Why, Mum ? It's very harmless.

MRS. L. Out of your room, when you should be in bed, and asleep.

DIANA. Well, Mum—this is Paris.

BRYN. Just seeing " life," you know.

MRS. L. Monkeys ! [*Seeing pillows tossed about.*] Have you been pillow-fighting ?

DIANA. Only softening them, Mum. Feel ! They're awfully hard.

MRS. L. It'll be a relief to get you home.

BRYN. Are we going to-morrow ?

MRS. L. If Father's well enough to travel. What's this odol doing here ?

BRYN. What is it doing there, Di ?

DIANA. Oh ! It just strayed in.

MRS. L. Go and get that screen back.

[*The children go out and bring back the screen.* MRS. LENNOX *tidies their beds.*

DIANA. Listen !

BRYN. [*At the window*] Doesn't he play beautifully ?

[*She leans against the drawn back curtain, at first feigning reverence then genuinely moved. The violinist is playing Poise's " Joli Gilles."*

MRS. L. [*Not to be put off—to* DIANA] You girls are altogether too young for your age.

DIANA. Well, Mum ! We've got to be old some day. It's no use beginning before we need.

MRS. L. It's time *you* were getting serious, Di.

DIANA. Oh ! no, not yet, Mum. *You* never have any fun. No one seems to have any fun after they're grown-up.

MRS. L. All right, duckie. Keep your fun as long as you can.

DIANA. Yes, that's what I thought. Dad's kept some, hasn't he ?

MRS. L. Yes, you both take more after him than after me.

DIANA. Girls do. And boys take after their mothers. Dad's got a little joke inside that you couldn't put out, could you ? He bubbles.   [MRS. LENNOX *cannot answer.*] You don't want to put it out, do you ?

MRS. L. Heavens! No, child.

BRYN. Mum! I suppose all the people in this hotel have come to see " life," haven't they? Why is there more " life " in Paris than in other places?

MRS. L. It's a superstition, Bryn.

BRYN. And what is " life," anyway?

MRS. L. A very ugly thing.

BRYN. Really?

DIANA. *I* know what it is—cocktails and dancing, and that.

BRYN. That tune gave me a funny feeling—here. [*She puts her hand on the middle of her waist.*] It squeezed me.

DIANA. Don't be soppy, Bryn. Besides, your heart isn't there, it's higher, to the left.

BRYN. Mum, it's in your middle, isn't it?

MRS. L. Anatomically—yes.

DIANA, Not in the tummy, Mum.

BRYN. It isn't my tummy. It's higher, in the diaphragum.

MRS. L. Diaphragm, Bryn.

BRYN. Tell us more about " life," Mum.

MRS. L. " Life " as they call it, has nothing to do with the heart, anyway.

BRYN. What has it to do with, then?

MRS. L. The appetites. And it's the shortest way to destroy them.

DIANA. Does Dad say that, too? Or would he only just say it to *us* for fear that we might want to " see life "?

BRYN. But *can* you have too much dancing, Mum?

MRS. L. Of this modern dancing, much too much.

BRYN. Was ancient dancing more virtuous?

DIANA. I bet it wasn't. Dad says human nature doesn't change.

BRYN. When you used to dance, Mum, did it destroy your appetite?

MRS. L. [*Laughing*] No, increased it.

DIANA. There you are then!

MRS. L. You don't understand, my dears.

DIANA. But, Mum—*you* haven't seen any " life," have you?

MRS. L. Not in that sense, perhaps. But you can take it from me, that it's silly, all the same.

BRYN. [*With a deep sigh*] I think it's so sad having to take things from other people.

MRS. L. Now, darlings, you really must go to bed. I'll tuck you up.

BRYN. [*With suspicious readiness*] All right, Mum, we were waiting up for that. Come on, Di!

[*They race into bed.* MRS. LENNOX *tucks up and kisses first one and then the other.*

MRS. L. Now be good, won't you?

36

BOTH. Oh! rather!

[MRS. LENNOX, *with a look back, goes out, switching off the light; as she opens the door the cry,* " We want cocktails! " *from below comes in.*

BRYN. [*In the dark*] Di, I'm jolly thirsty.

DIANA. So'm I. Let's ring! The bell's over you—three times for the waiter.   [BRYN *rings emphatically.*]
We'd better put our undies away. He's very old. Turn up!

[BRYN *turns the light up. They both scramble out of bed and tidy away their undies. They have barely got back to bed, when* GUSTAVE *is seen in the corridor and there is a knock.*

DIANA. Entrez!   [GUSTAVE *appears.*

GUSTAVE. Ye-es, Mees?

BRYN. Oh! Gustave, we're *so* thirsty. Could you bring us some ginger-ale?

GUSTAVE. Ye-es, Mees. I bring it—veree sweet, veree cool.

DIANA. Are you always busy, Gustave?

GUSTAVE. 'Ave some gentlemen down there, Mees.

DIANA. Yes, we heard them calling for cocktails. I suppose they're seeing " life "?

GUSTAVE. Ye-es, Mees—a leetle life—veree nice.

DIANA. I suppose we couldn't have a little " life " up here, could we, Gustave?

GUSTAVE. [*Interrogating*] Excuse, Mees—life?

BRYN. She means cocktails.

GUSTAVE. [*With his smile*] No, Mees, not for young ladies.

BRYN. We like you, Gustave.

GUSTAVE. [*With his patient ghost of a smile*] Veree glad, Mees. Excuse!

[*He turns to go; the* CHILDREN *chant softly :* " We like Gustave —we like Gustave—we like Gustave! " GUSTAVE *gives them his patient, smiling look back and goes.*

DIANA. Doesn't he look tired, Bryn? He's so old, and he has to run about like a rabbit. It's a shame. I'm sorry we rang, you know.

BRYN. I *am* thirsty, Di, and Mum makes such a fuss about water.

DIANA. Well, look here, *I'll* go down and get the ginger ale. That'll save him.   [*Opens the door.*

[*The violinist has begun to play a tango called " Cumparsita."*

DIANA. It's a tango; while I'm gone you can practise, then we can dance it together.

BRYN. All right. Hurry up!

[DIANA *goes out, closing the door, and can be seen stopping and sniffing in the corridor.*

[*The music comes in at the window,* BRYN, *who has quite a good*

notion of a tango, stands a moment and then begins to dance.
She soon becomes quite absorbed, and dances till the tune stops.
Then she runs to the window and leans out ; almost at once
she recoils, sniffing ; as she does so the light goes out in the room
and corridor. She gasps, gropes to the door in the dim light
from the open window, and after trying the switch, opens the
door and calls softly, then more loudly.]

Di ! Di !   [DIANA *appears from the corridor with a candle.*

DIANA. [*Excitedly*] Bryn, the house is on fire. Are there any candles ?

BRYN. I say ! That'll be the first fire I've seen. Is it a real one ?

DIANA. It's all over the place downstairs, and coming up fast.

BRYN. Up the stairs ? Can't we get down, then ?

DIANA. No. Hurry up ! They can't put it out. [*She finds and lights two candles.*] There are four men and Gustave trying to.

BRYN. Shall we go down and help ?

DIANA. No. We're to go on the roof. The engines are coming. Buck up !

BRYN. Have we got to dress ?

DIANA. No ; bung on your mack and shoes.
                              [*She is herself doing this.*

BRYN. [*Beginning to bung*] But we shall miss it all on the roof, Di.

DIANA. We shall see the engines, and we can find a way down— there'll be iron stairs, I expect.

BRYN. Does Mum know ?

DIANA. Of course she knows. I told them.

BRYN. [*Suddenly*] Listen ! He's still playing—he can't know.

     [*The violinist indeed is letting himself go on a Vivaldi—Bach*
          Andante.

DIANA. We'll tell him as we go up. I routed out those stuffy old things.

BRYN. It's jolly exciting, isn't it ? Is Dad helping to put it out ?

DIANA. No, he's not well enough.

BRYN. Oh ! Di, I must go down and see.

DIANA. [*Holding her*] No.

BRYN. It's not fair. You've had your go—— Well, let me startle those honeyspooners.

DIANA. All right ! But hurry up !

     [BRYN *rushes out with a candle into the corridor, where it is dark.*
          The sound of a fire engine is heard. DIANA *puts on a cap and*
          runs to the window. MRS. LENNOX *enters from the corridor*
          with her dressing bag.

MRS. L. Where's Bryn, Di ?

DIANA. [*Turning*] Oh ! she's just stirring-up the honeyspooners close by.

MRS. L. The what! [*Seizing a suit-case.*] Help me put things in —everything will be spoiled by the water.

[DIANA *and she throw things into the suit-case.* BRYN *runs in.*
BRYN. I say! The door *wasn't* locked. They were *eating*—in the dark. Didn't they stare just! Oh! Mum! Isn't it exciting!

MRS. L. Have you got your stockings on, Bryn?

BRYN. No.

MRS. L. Put them on, then.

BRYN. Over my pys, or under?

MRS. L. Under. And then get your sponge and things. Hurry! Now, listen! You're both to go quietly up on the roof, take this bag up—and stay there till we come. Diana, take care of Bryn, and don't let her look over the edge. I must go back to Dad.

[*The two* CHILDREN *are gazing at her,* BRYN *putting on her stockings.*
DIANA. [*Awed*] Is Dad really ill, Mum?

MRS. L. Yes.

BRYN. Oh! Isn't it awful, then!

MRS. L. [*At the door*] Now, my darlings, be good, and do what I say.

DIANA. Yes, rather!

BRYN. Can't we help at all?

MRS. L. No, only by doing what I say.

BRYN. All right then, we will.

MRS. L. Good girls. Bless you!   [*She goes.*

BRYN. Di, this is seeing " life," isn't it?

DIANA. You bet! Listen! He's still playing! Come on, Bryn

[*Each with a candle in one hand, bag, suit-case and sponge-bags in the other, they go out and down the corridor.*
BRYN. Look at our shadows, Di! Aren't they long!

The curtain falls.

SCENE IV

SECOND FLOOR

The same evening : eleven o'clock.

The adjoining bedroom. In the two beds side by side facing the footlights, are MR. *and* MRS. BEETON.

[MRS. BEETON *is a large decided-looking lady of about sixty reading by the light of a bed lamp.* MR. BEETON, *perhaps sixty-six, is asleep on his back with his mouth open beneath his stubby moustache, from it are issuing faint but deepening snores.*
MRS. B. [*Lowering her book*] Tom!

[MR. B. *utters one of those louder snores cut off in the middle which mark the return to consciousness.*

MR. B. Eh ? What ?

MRS. B. You were snoring.

MR. B. What ! I wasn't.

MRS. B. You were.

MR. B. Well, why didn't you tell me ? You know it gives me a sore throat.

MRS. B. I have told you.

MR. B. [*After a pause*] I suppose you think you *never* snore.

MRS. B. I know I don't.

MR. B. My hat !

MRS. B. You shouldn't lie on your back.

MR. B. [*Turning on his side*] I don't. It doesn't suit me.

MRS. B. I wish you wouldn't contradict me, Tom.

MR. B. Contradict ? I——?

MRS. B. Yes, say you don't !   [*Pause.*

MR. B. I suppose you think you never contradict me.

MRS. B. Only when I have to.

MR. B. My Aunt ! [*A pause.*] What's the time ?

MRS. B. Just struck eleven.

MR. B. What are you reading there ?

MRS. B. A very silly book.

MR. B. Then why do you read it ?

MRS. B. Because I'm not sleepy.

MR. B. I told you not to drink that coffee. That's why you drank it, I suppose.

MRS. B. Oh ! go to sleep and let me read !

[MR. B. *turns his back on her with a grunt. A silence. Then* MRS. B. *puts her book down.*

MRS. B. [*Softly*] Tom ! Are you asleep ?

MR. B. Yes. Why ?

MRS. B. What made you choose this hotel ?

MR. B. It's got a name for cooking. The dinner was first chop.

MRS. B. There's illness in the house. I saw a nurse.

MR. B. Where ?

MRS. B. Close by.

MR. B. Infectious ?

MRS. B. How should I know ?

MR. B. Didn't you ask ?

MRS. B. No.

MR. B. If you'd told me, I'd——

MRS. B. Yes, what would you have done ?

MR. B. Made a point of finding out, of course.

Mrs. B. Exactly!

Mr. B. [*Turning to her*] Well, d'you want to catch the 'flu?

Mrs. B. Now, of course, you're in a stew!

Mr. B. Fiddlesticks! I wish you wouldn't make me out an old woman.

Mrs. B. I don't need to.

Mr. B. Don't be funny.

Mrs. B. It's a man who's ill.

Mr. B. How d'you know?

Mrs. B. The nurse was pretty.

Mr. B. That's no proof. You got me a perfect hag last winter.

Mrs. B. Naturally. There's a wife. She's very pale.

Mr. B. You seem to see everything.

Mrs. B. Listen, Tom! [*Pause.*] What's that tapping?

Mr. B. I don't hear anything.

Mrs. B. Of course you don't, with your head under the bedclothes like that.

Mr. B. Look here! Do you want me to go to sleep or not?

Mrs. B. Yes, or you'll be fit for nothing to-morrow. I don't want to have to drag you round half awake.

Mr. B. All right, then! Good-night!   [*Turns his back on her.*

Mrs. B. There *is* a tapping, Tom. It's on this wall.

Mr. B. [*Stirring*] Oh! damn!   [*He frees his head.*

Mrs. B. There!   [*A tapping sound.*

Mr. B. [*Screwing round towards the wall*] Here! What blasted lunatic——?

Mrs. B. I wish you wouldn't swear, Tom.

Mr. B. [*Thumping his fist on the wall*] Who is it next door?

Mrs. B. It's those children.

Mr. B. Children! Oh! Ah! Pretty couple! Well, I've stopped it.

Mrs. B. I wonder you didn't tap back.

Mr. B. [*Snuggling down*] I wish the deuce, you—you——!

[*A silence, during which* Mrs. B. *takes up her book.*

Mrs. B. [*Softly*] Tom! You're not asleep yet, are you?

Mr. B. Yes.

Mrs. B. You couldn't have been.

Mr. B. Why not?

Mrs. B. You weren't breathing.

Mr. B. Well, I can sleep without breathing.

Mrs. B. I can always tell when you're asleep. When you don't snore, you make a funny little ticking noise.

[*Clucks with her tongue, like the tick of a clock.*

Mr. B. Well, then why d'you ask me?

Mrs. B. I didn't want to wake you.

Mr. B. Well, you have.

Mrs. B. Did you fasten the door?

Mr. B. Yes.   No.

Mrs. B. Hadn't you better, then?

Mr. B. What's it matter?

Mrs. B. You wouldn't like it if my pearls were stolen.

> [Mr. B. *gets out of bed and goes to the lower door, which he opens.   He shuts the door and turns the key.*]

Mr. B. Rowdy lot down there!

Mrs. B. If you will choose little out-of-the-way hotels like this. I saw a young man with hair that stood out like a tea-tray.

Mr. B. Black japanned hair.   That's rather good.   What! [*Getting into bed again.*]   Let's go to sleep!

Mrs. B. Is the window open?

Mr. B. About eight inches.

Mrs. B. That's not enough.   It's very stuffy to-night.

Mr. B. [*Sighing*] All right!   All right! [*Gets out of bed again and going to the window, opens it wider.*]   Now I suppose you'll say there's a draught.

Mrs. B. Don't be cross!

Mr. B. I'm not cross.   [*Gets into bed.*]   Are you going to put that light out?

Mrs. B. Give me a kiss, Tom.

> [*He jerks himself up, kisses her cheek perfunctorily and subsides.* Mrs. B. *turns out the lamp.   Darkness and silence.   A sound of breathing rises.*]

Mrs. B. Tom!

Mr. B. Um?

Mrs. B. There's a mosquito!

Mr. B. [*Sitting up alert*] What!   No!

Mrs. B. Listen! [*Pause.*]   There!   Now!

Mr. B. [*The sportsman roused*] By Jove, there is!   Turn up! [Mrs. B. *turns up the light.*]   I must get my specs. [*He gets out of bed, puts on a pair of spectacles, takes up a slipper, turns on the full light and proceeds to revolve slowly on his heels, scrutinizing the ceiling and the walls.*] There he is! [*Pointing.*]   No, it's a fly.

Mrs. B. [*Whose ears are also standing up*] Tom!   What's that?
> [*Points.*

Mr. B. [*Approaching mark on wall*] It's an old one, squashed. [*Pointing.*]   There he goes!   Brute!   Keep your eye on him!

Mrs. B. How can I?   I haven't seen him.

Mr. B. There, there!

Mrs. B. I see him.   He's settled.

Mr. B. Where?

Mrs. B. [*Pointing*] Over that chest of drawers.   Look!   Right above—about five feet from the ceiling.

Mr. B. Right-o! I'll get on the drawers. Keep him spotted! [*With the help of a chair he climbs cumbrously on to the chest of drawers, cautiously raises his arm; aims, and slaps the slipper on the wall.*] God! I've missed him. [*Pauses, perched on chest of drawers, gazing round.*] Lost him now—lost him—lost him! Where'd he go?

Mrs. B. There he is, Tom!

Mr. B. Where?

Mrs. B. On the ceiling.

Mr. B. [*Climbing down*] I'll fetch him off with a slipper. Where?

Mrs. B. [*Pointing*] There!

Mr. B. I spot him. [*Hurls slipper*] He's off! Now! [*Both stare blankly.*] They're so damned invisible.

Mrs. B. Look! He's settled over your bed. Take a towel.

[*Mr. B. gets a towel.*

Mr. B. Watch him, old girl. [*Climbs on to his bed.*] I believe I could reach him with the slipper.

Mrs. B. The towel will be safer.

Mr. B. Might flap him off.

Mrs. B. You'll overbalance. Take good aim, Tom. Make sure of him this time!

Mr. B. I'll get on the bolster.

[*He cautiously extends his arm upwards, makes a sudden furious dab with the slipper, and falls backwards on to the bed.*

Mrs. B. There now! I told you.

Mr. B. [*On his back, with triumph*] Got him though! [*He scrutinizes the sole of the slipper.*] Look! [*Scrambling forward and showing it to her.*] No blood in him, thank God!

Mrs. B. I must say, you're splendid with mosquitoes, Tom.

Mr. B. [*Resuming an upright posture on the floor*] Um, wasn't a bad shot—considering. Think there are any more?

[*He stands gazing around.*

Mrs. B. Tom!

Mr. B. Hallo?

Mrs. B. That very young man at dinner was the son of Lady Ilfracombe.

Mr. B. How d'you know that?

Mrs. B. Looked in the register. The Honourable Reginald Fanning.

Mr. B. Looked rather a young juggins, I thought.

Mrs. B. Two of the men he was with were very Stock-Exchangey. The other one leads him about, a Major Moulteney.

Mr. B. How on earth you hear everything—I don't know!

Mrs. B. *I* use my ears.

Mr. B. You jolly well do! [*Turning out main light and moving towards his bed.*] There aren't any more. [*He prepares to get into bed.*

MRS. B. Tom! There's a tap dripping in the bathroom.

MR. B. Well, let it!

MRS. B. You know if you once begin to hear it, it'll get on your nerves.

MR. B. Oh! All right. [*Gets out of bed and opens door into bathroom.*] It isn't dripping.

MRS. B. I heard it, I tell you.

MR. B. You've got noises on the brain.

MRS. B. Will you go and look at the taps, instead of standing there, arguing.   [MR. BEETON *disappears into the bathroom.*

MRS. B. [*As he reappears*] Well?

MR. B. I suppose you might call it a drip with luck.

MRS. B. There!

MR. B. You needn't rub it in.

MRS. B. I never rub it in.

MR. B. My Sam!   [*Prepares to get into bed.*
                [*The* NURSE *is seen in the corridor knocking at the door.*

MRS. B. There's somebody knocking, Tom.

MR. B. Oh! Great Scott! [*Gets out of bed.*] What is it?
                                                        [*Renewed knock.*

[*He puts on a dressing gown and slippers, goes to the door and opens it.*]

Yes?

NURSE. [*Outside*] My patient has severe heart pain. You haven't such a thing as a hypodermic needle? Mine's out of action.

MR. B. [*Leaning in*] It's the nurse—wants to know if we've got a hypodermic needle. Haven't, have we?

MRS. B. Of course not. What's the matter? Shall I——?

MR. B. [*To the* NURSE] Awfully sorry—afraid we haven't.
                [*The* NURSE *is seen going back down the corridor.*
                                                        [*To his wife.*]

It's a heart case—so that's all right. Poor devil! I suppose one ought to have one of those things handy. Nice-looking woman, what!

MRS. B. I thought you'd think so.

MR. B. There you go!

MRS. B. What do you mean by: "There you go!"

MR. B. Nothing—nothing!   [*Prepares to get into bed.*

MRS. B. [*Ineffably*] Nothing, indeed!

MR. B. Oh, let's get to sleep.
                [*Gets into bed and settles down with his back to her.*

[MRS. B., *after contemplating the back of his head with a certain acidity, turns out the lamp. Dark silence. Then a sound of sniffing.*

36*

Mrs. B. [*Sharply*] Tom !

Mr. B. Good Lord ! What now ?

Mrs. B. There's a smell of burning.

[*The light in the corridor goes out.*

Mr. B. What next ! It's your nose, now.

Mrs. B. [*Sniffing*] Can't you smell it ?

Mr. B. [*Sniffing*] Um ? Yes—yes—distinct. Now, what the deuce ?

Mrs. B. You didn't throw a match or a cigarette into——?

Mr. B. I like that, when you wouldn't let me smoke !

Mrs. B. It's getting worse. [*Tries to turn up lamp.*] Tom ! The light's off !

Mr. B. Nonsense ! You imagine things.

Mrs. B. It is, I tell you.

Mr. B. I'll try the other switch. [*Gets out of bed in the dark and stubs his toe.*] Damn ! Stubbed my toe ! Where is that switch ?

Mrs. B. By the door.

Mr. B. [*Feeling the wall*] Can't find it. Oh ! Here it is ! Doesn't work.

Mrs. B. What did I say ?

Mr. B. Fuse must have blown out.

Mrs. B. Where are your matches ?

Mr. B. How should I know ? Dash it ! [*Groping.*] Ow-w ! Done it again !

Mrs. B. Pull the curtains, there'll be some light. [*Sniffs.*] It's getting worse, Tom. [*Gets out of bed.*

Mr. B. [*Pulling the curtains. A feeble light comes in.*] Here they are, on the chest of drawers. Who put 'em there ?

Mrs. B. You did. [*Donning dressing-gown and slippers.*] Light a candle.

[Mr. B. *strikes a match and gropes round, seeking.* Mrs. B. *stands at the bottom of her bed sniffing.*

Mr. B. Where—where are they ? Oh ! Here's one ! [*Lighting candle and gazing round.*] Nothing wrong here, I'll go and scout.

[*He goes towards the door.*

[*The pyjamad figure of the child* Diana Lennox *is seen outside in the corridor.*

Mrs. B. Be careful, Tom !

Mr. B. All right, all right ! Hallo !

[*The door is burst open in his face by* Diana, *with a lighted candle in her hand.*

Mrs. B. There ! You never fastened the door again. Tom !

Diana. Awfully sorry ! But the house is on fire. Isn't it exciting ?

Mrs. B. On fire ? What d'you mean, on fire ?

DIANA. On fire. You can't get down. It's caught the stairs. We're to go on the roof. They've telephoned for the engines.

MRS. B. Tom! [*Pointing.*] Look!

[*A flicker as of flame from below is dimly seen through the window.*

MR. B. She's right! Here's a mess! Where are my trousers? Keep cool! [*To the* CHILD.] You keep your head, young woman. [*Seeking.*] Damn it, where *are* my trousers?

[DIANA *has flitted, with her candle, and her figure is seen flying up the corridor, which is now dark again.* MRS. B., *in the dim light is hitching up her nightgown under a skirt.*]

Keep cool, old girl, keep cool! [*Drawing trousers over his pyjamas.*] We'll pack. Put on your long coat! Where the hell is everything? Put your pearls on. Where's my watch?

MRS. B. [*Cooler than he*] Under your pillow, of course, Tom.

[*The door is again opened,* GUSTAVE *enters.*

GUSTAVE. [*Gently*] Sare, Madame! The 'ouse is fired.

MR. B. Yes, yes, we know. Who's responsible? Why don't you put it out?

GUSTAVE. A beeg fire.

MRS. B. Can't we get downstairs?

GUSTAVE. Non, Madame—the roof. Excuse! The sick gentleman.   [*He vanishes down the dark corridor.*

MR. B. Where are the passports—in your dressing-case?

MRS. B. Yes. I must do my hair, Tom. I'm not going out like a fright.

MR. B. Nonsense! What does your appearance matter?

MRS. B. You never think of my appearance.

MR. B. Stuff it under your collar. They'll think you're shingled.

MRS. B. [*With finality*] I'm going to do my hair.

MR. B. All right, all right! Hurry up with it, then! The house'll burn like tinder. These French houses are all wood and paint.

MRS. B. [*Before glass*] I must have the candle, Tom. Put it there. I call it frightfully careless not letting us know until the stairs were caught.

MR. B. [*Packing*] I've got my dress things anyway. You won't have time to pack.

MRS. B. I shall take my dressing-bag.

MR. B. Got your keys, and your watch? Right. I'll get my shaving things.   [*Sound of a fire engine.*] By George! There's an engine!   [*Goes into bathroom.*

MRS. B. Don't forget the toothbrushes. [*Twisting and rolling her hair; to herself.*] Tt, tt, it really is annoying! [*Turns suddenly at a knock, with pins in her mouth.*] Come in!

[GUSTAVE's *figure is dimly seen in the dark corridor.*

GUSTAVE. [*At the door*] Madame! Time to go on the roof Madame.

MRS. B. [*Through the pins*] Yes, yes! I can't be hurried.

GUSTAVE. I carry bag, Madame?

MRS. B. [*Putting hairpinned hand on her dressing bag*] No, don't you touch that. Take this suit-case—— [GUSTAVE *takes the suit-case.*
[*There comes a howl from the bathroom.*

VOICE OF MR. B. Wow! I——! It's so damned dark!

MRS. B. Come along, Tom—never mind——

MR. B. [*Reappearing with sponge-bags, etc.*] Can't find my shaving brush. [*To* GUSTAVE.] Hi, here's a soaked bath towel—might come in handy. [*Throws it to* GUSTAVE, *who places it over his arm like a napkin.*

GUSTAVE. Yes, Sare! Please come, queeck, Sare and Madame.

MR. B. All right, all right! Ready, old girl!

MRS. B. [*With a final pin and pat*] I've never done my hair so quickly —how does it look, Tom?

MR. B. Jolly fine—jolly fine! Here's your coat. [*Puts it on her.*] Now then! [*He takes up the dressing-bag. The sound of a fire engine approaching is heard.*] There's another! Good biz!

GUSTAVE. Sare, Madame—please, queeck. [*He goes out.*

MR. B. All right, all right! Plenty of time! No good getting the wind up.

MRS. B. Now, Tom, give me your word not to be rash.

MR. B. Rash! I'm never rash.

[*They go to the door, pass out, leaving the room dark, and are seen in the corridor,* MRS. B. *carrying the candle.*

MR. B. [*Without*] Here, take these, I've forgotten my pipe.

[*Sound of engines; then voice of* MR. B. *in the dark, within the room again.*]

Where did I put the blasted thing?

MRS. B. [*Without*] Tom, I'm not going up without you.

VOICE OF MR. B. [*Within*] All right, all right, coming! [*To himself.*] I know—got it! Wow! My shin! [*Goes out.*

MR. B. [*In the corridor*] Come on, old girl, up we go!

VOICE OF MRS. B. Does my nightgown show, Tom?

VOICE OF MR. B. What? No! Yes! Yes! Looks jolly well!
[*Their voices die.*

The curtain falls.

SCENE V

SECOND FLOOR

The same evening : eleven o'clock.

Another bedroom.   The neighbouring clock is striking eleven.

> *The door opens and there enters a* YOUNG WOMAN *in evening dress with a wrap over her arm.*

YOUNG WOMAN. [*As the clock finishes*] Eleven !   How nice and early !

> [*She turns up the light.   The room is then seen to be in the disorder of a hurried unpacking, as of travellers just in from a train, hastening down to dinner.   She throws down her wrap and tidies the dressing-table, humming and whistling the " Habanera " from Carmen.   She lays some pyjamas on a bed, then stands before the glass.   She is an attractive young person.   Breaking into the song, she sits down before the glass and touches herself up.   The door is opened softly and the* YOUNG MAN *" Tony," in evening dress with a coat over his arm and a hat, comes in ; he puts them down, comes up, leans over and kisses her.*

YOUNG MAN. [*Fervently*] Darling !

YOUNG WOMAN. Oh !   Tony !   [*Puts her lips to his.   A pause.*

> [*The* YOUNG MAN *sits on the edge of the dressing table and lights a cigarette.*

YOUNG MAN. We took a chance, Nell—going to the opera.

YOUNG WOMAN. Ah !   but Carmen's worth it.   Gives you such a kick.

YOUNG MAN. D'you know, there's young Fanning in the hotel. Rotten luck !   A little out-of-the-way place like this !   I chose it so carefully.

YOUNG WOMAN. Fanning ?   D'you mean that babe Reggie ?   He was in pinafores last year—absolute mother's darling.

YOUNG MAN. Yes.   He's being bear-led to get him ready for the Guards.   It's all right.   He hasn't seen you, and he shan't.   I don't know the man he's with, luckily.

YOUNG WOMAN. No.   But perhaps I do.

YOUNG MAN. [*Gloomily*] That's the worst of good cooking.   You never know who'll be gathered round the fleshpots.

YOUNG WOMAN. I didn't have much of them to-night, after that crossing.   Ugh !

YOUNG MAN. [*Gazing at her and chanting under his breath*] Carmen ! Carmen !   Nell, I shall call you Carmen.

YOUNG WOMAN. [*Suddenly*] Tony! Tell me! Is *ours* a grand passion? Is it?

YOUNG MAN. If it wasn't, Nell, would you be here with me?

YOUNG WOMAN. [*Laying hold of his lapels*] But is it? Is there any such thing nowadays?

YOUNG MAN. Of course there is.

YOUNG WOMAN. I wonder! If it *is* a grand passion, it's going to be an awful life, Tony. Unless—I've got the pluck to cut the painter.

YOUNG MAN. What d'you mean, Nell? Of course you're going to cut the painter, or you wouldn't have come, and I wouldn't have asked you.

YOUNG WOMAN. [*Turning round and gazing past him*] But, Tony, this is only a try out. I thought you realized that?

YOUNG MAN. A try out? Yes. But there's only one end to it.

YOUNG WOMAN. My grandmother ran away for good in what she stood up in. But *this* isn't a run-away age, Tony. It's an age of calculated divorce.

YOUNG MAN. I don't care what the rotten age is. I'm in love.

YOUNG WOMAN. Besides, she hated her husband, and I don't hate Hugh. I've tried to, but I can't. He means nothing. You can't hate something that means nothing.

YOUNG MAN. Well, *I* hate him.

YOUNG WOMAN. Only because he has me. And not enough to stick a knife into me, like Don José, if I go back to him.

YOUNG MAN. I'd stick a knife into *him* fast enough, if you went back after this!

YOUNG WOMAN. [*Shaking her head*] Not done in the best circles, Tony.

YOUNG MAN. If I could without being hanged.

YOUNG WOMAN. That's mean.

YOUNG MAN. Passion makes you mean. I don't know what I'd have done if you hadn't come, Nell. I couldn't have stood it any more.

YOUNG WOMAN. No; but, Tony, for both our sakes—we really have got to find out; I couldn't go wrong a second time. Think of my reputation!

YOUNG MAN. Nell!

YOUNG WOMAN. No, don't look like that! I've been married and you haven't. I've seen a man flare up for me and go out. I've seen myself make a terrible bloomer. Who knows whether *we* shall have burned out or be still alight three weeks from now?

YOUNG MAN. [*Squeezing out his cigarette*] Alight, and flaming!

YOUNG WOMAN. I wonder.

YOUNG MAN. [*Putting his hands on her shoulders and turning her square to him*] You little doubter! No, I shan't call you Carmen. She didn't talk about try-outs.

YOUNG WOMAN. She was a prize vamp. I'm only an average vamp, Tony.

YOUNG MAN. You're not a vamp.

YOUNG WOMAN. Vamp; Siren; Enchantress; *vide* Dalilah: species of female given to pursuit of the male. Did I pursue you, Tony?

YOUNG MAN. No, darling.

YOUNG WOMAN. Did you pursue me?

YOUNG MAN. No, darling.

YOUNG WOMAN. What happened then?

YOUNG MAN. We looked, we touched, we loved. Could we help it?

YOUNG WOMAN. Of course we could have helped it—by being unhappy.

YOUNG MAN. In torment, Nell. You are all I want.

YOUNG WOMAN. Oh! what a stretcher! All—for the moment.

YOUNG MAN. For ever.

YOUNG WOMAN. Darling, what optimism! You're not selling a horse.

YOUNG MAN. No, I'm buying my life.

YOUNG WOMAN. So you think now.

YOUNG MAN. I know my mind.

YOUNG WOMAN. Doesn't the mind change? "When the cake is eaten the child begins to cry: 'I've got a pain, oh, such a pain, I wish that I could die.'" [*Taking his ears.*] I love you, Tony, but I don't know if I shall three weeks hence. And suppose I don't!

YOUNG MAN. You will.

YOUNG WOMAN. And suppose you don't!

YOUNG MAN. I shall.

YOUNG WOMAN. So speaks the hungry male. [*Rising and clasping her hands to her waist.*] Tony, I've got an awful sinking—not a moral sinking, a real one—you know, I practically had no dinner.

YOUNG MAN. My poor lamb! Where's the bell? How about caviare?   [*Rings.*

YOUNG WOMAN. Marvellous!

YOUNG MAN. And Chateau d'Yquem.

YOUNG WOMAN. Divine! I could live on them for months. Oh! Tony, I shall be awfully happy when I've had them.

YOUNG MAN. I thought there was something wrong with your blood-pressure.   [GUSTAVE *can be seen outside in the corridor*.

YOUNG WOMAN. It simply isn't pressing. Look! There's a nice little table.

[*As the* YOUNG MAN *places it and two chairs, there comes a knock.*]
Entrez !

GUSTAVE. [*Entering*] Sare—Madame ?

YOUNG MAN. Oh !—er—est ce que vous avez du caviare ?

GUSTAVE. Ye-es, Sare—veree good, veree fresh.

YOUNG MAN. Oh ! then bring a lot, will you, quick ; and lemon
and butter and bread—never mind toasting it.   Oh ! and a bottle
of Chateau d'Yquem.

GUSTAVE. [*Approving utterly*] Ye-es, Sare—veree nice.   An olive,
Sare—leetle olives veree black, veree good.

YOUNG MAN. Yes, olives ; but quick, please.

GUSTAVE. [*Nodding with his faint smile*] Ye-es, Sare.

[*He slides away and can be seen hastening down the corridor.*

YOUNG MAN. That old chap knows what's what.

YOUNG WOMAN. He has a charming face.   *I* should hate having
to bring nice things for other people to eat all day.   What's
that ?

[*She listens, leaning against the foot-rail of the bed.*
[*A sound of caterwauling from the corridor.*

YOUNG MAN. Cats—courting !   Jolly, isn't it ?   This is a queer
little old place, awfully French.

YOUNG WOMAN. [*As the sound swells and suddenly ceases*] Tony, I
was wondering—have *we* got any further than *that* ?

YOUNG MAN. I don't know and I don't care—I've got *you.*

[*But instead of seizing her, he only lifts her hand to his lips.*

YOUNG WOMAN. Thank you, dear, for that moderate gesture.   It
gives me hope.   Has it ever struck you, Tony, that the great thing
about love is that each should know by instinct what the other wants
at the moment ?

YOUNG MAN. Yes.   [*Hesitating.*] I've written a poem to you,
Nell.

YOUNG WOMAN. Tony !   How *thrilling !*   That is exactly what I
want at the moment.   Let's hear it.   Now !   At once !

YOUNG MAN. Not till you're stronger—you must be nourished.

[*A knock.*]

Here it comes.   [*Enter* GUSTAVE *with tray, which he disposes.*

GUSTAVE. Caviare, Sare—veree fresh.   The wine a leetle cold.

YOUNG MAN. Splendid !

[*The two seat themselves.*   GUSTAVE *helps them to caviare.*

GUSTAVE. A squeeze of lemon, Madame.   Ye-es.

YOUNG MAN. [*Apologetic*] Afraid this is rather late for you.   We've
been to the Opéra Comique.   [*They eat.*

GUSTAVE. Ye-es, Sare.   Carmen.   Veree nice.

YOUNG WOMAN. Oh !   Do you know it ?

GUSTAVE. Not in ze flesh, Madame.   I listen-in one time.

YOUNG WOMAN. You never get a chance in the evening, I suppose ?

GUSTAVE. Non, Madame.

YOUNG MAN. Don't you ever get off ?

GUSTAVE. Sundays.

YOUNG MAN. Sundays ? Can you get any fun then ?

GUSTAVE. I feesh, Sare. [*Pouring out wine.*] Veree old, Madame.

YOUNG WOMAN. [*Drinking*] Lovely !

GUSTAVE. [*Standing, patient*] Anyt'ing else, Sare ?

YOUNG MAN. Nothing, thank you. And never mind about the tray.

GUSTAVE. No, Sare. What time I bring the coffee, to-morrow morning ?

YOUNG MAN. Oh ! say—ten o'clock.

GUSTAVE. Veree good, Sare. Bon soir, Madame ! Bon soir, Monsieur !

BOTH. Bon soir !   [GUSTAVE *goes.*

YOUNG WOMAN. Nice old man ! " I feesh, Sare ! " This caviare's divine, Tony. It was an inspiration ; and the wine's perfect. Now for the poem—all about me !

YOUNG MAN. [*Producing a sheet of paper*] I know it by heart. Sure you're up to it, Nell ?

YOUNG WOMAN. Try me !

THE YOUNG MAN. [*Leaning a little towards her, begins*]

    " Avowal.

        " Thou art my Love, and I alway,
        That nothing rueful thee dismay,
        My every waking thought intend
        From this beginning to the end.
        And in my sleep I dream of thee
        That unto me thou linkéd art,
        And we are sailing, thou and I,
        To watch the silver fishes fly,
        The stars uncounted in the sky,
        And that great floorway of the sea."

YOUNG WOMAN. [*Under her breath*] I love that !

YOUNG MAN. " Be not afraid that I confess
        To love thee for thy loveliness,
        For in my choosing I am sure
        Thy loveliness will all endure.
        It has so fingered at my heart,
        And from it, like a lyre, has drawn
        A reeling tune on silver strings,
        That, brightest of all airy things,
        Thy life may rise on happy wings——
        A humming bird to spin and dart.

"I'll catch the bubbles Fortune blows
    For thee, if bright, but only those ;
    The buffets of the ruder breeze——
    Thou shalt have zephyrs—but not these.
    Yet I'll not keep thine hours in pawn,
    Thou shalt be free thy race to run ;
    And if thou tread the gipsy way
    I'll care not what the gossips say,
    So thou be not *too* far away
    From me, beneath or stars or sun."

[*He leans still more towards her, and she looks at him with parted lips.*

YOUNG MAN. " Then come with me if thou would'st know
    A summer that will never go,
    Flowers unfading and the tune
    Of sheep-bells wandering in June.
    And I will conjure till these seem
    Such part of elfin land to thee,
    That backed on swallow thou shalt fly
    And chase the thistle floating by,
    And ride on moonbeams thro' the sky
    To rob dark night of ecstasy.
        I am a world devoted quite,
        That lives but when thou'rt in my sight.
        Ah! dwell in me, and I will try
        To make thee happy till I die."

[*He drops the paper, from which indeed he has not been reading, and
    seizes her hand.*

YOUNG WOMAN. [*Emotionalized*] Oh! Tony! [*Looking at him.*]
All that?

YOUNG MAN. [*With her hand to his lips*] And more!

[*He kisses her hand till she draws it away.*

YOUNG WOMAN. [*Wistfully*] But are people ever faithful? Look
at me!

YOUNG MAN. You had no luck, Nell. The real thing's a divine
accident, and it's happened to us.

YOUNG WOMAN. So all lovers say until they've had enough. You
don't know me, Tony, you don't know me.

YOUNG MAN. Better than you know yourself.

YOUNG WOMAN. I'm a selfish baggage. I want my own way.

YOUNG MAN. More than you want me?

YOUNG WOMAN. Perhaps. I'll have to be tested.

YOUNG MAN. You *will* be.

YOUNG WOMAN. And suppose I don't stand fire?

YOUNG MAN. You will.

YOUNG WOMAN. But if I didn't!

YOUNG MAN. [*Sombrely*] " Who dares not put it to the touch ? "

YOUNG WOMAN. Do you despise me, Tony ?

YOUNG MAN. " Thou art my Love, and I alway—— "

YOUNG WOMAN. Tony, you're single-hearted, you ought to be exhibited. Listen !

[*They listen. The violinist has begun to play the " Cumparsita."*] " Cumparsita ! " My favourite tango.

YOUNG MAN. [*Filling the glasses and holding his up*] Nell ! Death to doubt !

YOUNG WOMAN. [*Raising her glass*] " Death to—— "

[*The light goes out.*

YOUNG MAN. Hallo !

YOUNG WOMAN. Is that an omen ?

YOUNG MAN. A good one. To our leap in the dark. No heel-taps.   [*Drinks.*

YOUNG WOMAN. [*Drinking—with a little laugh*] Well ! Light up ! There are some candles on the dressing-table.

YOUNG MAN. It'll come up again directly. There's light enough to eat by. Eat, pretty creature, eat !   [*They sit and eat.*

YOUNG WOMAN. Feasts in the dark at school ! Sardines on Bath olivers, rolling off on to the beds. This wine's going right down into my toes. D'you know that feeling ? Darling Tony ! You *have* been sweet to me to-day. After my exhibition on the boat ! If you could stand that, you can stand anything.

YOUNG MAN. From *you*, Nell.

YOUNG WOMAN. Tony, you're a fanatic ! [*Holding out her glass.*] My love to you !

[BRYN *with her candle is seen in the corridor. They clink glasses. The door is burst open ;* BRYN *with her lighted candle, stands before them.*

YOUNG MAN. Hallo !

BRYN. Oh ! You're eating ! Awfully sorry ! I thought you'd like to know the house is on fire. You can't get down. We've got to go on the roof.   [*She flies out again, banging the door.*

YOUNG WOMAN. [*In consternation*] Tony !

YOUNG MAN. [*Sniffing*] By Jove ! There *is* a fire ! What awful luck !   [*He jumps up, gropes, and lights candles.*

[*The* YOUNG WOMAN *has gone to the door and opened it.*

YOUNG WOMAN. I can see the flames down there. Tony, I'm scared—I'm scared.

YOUNG MAN. It'll be all right, darling. We've hardly taken any-thing out. Jam the things in. We'll take our bags up on the roof ; we can get the big luggage at the station and be off by the first train.

YOUNG WOMAN. I hate fire—we had a fire once, at home. It's awful.

YOUNG MAN. Don't worry, darling, we shall be all right up there —they'll soon get us down. Put on your travelling coat.

[*They are hurriedly putting things into a suit-case and dressing-bag.*

YOUNG WOMAN. But, Tony, you don't see. We shall be spotted! Reggie Fanning!

YOUNG MAN. Oh! damn him! Look here, put this scarf over your head, it'll hide your face if he comes up there. [*He winds it round her head.*] You look so sweet!

YOUNG WOMAN. Kiss me! I feel this is the end, Tony. We shall never——

YOUNG MAN. [*Kissing her*] Now, now, Nell! Stay here a minute.

[*He goes into the corridor.*

[*The* BEETONS *pass him in the corridor.*

MR. B. [*To him*] Awkward, isn't it? What! This hotel's dam' badly managed. We've got to go on the roof.

YOUNG MAN. So I hear, Sir. [*Into the room.*] Stout couple just gone up. Ready, Nell? It's all clear.

YOUNG WOMAN. " The stars in their courses fought against Sisera."

YOUNG MAN. Bosh! It's the test, Nell—and we'll see it through. Come on! [*Looking out again.*] Now, darling!

[*She goes out, he looks round him, catches up his coat and hat, and, candle in hand, follows.*

The curtain falls.

SCENE VI

SECOND FLOOR

The same evening : eleven o'clock.

A fourth and fully lighted bedroom.
On a sofa at the foot of the two beds HENRY LENNOX, *in a dressing gown, is lying facing the window, on the Right, which is wide open. He is a thin man of nearly sixty, with a pale whimsical wistful face, across which pass at times spasms of pain.* MRS. LENNOX *sits on a chair below the window, with the air of one expecting to rise at any moment.*

LENNOX. Look here, my dear. It's eleven. You go to bed.

MRS. L. [*Rising*] Are you easier, Harry?

LENNOX. M'm! Yes. Always easier. Some day very easy.

MRS. L. Don't!

LENNOX. My child, we all have to walk out, some time. [*Pointing to window.*] Look at that! Nice little square—I always liked Paris—it hath a pleasant stink.   But what I miss in this room is a view of the workers on the top floors—most characteristic thing in France, those workers on the top floors, busy as ants.

Mrs. L. Yes, what *do* they make ?

Lennox. Cotton, tape and laces.   Where's Nurse ?

Mrs. L. Having her supper downstairs.   She'll be up directly.

Lennox. Nice woman—not ordinary—got background, I should say.   The thing I most regret in life, Evelyn, is that I haven't known all about everybody I've ever met.

Mrs. L. [*With a smile*] That's modest.

Lennox. Modest but greedy.

Mrs. L. You're not greedy.

Lennox. Avid, my dear.   Haven't written half enough books, or half good enough.   Haven't loved half enough women.

Mrs. L. [*Dryly*] I'm sorry.

Lennox. Nothing personal, my love.   Never eaten at a sitting as many oysters as I should like—not by dozens.   Not ridden over a quarter of the fences a man ought to ; but as I say, what I regret most is not having been in the skin of everybody else.

Mrs. L. You *are* absurd.

Lennox. [*After lying still a moment with his eyes closed from pain*] Imagine !   You mayn't stare at people ; you mayn't listen to their private conversations ; you mayn't even get under their beds ; you mayn't do anything that would give you some real knowledge of them. It's tragic ; or rather it's a clean stopper on comedy.   And comedy is the saving grace, my love.

Mrs. L. No one can say you haven't kept your sense of comedy.

Lennox. Well, if Life wasn't essentially comic, it would be intolerable.   Take war—the most comic activity in which we indulge ; if one couldn't see what farcical midgets we are when we go to war, one would die of horror.

Mrs. L. Ought you to be talking ?

Lennox. No.   Religion !   A Mohammedan, a Buddhist, a Christian, a Confucian, all equally convinced their creeds are divine, each equally certain the others will be damned.   What's to be done if one can't smile at that ?

Mrs. L. Will you have another pillow ?

Lennox. Dress—all climate.   What's the lust of missionaries for putting other people into trousers, if it isn't comic.

Mrs. L. [*Putting pillow behind his head*] There !   Is that better ?

Lennox. Morals !   The rule of Home Secretaries by Home Secretaries, for Home Secretaries.   There's a twinkle in that.

Mrs. L. And love ?

Lennox. Passion ?   *Most* comic of all !   We don't take the sacrament every time we sit down to dinner.

MRS. L. I said *love*.

LENNOX. [*With eyes again closed*] Perhaps you're right, dear heart. But then love's the sheen on the wings, the scent of the rose, the flavour in the soup. I agree. It's not comic, but then—it's not essential.

MRS. L. Love *is* essential.

LENNOX. [*With a smile cut off by pain*] Well, well!
"He talked too much, and through his hat,
And all of it was gas;
But was it to be wondered at?
The fellow was an ass."

MRS. L. [*Rising*] You're in pain again.

LENNOX. No, but I should think you must be.

MRS. L. [*Going towards the door*] Why doesn't Nurse come?

LENNOX. Don't spoil her supper. They cook jolly well here.

MRS. L. As if her supper mattered!

LENNOX. That's where you're too English, my love, grasping at conscience and missing casseroles. That poor woman would come rushing up supperless, and what can she do? The digitalis is over there, [*Pointing*] if you want to give me some. [MRS. L. *measures a a dose*.] That's what I like about the French: by giving full spiritual attention to the body, they avoid starvation and repletion, and so are able to give full bodily attention to the spirit.

MRS. L. [*Bringing him the dose*] Better not talk any more.

LENNOX. I won't. [*Drinking*] We English you know still look on the body as the devil. It's bad form, until it's dead—then we're all over it. The body becomes sacred at once. We catch our deaths burying it—by the way, don't let anybody get pneumonia over me. We write books about it. We dig it up to search for arsenic; and sit on it for weeks together. And we assert that it's going to rise again. Considering how we treat it till it's dead, it's unreasonable, my dear. But after all what would the English be without their sweet unreasonableness.

MRS. L. Now that's enough, Harry!

LENNOX. [*Taking her hand*] Right you are, dear one. That stuff always goes to my head. Where are the girls sleeping?

MRS. L. Quite close. They're wildly excited about Paris. Harry, I *should* like to get home; d'you think you'll be able to travel the day after to-morrow?

LENNOX. [*Patting her hand*] I'll have a good stab at it, as my more genial colleagues say.

MRS. L. We can take Nurse on for the journey. Oh! Here she is!
[*The* NURSE *is seen outside in the corridor. She enters, attractive in her uniform, and with an unprofessional smile.*

NURSE. Very sorry I've been so long. There's only one waiter on duty, and he's on the run all the time, poor old fellow.

MRS. L. I think I'll go and see if the children are all right. He's just had a dose, Nurse.

> [*She goes out, and is seen going down the corridor.*

LENNOX. Nurse, there's someone playing the violin.

NURSE. I've been talking to the young man. He's a Yugo-Slav, who's been in America ten years. He says you're much loved in the States.

LENNOX. Yes, I've never been there.

> [*The strains of the violin float in through the open window. They*
> *listen. On* LENNOX's *face comes a smile at first, then a sombre*
> *melancholy. The playing stops.*

LENNOX. I know that little tune—" Le joli Gilles, " by Poise—used to hear Corsanego play it at Monte in the 'nineties. [*Suddenly to the* NURSE, *who is at the window looking out.*] Nurse, forgive an awkward question—but you must have seen a lot of death. Is it, or isn't it ?

NURSE. [*Turning*] The end ? I don't know, Mr. Lennox ; I don't think so.

LENNOX. I'm afraid it is.

NURSE. [*Turning to him*] I once saw an old lady die, she was all darkened and drawn, quite unconscious. Suddenly she smiled very faintly, very sweetly, and was gone. Why—why did she smile, if something hadn't opened to her ? It was so happy.

LENNOX.   " She got a crown—we got a crown—
                      All God's chillen got a crown."

But what if the crown is just relief at oblivion, Nurse ?

NURSE. Could one smile at nothingness ?

LENNOX. I wonder. This attack may finish me, you know. I've had three. One oughtn't to be so interested in one's own concerns, but then, you see, [*with a smile*] one is.

NURSE. [*Coming over to him*] Of course, one is. But it's going to be all right with care.

LENNOX. It'd be better for my wife if it were all over. It's terrible for her. Nothingness ! [*With a smile*] There's no realizing that one won't *be.*

NURSE. [*Eagerly*] But that's just it, Mr. Lennox. Surely if one can't realise nothingness, death *can't* be the end ?

LENNOX. [*Shaking his head*] I'm afraid that belief in the persistence of life is just natural to the state of being alive, Nurse. Under an anæsthetic one has no belief in anything ; and no life anywhere. The eternal anæsthetic ? I funk it, and I'm afraid of showing that I funk it. Do I show ?

NURSE. You certainly don't.

LENNOX. Good ! It's been a relief to confess. What made you take up nursing ?

NURSE. [*Simply*] I lost my husband.

LENNOX. Long?

NURSE. Three years ago—in a motor smash.

[LENNOX *puts out his hand and takes hers.*

LENNOX. Poor Nurse!

NURSE. [*Simply*] I don't like to think death's the end; I want to see him again. [LENNOX *nods.*] But I know that's not a reason. [*Looking into his face.*] You ought to have some nourishment, now. There's some very nice cold consommé downstairs. [*She rings.*] That old waiter Gustave is such a dear. When the French are nice, they're awfully nice.

LENNOX. I've always wanted to write the story of a waiter.

NURSE. Have a talk with him when he comes up.

LENNOX. [*With a sigh*] It won't tell me what he's thinking. And that's my job—to tell how people feel and think by the way they don't look and act. There's one thing, Nurse, we're all better, or at least more vivid than we seem. Life's a pagoda. We hatch in the basement and take wings on the roof, and in between we live masked in a sort of unending bluff, and who knows what we're really like?

NURSE. Gustave is transparent anyway—patient to the core, and looks it.

[GUSTAVE *is seen in the corridor.*

LENNOX. I envy people with patience—I never had any. [*There is a knock.*] Come in!

[*The door is opened and* GUSTAVE *appears.*

GUSTAVE. Sare?

NURSE. Monsieur would like some of that nice cold consommé, Gustave.

GUSTAVE. Ye-es, Sare. I get it. A biscuit, thin, and creesp. Ye-es?

LENNOX. What's the name of the violinist, Gustave?

GUSTAVE. Froba, Sare, veree clevare. He annoy you, Sare?

LENNOX. Not a bit! He's got a touch.

GUSTAVE. Ye-es, Sare. He make it speak.

NURSE. *I'll* get the consommé, Gustave. Stay and talk to Mr. Lennox.

GUSTAVE. *Merci*, Mademoiselle—veree kind.

[*The* NURSE *goes out and down the corridor.*

LENNOX. Sit down, Gustave. You must get tired.

GUSTAVE. [*Sitting; with his faint smile*] Ye-es, Sare—the feet a leetle.

LENNOX. Always a waiter?

GUSTAVE. From the cradle, as you say, Sare.

LENNOX. Good life?

GUSTAVE. One is accustomed.

LENNOX. Not married?

GUSTAVE. No, Sare, no time as yet.

LENNOX. But you must be my age, I should think.

GUSTAVE [*With his faint smile*] Yes, Sare. Perhaps I range myself some day—'oo know?

LENNOX. Well, you see every kind of type—that's something. But I suppose you haven't time to study them.

GUSTAVE. 'Ave a leetle fun some time, Sare.

LENNOX. You get human nature about at its worst—satisfying appetite. Ugly thing appetite, Gustave.

GUSTAVE. Veree natural, Sare.

LENNOX. Wasn't it Maupassant who said—the only way to avoid temptation was to yield to it. That the measure of the human being, Gustave?

GUSTAVE. No, Sare. But it need an occasion to show what else-more is dere.

LENNOX. Right you are there!

[*A noise is heard.* GUSTAVE *rises and opens the door. The sound resolves into a cry of* "*We* want cocktails—*we* want cocktails!*"

LENNOX. Voice crying in the wilderness? Um?

GUSTAVE. [*Smiling*] Ye-es, Sare. A gentleman—'e want cocktails.

LENNOX. And you've got to get 'em?

GUSTAVE. Ye-es, Sare; excuse! I bring the consommé—veree nice, veree cold.

[GUSTAVE *goes out and down the corridor, passing* MRS. LENNOX.

LENNOX. An occasion to show! [*To himself.*] O God! Let me not show fear! [*As* MRS. LENNOX *enters*] Chicks all right.

MRS. L. Wild as kittens. I left them in bed, but I'm sure they won't stay there. Where's Nurse?

LENNOX. Bringing me up some fodder. I've had the old waiter here. Such a type! [*Draws in his breath at sharp pain.*

MRS. L. [*Anxiously*] Harry!

LENNOX. [*Eyes shut, faintly*] It's all right, it's all right.

[*The* NURSE *is seen in the corridor.*

MRS. L. [*Going to the door*] Oh! Nurse, quick!

[*The* NURSE *enters with a cup and some biscuits, puts them down and goes quickly to* LENNOX. *She and* MRS. L. *stand close to him in great anxiety.*

MRS. L. Can't anything be done to stop that pain?

NURSE. Hypodermic—but I haven't a needle.

MRS. L. Perhaps the people next door?

NURSE. I'll try them.

[*Goes quickly to the door and out into the corridor. The spasm passes.* LENNOX *lies exhausted.*

LENNOX. [*Smiling faintly*] So sorry!

MRS. L. Oh! Harry.   [*The* NURSE *returns.*

NURSE. No luck! [*Looking at* LENNOX.] Thank Heaven, it's passed.

[MRS. L. *turns up to the window, crying quietly. The figure of the child* DIANA *is seen coming up the corridor. While the* NURSE *stands close, looking compassionately down at* LENNOX, *the door is softly opened and the head of* DIANA *is poked in.*

DIANA. [*Excitedly whispering*] May I come in, Nurse?

LENNOX. [*Overhearing*] Come on, rogue! [DIANA *comes in.*

DIANA. There's such a smell of burning, Daddy. I think something's on fire. Can I go down and see?

MRS. L. [*Turning sharply from the window*] 'Ssh! Diana—Daddy's not——

NURSE. [*Sniffing*] There *is* a smell of burning—*I'll* go.

DIANA. No please, Nurse—let me, let me! I simply must.

[*She flies to the door and goes out. She is hardly out of the room before the light goes out.*

MRS. L. How maddening!

LENNOX. Patience, my dear! *We* want patience—*we* want patience. My matches are on the chest of drawers, Nurse.

NURSE. I've got them [*Strikes one.*] Oh! *there* are some candles.

[*Lights two candles.*

MRS. L. [*Distracted*] Diana wandering about in the dark. I—[*She goes to the door. Sharply.*] Nurse! [*The* NURSE *goes to her.*] Look! Look! Whatever is that glare, and the noise! Ring the bell?

VOICE OF DIANA. [*Without*] Mum! [*She comes in.*] The house *is* on fire, Mum. It's down there. There are some men trying to put it out. They're buzzing about like bees. Isn't it exciting?

MRS. L. 'Ssh!

LENNOX. [*Sitting up*] All right, my dear. It's doing me good.

[*They turn towards him.*

DIANA. Oh! Nurse, give me a candle. I'll go and warn everybody. What fun if we have to go on the roof!

[*She snatches a candle and runs off down the corridor.*

LENNOX. [*Getting to a sitting position*] I'll get into marching order, Nurse.

[*The* NURSE *has found another candle, and lighted it.* MRS. L. *brings his coat and waistcoat, and helps him on with them. Through the still-open door come confused sounds.*

NURSE. [*Calmly*] They'll put it out all right. Don't move yet, Mr. Lennox. [LENNOX *sits clothed and passive.*

LENNOX. Don't worry about me. Get on with the salvage. Got the passports, dear? I'll put on my shoes, Nurse.

NURSE. No let me. [*She puts them on, while* MRS. L. *collects property.*

[GUSTAVE *is seen in the corridor.*

LENNOX. New cure for heart trouble? I feel fine.

GUSTAVE. [*Appearing in the doorway; gently*] Monsieur, Madame—

the 'ouse burn, Madame. Plentee time—a leetle journey to the roof, Sare—one flight onlee, Madame, and the iron steps.

LENNOX. Splendid, Gustave!

GUSTAVE. Beeg fire—flames veree 'igh; but soon the pompiers come. Excuse, Madame, I tell the ladee and gentleman next door, and come back.   [*He vanishes.*

MRS. L. This is terrible. Harry!

LENNOX. [*Calmly*] Go and see to the chicks, dear. Nurse and Gustave will give me a hand, eh, Nurse?

NURSE. It's all right, Mrs. Lennox, we can manage perfectly.

[MRS. L. *after a look at him, hurries out in her coat and with a bag in her hand.*

LENNOX. [*Leaning back with his eyes closed*] Nurse, I thought this was going to be good for me, but I'm afraid it isn't.

NURSE. [*Applying salts*] Gently! There's plenty of time.

LENNOX. [*Faintly*] All the time in the world, and a little over perhaps.

NURSE. [*Applying flask*] Drink some brandy.

LENNOX. [*After drinking*] Ah! That's better! Now, Nurse!
> [*She puts her arm round him, and he stands.*

[GUSTAVE *is seen in the corridor. As they move towards the door, he comes in.*

GUSTAVE. *Les pompiers*, the engines come, Sare.
> [*They stand listening to the approaching claxon of a fire engine.*

LENNOX. Nurse, I think I'd rather bet on the engines and just wait.

NURSE. Very well. Come back to the sofa. I'll wait with you.

GUSTAVE. Sare, we carry you. The flames march so queeck— better we carry you.

LENNOX. [*Sitting*] No, Gustave. Get your other folk up. I shall be all right.

GUSTAVE. [*Lifting his hands in patient protest*] I come back, Sare.
> [*He goes again, and is seen running down the corridor.*

LENNOX. Now, Nurse, trot along!

NURSE. [*With a smile*] Don't be silly.

LENNOX. The Nurse stood on the burning deck whence all but she had fled. First poem I ever learned; indelibly connected with strawberry jam. Well, I'm all for cremation and one will avoid the service. [*The swish of water is heard. Putting his hand to his heart.*] Yes, I've got to take the chance. I don't feel like moving. Nurse, there's a little photograph in the left-hand top drawer there—d'you mind? [*The* NURSE *gets it. Looking at it.*] My wife when she was three years old. Now, Nurse, please go! You'll find me here quite comfortable when they've put the fire out. Please!

NURSE. You know I can't leave you.

GUSTAVE [*Appearing from corridor*] Time to go, Sare.

LENNOX. Gustave, take Nurse away.

NURSE. Mr. Lennox, I think for your wife and children's sake we ought to have a try.   Lean all your weight on me.

> [*A pause.   The shadow of his fear passes over* LENNOX'S *face. He masters it and stands up.*

LENNOX. All right, Nurse, since you won't go.

GUSTAVE [*With suit-case in one hand*] The arm round my neck, Sare—round Mademoiselle's neck—veree comfortable, veree easy.   Now, Sare, we march.

> [*They move thus towards the door.   Just there* LENNOX'S *heart suddenly gives way, and he becomes dead weight.   They bend and halt in horror.*

NURSE. [*Looking in his face ; in a whisper*] I'm afraid he's——

GUSTAVE. Oh!   Oh!   I get 'elp, we carry 'eem.

NURSE. He's dead, Gustave.

> [*On* GUSTAVE, *dropping the suit-case to cross himself and hold up his hand in patient dismay,*

The curtain falls.

SCENE VII

THE ROOF

The same evening : twenty minutes past eleven.

The empty moonlit roof, shut in by much higher roofs on either side, with a trap door Centre.   There is a parapet at the back of the stage, and from over it one sees the roofs of houses and the stars in the sky.   Bright moonlight throws shadows, and a black cat is seen moving across.   The engines are playing on the fire below, with an intermittent hissing.

> [*The trap door is raised and the capped head of* MR. BEETON *is seen emerging.   He looks round him and calls down.*

MR. BEETON. It's all right—quite flat.   No smoke.   Up you come !

> [*He puts down a bag and stands reaching down his hand, takes his wife's dressing-case, deposits it, and reaches his hand down again.*

MRS. BEETON'S VOICE. No, Tom, you're only clawing me ; I can manage.   Is anybody up there ?

MR. BEETON. Not a cat.

> [MRS. BEETON'S *head and body, to the waist, emerge.*

Give us both hands.   Now then !   [MRS. BEETON *arrives.*

MRS. BEETON. Have you looked over ?

MR. BEETON. [*At the parapet*] M'm! It's a long way down! No flames yet this side. They'll rig something up. [*Looking at the high side walls.*] Why they built a little house in between two big ones like this I don't know. Perverse devils the French!

[*The head of* DIANA *has emerged from the trap.*]

Hallo! So *you've* got here, all right, young woman.

DIANA. [*Coming quickly up*] Oh! What a flat roof!

MR. BEETON. Where's your sister?

DIANA. [*Looking down the trap*] Come on, Bryn.

BRYN. [*Emerging rapidly*] I say, Di, isn't this topping? [*She runs to the parapet.*] Oo! It's beastly high! Shall we have to go down a rope? [*Turning to* MRS. BEETON.] Can you climb down ropes?

MRS. BEETON. I could when I was your age. But they'll put us into chutes or something—won't they, Tom? Do you see any firemen?

MR. BEETON. Not yet! This is the back of the house. Goodness knows if these French firemen are any good. What do they call 'em? Pomp——

DIANA. *Pompiers.*

MR. BEETON. Ah! Pompeers.

DIANA. Look, Bryn! [*Pointing to the trap; softly.*] The honey-spooners!

BRYN. [*Chanting the hymn*] "Who are these like stars appearing?"

DIANA. Shut up!

[*She and* BRYN *go to the far corner of the parapet.*
[*The* YOUNG WOMAN, *her head swathed in the scarf, emerges, followed by the* YOUNG MAN. *They both move over to the parapet.*

YOUNG WOMAN. [*Shuddering*] I do hate heights, Tony.

MR. BEETON. [*Approaching the* YOUNG MAN] This is too bad—what! The French are so theatrical. You never know what they'll do next. Let me introduce my wife. [*The* YOUNG PEOPLE *bow and the* YOUNG WOMAN *shrinks a little away, looking over the parapet.*] Shouldn't be surprised if it was all exaggerated. They bundled us up in such a hurry. [*To the* YOUNG MAN.] Shall we go down and see?

MRS. BEETON. You'll do nothing of the kind, Tom.

YOUNG WOMAN. [*Aside*] Tony, don't leave me!

YOUNG MAN. All right, darling.

MR. BEETON. They're always having fires in Paris. It's an inflammable place.

BRYN. [*Suddenly*] Di, we *must* go down and see about Mum and Dad.

MRS. BEETON. No, my dears, you'll just stay here.

BRYN. But suppose something's happened to them. Oh! here's somebody coming!   [*They go towards the trap.*

[FROBA's *hair appears.*]

Oh! It's only him!

[FROBA *emerges, violin under one arm and a bag in the other hand.*]

Did you see my father and mother?

DIANA. Yes, did you?

FROBA. No one passed up to my floor. I judge dey're still below.

[*He passes on to the parapet and looks over.*

MR. BEETON. [*Gazing at the side walls*] Looks to me as if we were in a trap up here. Why the deuce they couldn't have escape ladders up these walls!

MRS. BEETON. Don't talk like that, Tom—the children!

BRYN. Oh! It's awful!

YOUNG MAN. I'll go down and see.

[*The* YOUNG WOMAN *puts out her hand as if to keep him.*

DIANA. Oh! would you?

BRYN. We're sorry we miaowed.

DIANA. H'ssh!

BRYN. [*Who is at the trap*] Oh! Di! There's Mum! She's fainted. Nurse and Gustave have got her all stretched out. They can't get her up! And where's Dad?

YOUNG MAN. Nell?

YOUNG WOMAN. Yes, go!   [*He slips down the trap.*

[*They all gather round the trap.*

MR. BEETON. [*Directing into the aperture*] That's right! Get her under the arms! Good! Heave her legs. Don't let her slip! Capital! Top hole! She's coming!

[*He leans down, grips at something invisible, and staggers backward, the something having given way.*

MRS. BEETON. Don't fuss, Tom!

[*The* YOUNG MAN *is slowly emerging with* MRS. LENNOX *clasped to him.* DIANA *and* BRYN *tug under his arms, and he lands his burden and stands breathless.* GUSTAVE, *follows up, holding* MRS. LENNOX's *feet.*

DIANA AND BRYN. [*Hanging over their motionless mother*] Mum! Mum!

MRS. BEETON. [*At her dressing-case*] Here! Wait! I've got some sal volatile.

MR. BEETON. Bend her head down! Tickle her feet! Pinch her!

[*The* NURSE *emerges from the trap.* GUSTAVE *assisting her.*

GUSTAVE. Attend to the lady. I fetch the other gentlemen.

[*He goes down again. The* NURSE *takes the sal volatile from* MRS. BEETON *and sets to work on* MRS. LENNOX.

DIANA. Where's Dad, Nurse?

NURSE. H'ssh! Don't—your mother——

BRYN. But why did she faint? Mum never faints.

DIANA. [*Beginning to realize*] Nurse! Dad?

NURSE. 'Ssh! Look, she's coming to. Don't think of yourselves. Think of her!

> [MRS. LENNOX *is regaining consciousness. The* CHILDREN *gaze at her face. The others have withdrawn a little, except the* NURSE, *who holds her head.*

BRYN. [*Timidly*] We're here, Mum.

MRS. LENNOX. Where am I? Where——?

DIANA. On the roof, Mum. We're quite safe—only where's——?
> [*Checks herself.*

BRYN. Is Dad coming?

> [MRS. LENNOX *looks at one* CHILD *and the other, shakes her head and holds out her arms.* DIANA *throws herself down into them with a choked "* Oh! Mum! "*

BRYN. [*Frozen*] Why?

MRS. LENNOX. [*Very quietly over* DIANA'S *head*] Dad is dead.

BRYN. Oh-h-h!   [*Her face breaks up, and then she doesn't cry.*

MRS. BEETON. [*With a rapid movement circling her with an arm*] Brave child! Brave child! There, there! That's right! Don't cry!

DIANA. [*Wrenching free, on her knees*] Mum, how?

NURSE. His heart, dear.

MRS. LENNOX. Help me up.

> [*While the* CHILDREN *are helping her up,* BRICE *emerges from the trap; he is quite sobered and slinks apart; he is followed by young* FANNING, *who is also sobered, and stands staring round him dazedly. The* NURSE *and the* BEETONS *are grouped Left, she telling them of the death.* FROBA *and* BRICE *are looking over the parapet far apart. The* YOUNG MAN *and* WOMAN *are together forward on the Right.*

YOUNG MAN. Young Fanning! Keep your face turned, Nell. I'll go to him, or he may come over here.

> [*She turns, shrouded in her scarf; and he moves towards* FANNING.

YOUNG MAN. Hallo, Fanning!

FANNING. Oh! Hallo! I say, this is seeing " life," what!

YOUNG MAN. [*Low*] Seeing death. [*Pointing to the* CHILDREN *and their* MOTHER.] Their father's dead—heart failure.

FANNING. I say!

> [BAKER'S *head emerges and he comes up the trap, followed by* MOULTENEY.

BAKER. Where's the old waiter, Major?
> [BRICE *turns sharply round.*

MOULTENEY. By George, isn't he here? The flames are pretty well up to the second floor.

NURSE. [*Who has approached*] He must have gone back to Mr. Lennox.

MOULTENEY. What! Somebody else down there still?

NURSE. Dead—his heart failed. That poor lady!

            [MRS. LENNOX *comes rushing up to them.*

MRS. LENNOX. Nurse! Sir! I must—I can't let him stay.

BAKER. Steady, Ma'am! Of course not! We'll get him. Here, four of us! Who?   [*All cluster round.*] Reggie, you! I. [*To the* YOUNG MAN.] You!

YOUNG MAN. Rather! Just a second! [*He turns back to the* YOUNG WOMAN.] I must, Nell. I must.

        [BAKER *and the* MAJOR *are restraining* MRS. LENNOX.

YOUNG WOMAN. Of course!   [*Suddenly freeing her face.*

YOUNG MAN. Nell! Careful!

          [*He runs back to the trap and goes down.*

BAKER. Down you go, Reggie! [FANNING *descends.*] Major! Right!

MR. BEETON. [*Pushing forward*] Look here! I——

MOULTENEY. No, Sir. The younger men.

MR. BEETON. What! What are *you*, if it comes to that?

BRICE. [*Pushing suddenly between them*] Get out of the way!

            [*He descends.*

BAKER. [*Barring the way to the elder men*] Now, Major, you and our friend look after the ladies. We'll get him. Right!   [*He descends.*

MR. BEETON. Look here! I don't get any show. What!

MRS. BEETON. [*Taking his arm*] Tom, don't be foolish!

MR. BEETON. Damn!

     [MRS. LENNOX *turns up, covering her face with her hands. A hush has fallen.* FROBA *has gone back to the parapet. The* NURSE *stands beside* MRS. LENNOX *and* DIANA *is close to them.* MR. *and* MRS. BEETON *and the* MAJOR, *not far from them, are talking in low tones. The* YOUNG WOMAN *stands by herself, forward, on the Right, close to the trap.* BRYN *steals up to her and peers into the trap.*

BRYN. Oh! Isn't it hot? D'you think it's dangerous now?

YOUNG WOMAN. Yes.

BRYN. Dad wouldn't like them to risk their lives for him, now he's dead. [*She covers her face with her arm, and the* YOUNG WOMAN *puts an arm around her. In a choked voice.*] He was such a darling. [*Freeing her face and shaking her head.*] He'd much rather be left there. I know he would.

YOUNG WOMAN. But your mother, dear.

BRYN. Oh! Dad! [*The* YOUNG WOMAN *strokes the top of her head. Brokenly.*] Nasty stuffy coffin! [*Trying to break away.*] I want to go down.

YOUNG WOMAN. No, no, no! You might easily make one of them lose his life.

BRYN. Isn't it awful! We were having such a gorgeous time. And so were you I expect.

MR. BEETON. [*Voice suddenly raised*] These confounded old French houses—all wood, and no fire extinguishers. They ought to be prosecuted. Some paraffin left about, I'll bet.

BRYN. Suppose it all fell in! And they were killed!

YOUNG WOMAN. Don't!

BRYN. I'm going to cry.

YOUNG WOMAN. Cry, dear! You'll feel better.

BRYN. [*Suddenly slipping down and kneeling at the trap*] Listen!

[BAKER's *voice is heard.*

BAKER. Right!

BRYN. [*Excitedly*] They're coming! [*Recoiling.*] Oh! I don't want to see!

YOUNG WOMAN. [*Drawing her away*] No! There, there! Tuck your head into me.   [*She stands looking over the child's buried face.*

BRYN. [*In a smothered voice*] I feel—I feel all grown-up! It's awful!

[DIANA *and all, save* MRS. LENNOX *and the* NURSE, *are gathered round the trap*; BAKER *emerges slowly backwards, bearing one end of* LENNOX's *sheeted body. The* YOUNG MAN *emerges next bearing the other end. They lay it down on the left by* MRS. LENNOX, *who looks up at them for a moment, and then crouches silently beside it.* FANNING *and* BRICE *emerge, of whom the last steals away again to the parapet.*

FROBA. [*To him*] Say, Mister—is de fire gaining?

BRICE. Oh! Go to hell!

[*The* YOUNG MAN *goes to his* YOUNG WOMAN. BRYN *and* DIANA *are close to their* MOTHER.

MOULTENEY. Well?

BAKER. Only just in time. That floor's blazing.

MOULTENEY. [*To* FANNING, *who is feeling his arm*] Anything wrong, old chap?

FANNING. Caught my sleeve. It's nothing, Major.

BAKER. He was a brick. Great pluck!

MOULTENEY. It's an ill fire that tests no metal.

MR. BEETON. [*Coming up*] Pretty bad down there, what! Where are those damned pompeers? Are they going to let us roast up here. Phew! It's coming up now. [*He recoils from the heat emerging.*] Oughtn't we to make a rope with our trousers or something?

[*They all turn to the parapet.*

MOULTENEY. [*Calling to* BRICE] Any of them there?

BRICE. Not a blasted sign!

BAKER. Come and shout!

[*He and* FANNING *join* BRICE, *and all three begin shouting :* " We want ladders, we want ladders, we want ladders ! " *All are at the parapet now except* MRS. LENNOX *by the body of* LENNOX, *and the* YOUNG MAN *and* WOMAN, *who have been standing close together silent.*

YOUNG WOMAN. [*As the shouting stops*] Tony, if we get away, I'm coming—for good.

YOUNG MAN. You are, Nell ? You are ! The fire was worth it then. *I'd* rather we burned up here together, than go back.

DIANA. [*From the parapet*] Look ! There they are ! Look !

[" Ladders. We want ladders ! " *The shouting goes up once more, and then stops altogether.*

BRYN. [*Running back from the parapet*] They're coming ! Don't you care ? Oh ! I forgot—you're honey——!

MR. BEETON. [*Shouting down over the parapet*] No, put 'em *there !* The French are hopeless. They never understand a thing. [*To* MOULTENEY.] Here, Sir, call to 'em in their own confounded lingo.

MOULTENEY. We mustn't get rattled, Sir. They know their own business.

MR. BEETON. Well, I see no signs of it.

FANNING. [*Turning and suddenly coming on the young couple, who are approaching the parapet*] Why ! Why it's Mrs. Hugh——!

YOUNG WOMAN. It *was* Mrs. Hugh, Reggie.

YOUNG MAN. Yes, Fanning. This lady is going to be *my* wife in future.

FANNING. Oh ! Quite ! I see. Yes ! Of course ! Yes ! Er— it's all rather a—a turmoil, isn't it ?

YOUNG WOMAN. It is, Reggie.

FANNING. I mean, things are happening. What ! [*Still absorbed by the awkwardness of the meeting.*] Do you think we shall get down in time ? I say ! Look there ! [*Smoke is rising from the trap.*] Hadn't we better shut that ? It makes a draught, you know.

[*He and the* YOUNG MAN *close the trap door.*

BAKER. [*At the parapet*] Here come the ladders ! Up—up—up— up !

[FANNING, *running to the parapet, joins in the shout.*

MOULTENEY. [*Taking charge*] Now, please, all—steady ! Bring [*pointing*] *that* over here.

[BAKER, BRICE, FANNING *and the* YOUNG MAN *go across, lift the white-sheeted body and bring it to the parapet.*

MOULTENEY. Now, in order—ready. First this ! [*To* BRYN.] Then you, child, [*To* DIANA] and you. Then you, Mrs. Lennox—

yes, please; and you, Mrs. Beeton.   Please line up here, and don't
waste time !

> [*Two* POMPIERS, *one after the other, appear above the parapet.*
> [*To the* POMPIERS.]

Take this first !

> [*The* POMPIERS *lift the sheeted body over the parapet to lower it by
> a rope, invisibly.   All stand with bowed heads.*

MOULTENEY.   Now, child ; on the other ladder.

BRYN.   No ! Di and Mum !

MOULTENEY.   Do as you're told.   Baker, you and Brice get over
and help.

> [BAKER *and* BRICE *climb over to work with the* POMPIERS.

MRS. BEETON.   [*While* BRYN *is being handed down followed by* DIANA
and MRS. LENNOX] I'm not going without you, Tom.

MR. BEETON.   Stuff !   Don't be silly !

MRS. BEETON.   Couldn't they put us over together ?

MOULTENEY.   [*To* MRS. BEETON] Come along, Mrs. Beeton.

MRS. BEETON.   No, I prefer to wait with my husband.

MOULTENEY.   Come, you're only keeping us.   [*As she holds back,
looking round.*] Very well.   Nurse !   Down you go.

> [*The* NURSE *goes over and down.*
> [*To* MRS. BEETON.]

Now Mrs. Beeton.

> [BEETON *and he seize her and put her over the edge.*

MRS. BEETON.   [*As she goes over*] Tom, you're to come next.   D'you
hear me !   No !   Don't contradict !   Tom !   [*Disappears.*

BAKER.   [*His head appearing above parapet.   To* BEETON.] Now, Sir,
Race her down !

MR. BEETON.   There's another lady !   What !

YOUNG WOMAN.   [*From where she has been standing clinging to the*
YOUNG MAN *and half hidden*] Please go, I'm all right.

YOUNG MAN.   Nell !

YOUNG WOMAN.   No.   [*Clings to him.*

MR. BEETON.   Ladies first !   Here, I say—— !

MOULTENEY.   Over you get, Sir.   Shove him over !

> [FANNING, BRICE *and* BAKER *shove* MR. BEETON *over, protesting.*

MR. BEETON.   Well, I'm dashed !   It's most irregular——

> [*Disappears.*

MOULTENEY.   [*At the other ladder*] Ready here !   [*To the* YOUNG
MAN.] Bring her, please.

> [*The* YOUNG MAN *lifts the* YOUNG WOMAN *and carries her to
> the ladder.   She turns her head to him, and her face is seen pale,
> straining to his ; then she too vanishes over the edge.*

BAKER.   [*Above the parapet*] Now you, Sir, with the hair.   Got
your fiddle ?   Right !

FROBA. What about your oder guys?

BAKER. Get on! 　　　　　[FROBA *goes over onto the other ladder.*

YOUNG MAN. [*Leaning over*] Thank God! She's down.

BAKER. [*His head and thrown-up hands appearing above parapet*] By Gad! that ladder's gone! No! Yes! Ah! ha! He's all right, they caught him. Only one in action now, Major. Who's next? Good Lord! Now the other's loose. We must just wait.

　　　　[*He and* BRICE *climb back, and the five* MEN *wait, clustered at the parapet.*

MOULTENEY. How did this damned fire start? [BRICE *makes as if to speak and checks himself.*] Do you know?

BRICE. [*Sullenly*] How should I know?

MOULTENEY. Well, do you—that's the point?

BRICE. [*Defiantly*] Yes. It was a joke on the old waiter. Who could tell the damned thing would spread!

MOULTENEY. Good God! You lit it!

BAKER. Look out! Major! They've got your ladder right again. Let's send these bags down. 　　　　　　[*They tip the bags over.*

MOULTENEY. Reggie! You next.

FANNING. No, Major! Elders.

MOULTENEY. [*Quietly*] On the contrary, my boy—this isn't a war.

　　　　　　　　[*The head of one of the* POMPIERS *appears.*

FANNING. I say, Mr. Baker—make him!

BAKER. No, old son. Over you go. Right! [*They shove him over and he disappears.*] That boy's made good, Major!

MOULTENEY. [*To the* YOUNG MAN] Come on, Sir! You're next.

　　　　　　　　[*As the* YOUNG MAN *holds back.*

BAKER. Lovers first! You owe it to the lady. Come on! Over you go. [*The* YOUNG MAN *goes over.*] Right! Now, Major, don't let's have any fuss—your turn.

MOULTENEY. Let's send the old waiter down. Gustave! Where is he?

BAKER. [*Looking round*] Good God! Didn't he come up?

BRICE. What!

BAKER. Here! Get that trap open.

　　　　　　[*He and* BRICE *spring to the trap and wrench it off.*]
By God! He must be suffocated—it's hot as hell! Gustave!

BRICE. [*Agonized*] Gustave!

BAKER. What's to be done, Major? Can't let the poor old boy——

MOULTENEY. Steady! To go down is certain death! Call him!

　　　　　　　　　　　　[*They call* "Gustave!"

BAKER. He must be lying there!

BRICE. I'm going.

MOULTENEY. Stop him, Baker!

BRICE. [*Pushing* BAKER *aside*] To hell with you! I'm going.

[*He disappears headlong down the trap.*

BAKER. That's put the lid on. What now?

[*The* POMPIERS *appear on the parapet.*]

Here are these fellows again!

A POMPIER. Venez, Messieurs, venez. Vite!

BAKER. What about it, Major?

MOULTENEY. One or other of us—no good both staying. You go.

BAKER. [*Spinning a coin and calling*] Heads! Tails! Your shot.

[*The* MAJOR *climbs over and is assisted onto the ladder.*

POMPIERS. [*To* BAKER] Venez, Monsieur, venez!

BAKER. [*Pointing wildly*] Still below there! [*He looks down the trap shading his eyes.*] Brice! Brice!

[*The* POMPIERS *approach and seize him.*]

Get out! Damn it! Can't leave my friend. [*He breaks from them and calls down the trap.*] Brice!

POMPIER. Venez, Monsieur—rien à faire—vous nous perdrez tous!

[*A drift of smoke comes up. They seize* BAKER, *run him up to the parapet and force him over.*

[*A cheer rises from below. During this the smoke issuing from the trap has cleared for a moment, and* BRICE *is seen on the steps leading to the trap painfully thrusting* GUSTAVE *up so that his head and half his body are visible lying in the mouth of the trap.*

BRICE. [*Gasping*] There you are old sport—blast you! That's quits. God! I'm all in.   [*He reels and slips back down the steps.*

[*A* POMPIER *has turned from the parapet. He sees* GUSTAVE.

POMPIER. Ah! le voilà. Voyez, Jacques!

[*They rush to* GUSTAVE, *lift him and carry him to the parapet.*

FIRST POMPIER. Il est foutu.

SECOND POMPIER. [*Feeling his heart and lips*] Non, non, non! Il vit, il vit.

GUSTAVE. [*Recovering consciousness and looking round*] Un Monsieur —un Monsieur Anglais! [*Pointing to the trap.*] La bas—Vite! [*Wildly.*

[*He tries to escape from them and go back.*]

I fetch 'im—'e spek no French.

POMPIERS. Voyons—voyons!

[*They force him over the parapet. A cheer rises from below and another as* GUSTAVE *is lowered down. The* POMPIERS *reappear and go towards the trap.*

FIRST POMPIER. [*At the top—calling*] Monsieur! Hè! La bas!

SECOND POMPIER. Faut descendre!

[*He tries to go down the steps but is driven back by a blast of smoke and heat. Reappearing—gasping.*]

C'est impossible! Doit être mort!

[*The* FIRST POMPIER *tries, but is also driven back.*

SECOND POMPIER. Fini ! [*He sees the cat at the end of the parapet.*] Ah ! V'la le chat ! Prenez-le ! Pincez le bougre !

[*The* FIRST POMPIER *seizes the cat.*

SECOND POMPIER. [*At the parapet*] Vite, Jacques, vite !

[*They disappear over the parapet.*

[*A cry of " Oh ! La ! " A second shrill cheer. A glare and a flurry of water. Then in the smoke* BRICE *is seen emerging from the trap. He sways, suffocated, reels forward and subsides against the parapet. A spurt of flame shoots forth from the trap. He raises himself, looks over and round him and calls wildly. Flame and smoke top the parapet. With a groan and a despairing gesture he cries out.*

BRICE. Christ ! I'm done for ! To hell with it all ! Up—up—up !

[*And falls down into the drifting smoke.*

The curtain falls.

Printed in Great Britain
at
The Chapel River Press,
Kingston, Surrey